MANUAL

OF

ENGLISH PRONUNCIATION

AND

SPELLING:

CONTAINING

A FULL ALPHABETICAL VOCABULARY OF THE LANGUAGE

WITH A PRELIMINARY

EXPOSITION OF ENGLISH ORTHOËPY AND ORTHOGRAPHY;

AND

DESIGNED AS A WORK OF REFERENCE FOR GENERAL USE, AND AS A TEXT-BOOK IN SCHOOLS.

BY

RICHARD SOULE,

ASSOCIATE EDITOR OF WORCESTER'S QUARTO DICTIONARY,

AND

WILLIAM A. WHEELER,

ASSOCIATE EDITOR OF WEBSTER'S DICTIONARIES

BOSTON:

LEE AND SHEPARD, PUBLISHERS.

NEW YORK:

LEE, SHEPARD, AND DILLINGHAM

1875.

PREFACE.

THE design of this work is to provide a convenient manual for consultation, whenever a doubt arises in regard to the pronunciation or the spelling of any word now commonly or occasionally used in English speech, or often met with in modern writings; and also to furnish a text-book for teaching English pronunciation and orthography in a more systematic and thorough manner than has heretofore been possible by the use of the common spelling-books alone.

So difficult is it to become thoroughly versed in either of these branches of learning, that an English dictionary is probably quite as often consulted to ascertain the pronunciation or the spelling of a word, as to learn its meaning. As works of reference for this purpose, the smaller dictionaries are often found to be defective in their vocabularies, and the larger ones are too bulky for convenient use. In order that this volume might contain a very full vocabulary, and at the same time be kept within a small compass, definitions have been omitted, except when they seemed to be required for some purpose of distinction, as in the case of words pronounced alike but differently spelled, or of words spelled alike but differently pronounced.

The words which it has been thought best, as a general rule, to omit from the Vocabulary are all such as are obsolete, most of those that are very rarely used, or are exclusively technical and not Anglicized, and many derivatives ending in *-er*, *-ish*, *-ly*, *-less*, *-like*, *-ness*, or *-ship*, which present no difficulty either of pronunciation or of spelling. Most of the words compounded with the prefixes *all-*, *counter-*, *in-*, *out-*, *over-*, *sub-*, *super-*, *un-*, *under-*, as they are attended with no difficulty that is not explained under their simple forms, have also been omitted.

The Introduction contains a description of the organs of speech, preliminary definitions of a few terms, and an account of the elementary sounds of the language, with a statement of the views in respect to these sounds, held by the most eminent orthoëpists, and of the various ways in which they are represented by the letters of the alphabet. It also embraces, under distinct heads, a succinct treatment of the following topics; namely, syllables, the seat and the influence of the accent, the causes which render words liable to be mispronounced or misspelled, compound words, prefixes, and syllabication.

A marked feature of the plan is, that, though the words of the Vocabulary are arranged in alphabetical order, the more important of them are classified according to some prominent characteristics, either of pronunciation or of spelling, by means of figures referring them to the sections of the Introduction in which those characteristics are described and exemplified. This method of reference, so far as it relates to pronunciation, was introduced by Nares, in his "Elements of Orthoëpy," and has been adopted by Walker, Smart, Worcester, and Goodrich. Smart remarks: "I have . . . copied from Walker the method of referring, throughout the Dictionary, to principles of pronunciation laid down at the commencement; I believe his Dictionary owes its reputation to the obvious excellence of this plan." The attempt has not hitherto been made to apply the same method of reference, in a full alphabetical vocabulary of our language, to preliminary statements of the principles and difficulties of its orthography. It has been a gratifying result of such an attempt, on the part of the compilers, to find how easily the great mass of English words may be grouped under a comparatively few principles, and how readily the difficulties in the way of learning to spell may be overcome by classifying these difficulties and explaining their causes.

Particular attention has been paid to those words in regard to the pronunciation of which good authorities are at variance, and the method suggested and applied by Walker, and more completely and ingeniously carried out by Worcester, of exhibiting the different modes of pronunciation preferred or sanctioned by such authorities, has been adopted in this work. It has not been thought advisable, however, to record the opinions upon this point of others beside Walker and Smart, among English orthoëpists, and Webster, Worcester, and Goodrich, among American orthoëpists. A careful examination of their Dictionaries has been made with reference to the purposes of this Manual, and no pains has been spared to report accurately their modes of pronunciation, wherever there is any essential difference, though, in a very few cases, the precise sound intended by them may not be adequately represented by the notation used, which is, in some respects, different from theirs.

Of the English writers upon orthoëpy, Walker and Smart are the most eminent. The authority of the former, at the time he wrote, was very great; and, though polite usage in the pronunciation of some words has since much changed, and though later writers have shown that he was in error on several points, still his opinion in regard to the proper mode of pronouncing most words, founded, as it was, upon an attentive study of the analogies of the language, is too valuable to be altogether neglected. Smart is one of the most recent writers upon this subject, and, by general consent, is regarded as the highest single authority, at the present day, upon English orthoëpy and English usage in the matter of pronunciation.

Of American writers who have given a careful attention to the subject of pronunciation, Dr. Webster stands first in point of time, and probably first, also, as regards the extent to which the influence of authority upon this subject has prevailed in the United States, if we may judge from the large circulation in this country of his Dictionary and his Spelling-book. But it is to be observed that both these works have been subjected to considerable revision by their editors, since Dr. Webster's death, in 1843, with respect both to pronunciation and to orthography. In order, therefore, to ascertain the mode in which Dr. Webster himself pronounced words, the compilers of this Manual have examined very carefully the edition of his Dictionary published in 1841, which was the last issued during his lifetime. To this was appended, in 1843, shortly after the author's death, a Supplement of new words, which was prepared by his own hand, and which has accordingly been examined with the same object. By comparing this edition with that of 1859, edited by Dr. Goodrich, the changes of pronunciation introduced by the latter have been determined. They were made, according to the statement of Dr. Goodrich in reply to a letter addressed to him on the subject, in conformity with Dr. Webster's known principles, and in consultation with his son, Mr. William G. Webster, who had been associated with him in his literary labors. "We supposed ourselves," says Dr. Goodrich, "to be well acquainted with the *principles* on which he would have wished such a revision to be conducted. . . . It is matter of mere conjecture how far he might have been satisfied with each individual alteration. I am not certain he would have rejected any of them. I am sure he would have embraced nearly all, had he lived to understand the progress of the public mind as we have endeavored to do in his behalf. A dictionary, from the nature of the case, is a *progressive* thing. As the language is in a state of slow but continual progress, the volume that records it must from time to time undergo corresponding changes."

As it is chiefly the editions edited with eminent ability by Dr. Goodrich that are now much used or circulated, and that are regarded by the public as Webster's Dictionaries, it has not been deemed important to record pronunciations which, though originally adopted by Dr. Webster, were subsequently altered by his editor, with the view of conforming, as nearly as could be judged, to the principles by which the author himself would have been guided. Whenever, therefore, the name of Webster is given as an authority for pronunciation, it is accompanied with that of Goodrich, to show that the latter made no change; and whenever that of Goodrich is unaccompanied with that of Webster, it is to be inferred either that Dr. Goodrich introduced a change which he supposed Dr Webster would have sanctioned, or that the word in question was added by the editor. It is to be observed that the pronunciation of some words, as noted in the abridged Dictionaries of the series edited by Dr. Goodrich, does not correspond with that of the same words, as noted in the unabridged edition of 1859; but this, being the most recent and the most important work of the series, has been taken as the standard of reference.

To Dr. Worcester, the other distinguished American authority quoted for pronunciation, is justly awarded the praise of having bestowed great care upon this subject, and of having given the results of his extensive research in a condensed and simple form, well adapted to make them intelligible and useful. His method of exhibiting the opinions of various orthoëpists about words of disputed pronunciation is particularly valuable, as it enables an inquirer to select, without the labor of looking into many volumes, that mode of pronouncing any of these words which seems to be sustained by the greatest weight of authority. An English writer, Mr. Alexander J. Ellis, who has himself made the subject of orthoëpy a special study, truly remarks of what Dr. Worcester has contributed to this department of learning, that it is "deserving of great attention."

It should be stated that in most of the cases in which the name of Worcester appears, as quoted, to stand alone in support of any mode of pronunciation, his decision has apparently been influenced by the opinions of orthoëpists or lexicographers whose names he uses as authorities, but which it has not been thought advisable to cite in this work.

In regard to words of various orthography there seemed to be no better rule to follow than to record in their different forms all such, and only such, as are variously written by respectable English and American authors at the present day. There is not much difference of usage between England and the United States in the mode of spelling words, except in reference to a few words, mostly of French origin, which are still generally spelled, in England, with the termination *our*, as *colour*, *honour*, &c., instead of *or*, which is now the termination given to this class of words almost universally in the United States; and except, also, as respects those words in the orthography of which Dr. Webster made changes that have been extensively adopted in the United States, but which have not found equal favor in England. The number of words, however, which have a peculiar spelling in the latest edition of Webster's Dictionary, is comparatively small, amounting in all to only about two hundred and eighty. In the case of about sixty of this number, the spelling found in the Dictionaries of Walker, Smart, and Worcester, is allowed as an alternative mode; and of the rest, about one hundred and seventy are derivatives of words ending in *l*, not accented on the last syllable. In regard to Webster's mode of spelling these words, without doubling the *l*, on adding a syllable beginning with a vowel, Smart, Worcester, and almost all other recent lexicographers, though they do not consider that the prevailing usage warrants them in adopting this mode, agree that it is more in accordance with analogy than the practice by which the *l* is doubled. All the words referred to as having a peculiar spelling in the latest edition of Webster's Dictionary will be found recorded in this Manual in the same manner as other words are recorded in regard to the orthography of which there is any difference of usage, and they may be known by the abbreviations for the names of Webster and Goodrich which follow them.

The proper mode of joining the constituent parts of compound words is a subject necessary to be considered, in connection with that of spelling, in a complete and systematic exhibition of the principles of English orthography. This difficult subject has received special attention in this work. It has not been deemed advisable, however, to swell the Vocabulary with words of this class, which may be coined almost at will, and which exist, unregistered, by hundreds or thousands, in books of every description. Were the German method of writing compound words, without the hyphen, uniformly followed in our own language, such words would have no peculiar claim to be considered at all in a manual of orthography; but, as we compound words, sometimes with, and sometimes without, the hyphen, it is a matter of no small difficulty to know when to use this connecting mark, and when to omit it. The statement, in the Introduction, of a few simple rules of extensive application, and deduced from the best sources by a careful examination and comparison of authorities, has rendered it unnecessary to insert the greater number of compound words, while the exceptional cases, which are comparatively few, are entered in their proper alphabetical places. A few compounds of regular formation and very common occurrence have been retained for the purpose of illustrating the rules, in conformity with the general plan.

In this part of the work, and in what relates to the mode of joining prefixes, and to the principles of syllabication, — topics also concisely treated of as connected with orthography, — much assistance has been derived from Mr. John Wilson's valuable "Treatise on English Punctuation," in which the usage of the best writers of the present day, as ascertained by the ample observation of a practical printer and corrector of the press, is fully and clearly set forth.

It will, perhaps, be sufficiently obvious, without much explanation, how the present work may be used as a text-book for teaching English pronunciation and spelling. All the principles and all the difficulties which relate to either are stated, in distinct sections, in the Introduction, with illustrative examples. In order that pupils may make extended lists of such examples, and thus classify the more important words of the language for special study, according to their analogies of pronunciation or of orthography, these words in the Vocabulary are referred to the group to which they belong by having figures affixed corresponding to the figures prefixed to the section in which some characteristic of this group is treated of. In many cases, a word is thus distinguished by more than one numerical reference, for the reason that it has characteristics which ally it with different groups.

After pupils have become familiar, by careful study, with the principles contained in the earlier portions of the Introduction relating to the elementary sounds and the modes of representing them, and to the influence of accent on the vowel sounds, their attention may be called to what relates to pronunciation in Parts VI. and VII., or to what pertains to spelling in Parts VIII. and IX., as may be thought best. In either case, the mode of study recommended is, that, at first, the pupils should take up a single section at a time, either in its order or otherwise, as the teacher may direct, and, after committing it to memory, or reading it so attentively as to be able to repeat the substance of it, should turn to certain pages of the Vocabulary assigned for each exercise, and selecting there, by the aid of the figures corresponding to this section, the illustrative words, copy them on a slate or on paper.

In the lists copied for pronunciation, the accents and all other diacritical marks should be omitted, and the pupils should be required to pronounce the words from the lists by inspection merely of the forms which they ordinarily have in books. The lists copied for spelling are to serve the purpose, primarily, of training the eye to determine the correct orthographical forms of words; but, in order to impress these forms more distinctly on the memory, the words should also be given out by the teacher, either from the copied lists or from the Vocabulary itself, to be spelled orally. The words that are particularly difficult to spell, and which the teacher, therefore, would do well to assign most frequently for special attention, are those referred to by the figures 162, 169, 170, and 171. The classes of words referred to by the figures 160 and 161 will be especially useful in exemplifying the different modes in which the elementary sounds are represented by the letters of the alphabet.

Occasionally, the pupils may be separately called upon to copy words upon the blackboard to be used in a general exercise for the whole class or the whole school. The teacher, for example, may direct a pupil to copy upon the blackboard such words as may be found in any assigned portion of the Vocabulary having the reference figures 153, that is to say, words which afford examples of unauthorized or vulgar pronunciations. When the list is finished, this pupil, or any other, may be required to point out what errors are apt to be made in pronouncing these words. To take another example, some of the words distinguished by the numerical reference 155, as being of disputed pronunciation, may be advantageously copied in the same way, and made the subject of remark as to which mode is to be preferred. As an example of a similar exercise in spelling, the teacher may call out, or dictate, from the Vocabulary some of the words having the reference figures 171, as among those particularly difficult to spell, and any pupil, or several pupils in turn or simultaneously, may be required to write them down as they are uttered.

By this method of studying pronunciation and orthography, besides the advantage arising from the interest which the pupils will take in preparing lists of words for themselves, — thus making, in fact, their own Spelling-book, — they will also have the benefit of practice in writing them, which, so far as spelling is concerned, is the only sure way of becoming skilful in this difficult art. And it should not be forgotten that it is for the purpose of writing, chiefly, that spelling needs to be made a part of education. In order to insure a repetition of this practice, and to awaken anew the interest and attention of the pupils, it will be well to lay aside or to erase the lists, after they have once served the purpose of recitation, and to recur, at intervals, to the same exercise under each of the sections, or under such of them as relate to matters of the most importance.

The mode of study may be varied by taking up certain words which have figures affixed, and occasionally, also, some of those which are not so distinguished, and by considering them in reference to the several principles or points which they exemplify. For an examination of the pupils in order to test their knowledge of the subjects treated of in the Introduction, this method will perhaps be found to be the best. The teacher may accomplish the same object by writing words upon the blackboard, and requiring the pupils to refer each of them to the group or groups to which it belongs.

The sections in Parts X., XI., and XII., on Compound Words, Prefixes, and Syllabication, should be carefully read, and questions should be put to the pupils from time to time in regard to them, — though it has not been thought advisable to multiply references to these sections. Only a few compound words have been inserted, these having been selected, as before stated, merely for the sake of illustration. The matter of syllabication, it is obvious, may be amply exemplified by the words found on any page of the Vocabulary.

In the Table of Contents, a pretty full analysis of the several sections of the Introduction is given, not only to serve the purpose of an index, but to assist teachers in framing questions suitable to be put to their pupils in reference to the various matters treated of. Discretion must be used as to which of these should receive the most attention, or which may be most fitly studied by any class of pupils. The anatomical structure of the vocal organs, for example, need not be dwelt upon any farther than a natural curiosity prompts inquiry in regard to it. These organs are described, not in the belief that the processes of speech will be any better performed by knowing how they are performed, but merely with the view of explaining, to those who desire the information, the wonderful mechanism by which the phenomena of spoken language are produced.

A list of the principal works made use of in the preparation of the volume is appended to the Preface, both for the purpose of acknowledging indebtedness to their authors, and of furnishing the inquirer with the means of verifying any of the statements made by the compilers, or of examining the ground over which they have passed. Brief critical notices of such of these works as may not be generally known are quoted, to show in what estimation they are held by good judges.

BOSTON, *March*, 1861.

A LIST OF THE PRINCIPAL WORKS USED IN THE PREPARATION OF THIS MANUAL.

BELL, ALEX. M. A new Elucidation of the Principles of Speech and Elocution. 8vo., pp. viii, 311. Edinburgh, 1849.

BELL, SIR CHARLES. Article on the Organs of the Human Voice, in the Philosophical Transactions of the Royal Society of London, for the year 1832. Vol. 132, pp. 299–334.

BROWN, GOOLD. The Grammar of English Grammars. 8vo., pp. xx, 1070. New York, 1857.

ELLIS, ALEX. J. The Alphabet of Nature. 8vo., pp. v, 194. Bath, 1844–45.

"An excellent account of the researches of the most distinguished physiologists on the human voice and the formation of letters [sounds] is found in Ellis, *The Alphabet of Nature*, a work full of accurate observations and original thought."—*Prof. Max Müller of Oxford*, Proposals for a Missionary Alphabet. Appendix D. III., vol. 2 of *Chev. Bunsen's* Outlines of the Philosophy of Universal History.

ELLIS, ALEX. J. The Essentials of Phonetics. 8vo., pp. xvi, 275. London, 1848.

"Mr. Ellis's work, *The Essentials of Phonetics*, [is] by far the most complete and accurate of all. . . . Those who delight in phonetic investigations will find the subject almost exhausted in this treatise. . . . An invaluable work to those interested in the scientific part of the question."—*Westminster Review, April*, 1849.

ELLIS, ALEX. J. A Plea for Phonetic Spelling, [with an Appendix showing the inconsistencies of the common orthography.] 8vo., pp. ix, 180. London, 1848.

ELLIS, ALEX. J. English Phonetics. 12mo., pp. 16. London, 1854.

ELLIS, ALEX. J. Universal Writing and Printing with Ordinary Letters. 4to., pp. 22. Edinburgh and London, 1856.

"The very able writings of Mr. Alexander John Ellis, on phonetics, have done much to enlighten the public, and to awaken the attention of men of science to the alphabet of sounds as a practical question."—*Richard Cull*, Address to the Ethnological Society of London, 1854.

FOWLER, W. C. The English Language in its Elements and Forms. 8vo., pp. xxxii, 754. New York, 1857.

GOODRICH, C. A. A Pronouncing and Defining Dictionary of the English Language, abridged from Webster's American Dictionary. 8vo., pp. xxiv, 610. Philadelphia, 1856.

GOODWIN, D. R. The North American Review, No. CLIV. Article I., pp. 1–24. Boston, 1852.

"A paper in the North American Review (Jan., 1852) where the sounds of the English, and in general of the Teutonic and Pelasgic languages, are thoroughly and scientifically treated." — *Prof. F. J. Child*, Advertisement to the second American edition of *Latham's* Elementary English Grammar.

GRAY, HENRY. Anatomy, Descriptive and Surgical. 8vo., pp. xxxii, 750. London, 1858.

HUNT, JAMES. A Manual of the Philosophy of Voice and Speech. 12mo., pp. xvi, 422. London, 1859.

JENNISON, JAMES. Lessons in Orthoëpy. 16mo., pp. 68, 1856.

Printed for use in Harvard College, but not published, except in the form of an Introduction to Hillard's Readers.

LATHAM, R. G. A Handbook of the English Language. 12mo., pp. xxiv, 398. London, 1851.

"The . . . part . . . on the Phonology of the English language is a most valuable, and, in some respects, a highly original, contribution to this branch of English grammatical science." — *Rev. Dr. D. R. Goodwin.*

MULLER, J. Elements of Physiology, translated from the German, by William Baly. 2 vols. 8vo. Vol. I., pp. 848; Vol. II., pp. 889.

PHILOLOGICAL SOCIETY. Proceedings for 1850–51, and 1851–52. 8vo. London, 1854.

QUAIN, JONES, and WILSON, W. J. E. A Series of Anatomical Plates. Third Edition, Revised, with Additional Notes, by Joseph Pancoast, M. D. 4to. Five Parts, pp. 92, 104, 100, 88, 64. Philadelphia, 1845.

RUSH, JAMES. The Philosophy of the Human Voice, (fifth edition, enlarged.) 8vo., pp. lxv, 677. Philadelphia, 1859.

"For the advance which has been made in elocutionary science in modern times, we are indebted to the useful labors of Steele, Odell, Walker, Thelwell, Chapman, Smart, and *Rush*, especially to the last, who has done much to perfect what was begun by others, and whose 'Philosophy of the Human Voice' contains a more minute and satisfactory analysis of the subject than is to be found in any other work." — *Penny Cyclopædia.*

RUSSELL, WILLIAM. Orthophony, or the Cultivation of the Voice in Elocution. [With a Supplement on Purity of Tone, by G. J. Webb.] 12mo., pp. 300. Boston, 1855.

SMART, B. H. A Practical Grammar of English Pronunciation. 8vo., pp. xv, 397. London, 1810.

SMART, B. H. Walker's Pronouncing Dictionary of the English Language, adapted to the present state of Literature and Science. Fifth Edition. 8vo., pp. cxxviii, 792. London, 1857.

SMART, B. H. Pronouncing Dictionary of the English Language Epitomized, (second edition, revised.) 16mo., pp. xxxi, 694. London, 1846.

Smart thus alludes to his own qualifications for editing a Pronouncing Dictionary of the English Language: "I pretend to reflect the oral usage of English, such as it is at present [1846] among the sensible and well-educated in the British metropolis; and I am now to state what my opportunities have been of learning that usage. I am a Londoner, the son of a Londoner, and have lived nearly all my life in London. My early days were spent in preparing for a literary profession; and a 'Practical Grammar of English Pronunciation,' which I published thirty years ago, is an evidence of the length of time during which my attention has been fixed on the subject in view. It has been said that the example of pronunciation should be taken not exclusively from those who move only in the highest circles, nor yet from those who devote all their time to learning. I have been able to observe the usage of all classes. As a teacher of the English language and literature, I have been admitted into some of the first families of the kingdom; as one partial to books, I have come much into contact with bookish men; while, as a public reader and lecturer, I have been obliged to fashion my own pronunciation to the taste of the day. Thus prepared, I may not unwarrantably believe that my opinion may have some value with those who seek the opinion of another to regulate their pronunciation."

SPURRELL, WILLIAM. The Elementary Sounds of the English Language and their Classifications. 12mo., pp. 23. Carmarthen, 1850.

STEARNS, EDW. J. A Practical Guide to English Pronunciation. 12mo., pp. lxxx, 55. Boston, 1857.

STODDART, SIR JOHN. Glossology, or the Historical Relations of Languages. 8vo., pp. 387. London and Glasgow, 1858.

TODD, ROBERT B. The Cyclopædia of Anatomy and Physiology. 4 vols. 8vo. London, 1839–1852; and Supplement, 1 vol. London, 1859.

Todd, Robert Bentley, and Bowman, William. The Physiological Anatomy and Physiology of Man. 2 vols. 8vo. Vol. I., pp. xv, 448; Vol. II., pp. xxiv, 660. London, 1856.

Walker, John. A Critical and Pronouncing Expositor of the English Language. 4to., Introduction, pp. 87, Vocabulary, pp. 263. Fourth Edition. London, 1806.

☞ This edition of Walker's Dictionary was the last that was published during his lifetime.

Walker, John. A Rhyming Dictionary, . . . in which the whole Language is arranged according to its Terminations. (A New and Revised Edition.) 12mo., pp. xxiv, 684. London, 1851.

Webster, Noah. An American Dictionary of the English Language. 2 vols. 8vo. Vol. I., pp. lxxvi, 938; Vol. II., pp. 1004. New Haven, 1841.

Webster, Noah. The same, [with a Supplement by the author, first published in 1843, after his decease.] 2 vols. 8vo. Vol. I., pp. lxxvi, 944; Vol. II., pp. 1020. Springfield, 1845.

Webster, Noah. The same, revised and enlarged, by Chauncey A. Goodrich. (Pictorial Edition.) 4to., pp. ccxxxvi, 1512. Springfield, 1859.

Willis, Robert. Article on the Mechanism of the Larynx in the Transactions of the Cambridge Philosophical Society for the year 1829. Vol. IV., pp. 313–352.

"We strongly recommend any one who wishes to understand the operation of the muscles of the larynx, and the production of vocal sound by the glottis, to read Professor Willis's paper with great attention." — *Alexander John Ellis*, Essentials of Phonetics.

Wilson, Erasmus. A System of Human Anatomy, General and Special. Fourth American, from the last London Edition. Edited by Paul B. Goddard. 8vo., pp. xxiv, 576. Philadelphia, 1857.

Wilson, John. A Treatise on English Punctuation. 12mo., pp. xii, 334. Boston, 1855.

"We have a beautiful monograph on Punctuation, by John Wilson (Boston, 1850). It is thorough, so as to embrace his whole topic, and critical, so as to exclude what does not belong there." — *Prof. J. W. Gibbs.*

Worcester, Joseph E. A Dictionary of the English Language. 4to., pp. lxviii, 1786. Boston, 1860.

CONTENTS.

INTRODUCTION.

I in an Unaccented Syllable.

O in an Unaccented Syllable.

U in an Unaccented Syllable.

Y in an Unaccented Syllable.

AI in an Unaccented Syllable.

EI in an Unaccented Syllable.

EY in an Unaccented Syllable.

IE in an Unaccented Syllable.

OU in an Unaccented Syllable.

OW in an Unaccented Syllable.

Rules for Syllabication.

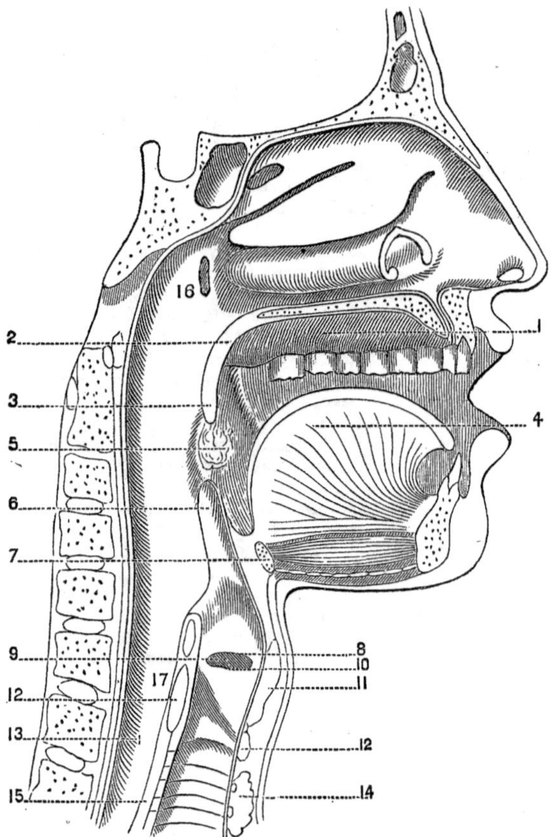

Fig. I. Section of the Head and Neck, showing the Organs of Speech.

1. Hard palate.
2. Soft palate.
3. Uvula.
4. Tongue.
5. Tonsil.
6. Epiglottis.
7. Hyoid or lingual bone.
8. Superior vocal chord of one side.
9. Ventricle of larynx on one side.
10. Inferior or true vocal chord of one side.
11. Thyroid cartilage.
12. Cricoid cartilage.
13. Œsophagus.
14. Thyroid gland.
15. Trachea.

16, 17, Pharynx.

INTRODUCTION.

I. DESCRIPTION OF THE ORGANS OF SPEECH, AND PRELIMINARY DEFINITIONS.

§ **1.** SPEECH consists of a series of significant sounds produced by emissions of breath, variously modified, and in the form either of whisper or of voice.

§ **2.** The ORGANS OF SPEECH are the *lungs*, the *trachea* or *windpipe*, the *larynx*, the *pharynx*, the *mouth*, and the *nasal passages*, with various appendages. The organs more directly concerned in modifying the sounds of which speech consists are the *lips*, the *tongue*, the *teeth*, the *hard palate*, and the *uvula*, which are parts of the mouth.

The *two lungs*, which are the essential organs of respiration, are placed one in each of the lateral cavities of the chest, separated from each other by the heart and the large arteries and veins connected with it. They are alternately dilated and compressed for the inspiration and expiration of air by the action of the diaphragm and certain muscles of the ribs.

The *trachea*, or *windpipe*, is a cartilaginous and membranous tube in the anterior part of the neck, extending from the lower part of the larynx downward about four inches to a point opposite the third dorsal vertebra, where it divides into two *bronchi*, or branches, which connect it, one with each lung. It is from three quarters of an inch to an inch in diameter, and is composed of from sixteen to twenty imperfect, elastic rings formed of cartilage and fibrous membrane, one above another, and separated by narrow strips of membrane. The cartilaginous and cylindrical portion of the rings occupies about two thirds of the circumference in front and on the sides, and the remaining part behind is nearly flat, and consists principally of fibrous membrane and a fine, very regular layer of muscular fibres on the outside. This structure enables it, while serving the purpose of an air-tube, to accommodate itself to the motions of the head and neck, and to yield, in the act of swallowing, to the distended œsophagus, or gullet, which is situated behind it. The *thyroid gland* — so called, though it has no excretory duct — is a firm, vascular substance, lying, like a cushion, in two lobes across the upper part of the trachea, to which it is capable of being braced by four flat muscles that pass over its surface. Its function is generally stated to be unknown; but Sir Charles Bell supposes that it is designed to check the vibrations of sound, "and so impede the motions originating in the larynx from being propagated downward." The thyroid gland is always larger in the female than in the male sex, and it is occasionally of an enormous size, constituting the disease called *goitre*, or *bronchocele*.

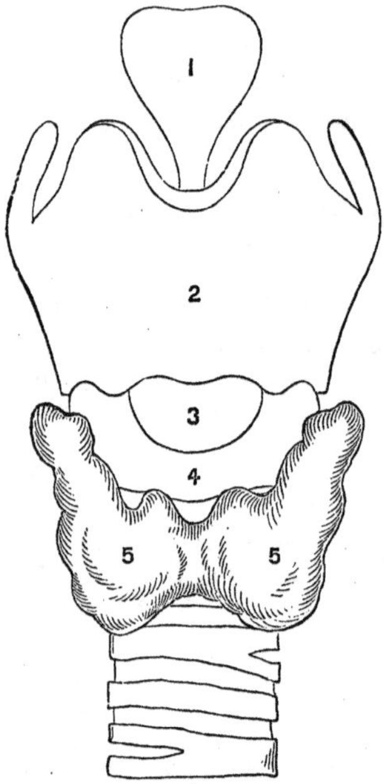

Fig. II. Front view of the Larynx and a part of the Trachea.

1. Epiglottis. — 2. Thyroid cartilage. — 3. Crico-thyroid membrane. — 4. Cricoid cartilage. — 5. Thyroid gland. — 6. Trachea.

The *larynx*, which is the immediate seat and instrument of sound, is situated between the trachea and the base of the tongue. It is a complex piece of mechanism, resembling, in its general form, a kind of box, or an irregular hollow body triangular at top, but approaching nearly to a circle at its junction with the trachea. It is composed of nine cartilages; three single, namely, the *cricoid* (or ring-shaped) *cartilage*, the *thyroid* (or shield-shaped) *cartilage*, and the *epiglottis*; and six in pairs, namely, two *arytenoid* (or pitcher-shaped) *cartilages*, two termed *cornicula laryngis* (or little horns of the larynx), and two *cuneiform* (or wedge-shaped) *cartilages.*

The *cricoid cartilage*, situated at the base of the larynx, which it supports, is thicker and stronger than the other cartilages, and is in the form of a ring slightly elliptical, and considerably deeper at the posterior part than in front. It is connected below to the first ring of the trachea by ligaments and mucous membrane, and is articulated posteriorly on the outer sides with the thyroid cartilage, and, on the upper margin, with the arytenoid cartilages.

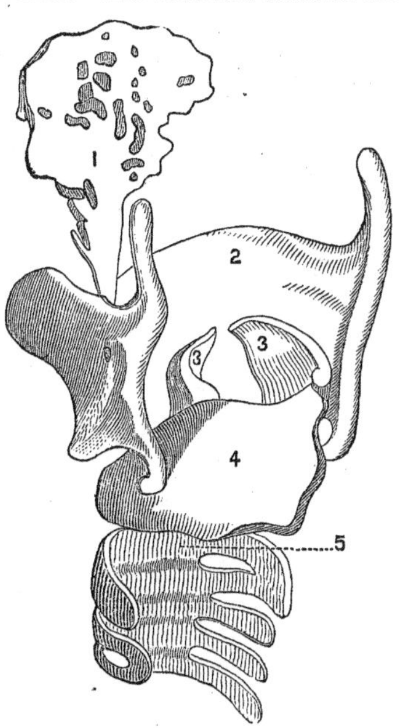

Fig. III. Principal Cartilages of the Larynx and upper part of the Trachea, seen from behind.

1. Epiglottis. — 2. Thyroid cartilage. — 3, 3. Arytenoid cartilages. — 4. Cricoid cartilage. — 5. Trachea.

The *thyroid cartilage* is the largest of the cartilages composing the larynx, and partially embraces the cricoid cartilage, with which it is articulated, and also otherwise connected by muscles and ligaments. It consists of two lateral, four-sided plates, or wings, open behind, but united at an acute angle in front, forming a vertical ridge, and terminating above in a prominence called the *pomum Adami*, or *Adam's-apple*, which is more developed in the male than in the female sex. On its four posterior angles, are situated four *cornua*, or horns, two superior and two inferior. The superior horns, being longer than the inferior, are called *great horns*, and are connected with the bone at the base of the tongue (lingual bone, hyoid bone, or *os hyoides*) by ligaments. The lateral and front portions of the upper border of the thyroid cartilage are connected with the same bone by what is called the *thyro-hyoid membrane.* The inferior horns are curved forward, and are articulated at their extremities to the cricoid cartilage by oblique planes directed forward and inward. The thyroid cartilage overlaps the cricoid cartilage on each side, but in front there is a space between the two, over which the *crico-thyroid membrane* extends. This space may be easily felt on applying the finger at the upper and front part of the neck.

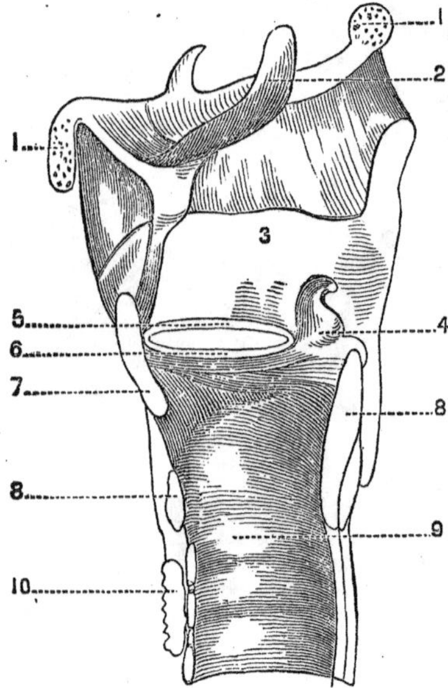

Fig. IV. Vertical section of the Larynx and a part of the Trachea.

1, 1. Hyoid or lingual bone, below which is seen the thyro-hyoid membrane extending to the thyroid cartilage. — 2. Epiglottis. — 3. One wing of the thyroid cartilage. — 4. Arytenoid cartilage of one side. — 5. Superior or false vocal chord of one side. — 6. Inferior or true vocal chord of one side. — 7. Thyroid cartilage in front. — 8, 8. Cricoid cartilage. — 9. Upper ring of the trachea. — 10. Thyroid gland.

The *epiglottis* is a thin, flexible plate of cartilage, having shallow pits upon its surface, and shaped like a cordate leaf, with a broad, rounded upper extremity, which is free to move. It is placed behind the tongue, to the bone of which it is connected by an elastic ligament, and it is attached below by a long, narrow ligament to the receding angle between the two plates of the thyroid cartilage. During respiration, its direction is nearly vertical, its free extremity curving forward towards the base of the tongue, above which it projects; but, when the larynx is drawn upward in the act of swallowing, the epiglottis is carried downward and backward, so as to serve the purpose of a valve and completely close the glottis, or opening of the larynx.

The two *arytenoid cartilages* are situated on the posterior inner and upper margin of the cricoid cartilage in such a manner as to resemble, when approximated, the mouth of a pitcher, from which circumstance they take their name. They are of an irregular shape, but may be considered as having the form of a pyramid with a broad base, and presenting surfaces for the attachment of muscles and ligaments. The posterior surfaces are triangular, smooth, and concave, and give attachment to the *arytenoideus* muscle. The anterior surfaces are somewhat convex and rough, and give attachment to the *thyro-arytenoid* muscles and to the superior, or false, vocal chords. The interior surfaces are narrow, smooth, and flattened, and form a part of the lateral wall of the larynx. Of the three corners of the bases, the external one is short, rounded, and prominent, and gives attachment to the posterior and lateral *crico-arytenoid muscles;* and the anterior one, also prominent, but more pointed, gives attachment to the true vocal chord. The apex of each of these cartilages is pointed and curved backward and inward. The two small cartilages termed *cornicula laryngis* are situated on the apexes of the arytenoid cartilages, with which they are sometimes united, and serve to prolong them backward and inward.

The *cuneiform cartilages* are two small, elongated bodies, placed one on each side in the fold of mucous membrane which extends from the apex of the arytenoid cartilage to the side of the epiglottis.

The cavity of the larynx is divided into two parts, with a narrow, oblong opening between them, by the *thyro-arytenoid ligaments*, or *vocal chords*, on each side, and the *thyro-arytenoid muscles* parallel with these chords, both of which are enclosed in folds of mucous membrane, stretched between the sides of the epiglottis and the apexes of the arytenoid cartilages, and are attached in front to the thyroid cartilage at the angle formed by the meeting of its two plates, or wings, and behind to the arytenoid cartilages. The form of this cavity is broad and triangular at top, and becomes gradually narrower downward towards the vocal chords, below which it becomes gradually broader and nearly cylindrical, its circumference coinciding below with the inner part of the ring of the cricoid cartilage. The vocal chords are in pairs on each side, one over the other. The superior chords (called the *false vocal chords*, because they are supposed not to be concerned, or to have only a subordinate part, in the production of voice) are delicate, narrow, fibrous bands, enclosed in thick folds of the mucous membrane, and attached, in front, to the receding angle of the thyroid cartilage below the epiglottis, and behind, to the interior surface of the arytenoid cartilage. The inferior vocal chords (called the *true vocal chords*, because they are chiefly concerned in the production of voice by their vibrations) are two thick and strong fibrous bands, covered externally by a thin and delicate mucous membrane. They are attached, in front, to the centre of the depression between the two plates or wings of the thyroid cartilage, and behind, to the anterior angle of the base of the arytenoid cartilage. On their outer sides, they are connected with the thyro-arytenoid muscles. The lower borders of the superior vocal chords have the form of a crescent, and constitute the upper boundaries of the *ventricles of the larynx*, of which the lower boundaries are the superior straight borders of the inferior vocal chords.

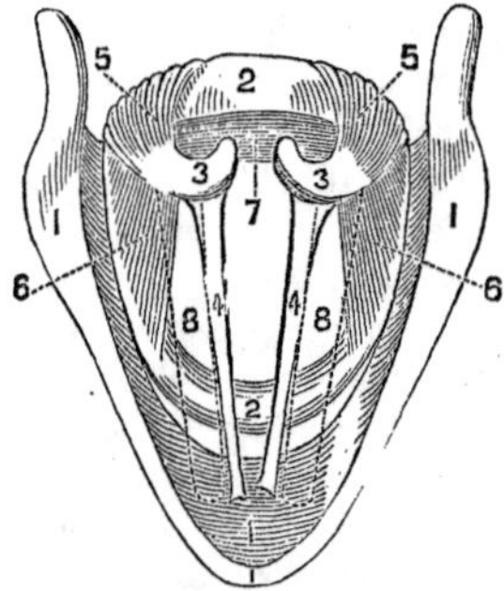

Fig. V. Interior of the Larynx, seen from above.

1. Thyroid cartilage. — 2. Cricoid cartilage. — 3, 3. Arytenoid cartilages. — 4, 4. Inferior or true vocal chords. — 5. Posterior crico-arytenoid muscles. — 6. Lateral crico-arytenoid muscles. — 7. Arytenoideus muscle. — 8. Thyro-arytenoid muscles, within the dotted lines.

The *ventricles of the larynx* are two oblong, oval cavities between the superior and inferior vocal chords, extending nearly their entire length, one on each side, and formed by the folding inward of the mucous membrane which covers them. The chief office of these cavities is to afford sufficient space for the vibrations of the inferior, or true, vocal chords.

Each of the ventricles of the larynx leads upward on the outer side of the superior vocal chord into the *sacculus laryngis*, or laryngeal pouch, which is a membranous sac of a conical form, and of a variable size between this chord and the inner surface of the thyroid cartilage.

The narrow opening between the inferior, or true, vocal chords is called the *glottis*, or *chink of the glottis.* Its length in the adult male is rather less than an inch, and it varies in breadth at its widest part from a third of an inch to half an inch. In the female, these dimensions are somewhat less. The form of the aperture is variable. In a state of repose, or that of ordinary respiration, it is triangular, or narrower in front than behind, dilating somewhat during inspiration and contracting during expiration. In the act of producing voice, as in speaking or in singing, the glottis is nearly closed, the true vocal chords being brought into a nearly parallel position, and separated only about one tenth of an inch by the approximation of the anterior angles of the bases of the arytenoid cartilages to which they are attached. The breath being forced through the glottis when these chords are in this position, causes them to vibrate and produce a sound, the pitch of which depends entirely upon their tension. The aperture between the superior, or false, vocal chords is sometimes called the *false glottis.*

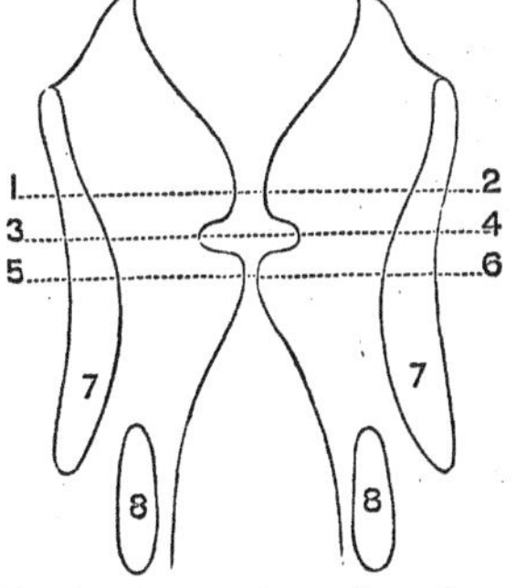

Fig. VI. Transverse section, showing the form of the cavity of the Larynx, the true vocal chords being nearly parallel, or in a position to vibrate.

1-2. Line through the superior or false vocal chords and false glottis. — 3-4. Line through the ventricles of the larynx. — 5-6. Line through the inferior or true vocal chords and true glottis. — 7, 7. Section of the thyroid cartilage. — 8, 8. Section of the cricoid cartilage.

The mucous membrane of the larynx is continuous with that which lines the pharynx and mouth above, and it is prolonged downward through the trachea and bronchial tubes into the lungs. The whole apparatus of the larynx, being suspended loosely in front of the pharynx and the œsophagus, may be moved freely up and down in the neck, approximating to, or receding from, the lower jaw by means of what are called the *extrinsic muscles,* while the movements of its various segments are controlled by what are called the *intrinsic muscles.*

The *intrinsic muscles* are arranged symmetrically, and are attached to corresponding points on each side of the glottis.

Those of them which open or close the glottis, or regulate the tension of the vocal chords, are the following: the *posterior crico-arytenoid*, the *lateral crico-arytenoid*, the *arytenoideus*, the *crico-thyroid*, and the *thyro-arytenoid.*

The two *posterior crico-arytenoid muscles* are attached to the posterior surface of the cricoid cartilage, and passing obliquely upward and outward, converge to be inserted into the outer angles of the bases of the arytenoid cartilages. They open the glottis by drawing the bases of the arytenoid cartilages outward and backward.

The two *lateral crico-arytenoid muscles* arise from the upper borders of the sides of the cricoid cartilage, and passing obliquely upward and backward, are inserted into the outer angles of the bases of the arytenoid cartilages in front of the posterior crico-arytenoid muscles. They close the glottis by drawing the bases of the arytenoid cartilages inward and forward.

The *arytenoideus muscle* is single, though it consists of three planes of fibres, two oblique and one transverse. It fills up the posterior concave surface of the arytenoid cartilages, arising from the posterior surface and outer border of one of them, and being inserted into the corresponding parts of the other. It approximates these cartilages, and thus closes the glottis.

The two *crico-thyroid muscles* arise from the front and lateral parts of the cricoid cartilage, and diverging, pass obliquely upward and outward, to be inserted into the lower and inner borders of the thyroid cartilage from near the median line in front as far back as the inferior horns. They stretch the vocal chords by rotating the cricoid cartilage on the inferior horns of the thyroid cartilage.

The two *thyro-arytenoid muscles* are broad and flat, and lie parallel with the outer side of the true vocal chords. They are attached in front to the receding angle of the thyroid cartilage, and passing horizontally backward and outward, are inserted into the bases and anterior and outer surfaces of the arytenoid cartilages. They approximate the anterior angles of these cartilages, and thus close the glottis. According to Willis, they also draw the arytenoid cartilages, together with the cricoid cartilage, forward, and thus shorten and relax the vocal chords.

The *pharynx* is a kind of dilatable bag, and consists of all that funnel-shaped cavity, lined with mucous membrane and acted on by many muscles, which is situated in front of the cervical vertebræ behind the nose, mouth, and larynx, and above the œsophagus, with which it is continuous. It is about four inches and a half in length, extending from the base of the skull to a point between the cricoid cartilage in front and the fifth cervical vertebra behind. There are seven openings communicating with it, namely, the two posterior nares or nostrils, the two Eustachian tubes (canals leading from the tympana of the ears), the mouth, the larynx, and the œsophagus. The pharynx exercises a considerable influence on the modulation of the voice; and, according to Sir Charles Bell, it is a very important agent in the articulation of the consonants, especially the explosive consonants. Being dilated at the moment when the articulating organs come in contact, it "is prepared," he remarks, "to give an appulse by its muscular action, exactly in time" with the separation of these organs. The guttural murmur which is heard before the mouth is opened to pronounce certain consonants, as *b*, *d*, and *g*, is due, in the opinion of this author, to the vibration of the vocal chords by the ascent of air from the lungs in consequence of the dilation of the pharynx, the nasal passages being closed, by the soft palate. In the process of articulation, "this smaller cavity [the pharynx]," he remarks, "is substituted for the larger cavity of the chest, to the great relief of the speaker."

The *mouth* is a nearly oval-shaped cavity, bounded in front by the lips; laterally by the internal surface of the cheeks; above by the hard palate and the teeth of the upper jaw; below by the tongue, by the mucous membrane stretched between the lower surface of the tongue and the inner surface of the lower jaw, and by the teeth of this jaw; and behind by the *soft palate*, which is a movable fold of mucous membrane containing muscular fibres and glands suspended from the posterior border of the hard palate between the mouth and the pharynx. Hanging from the middle of its lower border, is a small, rounded process called the *uvula*. Passing outward from the uvula, on each side are two curved folds of the mucous membrane called the *arches of the palate*, or the *pillars of the palate*. The anterior arches run downward and forward from the base of the uvula to the sides of the base of the tongue. The posterior arches approach nearer to each other, are longer than the anterior, and run downward and backward from the base of the uvula to the sides of the pharynx. In the triangular intervals between the arches of the palate are situated the *tonsils*, one on each side. These are glandular organs, varying in size in different individuals. When enlarged from inflammation, they give to the voice a peculiar nasal tone.

The *tongue*, being chiefly composed of muscular fibres, and having a thin, flexible tip and a large, fleshy root, is capable of taking a great variety of positions and shapes. It is connected by muscles to the soft palate, to the hyoid bone, and to the lower jaw. It is also connected by the mucous membrane with the soft palate, as well as with the epiglottis and the pharynx.

The lingual bone, or bone at the base of the tongue, — called also the *os hyoides*, or *hyoid bone*, on account of its resemblance to the Greek letter *υ*, — consists of a bony arch, with a curvature nearly approaching a parabola, convex in front and concave behind. Situated in an almost horizontal position behind, and rather below, the lower jaw, it performs the triple office of a basis of the tongue, a point of support to the larynx, and a fulcrum by which the contractions of the intrinsic muscles of the tongue and the larynx may be impressed on these organs. It is not immediately joined to any other bone, but the muscles and ligaments which converge to it from different directions effectually prevent its displacement. Being thus suspended between the tongue and the larynx, it impresses on each the movement of the other, and is the medium by which these two organs are so intimately associated.

The *nasal passages* consist of several channels among the bones of the head in front, terminating externally in the anterior nares, or nostrils, and internally in the posterior nares, or nostrils, which are two nearly oval apertures opening into the pharynx, and capable of being closed by the soft palate.

§ **3.** Whisper is the sound, or series of sounds, produced by an emission of breath through the larynx, when the vocal chords are relaxed, or in such a position that they will not vibrate.

§ **4.** Voice is the sound, or series of sounds, produced by an emission of breath through the larynx, when the vocal chords are tense, or in a position very nearly parallel to each other, so as to be made to vibrate.

§ **5.** A VOWEL SOUND is a sound produced by an unobstructed utterance of the breath (as in whispering), or of the voice (as in speaking aloud), more or less modified by the position of the tongue, the soft palate, and the lips, or by the motions of the lower jaw in varying the cavity of the mouth. The letter which represents such a sound is called a *vowel*; but this term is sometimes applied to the sound itself.

§ **6.** A COMPOUND VOWEL SOUND, or DIPHTHONG, consists of two simple vowel sounds connected by a glide, or continuous emission of the breath or the voice, while the organs of speech are rapidly changing from their position in forming the first to that necessary for forming the second.

§ **7.** A CONSONANT SOUND is a sound produced by the partial or the total obstruction of the breath or the voice, on passing through the mouth or the nose, by the contact or the approximation of two of the organs of speech, as the two lips (*b*, *wh*, *m*), the lower lip and the upper teeth (*f*, *v*), the tip of the tongue and the upper teeth (*th* as in *thin*, *th* as in *this*), the tip of the tongue and the hard palate (*sh*, *zh*), the back of the tongue and the soft palate (*g*, *ng*); or it is a sound produced by an utterance of the breath at the moment of separating two of these organs (*k*, *p*, *t*). The letter which represents such a sound, and sometimes the sound itself, is called a *consonant* (from the Latin *consonans*, meaning literally *sounding with*), a name probably suggested by the fact that a vowel sound is usually joined with a consonant sound in forming syllables, though not meant to imply, as some writers seem to have supposed, that no consonant sound can be uttered without being joined with a vowel sound.

§ **8.** A DIGRAPH is a combination of two letters to represent a single sound; as, *ea* in *fear*, *ei* in *vein*, *ow* in *slow*, *ch* in *church*, *th* in *thin*, *this*, *ng* in *thing*.

§ **9.** An ELEMENTARY SOUND, or element of speech, is a sound which is, in its nature, essentially simple, or which cannot be shown to consist of any other sounds.

II. ELEMENTARY SOUNDS.

The following is a Table of the Elementary Sounds of the English Language, with the letters or characters used in this work to indicate them: —

1. Simple Vowel Sounds.

1. Sound of *a* in *and*, indicated by *ă* . . . . . . § 10
2. “ “ *a* “ *far*, “ “ *ä* (before *r*, by *a*) . § 11
3. “ “ *a* “ *fast*, “ “ *ȧ* . . . . . . § 12
4. “ “ *e* “ *me*, “ “ *ē* . . . . . . § 13
5. “ “ *e* “ *there*, “ “ *ê* . . . . . . § 14
6. “ “ *e* “ *then*, “ “ *ĕ* . . . . . . § 15
7. “ “ *i* “ *ill*, “ “ *ĭ* . . . . . . § 16
8. “ “ *o* “ *orb*, (or *a* in *all*) *aw*, *â* (before *r*, by *o*) . § 17
9. “ “ *o* “ *on*, “ “ *ŏ* . . . . . . § 18
10. “ “ *oo* “ *food*, “ “ *oo* . . . . . . § 19
11. “ “ *oo* “ *foot*, “ “ *o͝o* . . . . . . § 20
12. “ “ *u* “ *urn*, “ “ *uh* (before *r*, by *u*) . § 21
13. “ “ *u* “ *up*, “ “ *ŭ* . . . . . . § 22

2. Compound Vowel Sounds.

14. Sound of *a* in *ale*, indicated by *ā* . . . . . . § 23
15. “ “ *o* “ *old*, “ “ *ō* . . . . . . § 24
16. “ “ *i* “ *time*, “ “ *ī* . . . . . . § 25
17. “ “ *u* “ *use*, *cube*, “ *ū*, or *yoo* . . . . § 26
18. “ “ *oi* “ *oil*, “ “ *oi*, or *oy* . . . . § 27
19. “ “ *ou* “ *ounce*, “ “ *ou*, or *ow* . . . . § 28

3. Aspirate Sound.

20. Sound of *h* in *home*, indicated by *h* . . . . . . § 29

4. Consonant Sounds.

21. Sound of *p* in *pet*, indicated by *p* . . . . . . § 30
22. “ “ *b* “ *bet*, “ “ *b* . . . . . . § 31
23. “ “ *m* “ *man*, “ “ *m* . . . . . . § 32
24. “ “ *wh* “ *when*, “ “ *wh* . . . . . . § 33
25. “ “ *w* “ *wen*, “ “ *w* . . . . . . § 34

26.	Sound of *f*	in *feel*,	indicated by *f*			§ 35
27.	" " *v*	" *veal*,	" " *v*			§ 36
28.	" " *th*	" *thin*,	" " *th*			§ 37
29.	" " *th*	" *this*,	" " *th̲*			§ 38
30.	" " *s*	" *seal*,	" " *s*			§ 39
31.	" " *z*	" *zeal*,	" " *z*			§ 40
32.	" " *t*	" *tale*,	" " *t*			§ 41
33.	" " *d*	" *dale*,	" " *d*			§ 42
34.	" " *n*	" *name*,	" " *n*			§ 43
35.	" " *ch*	" *church*,	" " *ch*			§ 44
36.	" " *j*	" *just*,	" " *j*			§ 45
37.	" " *sh*	" *shall*,	" " *sh*			§ 46
38.	" " *z*	" *azure*,	" " *zh*			§ 47
39.	" " *r*	" *roam*, *florid*,	" *r*			§ 48
40.	" " *r*	" *nor*, *sort*,	" *r*			§ 49
41.	" " *l*	" *low*,	" " *l*			§ 50
42.	" " *y*	" *yet*,	" " *y*			§ 51
43.	" " *k*	" *kill*,	" " *k*			§ 52
44.	" " *g*	" *go*,	" " *g* (before *e*, *i*, or *y*, by *gh*)			§ 53
45.	" " *ng*	" *sing*,	" " *ng*			§ 54

Remarks on the Elementary Sounds.

In the following remarks, the elementary sounds are treated in the order in which they are given in the Table, and the modes in which they are represented in the established system of orthography, as they occur in monosyllables or in accented syllables, are illustrated by examples.

1. Simple Vowel Sounds.

§ **10.** (1.) The sound of *a* in *and* (short *a*, marked *ă*).

This sound, which is peculiarly English, is commonly reckoned the short form of *a* in *far* (No. 2, § 11), differing from it only in duration; but between these two sounds, as Bell remarks, "there is a great organic difference," the tongue being raised higher for the former than for the latter. Smart says of *a* in *and*, that "it differs in quality as well as in quantity both from *a* [in *ale*] and *a* [in *far*]. It is much nearer the latter than the former." According to Ellis, the long, or protracted, sound of this element occurs as a provincialism in the west of England, in Ireland, and in New England. — See No. 5, § 14.

It is represented by *a*, and also by *ai* (*plaid*). — See § 11, NOTE.

§ **11.** (2.) The sound of *a* in *far* (the Italian *a*, marked ä).

This sound is represented by *a* before *h* in the same syllable (*ah*), and before *r* (*car*, *cart*, *martyr*), except in the cases mentioned in the Note; also by *au* (*aunt*), *ea* (*heart*), and *ua* (*guard*). — See § 72.

NOTE.—The vowel *a* represents the sound of *a* in *far* before *r* in a monosyllable or an accented syllable of some words, and in their derivatives (as in *star*, *star'ry*, *tar*, *tar'ry*, *de-bar'*, *de-bar'ring*); but when *a* comes before *r* in an accented syllable of a word not a derivative, and is followed by a syllable commencing with another *r* or with a vowel, it has its short sound (as in *mar'ry*, *ar'id*).

§ **12.** (3.) The sound of *a* in *fast* (intermediate *a*, marked ȧ).

There is a class of words, mostly monosyllables, ending in *aff*, *aft*, *ass*, *ast*, *ask*, *asp*, with a few ending in *ance* and *ant*, (as *staff*, *graft*, *glass*, *fast*, *bask*, *grasp*, *dance*, *chant*) in the pronunciation of which good usage, both in England and in America, is far from being uniform, some speakers giving them the long, full sound of *a* in *far* (No. 2, § 11), while others — including most of the orthoëpists — pronounce them with the extreme short sound of *a* in *and* (No. 1, § 10). According to Smart, as stated by Goodrich, the sound of *a* in *and* is, in such words, "at present [1856] the pronunciation of well-educated London people under sixty-five or sixty years of age." Ellis, however, maintains that "it is usual," in such words, "to pronounce the clear vowel *ah*," not only in London, but throughout the south of England, and that the sound of short *a* is "seldom or never heard" instead of it. This conclusion he arrived at, he says, "after many observations on the pronunciation of different speakers, instituted solely with a view of discovering whether this was or was not the case." Bell remarks: "The extreme pronunciations [*a* in *and*, and *a* in *far*] are, at the present day [1849], comparatively seldom heard. The precise quality of the prevailing intermediate sound cannot be correctly noted; for it ranges among different speakers through every practicable shade within these limits." The orthoëpists Fulton and Knight regard this intermediate sound as a shortened form of the Italian *a* (No. 2,

§ 11), and Worcester and Goodrich adopt substantially the same view.

This sound is always represented by *a*, as in the class of words above mentioned (*staff*, *grass*, *dance*, &c.).

§ **13.** (4.) The sound of *e* in *me* (long *e*, marked ē).

This sound is represented by *e* and also by *æ* (Cæsar), *ea* (s*ea*l), *ee* (s*ee*), *ei* (s*ei*ze), *eo* (p*eo*ple), *ey* (k*ey*), *i* (rav*i*ne), *ie* (f*ie*ld), *œ* (fœtus), *uay* (q*uay*).— See No. 7, § 16.

§ **14.** (5.) The sound of *e* in *there* (marked ê).

This sound is heard, in English, only before that of *r* (No. 40, § 49) in the same syllable, and it is considered by Walker, Smart, and most orthoëpists, to be the same as that of long *a* (No. 14, § 23). Worcester characterizes it as the sound of long *a* "qualified by being followed by the letter *r*." But Bell and Spurrell regard it as a lengthened form of short *e* (No. 6, § 15). The former remarks: "An ear unaccustomed to analyze vocal sounds may possibly, at first, fail to recognize the same vowel formation in the words *ell*, *ere*, *air*, *heir*, arising from its combination in the [three] latter words with the open *r*" (No. 40, § 49); "but close observation and careful experiment will satisfy the demurring ear of the correctness of our classification." Russell describes the sound in question as "approaching to the *e* in *end*," and Smart, though he maintains its identity with that of long *a*, approves, according to the statement of Goodrich, the mode of obtaining it by "prolonging our short *e* before *r*." It is a common practice in some parts of the United States to substitute for the true sound of the first *e* in *there* a protracted sound of *a* in *and* (No. 1, § 10); but this pronunciation is countenanced by no good authority.

This sound is represented by *e*, and also by *a* (f*a*re), *ai* (*ai*r), *aye* (pr*aye*r, in the sense of a *petition*), *ea* (b*ea*r), and *ei* (h*ei*r).

§ **15.** (6.) The sound of *e* in *then* (short *e*, marked ĕ).

This sound is merely a shortened form of the first *e* in *there* (No. 5, § 14).

It is represented by *e*, and also by *a* (*a*ny), *æ* (di*æ*resis), *ai* (s*ai*d), *ay* (s*ay*s), *ea* (h*ea*d), *ei* (h*ei*fer), *eo* (l*eo*pard), *ie* (fr*ie*nd), *œ* (asafœtida), *u* (b*u*ry), and *ue* (g*ue*st).

§ **16.** (7.) The sound of *i* in *ill* (short *i*, marked ĭ).

This sound has been considered by many writers to be an extremely shortened form of *e* in *me* (No. 4, § 13); but by Rush, Bell, Ellis, and Goodrich, it is regarded as a distinct element. Bell remarks: "The shortest utterance of *e* [in *me*] will be a distinctly different sound from this [short *ĭ*]. . . . There is no longer form of this vowel [*ĭ*] in English, than that of the word *hinge*; but the prolongation of the sound is, of course, quite practicable. . . . The tendency of all vowels is to open in prolongation; but 'short *i*' is more open than *e*, and would not, therefore, naturally be lengthened into *e*. On the contrary, if any person, guided by his ears, and not by preconceived classifications, strive to lengthen the generally short vowel *i*, as in *vision*, *him*, *ill*, &c., he will find that the tendency of the prolonged sound will be towards *a* [in *ale*] rather than *e* [in *me*]. This may be well tested by singing the words to long notes." Ellis notices the fact "that almost all English orthoëpists, as Walker, Smart, and Worcester, confound [long] *e* and [short] *i*, in unaccented syllables."

This sound is represented by *i*, and also by *e* (pr*e*tty), *eau* (b*eau*fin), *ee* (b*ee*n), *ie* (s*ie*ve), *o* (w*o*men), *u* (b*u*sy), *ui* (g*ui*lt), and *y* (m*y*th).

§ **17.** (8.) The sound of *o* in *orb* (or of *aw* in *awl*, or of *a* in *fall*, called broad *a*, or German *a*, marked *ȧ*).

This sound is represented by *o* (before *r*), and also by *a* (f*a*ll), *ao* (extr*ao*rdinary), *au* (h*au*l), *aw* (*aw*l), *awe* (*awe*), *eo* (g*eo*rgic), *oa* (br*oa*d), and *ou* (*ou*ght).

§ **18.** (9.) The sound of *o* in *on* (short *o*, marked *ŏ*).

This sound is the shortened form of *o* in *orb* (No. 8, § 17).

It is represented by *o*, and also by *a* (w*a*sh), *ou* (c*ou*gh), and *ow* (kn*ow*ledge).

NOTE.—According to the marking of most orthoëpists, this short sound of *o* occurs before the sound of *f*, *s*, or *th* in the same syllable (as in *off*, *cough*, *soft*, *cross*, *cost*, *broth*), though some authorities give to *o* in this situation its broad sound of *o* in *orb* (the same as that of *aw* in *awl*, No. 8, § 17). In regard to the pronunciation of words of this class, Smart remarks that "a medium between the extremes is the practice of the best speakers." Worcester observes that "this sound [*ŏ*] is somewhat prolonged also in *gone* and *begone*, and in some words ending in *ng*, as, *long*, *along*, *prong*, *song*, *strong*, *thong*, *throng*, *wrong*."

§ **19.** (10.) The sound of *oo* in *food*.

This sound is represented by *oo*, and also by *eu* (rh*eu*matism), *ew* (br*ew*), *o* (d*o*), *oe* (sh*oe*), *œu* (man*œu*vre), *ou* (s*ou*p), *u* (r*u*le), *ue* (tr*ue*), and *ui* (fr*ui*t); the digraphs *eu*, *ew*, *ue*, and *ui*, having this sound when that of *r* immediately precedes them, and the vowel *u* having this sound when it is immediately preceded by that of *r*, and followed by a consonant and a silent *e* final, or when it is immediately preceded by the sound of *sh* (*su*re).

§ **20.** (11.) The sound of *oo* in *foot* (marked ŏŏ).

This sound is the shortened form of *oo* in *food* (No. 10, § 19).

It is represented by *oo*, and also by *o* (w*o*lf), *ou* (c*ou*ld), and *u* (f*u*ll).

§ **21.** (12.) The sound of *u* in *urn* (called the *natural vowel*).

This sound is heard only before that of *smooth r* (No. 40, § 49). By most orthoëpists it is not distinguished from the sound of *u* in *up* (No. 13, § 22).

It is represented by *u*, and also by *o* (w*o*rk), and *ou* (j*ou*rnal); the vowel *u* having this sound before *r* in a monosyllable or an accented syllable of some words and in their derivatives (as in *fur*, *fur'ry*, *in-cur'*, *in-cur'ring*); but when *u* comes before *r* in an accented syllable of a word not a derivative, and is followed by another *r*, in the next syllable, it has its short sound; as in *cur'ry*, *hur'ry*.

NOTE. — According to the common practice in the United States, the sound of *u* in *urn* is represented also in monosyllables, and in accented syllables, before *r* (when not occurring before another *r*, in a word not a derivative, as in *mer'ry*, or before a vowel, in the next syllable, as in *mer'it*), by *e* (t*e*rm, s*e*r'vant, de-f*e*r', de-f*e*r'ring), by *ea* (*ea*rth, *ea*r'ly), by *i* (g*i*rl, *i*rk'some, st*i*r'ring), and by *y* (m*y*rrh, m*y*r'tle). But the best English speakers give a somewhat different sound to the vowels *e*, *i*, and *y*, and the digraph *ea*, when they occur before *r*, as stated above. Sheridan, Walker, Knowles, and some other writers, erroneously identify this peculiar English sound with that of *e* in *then* (No. 6, § 15). Goodrich considers it as intermediate between the sound of *e* in *then*, and that of *u* in *up* (No. 13, § 22), or rather of *u* in *urn* (No. 12, § 21), which is merely a lengthened quantity of *u* in *up*. "In a correct pronunciation," he says, "the organs are placed in a position for forming the short *e*, and then open instantly (as the sound begins to form) into the short *u* [or the *u* in *urn*], thus making (as Smart observes) 'a *compromise* between the two.'" Smart speaks of this peculiarity of English pronunciation as a delicacy which prevails only in the more refined classes of society. "Even in these classes," he says, "*sur*, *durt*, *burd*, &c., are the current pronunciation of *sir*, *dirt*, *bird*, &c.; and, indeed, in all very common words it would be somewhat affected to insist on the delicacy referred to." "It is only very careful speakers," says Ellis, "who make this distinction; and only a very small minority of those who do make it at all, keep up the distinction in unaccented syllables." In the opinion of Worcester, "there is little or no difference" in the vowel sounds of such words as *her*, *earn*, *fir*, *fur*, *myrrh*; and Spurrell says that "the distinction, if any, is so slight that writers of the best authority disregard it." — See No. 40, § 49.

§ **22.** (13.) The sound of *u* in *up* (short *u*, marked *ŭ*).

This sound is the shortened form of *u* in *urn* (No. 12, § 21).

It is represented by *u*, and also by *o* (s*o*n), *oe* (d*oe*s), *oo* (bl*oo*d), and *ou* (t*ou*ch). — See § 21.

2. Compound Vowel Sounds.

§ **23.** (14.) The sound of *a* in *ale* (long *a*, marked *ā*).

This sound is generally regarded by English orthoëpists as a simple element; but Rush, Smart, Goodrich, Bell, Spurrell, and some other writers regard it as ending in a brief sound of *e* in *me* (No. 4, § 13). Spurrell, moreover, considers its initial or radical part to be the sound of the first *e* in *there* (No. 5, § 14). Bell remarks that the omission of the "vanishing sound" of *ē* is "a marked provincialism, and is one of the leading features of the Scottish dialect." Ellis, on the contrary, asserts that the addition of this vanishing sound "is a peculiarly English mispronunciation," and maintains that the vowel should be "kept pure"; though he admits that "it is very common to let it glide almost imperceptibly into the distinctive vowel *e*."

This sound is represented by *a*, and also by *ai* (*ai*m), *ao* (g*ao*l), *au* (g*au*ge), *ay* (d*ay*), *aye* (*aye*), *ea* (gr*ea*t), *ei* (v*ei*l), and *ey* (th*ey*).

§ **24.** (15.) The sound of *o* in *old* (long *o*, marked *ō*).

This sound is regarded by some writers as simple, by others as ending in a slight sound of *oo* in *food* (No. 10, § 19). The former view is that taken by Walker, Ellis, and most other writers; the latter that adopted by Rush, Smart, Bell, Russell, Spurrell, Goodrich, and others. Ellis allows that the sound of *o* is often made to taper off into that of *oo*, but this practice he characterizes as an error. Bell, on the other hand, remarks that "with less or more distinctness, its compound quality should be heard in every combination, in careful reading." Smart and Goodrich observe that the final *oo* sound is omitted in unaccented syllables; as in *o*-pin′ion, to-bac′*co*, fel′l*ow*.

It is a very common practice, in the United States, to shorten the sound of long *o* in some words, chiefly, if not exclusively, the following: *boat, bolster, bolt, bone, both, broke, broken, choke, cloak, close* (the adjective), *coach, coat, colt, comb, dolt, holster, home, homely, hope, jolt, load, molten, moult, only, open, poultice, road, rode, rogue, smoke, spoke, spoken, stone, throat, toad, upholsterer, whole, wholly, wholesome, wrote.* The effect thus produced is due, in the opinion of Goodrich, to the omission of the brief sound of *oo*, which should properly be preserved. The shortening of long *o* in the words here enumerated, is contrary to English usage, and is not sanctioned by any orthoëpist.

This sound is represented by *o*, and also by *au* (h*au*tboy), *eau* (b*eau*), *eo* (y*eo*man), *ew* (s*ew*), *oa* (*oa*k), *oe* (f*oe*), *oo* (br*ōō*ch), *ou* (s*ou*l), *ow* (sn*ow*), *owe* (*owe*).

§ **25.** (16.) The sound of *i* in *time* (long *i*, marked ī).

With regard to the composition of this sound, considerable difference of opinion exists. Some writers, as Smart, consider it to be compounded of *u* in *urn* (No. 12, § 21) and *e* in *me* (No. 4, § 13). Ellis resolves it into *a* in *and* (No. 1, § 10) and *i* in *ill* (No. 7, § 16). But Walker, Bell, and most other orthoëpists maintain that it is composed of *a* in *far* (No. 2, § 11) and *e* in *me* (No. 4, § 13).

It is represented by *i*, and also by *ai* (*ai*sle), *ei* (h*ei*ght), *ey* (*ey*ing), *eye* (*eye*), *ie* (t*ie*), *ui* (g*ui*de), *uy* (b*uy*), *y* (b*y*), and *ye* (r*ye*).

§ **26.** (17.) The sound of *u* in *use, cube* (long *u*, marked ū).

All orthoëpists, except Webster, agree that this sound terminates in the sound of *oo* in *food* (No. 10, § 19), and a majority of them agree that, when it begins a word or a syllable, its initial element is the sound of consonant *y*, being equivalent, in that case, to the syllable *yoo*. As to its composition when it follows a consonant in the same syllable, there is a difference of opinion, some writers, as Smart, Bell, and Goodrich, considering that its initial element remains, as before, the sound of consonant *y* slightly uttered, and others, as Walker and Spurrell, that it is rather the sound of long *e*. The former orthoëpists, however, admit that the initial element *y* is heard less distinctly after some consonants, as *j* and *l* (*jew, lute*), than after others, as *c* and *m* (*cube, mute*). Smart describes the sound which is properly heard as the initial element of long *u* after *j* and *l*, as "a slight semi-consonant sound [noted in his Dictionary by an apostrophe (')] between ĕ [shortened quantity of ē] and *y* consonant, — a sound so short and slight as to be lost altogether in the mouth of an unpolished speaker, who says *loot, joo*, &c., for *l'oot, j'oo*, &c." "On the other hand," he adds, "there are persons who, to distinguish themselves from the vulgar, pronounce *y* consonant distinctly on the occasions which call for this slighter sound. . . . To say *lūte, lū'cid, lū'natic*, with the *u* as perfect [i. e. with the consonant element *y* as distinct] as in *cūbe, cū'bic*, is Northern or laboriously pedantic in effect; and the practice of good society is *l'oot, l'oo'cid, l'oo'na-tic*, &c.; avoiding, at the same time, the vulgar extreme *loot, loo'cid, loo'na-tic*, &c." It is, perhaps, not of much practical importance whether the initial element of long *u*, after a consonant, be considered as the sound of consonant *y* or as that of the vowel ē, since, in either case, it is only slightly pronounced, and, especially, since these sounds are nearly alike in their organic formation. (See No. 42, § 51.) It is more important to observe that the compound sound of long *u* is not properly heard after the sound of either *r*, *ch*, or *sh*, the letter *u* taking, when so situated, the simple sound of *oo* in *food*, or in *foot*. The words *rule, truth, chew, sure, sugar*, for example, should be pronounced *rool, trooth, choo, shoor, shŏŏg'ar*.

According to Webster, the sound of long *u*, when it follows a consonant in the same syllable, is not compound, but a distinct and simple element. "Dr. Webster," says Goodrich, "did not consider it to be diphthongal, except at the commencement of a syllable, as in *unite*. In all other cases, he regarded our long *u* as a distinct elementary sound."

The sound of long *u* is represented by *u*, and also by *eau* (b*eau*ty), *eo* (feodal), *eu* (f*eu*d), *ew* (f*ew*), *ewe* (*ewe*), *ieu* (l*ieu*), *iew* (v*iew*), *ue* (d*ue*), *ui* (s*ui*t), *yew* (*yew*), *you* (*you*th), and *yu* (*yu*le).

§ **27.** (18.) The sound of *oi* in *oil*.

This sound is compounded, according to Smart, Bell, Spurrell, and most orthoëpists, of that of *o* in *orb* (No. 8, § 17), and that of *e* in *me* (No. 4, § 13). Some writers, as Walker and Worcester, consider its final element to be the sound of *i* in *ill*, which, however, they regard as only a shortened quantity of long ē. — See No. 7, § 16.

It is represented by *oi*, and also by *oy* (b*oy*), and *eoi* (burg*eoi*s).

§ **28.** (19.) The sound of *ou* in *ounce*.

The final element in this compound sound, as all orthoëpists agree, is the sound of *oo* in *food* (No. 10, § 19), or its shortened form in *foot* (No. 11, § 20); and most writers, as Smart, Bell, Spurrell, and others, consider its initial element to be the sound of *a* in *far* (No. 2, § 11). But, according to Walker and Worcester, its initial element is the sound of *o* in *orb* (No. 8, § 17); according to Russell, the sound of *u* in *up* (No. 13, § 22); and, according to Ellis, the sound of *a* in *and* (No. 1, § 10), or of *u* in *up* (No. 13, § 22). Bell characterizes the combination *ŭ-oo* as peculiar to Scotland.

This sound is represented by *ou*, and also by *ow* (n*ow*), and *eo* (Macl*eo*d).

NOTE A. — The preceding vowel sounds may be arranged in such a manner as to show their organic relation to each other. We may consider them as forming two series extending (1) from the palate to the throat, and (2) from the throat to the lips. The vowels which derive their characteristic quality from the influence of the pharynx and posterior part of the mouth may be termed *guttural* (L. *guttur*, the throat); those which receive their peculiar modification from the gradual elevation of the tongue towards the palate may be termed *palatal*; and those which are due, in some measure, to the position of the lips, may be termed *labial*. The following diagram will make this classification more evident. It will be observed that the short forms of some of the vowels, namely, *oo* in *foot* (ŏŏ), *o* in *on* (ŏ), *u* in *up* (ŭ), *a* in *fast* (ȧ), *e* in *then* (ĕ), — shortened forms respectively of *oo* in *food* (oo), *o* in *orb* or *a* in *all* (â), *u* in *urn* (uh), *a* in *far* (ä), and *e* in *there* (ê), — are not represented, regard being had to the *quality* of the sounds, rather than to simple differences of *quantity*. The vowels ă (No. 14, § 23) and ŏ (No. 15, § 24) are included in this scheme, because, in foreign languages, they represent simple sounds, and because they are considered to do so, in English also, by many orthoëpists of high authority.

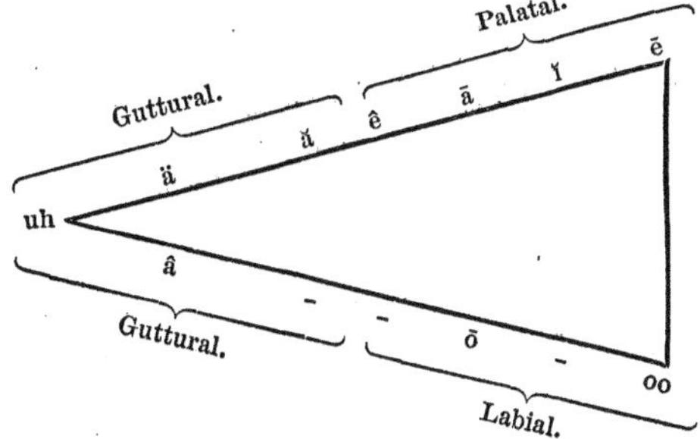

3. Aspirate Sound.

§ **29.** (20.) The sound of *h* in *home*.

As no contact of the articulating organs is necessary for the formation of this elementary sound, it is clearly distinguished from the consonants. It is a mere aspiration, or, as Bell describes it, "simply a breathing of the vowels"; and, in forming it, "the organs," he says, "are adjusted to the vowel position before the breathing of *h* is emitted."

It is always represented by *h*.

4. Consonant Sounds.

§ **30.** (21.) The sound of *p* in *pet*.

This sound is formed by a firm contact of the edges of both lips, and a compression of the breath within the mouth and pharynx, followed by a sudden separation of the lips, allowing the compressed breath to escape. — See Rem. 2, p. 34.

It is represented by *p*, and also by *ph* (di*ph*thong), *gh* (hiccou*gh*), and *pp* (ste*pp*e).

§ **31.** (22.) The sound of *b* in *bet*.

This sound differs in the mode of its formation from that of *p* in *pet* only in a slighter contact of the edges of the lips, and in the compression of the *voice*, instead of simple *breath*, within the mouth and pharynx, causing a muffled sound or murmur to precede the separation of the lips. — See Rem. 2, p. 34.

It is represented by *b*, and also by *bb* (e*bb*).

§ **32.** (23.) The sound of *m* in *man*.

In the production of this sound, the lips are closed as for *b*, but the nasal passages are uncovered, and the voice, instead of being compressed within the mouth and pharynx, flows continuously through the nostrils. — See Rem. 1, p. 34.

It is represented by *m*, and also by *mm* (ra*mm*ed).

§ **33.** (24.) The sound of *wh* in *when*.

In the digraph *wh*, the *h* is regarded by many orthoëpists as representing a simple aspiration preceding the sound of *w*, as if the letters *wh* were written, according to the original Anglo-Saxon mode, *hw*. But by Rush, Ellis, Bell, Spurrell, and some other recent writers of high authority, this digraph is regarded, with good reason, as representing a simple elementary sound which consists of a mere emission of breath when the lips have been placed in a position to sound *w* (No. 25, § 34), the voice not being heard till the following vowel is commenced. "We doubt not," says Dr. D. R. Goodwin, "that, if a man will observe carefully for himself how and with what difference he pronounces *wit* and *whit*, he will be satisfied that the *h* is really pronounced neither before nor after the *w*, but in a sort of constant combination with it. Whether the *h*, therefore, should be printed before or after the *w*, is a matter of indifference, except so far as consistency in the notation of a given alphabet is concerned. *Wh* is certainly the most consistent with the rest of the English alphabet." Upon this subject, Bell remarks: "This element [*wh*] is a whispered form of *w*. In its formation, the lips are closely approximated, and then rapidly separated: the breath is not obstructed."

This sound is always represented by *wh*.

§ **34.** (25.) The sound of *w* in *wen*.

This sound nearly resembles that of *oo* in *food* (No. 10, § 19), and by some writers, as Lowth, Webster, and Latham, is considered identical with it. But in forming it the lips are more closely approximated than for the sound of *oo*. Besides, it is to be observed that the sound of *w* occurs in some words before the sound of *oo* in the same syllable, as in *woof*, *wood*; and it is generally admitted that two and the same vowel sounds cannot occur in succession without forming two syllables. "This letter [*w*]," says Bell, "has been called a vowel by some orthoëpists, by others a consonant, and by others both. When before a vowel, it is unquestionably an articulation [or consonant]; and when in other situations, it is either a redundant letter, as in *flow*, or merely an auxiliary mark to make up the writing of some sound which has no fixed simple symbol." Smart remarks in regard to *w*, when it occurs before a vowel, that it "is a consonant having for its basis the most contracted of the vowel sounds, namely *oo*, which sound, being partially obstructed by an inward action of the lips, and then given off by an outward action, is changed from a vowel to a consonant." — See No. 42, § 51.

This sound is represented by *w*, at the beginning of a word or a syllable, and also by *u*, when *q* precedes it (q*u*it), and, in some words, by *u*, when *g* or *s* precedes it (ang*u*ish, pers*u*ade).

§ **35.** (26.) The sound of *f* in *feel.*

This sound is formed by placing the under lip against the edges of the upper front-teeth, so as partially to intercept the passing of the breath.

It is represented by *f*, and also by *ff* (sti*ff*), *gh* (lau*gh*), and *ph* (syl*ph*).

§ **36.** (27.) The sound of *v* in *veal.*

The formation of this sound differs from that of *f* in *feel* only in the substitution of *voice* for *breath.*

It is represented by *v*, and also by *f* (in the word o*f*, only), and by *ph* (in the proper name Ste*ph*en).

§ **37.** (28.) The sound of *th* in *thin.*

This sound is produced by placing the tip of the tongue against the inner surface of the upper front-teeth, while the breath escapes over the sides of the forepart of the tongue.

It is always represented by *th.*

§ **38.** (29.) The sound of *th* in *this* (marked t͟h).

The distinction between this sound and that of *th* in *thin* consists only in the substitution of *voice* for *breath*, producing a spoken instead of a whispered articulation.

It is always represented by *th.*

§ **39.** (30.) The sound of *s* in *seal.*

In the formation of this sound, the tip of the tongue is rounded and brought near the upper front-teeth, while its sides are pressed firmly against the inner surface of the upper side-teeth, leaving a very narrow channel for the passing of the breath.

It is represented by *s*, and also by *ss* (gra*ss*), by *c* (called *soft c*) before *e*, *i*, or *y* in the same syllable (*c*ent, ni*c*e, *c*ite, *c*yst), or between two vowels the second of which is *e*, *i*, or *y* (ra*c*er, fa*c*ile, spi*c*y); and also by *z* when it follows the sound of *t* (walt*z*). — See NOTE C, p. 34.

NOTE. — The sound of *s*, combined with that of *k* before it, is represented, in some words, by *x*, as in wa*x* (pronounced wa*ks*). — See § 40, NOTE, and § 52, NOTE.

§ **40.** (31.) The sound of *z* in *zeal.*

To form this element, it is necessary only to place the tongue in the proper position for making the sound of *s*, and allow the passing of *voice* instead of *breath.*

It is represented by *z*, and also by *zz* (bu*zz*), *c* (suffi*c*e), *s* (ha*s*), *sc* (dis*c*ern), *ss* (hu*ss*ar), and, at the beginning of words, by *x* (Xenophon).

NOTE. — The sound of *z* in *zeal*, combined with that of *g* in *go* preceding it, is represented by *x* at the end of a syllable, in some words, before an accented syllable beginning with a vowel, as in e*x*-act′ (e*gz*-act′), lu*x*-u′ri-ous (lu*gz*-u′ri-ous). It is also represented by *x*, immediately after the sound of *ng*, in the word an*x*-i′e-ty (an*g*-*zi*′e-ty). — See § 39, NOTE, and § 52, NOTE.

§ **41.** (32.) The sound of *t* in *tale*.

This sound is produced by placing the margin of the forepart of the tongue firmly against the inside of the upper teeth, so as perfectly to obstruct the breath, till, by continued pressure, it removes some part of the obstructing edge, and thus escapes. — See REM. 2, p. 34.

It is represented by *t*, and also by *tt* (bu*tt*), by *d* (looke*d*, pronounced look*t*. — See NOTE C, p. 34), and by *th* (*th*yme).

§ **42.** (33.) The sound of *d* in *dale*.

This element differs from that of *t* in *tale*, just as *b* does from *p*; that is to say, *voice* instead of *breath* is compressed within the mouth and pharynx, while the organs remain in the same position as for *t*. — See REM. 2, p. 34.

It is represented by *d*, and also by *dd* (o*dd*).

§ **43.** (34.) The sound of *n* in *name*.

In the formation of this element, the tongue is placed in the same position as for *t* and *d*, but the nasal passages are uncovered, and the voice, instead of being compressed within the mouth and pharynx, passes freely through the nostrils. — See REM. 1, p. 34.

It is represented by *n*, and also by *nn* (i*nn*).

§ **44.** (35.) The sound of *ch* in *church*.

This sound has been regarded by most orthoëpists as compounded of the sound of *t* and that of *sh*. But this view seems not to be correct. "It is produced," says Goodwin, "by placing a certain portion of the tongue near the tip, but not the tip itself, against a certain part of the palate, and, after pressure, suddenly withdrawing it with a violent emission of breath. It has no *t*-sound in its composition, for neither the tip of the tongue nor the teeth are used in its production. Neither does it end in an *sh*-sound; for, in that case, it could be prolonged *ad libitum*, which the true English *ch* cannot be. Moreover, it does not begin with any one sound and end with another, but is the same simple sound throughout its whole extent."

It is represented by *ch*, and also by *tch* (la*tch*). — See NOTE D, p. 37.

NOTE 1. — When the aspirate sound represented by *t* immediately precedes, in an accented syllable, the sound of consonant *y* (as represented in long *u*, or by one of the letters *e*, *i*) in the next syllable, the two sounds are apt to be exchanged for the similar aspirate sound represented by *ch*, as in the words *nat'ure* (năt'yur), *right'eous* (rīt'yus), *Christ'ian* (Christ'yan), which are often pronounced, and, according to some orthoepists, correctly pronounced, *na'chur*, *ri'chus*, *Chris'chan*. This substitution of *ch* for *t-y*, is due to the difficulty with which, in rapid utterance, the tongue passes from its position in sounding *t* (with the margin of the forepart against the inside of the upper teeth) to its position in sounding *y* (being raised toward the hard palate and dilated against the upper side-teeth), and the greater ease with which it assumes the intermediate position necessary for sounding *ch* (with its upper surface, near the tip, against the upper part of the hard palate). — See § 45, NOTE; § 46, NOTE 2; and § 47, NOTE.

NOTE 2. — When the digraph *ch* is preceded by *l* or *n*, as in bel*ch*, ben*ch*, fil*ch*, fin*ch*, it is marked with the sound of *sh* by Walker and some other orthoëpists, as if pronounced bel*sh*, ben*sh*, fil*sh*, fin*sh*; but by Smart, Worcester, Webster, Goodrich, and most other authorities, the regular sound of *ch* in *church* is given to words of this class.

§ **45.** (36.) The sound of *j* in *just*.

This sound is produced in the same way as that of *ch*, and differs from it only in being vocal instead of aspirate. It has been regarded by most orthoëpists as compounded of the sound of *d* in *dale* (No. 33, § 42), and that of *z* in *azure* (No. 38, § 47). But "it may be shown," says Goodwin, "by a similar experiment and proof [referring to his remark, above quoted, in regard to the sound of *ch*] that *j* is a simple elementary sound."

It is represented by *j*, and also by *ch* (sandwi*ch*), *dg* (ju*dg*ment), *di* (sol*di*er), *g* (called *soft g*) before *e*, *i*, and *y* (*g*em, a*g*e, *g*ibe, le*g*ion, *g*yve), and by *gg* (exa*gg*erate).

NOTE. — When the vocal sound represented by *d* immediately precedes, in an accented syllable, the sound of consonant *y* in the next syllable, the two sounds are apt to be exchanged for the similar vocal sound represented by *j*, for the same reason that the sounds of *t* and *y*, when so situated, are apt to be exchanged for the corresponding aspirate sound represented by *ch*; as in the word *grand'eur* (grand'yur), which is often pronounced, and, according to Walker, rightly pronounced, *gran'jur*. So the word *soldier* may be supposed to have been originally pronounced *sold'yur*, and, for the reason indicated, to have subsequently taken the pronunciation *sōl'jur*, as at present sanctioned by all the orthoëpists. — See § 44, NOTE 1; § 46, NOTE 2; and § 47, NOTE.

§ **46.** (37.) The sound of *sh* in *shall.*

This sound is produced by drawing the tip of the tongue inward from the position it takes to sound *s* in *seal* (No. 30, § 39), slightly enlarging the aperture through which the breath issues, while, at the same time, the middle of the tongue rises within the arch of the palate.

It is represented by *sh*, and also by *c* (acacia); by *ce, ci, se, si, sci, ti,* before a vowel in a syllable following an accented syllable (o'*ce*an, so'*ci*al, nau'*se*ous, pen'*si*on, con'*sci*ence, ac'*ti*on), by *s* before *e* or *u* (nau'*s*e-a, *s*u'gar, in-*s*ure'), by *sch* (*sch*ist), and by *ch*, especially in words derived from the French (*ch*aise, *ch*a-rade', av'a-lan*ch*e).

NOTE 1. — The sound of *sh* in *shall* (No. 37, § 46), combined with that of *k* in *kill* preceding it (No. 43, § 52), is represented by *x* in the words an*x*'ious, no*x*'ious (angk-*sh*us, nok-*sh*us), and their derivatives. — See § 40, NOTE, and § 52, NOTE.

NOTE 2. — It is suggested by Smart, Latham, Ellis, and others, that the sound of *sh* may have replaced, in many words, the sounds of *s* and consonant *y*, in the same manner, and for the same reason, that *ch* tends to replace *t* and *y*. Thus, the words *noxious, ocean, social, notion, sure,* may have been originally pronounced *noks'yus, ōs'yan, sōs'yal, nōs'yun, syoor,* and subsequently have come to be pronounced, as at present, *nok'shus, o'shan, so'shal, no'shun, shoor.* — See § 44, NOTE 1, § 45, NOTE, and § 47, NOTE.

§ **47.** (38.) The sound of *z* in *azure* (indicated by *zh*).

This sound differs from the preceding in a manner analogous to the difference between the sounds of *s* and *z*. (See No. 30, § 39, and No. 31, § 40.) It is never found at the beginning, or at the end, of any purely English word.

It is represented by *z*, and also by *si, ti, zi* before a vowel in a syllable following an accented syllable (fu'*si*on, tran-si'*ti*on, gla'*zi*er), by *g* (rou*g*e), and by *s* (mea'*s*ure, u'*s*u-al).

NOTE. — It is suggested by Smart, Latham, Ellis, and others, that the sound of *zh* may have replaced, in all English words, the sounds of *z* and consonant *y* (the former occurring in an accented syllable immediately before the latter in the next syllable), in the same manner, and for the same reason, that *j* tends to replace *d* and *y*, when so situated. Thus, the words *brazier, glazier, pleasure, vision,* may have been originally pronounced *brāz'yur, glāz'yur, plez'yur, viz'yun,* and subsequently have come to be pronounced, as at present, *bra'zhur*, *gla'zhur*, *plezh'ur*, *vizh'un*. — See § 44, NOTE 1; § 45, NOTE; and § 46, NOTE 2.

§ **48.** (39.) The sound of *r* in *roam*, *florid* (called *trilled r*, or *rough r*).

This sound is produced by a more or less forcible vibration of the tip of the tongue against the inner gum of the upper teeth. It occurs only before vowels, or between two vowels of which the first is short, and is thus distinguished from the sound of *r* in *nor*, *sort* (No. 40, § 49). — See REM. 1, p. 34; see also § 66.

It is always represented by *r*.

§ **49.** (40.) The sound of *r* in *nor*, *sort* (called *untrilled r*, or *smooth r*).

This sound, which occurs only after a vowel in the same syllable, is much softer than that of initial *r* (No. 39, § 48), and is regarded by all the best modern orthoëpists as a distinct element. As to its true nature and its proper position in the scale of sounds, authorities are widely at variance. By Bell it is considered to be a *vowel*. "When the tongue is so placed," says this writer, "as just to *feel* the passing stream of air, *not yield to it*, we have the condition of the *final r*. The aperture for the emission of the voice is so free that the vowel quality of the sound is scarcely — if at all — affected. . . . The formation of this vowel differs but slightly from that of vowel [*u* in *urn*, No. 12, § 21]; and the difference between these sounds is, therefore, though clearly appreciable, not very strongly marked. This leads to a confusion, on the part of ordinary speakers, of such words as *fir* and *fur*, *earn* and *urn*, &c., but the audible distinction, though slight, should always be preserved." [See § 21, NOTE.] Bell states that the visible difference between the formation of this element and that of *u* in *urn* (No. 12, § 21) is "a *slight depression* of the *posterior part of the tongue*, which directs the breath against the palate somewhat *farther back* for the latter than for the former." Ellis regards the final *r* as a consonant sound produced by a greater or less elevation of the tongue, and an indistinct or very slight vibration of the uvula; but he admits that the sound partakes so much of the nature of a vowel as to form distinct syllables. "The letter *r*," says Smart, "is sometimes a consonant, as in *ray*, *tray*, *stray*, &c., and sometimes a guttural vowel sound [i. e. when it follows a vowel, as in the terminations *ar*, *er*, *ir*, *or*, *ur, yr, are, ere, ire, ore, ure, oor, ower*]. In the former capacity, it is formed by a strong trill of the tongue against the upper gum ; in the latter case, there is no trill, but, the tongue being curled back during the progress of the vowel preceding it, the sound becomes guttural, while a slight vibration of the back part of the tongue is perceptible in the sound." This author, accordingly, speaks of the vowels, when followed by *r*, as "terminating in guttural vibration." "A vowel," he says, "terminating in this manner, according to the idiomatic pronunciation of the English language as heard in well-bred London society, is properly considered as a single, though not a simple, element [i. e. though of a com̆pound nature, going to form one and the same syllable]. . . . Of this blending of the *r* with the previous vowel, it is further to be observed that the union is so smooth, in polite utterance, as to make it imperceptible where one ends and the other begins."

Smooth *r* is represented by *r*, and also by *rr* (e*rr*).

NOTE. — It is a marked peculiarity of English usage, as stated by Smart, Bell, Ellis, and Spurrell, that the letter *r*, when it is followed by a vowel, and is, at the same time, preceded, in an accented syllable, by a long vowel or a compound vowel, has always both its final and its initial value, or, in other words, is pronounced as if it both ended the former syllable with its smooth sound and began the latter syllable with its rough, or trilled, sound. To use the language of Smart, "the *r*," in this situation, "besides blending itself with the previous vowel, is also heard [with its initial value] in the articulation of the vowel which begins the following syllable." Thus, the words *serious*, *pirate*, *tory*, *fury*, are pronounced, according to this orthoëpist, as if spelled *sēr′ri-ous*, *pīr′rate*, *tōr′ry*, *fūr′ry*. In such cases, the omission of the final or smooth *r*, in the pronunciation, is, according to him, "decidedly provincial"; and Ellis states that it is a Scottish peculiarity. Yet, in the United States, it is, in many words, — chiefly primitives, — the common practice to sound the *r*, thus situated, as if it had merely its initial value, or was united only to the following syllable; for example, the words above mentioned are here usually pronounced *sē′rious*, *pī′rate*, *tō′ry*, *fū′ry*. The best speakers in this country, however, follow the English usage in pronouncing a few primitive words of this class, as *fairy*, *parent*, *apparent*, *transparent*, and especially almost all words derived from primitives ending in the sound of smooth *r*, as *desirous* (from *desire*), *poring* (from *pore*), *sourish* (from *sour*), &c., giving the *r* both its final and its initial value; thus, *fêr′ry*, *pêr′rent*, *ap-pêr′rent*, *trans-pêr′rent*, *de-sīr′rous*, *pōr′ring*, *sour′rish*.

§ **50.** (41.) The sound of *l* in *low*.

This sound, which Smart characterizes as being "the most harmonious of the consonants," is produced by a simple contact between the tip of the tongue and the upper gum, while the sides of the tongue remain free for the continuous passage of the voice. — See REM. 1, p. 34.

It is represented by *l*, and also by *ll* (ba*ll*).

§ **51.** (42.) The sound of *y* in *yet*.

In forming this element, the tongue is raised toward the hard palate and dilated against the upper side-teeth, being placed very nearly in the same position as for the vowel *ē*, with which, by some writers, it has been confounded, as *w* has also been with *oo*. (See No. 25, § 34.) But the tongue is brought closer to the palate for *y* than for *ē*, and the aperture through which the voice passes is, in consequence, still further diminished. In relation to the sounds of *y* and *w*, Goodwin remarks: "In *yarn*, *wit*, we may give first the full sounds *ee'-arn*, *oo'-it*, where, between the initial vowel sounds, *ee*, *oo*, and the following vowel sounds, the organs pass through a certain momentary but definite position, which gives the character of a consonant sound, and which we have denominated a fulcrum or pivot. If now the vowel part, the *ee* or *oo* sound, be reduced to a minimum, and we begin immediately upon this pivot or fulcrum, and pronounce *yard*, *wit*, we shall have *y* and *w* representing sounds of a proper consonant character."

This sound is represented by *y*, when it begins a syllable before a vowel, and also by *i*, when it begins an unaccented syllable immediately following an accented syllable (*fil'ial*, *pin'ion*), and by *j* in *hallelujah*.

NOTE.—In the opinion of most orthoëpists, the sound of consonant *y* is heard as the initial element of long *u*, especially when long *u* begins a word or a syllable. According to Bell, Ellis, and Spurrell, it is also heard, in an aspirated form, before long *u* preceded by *h* at the beginning of a syllable, as in *hue*, *hu'mid*, *post'humous*, where *u*, as has been already explained (See § 26), is equivalent to *yoo*; and, in this form, it is regarded by them as a distinct element of the English language, and is represented by the digraph *yh*, which bears the same relation to *y* that *wh* bears to *w*. (See § 33). By some authorities, however, the compound sound of long *u* is, in all situations, resolved into the elements *ē-oo*, and this analysis would make *u* preceded by *h* to be equivalent in sound to *hē-oo*. As this diversity of opinion respecting the composition of long *u* affects the question of the existence, in English speech, of such a sound as *yh*, no aspirate correspondent of *y* is given in the Table of Elementary Sounds, on p. 12, but it is recognized in the tabular classification on p. 34.

§ **52.** (43.) The sound of *k* in *kill.*

This sound is formed by bringing the back of the tongue into close contact with the posterior part of the palate, and then separating it by a continued pressure of the breath. — See REM. 2, p. 34.

When the sound of *k* (or of the corresponding vocal element *g*, No. 44, § 53) precedes the sound of Italian *a* (No. 2, § 11), of long *i* (No. 16, § 25), or of *e* or *i* before *r* in certain cases (§ 21, NOTE), (as in the words *card*, *guard*, *kind*, *sky*, *guide*, *kerchief*, *girl*), many speakers suffer a very delicate and slight sound, which resembles that of *y* in *yet* (No. 42, § 51) or of *e* in *me* (No. 4, § 13), to intervene between the sound of the consonant and that of the following vowel; and this practice is sanctioned by the authority of some eminent orthoëpists, as Bell and Smart. By some speakers, a full and distinct sound of *ē* or of consonant *y* is interposed between the sound of *k* or of *g* and that of the following vowel (as *kēärd*, *ghēärd*, or *k-yard*, *gh-yard*, &c.); but this style of speech — though sanctioned by Walker as "a polite pronunciation" — is strongly condemned by the best orthoëpists at the present day. Ellis, indeed, asserts that "it is now considered better to pronounce the pure *k*, *g*," in all such words, — by which he means that neither long *e*, consonant *y*, nor any sound approximating to either of these, should be allowed to slide in between the sound of *k* or *g* and that of the succeeding vowel. The best American usage inclines to the easy and natural way of pronouncing words of this class indicated by Ellis, though some speakers go so far as to adopt the affected mode recommended by Walker.

This sound is represented by *k*, and also by *ck* at the end of a word or a syllable (do*ck*, froli*ck*-ing), by *c* at the end of a word (ar*c*), at the end of a syllable when the next syllable begins with the sound of a consonant (fla*c*′cid, he*c*′tic), and before *a*, *o*, *u*, *l*, *r*, and final *t* (*c*at, *c*ot, *c*up, *c*loud, *c*rown, a*c*t), by *kh* (*kh*an), by *q* before *u* (*qu*ail, pi*qu*e), by *cq* (la*cq*uer), by *ch* (*ch*asm, e*ch*o, bald a-*ch*in, and other words of Greek and Italian origin), and by *gh* (lou*gh*).

NOTE. — The sound of *k*, combined with that of *s* in *seal* (No. 30, § 39) following it, is represented in some words by *x*, as in wa*x* (pronounced wa*ks*). — See § 39, NOTE, and § 40, NOTE.

§ **53.** (44.) The sound of *g* in *go* (called *hard g*).

This sound is formed by the same contact of the tongue and the palate as that for the sound of *k*, with the substitution of an effort of *voice* instead of simple *breath*. — See Rem. 2, p. 34.

The views of orthoëpists respecting the pronunciation of words in which *g* precedes the sound of the Italian *a*, of long *i*, or of *e* or *i* before *r* in certain cases, are given in the preceding section, as they apply equally to words in which the corresponding aspirate element *k* precedes any one of these sounds.

This sound is represented by *g*, and also by *gg* (e*gg*), *gh* (*gh*erkin), and, in combination with the sound of *z* in *zeal* (No. 31, § 40) following it, by *x*, in certain words. — See § 39, Note, and § 40, Note.

§ **54.** (45.) The sound of *ng* in *sing*.

This sound, which never occurs at the beginning of a syllable, is related to the sound of *g* in *go* (No. 44, § 53) as that of *m* (No. 23, § 32) to that of *b* (No. 22, § 31) and as that of *n* (No. 34, § 43) to that of *d* (No 33, § 42). (See Table, p. 34.) In its formation, the back of the tongue is applied to the soft palate, but the voice, instead of being retained and compressed in the pharynx, is allowed to pass freely out of the nostrils.

It is represented by *ng*, and also by *n* before the sound of *k*, in a monosyllable (dri*n*k) or in an unaccented syllable (lar′y*n*x), and at the end of an accented syllable (except in words in which this syllable is one of the prefixes *in*, *non*, or *un*) before the sound of *k* or of hard *g* at the beginning of the next syllable (tri*n*′ket, ba*n*′quet, co*n*′cord, a*n*′gle, hu*n*′ger).

Note 1. — By Webster and Goodrich, the letters *nk* occurring in the same syllable are considered to represent "a simple elementary sound," or a sound entirely distinct from that represented by *ngk*. "It is, therefore," says the latter, "undesirable to respell such words as *sink*, *brink*, by the use of *ng* [*singk*, *bringk*]. They are not so pronounced." But this view is supported by no other authorities.

Note 2. — In most words formed by adding the terminations *er*, *ing*, *y*, &c., to primitives in which *ng* is final, the *ng* retains its simple sound; as in *hang′er* (from *hang*), *ring′ing* (from *ring*), *spring′y* (from *spring*). But in the following words of this class, the *n* alone is made to represent the sound of *ng*, while the second letter of this digraph is pronounced with the next syllable; namely, *lon′ger*, *stron′ger*, *youn′ger*, *lon′gest*, *stron′gest*, *youn′gest*, *diph-thon′gal*, *triph-thon′gal*. These words would analogically be pronounced *long'er*, *strong'er*, *young'er*, &c., and Walker states that in Ireland this is the customary pronunciation.

NOTE B. — The consonants are capable of four distinct classifications: —

1. They may be classed according to the organs by which they are formed.

Those in pronouncing which the lips are used, are called *labials*. They are *p*, *b*, *wh*, *w*, *m*.

Those in forming which the lower lip touches the upper teeth, are called *labio-dentals*. They are *f*, *v*.

Those in forming which the tongue touches the teeth, are called *dentals*. They are *th*, *t̲h̲*.

Those in pronouncing which the tongue touches the upper gum at various points between the teeth and the hard palate, may be called *dento-palatals*. They are *t*, *d*, *s*, *z*, *n*.

Those formed near the roof of the mouth are called *palatals*. They are *ch*, *j*, *sh*, *zh*, *r*- (rough, or trilled), *l*, *yh*, *y*.

Those formed in the throat are called *gutturals*. They are *k*, *g*, -*r* (smooth, or untrilled), *ng*.

2. They may be classed according to the channel through which the air from the lungs passes in pronouncing them.

Those in pronouncing which the air passes through the mouth, are *oral* consonants. They are *p*, *b*, *t*, *d*, *ch*, *j*, *k*, *g*, *wh*, *w*, *f*, *v*, *th*, *t̲h̲*, *s*, *z*, *sh*, *zh*, *r*- (rough, or trilled), *l*, *yh*, *y*, -*r* (smooth, or untrilled).

Those in pronouncing which the air passes through the nose, are *nasal* consonants. They are *m*, *n*, *ng*.

3. They may be classed according to the manner in which they are pronounced.

Those which are incapable of being pronounced continuously, the air being first stopped in its passage, and then issuing with a sort of burst, may be called *explosive* consonants. They are *p*, *b*, *t*, *d*, *ch*, *j*, *k*, *g*.

Those in pronouncing which the air passes continuously may be called *continuous* consonants. Most of them have more or less of a hissing or buzzing sound. They are *wh*, *w*, *f*, *v*, *th*, *t̲h̲*, *s*, *z*, *sh*, *zh*, *r*- (rough, or trilled), *l*, *yh*, *y*, -*r* (smooth, or untrilled).

4. The consonants may again be classed into those which are formed without any vibration of the vocal chords, and those which are formed with a vibration of these chords; that is, those in which the whisper, or pure breath alone (§ 3) is heard, and those in which the voice (§ 4) is heard. They may be distinguished by applying the term *aspirate* to the former and the term *vocal* to the latter.

The *aspirate* consonants are *p*, *t*, *ch*, *k*, *wh*, *f*, *th*, *s*, *sh*, *yh*.

The *vocal* consonants are *b*, *d*, *j*, *g*, *w*, *v*, *t̲h̲*, *z*, *zh*, *r*- (rough, or trilled), *l*, *y*, -*r* (smooth, or untrilled), *m*, *n*, *ng*.

The following Table exhibits the four systems of classification at one view:—

CLASSES.		ORAL.				NASAL.	
		EXPLOSIVE.		CONTINUOUS.		CONTINUOUS.	
		Aspirate.	Vocal.	Aspirate.	Vocal.	Aspirate.	Vocal.
	Labial.	p	b	wh	w	—	m
	Labio-dental.			f	v		
Lingual.	Dental.			th	th		
	Dento-palatal.	t	d	s	z	—	n
	Palatal.	ch	j	sh	zh		
	"			—	r-		
	"			—	l		
	"			yh	y		
	Guttural.	k	g		-r	—	ng

REMARKS.—**1.** The consonant elements *l*, *m*, *n*, *r*, which are both continuous and vocal, are often called *liquids*, from their smooth and flowing sound.

2. The explosive consonants *p*, *b*, *t*, *d*, *k*, *g*, are frequently termed *mutes*. For the vocal forms *b*, *d*, *g*, the voice is heard only while the air from the lungs is compressed in the mouth and pharynx, and all sound ceases as soon as the articulating organs separate. For the aspirate forms *p*, *t*, *k*, the breath only is compressed, producing no sound till the articulating organs are separated (hence these three last consonants are termed *pure mutes*), when it issues as simple whisper, if the consonant is final, as in *up*, *at*, *eke*, or as vocalized breath, or voice, if followed by a vowel, as in *paw*, *too*, *key*.

3. The oral consonants *l* and *r*- (rough, or trilled, *r*), and the three nasal consonants *m*, *n*, and *ng*, are, in English speech, all vocal. In some languages, however, as the Welsh, *l* and *r*-have corresponding aspirates, produced by pronouncing them forcibly with the breath alone. It is possible to whisper *m*, *n*, *ng*, in like manner, but the breath passing freely through the nose, without the voice, would be both very indistinct and incapable of variation. Yet the aspirates of these sounds, though not acknowledged elements of any language, are, as Rush remarks, "constantly used before the vocality of *m* or *n* or *ng*, as the inarticulate symbol of a sneer." The vocal element -*r* (smooth, or untrilled), which, indeed, is by some writers considered to be truly a vowel, has no related aspirate whatever.—See § 49.

NOTE C.—The aspirate and vocal consonants are so related that generally two of the same class are more easily united in pronunciation than two of a different class. In English, the difficulty of pronouncing an aspirate and a vocal consonant together is so great that when they meet in a word, one is often changed from vocal to aspirate, or the reverse, to suit the sound of the other. Thus, the letter *s*, in the third person singular of verbs, and in the plural of nouns, is pronounced as *s* or as *z*, according as it is preceded by an aspirate or a vocal consonant. In the verbs *leaps*, *beats*, and the nouns *caps*, *hats*, for example, the *s* is sounded as *s* in *seal* (No. 30, § 39), because it follows an aspirate consonant; but in the verbs *robs*, *bids*, and the nouns *tubs*, *bags*, the *s* is sounded as *z* in *zeal* (No. 31, § 40), because it follows a vocal consonant. So also in the past tense and past participle of verbs, when either ends in *d* after a silent *e*, this consonant takes the sound of *t* or of *d* according as it is preceded by an aspirate or a vocal consonant. It takes the sound of *t*, for example, in *walked*, *washed*, because it follows the aspirate sounds represented by *k* and *sh*; and in *judged*, *moved*, it retains the sound of *d*, because it follows the vocal sounds represented by *j* and *v*.

The difficulty experienced in pronouncing consonants of opposite characters is much less when an aspirate follows a vocal than when it precedes it; and less after some vocal consonants than after others. The words *width*, *breadth*, &c., in which the *d* is vocal and the *th* aspirate, are easily pronounced; and such combinations as *lp* (he*lp*), *ls* (fa*ls*e), *lt* (be*lt*), *mp* (he*mp*), *ns* (o*n*ce), *nt* (we*nt*), *ngk* (i*nk*), *rs* (cu*rs*e), *rt* (ma*rt*), together with various others, are of very frequent occurrence.

III. NUMBER OF SOUNDS REPRESENTED BY THE SEVERAL LETTERS OF THE ALPHABET, OR BY COMBINATIONS OF THESE LETTERS.

The following summary includes only such of the representatives of vowel sounds as are uttered distinctly in monosyllables or in accented syllables. — See *Influence of Accent on the Vowel Sounds*, p. 40.

§ **55.** Of the vowels, *a* has 8 sounds (*a*nd, *a*le, f*a*r, f*a*st, f*a*re, f*a*ll, w*a*sh, *a*ny); *e*, 5 (m*e*, th*e*re, th*e*n, pr*e*tty, m*e*rcy); *i*, 5 (t*i*me, *i*ll, *i*rksome, rav*i*ne, fil*i*al); *o*, 9 (*o*ld, *o*rb, *o*n, d*o*, w*o*rk, s*o*n, w*o*lf, w*o*men, *o*ne); *u*, 8 (*u*se, r*u*le, *u*rn, *u*p, f*u*ll, b*u*ry, b*u*sy, q*u*it); *y*, 3 (b*y*, m*y*th, m*y*rtle).

§ **56.** Of the combinations representing vowel sounds, *æ* has 2 sounds (C*æ*sar, di*æ*resis); *ai*, 5 (*ai*m, *ai*r, s*ai*d, pl*ai*d, *ai*sle); *ao*, 2 (g*ao*l, extr*ao*rdinary); *au*, 4 (h*au*l, *au*nt, g*au*ge, h*au*tboy); *aw*, 1 sound (*aw*l); *awe*, 1 (*awe*); *ay*, 2 sounds (d*ay*, s*ay*s); *aye*,

2 (*aye*, *prayer*); *ea*, 6 (*sea*l, h*ea*d, b*ea*r, *ea*rth, gr*ea*t, h*ea*rt); *eau*, 3 (b*eau*ty, b*eau*, b*eau*fin); *ee*, 2 (s*ee*, b*ee*n); *ei*, 5 (s*ei*ze, h*ei*ght, v*ei*l, h*ei*r, h*ei*fer); *eo*, 6 (p*eo*ple, y*eo*man, l*eo*pard, g*eo*rgic, f*eo*dal, Macl*eo*d); *eoi*, 1 sound (burg*eoi*s); *eu*, 2 sounds (f*eu*d, rh*eu*matism); *ew*, 3 (br*ew*, f*ew*, s*ew*); *ewe*, 1 sound (*ewe*); *ey*, 3 sounds (th*ey*, k*ey*, *ey*ing); *eye*, 1 sound (*eye*); *ie*, 4 sounds (f*ie*ld, t*ie*, fr*ie*nd, s*ie*ve); *ieu*, 1 sound (l*ieu*); *iew*, 1 (v*iew*); *oa*, 2 sounds (*oa*k, br*oa*d); *oe*, 3 (f*oe*, d*oe*s, sh*oe*); *œ*, 2 (f*œ*tus, asaf*œ*tida); *œu*, 1 sound (man*œu*vre); *oi*, 2 sounds (*oi*l, ch*oi*r); *oo*, 4 (f*oo*d, f*oo*t, bl*oo*d, br*oo*ch); *ou*, 8 (*ou*nce, s*ou*p, s*ou*l, t*ou*ch, *ou*ght, c*ou*ld, j*ou*rnal, c*ou*gh); *ow*, 3 (n*ow*, sn*ow*, kn*ow*ledge); *owe*, 1 sound (*owe*); *oy*, 1 (b*oy*); *ua*, 1 (g*ua*rd); *uay*, 1 (q*uay*); *ue*, 3 sounds (d*ue*, tr*ue*, g*ue*st); *ui*, 4 (s*ui*t, fr*ui*t, g*ui*de, g*ui*lt); *uy*, 1 sound (b*uy*); *ye*, 1 (r*ye*); *yew*, 1 (*yew*); *you*, 1 (*you*); *yu*, 1 (*yu*le).

Remark. — The combinations *ay*, *ey*, *oy*, and *uy* should not be regarded as distinct digraphs, but simply as the forms which *ai*, *ei*, *oi*, and *ui* take respectively, when written at the end of a word, the vowel *i* not being used at the end of any word purely English.

§ **57.** Of the aspirate letter, *h*, there is but one sound (*h*ome).

§ **58.** Of the consonants, *b* has 1 sound (*b*et); *c*, 4 sounds (*c*at, *c*ent, suffi*c*e, aca*c*ia); *d*, 2 (*d*ale, looke*d*); *f*, 2 (*f*eel, o*f*); *g*, 3 (*g*o, *g*em, rou*g*e); *j*, 2 (*j*ust, hallelu*j*ah); *k*, 1 sound (*k*ill); *l*, 1 (*l*ow); *m*, 1 (*m*an); *n*, 2 sounds (*n*ame, dri*n*k); *p*, 1 sound (*p*et); *q*, 1 (*q*uail); *r*, 2 sounds (*r*oam, no*r*); *s*, 4 (*s*eal, ha*s*, *s*ugar, mea*s*ure); *t*, 1 sound (*t*ale); *v*, 1 (*v*eal); *w*, 1 (*w*en); *x*, 4 sounds (wa*x*, *X*enophon, e*x*act, an*x*ious); *y*, 1 sound (*y*et); *z*, 3 sounds (*z*eal, a*z*ure, walt*z*).

§ **59.** Of the combinations representing consonant sounds, *bb* has 1 sound (e*bb*); *ce*, 1 (o*ce*an); *ch*, 4 sounds (*ch*urch, *ch*aise, *ch*asm, sandwi*ch*); *ci*, 1 sound (so*ci*al); *ck*, 1 (do*ck*); *cq*, 1 (la*cq*uer); *dd*, 1 (a*dd*); *dg*, 1 (ju*dg*ment); *di*, 1 (sol*di*er); *ff*, 1 (sta*ff*); *gg*, 2 sounds (e*gg*, exa*gg*erate); *gh*, 3 (*gh*erkin, hiccou*gh*, lau*gh*); *kh*, 1 sound (*kh*an); *ll*, 1 (ba*ll*); *mm*, 1 (ra*mm*ed); *nn*, 1 (i*nn*); *ng*, 1 (si*ng*); *ph*, 3 sounds (*ph*rase, Ste*ph*en, di*ph*thong); *pp*, 1 sound (ste*pp*e); *rr*, 1 (e*rr*); *sc*, 1 (di*sc*ern); *sch*, 1 (*sch*ist); *sci*, 1 (con*sci*ence); *se*, 1 (nau*se*ous); *sh*, 1 (*sh*all); *si*, 2 sounds (pen*si*on, fu*si*on); *ss*, 2 sounds (gra*ss*, hu*ss*ar); *tch*, 1 sound (la*tch*); *th*, 3 sounds (*th*in, *th*is, *th*yme); *ti*, 2 (ac*ti*on, transi*ti*on); *wh*, 1 sound (*wh*en); *tt*, 1 (bu*tt*); *zz*, 1 (bu*zz*).

REMARK. — When the sound expressed by a digraph is the same as that which either of its letters is generally used to represent alone, that letter may be regarded as significant of the sound; and the other as silent. Thus, the letter having the diacritical mark in each of the digraphs *ai*, *ea*, *ie*, *oe*, *ui*, as they occur in the words *āim*, *plăid*, *sēal*, *hĕad*, *tīe*, *friĕnd*, *fōe*, *sūit*, *guīde*, may be taken to signify the vowel sound which that digraph has in those words. So also in the consonant digraphs *bb*, *ck*, *dd*, *ff*, *gg*, as they occur in the words *ebb*, *dock*, *add*, *staff*, *egg*, only one of the letters is to be taken as significant of the sound intended, the other being necessarily silent. Some digraphs, it is to be observed, express simple sounds quite different from the sound regularly expressed by either of their letters taken singly; as, *ei* in *veil*, *ey* in *they*, *th* in *thin*, *this*, *wh* in *when*, *ng* in *sing*.

NOTE D. — In some words, certain letters of the English alphabet, though not in themselves representing any sound, have an effect upon the sound of another letter that precedes any one of them in the same syllable. Thus, a silent final *e*, when it follows a single consonant, a consonant digraph, or the combined consonants *st* in a monosyllable, or an accented syllable, lengthens the preceding vowel, as in *babe*, *bathe*, *paste*, *a-bate'* (See § 163), and when it follows *c* or *g*, it gives to each its soft sound, as in *voice*, *peaceable*, *scarce*, *trance*, *stage*, *changeable*, *georgic*, *range*, *surge*. A silent final *e* also prevents the letter *s* following a liquid consonant from taking the sound of *z*, as in *else*, *nurse*, *rinse*; and it always gives to *th* its vocal sound, as in *bathe*, *breathe*, *blithe*, except in the word *withe*, in which most orthoëpists give to *th* its aspirate sound, to distinguish this word from the preposition *with*. In some words, as *browse*, *lapse*, *tease*, the final *e* appears at first sight to be useless, yet, without it, the *s* would seem to be the sign of the plural number. So the letter *k* after *c* and before *e* or *i*, as in *trafficker*, *trafficking*, the letter *u* after *c* or *g*, and the letter *h* after *g* and before *e* or *i*, as in *biscuit*, *guest*, *guide*, *gherkin*, may be regarded as mere orthographical expedients to keep the *c* or the *g* hard. In some words which have the termination *gue*, as *fugue*, *plague*, *vogue*, both *e* and *u*, though silent, have the influence referred to, the *e* serving to lengthen the vowel that precedes *g*, and the *u* serving to keep *g* hard.

In the combination *tch* used to represent the sound of *ch* in *church*, the *t* serves to prevent this sound from being changed into that of *k* (as in *ache*), or of *sh* (as in *cartouch*).

IV. SYLLABLES.

§ **60.** A syllable consists of an elementary sound or a combination of elementary sounds uttered by a single impulse of the voice, and forms either a word or a part of a word. — See § 65.

NOTE. — A word of one syllable is called a *monosyllable*; of two syllables, a *dissyllable*; of three syllables, a *trisyllable*; and of more than three syllables, a *polysyllable*.

§ **61.** Every syllable must contain at least one vowel sound, — either simple or compound, — or one liquid sound, before and after which may be placed various combinations of consonant sounds; as, *a*, *an*, *man*, *sev-en* (sev-n), *a-ble* (a-bl), *en-a-bled* (en-a-bld), *re-voked'st* (re-voktst), *plunged* (plunjd), *strength*, *twelfths*.

§ **62.** An aspirate sound cannot, alone, form a syllable.

§ **63.** Two vowel sounds cannot come together in the same syllable, unless they form a compound vowel, or diphthong (§ 6). — See § 229.

§ **64.** The consonant sounds in a syllable are arranged according to a determinate and invariable law; namely, Aspirate consonants precede vocal consonants, in beginning a syllable, and follow them in closing one; as, *fledst*, *shrunk*, *strength*.

§ **65.** In general, the closest contact, or the smallest opening, of the organs of speech that occurs in uttering any combination of elementary sounds, is a point of separation between syllables. Thus, in *priest-ly*, *joy-ous*, the consonant *t* and the final element of the diphthong *oy* (No. 18, § 27) respectively require for their enunciation a closer contact and a smaller opening of the organs than either the sounds which immediately precede or those which immediately follow; hence the voice, or vocal sound formed in the larynx (§ 4), instead of flowing freely and continuously through the throat and mouth, is more or less interrupted in its passage, and issues in the separate impulses which form the essential characteristic of syllables.

NOTE. — In one class of cases, the principle laid down in this section does not hold true. It has already been stated (§ 62) that an aspirate sound cannot, of itself, form a syllable: it follows, therefore, that such a word as *casks* consists of one syllable only, though a closer contact of the articulating organs is necessary for the sound of *k* than for that of *s*.

§ **66.** When a consonant sound, whether represented by a single letter, a double letter, or a digraph, occurs between two vowels, half of the sound belongs to one syllable and half to the other. Thus, in *hap-py*, the first syllable is ended by the closure of the lips which is necessary to form the articulation of *p*, and the next syllable begins with the opening of the lips which gives to *p* its peculiar explosive character.

NOTE.—It must be observed that, in such cases, there is but one contact of the organs of speech. The reduplication of the consonant in the written word, as in *happy*, is a mere orthographical expedient to keep the preceding vowel short, which otherwise would be liable to have a long sound given to it. But in compound words, in which one word ends with the same consonant sound as that with which the next begins (as in *book-case*, *boot-tree*, *fish-shop*), and in most derivatives having a prefix of English origin that ends, or a suffix of English origin that begins, with the same consonant sound as that with which the primitive respectively begins or ends (as in *misspell*, *outtalk*, *soulless*, *meanness*, *vilely*), though there is still but one articulation, or contact of the organs, yet, as the sound of the consonant, or the contact necessary for its formation, is dwelt upon for some little time, the final and initial effects are clearly separated, and the division of the written syllables accordingly falls between the two letters.

§ **67.** When the consonant called "the smooth *r*," which partakes largely of the nature of a vowel (See § 49), is immediately preceded by the sound of a long vowel, the combination is uttered by one impulse of the voice, and forms, or helps to form, a single syllable; as in *pair*, *hire*, *more*. If, however, the sound of "the natural vowel" (*u* in *urn*, No. 12, § 21) intervenes between the smooth *r* and a preceding vowel, it becomes impossible to avoid a double impulse of the voice, and the combination is therefore resolved into two syllables; as in *pay-er*, *high-er*, *mow-er*.

NOTE.—These doubtful combinations may obviously be made, as Smart remarks, to "pass on the ear as either one or two syllables." Hence it is important to observe that derivative words, like *payer*, *higher*, *mower* (from *pay*, *high*, *mow*), are properly pronounced as dissyllables. But primitive words, like *ewer*, *flower*, *tower*, should be pronounced, *in prose*, as monosyllables. By the poets, however, they are sometimes made to form two syllables.

☞ For the Rules which govern the division of words into syllables, in writing and printing, see pp. 76 to 79.

V. INFLUENCE OF ACCENT ON THE VOWEL SOUNDS.

§ **68.** In the English language, every word of more than one syllable is pronounced with a stress of the voice, called *accent*, upon one of its syllables, and many words, besides this primary accent, have a slighter, or secondary, accent upon another syllable or upon two other syllables. Thus, the words *cab'in*, *e-vent'*, *ar'dent*, *ob-scure'*, *va'cate*, *de-cide'*, have one accent; the words *ad''ver-tise'*, *com''pre-hend'*, *con''tra-vene'*, *ag'ri-cult''ure*, *al'a-bas''ter*, and *ol'i-gar''chy*, have two accents, one primary and one secondary; and the words *in''com-pat''i-bil'i-ty* and *in-com''pre-hen''si-bil'i-ty* have three accents, one primary and two secondary, — the mark (') being used in this Introduction to denote the primary accent, and the mark (''), to denote the secondary accent.

§ **69.** The vowel sounds are always uttered with distinctness in those syllables of a word which have an accent either primary or secondary; and they are also uttered distinctly in monosyllables, except some of the particles, as, *a*, *an*, *the*, *and*, *at*, *of*, &c., the vowel sounds of which are usually pronounced somewhat indistinctly in ordinary discourse.

§ **70.** When a syllable has no accent, its vowel sound is, in some cases, uttered distinctly, and, in others, it is pronounced with so much indefiniteness as hardly to be distinguished from some other vowel sound. Thus, the sounds of the vowels are uttered distinctly in the unaccented syllables of the following words: *ăd-vert'*, *as'pĕct*, *bī-sect'*, *bra'vō*, *cav'īl*, *clas'sĭc*, *graph'īte*, *e'păct*, *prō-vide'*, *wid'ōw*. But the sounds of the vowels *a* and *e*, and of the digraphs *ai*, *ei*, *ia*, and *ie*, in the unaccented syllables of the words *cab'bage*, *col'lege*, *fount'ain*, *for'feit*, *car'riage*, *cit'ies*, are scarcely distinguishable from the sound of *i* in the word *ves'tige*. And in the terminations *ar*, *er*, *ir*, *or*, *ur*, *yr*, of final unaccented syllables, all the vowels are sounded exactly alike; as in *dol'lar*, *mem'ber*, *na'dir*, *au'thor*, *sul'phur*, *mar'tyr*. "Unaccented sounds," says Smart, "will generally verge towards other sounds of easier utterance, and this will take place in a greater or less degree according as the pronunciation is colloquial or solemn."

§ **71.** It is obviously impossible to give precise rules for the proper sounds of the vowels in all cases when not under the accent, or to express all these sounds accurately by any system of notation. They can be learned only by the ear from the lips of good speakers. "Those who wish to pronounce elegantly," as Walker truly remarks, "must be particularly attentive to the unaccented vowels, as a neat pronunciation of these forms one of the greatest beauties of speaking." Though the ear must be chiefly trusted in attaining this accomplishment, some assistance may be derived from the following general rules and remarks drawn from writers of the highest authority upon this subject.

A in an unaccented syllable.

§ **72.** The vowel *a*, when it is final in a syllable not having an accent primary or secondary, and is followed, in the next syllable, by any consonant except *n* and *r*, or when it is at the end of a word, has the sound of *a* in *far* (Italian *a*, No. 2, § 11) somewhat shortened; as in *a-bound'*, *tra-duce'*, *ag'gra-vate*, *i-de'a*, *com'ma*. This shortened sound of the Italian *a*, as commonly uttered, resembles very nearly that of short *u* (No. 13, § 22).

When *a*, at the end of an unaccented syllable, is followed, in the next syllable, by *n* or by *r*, it has nearly the sound of short *e* (No. 6, § 15); as in *mis'cel-la-ny*, *cus'tom-a-ry*. When it is followed by a vowel in the next syllable it has the sound of long *a* (No. 14, § 23) somewhat shortened, or without its vanishing element *ē*; as in *a-e'ri-al*, *cha-ot'ic*.

When *a* is not final in an unaccented syllable, it is apt to fall into the sound of short *u* (No. 13, § 22); as in *hag'gard*, *mor'al*, *ty'rant*, *wom'an*.

When the aspirate *h* follows *a* in a final unaccented syllable, as in *Je-ho'vah*, *Mes-si'ah*, this vowel is considered by all the orthoëpists, except Worcester, to have the same sound as when final in a syllable. Worcester remarks that "*a* unaccented at the end of a word approaches the Italian sound of *a*," but adds that "*ah* final partakes still more of the Italian sound."

§ **73.** In the unaccented final syllable *ate*, the vowel *ā* has generally a shorter sound, — approaching that of short *e* (No. 6, § 15), — in adjectives and nouns than in verbs. Thus, it is shorter in *del'i-cate*, *in'tri-cate*, *pri'mate*, than in *cal'cu-late*, *ded'i-cate*, *reg'u-late*.

§ **74.** In the unaccented final syllable *ar*, the vowel *a* has the sound of *u* in *urn* (No. 12, § 21), but less prolonged; as in *dol'lar, pil'lar, schol'ar.*

E in an unaccented syllable.

§ **75.** The vowel *e*, when final in an unaccented syllable, and not silent, has the sound of *e* in *me* (No. 4, § 13), but less prolonged; as in *e-ject', ce-ment', pre-fer', ap'pe-tite, el'e-gant.*

§ **76.** The vowel *e*, in an unaccented syllable ending in a consonant, has properly, in most cases, the sound of *e* in *then* (No. 6, § 15); as in *ab'sent, e'gress, prob'lem, pre'fect*: though, in some words, it is liable to be sounded like short *i* (No. 7, § 16); as in *hel'met, du'el, box'es.*

§ **77.** In the unaccented final syllable *er*, the vowel *e* has the sound of *u* in *urn* (No. 12, § 21), but less prolonged; as in *bar'ber, of'fer, rob'ber, suf'fer.*

I in an unaccented syllable.

§ **78.** The vowel *i*, when final in an unaccented syllable that immediately follows an accented syllable, has the sound of *i* in *ill* (No. 7, § 16); as in *a-bil'i-ty, dif'fi-dent, fal'li-ble, wit'ti-cism.* — See § 16.

§ **79.** The vowel *i*, when final in an unaccented syllable that immediately precedes an accented syllable, is sometimes short, or has the sound of *i* in *ill* (No. 7, § 16); as in *di-gest', di-min'ish, fi-del'i-ty, I-tal'ian*: and sometimes it is long, or has the sound of *i* in *time* (No. 16, § 25); as in *dī-op'trics, dī-ur'nal.* In the prefixes *bi* and *tri*, it is generally long.

§ **80.** The vowel *i* in an unaccented syllable ending in a consonant is short; as in *art'ist, clas'sic, pump'kin, viv'id.*

§ **81.** The vowel *i* in the final syllable *ile*, when not under the primary accent, is generally short; as in *fer'tile, hos'tile, rep'tile, sub'tile.* It is long only in a few words; as in *e'dile, ex'ile, gen'tile, cham'o-mile, e-ol'i-pile, rec'on-cile.*

§ **82.** The vowel *i* in the final syllable *ine*, when not under the primary accent, is generally long in words accented on the antepenult; as in *as'i-nine, crys'tal-line, tur'pen-tine*: but in many words, — especially those accented on the penult, — it is short, as in *dis'ci-pline, her'o-ine, doc'trine, de-ter'mine.*

§ **83.** The vowel *i* in the final syllable *ite*, when not under the primary accent, is long in some words; as in *ac'o-nite, ap'pe-tite, par'a-site*: and in some words it is short; as in *def'i-nite, fa'vor-ite, op'po-site.*

§ **84.** The vowel *i* in the unaccented final syllable *ive* is short; as in *ac'tive, pas'sive, ad'jec-tive, gen'i-tive.*

§ **85.** In the unaccented final syllable *ir*, the vowel *i* has the sound of *u* in *urn* (No. 12, § 21), but less prolonged; as in *e-lix'ir, na'dir.*

O in an unaccented syllable.

§ **86.** The vowel *o*, when final in an unaccented syllable, has its long sound (No. 15, § 24) without the vanishing element *oo*; as in *croc'o-dile, he'ro, mot'to, o-bey', syl'lo-gism, to-bac'co, vol-ca'no.* But before the final syllables *ny* and *ry* this modified sound is so much shortened as to resemble the sound of short *u* (No. 13, § 22); as in *ac'ri-mo-ny, ter'ri-to-ry.* When not final in an unaccented syllable, it is apt to fall into the sound of short *u*; as in *big'ot, căr'ol, wan'ton.*

§ **87.** The vowel *o* in the unaccented final syllable *ogue* has its short sound (No. 9, § 18); as in *di'a-lŏgue, ep'i-lŏgue, mon'o-lŏgue, prol'ŏgue.*

§ **88.** In the unaccented final syllable *or*, the vowel *o* has, in most words, the sound of *u* in *urn* (No. 12, § 21), but less prolonged; as in *au'thor, er'ror, fer'vor, la'bor, ter'ror.* "This sound [*or* unaccented]," says Smart, "which, under the remission of accent always verges towards *ur*, in most cases sinks completely into it." "We may be justified," he adds, "in saying *ca'lor, stu'por*, &c., with that attention to the final syllable which preserves the sound; but the same care would be pedantic or puerile in *error, orator*, &c."

U in an unaccented syllable.

§ **89.** The vowel *u*, when final in an unaccented syllable, has its long sound (No. 17, § 26), and when it forms a syllable by itself, its initial element *y* is very distinctly pronounced, except when the preceding syllable ends with *r*; as in *bu-col'ic, cu-ra'tor, ed'u-cate, nat'u-ral, u-surp'.* When this vowel forms a syllable by itself and the preceding syllable ends with *r*, it has its long sound, according to Smart, with the initial element *y* very slightly pronounced; as in *er'u-dite, vĭr'u-lent.* "It is not possible," says this author, "to give the distinct sound [*yoo* to the vowel *u* so situated] without pedantic effort, and an approach to the sound signified by *'oo* is all that correct utterance requires." (See § 26.) But some writers are of the opinion that the vowel *u* in this case has the simple sound of *oo* in *food* (No. 10, § 19), precisely as it does when *r* precedes it in the same syllable.

§ **90.** The vowel *u*, when it precedes any consonant in an unaccented syllable ending with a silent *e*, except the consonant *r* in such a syllable immediately following an accented syllable, has generally its long sound (No. 17, § 26); as in *del'uge, fort'une, stat'ute, lit'er-a-ture.* The only exceptions are the words *fer'rule, let'tuce, min'ute,* in which *u* has the sound of short *i* (No. 7, § 16), and the word *ar'que-buse* (spelled also *ar'que-bus*), in which this vowel, according to most orthoëpists, has its short sound (No. 13, § 22).

§ **91.** The vowel *u*, when it precedes *r* in an unaccented syllable ending with a silent *e* and immediately following a syllable that is under the accent, primary or secondary, has a sound considered by Smart and some other orthoëpists to be identical in quality with that of long *u* (No. 17, § 26), though somewhat shortened in quantity; as in *fig'ure, ten'ure, verd'ure, ar'chi-tect''ure.* This shortened sound of long *u* resembles the shortened sound of *u* in *urn* (No. 12, § 21) with the sound of consonant *y* prefixed, except when the sound of *j, sh,* or *zh* precedes the *u*, in which case that of *y* is omitted; as in *in'jure, cen'sure, treas'ure.* The same remark applies to derivatives, although the final *e* of the syllable *ure* is omitted on adding a syllable beginning with a vowel; as in *ad-vent'ur-er, man-u-fact'ur-er, pleas'ur-a-ble.*

§ **92.** In the unaccented final syllable *ur* the vowel *u* has the sound of *u* in *urn* (No. 12, § 21), but less prolonged; as in *mur'mur, sul'phur.*

Y in an unaccented syllable.

§ **93.** The vowel *y* in an unaccented syllable, except the cases noticed in §§ 94, 95, has the sound of short *i* (No. 7, § 16); as in *a-nal'y-sis, a-poc'ry-pha, ap'a-thy, pit'y, o'nyx, phar'ynx.*

§ **94.** The vowel *y* in the unaccented final syllable *fy* of verbs has the sound of long *i* (No. 16, § 25); as in *clar'i-fy, grat'i-fy,* *pu'ri-fy, tes'ti-fy.* The vowel *y* has also the sound of long *i* in the unaccented final syllable of the following verbs; namely, *mul'ti-ply, oc'cu-py, proph'e-sy.*

§ **95.** In the unaccented final syllable *yr*, the vowel *y* has the sound of *u* in *urn* (No. 12, § 21), but less prolonged; as in *mar'tyr, zeph'yr.*

AI in an unaccented syllable.

§ **96.** The digraph *ai* in an unaccented syllable has the sound of short *i* (No. 7, § 16); as in *cap'tain, cer'tain, cur'tain, fount'ain, mount'ain.*

EI in an unaccented syllable.

§ **97.** The digraph *ei* in an unaccented syllable has the sound of short *i* (No. 7, § 16); as in *coun'ter-feit, for'eign, for'eign-er, for'feit, mul'lein, sur'feit.*

EY in an unaccented syllable.

§ **98.** The digraph *ey* in an unaccented final syllable has the sound of short *i* (No. 7, § 16); as in *al'ley, gal'ley, hon'ey, jour'ney, mon'ey, val'ley.* The noun *sur'vey* (*sur'vā*), as pronounced by most orthoëpists with the accent on the first syllable, is an exception to this rule.

IE in an unaccented syllable.

§ **99.** The digraph *ie* in an unaccented final syllable, as in the plurals of nouns ending in *y* preceded by a consonant, and in the third person singular present tense, and the imperfect tense and past participle of most of the verbs that end in *y* preceded by a consonant, has the sound of short *i* (No. 7, § 16); as in *cit'ies, du'ties, car'ries, mar'ried.* But in the third person singular present tense, and in the imperfect tense and past participle of verbs ending in *fy*, and of the verbs *multiply, occupy, prophesy,* this digraph has the sound of long *i* (No. 16, § 25).

OU in an unaccented syllable.

§ **100.** The digraph *ou* in the unaccented final syllable *ous* has the sound of *u* in *up* (No. 13, § 22); as in *cal'lous, fa'mous, em'u-lous, ob'vi-ous.*

OW in an unaccented syllable.

§ **101.** The digraph *ow* in an unaccented final syllable has the sound of long *o* (No. 15, § 24), without the vanishing element *oo*; as in *bŏr′row, fel′lōw, sŏr′row, win′dow.*

VI. SEAT OF THE ACCENT.

§ **102.** The seat of the accent in English words is governed by the following general laws or principles, of which sometimes one predominates and sometimes another.

§ **103.** Of words of two syllables, nouns and adjectives, for the most part, have the accent on the first syllable, and verbs on the second syllable. Thus, some nouns and some adjectives are distinguished from verbs of the same spelling by this difference of accent, as the following: —

Nouns.	*Verbs.*	*Adjectives.*	*Verbs.*
Ac′cent	ac-cent′	Ab′sent	ab-sent′
Con′duct	con-duct′	Com′pound	com-pound′
Con′tract	con-tract′	Con′crete	con-crete′
In′sult	in-sult′	Fre′quent	fre-quent′
Tor′ment	tor-ment′	Pres′ent	pre-sent′

§ **104.** Verbs of two or more syllables having the following endings are accented on the penult, or last syllable but one; namely, *en* (fright′en, en-light′en); *er* preceded by a consonant (al′ter, dif′fer, con-sid′er, &c., except a few ending in *fer*, as *de-fer′*, *pre-fer′*, &c., *min′is-ter*, *reg′is-ter*, and *de-ter′*); *ish* (per′ish, es-tab′lish); *om* (fath′om, ac-cus′tom); *on* (beck′on, a-ban′don); *op* (gal′lop, de-vel′op); *ry* (car′ry); *le* preceded by a consonant (am′ble, as-sem′ble, cir′cle, çur′dle, sti′fle, strug′gle, in-vei′gle, pick′le, grap′ple, bot′tle, puz′zle, &c., except a few derived from nouns or adjectives, as *ar′ti-cle, chron′i-cle, man′a-cle, quad′ru-ple*).

§ **105.** Words of more than two syllables have the primary accent, for the most part, on the antepenult, or last syllable but two, this being, as Walker expresses it, "the favorite accent of the language"; as, *dis'pu-tant, ef'flu-ence, in'dus-try, post'hu-mous, cen-trif'u-gal, cen-trip'e-tal, in-ter'po-late, mis-an'thro-py.*

§ **106.** Words derived from other words in the language generally retain the accent of their primitives. Thus, the derivatives *ser'vice-a-ble, ser'vice-a-ble-ness, hap'pi-ness, un-hap'pi-ness, mis'chiev-ous, ad'mi-ral-ty, sim'i-lar-ly,* have the accent respectively on the same syllable as the primitives *ser'vice, hap'py, mis'chief, ad'mi-ral, sim'i-lar.*

§ **107.** With regard to some words, in the accentuation of which there is at any time a diversity of usage, that mode is most likely to prevail which most favors ease of utterance. Thus, as stated by Goodrich, the mode of accentuating the words *ac'cept-a-ble, reç'ept-a-cle,* and *u'ten-sil* on the first syllable, — a pronunciation fashionable in the time of Walker, — has given place to the easier accentuation on the second syllable (*ac-cept'a-ble, re-cept'a-cle, u-ten'sil*). So, for the same reason, there is a strong tendency to transfer the accent from the first syllable of the words *an'ces-tral, dis'crep-an-cy, ex'em-pla-ry, in'ven-to-ry,* — as they are pronounced by most of the orthoëpists, — to the second syllable (*an-ces'tral, dis-crep'an-cy, ex-em'pla-ry, in-ven'to-ry*).

§ **108.** Words which have a common termination, such as *i-ble, ic-al, lo-gy, ic, tion,* &c., generally have the primary accent on the syllable which precedes this termination or which marks the limit where it begins.

Words of more than two syllables, having the following endings, take the primary accent on the antepenult, thus conforming to the general rule (§ 105); namely, *ac-al* (he-li'ac-al); *cra-cy* (de-moc'ra-cy); *e-fy* (răr'e-fy); *e-gate* (del'e-gate); *e-ous* (ex-tra'ne-ous, &c., except when the sound of *sh* or of *g soft* precedes *ous*, as in *crus-ta'ceous, cour-a'geous*); *er-al* (gen'er-al); *er-ate* (mod'er-ate); *er-ous* (gen'er-ous); *e-tude* (qui'e-tude); *e-ty* (so-ci'e-ty); *flu-ent* (af'flu-ent); *flu-ous* (su-per'flu-ous); *go-nal* (di-ag'o-nal); *go-ny* (cos-mog'o-ny); *gra-pher* (bi-og'ra-pher); *gra-phist* (chi-rog'ra-phist); *gra-phy* (ge-og'ra-phy); *i-ac* (ma'ni-ac, &c., except, according to some orthoëpists, *el-e-gi'ac*); *i-ate* (ra'di-ate); *i-ble* (cred'i-ble, &c., except *el'i-gi-ble, in-el'i-gi-ble, in-tel'li-gi-ble, cor'ri-gi-ble*); *ic-al* (log'ic-al); *i-cate* (ded'i-cate, &c., except *nid'i-fi-cate*) ; *i-cide* (hom'i-cide) ; *i-date* (can'di-date) ; *i-dence* (dif'fi-dence) ; *i-dent* (ac'ci-dent) ; *i-form* (u'ni-form) ; *i-fy* (paç'i-fy) ; *i-gate* (nav'i-gate) ; *i-late* (ven'ti-late) ; *i-mate* (an'i-mate) ; *i-ment* (con'di-ment) ; *i-nate* (cul'mi-nate) ; *i-nence* (em'i-nence) ; *i-nent* (per'ti-nent) ; *in-ous* (om'in-ous) ; *i-tant* (in-hab'i-tant) ; *i-tate* (ag'i-tate) ; *i-tive* (gen'i-tive) ; *i-ty* (a-bil'i-ty) ; *i-um* (o'di-um) ; *lo-ger* (as-trol'o-ger) ; *lo-gist* (ge-ol'o-gist) ; *lo-gy* (phi-lol'o-gy) ; *lo-quy* (col'lo-quy) ; *ma-chy* (lo-gom'a-chy) ; *ma-thy* (po-lym'a-thy) ; *me-ter* (ba-rom'e-ter) ; *me-try* (ge-om'e-try) ; *no-my* (e-con'o-my) ; *o-la* (pa-rab'o-la) ; *or-ous* (rig'or-ous, &c., except *ca-no'rous, so-no'rous*, and, according to some orthoëpists, *de-co'rous* and *in-de-co'rous*) ; *pa-rous* (o-vip'a-rous) ; *path-y* (ho-mœ-op'a-thy) ; *pho-ny* (sym'pho-ny, &c., except, according to some orthoëpists, *col'o-pho-ny*) ; *sco-py* (a-e-ros'co-py) ; *po-tent* (om-nip'o-tent) ; *so-nant* (con'so-nant) ; *stro-phe* (a-pos'tro-phe) ; *to-my* (a-nat'o-my) ; *u-al* (an'nu-al) ; *u-ence* (af'flu-ence) ; *u-ent* (con'flu-ent) ; *u-la* (neb'u-la) ; *u-lar* (sec'u-lar) ; *u-late* (cir'cu-late) ; *u-lent* (op'u-lent) ; *u-lous* (fab'u-lous) ; *u-ous* (sumpt'u-ous) ; *u-ral* (nat'u-ral) ; *u-tive* (con-sec'u-tive, &c., except *con'sti-tūt-ive*) ; *y-sis* (a-nal'y-sis).

§ **109.** Words of more than two syllables, having the following endings, take the primary accent on the penult, or last syllable but one ; namely, *ent-al* (or-na-ment'al) ; *ic* (an-gel'ic, &c., except *ag'ar-ic, Ar'a-bic, a-rith'me-tic, ar'se-nic*, the noun, *bish'-op-ric, cath'o-lic, chol'er-ic, cli-mac'ter-ic, em'pir-ic*, the noun, — as the last two are often pronounced, — *e-phem'e-ric, her'e-tic, im-pol'i-tic, lu'na-tic, pol'i-tic, rhet'o-ric, schis'mat-ic*, — as some orthoëpists pronounce the *noun*, — *splen'e-tic, tur'mer-ic*) ; *ics* (me-chan'-ics, &c., except *pol'i-tics*) ; *o-sis* (a-nas-to-mo'sis, &c., except *ap-o-the'o-sis* and *met-a-mor'pho-sis*) ; *sive* (ad-he'sive). — See § 104.

§ **110.** Of the words ending in *e-an*, some have the primary accent on the penult, as, *ad-a-man-te'an, At-lan-te'an, co-los-se'an, em-py-re'an, ep-i-cu-re'an, Eu-ro-pe'an, hy-me-ne'an, pyg-me'an* ; and some on the antepenult, as, *ce-ru'le-an, her-cu'le-an, Med-i-ter-ra'ne-an, sub-ter-ra'ne-an, tar-ta're-an.*

§ **111.** Of the words ending in *e-um*, some have the primary accent on the penult, as, *ly-ce'um, mau-so-le'um, mu-se'um* ; and some on the antepenult, as, *cas-to're-um, suc-ce-da'ne-um, per-i-os'te-um.*

§ **112.** Words the last syllable of which begins with the sound of *sh* (except when *ch* has this sound, as in *ma-chine'*), of *z* as in *a'zure* (*zh*), or of *y* consonant, constituting a very large class, have the primary accent on the penult (ab-lu'tion, ad-di'tion, ac-ces'sion, a-tro'cious, pro-vin'cial, mu-si'cian, cre-ta'ceous, ex-plo'sion, se-clu'sion, de-ci'sion, ex-pō'ure, ci-vil'ian, com-pan'ion).

§ **113.** Many words, especially scientific words derived from the Greek or the Latin with no change or only a slight change of orthography, retain the accent given to them by the rule according to which those languages are pronounced by modern scholars; namely, that words of two syllables are invariably accented on the first syllable; and that, in words of more than two syllables, if the penult is long, it is accented, but if the penult is short, the accent falls upon the antepenult. The following are examples of words which belong to this class: *a-cu'men, a-sy'lum, bi-tu'men, de-co'rum, ho-ri'zon, cat-a-chre'sis, ex-e-ge'sis, par-a-go'ge, pros-o-po-pœ'ia.* But the analogy of the English prevails over what may be termed the classical accent in many words of common occurrence; as, *au'di-tor, or'a-tor, min'is-ter, sen'a-tor.*

§ **114.** Many words derived without change of orthography from the French are accented on the last syllable; as, *an-tique', bas-tile', bour-geois', cha-teau', cor-vette', fi-nesse', gi-raffe', chev-a-lier', cui-ras-sier', gon-do-lier'.*

§ **115.** When two words, which differ only or chiefly in one of their syllables, are used antithetically, the primary accent is transferred to that syllable. Thus, the accent of the words *for-bear'ing, in-jus'tice, un-done',* is transferred to the first syllable when *for'bear-ing* is contrasted with *bear'ing, in'jus-tice* with *jus'tice, un'done* with *done.*

§ **116.** With respect to the secondary accent, Smart remarks that, though it is not indispensable, "its effect is very *generally* felt in the rhythm of the word, and still more generally in the distinctness it gives to the syllable under it." The place of this accent may, in most cases, be easily determined by the ear, when that of the primary accent is known.

§ **117.** The secondary accent is generally separated from the primary by the intervention of an unaccented syllable or of two unaccented syllables; as in *ac''ci-dent'al, căr''i-ca-ture'.* But the two accents are sometimes consecutive; as in the words *a''men'*, *co''e'qual*, *re''ech'o*, and in those with a negative prefix in the following lines: —

> And, doubly dying, shall go down
> To the vile dust from whence he sprung,
> Un''wept', un''hon'ored, and un''sung'.

§ **118.** When two words are used antithetically with respect to their prefixes or suffixes, the prefix or the suffix takes a primary accent, and the syllable which is ordinarily accented takes a secondary accent; as, *in'crease''* when opposed to *de'crease''*, *pro'ceed''* to *pre'cede''*, *im'pul''sion* to *ex'pul''sion*, *ex'te''ri-or* to *in'te''ri-or*; *de-pend''ant'* to *de-pend''ent'*, *les''see'* to *les''sor'*.

§ **119.** The accents primary and secondary sometimes change places when two words are used antithetically with respect to a syllable which ordinarily has the secondary accent; as in *prop'o-si''tion* when opposed to *prep'o-si''tion*, *al'lo-cu''tion* to *el'o-cu''tion*, *prob'a-bil''i-ty* to *plaus'i-bil''i-ty*.

VII. CLASSES OF WORDS LIABLE TO BE MISPRONOUNCED.

§ **120.** In acquiring a correct pronunciation, attention should be directed especially to such words as form exceptions to any of the general principles in regard to the seat of the accent, or to such as, being exceptional under one law, are embraced under another. It will be well to point out, also, for particular consideration, all other words or classes of words in pronouncing which errors of any kind are apt to be made.

§ **121.** Some nouns and adjectives accented on the second syllable, contrary to the principle stated in § 103, are often mispronounced; as, *ca-nine'*, *con-dign'*, *con-junct'*, *mo-rass'*, *re-cess'*, *re-search'*, *re-source'*, *ro-mance'*, *ro-bust'*, *ver-bose'*.

§ **122.** Many words of three or more syllables, not accented on the antepenult according to the principle stated in § 105, are liable to be mispronounced; as, *man-u-mit'*, *mar-mo-set'*, *mag-a-*

zine', *pan-ta-loons'*; *con-tem'plate*, *de-mon'strate*, *ex-po'nent*, *op-po'-nent*; *leg'is-lāt-ure*, *or'tho-e-py*, *per'emp-to-ry*.

§ **123.** Some derivative words are frequently mispronounced on account of not being accented like their primitives, in conformity with the principle stated in § 106; as, *chas'tise-ment*, *com'pa-ra-ble*, *dis'pu-ta-ble*, *lam'ent-a-ble*.

§ **124.** Care should be taken to discriminate by the right accent two such words as, being of the same spelling, have different meanings, or are classed under different parts of speech; as, *con'-jure* and *con-jure'*, *pre-cēd'ent* and *preç'e-dent*. — See § 103.

§ **125.** Persons unacquainted with the classical languages are apt to mispronounce such words as, being derived from these languages, retain the accent given to them in the original by scholars; as, *ag-no'men*, *al-bur'num*, *ca-no'rous*, *ly-ce'um*, *mu-se'um*. — See § 113.

§ **126.** The secondary accent is sometimes placed upon a syllable which should properly have no accent, as in *dif'fi-cul''ty*, *mem'bra''nous*, *pen'e-tra''ble*, *ter'ri-to''ry*; and sometimes it is very improperly made to change places with the primary, as in *al''a-bas'ter*, *in''ter-est'ing* (properly *al'a-bas''ter*, *in'ter-est''ing*).

§ **127.** It is a common error of pronunciation to substitute one vowel sound for another; as in saying *ăn'gel* for *ān'gel*, *crik* for *creek*, *cu'pa-lō* for *cu'po-la*, *dĕf* for *dēaf*, *jest* for *just*, *par'a-grăph* for *par'a-grȧph*, *plĕt* for *plāit*, *si'lunt* for *si'lent*, *sens* for *since*, *sŏŏn* for *soon*, *tos'sel* for *tas'sel*, *yal'ur* for *yel'lōw*, *yis* for *yes*.

§ **128.** The vowel *u*, or the digraph *ew*, when it follows the sound of *r* or of *sh*, is sometimes erroneously pronounced with the sound of long *u* (No. 17, § 26), instead of its proper sound of *oo*. Thus, the words *rule*, *true*, *shrew*, are sometimes pronounced as if they were written *r-yool*, *tr-yoo*, *shr-yoo*, or *reool*, *treoo*, *shreoo*, and not, as they should be to represent their correct pronunciation, *rool*, *troo*, *shroo*.

§ **129.** An affected pronunciation is sometimes given to *e*, *i*, and *ea* before *r*; as in saying *mêr'cy* for *mer'cy*, *sêr'vant* for *ser'vant*, *vêrt'ue* for *virt'ue*, *êarn* for *earn*, *êrth* for *earth*. — See § 21, Note.

§ **130.** The practice, common in the United States, of shortening the sound of long *o* in some words, as *coat*, *home*, *stone*, &c., is condemned by the best orthoëpists. — See § 24.

§ **131.** Particular attention should be paid to those words in which the vowel *a* is sounded as in *fast* (No. 3, § 12).

§ **132.** It is a common error of careless speakers to suppress the sounds of vowels in unaccented syllables; as in saying *comf'-ta-ble* for *com'fort-a-ble*, *des'prate* for *des'per-ate*, *ev'ry* for *ev'er-y*, *his'try* for *his'to-ry*, *mem'ry* for *mem'o-ry*, *part'ci-ple* for *part'i-ci-ple*.

§ **133.** The sound of short *u* should not be interposed between that of a final *m* and that of *l*, *s*, or *th* which precedes it; as in saying *hel'lum* for *helm*, *chaz'um* for *chasm*, *rhyth'um* for *rhythm*.

§ **134.** The sound of *t*, when it immediately precedes *e* in a syllable immediately following an accented syllable, is sometimes improperly changed into the sound of *ch*; and the sound of *d*, when so situated before *e* or *i*, is sometimes improperly changed into the sound of *j*; as in pronouncing the words *bounteous*, *plenteous*, *hideous*, *odious*, as if they were written *boun'che-us*, *plen'che-us*, *hij'e-us*, *o'ji-us*. This mode of pronouncing these and similar words was sanctioned by Walker, but it is now generally agreed that he was in error; inasmuch as such a substitution of *ch* for *t* and of *j* for *d* cannot take place, in conformity with the principle by which the sounds of *t* and consonant *y*, or of *d* and consonant *y* are sometimes properly exchanged for the sounds of *ch* and *j* (See § 44, Note 1, and § 45, Note), without making *e* or *i* do double duty, in representing the sound of consonant *y*, and at the same time retaining its vowel character. An error equally great, and of which the like pernicious influence may be observed in some modern mispronunciations, was made by Sheridan, as pointed out by Walker himself, in allowing the sound of *t* to be changed into that of *ch* when it occurred before long *u* in the same syllable, as in the words *tune*, *Tues'day*, *tu'mult*, which, according to Sheridan, should be pronounced *choon*, *chooz'dā*, *choo'mult*.

§ **135.** The smooth *r* (No. 40, § 49), should never be trilled, as in saying *faw-rm* for *form*, *wuh-rld* for *world*; nor should it be suppressed, as in saying *faw* instead of *for*, *cawd* for *cord*, *lawd* for *lord*, *nus* for *nurse*; nor sounded where it does not properly belong, as in saying *lawr* for *law*, *sawr* for *saw*.

§ **136.** The consonant *s* is frequently sounded like *s* in *seal* when it should have the sound of *z* in *zeal*; as in *dis-arm'* (diz-arm'), *flim'sy* (flim'zy), *greas'y* (greaz'y), *na'sal* (na'zal), *pos-sess'* (poz-zes'). It will be well to remember that *s* has always the sound of *z*; 1st, when it immediately follows a vocal consonant or a vocal consonant and a silent *e* in the same syllable, as in *tubs* (tubz), *drags* (dragz), *fades* (fādz); 2d, when it comes immediately before the liquid consonant *m* in the same syllable, as in *chasm* (kazm), *prism* (prizm); 3d, in the additional syllable *es* forming the plural of nouns and the third person singular of verbs, as in *box'es* (boks'ez), *prīz'es* (prīz'ez), *pleas'es* (plēz'ez); 4th, at the end of all plural nouns whose singular ends with the sound of a vowel, as in *op'er-as* (op'er-az), *shoes* (shooz); in the final syllable of verbs that end in *se* preceded by *u*, as in *a-buse'* (a-būz'), *ac-cuse'* (ak-kuz'); also of verbs that end in *se* preceded by *i*, as in *ad-vise'* (ad-vīz'), *de-spise'* (de-spīz'), except *mor'tise, prac'tise, prom'ise*; and in the third person singular of verbs that end with the sound of a vowel, as in *be-trays'* (be-trāz'), *sees* (sēz); 5th, in some verbs, in order to distinguish them from nouns of the same spelling, as in the verbs to *grease* (grēz), to *house* (howz), to *use* (ūz).

The letter *s* has the sound of *z*, generally, when it follows an accented syllable ending with a vowel or a liquid; as in *ea'sy* (ē'zy), *ro'sy* (ro'zy), *clum'sy* (klum'zy), *pâl'sy* (pâl'zy), *tan'sy* (tan'zy).

This letter has also the sound of *z* in the prefix *dis*, according to Smart, when the following syllable is accented and begins with a vocal consonant, or with any vowel sound except that of long *u*; as in *dis-gust'* (diz-gust'), *dis-own'* (diz-ōn'), *dis-hon'or* (diz-on'ur). Walker gives substantially the same rule; and Worcester follows it in marking the pronunciation of those words to which it applies. But Perry, Knowles, Webster, Goodrich, and some other orthoëpists, not adopting this rule, pronounce *dis* as *diz* in a very few words only.

The consonant *s* is also sometimes sounded like *z* when it should have its aspirate sound; as in saying *ad-he'ziv* for *ad-he'sĭve, met-a-mor'phōz* for *met-a-mor'phose, pre-cīz'ly* for *pre-cise'ly*.

§ **137.** The consonant *x* is sometimes sounded like *ks* when it should have the sound of *gz*. The general rule is, that *x* has the sound of *ks* when it ends an accented syllable, as in *ex'er-cise* (eks'-er-siz), *ex'e-crate* (eks'e-krāt), and when it ends an unaccented syllable, if the next syllable is accented and begins with a consonant, as in *ex-cuse'* (eks-kūs'), *ex-pense'* (eks-pens'); and that it has the sound of *gz* when it ends an unaccented syllable, and the next syllable, having the accent, begins with a vowel or the letter *h*, as in *ex-am'ple* (egz-am'pl), *ex-ert'* (egz-ert'), *ex-hort'* (egz-hort'), *lux-u'ri-ous* (lugz-yoo'ri-us). The word *ex'em-pla-ry*, pronounced *egz'em-pla-ry* according to most orthoëpists, and the word *ex-ude'*, pronounced *eks-ūd'*, are exceptions.

§ **138.** Care should be taken to note those words in which *g*, usually sounded like *j* before *e*, *i*, or *y*, has its hard sound, or the sound of *g* in *go* (No. 44, § 53), before any one of these vowels; as in *gear*, *geese*, *gew'gaw*, *gib'cat*, *gib'bous*, *brag'ger*, *rag'ged*, *drug'gist*, *rig'ging*, *crag'gy*, *fog'gy*. This consonant has necessarily its hard sound (See § 66) when it occurs, as in the last six examples, at the beginning of a syllable before *e*, *i*, or *y*, in consequence of being doubled at the end of a word, in which it has its hard sound, on adding a termination that begins with any one of these vowels. — See § 176.

§ **139.** The cases in which the letter *h* is silent at the beginning of a word, as in *hour* (our), *hon'or* (on'or), should be carefully discriminated from those in which it is sounded, as in *hos'pi-tal*, *hos'tage*. It is to be observed that *h* must always be sounded when it begins a syllable not initial, as in *ab-hor'*, *be-hest'*, *per-haps'*, *ve'he-ment*; and that it is always silent when it does not begin a syllable, as in *ah*, *eh*, *Brah'ma*, *Mes-si'ah*.

§ **140.** It is important to distinguish those words in which the digraph *th* has its aspirate sound (*th* in *thin*, No. 28, § 37), as in *path* (singular), *truth*, *truths* (singular and plural), *breath*, &c., from those in which it has its vocal sound (*th* in *this*, No. 29, § 38), as in *beneath*, *breathe*, *lithe*, *paths* (plural). The plural of *truth* should be especially noted in respect to the sound of *th*, as it is frequently mispronounced by giving to *th* the same vocal sound which it properly has in the plural of *path* (paths).

§ **141.** Some consonant sounds are apt to be confounded; as those of *sh* and *s* in saying *srink* for *shrink*, *srub* for *shrub*; of *d* and *g*, in saying *dloom* for *gloom*; of *t* and *k*, in saying *tlaim* for claim; of *ph* (equivalent to *f*) and *p*, in saying *ty'pus* for *ty'phus*; of *th* and *gh* (equivalent to *f*), in saying *troth* for *trough* (*trof*); of *wh* and *w*, in saying *weth'er* for *wheth'er*; of *n* and *ng*, in saying *sing'in* for *sing'ing*, and *van'quish* for *vang'quish*; of *w* and *r*, in saying *betreen* for *between*.

§ **142.** Consonant sounds are sometimes omitted where they should be heard; as in saying *con-dem'er* for *con-dem'ner*, *east'ard* for *east'ward*, *Feb'u-a-ry* for *Feb'ru-a-ry*, *han'ful* for *hand'ful*.

§ **143.** Derivative words that have a short vowel in one syllable answering to a long one in the primitive are apt to be mispronounced; as in saying *hē'ro-ine*, *hē'ro-ism* (from *hē'ro*) instead of *hĕr'o-ine*, *hĕr'o-ism*, and in saying *zēal'ot*, *zēal'ous* (from *zēal*) instead of *zĕal'ot*, *zĕal'ous*.

§ **144.** Some words are erroneously pronounced in consequence of blending two syllables into one; as in saying *an'ti-podes* for *an-tip'o-des*, *ex-tem'pore* for *ex-tem'po-re*, *se'ries* for *se'ri-es*.

§ **145.** Some words are mispronounced by dividing them into more syllables than properly belong to them; as in saying *brev'i-a-ry* for *brev'ia-ry* (brev'ya-ry), *en'gin-er-y* for *en'gine-ry*, *sav'a-ger-y* for *sav'age-ry*.

§ **146.** The sound of *y* consonant is sometimes wrongly interposed between that of one of the guttural consonants, *k* (or *c* hard) and *g*, and that of *a* in *far* (No. 2, § 11), *i* long, *er* or *ir*; as in saying *c-yar* for *car*, *k-yind* for *kind*, *k-yer'chief* for *ker'chief*, *g-yirl* for *girl*. — See § 52.

§ **147.** Mistakes are sometimes made in pronunciation through inattention to the meaning of two words which though spelled alike, are differently pronounced; as, *clĕan'ly* and *clēan'ly*, *hĭn'der* and *hīnd'er*, *slāv'er* and *slăv'er*. — See § 161.

§ **148.** Words nearly alike in spelling are sometimes confounded in pronunciation; as, *corps* (kōr) and *corpse*, *nap* and *nape*, *stalk* and *stork*, *subt'le* (sut'l) and *sub'tile*. — See § 67.

§ **149.** Of words ending in *el*, *en*, *il*, *in*, or *on*, the cases in which the vowels *e*, *i*, and *o* ought to be sounded, as in *civ'il*, *kitch'en*, *ros'in*, *ten'don*, *trav'el*, should be carefully discriminated from those in which they ought not to be sounded, as in *ba'sin* (ba'sn), *but'ton* (but'n), *e'vil* (e'vl), *ha'zel* (ha'zl), *of'ten* (of'n).

§ **150.** Of words ending in *ed* it should be observed that the *e* is generally suppressed in those which are verbs or participles, the root of which does not end in the sound of *d* or of *t*; as in *blamed*, *framed*, *believed*, *possessed*. When the root ends in *d* or in *t*, the *e* is necessarily sounded before *d* following it, as in *ac-ced'ed*, *col-lect'ed*, *ex-pect'ed*, because two consonant sounds uttered through the same position of the organs cannot be easily blended. The *e* of this termination is sounded in most adjectives, as *a'ged, crab'bed, dog'ged, na'ked, rag'ged, wretch'ed*; unless it is preceded by *l* and another consonant, when it is suppressed, as in *brin'dled, cir'cled, dim'pled, freck'led, mot'tled, griz'zled.* It is sounded also in a few participles used as adjectives, as *be-lov'ed, bless'ed, crook'ed, learn'ed, streak'ed, wing'ed.* Thus, the *e* of the termination *ed* is suppressed in the past tense and past participle of the verb *pick*, as in the expressions, "He *picked* his men," "A hundred *picked* men"; but it is sounded in the adjective *pick'ed* (point'ed), as in the phrase, "A *picked* stake." So, also, it is suppressed in the word *beloved*, used participially, as in the sentence, "He is much *beloved*"; but it is sounded when the same word becomes an adjective, as in the expression, "A *be-lov'ed* son."

The termination *ed* is sometimes sounded as a distinct syllable in poetry, for the sake of the metre, though the word in which it occurs is not so pronounced in prose; as in the following lines:

> Arrivèd there, the little house they fill. *Spenser.*
>
> 'T is mightiest in the mightiest; it becomes
> The thronèd monarch better than his crown. *Shakespeare.*
>
> In notes, with many a winding bout
> Of linkèd sweetness long drawn out. *Milton.*
>
> Or hear old Triton blow his wreathèd horn. *Wordsworth.*

In a derivative formed by adding either of the syllables *ly, ness*, to a word ending in *ed*, this termination is pronounced as a distinct syllable, though the *e* is suppressed in the primitive; as in *con-fess'ed-ly, de-sign'ed-ly, blear'ed-ness, pre-par'ed-ness.*

§ **151.** Of words which have an unaccented syllable ending in the vowel *i* immediately preceding an accented syllable, the cases in which *i* is long (No. 16, § 25), as in *bī-lin'gual, dī-am'e-ter, vī-vip'a-rous*, should be carefully discriminated from those in which it is short (No. 7, § 16), as in *bĭ-tu men, dĭ-vide', quĭ-nine'.*

§ **152.** Of words ending in *ile, ine,* and *ite*, the cases in which the vowel *i*, when not under the accent in these terminations, is long (No. 16, § 25), as in *ac'o-nite, crys'tal-line, gen'tile*, should be carefully discriminated from those in which it is short (No. 7, § 16), as in *def'i-nite, doc'trine, fer'tile.*

§ **153.** No pains should be spared to correct such vulgar errors, or unauthorized modes, of pronunciation as these: *cram'-*

ber-ry for *cran'ber-ry*, *scurs* for *scarce* (skêrs), *sahs* for *sâuce*, *voi'lunt* for *vi'o-lent*, *win'dur* for *win'dōw*, *ad'ult* for *a-dult'*, *ad-verse'* for *ad'verse*, *a-men'a-ble* for *a-me'na-ble*, &c.; and all words that exemplify this kind of pronunciation should be carefully noted.

§ **154.** With regard to the pronunciation of foreign words sometimes used in English speech, as those from the French and the Italian, Smart remarks: "At their first introduction, such words are pronounced, or attempted to be pronounced, without corruption of their original sounds; by being much used, they gradually resign their foreign cast, and some of them at length become quite English. It must therefore happen, while in transition from one of these states to the other, that they will be neither English nor foreign, — a condition it were bootless to complain of, injudicious to alter by going back to the original pronunciation, and quixotic to amend by reducing them at once to the state of English words." The same author says: "With regard to Latinized names in modern science, many of which have a form half Latin, half English, it is absurd to tie them to any classical law: their current will be their proper pronunciation, be it, in other respects, what it may."

§ **155.** There are many words in regard to the pronunciation of which both good speakers and the best orthoëpists differ. In such cases, individual taste must be consulted, or, if that is distrusted, the safest course will be to adopt that mode of pronunciation which seems to be supported by the greatest weight of authority.

In estimating authorities, caution should be observed with respect to the name of Walker, whose peculiarities of pronunciation, or the modes recommended by him, in certain cases, have been condemned by the best modern orthoëpists. — See §§ 52, 107, 134.

§ **156.** The number of this section (156) is affixed to such words in the Vocabulary as may, for any of the causes enumerated in the preceding sections, or for any other cause, be especially liable to be mispronounced.

VIII. CLASSES OF WORDS LIABLE TO BE MISSPELLED.

§ **157.** The difficulties usually experienced in learning to spell English words correctly, arise from various causes. These are separately enumerated in the following sections, with examples illustrating several classes of words. Other examples may be collected from the Vocabulary by means of the numbers which refer to the corresponding sections of this Introduction.

§ **158.** Several letters or several combinations of letters are used to represent the same sound; as, *a, ai, ao, au, ay, aye, ea, ei,* and *ey* to represent the sound of long *a*, respectively, in the words *ale, aim, gaol, gauge, day, aye, great, veil, they.* Numerous similar examples for each of the elementary sounds, especially the vowel sounds, may be collected from the Vocabulary by means of the numbers there inserted corresponding to the sections in which the several elementary sounds are treated of.

§ **159.** The same letter or the same combination of letters is used to represent different sounds; as, the letter *o* for the different sounds it has in *old, on, orb, do, work, son, wolf, wom'en,* and the combination *ou* for the different sounds it has in *ounce, soup, four, touch, ought, could, jour'nal, cough.* So the letter *x* is sometimes equivalent in sound to *ks* (wa*x*), sometimes to *ksh* (an*x*'ious), sometimes to *gz* (e*x*-act'), and sometimes to *z* (an*x*-i'e-ty). Other examples may be found in §§ 55, 56, 57, 58, 59, and more may be added to these by a comparison of the words noted by numbers in the Vocabulary as illustrating the several elementary sounds.

§ **160.** There are many pairs or groups of words pronounced alike, but differently spelled; as, *ail* and *ale*; *all* and *awl*; *cere, sear,* and *seer.* Similar examples are noted in the Vocabulary by the number of this section (160).

§ **161.** There are several pairs of words spelled alike but differently pronounced; as, *lead* (lĕd) and *lead* (lēd); *slough* (slou) and *slough* (sluf). — See § 147.

§ **162.** There are many words in the orthography of which silent letters occur, that is, letters which represent no sound; as, *b* in *debt* and *doubt*, *s* in *island*, *ch* in *yacht.* The consonants, single or combined, which are sometimes silent are *b* (de*b*t), *c* (vic*t*'uals), *d* (We*d*nes'day), *g* (fei*g*n, *g*nat), *h* (g*h*ost, *h*our), *k* (*k*nife), *l* (ta*l*k, sa*l*m'on), *m* (*m*ne-mon'ics), *n* (hym*n*, con-tem*n*'), *p* (*p*salm), *s* (i*s*'land), *t* (of'*t*en, cas'*t*le), *w* (*w*rite), *ch* (dra*ch*m), *gh* (ri*gh*t), *ph* (*ph*this'ic), *rh* (myr*rh*).

"When two consonant letters," says Smart, "come together that are articulated by contact in the same part of the mouth, as *m* and *b* [la*mb*], *m* and *p* [ade*mp*tion], *l* and *n* [ki*ln*]; or that are sounded in the same region, as *m* and *n* [hy*mn*]; or that are followed by a sound that more readily joins itself to the former of the two consonants than the latter, as *l* when it follows *sc* or *st* [mu*sc*le, bu*st*le], *m* or *n* when it follows *ft* or *st* [Chri*stm*as, che*stn*ut], *g* when it follows *rt* [mo*rtg*age], and *o* when it follows *sw* or *tw* [*sw*ord, *two*]; — in such cases the *latter* of the two consonants is generally dropped in the pronunciation."

From similar causes having reference to ease of utterance, and from the tendency, in adopting foreign words, to make the combinations of consonant sounds conform to English analogies, the *former* of two consonants, as the same author remarks, is dropped in pronouncing some words; as, *b* in *bd*ellium, de*bt*; *c* in *cz*ar, indi*ct*; *g* in *gn*ome, phle*gm*, si*gn*; *k* in *kn*eel; *l* in ca*lm*, fo*lk*, ta*lk*; *m* in *mn*emonics; *p* in *ps*alm, recei*pt*; *s* in deme*sn*e, i*sl*e.

Silent letters, especially silent consonants, may be traced, in most cases, to the original languages from which the words containing them were derived. Thus the silent *b* in the words *debt* and *doubt* may be traced to the Latin words *debitum* and *dubito*, in which *b* is sounded.

§ **163.** Of the vowels, *e* is always silent at the end of words, except a few derived from the Greek, the Latin, or other foreign languages; as, *apocope*, *apostrophe*, *catastrophe*, *epitome*, *recipe*, *simile*, *systole*, *syncope*, *anime*, *cicerone*, *protegé*. The usual effect of the final *e*, when it follows a single consonant, a consonant digraph, or the combined consonants *st*, in a monosyllable or in an accented syllable, is to lengthen the preceding vowel; as in *babe*, *here*, *mile*, *bone*, *lute*, *bathe*, *paste*, *a-bate'*, *com-plete'*, *re-voke'*, *tra-duce'*, *im-bathe'*, *dis-taste'*. The reason of this is, as Smart remarks, "that the *e* was originally sounded, and made with the consonant a distinct syllable, leaving the previous vowel final in the foregoing syllable. Thus, too, the vowel is long in *chaste*, *taste*, &c., because the words were originally *chă-ste*, *tă-ste*, &c.; so, likewise, in *bathe*, &c., because the consonant is double only to the eye."

The following monosyllables are exceptions to the lengthening effect of final *e* preceded by a single consonant; namely, *are*, *axe*, *bade*, *come*, *done*, *dove*, *give*, *glove*, *gone*, *have*, *live*, *love*, *none*, *one*, *sate* (as the past tense of *sit* is sometimes spelled), *shove*, *some*, *were*, and *withe*. In the accented syllables of the words *a-bove'*, *be-come'*, *for-bade'*, *for-give'*, and in the unaccented syllables of many other words, as *doc'trine*, *fer'tile*, *pas'sive*, *op'po-site*, the final *e* does not show the quantity of the preceding vowel, being, as Smart expresses it, "idle as well as silent."

§ **164.** There is a large class of words in which the vowel *e* final is silent after the combined consonants *bl* (bi'*ble*), *cl* (cir'*cle*), *dl* (bri'*dle*), *fl* (tri'*fle*), *gl* (ea'*gle*), *kl* (pic'*kle*), *pl* (ap'*ple*), *tl* (bot'*tle*), *zl* (puz'*zle*).

When *e* terminates the last syllable of a word after *r*, this syllable is pronounced as if *e*, or its equivalent before *r*, the natural vowel *u* (No. 12, § 21), preceded the *r*, as in *lu'cre* (lu'kur), *o'chre* (o'kur), *o'gre* (o'gur), *sa'bre* (sa'bur), *the'a-tre* (the'a-tur). Webster and Goodrich recommend that words of this class should be written with the *e* preceding the *r*, except when the *e* would thus be made to follow *c* or *g*, as in *lu'cre*, *o'gre*, which, if written *lu'cer*, *o'ger*, would be liable to be mispronounced by giving to *c* and *g* their soft sound.

§ **165.** The vowel *e* is usually silent in the termination *ed* of the imperfect tense and the past participle of regular verbs that do not end with the sound of *d* or of *t*; as in *caused* (kauzd), *de-ceived'* (de-sēvd'), *trans-gressed'* (trans-grest'). But it is sounded in most adjectives, in some participles used as adjectives, and sometimes also in poetry for the sake of the metre. — See § 150.

A few words, derived regularly from primitives ending in *ll* or in *ss* by adding *ed*, are also written by dropping this termination, as well as the final consonant of the primitive, and substituting *t*; as, *spelled*, *blessed*, which are frequently written *spelt*, *blest*. When the sound of *d*, which is vocal, follows that of *s*, which is aspirate, it is naturally changed into the sound of *t*. (See Note C, p. 34.) But when the sound of *d* follows that of *l*, as these sounds are both vocal, they may be easily uttered together; though the sound of *l*, being liquid as well as vocal, may also be easily made to blend with that of *t*. So, too, when the termination *ed* follows the liquid and vocal consonant *n*, in the regular form of a verb, there is a tendency to replace the sound of *d* by that of *t*; as in the words *burned, learned*, which are also sometimes written *burnt, learnt*.

§ **166.** The vowel *e* is silent in the termination *es* of the plural of nouns and the third person singular of the present tense of verbs, as in *lakes* (lāks), *apples* (ap'plz), *hastes* (hāsts), *craves* (krāvz), *trem'bles* (trem'blz); except when it follows a consonant that does not blend with the sound of *s* or of *z* (as *c* soft, *g* soft, *s* and *x*), as in *ra'ces* (ra'sez), *sta'ges* (sta'jez), *gas'es* (gas'ez), *box'es* (boks'ez).

§ **167.** The vowels *e*, *i*, and *o* are silent before *n* in the final syllable of some words, as in *heaven* (hev'n), *cous'in* (kuz'n), *but'ton* (but'n); and the vowels *e* and *i* are also silent before *l* in the final syllable of some words, as in *shov'el* (shuv'l), *e'vil* (e'vl).

§ **168.** The digraph *ue*, when final, is silent in some words after *g* and after *q*; as in *tongue* (tung), *u-nique'* (u-nēk').

§ **169.** There are numerous classes of words difficult to spell on account of the resemblance in sound of syllables or parts of syllables that are spelled differently, or on account of the indistinctness of the vowel sound in the penultimate syllable; as,

Words beginning with the following syllables: —

Ante, anti (*ante*cedent, *anti*thetical; *ante*penult, *anti*christian)

Cer, cir, ser, sur (*cer*tain, *cir*cle, *ser*vant, *sur*name).

De, di (*de*bate, *di*vide; *de*cline, *di*vine; *de*ception, *di*plomacy).

Fer, fir, fur (*fer*tile, *fir*kin, *fur*tive; *fer*vid, *fir*man, *fur*nace).

Mer, mur, myr (*mer*chant, *mur*mur, *myr*tle).

Per, pur (*per*fect, *pur*pose; *per*vade, *pur*sue).

Ter, tur (*ter*minate, *tur*pentine; *ter*tiary, *tur*binate).

Words ending in the following syllables: —

Age, ege, iage, idge, ige (ad*age*, coll*ege*, marr*iage*, porr*idge*, vest*ige*).

Ance, ence, (abund*ance*, resid*ence*; utter*ance*, differ*ence*).

Ant, ent (attend*ant*, impend*ent*; suppli*ant*, recipi*ent*).

Ar, er, ir, or, ur, yr, re (doll*ar*, mill*er*, tap*ir*, sail*or*, sulph*ur*, zeph*yr*, lust*re*).

Cede, ceed, sede (se*cede*, suc*ceed*, super*sede*).

Cial, *sial*, *tial* (bene*ficial*, controver*sial*, providen*tial*).
Cian, *sion*, *tion* (politi*cian*, apprehen*sion*, satisfac*tion*).
Ceous, *cious*, *tious* (herba*ceous*, saga*cious*, vexa*tious*).
City, *sity* (atro*city*, verbo*sity*; feli*city*, neces*sity*).
Cy, *sy* (poli*cy*, here*sy*; secre*cy*, courte*sy*).
Ear, *eer*, *ere*, *ier* (app*ear*, engin*eer*, persev*ere*, brigad*ier*).
Geous, *gious* (coura*geous*, reli*gious*; outra*geous*, conta*gious*).
Ice, *ise*, *is* (bod*ice*, treat*ise*, trell*is*; off*ice*, prom*ise*, bas*is*).
Om, *ome*, *um* (at*om*, welc*ome*, al*um*; idi*om*, lones*ome*, vacu*um*).
Ous, *us* (por*ous*, chor*us*; odi*ous*, radi*us*; peril*ous*, nautil*us*).
Phe, *phy* (apostro*phe*, philoso*phy*; catastro*phe*, biogra*phy*).
Sy, *zy* (dai*sy*, la*zy*; ea*sy*, bree*zy*; drow*sy*, blow*zy*).
Y, *ey* (lad*y*, barl*ey*; stud*y*, hon*ey*; sand*y*, turk*ey*).

Words in which the penultimate syllable is unaccented and ends in *a*, *e*, or *i*, or in *r* preceded by *e* (laud*a*ble, ed*i*ble, orn*a*ment, ten*e*ment, lin*i*ment, rar*e*fy, clar*i*fy, vitr*e*ous, var*i*ous, sol*i*tude, qui*e*tude, la*i*ty, pi*e*ty, del*e*gate, profl*i*gate, culin*a*ry, millin*e*ry).

Words in which the sound of long *e* is represented by *ei* or *ie* (s*ei*ze, p*ie*ce, w*ei*rd, ch*ie*f, rec*ei*ve, bel*ie*ve, conc*ei*t, bes*ie*ge).

NOTE.—It will obviate most of the difficulty of spelling words in which the sound of long *e* is represented by *ei* or *ie*, to remember that *ei* is always used for this purpose rather than *ie*, when this sound occurs immediately after *c*; and that *ie* is used rather than *ei* after most other consonants. The words in which *ei* represents the sound of long *e* after other consonants beside *c*, are chiefly the following,—*inveigle*, *leisure*, *neither*, *seignior*, *seine*, *seize*, *weird*, and such other words as are derivatives of any of these.

§ **170.** A doubt frequently arises as to the proper mode of spelling a word in which a consonant sound occurs between two vowel sounds in different syllables; a consonant sound so situated being, in some words, represented by a single letter, as in *ar'id*, *big'ot*, *pan'el*, *trip'le*, and, in others, by a double letter, as in *car'ried*, *fag'got*, *chan'nel*, *rip'ple*.—See §§ 66, 176.

§ **171.** The number of this section (171) is affixed to such words in the Vocabulary as may, for any of the causes enumerated in the preceding sections, or for any other cause, be peculiarly difficult to spell.

IX. RULES FOR SPELLING CERTAIN CLASSES OF WORDS.

§ **172.** (1.) The letter *l*, when preceded by a single vowel, is always doubled at the end of a monosyllable; as in *ball*, *bell*, *dell*, *mill*, *shall*, *will*.

§ **173.** (2.) The letter *f*, when preceded by a single vowel, is generally doubled at the end of a monosyllable; as in *bluff*, *cliff*, *muff*, *puff*, *snuff*, *stuff*. The words *clef*, *if*, and *of* are the only exceptions.

§ **174.** (3.) The letter *s*, when preceded by a single vowel, and when it is not the sign of the possessive case or of the plural of a noun, or of the third person singular of a verb, is generally doubled at the end of a monosyllable; as in *brass*, *class*, *dress*, *glass*, *kiss*, *moss*, *press*. The following words are the only exceptions, — *as*, *gas*, *has*, *his*, *is*, *pus*, *this*, *thus*, *us*, *was*, *yes*.

§ **175.** (4.) The only consonants, except *l*, *f*, and *s*, that are ever doubled at the end of a word, are; *b* in *abb*, *ebb*; *d* in *add*, *odd*, *rudd*; *g* in *egg*; *m* in *lamm*, *mumm* (verb); *n* in *bunn*, *inn*; *r* in *burr*, *err*, *murr*, *parr*, *purr*, *shirr*; *t* in *butt*; *z* in *buzz*, *fuzz*. These consonants are doubled, when final, only in the words enumerated.

§ **176.** (5.) In a derivative formed by adding a syllable beginning with a vowel to a monosyllable, or to a final accented syllable, ending in a single consonant (except *h*, and also *s* in the derivatives of *gas*, as *gaseous*, *gasify*) preceded by a vowel sound represented by a single letter, that consonant is doubled; as in *rob'ber*, *propel'ling*, *quit'ted*, formed by adding the syllables *er*, *ing*, *ed* to *rob*, *propel*, *quit*, respectively. In the last of these words (*quit*), the letter *u*, it will be observed, is a vowel to the eye only, being really equivalent to consonant *w*. If the primitive ends in two consonants (as in *act*, *reform*), or if, though ending in a single consonant, this consonant is preceded by a vowel sound represented by a digraph (as in *boil*, *feel*, *con-ceal'*), the final letter is not doubled in the derivative. So also if the accent is not on the final syllable of the primitive (as in *big'ot*, *prof'it*, *lim'it*), or if the accent of the primitive is thrown back in the derivative (as in *ref'erence* from *re-fer'*), the final consonant is not doubled in the derivative, except in the cases mentioned in the next section.

The reduplication of the consonant, according to the rule here given, is obviously an orthographical expedient to keep the preceding vowel short, in conformity with the general principle that the vowels have their short sound when followed by a consonant in the same syllable. If the final consonant of the primitives were not doubled in *robber*, *propelling*, *quitted*, for example, these words would be liable to be mispronounced in consequence of having their syllables wrongly divided; thus, *ro'ber*, *pro-pe'ling*, *qui'ted*.

§ **177.** (6.) In derivatives formed by adding a syllable beginning with a vowel to most words that end in *l*, this letter is doubled, by most writers, in conformity with a practice long prevalent, though the final syllable is not accented; as in *trav'el-ler*, *trav'el-ling*, *trav'elled* (from *trav'el*). But many persons in the United States now write the derivatives of such words with one *l*, as recommended by Lowth, Perry, Walker, Webster, and Goodrich, who justly maintain that this mode is more in accordance with analogy than the other. Both parties, however, agree in writing the derivatives of *par'al-lel* with one *l*. There is a diversity of usage, also, with respect to doubling the final consonant in the derivatives formed by adding a syllable beginning with a vowel to the words *bi'as*, *car'bu-ret*, *com'pro-mit*, *sul'phu-ret*, and *wor'ship*. The derivatives of *kid'nap* are uniformly written with the *p* doubled. The word *excellence* (from L. *excellentia*) is uniformly written with the *l* doubled, though the accent is on the first syllable. Smart remarks: "The double *p* in *worshipped*, *worshipper*, &c., the double *l* in *travelling*, *traveller*, &c., are quite unnecessary on any other score than to satisfy the prejudices of the eye." — See Note E, p. 70.

§ **178.** (7.) Derivatives formed by adding a syllable to words that end in a double consonant generally retain both consonants; as, *bliss'ful*, *gruff'ly*, *still'ness*. There are some exceptions in the derivatives of words ending in *ll*. When the syllable *less* or *ly* is added to a word of this termination, one *l* is omitted by all lexicographers, — as in *skil'less*, *ful'ly*, — in order to prevent the meeting of three letters that represent the same sound. So also in the derivatives formed by adding the syllable *ful* or *ness* to the words *dull*, *full*, *skill*, *will* (*dul'ness*, *ful'ness*, *skil'ful*, *wil'ful*), and in those formed by adding the syllable *ment* to *en-roll'*, *in-stall'*, *in-thrall'*, or the syllable *dom* to *thrall* (*en-rol'ment*, *in-stal'ment*, *in-thral'ment*, *thral'dom*), one *l*, according to Worcester, and most other lexicographers, should be omitted; but, according to Webster and Goodrich, these words should be spelled with the *l* doubled, as in the primitives. The derivatives of *pontiff*, which have only one *f*, as *pon-tif'i-cal*, are also exceptions.

§ **179.** (8.) Derivatives formed by prefixing a syllable to words that end in a double consonant generally retain both consonants, as, *be-fall'*, *un-well'*, *de-press'*; though some of this class of derivatives from primitives ending in *ll* are spelled in some modern dictionaries, as Smart's, with one *l*, as, *be-fal'*, *en-rol'*, *fore-tel'*, *in-thral'*. The words *dis-til'*, *ful-fil'*, *in-stil'*, and *un-til'*, are generally thus written with one *l*; but, according to Webster and Goodrich, all of these, except the last, should be spelled with the *l* doubled.

§ **180.** (9.) Compound words generally retain all the letters which are used in writing the simple words that compose them; as, *all-wise*, *well-bred*. The exceptions are some of the compounds of *all*; as, *al-mighty*, *almost*, *already*, *also*, *although*, *altogether*, *always*, *withal*, *therewithal*, *wherewithal*; the word *wherever* (where-ever); the words *chilblain*, *welfare*, *Christmas*, *candlemas*, and others compounded with the word *mass*; the words *artful*, *awful*, *sinful*, and all others similarly compounded with the word *full*; and, according to most lexicographers, the words *fulfil* and *instil*, though, according to Webster and Goodrich, these should be written with the *l* doubled in conformity with the general rule.

§ **181.** (10.) The letter *c* is generally followed by *k* to represent the sound of *k* at the end of a monosyllable; as in *back*, *brick*, *thick*, *sick*. The words *arc*, *fisc*, *lac*, *marc*, *orc*, *sac*, *talc*, *zinc*, are exceptions.

§ **182.** (11.) In derivatives formed by adding a syllable beginning with *e* or *i* to a word ending with *c*, the letter *k* is inserted after *c*, in order to prevent it from taking the sound of *s*; as in *trafficker*, *trafficking*, *trafficked* (from *traffic*).

§ **183.** (12.) In derivatives formed by adding a syllable beginning with a vowel to words that end in a silent *e*, the *e* is omitted, except when it serves to keep *c* or *g* soft, or when its omission would obscure the pronunciation or the meaning. Thus it is omitted in *com'ing*, *hōp'ing*, *sen'si-ble*, *spi'cy*, *su'ing* (from *come*, *hope*, *sense*, *spice*, *sue*); but it is retained in *peace'a-ble*, *change'a-*

ble (from *peace, change*), because, otherwise, *c* and *g*, coming immediately before *a*, would have their hard sound. It is also retained in *hoe'ing, shoe'ing* (from *hoe, shoe*), to prevent the doubt that might arise about their pronunciation, if these words were written *hoing, shoing*; and in *dye'ing, singe'ing, springe'ing, swinge'ing, tinge'ing* (from *dye, singe, springe, swinge, tinge*), in order that these participles may not be confounded with *dy'ing, sing'ing, spring'ing, swing'ing, ting'ing* (from *die, sing, spring, swing, ting*). The *e* is generally retained in the word *mileage*; and it was retained by Johnson and Walker in the derivatives formed by adding *able* to the words *move, prove*, and *sale*, but these derivatives are now more commonly written according to the rule, *movable, provable, salable.*

§ **184.** (13.) In the present participles of verbs that end in *ie*, not only is the final *e* omitted on adding the syllable *ing*, but the *i* is changed into *y*; as in *dy'ing, ly'ing, ty'ing, vy'ing* (from *die, lie, tie, vie*).

§ **185.** (14.) In derivatives formed by adding a syllable beginning with a consonant to words that end in a silent *e*, the *e* is generally retained; as in *peace'ful, tune'less, move'ment, vile'ly.* There are some exceptions; as, *aw'ful, ar'gument, a-bridg'ment, ac-knowl'edg-ment, judg'ment, du'ly, tru'ly, whol'ly, nurs'ling, wis'dom*, and such words as are derivatives of any of these. The words *abridgment, acknowledgment*, and the word *judgment*, with its derivatives, are, however, by Walker, Smart, and many others, conformed to the rule, and spelled *abridgement, acknowledgement, judgement, adjudgement, misjudgement, prejudgement.* The word *lodgement* is thus spelled, with a silent *e* in the first syllable, by Johnson, Walker, Smart, Worcester, and most other lexicographers; but, by Webster and Goodrich, the *e* is omitted in this word as well as in the others just enumerated.

§ **186.** (15.) In derivatives formed by adding any termination, except one that begins with *i*, to words that end in *y* preceded by a consonant, the *y* is generally changed into *i*; as in *ed'i-fies, ed'i-fied, ea'si-ly, ea'si-er, fan'ci-ful* (from *ed'i-fy, ea'sy, fan'cy*). The derivatives of *dry, shy*, and *sky* retain the *y*, as in *dry'ly, shy'ness, sky'ey.* In the derivatives of *sly*, the *y* is retained by Worcester and some other lexicographers; but Smart, Webster, and Goodrich spell these words with *i* instead of *y*. The *y* is also retained when an apostrophe and the letter *s* are added to form the possessive case singular of nouns; as in *city's*, *daisy's*, *sky's*.

§ **187.** (16.) In derivatives formed by adding any termination to words that end in *y* preceded by a vowel, the *y* remains, in most cases, unchanged; as in *dis-played'*, *gay'er*, *de-lays'*. The words, *daily*, *laid*, *lain*, *saith*, *said* (from *day*, *lay*, *say*), and *staid* (the past tense and past participle of *stay*, — written also *stayed*), together with their compounds, are exceptions.

§ **188.** (17.) In derivatives formed by adding a syllable beginning with a vowel to words that end in any vowel sound, the letter or letters representing this sound are generally retained; as in *sub-pœ'naed*, *a-gree'ing*, *a-gree'a-ble*, *em-bar'goed*, *wooed*, *be-stowed'*. When, however, the syllable *ed* is added to verbs that end in *ee*, one *e* is omitted; as in *a-greed'*, *de-creed'*, *freed*.

§ **189.** (18.) The plural of nouns is formed regularly by adding the letter *s* to the singular, when ending in a vowel, or by adding the letter *s*, or the syllable *es*, when ending in a consonant. The letter *s* only is added, when the singular ends in a sound which will blend with that of *s*; as in *adieus*, *ideas*, *solos*, *toys*, *cars*, *caves*, *cliffs*, *ducks*, *hills*, *kegs*, *lads*, *pans*, *paths*, *webs* (See NOTE C, p. 34). The syllable *es* is added, when the singular ends in a sound which will not blend with that of *s*, as in *boxes*, *bushes*, *churches*, *crosses*; but in case the singular ends in a silent *e* preceded by soft *c*, by soft *g*, or by *s*, the final *e* is sounded to form the syllable *es*; as in *faces*, *stages*, *vases*. Letters and figures used as nouns plural, and words so used without reference to their meaning, commonly have the plural form indicated by an apostrophe and the letter *s*; as in the expressions, "Dot your *i's*"; "In 44 there are two 4's"; "You use too many *also's*."

§ **190.** (19.) The plural of nouns that end in *y* preceded by a consonant or the sound of a consonant, is formed by changing *y* into *ies*, as in *fancies*, *ladies*, *mercies*, *colloquies* (from *fancy*, *lady*, *mercy*, *colloquy*); but the plural of nouns ending in *y* preceded by any vowel (except *u* sounded as *w*, as in *colloquy*) is formed regularly by adding *s* to the singular; as in *boys*, *days*, *attorneys*, *journeys*, *moneys*, *valleys*. Nouns which now end in *y* formerly ended in *ie*, as, *ladie*, *mercie*; so that the plural termination *ies* was once regular.

§ **191.** (20.) The plural of nouns that end in *i* is generally formed by adding *es* to the singular, as in *alkalies, rabbies* (from *alkali, rabbi*); but some writers add *s* only.

§ **192.** (21.) The plural of nouns that end in *o* is formed regularly by adding *s* to the singular, when the *o* is preceded by a vowel (See § 189), as in *cameos, folios* (from *cameo, folio*); but, when the *o* is preceded by a consonant, the plural is sometimes formed by adding *s* only, as in *bravos, centos, zeros*, and sometimes by adding *es*, as in *cargoes, echoes, mottoes, potatoes.*

§ **193.** (22.) The plural of the following nouns is formed by changing the final *f* or *fe* into *ves*; namely, *beef, calf, elf, half, knife, leaf, life, loaf, self, sheaf, shelf, thief, wife, wolf* (beeves, calves, elves, &c.). The plural of *staff* (staves) is formed by changing *ff* into *ves*; though the plural of its compounds is regular, as in *flagstaffs.* The plural of *wharf*, according to English usage, is *wharfs*, but in the United States it is generally written, as well as pronounced, *wharves.* All other nouns ending in *f, ff*, or *fe* have the plural formed regularly by the addition of *s* to the singular.

§ **194.** (23.) The plural of the nouns *brother, die, pea*, and *penny* is formed in two ways, to distinguish different meanings. Thus, that of *brother* is *brothers*, when children of the same parent are referred to, but *brethren*, when the reference is to members of the same society, or congregation, or of the same profession; that of *die* is *dies*, when used in the sense of stamps for coining, but *dice*, if implements for playing are meant; that of *pea* is *pease* for the fruit taken collectively, but *peas* for a number of individual seeds; that of *penny* is *pennies*, when a number of individual coins is spoken of, but *pence*, if reference is made to an aggregate sum, or to a coin, equal in value to a certain number of pennies.

§ **195.** (24.) The plural of the following nouns is irregularly formed; namely, *child* (children), *foot* (feet), *goose* (geese), *louse* (lice), *man* (men), *mouse* (mice), *ox* (oxen), *tooth* (teeth), *woman* (women).

§ **196.** (25.) The plural of compounds of which the word *man* is the final constituent is formed, after the analogy of this primitive, by changing *man* into *men*, as in *freemen, Dutchmen* (from *freeman, Dutchman*); but nouns not compound, and ending in the syllable *man*, have the plural formed regularly by adding *s* to the singular; as, *Germans*, *Mussulmans*, *caymans*, *firmans* (from *German*, *Mussulman*, *cayman*, *firman*).

§ **197.** (26.) The plural of compounds consisting of a noun and an adjective is generally indicated by the same change in the noun which it undergoes for the plural when single; as in *knight-errant* (knight*s*-errant), *son-in-law* (son*s*-in-law). But those compounds of which the adjective *full* — as a suffix, written *ful* — constitutes the last part, have their plural formed by adding *s* to the adjective; as, *handful* (handful*s*), *spoonful* (spoonful*s*).

§ **198.** (27.) Some nouns from foreign languages retain their original plural, as, *antithesis* (antith*e*ses), *axis* (ax*e*s), *cherub* (cherub*im*), *focus* (foc*i*), *larva* (larv*æ*), *stratum* (strat*a*), *monsieur* (*messieurs*); and some nouns of this class have two plurals, one after the foreign form and the other after the English form, as, *formula* (formul*æ* or formula*s*), *medium* (medi*a* or medium*s*), *memorandum* (memorand*a* or memorandum*s*), *seraph* (seraph*im* or seraph*s*).

§ **199.** (28.) There is a class of words, which it was formerly the general usage to write with the termination *our*, that are now commonly written in the United States with the termination *or*, the *u* being omitted; as, *candor*, *color*, *error*, *honor*, *rigor*. Many of these words, however, are still written in England with the *u*.

§ **200.** (29.) Most words of two or more syllables which were formerly written with the termination *ick* are now written with the termination *ic*, the *k* being omitted; as, *mimic*, *music*, *public*, *traffic*. When, however, a syllable beginning with *e* or *i* is added to any of these words in forming a derivative, the letter *k* is inserted to keep the *c* hard. — See § 182, Rule 11.

§ **201.** (30.) Several words derived from the Latin through the French are variously written with the prefix *en* or *in*; as, *enquire* or *inquire*, *enclose* or *inclose*, *endorse* or *indorse*, — the prefix *en* being the French form of the Latin *in*.

§ **202.** (31.) There is a diversity of usage in regard to the mode of spelling the last syllable of many of the verbs which terminate in the sound of *z* preceded by that of long *i*; some writers spelling this syllable *ize*, and others, *ise*; as, *catechize* or *catechise*, *patronize* or *patronise*, *recognize* or *recognise*. As a general rule, though with a few exceptions, those verbs of this class which are derived from Greek verbs ending in ιζω (*izo*), or which are formed after the analogy of these verbs, have this final syllable spelled *ize*, and in those derived from the French verb *prendre* or its participle *pris* or *prise*, it is written *ise*.

§ **203.** (32.) With respect to those words in the spelling of which usage is divided at the present time, both forms, or, if there are more than two, the various forms, are given in this work with references from one to the other; and those modes of spelling which seem to be least supported by usage and by the weight of authority are indicated by printing the words in spaced letters within brackets; though, in some cases, it is very difficult to determine whether one form or another is to be preferred.

NOTE E. — It is well known that Dr. Webster, in his Dictionary of the English Language, made changes in the orthography of many words, some of which he advocated on the ground of etymology, others on that of analogy. Dr. Goodrich, his son-in-law and the editor of the revised edition of that work, published in 1847, four years after the death of Dr. Webster, candidly states that such of these changes as were based on etymology (e. g. *bridegoom* for *bridegroom*, *fether* for *feather*) were never received with favor by the public, and that, Dr. Webster having restored the old orthography in a considerable number of cases after an experiment of twelve years (1828 to 1840), he himself had restored it, in the revised edition, to nearly all that remained. Most of those changes of orthography which seemed to Dr. Webster to be desirable on the ground of analogy have been retained in the editions of his Dictionary published under the editorial care of Dr. Goodrich. They have been extensively adopted in the United States, but they cannot yet be said to have the sanction of any considerable portion of the British public. The following is a brief statement of the modes of spelling which constitute peculiar features of the latest edition of Webster's Dictionary, edited by Goodrich, and published in 1859, and of the reasons assigned for them.

1. Words terminating in *re*, as *centre*, *theatre*, have the termination changed to *er* (*center*, *theater*), except *acre*, *chancre*, *massacre*, and *ogre*, in which the change would lead to an erroneous pronunciation. Words of this class, however, are given in both modes of spelling, a preference only being expressed for the termination *er*, on the ground that other words of like termination, as *chamber*, *cider*, have already undergone this change.

2. Most of those words which by long usage have formed exceptions to the general rule that a final consonant preceded by a single vowel in the primitive is not doubled in the derivative, on adding a syllable beginning with a vowel, unless the accent is on the last syllable, as the derivatives of *trav'el* (usually spelt *trav'el-ler*, *trav'el-ling*, *trav'elled*, &c.) and about fifty other words ending in *l*, together with the derivatives of *bi'as*, *car'bu-ret*, *com'pro-mit*, *sul'phu-ret*, and *wor'ship*, are spelled without doubling the final consonant of the primitive, in order that they may conform to the general rule. (See § 176.) The final consonant, however, is doubled in the derivatives of *kidnap*. It should be observed that some words in which the letter *l* is doubled are derived from other languages, as *tranquillity* (from L. *tranquillitas*), *crystallize* (from Gr. *κρύσταλλος*), *chancellor* (from L. *cancellarius*, through the French), and do not, therefore, come under the operation of the rule referred to, which applies only to English formatives.

3. The words *enrollment*, *installment*, *inthrall*, *inthrallment*, *thralldom*, are spelled in this manner, with a double *l*, for the reason that, if spelled with a single *l*, they are liable to be mispronounced by giving to the vowel that precedes this letter its short sound.

4. The words *distill*, *instill*, *fulfill*, are spelled in this manner, with a double *l*, because their derivatives, as *distiller*, *instilling*, *fulfilled*, &c., must be written with the *l* doubled.

5. The derivatives of *dull*, *full*, *skill*, and *will* are spelled with double *l*, as in *dullness*, *fullness*, *skillful*, *willful*, to prevent the inconvenience of exceptions to a general rule. — See § 178.

6. The words *defense*, *offense*, and *pretense* are thus spelled, with *s* instead of *c*, because *s* is used in the derivatives, as in *defensive*, *offensive*, *pretension*, and because the same change has already been made in the words *expense*, *license*, and *recompense*.

7. The verb *practice* is thus spelled, with *c* instead of *s* before the final *e*, 1st, because similar verbs, as *notice*, *apprentice*, in which the accent is not on the last syllable, are so spelled; 2d, because a distinction of spelling between a noun and a verb of like origin belongs properly to words accented on the last syllable, as *device*, *n.*, *devise*, *v.*; 3d, because such a distinction in spelling this verb with an *s* (*practise*) leads to a wrong pronunciation, the termination *ise* in verbs being usually sounded the same as *ize*. Though this spelling (*practice*) is proposed as the preferable one, the other form (*practise*) is also given.

8. The words *mould* and *moult* are given in this spelling, but a preference is expressed for the forms *mold* and *molt*, on the ground that they belong to the same class of words as *bold*, *colt*, *fold*, *gold*, &c., in which the *u* has either been dropped or was never introduced.

9. *Drought* and *height* are given as the established orthography of these words, but the forms *drouth* and *hight* are, on some accounts, considered preferable, and are given as alternative modes of spelling.

X. COMPOUND WORDS.

§ **204.** A compound word is one that consists of two or more simple words, each of which is separately current in the language. The simple words of which a compound is formed are either consolidated in writing or are joined by a hyphen.

Rules for writing Compound Words.

§ **205.** I. When each of the parts of a compound word is pronounced with a distinct accent, they should be joined with a hyphen; as, *fel'low-crea'ture*, *man'na-drop'ping*, *twen'ty-one'*.

EXCEPTIONS.

1. Compounds beginning with the prepositions *over*, *under*, unless the second part of the compound commences with the letter *r*; as, *o'verbear'-ing*, *un'dertak'ing*, *o'ver-rule'*, *un'der-rate'*.
2. A few compounds, mostly pronouns or adverbs, of very common occurrence; as, *here'upon'*, *nev'ertheless'*, *what'soev'er*.
3. Compounds terminating in *monger*; as, *ir'onmon'ger*.

§ **206.** II. When one of the words of which a compound is formed is pronounced without a distinct accent, no hyphen should be inserted between them; as, *black'smith*, *cler'gyman*, *earth'quake*, *ink'stand*.

EXCEPTIONS.

1. Compounds in which the first word ends with the same letter or digraph as that with which the second begins; as, *fish'-shop*, *flag'-grass*, *head'-dress*, *hop'-pole*, *post'-town*, *sail'-loft*, *snow'-white*, *stair'-rod*.
2. Compounds in which the first word ends, and the second begins, with a vowel; as, *love'-apple*, *pale'-eyed*, *sea'-egg*.
3. Compounds whose meaning or pronunciation would be obscured by writing the parts continuously; as, *gas'-holder*, *loop'-hole*, *pot'-house*, *tea'-chest*. In the first three of these words, if the hyphen were omitted, the letters *s-h*, *p-h*, *t-h*, might be mistaken for the digraphs *sh*, *ph*, *th*, and the words be improperly pronounced *gash'older*, *loo'phole*, *poth'ouse*. In the last of the examples, the omission of the hyphen would confound the word intended with the second person singular of the present indicative active of the verb to *teach* (teach'est).
4. Compounds formed by uniting a verb with an adverb, a preposition, or a noun; also those ending in *book* or *tree*; as, *get'-off*, *make'-shift*, *pla'ning-mill*, *set'-to*; *blank'-book*, *blue'-book*, *scrap'-book*; *fir'-tree*, *palm'-tree*, *pine'-tree*.
5. Almost all compound adjectives of whatever mode of formation;

as, *God'-fearing*, *heart'-sick*, *ill'-bred*, *knee'-deep*, *odd'-looking*, *one'-eyed*, *unhoped'-for*, *worn'-out*. But such adjectives as are formed from compound nouns of one accent, either by the addition of *ed* or *ing*, or by changing *er* into one of these terminations, or which end with one of the words *faced*, *coming*, *like*, follow the general rule, and omit the hyphen; as *cob'webbed* (from *cob'web*), *slave'holding* (from *slave'holder*), *bare'faced*, *forth'coming*, *bird'like*, &c.

Distinctions between words which are, and words which are not, to be considered as Compounds.

§ **207.** It is sometimes difficult to determine whether certain words should be compounded or written separately; and the decision of the question is often made more difficult by the conflicting practice of printers and authors, particularly lexicographers, who are not only at variance with each other in innumerable instances, but, from their frequent inconsistencies, seem to have consulted only their fancy or their convenience in regard to words of this description. The remarks which follow are intended to aid the reader in discriminating between combinations of words which are, and those which are not, properly written as compounds.

§ **208.** When two nouns, or a pronoun and a noun, are in apposition, and either of the two is separately applicable to the person or thing designated, they are to be regarded as not constituting a compound word; as, *King David*, *Lord Byron*, *Viscount Palmerston*, the *poet Wordsworth*, *I Paul*, &c.

Exception. — The pronouns *he* and *she*, used merely to express sex, are united by a hyphen to the nouns which they precede and qualify; as, *he-calf*, *she-bear*.

§ **209.** Nouns not in apposition, and of which only one is separately applicable to the person or thing designated, — or of which the first may be placed after the second with a preposition or phrase expressing the relation of the two words, — are properly regarded and written as compound words; as, *bedtime*, the time for going to bed; *bookseller*, a seller of books; *corkscrew*, a screw for drawing corks; *wine-merchant*, a merchant who deals in wine; *workshop*, a shop for work.

§ **210.** When the first of two nouns is used adjectively to express the matter or substance of which the thing designated by the second is made, each word preserving its proper accent, they are to be regarded as not forming a compound word; as, *brass key, cotton cloth, glass dish, gold ring, stone jar, silk dress, tin pan.*

§ **211.** When a noun, either simple or compound, is used before another noun, instead of an adjective, or to supply the place of one, the two nouns are properly written as distinct words; as, *angel visitant* (for *angelic visitant*), *church government* (for *ecclesiastical government*), a *custom-house officer*, *noonday sun* (for *meridian sun*), *party hatred, summer flowers.*

§ **212.** Two words, of which the latter is a noun, though in their usual construction separate, are compounded with a hyphen, when put before a noun which they qualify, but are set apart from the word qualified; as, a *bird's-eye* view, a *first-class* hotel, *high-water* mark, *Bowdoin-square* church, *New-England* scenery, *New-London* bridge.

§ **213.** If a noun in the possessive case, and the noun governing it, no longer retain the idea of property or ownership which the words, when literally taken, convey, they should be written as a compound word, with an apostrophe and a hyphen; as, *bishop's-cap, king's-evil, lady's-finger, Solomon's-seal.* But such phrases as *Baffin's Bay, Blackfriars' Bridge, King's College, Regent's Park, St. James's Palace,* and other titles of honor or distinction, are properly written as separate words.

§ **214.** If a noun in the possessive case, and the noun governing it, are used in their literal sense, and at the same time have but one accent, they should be written as compound words, without a hyphen and without any apostrophe; as, *beeswax, doomsday, townsman.*

§ **215.** Compound nouns are sometimes formed by uniting with a hyphen a verb and an adverb, preposition, or noun; as, a *break-down*, a *pulling-up*, a *take-off*, a *spelling-book.*

§ **216.** Adjectives are frequently compounded with nouns, when the compound thus formed admits of but one accent. If the adjective precedes the noun, the two words are properly written continuously, or without a hyphen; as, *black'bird, blue'bell, fore'ground, red'breast, strong'hold, wild'fire.* When the adjective follows the noun, the two words should be joined with a hyphen; as, *an'kle-deep, blood'-red, foot'-sore, stone'-cold,* except words ending with one of the adjectives *faced, coming, like.* (See § 206, Exc. 5.) But when the noun and the adjective which qualifies it are pronounced each with a distinct accent, the two words should be written separately (as, *church visitant, common sense, high sheriff,* *life eternal, prime minister*), unless they are used as epithets; as, *common sense*, in the phrase *common-sense* philosophy.

§ **217.** Two numerals expressing a number which is the sum of the two are connected with a hyphen (as, *thirty-four*); otherwise, no hyphen is used, and the two numerals are written as separate words; as, *four hundred.* Monosyllabic cardinal numerals denoting more than *one*, and followed by either of the words *fold* or *penny*, are consolidated with it; as, *threefold, threepenny*: if of more than one syllable, they are joined with a hyphen; as, *sixteen-fold, sixteen-penny. Pence*, preceded by a monosyllabic numeral, is consolidated with it; as, *sixpence, ninepence*: if preceded by a numeral of more than one syllable, the two words are written separately; as, *fourteen pence.* Such fractional terms as *one-half, four-fifths, five-sevenths*, &c., are commonly written with a hyphen, as compound words; so also such expressions as a *half-dollar*, a *quarter-box*, &c.

§ **218.** Epithets formed of an adverb ending in *ly*, and a past participle, are generally written as two separate words; as, a *cunningly contrived* scheme, a *newly married* man, a *poorly built* house.

§ **219.** When an adverb and a participle, or a preposition and a participle, are placed after the noun they qualify, they should be written separately, as distinct words; as, the sentence *above cited*, a passage *much admired*, a matter *soon settled.*

§ **220.** When words form only a phrase, — an idiomatic expression, or a compound term in which each word is taken literally, — they should be written as separate words (as, *after all, by and by, for ever, hand in hand, one's self, on high*), unless they are used adjectively and placed before the nouns they qualify, when they should be joined by the hyphen; as, the *never-to-be-forgotten* hero, an *out-of-the-way* place.

§ **221.** It is impossible to lay down principles by which the inquirer may be enabled, in every case, to decide whether words should be compounded or not; but, as most anomalous compounds are given in their proper places in the Vocabulary, it will be sufficient to remember the following general rule given by Goold Brown, in his "Grammar of English Grammars": "Words otherwise liable to be misunderstood, must be joined together or written separately, as the sense and construction may happen to require." Thus, *negro-merchant* will mean a merchant who buys and sells negroes, but *negro merchant*, a merchant who is a negro.

XI. PREFIXES.

§ **222.** When a prefix ends with a different letter from that with which the radical part of the word begins, the combination thus formed should be written continuously, as one unbroken word; as in *contradict, preternatural, substantial, transaction.*

NOTE.—The prefixes *ex* and *vice* are sometimes followed by a hyphen, as in *ex-president, vice-legate, vice-president*; but *vicegerent, vicegerency, viceroy, viceroyal, viceroyalty*, follow the rule.

§ **223.** When a prefix ends with a vowel, and the radical word with which it is combined begins with a vowel, the hyphen is used between them to denote that both vowels are pronounced separately; as in *co-operate, fore-ordain, pre-occupy, re-instate.*

NOTE.—Instead of the hyphen between the adjacent vowels, in such cases, many printers and authors use a diæresis over the second vowel. The prefixes *bi* and *tri* are exempted from the operation of this rule; as in *biennial, triune.*

§ **224.** When a dissyllabic prefix ends with the same consonant as that with which the radical part of a word of several syllables begins, it is followed by a hyphen; as in *counter-revolution, inter-radial.* The hyphen is also used after prefixes of rare occurrence ending with a vowel, even when the radical word begins with a consonant; as, *electro-magnetic, centro-lineal, mucoso-saccharine.*

XII. SYLLABICATION.

§ **225.** A syllable, in the spoken language, has already (§ 60) been defined to be an elementary sound or a combination of elementary sounds uttered by a single impulse of the voice. A syllable, in the written language, is a letter or a combination of letters representing a syllable in the spoken language.

§ **226.** Syllabication, in writing and printing, is the art of arranging the letters of words in groups corresponding to the natural divisions of the spoken words caused by the action of the organs of speech. A practical acquaintance with this subject is very necessary, in order to be able to divide words correctly at the end of a line, when, from want of space, one or more syllables must be carried over to the beginning of the next line. The following rules are observed, in this case, by the best writers; and they are also generally observed, in this work, in dividing words into syllables for the purpose of exhibiting their exact pronunciation. — See NOTE F, p. 79.

Rules for Syllabication.

§ **227.** (1.) Compound words should be separated, at the end of a line, into the simple words which compose them; as, *apple-tree* (not *ap-ple-tree*), *no-body* (not *nobod-y*), *what-ever* (not *whatev-er*).

§ **228.** (2.) Prefixes, suffixes, and grammatical terminations should be separated from the radical words to which they belong, whenever this can be done without misrepresenting the pronunciation; as in *trans*-mit, lead-*er*, rend-*ing* (not *tran*-smit, lea-*der*, ren-*ding*).

NOTE. — The application of this rule frequently enables us to distinguish words of like spelling but of unlike pronunciation and meaning; as, *re-petition* (to petition again) and *rep-etition* (iteration); *bless-ed* (*adjective*) and *blessed* (*past tense and past participle of the verb* to bless); *hind-er* (in the rear) and *hin-der* (to retard).

In ordinary writing and printing, when a suffix or a grammatical termination beginning with a vowel follows a single consonant preceded by a single vowel having its long sound, the consonant is attached to the suffix or termination, in order that the preceding vowel may not seem to have its short sound; as in fra-*mer*, gra-*cest*, ta-*keth*, vi-*ny*, wa-*ging*, advi-*sory*. In some pronouncing dictionaries, however, which indicate the various sounds of the vowels and consonants by means of diacritical marks, the suffix is generally separated from the consonant, in order that the root of the word may be more clearly presented to the eye.

When a suffix or a grammatical termination beginning with a vowel is added to a word of one syllable ending with a single consonant preceded by a single vowel (as *glad*, *plan*), or to a word of more than one syllable, ending in the same manner, and accented on the last syllable (as *allot'*, *begin'*), that consonant is doubled according to § 176, and the latter of the two consonants must be joined to the suffix or the termination; as in glad-*der*, glad-*dest*, plan-*ner*, plan-*nest*, plan-*neth*, allot-*ted*, begin-*ning*. — See Rule 4, § 230.

§ **229.** (3.) Two vowels coming together, and neither forming a digraph nor representing a compound vowel sound (See § 6), must be divided into separate syllables; as in *a-orta, curi-osity, o-olite, ortho-epy.*

§ **230.** (4.) When two or more consonants, capable of beginning a syllable, come between two vowels of which the first is long, they are joined to the second (as in fa-*ble*, tri-*fle*, be-*stride*), unless the second vowel begins a suffix, when they are joined to the first vowel (as in wa*st*-ed, wa*st*-ing). (See Rule 2.) When the consonants are not capable of beginning a syllable, or when the vowel preceding them is short, the first consonant must be joined to the former vowel; as in a*n*-*g*el, ba*n*-*n*er, ca*m*-*b*ric, fe*r*-*t*ile, o*c*-*t*ave, sy*m*-*b*ol; pe*t*-*r*ify, sa*c*-*r*ament, mi*n*-*str*el.

§ **231.** (5.) When a single consonant or a consonant digraph occurs between two vowels, the first of which is under the accent, it is joined to the former vowel, if that is short, as in hă*b*′-it, prŏ*ph*′-et, vĭ*v*′-id, ĕ*p*′′-idĕ*m*′-ic, except when the consonant and the following vowel have together the sound of *sh* in *shall* (No. 37, § 46), or of *z* in *azure* (No. 38, § 47), as in of-fĭ′*ci*al, vĭ′*si*on. (See § 234, Rule 8.) If the former vowel is not short, and is under the accent, the consonant or digraph is joined to the latter vowel; as in fa′*th*er, fē′*v*er, vī′*t*al, hō′*l*y, dū′*t*y.

Note. — In all the cases embraced by this rule, the single consonant or the consonant digraph between two vowels has the effect described in § 66.

§ **232.** (6.) When a single consonant or a consonant digraph occurs between two vowels, the second of which is under the accent, the consonant or digraph is joined to that vowel; as in a-*s*ide′, be-*n*eath′, de-*c*eive′, epi-*d*em′ic, e-*ph*em′eral.

Exception. — The letter *x*, so situated, is joined to the former vowel (as in *lux-u′ri-ous*), both to keep the vowel in its short sound, and because this consonant, when initial, always represents the sound of *z* in *zeal*. — See § 40.

§ **233.** (7.) When a single consonant occurs between two vowels not under the accent, it is joined to the latter; as in ni′ce-*t*y, mem′o-*r*y, mod′′i-*f*i-ca′tion.

Exceptions. — If the latter vowel begins a termination, the consonant is joined to the preceding vowel; as in *rig′or-ous*. (See Rule 2, § 228.) When the vowel *e* succeeds an accented syllable, and is followed by the single consonant *r*, these two letters are joined in the same syllable; as in lit′*er*-al, gen′*er*-al, mis′*er*-y, &c. These words, as Walker remarks, "can never be pronounced lit-*e*-ral, gen-*e*-ral, mis-*e*-ry, &c., without the appearance of affectation."

§ **234.** (8.) The terminations *cean*, *cian*, *cial*, *tial*, *ceous*, *cious*, *geous*, *tious*, *sion*, *tion*, and others of similar formation, must not be divided; as in the words o-*cean*, physi-*cian*, so-*cial*, par-*tial*, preda-*ceous*, gra-*cious*, coura-*geous*, ambi-*tious*, man-*sion*, na-*tion*.

§ **235.** (9.) Some words cannot be so divided, at the end of a line, as unequivocally to show their true pronunciation; as, *acid*, *docile*, *luring*, *miry*, *poring*, *register*. It is, therefore, desirable to avoid the division of such words.

§ **236.** (10.) The letters which form a syllable must never, from want of space, be separated at the end of a line.

NOTE F. — As the word *syllable* (Gr. συλλαβή, from σύν, with, together, and λαμβάνω, to take) literally means only a *collection*, it is not necessarily restricted either to a combination of sounds produced by a single impulse of the voice, or to the collection of letters by which such a combination of sounds is represented. Syllabication may, therefore, be a very different operation, according to the different ends proposed by it. In spelling-books, in which the sound of words forms a main object of attention, the division into syllables is intended to represent the true pronunciation as accurately as possible, no regard being paid to the derivation or mode of composition. Etymological syllabication is a different operation; it is a division of words into such parts as serve to show their origin and primary meaning; as, *ortho-graphy*, *theo-logy*, &c. In the division of words at the end of a line, the etymological principle of syllabication is generally allowed to prevail over the orthoëpical, unless the pronunciation is misrepresented by it. The rules generally adopted, in this case, by American writers and printers, are those given above; and it will be observed that, in every instance in which an etymological division would corrupt or obscure the pronunciation, the orthoëpical mode prevails over it. In English practice, however, the etymological principle is followed to a somewhat greater extent than in the United States, derivative words being resolved into their primitives (as *apo-strophe*, *carni-vorous*), and a single consonant or a consonant digraph between two vowels being joined to the latter (as ba-*l*ance, le-*v*el, spi-*r*it, pro-*ph*et, sy-*n*od, mo-*no*-*po*-*ly*). The letter *x*, however, and single consonants belonging to the former part of a compound or derivative word, are exempted from the operation of the latter rule (as e*x*-ist, u*p*-on, di*s*-arm).

EXPLANATIONS.

In addition to what appears in the Table of Elementary Sounds (p. 12) and in the key-line at the bottom of each page of the Vocabulary, the following explanations will be needed for understanding the notation made use of in this Manual:—

Words are not respelled for pronunciation except when the sound of a letter or of letters in the ordinary orthography is liable to be mistaken for some other sound; and often, when such a case occurs, the single syllable only which presents the difficulty is respelled.

As *e* final is, in most cases, silent, and usually has the effect, when following a single consonant, to lengthen the vowel that precedes it, as in *ale, glebe, site, tone, tune,* words and syllables in which a silent *e* final follows a single consonant and a single vowel are not generally marked nor respelled for pronunciation, except when the vowel that precedes the consonant is short.

When one letter of a vowel digraph is marked, it is to be considered as representing the sound of that digraph, and the other letter is to be regarded as silent; as in *gāin, dāy, plăid, brĕad, dīe, sĭeve, bōwl, fōur, dōor, dūe, feūd.* No mark is used for the digraph *ee* for the reason that its sound is almost invariably that of long *e*.

The combined letters *ou* and *ow*, when unmarked, and when the word in which they occur is not respelled, are sounded as in *our, now.*

As it is a general rule of the language that the vowels *a, e, i, o, u, y* have their long sound at the end of an accented syllable, as in *fa'tal, le'gal, li'on, to'tal, tu'tor, ty'rant,* and their short sound when followed by a consonant in the same syllable, as in *an'tic, hel'met, fin'ish, frol'ic, mus'ket, mys'tic,* they are not generally marked in either of these situations, except in cases that do not conform to the rule.

The letter *c* is hard, or has the sound of *k*, before *a, o, u, l,* and *r*, and also before *t* when final; as in *cap, cold, cup, cloak, crag, act:* it is hard at the end of a word, and also at the end of a syllable unless the next syllable begins with *e, i,* or *y* as in *arc, hav'oc, sec'ond.* It is soft, or has the sound of *s* before *e, i,* or *y* in the same syllable, and also at the end of a syllable, if the next syllable begins with any one of these letters, in which case it is represented by *ç*; as in *cent, cite, face, cy'press, fan'cy, aç'id.*

The letter *g* is hard, or has the sound of *g* in *go*, before *a, o, u, h, l, r,* and *w*: it is hard also at the end of a word and at the end of a syllable, unless the next syllable begins with *e, i,* or *y*. It is soft, or has the sound of *j*, before *e, i,* or *y*, unless the respelling indicates a different sound.

The letter *q* has always the sound of *k*, and it is always followed by *u*; and these letters have together the sound of *kw*, as in *quail* (kwāl), *quit* (kwit), except in some words from the French in which the *u* is silent, as in *pique* (pēk), *co-quette'* (ko-ket').

The letter *x* has the sound of *ks*, as in *tax, wax,* except when the respelling indicates a different sound.

The digraph *ph* has generally the sound of *f*, as in *phrase, seraph.* The few words in which it has not this sound are respelled.

The syllable *tion* is generally pronounced *shun*, as in *na'tion*; and the syllable *sion* has also the same sound, except when it is preceded by a vowel, in which case it has the sound of *zhun*, as in *e-va'sion, ad-he'sion, de-ci'sion, ex-plo'sion, con-fu'sion.*

The vowels *e, i,* and *y*, before *r* in a monosyllable or in an accented syllable, are sounded as in *her, mer'cy, vir'tue, myr'tle.* — See § 21, NOTE.

The combined consonants *ng* are used, in the respelling of French words, to replace *n* or *m*, as a mere sign of nasality in the preceding vowel sound. The French nasal vowel sounds differ from the sounds of the English syllables *ăng, ŏng, ōng, ŭng*, in being formed by allowing the voice to pass simultaneously through the nose and the mouth, and without any contact of the tongue and the soft palate.

Words from foreign languages, often used in English, but not thoroughly Anglicized, as *Ennui, Verbatim*, are printed in Italics.

Spaced Roman letters are used, within brackets, to distinguish modes of spelling that are not so generally prevalent or so well authorized as the other form given in the Vocabulary, but which are sanctioned or recorded as modern by one or more of the eminent lexicographers whose names are given below in the list of abbreviations. (See Abridgement.) A few words, in regard to which there may be a doubt whether one or the other of two modes of spelling them is the more common or the better authorized, are printed in both forms, — in spaced letters within brackets, as well as in close type without brackets. (See Apophthegm and Apothegm.)

A heavy hyphen (-) is used to distinguish such compound words as should have their parts connected by a hyphen in ordinary writing and printing; as, *to-morrow*. Such derivative words as have prefixes that are commonly joined to the primitive by a hyphen are distinguished in the same way; as, *co-operate.*

The exhibition of authorities for the different pronunciations of a word applies to all the derivative or related words, unless some intimation is given to the contrary.

The figures which follow words in the Vocabulary refer to corresponding sections in the Introduction.

ABBREVIATIONS.

a.	adjective.	*N.*	note.	*Gr.*	Greek.
adv.	adverb.	*part.*	participle.	*Heb.*	Hebrew.
coll.	colloquial.	*pl.*	plural.	*It.*	Italian.
conj.	conjunction.	*prep.*	preposition.	*L.*	Latin.
Eng.	English *or* England.	*pron.*	pronoun.	*Sp.*	Spanish.
		Rem.	Remark.		
Exc.	exception.	*v.*	verb.	*Gd.*	Goodrich.
fem.	feminine.			*Sm.*	Smart.
int.	interjection.	*Ar.*	Arabic.	*Wb.*	Webster.
mas.	masculine.	*Fr.*	French.	*Wk.*	Walker.
n.	noun.	*Ger.*	German.	*Wr.*	Worcester.

A

MANUAL

OF

ENGLISH PRONUNCIATION

AND

SPELLING.

Aa-ron′ic (*a-ron′ik*), 109.
Aa-ron′ic-al, 108, 171.
Ab′a-ca, 72.
Ab′a-cist.
A-back′.
Ab′a-cus, 105, 170.
A-bȧft′, 12, 131.
Ab-āl′ien-ate (*-āl′yen-*).
Ab-āl′ien-āt-ed, 183, 228.
Ab-āl′ien-āt-ing.
Ab-āl-ien-a′tion, 46, 112.
A-ban′don, 86.
A-ban′doned (*-dund*),
A-ban-don-ee′, 122. [105.
A-ban′don-er, 77.
A-ban′don-ing.
A-ban′don-ment.
Ab′a-net, 170.
Ab-ar-tic-u-la′tion, 112.
A-base′, 23.
A-based′ (*-bāst′*), Note C, p. 34.
A-base′ment.
A-bash′, 10.
A-bash′ment.
A-bās′ing, 183.
A-bāt′a-ble, 164, 183.
A-bate′, 23.
A-bāt′ed, 183.
A-bate′ment.
A-bāt′er, *n.* one who abates. [*See* Abator, 160.]
A-bāt′ing.
Abatis (Fr.) (*ab′a-tis* or *ab-a-te′*, 154) (161), *n.* a kind of intrenchment.
A-ba′tis (161), *n.* an officer of the stables.
Ab′a-tised (*-tīzd*).
A-bāt′or, *n.* one who abates. [Law term. *See* Abater, 160.]
Abattoir (Fr.) (*ab-a-twor′*).
Abb, 31, 175.
Ab′ba (Heb.), 66, 72.
Ab′ba-cy, 169, 170.
Ab-ba′tial (*-ba′shal*), 46.
Ab-bat′ic-al.
Abbé (Fr.) (*ab′bā*).
Ab′bess.
Ab′bey, 98.
Ab′bot, 66, 86.
Ab′bot-ship.
Ab-bre′vi-ate.
Ab-bre′vi-āt-ed, 183.
Ab-bre-vi-a′tion.
Ab-bre′vi-āt-or, 88.
Ab-bre′vi-a-to-ry, 86.
Ab-bre′vi-a-ture.
Ab′dals (*-dalz*), Note C, [p. 34.
Ab′de-rite, 105.
Ab′dest.
Ab′di-cant.
Ab′di-cate, 73.
Ab′di-cāt-ed, 183.
Ab′di-cāt-ing.
Ab-di-ca′tion, 112.
Ab′di-cāt-ĭve [so Wk. Sm. Wr.; *ab′di-ka-tiv* or *ab-dik′a-tiv*, Gd. 155].
Ab′di-to-ry, 86.
Ab-do′men [so Wk. Sm. Wr.; *ab-do′men* or *ab′do-men*, Gd. 155].
Ab-dom′in-al, 228.
Ab-dom-in-os′co-py.
Ab-dom′in-oŭs.
Ab-duce′, 26, 103.
Ab-duced′ (*-dūst′*), Note [C, p. 34.
Ab-du′cent.
Ab-du′cing.
Ab-duct′, 22, 103.
Ab-duc′tion.
Ab-duct′or (L.).
A-bêar′ance, 14, 169.
Ā-be-ce-da′ri-an, 49, N.
Ā-be-ce′da-ry, 72.
A-bed′, 15.
A-bēle′.
A-bēl′ian (*-bēl′yan*), 51.
A′bel-ite, 83, 152.
Ā-bel-o′ni-an.
A′bel-mosk.
A-ber′de-vīne, 21, N.
Ab-ĕr′rance, 170.
Ab-ĕr′ran-cy, 169.
Ab-ĕr′rant.
Ab-er-ra′tion, 112.
Ab-e-run′cāt-or (*-rung-*), [54.
A-bet′, 15, 103.
A-bet′tal, 176.
A-bet′ted.
A-bet′ting.
A-bet′tor, 88, 169.
A-bey′ance (*-ba′ans*).
A-bey′ant (*-ba′-*), 23, 169.
Ab-hor′, 17, 135.
Ab-horred′, 165, 176.
Ab-hŏr′rence, 169.

ā, ē, ī, ō, ū, ȳ, *long*; ă, ĕ, ĭ, ŏ, ŭ, y̆, *short*; ä *as in* far, ȧ *as in* fast, â *as in* fall; ê *as in* there; ŏŏ *as in* foot; ç *as in* facile; gh *as* g *in* go; t͟h *as in* this.

Ab-hŏr'ren-cy, 93.
Ab-hor'rer.
Ab-hŏr'ri-ble, 48, 164.
Ab-hor'ring, 176.
A-bīd'ance, 183.
A-bīde', 25.
A-bīd'er, 228.
A-bīd'ing.
A'bi-es (L.) (*ā'bi-ēz*).
A-bi'e-tīne, 152.
Ab'i-gail, 70, 170.
A-bil'i-ty, 108, 169.
Ab-in-tes'tate.
Ab-ir-ri-ta'tion.
Ab'ject, *a.* & *n.* 161.
Ab-ject', *v.* 103.
Ab-ject'ed-ness.
Ab-jec'tion.
Ab-ju-di-ca'tion.
Ab-ju-ra'tion, 49, N; 112.
Ab-jure', 26.
Ab-jūred'.
Ab-jūr'er, 77, 183.
Ab-jūr'ing.
Ab-lac-ta'tion, 112.
Ab-lā-que-a'tion [so Wk. Wr.; *ab-lak-we-a'-shun*, Sm. Wb. Gd., 155].
Ab-la'tion.
Ab'la-tīve (84) [*not* ab'-l-tīv, 132, 153].
A-blaze', 23.
A'ble, 164.
Ab'lep-sy, 169.
Ab'lu-ent, 89, 105.
Ab-lu'tion, 112.
Ab-lu'tion-a-ry, 72, 171.
Ab-lu'vi-on.
A'bly, 93.
Ab'ne-gate.
Ab'ne-gāt-ed, 183.
Ab'ne-gāt-ing.
Ab-ne-ga'tion, 112.
Ab'ne-ga-tīve, 106.
Ab-norm'al.
Ab-norm'i-ty, 108.
A-bōard', 24.
A-bode', 24.
A-bol'ish, 66, 104, 170.
A-bol'ish-a-ble, 164.
A-bol'ished (*-isht*), Note [C, p. 34.
A-bol'ish-er.
A-bol'ish-ing.
A-bol'ish-ment. [112.
Ab-o-lī'tion (*-lish'un*),
Ab-o-lī'tion-ism (*-lish'-un-izm*), 133, 136.
Ab-o-lī'tion-ist.
A-bom'i-na-ble, 164, 169.
A-bom'i-na-bly.
A-bom'i-nate.
A-bom-i-na'tion.

Ab-o-rig'in-al (*-rij-*).
Ab-o-rig'i-nēs (L. pl.) (*rij'i-nēz*).
A-bor'tion, 112.
A-bor'tīve, 84.
A-bound', 28.
A-bound'ed, 228.
A-bound'ing.
A-bout', 28.
A-bove' (*a-buv'*), 22, 163.
Ā-bra-ca-dab'ra, 72, 116.
A-brade', 23.
A-brād'ed, 183.
A-brād'ing.
Ā-bra-ham'ic, 109.
Ā-bra-ham-it'ic-al, 108.
A-bran'chi-an (*-brang'-ki-an*), 52, 54.
A-bran'chi-ate (*brang'-ki-*).
Ab-ra'sion (*-ra'zhun*), 112.
A-brâum'; 17.
A-brĕast', 15, 232.
Abreuvoir (Fr.) (*ab-ruh-vwor'*).
A-bridge' (*-brij'*), 16, 45.
A-bridged' (*-brijd'*), 183.
A-bridg'er, 77.
A-bridg'ing.
A-bridg'ment (171, 185) [Abridgement, 203].

☞ The prevailing usage is to omit the *e* after the *g* in this word, as also in *acknowledgment*, *judgment*, though its insertion is more in accordance with analogy. Todd, in his edition of Johnson's Dictionary, restores the *e* to these words from which Johnson had omitted it, "in order," as Smart remarks, "that they may not exhibit the otherwise unexampled irregularity of *g* soft before a consonant." For the same reason Smart spells these words in his Dictionary with an e following *g*.

A-brōach', 24.
A-brōach'ment.
A-broâd', 17.
Ab'ro-gate, 73.
Ab'ro-gāt-ed, 183.
Ab'ro-gāt-ing.
Ab-ro-ga'tion, 112.
Ab-rupt', 22, 121.
Ab-rup'tion.
Ab'scess (*ab'ses*), 162.
Ab-scind' (*-sind'*), 162.
Ab'sciss (*-sis*) [pl. *ab'-sciss-es*], 171.
Ab-scis'sa (L.) (*ab-sis'a*) [pl. *Ab-scis'sæ*, 198.]
Ab-scis'sion (*-sizh'un*), 112, 162, 171. [*See* Transition.]
Ab-scond', 18, 103.
Ab-scond'ed.
Ab-scond'ing.
Ab'sence.
Ab'sent, *a.* 103, 161.
Ab-sent', *v.* 103, 161.
Ab-sen-ta'tion, 112.
Ab-sent'ed.
Ab-sent-ee', 122.
Ab-sent-ee'ism (*-izm*), [133.
Ab-sent'er, 77.
Ab-sent'ing.
Ab'sinthe (*-sinth*).
Ab-sin'thi-an, 169.
Ab-sin'thi-āt-ed.
Ab-sin'thīne, 152, 171.
Ab'so-lute, 105.
Ab-so-lu'tion, 112.
Ab'so-lūt-ism (*-izm*).
Ab'so-lūt-ist, 106.
Ab-sol'u-to-ry (86) [so Wk. Sm. Wr.; *ab'-so-lu-to-ry* or *ab-sol'-u-to-ry*, Gd. 155].
Ab-solv'a-to-ry, 86, 171.
Ab-solve' (*-zolv'*), 40.
Ab-solved (*-zolvd'*).
Ab-solv'ing (*-zolv'ing*),
Ab-sorb', 17, 103. [183.
Ab-sorb-a-bil'i-ty, 108.
Ab-sorb'a-ble, 164, 169.
Ab-sorbed' (*ab-sorbd'*),
Ab-sorb'ent. [165.
Ab-sorb'ing.
Ab-sorp'tion, 112.
Ab-sorp'tīve, 84.
Ab-stāin', 23, 103.
Ab-stāined', 165.
Ab-stāin'ing.
Ab-ste'mi-oŭs, 171.
Ab-sterge', 21, N.; 129.
Ab-sterged', 165.
Ab-ster'gent, 183, 171.
Ab-ster'ging, 183.
Ab-ster'sion.
Ab-ster'sīve, 84.
Ab'sti-nence, 171.
Ab'sti-nent, 169.
Ab-stract', *v.* 103, 161.
Ab'stract, *a.* & *n.* 103,
Ab-stract'ed. [161.
Ab-stract'er, 77.
Ab-stract'ing.
Ab-strac'tion, 234.
Ab-stract'īve, 84.
Ab'stract-ly, *or* Ab-stract'ly [*ab'strakt-ly*, Wr. Wb. Gd.; *ab-*

strakt'ly, Wk. Sm. 155].
Ab'stract-ness, 106.
Ab-struse' (*ab-stroos'*), 19, 121.
Ab-surd', 21, 121.
Ab-surd'i-ty, 169, 171.
A-bun'dance, 169, 230.
A-bun'dant, 169.
A-buse' (*-būz'*), *v.* 136, 161.
A-buse', *n.* 161.
A-bused' (*-būzd'*), 183.
A-būs'er (*-būz'-*).
A-būs'ing (*-būz'-*).
A-bu'sīve, 84.
A-but', 22.
A-but'ment.
A-but'tal, 176.
A-but'ted, 171.
A-but'ter.
A-but'ting.
A-byss', 16, 171.
Ab-ys-sin'i-an, 171.
A-ca'ci-a (L.) (*-ka'shĭ-*), 46.
A-ca'cian (*-ka'shan*), 46.
Ac-a-dem'ic, 52, 109.
Ac-a-dem'ic-al, 108.
Ac-a-de-mĭ'cian (*-mish'-an*), 171.
A-cad'e-my [so Sm. Wr. Wb. Gd.; *a-kad'e-my* or *ak'a-dem-y*, Wk. 155].
Ac-a-le'phan, 35, 122.
A-cal-y'cīne, 82, 152.
Ac-a-lyç'i-noŭs, 39, 171.
Ac-a-na'ceous (*-shus*), 112.
A-can'tha, 72.
A-can-tha'ceoŭs (*-shus*), 112, 169.
A-can'thīne, 82, 152.
A-can-tho-ceph'a-lan, 35, 116.
A-can'tho-pod.
A-can-thop-te-ryg'i-oŭs (*-rij'ĭ-us*), 116, 171.
A-can'thus (L.).
A-car'di-ac, 108.
A-căr'i-dan, 169.
A-car'poŭs.
Ac'a-rus (L.) [pl. *Ac'a-ri*, 198].
A-cat-a-lec'tic, 109.
A-cat'a-lep-sy, 169.
A-cat-a-lep'tic, 109.
A-cau-les'cent, 171.
A-cau'līne, 82, 152.
A-cau'loŭs, 100.
Ac-cede', 39, 169.
Ac-cēd'ed, 183.
Ac-cēd'ing.
Ac-cel'er-ate, 171, 233.
Ac-cel'er-āt-ed.
Ac-cel'er-āt-ing.
Ac-cel-er-a'tion, 112.
Ac-cel'er-āt-īve, 84, 106.
Ac-cel'er-a-to-ry, 86, 106.
Ac-cend-i-bil'i-ty, 108.
Ac-cend'i-ble, 108, 164.
Ac'cent, *n.* 103, 161.
Ac-cent', *v.* 103, 161.
Ac-cent'ed.
Ac-cent'ing.
Ac-cent'or, 88, 169.
Ac-cent'u-al, 89.
Ac-cent'u-ate, 73, 89.
Ac-cent-u-a'tion, 112.
Ac-cept', 15, 103.
Ac-cept-a-bil'i-ty, 108, 171.
Ac-cept'a-ble (169) [so Sm. Wr. Wb. Gd.; *ak'sept-a-bl*, Wk. 155].
Ac-cept'a-bly, 93.
Ac-cept'ance, 169.
Ac-cept-a'tion, 112, 228.
Ac-cept'ed.
Ac-cept'er, *n.* one who accepts. [*See* Acceptor, 160].
Ac-cept'ing.
Ac-cept'or, *n.* one who accepts a draft, &c. [Law term.— *See* Accepter, 160].
Ac-cess', *or* Ac'cess [so Wr. Gd.; *ak-ses'*, Wk. Sm. 155].
Ac'ces-sa-ri-ly, 106.
Ac'ces-sa-ry (72) [A c c e s s o r y, 203.]
Ac-ces-si-bil'i-ty.
Ac-ces'si-ble, 164, 171.
Ac-ces'si-bly, 93.
Ac-ces'sion, 112.
Ac-ces'sion-al.
Ac-cess'īve, 84.
Ac-ces-so'ri-al.
Ac'ces-so-ri-ly.
Ac'ces-so-ry (86) A c c e s s a r y, 203].

☞ "*Accessory* claims a slight etymological preference, but is less usual." *Smart.*

Ac'ci-dence, 105, 171.
Ac'ci-dent.
Ac-ci-dent'al, 228.
Ac-cip'i-trīne, 82, 152.
Ac-claim', 23, 52.
Ac-cla-ma'tion (112). [*See* Acclimation, 148.]
Ac-clam'a-to-ry, 86.
Ac-cli'mate, 122.
Ac-cli'māt-ed, 183.
Ac-cli'māt-ing.
Ac-cli-ma'tion. [*See* Acclamation, 148.]
Ac-cli'ma-tize, 202.
Ac-cli'ma-tized, 165.
Ac-cli'ma-tīz-ing, 183.
Ac-cliv'i-ty, 108.
Ac-cli'voŭs.
Ac-co-lāde', *or* Ac-co-läde' [so Wr.; *ak-o-lād'*, Wb. Gd.; *ak-o-läd*, Sm. 155].
Ac-com'mo-date, 170.
Ac-com'mo-dāt-ed.
Ac-com'mo-dāt-ing.
Ac-com-mo-da'tion, 116.
Ac-com'mo-dāt-īve, 84.
Ac-com'mo-dāt-or, 88
Ac-com'pa-nĭed (*-nid*), 171, 186.
Ac-com'pa-ni-er (*-kum'-*)
Ac-com'pa-ni-ment (*-kum'-*), 169.
Ac-com'pa-nist (*-kum'-*).
Ac-com'pa-ny (*-kum'-*), 171.
Ac-com'pa-ny-ing (*-kum'-*).
Ac-com'plīce, 169, 171.
Ac-com'plish.
Ac-com'plish-a-ble, 164.
Ac-com'plished (*-kom'-plisht*), Note C, p. 34.
Ac-com'plish-er.
Ac-com'plish-ing.
Ac-com'plish-ment.
Ac-cord', 17.
Ac-cord'ance, 169.
Ac-cord'ant, 169.
Ac-cord'ed.
Ac-cord'ing.
Ac-cord'i-on, 171.
Ac-cŏst', 18, Note.
Ac-cŏst'a-ble, 164.
Ac-cŏst'ed.
Ac-cŏst'ing.
Accouchement (Fr.) *ak-koosh'mong*, 154).
Ac-count', 28.
Ac-count-a-bil'i-ty.
Ac-count'a-ble, 164, 171.
Ac-count'ant.

☞ Sometimes spelled Accomptant when used in a technical sense, as in the term *Accomptant-General*, an officer in the English Court of Chancery.

Ac-count'-bo͝ok, 206, Exc. 4.
Ac-count'ed.
Ac-count'ing.

Ac-coŭp'le (-*kup'l*), 164.
Ac-coŭp'led (-*kup'ld*).
Ac-coŭp'le-ment (-*kup'-l-ment*).
Ac-coŭp'ling(-*kup'ling*)
Ac-cou'tre (*ak-koo'tur*), (169, 171) [Accouter preferred by Wb. and Gd. — *See* Note E, p. 70.]
Ac-cou'tred (-*terd*), 183.
Ac-cou'tre-ment (-*koo'-tur-*).
Ac-cou'tring(-*koo'*-),183
Ac-cred'it.
Ac-cred'it-ed.
Ac-cres'cence.
Ac-cres'cent, 171.
Ac-cre'tion, 112.
Ac-cre'tive, 84.
Ac-crue' (-*kroo'*), 91.
Ac-crued' (-*krood'*), 183.
Ac-cru'ing (-*kroo'*-).
Ac-cu-ba'tion.
Ac-cum'ben-cy.
Ac-cum'bent, 169.
Ac-cu'mu-late, 73.
Ac-cu'mu-lāt-ed.
Ac-cu'mu-lāt-ing, 183.
Ac-cu-mu-la'tion, 112.
Ac-cu'mu-lāt-īve, 84.
Ac-cu'mu-lāt-or, 169.
Ac'cu-ra-cy, 169, 171.
Ac'cu-rate, 73, 89.
Ac-curse', 21, 103.
Ac-cursed' (*ak-kurst'*), Note C, p. 34.
Ac-curs'ing.
Ac-cūs'a-ble (-*kuz'*-), 164, 169.
Ac-cu-sa'tion (-*za'-shun*), 112.
Ac-cūs'a-tīve(-*kūz'*-),84.
Ac-cūs'a-to-ry, (-*kūz'*-) 86.
Ac-cuse' (-*kūz'*), 26.
Ac-cūs'er (-*kūz'er*), 183.
Ac-cūs'ing (-*kūz'ing*).
Ac-cus'tom, 86.
Ac-cus'tom-a-ri-ly, 72, 106.
Ac-cus'tom-a-ry, 72,169.
Ac-cus'tomed (-*kus'-tumd*), 165.
Ac-cus'tom-ing.
Ace, 23, 39.
A-cel'da-ma (Heb.), 72.
A-ceph'a-lan, 35.
A-ceph'a-loŭs, 35, 171.
Ace'point, 206.
A-cerb', 21, Note.
A-cerb'i-ty, 78, 108, 169.
Aç-er-ose' (233, Exc.) [so Sm. Wr.; *as'er-ōs*, Wb. Gd. 155.]
Aç'er-oŭs.
A-ces'cen-cy, 169, 171.
A-ces'cent, 171.
Aç-e-ta'ri-oŭs.
Aç'e-ta-ry, 72, 169.
Aç'e-tate, 171.
A-cet'ic, *or* A-ce'tic [*a-set'ik*, Sm. Wr.; *a-se'-tik*, Wb. Gd. 155.]
A-cet'i-fīed, *or* A-ce'ti-fīed, 165.
A-cet'i-fȳ, *or* A-ce'ti-fȳ, 94, 108.
A-cet'i-fy-ing, *or* A-ce'-ti-fy-ing.
Aç-e-tim'e-ter, 169.
Aç-e-tim'e-try.
Aç'e-tone, 169.
Aç-e-tose'.
A-ce'toŭs, 171.
A-chæ'an (*a-ke'an*) (52) [Achean, Wb. Gd. 203.]
A-cha'ian (*a-ka'yan*), 52, 51.
Ache (*āk*), 52, 171.
Ached (*ākt*), Note C, p. 34.
Ach'ing (*āk'ing*), 183.
A-che'ni-um (*a-ke'ni-um*), 169.
Ach'e-ron (*ak'e-ron*).
A-chiēv'a-ble, 169, 183.
A-chiēve', 13, 171.
A-chiēved', 150.
A-chiēve'ment, 185.
A-chiēv'er.
A-chiēv'ing, 183.
Āch'ing (*āk'ing*), 183.
A'chor (*a'kor*). [*See* Acre, 148.]
Ach-ro-mat'ic (*ak-ro-*), *or* Ā-chro-mat'ic (*ā'-kro-*) (171) [*ak-ro-mat'ik*, Wr. Gd.; *ā-kro-mat'ik*, Sm. 155.]
Ach-ro'ma-tism (*ak-ro'-ma-tizm*), *or* Ā-chro'-ma-tism (*ā-kro'ma-tizm*) [*ak-ro'ma-tizm*, Gd.; *ā-kro'ma-tizm*, Sm. Wr. 155.]
Ach-ro'ma-tize (*ak-ro'*-) *or* Ā-chro'ma-tize (*ā-kro'*-), 202.
A-cic'u-lar, 89, 108, 171.
A-cic'u-late, 73, 89.
A-cic'u-li-form.
Aç'id, 39, 171, 235.
Aç-id-if'er-oŭs, 108.
A-cid'i-fī-a-ble, 169.
A-cid-i-fi-ca'tion.
A-cid'i-fīed, 171.
A-cid'i-fī-er.
A-cid'i-fȳ, 94, 108.
A-cid'i-fȳ-ing.
Aç-id-im'e-ter, 169.
Aç-id-im'e-try, 170.
A-cid'i-ty, 171.
A-cid'u-late, 73, 89.
A-cid'u-lāt-ed.
A-cid'u-lāt-ing.
A-cid-u-la'tion, 112.
A-cid'u-loŭs, 89, 108.
Aç'i-form, 169.
Aç-i-na'ceoŭs (-*na'shus*) 112, 169.
Aç-i-naç'i-form, 171.
A-cin'i-form, 169.
Aç-i-nose' [so Wr.; *as'-i-nōs*, Sm. Wb. Gd. 155.]
Aç'i-noŭs.
Ac-knŏwl'edge(-*nol'ej*), 171. [*ejd*).
Ac-knŏwl'edged (-*nol'*-
Ac-knŏwl'edg-er.
Ac-knŏwl'edg-ing.
Ac-knŏwl'edg-ment (171, 185). [*See* Abridgment.]
Ac'me, 163.
A-col'o-gy, 108.
A-col'o-thist.
Ac'o-lȳte.
Ac'o-lȳth, 170.
A-con-dy-lose'.
A-con'dy-loŭs.
Ac'o-nīte, 83, 152.
A'corn.
A'corned, 150.
Ā-co-tyl-e'don, 122.
Ā-co-tyl-e'don-oŭs [so Sm. Wb. Gd.; *ā-cŏt-y-led'o-nus*, Wr. 155.]
A-cou'chy (*a-koo'chy*).
A-cous'tic, 28, 109.
A-cous'tics, 28, 109.
Ac-quāint', 34, 171.
Ac-quāint'ance, 169.
Ac-quāint'ed.
Ac-quāint'ing.
Ac-quest', 34.
Ac-qui-esce' (*ak-wi-es'*), 162, 163, 171.
Ac-qui-esced' (-*est'*), Note C, p. 34.
Ac-qui-es'cence, 171.
Ac-qui-es'cent.
Ac-qui-es'cing.
Ac-quīr-a-bil'i-ty.
Ac-quīr'a-ble, 164.
Ac-quire', 25.

Ac-quired′, 150.
Ac-quire′ment.
Ac-quīr′er, 77, 169.
Ac-quīr′ing.
Ac-qui-si′tion (*ak-wĭ-zish′un*), 171.
Ac-quis′i-tĭve (*kwiz′ĭ-*), 108, 171.
Ac-quis′i-tĭve-ness (*ac-kwiz′ĭ-*).
Ac-quit′, 16, 34.
Ac-quit′tal, 176.
Ac-quit′tance.
Ac-quit′ted.
Ac-quit′ting.
Ac′ra-sy (169) [so Wr. Wb. Gd.; *ā′cra-sy*, Sm. 155.]
A′cre (*a′kur*) (164, 171). [*See* Achor, 148.]
A′cre-age (*a′kur-*).
A′cred (*a′kurd*), 165, 183.
Ac′rid, 10.
Ac-ri-mo′ni-oŭs, 171.
Ac′ri-mo-ny, 86, 93, 171.
A-crit′ic-al.
Ac′ri-tude, 169.
Ac-ro-a-mat′ic, 109.
Ac-ro-a-mat′ic-al, 108.
Ac-ro-a-mat′ics.
Ac-ro-at′ic.
Ac-ro-at′ics.
Ac′ro bat [so Gd.; A c r o b a t e, Wr. 203.]
Ac-ro-ce-rau′ni-an, 171.
Ac′ro-gen.
Ac-rog′e-noŭs (*-roj′-*).
Ac′ro-lith.
A-crol′ith-an.
A-cro′mi-al.
A-cro′mi-on, 169.
A-cron′ic.
A-cron′y-cal [A c r o n i c a l, 203.]
A-cron′y-cal-ly, 93.
A-crop′o-lis, 170.
Ac′ro-spire.
Ac′ro-spired, 165.
A-crŏss′, 18, Note.
A-cros′tic, 109, 171.
A-cros′tic-al.
Ac-ro-te′ri-um (L.) [pl. *Ac-ro-te′ri-a*, 198.]
Act, 10, 52.
Act′ed.
Ac′ti-an.
Act′ing.
Ac-tin′i-a (L.) [pl. *Ac-tin′i-æ*, 198.]
Ac-tin′i-form, 169.
Ac-tin′ic.
Ac′tin-ism (*-izm*), 133.
Ac-tin′o-grăph, 127.
Ac-tin′o-līte.
Ac-tin-o-lit′ic.
Ac-tin-ol′o-gy.
Ac-tin-om′e-ter, 108.
Ac′tion, 10, 46.
Ac′tion-a-ble, 164.
Ac′tion-a-bly, 93.
Ac′tion-a-ry, 72.
Ac′tion-ist.
Act′ĭve, 84.
Ac-tiv′i-ty.
Act′or, 88, 169.
Act′ress, 228.
Act′u-al, 89.
Act-u-al′i-ty, 169.
Act′u-al-ize, 202.
Act′u-al-ly, 93.
Act′u-a-ry, 72.
Act′u-ate, 73, 89.
Act′u-āt-ed, 183.
Act′u-āt-ing.
A-cu′le-ate.
A-cu′le-āt-ed.
A-cu′le-oŭs.
A-cu′men, 113, 125.
A-cu′min-ate, 171.
A-cu′min-āt-ed.
A-cu′min-āt-ing.
A-cu-min-a′tion.
A-cu′min-oŭs.
Ac-u-punct-u-ra′tion, 112, 11?.
Ac-u-punct′ure, 91.
A-cute′, 26.
A-dac′tyl.
Ad′age, 169.
Ad′a-mant, 171.
Ad-a-mant-e′an, 110.
Ad-a-mant′īne, 84, 152, 171.
Ad-am′ic, 109.
Ad′am-īte, 152.
Ad-am it′ic, 109.
Ad′am's-Ap′ple, 213.
A-dapt′, 10, 103.
A-dapt-a-bil′i-ty, 108.
A-dapt′a-ble, 164, 169.
Ad-apt-a′tion, 112.
A-dapt′ed.
A-dapt′er, 169.
A-dapt′ing.
A-dapt′ĭve, 84.
Add, 10, 175.
Ad-den′dum (L.) [pl. *Ad-den′da*, 198.]
Ad′der, 66, 170.
Ad-di-bil′i-ty.
Ad′di-ble, 164, 169.
Ad-dict′, 16, 103.
Ad-dict′ed.
Ad-dic′tion.
Add′ing, 228.
Ad-dit′a-ment, 169.
Ad-di′tion (*-dish′un*), 112, 171, 231.
Ad-di′tion-al (*-dish′un-*)
Ad′dle, 164.
Ad′dle-hĕad′ed, 205, Exc. 5.
Ad′dling, 230.
Ad-dress′, *n.* & *v.*
Ad-dressed′ (*-drest′*), 165, Note C, p. 34.
Ad-dress′er, 77, 169.
Ad-dress′ing.
Ad-duce′, 26, 103.
Ad-duced′ (*-dūst′*), Note C, p. 34.
Ad-du′cent.
Ad-du′cer.
Ad-du′ci-ble, 164.
Ad-du′cing.
Ad-duc′tion.
Ad-duc′tĭve, 84.
Ad-duc′tor, 88, 169.
A-del′o-pod, 105.
A-demp′tion.
Ad-e-nog′ra-phy, 108.
Ad′e-noid.
Ad-e-no-log′ic-al (*-loj′-*).
Ad-e-nol′o-gy, 108.
Ad-e-no-phyl′loŭs, *or* Ad-e-noph′yl-loŭs [so Wr.]

☞ Worcester is the only lexicographer, except Knowles, who is uniform in his mode of pronouncing words that end in *phyllous*. Knowles pl ces the accent on the antepenult. Of the *fourteen* words of this class found in Smart's Dictionary, *six* are accented on the antepenult, and *eight* on the penult. Of the *seventeen* found in the last edition of Webster's Dictionary, edited by Goodrich, *fifteen* have the accent on the antepenult, and *two*, which are added in the Appendix, on the penult.

Ad-e-nose′ [so Wr.; *ad′e-nōs*, Sm. Gd. 155.]
Ad′e-noŭs.
Ad-e-not′o-my, 108.
A-dept′, 15, 232.
Ad′e-qua-cy, 169, 171.
Ad′e-quate, 73.
Ad-es-se-na′ri-an, 49, N.
Ad-here′, 13, 103.
Ad-hered′, 165, 183.
Ad-hēr′ence, 169, 183.
Ad-hēr′ent, 169.
Ad-hēr′er.
Ad-hēr′ing, 183.

Ad-he'sion (*-he'zhun*), 112.
Ad-he'sĭve, 84.
Ad-hor'ta-to-ry, 233.
A-dieu' (*a-du'*), 26.
Ad-i-poç'er-ate.
Ad-i-poç'er-āt-ed.
Ad-i-poç'er-āt-ing.
Ad-i-poç-er-a'tion, 171.
Ad'i-po-cēre, 169, 171.
Ad-i-poç'er-oŭs, 171.
Ad-i-pose' [so Wr.; *ad'-i-pōs*, Sm. Gd. 155.]
Ad'ip-sy, 169.
Ad'it, 170.
Ad-ja'cence.
Ad-ja'cen-cy, 169.
Ad-ja'cent, 171.
Ad'jec-tĭve, 84.
Ad'jec-tiv-al [so Wr.; *ad-jec-tīv'al*, Gd. 155.]
Ad-join', 27, 103.
Ad-joined', 165.
Ad-join'ing.
Ad-journ' (*ad-jurn'*),21.
Ad-journed' (*-jurnd'*).
Ad-journ'ing (*-jurn'-*).
Ad-journ'ment(*-jurn'-*).
Ad-judge' (*-juj'*), 45.
Ad-judged' (*-jujd'*), 165.
Ad-judg'ing (*-juj'-*),183.
Ad-judg'ment (185). [*See* Abridgment.]
Ad-ju'di-cate, 73, 108.
Ad-ju'di-cāt-ed, 228.
Ad-ju'di-cāt-ing.
Ad-ju-di-ca'tion.
Ad-ju'di-cāt-or, 169.
Ad'junct, 103.
Ad-junc'tion.
Ad-junct'ĭve, 84.
Ad-junct'ly, 93.
Ad-ju-rā'tion.
Ad-ju'ra-to-ry, 86.
Ad-jure', 26, 103.
Ad-jured', 150, 165.
Ad-jūr'er, 77, 183.
Ad-jūr'ing.
Ad-just', 22, 103.
Ad-just'a-ble, 164.
Ad-just'ed.
Ad-just'er.
Ad-just'ing.
Ad-just'ĭve, 84.
[Adjutage.—*See* Ajutage, 203.]
Ad'ju-tan-cy, 169.
Ad'ju-tant, 169, 171.
Ad'ju-tant-General, 216.
Ad'ju-vant [so Wk. Sm. Wr.; *ad-ju'vant*, Wb. Gd. 155.]

Ad-meas'ure-ment (*ad-mezh'ur-*), 91, 171.
Ad-min'is-ter, 77, 170.
Ad-min'is-tered, 165.
Ad-min-is-te'ri-al, 116.
Ad-min'is-ter-ing.
Ad-min-is-tra'tion, 112.
Ad-min'is-trāt-or, 228.
Ad-min-is-tra'trix.
Ad-mi-ra-bil'i-ty.
Ad'mi-ra-ble, 122, 143, 164.
Ad'mi-ra-bly, 93.
Ad'mi-ral, 105.
Ad'mi-ral-ty, 106, 145.
Ad-mi-ra'tion, 112.
Ad-mire', 25, 103.
Ad-mired', 165, 183.
Ad-mir'er, 169.
Ad-mīr'ing.
Ad-mis-si-bil'i-ty, 170.
Ad-mis'si-ble, 78, 164.
Ad-mis'si-bly, 93.
Ad-mis'sion (*-mish'un*), 46.
Ad-mis'so-ry, 86, 93.
Ad-mit', 16, 103.
Ad-mit'tance, 176.
Ad-mit'ted.
Ad-mit'ter.
Ad-mit'ting.
Ad-mix', 16, 103.
Ad-mixed' (*ad-mixt'*), Note C, p. 34.
Ad-mix'ing.
Ad-mix'tion (*ad-miks'-chun*), 44, Note 1.
Ad-mixt'ure, 91.
Ad-mon'ish, 104.
Ad-mon'ished (*-isht*), Note C, p. 34.
Ad-mon'ish-er.
Ad-mon'ish-ing.
Ad-mo-ni'tion (*-nish'-un*), 46, 171.
Ad-mon'i-tĭve, 108.
Ad-mon'i-tor, 78.
Ad-mon'i-to-ry, 86, 93.
Ad-mor-ti-za'tion.
Ad-nas'cent, 171.
Ad-nate', 121.
Ad-nom'in-al.
Ad'noun.
A-do' (*a-doo'*), 19.
Ad-o-les'cence, 171.
Ad-o-les'cen-cy, 169.
Ad-o-les'cent.
Ad-o-ne'an, 110.
A-don'ic.
A-dopt', 18, 103.
A-dopt'ed.
A-dopt'er.
A-dopt'ing.

A-dop'tion, 46.
A-dopt'ĭve, 84.
A-dōr'a-ble, 49, N.; 164.
A-dōr'a-bly.
Ad-o-ra'tion, 112.
A-dore', 24, 103.
A-dōred', 150, 183.
A-dōr'er.
A-dōr'ing.
A-dorn', 17, 103, 135.
A-dorned', 165.
A-dorn'ing.
Ad-os-cu-la'tion.
A-down', 28.
A-drift', 16.
Ad-ro-ga'tion.
A-droit', 27.
A-dry', 25.
Ad-sci-tĭ'tioŭs (*-sĭ-tish'-us*), 46, 171.
Ad'script.
Ad-u-la'tion, 112.
Ad'u-la-to-ry, 86, 171.
A-dult' [*not* ad'ult, 153.]
A-dul'ter-ant.
A-dul'ter-ate, *v.* & *a.* 73.
A-dul'ter-āt-ed, 183.
A-dul'ter-āt-ing.
A-dul-ter-a'tion.
A-dul'ter-er.
A-dul'ter-ess.
A-dul'ter-īne [so Wk. Sm. Wr.; *a-dul'ter-in*, Wb. Gd. 155.]
A-dul'ter-oŭs.
A-dul'ter-y, 233.
Ad-um'brant.
Ad-um'brate.
Ad-um'brāt-ed, 183.
Ad-um'brāt-ing.
Ad-um-bra'tion, 112.
A-dun'ci-ty, 169.
A-dun'coŭs (*a-dung'-kus*), 54.
A-dust', 22.
A-dust'ion (*-yun*), 51.
Ad-vȧnce', *n.*& *v.*12,131.
Ad-vȧnced' (*-vȧnst'*).
Ad-vȧnce'ment.
Ad-vȧn'cer, 183.
Ad-vȧn'cing.
Ad-vȧn'cĭve.
Ad-vȧn'tage, 70, 131, 169.
Ad-vȧn'taged, 150, 183.
Ad-van-ta'geoŭs (*-ta'-jus*), 45, 169, 171.
Ad-van'ta-ging.
Ad-vene', 13, 103.
Ad'vent, 10, 103.
Ad-ven-tĭ'tious (*-tish'-us*), 46, 171.
Ad-vent'u-al, 89.

Ad-vent′ure, 91.
Ad-vent′ured, 165.
Ad-vent′ure-ful (-*fōōl*), 180.
Ad-vent′ur-er, 91, 183.
Ad-vent′ure-some (-*sum*).
Ad-vent′ur-ing, 91, 183.
Ad-vent′ur-oŭs.
Ad′verb, 10, 103.
Ad-verb′i-al, 123.
Ad-ver-sa′ri-a (L. pl.).
Ad′ver-sa-ry, 72, 93.
Ad-ver′sa-tĭve, 84.
Ad′verse [*not* ad-verse′, 153.]
Ad′verse-ly [so Sm. Wk. Wb. Gd.; *ad-vers′ly*, Wr. 155.]
Ad-ver′si-ty, 21, N.; 93.
Ad-vert′, 21, Note.
Ad-vert′ed.
Ad-vert′ence, 169.
Ad-vert′en-cy, 169.
Ad-vert′ent.
Ad-vert′ing.
Ad-ver-tise′, *or* Ad′ver-tise (-*tīz*) (136, 202) [so Wr.; *ad-ver-tīz′*, Wk. Wb. Gd.; *ad′ver-tīz*, Sm. 155.]
Ad-ver-tised′ (-*tīzd′*).
Ad-ver′tise-ment (-*tīz*-), *or* Ad-ver-tīse′ment (-*tīz*-) [so Wk. Wr.; *ad-ver′tīz-ment*, Sm. Wb. Gd. 155.]
Ad-ver-tīs′er (-*tīz′*-), 183.
Ad-ver-tīs′ing (-*tīz′*-).
Ad-vice′, 25.
Ad-vīs-a-bil′i-ty (-*vīz*-), 116.
Ad-vīs′a-ble (*vīz′a-bl*), 40, 164.
Ad-vīs′a-bly (*ad-vīz′a-bly*), 93.
Ad-vise′ (-*vīz′*), 103, 136, 202.
Ad-vised′ (-*vīzd′*), 165.
Ad-vis′er (-*vīz′er*), 183.
Ad-vis′ing (-*vīz′ing*).
Ad′vo-ca-cy, 169.
Ad′vo-cate, *n.* & *v.* 105.
Ad′vo-cāt-ed, 228, Note.
Ad′vo-cāt-ing.
Ad-vo-ca′tion, 112.
Ad-vow-ee′, 122, 171.
Ad-vow′son, 28.
Ad-y-nam′ic [so Wr.; *ā-dy-nam′ik*, Wb. Gd. 155.]
Ad-y-nam′ic-al.
Ad′y-tum (L.) [pl. *Ad′y-ta*, 198] [so Wr.; *a-dy′tum*, Wb. Gd. 155.]
Adze (*adz*), (10, 40) [A d z, 203.]
Æ′dile (*e′*-), (13) [E d i l e, 203.]
Æ-ge′an (*e-je′an*), 110
Æ′gi-lops (*e′ji-lops*), *or* Æg′i-lops (*ej′i-lops*) [*e′ji-lops*, Sm. Wb. Gd.; *ej′i-lops*, Wr. 155.]
Æ′gis (L.) (*e′jis*).
Æ-ne′id (*e-ne′id*), *or* Æ′ne-id (*e′ne-id*) [so Wr.; *e-ne′id*, Sm. Gd 155.] [E n e i d, 203.]
Æ-o′li-an (*e-o′li-an*) [E o l i a n, 203.]
Æ-ol′ic, (*e-ol′ik*) [E o l′-i c, 203.]
Æ-ol′i-pile (*e-ol′i-pīl*) [E o l i p i l e, 203.]
Æ′on (*e′on*) [E o n, 203.]
A′er-ate, 233.
A′er-āt-ed, 183.
A′er-āt-ing.
A-er-a′tion.
A-e′ri-al, 78, 171.
Ae′rie (*e′ry*), *or* A′er-ie (*a′er-y*) [so Wr.; *e′ry*, Wk. Sm.; *a′er-y*, or *e′ry*, Gd. 155.] [A y-r y, E y r y, 203.]
Ā-er-i-fi-ca′tion, 116.
Ā′er-i-form [so Wb. Gd.; *ār′i-form*, Sm., *a′e-ri-form*, Wr. 155.]
A′er-i-fȳ, 94, 169.
Ā-er-o-dȳ-nam′ics, 116, 171.
Ā-er-og′ra-phy, 108.
Ā′er-o-lite, 152.
Ā-er-o-lit′ic.
Ā-er-o-log′ic (-*loj′ik*).
Ā-er-o-log′i-cal (-*loj′ik*-).
Ā-er-ol′o-gist.
Ā-er-ol′o-gy, 108.
A′er-o-man-cy, 122, 169.
Ā-er-om′e-ter, 108.
Ā-er-o-met′ric.
Ā-er-om′e-try, 93.
A′er-o-nâut, 122.
Ā-er-o-nâut′ic, 109.
Ā-er-o-nâut′ic-al, 108.
Ā-er-o-nâut′ics, 109.
A′er-o-phyte, 171.
Ā-er-os′co-py, 93, 108.
Ā′er-o-stat.
Ā-er-o-stat′ic, 109.
Ā-er-o-stat′ic-al, 108.
Ā-er-o-stat′ics, 109.
Ā-er-os-ta′tion.
Æ-ru′gi-noŭs (*e-roo′ji-nus*) [E r u g i n o u s, 203.]
Æs-thet′ic (*es-thet′ik*) (171) [E s t h e t i c, 203.]
Æs-thet′ic-al (*es-thet′-i-kal*).
Æs-thet′ics (*es-thet′-iks*), 109, 171.
[Æ s t i v a t i o n. — *See* Estivation, 203.]
Ā e-the-og′a-mous, 116.
A-far′, 11.
Af-fa-bil′i-ty, 108, 169.
Af′fa-ble, 66, 164, 170.
Af′fa-broŭs [so Wk. Wr.; *af-fa′brus*, Sm. 155.]
Af-fair′ (*af-fêr′*), 14, 66.
Af-fect′, 15, 103.
Af-fect-a′tion, 228.
Af-fect′ed.
Af-fect′er.
Af-fect-i-bil′i-ty, 116.
Af-fect′i-ble, 164, 169.
Af-fect′ing.
Af-fec′tion.
Af-fec′tion-al.
Af-fec′tion-ate, 73.
Af-fec′tioned (*af-fek′-shund*), 165.
Af-fec′tĭve, 84.
Af-fēar′.
Af-fēar′er.
Af-fēar′ment.
Af′fer-ent.
Af-fi′ance, 122.
Af-fi′anced (-*fī′anst*), Note C, p. 34.
Af-fi′an-cer.
Af-fi′an-cing.
Af-fi-da′vit, 170.
Af-fīed′.
Af-fil′i-ate, 73.
Af-fil′i-āt-ed, 183.
Af-fil′i-āt-ing.
Af-fil-i-a′tion, 170.
Af′fin-age.
Af-fin′i-ty, 171.
Af-firm′, 21, Note.
Af-firm′a-ble, 169.
Af-firm′ant.
Af-firm-a′tion.
Af-firm′a-tĭve, 108, 171.
Af-firmed′, 165.
Af-firm′er, 77, 169.
Af-firm′ing.
Af-fix′, *v.* 161.
Af′fix, *n.* 161.
Af-fixt′ure, 91.

Af-fla′tion.
Af-fla′tus (L.) (125) [*not* af-flā′tus, 153.]
Af-flict′, 16, 52, 103.
Af-flict′er, 77, 169.
Af-flict′ing.
Af-flic′tion.
Af-flict′ĭve, 84.
Af′flu-ence, 105, 169.
Af′flu-ent, 89.
Af′flux.
Af-flux′ion (*-fluk′shun*) 46, Note.
Af-fōrd′, 24, 103.
Af-fōrd′ed.
Af-fōrd′ing.
Af-fŏr′est, 170.
Af-fŏr-est-a′tion.
Af-fran′chīse (*-frăn′-chĭz*), 202.
Af-fran′chīse-ment (*af-frăn′chĭz-ment*), 123.
Af-frāy′, 23.
Af-freight′ (*af-frāt′*), 162, 171.
Af-fright′ (*af-frīt′*), 162.
Af-fright′ed (*-frīt′ed*).
Af-fright′ing (*-frīt′-*).
Af-front′ (*af-frunt′*), *n.* (22). [*See* Afront, 148.]
Af-front′ed (*-frunt′ed*).
Af-front′ing (*af-frunt′-ing*).
Af-fuse′ (*af-fūz′*), 26, 40.
Af-fu′sion (*-fu′zhun*), 47.
Af-fy′, 25.
Af-fy′ing.
Af′ghan, 53.
A-fire′, 25.
A-float′, 24.
A-fōōt′, 20.
A-fore′, 24.
A-fore′hand.
A-fore′said (*-fŏr′sed*).
A-fore′thought (*-thawt*).
A-fore′time.
A-foul′, 28.
A-frāid′, 23.
A-fresh′, 15.
Af′ric, 10.
Af′ric-an.
A-front′ (*a-frunt′*), *ad.* [*See* Affront, 148.]
Aft, 12, 131.
Aft′er.
Aft′er-mōst, 206.
Aft′er-noon.
Aft′er-piēce.
Aft′er-ward.
Aft′er-wards (*-wardz*), Note C, p. 34.
A-gain′ (*a-ghen′*) (15, 171) [*not* a-gān′, 127, 153.]
A-gainst′ (*a-ghenst′*) (15, 171) [*not* a-gānst′, 127, 153.]
Ag′al-loch (*-lok*), 52.
A-gal′lo-chum (*-kum*), 52.
Ag′a-mist, 170.
Ag′a-moŭs.
Ag′a-pœ (L. pl.) (*ag′a-pē*).
A-gäpe′ [so Wr. Wb. Gd.; *a-găp′*, Wk. Sm. 155.]
Ag′a-ric, 109, 170.
[Agast.—*See* Aghast, 203.]
Ag′ate, 73, 170.
Ag′a-tīze, 202.
Ag′a-tīzed, 150, 165.
Ag′a-tīz-ing, 183.
Ag′a-ty, 93.
Age, 23, 45.
A′ged, 150, 165.

☞ Pronounced *a′jed*, except in compound words, as *full-aged*, in which it is pronounced *ājd*.

A′gen-cy, 169.
A′gent, 23, 45.
A′gent-ship.
Ag-ger-a′tion (*aj′er-*).
Ag-glom′er-ate, 73.
Ag-glom′er-āt-ed, 228, [N.
Ag-glom′er-āt-ing.
Ag-glom-er-a′tion, 116.
Ag-glu′ti-nant, 169.
Ag-glu′ti-nate, 78.
Ag-glu′ti-nāt-ed.
Ag-glu′ti-nāt-ing.
Ag-glu-ti-na′tion, 112, 116.
Ag-glu′ti-nāt-ĭve, 84, 116.
Ag′gran-dīze (202) [*not* ag-gran′dīze, 153.]
Ag′gran-dīzed, 165.
Ag′gran-dīze-ment, *or* Ag-gran′dīze-ment [so Wr.; *ag′gran-dīz-ment*, Wk. Sm.; *ag-gran′dĭz-ment*, or *ag′-gran-dĭz-ment*, Gd. 155.]
Ag′gran-dīz-ing, 183.
Ag′gra-vate.
Ag′gra-vāt-ed.
Ag′gra-vāt-ing.
Ag-gra-va′tion.
Ag′gre-gate, *a.* & *v.* 73, 170.
Ag′gre-gāt-ed.
Ag′gre-gāt-ing.
Ag′gre-gāt-ĭve, 84.
Ag′gre-gāt-or, 169.
Ag-gress′.
Ag-gressed′ (*ag-grest′*), 165.
Ag-gress′ing.
Ag-gres′sion (*-gresh′-un*), 46.
Ag-gress′ĭve, 84.
Ag-gress′or, 88, 169.
Ag-griēve′, 13, 171.
Ag-griēved′, 165.
Ag-griēv′ing, 171, 183.
Ag-group′ (*-groop′*), 19.
Ag-groupt′ (*-groopt′*), Note C, p. 34.
Ag-group′ing (*groop′-ing*).
A-ghast′ (12, 53, 131) [Agast, 203.]
Ag′ĭle (*aj′il*), 45, 152, [171.
A-gil′i-ty, 169.
Agio (It.) (*a′je-o*, or *ad′-je-o*) [so Wr.; *a′je-o*, Wb. Gd.; *ad′je-o*, Sm. 155.]
A′gi-o-tāge, *or* Ag′i-o-tāge (*aj′i-o-tāj*) [*a′ji-o-tāj*, Gd.; *aj′i-o-taj*, Wr. 155.]
A-gist′.
A-gist′ment.
A-gist′or.
Ag′i-tate (*aj′i-tāt*), 169.
Ag′i-tāt-ed (*aj′i-*), 183.
Ag′i-tāt-ing (*aj′i-*).
Ag-i-ta′tion (*aj-i-*).
Ag′i-tāt-ĭve (*aj′i-*).
Ag′i-tāt-or, 169.
Ag′let [Aiglet, 203.]
A-glōw′, 24.
Ag′nāil.
Ag′nate.
Ag-nat′ic, 109.
Ag-na′tion.
Ag-no′men (L.), 125.
Ag-nom-in-a′tion.
A-go′, 24.
A-gog′, 18.
A-go′ing.
A-gon′ic.
Ag′o-nist, 170.
Ag-o-nist′ic, 109.
Ag-o-nist′ic-al, 108.
Ag-o-nist′ics.
Ag′o-nize, 202.
Ag′o-nīzed, 150.
Ag′o-nīz-ing, 183.
Ag′o-ny, 170.
A-gou′ti (*a-goo′ty*), 19, 171.
A-gra′ri-an, 49, Note.

A-gra'ri-an-ism (*-izm*), 133, 136.
A-gra'ri-an-īze, 202.
A-gree', 13.
A-gree-a-bil'i-ty, 108.
A-gree'a-ble, 164, 171.
A-greed', 188.
A-gree'ing.
A-gree'ment.
A-gres'tic.
A-gres'tic-al.
A-gric'o-list, 105.
A-gric'o-loŭs.
Ag'ri-cult-or, 88.
Ag-ri-cult'u-ral, 89.
Ag'ri-cult-ure, 91.
Ag-ri-cult'ur-ist, 91.
Ag'ri-mo-ny, 86.
Ag-ro-nom'ic.
Ag-ro-nom'ic-al.
A-gron'o-my, 108.
Ag-ros-tog'ra-phy.
Ag-ros-tol'o-gy, 108.
A-ground', 28.
A'gūe, 171.
A'gūed, 183. [5.
A'gūe-proof, 206, Exc.
A'gu-ish.
A-hä'.
A-hä', 72.
A-hĕad', 15.
A-hōld'.
A-hoy', 27.
A-hull'.
Āid, 23.
Aide-de-camp (Fr.) (*ād-de-kŏng*, 154) [so Wr.; Aid-de-camp, Wk. Sm. Wb. Gd. 203.]
Āid'ed.
Āid'er, 169.
Āid'ful (*-fōōl*, 180).
Āid'ing.
[Aiglet.—*See* Aglet, 203.]
Āi'gret.
Āil, *v.* to be ill. [*See* Ale, 160.]
Āiled, 165.
Āil'ing.
Āil'ment.
Āim, 23.
Āimed, 165.
Āim'er, 169.
Āim'ing.
Āim'less.
Air (*êr*) (14), *n.* the atmosphere. [*See* Ere, Heir, 160.]
Aired (*êrd*).
Air'er (*êr'ur*).
Air'-hole (*êr'hōl*), 221.
Air'i-ly (*êr'i-ly*), 78, 93.
Air'i-ness (*êr'i-*), 171.
Air'ing (*êr'ing*).
Air'pump (*êr-*), 206.
Air'tight (*êr'tīt*), 216.
Air'y (*êr'y*), 93.
Aisle (*īl*) (162), *n.* a walk in a church. [*See* Isle, 160.]
A-jar', 11.
Aj'u-tage [Adjutage, 203.]
A-kim'bo, 86.
A-kin', 16.
Al'a-bas-ter (131, 170) [*not* al-a-bas'ter, 153.]
A-lack'.
A-lac'ri-ty, 171.
À-la-mode' (Fr.) [so Sm.; *àl-a-mōd'*, Wb. Gd. Wr. 155.]
A'lar, 169.
A-larm', 135.
A-larmed', 165.
A-larm'ing.
A-larm'ist.
A-lär'um [so Sm.; *a-lar'um*, Wr. Gd. 155.]
A-las', 12, 131.
A'late, *a.* 161.
A-late', *ad.* 161.
Alb, 10.
Al'ba-core [so Wr.; Albicore, Gd. 203.]
Al-ba'ni-an.
Al'ba-tross, 171.
Âl-be'it, 17, 171, 180.
Al-bes'cent.
Al-bi-gen'sēs (L. pl.) (*-jen'sēz*).
Al'bin-ism (*-izm*) [so Gd.; *al-bī'nizm*, or *al'bin-izm*, Wr. 155.]
Al-bī'no [so Sm. Wb. Gd.; *al-bī'no*, or *al-bē'no*, Wr. 155.]
Al-bi'no-ism (*-izm*), 133, 136.
Al-bu-gin'e-oŭs.
Al-bu'go (L.) [pl. *Al-bu'gi-nēs* (*-nēz*), 198.
Al'bum.
Al-bu'men (L.) [*not* al'-bu-men, 125, 153.]
Al-bu'men-īze, 202.
Al-bu'min-oŭs, 171.
Al-bur'num (L.), 125.
[Alcade.—*See* Alcaid, 203.]
[Alcahest.—*See* Alkahest, 203.]
Al-ca'ic.
Al-cāid' [Alcade, 203.]
Al-cal'de (Sp.) (*al-kal'-dā*).
Al-chem'ic (*-kem'ik*).
Al-chem'ic-al (*-kem'ik-*).
Al'che-mist (*-ke-mist*),
Al'che-my (*ke*), 171. [52.
Al'co-hol, 171.
Al'co-hol-ate.
Al-co-hol'ic, 109.
Al-co-hol-ī-za'tion, 116.
Al'co-hol-ize, 202.
Al-co-hol'me-ter.
Al-co-hol-met'ric-al, 116.
Al'co-ran [Alkoran, 203.]

☞ "Orientalists generally pronounce this word *al-ko-rawn'*." *Smart.*

Al-co-ran'ic, 109.
Al'co-ran-ist [so Gd.; *al-co-ran'ist*, Wr. 155.]
Al'cove, *or* Al-cove' [so Gd.; *al-kōv'*, Wk. Sm. Wr. 155.]
Al-de-ba'ran [so Gd.; *al-deb'a-ran*, Wr. 155.]
Al'de-hyde, 171.
Âl'der, 17, 169.
Âl'der-man, 196.
Âl-der-man'ic, 170.
Al'dīne, *or* Al'dīne [*al'-dīn*, Wr. Gd.; *al'dīn*, Sm. 155.]
Ale (23), *n.* a liquor made from fermented malt. [*See* Ail, 160.]
A-lĕak', 13.
Al'e-a-to-ry, 86.
A-lec'try-o-man-cy, 169.
A-lee', 13.
Ale'hoof, 206.
Al-e-man'nic, 170.
A-lem'bic.
A-lem'broth, 122.
A-lert', 21, Note.
Al-eu'ro-man-cy (*-u'ro-*)
A-leū'ti-an [so Sm. Wr.; *a-lu'shan*, Wb. Gd. 155.]
A-leū'tic.
Ale'wife, 206.
Al-ex-an'drīne [so Sm. Wr.; *al-ex-an'drīn*, Wb. Gd. 155.]
A-lex-i-phar'mic.
A-lex-i-tĕr'ic.
A-lex-i-tĕr'ic-al.
A-lex-i-tĕr'ics.
Al'ga (L.) [pl. *Al'gæ* (*-je*), 198.]
Al'ge-bra (72) [*not* je-brā, 153.]
Al-ge-bra'ic, 109.

Al-ge-bra′ic-al, 108.
Al′ge-brā-ist [so Sm. Wr.; *al-je-bra′ist*, Gd. 155.]
Al′ge-neb.
Al-ge-rine′ (*-rēn′*), 171.
Al′gol.
Al′go-rab.
Al′go-rithm, 133.
Al′gua-zil (*al′ga-zēl*) [so Sm. Wr.; *al-gwa-zil′*, Wb. Gd. 155.]
Al-ham′bra (Ar.).
A′li-as (L.).
Al′i-bī (L.).
Āl′ien (*āl′yen*), 23, 51.
Āl-ien-a-bil′i-ty (*āl-yen-*).
Āl′ien-a-ble (*āl′yen-*), 171.
Āl′ien-age (*āl′yen-aj*).
Āl′ien-ate (*āl′yen-āt*).
Āl′ien-āt-ed (*-yen-*), 183.
Āl′ien-āt-ing (*āl′yen-*).
Āl-ien-a′tion (*āl-yen-*).
Āl′ien-āt-or (*āl′yen-*).
Āl-iēne′ (*āl-yēn′*), 51, 171.
Āl-ien-ee′ (*-yen-*), 122.
Āl′ien-ism (*āl′yen-izm*).
Āl-ien-or′ (*āl-ien-or′*), [122.
Al′i-form, 78.
A-līght′ (*a-līt′*), 162.
A-light′ed (*-līt′-*).
A-lign′ (*a-līn′*), 162.
A-lign′ment (*-līn′-*), 162.
A-like′, 25.
Al′i-ment, 170.
Al-i-ment′al.
Al-i-ment′a-ry, 72, 170.
Al-i-ment-a′tion.
Al-i-ment′ĭve-ness.
Al-i-mo′ni-oŭs, 169.
Al′i-mo-ny, 126.
A′li-oth [so Wr.; *al′i-oth*, Gd. 155.]
Al′i-ped.
Al′i-quănt [so Sm. Wr. Wb. Gd.; *al′i-kwŏnt*, Wk. 155.]
Al′i-quot, 170.
Āl′ish, 183.
A-live′, 25.
A-liz′a-rĭne [Alizarin, Sm. 203.]
Al′ka-hest [Alcahest, 203.]
Al-ka-hest′ic.
Al-ka-les′cen-cy, 171.
Al′ka-lĭ, *or* Al′ka-lī [so Wr.; *al′ka-lĭ*, Wk. Sm.; *al′ka-lī*, or *al′-ka-lĭ*, Gd. 155.]
Al′ka-li-fī-a-ble (116) [so Wb. Gd.; *al-kal′i-fī-a-bl*, Wr. 155.]
Al′ka-li-fīed, 186.
Al′ka-li-fȳ (94) [so Wb. Gd.; *al-kal′i-fȳ*, Sm. Wr. 155.]
Al′ka-li-fȳ-ing, 116.
Al-ka-lig′e-noŭs (*-lij′-*).
Al-ka-lim′e-ter, 108.
Al-kal-i-met′ric.
Al-kal-i-met′ric-al.
Al-ka-lim′e-try, 169.
Al′ka-lĭne, *or* Al′ka-līne [so Wr.; *al′ka-lĭn*, Wk. Sm.; *al′ka-līn*, or *al′ka-lĭn*, Gd. 155.]
Al-ka-lin′i-ty, 171.
Al-ka′li-oŭs.
Al′ka-lize, 202.
Al′ka-loid.
Al′ka-net.
Al-ker′mēs (*-mēz*), 21, Note.
[Alkoran.—*See* Alcoran, 203.]
Âll, (17, 172,) *a.* the whole. [*See* Awl, 160.]
Al′lah (Ar.), 72.
Al-lan-to′ic, 109.
Al-lan′toid, *or* Al-lan-toid′ [so Wr.; *al-lan-toid′*, Wb. Gd. 155.]
Al-lan′to-is, *or* Al-lan-tois′ [so Wr.; *al-lan-tois′*, Wb. Gd. 155.]
Al-lāy′, 23, 170.
Al-lāyed′, 165.
Al-lāy′er.
Al-lāy′ing.
Al-le-gā′tion (170). [*See* Alligation, 148.]
Al-lĕge′ (*al-lej′*), 45, 171.
Al-lĕge′a-ble, 171, 183.
Al-lĕged′ (*-lejd′*), 165.
Al-leg′er (*-lej′-*), 183.
Al-le′giance (*al-le′jans*) [so Wk. Wr.; *al-le′-gi-ans*, Wb. Gd. 155.]

☞ Smart respells this word thus, *al-le′j′ance*; the apostrophe being used by him to represent a slight sound resembling that of consonant *y*.—*See* § 26.

Al-leg′ing (*-lej′-*), 171.
Al-le-gŏr′ic, 48, 109, 170.
Al-le-gŏr′ic-al, 108.
Al′le-go-rist, 126.
Al′le-go-rize, 202.
Al′le-go-rīzed, 165.
Al′le-go-rīz-er.
Al′le-go-rīz-ing.
Al′le-go-ry, 86, 170.
Al-le-gret′to (It.).
Al-le′gro (It.), 154.
[Alleluiah, Allelujah.—*See* Hallelujah, 203.]
Al-le′vi-ate, 169, 170.
Al-le′vi-āt-ed, 183.
Al-le′vi-āt-ing.
Al-le-vi-a′tion.
Al′ley, 98, 169 [pl. Al′-leys, 187.]
Al-li-a′ceous (*-a′shus*), 112, 170.
Al-li′ance.
Al-līed′, 186.
Al-li-ga′tion (170) [*See* Allegation, 148.]
Al′li-ga-tor, 116, 170.
Al-lĭ′sion (*-lizh′un*), 47, 234.
Al-lit-er-a′tion, 170.
Al-lit′er-a-tĭve.
Al′lo-cate.
Al-lo-ca′tion.
Al-lo-ca′tur (L.).
Al′lo-chro-ite (*-kro-īt*) [so Sm. Wb. Gd.; *al-lok′ro-īt*, Wr. 155.]
Al-lo-cu′tion [*See* Elocution, 148.]
Al-lo′di-al, 169, 170.
Al-lo′di-um, 78, 169.
Al-longe′ (*al-lunj′*), 22.
Al-lo-path′ic, 126, 170.
Al-lop′a-thist.
Al-lop′a-thy (108) [*not* al′lo-păth-y, 153.]
Al′lo-phane.
Al-lot′, 18.
Al-lot′ment.
Al-lo-trop′ic.
Al-lot′ro-pism (*-pizm*), [136.
Al-lot′ro-py, 93.
Al-lot′ted, 176.
Al-lot′ting.
Al-low′, 24, 66.
Al-low′a-ble, 164.
Al-low′ance.
Al-low′anced (*-anst*), Note C, p. 34.
Al-low′an-cing.
Al-lowed. [*See* Aloud, 148.]
Al-low′er, 77.
Al-low′ing.
Al-loy′, 27.
Al-loy′age, 169.
Al-loyed′, 188.
Âll′spice, 171, 206.
Al-lude′, 26.
Al-lūd′ed, 183.
Al-lūd′ing.

Al-lure′, 26.
Al-lured′, 183.
Al-lure′ment.
Al-lūr′er, 77.
Al-lūr′ing.
Al-lu′sion(-*lu′zhun*),47, 112.
Al-lu′sĭve, 84.
Al-lu′so-ry, 93.
Al-lu′vi-al, 78, 169.
Al-lu′vi-on.
Al-lu′vi-um (L.) [pl. *Al-lu′vi-a*, 198.]
Al-ly′, *n.* & *v.* [pl. of *n.* Al-lies′, 190] [*not* al′lȳ, al′līes, 153.]
Al-ly′ing.
Ăl′ma-gest.
Âl′ma-nac (171) [so Wk. Wr. Gd.; *ăl′ma-nac*, Sm. 155.] [Alma-nack, 203.]
Ăl′man-dīne [so Sm. Wr.; *ăl′man-dĭn*, Wb. Gd. 155.]
Âl-might′i-ness (*awl-mīt′-*), 162, 171.
Âl-might′y (*-mīt′y*), 162.
Ä′mond (*ä′mund*) [so Wk. Sm. Wr.; *al′-mund*, popularly, *ä′mund*, Wb. Gd.155.]
Ä′mond-tree (*ä′mund-trē*), 206, Exc. 4.
Ăl′mo-ner.
Ăl′mon-ry, 93.
Âl′most, 180.
Älms (*ämz*), 162; Note C, p. 34.
Älms′house (*ämz′hous*), 206.
Al′na-ger [Alnagar, Aulnager, 203.]
Al′ōe (170) [pl. Al′ōes (*al′ōz*).]
Al-o-et′ic.
Al-o-et′ic-al.
Al-o-et′ics.
A-lŏft′, 18, Note.
Al-o-got′ro-phy [so Wr.; *al′lo-go-trō-phy*, Wb. Gd. 155.]
Al′o-man-cy, 170.
A-lone′, 24.
A-lŏng′ 18, Note.
A-loof′, 19.
Al′o-pe-cy, 169, 170.
Alp, 10, 30, 50.
Al-pac′a, 145, 170.
Al′pha (Gr.), 35.
Al′pha-bet, 35.
Al-pha-bet-a′ri-an, 116.
Al-pha-bet′ic, 109.
Al-pha-bet′ic-al, 108.
Al-phe′nic [so Wr.; Alphenix, Wb. Gd. 203.]
Al-phit′o-man-cy.
Al-phon′sin, *n.* [so Wb. Gd. Wr.; Alphonsine, Sm. 203.]
Al-phon′sīne, *a.* [so Sm. Wr.; Alphonsin, Wb. Gd. 203.]
Al′pīne, *or* Al′pīne [so Wr.; *al′pĭn*, Sm.; *al′-pīn*, or *al′pĭn*, Gd. 155.]
Âl-rĕad′y, 93, 180.
Âl′so, (180) [*not* ŏl′so, 145, 153.]
Âl′tar, *n.* a place for sacrifices. [*See* Alter, 160.]
Âl′tar-age, 169.
Âl′ter, *v.* to change. [*See* Altar, 160.]
Âl-ter-a-bil′i-ty, 171.
Âl′ter-a-ble, 164.
Âl′ter-ant, 169.
Âl-ter-a′tion, 112.
Âl′ter-a-tĭve, 84, 171.
Al′ter-cate, 73.
Al′ter-căt-ing, 183.
Al-ter-ca′tion [*not* âl-ter-ka′shun, *nor* ŏl-ter-ka′shun, 153.]
Al-tern′.
Al-tern′a-cy, 169.
Al-tern′ate, *a.* 73.
Al-tern′ate, *or* Al′tern-ate, *v.* [so Wr.; *al-tern′āt*, Wk. Sm.; *al′-tern-āt*, Gd. 155.]
Al-tern′āt-ed, *or* Al′-tern-āt-ed, 183.
Al-tern′ate-ly, 93.
Al-tern′āt-ing, *or* Al′-tern-āt-ing.
Al-tern-a′tion, 112.
Al-tern′a-tĭve, 84, 171.
Al-the′a [*Althœa* (L.), 203.]
Âl-though′ (*-thō′*), 162, 171, 180.
Al-tim′e-ter, 169.
Al-tim′e-try, 93.
Al′ti-tude, 108, 171.
Al′to (It.).
Âl-to-geth′er, 180.
Al′u-del, 89.
Al′um, 169, 170, 231.
A-lu′mi-na, 78, 171.
A-lu′mi-nate.
Al′u-mĭne, 82, 152.
A-lu-mi-nif′er-oŭs, 108, 116.
A-lu′mi-nīte.
A-lu′mi-noŭs, 169.
A-lu′mi-num.
Al′um-ish.
A-lum′nus (L.) [pl. A-lum′nī, 198.]
Al′ve-a-ry, 72.
Al′ve-āt-ed.
Al′ve-o-lar [so Sm.Wb. Gd.; *al-ve′o-lar*, or *al′ve-o-lar*, Wr. 155.]
Al′ve-o-la-ry, 72.
Al′ve-o-late [so Wb. Gd.; *al-ve′o-lāt*, or *al′-ve-o-lāt*, Wr. 155.]
Al′ve-o-līte.
Al-ve′o-lus (L.) [pl. Al-ve′o-lī, 198.]
Al′vīne [so Sm. Wr.; *al′vĭn*, Gd. 155.]
Âl′wāy, 230.
Âl′wāys (*-wāz*), 180.
Am, 10, 32.
Am-a-dou′ (Fr.) (*am-a-doo′*) [so Wr.; *am′a-doo*, Gd.; *am′a-dow*, Sm. 155.]
A-māin′, 23.
A-mal′gam, 171.
A-mal′gam-ate.
A-mal′gam-āt-ed.
A-mal′gam-āt-ing.
A-mal-gam-ā′tion, 112.
A-man-u-en′sis (L.) [pl. A-man-u-en′sēs (*-en′-sēz*), 198.]
Am′a-ranth, 170.
Am-a-ranth′ĭne, 171.
A-măss′, 12, 131.
A-măssed′ (*a-măst′*), Note C, p. 34.
A-măss′ing.
A-măss′ment.
Amateur (Fr.) (*am-a-tūr′*, or *a-ma-tūr′*) [so Wr.; *am-a-tūr′*, Wk. Wb. Gd.; *a-ma-tur′*, Sm. 154, 155.]
Am′a-tĭve-ness, 156.
Am-a-to′ri-al.
Am′a-to-ry, 86.
A-māze′, 23.
A-māzed′, 165, 183.
A-māze′ment.
A-māz′ing, 183.
Am′a-zon, 170.
Am-a-zo′ni-an.
Am-bas′sa-dor (86, 170) [Embassador, 203.]

☞ Smart says, "*Embassador* is consistent with *embassy*, but is not usual." Worcester remarks, "The immediate derivation of the word from the French is a reason for preferring *ambassador*." Webster and Goodrich allow that *ambassador* is more common, but they prefer *embassador* for the reason that this form corresponds with *embassy*.

Am-bas′sa-dress, 170.
Am′ber, 10, 77.
Am′ber-gris (*am′ber-grēs*), 156, 171.
Am-bi-dex-ter′i-ty, 116.
Am-bi-dex′troŭs.
Am′bi-ent, 169.
Am-big′e-nal(-*bij′*-),171.
Am-bi-gu′i-ty.
Am-big′u-oŭs.
Am′bit, 230.
Am-bi′tion (-*bish′un*), 171.
Am-bi′tious (-*bish′us*).
Am′ble, 10, 104, 164.
Am′bled (*am′bld*), 171, 183.
Am′bler, 77.
Am′bling.
Am′bly-gon, 171.
Am-blyg′on-al.
Am′bly-o-py, 122, 126.
Am-bro′si-a (L.) (*am-bro′zhĭ-a*) [so Wk. Sm. Wr.; *am-bro′zha*, Wb. Gd. 155.]
Am-bro′si-al (-*zhĭ*-),171.
Am-bro′si-an (-*zhĭ*-).
Am′bro-type, 105.
Am′bry, 93.
Āmbs′ace (*āmz′ās*) [so Sm. Wb. Gd.; *āmz-ās′*, Wk. Wr. 155.] [Amesace, 203.]
Am′bu-lance, 169.
Am′bu-lant, 169.
Am′bu-la-to-ry, 86.
Am′bu-ry, 89, 93.
Am-bus-cade′, *n.* & *v.* [so Wk. Sm. Wr.; *am′bus-kād*, Wb. Gd. 155.]
Am-bus-cād′ed.
Am-bus-cād′ing.
Am′bush (*am′bo͝osh*).
A-mēl′io-rate (-*mēl′yo*-), 51, 171.
A-mēl′io-rāt-ed (-*yo*-).
A-mēl′io-rāt-ing (-*yo*-).
A-mel-io-ra′tion (-*yo*-).
Ā-men′, 15, 23, 117, 232.
A-mē-na-bil′i-ty, 108.
A-me′na-ble (164) [*not* a-men′a-ble, 153.]
A-mend′, 15, 232.
A-mend′a-ble, 164.
A-mend′a-to-ry, 86, 171.
A-mend′ed.
A-mend′er.
A-mend′ing.
A mend′ment.
A-mends′ (-*mendz′*), 15, 72, Note C, p. 34.
A-men′i-ty (169) [*not* a-me′ni-ty, 153.]
Am′ent, 156, 170.
A-ment′um (L.) [pl. *A-ment′a*, 198.]
Am-en-ta′ceous (-*ta′shus*), 112, 169.
A-merce′, 21, Note.
A-merce′a-ble, 164, 183.
A-merced′ (-*merst′*).
A-merce′ment, 185.
A-mer′cer.
A-mer′cing.
A-mĕr′i-can, 78.
A-mĕr′i-can-ism (-*izm*), 133.
A-mĕr′i-can-īze, 202.
[Amesace.—*See* Ambsace, 203.]
A-met-a-bo′li-an.
Am′e-thyst, 170.
Am-e-thyst′ĭne, 84, 152.
Ā-mi-a-bil′i-ty, 108.
Ā′mi-a-ble, 164, 171.
Ā′mi-a-bly, 93.
Am-i-an′thi-form, 169.
Am-i-an′thus, 170.
Am-i-ca-bil′i-ty, 116.
Am′i-ca-ble, 164, 171.
Am′i-ca-bly, 93.
Am′ĭce (*am′is*), 169, 170.
A-mid′, 16.
A-midst′, 232.
Am′ĭde [Ammid, 203.]
Am′i-dĭne, 82, 152.
A-mid′ships.
A-miss′, 16.
Am′i-ty, 93, 170.
[Ammid, 203.—*See* Amide.]
Am-mo′ni-a, 169, 170.
Am-mo′ni-ac, 108.
Am-mo-ni′ac-al, 108,171.
Am′mo-nīte, 152.
Am-mo′ni-um, 108.
Am-mo-ni′u-ret, 105.
Am-mu-ni′tion (-*nish′un*), 112, 170.
Am′nes-ty, 93.
Am′ni-on, *or* Am′ni-os.
Am-ni ot′ic.
Am-œ-be′an (*am-e-be′an*), 110, 171.
A-mong′ (*a-mung′*), 22.
A-mongst′ (*a-mungst′*).
Am′o-roŭs.
A-mor′phism (-*fizm*),35.
A-mor′phoŭs.
A-mort′.
A-mor′tīse (*a-mor′tĭz*) [so Wk. Sm. Wr.; (*a-mor′tīz*), Wb. Gd. 155.] [Amortize, 203.]
A-mor-ti-za′tion.
A-mor′tīze-ment.
A-mount′, 28.
A-mour′ (-*moor′*), 114, 171.
Am′per-sand.
Am-phib′i-an, 35, 169.
Am-phib-i-o-log′ic-al (-*loj′ik-al*), 116.
Am-phi-bol′o-gy, 108.
Am-phib′o-loŭs.
Am′phi-brach (*am′fi-brak*), 35, 52.
Am-phic-ty-on′ic, 171.
Am-phic′ty-o-ny,93,171.
Am-phic′ty-ons (-*onz*), 136.
Am-phig′a-moŭs.
Am-phi-hex-a-he′dral, 116.
Am-phil′o-gy, 108.
Am′phi-pod.
Am-phip′o-doŭs.
Am-phip′ro-style.
Am-phis-bæ′na (*be′na*), 171.
Am-phĭ′scian (-*fish′an*), 171.
Am-phĭ′sci-ī (L. pl.) (*am-fish′i-ī*).
Am-phi-the′a-tre (116; 164, 171) [Amphitheater, preferred by Wb. and Gd.—*See* Note E, p. 70.]
Am-phi-the-at′ric.
Am-phi-the-at′ric-al.
Am-phit′ro-pal.
Am′pho-ra (L.) [pl. *Am′pho-ræ*, 198.]
Am′pho-ral.
Am-pho-tĕr′ic.
Am′ple, 10, 164.
Am-plex′i-câul, 169.
Am-pli-fi-ca′tion, 112, 116.
Am′pli-fi-cā-tĭve, 116.
Am′pli-fīed, 186.
Am′pli-fī-er.
Am′pli-fȳ, 94, 108.
Am′pli-fȳ-ing.
Am′pli-tude, 108, 171.
Am′ply, 10, 93.
Am-pul′la (L.) [pl. *Am-pul′læ*, 198.]

Am-pul-la'ceoŭs (*-la'-shus*).
Am'pu-tate, 89.
Am'pu-tāt-ed, 183.
Am'pu-tāt-ing.
Am-pu-ta'tion.
Am'u-let, 170.
A-mūs'a-ble (*a-mūz'a-bl*), 169, 183.
A-muse' (*a-mūz'*), 40, 136.
A-mused' (*a-mūzd'*), 183.
A-muse'ment (*-mūz'-*).
A-mūs'er (*-mūz'-*).
A-mūs'ing (*-mūz'-*).
A-mu'sīve, 84.
A-myg'da-late.
A-myg'da-līne, 152, 171.
A-myg'da-loid, 171.
Am-y-la'ceous (*-shus*), 112.
Am'ȳle (*am'il*), 171.
Am'yl-īne, 152.
An-a-bap'tism (*-tizm*), 133, 136.
An-a-bap'tist, 170.
An-a-bap-tist'ic, 109.
An-a-bap-tist'ic-al, 108, 116.
An-a-car'dic, 170.
An-a-ca-thar'tic.
An-a-ceph-a-lœ-o'sis (Gr.) (*an-a-sef-a-le-o'-sis*) [so Gd.; *an-a-sef-a-le'o-sis*, Sm. Wr. 155.]
An-ach'ro-nism (*an-ak'-ro-nizm*), 52, 133.
An-ach-ro-nist'ic (*-ak-*).
An-ach-ro-nist'ic-al (*-ak-*), 108.
An-a-clas'tic.
An-a-clas'tics.
An-a-co-lu'thic.
An-a-co-lu'thon (Gr.).
An-a-con'da, 72, 170.
A-nac-re-on'tic.
An'a-dem.
A-nad'ro-moŭs.
An-æs-the'si-ȧ (Gr.)(*an-es-the'zhi-a*).
An-æs-thet'ic (*an-es-*), 171.
An'a-glyph, 35, 170.
An-a-glyph'ic.
An-a-glyph'ic-al.
An-a-glyp'tic.
An-a-glyp-tog'ra-phy, 93, 108, 116.
An'a-go-gē (Gr.), 163.
An-a-gog'ic-al (*-goj'-*).
An-a-gog'ics (*-goj'-*).
An'a-gram, 170.
An-a-gram-mat'ic.
An-a-gram-mat'ic-al.
An-a-gram'ma-tism (*-tizm*).
An-a-gram'ma-tist, 170.
An-a-gram'ma-tize, 202.
An'a-grăph, 35, 170.
An-a-lec'tic.
An'a-lects, 170.
An-a-lem'ma (L.) [so Wr.; *an'a-lem-ma*, Sm. Wb. Gd. 155.]
An-a-lep'sy, 169.
An-a-lep'tic.
An-a-log'ic-al (*-loj'-*).
A-nal'o-gism (*-jizm*), 133, 136.
A-nal'o-gist, 170.
A-nal'o-gize, 202.
A-nal'o-goŭs.
An'a-lŏgue, 87, 168, 171.
A-nal'o-gy, 170.
A-nal'y-sis, 171.
An'a-lyst (171), *n.* one skilled in analysis. [*See* Annalist, 160.]
An-a-lyt'ic, 109.
An-a-lyt'ic-al, 108.
An-a-lyt'ics.
An-a-lȳz'a-ble, 164.
An-a-lȳz-a'tion.
An'a-lȳze (171), *v.* to resolve by analysis. [*See* Annalize, 160.]
An'a-lȳzed, 165.
An'a-lȳz-er, 169.
An'a-lȳz-ing.
An-a-mor-pho'sis, or *An-a-mor'pho-sis*(Gr.) [so Wr.; *an-a-mor-fo'sis*, Wk.; *an-a-mor'fo-sis*, Sm.; *an-a-mor-fo'sis*, or *an-a-mor'fo-sis*, Gd. 154, 155.]
A-na'nas.
A-nan'droŭs.
An'a-pest [Anapæst, 203.]
An-a-pest'ic.
An-a-pest'ic-al.
A-narch'ic (*a-nark'ik*), 52.
A-narch'ic-al (*-nark'ik-*)
An'arch-ism (*-ark-izm*), 133, 136.
An'arch-ist (*-ark-ist*).
An'ar-chy (*an'ar-ky*), 52, 93.
An-ar'throŭs.
An-a-sar'coŭs.
An-a-stal'tic, 109.
An-a-stat'ic.
A-nas'to-mōse (*-mōz*).
A-nas'to-mosed (*-to-mōzd*), 156.
A-nas'to-mōs-ing (*-mōz-ing*).
A-nas-to-mo'sis (Gr.), 154.
A-nas-to-mot'ic.
A-nas'tro-phē (Gr.), 163.
An'a-tase, 170.
A-nath'e-ma, 169, 171.
A-nath-e-mat'ic-al, 116.
A-nath'e-ma-tism (*-tizm*), 133, 136.
A-nath-e-mat-i-za'tion, 116.
A-nath'e-ma-tīze, 202.
A-nath'e-ma-tīzed, 165.
A-nath'e-ma-tīz-er.
A-nath'e-ma-tīz-ing.
An-a-tif'er-oŭs, 108, 233.
An-a-tom'ic, 109.
An-a-tom'ic-al, 108.
A-nat'o-mist, 170.
A-nat-o-mi-za'tion.
A-nat'o-mīze, 202.
A-nat'o-my, 93, 108, 170.
An-a-trep'tic.
An-a-trip-sol'o-gy, 108.
An'a-tron, 170.
A-nat'ro-poŭs.
An'bu-ry.
An'ces-tor, 105, 169.
An-ces-to'ri-al.
An'ces-tral(107)[so Wk. Sm. Wr.; *an-ces'tral*, Wb. Gd. 155.]
An'ces-tress [so Wr.; *an-ces'tres*, Gd. 155.]
Anch'or (*angk'ur*) (52, 54), *n.* an instrument to hold a vessel. [*See* Anker, 160.]
Anch'or-a-ble (*angk'-*).
Anch'or-age (*angk'ur-aj*), 171.
Anch'ored (*angk'urd*), 165.
Anch'o-ress (*angk'-*).
Anch'o-ret (*angk'-*).
Anch-o-ret'ic (*angk-*).
Anch-o-ret'ic-al(*angk-*).
Anch'or-ing (*angk-*).
Anch'o-rite (*angk'-*).
An-cho'vy (44) [*not* an'-cho-vy, 153.]
Anch'y-lose (*angk'i-lōs*).
Anch'y-losed (*angk'i-lōst*) [so Gd.; *angk'i-lōzd*, Wr. 155.]
Anch'y-lōs-ing (*angk'i-lōs-*).

Anch-y-lo′sis (*angk-i-*) (109) [Ankylosis, 203.]
Anch-y-lot′ic (*angk-i-*).
Ān′cient (*ān′shent*), 46, Note 2; 171.
Ān′cient-ry (*ān′shent-*).
An′cil-la-ry, 72, 171.
An-cip′i-tal, 169, 171.
An-cip′i-toŭs.
An′con, 230.
An′cone.
And, 10, 42, 43.
An-de′an (110, 169) [so Wr.; *an′de-an*, Gd. 155.]
And′ī-ron (*and′ī-urn*), 171.
An-dra-nat′o-my, 108.
An-drog′y-nal (*-droj′i-*).
An-drog′y-noŭs (*-droj′-i-nŭs*).
An′droid.
An-droid′ēs (*-droid′ēz*) [so Gd.; *an-dro′i-dēz*, Wr. 155.]
An′dron.
An′droŭs.
An′ec-dōt-al.
An′ec-dote, 170.
An-ec-dot′ic, 143.
An-ec-dot′ic-al.
An′ec-dōt-ist.
A-nel′li-dan [Annel-lidan, Anneli-dan, 203.]
An-e-mog′ra-phy, 108.
An-e-mol′o-gy, 108.
An-e-mom′e-ter, 169.
An-e-mom′e-try.
A-nem′o-nē, (163, 170) [*not* an-e-mo′nē, 153.]
A-nem′o-scope.
An′er-oid, 170, 233.
An′eu-rism (*an′u-rizm*), 133.
A-new′ (*a-nu′*), 26.
An-fract′u-ose.
An-fract-u-os′i-ty, 108.
An-fract′u-oŭs, 89.
[Angeiography.—*See* Angiography, 203.]
Ān′gel [*not* ăn′jel, *nor* ān′jl, 127, 153.]
An-gel′ic, 109, 170.
An-gel′ic-al.
Ān′gel-winged (*-jel-wingd*), 205, Exc. 5.
An′ger (*ang′gur*) (54, 138), *n.* wrath. [*See* Angor, 148.]
An-gi-o-car′poŭs.
An-gi-og′ra-phy (108) [Angeiography, 203.]
An-gi-ol′o-gy.
An-gi-o-mon-o-sperm′-oŭs, 116.
An′gi-o-sperm.
An-gi-o-sperm′oŭs.
An-gi-ot′o-my, 108.
An′gle (*ang′gl*), 54, 164.
An′gled (*ang′gld*).
An′gler (*ang′glur*), 54, 77.
An′gli-can (*ang′-*), 54.
An′gli-can-ism (*-izm*), 133.
An′gli-cē (L.) (*ang′-*).
An′gli-cism (*-sizm*), 136.
An′gli-cīze, 202.
An′glo-Sax′on, 224.
An′gor (*ang′gawr*) (88), *n.* intense pain. [*See* An′ger, 148.]
An′grĭ-ly (*ang′-*), 171.
An′gry (*ang′-*), 54, 93.
An-guil′li-form (*-gwil-*), 34, 178.
An′guish (*ang′gwish*), 34, 54.
An′gu-lar (*ang′gu-*), 89.
An-gu-lăr′i-ty, 54, 108.
An′gu-lāt-ed (*ang′gu-*).
An-har-mon′ic.
An-har-mon′ic-al.
An-he-la′tion, 112.
An-hy′droŭs.
An′il, 170, 231.
An′īle, 81, 152.
A-nĭl′i-ty, 143, 169.
An-i-mad-ver′sion, 116.
An-i-mad-vert′, 122.
An-i-mad-vert′ed.
An-i-mad-vert′er.
An-i-mad-vert′ing.
An′i-mal, 169, 170.
An-i-mal′cu-lar, 169.
An-i-mal′cu-līne, 152.
An-i-mal′cule.
An-i mal′cu-list, 89.
An-i-mal′cu-lum (L.) [pl. *An-i-mal′cu-la.*]

☞ The plural form, *Animalculæ*, sometimes used, is erroneous.

An′i-mal-ism (*-izm*), 133.
An-i-mal′i-ty, 108, 169.
An-i-mal-ĭ-za′tion, 116.
An′i-mal-ize, 202.
An′i-mate, 170.
An′i-māt-ed, 183.
An′i-māt-ing.
An-i-ma′tion, 112, 170.
An′i-māt-ĭve, 84.
An′i-māt-or, 169.
An′i-mē (Sp.), 163.
An′i-mism (*-mizm*), 136.
An′i-mist.
An-i-mos′i-ty, 108, 171.
An′i-on.
An′īse, 169, 170, 231.
An′īse-seed, 206, Exc. 3.
An-i-sette′ (Fr.), 114.
An′ker (*ang′kur*) (54, 77), *n.* a Dutch liquid measure. [*See* Anchor, 160.]
An′kle (*ang′kl*), 54, 164.
An′kle-deep, 216.
[Ankylosis.—*See* Anchylosis, 203.]
An′nal-ist (170), *n.* a writer of annals. [*See* Analyst, 160.]
An′nal-īze (170), *n.* to record in annals. [*See* Analyze, 160.]
An′nals (*an′nalz*), 136, 230.
An′nats, 170.
An-nēal′, 13, 103.
An-nēaled′, 165.
An-nēal′ing.
[Annelidan, Annellidan.—*See* Anellidan, 203.]
An-nex′, 15, 39, Note.
An-nex-a′tion, 170.
An-nexed′ (*-next′*), Note C, p. 34.
An-nex′ing.
An-ni′hi-la-ble, 164.
An-ni′hi-late, 171.
An-ni′hi-lāt-ed.
An-ni′hi-lāt-ing.
An-nī-hi-la′tion, 112, 116.
An-ni′hi-lāt-or, 169.
An-ni-ver′sa-ry, 72, 171.
An′no-tate, 170.
An′no-tāt-ed, 183.
An′no-tāt-ing.
An-no-ta′tion.
An-no-tāt′or, 169.
An-no′ta-to-ry, 86.
An-not′i-noŭs, 108, 169.
An-not′to (170) [Annotta, Anotta, Arnotto, Arnotta, Arnatto, 203.]
An-nounce′, 28, 39.
An-nounced′ (*-nounst′*), Note C, p. 34.
An-nounce′ment, 185.
An-noun′cer, 183.
An-noun′cing.
An-noy′, 27.
An-noy′ance, 169.

An-noyed', 165.
An-noy'er.
An-noy'ing.
An'nu-al, 170.
An'nu-al-ly, 93, 170.
An'nu-ent, 91, 169.
An-nu'i-tant, 170.
An-nu'i-ty, 93, 169, 170.
An-nul', 22, 170.
An'nu-lar, 169.
An'nu-late, 73.
An'nu-lāt-ed, 183.
An-nu-la'tion.
An'nu-let, 170.
An-nulled' (*-nuld'*), 176,
An-nul'ling, 176. [183.
An-nul'ment.
An'nu-lose [so Gd.; *an-nu-lōs'*, Sm. Wr. 155.]
An-nu'mer-ate, 73.
An-nun'ci-ate (*an-nun'-she-āt*) (46) [so Sm. Wr.; *an-nun'shāt*, Wb. Gd. 155.]
An-nun'ci-āt-ed (*-shĭ-*).
An-nun'ci-āt-ing (*-shĭ-*).
An-nun-ci-a'tion (*-shĭ-ā'shun*).
An-nun'ci-āt-or (*-shĭ-*).
An-nun'ci-a-to-ry(*-shĭ-*)
An'ode, 170.
An'o-dyne, 170.
An'o-dyn-oŭs, 106.
A-noint', 27.
A-noint'ed.
A-noint'er.
A-noint'ing.
A-noint'ment.
A-no'lis, 156.
A-nom'a-li-ped.
A-nom'a-lism (*-lizm*), 133.
A nom-a-list'ic, 109.
A-nom-a-list'ic-al, 108.
A-nom'a-loŭs, 170.
A-nom'a-ly, 93, 170.
A-non', 18.
A-no'na.
A-non'y-moŭs, 171.
A-norm'al.
An-oth'er (*an-uth'er*), 22, 156.
[A n o t t a. — *See* Annotto, 203.]
An'ser-āt-ed.
An'ser-īne, 82, 152.
An'swer (*an'sur*), 162, 171.
An'swer-a-ble (*-sur-*), 171.
An'swer-a-bly (*-sur-*), 93.
An'swered (*-surd*), 165.
An'swer-er (*-sur-er*),77.
An'swer-ing (*-sur-*).
Ant (12, 131), *n.* an emmet. [*See* Aunt, 160.]
An'ta (L.) [pl. *An'tæ*, 198.]
Ant-aç'id, 235.
An-tag'o-nism (*-nizm*), 133, 136.
An-tag'o-nist, 170.
An-tag-o-nist'ic, 109.
An-tag-o-nist'ic-al, 108.
Ant-al'gic, 171.
Ant-al'ka-lī, *or* Ant-al'-ka-lī.
Ant-an-a-go'gē (Gr.), 163.
Ant-aph-ro-dĭ'si-ac (*-af-ro-diz'i-ak*).
Ant-aph-ro-dit'ic.
Ant-ap-o-plec'tic.
Ant-arc'tic, 142.
Ant-ar-thrit'ic.
Ant-asth-mat'ic (*-ast-mat'ik*), 162.
Ant-a-troph'ic.
An'te (L.), *prep.* before. [*See* Anti, 160.]
An-te-ce'dence.
An-te-ce'dent, 169.
An-te-ces'sor.
An'te-chām-ber.

☞ Sometimes incorrectly written A n t i - c h a m b e r.

An'te-chap-el.
An-te'cian (*-te'shan*),46.
An'te-date.
An'te-dāt-ed, 183.
An'te-dāt-ing.
An-te-dĭ-lu'vi-an, 169.
An'te-fix-æ (L. pl.), 198.
An'te-lope [A n t i - l o p e, 203.]
An-te-lu'can, 169.
An-te-me-rid'i-an.
[A n t e m e t i c. — *See* Antiemetic, 203.]
An-te-mun'dane.
An-te-mu'ral.
An-te-ni-cene' [so Wk.; *an-te-ni'cēn*, Gd. 155.]
An-ten'na (L.) [pl. *An-ten'næ*, 198.]
An-ten-nif'er-oŭs, 170.
An-ten'ni-form, 170.
An-te-nup'tial(*-shal*),46.
An-te-pas'chal (*-kal*),52.
An'te-pāst, 12, 131.
An-te-pe-nult', 122.
An-te-pe-nult'i-mate, 116, 169.
Ant-ep-i-lep'tic.
An-te-po-sĭ'tion (*-zish'-un*), 40, 112.
An-te-pre-dic'a-ment.
An-te'ri-or, 49, Note.
An-te-ri-or'i-ty, 93.
An'te-room, 169.
Ant-hēl'i-on (Gr.) [pl. *Ant-hēl'i-a*, 198.]
Ant-he'lix.
An-thel-min'tic [so Sm. Wb. Gd.; *ant-hel-min'tik*, Wr. 155.]
An'them, 10, 37.
An'ther, 10, 37, 77.
An'ther-al.
An-ther-if'er-oŭs, 108.
An'ther-oid.
An tho'di-um, 108, 169.
An-tho-log'ic-al (*-loj'-*).
An-thol'o-gy, 108, 170.
An-tho-phyl'lite,*or* An-thoph'yl-lite [so Wr.; *an-thoph'yl-līte*, Gd. 155.]
An'tho-rism (*-rizm*) [so Sm. Gd.; *ant'ho-rizm*, Wr. 155.]
An'thra-cite, 171.
An-thra-cit'ic.
An-throp'o-glot.
An-thro-pog'ra-phy.
An-throp'o-lite.
An-thro-po-log'ic-al (*-loj'ik-*).
An-thro-pol'o-gist, 108.
An-thro-pol'o-gy, 108.
An'thro-po-man-cy [so Gd.; *ăn-thro-pom'an-cy*, Wr. 155.]
An-thro-pom'e-try.
An-thro-po-mor'phism (*-mor'fizm*), 116, 133.
An-thro-po-mor'phist.
An-thro-po-mor'phīte.
An-thro-po-mor-phit'ic
An-thro-po-mor'phit-ism (*-mor'fit-izm*), 116.
An-thro-po-mor'phoŭs.
An-thro-pop'a-thy.
An-thro-poph'a-gī,*n. pl.* 198.
An-thro-poph'a-goŭs.
An-thro-poph'a-gy, 93.
An-thro-pos'o-phy.
An-thro-pot'o-my.
Ant-hyp-not'ic [A n t i - h y p n o t i c, 203.]
Ant-hyp-o-chon'dri-ac (*-hip-o-kon'-*) (108,116) [A n t i h y p o c h o n - d r i a c, 203.]
Ant-hys-ter'ic [A n t i - h y s t e r i c, 203.]

An′tī (Gr.), *prep.* against [*See* Ante, 160.]
An-ti-aç′id.
An-ti-asth-mat′ic (*-ast-mat′-*).
An-ti-bac-chī′us (L.) (*-bak-kī′us*) [so Wr., *an-ti-bak′kī-us*, Sm. Gd. 155.]
An-ti-brach′i-al (*-brak′-i-al*, or *-bra′ki-al*) [*-brak′i-al*, Gd.; *bra′-ki-al*, Wr. 155.]
An′tic, 10, 52, 230.
[Antichamber.—*See* Antechamber, 203.]
An′ti-chrīst (*-krīst*), 52, 169.
An-tich′ro-nism (*-tik′-ro-nizm*).
An-tiç′i-pant.
An-tiç′i-pate, 169, 171.
An-tiç′i-pāt-ed, 183.
An-tiç′i-pāt-ing.
An-tiç-i-pa′tion, 112, 171.
An-tiç′i-pāt-ĭve.
An-tiç′i-pāt-or, 88.
An-tiç′i-pa-to-ry, 86.
An-ti-cli′max.
An-ti-cli′nal, 169.
An′ti-cor.
An-ti′coŭs.
An-ti-dōt′al, 228.
An′ti-dote, 169.
An-ti-dōt′ic-al [so Wr.; *an-ti-dōt′ik-al*, Gd. 155.]
An-ti-dys′u-ric [so Gd.; *an-ti-diz′u-rik*, Wr. 155.]
An-ti-feb′rīle [so Wk. Sm. Wr.; *an-ti-fe′bril*, or *an-ti-feb′ril*, Gd. 155.]
An-ti-fed′er-al, 233.
An-ti-fed′er-al-ism (*-al-izm*), 136.
An-ti-fed′er-al-ist, 171.
An′ti-grăph, 35.
An-ti-hyp-not′ic [Anthypnotic, 203.]
An-ti-hyp-o-chon′dri-ac (*-kon′-*) [Anthypochondriac, 203.]
An-ti-hys-ter′ic [Anthysteric, 203.]
An-ti-log′a-rithm, 133.
An-ti-loi′mic
[Antilope.—*See* Antelope, 203.]
An′ti-măsk.
An-ti-ma′son (*-ma′sn*).
An-ti-ma-son′ic, 109.
An-ti-ma′son-ry, 93.
An-ti-me-tab′o-lē (Gr.), [163.
An-tim′e-ter, 170.
An-ti-mo′ni-al.
An-ti-mo′ni-ate.
An-ti-mon′ic.
An-ti-mo′ni-oŭs.
An′ti-mo-ny, 169, 171.
An-ti-ne-phrit′ic.
An-ti-no′mi-an, 169.
An-ti-no′mi-an-ism (*-izm*), 136.
An′ti-no-my [so Sm. Wb. Gd.; *an-tin′o-my*, Wk.; *an′ti-no-my*, or *an-tin′o-my*, Wr. 155.]
An-ti-o′chi-an (*-o′kī-*).
An-ti-o-don-tal′gic, 109, 116.
An-ti-path′ic.
An-tip′a-thy, 171.
An-ti-pe-ris′ta-sis (Gr.).
An-ti-phlo-gis′tic.
An′ti-phon.
An-tiph′o-nal, 35.
An-tiph′o-na-ry, 35, 72.
An-ti-phon′ic-al.
An-tiph′o-ny, 35, 93.
An-tiph′ra-sis, 35.
An-ti-phras′tic.
An-ti-phras′tic-al.
An-tip′o-dal, 170.
An′ti-pode, 169.
An-ti-po′de-an, 110, 169.
An-tip′o-dēs (*-dēz*) (L. pl.), 156.
An-tip-to′sis (Gr.), 109.
An-ti-qua′ri-an, 49, N.
An-ti-qua′ri-an-ism (*-izm*), 136.
An′ti-qua-ry, 72, 171.
An′ti-quate.
An′ti-quāt-ed, 183.
An-ti-qua′tion.
An-tique′ (*an-tēk′*), 114.
An-tique′ness (*-tēk′-*).
An-tiq′ui-ty (*-tik′we-ty*), 171. [46.
An-tĭ′scian (*-tish′an*),
An-tĭ′sci-ī (L. pl.) (*tish′-i-ī*), 171.
An-ti-scor-bu′tic [*not* an-ti-skor-but′ik, 153.]
An-ti-script′u-ral, 91.
An-ti-sep′tic.
An-ti-slāv′er-y, 233.
An-tis′ta-sis (Gr.).
An-tis′tro-phē (Gr.), 163.
An-ti-stroph′ic.
An-tith′e-sis (Gr.) [pl. An-tith′e-sēs (*-e-sēz*), 198.]
An-ti-thet′ic, 169.
An-ti-thet′ic-al.
An-tit′ro-pal.
An-tit′ro-poŭs.
An′ti-type, 169.
An-ti-typ′ic-al, 143.
Ant′ler, 10, 77.
Ant′lered (*ant′lurd*), [165.
Ant′like, 13, 131.
An-to-no-ma′si-a (L.) (*an-to-no-ma′zhi-a*) [so Wr.; *an-to-no-ma′-zha*, Gd. 155.]
An′vil, 10, 230.
Anx-i′e-ty (*ang-zi′e-ty*), 40, N.; 171.
Anx′ious (*angk′shus*), 46, N.; 171.
An′y (*en′y*), 15, 93 [*See* Note under *Many*.]
An′y-how (*en′y-*).
An′y-whêre (*en′y-*), 15.
An′y-wise (*en′y-wīz*), 34.
Ā-o′ni-an, 72.
A′o-rist.
Ā-o-rist′ic, 109.
Ā-o-rist′ic-al, 108.
Ā-or′ta, 72.
Ā-or′tal.
Ā-or′tic.
Ap′a-go-gē (Gr.), 163.
Ap-a-gog′ic-al (*-goj′ik-*), 143, 171.
Ap′a-nage [Appanage, Appenage, 203.]
Ap-a-rith′me-sis (Gr.).
A-part′, 11
A-part′ment.
Ap-a-thet′ic, 109.
Ap-a-thet′ic-al, 108.
Ap′a-thist, 170.
Ap-a-thist′ic-al.
Ap′a-thy, 93, 170.
Ap′a-tīte [*See* Appetite, 148.]
Ape, 23.
A-pēak′, 13.
A-pel′loŭs, 170.
Ap′en-nīne, 152, 170.
A-pep′sy (169) [so Sm. Wb. Gd.; *ap′ep-sy*, Wk. Wr. 155.]
Āp′er, 183.
A-pe′ri-ent, 49, N.; 169.
A-pĕr′i-tĭve, 84, 170.
Ap′er-ture, 170.
A-pet′a-loŭs, 170.
A′pex [L. pl. *Ap′i-cēs* (*-sēz*); Eng. pl A′pex-es (*-ĕz*).]

A-phær′e-sis (*a-fĕr′e-sis*) [so Wk. Wr. Gd; *a-fe′re-sis*, Sm. 155] [Apheresis, 203.]
A-phe′li-on [so Wk. Sm. Wr.; *a-fēl′yon*, Wb. Gd. 155.] [pl. A-phe′-li-a, 198.]
A-phid′i-an, 35, 169.
Aph-i-lan′thro-py.
A′phis [pl. *Aph′i-dēs* (*-dēz*), 198.]
Aph-lo-gis′tic.
Aph′o-noŭs, 35.
Aph′o-ny, 35, 93.
Aph′o-rism (*-rizm*), 133, 136.
Aph-o-ris′mic (*-riz′-*).
Aph′o-rist.
Aph-o-rist′ic, 109.
Aph-o-rist′ic-al, 108.
Aph′rīte, 35, 152.
Aph-ro-dĭ′si-ac (*-dizh′i-ak*).
Aph-ro-di-si′ac-al (*-zi′-ak-*).
Aph′ro-dīte, 35, 152.
Aph′thæ (L. pl.) (*af′-thē*).
Aph′thong (*ap′thong*) [so Sm. Wr.; *af′-thong*, Wb. Gd. 155.]
Aph′thoŭs.
A-phyl′lous, *or* Aph′-yl-lous [*See* Adeno-phyllous.]
Ā-pi-a′ri-an, 49, N.
Ā′pi-a-rist.
A′pi-a-ry, 72.
Ap′i-cēs (L. pl.) (*ap′i-sēz*) [*See* Apex.]
A-pic′u-late, 89.
A-pic′u-lāt-ed, 183.
A-piēce′, 13.
A′pi-īne, 152.
A′pis (L.).
Āp′ish, 23, 183.
Ap-la-nat′ic.
A-plăs′tic.
Ap′lome [so Gd.; *a-plōm′*, Wr. 155.]
A-plot′o-my, 108.
A-plus′tre (L.), 164.
A-poc′a-lȳpse, 171.
A-poc-a-lyp′tic.
A-poc-a-lyp′tic-al.
Ap-o-car′poŭs.
A-poc′o-pate, 170.
A-poc′o-pē (Gr.), 163.
Ap-o-crus′tic.
A-poc′ry-pha, 171.
A-poc′ry-phal.
A-poc′ry-phal-ly, 93, 171.
Ap′o-dal, 170.
Ap′ode.
Ap-o-dic′tic.
Ap-o-dic′tic-al.
Ap′o-don (L.) [pl. *Ap′o-da*, 198.]
A-pod′o-sis (L.), 170.
Ap′o-gee, 170.
Ap′o-grăph.
A-pog′ra-phal.
A-pol-li-na′ri-an, 49, N.
A-pol′lō-Bel-ve-dēre′ (210) [so Gd.; *A-pol′-lo-Bel′ve-dēr*, Wr. 155.]
A-pol′ly-on, 170.
A-pol-o-get′ic, 109, 170.
A-pol-o-get′ic-al, 108.
A-pol-o-get′ics, 109.
A-pol′o-gist, 170.
A-pol′o-gize, 170, 202.
Ap′o-lŏgue, 87, 170.
A-pol′o-gy, 170.
Ap-o-me-com′e-try.
Ap-o-neū-rog′ra-phy.
Ap-o-neū-rol′o-gy.
Ap-o-neū-ro′sis (Gr.) [pl. *Ap-o-neū-ro′sēs* (*-sēz*), 198.]
Ap-o-neū-rot′ic.
Ap-o-neū-rot′o-my.
Ap-o-pemp′tic.
A-poph′a-sis (Gr.) [pl. *A-poph′a-sēs* (*-sēz*), 198.]
Ap-o-phleg-mat′ic [so Sm. Wb. Gd.; *ap-o-fleg′ma-tik*, Wk. Wr. 155.]
Ap-o-phleg′ma-tism, (*-tizm*).
Ap-o-phleg-mat′i-zant, 116.
Ap′oph-thegm (*ap′o-them*) (162) [Apothegm, 203.]

☞ Both modes of spelling this word have the sanction of good authority. *Apophthegm* is favored by the etymology (Gr. ἀπόφθεγμα), but *Apothegm*, says Worcester, "is perhaps best supported by common usage."

A-poph′y-gē, 163.
Ap-o-phyl′līte, *or* A-poph′yl-līte [so Wr.; *a-pof′il-līt*, Gd. 155.]
Ap-o-plec′tic, 109.
Ap-o-plec′tic-al, 108.
Ap′o-plex-y, 93, 170.
A-pos′ta-sy, 169.
A-pos′tate.
A-pos′ta-tīze, 202.
A-pos′ta-tīzed, 183.
A-pos′ta-tīz-ing.
Ap′o-steme, 170.
A-pos′til.
A-pos′tle (*-pos′sl*), 162, 171.
A-pos′to-late.
Ap-os-tol′ic.
Ap-os-tol′ic-al.
A-pos-to-liç′i-ty.
A-pos′tro-phē, 163, 171.
Ap-os-troph′ic.
A-pos′tro-phīze, 202.
A-pos′tro-phīzed, 183.
A-pos′tro-phīz-ing.
A-poth′e-ca-ry, 72, 171.
Ap′o-thegm (*ap′o-them*) (162) [Apophthegm, 203.]

☞ *See* Note under Apophthegm.

Ap-o-theg-mat′ic.
Ap-o-theg-mat′ic-al.
Ap-o-theg′ma-tist, 171.
Ap-o-theg′ma-tīze, 202.
Ap-o-the′o-sis, 109.
Ap-o-the′o-sīze, 202.
A-pot′o-mē, 163.
Ap′o-zem.
Ap-o-zem′ic-al.
Ap-pa-la′chi-an, 170.
Ap-pâll′ (17) [Appal, Sm. 203.]
Ap-pâlled′, 165.
Ap-pâll′ing.
[Appanage.— *See* Apanage, 203.]
Ap-pa-ra′tus (170) [pl. Ap-pa-ra′tus, *or* Ap-pa-ra′tus-es, 198.]
Ap-păr′el, 170.
Ap-păr′elled (*-păr′eld*) (177) [Appareled, Wb. Gd. 203.—*See* 177, and Note E, p. 70.]
Ap-păr′el-ling [Appareling, Wb. Gd. 203.]
Ap-par′ent (*ap-pêr′ent*) (14, 171) [*not* ap-pā′-rent, 153.]
Ap-pa-rĭ′tion (*-rish′un*), 46, 170.
Ap-păr′i-tor.
Ap-pēal′, 13.
Ap-pēal′a-ble, 164, 169.
Ap-pēaled′, 165.
Ap-pēal′er.
Ap-pēal′ing.
Ap-pēar′, 13.

Ap-pēar'ance, 169.
Ap-pēared', 165.
Ap-pēar'ing, 49, N.
Ap-pēas'a-ble (-*pēz'*-).
Ap-pēase' (-*pēz'*), 40, 136.
Ap-peased' (-*pēzd'*), 165.
Ap-pēase'ment (-*pēz'*).
Ap-pēas'er (-*pēz'ur*), 77, 183.
Ap-pēas'ĭve (-*pēz'*-).
Ap-pel'lant, 170.
Ap-pel'late, 170.
Ap-pel'la-tĭve, 170.
Ap-pel'la-to-ry, 86.
Ap-pel-lee', 122, 170.
Ap-pel-lor' (118) [so Wb. Gd.; *ap-pel'lor*, Sm.; *ap-pel'lor*, or *ap-pel-lor'*, Wr. 155.]
[Ap pen a ge, 203.—*See* Apanage.]
Ap-pend', 15, 103.
Ap-pend'age, 171.
Ap-pend'ant, 169.
Ap-pen'di-cle, 164, 169.
Ap-pen-dic'u-late.
Ap-pen'dix (170) [pl. Ap-pen'di-cēs (-*sēz*), *or* Ap-pen'dix-es, 198.]
Ap-per-cep'tion, 170.
Ap-per-tāin', 122, 170.
Ap'pe-tence, 169.
Ap'pe-ten-cy, 169.
Ap'pe-tīte (152, 170) [*See* Apatite, 148.]
Ap'pe-tĭ-tĭve, 84, 170.
Ap'pe-tīze, 170, 202.
Ap'pe-tīz-er, 183.
Ap'pi-an, 169, 170.
Ap-plâud', 17, 103.
Ap-plâud'ed.
Ap-plâud'er.
Ap-plâud'ing.
Ap-plâuse' (-*plawz'*), 17.
Ap-plâu'sĭve, 156.
Ap'ple (*ap'l*), 10, 164.
Ap'ple-tree, 206, Exc.4.
Ap-plī'a-ble, 164.
Ap-plī'ance, 169.
Ap-plī'an-cy, 169.
Ap-pli-ca-bil'i-ty, 171.
Ap'pli-ca-ble, 164, 170.
Ap'pli-can-cy, 169.
Ap'pli-cant, 170.
Ap'pli-cate.
Ap-pli-ca'tion, 112.
Ap'pli-ca-tĭve, 84.
Ap'pli-ca-to-ry, 86.
Ap-plīed', 186.
Ap-plī'er.
Ap-ply', 25.
Ap-ply'ing.
Appogiatura (It.) (*ap-poj-a-too'ra*).
Ap-point', 27.
Ap-point'a-ble, 164, 169.
Ap-point'ed.
Ap-point-ee', 122.
Ap-point'er.
Ap-point'ing.
Ap-point'ment.
Ap-pōr'tion, 67.
Ap-pōr'tioned (-*pōr'-shund*.)
Ap-pōr'tion-er.
Ap-pōr'tion-ing.
Ap-pōr'tion-ment.
Ap-pōs'er (-*pōz'*-).
Ap'po-sĭte (-*zĭt*), 83, 170.
Ap-po-sĭ'tion (-*zish'un*), 40.
Ap-pos'i-tive (-*poz'*-).
Ap-prāise' (-*prāz'*), 40, 43, 136.
Ap-prāised' (-*prāzd'*), 165.
Ap-praise'ment (-*prāz'-ment*.)
Ap-prāis'er (-*prāz'*-).
Ap-prāis'ing (-*prāz'*-).
Ap-pre'ci-a-ble (-*pre'-shĭ-a-bl*), 46, 169, 171.
Ap-pre'ci-ate (*ap-pre'-shĭ-āt*) (171) [so Wk. Sm. Wr.; *ap-pre'shāt*, Wb. Gd. 155.]
Ap-pre'ci-āt-ed (-*shĭ*-).
Ap-pre'ci-āt-ing (-*shĭ-āt*-).
Ap-pre-ci-a'tion (-*pre-shĭ-a'shun*), 171.
Ap-pre'ci-a-tĭve (-*shĭ-a*-)
Ap-pre'ci-a-to-ry (-*shĭ*-), 86, 93.
Ap-pre-hend', 170.
Ap-pre-hend'ed.
Ap-pre-hend'er.
Ap-pre-hend'ing.
Ap-pre-hen'si-ble, 164.
Ap-pre-hen'sion.
Ap-pre-hen'sĭve.
Ap-pren'tĭce, 169, 171.
Ap-pren'tĭced (-*tist*), Note C, p. 34.
Ap-pren'ti-cing, 183.
Ap-pressed' (-*prest'*), *or* Ap-prest'.
Ap-prise' (-*prīz'*) (25, 136), *v.* to inform [*See* Apprize, 160.]
Ap-prīze', *v.* to set a price upon [*See* Apprise, 160.]
Ap-prīzed', 150.
Ap-prize'ment.
Ap-prīz'er.
Ap-prōach', *n.* & *v.* 24.
Ap-prōach'a-ble, 164.
Ap-prōached' (-*prōcht'*), Note C, p. 34.
Ap-prōach'er.
Ap-prōach'ing.
Ap'pro-bate.
Ap'pro-bāt-ed, 183.
Ap'pro-bāt-ing.
Ap-pro-bā'tion, 112.
Ap'pro-bāt-ĭve [so Sm. Wb. Gd.; *ap'pro-ba-tĭv*, Wr. 155.]
Ap'pro-ba-to-ry, 86.
Ap-pro'pri-a-ble, 164.
Ap-pro'pri-ate, 171.
Ap-pro'pri-āt ed, 183.
Ap-pro-pri-a'tion.
Ap-pro'pri-a-tĭve, 84.
Ap-pro'pri-āt-or.
Ap-pro'pri-e-ta-ry (72) [so Wb. Gd.; *ap-pro-pri'e-ta-ry*, Wr. 155.]
Ap-prov'a-ble (-*proov'-a-bl*), 169.
Ap-prov'al (-*proov'al*), 183.
Ap-prove' (-*proov'*), 19.
Ap-proved' (-*proovd'*), 183.
Ap-prove'ment (*ap-proov'*-), 185.
Ap-prov'er (-*proov'ur*).
Ap-prov'ing (-*proov'*-).
Ap-prox'i-mate, *a.* & *v.*
Ap-prox'i-māt-ed. [73.
Ap-prox'i-māt-ing.
Ap-prox-i-ma'tion, 112.
Ap-prox'i-ma-tĭve.
Ap-pulse' [so Sm. Wb. Gd.; *ap'puls*, Wk.; *ap'puls* or *ap-puls'*, Wr. 155.]
Ap-pul'sion.
Ap-pul'sĭve.
Ap-pur'te-nance, 169.
Ap-pur'te-nant, 72, 169.
Ā'pri-cot (171) [*not* ap'-ri-cot, 153.]
A'pril, 23, 230.
A'pron (17) (*a'purn* or *a'prun*) [so Wr.; *a'-purn*, Wk. Gd.; *a'-prun*, colloquially *a'purn*, Sm. 155.]
A'proned (*a'purnd*), 171.
Ap'ro-pos (Fr.) (*ap'ro-po*) [so Sm. Gd.; *ap-ro po'*, Wr. 155.]
Ap'si-dal.
Ap'sis (Gr.) [pl. *Ap'si-dēs* (-*dēz*), 198.]

Apt, 10, 30, 41.
Ap'ter-al, 233.
Ap'ter-an.
Ap'ter-oŭs.
Ap'ter-ȳx, 171.
Apt'i-tude, 169, 171.
Ap'tote, 230.
Ā-pȳ-ret'ic [so Gd.; *ap-y-ret'ic*, Wr. 155.]
Ap'y-rex-y, 93, 171.
Ap'y-roŭs [so Wr.; *a'-pĭr-us*, Sm.; *a-pi'rus*, Gd. 155.]
A'qua (L.) (*a'kwa*).
A-qua'ri-al, 49, N.
A-qua'ri-an, 169.
A-qua'ri-um (L.) [pl. *A-qua'ri-a*, 198.]
A-qua'ri-us (L.).
A-quat'ic.
A'qua-tint.
Aq'ue-duct (*ak'we-*),171.
A'que-oŭs, 171.
A'qui-form (*a'kwĭ-*) [so Wb. Gd.; *ak'we-form*, Wr. 155.]
Aq'ui-līne (*ak'wi-līn*), *or* Aq'ui-līne (*ak'wi-lĭn*) [so Wr. Gd.; *ak'-wi-lĭn*, Wk. Sm. 155.]
Aq'ui-lon (*ak'wi-lon*).
Ăr'ab *or* Ā'rab (170) [so Wr.; *ăr'ab*, Gd. 155.]
Ăr-a-besque'(*-besk'*),168.
Ăr-a-besqued' (*-beskt'*), Note C, p. 34.
A-ra'bi-an, 78.
Ar'a-bic, 109, 156, 170.
A-rab'ic-al, 108.
Ar'a-bĭne [Arabin, 203.]
Ăr'a-bism (*-bizm*).
Ăr'a-bist.
Ăr'a-ble, 164, 170.
A-ra'ceous (*-ra'shus*).
A-rach'ni-dan (*-rak'-*), 52.
A-rach'noid (*-rak'-*).
A-rach-nol'o-gist (*-rak-nol'-*), 108.
A-rach-nol'o-gy (*-rak-*), 108.
Ăr'a-gon-ite [Arragonite, 203.]
Ăr-a-mæ'an (*-me'an*).
Ăr-a-ma'ic.
Ăr-a-ne'i-dan.
Ăr-a-ne'i-form, 108.
A-ra'ne-oŭs.
A-ra'tion.
Ar'bal-ist.
Ar'bal-ist-er.
Ar'bi-ter, 77.
Ar'bi-tra-ble, 164.
Ar-bit'ra-ment [Arbitrement, 203.]
Ar'bi-tra-ri-ly.
Ar'bi-tra-ry, 72, 93.
Ar'bi-trate, 73.
Ar'bi-trăt-ed, 183.
Ar'bi-trăt-ing.
Ar-bi-tra'tion.
Ar'bi-trăt-or.
Ar'bi-trăt-rix [so Sm. Wr.; *ar-bi-trăt'rix*, Wb. Gd. 155.]
[Arbitrement. — *See* Arbitrament,203.]
Ar'bi-tress.
Ar'bor (11, 169) [Ar'-bour, Sm. 199, 203.]
Ar'bored (*ar'burd*).
Ar-bo're-oŭs, 169.
Ar-bo-res'cent, 171.
Ar'bo-ret.
Ar-bor-i-cult'ur-al, 91.
Ar-bor-i-cult'ure, 91.
Ar-bor-i-cult'u-ist.
Ar-bŏr'i-form, 143.
Ar'bor-ist.
Ar-bor-i-za'tion.
Ar'bor-oŭs.
Ar-bus'cle (*-bus'sl*), 162.
Ar-bus'cu-lar, 108.
Ar-bust'ĭve.
Ar'bute, 11, 26.
Ar-bu'te-an, 110.
Arc (11, 49, 52), *n.* a part of a circumference [*See* Ark, 160.]
Ar-cade', 11, 23.
Ar-căd'ed, 183.
Ar-ca'di-an, 169.
Arch, 11, 44.
Ar-chæ-og'ra-phy (*-ke-og'-*), 108.
Ar-chæ-o-lo'gi-an (*ar-ke-*).
Ar-chæ-o-log'ic (*-ke-o-loj'ik*).
Ar-chæ-o-log'ic-al (*-ke-o-loj'ik-*).
Ar-chæ-ol'o-gist (*-ke-ol'-*), 108.
Ar-chæ-ol'o-gy (*-ke-*), 108. [Archaiology, 203.]
Ar-cha'ic (*-ka'ik*), 52.
Ar'cha-ism (*ar'ka-izm*).
Arch-an'gel (*ark-*), 171.
Arch-an-gel'ic (*-ark-*).
Arch-a-pos'tle (*-pos'sl*).
Arch-bish'op.
Arch-bish'op-ric.
Arch-chem'ic (*arch-kem'ik*), 44, 52.
Arch-dēa'con (*-de'kn*), 167.
Arch-dēa'con-ry (*-dē'-kn-*), 93.
Arch-di'o-cēse (*-o-cēs*),
Arch-du'cal. [171.
Arch-duch'ess, 44.
Arch-duch'y, 44, 93.
Arch-duke'.
Arch-duke'dom.
Arched (*archt*, or *arch'-ed*), 150.
Ar-chel'o-gy (*-kel'o-jy*).
Arch'er, 77.
Arch'er-ess.
Arch'er-y, 93.
Ar-che-tȳp'al (*ar-ke-*), 183.
Ar'che-type(*ar'ke-*),171.
Ar-che-typ'ic-al(*ar-ke-*).
Arch-fiend', 206.
Ar-chi'a-ter (*ar-ki'a-tur*) [so Wr.; *ar'ki-a-tur*, Wb. Gd. 155.]
Arch'ic-al (*ark'ik-*).
Ar-chĭ-dĭ-ac'o-nal (*ar-kĭ-*).
A-chĭ-e-pis'co-pa-cy(*ar-kĭ'-*), 171.
Ar-chĭ-e-pis'co-pal (*ar-kĭ-*).
Ar'chil (*ar'chil* or *ar'-kil*) [so Wr.; *ar'chil*, Sm.; *ark'il*, Wb. Gd. 155.]
Ar-chi-lo'chi-an (*ar-kĭ-lo'ki-an*), 52, 171.
Ar-chi-man'drīte (*ar-kĭ-*).
Ar-chim-e-de'an (*-kim-e-*), 110, 171.
Arch'ing.
Ar-chi-pe-lag'ic (*ar-kĭ-pe-laj'ik*), 171.
Ar-chi-pel'a-go (*ar-kĭ-pel'a-go*) (171) [*not* arch-i-pel'a-go, 153.]
Ar'chi-tect (*ar'ki-tekt*) (171) [*not* arch'i-tekt, 153.]
Ar-chi-tect'ĭve (*ar-kĭ-*).
Ar-chi-tec-ton'ic (*ar-kĭ-*).
Ar-chi-tec-ton'ic-al (*ar-kĭ-*).
Ar'chi-tect-ress (*ar'kĭ-tekt-res*) [so Wr.; *ar-kĭ-tekt'res*, Wb. Gd. 155.]
Ar-chi-tect'ur-al (*ar-kĭ-*).
Ar'chi-tect-ure (*ar'kĭ-tekt-yur*) (52, 91, 171)

[*not* arch'i-tect-yur, 153.]
Ar'chi-trave (*ar'kĭ-*),171
Ar-chiv'al (*ar-kīv'al*) [so Wr.; *ark'i-val*, Wb. Gd. 155.]
Ar chives (*ar'kīvz*) [*not* ar'chīvz, 153.]
Ar'chi-vist (*ar'kĭ-*).
Ar'chi-volt (*ar'kĭ-*).
Ar'chon (*ar'kon*).
Arch-pres'by-ter (*-prĕz'-*) [so Wk.Wr.; *arch-pres'by-tur*, Gd. 155.]
Arch-pres'by-ter-y, (*-prĕz'-*), 171.
Arch-priēst', 206.
Arch-pri'mate.
Arch'stōne, 24, 206.
Arch'wāy, 206.
Arch'wise (*-wīz*).
Ar'co-grăph.
Arc-ta'tion.
Arc'tic, 49, 52.
Arc-tu'rus, 49, N.
Ar'cu-ate, 89.
Ar-cu-a'tion.
Ar'cu-bal-ist.
Ar-cu-bal-ist'er, *or* Ar-cu-bal'ist-er [so Wr.; *ar-cu-bal-ist'ur*, Sm.; *ar-cu-bal'ist-ur*, Wb. Gd. 155.]
Ar'den-cy, 169.
Ar'dent, 169, 230.
Ar'dor (11, 88) [Ardour, Sm. 199, 203.]
Ard'u-oŭs [so Sm. Gd.; *ar'du-us*, Wr.; *ar'ju-us*, Wk. 155.]
Are (*är*), 11, 163.
A're-a, 49, N.; 171.
A-reek'.
Ar-e-fac'tion.
Ar'e-fȳ, 94, 169.
A-re'na, 171.
Ar-e-na'ceous (*-na'shus*), 112, 169.
Ar-e-na'ri-oŭs, 49, N.
Ar-e-na'tion.
A-ren-i-lit'ic.
Ar-e-nose'.
Ar'e-noŭs.
A-re'o-la (L.) [pl. *A-re'o-læ*, 198.]
A-re'o-lar, 74.
A-re'o-late, 73.
A-re-o-la'tion.
Ā-re-om'e-ter (49, N.) [so Sm. Wr.; *ăr-e-om'e-tur*, Wb. Gd. 155.]
Ā-re-o-met'ric.
Ā-re-o-met'ric-al.
Ā-re-om'e-try.
Ăr-e-op'a-gist.
Ăr-e-op'a-gīte [so Wk. Wr. Wb. Gd.; *ăr-e-op'a-jīt*, Sm. 155.]
Ăr-e-op'a-gus (170) [so Wr. Wb, Gd.; *ēr-e-op'a-gus*, Sm. 155.]
Ar'gal.
Ar'gand.
Ar'gent.
Ar-gent'al [so Gd.; *ar'-jent-al*, Wr. 155.]
Ar-gent'ic.
Ar-gen-tif'er-oŭs.
Ar'gent-ine [so Wr.Gd.; *ar'jent-īn*, Sm. 155.]
Ar'gil, 171.
Ar-gil-la'ceous (*-shus*), 169, 171.
Ar-gil-lif'er-oŭs.
Ar-gil'lo-cal-ca're-oŭs.
Ar-gil'loŭs [so Wk.Wr. Wb. Gd.; *ar'jil-lus*, Sm. 155.]
Ar'gol.
Ar-gol'ic.
Ar'go-nâut.
Ar-go-nâut'ic, 108.
Ar'go-sy, 169.
Ar'gūe.
Ar'gūed, 183.
Ar'gu-er, 77, 89.
Ar'gu-ing.
Ar'gu-ment.
Ar-gu-ment-a'tion.
Ar-gu-ment'a-tĭve, 171.
A'ri-an, 49, N.; 169.
A'ri-an-ism (*-izm*), 133.
Ăr'id, 66, 170, 231.
A-rid'i-ty, 108, 171.
A'ri-ēs (L.) (*a'ri-ēz*).
A-rīght' (*a-rīt'*), 162.
Ar'il, 170, 231.
Ar'il-late.
Ar'il-lāt-ed.
Ăr'i-ose, 170.
A-rīse' (*a-rīz'*), 25, 40.
A-rīs'ing (*a-rīz'ing*),183
Ar'is-tarch (*-tark*).
Ar-is-tarch'i-an (*-tark'-*).
A-ris'tate.
Ar-is-toc'ra-cy, 108, 169.
A-ris'to-crat, *or* Ăr'is-to-crat [so Wr.; *ar-is-to-krat'*, Wk.; *ar'-is-to-krat*, Sm.; *ar'is-to-krat* or *a-ris'to-krat*, Gd. 155.]
Ăr-is-to-crat'ic, 109.
Ăr-is-to-crat'ic-al, 108.
Ăr-is-to-te'li-an [so Wr. Wb. Gd.; *ar-is-to-tēl'-yan*, Sm. 155.]
Ăr-is-to-tel'ic, 170.
A-rith'man-cy (169) [so Wk. Wr.; *ar'ith-man-sy*, Sm.; *ar'ith-man-sy* or *a-rith'man-sy*, Gd. 155.]
A-rith'me-tic, 109, 171.
Ăr-ith-met'ic-al, 108.
A-rith-me-tĭ'cian (*-tish'-an*), 46, 112, 171.
Ark (11, 49, 52), *n.* a kind of vessel. [*See* Arc, 160.]
Arm, 11, 32, 49.
Ar-mā'da (Sp.).
Ar-ma-dil'lo (170) [pl. Ar-ma-dil'los (*-lōz*), 192.]
Ar'ma-ment.
Ar'ma-ture, 171.
Armed, 165.
Ar-me'ni-an [*See* Ar-min'i an, 148.]
Arm'ful (*-fŏŏl*) (180, 197).
Arm'il-la-ry, 72, 170.
Arm'ing.
Ar-min'ian (*ar-min'-yan*) [*See* Armenian, 148.]
Ar-min'ian ism (*-min'-yan-izm*), 133, 136.
Arm'is-tĭce, 169, 171.
Ar'mor (11, 88) [Armour, Sm. 199, 203.]
Ar'mor-er, 77, 88.
Ar-mo'ri-al.
Ar-mŏr'ic, 109.
Ar-mŏr'ic-an.
Arm'o-ry, 86, 93.
Arms (*ärmz*), 136.
Ar'my, 93.
Ar'ni-ca, 169, 171.
[Arnotto.—*See* Annotto, 203.]
A-ro'ma, 72, 171.
Ar-o-mat'ic, 109, 170.
Ar-o-mat'ics.
A-ro'ma-tīze, *or* Ăr'o-ma-tize (202) [*a-ro'ma-tīz*, Sm. Wb. Gd.; *ăr'o-ma-tīz*, Wk.; *ar'-o-ma-tīz* or *ă-ro'ma-tīz*, Wr. 155.]
A-ro'ma-tīz-er, *or* Ăr'-o-ma-tīz-er.
A-ro'ma-toŭs.
A-rōse' (*a-rōz'*), 136.
A-round', 28.
A-rouse' (*a-rouz'*), 28, 136.

A-roused′ (*a-rouzd′*), 165, 183.
A-rous′ing(*a-rouz′ing*).
A-roynt′, 27.
Ar-peg′gio (It.) (*ar-ped′jo*).
Ar′pent.
Ar-que-bus-ade′.
Ar′que-büse (*ar′kwe-bus*) [so Wk. Wr.; *ar′kwe-bŭs*, Wb. Gd.; *ar′kwe-bōōz*, Sm. 155.]
Ar-que-bus-iēr′(*ar-kwe-bus-ēr′*), 114, 169.
Ăr-rack′ (170) [so Wk. Wr. Wb. Gd.; *ăr′ak*, Sm. 155.]
[Arragonite, 203.—*See* Aragonite.]
Ar-rāign′ (*a-rān′*), 162, 171.
Ar-rāigned′ (*a-rānd′*).
Ar-rāign′ing (*a-rān′-ing*).
Ar-rāign′ment (*-rān′*).
Ar-rānge′, 48, 66, N.; 170.
Ar-rānged′, 165, 183.
Ar-rānge′ment.
Ar-rān′ger.
Ar-rān′ging.
Ăr′rant, 48, 170.
Ăr′ras, 170.
Ar-rāy′, *n.* & *v.*
Ar-rāyed′, 150, 187.
Ar-rāy′er.
Ar-rāy′ing.
Ar-rēar′, 171.
Ar-rēar′age, 169, 171.
Ar-rect′.
Ar-rest′, 15, 103.
Ar-rest′ed.
Ar-rest′er, *or* Ar-rest′-or, 77, 88.
Arrêt (Fr.) (*ar-ret′* or *ar-rā′*) [so Wr.; *ar-ret′*, Gd. 154, 155.]
Ar-rière′ (Fr.) (*ar-rēr′*).
Ar′ris, 170.
Ar-rīv′al, 228.
Ar-rive′, 25.
Ar-rived′, 165, 183.
Ar-rīv′ing.
Ar-ro′ba (Sp.).
Ăr′ro-gance, 170.
Ăr′ro-gant, 170.
Ăr′ro-gate, 73.
Ăr′ro-gāt-ed, 183.
Ăr′ro-gāt-ing.
Ăr-ro-ga′tion.
Ăr′ro-ga-tĭve, 84.
Arrondissement (Fr.) (*ar-ron′dēs-mäng*).

Ăr′rōw, 48, 66, N.; 170.
Ăr′rōw-root.
Ăr′rōw-shaped(*-shapt*), 2 5.
Ăr′rōw-y, 93.
Ar′se-nal, 171.
Ar-se′ni-ate.
Ar′sen-ic, *n.* (161) [so Sm. Wb. Gd.; *ars′-nik*, Wk.; *ar′sen-ik* or *ars′nik*, Wr. 155.]
Ar-sen′ic, *a.* 161.
Ar-sen′ic-al.
Ar-sen′i-cate.
Ar-se′ni-oŭs, 169.
Ar′se-nīte.
Ar-se-ni′u-ret.
Ar-se-ni′u-ret-ted.
[Arseniureted, 203]
Ar′son, 171.
Art, 11, 41, 49.
Ar-te′ri-ac.
Ar-te′ri-al, 49, N.
Ar-te-ri-al-ĭ-za′tion, 112.
Ar-te′ri-al-īze, 202.
Ar-te-ri-og′ra-phy, 108.
Ar-te-ri-ol′o-gy, 108.
Ar-te-ri-ot′o-my, 108.
Ar′ter-y, 93, 233.
Ar-te′sian (*ar-te′zhan*), 112.
Art′ful (*art′fōōl*).
Ar-thrit′ic.
Ar-thri′tis (Gr.).
Ar-throd′ic.
Ar-thro-dyn′ic.
Ar-throl′o-gy, 108.
Ar′ti-chōke, 171.
Ar′ti-cle, 78, 164.
Ar′ti-cled (*ar′ti-kld*), 165, 183.
Ar′ti-cling, 183.
Ar-tic′u-lar, 89.
Ar-tic′u-late, *a.* & *v.* 72.
Ar-tic′u-lāt-ed.
Ar-tic′u-lāt-ing.
Ar-tic-u-la′tion, 112.
Art′i-fĭce, 169, 171.
Ar-tif′i-cer.
Art-i-fĭ′cial (*-fish′al*) (169) [so Wk. Wr. Wb. Gd.; *art-i-fish′yal*, Sm. 155.]
Ar-ti-fĭ-ci-al′i-ty (*-fish-i-al′i-ty*), 108, 116.
Ar-til′ler-ist, 170.
Ar-til′ler-y, 93, 170.
Art′i-san (*-zan*) [so Sm. Wb. Gd.; *art-i-zan′*, Wk.; *art′i-zan* or *art-i-zan′*, Wr. 155.]
Art′ist, 80.

Artiste (Fr.) (*ar-tēst′*).
Art-ist′ic, 109.
Ar-to-car′poŭs.
Ăr-un-dēl′ian (*ăr-un-dēl′yan*) [so Sm. Gd.; *ăr-un-dē′li-an*, Wr. 155.]
Ăr-un-dif′er-oŭs, 108.
A-run-di-na′ceous (*na′-shus*), 169.
A-run-din′e-oŭs.
A-rus′pĭce, 169.
A-rus′pi-cy, 169.
A-ryt′e-noid.
As (L.) (161), *n.* a Roman coin.
As (*az*) (161), *ad.* & *conj.* in the manner that; because.
As-a-fœt′i-da [Assafœtida, 203.]

☞ Walker, Smart, and Goodrich, prefer the first form; Worcester the second. Goodrich gives also the forms Asafetida, and Assafetida.

As-bes′tic.
As-bes′ti-form, 171.
As-bes′tĭne, 82, 152.
As-bes′toid.
As-bes′tos, *or* As-bes′-tus, 203.
As′ca-ris (L.) [pl. *As-car′i-dēs* (*-dēz*), 198.]
As-cend′, 39, 230.
As-cend′a-ble, 164.
As-cend′an-cy [Ascendency, 203.]
As-cend′ant [Ascendent, 203.]
As-cend′ed.
As-cend′en-cy [Ascendancy, 203.]
As-cend′ent [Ascendant, 203.]
As-cend′ing.
As-cen′sion, 171.
As-cen′sion-al.
As-cent′, *n.* act of rising [*See* Assent, 160.]
As-cer-tāin′, 171.
As-cer-tāin′a-ble, 169.
As-cer-tāined′, 165.
As-cer-tāin′er.
As-cer-tāin′ing.
As-cer-tāin′ment.
As-cet′ic, 39, 171.
As-cet′i-cism (*-sizm*), 133, 136.
As′ci-an (*ash′ĭ-an*) [so Gd., *ash′yan*), Wr. 155.]

As-cid'i-an, 169.
As'ci-ī (L. pl.) (*ash'ĭ-ī*) [so Wr. Gd.; *ash'yī*, Sm. 155.]
As-cit'ic.
As-ci-tĭ'cious (*-tish'us*), 169, 231, Exc.
As-cle'pi-ad.
As-crīb'a-ble, 164.
As-cribe', 25.
As-cribed', 165.
As-crīb'ing, 183.
As-crip'tion.
A-sep'tic.
Ash, 10, 46.
A-shamed' (*a-shāmd'*), [150.
Ash'en.
Ash'er-y, 93, 233.
Ash'es (*ash'ez*), 40, 46.
Ash'lar, *or* Ash'ler, 74, [77.
Ash'ler-ing.
A-shōre', 24.
Ash'y, 93.
A'sian (*a'shan*) [so Wb. Gd.; *āsh'yan*, Sm. Wr. 155.]
A'si-arch (*a'shĭ-ark*).
Ā-si-at'ic (*ā-shĭ-at'ik*), 109.
Ā-si-at'i-cism (*ā-shĭ-at'ĭ-sizm*), 133, 136.
A-side', 25.
As'i-nine, 78, 170
Ȧsk, 12, 131.
A-skānce', 11.
A-skānt', 11.
Ȧsked (*ȧskt*), 150, Note C, p. 34.
Ȧsk'er.
A-skew' (*a-sku'*), 26.
Ȧsk'ing.
A-slănt', 11.
A-sleep', 13.
A-slope', 24.
As-mo-næ'an (*-ne'an*) [Asmonean, 203.]
Asp, 12, 131.
As-păr'a-gus (170).

☞ This word has been vulgarly corrupted into *sparrow-grass*. Walker remarks of this form of the word: "It may be observed that such words as the vulgar do not know how to spell, and which convey no definite idea of the thing, are frequently changed by them into such words as they do know how to spell, and which do convey some definite idea. The word in question is an instance of it."

As'pect, 10.
As'pen, 10, 149.
As-pĕr'i-ty, 169, 170.
A-sperm'oŭs.
As-perse', 21, Note.
As-persed' (*-perst'*), 165, Note C, p. 34.
As-pers'er, 183.
As-pers'ing.
As-per'sion, 171.
As-pers'īve, 84.
As-phalt', 121.
As-phalt'ic, 35.
As-phal'tum, 35.
As'pho-del.
As-phyx'i-a, 16, 171.
As-phyx'y, 93, 169.
As-pīr'ant (49 N.) [so Sm. Wb. Gd.; *as-pīr'ant*, or *as'pi-rant*, Wr. 155.]
As'pi-rate, *n.* & *v.* 73.
As'pi-rāt-ed.
As'pi-rāt-ing.
As-pire', 25.
As-pired', 165, 183.
As-pīr'ing, 49, Note.
A-squint', 34, 52.
Ȧss, 12, 131, 174.
[Assafœtida, 203.—*See* Asafœtida.]
As-sāil', 23.
As-sāil'a-ble, 164.
As-sāil'ant, 169.
As-sāiled', 165.
As-sāil'er.
As-sāil'ing.
As-sas'sin, 170, 230.
As-sas'sin-ate, 169.
As-sas'sin-āt-ed, 183.
As-sas'sin-āt-ing.
As-sas-sin-a'tion.
As-sas'sin-āt-or.
As-sâult', 17.
As-sâult'ed.
As-sȧult'er.
As-sâult'ing.
As-sāy', *n.* & *v.* 23.
As-sāyed', 165.
As-sāy'er.
As-sāy'ing.
As-sem'blage.
As-sem'ble, 164.
As-sem'bled (*-bld*), 183.
As-sem'bler.
As-sem'bling.
As-sem'bly, 93.
As-sent' (15), *n.* agreement:—*v.* to agree; to consent. [*See* Ascent, 160.]
As-sent-a'tion.
As-sent'ed.
As-sent'er.
As-sen'tient (*-shent*), 46
As-sent'ing.
As-sert', 21, Note.
As-sert'ed.
As-sert'ing.
As-ser'tion.
As-sert'īve, 84.
As-sert'or, 169.
As-sert'o-ry [so Sm. Wb. Gd.; *as'ser-to-ry*, Wr. 155.]
As-sess', 15, 174.
As-sess'a-ble, 164.
As-sessed' (*-sest'*), 165, Note C, p. 34.
As-sess'ing.
As-ses'sion-a-ry (*-sesh'un-*), 46, 72.
As-sess'ment.
As-sess'or, 169.
As'sets, 170.
As-sev'er-ate, 72.
As-sev'er-āt-ed, 183.
As-sev'er-āt-ing.
As-sev-er-a'tion.
As'si-dent, 169, 170.
As-si-du'i-ty, 103, 170.
As-sid'u-oŭs, 91, 170.
As-sign' (*as-sīn'*), 162.
As-sign'a-ble (*-sīn'a-bl*), 162, 164.
Assignat (Fr.) (*as-sēn-yä'*) [so Sm.; *äs-in-yä'*, or *as-ig-nat'*, Wr.; *as'-sig-nat*, Gd. 154, 155.]
As-sig-na'tion, 170.
As-signed' (*-sīnd'*), 165.
As-sign-ee' (*-sīn-e'*), 122, 162.
As-sign'er (*-sīn'ur*).
As-sign'ing (*-sīn'ing*).
As-sign'ment (*-sīn'-*).
As-sign-or' (*-sīn-or'*), (118, 122) [correlative of *Assignee*.]
As-signs' (*as-sīnz'*), 136.
As-sim'i-la-ble, 164.
As-sim'i-late, 169, 170.
As-sim'i-lāt-ed.
As-sim'i-lāt-ing.
As-sim-i-la'tion.
As-sim'i-la-tīve, 84.
As-sim'i-la-to-ry.
As-sist', 16.
As-sist'ance, 169.
As-sist'ant, 169.
As-sist'ed.
As-sist'ing.
As-size', 16.
As-sīz'er, 183.
As-so-ci-a-bil'i-ty (*so-shĭ-*).
As-so'ci-a-ble (*-so'shĭ-a-*

bl) [so Wk. Sm. Wr.; (*as-so'sha-bl*), Wb. Gd. 155.]
As-so'ci-ate, *n.* & *v.* (*so'shĭ-āt*) [so Wk. Sm. Wr.; *as-so'shāt*, Wb. Gd. 155.]
As-so'ci-āt-ed (*-shĭ-āt-*), 183.
As-so'ci-āt-ing (*-shĭ-āt-*)
As-so-ci-a'tion(*-shĭ-a'-*).
As'so-nance, 169, 170.
As'so-nant.
As-sort', 17, 103.
As-sort'ed.
As-sort'ing.
As-sort'ment.
As-suage' (*as-swāj'*), 34, 45, 171.
As-suaged' (*-swājd'*), 165.
As-suāg'er (*-swāj'-*), 183.
As-suāg'ing (*-swāj'-*).
As-sua'sĭve (*-swa'-*), 171.
As'sue-tude (*as'swe-tūd*), 174.
As-sume', 26, 103.
As-sumed', 165, 183.
As-sūm'er.
As-sūm'ing.
As-sump'sit (L.).
As-sump'tion (*-sum'-*), 162.
As-sump'tĭve (*-sum'-*), 162.
As-sur'ance (*a-shoor'-*), 171.
As-sure' (*a-shoor'*), 46.
As-sured' (*a-shoord'*).
As-sur'ed-ly (*a-shoor'-ed-ly*), 150.
As-sur'er (*a-shoor'er*).
As-sur'ing(*a-shoor'ing*)
As-tat'ic.
As'te-ism (*-izm*), 136, 169.
As-te'ri-āt-ed, 49, N.
As'ter-isk, 171.
As'ter-ism (*-izm*), 133.
As'ter-īte, 152.
A-stern', 21, N.
As'ter-oid, 171, 233.
As-ter-oid'al.
As'the-ny.
As-then'ic.
Asth'ma (*ast'ma*), 41, 72, 171.
Asth-mat'ic (*ast-*).
A-stir', 21, N.
As-ton'ish, 104.
As-ton'ished (*-isht*).
As-ton'ish-ing.
As-ton'ish-ment.
As-tound', 28, 103.
As-tound'ed.
As-tound'ing.
A-strad'dle, 164.
As-træ'a (L.) (*as-tre'a*)
As'tra-gal.
As'tral, 10, 230.
A-strāy', 23, 232.
As-tric'tion.
As-tric'tĭve.
A-stride', 25.
As-trin'gen-cy, 169.
As-trin'gent.
As-trog'ra-phy, 108.
As'tro-īte, 152.
As'tro-labe.
As-trol'o-ger.
As-tro-log'ic (*-loj'ik*).
As-trol'o-gy, 93, 108.
As-tron'o-mer, 170.
As-tro-nom'ic, 109.
As-tro-nom'ic-al, 108.
As-tro-nom'ic-al-ly.
As-tron'o-my, 170.
As'tro-scope.
As'tro-the-ol'o-gy, 224.
A-strut'.
As-tute', 26.
A-sun'der.
A-sy'lum (125, 171) [*not* as'y-lum, 153.]
A-sym'me-tral, 169, 170.
As-ym-met'ric-al, 116.
A-sym'me-try.
As'ymp-tote (*as'im-*), 162, 171.
As-ymp-tot'ic (*as'im-*).
As-ymp-tot'ic-al (*as'-im-*).
A-syn'de ton (Gr.) [pl. *A-syn'de-ta*, 198.]
At, 10.
At'a-bal, 170. [203.]
At'a-ghan [Yataghan,
A-tax'ic.
Ate (*āt*, or *ĕt*) [so Wr.; *āt*, Wk. Wb. Gd.; *ĕt*, Sm. 203.]
At'e-lene, 170.
Atelier (Fr.) (*at'le-ā*), 154.
A-thal'a-moŭs.
Ath-a-na'sian (*ath-a-na'shan*, or *ath-a-na'-zhan*) [*ath-a-na'shan*, Wb. Gd.; *ath-a-na'-zhan*, Wr.; *ath-a-năzh'i-an*, Sm. 155.]
A'the-ism (*-izm*), 133.
A'the-ist.
A-the-ist'ic, 109.
A-the-ist'ic-al, 108.
Ath-e-næ'um (L.), *or* Ath-e-ne'um (Eng.) (111) [L. pl. *Ath-e-næ'a*; Eng. pl. Ath-e-ne'ums, 198.]
A-the'ni-an.
A-thirst', 232.
Ath'lete, (171, 231) [so Wr. Gd.; *ath-lēt'*, Sm. 155.]
Ath-let'ic, 170.
A-thwârt', 17, 171.
A-tilt'.
At-lan-te'an, 110.
At-lan'tēs (*-tēz*) (L. pl.).
At-lan'tic.
At-lan'ti-dēs (*-dēz*) (L. pl.).
At'las.
At-mom'e-ter.
At'mos-phere, 35, 171.
At-mos-phĕr'ic, 143.
At-mos-phĕr'ic-al.
At'om, 169, 170.
A-tom'ic, 109.
A-tom'ic-al, 108.
At'om-ism (*-izm*).
At'om-ist.
At'om-ize, 202.
At-om-ol'o-gy, 108.
A-tone', 24.
A-toned', 165, 183.
A-tone'ment.
A-tōn'er.
A-ton'ic.
A-tōn'ing.
At'o-ny, 93, 170.
A-top'.
At-ra-bil-a'ri-an.
At-ra-bil-a'ri-oŭs, 171.
At-ra-bil'ia-ry (*-bil'ya-ry*).
At-ra-bil'ious (*-bil'yus*).
At-ra-ment-a'ceous (*-shus*), 112.
At-ra-ment'al.
At-ra-ment-a'ri-oŭs.
At-ra-ment'oŭs.
A-trip'.
A-tro'cious (*-shus*), 46, 169, 171.
A-troç'i-ty, 39, 171.
At'ro-phĭed (*-fid*), 171.
At'ro-phy, 93, 170.
At-tach', 10, 103.
At-tach'a-ble, 164.
Attaché (Fr.) (*at-ta-shā'*).
At-tached' (*-tacht'*), 165, Note C, p. 34.
At-tach'ing.
At-tach'ment.
At-tack', *n.* & *v.* 10, 52.

At-tack'a-ble, 164.
At-tack'er.
At-tāin', 23.
At-tāin'a-ble, 164.
At-tāin'der.
At-tāined', 165.
At-tāin'ing.
At-tāin'ment.
At-tāint', 23.
At-tāint'ed.
At-tāint'ing.
At-tāint'ment.
At-tāint'ure (-yur), 91.
[Attar, 203.— See Ottar and Otto.]
At-tem'per.
At-tem'pered (-purd).
At-tem'per-ing.
At-tem'per-ment.
At-tempt' (-temt'), 162.
At-tempt'ed (-temt'-).
At-tempt'ing (-temt'-).
At-tend', 15.
At-tend'ance, 169
At-tend'ant, 169
At-tend'ed.
At-tend'er.
At-tend'ing.
At-tent'.
At-ten'tion.
At-ten'tĭve, 84.
At-ten'u-ant, 91.
At-ten'u-ate, *a.* & *v.* 73.
At-ten'u-āt-ed, 183.
At-ten'u-āt-ing.
At-ten-u-a'tion.
At-test', 15.
At-test-a'tion, 112.
At-test'ed.
At-test'er, *or* At-test'-or, 169.
At-test'ing.
At'tic, 170.
At'ti-cism (-sizm), 133.
At'ti-cize, 202.
At-tire', *n.* & *v.*
At-tired', 165, 183.
At-tīr'er.
At-tīr'ing.
At'ti-tude.
At-ti-tu'di-nal.
At-tŏl'lent, 170.
At-torn' (*at-turn'*)[Atturn, 203.]
At-tor'ney(-*tur'ny*),156.
[pl. At-tor'neys, 190.]
At-tor'ney-gen'er-al, 216.
At-tract', 10, 103.
At-tract-a-bil'i-ty.
At-tract'a-ble, 164.
At-tract'ed.
At-tract'ĭle, 152.
At-tract'ing.
At-trac'tion.
At-tract'ĭve, 94.
At-tract'or.
At'tra-hent [so Wk. Sm. Wr; *at-tra'hent*, Wb. Gd. 155.]
At-trib'u-ta-ble, 164.
At'tri-bute, *n.* 161.
At-trib'ute, *v.* 161.
At-trib'ūt-ed, 183
At-trib'ūt-ing.
At-tri-bu'tion.
At-trib'u-tĭve.
At-trite'.
At-trĭ'tion (-*trish'un*), 112.
At-tune', 26.
[Atturn, 203. — *See* Attorn.]
A-typ'ic.
Âu'burn, 17, 171.
Âuc'tion, 17.
Âuc'tion-a-ry 72.
Âuc-tion-eer', 122, 169.
Âu-da'cious (-*da'shus*), 112, 169.
Âu-daç'i-ty, 169, 171, 235.
Âu'di-ble, 164, 169.
Âu'di-bly, 93.
Âu'di-ence (169) [so Sm. Wr. Wb. Gd.; *aw'jĭ-ens*, Wk. 134, 155.]
Âu'dit, *n.* & *v.*
Âu'dit-ed.
Âu'dit-ing.
Âu'di-tor, 88, 169.
Âu-di-to'ri-al, 49, N.
Âu'di-to-ry, 86, 93.
Âu'di-tress.
Âu-ge'an, 110.
Âu'ger (*aw'gur*) (138), *n.* an instrument for boring. [*See* Augur, 160.]
Âught (*awt*) (162), *n.* any thing.

☞ Incorrectly written Ought. — *See* Ought, 160.

Âu'gite, 45.
Âug'ment, *n.* 103, 161.
Âug-ment', *v.* 103, 161.
Âug-ment'a-ble, 164.
Âug-ment-a'tion.
Âug-ment'a-tĭve.
Âug-ment'er, 77.
Âu'gur (169), *n.* a soothsayer: — *v.* to foretell. [*See* Auger, 160.]
Âu'gured (*aw'gurd*), 165.
Âu'gur-er.
Âu-gu'ri-al.
Âu'gu-ry, 91, 93.
Âu'gust, *n.* 161.
Âu-gust', *a.* 161.
Âu-gus'tan.
Âu-gus'tĭnes (-*tĭnz*), *n.* [*pl.*
Âuk, 17.
Âu-la'ri-an, 49, N.
Âu'lic.
Âuln (*awn*) (162), *n.* an ell. [*See* Awn, 160.] [Aune, 203.]
Âul'na-ger (*aw'na-jur*) (162) [Aulnager, 203. — *See* Alnager.]
Aunt (*änt*) (11), *n.* a female related to a person by being the sister of that person's father or mother. [*See* Ant, 160.]
Âu'rate.
Âu'rāt-ed.
Âu're-ate, 169.
Âu-re'li-a.
Âu-re'li-an.
Âu-re'o-la (L.).
Âu'ric.
Âu'ri-cle, 164.
Âu-ric'u-lar, 89, 108.
Âu-ric'u-late.
Âu-ric'u-lāt-ed.
Âu-rif'er-oŭs, 108, 171.
Âu'ri-form, 169.
Âu-ri'gal.
Âu-rig'ra-phy, 108.
Âu'ri-scalp.
Âu'rist.
Âu'rochs (*aw'roks*), 171.
Âu-ro'ra, 49, N.; 72.
Âus-cul-ta'tion.
Âus-cul-ta'tor, 169.
Âus-cul'ta-to-ry, 86, 93.
Âu'spi-cate.
Âu'spĭce, 169.
Âu-spĭ'cioŭs (-*spish'us*), 112, 169, 171.
Âu-stere', 169.
Âu-stĕr'i-ty, 143.
Âu'stral.
Âu-stra'li-an.
Âus'tri-an, 78, 169.
Âus'tro-man-cy, 169.
Âu-then'tic.
Âu-then'tic-al.
Âu-then'ti-cate, 169.
Âu-then'ti-cāt-ed, 183.
Âu-then'ti-cāt-ing.
Âu-then-ti-ca'tion.
Âu-then-tiç'i-ty, 171.
Âu-then'tics.
Âu'thor, 88, 169.
Âu'thor-ess.

Âu-thŏr′i-ta-tĭve, 171.
Âu-thŏr′i-ty, 169, 170.
Âu′thor-iz-a-ble, 183.
Âu-thor-ī-za′tion.
Âu′thor-ize, 202.
Âu′thor-īzed, 165, 183.
Âu′thor-īz-ing.
Âu′thor-ship.
Âu-to-bī-og′ra-pher.
Âu-to-bi-o-graph′ic.
Âu-to-bī-o-graph′ic-al.
Âu-to-bi-og′ra-phy, 108.
Âu-to-car′poŭs.
Âu-toch′thon (Gr.) (*aw-tok′*-) [pl. *Âu-toch-tho-nēs* (-*nēz*), 198.]
Âu-toch′tho-nal (-*tok′*-).
Âu-toch′tho-noŭs (-*tok′*-).
Âu-toc′ra-cy, 108, 169.
Âu′to-crat.
Âu-to-crat′ic, 109.
Âu-to-crat′ic-al, 108.
Âu-toc′ra-trĭce, 160.
Âu-toc′ra-trix.
Âuto-da-fe (Port.) (*aw′-to-dä-fā′*) [pl. *Âutos-da-fe*, 198.]
Âuto-de-fe (Sp.) (*aw′to-dā-fā′*) [pl. *Âutos-de-fe*, 198.]
Âu-tog′e-noŭs (-*toj′e*-).
Âu′to-grăph, 171.
Âu-to-graph′ic.
Âu-to-graph′ic-al.
Âu-tog′ra-phy, 108.
Âu′to-math.
Âu-to-mat′ic, 109.
Âu-to-mat′ic-al, 108.
Âu-tom′a-tism (-*tizm*).
Âu-tom′a-ton (170) [L. pl. *Âu-tom′a-ta*; Eng. pl. Âu-tom′a-tons (-*tonz*), 198.]
Âu-tom′a-toŭs.
Âu-tom′e-ter, 108.
Âu-to-nom′ic.
Âu-ton′o-my.
Âu-top′sic.
Âu-top′sic-al.
Âu′top-sy, 169.
Âu′tumn (*aw′tum*), 162.
Âu-tum′nal, 171.
Âux-il′iar (*awg-zil′yar*).
Âux-il′ia-ry (*awg-zil′-ya-ry*), 40, N.; 171.
A-vāil′, 23.
A-vāil-a-bil′i-ty.
A-vāil′a-ble, 164.
A-vāiled′, 165.
A-vāil′ing.
Av-a-lănche′ (*av-a-lănsh′*) (171) [so Wr.; *av′a-lŏngsh*, Sm.; *av-a-lanch′*, Wb. Gd. 155.]
Avant-courier (Fr.) (*a-vang′koo-rēr*) [so Wr. Gd.; *av-ŏng′koo-rēr*, Sm. 154, 155.]
A-vănt′guärd (*a-vănt′-gard*, or *a-văng′gärd*) [*a-vant′gard*, Wb. Gd.; *a-vant′gard*, or *a-vang′gärd*, Wr.; *a-vant′gärd*, Wk.; *a-vong′gard*, Sm. 154, 155.]
Av′a-rĭce, 169, 170.
Av-a-rĭ′cious (-*rish′us*), 169, 171.
Av-a-tar′ [so Sm. Wr.; *av-a-tar′*, or *a-vä′tar*, Gd. 154, 155.]
A-vâunt′, 17.
A′vē (L.).
Av′en-age.
A-venge′, 15, 45.
A-venged′ (-*venjd′*), 165, 183.
A-veng′er (-*venj′*-).
A-veng′ing (-*venj′*).
Av′ens (*av′enz*).
Av′en-tāil [Aven-taile, 203.]
A-vent′u-rĭne.
Av′e-nūe, 169, 170.
A-ver′, 21, N.
Av′er-age, 170.
A-ver′ment.
A-verred′ (-*verd′*), 165, 176.
A-ver′ring.
A-vĕr′ro-ist.
Av-er-run-ca′tor.
A-verse′, 21, N.
A-ver′sion, 171.
A-vert′, 21, N.
A-vert′ed.
A-vert′ing.
A-vid′i-ty, 170.
Av-o-ca′tion, 170.
Av′o-cā-tĭve [so Sm.; *a-vok′a-tiv*, Wr.; *a-vo′ka-tiv*, Wb. Gd. 155.]
A-void′, 27.
A-void′a-ble, 164.
A-void′ance, 169.
A-void′ed.
A-void′er.
A-void′ing.
Av-oir-du-pois′ (*av-ur-du-poiz′*, 171).
Av′o-set, 170.
A-vouch′, 28.
A-vouched′ (-*voucht′*), 165; Note C, p. 34.
A-vouch′er.
A-vouch′ing.
A-vow′, 28.
A-vow′al.
A-vowed′, 165.
A-vow-ee′, 122.
A-vow′er.
A-vow′ry.
A-vulsed′ (-*vulst′*), Note C, p. 34.
A-vul′sion.
A-vun′cu-lar (-*vung′*-), 54, 108.
A-wāit′, 23.
A-wāit′ed.
A-wāit′ing.
A-wake′, 23.
A-wa′ken (-*wa′kn*), 149.
A-wa′kened (-*wa′knd*).
A-wa′ken-ing (-*wa′kn*-).
A-wârd′, 17.
A-wârd′ed.
A-wârd′er.
A-wârd′ing.
A-ware′ (*a-wêr′*), 14.
A-wāy′ (23, 160), *ad.* at a distance. [*See* A-weigh.]
Âwe (*aw*), 171.
A-wĕath′er.
A-weigh′ (*a-wa′*) (23, 162), *ad.* denoting the position of an anchor when it is raised from the ground and is hanging by the cable. [*See* Away, 160.]
Âwe′-struck, 215.
Âw′ful (-*fŏŏl*), 180, 185.
Âw′ful-ly (-*fŏŏl*-), 93.
A-while′, 25, 33.
Âwk′ward, 171.
Âwl (17), *n.* a small pointed instrument to bore holes with. [*See* All, 160.]
Âwn.
A-woke′, 24.
A-wry′ (-*rī′*), 162.
Ax′al.
Ăxe (*ax*) [Ax, 203.]
Ăxe′hĕad, 206.
Ax′i-al.
Ax-if′er-oŭs, 108, 233.
Ax′il, *n.* 160.
Ax′īle, *a.* 160.
Ax-il′la (L.) [pl. *Ax-il′-læ*, 198.]
Ax′il-la-ry, 72, 93.
Ax′in-īte, 152.
Ax-in′o-man-cy.
Ax′i-om (*aks′i-um*), or Ax′iom (*aks′yum*)

[*aks'i-um*, Sm.; *aks'-yum*, Wr. Wb. Gd.; *ak'shum*, Wk. 155.]
Ax-i-o-mat'ic, 109.
Ax-i-o-mat'ic-al, 108.
Ax'is, 10.
Ax'le (*aks'l*), 171.
Ax'le-tree, 206.
Ax'led (*aks'ld*), 183.
Ax'o-lotl, 171.
Äy, *or* Äye (*äÿ*), *n.* & *ad.* (160), yes. [pl. of *n.* Äys, *or* Äyes (*äīz*).]
Āye (*ā*), *ad.* (160), always.
[Ayry, 203. — *See* Aerie.]
A-za'le-a.
Az'i-muth, 169, 170.
Az'i-muth-al [so Wb. Gd.; *az-i-mu'thal*, Wr. 155.]
A-zo'ic.
Az'ote, *or* A'zote [*az'ōt*, Sm. Wr.; *a'zōt*, Wb. Gd. 155.]
A-zot'ic.
Az'tec.
Āz'ure (*āzh'ur*), or Ăz'ure (*ăzh'ur*) (47, 171) [so Wr.; *āzh'ur*, or *ā'zhur*, Wb. Gd.; *ā'zhūr*, Wk.; *ā'zh'oor*, Sm. 26, 155.]
Āz'ured (*āzh'urd*), *or* Ăz'ured (*ăzh'urd*).
Az'y-goŭs.
Az'y-mite, 170.
Az'y-moŭs.

B.

Bäa (*bä*), *n.* & *v.*
Ba'al.
Bab'ble, 10, 164.
Bab'bled (*bab'bld*), 183.
Bab'bler, 170.
Bab'bling.
Babe, 23.
Ba'bel.
Băb'er-y.
Bab-oon', 121, 171, 231.
Ba'by, 93.
Ba'by-hŏŏd.
Ba'by-ish.
Bab-y-lo'ni-an, 171.
Bab-y-lon'ic.
Bab-y-lon'ic-al.
Bab-y-lo'nish.
Bac, *n.* a brewer's vat. [*See* Back, 160.]
Bac-ca-lâu're-ate, 169.
Bac'cate.
Bac'cāt-ed.
Bac'cha-nal (*-ka-*), 171.
Bac-cha-na'li-an (*-ka-*).
Bac'chant (*-kant*) (160), *n.* a priest of Bacchus.
Bac'chante (*-kant*) (160), *n.* a priestess of Bacchus.
Bac'chic (*-kik*), 52.
Bac'chic-al (*-kik-*).
Bac-cif'er-ous, 108, 148, 171.
Bac-civ'o-roŭs, 108, 148.
Bach'el-or, 169, 171.
Back (10), *n.* the part of the body in which the spine is. [*See* Bac, 160.]
Back'bar.
Back'bite.
Back-bīt'er, 183.
Back-bīt'ing.
Back-bit'ten (*bĭt'n*).
Back'bōne.
Back'dōor (*-dōr*), 206.
Băcked (*băkt*), Note C, p. 34.
Back'er.
Back-gam'mon, 170.
Back'ground, 206.
Back'hand-ed, 206.
Back'ing.
Back'lash, 206.
Back'sight (*-sīt*), 162.
Back-slīd'.
Back-slide'.
Back-slīd'er.
Back-slīd'ing.
Back-slid'den (*-slid'n*).
Back'stāy.
Back'swōrd (*-sōrd*), 162.
Back'ward.
Back'wards (*-wardz*).
Ba'con (*ba'kn*), 149.
Ba-co'ni-an.
Bad (10, 160), *a.* not good.
Băde, *v.* (160), did bid.
Badge (*baj*), 10, 45.
Badg'er (*baj'ur*), 169.
Ba-dige'on (*ba-dij'un*) [so Sm. Wr.; *bad-i-je'on*, Wb. Gd. 155.]
Bad-i-näge' (Fr.) (*bad-i-näzh'*).
Baf'fle, 164.
Baf'fled (*baf'fld*), 183.
Baf'fler.
Baf'fling.
Bag, 10, 31, 53.
Ba-gässe' (Fr.).
Bag-a-tĕlle' (Fr.), 171.
Bag'gage, 170.
Bagged (*bagd*), 165, 176.
Bag'ging (*-ghing*).
Bag'pipe, 206.
Bāil, *n.* surety. [*See* Bale, 160.]
Bāil'a-ble, 164.
Bāiled, 165.
Bāil-ee', 121.
Bāil'er [Bailor, 203.]
Bāil'iff, 171.
Bāil'ing.
Bāil'ment.
Bāil'or, *or* Bāil-or'.

☞ It is pronounced *bail-or'* when contrasted with *bail-ee'*, 118.

Bāit, *v.* to put food upon, as upon a hook to lure fish: — *n.* a lure. [*See* Bate, 160.]
Bāit'ed.
Bāit'ing.
Bāize, *n.* a coarse woollen stuff. [*See* Bays, 160.]
Bake, 23.
Baked (*bākt*), 183.
Bake'house, 206.
Bāk'er, 171, 183.
Bāk'er-y.
Bāk'ing.
Bak'shish (Ar.) (*bak'sheesh*) [Bukshish, Backshish, and Buckshish, 203.]
Bal'a-chŏng.
Bal'ance, 170.
Bal'anced (*bal'anst*).
Bal'anç-ing.
Bal'co-nied (*-nid*).
Bal'co-ny, *or* Bal-co'ny [so Wr. Gd.; *bal'ko-ny*, Sm.; *bal-ko'ny*, Wk. 155.]
Bâld, *a.* without hair on the head. [*See* Bawled, 160.]
Bal'da-chin (*-kin*).
Bâl'der-dash, 171.
Bâl'dric, 171.
Bale, *n.* a bundle. [*See* Bail, 160.]
Bal-e-a'ri-an.
Bal-e-ăr'ic, 170.
Bāled, 165, 183.
Ba-leen', 121.
Bale'ful (*-fŏŏl*), 180.
Bāl'ing, 183.
[Balister, 203. — *See* Ballister.]
Ba-lize' (*ba-lēz'*), 121.
Bâlk, *n.* & *v.* (*bawk*) (162) [the noun and

verb are sometimes written B a u l k; the noun also B a u k, and B a w k, 203.]
Bâlked (*bawkt*), 165, Note C, p. 34.
Bâlk'er (*bawk'er*).
Bâlk'ing (*bawk'-*).
Bâll, *n.* any thing globular. [*See* Bawl, 160.]
Bal'lad, 170.
Bal'lad-mong'er (*-lad-mung'gher*), 54, N.; 205.
Bal'lan, 170.
Bal'last, 170.
Bal'last-ed.
Bal'last-ing.
Bâll'cock, 206.
Bal'let (Fr.) (*bal'lā*, or *bal'let* [*bal'lā*, Sm.; *bal'let*, Wb. Gd.; *bal-lā'*, or *bal'let*, Wr. 155.]
Bal'li-age, 170.
Bal-lis'ta (L.) [pl. *Bal-lis'tæ*, 198.]
Bal-lis'ter [so Sm. Wb. Gd.; *bal'lis-tur*, Wr. 155.]
Bal-lis'tic.
Bal-lis'tics, 109.
Bal-loon', 121, 171.
Bal-loon'ist.
Bal'lot, 170.
Bal'lo-tāde (Fr.) [so Sm. Wr.; *bal'lo-tād*, Wb. Gd. 155] [B a l o t a d e, 203.]
Bal'lot-box, 209.
Bal'lot-ed.
Bal'lot-ing.
Bâll'room, 206.
Bälm (*bäm*), 162, 171.
Bälm'y (*bäm'y*), 93.
[B a l o t a d e, 203.— *See* Ballotade.]
Bâl'sam, 171.
Băl-sam'ic.
Băl-sam'ic-al.
Băl-sam-if'er-ous, 108.
Bâl-sam-īne', 152.
Bâl'tic.
Bal'us-ter, 170.
Bal'us-tered, 165.
Bal'us-trade, 170.
Bal-za-rine' (*-rēn'*), 122.
Bam-boo'.
Bam-boo'zle, 164.
Bam-boo'zled (*-boo'zld*).
Bam-boo'zling, 183.
Ban, 10.
Ba-nä'na, *or* Ba-nā'na [*ba-na'na*, Wb. Gd.; *ba-nā'na*, Sm.; *ba-nā'-na*, or *ba-na'na*, Wr. 155.]
Band, 10.
Band'age, 169.
Ban-dan'a, *or* Ban-dan'-na.
Band'box, 206.
Band'ed.
Ban'de-role [B a n d r o l, 203.]
Ban'di-coot.
Band'ing.
Ban'died (*ban'dĭd*), 186.
Ban'dit.
Ban-dit'tī, *n. pl.* 170.
Ban'dog, 206.
Ban-do-leer' (122) [B a n-d o l i e r, 283.]
Ban-dore' [so Wr.; *ban'dōr*, Gd. 155] [P a n d o r e, 203.]
Band'rōl [B a n d e r o l e, 203.]
Ban'dy.
Ban'dy-ing.
Ban'dy-leg, 206.
Ban'dy-legged (*-legd*), 206, Exc. 5.
Bane, 23.
Bane'ful (*-fōōl*), 180.
Bang, 10, 54.
Banged (*bangd*), 165.
Bang'ing.
Ban'gle (*bang'gl*), 54, 164.
Ban'ian (*ban'yan*), or Ban-ian' (*ban-yan'*) [*ban'yan*, Wb. Gd.; *ban-yan'*, Wk. Sm. Wr. 155] [B a n n i a n, B a n y a n, 203.]
Ban'ish, 170.
Ban'ished (*-isht*), 150.
Ban'ish-ing.
Ban'ish-ment, 170.
Ban'is-ter.

☞ This word is a corruption of *Baluster*.

Ban'jo [B a n j e r, 203.]
Bank, 54.
Bank'a-ble, 169.
Banked (*bangkt*), Note C, p. 34.
Bank'er.
Bank'ing.
Bank'rupt.
Bank'rupt-cy, 169.
Ban'ner, 170.
Ban'nered (*-nurd*), 165.
Ban'ner-et.
Ban'ner-ōl.
[B a n n i a n, 203.— *See* Banian.]
Ban'ning, 176.
Ban'nock, 170.
Banns (*banz*), *n. pl.* 136.
Ban'quet (*bang'kwet*), 54, 171.
Ban'quet-ed.
Ban'quet-er.
Ban'quet-ing.
Banquette (Fr.) (*bang-ket'*).
Ban'tam.
Ban'ter, 10, 77.
Ban'tered, 165.
Ban'ter-er.
Ban'ter-ing.
Bant'ling.
[B a n y a n, 203.— *See* Banian.]
Ba'o-bab.
Baph'o-met, 35.
Bap'tism (*-tizm*), 133, 136.
Bap'tist-er-y, 171.
Bap-tist'ic, 109.
Bap-tist'ic-al, 108.
Bap-tīz'a-ble, 164.
Bap-tize', 202.
Bap-tized', 165.
Bap-tīz'er, 183.
Bap-tīz'ing.
Bar, 11, 49.
Barb, 11, 49.
Bar'ba-can [B a r b i-c a n, 203.]
Bar-ba'di-an.
Bar-ba'ri-an, 49, N.
Bar-băr'ic, 170.
Bar'ba-rism (*-rizm*), 136.
Bar-băr'i-ty, 108, 170.
Bar'bar-ize, 202.
Bar'bar-oŭs.
Bar'bate.
Bar'bāt-ed.
Bar'be-cūe, 171.
Bar'be-cūed, 165, 171.
Bar'be-cu-ing, 183.
Barbed, 165.
Bar'bel.
Bar'bel-late, 170.
Bar'ber, 77, 169.
Bar'bered (*-burd*).
Bar'ber-ry, 93.
Bar'bet.
[B a r b i c a n, 203.— *See* Barbacan.]
Barb'ing.
Bar'bule.
Bard (11), *n.* a poet. [*See* Barred, 160.]
Bard'ic.
Bare (*bêr*), *a.* naked. [*See* Bear, 160.]
Bared (*bêrd*), 165, 183.
Bare'faced (*bêr'fāst*), 206
Bare'fōōt (*bêr-*), 206.
Bare'fōōt-ed (*bêr'-*).

Barege (Fr.) (*ba-rāzh'*).
Bar'gain (*bar'ghin*), 171.
Bar'gained (*-ghĭnd*).
Bar-gain-ee', 122.
Bar'gain-er. [*See* Bargainor.]
Bar'gain-ing.
Bar-gain-or'.

☞ So written and pronounced, when contrasted with *Bargainee*.

Barge, 11, 45.
Ba-ril'la, 170.
Bar'ing (*bêr'ing*), *part.* making bare. [*See* Bear'ing, 160.]
[Baritone, 203.—*See* Barytone.]
Ba'ri-um, 78, 169.
Bark, 11.
Bar'keep-er, 206.
Barked (*barkt*), 165.
Bark'er.
Bark'er-y, 93.
Bark'ing.
Bark'y, 93.
Bar'ley, 98, 169.
Barm, 11, 135.
Barn, 11, 135.
Bar'na-cle, 164.
Băr'o-lite, 152.
Ba-rom'e-ter, 170.
Băr-o-met'ric, 109.
Băr-o-met'ric-al, 108.
Băr'on, 170.
Băr'on-age.
Băr'on-ess.
Băr'o-net, 170.
Băr'o-net-age.
Băr'o-net-cy, 169.
Ba-ro'ni-al, 79.
Băr'o-ny, 93, 170.
Băr'o-scope.
Băr-o-scop'ic, 109.
Băr-o-scop'ic-al, 108.
Băr-o-sel'e-nite.
Ba-rouche' (*ba-roosh'*), 156, 171.
Băr'ra-can.
Băr'rack, 170.
Băr-ra-coon', 122.
Băr'ras.
Băr'ra-tor, 169, 170.
Băr'ra-troŭs.
Băr'ra-try, 170.
Barred (*bard*)(176), *part.* did bar [*See* Bard, 160.]
Băr'rel.
Băr'relled (165) [Barreled, 203.—*See* 177, and Note E, p. 70.]
Băr'ren, 149, 171.
Băr'ren-ness, 170.
Băr-ri-cade', *n.* & *v.* 170.
Băr-ri-căd'ed, 183.
Băr-ri-căd'ing.
Băr'ri-er, 170.
Băr'ring, 176.
Băr'ris-ter, 170.
Băr'row, 101.
Bar'ter, *n.* & *v.*
Bar'tered, 165.
Bar'ter-er.
Bar'ter-ing.
Bar'ti-zan [so Gd.; *bar-ti-zan'*, Wr. 155.]
Ba-ry'ta, 171.
Ba-ry'tēs (*-tēz*).
Ba-ryt'ic.
Băr'y-tone, 93, 170.
Ba'sal.
Ba-sâlt' (171) [so Sm. Wr.; *ba-zŏlt'*, Wb. Gd. 155.]
Ba-sâlt'ic [so Sm. Wr.; *ba-zŏlt'ik*, Wb. Gd. 155.]
Ba-sâlt'i-form [*ba-săl'-ti-form*, Wr.; *ba-zŏlt'-i-form*, Gd. 155.]
Ba-sâlt'īne, 152.
Bas'a-nīte (*baz'a-nīt*) [so Sm. Gd.; *bas'a-nīt*, Wr. 155.]
Base (23), *a. n.* & *v.* [*See* Băss, 160.]
Based (*bāst*), 165, 183.
Base'ment.
Ba-shaw', 121.
Bash'ful (*-fŏŏl*), 180.
Ba'sic.
Ba'si-fī-er, 186.
Ba'si-fȳ, 94.
Bas'il (*baz'il*).
Bas'i-lar (*baz'i-lar*) [so Sm. Wb. Gd.; *bas'i-lar*, Wr. 155.]
Bas'i-la-ry (*baz'i-la-ry*) [so Sm. Wb. Gd.; *bas'i-la-ry*, Wr. 155.]
Ba-sil'ic (*-zil'ik*), *n.* & *a.*
Ba-sil'ic-al (*-zil'ik-*).
Ba-sil'i-ca (*-zil'ĭ-ka*).
Ba-sil'i-con (*-zil'ĭ-kon*).
Bas'i-lisk (*baz'-*), 78, 171.
Ba'sin (*ba'sn*), 149.
Ba'sis (L.) [pl. Ba'ses, 198.]
Ba-sis'o-lute.
Bȧsk, 12, 131.
Bȧsked (*bȧskt*), 165, 183.
Bȧs'ket, 131.
Bȧsk'ing.
Băsque (Fr.) (*bask*).
Bȧss, 12, 131, 161.
Bāss (161), *n.* the lowest part in harmony. [Sometimes written Base, 160, 203.]
Bas'set, *n.* & *v.*
Bas'set-ing, *a.* & *n.* 170.
Bas-soon', 66, N.; 121.
Bas-soon'ist.
Băss-re-liēf' (*-lēf'*).
Băss-vi'ol, 205.
Băss'wŏŏd, 206.
Băst.
Bas'tard, 131.
Bas'tard-ize, 202.
Bas'tard-īzed, 165, 183.
Bas'tard-īz-ing.
Bas'tard-y, 93.
Bāste, 163.
Bāst'ed.
Bas-tile' (*bas-tēl'*), 121.
Bas-ti-nade', 122.
Bas-ti-na'do, *n.* & *v.* 79 [pl. of *n.* Bas-ti-na'does (*-dōz*).]
Bas-ti-na'dōed, 188.
Bas-ti-na'do-ing.
Bāst'ing.
Băst'ion (*bast'yun*), 51.
Bas'ȳle (*bas'il*), 171.
Bat, 10.
Bāt'a-ble, 164, 169.
Ba-ta'tas.
Batch, 10, 44.
Bate, *v.* to abate. [*See* Bait, 160.]
Bȧth [pl. Bȧths (*baṯẖz*).]
Bāthe.
Bāthed, 165, 183.
Bāth'er.
Bāth'ing.
Bāth'ing-room, 215.
Ba'thos.
Bāt'ing, 183.
Bat-iste' (Fr.) (*bat-ēst'*) [Batist, 203.]
Bat'let.
Ba-ton' (Fr.) (*ba-tŏng'*) [so Gd.; *ba-tŏng'* or *bat'on*, Wr.; *bä'tŏng*, Sm. 154, 155.]
Ba-tra'chi-an (*-tra'kĭ-*).
Bat'ra-chīte (*-kīt*). [171.
Bat'ra-choid (*-koid*).
Băt-ra-chŏm-y-om'a-chy (*-kŏm-ĭ-om'a-ky*), 116, 171.
Băt-ra-coph'a-goŭs (*-kof'-*).
Bats'man, 214.
Bat-tăl'ia (*-tăl'ya*), 156.
Bat-tal'ion (*-tal'yun*), 171.
Bat-tal'ioned (*-yund*),
Bat'tel, 149. [165.

Bat′tel-ler [Bateler, Wb. Gd. *See* 177, and Note E, p. 70.—Batt-ler, 203.]
Bat′ten, *n.* & *v.* (*bat′n*), 149.
Bat′ten-ing (*bat′n-*).
Bat′ter.
Bat′tered, 165.
Bat′ter-er.
Bat′ter-ing.
Bat′ter-y, 93, 170.
Bat′ting, 170.
Bat′tish, 176.
Bat′tle, 164.
Bat′tled (*bat′ld*), 164, 183.
Bat′tle-dōōr (*-dōr*).
Bat′tle-ment.
[Battler, 203.—*See* Batteller.]
Bat′tling.
Bat-tol′o-gy, 108.
[Bauble, 203.—*See* Bawble.]
[Bauk, Baulk, 203.—*See* Balk.]
Ba-va′ri-an.
Bav′a-roy [so Wb. Gd.; *bav-a-roy′*, Wr. 155.]
Bav′in.
Baw′ble [Bauble, 203.]
Bawd.
Bawd′i-ly.
Bawd′ry.
Bawd′y.
[Bawk, 203.—*See* Balk.]
Bawl, *v.* to make a clamorous outcry. [*See* Ball, 160.]
Bawled, 165.
Bawl′er.
Bawl′ing.
Bāy (23), *n.* an inlet of the sea. [*See* Bey, 160.] [pl. Bays.—*See* Baize, 160.]
Bāy-a-dere′ (Fr.) (114) [so Gd.; *ba′ya-dēr*, Sm. Wr. 154, 155.]
Bāy′ard.
Bāy′ber-ry.
Bāy′o-net [so Wr. Gd.; *ba′yun-et*, Wk. Sm. 155.]
Bayou (Fr.) (*bī′oo*) [so Gd.; *bī′oo*, or *bī′ō*, Wr. 155.]
Ba-zäar′ (*-zar′*), *or* Ba-zar′. [171.
Bdell′ium (*del′yum*), 162.
Be (13), *v.* to exist. [*See* Bee, 160.]

Bēach, *n.* the shore. [*See* Beech, 160.]
Bēach′y, 93.
Bēa′con (*be′kn*), 149.
Bēa′coned (*be′knd*).
Bēa′con-ing (*be′kn-*).
Bēad, 13.
Bēa′dle, 164.
Bēad′rōll, 206.
Bēads′man (*bēdz-*), 214.
Bēa′gle, 164.
Bēak, 13.
Beaked (*bēkt*).
Bēak′er, 13, 77.
Bēam, *n.* & *v.* 13.
Bēam′ful (*-fōōl*).
Bēam′ing.
Bēam′y.
Bēan, 13.
Bêar, *n.* & *v.* (14). [*See* Bare, 160.]
Bêar′a-ble, 164.
Bēard, *n.* & *v.* 13.
Bēard′ed.
Bēard′ing.
Bêar′er, 14, 77.
Bêar′ing, *part.* supporting. [*See* Baring, 160.]
Bêar′ish.
Bēast, 13.
Bēast′li-ness, 78, 171.
Bēast′ly, 93.
Bēat (13), *v.* to strike: —*n.* a stroke. [*See* Beet, 160.]
Bēat′en (*bēt′n*), 149.
Bēat′er.
Bē-a-tif′ic, 109.
Bē-a-tif′ic-al, 108.
Bē-at-ĭ-fĭ-ca′tion, 171.
Bē-at′i-fȳ, 79, 94.
Bēat′ing.
Bē-at′i-tude, 171.
Beau (Fr.) (*bō*), *n.* a gallant. [*See* Bow, 169;] [Fr. pl. *beaux* (*bōz*); Eng. pl. Beaux, *or* Beaus (*bōz*), 198.]
Beau′fet (*bo′fet*).
Beauf′in (*bif′in*) [*bo′fin*, Wr.]

☞ Ellis says, "There is no doubt as to the pronunciation [*bif′in*]," and that the word is often spelled Biffin.

Beau ideal (Fr.) (*bō-e-dā′āl*, or *bō-ī-de′al*) [so Wr.; *bō-e-dā′āl*, Sm.; *bō-ī-de′al*, Wb. Gd. 154, 155.]
Beau monde (Fr.) (*bo-mōnd′*, or *bo-mŏnd′*).

Beaū′te-oŭs (*bu′te-us*) [so Wr. Gd.; *bu′te-us*, or *but′yus*, Sm.; *bu′che-us*, Wk. 134, 155.]
Beaū′ti-fīed, 186.
Beaū′ti-fī-er (*bū′-*).
Beaū′ti-ful (*bu′ti-fōōl*).
Beaū′ti-fȳ (*bū′-*), 94.
Beaū′ti-fȳ-ing.
Beaū′ty (*bu′ty*), 26, 93.
Bēa′ver, 13, 77.
Bec-a-fī′co (*-fē′ko*).
Be-cälm′ (*-käm′*), 162.
Be-cälmed′ (*-kämd′*), 165.
Be-cälm′ing (*-käm*).
Be-came′.
Be-cause′ (*-kawz′*).
B-chânce′.
Bêche de mer (Fr.) (*bāsh-duh-mêr′*).
Beck.
Beck′et.
Beck′on (*bek′n*), 149.
Be-cloud′, 28.
Be-come′ (*-kum′*), 22, 163.
Be-com′ing (*-kum′-*), 183.
Bed, 15.
Be-dab′ble, 164.
Be-dag′gle, 164.
Be-dark′en (*-dark′n*).
Be-däsh′.
Be-dâub′.
Be-daz′zle, 164.
Bed′clōthes (*-klōthz*) [so Sm. Wb. Gd.; *bed′klōz*, Wk.; *bed′klōthz*, or *bed′klōz*, Wr. 155.]

☞ Smart says that the pronunciation *bed′klōz* is *colloquial*. *See* Clothes.

Bed′ded, 176.
Bed′ding.
Bed′e-guar (*-gar*) [Bedegar, 203.]
Be-dew′ (*be-du′*).
Be-dewed′ (*-dūd′*), 165.
Be-dew′ing.
Be-di′zen (*be-dī′zn*), or Be-diz′en (*be-diz′n*) [*be-dī′zn*, Wk. Sm. Wr.; *be-diz′n*, Wb. Gd. 155.]
Bed′lam.
Bed′lam-īte, 152.
Bed′ou-ins (*bed′oo-ēnz*) [so Gd.; *bed′oo-ĭnz*, Wr. 155.]
Bed′plate, 206.
Bed′pōst.
Bed′quilt.
Bed′rid.
Bed-rid′den (*-rid′n*).
Bed′room, 206.

Bed′stĕad.
Bed′ward.
Bee (13), *n.* an insect that makes honey. [*See* Be, 160.]
Beech (13), *n.* a forest tree. [*See* Beach, 160.]
Beef, 13.
Beef′steāk (-*stāk*), 14, [171.
Bee′hive.
Be-el′ze-bub, 171.
Been (*bin*), [*not* bēn, 153] *part.* of *Be.* [*See* Bin, 160.]
Beer (13), *n.* a fermented liquor. [*See* Bier, 160.]
Bees′wax (*bēz′*-), 214.
Beet (13), *n.* a kind of vegetable. [*See* Beat, 160.]
Bee′tle (164), *n.* a coleopterous insect. [*See* Betel, 160.]
Bee′tling, 183.
Beeves (*bēvz*), *n. pl.* Note C, p. 34.
Be-fâll′ [Befal, Sm. 203.]
Be-fâllen′ (-*fawln′*).
Be-fâll′ing.
Be-fit′.
Be-fit′ted, 176.
Be-fit′ting.
Be-fool′, 19.
Be-fōre′, 24.
Be-friĕnd′.
Be-friĕnd′ed.
Be-friĕnd′ing.
Beg, 15.
Be-gan′.
Be-get′ (-*ghet′*), 138.
Be-get′ter, 176.
Be-get′ting.
Beg′gar, 169, 170, 171.
Beg′gar-y, 93, 171.
Begged (*begd*), 176, 183.
Beg′ging (-*ghing*), 138.
Be-ghard′, 121.
Be-gin′ (-*ghin′*), 138.
Be-gin′ner (-*ghin′*-), 176.
Be-gin′ning (-*ghin′*-).
Be-gird′ (-*ghird′*), 21.
Be-gird′ed (-*ghird′*-).
Be-gird′ing (-*ghird′*-).
Be-girt′ (-*ghirt′*).
Be-gōne′ (18, N.) [so Wr.; *be-gawn′*, Wb. Gd. 155.]
Be-got′.
Be-got′ten (-*got′n*), 149.
Be-grime′.
Be-grīmed′, 150, 183.
Be-grīm′ing.
Be-grudge′, 45.
Be-grudged′, 150, 183.
Be-grudg′ing.
Be-guile′ (-*ghīl′*), 171.
Be-guiled′ (-*ghīld′*).
Be-guil′ing (-*ghīl′*-).
Be-guil′er (-*ghīl′*-).
Béguin (Fr.), *n. mas.* (*bā-gang′*, or *beg-win′*).
Béguine (Fr.), *n. fem.* (*bā-ghēn′*).
Be-gun′.
Be-hälf′ (-*häf′*), 162.
Be-hāve′.
Be-hāved′, 165.
Be-hāv′ing, 183.
Be-hāv′ior (-*hāv′yur*) [Behaviour, Sm. 199, 203.]
Be-hĕad′, 15.
Be-hĕad′ed.
Be-hĕad′ing.
Be-held′.
Be′he-moth, 156.
Be′hen.
Be-hest′, 122.
Be-hīnd′, 25.
Be-hōld′, 24.
Be-hōld′en(-*hōld′n*),149.
Be-hōld′er.
Be-hōld′ing.
Be-hoof′, 19.
Be-hoove′ [Behove, 203.]
Be-hooved′,150, 183.
Be-hoov′ing.
[Behove, 203.]
☞ Properly written *Behoove. Smart.*
Be′ing.
Be-la′bor, 169.
Be-la′bored (-*la′burd*).
Be-la′bor-ing.
Be-lāid′ [Belayed, 203.]
Be-lāt′ed.
Be-lāy′.
Be-lāyed′ (187) [Belaid, 203.]
Be-lāy′ing.
Belch, 15, 44, Note 2.
Belched (*belcht*), Note C, p. 34.
Belch′ing.
Bel′dăm.
Be-lēa′guer (-*le′gher*), 171.
Be-lēa′guered, 150.
Be-lēa′guer-ing.
Be-lem′nite, 152.
Bel es-prit (Fr.) (*bel es-prē′*) [pl. *Beaux es-prits* (*bōz es-pre′*), 198.]
Bel′fry, 93.
Bel′gi-an, 78.
Bel′gic.
Bē′lial (*bēl′yal*), *or* Be′li-al [*bēl′yal*, Sm.; *be′li-al*, Wr. Wb. Gd. 155.]
Be-lie′, 25.
Be-līed′, 165, 183.
Be-lief′, 13, 171.
Be-liēv′a-ble, 164.
Be-liēve′, 13, 171.
Be-lieved′, 165.
Be-liēv′er, 183.
Be-liēv′ing.
Be-lit′tle, 164.
Be-lit′tled, 165.
Be-lit′tling.
Bell (15), *n.* a hollow vessel used for making a ringing sound. [*See* Belle, 160.]
Bel-la-don′na, 72, 170.
Bĕlle *n.* a gay young lady. [*See* Bell, 160.]
Belles-lettres (Fr.) (*bel-let′tur*) [so Sm. Gd.; *bel-let′r*, Wr.; *bel-lā′-tur*, Wk. 154, 155.]
Bel′li-cose [so Gd.; *bel-i-kōs′*, Wr. 155.]
Bel′līed (*bel′id*), 186.
Bel-lig′er-ent (-*lij′*-),171
Bell′-met′al (-*met′l*, or *met′al*), 205.
Bel′lōw, 101.
Bel′lōwed, 165, 188.
Bel′lōw-er.
Bel′lōw-ing.
Bel′lows (*bel′us*), 171.
Bel′lu-īne, 152.
Bel′ly, *n.* & *v.*
Bel′ly-ing.
Bel′o-man-cy, 169.
Be-lŏng′, 18, N.
Be-lŏnged′(-*longd′*),165.
Be-lŏng′ing.
Be-loved′ (*be-luvd′*), *part.* 150.
Be-lov′ed (*be-luv′ed*), *part. a.* 150.
Be-lōw′, 24.
Belt, 15.
Bel′tane [Beltein, Beltin, 203.]
Belt′ing.
Be-ly′ing.
Bel′ve-dēre, 171.
Be-mōan′, 24.
Be-mōaned′, 165.
Be-mōan′ing.
Be-mused′ (-*muzd′*).

Ben, 15.
Ben′-nut, 66, N.; 209.
Bench, 15, 44, Note 2.
Bench′er.
Bend, 15.
Bend′a-ble, 164, 169.
Bend′ed.
Bend′er.
Bend′ing.
Bend′let.
Bend′y, 93, 169.
Be-neath′, 38.
Ben′e-dict, 171.
Ben-e-dict′ĭne, 152.
Ben-e-dic′tion, 171.
Ben-e-dic′tĭve, 84.
Ben-e-dic′to-ry, 86.
Ben-e-fac′tion, 171.
Ben-e-fac′tor.
Ben-e-fac′tress.
Ben′e-fĭce, 169, 171.
Ben′e-fĭced (*-fist*).
Be-nef′i-cence, 170.
Be-nef′i-cent, 171.
Ben-e-fĭ′cial (*-fish′al*), 46, N. 2; 171.
Ben-e-fĭ′cia-ry (*-fish′ya-ry*) [so Wk. Sm. Wr.; *ben-e-fish′a-ry*, Wb. Gd. 155.]
Ben′e-fit, 170.
Ben′e-fit-ed, 176.
Ben′e-fit-ing.
Be-nev′o-lence, 169, 171.
Be-nev′o-lent.
Ben-gal-ee′, 122.
Ben-gal-ēse′ (*-ēz′*), *n. sing. & pl.*
Be-nīght′ (*-nīt′*), 162.
Be-nīght′ed (*-nīt′ed*).
Be-nīght′ing (*-nīt′ing*).
Be-nign′ (*be-nīn′*), 162, 171.
Be-nig′nant, 169.
Be-nig′ni-ty, 93, 171.
Ben′net, 170.
Bent, 15.
Be-numb′ (*be-num′*), 162.
Be-numbed′ (*-numd′*), 165.
Be-numb′ment (*-num′-*).
Ben-zo′ic, 109.
Ben-zoin′, 21, 121.
Ben′zole.
Ben′zo-lĭne, 152.
Be-quēath′, 38, 140, 171.
Be-quēathed′, 165.
Be-quēath′er.
Be-queath′ing.
Be-quest′, 34, 52.
Be-rate′, 23.
Be-răt′ed, 183.
Be-răt′ing.
Ber′ber-ĭne, 152.
[Berberry, 203.—*See* Barberry.]
Be-re′an, 110.
Be-rēave′, 13.
Be-rēaved′, 150, 183.
Be-rēave′ment, 185.
Be-rēav′er.
Be-rēav′ing.
Be-reft′.
Ber′ga-mot, 21, N.
[Burgamot, 203.]
Ber′gan-der.
Ber′lin [so Sm. Wb. Gd.; *ber-lin′*, Wk.; *ber-lin′*, or *ber′lin*, Wr. 155.]
Berme (*berm*), 21, N.
Ber′nard-ĭne, 152.
Bĕr′o-ē (L.), 163.
Bĕr′rĭed (*ber′id*), *a.* having berries. [*See* Buried, 160.]
Bĕr′ry, *n.* a small fruit. [*See* Bury, 160.]
Berth (21 N.), *n.* a place in a ship to sleep in. [*See* Birth, 160.]
Bĕr′yl, 170.
Bĕr′yl-lĭne, 152.
Be-şāyle′.
Be-seech′, 13, 44.
Be-seech′ing.
Be-seem′.
Be-seem′ing.
Be-set′.
Be-set′ting, 176.
Be-shrew′ (*be-shroo′*), 19.
Be-side′.
Be-sides′ (*-sīdz′*), Note C, p. 34.
Be-siege′, 13
Be-sieged′, 150, 183.
Be-sieg′er (*-sēj′-*), 183.
Be-sieg′ing (*-sēj′-*).
Be-smēar′, 13.
Be-smēared′, 150.
Be-smēar′ing.
Be′som (*be′zum*), 40, 171.
Be-sot′, 18.
Be-sot′ted, 176.
Be-sot′ting.
Be-sought′ (*-sawt′*), 162.
Be-spat′ter, 170.
Be-spat′tered, 150.
Be-spat′ter-ing.
Be-spēak′, 13.
Be-spēak′er.
Be-spēak′ing.
Be-spoke′, 24.
Be-spōk′en (*spōk′n*), 149.
Be-sprĕad′.
Best, 15.
Best′ial (*best′yal*) (156) [so Wr. Wb. Gd.; *best′i-al*, Sm.; *bes′chi-al*, Wk. 134, 155.]
Best-ial′i-ty (*best-yal′i-ty*) [so Wb. Gd.; *best-i-al′i-ty*, Sm.; *best-yi-al′i-ty*, Wr.; *bes-chi-al′i-ty*, Wk. 134, 155.]
Best′ial-ize (*best′yal-īz*).
Be-stir′, 21, N.
Be-stirred′, 150, 176.
Be-stir′ring.
Be-stōw′, 24.
Be-stōw′al.
Be-stōwed′, 150, 183.
Be-stōw′er.
Be-stōw′ment.
Be-strew′ (*be-stroo′*, or *be-strō′*) [so Wr. Gd.; *be-stroo′*, Sm.; *be-strō′*, Wk. 155.]
Be-strew′ing.
Be-strid′.
Be-strid′den (*-strid′n*), 167, 170.
Be-stride′, 25.
Be-strīd′ing.
Bet, 15.
Be-take′, 23.
Be′tel (*be′tl*) (149), an aromatic shrub of the East Indies. [*See* Beetle, 160.] [Betle, 203.]
Beth′el.
Be-think′.
Be-think′ing.
Be-thought′ (*-thawt′*), 162, 171.
Be-tid′, 16.
Be-tide′, 25.
Be-tīmes′ (*-tīmz′*).
[Betle, 203.—*See* Betel.]
Be-to′ken (*-to′kn*), 149.
Be-to′kened (*-to′knd*), 150.
Be-to′ken-ing (*-to′kn-*).
Bet′o-ny, 93, 170.
Be-tōok′, 21.
Be-trāy′, 23.
Be-trāy′al.
Be-trāyed′, 150, 187.
Be-trāy′er.
Be-trŏth′, 18, 37.
Be-trŏth′al.
Be-trŏthed′ (*-trŏtht′*), Note C, p. 34.
Be-trŏth′ing.
Be-trŏth′ment.
Bet′ted, 176.
Bet′ter, *a.* comparative

of *good*. [*See* Bettor, 160.]
Bet′tered, 150.
Bet′ter-ing.
Bet′ter-ment.
Bet′ting.
Bet′tor, *n.* one who bets. [*See* Better, 160.]
Bet′ty, 170.
Be-tween′, 13.
Be-twixt′.
Bev′el [Wk. Wr. Wb. Gd.; *bev′l*, Sm. 155.]
Bev′elled (150) [Beveled, Wb. Gd. 203. — *See* 177, and Note E, p. 70.]
Bev′el-ling [Beveling, Wb. Gd. 203.]
Bev′er-age, 170.
Bev′y, 93, 170.
Be-wāil′, 23.
Be-wāiled′, 150.
Be-wāil′er.
Be-wāil′ing.
Be-ware′ (*-wêr′*), 14.
Be-wil′der.
Be-wil′dered (*-durd*), 150.
Be-wil′der-ing.
Be-witch′, 44.
Be-witched′ (*-wicht′*), Note C, p. 34.
Be-witch′er.
Be-witch′er-y, 233.
Be-witch′ing.
Be-witch′ment.
Be-wrāy′ (*be-ra′*), 162.
Bey (*ba*), *n.* a Turkish or Tartar governor. [*See* Bay, 160.]
Be-yond′, 18.
Be-zant′ [so Wr. Wb. Gd.; *bez′ant*, Sm. 155.]
Bez′el (*bez′el*, or *bez′l*) [so Wr.; *bez′el*, Wb. Gd.; *bez′l*, Sm. 155.]
Be-zōar′, 24, 171.
Bez-o-ar′dic, 109.
Bi′as.
Bi′assed, *or* Bi′ased (*bi′-ast*), Note C, p. 34.

☞ "This [*biassed*] is the common spelling, but it should be *biased*." *Smart.*

Bi′as-sing, *or* Bi′as-ing.
Bī-âu-ric′u-late, 116.
Bi-ax′al, 39 N.; 79.
Bib, 16, 31.
Bī-ba′cious (*-ba′shus*), 169.
Bib′ber, 170.
Bib′i-to-ry, 86, 170.
Bi′ble, 25, 164.
Bib′ler.
Bib′lic-al, 108, 169.
Bib′li-cist, 78, 171.
Bib-li-og′ra-pher.
Bib-li-o-graph′ic.
Bib-li-o-graph′ic-al.
Bib-li-og′ra-phy, 108.
Bib-li-ol′a-try, 170.
Bib′li-o-līte, 152.
Bib-li-o-log′ic-al (*-loj′-*).
Bib-li-ol′o-gy, 108.
Bib′li-o-man-cy.
Bib-li-o-ma′ni-a.
Bib-li-o-ma′ni-ac, 116.
Bib-li-o-ma-ni′ac-al.
Bib-li-o-ma′ni-an-ism (*-izm*), 136.
Bib-li-o-peg′ic (*-pej′ik*).
Bib-li-op′e-gy.
Bib′li-o-phīle.
Bib-li-oph′i-lĭsm (*-lizm*).
Bib-li-oph′i-lĭst.
Bib-li-o-pho′bi-a.
Bib-li-op′o-lar.
Bib′li-o-pole.
Bib-li-op′o-lism (*-lizm*).
Bib-li-op′o-list.
Bib-li-op-o-list′ic.
Bib′li-o-theke.
Bib′list, 16.
Bib′u-loŭs, 89, 108.
Bī-cal′car-āte, 79.
Bī-cap′su-lar, 79, 89.
Bī-car′bon-ate, 73, 79.
Bice, 25.
Bī-ceph′a-loŭs.
Bī-chro′mate (*-krō′-*).
Bī-cip′i-tal, 78, 169.
Bī-cip′i-toŭs.
Bick′er.
Bick′ered (*-urd*), 150.
Bick′er-er, 77.
Bick′er-ing.
Bick′ern (*-urn*).
Bī-con′ju-gate.
Bī-corn′oŭs.
Bī-cor′po-ral.
Bī-cru′ral (*-kroo′-*).
Bid, 16.
Bid′den (*bid′n*), 149.
Bid′der, 176.
Bid′ding.
Bide, 25.
Bī-dent′al, 79.
Bī-dent′ate.
Bī-dent′āt-ed.
Bī-det′ (Fr.) (*bī-det′*, or *bī-da′* [so Wr.; *bī-det′*, Wb. Gd.; *bī-da′*, Sm. 155.]
Bī-en′ni-al, 170.
Biēr (13), *n.* a kind of frame for carrying a dead body to the grave [*See* Beer, 160.]
Biēst′ings (*-ingz*).
Bī-fa′ri-oŭs.
Bif′er-oŭs.
Bif′fin [Beaufin.—*See* Beaufin, 203.]
Bī′fid.
Bif′i-date, 170.
Bif′i-dāt-ed.
Bif′i-lar.
Bī′fōld.
Bī-fo′li-ate.
Bī′fo-rate [so Sm. Wb. Gd.; *bī-fo′rate*, Wr. 155.]
Bif′o-rīne [Biforin, 203.]
Bī′form.
Bī′formed, 150.
Bī-front′ed (*-frunt′-*).
Bī-fur′cate.
Bī-fur′cāt-ed.
Bī-fur-ca′tion.
Bī-fur′coŭs.
Big, 16.
Big′a-mist, 170.
Big′a-my, 93, 170.
Big′e-ner (*bij′-*).
Big′gin (*-ghin*), 138.
Bight (*bīt*), *n.* a small inlet of the sea. [*See* Bite, 160.]
Big′ot, 86, 170.
Big′ot-ed, 176.
Big′ot-ry.
Bi-jou′try (*bē-zhoo′try*).
Bī-ju′gate.
Bī-ju′goŭs [so Wr. Wb. Gd.; *bī′ju-gus*, Sm. 155.]
Bī-la′bi-ate, 78, 169.
Bī-lam′el-late.
Bī-lam′el-lāt-ed.
Bil′an-der.
Bī-lat′er-al.
Bil′bĕr-ry.
Bil′bo [pl. Bil′boes (*bil′-bōz*, 192).]
Bilboquet (Fr.) *bil′bo-kā*, or *bil′bo-ket*) [*bil′-bo-kā*, Wr.; *bil′bo-ket*, Wb. Gd. 154, 155.]
Bild′stein.
Bile, *n.* the fluid secreted by the liver.
Bile, *n.* a painful tumor [Boil, 203.]

☞ Of these two forms of spelling this word, *bile* is more in conformity with its etymology (Anglo-Saxon *byl* or *bile*), and it is so spelled in the oldest English Dictionaries. Johnson and Walker give both forms, but prefer *bile*. Smart, Webster, and Goodrich give the preference to *boil*. Worcester says, "Both [forms] are still more or less in use;" and he remarks also that the word is "more commonly spelt *boil*."

Bilge, 16, 45.
Bilged (*biljd*), 150, 183.
Bil′ia-ry (*bil′ya-ry*).
Bī-lin′gual (*-ling′gwal*), 34, 54.
Bī-lin′guist (*bī-ling′-gwist*).
Bī-lin′guoŭs (*bī-ling′-gwus*).
Bil′ioŭs (*bil′yus*), 51, 171.
Bī-lit′er-al, 79.
Bilk, 16.
Bilked (*bilkt*), Note C, p. 34.
Bilk′ing.
Bill, 16, 172.
Bill′bŏŏk, 206.
Billed (*bild*), *a.* having a bill. [*See* Build, 160.]
Bil′let, 170.
Bil′let-doux (Fr.) (*bil′le-doo*) [pl. *Bil′lets-doux* (*bil-le-dooz′*), 198.]
Bil′let-ed, 176.
Bil′let-ing.
Bill′iard (*bil′yard*).
Bill′iards (*bil′yardz*), 136, 171.
Bil′lings-gate (*-lingz-*).
Bill′ion (*bil′yun*), 171.
Bil′lot, 170.
Bil′lōw, 101.
Bī-lo′bate [so Wr. Wb. Gd.; *bī′lo-bate*, Sm. 195.]
Bī′lōbed, 165.
Bī-loc′u-lar, 79, 89.
Bī-mac′u-late.
Bī-ma′na.
Bī′mane.
Bī-ma′noŭs, 79.
Bī-mar′gin-ate.
Bī-me′di-al [so Wr. Wb. Gd.; *bī-mĕd′yal*, Sm. 155.]
Bī-men′sal.
Bī-mes′tri-al.
Bī-month′ly (*-munth′-*), 93, 169.
Bin (16), *n.* a chest or cell for grain. [*See* Been, 160.]
Bī′na-ry, 72, 171.
Bī′nate.
Bīnd, 25.
Bīnd′er.
Bīnd′er-y, 93, 233.
Bīnd′ing.
Bī-nerv′ate.
Bin′na-cle, 148, 164, 170.
Bin′o-cle, 148, 164, 170.
Bī-noc′u-lar, 74, 89.
Bī-no′mi-al, 79, 169.
Bī-nom′i-noŭs.
Bī-not′o-noŭs.
Bī′noŭs.
Bī-nox′id [Binoxyd, 203. — *See* Oxide.]
Bī-oç′el-late, 170.
Bī-o-dȳ-nam′ics.
Bī-og′ra-pher, 108.
Bī-o-graph′ic.
Bī-o-graph′ic-al.
Bī-og′ra-phy, 79, 108, 171.
Bī-ol′o-gy, 108.
Bī′o-tīne, 152.
Bip′a-roŭs.
Bī-part′i-ble, 164.
Bip′ar-tīle [so Gd.; *bī-par′tīle*, Wr. 155.]
Bī-par′tient (*-par′shent*)
Bip′ar-tite, 171.
Bī-par-tī′tion (*-tish′un*).
Bī-pec′tin-ate.
Bī′ped, 25.
Bī-pel′tate.
Bī-pen′nate, 170.
Bī-pen′năt-ed.
Bī-pet′al-oŭs, 170.
Bī-pin′nate, 170.
Bī-pin-nat′i-fid.
Bī-pli′cate [so Gd.; *bī′-plī-căt*, Wr. 155.]
Bī-pliç′i-ty, 171.
Bī-po′lar, 74, 79.
Bī-po-lär′i-ty, 108.
Bī′pont.
Bī-pont′īne, 152.
Bī-punct′u-al.
Bī-pu′pil-late, 170.
Bī-quad′rate (*bī-kwod′-rāt*) [so Sm. Wr. Wb. Gd.; *bī-kwaw′drāt* Wk. 155.]
Bī-qua-drat′ic.
Bī-quin′tīle, 152.
Bī-ra′di-ate.
Bī-ra′di-āt-ed.
Birch, 21, N.
Birch′en (*birch′n*), 149.
Bird, 21, N.
Bird′-like, 216.
Bird′lime, 206.
Bī-rhom-boid′al (*-rom-*), 162.
Bī-ros′trate.
Bī-ros′trăt-ed.
Birth (21, N.), *n.* a coming into life. [*See* Berth, 160.]
Birth′day, 206.
Bis′co-tin.
Bis′cuit (*bis′kit*), 171.
Bise (Fr.) (*bēz*).
Bī-sect′, 15, 79.
Bī-sect′ed.
Bī-sect′ing.
Bī-sec′tion.
Bī-seg′ment.
Bī-se′ri-al, 49, N.
Bī-sĕr′rate, 170.
Bī-se′tose.
Bī-se′toŭs.
Bī-sex′u-al, 89.
Bish′op, 171.
Bish′op-ric.
Bisk.
Bis′muth (*biz′-*), 171.
Bis′muth-al (*biz′-*).
Bis′muth-ic (*biz′-*), 106.
Bī′son (149) [so Wb. Gd.; *biz′un*, Sm.; *bī′-son*, or *biz′un*, Wr. 155.]
Bisque (Fr.) (*bisk*).
Bis-sex′tīle (171) [so Wk. Sm. Wr.; *bis-seks′tĭl*, Wb. Gd. 155.]
Bī-stip′uled (*-ūld*).
Bis′tort.
Bis′tou-ry (*bis′too-*).
Bis′tre (164) [Bister, Wb. Gd. — *See* 164, and Note E, p. 70.]
Bī-sul′cate.
Bī-sul′coŭs.
Bī-sul′phate.
Bit (16), *n.* a part of a bridle; a tool for boring, &c. [*See* Bitt, 160.]
Bitch, 16, 44.
Bīte (25), *v.* to wound with the teeth. [*See* Bight, 160.]
Bīt′er, 183.
Bī-tern′ate, 21, N.
Bīt′ing, 183.
Bitt, *n.* a piece of timber projecting perpendicularly from a deck. [*See* Bit, 160.]
Bit′ted, 176.
Bit′ten (*bit′n*), 66, 149.
Bit′ter, 170.
Bit′tern, 66, N.; 170.
Bit′ters (*bit′urz*), 76.
Bit′ting, 176.

Bĭ-tu'men (L.), 125.
Bĭ-tu'mi-nate, 171.
Bĭ-tu'mi-nāt-ed, 183.
Bĭ-tu'mi-nāt-ing.
Bĭ-tū-mi-nif'er-oŭs, 108.
Bĭ-tu'mi-nize, 202.
Bĭ-tu'mi-nized.
Bĭ-tu'mi-nīz-ing.
Bĭ-tu'mi-noŭs, 171.
Bi'vălve.
Bī-valv'oŭs.
Bī-valv'u-lar, 89.
Bī-vâult'ed.
Bī-ven'tral.
Biv'i-oŭs, *or* Bī'vi-oŭs [*biv'i-us*, Wb. Gd.; *bī'vi-us*, Sm. Wr. 155.]
Biv'ouac, *n*. (Fr.) (*biv'-wak*, or *bīv'oo-ak*) [*bīv-wak*, Wr. Wb. Gd.; *bīv'oo-ak*, Sm. 155.]
[Bizantine, 203.— *See* Byzantine.]
Bi-zărre' (Fr.).
Blab, 10.
Blabbed (*blabd*), 165, 176.
Blab'ber.
Blab'bing.
Black, 10, 181.
Black'a-moor [so Sm. Wr. Wb. Gd.; *blak'-a-mōr*, Wk. 155.]
Black'bâll, *n*. & *v*.
Black'bâlled (*-bawld*), 165.
Black'bâll-ing.
Black'bĕr-ry.
Black'bird, 206.
Black'bōard.
Black'cap.
Blacked (*blakt*), 165; Note C, p. 34.
Black'en (*blak'n*), 149.
Black'ened (*blak'nd*).
Black'en-ing (*blak'n-*).
Black'en-er (*blak'n-ur*), 77.
Black'-eyed (*-īd*), 171.
Black'fish, 206.
Black'guärd (*blag'gard*) 171; Note C, p. 34.
Black'ing.
Black-lĕad' [so Wr.; *blak'lĕd*, Gd. 155.]
Black'-let'ter, *a*. & *n*.
Black'smith, 206.
Blad'der, 170.
Blad'der-y, 93.
Blade, 23.
Blād'ed, 183.
Blāin, 23.
Blām'a-ble, 164, 183.
Blām'a-bly, 93.
Blame, 23.
Blamed, 165.
Blām'er.
Blame'wor-thy (*-wur-thy*), 215.
Blànch, 12, 131.
Blànched (*blàncht*), Note C, p. 34.
Blànch-im'e-ter, 170.
Blànch'ing.
Blanc-mange } (Fr.)
Blanc-manger } (Fr.)
(*blä-monj'*) [so Wr.; *blong-mongzh'*, Sm.; *blo-monj'*, Wb. Gd. 154, 155.]
Bland, 10.
Bland'ish, *v*. 104.
Bland'ished (*-isht*), Note C, p. 34.
Bland'ish-ing.
Bland'ish-ment.
Blank, 10, 54.
Blanked (*blangkt*), Note C, p. 34.
Blank'et, 54.
Blank'et-ed, 176.
Blank'et-ing.
Blank-verse' (216) [so Wr.; *blank'vurs*, Gd. 155.]
Blare (*blâr*), 14.
Blar'ney, 98.
Blas-pheme', 35, 171.
Blas-phemed', 150, 183.
Blas-phēm'er.
Blas-phēm'ing.
Blas'phe-moŭs, 171.
Blas'phe-my, 93, 171.
Blàst.
Blàst'ed.
Blas-te'ma (Gr.).
Blas-te'mal.
Blàst'er.
Blàst'-fur-nace, 209.
Blàst'ing.
Blăs-to-car'poŭs.
Blas'to-derm.
Bla'tant, 169.
Blāy, 23.
Blāze, 23.
Blāzed, 150, 183.
Blāz'er.
Blāz'ing.
Bla'zon (*bla'zn*), 149.
Bla'zoned (*bla'znd*), 165.
Bla'zon-er (*bla'zn-*).
Bla'zon-ing (*bla'zn-*).
Bla'zon-ry (*bla'zn-*), 171.
Blēa'bĕr-ry.
Blēach, 13, 44.
Blēached (*blēcht*), Note C, p. 34.
Blēach'er-y, 93.
Blēach'ing.
Blēak, 13.
Blēar, 13, 67.
Blēared, 150.
Blēar'-eyed (*-īd*).
Blēat, 13.
Blēat'ed.
Blēat'ing.
Bleb, 15.
Bled, 15.
Bleed, 13.
Bleed'ing.
Blem'ish, 170.
Blem'ished (*-isht*).
Blem'ish-ing.
Blench, 15, 44, Note 2.
Blend (15), *v*. to mingle. [*See* Blende, 160.]
Blende, *n*. sulphuret of zinc. [*See* Blend, 160.]
Blend'ed.
Blend'ing.
Blend'oŭs, 183.
Blen'ny, 170.
Blent, 15.
Bless, 15, 174.
Blessed (*blest*), *part*. 165.
Bless'ed, *a*. 150.
Bless'er, 169.
Bless'ing.
Blest. [*See* Blessed.]
Blet, 15.
Ble'ton-ism (*-izm*), 133, 136.
Ble'ton-ist.
Blet'ting, 176.
Blew, *v*. (*blū*), did blow. [*See* Blue, 160.]
Blīght (*blīt*), 162.
Blīght'ed (*blīt'ed*).
Blīght'ing (*blīt'ing*).
Blīnd, 25.
Blīnd'age.
Blīnd'ed.
Blīnd'er, 77.
Blīnd'fōld.
Blīnd'fōld-ed.
Blīnd'fōld-ing.
Blīnd'ing.
Blīnd'side (206) [so Sm. Wr. Gd.; *blīnd-sīd'*, Wk. 155.]
Blink (*blingk*), 16, 54.
Blink'ard.
Blinked (*blingkt*), Note C, p. 34.
Blink'er, 77.
Blink'ing.
Bliss, 16, 174.
Bliss'ful (*-fo͞ol*), 180.
Blis'ter, 16, 77.

Blis'tered, 150.
Blis'ter-ing.
Blis'ter-y, 93.
Blīthe, 25, 38.
Blīthe'some (blīth'sum).
Blōat (24, 130), v. to swell. [See Blote, 160.]
Blōat'ed.
Blōat'er.
Blōat'ing.
Blob, 18.
Blob'ber, 170.
Blob'ber-lipped (-lipt), [205.
Block, 18, 181.
Block-ade'.
Block-ād'ed, 183.
Block-ād'ing.
Block'hĕad, 206.
Block'ing.
Block-tin' (209)[so Wr.; blok'tin, Wb. Gd. 155.]
Blom'a-ry (bloom'-) (72) [Bloomary, 203.]
Blond, a. 18.
Blonde, n. (Fr.) (blond).
Blood (blud), 22.
Blood'ed (blud'-). [209.
Blood'hound (blud'-),
Blood'i-ly, 171.
Blood'i-ness (blud'-).
Blood'ing (blud'-).
Blood'root (blud'-), 206.
Blood'shed (blud'-).
Blood'shot (blud'-).
Blood'shot-ten (blud'-shot-n), 149, 171.
Blood'-ves-sel, 209.
Blood'wort (blud'wurt).
Blood'y (blud'y), 93.
Bloom, 19.
Bloom'a-ry [Blomary, 203.]
Bloomed, 150.
Bloom'er.
Bloom'ing.
Bloom'y, 93, 169.
Blos'som, 170.
Blos'somed (-sumd), 150.
Blos'som-ing.
Blos'som-y.
Blot, 18.
Blotch, 18, 44.
Blote, v. to dry and smoke [See Bloat, 160.]
Blot'ted, 176.
Blot'ter.
Blot'ting.
Blouse (blouz) [Blowze, 203.]
Blōw, 24.
Blōw'er.
Blōw'ing.
Blōwn.
Blowze (28) [Blouse, 203.]
Blowzed (blouzd).
Blowz'y.
Blub'ber, 170.
Blub'bered, 165.
Blub'ber-ing.
Blud'geon (bluj'un), 171.
Blūe (26), n. a kind of color. [See Blew, 160.]
Blūe'bĕr-ry, 206.
Blūe'bird.
Blūe'y, 93, 171.
Bluff, 22, 173.
Bluff'y, 93.
Blu'ing, 183.
Blu'ish, 171.
Blun'der.
Blun'dered (-durd), 150.
Blun'der-er, 77.
Blun'der-ing.
Blunt, 22.
Blunt'ed.
Blunt'ing.
Blur, 21.
Blurred, 150, 176.
Blur'ring.
Blurt, 21.
Blush, 22, 46.
Blushed (blusht), Note C, p. 34.
Blush'ing.
Blus'ter, 22, 77.
Blus'tered, 150.
Blus'ter-er, 77.
Blus'ter-ing.
Bōar, n. the male of the hog. [See Bore, 160.]
Bōard, n. a thin piece of sawed timber. [See Bored, 160.]
Bōard'a-ble, 164.
Bōard'ed.
Bōard'er.
Bōard'ing.
Bōast, 24.
Bōast'ed.
Bōast'er.
Bōast'ful (-fo͝ol), 180.
Bōast'ing.
Bōat, 24, 130.
Bōat'a-ble, 169.
Bōat'bill, 206.
Bōat'-build'er (-bild'-ur), 209.
Bōat'ing.
Bōat'swain (bo'sn, in seaman's language) [so Wb. Gd.; bōt'-swān, colloquially bo'-sn, Sm.; bōt'swān, or bo'sn, Wr. 155.]
Bob, 18, 31.
Bobbed (bobd), 150, 176.
Bob'bin, 170.
Bob-bin-et' [so Gd.; bob'bi-net, Wr. 155.]
Bob'bing.
Bob'o-link, 171.
Bob'stāy, 206.
Bob'tāil.
Bob'tāiled (-tāld), 150.
Boc'a-sīne, 152.
Bock'ing.
Bock'land [Bookland, 203.]
Bode, 24.
Bōd'ed.
Bod'īce (bod'is), 169, 171.
Bod'īed (bod'id), 99, 186.
Bod'i-less, 169, 171.
Bod'i-ly, 78, 93.
Bōd'ing.
Bod'kin.
Bod'lēi-an (-lē-), 171.
Bod'y, 93, 170.
Bod'y-ing.
Bœ-o'tian (be-o'shan).
Bog, 18.
Bog'gle, 164.
Bog'gled (bog'ld), 165.
Bog'gler.
Bog'gling.
Bog'gȳ (-ghy), 138.
Bō-hēa' (bō-hē'), 171.
Bo-he'mi-an.
Boil, v. 27.
Boil, n. [Bile, 203.—See Bile.]
Boiled, 150.
Boil'er.
Boil'er-y.
Boil'ing.
Bois'ter-oŭs.
Bo'la-ry, 72.
Bōld, (24) a. daring, fearless. [See Bowled, 160]
Bōld'-faced (-fāst), 216.
Bole, n. a kind of mineral. [See Boll, and Bowl, 160.]
Bolero (Sp.) (bo-lā'ro).
Bōll, n. the capsule of a plant. [See Bole, and Bowl, 160.]
Bol'lard.
Bōll'ing [so Wr.; bŏl'-ing, Gd. 155.]
Bō-logn-ēse' (bō-lon-yēz'), 171.
Bo-lōgn'ian (-lōn'yan), [171.
Bōl'ster.
Bōl'stered (-sturd), 150.
Bōl'ster-ing.
Bōlt, 24, 130.
Bōlt'ed.

Bōlt'er.
Bōlt'ing.
Bo'lus.
Bomb (*bum*), 162.
Bom'bard, *n.* (*bum'-bard*), 161.
Bom-bard', *v.* (*bum-bard'*), 161, 171.
Bom-bard'ed (*bum-*).
Bom-bard-ier' (*bum-bard-ēr'*), 169, 171.
Bom-bard'ing (*bum-*).
Bom-bard'ment (*bum-*).
[Bombasin, 203. — *See* Bombazine.]
Bom'bast (*bum'-*), *or* Bom-bast' (*bum-*), *n.* [*bum'bast*, Wk. Wb. Gd.; *bum-bast'*, Sm.; *bum-bȧst'*, or *bum'-bȧst*, Wr.]

☞ Walker pronounces this word, when used as an adjective, *bum-bast'*.

Bom-bast'ic (*bum-*), 109.
Bom-ba-zette' (*bum-*).
Bom-ba-zine' (*bum-ba-zēn'*) (171) [Bombasin, 203.]
Bom'bi-late.
Bomb'-shell (*bum-*).
Bom-byç'i-noŭs, 171.
Bom'byx (L.).
Bo-na-part'e-an, 110.
Bo'na-part-ism (*-izm*) (133, 136) [so Gd.; *bo-na-part'izm*, Wr. 155.]
Bo-na'sus.
Bon'bon (Fr.) (*bong'-bong*).
Bon-chret'ien (Fr.) (*bon-kret'yen*).
Bond, 18.
Bond'age.
Bond'ed.
Bond'ing.
Bond'man, 206.
Bonds'man (*bondz'-man*), 136, 214.
Bone, 24.
Boned, 150.
Bone'set.
Bone'set-ting, 176.
Bon'fire.
Bōn'ing, 183.
Bo-ni'to (Sp.) (*bo-ne'to*).
Bon-mot' (Fr.) (*bong-mo'*).
Bŏn'net (170) [*not* bun'-et, 153.]
Bŏn'net-ed.
Bon'ny.
Bon'ny-clab'ber, *or* Bon-ny-clap'per
Bon-ton' (Fr.) (*bong-tong'*).
Bo'nus.
Bon-vi-vant' (Fr.) (*bong-ve-vȧng'*).
Bōn'y, 93.
Boo'by.
Bŏŏk (20), *n.* & *v.* [so Sm. Wr. Wb. Gd.; *book*, Wk. 155.]

☞ "My prototype Walker, I am informed, was a Yorkshireman; and the information must be correct, or surely he would not have marked all words in *ook*, — book, cook, look, &c., — to be pronounced with the long sound of the vowel digraph, as in food, pool, boot, &c., and not, as we always hear those words in London, with the short sound, as in good, wool, foot, &c." *Smart.* — Yet Walker says of himself, — "To a man born, as I was, within a few miles of the capital [at Colney-Hatch, county of Middlesex], living in the capital almost my whole life, and exercising myself there in public speaking for many years, — to such a person, if to any one, the true pronunciation of the language must be very familiar."

Bŏŏk'bīnd-er, 206.
Bŏŏk'bīnd-er-y.
Bŏŏk'bīnd-ing.
Bŏŏk'case, 66, N.
Bŏŏk'-keep'er.
Bŏŏk'-keep'ing.
Bŏŏk'land [Bockland, 203.]
Bŏŏk'mon-ger (*-mung-gher*).
Bŏŏk'sell-er.
Bŏŏk'sell-ing.
Bŏŏk'worm (*-wurm*).
Boom, 19.
Boomed, 150.
Boom'er-ang, 233.
Boom'ing.
Boon, 19.
Bo'ops.
Boor, 19.
Boose (*booz*) [Bouse, Booze, 203.]
Boo'sy (*boo'zy*) [Bousy, Boozy, 203.]
Boot, 19.
Boot'ed.
Boot-ee', 121.
Bo-o'tēs (L.) (*-tēz*).
Booth, 19, 38.
Boot'i-kin, 171.
Boo'ty, 19, 93.
[Booze, 203. — *See* Boose.]
[Boozy, 203. — *See* Boosy.]
Bo-peep'.
Bōr'a-ble, 164, 183.
Bo-raç'ic, 235.
Bor'age (*bur'aj*) (171) [so Wk. Wr. Wb. Gd.; *bŏr'aj*, Sm. 155.]
Bo'rate, 49, N.
Bo'rax, 24.
Bor'der.
Bor'dered (*-durd*), 150.
Bor'der-er, 77.
Bor'der-ing.
Bor'dure.
Bore, *v.* to perforate by giving to some pointed instrument a circular motion. [*See* Boar, 160.]
Bo're-al, 49, N.; 169.
Bo're-as (L.).
Bōred (*bōrd*), *part.* of *Bore*. [*See* Board, 160.]
Bōr'el, 170.
Bōr'er, 49, N.
Bōr'ing.
Born, *part.* of *Bear*, to bring forth.
Bōrne, *part.* of *Bear*, to carry [*See* Bourn, 60.]
Bo'ron, 24.
Bor'ough (*bŭr'ō*), 22, 162, 171.
Bŏr'rōw, 101, 170.
Bŏr'rōwed (*bŏr'rōd*), 188
Bŏr'row-er, 171.
Bos'cage.
Bosh.
Bosk'et [Busket, 203.]
Bosk'y.
Bos'om (*bŏŏz'um*, or *boo'zum*) [so Wr.; *bŏŏz'um*, Sm.; *boo'-zum*, Wb. Gd. 155.]
Boss, 18, 174.
Boss'age.
Bossed (*bŏst*), 150; Note C, p. 34.
Bos'sy.
Bot, 18.
Bo-tan'ic, 109, 170.
Bo-tan'ic-al, 108.
Bot'a-nist.
Bot'a-nize, 202.
Bot-a-nol'o-gy.
Bot'a-no-man-cy.
Bot'a-ny, 171.
Bo-tar'go.

Botch, 18, 44.
Botched (*bocht*), 150; Note C, p. 34.
Botch'er.
Botch'er-y.
Botch'y, 93.
Bōth, 24, 37.
Bŏth'er.
Bŏth'ni-an.
Bŏth'nic.
Bot'ry-oid, 93, 171.
Bot-ry-oid'al.
Bot'ry-o-līte, 152.
Bot'tle, 164.
Bot'tled (*bot'ld*), 183.
Bot'tling.
Bot'tom.
Bot'tomed (*bot'umd*), [150.
Bot'tom-ing.
Bot'tom-ry, 171.
Bouchet (Fr.) (*boo-shā'*, or *boo-shet'*).
Bou-doir' (Fr.) (*boo-dwor'*), 171.
Bough (*bou*) (162, 171), *n.* a branch of a tree. [*See* Bow, 160.]
Bought (*bawt*)(162, 171).
Bougie (Fr.) (*boo-zhē'*) [so Gd.; *boo'zhē*, Wr. 154, 155.]
Bouilli (Fr.) (*bool-yē'*).
Bouillon (Fr.) (*bool-yong'*).
Bōul'der (*bōl'dur*) [Bowlder, 203.]
Boulevard (Fr.) (*bool'e-var*, or *boo'le-vard*, 154).
Bounce, 28.
Bounced (*bounst*), 150.
Boun'cer, 183.
Boun'cing.
Bound, 28.
Bound'a-ry, 72, 171.
Bound'ed.
Bound'en (*bound'n*) [so Sm. Wb. Gd.; *bound'-en*, Wk. Wr. 155.]
Bound'ing.
Boun'te-oŭs [so Wr. Wb. Gd.; *boun'te-us*, or *bount'yus*, colloquially, *bount'che-us*, Sm.; *boun'che-us*, Wk. 134, 155.]
Boun'ti-ful (*-fŏŏl*), 78, 171.
Boun'ty, 28, 93.
Bouquet (Fr.) (*boo-kā'*) [so Wb. Gd.; *boo-kā'*, or *boo'ka*, Wr.; *boo'-ka*, Sm. 154, 155.]
Bour'bon-ism(*boor'bon-izm*).
Bour'bon-ist (*boor'-*).
Bourgeois (Fr.) (*boor-zhwä'*) (161), *n.* a citizen.
Bour-geois' (*bur-jois'*) (161), *n.* a kind of printing type. [Burgeois, 203.]
Bourgeoisie (Fr.) (*boor-zhwâ-zē'*).
Bōurn (*bōrn*) [so Wk. Sm. Wb. Gd.; *bōrn*, or *boorn*, Wr. 155], *n.* a limit. [*See* Borne, 160.]
Bourse (Fr.) (*boors*).
Bouse (*booz*) [Boose, 203.]
Bou-stro-phe'don [so Wr. Gd.; *bou-stroph'-e-don*, Sm. 155.]
[Bousy, 203. — *See* Boosy.]
Bout, 28.
Bouts-rimés (Fr.) (*boo-re-mā'*).
Bo'vate.
Bo'vīne, 152.
Bow (28), *n.* an inclination of the head or of the head and body in token of respect, or of recognition: — the round part of a ship's side forward. [*See* Bough, 160.]
Bōw (*bo*), *n.* an instrument for shooting arrows. [*See* Beau, 160.]
Bow'els (*-elz*), 28, 136.
Bower (*bour*), 67.
Bower'y (*bour'-*).
Bōw'-knot (*-not*), 206, Exc. 3.
Bōwl (*bōl*), *n.* a vessel to hold liquids: — a ball of wood used for play. [*See* Bole, *and* Boll, 160.]
Bōwl'der (*bōl'dur*) [Boulder, 203.]
Bōwled (*bōld*), *v.* did bowl. [*See* Bold, 160.]
Bōw'-legged (*bo'legd*), 206, Exc. 4.
Bōwl'er.
Bōw'līne (*bo'lĭn*) [so Sm.; *bo'lĭn*, Wb. Gd.; *bou'lĭn*, Wk.; *bo'lĭn*, or *bou'lĭn*, Wr. 155.]
Bōwl'ing.
Bōwl'ing-al-ley, 206, Exc. 4.
Bow'-ōar, 206, Exc. 3.
Bōw'pen, 206.
Bowse.
Bōw'sprit, 171.
Bōw-win'dōw, 206, Exc. 1.
Box, 18, 39, N.
Boxed (*bokst*), 150.
Box'en (*boks'n*), 149.
Box'er, 77.
Box'hâul.
Box'hâul-ing.
Box'ing.
Box'-tree, 206, Exc. 4.
Box'wŏŏd, 206.
Boy, 27.
Boyau (Fr.) (*boy'o*) [so Wb. Gd.; *bo-yō'*, Wr. 155.] [pl. *Boyaux* (*boy-ōz'*).]
Boy'hŏŏd.
Boy'ish.
Brac'cāte, 170.
Brace, 23, 39.
Braced (*brāst*), 165; Note C, p. 34.
Brāce'let.
Bra'cer, 183.
Brach'i-al (*brak'ĭ-al*), *or* Bra'chi-al (*bra'kĭ-al*) [*brak'ĭ-al*, Wb. Gd.; *brā'kĭ-al*, Sm.; *brăk'-yal*, Wk.; *brăk'yal* or *brā'kĭ-al*, Wr. 155.]
Brach'i-ate (*brak'-*).
Brach'i-o-pod (*brak'-*).
Brăch-y-cat-a-lec'tic (*brak-*), 116.
Bra-chyg'ra-pher (*-kig'-*).
Bra-chyg'ra-phy (*-kig'-*)
Bra-chyl'o-gy (*-kil'-*).
Bra-chyp'ter-oŭs (*-kip'-*)
Bra-chys'to-chrone (*-kis'to-krōn.*)
Bra'cing.
Brack'et.
Brack'et-ed.
Brack'et-ing.
Bract, 10, 52.
Bract'e-al, 169, 171.
Bract'e-ate.
Bract'e-o-late.
Brad, 10.
Brad'y-pod, 171.
Brag, 10.
Brag-ga-do'ci-o (*-shĭ-o*) (170) [so Wk. Sm. Wr.; *brag-a-do'sho*, Wb. Gd. 155.]
Brag'gart, 170.

Bragged (*bragd*), 150, 176.
Brag'ger (*-gur*), 138.
Brag'ging (*-ghing*).
Brah'ma [Brama, 203.]
Brah'min [Bramin, 203.]
Brāid (*brād*) (23), *v.* to weave together. [*See* Brayed, 160.]
Brāil, 23.
Brāin, 23.
Brāined (*brānd*), 150.
Brāit, 23.
Brake (23), *n.* an apparatus for checking the motion of a wheel. [*See* Break, 160.]
Brake'man, 206.
Brāk'y, 93.
Bram'ble, 164.
Bram'bling, 183.
Bram'bly.
Brä'min [Brahmin, 203.]
Bra-min'ic-al, 108.
Bran, 10.
Brȧnch, 131.
Brȧnched (*brȧncht*), 150.
Bran'chi-al (*brang'-kĭ-*), 54, 171.
Bran'chi-æ (L.) (*brang'-ki-ē*).
Brȧnch'ing.
Bran'chi-o-pod (*brang'-kĭ-*).
Brȧnch'y, 93, 169.
Brand, 10.
Brand'ed.
Brand'er.
Brand'ing.
Bran'dish, 104.
Bran'dished (*-disht*), 150.
Bran'dish-ing.
Brand'ling.
Bran'dy, 10, 93.
Bran'gle (*brang'gl*), 54, 164.
Brang'gled (*bran'gld*).
Bran'gler (*brang'-*).
Bran'gling (*brang'-*).
Bran'lin.
Bran'ny, 170, 176.
Brant, 10.
Brash.
Bra'sier (*bra'zhur*) (171) [Brazier, 203.]
Brȧss, 12, 131, 174.
Bras'sart.
Bras'set.
Bras'si-ca (L.).
Brȧss'i-ness, 169.
Brȧss'y, 93.
Brat, 10.
Bra-vā'do [*not* bra-vä'-do, 153.]
Brave, 23.
Braved, 150, 183.
Brāv'er-y, 171.
Brāv'ing.
Brä'vo, *or* Brā'vo, *interj.* [so Wr.; *bra'vo*, Wb. Gd.; *brā'vo*, Sm. 155.]

☞ "The proper *English* exclamation is 'Oh! brave!' or 'Brave! O!'" *Smart.*

Brä'vo, *or* Brā'vo, *n.* [so Wr.; *bra'vo*, Wk.; *brā'vo*, Sm. Wb. Gd. 155.] [pl. Bravoes, (*-vōz*), 192.]
Bra-vu'ra (It.).
Brawl, 17.
Brawled, 150.
Brawl'er.
Brawl'ing.
Brawn, 17.
Brawn'y, 93.
Brāy, 23.
Brāyed (*brād*), *v.* did bray. [*See* Braid, 160.]
Brāy'er.
Brāy'ing.
[Brayle, 203. — *See* Brail.]
Braze, 23.
Bra'zen, (*bra'zn*), 149.
Bra'zen-faced (*bra'zn-fāst*), 216.
Bra'zier (*bra'zhur*) [Brasier, 203.]
Bra-zil'-wōōd (*bra-zĭl'-wōōd*) [so Wb. Gd.; *bra-zēl'wōōd*, Wr. 155]
Brāz'ing, 183.
Brēach (13), *n.* a fracture. [*See* Breech, 160.]
Brĕad (15), *n.* food made of grain. [*See* Bred, 160.]
Brĕadth, 15, Note C, p. 34.
Breāk (*brāk*), *v.* to rend. [*See* Brake, 160.]
Breāk'age.
Breāk'er.
Brĕak'fast (*brek'-*), 143, 171.
Brĕak'fast-ed.
Brĕak'fast-ing.
Breāk'wâ-ter, 206.
Brēam, 13.
Brēam'ing.
Brĕast (*brest*), 15.
Brĕast'ed.
Brĕast'fȧst.
Brĕast'ing.
Brĕast'-wheel.
Brĕast'work (*brest'-wurk*), 206.
Brĕath, 15.
Brēath'a-ble, 164.
Brēathe, 13, 38.
Brēathed, 150, 183.
Brēath'er.
Brēath'ing.
Brec'cia (It.) (*bret'cha*) [so Sm. Wr.; *brek'-sha*, Wb. Gd. 155.]
Brec'ciāt-ed (*brek'shāt-ed*) [so Sm. Wb. Gd.; *brek'shĭ-āt-ed*, Wr. 155.]
Bred, *v.* did breed. [*See* Bread, 160.]
Breech, *n.* the thick end of a firearm behind the bore. [*See* Breach, 160.]
Breeched (*brēcht*), Note C, p. 34.
Breech'es (*brich'ez*), 171.
Breech'ing (*brich'ing*), 171.
Breed, 13.
Breed'er.
Breed'ing.
Breese (*brēz*) (160), *n.* the gadfly. [Breeze, Brize, 203.]
Breeze (160), *n.* a gentle gale.
Breez'y, 93.
Brent, 15.
Bret, 15.
Breth'ren (127, 145) [pl. of Brother, 194.]
Breve (*brēv*).
Bre-vet', *n.* [so Sm. Wb. Gd.; *bre-vet'* or *brev'-et*, Wr. 155.]
Bre-vet', *a.* [*bre-vet'*, or *brev'et*, Wr.; *brev'et*, Sm. 155.]
Bre-vet', *v.*
Bre-vet'ted, 176.
Bre-vet'ting.
Brēv'ia-ry (*brēv'ya-ry*) [so Wk. Sm. Wr.; *bre'vĭ-ȧ-ry*, Wb. Gd. 155.]
Bre'vi-ate [so Sm. Wb. Gd.; *brēv'yāt*, or *brē'-vĭ-āt*, Wr. 155.]
Bre'vi-a-ture [so Sm. Wb. Gd.; *brēv'ya-tūr*, Wr.; *brēv'ya-chūr*, 134, 155.]
Bre-viēr' (*bre-vēr'*).
Brev'i-ped.
Brev-i-pen'nate.

Brev'i-ty, 169, 171.
Brew (*broo*), 19.
Brew'age (*broo'*).
Brewed (*brood*), *v.* did brew. [*See* Brood, 160.]
Brew'er (*broo-*), 19, 77.
Brew'er-y (*broo'-*), 171.
Brew'ing (*broo'-*).
Brew'is (*broo'-*).
[Briar, 203. — *See* Brier.]
Brī-a're-an, 110, 169.
Bribe, 25.
Brībed, 150, 183.
Brīb'ing.
Brīb'er.
Brīb'er-y, 171.
Brick, 16, 181.
Brick'kiln (*-kil*), 162, 171.
Brick'lāy-ing.
Brick'māk-er.
Brick'work (*-wurk*).
Brīd'al [*See* Bridle, 148.]
Bride, 25.
Bride'groom, 206.
Bride'māid.
Bride'man.
Bride'well.
Bridge (*brij*), 16, 45.
Bridged (*brijd*), 150, 183.
Bridg'ing (*brij'-*).
Bridg'y (*brij'-*).
Brī'dle (164) [*See* Bridal, 148.]
Brī'dled (*brī'dld*), 183.
Brī'dler.
Brī'dling.
Bri-doon', 121.
Brief, 13.
Brī'er, (169) [Briar, 203.]
Brī'ered (*-urd*), 150.
Brī'er-y, 171.
Brig, 16.
Brī-gade', 121.
Brig-a-diēr', 122, 169, 171.
Brig'and, 156, 170.
Brig'an-dīne [so Wk. Wr. Wb. Gd.; *brig'-an-dīn*, Sm. 155.]
Brig'an-tīne [so Wk. Wr. Wb. Gd.; *brig'-an-tīn*, Sm. 155.]
Bright (*brīt*), 162.
Bright'en (*brīt'n*), 149, 162. [150.
Bright'ened (*brīt'nd*),
Bright'en-ing (*brīt'n-ing*).
Bright'-eyed (*brīt'īd*), 206, Exc. 5.
Brill, 16, 172.
Brill'ian-cy (*-yan-sy*), 171
Brill'iant (*-yant*), 171.
Brim, 16.
Brimmed (*brimd*), 150, 176.
Brim'ful (*-fōōl*).
Brim'mer, 176.
Brim'ming.
Brim'stōne, 130.
Brīnd'ed.
Brin'dled (*brin'dld*), 171,
Brine, 25. [183.
Bring, 16, 54.
Bring'er.
Brīn'ish, 183.
Brink, 16, 54.
Brīn'y, 93.
Brisk, 16.
Brisk'et.
Bris'tle (*bris'l*), 162, 171.
Bris'tled (*bris'ld*).
Bris'tling (*bris'ling*), 162.
Bris'tly (*bris'ly*), 171.
Brit, 16.
Bri-tan'ni-a [so Wr.; *bri-tan'ya*, Wb. Gd. 155.]
Bri-tan'nic.
Brit'ish, 170.
Brit'on.
Brit'tle (*-brit'l*), 164.
Brĭtz'ska (*brĭs'ka*), 171.
Brize [Breese, 203.]
Brōach, *v.* to pierce. [*See* Brooch, 160.]
Brōached (*brōcht*), 150.
Brōach'er.
Brōach'ing.
Broad (*brawd*), 17, 171.
Broad'āxe, 171, 206.
Broad'cȧst.
Broad'clŏth, 18.
Broad'en (*brawd'n*), 149.
Broad'side.
Brob-dig-na'gi-an.
Bro-cade', 121.
Bro-cād'ed, 183.
Bro'cage [Brokage, 203.]
Broc'co-lĭ, 170.
Bro-chure' (Fr.) (*bro-shūr'*).
Brod'e-kin [so Wb. Gd.; *brōd'kin*, Wr.; *brŏd'-e-kin*, Sm. 155.]
Bro'gan.

☞ *Bro-gan'*, as it is often pronounced, is not sanctioned by any orthoëpist.

Brōgue (*brōg*), 168.
Broil, 27.
Broiled, 150.
Broil'ing.
Brōke, 24, 130.
Brōk'en (*brōk'n*), 24, 149.
Bro'ker, 24, 77.
Bro'ker-age.
Bro'ma.
Bro'mal, 72.
Brō-ma-tol'o-gy [so Gd.; *brŏm-a-tol'o-gy*, Wr. 155.]
Bro'mīde [Bromid, 203.]
Bro'mīne, 152.
Bron'chi-a, *n. pl.* (*brŏng'kĭ-a*).
Bron'chi-al (*brong'kĭ-*).
Bron'chĭ-æ (*brong'kĭ-ē*).
Bron-chī'tis (*bron-kī'tis*) [*not* brong-kē'tis, 153.]
Bron'chus (*brong'kus*) [pl. Bron'chī (*brong'-kī*, 198.]
Brŏnze, *or* Brōnze, *n.* & *v.* [so Wr. Gd.; *brŏnz*, Wk. Sm., 155.]
Brŏnzed, 165, 183.
Brŏnz'ing.
Brooch (*brōch*), *n.* an ornamented pin used to fasten parts of a dress. [*See* Brōach, 160.]
Brood, *n.* the young birds hatched at one time by the same mother. [*See* Brewed, 160.]
Brood'ed.
Brood'ing.
Brŏŏk, *n.* & *v.* [so Sm. Wr. Wb. Gd.; *brook*, Wk. 155. — *See* Book.]
Brŏŏked (*brŏŏkt*), Note C, p. 34.
Brŏŏk'ing.
Broom, 19.
Broom'stick, 206.
Broom'y, 93.
Brose.
Broth (*brawth*, or *brŏth*) [so Wr.; *brawth*, Wb. Gd.; *brŏth*, Wk. Sm. 155.]
Brŏth'el, 149.
Broth'el-ler [Brotheler, Wb. Gd. — *See* 177, and Note E, p. 70.]
Brot͟h'er (*brut͟h'ur*) (171) [pl. Brot͟h'ers, *or* Bret͟h'ren, 194.]
Brot͟h'er-hŏŏd.
Brough'am (*broo'am*, or

broom) [*broo'am*, Wr.; *broom*, Gd. 155], *n.* a kind of carriage.
Brought (*brawt*), 162, 171
Brow, 28 [pl. Brows (*browz*), 136. — *See* Browse, 160.]
Brow'bēat.
Brow'bēat-en (*-bēt-n*).
Brow'bēat-ing.
Brown, 28.
Browned, 150.
Brown'ing.
Browse (*browz*), *v.* to nibble [*See* Brow, 160.]
Browsed (*browzd*), 150.
Brows'er (*browz'ur*).
Brows'ing (*browz'ing*), 183.
Bru'in (*broo'in*), 19.
Bruise (*brooz*), 19, 171.
Bruised (*broozd*), 150, 183
Bruis'er (*brooz'ur*)
Bruis'ing (*brooz'ing*)
Bruit (*broot*), *n.* a rumor. [*See* Brute, 160.]
Bru'mal (*broo'mal*).
Bru-nette' (*broo-net'*), 121.
Brun'ion (*brun'yun*) [so Wr. Gd., *broon'yun*, Sm. 155.]
Brunt, 22.
Brush, 22, 46.
Brushed (*brusht*).
Brush'ing.
Brush'-wheel.
Brusque (Fr.) (*broosk*).
Bru'tal (*broo'tal*).
Bru-tal'i-ty (*broo-*), 108, 169.
Bru'tal-ize (*broo-*), 202.
Bru'tal-ized (*broo-*), 150, 183.
Bru'tal-īz-ing (*broo-*).
Bru'tal-ly (*broo-*), 93.
Brute (*broot*), *n.* an irrational animal. [*See* Bruit, 160.]
Bru'ti-fīed (*broo'-*), 186.
Bru'ti-fȳ (*broo'-*), 94.
Bru'ti-fȳ-ing (*broo'-*).
Brut'ish (*broot'-*).
Bry'o-ny, 93, 171.
Bub'ble, 164.
Bub'bled (*bub'ld*), 183.
Bub'bling.
Bub'bly.
Bu'bo.
Bu-bon'o-cēle [so Wk. Wr. Gd.; *bu'bo-no-sēl*, Sm. 155.]
Buc'cal, 170.
Buc-ca-neer', 122, 169.
Buc-ca-neer'ing, 170.
Buc-cel-la'tion.
Buc'ci-nal, 78, 169.
Bu-cen tâur [so Wb. Gd.; *bu'sen-taur*, Sm.; *bu-sen'tâur*, or *bu'sen-tâur*, Wr. 155.]
Bu'ce-ros.
Buck, 22, 181.
Buck'et, 22.
Buck'ing.
Buc'kle (*buk'l*), 164.
Buc'kled (*buk'ld*), 183.
Buck'ler.
Buc'kling.
Buck'ram.
Buck'skin, 206.
Buck'whēat.
Bu-col'ic, 109.
Bu-col'ic-al, 108.
Bud, 22.
Bud'ded, 176.
Buddh'a (*bood'a*) [so Wr.; *bŭd'a*, Gd. 155.]
Buddh'ism (*bood'izm*) [so Wr.; *bŭd'izm*, Sm.; *bŭd'izm*, Gd.]
Buddh'ist (*bood'ist*), 171.
Buddh-ist'ic (*bood-*).
Bud'ding, 176.
Bud'dle, 164.
Budge (*buj*), 22, 45.
Budged (*bujd*), 150.
Budg'et (*buj'et*).
Bud'let.
Buff, 22, 173.
Buf'fa-lō, 170.
Buf'fel, 170.
Buf'fer, 170.
Buf'fet.
Buf'fet-ed, 176.
Buf'fet-er.
Buf'fet ing.
Buf-foon', 121.
Buf-foon'er-y.
Buf-foon'ing.
Buf'fy.
Bug, 22.
Bug'bêar.
Bug'gi-ness (*-ghĭ-*), 78.
Bug'gy, *a.* & *n.* (*-ghy*), Bu'gle, 164. [138.
Bu'gloss.
Bŭhl (*bŭl*), 162.
Bŭhl'work (*bŭl'work*).
Buhr'-stone.
Buĭld (*bild*) (16, 171), *v.* to construct. [*See* Billed, 160.]
Buĭld'ed.
Buĭld'er.
Buĭld'ing.
Buĭlt, 16, 171.
Bulb, 22.
Bulbed, 150.
Bulb-if'er-oŭs, 108
Bulb'let.
Bulb'oŭs.
Bŭl'bŭl, 22.
Bŭl'būle.
Bulge, 22, 45.
Bulged, 150, 183.
Bulg'ing (*bulj'-*).
Bu'li-my.
Bulk, 22.
Bulk'hĕad, 206.
Bulk'i-ness.
Bulk'y, 93.
Bull (*bo͝ol*), 20, 172.
Bul-lan'tic (*bo͝ol-*), 170.
Bul'la-ry (*bo͝ol-*), 72.
Bŭl'late.
Bull'-dog.
Bul'let (*bo͝ol'et*), 170.
Bul'le-tin (*bo͝ol'e-tēn*, or *bo͝ol'e-tĭn*) (171) [so Wr.; *bo͝ol'e-tēn*, Sm.; *bo͝ol'e-tĭn*, Wb. Gd. 155.]
Bull'-fight (*bo͝ol'fīt*).
Bull'-frog (*bo͝ol'-*).
Bull'ied (*bo͝ol'id*), 99, 186.
Bull'ion (*bo͝ol'yun*), 171.
Bull'ion-ist (*bo͝ol'yun-*).
Bull'ist (*bo͝ol'ist*).
Bul'lock *bo͝ol'ok*), 171.
Bull's-eye (*bo͝olz'ī*), 214.
Bull'y (*bo͝ol'y*), 93.
Bull'y-ing (*bo͝ol'y-*), 186.
Bul'rush (*bo͝ol'-*), 171.
Bulse (*bŭls*).
Bŭl'tel.
Bul'tōw (*bo͝ol'tō*).
Bul'wark (*bo͝ol'-*), 171.
Bum'ble-bee (*bum'bl-*).
Bum'bōat.
Bum'kin, *n.* a short boom. [*See* Bumpkin, 148.]
Bump, 22.
Bumped (*bumpt*), 150, Note C, p. 34.
Bump'er.
Bump'kin, *n.* a clown. [*See* Bumkin, 148.]
Bun [Bunn, 203.]
Bunch, 22, 44.
Bunch'i-ness, 78, 171.
Bunch'y, 93.
Bun'dle, 164.
Bun'dled (*bun'dld*), 183.
Bun'dling.
Bung, 22, 54.
Bun'ga-lōw (*bung'-*).

Bung′-hole, 206, Exc. 3.
Bun′gle (*bung′gl*), 54, 164.
Bun′gled(*bung′gld*),183.
Bun′gler (*bung′glur*).
Bun′gling (*bung′gling*).
Bun′ion (*bun′yun*) [Bunyon, 203.]
Bunk (*bungk*), 22, 54.
Bunn [Bun, 203.]
Bunt, 22.
Bunt′ĭne, 82, 152.
Bunt′ing.
Bunt′lĭne [so Wr.; *bunt′lĭn*, Wb. Gd.155.]
Bun′yon [Bunion, 203.]
Buoy (*bwoy*), 171.

☞ "On board of ship, where the word *buoy* is always occurring, it is called a '*boy*,' though the slow, correct pronunciation is *bwoy*." *Smart*.

Buoyed (*bwoyd*) 150,188.
Buoy′age (*bwoy′-*).
Buoy′an-cy (*bwoy-*), 171.
Buoy′ant (*bwoy-*), 169.
[Bur, 203.— *See* Burr.]
Bur′bot.
Bur′den (*bur′dn*), 149.
Bur′dened (*bur′dnd*).
Bur′den-ing (*bur′dn-*).
Bur′den-some (*bur′dn-sum.*)
Bur′dock.
Bu′reau (Fr.) (*bu′rō*, or *bu-ro′*) [*bu′ro*, Wb. Gd.; *bu-ro′*, Wk. Sm.; *bu-ro′*, or *bu′ro*, Wr. 155.] [Fr. pl. *Bureaux* (*-rōz*); Eng. pl. Bureaus (*-rōz*), 198.]
Bu-reau′cra-cy (*-ro′-*), 169.
Bū-reau-crat′ic (*-ro-*).
Bu-reau-crat′ic-al (*-ro-*).
Bu-reau′crat-ist (*-ro′-*).
Bu-rette′ (Fr.).
[Burg, 203.— *See* Burgh.]
Burg′age.
Bur′gâll.
Bur′ga-mot [Bergamot, 203.— *See* Bergamot.]
Bur-gee′ [so Gd.; *bur′-jē*, Wr. 155.]
[Burgeois, 203.— *See* Bourgeois.]
Bur′gess.
Burgh (*burg*) (162) [Burg, 203.]
Burgh′er (*burg′-*), 171.
Burgh′ist (*burg′-*).
Burg′lar.
Burg-la′ri-oŭs.
Burg′la-ry, 72, 171.
Burg′mote.
Bur′go-mȧs-ter.
Bur-goo′, *or* Bur-gout′ (*-goo′-*) [so Wr.; *bur′-goo*, Wb. Gd. 155.]
Bur′grave.
Bur′gun-dy.
Bur′ĭ-al (*bĕr′i-*), 171.
Bur′ĭed (*bĕr′id*) (186), *part.* put into a grave, or covered with earth. [*See* Berried, 160.]
Bur′i-er (*bĕr′ĭ-*).
Bu′rin, 25.
Burke (*burk*).
Burked (*burkt*), 150, Note C, p. 34.
Burk′er, 183.
Burk′ing.
Burk′ism (*-izm*),133,136.
Burl, 21.
Bur′lap.
Bur-lesque′ (*-lesk′*), 121.
Bur-lesqued′ (*-leskt′*), 165.
Bur-lesqu′ing (*-lesk′-ing*), 183.
Bur′li-ness, 78, 171.
Bur′ly.
Burn, 21.
Burned, 150.
Burn′er.
Burn′ing.
Bur′nish, 21, 104.
Bur′nished (*-nisht*), 150.
Bur′nish-er.
Bur′nish-ing.
Burnt, 21.
Burr (21, 175) [Bur, 203.]
Bŭr′rel, 170.
Bŭr′rock, 170.
Bŭr′rōw (170), *n.* a hole in the ground for rabbits, &c. [*See* Borough, 160.]
Bŭr′rōwed, 150, 188.
Bŭr′rōw-ing.
Burr′y, 93.
Bur′sar.
Bur′sa-ry, 72.
Bursch (Ger.) (*boorsch*) [pl. *Bursch′en*, 198.]
Burst, 21, 49.
Burst′ing.
Bur′then (*bur′thn*), 149.
Bur′ton (*bur′tn*), 149.
Bur′y (*bĕr′y*) (171), *v.* to put into a grave: — to cover with earth. [*See* Berry, 160.]
Bur′y-ing (*bĕr′y-ing*).
Bush (*bo͝osh*), 20.
Bush′el (*bo͝osh′el*), 149.
Bush′el-age (*bo͝osh-*).
Bush′i-ness (*bo͝osh-*), 78.
Bush′ing (*bo͝osh′ing*).
Bush′man (*bo͝osh′-*), 206.
Bush′y (*bo͝osh′y*).
Bus′ĭed (*bĭz′id*), 171, 186.
Bus′i-ly (*bĭz′ĭ-*).
Business (*biz′nes*), 171.
Busk, 22.
Busk′et.
Busk′in.
Busk′ĭned (*-ĭnd*), 150.
Busk′y, 93.
Buss, 22, 174.
Bust, 22.
Bus′tard.
Bus′tle (*bus′l*), 162, 164.
Bus′tled (*bus′ld*), 183.
Bus′tler (*bus′lur*).
Bus′tling (*bus′ling*).
Bus′y (*biz′y*), 171.
But (22), *conj.* on the other hand: — *prep.* excepting: — *n.* end of any thing. [*See* Butt, 160.]
Butch′er (*bo͝och′ur*), 20, 77. [150.
Butch′ered (*bo͝och′urd*),
Butch′er-ing (*bo͝och′-*).
Butch′er-y (*bo͝och′-*).
But′-hĭnge.
But′ler.
But′ler-age.
But′ment.
Butt, *n.* a mark to be shot at: — *v.* to strike with the head. [*See* But, 160.]
Butt′ed.
But′ter, 170.
But′tered, 150.
But′ter-cup, 206.
But′ter-flȳ.
But′ter-y, 170.
But′tock.
But′ton (*but′n*), 149.
But′toned (*but′nd*).
But′ton-ing (*but′n-*).
But′tress, 170.
But′tressed (*but′rest*), 150.
But′tress-ing.
Bū-ty-ra′ceous (*-ra′-shus*) [so Sm. Wr.; *bŭt-y-ra′shus*, Wb. Gd. 155.]
Bu-tyr′ic.

Bu′tyr-ĭne, 152.
Bu′ty-roŭs [so Sm. Wr.; *bŭt′y-rus*, Wb. Gd. 155.]
Bux′e-oŭs.
Bux′ĭne, 152.
Bux′om, 169.
Buȳ (*bī*) (171), *v.* to purchase. [*See* By, 160.]
Buȳ′er (*by′-*).
Buȳ′ing (*by′-*).
Buzz, 22, 175.
Buz′zard, 170.
Buzzed (*buzd*), 150.
Buzz′ing.
By (*bī*, colloquially *bĭ*), *prep.* through or with, &c. [*See* Buy, 160.]
Bȳ, *or* Bȳe, *n.* something aside from the main subject. [*See* Bye, 160.]
Bȳe, *n.* a village. [*See* By, 160.]
Bȳ′-gōne, 206, Exc. 4.
By′-law.
Bys′sĭne, 152.
Bys′sus (L.).
By′word (*-wurd*).
By-zan′tian (*-shan*).
Byz′an-tīne, *a.* & *n.* [so Wr.; *byz-an′tin*, Gd. 155.]

C.

Cab, 10.
Ca-bal′, *n.* & *v.* 121.
Cab′a-la, 72.
Cab′al-ism (*-izm*), 136.
Cab′al-ist.
Cab-al-ist′ic, 109.
Cab-al-ist′ic-al, 108.
Ca-bal′ler, 176.
Cab′al-līne, *a.* & *n.* 82.
Cab′a-ret (*kab′a-rā*, or *kab′a-ret*) [so Wr.; *kab′a-rā*, Sm.; *kab′a-ret*, Wb. Gd. 155.]
Cab′bage, 70, 170.
Cab′in, 170.
Cab′ined (*-ĭnd*), 150.
Cab′i-net, 170.
Cab′in-ing.
Ca-bĭr′i-an, 78.
Ca-bĭr′ic.
Ca′ble, 164.
Ca′bled (*ka′bld*), 183.
Ca′bling.
Ca-boose′ (121) [Camboose, Coboose, 203.]
Cab′ot-age.
Cab-ri-o-let′ (Fr.) (*kab-ri-o-lā′*).
Cab′urns (*-urnz*).
Cac′a-gōgue (*-gog*), 87.
Ca′caō (*ka′kō*) [so Wr.; *ka-ka′o*, Wb. Gd. 155.]
Cach′a-lot (*kash′a-lot*) [so Wr.; *kach′a-lot*, Wb. Gd. 155.]
Cache (Fr.) (*kash*), *n.* a hole dug in the ground for concealing and preserving provisions [*See* Cash, 160.]
Ca-chet′ic (*-ket′-*), 109.
Ca-chet′ic-al (*-ket′-*), 108.
Ca-chex′y (*ka-kex′y*) [so Sm. Wr. Wb. Gd.; *kak′ek-sy*, Wk. 155.]
Cach-in-na′tion (*kak-*).
Cach′o-long (*kash′-*).
Ca-cique′ (Fr.) (*ka-sēk′*).
Cack′er-el.
Cac′kle (*kak′l*), 164.
Cac′kled (*kak′ld*), 150, 183.
Cac′kler.
Cac′kling.
Cac-o-chym′ic (*-kim′-*).
Cac-o-chym′ic-al (*-kim′-*)
Cac′o-chym-y (*-kim-y*).
Cac-o-de′mon.
Cac-o-e′thēs (L.) (*-thēz*), 113.
Ca-cog′ra-phy.
Ca-col′o-gy, 93.
Cac-o-phon′ic, 109.
Cac-o-phon′ic-al, 108.
Cac-o-pho′ni-oŭs.
Ca-coph′o-ny, 108.
Cac-o-tech′ny (*-tek′-*).
Ca-cot′ro-phy.
Cac-ta′ceous (*-shus*).
Cac′tus.
Cad, 10.
Ca-dav′er-oŭs.
Cad′dīce (*kad′is*) [Cadis, 203.]
Cad′dis [so spelled invariably when it means *a kind of ribbon*; but, in the sense of *a case-worm*, it is written also Caddice, 203.]
Cad′dōw, 101.
Cad′dy, 93.
Cade, 23.
Ca′dence, 169.
Ca′denced (*-denst*), 150.
Ca′denç-ing, 183.
Ca-det′, 121.
Ca′dew (*ka′du*).
Cadge (*kaj*), 45.
Cadg′er (*kaj′ur*) [so Sm. Wr. Wb. Gd.; *kej′ur*, Wk. 155.]
Ca′dī (Ar.).
Ca-dil′lac.
Cad-me′an, 110.
Cad′mi-a.
Cad′mi-um, 169.
Cad-u-ce′an [so Sm. Wr.; *ka-du′ce-an*, Wb. Gd. 155.]
Ca-du′ceus (L.) (*ka-du′shus*) [so Wr.; *ka-du′she-us*, Wk. Sm.; *ka-du′ce-us*, Wb. Gd. 155.]
Ca-du′coŭs.
Cæ′cum (*se′cum*).
[Cæsarean, 203.— *See* Cesarean.]
Cæs-pi-tose′ (*sĕs-*).
Cæ-su′ra (*se-zu′ra*) [so Wk. Sm. Wr; *se-zu′ra*, or *se-su′ra*, Gd. 155.] [Cesura, Sm. 203.]
Cæ-su′ral (*se-zu′ral*).
Café (Fr.) (*kaf′ā*).
Caf-fe′ic, 109.
Caf-fe′ĭne [Caffein, 203.]
Caf′fre (*kaf′ur*), 164.
Cag [Keg, 203.]
Cage, 23.
Caged, 150, 183.
Cag′ing (*kāj′-*).
Cahier (Fr.) (*kä′e-yā*) [so Sm. Wr.; *ka-hēr′*, Gd. 155.]
Ca-hoot′.
[Caic, 203.— *See* Caique.]
[Caiman, 203.— *See* Cayman.]
Cairn (*kêrn*).
Cāis′son [so Sm. Gd.; *ka-soon′*, Wr. 155.] [Caissoon, Sm. 203]

☞ When spelled *caissoon*, Smart pronounces it *ka-soon′*.

Cāi′tiff, 23.
Caj′e-put, 169.
Ca-jole′.
Ca-joled′, 150, 183.
Ca-jōl′er.
Ca-jōl′er-y.
Ca-jōl′ing.
Cake, 23.
Caked (*kākt*), Note C, p. 34.
Cāk′ing, 183.

Cal′a-bash.
Cal′a-boose, 169.
Cal-a-man′co(*-mang′ko*)
Cal′a-ma-ry, 72.
Cal′am-bac.
Cal-a-mif′er-oŭs, 108.
Cal′a-mīne [so Sm. Wb. Gd.; *kal′a-mĭn*, or *kal′a-min*, Wr. 155.]
Cal′a-mite.
Ca-lam′i-toŭs.
Ca-lam′i-ty, 108, 169.
Cal′a-mus [L. pl. *Calami*; Eng. pl. Cal′a-mus-es.]
Ca-lash′, 121.
Cal′car.
Cal′car-ate.
Cal-ca′re-oŭs, 169.
Cal′ce-āt-ed [so Sm. Wr. Wb. Gd.; *kal′she-āt-ed*, Wk. 134, 155.]
Cal′ce-don.
[Calcedony, 203. — *See* Chalcedony.]
Cal-ce′i-form, 169.
Cal-cif′er-oŭs, 108.
Cal′ci-form, 169.
Cal-cin′a-ble (164) [so Sm. Wb. Gd.; *kal-sĭn′a-bl*, or *kal′si-na-bl*, Wr. 155.]
Cal-ci-na′tion, 112.
Cal-cin′a-to-ry, 86.
Cal-cīne′, *or* Cal′cīne [so Gd.; *kal-sĭn′*, Wk. Sm. Wr. 155.]
Cal′cite.
Cal′ci-um [so Sm. Wb. Gd.; *kal′she-um*, Wr. 134, 155.]
Calc′-sin-ter [so Gd.; *kalk-sin′tur*, Wr. 155.]
Calc′-spar, 224.
Calc′-tŭff.
Cal′cu-la-ble, 164.
Cal′cu-la-ry, 72.
Cal′cu-late.
Cal′cu-lāt-ed, 183.
Cal′cu-lāt-ing.
Cal-cu-la′tion, 112.
Cal′cu-lāt-ĭve, 84.
Cal′cu-lāt-or.
Cal′cu-la-to-ry, 86.
Cal′cu-lus [L. pl. *Calculi* (used when the word has its medical sense of *a morbid concretion*); Eng. pl. Calculuses (used when the word means *a method of computation*), 198.]

Câl′dron, 17.
Ca-lèche′ (Fr.)(*ka-lāsh′*)
Cal-e-do′ni-an, 169.
Cal-e-fa′cient (*-fa′shent*)
Cal-e-fac′tion.
Cal-e-fac′to-ry, 86.
Cal′em-bourg (Fr.) (*-boorg*).
Cal′en-dar, *n.* a register of the year. [*See* Calender, 160.]
Cal′en-der, *n.* a hot press for cloth: — *v.* to dress, as cloth, by hot pressing. [*See* Calendar, 160.]
Cal′en-dered (*-durd*), 150
Cal′en-der-ing.
Cal′en-drer.
Cal′ends (*-endz*), 136.
Cal′en-ture.
Ca-les′cence.
Cälf (*käf*) (162) [pl. Calves (*kävz*), 193.]
Cal′i-ber, *or* Cal′i-bre (*kal′i-bur*) [so Wr. Gd.]

☞ Walker and Webster give this word only in the first spelling. Smart spells it *caliber*, when it means *the bore of a gun*, and *calibre*, when it means *mental capacity*. In the first form he pronounces it *kal′i-bur*, and in the second *ka-le′br*.

Cal′ice (*-ĭs*), 169.
Cal′i-co [pl. Cal′i-coes, 192.]
[Calif, 203. — *See* Caliph.]
[Califate, 203. — *See* Caliphate.]
Cal-i-pash′, *or* Cal′i-pash [*kal-i-pash′*, Sm. Wr.; *kal′i-pash*, Wb. Gd. 155.] [Callipash. 203.]
Cal-i-pee′, *or* Cal′i-pee [*kal-i-pē′*, Sm. Wr.; *kal′i-pē*, Wb. Gd. 155.] [Callipee, 203.]
Cal′i-pers (*-purz*), 78, 136 [Callipers, 202.]
Ca′liph (*ka′lif*) [Calif, Kalif, 203.]
Cal′iph-ate [Califate, Kalifate, 203.]
Cal-is-then′ic [*not* Ca-lis′then-ic, 153.] [Callisthenic, 203.]
Cal-is-then′ics.
Cal′i-ver.

[Calix, 203. — *See* Calyx.]
Câlk (*kawk*) (148, 161, 162) [Caulk, 203.]
Călk, 161.
Câlked (*kawkt*), Note C, p. 34.
Câlk′er (*kawk′er*).
Cal′kin, *or* Câlk′in (*kal′kin*, or *kawk′in*) [so Wr.; *kal′kin*, vulgarly *kawk′in*, Sm.; *kawk′in*, Wb. Gd. 155.]
Câlk′ing(*kawk′ing*), 162.
Câll, 17, 172.
Câlled, 150.
Câll′er.
Cal-lig′ra-pher.
Cal-li-graph′ic, 109.
Cal-li-graph′ic-al, 108.
Cal-lig′ra-phist.
Cal-lig′ra-phy, 108.
Câll′ing.
Cal-li′o-pē, 170.
[Callipash, 203. — *See* Calipash.]
[Callipee, 203. — *See* Calipee.]
[Callipers, 203. — *See* Calipers.]
[Callisthenic, 203. — *See* Calisthenic.]
Cal-los′i-ty, 78, 169.
Cal′loŭs.
Cal′lōw, 170.
Cälm (*käm*), 162.
Cälmed (*kämd*), 156.
Cälm′er (*käm′-*).
Cälm′ing (*kam′-*).
Ca-log′ra-phy, 108.
Cal′o-mel.
Ca-lŏr′ic [so Wr. Wb. Gd.; *ka-lo′rik*, Sm. 155.]
Cal-o-rif′ic, 109.
Ca-lŏr-i-fĭ-ca′tion.
Cal-o-rim′e-ter, 108.
Ca-lŏr-i-mo′tor [so Gd.; *ka-lŏr′i-mo-tor*, Sm; *kal-o-ri-mo′tor*, Wr. 155.]
Cal′o-type, 170.
Ca-loy′er.
Calp, 10.
Cal′trop.
Ca-lum′ba.
Cal′u-met, 89.
Ca-lum′ni-ate, 78.
Ca-lum′ni-āt-ed, 183.
Ca-lum′ni-āt-ing.
Ca-lum-ni-a′tion, 112.
Ca-lum′ni-āt-or.
Ca-lum′ni-a-to-ry, 86.

Ca-lum'ni-oŭs.
Cal'um-ny, 93.
Cal'va-ry, 72.
Cälve (*kav*), 162.
Cälved (*kävd*), 150.
Cälv'ing (*kav'*-), 183.
Cal'vin-ism (-*izm*), 133, 136.
Cal'vin-ist.
Cal-vin-ist'ic, 109.
Cal-vin-ist'ic-al, 108.
Calx (L.) [L. pl. *Calces*; Eng. pl. Calxes, 198.]
Ca-lyç'i-nal [so Wb. Gd.; *kal-i-si'nal*, Wr. 155.]
Cal'y-cine [so Wr. Wb. Gd.; *kal'y-sin*, Sm. 155.]
Cal'y-cle (*kal'i-kl*), 164.
Cal'y-cled (*kal'i-kld*), 183
Ca-lyc'u-late.
Ca-lyc'u-lāt-ed.
Ca-lyp'tra [Calypter, 203.]
Ca-lyp'tri-form.
Ca'lyx [L. pl. *Cal'y-cēs* (-*sēz*); Eng. pl. Ca'-lyx-es, 198.]
Cam (10), *n.* a contrivance to produce alternating motion. [*See* Cham, 160.]
Ca-ma'ieu (-*ma'yoo*), 171.
Cam'ber.
Cam'ber-ing.
Cam'bi-al, 169.
Cam'bist.
Cam'bi-um.
Cam-boose' [Caboose, 203.]
[Cambrel, 203. — *See* Gambrel.]
Cam'bri-an.
Cām'bric.
Came, 23.
Cam'el, 170.
Ca-me'le-on, 169.
Ca-mel'o-pard, *or* Cam'-el-o-pard [so Wr. Gd.; *ka-mel'o-pard*, Wk.; *kam'el-o-pard*, Sm. 155.]
Cam'e-ō, 170.
Cam'e-ra.
Cam-e-ra-list'ic.
Cam-e-ra-list'ics.
Cam'er-āt-ed.
Cam-er-a'tion.
Cam-is-ade'.
Cam-i-sa'do.
Cam'i-sāt ed.
Cam'let.
[Camomile, 203.—*See* Chamomile.]
Ca'moŭs.
Camp, 10.
Cam-pag'nol.
Cam-paign' (-*pān'*), 162.
Cam-paign'er (-*pān'*-).
Cam-pan'i-form, 169.
Cam-pa-ni'lē (-*ne'lē*), 163.
Cam-pa-nil'i-form.
Cam-pa-nol'o-gist.
Cam-pa-nol'o-gy, 108.
Cam-pan'u-late.
Cam-pes'tral.
Cam-pes'tri-an.
Cam-phene' [so Wr.; *kam'fēn*, Sm. Wb. Gd. 155.]
Cam'pho-gen.
Cam'phor.
Cam'phor-ate.
Cam'phor-āt-ed.
Cam'phor-āt-ing.
Cam'pi-on, 169.
Can (10), *n.* a vessel for liquor:—*v.* to be able. [*See* Khan, 160.]
Ca'naan-īte (-*nan*-), 171.
Ca-naan-īt'ish (-*nan*-),
Ca-na'di-an, 169. [183.
Canaille (Fr.) (*ka-nä'il*) [so Sm.; *ka-nāl'*, Wk. Wr. 154, 155.]
Can'a-kin.
Ca-nal'.
[Canal-coal, 203. — *See* Cannel-coal.]
Can-a-lic'u-late.
Can-a-lic'u-lāt-ed.
Ca-na'ry.
Can'cel.
Can'cel-late.
Can'cel-lāt-ed.
Can-cel-la'tion, 112.
Can'celled (-*seld*) [Canceled, Wb. Gd. 203. — *See* 177, and Note E, p. 70.]
Can'cel-ling [Canceling, Wb. Gd. 203.]
Can'cer.
Can'cer-ate.
Can'cer-āt-ed.
Can-cer-a'tion.
Can'cer-īte.
Can'cer-oŭs.
Can'cri-form (*kang'*-), 54
Can'crīne (*kang'*-).
Can'crite (*kang'*-).
Can-de-la'brum (L.) [L. pl. *Can-de-la'bra*; Eng. pl. Can-de-la'-brums, 198.]
Can'dent.
Can-des'cence, 171.
Can'did, *a.* honest. [*See* Candied, 160.]
Can'di-da-cy, 171.
Can'di-date, 78, 169.
Can'died (-*did*), *a.* incrusted with sugar. [*See* Candid, 160.]
Can'dle, 164.
Can'dle-mas, 180.
Can'dor [Candour, Sm. 199, 203.]
Can'dy, 93.
Cane, 23.
Caned, 150, 183.
Ca-nic'u-lar.
Can'i-cule.
Ca-nine', 121, 156.
Cān'ing, 183.
Can'is-ter, 170.
Can'ker (*kang'*-), 54.
Can'kered (*kang'kurd*), 150.
Can'ker-ing (*kang'*-).
Can'ker-oŭs (*kang'*-).
Can'ker-rash, 206, Exc. 1.
Can'ker-y (*kang'*-).
Can'nel-coal [Canal-coal, 203.]
Can'ni-bal, 78, 170.
Can'ni-bal-ism (-*izm*).
Can'non (170), *n.* a great gun. [*See* Canon, 160.]
Can-non-ade', *n.* & *v.*
Can-non-ād'ed, 183.
Can-non-ād'ing.
Can-non-eer', *or* Can-non-iēr', 122.
Can'not, 170.

☞ According to Webster and Worcester it would be more analogical to write *can* and *not* separately. But to join them is more consistent with their usual pronunciation as a simple word (*can'ot*), the two *n's* having the effect described in § 66.

Can'nu-lar, 89.
Can'ny, 93, 170.
Ca-noe' (-*noo'*), 19.
Can'on (170), *n.* a rule or law. [*See* Cannon, 160.]
Cañon (*kan'yun*) (Sp.), *n.* a deep gorge worn by a water-course. [*See Canon*, 161.] [Canyon, 203.]
Can'on-ess, 170.
Ca-non'ic, 109.

Ca-non′ic-al, 108.
Ca-non′i-cāte, 73.
Can′on-ist.
Can-on-ist′ic, 109.
Can-on-ī-za′tion, 112.
Can′on-ize, 203.
Can′on-ized, 150, 183.
Can′on-īz-ing.
Can′o-pīed (-*pīd*), 99.
Can′o-py, 93, 170.
Can′o-py-ing, 186.
Ca-no′roŭs, 125.
Cant, 10.
Can-ta′bri-an.
Can ta-brig′i-an(-*brij′*-).
[Cantaliver, 203. — *See* Cantilever.]
Can′ta-loupe (-*loop*).
[Cantaleup, 203.]
Can-tan′ker-oŭs (-*tang′*-).
Can-ta′ta, or *Can-tä′ta* (It.) [so Wr.; *kan-ta′-ta*, Wk. Sm.; *kan-ta′-ta*, Gd. 155.]
Can-ta-tri′ce (It.) (-*ta-trē′chē*) [so Wr.; *kan′-ta-tris*, Gd. 155.]
Cant′ed.
Can-teen′, 121.
Can′tel [Cantle, 203.]
[Canteliver, 203. — *See* Cantilever.]
Can′ter.
Can′ter-bur-y (-*bĕr-y*).
Can′tered, 150.
Can′ter-ing.
Can′tha-ris (Gr.) [pl. *Can-thăr′i-dēs* (-*dēz*), 198.]
Can′ti-cle, 164.
Can′ti-late [Cantillate, 203.]
Can-ti-la′tion [Cantillation, 203.]
Can′ti-le-ver [so Wr.; *kan-ti-le′vur*, Sm.; *kan′ti-lev ur*, Gd. 155.] [Cantaliver, Canteliver, Cantiliver, 203.]
Cant′ing.
Can′tle (164) [Cantel, 203.]
Can′to [pl. Can′tōs (-*tōz*), 192.]
Can′ton.
Can′ton-al.
Can′toned (-*tund*), 150.
Can′ton-ing.
Can′ton-ize, 202.
Can′ton-ment.
Can′vas, *n.* a coarse cloth of hemp or of flax. [*See* Canvass, 160.]
Can′vass, *v.* to examine: — to discuss: — to solicit votes. [*See* Canvas, 160.]
Can′vassed, 150.
Can′vass-er.
Can′vass-ing.
Ca′ny, 93.
Can′yon [Cañon, 203.]
Can-zo′nē (It.), 163.
Can-zo-net′.
Caout′chouc(*koo′chŏŏk*) [so Sm. Wr.; *koo′-chook*, Wb. Gd. 155.]
Caout′chou-sĭne (*koo′-choo-sin*).
Cap, 10.
Ca-pa-bil′i-ty, 108, 169.
Ca′pa-ble, 164.
Ca-pa′cious (-*shus*), 112.
Ca-paç′i-tate.
Ca-paç′i-tāt-ed, 183.
Ca-paç′i-tāt-ing.
Ca-paç′i-ty, 108, 169.
Ca-păr′i-son, 78, 169.
Ca-păr′i-soned (-*sund*), 150.
Ca-păr′i-son-ing.
Cape, 23.
Cap′e-lon, 169.
Ca-pel′la, 170.
Cap′el-let [so Wb. Gd.; *kap′el-et*, or *ka-pel′et*, Wr. 155.]
Ca′per.
Ca′pered (-*purd*), 150.
Ca′per-er.
Ca′per-ing.
Cap-il-laire′ (-*lêr*), 154.
Ca-pil′la-ment.
Cap-il-lăr′i-ty, 170.
Cap′il-la-ry, *or* Ca-pil′-la-ry [so Wr. Gd.; *kap′il-a-ry*, Wk. Sm. 155.]
Ca-pil′li-form, 78, 169.
Cap′i-tal, *a.* (169) relating to the head: — *n.* the upper part of a pillar. [*See* Capitol, 160.]
Cap′i-tal-ist.
Cap′i-tate.
Cap-ĭ-ta′tion.
Cap′i-tol, *n.* a public edifice for a legislative body. [*See* Capital, 160.]
Cap-ĭ-to′li-an.
Cap′i-tol-ĭne.
Ca-pit′u-lar, 89.
Ca-pit′u-la-ry, 72.
Ca-pit′u-late.
Ca-pit′u-lāt-ed, 183.
Ca-pit′u-lāt-ing.
Ca-pit-u-la′tion.
Ca-pit′u-lāt-or.
Ca-pit′u-lum.
Ca-pi′vi (-*pe′vē*) [Copaiba, 203. — *See* Copaiba.]
Cap′lin.
Cap′no-man-cy.
Cap′no-mor.
Ca′pon (*ka′pn*), 149.
Ca-poch′ (-*pooch′*) [Capouch, 203.]
Caponniere (Fr.) (*kap-o-nēr′*) [Caponiere, 203.]
Ca-pot′.
Ca-pote′.
Ca-pouch′(-*pooch′*)[Capoch, 203.]
Capped (*kapt*), 176, Note C, p. 34.
Cap′per, 176.
Cap′ping.
Ca-pre′o-late [so Wr.; *ka′pre-o-lāt*, Sm.; *kap′re-o-lāt*, Wb. Gd. 155.]
Ca-price′(-*prēs′*) [so Sm. Wr. Wb. Gd.; *ka-prēs′*, or *kap′rēs*, Wk. 155.]
Ca-prĭ′cious (-*prish′us*), 112, 231, Exc.
Cap′ri-corn, 78, 169.
Cap′rid.
Cap-rĭ-fi-ca′tion.
Cap′ri-form.
Ca-prig′e-noŭs (-*prij′*-).
Cap′rĭne, *or* Ca′prĭne, [so Wr.; *kap′rin*, Gd.; *kā′prīn*, Sm. 155.]
Cap′ri-ole [so Wr. Wb. Gd.; *ka′pri-ōl*, Sm. 155.]
Cap′ro-mȳs.
Cap′si-cum, 78, 169.
Cap-size′, *v.*
Cap′size, *n.*
Cap′stan.
Cap′su-lar, 72, 89.
Cap′su-la-ry, 72.
Cap′su-late, 73.
Cap′su-lāt-ed.
Cap′sule.
Cap′taĭn (-*tin*), 96.
Cap′taĭn-cy (-*tin*-), 169.
Cap′tion.
Cap′tioŭs (-*shus*).

Cap′ti-vate, 73.
Cap′ti-vāt-ed, 183.
Cap′ti-vāt-ing.
Cap-ti-va′tion.
Cap′tĭve, 84.
Cap-tiv′i-ty, 108, 169.
Cap′tor, 88.
Capt′ure (*-yur*), 91.
Capt′ured (*-yurd*), 150, 183.
Capt′ur-ing (*-yur-*), 91.
Cap-u-chin′ (*-shēn′*), 46.
Cap′u-let.
Car, 11.
Căr′a-bīne [so Wb. Gd.; *kar′a-bin*, Wr. 155.] [Carbine, 203.]
Căr-a-bi-neer′, 122.
Căr′ack [Carac, 203.]
Căr′a-căl, 170.
Căr′a-cole [Caracol, 203.]
Căr′a-co-ly [Caracoli, 203.]
[Caragheen, 203.—*See* Carrageen.]
Căr′a-mel [Caromel, 203.]
Căr′at, *n.* a weight of four grains. [*See* Carrot, 160.]
Căr-a-van′, *or* Căr′a-van (170) [*kăr-a-van′*, Wk. Sm. Wr.; *kăr′a-van*, Wb. Gd. 155.]
Căr-a-van-eer′.
Căr-a-van′sa-ry (72) [Caravansera, 203.]
Căr′a-vel [Carvel, 203.]
Căr′a-wāy (170) [Carraway, 203.]
Car′bīne [so Sm. Gd.; *kar-bīn′*, Wk.; *kar′-bīn*, or *kar-bīn′*, Wr. 155.][Carabine, 203]
Car-bi-neer′.
Car′bŏn.
Car-bon-a′ceous (*-shus*), 112.
Car′bon-ate, 73.
Car′bon-āt-ed.
Car-bon′ic, 109.
Car-bon-if′er-ous, 108.
Car-bon-i-za′tion.
Car′bon-ize, 202.
Car′bon-ized, 150, 183.
Car′bon-īz-ing.
Car′boy.
Car′bun-cle (*-bung-kl*), 54
Car′bun-cled (*-bung-kld*)
Car-bun′cu-lar (*-bung′-*).
Car-bun-cu-la′tion (*-bung-*).
Car′bu-ret-ted [Carbureted, Wb. Gd. 203.]
Car′ca-jou (*-joo*).
Car′ca-net.
Car′cass [Carcase, 203.]
Car-ci-no′ma.
Car-ci-nom′a-toŭs.
Card, 11.
Car′da-mīne, 152.
Car′da-mom.
Card′ed.
Card′er.
Car′di-a.
Car′di-ac, 78.
Car-di′ac-al (108) [so Wk. Wr. Wb. Gd.; *kar′di-ak-al*, Sm. 155.]
Car-di-ag′ra-phy, 108.
Car-di-al′gi-a.
Car′di-al-gy.
Car′di-nal, 78, 169.
Car′di-nal-ate.
Card′ing.
Car′di-oid.
Car-di-ol′o-gy, 108.
Car-di′tis.
Car-doon′, 121.
Care (*kêr*), 14.
Cared (*kêrd*), 165, 183.
Ca-reen′.
Ca-reen′age, 169.
Ca-reened, 150.
Ca-reen′ing.
Ca-reer′, 171.
Care′ful (*kêr′fo͝ol*).
Ca-ress′.
Ca-ressed′ (*ka-rest′*), Note C, p. 34.
Ca-ress′ing.
Ca′ret, 49, N.
Care′wōrn (*kêr′-*).
Car′go [pl. Car′goes, 192.]
Car′goose.
Căr′ib.
Căr-ib-be′an, 110.
Căr′i-bou (*-boo*) (Fr.) [Cariboo, 203.]
Căr′i-ca-ture, *n.* (161) [so Sm. Wr. Wb. Gd.; *kăr-i-ka-tūr′*, Sm.; *kăr-i-ka-chūr′*, Wk. 134, 155.]
Căr-i-ca-ture′, *v.* 122, 161.
Căr-i-ca-tured′, 165, 183.
Căr-i-ca-tūr′ing.
Căr-i-ca-tūr′ist.
Căr-i-cog′ra-phy, 108.
Căr′i-coŭs, 170.
Ca′ri-ēs (*-ēz*), 171.
Căr′il-lon [so Wb. Gd.; *ka-ril′on*, Wr. 155.]
Căr′i-nate, 169.
Căr′i-nāt-ed.
Car′ing (*kêr′-*), 183.
Căr′i-ole.
[Cariopsis, 203.—*See* Caryopsis.]
Ca-ri-os′i-ty, 108, 169.
Ca′ri-oŭs, 78.
Car′lings (*-lingz*), *n. pl.*
Car′lock.
Car-lo-vin′gi-an.
Car′man, 196.
Car′mel-ite, 83.
Car-min′a-tĭve, 84, 170.
Car′mīne, *or* Car-mīne′ [so Wr.; *kar′mīn*, Wb. Gd.; *kar-mīn′*, Wk. Sm. 155.]
Car′nage, 169.
Car′nal.
Car-nal′i-ty, 108.
Car-na′tion, 112.
Car-na′tioned (*-shund*).
Car-nĕl′ian (*-yan*), 51.
Car′ne-oŭs.
Car′ney, 98, 169.
Car-ni-fi-ca′tion.
Car′ni-fīed, 186.
Car′ni-fȳ, 78, 94.
Car′ni-fȳ-ing.
Car′ni-val, 169.
Car-niv′o-ra, *n. pl.*
Car-niv′o-roŭs, 108.
Car-nose′.
Car-nos′i-ty, 108, 169.
Căr′ol, 170.
Căr-o-lin′i-an, 169.
Căr′olled (*-uld*) (150) [Caroled, Wb. Gd. 203.]
Căr′ol-ling [Caroling, Wb. Gd. 203.]
Căr-o-lyt′ic [Carolitic, 203.]
[Caromel, 203.—*See* Caramel.]
Ca-rot′id, 170.
Ca-rous′al (*-rouz′-*), 72.
Ca-rouse′ (*-rouz′*).
Carp, 11.
Car′pal, 72.
Car-pa′thi-an.
Carped (*karpt*), Note C, p. 34.
Car′pel.
Car′pel-la-ry, 72.
Car-pel′lum, 170.
Car′pen-ter.
Car′pen-try, 93.
Carp′er.
Car′pet.

Car′pet-ed.
Car′pet-ing.
Car-phol′o-gy.
Carp′ing.
Car′po-lite, 83.
Ca-pol′o-gist, 108.
Car-pol′o-gy, 108.
Căr′ra-geen (-ghēn) [Carragheen, 203.]
[Carraway, 203.—*See* Caraway.]
Căr′rel.
Căr′riage (-rij), 169, 171.
Căr′ried, 99, 186.
Căr′ri-er, 170.
Căr′ri-on, 170.
Căr′rom.
Căr′ron-ade.
Căr′rot (170), *n.* a plant. [*See* Ca′rat, 160.]
Căr′rot-y, 93.
Căr′ry, 170.
Căr′ry-âll, 206, Exc. 3.
Căr′ry-ing.
Cart, 11.
Cart′age.
Carte-blanche′ (*kart-blongsh′*) [so Sm.; *kart-blänsh′*, Wk.; *kärt-blänch′*, Wr.; *kärt-blänsh′*, Gd. 154, 155.]
Cart′ed.
Car-tel′, *n.* [so Wk. Sm. Wr.; *kar-tel′*, or *kar′-tel*, Gd. 155.]
Cart′er.
Car-te′sian (-zhan), 112.
Car-tha-gin′i-an.
Car′tha-mine, 82.
Car-thu′sian (-zhan).
Car′ti-lage, 169.
Car-ti-lag′i-noŭs (-laj′-).
Cart′ing.
Car-tog′ra-pher, 108.
Car-to-graph′ic.
Car-to-graph′ic-al.
Car-tog′ra-phy.
Car-toon′, 121.
Car-touch′ (-tooch′), 121.
Car′tridge (-trij), 169,
Cart′u-la-ry, 72. [171.
Căr′u-cage.
Căr′u-cate.
Căr′un-cle (-ung-kl), 54.
Ca-run′cu-lar (-rung′-).
Ca-run′cu-late (-rung′-).
Ca-run′cu-lāt-ed (-rung′-).
Ca-run′cu-loŭs (-rung′).
Carve, 11.
Carved, 165, 183.
Car′vel [Caravel, 203]
Carv′er, 77.
Carv′ing.
Căr-y-a′tēs (-tēz), *n. pl.*
Căr-y-at′ic, 109.
Căr-y-at′id.
Căr-y-at′i-dēs (-dēz), *n. pl.* 171.
Căr-y-oph-yl-la′ceous (-of-il-a′shus), 171.
Căr-y-o-phyl′loŭs, *or* Căr-y-oph′yl-lous [*See* Adenophyllous.]
Căr-y-op′sis, *or* Că-ry-op′sis [so Wr.; *kar-y-op′sis*, Sm.; *kā-ry-op′sis*, Gd. 155.]
Ca′sal.
Cas′ca-bel.
Cas-cade′, 121.
Cas-ca-ril′la, 170.
Case, 23.
Cased (*kāst*), 150, 183, Note C, p. 34.
Case′hard-en (-hard-n).
Case′hard-ened (-hard-nd), 165.
Case′hard-en-ing (-hard-n-), 149.
Ca′se-ïne [Casein, 203]
Case′mate.
Case′māt-ed.
Case′ment (*kāz′ment*, or *kās′ment*) [*kāz′ment*, Wk. Sm. Wr.; *kās′-ment*, Wb. Gd. 155.]
Ca′se-oŭs [so Wb. Gd.; *ka′se-us*, or *ka′she-us*, Wr.; *ka′sh′us*, Sm. 26, 155.]
Ca′sern (-zurn), 136, 171.
Cash (10), *n.* ready money. [*See* Cache, 160.]
Cashed (*kasht*), Note C, p. 34.
Ca-shew′ (*ka-shoo′*), *or* Cash′ew (*kash′oo*) [*ka-shoo′*, Wk. Sm.; *ka-shu′*, or *kash′u*, Wr.; *kash′u*, Wb. Gd. 155.]
Cash-iēr′ (*kash-ēr′*), *n.* [so Wb. Gd.; *ka-shēr′*, Wk. Sm. Wr. 155.]
Ca-shiēr′ (*ka-shēr′*), *v.* [Wk. Sm. Wr.; *kash-ēr′*, Wb. Gd. 155.]
Ca-shiēred′ (-shērd′), 150.
Ca-shiēr′ing (-shēr′-).
Cash′mere (171) [so Wb. Gd.; *kash′mēr*, or *kash-mēr′*, Wr. 155.]
Cash′oo.
Cās′ing.
Càsk (12, 131) [Casque (in the sense of *a helmet*), 203.]
Càsk′et.
Cas′pi-an, 78.
Casque (Fr.) (*kàsk*) [Cask, 203.]
Cas′sa-da, *or* Cas-sa′da [*kas′a-da*, Wk. Sm. Wb. Gd.; *kas-a′da*, or *kas′a da*, Wr. 155.] [Cassava, Cassavi, 203.]
Cas-sa′tion.
Cas′sa-va, *or* Cas-sa′va [*kas′a-va*, Gd.; *kas-a′va*, or *kas′a-va*, Wr. 155.] [203.]
[Cassada, Cassavi,
Cas′sia (*kash′ya*) [so Sm. Wb. Gd.; *kash′-she-a*, Wk. Wr. 155.]
Cas-sid′e-oŭs.
Cas′si-do-ny, 170.
Cas′si-mere [so Wr. Wb. Gd.; *kas-i-mēr′*, Sm. 155.]
Cas-si-o-pe′a, 169, 170.
Cas′sock, 170.
Cas′socked (-sokt).
Caṣ-son-ade′ [so Gd.; *kas′on-ād*, Wr. 155.]
Cas′so-wā-ry, 170.
Càst (12, 131), *v.* to throw: — *n.* a throw. [*See* Caste, 160.]
Cas-ta′li-an, 169.
Cas-ta-net′, *or* Cas′ta-net [*kas-ta-net′*, Sm.; *kas′-ta-net*, Wk. Wr. Wb. Gd. 155.]
Càst′a-way.
Càste (*kàst*) *n.* class. [*See* Cast, 160.]
Cas′tel-lan, 170.
Cas′tel-la-ny, 72.
Cas′tel-lāt-ed.
Càst′er.
Cas′ti-gate, 78, 169.
Cas′ti-gāt-ed, 183.
Cas′ti-gāt-ing.
Cas-ti-ga′tion.
Cas′ti-gāt-or.
Cas′ti-ga-to-ry.
Cas-til′ian (-til′yan).
Càst′ing.
Càst′-ī-ron (-ī-urn).
Cas′tle (*kas′l*), 162, 154.
Cas′tled (*kas′ld*).
Cas′tle-ry (*kas′l-ry*).
Càst′ling.
Càs′tor, 88.
Càs-to′re-um, 169.

Căs′to-rīne [Castorin, 203.]
Cas′tor-oil, 206, Exc. 3.
Cas-tra-me-ta′tion.
Căs′trate.
Căs′trăt-ed.
Căs′trāt-ing.
Căs-tra′tion.
Căs′trel [Kestrel, 203]
Cas′u-al (kazh′-), 47.
Cas′u-al-ty (kazh′-), 171.
Cas′u-ist (kazh′-).
Cas-u-ist′ic (kazh-), 109.
Cas-u-ist′ic-al (kazh-), 108.
Cas′u-ist-ry (kazh′-), 171
Cat, 10.
Cat-a-câus′tic.
Cat-a-chre′sis (-kre′-).
Cat-a-chres′tic (-kres′-).
Cat-a-chres′tic-al.
Cat′a-clysm(-klizm),136.
Cat′a-cōmb (-kōm), 162.
Cat-a-cous′tics, 28.
Cat-a-di-op′tric.
Cat-a-di-op′tric′al.
Cat′a-drome.
Cat-a-fal′co (It.).
Cat-a-falque′ (Fr.) (-falk′).
Cat-ag-mat′ic.
Cat′a-grăph, 127.
Cat′a-lan.
Cat-a-lec′tic, 109.
Cat-a-lep′sis.
Cat′a-lep-sy, 169.
Cat-a-lep′tic.
Cat′a-lŏgue, 87.
Cat′a-lŏgued (-logd),150.
Cat′a-lŏgu-ing (-log-), 183.
Cat-a-lo′ni-an, 169.
Ca-tal′pa, 72.
Ca-tal′y-sis, 171.
Cat-a-lyt′ic, 109.
Cat-a-ma-ran′, 122.
Cat-a-me′ni-a.
Cat-a-me′ni-al.
Cat′a-mite.
Cat′a-mount.
Cat-an-ad′ro-moŭs.
Cat′a-pasm (-pazm), 136.
Cat-a-pelt′ic.
Cat-a-pet′a-loŭs.
Cat-a-phon′ics.
Cat′a-phract, 35.
Cat′a-phract-ed.
Cat-a-phract′ic.
Cat′a-plasm(-plazm),136
Cat′a-pult.
Cat-a-pult′ic, 109.
Cat′a-răct.
Cat-a-ract′oŭs.
Ca-tärrh′ (-tär′),162, 171.
Ca-tärrh′al (-tär′-).
Cat′ar-rhīne, 162.
Ca-tärrh′oŭs (-tär′-).
Cat-a-stalt′ic.
Ca-tas′ter-ism (-izm).
Ca-tas′tro-phē, 163, 169.
Ca-taw′ba.
Cat′câll.
Catch, 10, 44, Note D, p. [37.
Catched (kacht).
Catch′er.
Catch′fly, 206.
Catch′ing.
Catch′pen-ny. [203.]
Catch′up [Catsup,
Cat-e-chet′ic (-ket′-),171.
Cat-e-chet′ic-al (-ket′-).
Cat′e-chīne (-kin).
Cat′e-chise (-kīz) (169) [Catechize, 202,203]
Cat′e-chised (-kīzd), 183.
Cat′e-chīs′er (-kīz′-)
Cat′e-chīs-ing (-kīz-).
Cat′e-chism (-kizm), 136.
Cat-e-chis′mal (-kiz′-).
Cat′e-chist (-kist).
Cat-e-chist′ic, 109.
Cat-e-chist′ic-al, 108.
Cat′e-chu (-ku).
Cat-e-chu′men (-ku′-).
Cat-e-chu-men′ic (-ku-).
Cat-e-chu-men′ic-al (-ku-).
Cat-e-gŏr-e-mat′ic.
Cat-e-gŏr′ic-al.
Cat′e-go-ry, 171.
Cat-e-na′ri-an, 169.
Cat′e-na-ry, 72.
Cat-e-na′tion.
Ca′ter.
Ca′tered, 165.
Ca′ter-er.
Ca′ter-ing.
Cat′er-pil-lar, 170, 171.
Cat′er-wâul.
Cat′er-wâuled, 165.
Cat′er-wâul-ing.
Cātes, *n. pl.*
Cat′fish, 206.
Cat′gut. [*n. pl.*
Cat′harp-ings (-ingz),
Ca-thar′sis.
Ca-thar′tic.
Ca-thar′tic-al.
Ca-thar′tīne [Cathartin, 203.]
Cat′hĕad.
Ca-the′dra, or *Cath′e-dra* (L.) [so Wr.; *kath′e-dra*, Wb. Gd. 155.] [*See* Ex cathedra.]
Ca-the′dral.
Cath′e-ter, 169.
Cath-e-tom′e-ter, 108.
Cath′ode [so Sm. Wr.; *kat′ōd*, Gd. 155.]
Cath′o-lic, 109.
Ca-thol′i-cism (-sizm) [so Wk. Sm.; *ka-thol′-i-sizm*, or *kath′o-li-sizm*, Gd. 155.]
Cath-o-liç′i-ty, 169, 171.
Ca-thol′i-con.
Cat′i-lin-ism (-izm), 171.
Cat′kin.
Cat′ling.
Cat′mint.
Cat′nip.
Ca-to′ni-an, 169.
Ca-top′ter.
Ca-top′tric, 169.
Ca-top′tric-al, 108.
Ca-top′tro-man-cy.
Ca-top′tron.
Cat′stick, 206.
Cat′sup [Catchup, 203.]
Cat′tish, 176.
Cat′tle (kat′tl), 164.
Câu-ca′sian (-shan).
Câu′cus, 169.
Câu′dal.
Câu′date, 73.
Câu′dăt-ed.
Câu′dle, 164.
Câu′dled (kaw′dld), 150.
Câu′dling.
Câuf, 17.
[Caufle, 203. — *See* Coffle.]
Câught (kawt), 162.
Câuk, *n.* [Cawk, 203.]
Câul (17), *n.* a membrane covering the intestines. [*See* Call, 160.]
Câu-les′cent.
Câu′li-cle, 164.
Câu′li-cule, 78.
Câu-lif′er-ous, 108.
Câu′li-flow-er.
Câu′li-form, 169.
Câu′līne (84) [Caulin, 203.]
[Caulk, 203. — *See* Calk.]
Câu′sal (-zal), 136.
Câu-sal′i-ty (-zal′-), 108.
Câu′sal-ty (-zal-).
Câu-sa′tion (-za′-).
Câu′sa-tīve (-za-).
Câuse (kawz), 17.
Câused (kawzd),150,183.
Câus′er (kawz′-).
Câu′sey (kaw′zy), 98.

Câuse′wāy (*kawz′-*).
Câu′seyed (*kaw′zid*).
Câu-sid′ic-al (*-zid′-*).
Câus′ing (*kawz′-*).
Câus′tic.
Câus-tiç′i-ty, 171.
Câu′ter-ant.
Câu′ter-ism (*-izm*).
Câu-ter-i-za′tion.
Câu′ter-ize, 202.
Câu′ter-ized, 150, 183.
Câu′ter-īz-ing.
Câu′ter-y.
Câu′tion.
Câu′tion-a-ry, 72.
Câu′tioned (*-shund*), 150.
Câu′tion-er.
Câu′tion-ing.
Câu′tioŭs (*-shus*).
Cav-al-cade′ [so Wk. Sm. Wr.; *kav′al-kād*, Wb. Gd. 155.]
Cav-al-iēr′, 114, 122, 169.
Cav′al-ry.
Ca-vass′ (Turkish), 121.
Cave, 23.
Ca′ve-at.
Caved, 150, 183.
Căv′er.
Cav′ern.
Cav′erned (*-urnd*).
Cav′ern-oŭs.
Cav′es-son (170) [C a v - e z o n, 203.]
Ca-vet′to.
[C a v e z o n, 203. — *See* Cavesson.]
Ca-viare′ (*ka-vēr′*, or *kav-yēr′*) [so Wr.; *ka-vēr′*, Wk. Gd.; *kav-yēr′*, Sm.]

☞ Goodrich gives also the form C a v i a r, which he pronounces *kav′i-ar*.

Cav′i-corn.
Cav′il, 170.
Cav′illed (150) [C a v - i l e d, Wb. Gd. 203. — *See* 177 and Note E, p. 70.]
Cav′il-ler [C a v i l e r, Wb. Gd. 177, 203.]
Cav′il-ling [C a v i l - i n g, Wb. Gd. 177, 203.]
Cav′in, 170.
Căv′ing, 183.
Cav′i-ty, 78, 108, 169.
Ca′vy, 93.
Caw, 17.
Cawed, 150.
Caw′ing.
Cawk [C a u k, 203.]
Cax′ou (*kaks′oo*).
Cāy-enne′ (*kā-ĕn′*) [so Wr. Wb. Gd.; *kā-yĕn′*, Sm. 155.]
Cay′man (196) [C a i - m a n, 203.]
Ca-zique′ (*-zēk′*) [C a - z i c, 203.]
Cēase (*sēs*), 13.
Cēased (*sēst*), 150, 183.
Cēas′ing.
Cec-chin′ (*che-kēn′*) [C h e q u i n, S e - q u i n, C e c h i n, 203.]
Ce′ci-ty [so Sm. Wb. Gd.; *ses′i-ty*, Wk.; *ses′i-ty*, or *se′si-ty*, Wr. 155.]
Ce′dar, *n.* a genus of trees. [*See* Ceder, 160.]
Ce′dared (*-dard*), 150.
Ce′darn.
Cede, *v.* to yield. [*See* Seed, *and* Seid, 160.]
Cēd′er, *n.* one who cedes, or yields. [*See* Cedar, 160.]
Ce-dil′la, 170.
Cēd′ing, 183.
Ce′drat.
Ce′drīne [so Sm. Wr. Gd.; *se′drin*, Wk. 155.]
Ce′dry.
Cēil, *v.* to cover, as the upper surface of an apartment. [*See* Seal, *and* Seel, 160.]
Cēil′ing, *n.* the upper surface of an apartment. [*See* Sealing, 160.]
Cel′an-dīne, 152.
Cel′a-ture.
Cel′e-brate, 169.
Cel′e-brāt-ed, 183.
Cel′e-brāt-ing.
Cel-e-bra′tion, 112.
Cel′e-brāt-or.
Ce-leb′ri-ty.
Ce-le′ri-ac.
Ce-lĕr′i-ty, 108, 169.
Cel′er-y, 233.
Ce-lest′ial (*-lest′yal*).
Cel′es-tīn, *n.* one of an order of monks. [*See* Celestine, 160.] [C e l - e s t i n e, Wr. 203.]
Cel′es-tīne [so Wr. Wb. Gd.; *se-les′tin*, Sm. 155.] *n.* sulphate of strontia. [*See* Celestin, 160.] [C e l e s t i n, 203.]
[C e l i a c, 203. — *See* Cœliac.]
Cel′i-ba-cy (169) [so Wk. Sm. Wr.; *sel′i-ba-cy*, or *se-lib′a-cy*, Gd. 155.]
Cel′i-bate, *n.* & *a.* 169.
Cel-i-dog′ra-phy, 108.
Cell, *n.* a small apartment. [*See* Sell, 160.]
Cel′lar (170), *n.* a room under a house. [*See* Seller, 160.]
Cel′lar-age, 169.
Cel′lar-et.
Cel′lar-ist.
Cel′lu-lar, 74, 89, 108.
Cel′lu-lāt-ed.
Cel′lule.
Cel-lu-lif′er-oŭs, 108.
Cel′lu-līne, 82.
Cel′lu-lose.
Celt, 15.
Celt-i-be′ri-an.
Celt′ic.
Celt′i-cism (*-sizm*).
Celt′ish.
Cem′ent, *or* Ce-ment′, *n.* [*sem′ent*, Wr. Wb. Gd.; *se-ment′*, Sm.; *se′ment*, Wk. 155.]
Ce-ment′, *v.*
Cem-en-ta′tion.
Ce-ment′a-to-ry.
Ce-ment′ed.
Ce-ment′er.
Ce-ment′ing.
Cem-en-ti′tious (*-tish′-us*), 169.
Cem-e-te′ri-al.
Cem′e-ter-y, 171.
Cen′a-to-ry [so Wk. Wr. Wb. Gd.; *se′na-tur-y*, Sm. 155.]
Cen′o-bite, 171.
Cen-o-bit′ic, 109.
Cen-o-bit′ic-al, 108.
Cen′o-bit-ism (*-izm*).
Cen-o′bi-um, 169.
Ce′no-by [so Sm. Wb. Gd.; *se′no-by*, or *sen′-o-by*, Wr. 155.]
Cen′o-taph, 35, 127, 171.
Cense, *v.* to perfume. [*See* Sense, 160.]
Censed (*senst*), 150, 183.
Cen′ser, *n.* a vessel for burning incense. [*See* Censor, 160.]
Cens′ing.
Cen′sor (88), *n.* a censurer. [*See* Censer, 160.]
Cen-so′ri-al, 49, N.

Cen-so′ri-oŭs, 169.
Cen′su-al, *a.* relating to a census. [*See* Sensu-al, 160.] [164.
Cen′sur-a-ble (*-shur-*),
Cen′sure (*-shur.*)
Cen′sured (*-shurd*).
Cen′sur-er (*-shur*).
Cen′sur-ing (*-shur-*).
Cen′sus.
Cent, *n.* a hundredth part of a dollar. [*See* Scent, and Sent, 160.]
Cent′age.
Cen′tâur, 171.
Cen′tâu-ry, 171.
Cen-te-na′ri-an, 169.
Cen-te-na′ri-oŭs.
Cen′te-na-ry, 72.
Cen-ten′ni-al, 169, 170.
Cen-tes′i-mal, 78.
Cen-tes-i-ma′tion.
Cen-ti-cip′i-toŭs, 169.
Cen-tif′i-doŭs.
Cen-ti-fo′li-oŭs.
Cen′ti-grade, 169.
Cen′ti-gramme (Fr.).
Cen-ti-li′tre (Fr.) (*säng-ti-le′tr*) [Centiliter (*sen-til′i-tur*), Wb. Gd. 203.]
Cen′time (Fr.) (*säng-tēm′*).
Cen-tim′e-ter, 108.
Cen-ti-mètre(Fr.) (*säng-ti-ma′tr*).
Cen′ti-ped [Centipede (*sen′ti-pēd*), [203.]
Cent′ner.
Cen′to [pl. Cen′tos, 192]
Cen′to-nism (*-nizm*),136
Cen′tral, 72.
Cen′tral-ism (*-izm*), 133.
Cen-tral′i-ty, 108, 169.
Cen-tral-i-za′tion.
Cen′tral-ize, 202.
Cen′tral-ized, 183.
Cen′tral-īz-ing.
Cen′tre (164) [Center, Wb. Gd. 203. — *See* Note E, p. 70.]
Cen′tred (*-terd*),164,183.
Cen′tric.
Cen′tric-al.
Cen-tric′i-ty, 169.
Cen-trif′u-gal, 89, 170.
Cen′tring.
Cen-trip′e-tal, 169.
Cen-tro-băr′ic.
Cen-tum′vir (L.) [pl. *Cen-tum′vi-rī*, 198.]
Cen-tum′vi-rate.
Cen′tu-ple, 164.

Cen-tu′ri-al.
Cen-tu′ri-on, 49, N.; 169.
Cen′tu-ry, 171.
Ceph-a-lal′gic, 109.
Ceph′a-lăl-gy.
Ce-phal′ic, *a.* & *n.*
Ceph-a-li′tis.
Ceph-a-lol′o-gy, 169.
Ce-phal′o-pod [so Sm. Wr.; *sef-al′o-pod*, Gd. 155.]
Ceph-al-o-pod′ic.
Ceph-a-lop′o-doŭs.
Ce′pheŭs (*-fūs*) [so Wr.; *se-fe′us*, Wb. Gd. 155.]
Ce-ra′ceous (*-shus*), 112.
Ce-ram′ic, 109, 170.
Cĕr′a-sīne [Cerasin, 203.]
Cĕr′a-sīte, 83, 152.
Ce′rate.
Ce-rāt′ed, 183.
Cĕr′a-trīne [Ceratrin, 203.]
Cer-be′re-an, 110, 169.
Cer′be-rus (L.).
Cēre, *n.* the naked skin that covers the base of the bill of some birds: — *v.* to cover with wax. [*See* Sear, Seer, Sere, 160.]
Ce′re-al, 49, N.; 169.
Cĕr-e-bel′lum (L.) [pl. *Cĕr-e-bel′la.*]
Cĕr′e-bral, 156.
Cĕr′e-brum (L.).
Cere′cloth, 206.
Cere′ment, 171.
Cĕr-e-mo′ni-al, 169.
Cĕr-e-mo′ni-oŭs.
Cĕr′e-mo-ny, 171.
Ce′re-oŭs, *a.* waxen. [*See* Serious, 160.]
Ce′rēs (*-rēz*) (L.).
Ce′rīne [Cerin, 203.]
Ce′rite.
Ce′ri-um, 169.
Cer′nu-oŭs.
Cĕr-o-graph′ic.
Cĕr-o-graph′ic-al [so Wr.; *se-ro-graf′ik-al*, Wb. Gd. 155.]
Ce-rog′ra-phist.
Ce-rog′ra-phy, 108.
Cĕr′o-man-cy.
Ce-roon′ [Seroon, Seron, 203.]
Ce-ro-plas′tic.
Cĕr′ri-al, 170. [96.
Cer′taĭn (*-tin*), 21, N.;
Cer′taĭn-ty (*ser′tin-*).
Cer-tif′i-cate, 169.

Cer-ti-fi-ca′tion.
Cer′ti-fīed, 186.
Cer′ti-fī-er.
Cer′ti-fȳ, 78, 94, 169.
Cer′ti-fȳ-ing.
Ce-ru′le-an, 110, 169.
Ce′ruse (*-roos*) [so Sm. Wr.; *sē′rūs*, Wk. Gd. 155.]
Ce′rused (*-roost*).
Cer′vi-cal, 110, 169.
Cer′vīne (82, 152) [so Sm. Wb. Gd.; *ser′vin*, Wr. 155.]
Ce-sa′re-an (*-za′-*), 169.
Ces-pi-tĭ′tious(*-tish′us*).
Ces′pi-tose.
Ces′pi-toŭs.
Ces-sa′tion.
Ces′sion (*sesh′un*), *n.* the act of ceding. [*See* Session, 160.]
Ces′sion-a-ry (*sesh′un-*), 169.
Ces′sor, 88.
Cess′pool [Sesspool, 203.]
Ces′tus.
[Cesura, 203. — *See* Cæsura.]
Ce-ta′ce-a (*-she-a*), 171.
Ce ta′cean (*-shan*).
Ce-ta′ceous (*-shus*), *a.* relating to the Cetacea. [*See* Setaceous, 160.]
Ce′tīne [Cetin, 203.]
Ce-to-log′ic-al (*-loj′-*), 108.
Ce-tol′o-gist, 108.
Ce-tol′o-gy, 108, 170.
Cēy-lon-ēse′ (*-ēz′*).
Chab′a-siē (*kab′a-sē*, or *shab′a-sē*) [so Wr.; *kab′a-sē*, Wb. Gd.; *shab′a-sē*, Sm. 155.]
Chab′a-site (*kab′-*).
[Chad (*shad*), Sm. 203. — *See* Shad.]
Chafe, 23.
Chāfed (*chāft*), Note C, p. 34.
Chāf′er.
Chaff, 12, 131.
Chăf′fer, 170.
Chăf′fered (*-furd*), 150.
Chăf′fer-er.
Chăf′fer-ing.
Chăf′finch, 170.
Chăf′fy, 131, 170.
Chāf′ing, 183.
[Chagreen, 203.— *See* Shagreen.]

Cha-grin′ (*sha-grēn′*) [so Wk. Sm. Wr.; *sha-grĭn′*, Wb. Gd. 155.] *n.* vexation. [*See* Shagreen, 160.]
Cha-grined′(*sha-grēnd′*)
Cha-grin′ing (*sha-grēn′-*).
Chāin, 23.
Chāined, 150.
Chāin′ing.
Chāin′-pump.
Chair (*chêr*), 14.
Chaired (*chêrd*).
Chair′man (*chêr′-*), 206.
Chāise (*shāz*), 46.
Cha-laze′ (*ka-*).
Cha-la′za (*ka-*).
Chal-ce-don′ic(*kal-*),109.
Chal-ced′o-ny, *or* Chal′-ce-dō-ny (*kal′-*) [so Wr. Gd.; *kal-sed′o-ny*, Sm. 155.]
Chal-cog′ra-pher (*kal-*), 108.
Chal-cog′ra-phist (*kal-*).
Chal-cog′ra-phy (*kal-*).
Chal-da′ic (*kal-*), 109.
Chal′da-ism (*kal′da-izm*).
Chal-de′an (*kal-*), 110.
Chal-dee′ (*kal-*), 121.
Chal′der.
Châl′dron, *or* Chăl′dron [*chawl′dron*, Sm.; *chal′dron*, Wb. Gd.; *chawl′dron*, or *chal′-dron*, Wr. 155.]
Chal′ice (*chal′is*), 169.
Chal′iced (*chal′ist*).
Châlk (*chawk*), 162.
Châlked (*chawkt*), Note C, p. 34.
Châlk′i-ness (*chawk′-*), 169.
Châlk′ing (*chawk′-*).
Châlk′y (*chawk′y*), 93, 171.
Chal′lenge, 170.
Chal′lenge-a-ble, 183.
Chal′lenged, 150, 183.
Chal′len-ger.
Chal′len-ging.
Cha-lyb′e-ate (*ka-*), 169.
Cham (*kam*), *n.* the sovereign of Turkey. [*See* Cam, 160.]
Cha-made′ (Fr.) (*sha-mād′*).
Chām′ber.
Chām′bered (*-burd*),150.
Chām′ber-er.
Chām′ber-lain (*-lin*).
[Chambril (*kam-*), 203. — *See* Gambrel.]
Cha-me′le-on (*ka-*), 169.
Cham′fer.
Cham′fered (*-furd*), 150.
Chamois (Fr.) (*sham′y*, or *sha-moi′*) [so Wr. Gd.; *sha-moi′*, Wk.; *sham′wä*, Sm.154,155.] [Shamois, 203.]
Cham′o-mile (*kam′-*) [Camomile, 203.]
Chămp, 10, 44.
Cham-pagne′ (*sham-pān′*),*n.* a light sparkling wine. [*See* Champaign, *and* Champain, 160.]
Cham-paign′ (*sham-pān′*), *n.* a flat, open country. [*See* Champagne, *and* Champain, 160.]
Cham-pāin′, *n.* a mark of dishonor in an escutcheon. [*See* Champagne, *and* Champaign, 160.]
Chămped (*chămpt*).
Chăm′per-tor (*sham′-per-tor*) [so Sm. Wr.; *cham′per-tor*,Wb. Gd. 155.]
Cham′per-ty (*sham′per-ty*) [so Sm. Wr.; *cham′per-ty*, Wb. Gd. 155.]
Cham-pign′on (Fr.) (*sham-pin′yun*).
Cham′pi-on, 78, 169.
Chȧnce, 12, 131.
Chȧnced (*chȧnst*), Note C, p. 34.
Chăn′cel, 171.
Chan′cel-lor, 170.
Chȧn′cer-y, 131, 171.
Chȧnç′ing.
Chăn′cre (*shang′kur*).
Chăn′croŭs (*shang′-*).
Chăn-de-lier′ (*shan-de-lēr′*), 169.
Chȧnd′ler, 131.
Chȧnd′ler-y.
Chānge, 23.
Chānge-a-bil′i-ty, 183.
Chānge′a-ble, 164.
Chānge′a-bly.
Chānged, 183.
Chānge′ful (*-fo͝ol*), 180.
Chānge′ling.
Chāng′er (*chānj′-*), 183.
Chāng′ing (*chānj′-*).
Chan′nel, 170.
Chan′nelled (150) [Channeled, Wb. Gd. 203.—*See* 177, and Note E, p. 70.]
Chan′nel-ling [Channeling, Wb. Gd. 203.]
Chant, 12, 131.
Chȧnt′ed.
Chȧnt′er.
Chant′i-cleer, 156, 169.
Chȧnt′ing.
Chȧnt′ry.
Cha′os (*ka′-*), 52.
Cha-ot′ic (*ka-*), 109.
Chap, (*chap*, or *chop*), *v.* [so Wr. Gd.; *chap*, Sm.; *chop*, Wk. 155.]
Chap (*chap*, or *chop*), *n.* a cleft.
Chap (*chop*), *n.* the jaw.
Chăp, *n.* a boy.
Chafe.
Chapeau (Fr.) (*shap′o*) [pl. *Chapeaux* (*shap′-ōz*), 198.]
Chap′el.
Chap′el-la-ry, 72, 170.
Chap′el-ling [Chapeling, Wb. Gd. 155.— *See* 177, and Note E, p. 70.]
Chap′el-ry.
Chap′er-on (Fr.) (*shap′-er-ōng*) [so Sm.; *shap-er-oon′*, Wk.; *shap′er-on*, Wr. Gd. 155.]
Chap′fȧllen (*chop′-fawln*).
Chap′i-ter, 169.
Chap′lain (*-lin*), 171.
Chap′lain-cy (*-lin-*), 169.
Chap′let.
Chap′man.
Chapped (*chapt*, or *chopt*).
Chap′py, 170.
Chaps (*chops*) [Chops, 203.]
Chap′ter.
Chap′trel.
Chăr (161), *n.* a small fish: — *v.* to burn partially.
Char (*chêr*) (161), *n.* a small job. [Chare, Chore, 203.]
Chăr′ac-ter (*kăr′*).
Chăr-ac-ter-ist′ic (*kăr-*), 109, 126.
Chăr-ac-ter-ist′ic-al (*kăr-*), 108.

Chăr-ac-ter-i-za′tion (kar-), 112.
Chăr′ac-ter-īze (kar′-).
Chăr′ac-ter-īzed, 150, 183.
Chăr′ac-ter-īz-ing.
Charade′ (Fr.) (*sha-räd′*).
Char′cōal.
Chard, *n.* the blanched footstalk and midrib of the artichoke, &c.; — the white beet. [*See* Charred, 160.]
[Chare, 203. — *See* Char, *and* Chore.]
Charge, 11.
Charge-a-bil′i-ty, 183.
Charge′a-ble, 164, 169.
Charge′a-bly.
Charged (*charjd*), 150, 183.
Charg′er (*charj′-*).
Charg′ing (*charj′-*).
Char′i-ly (*chêr-*) [so Wk. Sm. Wb. Gd.; *chêr′-i-ly*, or *cha′ri-ly*, Wr. 155.]
Char′i-ness (*chêr′-*), 169.
Chăr′i-ot, 78.
Chăr-i-ot-eer′, 122.
Chăr′i-ta-ble, 164, 169.
Chăr′i-ty, 78, 108, 169.
Cha-ri-va-ri (Fr.) (*shä-re-vä-rē′*).
Char′la-tan (*shar′-*).
Char-la-tan′ic (*shar-*), 109.
Char-la-tan′ic-al (*shar-*).
Char′la-tan-ism (*shar′-la-tan-izm*), 131.
Char′la-tan-ry (*shar′-*).
Char′lock.
Char′lotte-Russe′ (Fr.) (*shar′lot-roos′*).
Charm, 11.
Charmed, 150.
Charm′er.
Charm′ing.
Char′nel.
Char′pīe (Fr.) (*shar′pē*).
Charred (*chard*) (170), *part.* from *Char.* [*See* Chard, 160.]
Chăr′ring, 11, N.
Chăr′ry, 11, 170.
Chart, 11.
Char′ta (L.) (*kar′ta*).
Char-ta′ceous (*kar-ta′-shus*).
Char′ter.
Char′tered, 165.
Char′ter-er.
Char′ter-par′ty.
Chart′ism (*-izm*), 133, 136.
Chart′ist.
Char′y (*chêr′-*) [so Wk. Sm. Gd.; *chĕr′y*, or *chā′ry*, Wr. 155.]
Chās′a-ble, 164.
Chase, 23.
Chased (*chāst*), *part.* from *Chase.* [*See* Chaste, 160.]
Chās′er, 183.
[Chasible, 203. — *See* Chasuble.]
Chās′ing. [136.
Chasm (*kazm*), 52, 133, 143.
Chas-seur′ (Fr.) (*shas′-ur*) [so Wr.; *shas′-sūr*, Gd. 155.]
Chāste, *a.* pure. [*See* Chased, 160.]
Chāst′en (*chās′n*), (162) [*not* chăs′n, 153.]
Chāst′ened (*chās′nd*).
Chāst′en-er (*chās′n-*).
Chāst′en-ing (*chās′n-*).
Chas-tīs′a-ble (*-tīz′-*).
Chas-tise′ (*-tīz′*), 202.
Chas-tīsed′ (*-tīzd′*), 150, 183.
Chas′tĭse-ment (*-tiz-*),
Chas-tīs′er (*-tīz′*).
Chas-tīs′ing (*-tīz′-*).
Chas′ti-ty, 169.
Chas′u-ble (*chaz′-*) [Chasible, Chesible, 203.]
Chat, 10.
Château (Fr.) (*sha-tō′*) [pl. *Chateaux* (*sha-tōz′*), 198.]
Chat′el-la-ny (*shat′-*), 72.
Cha-toy′ant (*sha-toi′-ant*).
Cha-toy′ment (*sha-toi′-*)
Chat′tel (*chat′l*) (170) [so Wk. Sm. Wb. Gd.; *chat′l*, or *chat′-el*, Wr. 155.]
Chat′ter, 170.
Chat′tered, 150.
Chat′ter-er.
Chat′ter-ing.
Chat′ty, 170.
Chat′wŏŏd.
Chaud′-med′ley (*shōd′-*)
Chauf′fer [Chaufer, 203.]
Chav′en-der.
Chēap, 13.
Chēap′en (*chēp′n*), 149.
Chēap′ened (*chēp′nd*).
Chēap′en-er (*chēp′n-*).
Chēat, 13.
Chēat′a-ble. 164, 169.
Chēat′ed.
Chēat′er.
Chēat′ing.
Che-bac′co.
Check, *n.* [Cheque, 203.]

☞ Sometimes written *cheque*, when used in the sense of *an order for money.*

Check, *v.*
Check′-bŏŏk, 206, Exc. 4.
Checked (*chekt*), Note C, p. 34.
Check′er [Chequer, 203.]
Check′ered (*-urd*), 150.
Check′ers (*-urz*), *n. pl.* [Chequers, 203.]
Check′ing.
Check′mate, *n.* & *v.*
Check′māt-ed.
Check′māt-ing.
Check′y.
Cheek, 13.
Cheer, 13.
Cheered, 150.
Cheer′ful (*-fŏŏl*) [so Sm. Wr. Wb. Gd.; *chēr′-fŏŏl*, or *chĕr′fŏŏl*, Wk. 155.]
Cheer′i-ly, 78, 169.
Cheer′i-ness.
Cheer′ing.
Cheer′y.
Cheese (*chēz*).
Chees′y (*chēz′y*).
Chef-d'œuvre (Fr.) (*shā-doovr′*) [so Wr.; *shef-doovr′*, Wb. Gd. 154, 155.]
[Chegoe, Chegre, 203. — *See* Chigre.]
Chei-rop′ter-oŭs (*kī-*).
Che-ko′a [so Wr.; *chek-o′a*, Wb. Gd. 155.]
Che-lif′er-oŭs (*ke-*), 108.
Chel′i-form (*kel′-*), 169.
Che-lo′ni-an (*ke-*), 169.
Chem′ic (*kem′-*).
Chem′ic-al (*kem′-*) [*See* Chemistry.]
Che-mise′ (Fr.) (*she-mēz′*).
Chem-i-sette′ (Fr.) (*shem-i-zet′*).
Chem′ist (*kem′-*).
Chem′is-try (*kem′is-try*, or *kim′is-try*) [so Wr.; *kim′is-try*, or *kem′is-try*, Gd.; *kim′is-try*,

Sm. 155.] [Chymistry, 203.]

☞ The pronunciation *kim'is-try* is obviously derived from the obsolete spelling *Chymistry*.

[Cheque, 203. — *See* Check.]
[Chequer, 203. — *See* Checker.]
[Chequers, 203.—*See* Checkers.]
[Chequin, 203. — *See* Cecchin.]
[Cherif, 203. — *See* Sherif.]
Chĕr'ish, 48, 66.
Cher'ished (*-isht*).
Chĕr'isher.
Chĕr'ish-ing.
Che-root' (*she-root'*) [so Gd.; *che-root'*, Wr. 155.]
Chĕr'ris, 170.
Chĕr'ry, 170.
Cher'so-nēse (*ker'-*), 136
Chert, 21, N.
Chert'y.
Chĕr'ub, 170.
Che-ru'bic, 109.
Che-ru'bic-al, 108.
Chĕr'u-bim.
Chĕr-u-bim'ic.
Chĕr'up.
Cher'vil.
[Chesible, 203.— *See* Chasuble.]
Chess, 15, 174.
Chest, 15, 44.
Chest'ed.
Chest'nut (*ches'nut*), (162)[Chesnut,203.]
Che'tah.
Chevaux-de-frise (Fr.) (*shev'ō-duh-frēz'*)*n.pl.*
Chev-a-liēr'(*shev-a-lēr'*) 122, 169.
Chev'en, 149.
Chev'er-il.
Chev'i-sänce (*shev'i-zäns*).
Chev'ron (*shev'ron*).
Chev'roned (*shev'rond*).
Chev'ron-el (*shev'-*).
Chew (*choo*) [so Sm. Wr.; *chu*, Wb. Gd. 155.]
Chewed (*chood*).
Chew'ing (*choo'-*).
Chib'bal, 170.
Chi-bouque' (Turkish) (*che-book'*).
Chi-cane' (*shē-*).
Chi-cān'er (*she-*).
Chi-cān'er-y (*she-*).
Chic'co-ry, 170.
Chich, 16, 44.
Chich'ling.
Chick, 16.
Chick'a-dee.
Chick'a-ree.
Chick'en, 149.
Chick'ling.
Chick'pēa.
Chick'weed, 206.
Chide, 25.
Chīd'ed, 183.
Chīd'er.
Chīd'ing.
Chiēf, 13.
Chiēf'taĭn (*-tin*), 96.
Chig're (*chig'ur*) (164) [Chigger, Chigua, Chigoe, Chegoe, Cheger, Chegre, Jigger, 203.]
Chil'blāin, 180.
Chīld (25, 44), *n.* [pl. Children, 195.] a son or a daughter. [*See* Childe, 160.]
Chīld'bed.
Chīld'birth.
Chīlde, *or* Chĭlde [so Wr.; *chīld*, Gd.; *chĭld*, Sm. 155], *n.* the son of a nobleman. [*See* Child, 160.]
Chīld'hood.
Chīld'ing.
Chīld'ish.
Chīld'like, 206, Exc. 5.
Chil'dren, *n. pl.*
Chĭ-lese' (*-lēz'*).
Chil'i-ad (*kil'-*).
Chil'i-a-gon (*kil'-*).
Chil-i-a-he'dron (*kil-*) [pl. *Chil-i-a-he'dra*, 198.]
Chil'i-arch (*kil'i-ark*), 52.
Chil'i-arch-y(*kil'i-ark-*).
Chil'i-ǝsm (*kil'i-azm*),
Chil'i-ast (*kil'-*). [136.
Chil-i-ast'ic (*kil-*).
[Chilifactive, 203. — *See* Chylifactive.]
Chill, 16, 172.
Chilled, 150.
[Chilli, 203.— *See* Chilly, *n.*]
Chil'li-ness, 78, 169.
Chill'ing.
Chil'ly, *n.* the pod or fruit of Capsicum. [Chilli, 203.]
Chil'ly (178), *a.* cold.
Chĭ-lo'ni-an (*kī-*).
Chĭ-lon'ic (*kī-*).
Chil'o-pod (*kil'-*).
Chīmb (*chīm*) (162), *n.* the edge of a cask. [Chime, Chine, 203] [*See* Chime, 160.]
Chime, *n.* harmony of many instruments; a set of balls; the edge of a cask: — *v.* to sound in harmony. [*See* Chimb, 160.]
Chīmed, 150.
Chīm'er.
Chī-mē'ra (*kī-*).
Chī-mĕr'ic-al (*kī-*), 108.
Chim'in-age (*shim'-*).
Chīm'ing.
Chim'ney (98, 169) [pl. Chimneys, 190.]
Chim-pan'zee [so Wr. Wb. Gd.; *chim-pan-zē'*, Sm. 155.]
Chin, 16.
Chi'na [so Sm. Wr. Wb. Gd.; *cha'nē*, or *chi'-na*, Wk. 155.]

☞ Though Walker gives *cha'nē* as the most fashionable pronunciation of this word in his time, yet he says of it; —" What could induce us to so irregular a pronunciation of this word is scarcely to be conceived."

Chin'ca-pin (*ching'-*) (54) [Chinkapin, Chinquapin, 203.]
Chin-chil'la, 170.
Chin'cough (*-kof*).
Chine [Chimb (in the sense of *the edge of a cask*), 203.]
Chined, 183.
Chī-nese' (*-nēz'*), 136.
Chink (*chingk*), 54.
[Chinkapin, 203.— *See* Chincapin.]
Chinked (*chingkt*).
Chink'ing (*chingk'-*).
Chink'y (*chingk'y*).
Chinned (*chind*), 176.
[Chinquapin, 203.— *See* Chincapin.]
Chinse, *v.* to fill with oakum, as a seam. [*See* Chintz, 148.]
Chintz (*chints*) (Note C, p. 34), *n.* a kind of calico. [*See* Chinse, 148.]

Chip, 16.
Chip'monk [Chipmunk, Chipmuk, 203.]
Chipped (*chipt*), 150, 176.
Chip'per.
Chip'ping, 176.
Chip'py.
Chī-ra'grā (*kī*-).
Chī-rag'ric-al (*kī*-).
Chī'ro-grăph (*kī*-), 127.
Chī-rog'ra-pher (*kī*-).
Chī-ro-graph'ic (*kī*-), 109
Chī-ro-graph'ic-al (*kī*-), 108.
Chī-rog'ra-phist (*kī*-).
Chī-rog'ra-phy (*kī*-).
Chī-ro-log'ic-al (*kī-ro-loj'*-).
Chī-rol'o-gist (*kī*-).
Chī-rol'o-gy, 108.
Chī'ro-man-cer (*kī*-).
Chī'ro-man-cy (*kī'*-) [so Sm. Wb. Gd.; *kĭr'o-man-sy*, Wk.; *kī'ro-man-sy*, or *kĭr'o-man-sy*, Wr. 155.]
Chī-ro-man'tic (*kī*-).
Chī-ro-man'tic-al (*kī*-).
Chī-ro-nom'ic (*kī*-).
Chī-ron'o-my (*kī*-), 108.
Chī'ro-plast (*kī'*-).
Chī'ro-pod (*kī'*-).
Chī-rop'o-dist (*kī*-).
Chī-ros'o-phist (*kī*-).
Chirp, 21, N.
Chirped (*chirpt*), Note C, p. 34.
Chirp'er.
Chirp'ing.
Chĭr'rup, 170.
Chĭr'ruped (-*rupt*).
Chĭr'rup-ing.
Chis'el (*chiz'el*), 149.
Chis'elled (*chiz'eld*) [Chiseled, Wb. Gd. 203.— *See* 177, and Note E, p. 70.]
Chis'el-ling [Chiseling, Wb. Gd. 203.]
Chis'leū.
Chis'ley (*chiz'ly*).
Chis'sels (*chiz'zlz*), *n. pl.* [so Sm.; *chiz'zelz*, Wr. 155.]
Chit.
Chit'-chat, 206, Exc. 3.
Chit'ter-lings, *n. pl.* 170.
Chī-val'ric (*shī-val'rik*), *or* Chĭv'al-ric (*shiv'-al-rik*) [*shī-val'rik*, Sm. Wr.; *shiv'al-rik*, Wb. Gd. 155.]
Chiv'al-roŭs (*shiv'al-rus*) [so Sm. Wb. Gd.; *chiv'al-rus*, Wk.; *shiv'al-rus*, or *chiv'-al-rus*, Wr. 155.]
Chiv'al-ry (*shiv'al-ry*) [so Sm. Wb. Gd.; *chiv'al-ry*, Wk.; *shiv'-al-ry*, or *chiv'al-ry*, Wr. 155.]
Chives (*chīvz*), *n. pl.*
Chlam'y-phore (*klam'*-).
Chlo'ral (*klo'*-).
Chlo'rate (*klo'*-).
Chlo'ric (*klo'*-).
Chlo'rĭde (*klo'*-) [Chlorid, 203.]
Chlo'rĭne (*klo'*-) (82, 152) [Chlorin, 203.]
Chlo'rite (*klo'*-).
Chlo-rit'ic (*klo*-).
Chlo'ro-form (*klo'*-), 171.
Chlo-rom'e-ter (*klo*-), 108.
Chlo-rom'e-try (*klo*-).
Chlo'ro-phane (*klo'*-).
Chlo'ro-phȳl (*klo'*-).
Chlo-roph'ȳl-lite (*klo*-).
Chlo-ro'sis (*klo*-).
Chlo-rot'ic (*klo*-).
Chlo'roŭs (*klo*-).
Chlo'ru-ret (*klo*-).
Chock, 181.
Choc'o-late, 132, 171.
Choice, 27.
Choir (*kwīr*).
Chōke, 24.
Chōked (*chōkt*), Note C, p. 34.
Chōk'er, 183.
Chōk'ing.
Chōk'y.
Chol'er (*kol'ur*), *n.* anger. [*See* Collar, 160.]
Chol'er-a (*kol'*-), 171, 233.
Chol'er-ic (*kol'*-).
Cho-les'ter-ĭne (*ko*-).
Cho-li-am'bic (*ko*-).
Chon-drog'ra-phy (*kon*-)
Chon-drol'o-gy (*kon*-).
Chon-drop-te-ryg'i-an (*kon-drop-te rij'i-an*).
Chon-drot'o-my (*kon*-).
Choose (*chooz*).
Choos'er (*chooz'*-).
Choos'ing (*chooz'*-).
Chop, 18, 44.
Chopin (*chop'in*, or *cho-pēn'*) [so Wr.; *chop'-in*, Gd.; *cho-pēn'*, Wk. 155.]
Chopped (*chopt*), 176.
Chop'per.
Chop'ping.
[Chops, 203.— *See* Chaps.]
Chop'stick.
Cho-rag'ic (*ko-raj'*-).
Cho-ra'gus (L.) (*ko*-).
Cho'ral (*ko'*-).
Cho'ral-ist (*ko'*-).
Chord (*kord*), *n.* the string of a musical instrument; — tones that harmonize; — a right line joining the two ends of an arc. [*See* Cord, 160.]
Chord'ed (*kord'*-).
Chord'ing (*kord'*-).
Chore [Char, Chare, 203.]
Cho-re'a (*ko*).
Cho-ree' (*ko*-), 121.
Cho-re'us (*ko*-).
Cho'ri-ant (*ko'*-).
Cho-ri-am'bic (*ko*-).
Cho-ri-am'bus (L.) (*ko*-)
Cho'ri-on (*ko'*-).
Cho'rist, 21, N.
Chor'ist-er [so Sm. Wr. Wb. Gd.; *kwĭr'ist-ur*, Wk. 155.] [Quirister, 203.]
Cho-rog'ra-pher (*ko*-).
Cho-ro-graph'ic (*ko*-).
Cho-ro-graph'ic-al (*ko*-). [so Wb. Gd.; *kor-o-graf'ik-al*, Wr. 155.]
Cho-rog'ra-phy (*ko*-).
Cho'roid (*ko'*-).
Cho'rus (*ko'*-), 52, 169.
Chōse (*chōz*), 136, 161.
Chose (Fr.) (*shōz*), 161.
Chos'en (*chōz'n*), 149.
Choŭgh (*chuf*) (35), *n.* a kind of bird. [*See* Chuff, 160.]
[Choule, 203.— *See* Jowl.]
Chouse (*chous*), 28.
Choused (*choust*).
Chous'ing, 183.
Chow'der, 77.
Chre-ma-tis'tics (*krē*-).
Chres-tom'a-thy (*kres*-).
Chrism (*krizm*), 133, 136.
Chris'mal (*kriz'*-).
Chris'ma-to-ry (*kriz'*-).
Christ-cross-rōw' (*kris-kros-rō'*).
Christ'en (*kris'n*), 162.
Christ'ened (*kris'nd*), 150.
Christ'en-ing (*kris'n*).

Christ′ian (*krist′yan*), 44, Note 1; 51.
Christ′ian-ism (*krist′-yan-izm*).
Christ-ian′i-ty (*krist-yan′i-ty*) [so Sm. Wb. Gd.; *kris-chī-an′i-ty*, Wk.; *krist-yī-an′i-ty*, Wr. 155.]
Christ-ian-i-za′tion (*krist-yan-*).
Christ′ian-ize (*krist′-yan-*).
Christ′ian-īzed (*krist′-yan-īzd*), 183.
Christ′ian-īz-ing (*krist′-yan-*)
Christ′mas (*kris′mas*), 162, 180.
Chris-tol′o-gy (*kris-*), 108.
Chro′mate (*kro′-*).
Chro-mat′ic (*kro-*), 109.
Chro-mat′ics (*kro-*).
Chro-ma-tog′ra-phy (*kro-*).
Chro-ma-tol′o-gy (*kro-*).
Chrome (*krōm*).
Chro′mic (*kro-*).
Chro′mi-um (*kro′-*), 169.
Chro′mo-grăph (*kro′-*).
Chron′ic (*kron′-*).
Chron′ic-al (*kron′-*), 148.
Chron′i-cle (*kron′-*), 148, 164.
Chron′i-cled (*kron′i-kld*).
Chron′i-cler (*kron′-*).
Chron′i-cles (*kron′i-klz*), 171.
Chron′i-cling (*kron′-*), 183.
Chron′o-grăph (*kron′-*).
Chron′o-gram (*kron′-*).
Chron-o-gram-mat′ic
Chron-o-gram-mat′ic-al (*kron-*).
Chron-o-gram′ma-tist (*kron-*).
Chro-nog′ra-pher (*kro-*).
Chro-nog′ra-phy (*kro-*).
Chro-nol′o-ger (*kro-*).
Chro-no-log′ic (*kro-no-loj′-*).
Chro-no-log′ic-al (*kro-no-loj′ik-al*) [so Wk. Sm. Gd.; *kron-o-loj′-ik-al*, Wr. 155.]
Chro-nol′o-gist (*kro-*).
Chro-nol′o-gy (*kro-*).
Chro-nom′e-ter (*kro-*), 108, 169.
Chro-no-met′ric [so Gd.; *kron-o-met′rik*, Wr. 155.]
Chro-no-met′ric-al.
Chro-nom′e-try (*kro-*).
Chron′o-scope (*kron′-*).
Chrys′a-lid (*kris′-*).
Chrys′a-lis (*kris′-*) [pl. Chrys-al′i-dēs (*-dēz*), 198.]
Chrys-o-bĕr′yl (*kris-*).
Chrys′o-col-la (*kris′-*).
Chrys-og′ra-phy (*kris-*).
Chrys′o-līte (*kris′-*).
Chrys-ol′o-gy (*kris-*).
Chrys′o-prase (*kris′o-prās*) [so Sm. Wr.; *kris′-o-prāz*, Wb. Gd. 155.]
Chub, 22.
Chub′bed, 150.
Chuck, 22, 181.
Chucked (*chukt*).
Chuck′ing.
Chuc′kle (*chuk′l*), 164.
Chuc′kled (*chuk′ld*), 183.
Chuck′ling.
Chu′fa (*choo′-*).
Chuff, *n.* a clown. [*See* Chough, 160.]
Chuf′fi-ly, 93, 170.
Chuf′fi-ness, 169.
Chuf′fy, 93, 170.
Chum, 22, 44.
Chump.
Chunk.
Chunk′y.
Church, 44.
Churched (*churcht*).
Church′ing.
Church′man, 206.
Church′yard.
Churl, 21, 44, 135.
Churl′ish.
Churn, 21, 44.
Churned, 165.
Churn′ing. [171.
Churr′worm (*-wurm*).
Chȳ-la′ceous (*kī-la′-shus*).
Chȳle (*kīl*).
Chȳ-li-fac′tion (*kī-*).
Chȳ-li-fac′tīve (*kī-*), *or* Chyl′i-fac-tive (*kil′-*) [so Wr.; *kī-lĭ-fac′tiv*, Sm.; *kil′i-fac-tiv*, Wk. Wb. Gd. 155.] [Chil-ifactive, 203.]
Chȳ-lif′er-oŭs (*kī-*), 108.
Chȳ-li-fac′tion (*kī-*).
Chȳ-lo-po-et′ic (*kī-*).
Chȳl′oŭs (*kīl′-*).
Chȳme (*kīm*).
Chȳm-i-fi-ca′tion (*kim-*).
Chȳm′i-fȳ (*kīm′-*), 94.
[Chymistry, 203.— *See* Chemistry.]
Chȳm′oŭs (*kīm′-*).
Cī-ba′ri-oŭs.
Cib′ol, 170.
Cī-bo′ri-um (L.) [pl. *Cī-bo′ri-a*, 198.]
Cī-ca′da (L.) [pl. *Cī-ca′dæ*, 198.]
Cic′a-trīce, 169.
Cic′a-trī-sant (*-zant*) [Cicatrizant, 203.]
Cic-a-trī′sīve.
Cī-ca′trix (L.) [*Cic-a-trī′cēs* (*-sēz*), 198.]
[Cicatrizant, 203.— *See* Cicatrisant.]
Cic-a-tri-za′tion.
Cic′a-trize, 202.
Cic′a-trized, 150, 183.
Cic′a-trīz-ing.
Çiç′e-ly (*sis′e-ly*) [so Sm. Wr. Wb. Gd.; *sis′ly*, Wk. 155.]
Cicerone (It.) (*che-che-ro′ne*, or *sis-e-ro′ne*) [so Wr. Gd.; *chē-chā-ro′nā*, Sm. 154, 155.]
Ciç-e-ro′ni-an, 169.
Ciç-e-ro′ni-an-ism (*-izm*).
Cich-o-ra′shus (*sik-o-ra′shus*).
Cich′o-ry (*sik′-*), 52.
Cī-cis′be-ism (*-izm*).
Cicisbeo (It.) (*che-chis-ba′o*, or *se-sis′be-o*) [so Wr. Gd.; *che-chis-ba′o*, Sm. 154, 155.]
Cid, 16, 39.
Ci′der, 25, 77.
Ci′der-ist.
Ci′der-kin.
Ci-devant (Fr.) (*se-de-väng′*).
Cierge (Fr.) (*sērj*).
Cī-gar′ [Segar, 203.]
Cil′i-a (L.) *n. pl.*
Cil′ia-ry (*sil′ya-ry*), 51, 171.
Cil′i-ate, 169.
Cil′i-āt-ed.
Cī-lĭ′cian (*-lish′an*).
Cī-lĭ′cioŭs (*-lish′us*), *a.* made of hair. [*See* Silicious, 160.]
Cil′i-o-grade.
[Cima, 263.— *See* Cyma.]
[Cimar, 203.— *See* Simar.]
Cim′bal, *n.* a kind of cake. [*See* Cymbal, 160.]

Cim′bric.
Cim′e-ter [S c i m i t a r, 203.]
Ci′miss.
Cim-me′ri-an, 169, 170.
Cim′o-lite.
Cin-cho′na (-*ko′*-).
Cin-cho′ni-a (-*ko′*-).
Cin′cho-nīne (-*ko*-).
Cinct′ure, 91.
Cinct′ured (-*yurd*), 150.
Cin′der, 171.
Cin′der-y.
Cin′droŭs.
Cin-e-fac′tion.
Cin′er-a-ry, 72, 171, 233.
Cin-er-a′tion.
Cī-ne′ri-oŭs, 169.
Cin-er-ĭ′tious (-*ish′us*).
Cin-ga-lese′ (-*lēz*).
Cin′na-bar, 170.
Cin′na-bar-īne, 84.
Cin′na-mon, 170.
Cinque (Fr.) (*singk*).
Cinque′-foil (*singk′*-).
Ci′on [S c i o n, 203.]
Ci′pher, 25, 35.
Ci′phered (-*furd*), 150.
Ci′pher-ing.
Cip′o-lin, 170.
[C i r c æ a n, 203. — *See* Circean.]
Cir-cas′sian (*sur-kash′-an*) [so Gd.; *sur-kash′ĭ-an*, Wr. 155.]
Cir-ce′an (110) [C i r-c æ a n, 203.]
Cir-cen′sial (-*shal*).
Cir-cen′sian (-*shan*).
Cir′ci-nal, 78, 169.
Cir′ci-nate.
Cir′cle, 21, N.; 164.
Cir′cled (-*kld*), 150, 183.
Cir′cler.
Cir′clet.
Cir′cling.
Cir′cuit (-*kit*), 171.
Cir′cuit-ed (-*kit*-).
Cir-cuit-eer′ (-*kit*), 122.
Cir′cuit-er (-*kit*-).
Cir-cu′i-toŭs, 169.
Cir-cu′i-ty, 108.
Cir′cu-lar, 89, 108.
Cir-cu-lăr′i-ty.
Cir′cu-late, 171.
Cir′cu-lāt-ed, 183.
Cir′cu-lāt-ing.
Cir cu-la′tion, 112.
Cir′cu-la-tīve, 106.
Cir′cu-la-to-ry.
Cir-cum-am′bi-ent, 169.
Cir-cum-cell′ion (-*sel′-yun*) [so Wb. Gd.; *sur-cum-sel′i-on*, Wr. 155.]
Cir′cum-cise (-*sīz*), 202.
Cir′cum-cised (-*sīzd*), 150, 183.
Cir′cum-cīs-er (-*sīz*-).
Cir′cum-cis-ing (-*sīz*-).
Cir-cum-cĭ′sion (-*sizh′-un*).
Cir-cum′fer-ence, 169.
Cir-cum-fe-ren′tial (-*shal*).
Cir-cum-fe-ren′tor.
Cir′cum-flect.
Cir′cum-flex.
Cir-cum′flu-ence, 105.
Cir-cum′flu-ent.
Cir-cum′flu-oŭs.
Cir-cum-fo-ra′ne-oŭs.
Cir-cum-fuse′ (-*fūz′*).
Cir-cum-fused′ (-*fūzd′*).
Cir-cum-fū′sīle.
Cir-cum-fūs′ing (-*fūz′*-).
Cir-cum-fu′sion (-*zhun*).
Cir-cum′gy-rate, 105.
Cir-cum-gy-ra′tion.
Cir-cum-ja′cence.
Cir-cum-lo-cu′tion.
Cir-cum-loc′u-to-ry.
Cir-cum-mured′.
Cir-cum-nav′i-ga-ble.
Cir-cum-nav′i-gate.
Cir-cum-nav′i-gāt-ed, 183.
Cir-cum-nav′i-gāt-ing.
Cir-cum-nav-i-ga′tion.
Cir-cum-nav′i-gāt-or.
Cir-cum-po′lar.
Cir-cum-scis′sīle(-*sis′il*)
Cir-cum-scrīb′a-ble, 183.
Cir-cum-scribe′.
Cir-cum-scrībed′.
Cir-cum-scrīb′er.
Cir-cum-scrīb′ing.
Cir-cum-script′i-ble,169.
Cir-cum-scrip′tion.
Cir-cum-scrip′tīve.
Cir′cum-spect, 171.
Cir-cum-spec′tion.
Cir′cum-stănce, 171.
Cir′cum-stănced (-*stanst*).
Cir′cum-stanç-ing.
Cir-cum-stan′tial (-*shal*)
Cir-cum-stan′ti-ate (-*shĭ-āt*) [so Wk. Sm. Wr.; *sur-kum-stan′-shāt*, Wb. Gd. 155.]
Cir-cum-stan′ti-āt-ed (-*shĭ-āt*-).
Cir-cum-stan′ti-āt-ing (-*shĭ-āt*-).
Cir-cum-val′late, 170.
Cir-cum-val-la′tion
Cir-cum-vec′tion.
Cir-cum-vent′.
Cir-cum-vent′ed.
Cir cum-ven′tion.
Cir-cum-vent′īve, 84.
Cir-cum-vest′.
Cir-cum-vo-la′tion.
Cir-cum-volve′.
Cir-cum-volved′,150, 183
Cir-cum-volv′ing.
Cir′cus [pl. Cir′cus-es (-*ez*).]
Cĭr-rif′er-ous, 108, 170.
Cĭr′-ri-form, 169, 170.
Cĭr-rig′er-oŭs (-*rij′*-).
Cĭr′ri-ped, 78, 169, 170.
Cĭr-ro-cu′mu-lus.
Cĭr′rose.
Cĭr-ro-stra′tus.
Cĭr′roŭs (170) *a.* having tendrils. [*See* Cirrus, 160.]
Cĭr′rus (L.), *n.* [pl. *Cir-ri*, 98] a tendril. [*See* Cirrous, 160.]
Cir′so-cēle.
Cis-alp′īne [so Wr. Wb. Gd.; *siz-alp′in*, Sm. 155.]
Cis-at-lan′tic.
Cis-mon′tane.
Cis′pi-dane.
Cis′soid, 170.
Cist, *n.* a place of interment.
Cist, *n.* a pouch or sac. [C y s t, 203.]
Cist′ed [C y s t e d, 203.]
Cis-ter′cian (-*shan*).
Cis′tern, 171.
Cis′tic [C y s t i c, 203.]
Cit, 16.
Cīt′a-ble, 164.
Cit′a-del, 171.
Cīt′al.
Cī-ta′tion.
Ci′ta-to-ry, 86, 93.
Cite, *v.* to call: — to quote. [*See* Site, Sight, 160.]
Cīt′ed, 183.
Cīt′er.
Cīt′ing.
Cith-a-ris′tic, 109.
Cith′ern [C i t t e r n, 203]
Cit′i-zen (-*zn*), 78, 149.
Cit′rate.
Cit′rēne.
Cit′ric.
Cit′ril.
Cit′rīne, 82, 152.

Cit′ron, 86.
Cit′tern (170) [Cithern, 203.]
Cit′y, 169, 170, 190.
Cīves (*sīvz*), 136.
Civ′et, 170.
Civ′ic.
Civ′il, 149, 170.
Cĭ-vil′ian (*-yan*), 51.
Civ′il-ist.
Cĭ-vil′i-ty, 78, 108, 169.
Civ′il-īz-a-ble, 164, 169.
Civ-il-ĭ-za′tion, 112.
Civ′il-ize, 170, 202.
Civ′il-īzed, 150, 183.
Civ′il-īz-er.
Civ′il-īz-ing.
Civ′il-ly, 66, 170.
Clab′ber.
Clack, 181.
Clacked (*klakt*), Note C, p. 34.
Clack′er.
Clack′ing.
Clad, 10.
Clāim, 23.
Clāim′a-ble, 164.
Clāim′ant, *n.* one who claims. [*See* Clamant, 160.]
Clāimed, 150.
Clāim′er.
Clāim′ing.
Clair-voy′ance (*klêr-*).
Clair-voy′ant (*klêr-*).
Clam, *n.* & *v.* 10.
Cla′mant, *a.* crying. [*See* Claimant, 160.]
Clam′ber.
Clam′bered (*-burd*), 150.
Clam′ber-ing.
Clammed (*klamd*), 150, 176.
Clam′ming.
Clam′mi-ness, 169.
Clam′my, 170.
Clam′or [Clamour, Sm. 199, 203.]
Clam′ored (*-urd*), 150.
Clam′or-er.
Clam′or-ing.
Clam′or-oŭs, 171.
Clamp, 10.
Clamped (*klampt*).
Clamp′ing.
Clan, 10.
Clan-des′tĭne (82, 152) [*not* klan′des-tin, 153.]
Clang, 10, 54.
Clanged (*klangd*), 150.
Clang′ing.
Clan′gor (*klang′gor*), 54, Note 2.
Clan′gor-oŭs (*klang′-gor-*).
Clank (*klangk*), 10, 54.
Clanked (*klangkt*), Note C, p. 34.
Clank′ing (*klangk′-*).
Clannish, 176.
Clap, 10.
Clap′bōard (*klab′bōrd*), Note C, p. 34.
Clapped (*klapt*).
Clap′per, 176.
Clap′per-claw.
Clap′ping, 170, 176.
Clap′-trăp.
Clăr-en-ceux′, *or* Clăr-en-cieux′ (*klăr-en-shoo′*) [so Wr.; *klăr en-shu′*, Gd.; *klăr-ens-yoo′*, Sm.; 154, 155.]
Clare-ob-scure′ (*klêr-*).
Clăr′et, 170.
Clăr′i-chord (*-kord*).
Clăr-i-fi-ca′tion, 112, 171.
Clăr′i-fīed, 186.
Clăr′i-fī-er.
Clăr′i-fȳ, 78, 94, 169.
Clăr′i-fȳ-ing, 186.
Clăr′i-net [Clarionet, 203.]
Clăr′i-on (169, 170) [so Sm. Wr. Gd.; *klêr′-yun*, Wk. 155.]
Cla′ry, 49, N.
Clash, 10, 46.
Clashed (*klasht*).
Clash′ing.
Clȧsp, 12, 131.
Clȧsped (*klȧspt*), Note C, p. 34.
Clȧsp′er.
Clȧsp′ing.
Clȧsp′-knife.
Clȧss, 12, 131, 174.
Clȧssed (*klast*).
Clȧss′i-ble, 164, 169.
Clăs′sic.
Clăs′sic-al, 108, 170.
Clăs′si-cism (*-sizm*), 136.
Clăs′si-cist, 169, 170.
Clas-sif′ic, 109.
Clas-si-fi-ca′tion.
Clas′si-fīed, 186.
Clas′si-fȳ, 78, 94, 170.
Clas′si-fȳ-ing.
Clȧss′ing.
Clȧss′man.
Clȧss′mate.
Clat′ter, 170.
Clat′tered, 150.
Clat′ter-er.
Clat′ter-ing.
Clâuse (*klawz*), 17.
Clâus′tral.
Clâus′u-lar (*klawz′-*), 108
Cla′vate.
Cla′vāt-ed.
Clave, 23.
Clav′el-lāt-ed.
Cla′vi-a-ry, 72.
Clav′i-chord (*-kord*).
Clav′i-cle, 164, 170.
Cla-vic′u-lar, 108.
Clă′vi-er (Fr.) (*klă′vĭ-ā*) [so Wr.; *kla′vi-ur*, Gd.; 154, 155.]
Clav′i-ger.
Cla-vig′er-oŭs (*-vij′-*).
Cla′vis (L.) [L. pl. *Cla′vēs* (*-vēz*); Eng. pl. *Cla′vis-es*, 198.]
Cla′vy, 169.
Claw, 17.
Clawed, 150.
Claw′ing.
Clāy, 23.
Clāyed, 150, 187.
Clāyes (*klāz*).
Clāy′ey, 98, 169.
Clāy′ing.
Clāy′more [Glaymore, 203.]
Clĕad′ing.
Clēan, 13.
Clēaned, 150.
Clēan′ing.
Clĕan′li-ness, 169.
Clĕan′ly, *a.* (161) clean, neat.
Clēan′ly, *ad.* (161) neatly.
Clēan′ness, 66, N.; 170, 230.
Clĕanse (*klenz*), 15.
Clĕansed (*klenzd*), 183.
Clĕans′er (*klenz-*).
Clĕans′i-ble (*klenz′-*), 164, 169.
Clĕans′ing (*klenz′-*).
Clēar, 13.
Clēar′age.
Clēar′ance.
Clēared, 150.
Clēar′er.
Clēar′ing.
Clēat, 13.
Clēav′age.
Clēave, 13.
Clēaved, 150.
Clēav′er.
Clēav′ing.
Clĕdge.
Clĕdg′y (*klej′-*).
Clef (*klĕf*, or *klĭf*) [so

Wr.; *klĕf*, Wb. Gd.; *klĭf*, Wk. Sm. 155.]

☞ Though Walker gives only the pronunciation *klif*, yet he says, — "Even without the plea of brevity, *clef* is changed by musicians into *cliff*."

Cleft.
Clem'a-tis.
Clem'en-cy, 169.
Clem'ent, 169.
Clem'ent-ĭne, 84, 152.
Cle-op'ter-oŭs.
Clep'sy̆-dra [so Sm. Wb. Gd.; *klep'sy̆-dra*, or *klep-sy̆'dra*, Wr. 155.]
Cler'gy, 21, N.
Cler'gy-a-ble, 164.
Cler'gy-man, 196.
Clĕr'ic.
Clĕr'ic-al, 108.
Clĕr'i-sy, 169.
Clerk (*klerk*, or *klark*) [*klerk*, Wb. Gd.; *klark*, Wk. Sm.; *klark*, or *klerk*, Wr. 155.]

☞ The pronunciation *klark* is the prevailing one in England, but *klerk* is very generally preferred in the United States.

Clĕr'o-man-cy, 169.
Clev'er, 77, 170.
Clev'is.
Clev'y.
Clew (*klū*) (26) [Clue, 203.]
Click, 16, 181.
Clicked (*klikt*), Note C, p. 34.
Click'er.
Click'et.
Click'ing.
Cli'ent, 169.
Cli-ent'al.
Cli'ent-ed.
Cliff, 16, 173.
Clift, 16.
Clim-ac-tĕr'ic, *or* Clī-mac'ter-ic, *a.* & *n.* [so Wr.; *klim-ak-tĕr'ik*, Wk. Sm.; *klī-mak'-ter-ik*, Wb. Gd. 155.]
Clim-ac-tĕr'ic-al.
Cli'mate, 73.
Clī-mat'ic, 109.
Clī-mat'ic-al, 108.
Cli'ma-tize, 202.
Clī-ma-tog'ra-phy, 108.
Clī-ma-tol'o-gy, 108.
Cli'max.
Climb (*klīm*) (162), *v.* to mount by means of the hands and feet. [*See* Clime, 160.]
Clīmb'a-ble (*-klīm'-*).
Clīmbed (*klīmd*).
Clīmb'er (*klīm'-*).
Clīmb'ing (*klīm'-*).
Clime, *n.* climate, region. [*See* Climb, 160.]
Clinch, 16, 44.
Clinched (*klincht*), Note C, p. 34.
Clinch'er.
Clinch'er-built (*-bilt*) [Clinker-built, 203.]
Clinch'ing.
Cling, 16, 54.
Cling'stōne, 206.
Cling'y, 93.
Clin'ic.
Clin'ic-al.
Clinique (Fr.) (*klin-ēk'*).
Clink (*klingk*), 16, 54.
Clinked (*klingkt*).
Clink'er (*klingk'-*).
[Clinker-built, 203. — *See* Clincher-built]
Clink'ing (*klingk'-*).
Cli'noid.
Cli-nom'e-ter, 108.
Cli-no-met'ric.
Cli-no-met'ric-al.
Cli-nom'e-try, 108.
Clip, 16.
Clipped (*klipt*), 176.
Clip'per, 170, 176.
Clip'ping.
Clique (Fr.) (*klēk*).
Cliqu'ish (*klēk'-*).
Cliqu'ism (*klēk'izm*).
Cli'vers (*-vurz*).
Cliv'i-ty, 169.
Clo-a'ca (L.) [pl. *Clo-a'cæ*, 198.]
Clo-a'cal.
Clōak, 24, 130.
Clōaked (*klōkt*), 150.
Clōak'ing.
Clock, 18, 181.
Clock'-work (*-wurk*).
Clod, 18.
Clod'dy, 176.
Clod'hop-per.
Clod'pate, 206.
Clod'pāt-ed.
Clod'pōll [Clotpoll, 203.]
Clŏff [Clough, 203.]
Clog, 18.
Clogged (*klogd*), 165, 176.
Clog'gi-ness (*-ghĭ*), 138.
Clog'ging (*-ghing*).
Clog'gy (*-ghy*).
Clois'ter.
Clois'ter-al.
Clois'tered, 150.
Clois'ter-er.
Clois'ter-ing.
Clon'ic.
Clōse (*klōz*), *v.* & *n.* 24, 161.
Clōse (*klōs*), *n.*, *a.* & *ad.* 161.
Clōsed (*klōzd*).
Clōs'er (*klōz'-*).
Clos'et (*kloz'-*).
Clos'et-ed (*kloz'-*).
Clos'et-ing (*kloz'-*).
Clōs'ing (*klōz'-*).
Clōs'ure (*klōz'yur*), 91.
Clot, 18
Clot'bur, 206.
Cloth (*klŏth*, or *klawth*) (18 N.) [so Wr. Wb. Gd.; *kloth*, Wk. Sm. 155.]
Clothe, 24, 38.
Clothed (*klothd*), 150.
Clothes (*klōthz*) [so Sm.; *klōthz*, or *klōz*, Wr. Gd.; *klōz*, Wk. 155.]

☞ Though Walker gives only the pronunciation *klōz*, he speaks of it as "a corruption that is not incurable."

Clōth'ier (*kloth'yur*), 51.
Cloth'ing.
Clot'pōll [Clodpoll, 203.]
Clot'ted, 66, N.; 176.
Clot'ting.
Clot'ty, 93.
Cloud, 28.
Cloud'-capt.
Cloud'ed.
Cloud'i-ly, 169.
Cloud'i-ness.
Cloud'ing.
Cloud'y, 93, 169.
Clough (*kluf*, or *klof*) [so Wr.; *kluf*, Sm.; *klof*, Gd.; *klou*, Wk. 155.] [Cloff (in the sense of *an allowance in weight*), 203.]
Clout, 28.
Clout'ed.
Clout'ing.
Clout'-nāil.
Clo'vate.
Clove.
Clo'ven (*klo'vn*), 149.

Clo′ven-fŏŏt′ed.
Clo′ver.
Clo′vered (*-vurd*), 150.
Clown, 28.
Cloy, 27.
Cloyed (*kloid*), 150.
Cloy′ing.
Club, 22.
Clubbed (*klubd*), 150, 176.
Club′bist, 170.
Club′-fŏŏt.
Cluck, 22, 181.
Clucked (*klukt*), Note C, p. 34.
Cluck′ing.
[Clue, 203.—*See* Clew]
Clump, 22.
Clum′si-ly (*-zĭ-*), 169.
Clum′si-ness (*-zĭ-*), 78.
Clum-sy (*-zy*), 169.
Clunch, 22, 44.
Clung, 22, 54.
Clu′ni-al.
Clus′ter, 77.
Clus′tered, 150.
Clus′ter-ing.
Clutch, 22, 44.
Clutched (*klutcht*).
Clutch′ing.
Clut′ter, 170.
Clut′tered, 150.
Clut′ter-ing.
Clyp′e-ate, 169.
Clys′mi-an (*kliz′-*).
Clys′mic (*kliz′-*).
Clys′ter, 16, 77.
Co-a-cer′vate.
Cōach, 24, 44.
Cōach′man, 206.
Cō-ad′ju-tant, 169.
Cō-ad-ju′tor, 122.
Co-ag′u-la-ble, 164.
Co-ag′u-lant, 169.
Co-ag′u-late, 73.
Co-ag′u-lāt-ed, 183.
Co-ag′u-lāt-ing.
Co-ag-u-la′tion.
Co-ăg′u-la-tĭve, 84, 106.
Co-ag′u-lāt-or.
Co-ag′u-la-to-ry, 86.
Co-ag′u-lum (L.).
Cō-āid′, 223.
[Coak, 203.—*See* Coke.]
Cōal (24), *n.* a carbonaceous substance. [*See* Cole, 160.]
Cōaled (*kōld*), *part.* burnt to charcoal. [*See* Cold, 160.]
Cō-a-lesce′ (*-les′*), 171.
Cō-a-lesced′ (*-lest′*).
Cō-a-les′cing (*-les′ing*).
Cō-a-les′cence (*-les′ens*).
Cō-a-les′cent (*-les′ent*).
Cōal′ing.
Cō-a-lĭ′tion (*-lish′un*).
Cōal′y, 93, 169.
Cōam′ings.
Co-ap-ta′tion.
Cō-arc-ta′tion.
Cōarse (*kōrs*), *a.* not fine. [*See* Course, 160.]
Cōast, 24.
Cōast′ed.
Cōast′er.
Cōast′ing.
Cōast′wise (*-wīz*).
Cōat (24, 130), *n.* a kind of garment. [*See* Cote, 160.]
Cōat′ed.
Cōat-ee′, 121.
Cōat′ing.
Cōax, 24.
Cōaxed (*kōkst*).
Cōax′er.
Cob, 18.
Co′bâlt, *or* Co′balt (*-bŏlt*) [*ko′bawlt*, Sm.; *ko′bŏlt*, Gd.; *kŏb′alt*, Wk.; *ko′bawlt*, or *kob′alt*, Wr. 155.]
Cō′balt-īne (*ko′bawlt-in*) [*ko′bŏlt-in*, Gd.; *kob′-alt-in*, Wr. 155.]
Cob′bing, 170.
Cob′ble, *v.* 164.
Cob′ble, *n.* [Co′ble (in the sense of *a small fishing boat*), 203.]
Cob′bled (*kob′ld*), 150, 183.
Cob′bler.
Cob′bling, 183.
Cob′le (*kob′l*) [Cobble, 203.]
[Coboose, 203.—*See* Caboose.]
Cob′web, 206.
Cob′webbed (*-webd*).
Cob-web′by [Cobweby, Gd. 203.]
Coc-agne′ (Fr.) (*kok-ān′*)
Coc-cif′er-ous, 108.
Coc′cyx (*kok′siks*).
Coch′i-nēal (78, 169) [so Wr. Wb. Gd.; *koch-i-nēl′*), Sm.; *kuch′i-nēl*, Wk. 155.]
Coch′le-an (*ko*[illegible]*-*), 169.
Coch-le-a′ri-form (*kok-*).
Coch′le-a-ry (*kok′-*), 72.
Coch′le-ate (*kok′-*).
Coch′le-āt-ed (*kok′-*).
Coch′līte (*kok′-*).
Cock, 18, 181.
Cock-ade′, 121.
Cock-ād′ed.
Cock-a-too′, 122.
Cock-a-toon′.
Cock′a-trīce, (171) [*not* kok′a-tris, 153.]
Cock′bill.
Cock′bōat, 206.
Cock′chāf-er.
Cocked (*kokt*), 165.
Cock′er.
Cock′er-el.
Cock′et.
Cock′ing.
Coc′kle, 164.
Coc′kled (*kok′ld*), 165, 183.
Cock′ling.
Cock′ney, 98, 169, 190.
Cock′ney-ism (*-nĭ-izm*).
Cock′pit, 206.
Cock′rōach.
Cock's-cōmb (*-kōm*) (213) [Coxcomb, 203.]
Cock′spur.
Cock′swain (*kok′swān*), or *kok′sn*) [so Wr.; *kok′swān*, coll. *kok′-sn*, Wk. Sm.; *kok′-swān*, contracted into *kok′sn*, Wb. Gd. 155.]

☞ Seamen always pronounce this word *cok′sn.*

Co′cōa (*ko′kō*) (171) [Cacao, 203.]
Co′cōa-nut.
Co-coon′, 121.
Co-coon′er-y.
Coc′tĭle.
Coc′tion.
Cod, 18.
Cod′dle, 164.
Cod′dled (*kod′ld*), 150.
Cod′dling.
Code, 24.
Co-de′ia (*-de′ya*).
Co-de′īne [Codein, 203.]
Co′dex (L.) [pl. *Cod′i-cēs* (*-sēz*), 198.]
Cod′fish, 206.
Cod′ger (*koj′ur*).
Cod′i-cil, 169.
Cod-i-cil′la-ry, 72, 170.
Cod-i-fi-ca′tion.
Cod′i-fīed, 186.
Cod′i-fī-er.
Cod′i-fy, 78, 94.
Co-dille′ (*-dil′*).
Cod′ling.

Co-ef-fĭ′cient (-*fish′ent*), 171.
Cœ′li-ac (*se′*-) [Celiac, 203.]
Co-emp′tion (-*em′*-), 162.
Co-e′qual.
Co-erce′ (-*ers′*), 103, 171.
Co-erced′ (-*erst′*), 150, 183
Co-erç′i-ble, 164, 169.
Co-erç′ing.
Co-er′cion (-*shun*).
Co-erç′ĭve, 84.
Co-es sen′tial.
Co-es-sen-ti-al′i-ty (-*shĭ-al′*-) [so Wk. Sm. Wr.; *ko-es-sen-shal′i-ty*, Wb. Gd. 155.]
Co-e-ta′ne-oŭs.
Co-e-ter′nal, 21, N.
Co-e-ter′ni-ty, 108, 169.
Co-e′val.
Co-ex-ist′ (*egz*-).
Co-ex-ist′ed (-*egz*-).
Co-ex-ist′ence (-*egz*-), 169.
Co-ex-ist′ent (-*egz*-), 169.
Co-ex-ist′ing (-*egz*-).
Co-ex-ten′sĭve, 84.
Cof′fee, 66, N.; 170.
Cof′fer.
Cof′fer-dam.
Cof′fer-er.
Cof′fin, 170.
Cof′fined (-*fĭnd*), 150
Cof′fin-ing.
Cof′fle (164) [Caufle, 203.]
Cog, 18.
Co′gen-cy, 169.
Co′gent.
Cogged (*kogd*), 176.
Cog′ging, 138.
Cog-i-ta-bil′i-ty (*coj*-).
Cog′i-ta-ble (*coj′*-), 164.
Cog′i-tate (*coj′*-), 169.
Cog′i-tāt-ed (*coj′*-), 183.
Cog′i-tāt-ing (*coj′*-).
Cog-i-ta′tion (*coj*-), 112.
Cog′i-tāt-ĭve (*coj′*-), 84.
Cognac (Fr.) (*kōn′yak*) [Cogniac, 203.]
Cog′nate.
Cog-na′tion.
Cog-nĭ′tion (-*nish′un*).
Cog′ni-za-ble (*kog′ni-za-bl*, or *kon′i-za-bl*).
Cog′ni-zance (*kog′ni-zans*, or *kon′i-zans*) [so Wk. Wr. Gd.; *kon′i-zans*, Sm. 155.]
Cog′ni-zant, 78.
Cog-ni-zee′ (*kog-ni-ze′*, or *kon-i-ze′*).
Cog-ni-zor′ (*kog-ni-zor′*, or *kon-i-zor′*).
Cog-no′men (L.), 125.
Cog-nom′i-nal, 228.
Cog-nom-i-na′tion.
Cog-nos-cen′te (It.) [pl. *Cog-nos-cen′ti* (-*tē*), 198.]
Cog-nos′ci-ble, 164, 171.
Cog′-wheel.
Co-hab′it.
Co-hab′it-ant, 228.
Co-hab-it-a′tion.
Co-hab′it-ed.
Co-hab′it-er.
Co-hab′it-ing.
Co′-heir (-*ĕr*), 223.
Co-here′.
Co-hered′ (-*hērd′*), 150, 183.
Co-hēr′ence.
Co-hēr′en-cy, 169.
Co-hēr′ent, 49, N.
Co-hēr′ing.
Co-he-si-bil′i-ty.
Co-he′si-ble, 164, 169.
Co-he′sion (-*zhun*).
Co-he′sĭve, 84.
Co′hort, 139.
Coif, *n.* & *v.* (27) [Quoif, 203.]
Coifed (*koift*), 150.
Coif′fure [*koif′oor*, Sm. (*See* § 26); *koif′foor*, Wr. 155.]
Coigne (*koin*) (162), *n.* a corner; — a wedge. [*See* Coin, 160.] [Coin, Quoin, 203.]
Coil, 27.
Coiled, 159.
Coil′ing.
Coin, *n.* a corner; — a wedge. [Coigne, Quoin, 203.]
Coin, *n.* a piece of metal used as money: — *v.* to convert into money; to invent. [*See* Coigne, 160.]
Coin′age.
Co-in-cide′.
Co-in′ci-dence, 169.
Co-in′ci-dent, 169.
Coined, 150.
Coin′er.
Coir, 27.
Cois′tril.
[Coit, 203. — *See* Quoit]
Co-ĭ′tion (-*ish′un*).
Coke (24) [Coak, 203.]
Coked (*kōkt*).
Cōk′ing.
Col′an-der (*kul′*-) [Cullender, 203.]
Col-ber-tine′ (*kol-ber-tēn′*) [so Wk. Sm.; *kol′ber-tēn*, Wr.; *kol′ber-tĭn*, Wb. Gd. 155.]
Col′chi-cum (-*kĭ*-), 171.
Col′co-thar.
Cold, *a.* not warm. [*See* Coaled, 160.]
Cole (24), *n.* a plant of the cabbage family. [*See* Coal, 160.]
Co-le-op′ter-an.
Co-le-op′ter-oŭs.
Cole′seed, 206.
Cole′wort (-*wurt*).
Col′ic, 170.
Col′ick-y, 182.
Col′in.
Col-i-se′um (111) [Colosseum, 203.]
Col-lab-o-ra′tion.
Col-lab-o-ra′tor, 170.
Col-lapse′, 170.
Col-lapsed′ (-*lapst′*).
Col-laps′ing.
Col-lap′sion.
Col′lar, *n.* a neck-band. [*See* Choler, 160.]
Col′lared (-*lurd*), 150.
Col′lar-ing.
Col-lāt′a-ble, 164.
Col-late′.
Col-lāt′ed, 183.
Col lat′er-al, 170.
Col-lāt′ing.
Col-la′tion, 112.
Col-la′tion-er.
Col-lāt′ĭve, 84.
Col-lāt′or, 228.
Col′lēague (-*lēg*), 171.
Col-lect′, *v.* 161.
Col′lect, *n.* 161.
Col-lec-ta′ne-a (L. pl.).
Col-lec-ta′ne-oŭs.
Col-lect′ed.
Col-lect′i-ble, 164, 169
Col-lec′tion.
Col-lect′ĭve, 84.
Col-lect′or.
Col-leg′a-ta-ry, 72.
Col′lege (-*lej*), 169, 171.
Col-le′gi-an.
Col-le′gi-ate, 73.
Col′let, 170.
Col-lide′.
Col-lĭd′ed, 183.
Col-lĭd′ing.
Col′lier (*kol′yur*), 171.
Col′lier-y (*kol′yur-y*).
Col′li-māt-ing.
Col-li-ma′tion, 112.

Col-li-ma'tor.
Col-lin-e-a'tion.
Col-lin'gual, 170.
Col-lĭ-qua'tion.
Col-liq'ua-tĭve (*-lik'wa-*)
Col-liq'ue-fac-tion (*-lik'-we-*).
Col-lĭ'sion (*-lizh'un*).
Col'lo-cate, 170.
Col'lo-cāt-ed.
Col'lo-cāt-ing.
Col-lo-ca'tion, 112.
Col-lo'di-on, 169, 170.
Col'lop.
Col-lo'qui-al.
Col-lo'qui-al-ism (*-izm*).
Col'lo-quist.
Col'lo-quy, 170.
Col-lude'.
Col-lūd'ed, 183.
Col-lūd'er.
Col-lūd'ing.
Col-lu'sion (*-zhun*).
Col-lu'sĭve.
Col-lu'so-ry.
Col-lu'vi-ēs (*-ēz*) (L. sing. & pl.).
Col'ly, 93, 169.
Col-lyr'i-um (L.) [pl. *Col-lyr'i-a.*]
Col'o-cynth, 171.
Col-o-cynth'ĭne [Colocynthin, 203.]
Co-logne' (*ko-lōn'*).
Co'lon.
Colonel (*kur'nel*), 171.

☞ "The spelling is French; the pronunciation comes from the Spanish *Coronel.*" *Smart.*

Colonelcy (*kur'nel-sy*).
Co lo'ni-al.
Col'o-nist, 170.
Col-o-ni-za'tion, 112.
Col'o-nize, 170, 202.
Col'o-nīzed, 150, 183.
Col'o-nīz-ing.
Col-on-nade', 170.
Col'o-ny, 170.
Col'o-phon, 170.
Col o-pho'ni-an.
Col'o-pho-ny, *or* Co-loph'o-ny [*kol'o-fo-ny*, Wb. Gd.; *kol'o-fon-y*, Sm.; *ko-lof'o-ny*, Wk.; *ko-lof'o-ny*, or *kol'o-fo-ny*, Wr. 155.]
Col-o-quin'ti-da.
Col'or (*kul'ur*) (22) [Colour, Sm. 203.]
Col'or-a-ble (*kul'-*), 164.
Col'or-a-bly (*kul'-*).
Col-or-a'tion (*kul-*).
Col'or-a-ture (*kul'-*).
Col'ored (*kul'urd*), 171.
Col-or-if'ic (*kul-ur-if'-ik*) [so Sm. Wb. Gd.; *kol-or-if'ik*, Wk. Wr. 155.]
Col'or-ing (*kul'-*).
Col'or-ist (*kul'-*)
Col'ors (*kul'urz*).
Co-los'sal, 170.
Col-os-se'an, 110.
Col-os-se'um (L.) [Coliseum, 203.]
Co-los'sian (*ko-losh'an*).
Co-los'sus (L.) [L. pl. *Co-los'sī*; Eng. pl. Co-los'sus-es (*-ez*), 198.]
Col'pōrt-age [so Gd.; *kol-pōrt'aj*, Wr. 155.]
Col'pōrt-or [so Wb. Gd.; *kol-pōrt'or*. Wr. 155.]
Col'staff.
Cōlt, 24.
Cōlt'er [Coulter, 203.]
Colt's'-fōōt, 213.
Col'u-ber.
Col'u-brīne, 82, 152.
Co-lum'ba.
Col'um-ba-ry (72) [so Sm. Wb. Gd.; *ko-lum'ba-ry*, Wk.; *kol'-um-ba-ry*, or *ko-lum'-ba-ry*, Wr. 155.]
Co-lum'bi-an, 169.
Co-lum'bic.
Col-um-bif'er-ous, 108.
Col'um-bīne, 82, 152.
Col'um-bite.
Co-lum'bi-um, 169.
Col-u-mel'la, 170.
Col'umn (*-um*) (162) [*not* kol'yum, 153.]
Co-lum'nar.
Col'umned (*-umd*).
Co-lum-ni-a'tion.
Co-lure' (121) [*not* kōl'-yur, 153.]
Col'za.
Co'ma, 72.
Co-mate', *n.* [so Wk. Sm. Wr.; *kō'māt*, Gd. 155.]
Cōm'ate, *a.* [so Sm. Wr.; *ko'māt*, Wb. Gd. 155.]
Co'ma-tose [so Sm. Wb. Gd.; *kom-a-tōz'*, Wk. Wr. 155.]
Co'ma-toŭs [so Wb. Gd.; *kom'a-tus*, Wr. 155.]
Cōmb (*kōm*), 24, 162.
Com'bat (*kum'bat*, or *kom'bat*) [so Wr.; *kum'bat*, Wk. Sm.; *kom'bat*, Wb. Gd. 155.]
Com'bat-a-ble (*kum'-*, or *kom'-*) [so Wr.; *kom-bat'a-bl*, Gd. 155.]
Com'bat-ant (*kum'-*, or *kŏm'-*).
Com'bat-er (*kum'-*, or *kŏm'-*).
Com'bat-ĭve (*kum'-*, or *kŏm'-*).
Cōmbed (*kōmd*).
Com-bīn'a-ble, 164.
Com-bi-na'tion.
Com-bīn'a-to-ry, 72.
Com-bine'.
Com-bined', 150.
Com-bīn'er.
Cōmb'ing (*kōm'-*).
Com-bīn'ing.
Com-bust', 121.
Com-bus-ti-bil'i-ty.
Com-bus'ti-ble, 164, 169.
Com-bus'tion (*-bust'-yun*).
Com-bus'tĭve.
Come (*kum*), 22, 163.
Co-me'di-an, 169.
Com'e-dy, 171.
Come'li-ness (*kum'-*), 169
Come'ly (*kum'-*), 171.
Com'er (*kum'-*), 183.
Com'et, 18, 170.
Com-et-a'ri-um.
Com'et-a-ry, 72.
Com-et-og'ra-phy, 108.
Com'fit (*kum'-*), 22.
Com'fi-ture (*kum'-*).
Com'fort (*kum'-*), 135.
Com'fort-a-ble (*kum'-*), 132, 164.
Com'fort-ed (*kum'-*).
Com'fort-er (*kum'-*).
Com'fort-ing (*kum'-*).
Com'frey (*kum'fry*) [Cumfrey, Comfry, 203.]
Com'ic, 170.
Com'ic-al.
Com'ic-al-ly, 170.
Com'ing (*kum'-*), 183.
Co-mĭ'ti-a (L. pl.) (*ko-mish'ĭ-a*).
Co-mĭ'tial (*-mish'al*).
Com'i-ty, 169, 170.
Com'ma, 170.
Com-mand'.

☞ "Speakers of the old school, and the vulgar, universally pronounce the *a* broad [as in *far*] in both these words [*command* and *demand*]." *Smart*. They are very commonly pronounced, in the United States, *com-mănd'* and *de-mănd'*.

Com-man-dänt', 122.
Com-mand'ed.
Com-mand'er.
Com-mand'er-y [Commandry, 203.]
Com-mand'ing.
Com-mand'ment.
[Commandry, 203. — *See* Commandery.]
Com-mat'ic.
Com'ma-tism (*-tizm*).
Com-mĕas'ur-a-ble (*-mĕzh'-*), 164.
Com-mem'o-ra-ble, 164.
Com-mem'o-rate, 170.
Com-mem'o-rāt-ed.
Com-mem'o-rāt-ing.
Com-mem-o-ra'tion.
Com-mem'o-ra-tĭve, 84.
Com-mem'o-ra-to-ry.
Com-mence'.
Com-menced' (*-menst'*).
Com-mence'ment.
Com-menç'ing, 183.
Com-mend'.
Com-mend'a-ble [so Sm. Wr. Wb. Gd.; *kom'-men-da-bl*, or *kom-mend'a-bl*, Wk. 107,
Com-mend'a-bly. [155.]
Com-men'dam (L.).
Com-mend'a-ta-ry (72), *a*. holding in commendam. [*See* Commendatory, 148.]
Com-mend-a'tion.
Com-mend'a-tor.
Com-mend'a-to-ry, *a*. bestowing commendation. [*See* Commendatary, 148.]
Com-mend'ed.
Com-mend'ing.
Com-men-su-ra-bil'i-ty (*-shoo-*).
Com-men'su-ra-ble (*-shoo-*), 164, 171.
Com-men'su-rate (*-shoo-*).
Com-mĕn-su-ra'tion (*-shoo-*).
Com'ment, *v*. [so Wk. Sm. Wb. Gd.; *kom'-ent*, or *kom-ent'*, Wr. 155.]
Com'ment, *n*. 170.
Com'ment-a-ry, 72.
Com'ment-ā-tor.
Com-ment'ed.
Com'ment-er [so Sm. Wb. Gd.; *kom-ent'ur*, Wk.; *kom'ent ur*, or *kom-ent'ur*, Wr. 155.]
Com'merce (*-murs*), 170.
Com-mer'cial (*-shal*).
Com-mi-na'tion.
Com-min'a-to-ry.
Com-min'gle (*-ming'gl*), 54, 164. [*gld*).
Com-min'gled (*-ming'-*
Com-min'gling (*-ming'-gling*).
Com'mi-nate, 169, 170.
Com'mi-nāt-ed, 183.
Com'mi-nāt-ing.
Com-mi-nu'tion, 112.
Com-mis'er-a-ble (*-miz'-*), 164.
Com-mis'er-ate (*-miz'-*).
Com-mis'er-āt-ed (*-miz'-*).
Com-mis'er-āt-ing (*-miz'-*).
Com-mis-er-a'tion (*-miz-*).
Com-mis'er-a-tĭve (*-miz'-*).
Com-mis'er-āt-or (*-miz'-*).
Com-mis-sa'ri-al, 170.
Commissariat (Fr.) (*kom-is-sär'e-a*, or *kom-is-sa'ri-at*) [so Wr.; *kom-is-sär'e-a*, Sm.; *kom-is-sa'ri-at*, Wb. Gd.; 154, 155.]
Com'mis-sa-ry, 72, 170.
Com-mis'sion (*-mish'-un*). [*und*).
Com-mis'sioned (*-mish'-*
Com-mis'sion-er (*-mish'un-*).
Com-mis'sion-ing (*-mish'un-*).
Com-miss'ure (*-mish'-yur*), 91.
Com-mit', 170.
Com-mit'ment.
Com-mit'tal, 176.
Com-mit'ted.
Com-mit'tee (161, 170), *n*. a body of persons appointed for any purpose.
Com-mit-tee' (161), *n*. the person to whom the care of an idiot or a lunatic is committed.
Com-mit'ter (176) [Committor, 203.]
Com-mit'ti-ble, 164, 169.
Com-mit-tor', 118.

☞ This word is thus spelled and pronounced when it is contrasted with *Com-mit-tee'*.

Com-mix'.
Com-mixed' (*-mikst'*).
Com-mix'ing.
Com-mixt'ion (*-yun*).
Com-mixt'ure (*-yur*), 91.
Com-mode' [so Wk. Wr. Wb. Gd.; *kom'mud*, Sm. 155.]
Com-mo'di-oŭs [so Sm. Wr. Wb. Gd.; *kom-mo'di-us*, or *kom-mo'-ji-us*, Wk. 134, 155.]
Com-mod'i-ty, 169, 170.
Com'mo-dore (170) [so Sm. Gd.; *kom'mo-dōr*, or *kom-mo-dōr'*, Wk. Wr. 155.]
Com'mon, 170.
Com'mon-a-ble, 164, 169.
Com'mon-age.
Com'mon-al-ty, 145.
Com'mon-er, 170.
Com'mon-ness, 170.
Com'mon-place, *n*. & *a*.
Com-mon-place', *v*.
Com'mon-place-bŏŏk, 206, Exc. 4.
Com'mon-placed' (*-plāst'*).
Com-mon-plāç'ing.
Com'mons (*-munz*).
Com-mon-wēal'.
Com'mon-wĕalth, *or* Com-mon-wĕalth' [so Wr.; *kom'mon-welth*, Wk. Sm.; *kŏm-mon-welth'*, Wb. Gd. 155.]
Com-mon-wealths'man, 171, 214.
Com'mo-rance.
Com'mo-ran-cy.
Com-mo'tion.
Com-move' (*-moov'*).
Com-mune', 170.
Com-muned', 150.
Com-mu-ni-ca-bil'i-ty.
Com-mu'ni-ca-bly, 164.
Com-mu'ni-cant, 169.
Com-mu'ni-cate, 73, 78.
Com-mu'ni-cāt-ed, 183.
Com-mu'ni-cāt-ing.
Com-mu-ni-ca'tion.
Com-mu'ni-cāt-ĭve, 84.
Com-mu'ni-cāt-or.
Com-mu'ni-ca-to-ry.
Com-mūn'ing, 183.

Com-mūn′ion (-*yun*).
Com-mūn′ion-ist (-*yun*).
Com′mu-nism (-*nizm*).
Com′mu-nist.
Com-mu-nist′ic.
Com-mu′ni-ty, 169.
Com-mūt-a-bil′i-ty.
Com-mūt′a-ble, 164, 169.
Com-mu-ta′tion.
Com-mūt′a-tīve, 84.
Com-mūte′.
Com-mūt′ed.
Com-mūt′ing.
Com-mūt′u-al, 91, 170.
Co-mose′ [so Sm. Wr.; *ko′mōs*, Wb. Gd. 155.]
Com′pact, *n.* 103, 161.
Com-pact′, *a.* & *v.* 161.
Com-pact′ed.
Com-pact′i-ble, 164.
Com-pact′ing.
Com-pac′tion.
Com-pa′gēs (-*jēz*) [L. sing. & pl.]
Com-pan′ion (-*yun*), 51.
Com-pan′ion-a-ble (-*yun*-), 164, 169.
Com′pa-ny (*kum′*-).
Com′pa-ra-ble (122) [*not* kom-pêr′a-bl, 123, 153.]
Com′pa-rātes, *n. pl.*
Com-păr′a-tīve, 84, 170.
Com-pare′ (-*pêr′*), 14.
Com-pared′ (-*pêrd′*), 150, 183.
Com-par′er (-*pêr′*-).
Com-par′ing (-*pêr′*-).
Com-păr′i-son (*kom-păr′i-sun*, or *kom-păr′i-sn*) [so Wr.; *kom-păr′i-sun*, coll. *kom-păr′i-sn*, Sm.; *kom-păr′i-sun*, Wb. Gd.; *kom-păr′i-sn*, Wk. 156.]
Com-part′.
Com-part′ed.
Com-part′ing.
Com-part′ment.
Com′pass (*kum′*-), 22.
Com′pass-a-ble (*kum′*-), 164, 169.
Com′passed (*kum′past*).
Com′pass-es (*kum′pas-ez*), *n. pl.* 171.
Com′pass-ing (*kum′*-).
Com-pas′sion (-*pash′-un*).
Com-pas′sion-ate (-*pash′un*-).
Com-pas′sion-āt-ed (-*pash′un*-).
Com-pas′sion-āt-ing (-*pash′un*-).
Com-pat-i-bil′i-ty, 169.
Com-pat′i-ble, 164, 169.
Com-pa′tri-ot [so Wk. Sm. Wr.; *kom-pa′tri-ot*, or *kom-pat′ri-ot*, Gd. 155.]
Com-peer′, 121.
Com-pel′, 15.
Com-pel′la-ble, 164, 176.
Com-pel-la′tion, 112.
Com-pel′la-to-ry.
Com-pelled′ (-*peld′*), 150.
Com-pel′ler
Com-pel′ling.
Com′pend, 18
Com-pen′di-oŭs [so Sm. Wr. Wb. Gd.; *kom-pen′ji-us*, Wk. 134, 155.]
Com-pen′di-um, 169.
Com-pen′sate [so Wk. Sm. Wr.; *kom-pen′-sāt*, or *kom′pen-sāt*, Gd. 155.]
Com-pen′sāt-ed.
Com-pen′sāt-ing.
Com-pen-sa′tion.
Com-pen′sa-tīve.
Com-pen′sa-to-ry.
Com-pete′, 13.
Com-pēt′ed, 183.
Com′pe-tence.
Com′pe-ten-cy, 169.
Com′pe-tent.
Com-pēt′ing, 183.
Com-pe-tĭ′tion (-*tish′un*)
Com-pet′i-tīve, 84, 169.
Com-pet′i-tor, 171.
Com-pi-la′tion, 112.
Com-pile′, 25, 103.
Com-piled′, 150, 183.
Com-pīl′er.
Com-pīl′ing.
Com-pla′cence, 171.
Com-pla′cen-cy, 169.
Com-pla′cent.
Com-pla-cen′tial.
Com-plāin′, 23, 103.
Com-plāin′a-ble, 164.
Com-plāin′ant.
Com-plāined′, 150.
Com-plāin′er.
Com-plāin′ing.
Com-plāint′, 23.
Com-plāi-sance′ (-*zans′*) [so Wk. Sm. Wr.; *kom′pla-zans*, Wb. Gd. 155.]
Com-plāi-sant′ (-*zant′*) [so Wk. Sm. Wr.; *kom′plā-zant*, Wb. Gd. 155.]
Com′ple-ment, *n.* fulness. [*See* Compliment, 160.]
Com-ple-ment′al, *a.* that completes. [*See* Complimental, 160.]
Com-ple-ment′a-ry, *a.* completing. [*See* Complimental, 160.]
Com-plete′, 13, 103.
Com-plēt′ed.
Com-plēt′ing.
Com-ple′tion.
Com-plēt′īve.
Com-ple′to-ry, 86.
Com′plex [*not* kom-plex′, 153, 156.]
Com-plex′ion (-*plek′-shun*).
Com-plex′ion-a-ry (-*plek′shun*-), 72.
Com-plex′ioned (-*plek′-shund*).
Com-plex′i-ty, 169.
Com-pli′a-ble, 164.
Com-pli′ance.
Com-pli′ant, 169.
Com′pli-cate, 73, 78.
Com′pli-cāt-ed, 183.
Com′pli-cāt-ing.
Com-pli-ca′tion.
Com-pliç′i-ty, 169, 171.
Com-plied′, 186.
Com-pli′er.
Com′pli-ment, *n.* an act or an expression of civility. [*See* Complement, 160.]
Com-pli-ment′al, *a.* implying compliments. [*See* Complemental, 160.]
Com-pli-ment′a-ry, *a.* bestowing compliment. [*See* Complementary, 160.]
Com′pli-ment-er.
Com′plīne [Complin, 203.]
Com′plot, *n.* 161.
Com-plot′, *v.* 161.
Com-plot′ted, 176.
Com-plot′ting.
Com-plu-ten′sian (-*shan*).
Com-ply′, 25.
Com-pone′.
Com-po′nent [so Wk. Sm. Wr.; *kom-po′-nent*, or *kom′po-nent*, Gd. 155.]
Com-pōrt′.
Com-pōrt′a-ble, 164.

Com-pōrt′ed.
Com-pōrt′ing.
Com-pose′ (-pōz′), 24.
Com-posed′(-pōzd′),165, 183.
Com-pōs′er (-pōz′).
Com-pōs′ing (-pōz′-).
Com-pos′ĭte (-poz′it) (83, 152) [not kom′po-zit, 153.] [un).
Com-po-sĭ′tion (-zish′-
Com-pos′i-tĭve (-poz′-).
Com-pos′i-tor (-poz′-).
Com′pōst, n. 161.
Com-pōst′, v. 103, 161.
Com-pos′ure (-pōz′-),91.
Com′pote.
Com′pound, a. & n. 161.
Com-pound′, v. 161.
Com-pound′a-ble, 164.
Com-pound′ed.
Com-pound′er.
Com-pound′ing.
Com-pre-hend′, 122.
Com-pre-hend′ed.
Com-pre-hend′er.
Com-pre-hend′ing.
Com-pre-hen′si-ble, 164.
Com-pre-hen′si-bly.
Com-pre-hen′sion.
Com-pre-hen′sĭve.
Com-press′, v. 103, 161.
Com′press, n. 161.
Com-pressed′ (-prest′).
Com-pres-si-bil′i-ty,169.
Com-press′ing.
Com-press′ĭve.
Com-press′or.
Com-press′ure(-presh′-)
Com-print′, v. 161.
Com′print, n. 161.
Com-print′ed.
Com-print′ing.
Com-prise′ (-prīz′).
Com-prised′(-prīzd′)150
Com-prīs′ing (-prīz′-).
Com′pro-mise (-mīz).
Com′pro-mised (-mīzd).
Com′pro-mīs-er (-mīz-).
Com′pro-mīs-ing(-mīz-)
Com′pro-mit.
Com′pro-mit-ted[Compromited, Wb. Gd. 177, 203.]
Com′pro-mit-ting [Compromiting, Wb. Gd. 177, 203.]
Comp-trol′ler(kon-trōl′-ur) [Controller, 203.]

☞ This word is now written *Comptroller* only when used in a technical sense to denote *one who examines the accounts of other officers.*

Com-pul′sion.
Com-pul′sĭve.
Com-pul′so-ry, 86.
Com-punc′tion (-pungk′-).
Com-punc′tioŭs (-pungk′shus).
Com-pur-ga′tion.
Com′pur-gā-tor [so Sm. Wr.; kom-pur-ga′tor, Wb. Gd. 155.]
Com-pūt′a-ble, 164, 169.
Com-pu-ta′tion.
Com-pute′, 26.
Com-pūt′ed, 183.
Com-pūt′er.
Com-pūt′ing.
Com′rade [so Sm. Wb. Gd.; kum′răd, Wk.; kom′răd, or kum′răd, Wr. 155.]
Con, 18.
Con-cat′e-nate, 169.
Con-cat′e-nāt-ed.
Con-cat′e-nāt-ing.
Con-cat-e-na′tion.
Con′cave (kong′-), 54.
Con-cav′i ty, 108, 169.
Con-ca′voŭs.
Con-cēal′, 13.
Con-cēal′a-ble, 164, 169.
Con-cēaled′, 165.
Con-cēal′er.
Con-cēal′ing.
Con-cēal′ment.
Con-cede′.
Con-cēd′ed, 183.
Con-cēd′ing.
Con-cēit′, 121, 169, N.
Con-cēit′ed.
Con-ceit′ing.
Con-ceiv′a-ble, 164, 169.
Con′cēive′, 169.
Con-cēived′, 165, 183.
Con-cēiv′er.
Con-cēiv′ing.
Con-cent′, n. harmony. [See Consent, 160.]
Con-cen′trate.
Con-cen′trāt-ed, 183.
Con-cen′trāt-ing.
Con-cen-tra′tion.
Con-cen′tre [Concenter preferred by Wb. and Gd.—See Note E, p. 70.]
Con-cen′tric, 109.
Con-cen′tric-al, 108.
Con-cep′ta-cle, 164, 169.
Con-cep′tion.
Con-cep′tion-al-ist.
Con-cern′, 21, N.
Con-cerned′ (-sernd′), [165.
Con-cern′ing.
Con-cern′ment.
Con-cert′, v. 103, 161.
Con′cert, n. 103, 161.
Con-cert′ed.
Con-cert′ing.
Con-cer′to (It.) [pl. *Con-cer′tōs* (-tōz), 192.]
Con-ces′sion (-sesh′un).
Con-ces′sion-a-ry, 72.
Con-ces′sĭve.
Con-ces′so-ry.
Conch (kongk), 52, 54.
Conch′i-fer (kongk′-), 169.
Conch-if′er-oŭs (kongk-if′-), 108.
Conch′īte (kongk′-), 152.
Conch′oid (kongk′-).
Conch-oid′al (kongk-).
Conch-o-log′ic-al (kongk-o-loj′-), 108.
Conch-ol′o-gist(kongk-)
Conch-ol′o-gy (kongk-), 108.
Conch-yl-i-a′ceous (kongk-il-i-a′shus),112
Conch-yl-i-om′e-try (kongk-), 108.
Conch-yl′i-oŭs (kongk-)
Con-cierge (Fr.) (kon-sêrj′).
Con-cil′i-ate [so Sm. Wr. Wb. Gd.; kon-sil′yāt, Wk. 155.]
Con-cil′i-āt-ed, 183.
Con-cil′i-āt-ing.
Con-cil-i-a′tion.
Con-cil′i-āt-or.
Con-cil′i-a-to-ry[so Wk. Wr. Wb. Gd.; kon-sil′ya-tŭr-y, Sm. 155.]
Con-cise′, 121.
Con′clave (kong′-), 54.
Con′cla-vist (kong′-).
Con-clude′, 26.
Con-clūd′ed, 183.
Con-clūd′er.
Con-clūd′ing.
Con-clu′sion (-zhun).
Con-clu′sĭve, 84.
Con-clu′so-ry, 86.
Con-coct′, 103.
Con-coct′ed.
Con-coct′ing.
Con-coc′tion.
Con-coc′tĭve.
Con-com′i-tance, 78, 169.
Con-com′i-tan-cy, 169.
Con-com′i-tant, 169, 170.

Con′cord (*kong′-*), 54.
Con-cord′a-ble, 164.
Con-cord′ance, 169.
Con-cord′ant.
Con-cord′at.
Con-cord′ist.
Con′cōurse (*kong′kōrs*).
Con-cres′cence, 171.
Con-cres′ci-ble, 164, 169.
Con-crete′, *v.* 161.
Con′crete (*kong′krēt*), *n.* [so Sm. Wb. Gd.; *kon-krēt′*, Wk.; *kong′-krēt*, or *kon-krēt′*, Wr. 155.]
Con-crēt′ed, 183.
Con-crēt′ing.
Con-cre′tion.
Con-cre′tion-al.
Con-cre′tion-a-ry, 72.
Con-crēt′ĭve.
Con-cu′bin-age.
Con-cu′bin-a-ry, 72.
Con′cu-bīne (*kong′-*), 54.
Con-cu′pis-cence.
Con-cu′pis-cent.
Con-cur′, 21.
Con-curred, 150, 176.
Con-cŭr′rence, 169, 170.
Con-cŭr′rent.
Con-cur′ring.
Con-cus′sion(*-kush′un*).
Con-cus′sĭve, 84.
Con-demn′ (*-dem′*), 162.
Con-dem′na-ble, 164, 169.
Con-dem-na′tion.
Con-dem′na-to-ry.
Con-demned′ (*-demd′*), 162.
Con-dem′ner [*not* kon-dem′ur, 153.]
Con-dem′ning [*not* kon-dem′ing, 153.]
Con-den-sa-bil′i-ty.
Con-den′sa-ble, 164, 169.
Con-den-sa′tion.
Con-den′sa-tĭve.
Con-dense′, 103.
Con-densed′ (*-denst′*).
Con-dens′er.
Con-dens′ing.
Con′der, *n.* a pilot. [*See* Condor, 160.]
Con-de-scend′, 171.
Con-de-scend′ed.
Con-de-scend′ing.
Con-de-scen′sion.
Con-dign′ (*-dīn′*), 121, 162.
Con′di-ment, 160.
Con-dĭ′tion (*-dish′un*).
Con-dĭ′tion-al (*-dish′-un-*).
Con-dĭ′tioned (*-dish′-und*).
Con-do′la-to-ry, 86.
Con-dole′, 103.
Con-dōled′, 165, 183.
Con-dōle′ment.
Con-do′lence (169) [*not* kon′do-lens, 153.]
Con-dōl′er.
Con-dōl′ing.
Con′dor (88), *n.* a kind of vulture. [*See* Conder, 160.]
Con-duce′, 26.
Con-duced′ (*-dūst′*), Note C, p. 34.
Con-dūç′i-ble, 164, 169.
Con-duç′ĭve, 84.
Con′duct, *n.* 103, 161.
Con-duct′, *v.* 103, 161.
Con-duct′ed.
Con-duct-i-bil′i-ty, 108.
Con-duct′i-ble, 164, 169.
Con-duct′ing.
Con-duc′tion.
Con-duct′ĭve.
Con-duct-iv′i-ty.
Con-duct′or.
Con′duĭt (*kun′dit*, or *kon′dit*) [*kun′dit*, Wk. Sm. Wr.; *kon′dit*, Wb. Gd. 155.]
Con′dȳle, 171.
Con′dy-loid.
Cone, 24. [ny.]
[Coney, 203.— *See* Co-
Con-fab-u-la′tion.
Con-făr-re-a′tion.
Con-fect′, *v.* 103, 161.
Con′fect, *n.* 103, 161.
Con-fect′ed.
Con-fect′ing.
Con-fec′tion.
Con-fec′tion-er.
Con-fec′tion-er-y, 169.
Con-fed′er-a-cy, 169.
Con-fed′er-ate.
Con-fed′er-āt-ed, 183.
Con-fed′er-āt-er.
Con-fed′er-āt-ing.
Con-fed-er-a′tion.
Con-fer′, 21, N.
Con′fer-ence, 176.
Con-fer′ra-ble, 164, 170.
Con-ferred′, 150, 176.
Con-fer′rer, 21, N.
Con-fer′ring.
Con-fess′. 103.
Con-fessed′ (*-fest′*).
Con-fess′ing.
Con-fes′sion (*-fesh′un*).
Con-fes′sion-al (*-fesh′-un-*).
Con-fes′sion-a-ry, 72.
Con-fess′or, *or* Con′-fess-or [*kon-fes′ur*, Wb. Gd.; *kon′fes-ur*, Wk. Sm.; *kon′fes-ur*, or *kon-fes′ur*, Wr. 107, 155.]
Con-fi-dant′ (160), *n. mas.* [so Wk. Sm. Wr.; *kon′fi-dant*, Wb. Gd. 155.]
Con-fi-dante′ (160), *n. fem.* [so Sm. Wr.; *kon′fi-dant*, Gd. 155.]
Con-fide′, 25.
Con-fīd′ed, 183.
Con′fi-dence, 78, 169.
Con′fi-dent, 169.
Con-fi-den′tial (*-shal*).
Con-fīd′er.
Con-fīd′ing.
Con-fig-u-ra′tion.
Con-fīn′a-ble, 164, 169.
Con-fine′, *v.* (active), 103, 161.
Con′fine, *v.* (neuter) [so Sm. Wb. Gd.; *kon-fīn′*, Wk.; *kon-fīn′*, or *kon′fīn*, Wr. 155.]
Con′fine, *n.* 103, 161.
Con-fīned′, 165, 183.
Con-fine′ment.
Con-fīn′er (161), *n.* one who, or that which, confines.
Con′fīn-er (161), *n.* a borderer. [so Sm. Wb. Gd.; *kon-fīn′ur*, Wk.; *kon-fīn′ur*, or *kon′fi-nur*, Wr. 155.]
Con-fīn′ing.
Con-firm′, 21, N.
Con-firm′a-ble, 164.
Con-fir-ma′tion, 112.
Con-firm′a-tĭve.
Con-firm′a-to-ry, 86.
Con-firmed′, 165.
Con-firm-ee′ (122) [Law term.]
Con-firm′er.
Con-firm′ing.
Con-firm-or′ (118, 122) [Law term.]
Con-fis′ca-ble, 164.
Con-fis′cate, *v.* & *a.* [so Wk. Sm. Wr.; *kon-fis′kāt*, or *kon′fis-kāt*, Gd. 155.]
Con-fis′cāt-ed, 183.
Con-fis′cāt-ing.
Con-fis-ca′tion.
Con′fis-cāt-or.
Con-fis′ca-to-ry.

Con-fla-gra'tion.
Con-flict', *v.* 103, 161.
Con'flict, *n.* 103, 161.
Con-flict'ed.
Con-flict'ing.
Con-flict'ĭve.
Con'flu-ence, 169.
Con'flu-ent, *a.* & *n.* 169.
Con'flux.
Con-form'.
Con-form'a-ble, 164, 169.
Con-form'a-bly, 93.
Con-form-a'tion.
Con-formed', 165.
Con-form'ing.
Con-form'ist.
Con-form'i-ty, 169.
Con-found', 28.
Con found'ed.
Con-found'er.
Con-found'ing.
Con-fra-ter'ni-ty, 169.
Con-front' (*-frunt'*) [so Sm. Wb. Gd.; *kon-frŏnt'*, Wk.; *kon-frunt'*, or *kon-frŏnt'*, Wr. 155.]
Con-front'ed (*-frunt'-*).
Con-front'er (*-frunt'-*).
Con-front'ing (*-frunt'-*).
Con-fu'cian (*-shan*).
Con-fūs'a-ble (*-fūz'-*), 164.
Con-fuse' (*-fūz'*).
Con-fused' (*-fūzd'*), 183.
Con-fūs'ing (*-fūz'-*).
Con-fu'sion (*-zhun*).
Con-fūt'a-ble, 164.
Con-fūt'ant.
Con-fu-ta'tion.
Con-fūt'a-tĭve.
Con-fute', 26.
Con-fūt'ed.
Con-fūt'er.
Con-fūt'ing.
Con'gē (Fr.) [so Sm. Wr. Wb. Gd.; *kon-je'*, Wk. 155], *n.* leave.
Con'gē, *n.* a kind of moulding.
Con'gē, *v.* [so Sm. Gd.; *kon-je'*, Wk.; *kon'jē*, or *kon-je'*, Wr. 155.]
Con-gēal', 13.
Con-gēal'a-ble, 164, 169.
Con-gēaled'.
Con-gēal'ing.
Con-gēal'ment.
Con'geed, 188.
Con'gee-ing.
Con-ge-la'tion.
Con'ge-ner [so Sm. Wb. Gd.; *kon-je'nur*, Wk.; *kon'je-nur*, or *kon-je'-nur*, Wr. 155.]
Con-ge'ni-al, *or* Con-gēn'ial (*-yal*) [so Wr.; *kon-je'ni-al*, Wk. Sm. Wb. Gd. 155.]
Con-ge-ni-al'i-ty, 108, 169.
Con-gen'i-tal, 169.
Con'ger (*kong'gur*), 54, 138.
Con-ge'ri-ēs (*-ēz*), *n.* sing. & pl. 144.
Con-gest'.
Con-gest'ed.
Con-gest'ion (*-jest'yun*), 51.
Con-gest'ĭve, 84.
Con'gi-a-ry, 72.
Con-glo'bate [so Wk. Wr. Wb. Gd.; *kong'-glo bāt*, Sm. 155.]
Con-glo'bāt-ed, 183.
Con-glo'bāt-ing.
Con-glo-ba'tion.
Con-glob'u-late.
Con-glom'er-ate, 170.
Con-glom'er-āt-ed.
Con-glom'er-āt-ing.
Con-glom-er-a'tion.
Con-glu'ti-nant, 78, 169.
Con-glu'ti-nate.
Con-glu'ti-nāt-ed, 183.
Con-glu'ti-nāt-ing.
Con-glu-ti-na'tion.
Con-glu'ti-nāt-ĭve.
Con-glu'ti-nāt-or.
Con'go (*kong'gō*).
Con-grat'u-lant.
Con-grat'u-late, 108.
Con-grat'u-lāt-ed.
Con-grat'u-lāt-ing.
Con-grat-u-la'tion.
Con-grat'u-lāt-or.
Con-grat'u-la-to-ry, 171.
Con'gre-gate (*kong'-*), 169.
Con'gre-gāt-ed (*kong'-*).
Con'gre-gāt-ing (*kong'-*)
Con-gre-ga'tion (*kong-*).
Con-gre-ga'tion-al (*kong-*).
Con-gre ga'tion-al-ism (*-izm*).
Con-gre-ga'tion-al-ist (*kong-*).
Con'gress (*kong'-*), 54.
Con-gres'sion-al (*-gresh'un-*).
Con'gru-ence (*kong'-groo-*), 19, 54, 169.
Con-gru'en-cy (*-groo'-*), 169.
Con'gru-ent (*kong'-groo-*), 169.
Con-gru'i-ty (*-groo'-*), 19, 169.
Con'gru-oŭs (*kong'-groo-*).
Con'ic, 170.
Con'ic-al.
Co-nif'er-ous, 108.
Co'ni-form, 78, 169.
Co-ni-ros'tral.
Con-ject'ur-a-ble (*-yur-*), 91, 169. [183.
Con-ject'ur-al (*-yur-*),
Con-ject'ure, 91.
Con-ject'ured (*-yurd-*), 150.
Con-ject'ur-er (*-yur-*).
Con-ject'ur-ing (*-yur-*).
Con-join', 27.
Con-joined', 150.
Con-join'ing.
Con-joint', 121.
Con'ju-gal, 72.
Con'ju-gate, 73.
Con'ju-gāt-ed.
Con'ju-gāt-ing.
Con-ju-ga'tion-al.
Con-ju'gi-al.
Con-junct', 121.
Con-junc'tion, 171.
Con-junc'tion-al.
Con-junct'ĭve, 84.
Con-junct'ure, 91.
Con-ju-ra'tion.
Con-jure' (124, 161), *v.* to enjoin solemnly.
Con'jure (*kun'jur*) (124, 161), *v.* to practise magic.
Con-jured', 161, 183.
Con'jured (*kun'jurd*), 161.
Con-jūr'er (161), *n.* one who enjoins solemnly. [*See* Conjuror, 160.]
Con'jur-er (*kun'-*) (161), *n.* an enchanter.
Con-jūr'ing, 161, 183.
Con'jur-ing (*kun'-*), 161.
Con-jūr'or, *n.* one bound by oath with others. [Law term.—*See* Conjurer, 160.]
Con-nas'cence, 171.
Con-nas'cen-cy, 169.
Con-nas'cent.
Con-nate' [so Wk. Sm. Wr.; *kon'āt*, Wb. Gd. 155.]
Con-nat'u-ral.
Con-nect', 15, 103.

Con-nect'ed.
Con-nect'ing.
Con-nec'tion [Connexion, 203.]
Con-nect'ĭve, 84.
Con-nect'or.
Conned (*kŏnd*), 150, 176.
[Connexion, 203.—*See* Connection.]
Con'ning, 176.
Con-ni'vance, 169, 170.
Con-nive', 25, 103.
Con-nīved', 183.
Con-nīv'ent.
Con-nīv'er.
Con-nīv'ing.
Con-nois-seur' (Fr.) (*kon-is-sūr'*, or *kon-is-sur'*) [so Wr.; *kon-is-sūr'*, or *kon'is-sêr*, Gd.; *kon-nā-sur'*, Sm. 154, 155.]
Con-nu'bi-al, 169, 170.
Co'noid.
Co-noid'al, 72.
Co-noid'ic, 109.
Co noid'ic-al, 108.
Con'quer (*kong'kur*) (54) [so Sm. Wr.; *konk'ur*, Wb. Gd.; *kong'kur*, or *kong'kwur*, Wk. 155.]
Con'quer-a-ble (*kong'kur-*), 164, 169.
Con'quered(*kong'kurd*)
Con'quer ing (*kong'kur-*).
Con'quer-er (*kong'kur-*)
Con'quest (*kong'kwest*), 54.
Con-san-guin'e-oŭs, 169.
Con-san-guin'i-ty, 171.
Con'science (*-shens*), 171
Con'scienced (*-shenst*).
Con-sci-en'tioŭs (*-shĭ-en'shus*) [*not* kon-sĭ-en'shus, 153, 155.]
Con'scious (*-shus*).
Con'script.
Con-scrip'tion.
Con'se-crate, 169.
Con'se-crăt-ed.
Con'se-crăt-er.
Con'se-crăt-ing.
Con-se cra'tion.
Con-sec-ta'ne-oŭs, 169.
Con'sec-ta-ry, *or* Con sec'ta-ry [*kon'sek-ta-ry*, Wk. Wr. Wb. Gd.; *kon-sek'ta-ry*, Sm. 155]
Con-se-cu'tion.
Con-sec'u-tĭve.
Con-se-nes'cence.
Con-se-nes'cen-cy.
Con-sent', *n.* concurrence: — *v.* to agree. [*See* Concent, 160.]
Con-sen-ta'ne-ous, 169.
Con-sent'ed.
Con-sent'er.
Con-sen'tient (*-shent*).
Con-sent'ing.
Con'se-quence.
Con'se-quent.
Con-se-quen'tial (*-shal*).
Con-serv'a-ble, 164, 169.
Con-serv'an-cy.
Con-serv'ant.
Con-ser-va'tion.
Con-serv'a-tism (*-tizm*), 136.
Con-serv'a-tĭve.
Con'ser-vā-tor, *or* Con-ser-va'tor [*kon'ser-vā-tor*, Sm. Wr.; *kon-sur-va'tor*, Wk. Wb. Gd. 155.]
Con-serv'a-to-ry, 86.
Con-serve', *v.* 103, 161.
Con'serve, *n.* 103, 161.
Con-served', 150, 183.
Con-serv'er.
Con-serv'ing.
Con-sid'er, 104.
Con-sid'er-a-ble, 164, 169.
Con-sid'er-a-bly.
Con-sid'er-ate, 73.
Con-sid-er-a'tion.
Con-sid'ered (*-urd*), 150.
Con-sid'er-er.
Con-sid'er-ing.
Con-sign' (*-sīn'*), 162.
Con-signed' (*-sīnd'*).
Con-sign-ee' (*-sīn-*), 118.
Con-sign'er (*sīn'-*).
Con-sign'ing (*-sīn'-*).
Con-sign'ment (*-sīn'-*).
Con-sign-or' (*kon-sīn-or'*) [Law term, correlative to *Consignee*]
Con-sist', 16.
Con-sist'ed.
Con-sist'ence.
Con-sist'en-cy, 169.
Con-sist'ent.
Con-sist'ing.
Con-sis-to'ri-al, 49, N.
Con'sis-to-ry, *or* Con-sis'to-ry [so Wr.; *kon'sis-to-ry*, Wk. Sm.; *kon-sist'o-ry*, Wb. Gd. 155.]
Con-so'ci-ate (*-shĭ-*) (46, 73) [so Wk. Sm. Wr.; *kon-so'shăt*, Wb. Gd. 155.]
Con-so'ci-āt-ed, (*-shĭ-*).
Con-so'ci-āt-ing (*-shĭ-*).
Con-so-ci-a'tion (*-shĭ-*).
Con-sōl'a-ble, 164, 169.
Con-so-la'tion.
Con-sol'a-to-ry, 86.
Con-sole', *v.* 161.
Con'sole, *n.* 161.
Con-sōled', 150, 183.
Con-sōl'er.
Con-sol'i-dant, 169.
Con-sol'i-date, 169.
Con-sol'i-dāt-ed, 183.
Con-sol'i-dāt-ing.
Con-sol-i-da'tion.
Con-sōl'ing, 183.
Con-sols', *or* Con'sols (*-sŏlz*) [so Wr.; *kon-sŏlz'*, Sm.; *kon'solz*, Wb. Gd. 155.]

☞ "The uninitiated talk of selling *con'sols*, till they learn on the stock exchange that the technical pronunciation is *con-sols'*." *Smart.*

Con'so-nance.
Con'so-nan-cy.
Con'so-nant, 169.
Con-so-nant'al.
Con'so-noŭs.
Con'sort, *n.* 161.
Con-sort', *v.* 103, 161.
Con-sort'ed.
Con-sort'ing.
Con-spic'u-oŭs.
Con-spĭr'a-cy, 169.
Con-spi-ra'tion, 112.
Con-spĭr'a-tor.
Con-spire', 25.
Con-spīred', 150, 183.
Con-spīr'er, 49, N.
Con-spīr'ing.
Con'sta-ble (*kun'-*), 22, 164.
Con-stab'u-la-ry, 72.
Con'stan-cy, 164.
Con'stant.
Con'stel-late [so Sm. Wb. Gd.; *kon-stel'lāt*, Wk. Wr. 155.]
Con-stel-la'tion, 112, 170.
Con-ster-na'tion.
Con'sti-pate, 169.
Con'sti-pāt-ed, 183.
Con'sti-pāt-ing.
Con-sti-pa'tion.
Con-stit'u-en-cy, 169.
Con-stit'u-ent.
Con'sti-tute, 78.
Con'sti-tūt-ed, 183.
Con'sti-tūt-er.
Con'sti-tūt-ing.

Con-sti-tu′tion.
Con-sti-tu′tion-al.
Con-sti-tu′tion-al-ist.
Con-sti-tu-tion-al′i-ty.
Con-sti-tu′tioned (*-shund*), 171.
Con-sti-tu′tion-ist.
Con′sti-tūt-ĭve.
Con-strain′, 23.
Con-strāin′a-ble, 164.
Con-strāined′, 150.
Con-strāin′er.
Con-strāin′ing.
Con-strāint′.
Con-strict′.
Con-strict′ed.
Con-strict′ing.
Con-stric′tion.
Con-strict′ĭve, 84.
Con-strict′or.
Con-stringe′.
Con-stringed′(*-strinjd′*)
Con-string′ent (*-strinj′-ent*), 183.
Con-stringe′ing.
Con-struct′.
Con-struct′ed.
Con-struct′er [Constructor, 203.]
Con-struc′tion.
Con-struc′tion-al.
Con-struc′tion-ist.
Con-struct′ĭve.
Con-struct′or [Constructer, 203.]
Con′strue (*kon′stroo*) [so Sm. Wr.; *kon′-stru*, Wb. Gd.; *kon′-stru*, or *kon′stur*, Wk. 155.]

☞ "It is a scandal to seminaries of learning, that the latter pronunciation [*kon′stur*] should prevail there." *Walker.*

Con′strued (*-strood*), 183
Con′stru-ing (*-stroo-*).
Con-sub-stan′tial (*-shal*)
Con-sub-stan-ti-al′i-ty (*-shĭ-*).
Con-sub-stan′ti-ate (*-shĭ-āt*) [so Wk. Sm. Wr.; *kon-sub-stan′-shāt*, Wb. Gd. 155.]
Con-sub-stan-ti-a′tion (*-shĭ-*).
Con′sue-tude (*-swe-*), 171
Con-sue-tu′di-nal(*-swe-*)
Con-sue-tu′di-na-ry (*-swe-*), 72.
Con′sul, 18.
Con′sul-age.
Con′sul-ar [so Sm. Wr. Wb. Gd.; *kon′shu-lar*, Wk. 155.]
Con′sul-ate, 73.
Con-sult′, *v.*
Con-sult′, *or* Con′sult, *n.* [*kon-sult′*, Sm. Wb. Gd.; *kon′sult*, or *kon-sult′*, Wk. Wr. 155.]
Con-sult-a′tion.
Con-sult′ed.
Con-sult′er.
Con-sult′ing.
Con-sult′ĭve.
Con-sūm′a-ble, 164, 169.
Con-sume′.
Con-sumed′, 183.
Con-sūm′er.
Con-sūm′ing.
Con-sum′mate, *v.* [so Wk. Sm. Wr.; *kon-sum′āt*, or *kon′sum-āt*, Gd. 155.]
Con-sum′mate, *a.*
Con-sum′māt-ed.
Con-sum′māt-ing.
Con-sum-ma′tion.
Con-sump′tion (*-sum′-*), 162.
Con-sump′tĭve (*-sum′-*).
Con′tact, 18.
Con-tact′u-al.
Con-ta′gion (*-jun*), 171.
Con-ta′gion-ist (*-jun-*).
Con-ta′gioŭs (*-jus*).
Con-tāin′, 23.
Con-tāin′a-ble, 164, 169.
Con-tāin′ant.
Con-tāined′, 150.
Con-tāin′er.
Con-tāin′ing.
Con-tam′i-nate, 78, 169.
Con-tam′i-nāt-ed.
Con-tam′i-nāt-ing.
Con-tam-i-na′tion.
Con-temn′ (*-tem′*), 162.
Con-temned′ (*-temd′*).
Con-tem′ner.
Con-tem′ning.
Con-tem′plate (122) [so Wk. Sm.; *kon-tem′-plāt*, or *kon′tem-plāt*, Gd. 155.]
Con-tem′plāt-ed, 183.
Con-tem′plāt-ing.
Con-tem-pla′tion.
Con-tem′pla-tĭve.
Con-tem′plāt-or, *or* Con′tem-plāt-or [so Wr.; *kon-tem′plāt-or*, Wk.; *kon′tem-plāt-or*, Sm. Wb. Gd. 155.]
Con-tem-po-ra′ne-oŭs, 171.
Con-tem′po-ra-ry (72) [Cotemporary, 203.]

☞ Webster and Goodrich prefer *co-temporary*. But Smart, Worcester, and most writers give the preference to *con-temporary*. "I prefer *con-temporary*," says Dr. Campbell, 'to *co-temporary*. The general use in words compounded with the inseparable preposition *con* is to retain the *n* before a consonant, and expunge it before a vowel or an *h* mute." There are several exceptions to the rule referred to by Dr. Campbell, as *co-partner*, *co-parcener*, *co-regent*, *co-tidal*, *co-tenant*, *co-trustee*, *co-worker*.

Con-tempt′, 15.
Con-temp′ti-ble (*kon-tem′ti-bl*) (164, 169) [so Wk. Sm. Wr.; *kon-tempt′i-bl*, Wb. Gd. 155.]
Con-temp′ti-bly (*-tem′-*)
Con-tempt′u-oŭs, 89.
Con-tend′, 15.
Con-tend′ed.
Con-tend′er.
Con-tend′ing.
Con-tent′, *a. v. & n.* 15.
Con-tent′ed.
Con-tent′ing.
Con-ten′tion.
Con-ten′tious (*-shus*).
Con-tent′ment.
Con-tents′, *or* Con′-tents, *n. pl.* [so Wr.; *kon-tents′*, Wk. Sm.; *kon′tents*, or *kon-tents′*, Gd. 155.]

☞ Walker says of this word that it "is often heard with the accent on the first syllable."

Con-ter′mi-noŭs.
Con-test′, *v.* 15, 103, 161.
Con′test, *n.* 161.
Con-test′a-ble, 164, 169.
Con-test-a′tion.
Con-test′ed.
Con-test′ing.
Con′text, 18.
Con-text′u-ral.
Con-text′ure, 91.
Con-ti-gu′i-ty, 169.
Con-tig′u-oŭs.
Con′ti-nence, 78, 169.
Con′ti-nen-cy.

Con′ti-nent, 169.
Con-ti-nent′al.
Con-tin′gence.
Con-tin′gen-cy, 169.
Con-tin′gent.
Con-tin′u-a-bly, 164.
Con-tin′u-al.
Con-tin′u-ance.
Con-tin-u-a′tion.
Con-tin′u-a-tĭve, 84, 106.
Con-tin′ue (-*yoo*).
Con-tin′ued (-*yood*), 183.
Con-tin′u-er.
Con-tin′u-ing.
Con-ti-nu′i-ty, 169.
Con-tin′u-oŭs.
Con-tour′ (Fr.) (*kon-toor′*), 114, 121.
Con-tort′.
Con-tort′ed.
Con-tort′ing.
Con-tor′tion, 112.
Con′tra-band.
Con-tract′, *v.* 103, 161.
Con′tract, *n.* 103, 161.
Con-tract′ed.
Con-tract-i-bil′i-ty.
Con-tract′i-ble, 164, 169.
Con-tract′ĭle, 81, 152.
Con-tract′ing.
Con-trac′tion.
Con-tract′ĭve.
Con-tract′or.
Con′tra-dance [Coun-try-dance, 203. — *See* Country-dance.]
Con-tra-dict′, 122.
Con-tra-dict′ed.
Con-tra-dict′er.
Con-tra-dict′ing.
Con-tra-dic′tion.
Con-tra-dict′ĭve.
Con-tra-dict′or.
Con-tra-dict′o-ry, 86.
Con-tra-dis-tinc′tion.
Con-tra-dis-tin′guish (-*ting′gwish*), 54.
Con-tra-dis-tin′guished (-*ting′gwisht*), Note C, p. 34.
Con-tra-dis-tin′guish-ing (-*ting′gwish*-).
Con-tral′to (It.).
Con-tra-mure′, 122.
Con′tra-rĭes (-*rĭz*), *n. pl.*
Con-tra-ri′e-ty, 169.
Con′tra-ri-ly, 171.
Con′tra-ry, 72.
Con′trȧst, *n.* 103, 161.
Con-trȧst′, *v.* 103, 131, 161
Con-trȧst′ed.
Con-trȧst′ing.
Con-tra-val-la′tion.
Con-tra-vene′, 122.
Con-tra-vēned′, 165, 183.
Con-tra-vēn′er.
Con-tra-vēn′ing.
Con-tra-ven′tion.
Con-trib′u-ta-ry (72) [Contributory, 203.]
Con-trib′ute [*not* kon′-tri-būt, 153, 156.]
Con-trib′ūt-ed, 183.
Con-trib′ūt-ing.
Con-tri-bu′tion.
Con-trib′ūt-ĭve.
Con-trib′ut-or.
Con-trib′u-to-ry [Con-tributary, 203.]
Con′trite [so Wk. Wr. Wb. Gd.; *kon-trīt′*, Sm. 155.]

☞ "This word ought to have the accent on the last syllable." *Walker*. — "This word is accented both ways, more commonly on the first syllable, more consistently on the last." *Smart*.

Con-trĭ′tion (*trish′un*).
Con-trīv′a-ble, 164, 169.
Con-trīv′ance, 169.
Con-trive′.
Con-trīved′, 165, 183.
Con-trīv′er.
Con-trīv′ing.
Con-trōl′, 24.
Con-trōl′la-ble, 164, 176.
Con-trōlled′(-*trōld′*), 165
Con-trōl′ler [Comp-troller, 203. — *See* Comptroller.]
Con-trōl′ling.
Con-tro-ver′sial (-*shal*).
Con′tro-ver-sy, 169.
Con′tro-vert.
Con′tro-vert-ed.
Con′tro-vert-ing.
Con′tro-vert-ist.
Con-tu-ma′cious(-*shus*).
Con′tu-mȧ-cy, 122, 169.
Con-tu-me′li-oŭs.
Con′tu-me-ly, 122, 171.
Con-tuse′ (-*tūz′*).
Con-tused′ (-*tūzd′*), 183.
Con-tūs′ing (-*tūz′*-).
Con-tu′sion (-*zhun*).
Co-nun′drum, 86.
Con-va-lesce′ (-*les′*).
Con-va-lesced′ (-*lest′*).
Con-va-les′cence, 171.
Con-va-les′cent.
Con-va-les′cing.
Con-vec′tion.
Con-vēn′a-ble, 164, 169.
Con-vene′, 13.
Con-vened′, 165, 183.
Con-vēn′er.
Con-vēn′ience (-*yens*) (171) [so Wr. Gd.; *kon-ve′ni-ens*, Wk. Sm. 155.]
Con-vēn′ien-cy (-*yen*-), 169.
Con-vēn′ient (-*yent*-) [so Wr. Gd.; *kon-ve′ni-ent*, Wk. Sm. 155.]
Con′vent, *n.*
Con-ven′ti-cle, 164, 171.
Con-ven′ti-cler, 183.
Con-ven′tion.
Con-ven′tion-al.
Con-ven′tion-al-ism (-*izm*).
Con-ven′tion-a-ry, 72.
Con-vent′u-al.
Con-verge′, 21, N.
Con-verged′, 165, 183.
Con-verg′ence (-*verj′*-).
Con-verg′en-cy (-*verj′*-), 169.
Con-verg′ent (-*verj′*-).
Con-verg′ing (-*verj′*-).
Con-ver′sa-ble, 164, 169.
Con′ver-sance [so Gd.; *kon′ver-sans*, or *kon-ver′sans*, Wr. 155.]
Con′ver-sant (169) [so Sm. Wr. Wb. Gd.; *kon′ver-sant*, or *kon-ver′sant*, Wk. 155.]
Con-ver-sa′tion, 112.
Con-ver-sa′tion-al.
Con-ver-sa′tion-ist.
Con-ver′sa-tĭve, 72, 84.
Conversazione (It.) (*kon-ver-sat-se-o′nā*) [pl. *Conversazioni* (*kon-ver-sȧt-se-o′nē*).]
Con-verse′, 21, N.
Con-versed′ (-*verst′*), 183
Con-vers′er.
Con-vers′ing.
Con-ver′sion.
Con-vers′ĭve.
Con-vert′, 21, N.
Con-vert′ed.
Con-vert′er.
Con-vert-i-bil′i-ty, 169.
Con-vert′i-ble, 164, 169.
Con′vex [*not* kon-veks′, 153, 156.]
Con-vex′i-ty, 108, 169.
Con′vex-ly (93) [so Sm. Wr. Wb. Gd.; *kon-veks′ly*, Wk. 155.]
Con-vey′ (-*va′*), 23.
Con-vey′a-ble (-*va′*-), 169

Con-vey'ance(-va'-),169.
Con-vey'anç-er (-va'), 183
Con-vey'anç-ing (-va'-).
Con-veyed' (-vād'), 150.
Con-vey'er (-va'-).
Con-vey'ing (-va'-).
Con-vict', *v.* 16, 103, 161.
Con'vict, *n.* 103, 161.
Con-vict'ed.
Con-vict'ing.
Con-vic'tion.
Con-vict'ĭve.
Con-vince', 16, 103.
Con-vinced' (-*vinst'*), 165, 183.
Con-vinç'er.
Con-vinç'i-ble, 164, 169.
Con-vinç'ing.
Con-viv'i-al (169) [so Sm. Wb. Gd., *kon-viv'yal*, Wk. 155.]
Con-viv'i-al-ist.
Con-viv-i-al'i-ty, 108.
Con-vo-ca'tion.
Con-voke', 24, 103.
Con-voked' (-*vōkt'*), Note C, p. 34.
Con-vōk'ing, 183.
Con'vo-lute.
Con'vo-lūt-ed.
Con-vo-lu'tion, 112.
Con-volve', 18.
Con-volved' (-*volvd'*-), 183.
Con-vŏlv'ing.
Con-voy', *v.* 27, 103, 161.
Con'voy, *n.* 103, 161.
Con-vulse', 22, 163.
Con-vulsed' (-*vulst'*), [183.
Con-vuls'ing.
Con-vul'sion.
Con-vul'sion-a-ry, 72.
Con-vul'sĭve.
Co'ny, *or* Con'y (*kun'y*) [so Gd.; *ko'ny*, Sm.; *kun'y*, Wk., *kun'y*, or *ko'ny*, Wr. 155.]

☞ "It is familiarly pronounced *cun'ey*; the former or regular pronunciation [ko'ny] is that proper for solemn reading." *Smart.*

Coo, 19.
Cooed (*kood*), 188.
Coo'ing.
Cŏŏk (20) [*See* Book.]
Cŏŏked (*kŏŏkt*), Note C, p. 34.
Cŏŏk'er-y, 93.
Cŏŏk'ing.
Cŏŏk'y, 93.
Cool, 19.
Cooled, 165.
Cool'er.
Cool'ing.
Cool'ly, *ad.* 66, N.; 148.
Coo'ly, *n.* (148) [pl. Coolies, 190.]
Coom, *n.* dirt. [*See* Comb, 160.]
Coomb (*koam*), *n.* (162) a dry valley. [*See* Coom, 160.]
Coop, 19.
Coo-pee' [Coupee, 203.]
Coop'er, *or* Cŏŏper [so Sm. Wr.; *koop'er*, Wk.; *kŏŏp'ur*, Wb. Gd. 155.]
Coop'er-age.
Co-op'er-ate, 223.
Co-op'er-at-ed, 183.
Co-op'er-at-ing.
Co-op-er-a'tion.
Co-op'er-āt-ĭve.
Co-op'er-āt-or.
Coop'er-ing.
Coop'er-y.
Co-or'di-nate, 223.
Co-or-di-na'tion.
Coot, 19.
Co-pāi'ba (*ko-pa'ba*) [so Sm. Gd.; *ko-pe'ba*, Wr. 155.] [Copaiva, Copayva, Copivi, Capivi, 203.]
Co'pal.
Co-par'ce-na-ry, 72.
Co-par'ce-ny, 169.
Co-part'ner.
[Copayva, 203.—*See* Copaiba.]
Cope, 24.
Coped (*kōpt*), Note C, p. 34.
Co-per'ni-can, 21, N.; 169
Cop'ĭed (-*id*), 99, 186.
Cop'i-er [Copyer, 203.]
Cōp'ing.
Co'pi-oŭs, 78, 169.
[Copivi, 203.—*See* Copaiba.]
Copped (*kopt*).
[Coppel, 203.—*See* Cupel.]
Cop'per, 66, 170.
Cop'per-as, 171.
Cop'pered (-*purd*), 165.
Cop'per-ing.
Cop'per-plate, 206.
Cop'per-y, 93.
Cop'pis (*kop'is*), 169.
Cop'ple-crown.
Cop'ro-līte, 83, 152.
Cop-ro-lit'ic.
Co-proph'a-goŭs.
Cŏpse (*kops*), 171.
Cop'sy.
Copt.
Cop'tic.
Cop'u-la (L.) [pl. Cop'u-læ, 198.]
Cop'u-late.
Cop'u-lāt-ed.
Cop'u-lāt-ing.
Cop-u-la'tion.
Cop'u-la-tĭve, 84, 89
Cop'y, 169, 170.
[Copyer, 203.—*See* Copier.]
Cop'y-hōld.
Cop'y-ing, 186
Cop'y-ist.
Cop'y-right (-*rīt*), 162.
Co-quet' (*ko-ket'*), *v.*160.
Co-quet'ry (-*ket'*-), 156.
Co-quette' (*ko-ket'*), *n.* 160.
Co-quet'ted (-*ket'*-), 176.
Co-quet'ting (-*ket'*-).
Cŏr'a-cle, 164.
Cŏr'a-coid.
Cŏr'al (170), *n.* a hard substance found in the ocean, and formed of the skeletons of certain polypes. [*See* Corol, 160.]
Cŏr-al-lā'ceous (-*shus*).
Cŏr-al-lif'er-oŭs, 108.
Co-ral'li-form, 169.
Cŏr-al-lig'e-noŭs (-*lij'*-).
Cŏr'al-līne, 82, 152.
Cŏr'al-lite, 83, 152.
Cŏr-al loid'al.
Cŏr'a-nach(-*nak*) [Coranich, Coronach, 203.]
Corb.
Corb'an.
Cor'beil (*kor'bel*), *n.* a little basket to be filled with earth,—a term in fortification. [*See* Corbel, 160.]
Cor'bel, *n.* a sculptured basket,—a term in architecture. [*See* Corbeil, 160.]
Cord, *n.* a small rope. [*See* Chord, 160.]
Cord'age, 169.
Cor'date.
Cor'dāt-ed.
Cord'ed.
Cor'di-al, *or* Cord'ial

(*kord'yal*) [*kor'di-al*, Sm. Wb. Gd.; *kord'-yal*, or *kor'di-al*, Wr.; *kor'ji-al*, Wk. 134, 155.]
Cor-di-al'i-ty, *or* Cord-ial'i-ty (*-yal'-*) [*kor-di al'i-ty*, Sm. Wb. Gd.; *kord-yi-al'i-ty*, Wr.; *kor-ji-al'i-ty*, Wk. 134, 155.]
Cor'di-form, 169.
Cord'ing.
Cor'don (Fr.) (*kor'don*, or *kor'dŏng*) [*kor'don*, Wb. Gd.; *kor'dŏng*, Sm.; *kor'don*, or *kor'-dŏng*, Wr. 154, 155.]
Cor'do-van.
Cor'du-roy [so Sm.Wr.; *kor-du-roi'*, Wb. Gd. 155.]
Cord'wāin-er.
Core, 24, 163.
Cored (*kōrd*), 165, 183.
Co-ri-a'ceous (*-shus*), 112
Co-ri-an'der.
Co-rin'thi-an, 78, 169.
Cork, 17.
Corked (*korkt*), Note C, [p. 34.
Cork'ing.
Cork'-tree, 206, Exc. 4.
Cork'y, 93.
Cor'mo-rant.
Corn, 17.
Cor'ne-a, 75, 169.
Corned (*kornd*), 165.
Cor'nel, 149.
Cor'ner, 17, 77.
Cor'nered (*-nurd*), 165.
Cor'ner-ing.
Cor'net.
Cor'net-cy, 169.
Corn'fiēld, 206.
Cor'nīce (*-nis*), 169.
Cor'ni-cle, 78, 164.
Cor-nic'u-late, 73, 89.
Cor'ni-form, 169.
Cor'nist.
Corn'-laws (*-lawz*).
Cor-nu-co'pi-a (L.) [pl. *Cor-nu-co'pi-æ*(*-pĭ-ē*), 198.]
Cor-nute'.
Corn'y, 93.
Cŏr'o-dy [Corrody, 203.]
Cŏr'ol, *n.* a corolla. [*See* Coral, 160.]
Co-rol'la, 170.
Cŏr-ol-la'ceous (*-shus*).
Cŏr'ol-la-ry (72) [so Wk. Sm. Wb. Gd., *kor'-ol-a-ry*, or *ko-rol'a-ry*, Wr. 155.]
Cŏr'ol-late.
Cŏr'ol-lāt-ed.
Cŏr'ol-let.
Co-ro'na (L.) [pl. Co-ro'næ (*-nē*).]
[Coronach, 203. — *See* Coranach.]
Cŏr'o-nal, *n.* & *a.* [so Sm. Wb. Gd.; *ko-ro'-nal*, Wk.; *ko-ro'nal*, or *kŏr'o-nal*, Wr. 155.]
Cŏr'o-na-ry, 72.
Cŏr'o-nāt-ed.
Cŏr-o-na'tion.
Cŏr'o-ner, 77, 170.
Cŏr'o-net, 86, 170.
Cŏr'o-net-ed.
Co-ron'i-form, 78, 169.
Cŏr'o-noid.
Cŏr'o-nule.
Cor'po-ral.
Cor-po-ra'lē (L.), 163.
Cor'po-ral-ly, 170.
Cor'po-rate, 73.
Cor-po-ra'tion.
Cor'po-rāt-or.
Cor-po're-al, 169.
Cor-po're-al-ly.
Cor-po-re'i-ty, 108, 169.
Cor'po-sant (*-zant*).
Corps (Fr.) (*kōr*) (156), *n.* a body of troops. [*See* Core, 160.] [pl. Corps (*kōrz*).]
Corpse (*korps*), *n.* a dead human body. [*See* Corps, 148.]
Cor'pu-lence, 169.
Cor'pu-len-cy, 169.
Cor'pu-lent.
Cor-pus'cle (*-pus'l*), 162.
Cor-pus'cu-lar, 108.
Cor-rect', 15, 105.
Cŏr-rect'ed.
Cŏr-rect'ing.
Cŏr-rec'tion, 170.
Cŏr-rec'tion-al.
Cŏr-rect'īve, 84.
Cŏr-rect'or.
Cŏr-rect'o-ry, 86.
Cŏr're-late.
Cŏr-re-la'tion.
Cŏr-rel'a-tīve, 84, 170.
Cŏr-re-spond', 170.
Cŏr-re-spond'ed.
Cŏr-re-spond'ence, 169.
Cŏr-re-spond'ent.
Cŏr-re-spond'ing.
Cor'ri-dōr, 78, 170.
Cŏr-ri-gen'da (L.), *n.pl.*
Cŏr'ri-gent, 78.
Cŏr-ri-gi-bil'i-ty, 171.
Cŏr'ri-gi-ble, 164.
Cŏr-ri'val.
Cŏr-ri'val-ry.
Cŏr-rob'o-rant.
Cŏr-rob'o-rate, 170.
Cŏr-rob'o-rāt-ed.
Cŏr-rob'o-rāt-ing.
Cŏr-rob-o-ra'tion.
Cŏr-rob'o-ra-tīve.
Cŏr-rob'o-ra-to-ry, 86.
Cŏr-rode', 24.
Cŏr-rōd'ed, 183.
Cŏr-rōd'ent, 169.
Cŏr-rōd'ing.
Cŏr'ro-dy [Corody, 203.]
Cŏr-ro'sion (*-zhun*).
Cŏr-ro'sīve, 84.
Cŏr'ru-gant, 170.
Cŏr'ru-gate, 66, 89.
Cŏr'ru-gāt-ed, 183.
Cŏr'ru-gāt-ing.
Cŏr-ru-ga'tion, 112.
Cŏr'ru-gāt-or.
Cŏr-ru'gent (*-roo'-*), 26.
Cŏr-rupt', 22.
Cŏr-rupt'ed.
Cŏr-rupt'er.
Cŏr-rupt-i-bil'i-ty, 169.
Cŏr-rupt'i-ble, 78, 164.
Cŏr-rupt'i-bly.
Cŏr-rupt'ing.
Cŏr-rup'tion.
Cŏr-rupt'īve.
Cor'sair (*-sêr*), 171.
Corse (*kors*), *or* Cōrse (*kōrs*) [so Gd.; *kors*, Sm.; *kōrs*, Wk.; *kōrs*, or *kors*, Wr. 155.]
Corse'let (*kors'-*), 171.
Cor'set.
Cor'si-can, 78.
Cors'ned.
Cor'tege(Fr.)(*kor'tāzh*).
Cor'tes (Sp.) (*kor'tĕz*), *n. pl.*
Cor'ti-cal, 78.
Cor'ti-cate.
Cor'ti-cāt-ed.
Cor-ti-cif'er-oŭs 108,
Cor-tiç'i-form, 78, 169.
Co-nun'drum.
Co-rus'cant.
Co-rus'cate [so Sm. Wr.; *kŏr'us-kāt*, Wb. Gd. 155.]
Co-rus'cāt-ed, 183.
Co-rus'cāt-ing.
Cŏr-us-ca'tion.
Cor-vette' (Fr.), 114, 171.
Cor'vīne, 82, 152.
Cor-y-ban'tic.

Cŏr'ymb, 171.
Co-rym'bi-ate.
Co-rym'bi-āt-ed.
Cor-ym-bif'er-oŭs, 108.
Cŏr-ym-bose'.
Co-rym'boŭs.
Co-rym'bu-loŭs.
Co-rym'bus (L.).
Cŏr-y-phe'us (L.) [L. pl. *Cor-y-phæ'ī*; Eng. pl. Cor-y-phe'us-es (-ĕz).]
Co-se'cant.
Cos'en-age (*kuz'en-*) [Law term] [Cosinage, 203.]
Co'sey (*ko'zy*) [Cosy, Cozy, Cozey, 203.]
Co'si-ly (-zĭ-), 78, 93.
Co'sine, 152.
Cos-met'ic (*koz-*).
Cos-met'ic-al (*koz-*.
Cos'mic (*koz'-*).
Cos'mic-al (*koz'-*).
Cos'mic-al-ly (*koz'-*).
Cos-mog'o-nal (*koz-*).
Cos-mo-gon'ic (*koz-*).
Cos-mo-gon'ic-al (*koz-*).
Cos-mog'o-nist (*koz-*).
Cos-mog'o-ny (*koz-*).
Cos-mog'ra-pher (*koz-*), 108.
Cos-mo-graph'ic (*koz-*).
Cos-mo-graph'ic-al (*koz-*).
Cos-mog'ra-phy (*koz-*).
Cos'mo-labe (*koz'-*).
Cos-mol'a-try (*koz-*).
Cos-mo-log'ic-al (*koz-mo-loj'-*).
Cos-mol'o-gist (*koz-*).
Cos-mol'o-gy (*koz-*).
Cos-mom'e-try (*koz-*).
Cos-mo-plas'tic (*koz-*).
Cos-mo-pol'i-tan (*koz-*).
Cos-mop'o-lite (*koz-*).
Cos-mop'o-li-tism (*koz-mop'o-li-tizm*), 78, 136.
Cos-mo-ra'ma (*koz-*).
Cos-mo-ram'ic (*koz-*).
Cos'mŏs (*koz'-*).
Cos'mo-sphere (*koz'-*).
Cos'sack, 170.
Cos'set, 170.
Cos'set-ed.
Cos'set-ing.
Cost, 18, N.
Cos'tal, 72.
Cos'tard.
Cos'tate, 73.
Cos'tāt-ed.
Cos'tive.
Cost'li ness, 78, 169.
Cost'ly, 93.
Cost'ma-ry, 72.
Cos-tume' (121) [*not* kos'tŭm, 153, 156.]
[Cosy, 203. — *See* Cosey.]
Cot, 18.
Co-tan'gent.
Cote, *n.* a cot. [*See* Coat, 160.]
Co-tem'po-ra-ry (72) [Contemporary, 203. — *See* Contemporary.]
Co-te-rie (Fr.)(*kō-te-rē'*) [so Wk. Wr. Gd.; *kot-e-rē'*, Sm. 154,155.]
Co-thurn'ate.
Co-thurn'āt-ed.
Co-tic'u-lar, 108.
Co-tid'al.
Co-til'lon (*ko-til'yun*) [so Wr. Wb. Gd.; *ko-til'yŏng*, Sm.; *ko-til-yŏng'*, Wk. 154, 155.] [Cotilion, Cotillion, 203.]
Cot'quean.
Co-trus-tee'.
Cots'wōld.
Cot'tage, 70. 170.
Cot'taged, 183.
Cot'ta-ger.
Cot'ter.
Cot'ton (*kot'n*), 149.
Cot'ton-gin (*kot'n*).
Cot'ton-y (*kot'n-y*).
Co-tyl-e'don (171) [so Sm. Wb. Gd.; *kot-y-le'don*, Wr. 155.]
Co-tyl-e'don-oŭs [so Gd.; *kot-y-led'o-nŭs*, Sm. Wr. 155.]
Co-tyl'i-form, 78, 169.
Cot'y-loid.
[Cou'age, 203. — *See* Cowhage.]
Couch, 28.
Couch'an-cy.
Couch'ant, 169.
Couched (*koucht*).
Cou-chee' (Fr.)(*koo-she'*)
Couch'er.
Couch'ing.
Cou'gar (*koo'-*).
Cough (*kŏf*), 18, N.
Coughed (*kŏft*), Note C, p. 34.
[Couhage, 203. — *See* Cowhage.]
Could (*kood*), 162.
Cōul'ter [Colter, 203.]
Cōul'ter neb (*kōl'-*).
Coun'cil, *n.* an assembly for deliberation; a body of advisers. [*See*, Counsel, 148.]
Coun'cil-lor, *n.* a member of a council. [*See* Counsellor, 148.] [Councilor, Wb. Gd. 203.—*See* 177, and Note E, p. 70.]
Coun'sel, *n.* advice. [*See* Council, 148.]
Coun'selled (*-seld*) [Counseled, Wb. Gd. 203. — *See* 177, and Note E, p. 70.]
Coun'sel-ling [Counseling, Wb. Gd. 203.]
Coun'sel-lor, *n.* one who gives advice. [*See* Councillor, 148.] [Counselor, Wb. Gd. 203.]

☞ The words *Councillor* and *Counsellor* have often been used as synonymous; but, as Worcester remarks, "the proper distinction is now more frequently made than formerly."

Count, 28.
Count'a-ble, 164, 169.
Count'ed.
Coun'te-nance, 169.
Coun'te-nanced (*-nanst*)
Coun'te-nanç-er.
Coun'te-nanç-ing.
Coun'ter.
Coun'ter-act.
Coun-ter-bal'ance, *v.* 161.
Coun'ter-bal-ance, *n.* 161.

☞ "We may observe, in words composed of *counter*, an evident tendency to that distinction that obtains between the noun and the verb in dissyllables. Thus the word to *counterbalance* has the accent on the third syllable, and the noun of the same form on the first, and so of the rest." *Walker.*

Coun-ter-bal'anced (*-anst*).
Coun-ter-bal'anç-ing.
Coun'ter-brace, *n.*
Coun'ter-feit (*-fit*), 171.
Coun'ter-feit-ed.
Coun'ter-feit-er.
Coun'ter-feit-ing.
Coun-ter-mand', *v.* 156, 161.

Coun′ter-mand, *n.* 161.
Coun-ter-mand′ed.
Coun-ter-mand′ing.
Coun ter-march′, *v.* 161.
Coun′ter-march, *n.* 161.
Coun-ter-mark′, *v.* 161.
Coun′ter-mark, *n.* 161.
Coun-ter-mine′, *v.* 161.
Coun′ter-mine, *n.* 161.
Coun-ter-mure′, *v.* 161.
Coun′ter-mure, *n.* 161.
Coun′ter-pane.
Coun′ter-part.
Coun-ter-plot′, *v.* 161.
Coun′ter-plot, *n.* 161.
Coun-ter-plot′ted, 176.
Coun-ter-plot′ting.
Coun′ter-point.
Coun-ter-poise′ (*-poiz′*), *v.* 161.
Coun′ter-poise (*-poiz*), *n.* 161.
Coun-ter-poised′ (*-poizd′*), 165.
Coun-ter-pois′ing (*-poiz-*), 183.
Coun-ter-sīgn′ (*-sīn′*),*v.* 161, 162.
Coun′ter-sīgn (*-sīn*), *n.* [161.
Coun-ter-sīgned′ (*-sīnd′*), 165.
Coun-ter-sīgn′ing (*-sīn′-*).
Coun-ter-sink′, *v.*54,161.
Coun′ter-sink, *n.* 161.
Coun-ter-vāil′.
Coun ter-vāiled′, 165.
Coun-ter-vāil′ing.
Coun-ter-val-la′tion.
Coun-ter-weigh′ (*-wā′*).
Coun-ter-weighed′ (*-wād′*), 162, 165.
Coun-ter-weigh′ing (*-wā′-*).
Coun′ter-weight (*-wāt*).
Count′ess, 228.
Count′ing.
Coŭn′tri-fīed (*kun′-*), 78, 171.
Coŭn′try (*kun′-*), 22, 93.
Coŭn′try-dànce [Con-tra-dance, 203.]

☞ *Country-dance* is supposed to be corrupted from *Contra-dance* (a dance in which the parties stand opposite to one another), "as though," to use the words of Trench, "it were the dance of the country folk and rural districts, as contrasted with the quadrille and waltz, and more artificial dances of the town."

Coŭn′try-man (*kun′-*).
Coun′ty, 28, 93.
Coup de main (Fr.) (*koo′duh-mang′*).
Coup d'état (Fr.) (*koo′-dā-ta′*).
Coup d'œil′ (Fr.) (*koo-duhĭl′*) [so Sm.; *koo-dāl′*, Wr. Gd. 155.]
Cou-pé (Fr.) (*koo-pā′*).
Cou-pee′ (*koo-pē′*) [Coopee, 203.]
Coŭp′le (*kup′l*), 164.
Coŭp′led (*kup′ld*).
Coŭp′let (*kup′-*), 22.
Coŭp′ling (*kup′-*).
Cou-pon′ (Fr.) (*koo-pong′*).
Coŭr′age (*kur′-*), 169.
Coŭr-a′geous (*kŭr-a′-jus*), 171.
Cou-ränt′ (*koo-ränt′*) [so Wk. Wr. Gd.; *koo-rănt′*, Sm. 155.]
Cou′ri-er (Fr.) (*koo′rĭ-ur*) [so Sm. Gd.; *koo-rēr′*, Wk.; *koo′rēr*, Wr. 154, 155.]
Cōurse (*kōrs*), 24.
Cōursed (*kōrst*), 183.
Cōurs′er (*kōrs′-*).
Cōurs′ing (*kōrs′-*).
Cōurt (*kōrt*), 24.
Cōurt′ed.
Court′e-oŭs (*kurt′e-us*), *or* Cōurt′eoŭs (*kōrt′-yus*) [so Wr.; *kurt′e-us*, Gd.; *kōrt′yus*, Sm.; *kur′che-us*, Wk. 134, 155.]
Cōurt′er.
Coŭrt′e-san (*kurt-e-zan′*, or *kurt′e-zan*) [*kurt-e-zan′*, Wk. Sm. Wr.; *kur′te-zan*, Wb. Gd. 155.]
Coŭrt′sĭed (*kurt′sid*), 171, 186.
Coŭrt′e-sy (*kur′te-sy*) (148), *n.* civility.
Courte′sy (*kurt′sy*) (148), *n.* a bending and depression of the body by a woman or a girl, expressive of civility: — *v.* to make a courtesy. [Curtsy, 203.]
Coŭrte′sy-ing (*kurt′-*).
Cōurt′ier (*kōrt′yur*) [*not* kōrt′i-ur, 145, 153.]
Cōurt′li-ness, 78, 169.
Cōurt′ling.
Cōurt′ly, 193.
Cōurt′-mar′tial (*-shal*), 205, 216.
Coŭs′in (*kuz′n*) (149), *n.* one related to another, as the children of brothers and sisters. [*See* Cozen, 160.]
Coŭs′in-ger′man (*kuz′-n-*) [pl. Cous′ins-ger′-man (*kuz′nz-*), 197.]
Cove, 24.
Cov′e-nant (*kuv′-*), 169.
Cov′e-nant-ed (*kuv′-*).
Cov-e-nant-ee′ (*kuv-*).
Cov′e-nant-er (*kuv′-*), 160.
Cov′e-nant-ing (*kuv′-*).
Cov′e-nant-or (*kuv′-*), 160.
[Covenous, 203. — *See* Covinous.] [Law term.]
Cov′er (*kuv′ur*), 22, 77.
Cov′ered (*kuv′urd*), 165.
Cov′er-er (*kuv′-*).
Cov′er-ing (*kuv′-*).
Cov′er-let (*kuv′-*).
Cov′ert (*kuv′-*), 171.
Cov′ert-ure (*kuv′-*), 91.
Cov′et (*kuv′et*), 22.
Cov′et-a-ble (*kuv′-*), 164, [169.
Cov′et ed (*kuv′-*).
Cov′et-ing (*kuv′-*).
Cov′et-oŭs (*kuv′-*) [*not* kuv′e-chus, 153, 156.]
Cov′ey (*kuv′y*), 22, 98.
Cov′in (*kuv′in*).
Cōv′ing.
Cov′in-oŭs [Covenous, 203.]
Cow, 28.
Cow′ard, 72.
Cow′ard-ĭce (*-is*), 169.
Cowed (*kowd*), 165.
Cow′er.
Cow′ered (*-urd*), 165.
Cow′er-ing.
Cow′hage [Couage, Cowitch, 203.]
Cow′ing.
[Cowitch, 203. — *See* Cowhage.]
Cowl, 28.
Cowled (*kowld*).
Cow′lick, 206.
Co-work′er (*-wurk′-*).
Cow′-pox [Cow-pock, 203.]
Cow′ry, 190.
Cow′slip [Cow's-lip (*kowz′lip*), Wb. Gd. 203.]

Cox'cōmb (*koks'kōm*), 39, N.; 162.
Cox'comb-ry (*-kōm-*).
Cox-com'ic-al.
Coy, 27.
Coz'en (*kuz'n*) (149), *v.* to cheat. [*See* Cousin, 160.]
Coz'en-age (*kuz'n-*).
Coz'ened (*kuz'nd*).
Coz'en-er (*kuz'n-*).
Coz'en-ing (*kuz'n-*).
[Cozey, 203.—*See* Cosey.]
[Cozy, 203.—*See* Cosey.]
Crab, 10.
Crab'-ap'ple, 205.
Crab'bed, 66, N.; 170.
Crab'by.
Crab'-tree, 206, Exc. 4.
Crab'yaw.
Crack, 10, 181.
Cracked (*krakt*), Note C, p. 34.
Crack'er.
Crack'ing.
Crack'le (*krak'l*), 164.
Crack'led (*krak'ld*), 183.
Crack'ling.
Cra-co'vi-ĕnne (Fr.), 171.
Cra'dle, 164.
Cra'dled (*kra'dld*), 183.
Cra'dling.
Cráft, 12, 131.
Cráft'i-ly, 78, 93.
Cráft'i-ness, 169.
Cráft'y.
Crag, 10.
Crag'ged (*-ghed*), 138, 176.
Crag'gi-ness (*-ghĭ-*).
Crag'gy (*-ghy*), 138.
Cram, 10.
Cram'bo.
Crammed (*kramd*), 176.
Cram'mer.
Cram'ming.
Cramp, 10.
Cramped (*krampt*).
Cramp'ing.
Cramp'i-ron (*-ī'urn*).
Cram-poons' (*-poonz*), *n. pl.* 122.
Crān'age.
Cran'ber-ry [*not* kram'-bĕr-ry, 153, 156.]
[Cranch, 203.—*See* Craunch.]
Crane, 23.
Crānes'bill (*krānz'-*), 214
Cra'ni-al, 78, 169.
Crā-ni-og'no-my, 108.
Crā-ni-o-log'ic-al (*-loj'-*).
Crā-ni-ol'o-gist.
Crā-ni-ol'o-gy, 108.
Crā-ni-om'e-ter, 108.
Crā-ni-o-met'ric-al.
Crā-ni-om'e-try, 108, 169.
Crā-ni-os'co-py, 108.
Crā'ni-um, 78, 169.
Crank (*krangk*), 10, 54.
Crăn'kle (*krang'kl*), 54, 164.
Cran'kled (*krang'kld*), 183.
Cran'kling (*krang'-*).
Crank'y (*krangk'y*).
Cran'nied (*kran'id*), 171.
Cran'ny, 66, 170.
Crants.
Crap'au-dīne, 82, 152.
Crape, 23.
[Crapnel, 203.—*See* Grapnel.]
Cra'pu-la (L.) [so Sm.; *krap'u-la*, Wr. Wb. Gd. 154, 155.]
Crap'u-lence, 169.
Crap'u-lent, 108.
Crap'u-loŭs.
Crash, 10, 46.
Crashed (*krasht*), Note C, p. 34.
Crash'ing.
Cras'sa-ment, 170.
Cras'si-tude, 169, 170.
Cratch, 10, 44.
Cratch'-Cra'dle (205) [Scratch-Cradle, 203.]
Cratch'es (*-ez*), *n. pl.*
Crate, 23, 163.
Cra'ter, 23, 77.
Cra-tĕr'i-form, 78, 169.
Cräunch (*kränch*) [Cranch, 203.]
Cräunched (*kräncht*).
Cräunch'ing (*kränch'-*).
Cra-vat', 121.
Crave, 23, 163.
Craved, 165.
Cra'ven (*kra'vn*), 149.
Crāv'er.
Crāv'ing.
Craw, 17.
Craw'fish [Crayfish, 203.]
Crawl, 17.
Crawled, 165.
Crawl'er.
Crawl'ing.
[Crayfish, 203.—*See* Crawfish.]
Crāy'on, 23, 86.
Craze, 23.
Crazed, 165, 183.
Cra'zi-ly, 78, 93.
Cra'zi-ness, 169.
Crāz'ing.
Cra'zy, 169.
Crēak, *v.* to make a harsh, grating noise: —*n.* a harsh noise. [*See* Creek, 160.]
Creaked (*krēkt*).
Crēak'ing.
Crēam, 13.
Crēamed, 165.
Crēam'ing.
Crēam'y.
Cre'ance.
Crēase, 13.
Crēased (*krēst*), Note C, p. 34.
Cre-ate'.
Cre-āt'ed, 183.
Cre-āt'ing.
Cre-a'tion.
Cre-āt'ĭve, 84.
Cre-āt'or, 228.
Crēat'ur-al (*-yur-*), 91.
Crēat'ure (91) (*krēt'yur*) [so Wr. Gd.; *kre'ture*, coll. *krēt'sh'oor*, Sm.; *kre'chŭr*, Wk. 26; 44, Note 1; 155.]
Cre'dence, 169.
Cre-den'dum (L.) [pl. *Cre-den'da*, 198.]
Cre'dent.
Cre-den'tial (*-shal*).
Cred-i-bil'i-ty, 78, 169.
Cred'i-ble, 78, 164.
Cred'i-bly, 93.
Cred'it, 15, 170.
Cred'it-a-ble, 164, 169
Cred'it-a-bly.
Cred'it-ed.
Cred'it-ing.
Cred'it-or.
Cre-du'li-ty, 78, 93.
Cred'u-loŭs, 89.
Creed, 13.
Creek (13) [*not* krĭk, 127, 153], *n.* a rivulet. [*See* Creak, 160.]
Creek'y, 169.
Creep, 13.
Creep'er.
Creep'ing.
Cre'nate.
Cre'nāt-ed.
Cren'a-ture.
Cren'el-late, 170.
Cren'el-lāt-ed, 183.
Cren'el-lāt-ing.
Cren-el-la'tion.
Cre-nĕlle'.

Cren′elled (*-eld*).
Cren′u-late.
Cre′ole.
Cre′o-sote, 171.
Cre′pance.
Cre′pane.
Crep′i-tate, 169.
Crep′i-tāt-ed, 183.
Crep′i-tāt-ing.
Crep-i-ta′tion.
Crept, 15.
Cre-pus′cu-lar, 89, 108.
Cre-pus′cule.
Cres′cent, 171.
Cress, 15, 174.
Cres′set, 170.
Crest, 15.
Crest′ed.
Crest′fallen (*-fawln*).
Crest′ing.
Cre-ta′ceous (*-shus*), 112.
Cre′tic.
Cre′tin.
Cre′tin-ism (*-izm*), 136.
Cre-văsse′ (Fr.).
Crev′ice (*-is*), 169, 170.
Crew (*kroo*) (19) [pl. Crews (*krooz*). — *See* Cruise, 160.]
Crew′el (*kroo′-*), *n.* a kind of yarn or worsted. [*See* Cruel, 160.]
[Crewet, 203. — *See* Cruet.]
Crib, 16.
Crib′bage, 170.
Cribbed, 165, 176.
Crib′bing.
Crib′ble, 164.
Crib′bled (*krib′ld*), 183.
Crib′bling.
Crib′ri-form, 78.
Crich′ton-īte (*krik-*) [so Wr.; *krich′ton-īt*, Gd. 155.]

☞ Sometimes pronounced *kri′ton-īt*, or *kri′tn-īt*.

Crick.
Crick′et, 16.
Crick′et-er.
Cri′coid [so Sm. Wr.; *krik′oid*, Gd. 155.]
Cried, 186.
Cri′er.
Crime, 25.
Crim′i-nal, 143, 169.
Crim-i-nal′i-ty.
Crim′i-nal-ly, 170.
Crim′i-nate, 72, 169.
Crim′i-nāt-ed.
Crim′i-nāt-ing.
Crim-i-na′tion.
Crim′i-nāt-ive.
Crim′i-na-to-ry, 86.
Crimp, 16.
Crimped (*krimpt*).
Crimp′ing.
Crim′ple, 164.
Crim′pled (*krim′pld*).
Crim′pling.
Crim′son (*krim′zn*), 149.
Crim′soned (*-znd*), 165.
Crim′son-ing (*krim′zn-*)
Cri′nāt-ed.
Cringe, 16, 45.
Cringed (*krinjd*).
Cringe′ling.
Cring′er (*krinj′-*).
Cring′ing (*krinj′-*).
Crin′gle (*kring′gl*), 54.
Crin-i-cult′u-ral.
Crī-nig′er-ous (*-nij′-*).
Cri′nite.
Crin′kle (*kring′kl*), 54.
Crin′kled (*kring′kld*).
Crin′kling (*kring′-*).
Cri′noid.
Crī-noid′al.
Crī-noid′e-an, 169.
Crin′o-līne, 82, 152 [*not* krin′o-lin, 153.]
Crip′ling (170), *n.* a short spar used as a support. [*See* Crippling, 160.]
Crip′ple (*krip′l*), 164.
Crip′pled (*krip′ld*).
Crip′pling (170), *part.* from *Cripple.* [*See* Cripling, 160.]
Cri′sis, 25.
Crisp, 16.
Crisp′āt-ed.
Crisped (*krispt*).
Crisp′er.
Cris′pin.
Crisp′ing.
Crisp′y, 93.
Criss-crŏss-rōw′.
Cris′tate.
Cris′tāt-ed.
Cri-te′ri-on (Gr.) [Gr. pl. *Cri-te′ri-a*; Eng. pl. Criterions, 198.]

☞ "The Greek plural, *criteria*, is most commonly used." *Worcester.*

Crit′ic, 16, 170.
Crit′ic-al, 72, 108.
Crit′ic-al-ly.
Crit′i-cīse (*-sīz*), (78, 202).
[Criticize, Sm. 203.]
Crit′i-cīsed (*-sīzd*).
Crit′i-cīs-er (*-sīz*).
Crit′i-cīs-ing (*-sīz*).
Crit′i-cism (*-sizm*), 133.
Cri-tique′ (Fr.) (*kri-tēk′*) 121, 171.
Criz′zel (*kriz′l*) (149) [Crizzle, 203.]
Criz′zel-ing (*kriz′l-*).
Crōak, 24.
Crōaked (*krōkt*), Note C, p. 34.
Crōak′er, *n.* one who croaks. [*See* Croker, 160.]
Crōak′ing.
Cro′at.
Cro′ches (*-chĕz*), *n. pl.*
Cro-chet′ (Fr.) (*kro-sha′*).
Crock, 18, 181.
Crock′er-y, 233, Exc.
Crock′et.
Croc′o-dīle (152) [so Sm. Wb. Gd.; *krok′-o-dīl*, Wk.; *krok-o-dīl′*, or *krok′o-dīl*, Wr. 155.]
Croc-o-dil′i-an [so spelled by Gd. — Crocodilean, Wr. 203.]
Croc-o-dil′i-ty, 169.
Cro′cus.
Crŏft, 18, N.
Croi′ses (*-sĕz*), *n. pl.*
Cro′ker, *n.* a large water-fowl. [*See* Croaker, 160.]
Crom′lech (*-lek*), 171.
Crone, 24.
Cro′ny, 190.
Crŏŏk [*See* Book.]
Crŏŏk′ed.
Crŏŏk′ing.
Crop, 18.
Cropped (*kropt*).
Cro′sier (*-zhur*), 47.
Cro′siered (*-zhurd*), 165.
Cros′let [Crosslet, 203.]
Cross (18, N.).
Cross′bar, 206.
Cross′-billed.
Crossed (*krŏst*), Note C, p. 34.
Cross′-eyed (*-īd*).
Cross′ing.
Cross′-legged (*-legd*).
Cross′-trees (*-trēz*).
Cross′wise (*-wīz*).
Crotch, 18, 44.
Crotched (*krocht*), 165.
Crotch′et, 171.
Crotch′et-ed.
Crotch-et-y.
Crouch, 28.

Crouched (*kroucht*).
Crouch′ing.
Croup (*kroop*), 19.
Crou-pade′ (*kroo-*).
Crou′pi-er (*kroo′pĭ-ur*).
Crout [K r o u t, 203.]
Crōw, 24.
Crōwed (*krōd*), 188.
Crowd, 28.
Crowd′ed.
Crowd′er.
Crowd′ing.
Crōw′fōōt.
Crōw′ing.
Crown, 28.
Crowned, 165.
Crown′er.
Crown′ing.
Crown′-wheel.
Crōw's′-fōōt (*krōz′-*), 213.
Cru′ci-al (*kroo′shĭ-al*) [so Wk. Sm. Wr.; *krū′shal*, Wb. Gd. 155.]
Cru′ci-ate (*kroo′shĭ-āt*) [so Wk. Sm. Wr.; *krū′shāt*, Wb. Gd. 155.]
Cru′ci-ble (*kroo′-*), 78, 164.
Cru-cif′er-oŭs (*kroo-*), 108.
Cru′ci-fīed, 186.
Cru′ci-fi-er (*kroo′-*).
Cru′ci-fix (*kroo′-*), 78, 169.
Cru-ci-fix′ion (*kroo-sĭ-fik′shun*), 171.
Cru′ci-form (*kroo′-*).
Cru′ci-fȳ (*kroo′-*), 94.
Cru′ci-fȳ′ing (*kroo′-*).
Cru-cig′er-oŭs (*kroo-sij′-*), 108.
Cru′cite (*kroo′-*).
Crude (*krood*), 19.
Cru′di-ty (*kroo′-*), 78, 93.
Cru′el (*kroo′-*), *a.* unfeeling. [*See* Crewel, 160.]
Cru′el-ty (*kroo′-*).
Cru′et (*kroo′-*) [C r e w - e t, 203.]
[C r u i s e, *n.*—*See* Cruise, 203.]
Cruise (*krooz*) [*not* kroos, 136, 153], *v.* to rove over the sea:—*n.* a roving voyage. [*See* Crews, pl. of Crew, 160.]
Cruised (*kroozd*), 183.
Cruis′er (*krooz′-*).
Cruis′ing (*krooz′-*).
Crum [C r u m b, 203.]
Crumb (*krum*) (162) [C r u m, 203.]

☞ Though both these forms, *crum* and *crumb*, are well authorized, the form *crumb* is probably most in use. It is preferred by Worcester and Goodrich. Smart, however, gives only *crum*, and remarks: "It is often unnecessarily spelled *crumb*."

Crumbed (*krumd*) [C r u m m e d, 203.]
Crumb′ing (*krum′-*) [C r u m m i n g, 203.]
Crum′ble, 164.
Crum′bled (*krum′bld*).
Crum′bling.
Crum′ma-ble, 164, 170.
Crummed (*krumd*) [C r u m b e d, 203.]
Crum′ming [C r u m-m i n g, 203.]
Crum′my, 170.
Crump.
Crum′pet.
Crum′ple, 164.
Crum′pled (*krum′pld*), 183.
Crum′pling.
Crup′per (*krup′ur*, or *krōōp′ur*) [*krup′ur*, Wk. Sm. Wr.; *krōōp′-ur*, Wb. Gd. 155.]
Cru′ral (*kroo′-*).
Cru-sade′ (*kroo-*), 121.
Cru-sād′er (*kroo-*), 183.
Cru-sād′ing (*kroo-*).
Cruse, *n.* (*kroos*) [*not* krooz, 136, 153.]
Cru′set (*kroo′-*).
Crush, 22.
Crushed (*krusht*), Note C, p. 34.
Crush′er.
Crush′ing.
Crust, 22.
Crus-ta′cean (*-shan*).
Crus-tā-ce-ol′o-gy, 108.
Crus-ta′ceous (*-shus*), 112.
Crust′-āt-ed.
Crust′ed.
Crust′i-ly.
Crust′i-ness, 169.
Crust′ing.
Crust′y.
Crutch, 22, 44.
Crutched (*krucht*).
Crutch′ing.
Cry, 25.
Cry′ing, 186.
Cry-oph′o-rus (*-ŏf-*).
Crypt, 16.
Cryp′tic.
Cryp′tic-al, 108.
Cryp-to-gam′ic, 170.
Cryp-tog′a-moŭs.
Cryp-tog′a-mist.
Cryp-tog′ra-pher.
Cryp-to-graph′ic.
Cryp-to-graph′ic-al.
Cryp-tog′ra-phy, 108.
Cryp-tol′o-gy.
Crys′tal, 16, 72.
Crys′tal-line, *or* Crys′-tal-līne (170) [so Wk. Wr.; *kris′tal-ĭn*, Gd.; *kris′tal-īn*, Sm. 155.]
Crys′tal-lite.
Crys-tal-līz′a-ble, 164.
Crys-tal-lĭ-za′tion.
Crys′tal-lize, 170, 202.
Crys′tal-lized, 165, 183.
Crys-tal-log′ra-pher.
Crys-tal-lo-graph′ic, 109.
Crys-tal-lo-graph′ic-al, 108.
Crys-tal-log′ra-phy, 108, 170.
Crys-tal′lo-type, 170.
Cte′noid (*te′-*), 162.
Cub, 22.
Cu′ba-ture.
Cubbed (*kubd*,) 150, 176.
Cub′bing.
Cub′by-hole.
Cube, 26.
Cu′beb.
Cu′bic.
Cu′bic-al.
Cu′bi-form, 78.
Cu′bit, 26.
Cu′bit-al, 228.
Cu′bit-ed.
Cu′boid.
Cu-boid′al.
Cuck′ing-stool.
Cuck′old.
Cuck′oo (*kōōk′oo*), 20, 156, 171.
Cu-cul′late (170) [so Wk. Sm. Wr.; *ku′kul-āt*, Wb. Gd. 155.]
Cu-cul′lat-ed [so Wk. Sm. Wr.; *ku′kul-āt-ed*, Wb. Gd. 155.]
Cu′cum-ber [so Sm. Wr. Wb. Gd.; *kow′-kum-bur*, Wk. 155.]

☞ The pronunciation *kowkumbur*, though fashionable in the time of Walker, is now antiquated.

Cu'cur-bit [Cucurbite, 203.]
Cu-cur-bi-ta'ceous (-*shus*).
Cud, 22.
Cud'bear (-*bêr*), 171.
Cud'dle, 164.
Cud'dled (*kud'ld*), 183.
Cud'dling.
Cud'dy, 170.
Cud'gel, 149.
Cud'gelled (-*jeld*) (165) [Cudgeled, Wb. Gd. 203. — *See* 177, and Note E, p. 70.]
Cud'gel-ler [Cudgeler, Wb. Gd. 203.]
Cud'gel-ling [Cudgeling, Wb. Gd. 203.]
Cud'weed.
Cūe (*kū*), 26.
Cuff, 22, 173.
Cuffed (*kuft*), Note C, p. 34.
Cuff'ing.
Cui-rass (*kwē-răs'*, or *kwē'-răs*) (171) [so Wr.; *kwē-ras'*, Wk. Wb. Gd.; *kwē'răs*, Sm. 155.]
Cui-ras-sier', (*kwē-ras-sēr'*), 122, 171.
Cuish (*kwis*).
Cul-dee' (121) [so Wk. Sm. Wr.; *kul'dē*, Wb. Gd. 155.]
Cu-liç'i-form, 78, 169.
Cu'li-na-ry, 72, 171.
Cull, 22.
Culled, 165.
Cul'len-der [Colander, 203.]
Cull'er, *n.* one who culls, or selects. [*See* Color.]
Cull'ing.
Cull'ion (-*yun*).
Cul'lis.
Cul'ly, 170, 190.
Culm, 22, 133.
Cul-mif'er-oŭs, 108.
Cul'mi-nate.
Cul'mi-năt-ed, 183.
Cul'mi-năt-ing.
Cul-mi-na'tion.
Cul-pa-bil'i-ty, 108, 169.
Cul'pa-ble, 164.
Cul'prit, 22.
Cul'ti-va-ble, 164.
Cul'ti-văt-a-ble, 164.
Cul'ti-vate, 169.
Cul'ti-văt-ed, 183.
Cul-ti-va'tion, 112.
Cul'ti-văt-or.
Cul'trate.
Cul'trăt-ed.
Cul'tri-form, 169.
Cult'ure, 91.
Cul'ver-in.
Cul'vert, 22.
Cul'ver-tăil.
Cul'ver-tăiled.
Cum'bent, 169.
Cum'ber, 104.
Cum'bered (-*burd*), 165.
Cum'ber-ing.
Cum'ber-some (-*sum*).
Cum'brance, 169.
Cum'bri-an, 169.
Cum'broŭs.
Cum'frey (98, 169) [Comfrey, 203.]
Cum'in, 170.
Cu'mu-la-tĭve, 84.
Cu'mu-lose [so Wb. Gd.; *cu-mu-lōs'*, Wr. 155.]
Cu'mu-lo-cĭr-ro-stra'-tus.
Cu'mu-lo-stra'tus, 224.
Cu'mu-lus (L.) [pl. *Cu'mu-lī*, 198.]
Cu'ne-al, 169.
Cu'ne-ate.
Cu'ne-āt-ed.
Cu-ne'i-form, 169.
Cu'ni-form, 108.
Cun'ner, 170.
Cun'ning, 170.
Cup, 22.
Cup'board (*kub'burd*) (Note C, p. 34) [so Wk. Wr. Gd.; *kub'bōrd*, Sm. 155.]
Cu'pel [Coppel, 203.]
Cu-pel-la'tion, 170.
Cup'ful (-*fōōl*), 197.
Cu-pid'i-ty, 170.
Cu'po-la [*not* ku'pa-lō, 127, 153.]
Cupped (*kupt*), 176.
Cup'per.
Cup'ping.
Cu'pre-oŭs, 170.
Cu-prif'er-oŭs, 108.
Cu'pule.
Cu-pu-lif'er-oŭs.
Cur, 21.
Cūr-a-bil'i-ty, 169.
Cūr'a-ble, 164.
Cu-ra-çōa' (*ku-ra-so'*) (171) [so Sm. Gd.; *koo-ra-so'*, Wr. 155.]
Cu'ra-cy, 169.
Cu-ras'sōw, 170.
Cu'rate, 49, N.
Cūr'a-tĭve.
Cu-ra'tor, 88.
Curb, 21.
Curbed, 165.
Curbing.
Curb'roof, 206, Exc. 3.
Cur-cu'li-o, 169.
Cur'cu-ma.
Curd, 21.
Curd'ed.
Curd'i-ness, 169.
Curd'ing.
Cur'dle, 164.
Cur'dled (*kur'dld*), 183.
Cur'dling.
Curd'y, 93.
Cure, 26.
Cured, 165, 183.
Cūr'er.
Cur'few (-*fū*), 171.
Cūr'ing, 183.
Cu-ri-o-log'ic (-*loj'*-)
Cu-ri-os'i-ty, 108, 169.
Cu'ri-oŭs.
Curl, 21.
Curled (*kurld*), 165.
Curl'er, 77.
Cur'lew (-*lu*), 171.
Curl'i-ness, 169.
Curl'ing.
Curl'y, 93.
Cur-mud'geon (*muj'un*), 171.
Cŭr'rant (170) [so Sm. Wb. Gd. Wr.; *kŭr'an*, Wk. 155], *n.*
Cŭr'ren-cy, 169, 170.
Cŭr'rent, *a.* 169.
Cŭr-ri'cle, 164, 170.
Cŭr-ric'u-lum (L.) [pl. *Cŭr-ric'u-la*, 198.]
Cŭr'ried (*kŭr'id*), 186.
Cŭr'ri-er, 169.
Cur'rish, 21, 170.
Cŭr'ry, *n.* & *v.* 22.
Cŭr'ry-ing.
Curse, 21.
Cursed (*kurst*), Note C, p. 34.
Curs'ing.
Cur'sĭve.
Cur'so-ri-ly, 169.
Cur'so-ri-ness.
Cur'so-ry, 93.
Curt, 21.
Cur-tăil'.
Cur'tăil-dog.
Cur-tăiled' (-*tāld'*), 165.
Cur-tăil'er.
Cur-tăil'ing.
Cur'tain (*kur'tin*) [*not* kur'tn,] 153.
Cur'tained (-*tind*), 165.

Cur′tate.
Cur-ta′tion.
[C u r t s y , 203. — See Courtesy.]
Cu′rule (*-rool*), 19, 26.
Curv′ate.
Curv′āt ed.
Curv′ā-ture.
Curve (*kurv*), 21, 163.
Curved (*kurvd*), 165,183.
Cur′vet, *or* Cur-vet′, *v.* [*kur′vet*, Sm. Wb. Gd.; *kur-vet′*, Wk.; *kur-vet′*, or *kur′vet*, Wr. 155.]
Cur′vet, *n.* [so Sm. Wb. Gd.; *kur-vet′*, Wk.; *kur′vet*, or *kur-vet′*, Wr. 155.]
Cur-vi-lin′e-al, 169.
Cur-vi-lin′e-ar.
Curv′ing, 183.
Curv′i-ty, 108, 169.
Cush′at (*kŏŏsh′at*), 20.
Cush′ion (*kŏŏsh′un*), 171.
Cush′ioned (*kŏŏsh′und*).
Cush, 22.
Cusp, 22.
Cusp′i date, 169.
Cusp′i-dāt-ed.
Cus′tard, 135, 171.
Cus-to′di-al.
Cus-to′di-an, 169.
Cus′to-dy, 86, 93.
Cus′tom, 22, 169.
Cus′tom-a-ble, 164, 169.
Cus′tom-a-ri-ly.
Cus′tom-a-ry, *a.* 72.
Cus′tom-a-ry, *n.* [C u s - t u m a r y , 203.]
Cus′tomed (*-tumd*), 171.
Cus′tom-er.
Cus′tom-house.
[C u s t u m a r y , *n.* 203. — *See* Customary.]
Cut, 22.
Cu-ta′ne-oŭs, 169.
Cu′ti-cle, 164.
Cu-tic′u-lar, 108.
Cut′lass, 171.
Cut′ler.
Cut′ler-y, 156, 233. Exc.
Cut′let.
Cut′purse, 206.
Cut′ter, 176.
Cut′thrōat, 206.
Cut′ting, 176.
Cut′tle-fish.
Cut′-wâ-ter.
Cy′an-ate.
Cȳ-an′ic.
Cy′a-nīde [C y a n i d, 203.]
Cȳ-an′o-gen, 170.
Cȳ-a-nom′e-ter, 108.
Cȳ-an′u-ret.
Cȳ-an-u′ric.
Cyc′la-men.
Cy′cle, 164.
Cyc′lic.
Cyc′lic-al.
Cy′clo-grăph (127) [so Sm. Wr.; *sik′lo-graf*, Gd. 155.]
Cȳ′cloid.
Cȳ-cloid′al.
Cȳ-cloid′i-an.
Cȳ-clom′e-try, 108.
Cȳ-clo-pæ′di-a (*-pē′-*) [C y c l o p e d i a , 203.]
Cȳ-clo-pe′an, 110.
Cȳ-clo-ped′ic, 109.
Cȳ-clo-ped′ic-al, 108.
Cȳ-clop′ic.
Cyg′net, *n.* a young swan. [*See* Signet, 160.]
Cyl-in-der, 171.
Cyl-in′dric.
Cyl-in′dric-al, 108.
Cyl-in′dri-form, 169.
Cyl′in-droid.
Cyl-in-dro-met′ric.
Cy′ma [C i m a , 203.]
Cȳ-mar′ (121) [S i m a r , 203.]
Cym′bal, *n.* a kind of musical instrument. [*See* Cimbal, 160.]
Cym′bi-form, 169.
Cȳme, 25.
Cȳ′mose, *or* Cȳ-mose′ [*sī′mōs*, Wb. Gd.; *sī-mōs′*, Wr. 155.]
Cy′moŭs.
Cȳ-nan′che (*-nang′kē*).
Cȳ-nan′thro-py.
Cyn-arc-tom′a-chy(*-ky*).
Cyn′ic.
Cyn′ic-al.
Cyn′i-cism (*-sizm*), 136.
Cy′no-sūre, *or* Cȳn′o-sūre [so Wr.; *si′no-zūr*, or *si′no-zh′oor* (see § 26), Sm.; *sin′o-shūr*, or *sī′no-shūr*, Wk. Gd. 155.]

☞ Though Walker prefers *sin′o-shūr* to *si′no-shūr*, he says. "I am not sure, however, that the best usage is not against me."

Cyph′o-nism (*nizm*).
Cy′press (171), *n.* a kind of tree. [*See* Cyprus, 148.]
Cyp′ri-an.
Cyp′rīne, 82, 152.
Cy′prŭs, *n.* a thin, transparent, black stuff. [*See* Cypress, 148.]
Cȳr-e-nā′ic.
Cȳ-re′ni-an.
Cȳr-i-o-log′ic (*-loj′-*).
Cyst [C i s t , 203.]
Cyst′ic.
Cys′to-cēle.
Cyst′ose.
Cys-tot′o-my, 108.
Cyt′i-sīne [C y t i s i n , 203.]
Cyt′o-blăst.
Czar (*zar*) [T z a r , 203.]
Cza-ri′na (*za-rē′na*).
Czăr′o-wĭtz (*zăr′o-wits*).

D.

Dab, 10.
Dabbed (*dabd*), 150, 176.
Dab′bing.
Dab′ble, 164.
Dab′bled (*dab′ld*), 183.
Dab′bler.
Dab′bling.
Dace, 23.
Dac′tyl, 171.
Dac′tyl-ar.
Dac-tyl′ic.
Dac-tyl′i-o-glȳph [D a c t y l o g l y p h , 203.]
Dac-tyl-i-og′ra-phy.
Dac-tyl′i-o-man-cy [D a c t y l o m a n c y , 203.]
Dac′tyl-ist, 171.
Dac-tyl′o-glyph [D a c - t y l i o g l y p h , 203.]
Dac-tyl-ol′o-gy, 108.
Dac-tyl′o-man-cy [D a c t y l i o m a n - c y , 203.]
Dac-tyl-on′o-my, 108.
Dad, 10.
Dad′dy, 170.
Dä′do.
Dæ′dal (*dē-*) [D e d a l , 203.]
Dæ-da′li-an (*dē-*) (169) [D e d a l i a n , 203.]
Dæd′a-loŭs (*ded′-*) [D e d a l o u s , 203.]
Daf-fa-dil′ly, 170.
Daf′fo-dil, 170.
Dag′ger (*-gur*), 138.
Dag′gle, 164.

Da-guĕrre′i-an (*-ghĕr′-*) [so Gd.; Daguerrian, Wr. 203.]
Da-guĕrre′o-type (*-ghĕr′-*) [*not* da-ghĕr′-e-o-tīp, 153.]

☞ This word (formed from the name of the inventor, *Daguerre*) is most commonly spelled *daguerreotype*, as given by Goodrich in the Supplement to Webster's Dictionary. But in the Dictionaries of Smart and Worcester it is spelled *daguerrotype*. Smart pronounces it *da-gwĕr′o-tīp*; Worcester and Goodrich, *da-ghĕr′o-tīp*.

Dah′li-a [so Wr.; *dāl′-ya*, Wb. Gd.; *dā′lĭ-a*, Sm. 155] [*not* dal′ya, 153.]
Dăi′ly, 93.
Dăin′ti-ly.
Dăin′ti-ness, 169.
Dăin′ty.
Dăi′ry, 49, N.
Da′is [so Sm. Wr.; *da′is*, or *dās*, Gd. 155.]
Dăi′sĭed (*da′zid*).
Dăi′sy (*da′zy*), 169.
Da′ker [Dakir, 203.]
Dale, 23.
Dal′li-ance, 169, 170.
Dal′lĭed (*-lid*), 99, 186.
Dal′li-er.
Dal′ly, 93, 170.
Dal′ton-ism (*-izm*), 136.
Dam (10), *n.* a female parent, — used of beasts; — a bank to confine water. [*See* Damn, 160.]
Dam′age, 169.
Dam′age-a-ble, 164, 183.
Dam′aged, 165, 183.
Dam′a-ging.
Dam′as-cene, 171.
Dam′ask.
Dam′asked (*-askt*).
Dam′as-keen, *v.* [so Sm. Wr.; *dam-as-kēn′*, Wb. Gd. 155.] [Damasken, Damaskin, 203.]
Dam′as-keened, 165.
Dam′as-keen-ing.
Dam′as-kīn, *n.* [so Sm. Wb. Gd.; *dam′as-kēn*, Wr. 155.]
Dam′as-sin [so Wb. Gd.; *da-mas′sin*, Wr. 155.]
Dame, 23.
Damn (*dam*) (162), *v.* to condemn. [*See* Dam, 160.]
Dam-na-bil′i-ty, 169.
Dam′na-ble, 164.
Dam′na-bly, 72, 93.
Dam-na′tion, 112.
Dam′na-to-ry, 86.
Damned (*damd*), *part.* 165.
Dam′ned, *a.* 150.
Damp, 10.
Damped (*dampt*), Note C, p. 34.
Damp′en (*damp′n*), 149.
Damp′ened (*damp′nd*).
Damp′en-ing (*damp′n-*).
Damp′er.
Damp′ing.
Dam′sel (*-zel*), 136.
Dam′son (*dam′zn*), 136, 149.
Dȧnce, 12, 131.
Dȧnced (*dȧnst*).
Dȧnç′er.
Dȧnç′ing.
Dan′de-lī-on, *or* Dan-de-lī′on [*dan′de-lī-on*, Wb. Gd.; *dan-de-lī′-on*, Wk. Sm. Wr. 155.]
Dan′di-prat, 169.
Dan′dle, 164.
Dan′dled (*dan′dld*), 150.
Dan′dler.
Dan′dling.
Dan′druff, 171.
Dan′dy, 10, 93.
Dane′geld (*-gheld*) [Danegelt, 203.]
Dane′wort (*-wurt*).
Dān′ger, 23, 77.
Dān′ger-oŭs.
Dan′gle (*dan′gl*), 54, 164.
Dan′gled (*dang′gld*), 183.
Dan′gler (*dang′glur*).
Dan′gling (*dang′gling*).
Dank (*dangk*), 10, 54.
Dap′per, 170.
Dap′ple, 164.
Dap′pled (*dap′ld*), 183.
Dap′pling.
Dare (*dêr*), 14.
Dared (*dêrd*), 183.
Dar′er (*dêr′-*).
Dăr′ic.
Dar′ing (*dêr′-*), 183.
Dark, 11.
Dark′en (*dark′n*), 149.
Dark′ened (*dark′nd*).
Dark′en-er (*dark′n-*).
Dark′en-ing (*dark′n-*).
Dark′some (*-sum*), 169.
Dar′ling.
Darn, 11.
Darned, 165.
Dar′nel.
Darn′er.
Darn′ing.
Dart, 11.
Dart′ed.
Dart′er.
Dart′ing.
Dar′troŭs.
Dash, 10, 46.
Dashed (*dasht*), Note C, p. 34.
Dash′er.
Dash′ing.
Das′tard.
Das′y-ure.
Da′ta (L. pl.).
Da-ta′ri-a [Gd. 154, 155.]
Da′ta-ry, 72.
Date, 23.
Dăt′ed, 183.
Dăt′er.
Dăt′ing.
Da′tĭve, 84.
Da′tum (L.) [pl. *Da′ta*, 198.]
Da-tu′ri-a, 72.
Da-tu′rĭne, 82, 152.
Dȃub, 17.
Dȃubed (*dawbd*), 165.
Dȃub′er.
Dȃub′ing.
Dȃub′y.
Dȃugh′ter (*daw′-*), 162.
Dȃunt (*dänt*) (11) [*not* dawnt, 153.]
Dȃunt′ed (*dänt-*).
Dȃunt′er (*dänt′-*).
Dȃunt′ing (*dänt′-*).
Dȃu′phin, 17, 35.
Da′vit [so Sm. Wr.; *dav′it*, Wb. Gd. 155.]
Daw, 17.
Daw′dle, 164.
Daw′dled (*daw′dld*).
Daw′dler.
Daw′dling.
Dawn, 17.
Dawned, 150.
Dawn′ing.
Dāy, *n.* the time between the rising and the setting of the sun; the period of twenty-four hours. [*See* Dey, 160.]
Dāy′time, 206.
Daz′zle, 164.
Daz′zled (*daz′ld*), 183.
Daz′zling.

Dēa'con (*de'kn*), 149.
Dēa'con-ry (*de'kn-*).
Dĕad, 15.
Dĕad'en (*ded'n*), 149.
Dĕad'li-ness, 169.
Dĕad'ly, 93.
Dĕaf (*dĕf*) [so Wk. Sm. Wr.; *dēf* in England, more commonly *dēf* in America, Gd. 155.]

☞ *Dēf*, though common in the U. S., is not the pronunciation of the best speakers in this country.

Dĕaf'en (*def'n*) (149) [so Wk. Sm. Wr.; *dēf'n*, or *dĕf'n*, Gd. 155.]
Dĕaf'ened (*def'nd*), 150.
Dĕaf'en-ing (*dĕf'n-*).
Dēal, 13.
Dēal'er.
Dēal'ing.
Dēan, 13.
Dēan'er-y.
Dēar, *a.* costly, precious. [*See* Deer, 160.]
Dēar'born.
Dearth (*derth*), 21, Note.
Dēar'y.
Dĕath, 15, 37.
De-ba'cle (Fr.) (*dā-bä'-kl*) [so Sm.; *de-ba'kl*, Wr.; *de-bak'l*, Wb. Gd. 154, 155.]
De-bar', 11.
De-barred' (*-bard'*), 176.
De-bar'ring.
De-base', 23.
De-bāsed' (*-bāst'*), 183.
De-bās'er.
De-bās'ing.
De-base'ment.
De-bāt'a-ble, 164.
De-bate', 23.
De-bāt'ed, 183.
De-bāt'er.
De-bāt'ing.
De-bâuch', 17, 44.
De-bâuched' (*-bawcht'*).
Deb-au-chee' (*-o-shē'*), 122, 171.
De-bâuch'er.
De-bâuch'er-y.
De-bâuch'ing.
De-bent'ure, 91.
De-bent'ured (*-yurd*).
De-bil'i-tate, 169.
De-bil'i-tāt-ed, 183.
De-bil'i-tāt-ing.
De-bil'i-ty, 108, 169.
Deb'it, 170.
Deb'it-ed.
Deb'it-ing.
De-bi-tu-min-ĭ-za'tion.
De-bi-tu'min-ize, 202.
De-bi-tu'min-īzed, 183.
De-bi-tu'min-īz-ing.
Deb-o-nair' (*-nêr'*), 122.
De-bouch' (*-boosh'*), 46.
Débris (Fr.) (*dā-brē'*), *n. pl.*
Debt (*det*), 15, 162.
Debt-ee' (*det-ē'*), 121.
Debt'or (*det'ur*), 162.
Début (Fr.) (*dā-bu'*) [so Gd.; *dā-b'oo'*, Sm. (see § 26); *dā-boo'*, Wr. 154, 155.]
Debutant (Fr.) (*dā-bu-tang'*).
Dec'a-chord (*-kord*).
Dec'a-dal, 72.
Dec'ade, 171.
De-ca'dence, 122.
De-ca'den-cy, 169.
Dec'a-gon.
Dec'a-gram [Decagramme, 203.]
Dec-a-gyn'i-an (*-jin'-*).
De-cag'y-noŭs (*-kaj'-*).
Dec-a-he'dral.
Dec-a-he'dron [pl. Dec-a-he'dra, 198.]
Dec-a-li'tre (Fr.) (*-le'-tur*) [Decaliter (*dek'a-lī-tur*, Sm.; *dē-kal'i-tur*, Gd.), 203.]
De-cal'o-gist.
Dec'a-lŏgue (*-log*), 87.
De-cam'er-on, 105.
Dec'a-mē-tre (Fr.) (*-me-tur*) [Decameter (*de-kam'e-tur*, or *dek'-a-mē-tur*), Gd. 203.]
De-camp', 10, 103.
De-camped' (*-kampt'*).
De-camp'ing.
De-camp'ment, 185.
Dec'a-nal [so Sm. Wb. Gd.; *dek'a-nal*, or *de-ka'nal*, Wr. 155.]
De-can'dri-an, 169.
De-can'droŭs.
Dec-an'gu-lar (*-ang'-*).
De-cant', 10.
De-cant-a'tion [so Sm. Wb. Gd.; *dek-an-ta'-tion*, Wk. Wr. 155.]
De-cant'ed.
De-cant'er.
De-cant'ing.
Dec-a-phyl'loŭs, *or* De-caph'yl-loŭs. [*See* Adenophyllous.]
De-cap'i-tate, 169.
De-cap'i-tāt-ed, 183.
De-cap'i-tāt-ing.
De-cap-i-ta'tion.
Dec'a-pod, 169.
De-cap'o-doŭs, 105.
De-car-bon-ī-za'tion.
Dē-car'bon-īze, 202.
De-car'bon-īzed, 183.
De-car'bon-īz-ing.
Dec'a-stich (*-stik*).
Dec'a-stȳle.
De-cāy', 23.
De-cāyed' (*-kād'*), 187.
De-cāy'er.
De-cāy'ing.
De-cēase', 13.
De-cēased' (*-sēst'*).
De-cēas'ing.
De-cēit', 13, 169.
De-cēit'ful (*-fōōl*).
De-cēiv'a-ble, 164, 169.
De-cēive' (*-sēv'*), 13, 169.
De-cēived' (*-sēvd'*), 183.
De-cēiv'er.
De-cēiv'ing.
De-cem'ber, 126.
De-cem'fid, 122.
De-cem'vir (L.) [pl. *De-cem'vi-rī*, 198.]
De-cem'vi-ral, 72.
De-cem'vi-rate, 169.
De'cen-cy, 169.
De-cen'na-ry, 72, 170.
De-cen'ni-al, 169, 170.
De'cent, 171.
De-cep'tion.
De-cep'tĭve, 84.
De-cīd'a-ble, 164, 183.
De-cide', 25.
De-cīd'ed, 183.
De-cīd'er.
De-cīd'ing.
De-cid'u-oŭs, 89.
Deç'i-gram [Deçigramme, 203.]
Deç'i-li-tre (Fr.) (*-lē-tur*) [Deciliter (*de-sil'i-tur*), Gd. 203.]
De-cill'ion (*-yun*).
De-cill'ionth (*-yunth*).
Deç'i-mal, 171.
Deç'i-mate, 73.
Deç'i-māt-ed, 183.
Deç'i-māt-ing.
Deç-i-ma'tion, 112.
Deç'i-me-tre (Fr.) (*-mē-tur*) [Decimeter (*de-sim'e-tur*), Sm. Wb. Gd. 203.]
De-ci'pher.
De-ci'pher-a-ble, 164.
De-ci'phered (*-sī'furd*), 150.

De-ci'pher-er, 77.
De-ci'pher-ing.
De-cī'sion (-*sizh'un*).
De-ci'sīve, 84.
Deck, 15, 181.
Deck'ed (*dekt*), 149.
Deck'er.
Deck'ing.
De-clāim', 23, 103.
De-clāim'er.
De-clāim'ing.
Dec-la-ma'tion, 112.
De-clam'a-to-ry, 86.
De-clar'a-ble (-*klêr'*-), 164.
Dec-la-ra'tion.
De-clăr'a-tīve, 84, 143.
De-clăr'a-to-ry, 86.
De-clare' (-*klêr'*), 14.
De-clared' (-*klêrd'*), 183.
De-clar'er (-*klêr'*-).
De-clar'ing (-*klêr'*-).
De-clen'sion.
De-clīn'a-ble, 164.
Dec-li-na'tion.
Dec'li-nā-tor.
De-clin'a-to-ry.
De-cline', 25, 103.
De-clined', 165, 183.
De-clīn'er.
De-clīn'ing.
Dec-li-nom'e-ter, 108.
De-clīn'oŭs.
De-cliv'i-toŭs.
De-cliv'i-ty, 108, 169.
De-cli'voŭs.
De-coct', 18, 103.
De-coct'i-ble, 164, 169.
De-coc'tion.
De-coct'īve, 84.
De-col'late, 170.
Dē-col'lāt-ed.
De-col'lāt-ing.
De-col-la'tion.
De-col'or (-*kul'*-).
De-col'or-ant (-*kul'*-)
De-col-or-a'tion (-*kul*-).
De-col'ored (-*kul'urd*), 165.
De-col'or-ing (-*kul'*-).
De-col'or-īze (-*kul'*-), 202.
De-col'or-ized (-*kul'*-).
De-col'or-īz-ing (-*kul'*-).
De-com-pōs'a-ble (-*pōz*-), 164.
De-com-pose' (-*pōz'*), 122.
De-com-posed' (-*pōzd'*).
De-com-pōs'ing (-*pōz'*-).
De-com-po-sī'tion (-*zish'un*).
De-com-pound', *v.* & *a.*
Dec'o-rate.
Dec'o-rāt-ed, 183.
Dec'o-rāt-ing.
Dec-o-ra'tion, 112.
Dec'o-ra-tīve.
Dec'o-rāt-or.
De-co'roŭs, *or* Dec'o-roŭs [so Wr. Gd.; *de-ko'rous*, Wk. Sm. 125, 155.]
De-cor'ti-cate.
De-cor'ti-cāt-ed, 183.
De-cor'ti-cāt-ing.
De-cor-ti-ca'tion.
De-co'rum, 125, 169.
De-coy', 27.
De-coyed', 165, 187.
De-coy'ing.
De-crēase' (-*krēs'*), 13, 118.
De-creased' (-*krēst'*), 165.
De-crēas'ing, 183.
De-cree'.
De-creed', 188.
De-cre'er.
De-cree'ing.
Dec're-ment, 105.
De-crep'it [*not* de-krep'-id, 141, 153.]
De-crep'i-tate, 169.
De-crep'i-tāt-ed.
De-crep'i-tāt-ing.
De-crep-i-ta'tion.
De-crep'i-tude, 169.
De-cres'cent, 171.
De-cre'tal [so Sm. Wr. Wb. Gd.; *de-kre'tal*, or *dek're-tal*, Wk. 155.]
De-cre'tist.
De-cre'tīve.
Dec're-tō-ry, 72, 122.
De-cri'al.
De-crīed', 186.
De-cry', 25,
De-cum'bence, 169.
De-cum'ben-cy.
De-cum'bent.
De-cum'bi-ture.
Dec'u-ple, *a. n.* & *v.* 164.
Dec'u-pled (-*pld*), 183.
Dec'u-pling.
De-cu'ri-on, 169.
De-cŭr'rent.
De-cur'sīve.
De-cus'sate, 170.
De-cus'sāt-ed.
De-cus'sāt-ing.
De-cus-sa'tion.
[Dedal, 203.—*See* Dædal.]
[Dedalian, 203.—*See* Dædalian.]
[Dedalous, 203.—*See* Dædalous.]
Ded'i-cate, 169.
Ded'i-cāt-ed, 183.
Ded'i-cāt-ing.
Ded-i-ca'tion.
Ded'i-cāt-or.
Ded'i-ca-to-ry, 86.
De-duce', 26.
De-duced' (-*dūst'*).
De-dūç'ing.
De-dūç'i-ble, 164, 169.
De-duct', 22, 103.
De-duct'ed.
De-duct'ing.
De-duc'tion.
De-duct'īve, 84.
Deed, 13.
Deem, 13.
Deemed, 165.
Deem'ing.
Deem'ster, 77.
Deep, 13.
Deep'en (*dēp'n*), 149.
Deep'ened (*dēp'nd*), 150.
Deep'en-ing (*dēp'n*-).
Deep'-sēat-ed, 206, Exc. 5.
Deer (13), *n.* a quadruped of the genus *Cervus.* [*See* Dear, 160.]
De-face', 23.
De-faced' (-*fāst'*), 183
De-facē'ment.
De-fāç'er.
De-fāç'ing.
De-fal'cate.
De-fal'cāt-ed.
De-fal'cāt-ing.
Dē-fal-ca'tion [so Sm. Wb. Gd.; *def-al-ka'-shun*, Wk. Wr. 155.]
Def-a-ma'tion.
De-fam'a-to-ry, 86.
De-fame', 23.
De-famed', 165, 183.
De-fām'er.
De-fām'ing.
De-fâult', 17.
De-fâult'ed.
De-fâult'er.
De-fâult'ing.
De-fea'sance (-*zans*), 122.
De-fēa'si-ble (-*fe'zī*-), 164.
De-fēat', 13.
De-fēat'ed.
De-fēat'ing.

Def′e-cate, 169, 170.
Def′e-cāt-ed.
Def′e-cāt-ing.
Def-e-ca′tion.
De-fect′, 15.
De-fec′tion.
De-fect′ĭve, 84.
De-fence′ [Defense, Wb. Gd. 203.—*See* Note E, p. 70.]
De-fend′, 15, 103.
De-fend′ant, 169.
De-fend′ed.
De-fend′er.
De-fend′ing.
De-fen′si-ble, 164, 169.
De-fen′sĭve, 84.
De-fer′, 21, N.
Def′er-ence, 123, 169.
Def′er-ent.
Def-er-en′tial (*-shal*).
De-ferred′, 165, 176.
De-fer′rer, 21, N.
De-fer′ring.
De-fi′ance, 169.
De-fi′ant.
De-fĭ′cien-cy (*-fish′en-*).
De-fĭ′cient (*-fish′ent*).
Def′i-cit (L.).
De-fīed′, 186.
De-fi′er.
De-fīle′, *v.* 25.
De′file, *or* De-file′, *n.* [*de′fīl*, Sm.; *de-fīl′*, Wk. Wr. Wb. Gd. 155.]

☞ "*Defile*, as a noun, begins to lose its French accent on the ultimate, which till within a few years was universal." *Smart.*

De-fīled′, 165, 183.
De-file′ment.
De-fīl′er.
De-fīl′ing, 183.
De-fīn′a-ble, 164, 169.
De-fine′, 25.
De-fīned′, 165, 183.
De-fīn′er.
De-fīn′ing.
Def′i-nĭte, 152, 171.
Def-i-nĭ′tion (*-nish′un*).
De-fin′i-tĭve, 169.
Def-la-gra-bil′i-ty.
Def′la-gra-ble, *or* De-fla′gra-ble (164) [*def′-la-gra-bl*, Sm.; *de-fla′gra-bl*, Wk. Wb. Gd.; *de-fla′gra-bl*, or *def′la-gra-bl*, Wr.]
Def′la-grate.
Def′la-grāt-ed, 183.
Def′la-grāt-ing.
Def-la-gra′tion.
Def′la-grāt-or.
De-flect′, 15, 103.
De-flect′ed.
De-flect′ing.
De-flec′tion.
De-flo′rate, 122.
Def-lo-ra′tion.
De-flour′, 28.
De-floured′, 165.
De-flour′er.
De-flour′ing.
De-flux′ion (*-fluk′shun*), 46, Note 1.
De-fo-li-a′tion.
De-form′, 17.
De-formed′, 165.
De-form′er.
De-form′ing.
De-form′i-ty, 108, 169.
De-frâud′, 17.
De-frâud′ed.
De-frâud′er.
De-frâud′ing.
De-frāy′, 23.
De-frāyed′, 165, 187.
De-frāy′er.
De-frāy′ing.
Deft, 15.
De-funct′, 22.
De-fy′, 25.
De-fy′ing.
De-gen′er-a-cy, 171.
De-gen′er-ate, 73.
De-gen′er-āt-ed, 183.
De-gen′er-āt-ing.
De-gen-er-a′tion.
Deg-lu-tĭ′tion (*-tish′un*).
Deg-ra-da′tion.
De-grade′, 23.
De-grād′ed, 183.
De-grād′ing.
De-gree′.
De-hisce′ (*-his′*).
De-hisced′ (*-hist′*).
De-his′cence, 171.
De-his′cent.
De-his′cing, 183.
De-hor′ta-to-ry, 72.
De′i-cide, 169.
De-if′ic, 109.
De-if′ic-al, 108.
De-i-fĭ-ca′tion.
De′i-fīed, 186.
De′i-fī-er.
De′i-form, 169.
De′i-fȳ, 94.
Deign (*dān*), 23.
Deigned (*dānd*), 165.
Deign′ing.
De′ism (*-izm*), 133, 136.
De′ist.
De-ist′ic, 109.
De-ist′ic-al, 108.
De′i-ty, 169.
De-ject′, 15.
De-ject′ed.
De-ject′er.
De-ject′ing.
De-jec′tion.
De-ject′o-ry.
Déjeûner, or *Déjeûné* (Fr.) (*dā-zhuh-nā′*).
De-lāy′, 23.
De-lāyed′, 165, 187.
De-lāy′er.
De-lāy′ing.
De′lē (L.), *v.*
Del′e-ble (164, 169) [so Wr. Wb. Gd.; *de′le-bl*, Sm. 155.]
De-lec′ta-ble, 164.
De-lec-ta′tion [so Sm. Wb. Gd.; *del-ek-ta′-shun*, Wr. 155.]
Del′e-gate, 169.
Del′e-gāt-ed.
Del′e-gāt-ing.
Del-e-ga′tion, *n.* act of delegating; persons delegated. [*See* Del-igation, 160.]
Del-e-te′ri-oŭs, 169.
Delft′-ware (*-wêr*).
De′li-ac.
De-lib′er-ate, 73.
De-lib′er-āt-ed, 183.
De-lib′er-āt-ing.
De-lib-er-a′tion, 112.
De-lib′er-āt-ĭve [so Sm.; *de-lib′ur-a-tiv*, Wk. Wr. Wb. Gd. 155.]
Del′i-ca-cy, 171.
Del′i-cate, 73, 169.
De-lĭ′cioŭs (*lish′us*), 231.
Del-i-ga′tion, *n.* a binding up,—a term in surgery. [*See* Delegation, 160.]
De-light′ (*-līt′*), 162.
De-light′ed (*-līt′-*).
De-light′ful (*-līt′fōōl*).
De-light′ing (*-līt′-*).
De-lin′e-ate, 169.
De-lin′e-āt-ed, 183.
De-lin′e-āt-ing.
De-lin-e-a′tion.
De-lin′e-āt-or.
De-lin′quen-cy (*-ling′-*).
De-lin′quent (*-ling′-*).
Del-i-quesce′ (*-kwes′*), 171.
Del-i-quesced′ (*-kwest′*).
Del-i-ques′cence.
Del-i-ques′cent, 171.
Del-i-ques′cing, 183.

De-lĭ'qui-um (L.) (*-lik'-wi-um*).
De-lĭr'i-oŭs, 78.
De-lĭr'i-um, 169.
Del-i-tes'cence.
Del-i-tes'cent, 171.
De-liv'er, 104.
De-liv'er-a-ble, 164, 169.
De-liv'er-ance, 169.
De-liv'ered (*-urd*), 150.
De-liv'er-er, 77.
De-liv'er-ing.
De-liv'er-y.
Dell, 15, 172.
Del'phi-an, 78.
Del'phic.
Del'phĭne, 82, 152.
Del'ta, 72.
Del'toid.
De-lude', 26.
De-lūd'ed, 183.
De-lūd'er.
De-lūd'ing.
Del'uge, 15, 90.
Del'uged, 165, 183.
Del'ug-ing (*-ŭj-*).
De-lu'sion (*-zhun*).
De-lu'sive, 84.
De-lu'so-ry, 86.
Delve, 15.
Delved (*delvd*), 165, 183.
Delv'er.
Delv'ing.
Dem'a-gog-ism (*-izm*) [so Gd.; *dem'a-gog-izm*, or *dem'a-go-jizm*, Wr. 155.]
Dem'a-gŏgue (*-gog*), 87, 171.
De-main', *or* De-mesne' (*de-mēn'*) [so Wk. Sm. Gd.; *de-mān'*, or *de-mēn'*, Wr. 155.] [Demean, 203.]
De-mand'. [*See* Command'.]
De-mand'ant.
De-mand'ed.
De-mand'er.
De-mand'ing.
De-mar-ca'tion.
De-mēan', *v.*
[Demean, *n.* 203.—*See* Demain.]
De-mēaned', 165.
De-mēan'ing.
De-mēan'or.
De-ment'ed.
De-meph-i-tĭ-za'tion.
De-meph'i-tize, 202.
De-meph'i-tized, 183.
De-meph'i-tiz-ing.
De-mĕr'it.
De-mersed' (*-merst'*).
De-mesne' (*-mēn'*) [*See* Demain, 203.]
Dem'i-god. [169.
Dem'i-john (*-jon*), 162,
De-mĭs-a-bil'i-ty(*-mīz-*).
De-mĭs'a-ble (*-mīz*), 164.
De-mise' (*mīz'*), *n.* & *v.*
De-mīsed' (*-mīzd'*), 183.
De-mīs'ing (*-mīz'-*).
Dem'i-urge, 169.
De-moc'ra-cy, 169, 171.
Dem'o-crat.
Dem-o-crat'ic, 109.
Dem-o-crat'ic-al, 108.
De-mol'ish, 104.
De-mol'ished (*-isht*).
De-mol'ish-er.
De-mol'ish-ing.
Dem-o-lĭ'tion (*-lish'un*).
De'mon, 86.
De-mo'ni-ac, 169.
Dem-o-ni'ac-al.
De-mo-ni'a-cism (*-sizm*)
De-mo'ni-an.
De-mo'ni-an-ism (*-izm*).
De'mon-ism (*-izm*), 136.
De'mon-ist.
De'mon-ize, 202.
De'mon-ized, 183.
De'mon-iz-ing.
De-mon-ol'a-try.
De-mon ol'o-gy, *or* Dem-on-ol'o-gy (108) [so Wr.; *de-mon-ol'-o-gy*, Wb. Gd.; *dem-on-ol'o-gy*, Wk. Sm. 155.]
De-mon'stra-ble, 164.
De-mon'strate [so Wk. Sm. Wr.; *de-mon'-strāt*, or *dem'on-strāt*, Gd. 155.]
De-mon'strāt-ed.
De-mon'strāt-ing
Dem-on-stra'tion.
De-mon'stra-tive.
Dem'on-strāt-or, *or* De-mon'strāt-or [so Wr.; *dem'on-strāt-ur*, Sm. Wb. Gd.; *dem-on-strāt'ur*, or *de-mon'-strāt-ur*, Wk. 155.]

☞ Smart and Walker agree that when used in the general sense of "one who demonstrates," this word is properly pronounced *de-mon'strāt-ur*; but Smart spells it, when thus used, Demonstrater. The spelling *demonstrator* he restricts to the sense of "one who exhibits a matter of science," and he pronounces it *dem'on-strāt-ur*; whereas Walker pronounces the word, when it is used in this sense, *dem-on-strāt'ur*.

De-mon'stra-to-ry, 86.
De-mŏr-al-ĭ-za'tion.
De-mŏr'al-ize, 202.
De-mŏr'al-ized, 183.
De-mŏr'al-īz-ing.
Dem-os-then'ic.
De-mot'ic.
De-mul'cent, 171.
De-mur', 21.
De-mure', 26.
De-mur'rage, 170.
De-murred', 165, 176.
De-mur'rer, 77.
De-mur'ring.
De-my', 121.
Den, 15.
De-na'ri-us (L.) [pl. *De-na'ri-ī*, 198.]
Den'a-ry.
De-nă'tion-al-ize(*-nash'-un-*)[so Sm. Wr.; *-na'-shun-*, or *nash'un*, Gd. 155.]
De-nă'tion-al-ized, 183.
De-nă'tion-al-īz-ing.
Den'dri-form, 169.
Den'drite.
Den-drit'ic, 109.
Den-drit'ic-al, 108.
Den'droid.
Den-drol'o-gist.
Den-drol'o-gy, 108.
Den'gue (Sp.)(*deng'gā*).
De-ni'a-ble, 164.
De-ni'al.
De-nied', 186.
De-ni'er.
Den'i-grate [so Sm. Wr. Wb. Gd.; *den'i grāt*, or *de-ni'grāt*, Wk. 155.]
Den'i-grāt-ed, 183.
Den'i-grāt-ing.
Den-i-za'tion.
Den'i-zen (*-zn*), 149.
De-nom'i-nate.
De-nom'i-nāt-ed, 183.
De-nom'i-nāt-ing.
De-nom-i-na'tion.
De-nom-i-na'tion-al.
De-nom'i-nāt-ĭve [so Sm.; *de-nom'i-na-tiv*, Wk. Wr. Wb. Gd. 155.]
De-nom-i-nāt'or.
De-nŏt'a-ble, 164, 169.
De-note', 24.
De-nŏt'ed.
De-nŏt'ing.

Den-oue-ment(Fr.)(*den-oo-mang'*) [so Wr. Gd.; *den-oo-mŏng'*, Sm. 154, 155.]
De-nounce', 28.
De-nounced' (*-nounst'*).
De-nounce'ment.
De-nounc'er.
Dense (*dens*), 15; Note D, p. 37.
Den'si-ty, 169.
Dent, 15.
Den'tal.
Den'tate.
Den'tāt-ed.
Den-ta'tion.
Dent'ed.
Den'ti-cle, 164.
Den-tic'u-late, 73.
Den-tic'u-lāt-ed.
Den-tic-u-la'tion.
Den'ti-form, 78, 169.
Den'ti-frīce (*-fris*) (169) [*not* den'tri-fis, 153.]
Den'til.
Den-ti-ros'tral.
Den'tist, 15, 16.
Den-tist'ic, 109.
Den-tist'ic-al.
Den'tist-ry.
Den-tĭ'tion (*-tish'un*).
Den'toid.
De-nū'date, *a.*
De-nu-da'tion [so Wk. Wb. Gd.; *den-u-da'-shun*, Sm. Wr. 155.]
De-nude', 26.
De-nūd'ed, 183.
De-nūd'ing.
De-nun'ci-ate (*-shĭ-āt*) [so Sm. Wr.; *de-nun'-shāt*, Wb. Gd. 155.]
De-nun'ci-āt-ed (*-shĭ-*).
De-nun'ci-āt-ing (*-shĭ-*).
De-nun-ci-a'tion (*-shĭ-*).
De-nun'ci-āt-or (*-shĭ-*).
De-ny', 25.
De-ob'stru-ent.
De'o-dand.
De-o'dor-ize, 202.
De-o'dor-īzed, 183.
De-o'dor-īz-er.
De-o'dor-īz-ing.
De-on-tol'o-gy, 108.
De-ox'i-date [Deoxydate, 203.]
De-ox'i-dāt-ed.
De-ox'i-dāt-ing.
De-ox-i-da'tion.
De-ox'i-dize (202) [Deoxydize, 203.]
De-ox'i dīzed, 183.
De-ox'i-dīz-ing.
[Deoxydate, 203. — *See* Deoxidate.]
[Deoxydize, 203. — *See* Deoxidize.]
De-ox'y-gen-ate, 171.
De-ox'y-gen-āt-ed.
De-ox'y-gen-āt-ing.
De-ox-y-gen-a'tion.
De-part', 11, 135.
De-part'ed.
De-part'er.
De-part'ing.
De-part'ment.
De-part-ment'al, 122.
De-part'ure, 91.
De-pend', 15.
De-pend'ant, *n.* [Dependent, 203.]
[Dependant, *a.* 203. — *See* Dependent.]
De-pend'ence, 169.
De-pend'en-cy.
De-pend'ent, *a.* [Dependant, 203.]
[Dependent, *n.* 203. — *See* Dependant.]
De-pend'er.
De-pend'ing.
De-phleg'mate, 35.
De-phleg'māt-ed.
De-phleg'māt-ing.
De-phleg-ma'tion [so Sm. Wb. Gd.; *def-leg-ma'shun*, Wk. Wr. 155]
De-pict', 16.
De-pict'ed.
De-pict'ing.
De-pict'ure, 91.
De-pict'ured (*-yurd*).
De-pict'ur-ing (*-yur-*).
De-pil'a-to-ry, 86.
De-ple'tion.
De-ple'to-ry, 86.
De-plōr'a-ble, 164.
De-plōr'a-bly.
Dep-lo-ra'tion.
De-plore', 24.
De-plōred', 165, 183.
De-plōr'er, 49, N.
De-plōr'ing.
De-ploy', 27.
De-ployed', 165, 188.
De-ploy'ing.
De-po'nent, 169.
De-pop'u-late, 89.
De-pop'u-lāt-ed.
De-pop'u-lāt-ing.
De-pop-u-la'tion.
De-pōrt', 24.
De-pōr-ta'tion, *or* Dep-or-ta'tion [*de-pōr-ta'-shun*, Sm.; *dep-or-ta'-shun*, Wk. Wr. Gd. 155]
De-pōrt'ment.
De-pōs'a-ble (*-pōz'-*), 164.
De-pōs'al (*-pōz'-*), 183.
De-pose' (*-pōz'*), 24.
De-posed' (*-pōzd'*), 183.
De-pōs'er (*-pōz'-*).
De-pōs'ing (*-pōz'-*).
De-pōs'it (*-pŏz'-*), 170.
De-pos'i-ta-ry (*-pŏz'-*) (72) *n.* one with whom any thing is intrusted. [*See* Depository, 148.]
De-pos'it-ed (*-pŏz'-*).
De-pos'it-ing (*-pŏz'-*).
Dep-o-sĭ'tion (*-zish'un*) [so Wk. Wr. Wb. Gd.; *de-po-zish'un*, Sm. 155]
De-pos'it-or (*-pŏz'-*).
De-pos'i-to-ry (*-pŏz'-*) (86), *n.* the place where any thing is deposited. [*See* Depositary, 148.]
Depot (Fr.) (*de-pō'*, or *dā-pō'*) [*de-pō'*, Wb. Gd. Wr.; *dā-pō'*, Sm. 155.]

☞ This word is very often pronounced *dē'po*, in the United States.

Dep-ra-va'tion.
De-prave', 23.
De-prāved', 165.
De-prāv'er, 183.
De-prāv'ing.
De-prăv'i-ty, 123, 169.
Dep're-ca-ble, 164.
Dep're-cate, 169.
Dep're-cāt-ed, 183.
Dep're-cāt-ing.
Dep-re-ca'tion.
Dep're-cāt-or.
Dep're-ca-to-ry, 72, 86.
De-pre'ci-ate (*-shĭ-āt*) [so Wk. Sm. Wr.; *-pre'shāt*, Wb. Gd. 155.]
De-pre'ci-āt-ed (*-shĭ-*).
De-pre'ci-āt-ing (*-shĭ-*).
De-pre-ci-a'tion (*-shĭ-*).
De-pre'ci-āt-īve (*-shĭ-āt-*) [so Sm.; *de-pre'-shĭ-a-tiv*, Wr.; *de-pre'-sha-tiv*, Wb. Gd.]
De-pre'ci-āt-or (*-shĭ-*).
De-pre'ci-a-to-ry, (*-shĭ-*)
Dep're-date, 169.
Dep're-dāt-ed, 183.
Dep're-dāt-ing.
Dep-re-da'tion.
Dep're-dāt-or.
Dep're-da-to-ry, 86.
De-press', 15.

De-pressed′ (*-prest′*).
De-press′ing.
De-pres′sion(*-presh′un*)
De-press′ĭve, 84.
De-press′or.
De-prīv′a-ble, 164.
Dep-ri-va′tion.
De-prive′, 25.
De-prīved′, 165, 183.
De-prīv′er.
De-prīv′ing.
Depth, 15, 37.
Dep′u-rate, 73, 89.
Dep′u-rāt-ed.
Dep′u-rāt-ing.
Dep-u-ra′tion.
Dep′u-rāt-or.
Dep′u-ra-to-ry, 86.
Dep-u-ta′tion.
De-pute′, 26, 103.
De-pūt′ed.
De-pūt′ing.
Dep′u-ty, 89, 93.

☞ "This word is often mispronounced [*deb′bu-ty*] even by good speakers." — *Walker*.

De-rānge′, 23.
De-rānged′, 165, 183.
De-rāng′ing (*-rānj′-*).
De-rānge′ment, 185.
Dĕr′e-lict, 169, 171.
Dĕr-e-lic′tion.
De-ride′, 25, 103.
De-rīd′ed.
De-rīd′er.
De-rīd′ing.
De-rĭ′sion (*de-rizh′un*), 171.
De-ri′sĭve, 84.
De-ri′so-ry, 86, 93.
De-rīv′a-ble, 164.
Dĕr-i-va′tion.
Dĕr-i-va′tion-al.
De-riv′a-tĭve, 84, 169.
De-rive′, 25, 103.
De-rīved′, 165, 183.
De-rīv′er.
De-rīv′ing.
Derm, 21, N.
Derm′al.
Derm-at′ic.
Derm′a-toid.
Derm-a-tol′o-gy, 108.
Derm-og′ra-phy, 108.
Derm′oid.
Derm-ot′o-my, 108.
Dĕr′o-gate.
Dĕr′o-gāt-ed, 183.
Dĕr′o-gāt-ing.
Dĕr-o-ga′tion.
De-rog′a-to-ry, 86.
Dĕr′rick, 170.

Der′vis [Dervise, Dervish, 203.]
Des′cant, *n.* 103, 161.
Des-cant′, *v.* 103, 161.

☞ By the poets it is often accented on the first syllable.

Des-cant′ed.
Des-cant′er.
Des-cant′ing. [171.
De-scend′ (*-send′*), 39,
De-scend′ant, *n.* 148.
De-scend′ed.
De-scend′ent, *a.* 148.
De-scend′er.
De-scend-i-bil′i-ty.
De-scend′i-ble, 164, 169.
De-scend′ing.
De-scen′sion, 171.
De-scen′sion-al.
De-scent′ (*-sent′*), 15, 39.
De-scrīb′a-ble, 164, 169.
De-scribe′, 25, 103.
De-scrībed′, 165, 183.
De-scrīb′er.
De-scrīb′ing.
De-scrīed′, 186.
De-scrip′tion.
De-scrip′tĭve, 84.
De-scry′, 25.
De-scry′ing.
Des′e-crate, 169.
Des′e-crāt-ed, 183.
Des′e-crāt-ing.
Des-e-cra′tion.
Des′ert (*dez′urt*), *a.* waste; solitary: — *n.* an uninhabited place. [*See* De-sert′, *n.* & *v.* 161.]
De-sert′ (*de-zert′*) (21, N.), *n.* that which is deserved: — *v.* to forsake; to leave. [*See* Des′ert, *a.* & *n.* 161, and Des-sert′, *n.* 148.]
De-sert′ed (*-zert′-*).
De-sert′er (*-zert′-*).
De-sert′ing (*-zert′-*).
De-ser′tion (*-zer′-*).
De-serve′ (*-zerv′*), 21, N.
De-served′(*-zervd′*), 165.
De-serv′ed-ly (*-zerv′-*).
De-serv′er (*-zerv′-*).
De-serv′ing (*-zerv′-*).
[Deshabille, 203. — *See* Dishabille.]
De-sic′cant, *a.* & *n.*
De-sic′cate [so Wk. Sm. Wr.; *de-sik′āt*, or *des′i-kāt*, Gd. 155.]
De-sic′cāt-ed, 183.
De-sic′cāt-ing.

Des-ic-ca′tion, 170.
De-sic′ca-tĭve.
De-sid′er-a-tĭve.
De-sid-er-a′tum (L.)[pl. *De-sid-er-a′ta*, 198.]
De-sign′ (*de-sīn′*, or *de-zīn′*)(162)[so Wr. Gd.; *de-sīn′*, Wk. Sm. 155.]
Des′ig-nate [*not* dez′ig-nāt, *nor* de-sig′nāt, 153.]
Des′ig-nāt-ed, 183.
Des′ig-nāt-ing.
Des-ig-na′tion.
De-signed′ (*-sīnd′*, or *-zīnd′*), 162.
De-sign′er (*-sīn′-*, or *-zīn′-*).
De-sign′ing (*-sīn′-*, or [*-zīn′-*).
De-sip′i-ent.
De-sīr-a-bil′i-ty (*-zīr-*).
De-sīr′a-ble (*-zīr′-*), 164.
De-sīr′a-bly (*-zīr′-*).
De-sire′ (*-zīr′*).
De-sīred′ (*-zīrd′*), 183.
De-sīr′ing (*-zīr′-*).
De-sīr′oŭs (*-zīr′-*).
De-sist′, 16, 103, 136.
De-sist′ed.
De-sist′ing.
Desk, 15.
Des′man.
Des′o-late, 136.
Des′o-lāt-ed, 183.
Des′o-lāt-er.
Des′o-lāt-ing.
Des-o-la′tion.
Des′o-la-to-ry, 72.
De-spair′ (*-spêr′*), 14.
De-spaired′ (*-spêrd′*).
De-spair′ing (*-spêr′-*).
De-spatch′ [Dispatch, 203.]

☞ The spelling *despatch* is most in conformity with the etymology of this word (Fr. *dépêcher*), and is preferred by Walker, Smart, and Worcester: but Webster and Goodrich prefer *dispatch*. Worcester remarks: "Good usage, as well as the dictionaries, is much divided."

De-spatched′ (*-spacht′*) [Dispatched, 203.]
De-spatch′ing [Dispatching, 203.]
Des-pe-ra′do [pl. Des-pe-ra′does (*-dōz*), 192.]
Des′per-ate, 132.
Des-per-a′tion.
Des′pi-ca-ble (164) [*not* des-pik′a-bl, 153.]

Des'pi-ca-bly.
De-spise' (-spīz'), 25.
De-spised' (-spīzd'), 183.
De-spīs'er (-spīz'-).
De-spīz'ing (-spīz'-).
De-spite', *n.* & *prep.*
De-spoil', 27, 103.
De-spoiled', 165.
De-spoil'er.
De-spoil'ing.
De-spond', 18.
De-spond'ed.
De-spond'ence, 169.
De-spond'en-cy.
De-spond'ent.
De-spond'ing.
Des'pot.
Des-pot'ic, 109.
Des-pot'ic-al, 108. [136.
Des'pot-ism (-izm), 133,
De-spu'mate [so Sm. Wr.; *des'pu-māt*, Wb. Gd. 155.]
De-spu'māt-ed.
De-spu'māt-ing.
Des-pu-ma'tion, 112.
Des-qua-ma'tion.
Des-sert' (*dez-zert'*), *n.* a service of fruit, pastry, &c., at a meal. [*See* Desert, *n.* & *v.* 148.]
Des-ti-na'tion.
Des'tĭne, 152, 171.
Des'tĭned (-tind), 183.
Des'tin-ing.
Des'ti-ny, 169.
Des'ti-tute.
Des-ti-tu'tion.
De-stroy', 27.
De-stroyed', 165, 188.
De-stroy'er.
De-stroy'ing.
De-struct-i-bil'i-ty.
De-struct'i-ble, 164.
De-struc'tion.
De-struct'ĭve.
Des-u-da'tion.
Des'ue-tude (-we-), 171.
Des'ul-to-ri-ly.
Des'ul-to-ri-ness.
Des'ul-to-ry, 86.
De-tach', 10, 44.
De-tached' (-tacht').
De-tach'ing.
De-tach'ment.
De-tail', *v.* 23.
De-tāil', *or* De'tāil, *n.* [so Wr.; *de-tāl'*, Wk. Wb. Gd.; *de'tāl*, Sm. 155.]
De-tāiled', 150.
De-tāil'er.
De-tāil'ing.
De-tāin', 23.
De-tāin'der.
De-tāined', 165.
De-tāin'er.
De-tāin'ing.
De-tect', 15, 103.
De-tect'a-ble, 164, 169.
De-tect'er.
De-tect'ing.
De-tec'tion.
De-tect'ĭve, 84.
De-tent', 121.
De-ten'tion.
De-ter', 21, N.
De-terge'.
De-terged', 165, 183.
De-terg'ent (-terj'-).
De-terg'ing (-terj'-).
De-te'ri-o-rate, 49, N.
De-te'ri-o-rāt-ed.
De-te'ri-o-rāt-ing.
De-te-ri-o-ra'tion.
De-ter'ment.
De-ter'mi-na-ble, 164.
De-ter'mi-nate, *a.*
De-ter-mi-na'tion.
De-ter'mi-na-tĭve.
De-ter'mĭne.
De-ter'mĭned (-mĭnd), 150.
De-ter'min-er, 183.
De-ter'min-ing.
De-tĕr-ra'tion, 170.
De-terred', 165, 176.
De-ter'ring, 21, N.
De-ter'sĭve.
De-test', 14.
De-test'a-ble, 164.
Det-es-ta'tion, *or* De-tes-ta'tion [*det-es-ta'shun*, Wk. Wr. Gd.; *de-tes-ta'shun*, Sm. 155.]
De-test'ed.
De-test'er.
De-test'ing.
De-throne', 24.
De-throned', 165, 183.
De-throne'ment, 185.
De-thrōn'er.
De-thrōn'ing.
Det'i-nūe [so Sm. Wb. Gd.; *de-tin'u*, Wk.; *det'i-nu*, or *de-tin'u*, Wr. 155.]
Det'o-nate.
Det'o-nāt-ed, 183.
Det'o-nāt-ing.
Det-o-na'tion.
Det-o-nĭ-za'tion.
Det'o-nize, 105, 202.
Det'o-nized, 183.
Det'o-nīz-ing.
De-tract', 10.
De-tract'ed.
[Detracter, 203.—*See* Detractor.]
De-tract'ing.
De-trac'tion.
De-tract'ĭve.
De-tract'or [Detracter, 203.]
De-tract'o-ry, 86.
Det'ri-ment, 105, 169.
Det-ri-ment'al.
De-tri'tal.
De-trĭ'tion (-trish'un).
De-tri'tus.
De-trude' (-trood'), 19.
De-trud'ed(-trood'-),183
De-trud'ing (-trood'-).
De-trun'cate (-trung'-).
De-trun'cāt-ed(-trung'-)
De-trun-ca'tion.
De-tru'sion (-troo'zhun)
Deūce (*dūs*) [Duse, 203.]
Deū-ter-og'a-mist, 108.
Deū-ter-og'a-my.
Deū-ter-on'o-my, 108.
Deū-ter-op'a-thy.
Deū-ter-os'co-py.
Deū-tox'ĭde [so Wr.; *du-tox'ĭd*, Sm. 155.] [Deutoxyd, 203.]
De-vap-o-ra'tion.
De-văs'tate, *or* Dev'as-tate [*de-văs'tāt*, Wk. Sm.; *dev'as-tāt*, Wb. Gd.; *de-văs'tāt*, or *dev'as-tāt*, Wr. 155.]
De-văs'tāt-ed, *or* Dev'-as-tāt-ed.
De-văs'tāt-ing, *or* Dev'-as-tāt-ing.
Dev-as-ta'tion.
De-vel'op [Develope, 203.]
De-vel'oped (-opt).
De-vel'op-er.
De-vel'op-ing.
De-vel'op-ment.
De-vest' [Divest, 203.]

☞ Written *devest* as a technical term in law.

De'vi-ate, 73, 78.
De'vi-āt-ed, 183.
De'vi-āt-ing.
De-vi-a'tion.
De-vice', 25, 121.
Dev'il (*dev'l*), 149.
De'vi-oŭs, 78.
De-vīs'a-ble (-vīz'-), 164.
De-vīse' (-vīz'), 25, 103.

De-vīsed′ (-*vīzd′*), 183.
Dev-i-see′ (-*zē′*), 122.
De-vīs′er (-*vīz′*-), *n.* one who contrives. [*See* Devisor, 160.]
De-vīs′ing (-*vīz′*-).
De-vīs′or(-*vīz′*-)(118)[so Sm. Wb. Gd.; *dev-i-zor′*, or *de-vī′zur*, Wr. 155], *n.* one who bequeathes. [Law term, correlative of *devisee.* — *See* Deviser, 160.]
De-vit-ri-fi-ca′tion.
De-void′, 27, 121.
Devoir (Fr.) (*dev-wor′*).
De-volve′, 18, 103.
De-volved′, 165, 183.
De-volv′ing.
De-vote′, 24.
De-vōt′ed, 183.
Dev-o-tee′, 122.
De-vōt′er.
De-vōt′ing.
De-vo′tion.
De-vo′tion-al.
De-vour′, 28, 103.
De-voured′, 165.
De-vour′er.
De-vour′ing.
De-vout′, 28.
Dew (*dū*) (26) [*not* doo, 153], *n.* moisture deposited in consequence of the cooling of the atmosphere. [*See* Due, 160.]
Dew′drop (*dū′*-).
Dew′i-ness (*dū′*-), 169.
Dew′lap (*dū′*-), 206.
Dew′point (*dū′*-).
Dew′y (*dū′y*), 93.
Dex-tĕr′i-ty, 108, 169.
Dex′ter-oŭs [Dextrous, 203.]

☞ The spelling *dexterous* is the only form given by Walker and Smart; and it is preferred by Worcester. Webster and Goodrich, however, prefer the spelling *dextrous.*

Dex′tral.
Dex-tral′i-ty.
Dex′trīne, 82, 152.
Dex-tror′sal.
Dex′troŭs [Dexterous, 203.—*See* Dexterous.]
Dey (*dā*), *n.* a Turkish title of dignity. [*See* Day, 160.]
[Dhurra, 203. — *See* Doura.]
Dī-a-be′tēs (-*tēz*), *n. sing.* & *pl.*
Dī-a-bet′ic.
Dī-ab′ler-y (233, Exc.) [so Gd.; *dī-ab′l-rī*, Wr. 155.]
Dī-a-bol′ic, 109.
Dī-a-bol′ic-al.
Dī-ab′o-lism (-*lizm*),136.
Dī-a-ca-thol′i-con.
Dī-a-câus′tic.
Dī-ach′y-lon (-*ak′*-)[Diachylum, 203.]
Dī-ac′o-nal, 79.
Dī-ac′o-nate.
Dī-a-cous′tic, *a.* 28.
Dī-a-cous′tics, *n.* 28.
Dī-a-crit′ic.
Dī-a-crit′ic-al.
Dī-a-del′phi-an, 169.
Dī-a-del′phoŭs.
Dī′a-dem, 171.
Dī′a-demed (-*demd*),150.
Dī-ær′e-sis (-*ĕr′*-) [pl. Dī-ær′e-sēs(-*sēz*),198.] [Dieresis, 203.]
Dī-ag-no′sis, 125.
Dī-ag-nos′tic.
Dī-ag′o-nal, 79, 108, 170.
Dī′a-gram.
Dī′a-grăph, 127.
Dī-a-graph′ic.
Dī-a-graph′ic-al.
Dī-a-gryd′i-ate.
Dī′al, 25, 72.
Dī′a-lect, 171.
Dī-a-lect′ic, *a.* & *n.*
Dī-a-lect′ic-al.
Dī-a-lect′ics, *n.*
Dī-a-lec-tī′cian(-*tish′an*)
Dī′al-ing.
Dī′al-ist.
Dī-al′la-gē (161), *n.* a rhetorical figure by which arguments are placed in various points of view.
Dī′al-lage [so Wb. Gd.; *dī-al′la-jē*, Sm. Wr. 155] (161), *n.* a mineral of a foliated structure, whose joints and fractures present different lines.
Dī-al′o-gism (-*jizm*),136.
Dī-al′o-gist, 170.
Dī-al-o-gist′ic.
Dī-al-o-gist′ic-al.
Dī′a-lŏgue (-*log*), 87.
Dī-al′y-sis (171) [pl. Dī-al′y-sēs (-*sēz*), 198.
Dī-a-mag-net′ic.
Dī-am′e-ter, 79, 108.
Dī-a-met′ric.
Dī-a-met′ric-al.
Dī′a-mond (*dī′a-mond*, or *dī′mond*) [so Wr. Gd.; *dī′a-mond*, Wk.; *dī′a mond*, coll. *dī′-mond*, Sm. 155.]
Dī-an′dri-an.
Dī-an′droŭs.
Dī-a-pa′son (-*zun*), 156, 171.
Dī-a-pen′te, 163.
Dī′a-per, 77.
Dī-a-pha-ne′i-ty.
Dī-a-phan′ic.
Dī-aph′a-noŭs (-*af′*-).
Dī-a-phon′ic.
Dī-a-phon′ic-al.
Dī-a-phon′ics.
Dī-a-pho-re′sis, 125.
Dī-a-pho-ret′ic.
Dī′a-phragm (-*fram*), 105, 162.
Dī-a-phrag-mat′ic.
Dī-a-po-re′sis, 122, 125.
Dī-a′ri-an (169) [so Sm. Gd.; *dī-a′ri-an*, Wr. 155.]
Dī′a-rist.
Dī-ar-rhœ′a (-*rē′a*) (171) [Diarrhea, 203.]
Dī-ar-rhœt′ic (-*ret′*-) [Diarrhetic, 203.]

☞ Walker, Smart, and Worcester give only the forms *diarrhœa* and *diarrhœtic*. Webster and Goodrich give only the forms *diarrhea* and *diarrhetic.*

Dī-ar-thro′sis, 122, 125.
Dī′a-ry.
Dī′as-tase.
Dī-as′to-le, 163.
Dī′a-style.
Dī-a-tes′sa-ron, 170.
Dī-a-ther′mal, 21, N.
Dī-a-ther′ma-noŭs.
Dī-ath′e-sis.
Dī-a-ton′ic.
Dī′a-tribe [so Wb. Gd.; *dī′a-trī-be*, Sm.; *dī′a-trīb*, or *dī-at′ri-be*, Wr. 155.]
Dī-at′ro-bist, 105.
Dī-a-zeū′tic (-*zū′*-).
Dib′ble, 164.
Dib′bled (*dib′ld*), 183.
Dib′bler.
Dib′bling.
Dib′stōne, 206.
Dice (25), *n.* [pl. of Die, 194.]
Dī-ceph′a-loŭs.

Dīç′er, 183.
Dī-chla-myd′e-oŭs (-*kla*-).
Dī-chot′o-moŭs (-*kot*-).
Dī-chot′o-my (-*kot′*-).
Dī-chro-ism (-*kro-izm*).
Dī-chro-mat′ic (-*kro*-).
Dīç′ing.
Dick′y.
Dī-co-tyl-e′don [so Sm. Wb. Gd.; *dī-kot-y-le′-don*, Wr. 155.]
Dī-co-tyl-e′don-oŭs [so Sm. Gd.; *dī-kot-y-led′o-nus*, Wr. 155.]
Dic′tate, 16, 73.
Dic′tāt-ed, 183.
Dic′tāt-ing.
Dic-ta′tion, 112.
Dic-tāt′or.
Dic-ta-to′ri-al, 169.
Dic-tāt′ure (91) [so Sm. Wr.; *dik′ta-tūr*, Wb. Gd. 155.]
Dic′tion.
Dic′tion-a-ry, 72.
Dic′tum (L.) [pl. *Dic′-ta*, 198.]
Dĭ-dac′tic, 79, 108.
Dĭ-dac′tic-al, 109.
Dĭ-dac′tic-al-ly.
Dī-dac′tyl.
Dī-dac′tyl-oŭs.
Did-ap′per [so Wk. Sm. Wr.; *dī-dap′ur*, Wb. Gd. 155.]
Did-as-cal′ic [so Wk. Sm. Wr.; *dī-das-kal′-ik*, Wb. Gd. 155.]
Did′dle, 164.
Did′dled (*did′ld*), 183.
Did′dling.
Dī-dec-a-he′dral.
Dī-del′phic [D i d e l - p h y c, Gd. 203.]
Dī-del′phys [D i d e l - p h i s, Gd. 203.]
Dī-dym′i-um.
Did′y-moŭs.
Did-y-na′mi-an.
Dī-dyn′a-moŭs.
Die (*dī*), *v.* to cease to live. [*See* Dye, 160.]
[D i e c i a n, 203. — *See* Diœcian.]
[D i e c i o u s, 203. — *See* Diœcious.]
Dīed (*dīd*) (25, 186), *part.* from *Die.* [*See* Dyed, 160.]
[D i e r e s i s, 203. — *See* Diæresis.]
Di′e-sis.]

Di′et, 25, 76.
Di′et-a-ry, 72.
Di′et-er.
Di′et-ed.
Dī-e-tet′ic, 109.
Dī-e-tet′ic-al, 108.
Dī-e-tet′ics.
Di′et-īne, 82, 152.
Di′et-ing.
Dī-făr-re-a′tion, 170.
Dif′fer, 104, 170.
Dif′fered (-*furd*), 150.
Dif′fer-ence, 169.
Dif′fer-enced (-*enst*), 183.
Dif′fer-enç-ing.
Dif′fer-ent, 127, 169.
Dif-fer-en′tial, (-*shal*).
Dif-fer-en′ti-ate (-*shĭ-āt*).
Dif-fer-en-ti-a′tion (-*shĭ-a′*-).
Dif′fi-cult, 78, 170.
Dif′fi-cul-ty, 126.
Dif′fi-dence, 169.
Dif′fi-dent, 127.
Dif′form.
Dif-fract′.
Dif-fract′ed.
Dif-fract′ing.
Dif-frac′tion.
Dif-fuse′ (-*fūz′*), *v.* 161.
Dif-fused′ (-*fūzd′*), 183.
Dif-fūs′er (-*fūz′*-).
Dif-fu-si-bil′i-ty (-*zĭ*-).
Dif-fūs′i-ble (-*fūz′*-), 164, 183.
Dif-fūs′ing (-*fūz′*-).
Dif-fu′sion (-*zhun*).
Dif-fu′sīve, 84, 136.
Dig, 16.
Dī-gam′ma, 72.
Dī-gas′tric.
Dī′gest, *n.* 15, 25, 161.
Dĭ-gest′, *v.* 161.
Dĭ-gest′ed.
Dĭ-gest′er.
Dĭ-gest-i-bil′i-ty.
Dĭ-gest′i-ble, 164.
Dĭ-ges′tion (-*jest′yun*).
Dĭ-gest′īve, 84.
Digged (*digd*), 165, 176.
Dig′ger (-*gur*, 138.
Dig′ging (-*ghing*).
Dig′it (*dij′*-), 171.
Dīg′it-al (*dij′*-).
Dig′it-ate (*dij′*-).
Dig′it-āt-ed (*dij′*-).
Dig-it-ā′tion (*dij′*-).
Dig′it-i-grade (*dij′*-).
Dī′glyph.
Dig′ni-fīed.
Dig′ni-fȳ, 78, 94.
Dig′n-fȳ-ing.

Dig′ni-ta-ry, 72.
Dig′ni-ty, 169.
Dig′o-noŭs.
Dī′grăph, 127.
Dĭ-gress′, 79, 103.
Dĭ-gressed′(-*grest′*), 165.
Dĭ-gress′ing.
Dĭ-gres′sion (-*gresh′-un*).
Dĭ-gres′sion-al (-*gresh′-un*-).
Dĭ-gres′sīve.
Dī-gyn′i-an (-*jin′*-)
Dig′y-noŭs (*dij′*-) [so Gd.; *dī′jy-nus*, Wr. 155.]
Dī-he′dral.
Dī-he′dron.
Dike, 25.
Diked (*dīkt*), Note C, p. 34.
Dīk′ing, 183.
Dĭ-lap′i-date, 73, 169.
Dĭ-lap′i-dāt-ed.
Dĭ-lap′i-dāt-ing.
Dĭ-lap-i-da′tion.
Dĭ-lap′i-dāt-or.
Dĭ-late′, *or* Dī-late′ [so Wr.; *dĭ-lāt′*, Wk. Gd.; *dī-lāt′*, Sm. 155.]
Dĭ-lāt′ed, *or* Dī-lāted.
Dĭ-lāt′ing, *or* Dī-lāt′ing.
Dĭ-lāt′or, *or* Dī-lat′or.
Dil′a-to-ri-ly.
Dil′a-to-ri-ness 169.
Dil′a-to-ry, 86.
Dĭ-lem′ma, *or* Dī-lem′-ma (170) [*dĭ-lem′ma*, Wr. Gd.; *dī-lem′ma*, Wk. Sm. 155.]
Dil-et-tan′te (It.) (*tan′-tā*) [pl. *Dil-et-tan′ti* (-*tan′te*), 198.]
Dil-et-tan′te-ism (-*izm*).
Dil′i-gence, 169.
Dil′i-gent.
Dill, 16, 172.
Dil′u-ent, *a.* & *n.*
Dĭ-lute′, *a.* & *v.* 26, 104.
Dĭ-lūt′ed, 183.
Dĭ-lūt′er.
Dĭ-lūt′ing.
Dĭ-lu′tion.
Dĭ-lu′vi-al.
Dĭ-lu′vi-an.
Dĭ-lu′ vi-um (L.).
Dim, 16.
Dime, 25.
Dĭ-men′sion, 79.
Dim′e-ter [so Wr. Wb. Gd.; *dī′me-tur*, Sm. 155.]
Dĭ-mid′i-ate, *a.*

Dĭ-min′ish, 79, 104.
Dĭ-min′ished (*-isht*).
Dĭ-min′ish-ing.
Dim-i-nu′tion.
Dĭ-min′u-tĭve.
Dim′is-so-ry, 86.
Dim′i-ty, 169, 170.
Dimmed (*dimd*), 176.
Dim′ming.
Dim′mish, 170.
Dī-mor′phism (*-fizm*), 136.
Dī-mor′phoŭs.
Dim′ple, 164.
Dim′pled (*dim′pld*), 183.
Dim′pling.
Dim′ply, 93.
Din, 16.
Dine, 25,
Dined, 165, 183.
Ding, 16, 54.
Dinged (*dingd*), 165.
Din′gi-ness, 169.
Din′gy, 45, 93.
Dīn′ing.
Dīn′ing-room, 215.
Din′ner, 170.
Din′ning, 176.
Dint, 16.
Dī-oç′e-san, *or* Dī-o-ce′-san [so Wr.; *dī-os′e-zan*, Sm.; *dī′o-sē-san*, Wb. Gd. 155.]
Dī′o-cēse, *or* Dī′o-cēse [*dī′o-sēs*, Sm. Gd.; *dī′o-sēs*, Wk. Wr. 155.] [D i o c e s s, 203.]
Dī-œ′cian (*-e′shan*) [D i e c i a n, 203.]
Dī-œ′cioŭs (*-e′shus*) [D i e c i o u s, 203.]
Dī-op′tric.
Dī-op′tric-al, 108.
Dī-op′trics.
Dī-o-rä′ma, *or* Dī-o-rä′-ma [*dī-o-rä′ma*, Sm. Wr.; *dī-o-rä′ma*, Wb. Gd. 155.]
Dī-o-ram′ic.
Dī-or-tho′sis, 108, 125.
Dip, 16.
Dī-pet′a-loŭs.
Diph′thong (*dip′thong*) [so Wk. Sm. Wr.; *dif′thong*, Wb. Gd. 155.]

☞ "Though διφθογγος [*dif-thong′gus*] was the only way in which the word could be easily and gracefully pronounced by an ancient Greek, it does not follow that *dif′thong* is not a harsher and more uncouth pronunciation than *dip′thong*." — *Smart.*

Diph-thon′gal (*dip-thong′gal*) (54, N. 2.) [so Sm. Wr.; *dif-thong′gal*, Gd. 155.]
Dī-phyl′loŭs, *or* Diph′-yl-loŭs [*See* Adenophyllous.]
Dip′lo-ē, 163.
Dĭ-plo′ma, 79.
Dĭ-plo′ma-cy (169) [so Sm. Wr. Gd.; *dip′lo-ma-sy*, Wk. 155.]
Dip′lo-mate, *n.*
Dĭ-plo′māt-ed, *or* Dip′-lo-māt-ed, *a.* [so Wr.; *dī-plo′māt-ed*, Sm.; *dip-lo′mat-ed*, Wb. Gd. 155.]
Dip-lo-mat′ic.
Dip-lo-mat′ic-al-ly.
Dip-lo-mat′ics, *n.*
Dĭ-plo′ma-tist.
Dipped (*dipt*), 165, 176.
Dip′per, 170.
Dip′ping.
Dip′ter-al, 233, Exc.
Dip′tote.
Dip′tych (*-tik*).
Dī-rā-di-a′tion.
Dire (25, 67, Note), *a.* dreadful. [*See* Dyer, 160.]
Dĭ-rect′, *a.* & *v.* 79.
Dĭ-rect′ed.
[D i r e c t e r, 203. — *See* Director.]
Dĭ-rect′ing.
Dĭ-rect′ĭve.
Dĭ-rect′or [D i r e c t e r, 203.]
Dĭ-rec-to′ri-al.
Dĭ-rect′o-ry, 86.
Dĭ-rect′ress.
Dĭ-rect′rix.
Dire′ful (*-fōōl*).
Dirge, 21, Note.
Dĭr′i-gent.
Dirk, 21, Note.
Dirt, 21.
Dirt′ĭed (*-id*), 99, 186.
Dirt′i-ly.
Dirt′i-ness, 169.
Dirt′y, *a.* & *v.*
Dirt′y-ing.
Dis-a-bil′i-ty, 108, 169.
Dis-a′ble (*diz-*, or *dis-*) (136, 164) [*diz-a′bl*, Wk. Sm. Wr.; *dis-a′-bl*, Wb. Gd. 155.]
Dis-a′bled (*diz-a′bld*, or *dis-a′bld*), 136, 183.
Dis-a′bling(*diz-*,or*dis-*).
Dis-a-buse′ (*-būz′*).
Dis-a-būs′ing (*-būz′-*).
Dis-ad-van′tage, 131.
Dis-ad-van-tā′geous (*-jus*), 169.
Dis af-fect′.
Dis-af-fect′ed.
Dis-af-fect′ing.
Dis-af-fec′tion.
Dis-af-firm′.
Dis-af-firm′ance.
Dis-af-firmed′, 165.
Dis-af-firm′ing.
Dis-a-gree′.
Dis-a-gree′a-ble, 164.
Dis-a-gree′a-bly.
Dis-a-greed′, 188.
Dis-a-gree′ment.
Dis-a-gree′er.
Dis-a-gree′ing.
Dis-al-low′, 170.
Dis-al-lowed′, 165.
Dis-al-low′ing.
Dis-an-nul′.
Dis-an-nulled′, 165.
Dis-an-nul′ling.
Dis-ap-pēar′.
Dis-ap-pēar′ance, 169.
Dis-ap-pēared′, 165.
Dis-ap-pēar′ing.
Dis-ap-point′.
Dis-ap-point′ed.
Dis-ap-point′ing.
Dis-ap-point′ment.
Dis-ap-pro-ba′tion.
Dis-ap′pro-ba-to-ry, 86.
Dis-ap-prov′al (*-proov′-*), 183.
Dis-ap-prove′ (*-proov′*).
Dis-ap-proved′ (*-proovd′*).
Dis-arm′ (*diz-*), 136.
Dis-armed (*diz-armd′*).
Dis-arm′ing (*diz-*).
Dis-ar-rānge′, 170.
Dis-ar-rānged′, 183.
Dis-ar-range′ment, 185.
Dis-ar-rāng′ing (*-rānj′-*).
Dis-ar-rāy′.
Dis-ar-rāyed′, 188.
Dis-ar-rāy′ing.
Dis-as′ter (*diz-*).
Dis-as′troŭs (*diz-*).
Dis-a-vow′.
Dis-a-vow′al.
Dis-a-vowed′, 188.
Dis-a-vow′ing.
Dis-band′ (*diz-*, or *dis-*) (136) [*diz-band′*, Wk.

Sm. Wr.; *dis-band′*, Wb. Gd. 155.]
Dis-band′ed (*diz-*, or *dis*).
Dis-band′ing (*diz-*, or *dis-*).
Dis-be-lief′.
Dis-be-lieve′, 169.
Dis-be-lieved′, 150, 183.
Dis-be-liev′er.
Dis-be-liev′ing.
Dis-bur′den (*diz-bur′-dn*, or *dis-bur′dn*) (136) [*diz-bur′dn*, Wk. Sm. Wr.; *dis-bur′dn*, Wb. Gd. 155.] [Disburthen, 203.]
Dis-bur′dened (*diz-bur′dnd*, or *dis-bur′-dnd*).
Dis-bur′den-ing (*diz-bur′dn-ing*, or *dis-bur′dn-ing*).
Dis-burse′ (*diz-*, or *dis-*) [*diz-burs′*, Wk. Sm. Wr.; *dis-burs′*, Wb. Gd. 155.]
Dis-bursed′ (*diz-burst′*, or *dis-burst′*).
Dis-burse′ment (*diz-*, or *dis-*).
Dis-burs′er (*diz-*, or *dis-*), 183.
Dis-burs′ing (*diz-*, or *dis-*).
[Disburthen, 203. — *See* Disburden.]
Dis-card′, 11, 103.
Dis-card′ed.
Dis-card′ing.
Dis-cern′ (*diz-zern′*), 40, 156.
Dis-cerned′ (*diz-zernd′*), 150.
Dis-cern′er (*diz-zern′-*).
Dis-cern′i-ble (*diz-zern′-*), 164.
Dis-cern′i-bly (*diz-zern′-*).
Dis-cern′ing (*diz-zern′-*).
Dis-cern′ment (*diz-zern′-*).
Dis-charge′, 11.
Dis-charged′, 183.
Dis-charg′er (*-charj′-*).
Dis′ci-form, 78, 169.
Dis-ci′ple, 164.
Dis′ci-plin-a-ble, 164.
Dis-ci-pli-na′ri-an, 49, N.
Dis′ci-pli-na-ry, 72.
Dis′ci-plĭne, 82, 152.
Dis′ci-plĭned (*-plĭnd*), 183.
Dis′ci-plin-ing.
Dis-clāim′, 23.
Dis-clāimed′.
Dis-clāim′er.
Dis-clāim′ing.
Dis-close′ (*-klōz′*), 24.
Dis-closed′ (*-klōzd′*).
Dis-clōs′er (*-klōz′-*).
Dis-clōs′ing (*-klōz′-*).
Dis-clōs′ure (*-klōz′-*), 91.
Dis′coid, *a.* & *n.*
Dis-coid′al.
Dis-col′or (*-kul′ur*) [Discolour, Sm. 199, 203.]
Dis-col-or-a′tion (*-kul′-*), 112.
Dis-col′ored (*-kul′urd*), 150. [Discoloured, 199, 203.]
Dis-col′or-ing (*-kul′-*). [Discolouring, 199, 203.]
Dis-com′fit (*-kum′-*).
Dis-com′fit-ed (*-kum′-*), 171.
Dis-com′fit-ing (*-kum′-*).
Dis-com′fit-ure (*kum′-*).
Dis-com′fort (*-kum′-*), 135.
Dis-com-mode′.
Dis-com-mōd′ed, 183.
Dis-com-mōd′ing.
Dis-com-pose′ (*-pōz′*).
Dis-com-posed′ (*-pōzd′*).
Dis-com-pōs′ing (*-pōz′-*).
Dis-com-pōs′ure (*-pōz′-*), 91.
Dis-con-cert′, 21, Note; 171.
Dis-con-cert′ed.
Dis-con-cert′ing.
Dis-con-cer′tion.
Dis-con-nect′.
Dis-con-nect′ed.
Dis-con-nect′ing.
Dis-con-nec′tion.
Dis-con′so-late, 73.
Dis-con-tent′.
Dis-con-tent′ed.
Dis-con-tent′ing.
Dis-con-tin′u-ance, 169.
Dis-con-tin-u-a′tion.
Dis-con-tin′ūe.
Dis-con-tin′ūed (*-ūd*), 183.
Dis-con-tin′u-ing.
Dis-con-ti-nu′i-ty, 108.
Dis-con-tin′u-oŭs.
Dis′cord.
Dis-cord′ance, 169.
Dis-cord′an-cy.
Dis-cord′ant.
Dis′count, *n.*
Dis′count, *or* Dis-count′, *v.* [so Gd.; *dis-kount′*, Wk. Sm. Wr. 155.]

☞ "The accent [on the last syllable] is proper, but in the mercantile world the verb is very commonly made to bear the same accent as the noun." — *Smart.*

Dis-count′a-ble, 164.
Dis-coun′te-nance.
Dis-coun′te-nanced (*-nanst*).
Dis-coun′te-nanç-ing.
Dis′count-er, *or* Dis-count′er [*dis′kount-ur*, Gd.; *dis-kount′-ur*, Sm. Wr. 155.]
Dis-coŭr′age (*-kŭr′-*), 22, 171.
Dis-coŭr′aged (*-kŭr′-*), 183.
Dis-coŭr′age-ment (*-kŭr′-*), 185.
Dis-coŭr′a-ger.
Dis-cōurse′ (*-kōrs′*), *n.* & *v.*
Dis-cōursed′ (*-kōrst′*), 183.
Dis-cōurs′er (*-kōrs′-*).
Dis-cōurs′ing (*-kōrs′-*).
Dis-cōurs′ĭve, 84.
Dis-coŭrt′e-oŭs (*dis-kurt′e-us*), *or* Dis-cōurt′eoŭs (*dis-kōrt′-yus*) [so Wr.; *dis-kurt′e-us*, Gd.; *dis-kōrt′yus*, Sm.; *dis-kur′chus*, Wk. 155.]
Dis-cour′te-sy (*-kur′-*), 169.
Dis′coŭs, *a.* shaped like a disk. [*See* Discus, 160.]
Dis-cov′er (*-kuv′-*).
Dis-cov′er-a-ble (*-kuv′-*), 164.
Dis-cov′ered (*-kuv′urd*), 150.
Dis-cov′er-er (*-kuv′-*).
Dis-cov′er-ture (*-kuv′-*).
Dis-cov′er-y (*-kuv′-*), 171, 233, Exc.
Dis-cred′it.
Dis-cred′it-a-ble, 164.
Dis-cred′it-a-bly.
Dis-cred′it-ed.
Dis-cred′it-ing.
Dis-creet′ (13), *a.* pru-

dent. — *See* Discrete, 160.]
Dis′cre-pance [so Wk. Sm. Wr.; *dis-crep′-ans*, Wb. Gd. 107, 155.]
Dis′cre-pan-cy [so Wk. Sm. Wr.; *dis-krep′-an-sy*, Wb. Gd. 107, 155.]
Dis′cre-pant [so Wk. Sm. Wr.; *dis-krep′-ant*, Wb. Gd. 155.]
Dis-crete′ (13), *a.* separate, distinct. [*See* Discreet, 160.]
Dis-crĕ′tion (*-kresh′un*).
Dis-crĕ′tion-al (*-kresh′-un-*).
Dis-crĕ′tion-a-ry (*-kresh′un-*), 72.
Dis-cre′tīve.
Dis-crim′i-nate, 73.
Dis-crim′i-nāt-ed, 183.
Dis-crim′i-nāt-ing.
Dis-crim-i-na′tion.
Dis-crim′i-na-tīve.
Dis-crim′i-nāt-or.
Dis-crim′i-na-to-ry.
Dis-crown′, 28.
Dis-crowned′, 165.
Dis-crown′ing.
Dis-cur′sīve, 84.
Dis-cur′so-ry.
Dis′cus [L. pl. *Dis′cī*; Eng. pl. Dis′cus-es (*-ez*), 198], *n.* a quoit. [*See* Discous, 160.]
Dis-cuss′, 22, 103.
Dis-cussed′ (*-kust′*), 165.
Dis-cuss′er.
Dis-cuss′ing.
Dis-cus′sion (*-kush′un*).
Dis-dāin′ (*diz-dān′*), 23, 136.
Dis-dāined′ (*diz-dānd′*), 150.
Dis-dāin′ful (*diz-dān′-fŏŏl*).
Dis-dain′ing (*diz-*).
Dis-ēase′ (*diz-ēz′*), 136.
Dis-ēased′ (*diz-ēzd′*), 183.
Dis-ēas′ing (*-ēz′-*).
Dis-em-bark′.
Dis-em-bark-a′tion.
Dis-em-băr′rass, 170.
Dis-em-băr′rassed (*-rast*), 165.
Dis-em-băr′rass-ing.
Dis-em-bod′ĭed (*-id*), 171, 186.
Dis-em-bod′y.
Dis-em-bod′y-ing.
Dis-em-bōgue′ (*-bōg′*), 87, 171.
Dis-em-bōgued′ (*-bōgd′*), 183.
Dis-em-bōgue′ment (*-bōg′-*), 185.
Dis-em-bōgu′ing (*-bōg′-*).
Dis-em-bow′el.
Dis-em-bow′elled (*-eld*) [Disemboweled, Wb. Gd. 203. — *See* 177, and Note E, p. 70.]
Dis-em-bow′el-ling [Disemboweling, Wb. Gd. 203.]
Dis-em-broil′.
Dis-em-broiled′, 165.
Dis-em-broil′ing.
Dis-en-a′ble, 164.
Dis-en-a′bled (*-a′bld*), 183.
Dis-en-a′bling.
Dis-en-am′oured (*-am′urd*).
Dis-en-chȧnt′, 131.
Dis-en-chȧnt′ed.
Dis-en-chȧnt′er.
Dis-en-chȧnt′ing.
Dis-en-chȧnt′ment.
Dis-en-cum′ber.
Dis-en-cum′bered (*-burd*), 165.
Dis-en-cum′ber-ing.
Dis-en-cum′brance.
Dis-en-gage′.
Dis-en-gaged′, 183.
Dis-en-gage′ment.
Dis-en-gāġ′ing (*-gāj′-*).
Dis-en-no′ble, 164.
Dis-en-no′bled (*-no′bld*).
Dis-en-no′bling.
Dis-en-slave′.
Dis-en-slāved′, 183.
Dis-en-slāv′ing.
Dis-en-tan′gle (*-tang′-gl*), 54, 164.
Dis-en-tan′gled (*-tang′-gld*).
Dis-en-tan′gling (*-tang′-*).
[Disenthrall, 203. — *See* Disinthrall.]
Dis-es-teem′.
Dis-es-teemed′, 165.
Dis-es-teem′ing.
Dis-es-ti-ma′tion.
Dis-fa′vor [Disfavour, Sm. 199, 203.]
Dis-fa′vored (*-vurd*), 165.
Dis-fa′vor-ing.
Dis-fig-u-ra′tion.
Dis-fig′ure, 91.
Dis-fig′ured (*-yurd*), 183.
Dis-fig′ure-ment.
Dis-fig′ur-er (*-yur-*), 91.
Dis-fig′ur-ing (*-yur-*).
Dis-fran′chīse (*-chīz*) [*not* dis-fran′chiz, 153.]
Dis-fran′chīsed (*-chīzd*).
Dis-fran′chīse-ment (*-chīz-*).
Dis-gar′nish, 104.
Dis-gar′nished (*-nisht*).
Dis-gar′nish-ing.
Dis-gorge′ (*diz-*, or *dis-*) [*diz-gorj′*, Wk. Sm. Wr.; *dis-gorj′*, Wb. Gd. 155.]
Dis-gorged′ (*diz-*, or *dis-*), 165, 183.
Dis-gorge′ment (*diz-*, or *dis-*).
Dis-gorg′ing (*-gorj′-*), 183.
Dis-grace′ (*diz-*, or *dis-*) [*diz-grās′*, Wk. Sm. Wr.; *dis-grās′*, Wb. Gd. 155.]
Dis-graced′ (*diz-grāst′*, or *dis-grāst′*).
Dis-grace′ful (*diz-grās′-fŏŏl*, or *dis-grās′fŏŏl*).
Dis-grāç′ing.
Dis-guīse′ (*diz-ghīz′*, or *dis-ghīz′*) (171) [*diz-ghīz′*, Wr.; *dis-ghīz′*, Wb. Gd.; *dizg-yīz′*, Wk.; *diz-gu′īze*, Sm. 26, 53, 136, 155.]
Dis-guīsed′ (*diz-ghīzd′*, or *dis-ghīzd′*), 150, 183.
Dis-guīs′er (*diz-ghīz′-ur*, or *dis-ghīz′ur*).
Dis-guīs′ing (*diz-ghīz′-ing*, or *dis-ghīz′ing*).
Dis-gust′ (*diz-*, or *dis-*) [*diz-gust′*, Wk. Sm. Wr.; *dis-gust′*, Wb. Gd. 136, 155.]
Dis-gust′ed (*diz-*, or *dis-*).
Dis-gust′ing (*diz-*, or *dis-*).
Dish, 16, 46.
Dis-ha-bĭlle′ (*-bil′*) (171) [Deshabille, 203.]
Dish′clŏth, 206.
Dis-heart′en (*-hart′n*), 149.
Dis-heart′ened (*-hart′-nd*), 165.

Dis-heart′en-ing (*-hart′n-*).
Dished (*disht*), Note C, p. 34.
Dĭ-shev′el, 149.
Dĭ-shev′elled (*-eld*) (165) [Disheveled, Wb. Gd. 203. — *See* 177, and Note E, p. 70.]
Dĭ-shev′el-ling [Disheveling, Wb. Gd. 203.]
Dish′ing.
Dis-hon′est (*diz-on′-*), 136, 139.
Dis-hon′or (*diz-on′-*), (136, 139) [Dishonour, Sm. 203.]
Dis-hon′or-a-ble (*diz-on′-*), 164.
Dis-hon′or-a-bly (*diz-on′-*).
Dis-hon′or-a-ry (*diz-on′-*), 72.
Dis-hon′ored (*diz-on′-urd*), 165.
Dis-hon′or-er (*diz-on′-*), 77, 88.
Dis-hon′or-ing (*diz-on′-*).
Dis-in-cli-na′tion.
Dis-in-cline′.
Dis-in-clined′, 183.
Dis-in-clīn′ing.
Dis-in-cor′po-rate, *a.* & *v.* 73.
Dis-in-cor-po-rāt-ed, 183.
Dis-in-cor′po-rāt-ing.
Dis-in-cor-po-ra′tion.
Dis-in-fect′.
Dis-in-fect′ant.
Dis-in-fect′ed.
Dis-in-fec′tion.
Dis-in-gen′u-oŭs.
Dis-in-hĕr′it.
Dis-in-hĕr′it-ed.
Dis-in-her′it-ing.
Dis-in′te-gra-ble, 164.
Dis-in′te-grate.
Dis-in′te-grāt-ed.
Dis-in′te-grāt-ing.
Dis-in-te-gra′tion.
Dis-in-ter′, 21, Note.
Dis-in′ter-est-ed (*diz-*, or *dis-*) [*diz-in′ter-est-ed*, Wk. Sm. Wr.; *dis-in′ter-est-ed*, Wb. Gd. 136, 155.]
Dis-in-ter′ment.
Dis-in-thrâll′ [Disenthrall, Disinthral, Disenthral, Sm. 203.]
Dis-in-thrâlled′, 165.
Dis-in-thrâll′ing.
Dis-in-thrâl′ment [Disinthrallment, Wb. Gd. 155, 177.]
Dis-join′ (*diz-*, or *dis-*) [*diz-join′*, Wk. Sm. Wr.; *dis-join′*, Wb. Gd. 136, 155.]
Dis-joined′ (*diz-*, or *dis-*), 165.
Dis-join′ing (*diz-*, or *dis-*).
Dis-joint′ (*diz-*, or *dis-*) [*diz-joint′*, Wk. Sm. Wr.; *dis-joint′*, Wb. Gd. 136, 155.]
Dis-joint′ed (*diz-*, or *dis-*).
Dis-joint′ing (*diz-*, or *dis-*).
Dis-junct′ (*diz-*, or *dis-*), 136.
Dis-junct′ĭve (*diz-*, or *dis-*).
Disk, 16.
Dis-like′ (*diz-*, or *dis-*) [*diz-līk′*, Wk. Sm. Wr.; *dis-līk′*, Wb. Gd. 136, 155.]
Dis-liked′ (*diz-līkt′*, or *dis-līkt′*).
Dis-līk′ing (*diz-*, or *dis-*).
Dis′lo-cate.
Dis′lo-cāt-ed.
Dis′lo-cāt-ing.
Dis-lo-ca′tion.
Dis-lodge′ (*diz-*, or *dis-*) [*diz-loj′*, Wk. Sm. Wr.; *dis-loj′*, Wb. Gd. 136, 155.]
Dis-lodged′ (*diz-lojd′*, or *dis-lojd′*).
Dis-lodg′ing (*diz-*, or *dis-*), 183.
Dis-loy′al (*diz-*, or *dis-*) [*diz-loy′al*, Wk. Sm. Wr.; *dis-loy′al*, Wb. Gd. 136, 155.]
Dis-loy′al-ly (*diz-*, or *dis-*).
Dis-loy′al-ty (*diz-*, or *dis-*).
Dis′mal (*diz′-*), 136.
Dis′mal-ly (*diz′-*), 136, 170.
Dis-man′tle (*diz-*, or *dis-*) [*diz-man′tl*, Wk. Sm. Wr.; *dis-man′tl*, Wb. Gd. 136, 155.
Dis-man′tled (*diz-man′tld*, or *dis-man′tld*).
Dis-man′tling (*diz-*, or *dis-*).
Dis-mȧst′ (*diz-*, or *dis-*) [*diz-mȧst′*, Sm. Wr.; *dis mȧst′*, Wb. Gd. 136, 155.]
Dis-mȧst′ed (*diz-*, or *dis-*).
Dis-mȧst′ing (*diz-*, or *dis-*).
Dis-māy′ (*diz-*, or *dis-*) [*diz-mā′*, Wk. Sm. Wr.; *dis-mā′*, Wb. Gd. 136, 155.]
Dis-māyed′ (*diz-mād′*, or *dis-mād′*).
Dis-māy′ing (*diz-*, or *dis-*).
Dis-mem′ber (*diz-*, or *dis-*) [*diz-mem′bur*, Wk. Sm. Wr.; *dis-mem′bur*, Wb. Gd. 136, 155.]
Dis-mem′bered (*diz-mem′burd*, or *dis-mem′burd*).
Dis-mem′ber-ing (*diz-*, or *dis-*).
Dis-mem′ber-ment (*diz-*, or *dis-*).
Dis-miss′ (*diz-mis′*, or *dis-mis′*) [*diz-mis′*, Wk. Sm. Wr.; *dis-mis′*, Wb. Gd. 136, 155.]
Dis-mis′sal (*diz-*, or *dis-*).
Dis-missed′ (*diz-mist′*, or *dis-mist′*), 165; Note C, p. 34.
Dis-miss′ing (*diz-*, or *dis-*).
Dis-mis′sion (*diz-mish′-un*, or *dis-mish′un*).
Dis-mount′ (*diz-*, or *dis-*) (28) [*diz-mount′*, Wk. Sm. Wr.; *dis-mount′*, Wb. Gd. 136, 155.]
Dis-mount′ed (*diz-*, or *dis-*).
Dis-mount′ing (*diz-*, or *dis-*).
Dis-o-be′di-ence, 169.
Dis-o-be′di-ent.
Dis-o-bey′ (*-bā′*).
Dis-o-beyed′ (*-bād′*), 188.
Dis-o-bey′er (*-bā′-*).

Dis-o-bey'ing (-*bā'*-).
Dis-o-blige' [so Sm. Wr. Wb. Gd. ; *dis-o-blīj'*, or *dis-o-blēj'*, Wk. 155.]
Dis-o-bliged', 183.
Dis-o-blige'ment.
Dis-o-blīg-ing (-*blīj'*-).
Dis-or'der (*diz*-, or *dis*-) [*diz-or'dur*, Wk. Sm. Wr. ; *dis-or'dur*, Wb. Gd. 136, 155.]
Dis-or'dered (*diz-or'-durd*, or *dis-or'durd*), 150, 171.
Dis-or'der-ing (*diz*-, or *dis*-).
Dis-or'der-ly (*diz*-, or *dis*-).
Dis-or-gan-i-za'tion. (*diz*-, or *dis*-), 112.
Dis-or'gan-ize (*diz*-, or *dis*-) [*diz-or'gan-īz*, Sm. Wr. ; *dis-or'gan-īz*, Wb. Gd. 136, 155.]
Dis-or'gan-īzed (*diz*-, or *dis*-).
Dis-or'gan-īz-er (*diz*-, or *dis*-).
Dis-ōwn' (*diz-ōn'*, or *dis-ōn'*) [*diz-ōn'*, Wk. Sm. Wr. ; *dis-ōn'*, Wb. Gd. 136, 155.]
Dis-ōwned' (*diz-ōnd'*, or *dis-ōnd'*), 165.
Dis-păr'age, 70, 170.
Dis-păr'aged, 150, 183.
Dis-păr'age-ment.
Dis-păr'a-ger.
Dis-păr'a-ging.
Dis'pa-rate.
Dis-păr'i-ty, 108, 169.
Dis-part'.
Dis-part'ed.
Dis-part'ing.
Dis-pas'sion (-*pash'-un*).
Dis-pas'sion-ate (-*pash'-un*-).
Dis-patch' [Des-patch, 203. — *See* Despatch.]
Dis-patched' (-*patcht'*) [Despatched, 203.]
Dis-patch'ing [Despatching, 203.]
Dis-pel'.
Dis-pelled' (*peld'*), 176.
Dis-pel'ling.
Dis-pen'sa-ry, 72.
Dis-pen-sa'tion.
Dis'pen-sā-tor [so Sm. Wr. ; *dis-pen-sa'tor*, Wk. Wb. Gd. 155.]
Dis-pen'sa-to-ry, 86.
Dis-pense', 15 ; Note D, p. 36.
Dis-pensed' (-*penst'*), Note C, p. 34.
Dis-pens'er.
Dis-pens'ing, 183.
Dis-pēo'ple (-*pē'pl*), 164.
Dis-pēo'pled (-*pē'pld*), 183.
Dis-pēo'pler (-*pē'*-).
Dis-pēo'pling (-*pē'*-).
Dī-sperm'oŭs.
Dis-perse', 21, Note.
Dis-persed' (-*perst'*), 165.
Dis-pers'er, 183.
Dis-pers'ing.
Dis-per'sion.
Dis-pers'īve.
Dis-pĭr'it, 170.
Dis-pĭr'it-ed.
Dis-pĭr'it-ing.
Dis-place'.
Dis-placed' (-*plāst'*).
Dis-place'ment.
Dis-plāç'ing.
Dis-plănt'.
Dis-plănt'ed.
Dis-plănt'ing.
Dis-plāy', 23.
Dis-plāyed', 165, 188.
Dis-plāy'er.
Dis-plāy'ing.
Dis-plēase' (-*plēz'*).
Dis-plēased' (-*plēzd'*).
Dis-plēas'ing (-*plēz'*-).
Dis-plĕas'ure (-*plezh'*-), 91, 171.
Dis-plode'.
Dis-plōd'ed, 183.
Dis-plōd'ing.
Dis-plo'sion (-*zhun*).
Dis-plo'sīve, 84.
Dis-plume', 26.
Dis-plumed', 165.
Dis-plūm'ing.
Dis-pōrt'.
Dis-pōrt'ed.
Dis-pōrt'ing.
Dis-pōs'a-ble (-*pōz'*-), 164, 169.
Dis-pōs'al (-*pōz'*-).
Dis-pose', 136.
Dis-posed' (-*pōzd'*).
Dis-pōs'er (-*pōz'*-).
Dis-pōs'ing, (-*pōz'*-).
Dis-po-sĭ'tion (-*zish'-un*).
Dis-pos-sess' (-*poz-zes'*) [so Wk. Sm. Wr. ; *dis-pos-ses'*, Wb. Gd. 155. — *See* Possess.]
Dis-pos-sessed' (-*poz-zest'*).
Dis-pos-sess'ing (-*poz-zes'*-).
Dis-prāise' (-*prāz'*).
Dis-proof'.
Dis-pro-pōr'tion.
Dis-pro-pōr'tion-a-ble, 164.
Dis-pro-pōr'tion-a-bly.
Dis-pro-pōr'tion-al.
Dis-pro pōr'tion-al-ly.
Dis-pro-pōr'tion-ate, 73.
Dis-prov'a-ble (-*proov'-a-bl*), 164, 183.
Dis-prov'al (-*proov'*-).
Dis-prove' (-*proov'*-), 19.
Dis-proved' (-*proovd'*).
Dis-prov'er (-*proov'*-).
Dis-prov'ing (-*proov'*-).
Dis'pu-ta-ble (164) [so Sm. Wr. Wb. Gd. ; *dis'pu-ta-bl*, or *dis-pu'ta-bl*, Wk. 155.]
Dis'pu-tant.
Dis-pu-ta'tion, 112.
Dis-pu-ta'tioŭs (-*shus*).
Dis-pūt'a-tīve, 84.
Dis-pute', 26.
Dis-pūt'ed, 183.
Dis-pūt'er.
Dis-pūt'ing.
Dis-qual i-fi-ca'tion (*kwŏl*-), 112, 116.
Dis-qual'i-fīed (-*kwol'*-), 186.
Dis-qual'i-fȳ (-*kwol'*-).
Dis-qual'i-fȳ-ing (-*kwol'*-).
Dis-qui'et.
Dis-qui'et-ed.
Dis-qui'et-ing.
Dis-qui'e-tude, 108.
Dis-qui-sĭ'tion (-*zish'-un*).
Dis-re-gard'.
Dis-re-gard'ed.
Dis-re-gard'ful (-*fŏŏl*).
Dis-re-gard'ing.
Dis-rel'ish, 170.
Dis rel'ished (-*isht*), 165.
Dis-rel'ish-ing.
Dis-rep'u-ta-ble, 164.
Dis-rep'u-ta-bly.
Dis-re-pute'.
Dis-re-spect'.
Dis-re-spect'ful (-*fŏŏl*).
Dis-robe' (*diz*-, or *dis'*-) [*diz-rōb'*, Wk. Sm.

Wr.; *dis-rōb′*,Wb.Gd. 155.]
Dis-robed′ (*diz-rōbd′*, or *dis-rōbd′*), 165, 183.
Dis-rōb′ing (*diz-*, or *dis-*).
Dis-rup′tion (*diz-*, or *dis-*) [*diz-rup′shun*, Wk. Sm. Wr.; *dis-rup′shun*, Wb. Gd. 155.]
Dis-sat-is-fac′tion.
Dis-sat-is-fac′to-ry, 86.
Dis-sat′is-fīed, 186.
Dis-sat′is-fȳ, 94.
Dis-sat′is-fȳ-ing.
Dis-sect′, 15, 103.
Dis-sect′ed.
Dis-sect′i-ble, 164, 169.
Dis-sect′ing.
Dis-sec′tion.
Dis-sect′or.
Dis-sēis′in (*-sēz′in*), *or* Dis-sēiz′in.
Dis-sēize′, *or* Dis-sēise′ (*-sēz′*).
Dis-sēized′, *or* Dis-sēised′ (*-sēzd′*),150,183
Dis-sēiz′ing, *or* Dis-sēis′ing (*-sēz′-*).
Dis-sēiz-ee′, 118.
Dis-sēiz′or, 118.
Dis-sem′ble, 164.
Dis-sem′bled (*-sem′bld*), 183.
Dis-sem′bler.
Dis-sem′bling.
Dis-sem′i-nate, 73, 170.
Dis-sem′i-nāt-ed, 183.
Dis-sem′i-nāt-ing.
Dis-sem-i-na′tion.
Dis-sem′i-nāt-or.
Dis-sen′sion.
Dis-sent′, 15.
Dis-sent′ed.
Dis-sent′er.
Dis-sen′tient (*-shent*), 171.
Dis-sent′ing.
Dis-sep′i-ment, 169, 170.
Dis-ser-ta′tion.
Dis-serve′, 21, N.
Dis-served′, 165.
Dis-serv′īce, 169.
Dis-serv′īce-a-ble, 164, 183
Dis-serv′ing.
Dis-sev′er.
Dis-sev′er-ance, 169.
Dis-sev-er-a′tion.
Dis-sev′ered (*-urd*), 150.
Dis-sev′er-ing.
Dis′si-dence, 170.
Dis′si-dent.
Dis-sil′i-ence (169) [so Sm. Wb. Gd.; *dis-sil′yens*, Wk.; *dis-sil′yens*, or *dis-sil′ĭ-ens*, Wr. 155.]
Dis-sil′i-ent.
Dis-sim′i-lar, 169.
Dis-sim-i-lăr′i-ty.
Dis-si-mil′i-tude, 169.
Dis-sim-u-la′tion.
Dis′si-pate, 73, 170.
Dis′si-pāt-ed, 183.
Dis′si-pāt-ing.
Dis-si-pa′tion.
Dis-so′ci-ate (*-shĭ-āt*) [so Wk. Sm. Wr.; *dis so′shāt*, Wb. Gd. 155.]
Dis-so′ci-āt-ed(*-shĭ-āt-*).
Dis-so′ci-āt-ing.
Dis-so-ci-a′tion (*-so-shĭ-*).
Dis-so-lu-bil′i-ty.
Dis′so-lu-ble, 156, 164.
Dis′so-lute, 170.
Dis-so-lu′tion.
Dis-solv-a-bil′i-ty (*diz-zŏlv-*), 169.
Dis-solv′a-ble(*diz-zolv′-a-bl*), 136, 164, 183.
Dis-solve′ (*diz-zolv′*), 136, 171.
Dis-solved′ (*diz-zolvd′*), 183.
Dis-solv′ent(*diz-zolv′-*).
Dis-solv′ing(*diz-zolv′-*).
Dis′so-nance, 169.
Dis′so-nant.
Dis-suade′ (*-swād′*), 171.
Dis-suād′ed (*-swād′-*), 183.
Dis-swād′er (*-swād′-*).
Dis-suād′ing (*-swād′-*).
Dis-suā′sion (*-swā′-zhun*).
Dis-sua′sīve (*-swa′siv*).
Dis-syl-lab′ic, 109, 170.
Dis-syl′la-ble, *or* Dis′-syl-la-ble (164) [so Wr. Gd.; *dis-sil′a-bl*, Sm., *dis′sil-a-bl*, Wk. 155.]
Dis′taff, 171.
Dis-tāin′.
Dis-tāined′, 150.
Dis-tāin′ing.
Dis′tance, 169.
Dis′tanced (*-tanst*).
Dis′tanç-ing.
Dis′tant.
Dis-tāste′.
Dis-tāst′ed, 183.
Dis-tāste′ful (*-fōōl*).
Dis-tāst′ing.
Dis-tem′per.
Dis-tem′per-a-ture.
Dis-tem′pered (*-purd*), 150, 165.
Dis-tem′per-ing.
Dis-tend′, 15.
Dis-tend′ed.
Dis-tend′ing.
Dis-ten-si-bil′i-ty, 169.
Dis-ten′sīve.
Dis-ten′sion, 169.
Dis′tich (*-tik*) [*not* dis′-tich, 153.]
Dis′tich-oŭs (*-tik-*).
Dis-til′ [Distill, Wb. Gd. 203. — *See* 179, and Note E, p. 70.]
Dis-til′la-ble, 164, 176.
Dis-til-la′tion.
Dis-til′la-to-ry, 86.
Dis-tilled′ (*-tild′*), 176.
Dis-til′ler.
Dis-til′ler-ȳ, 170.
Dis-til′ling.
Dis-tinct′ (*-tingkt′*), 54.
Dis-tinc′tion (*-tingk′-*).
Dis-tinct′īve.
Dis-tin′guish (*-ting′-gwish*), 171.
Dis-tin′guish-a-ble (*ting′gwish-a-bl*), 169.
Dis-tin′guished (*-ting′-gwisht*), 165; Note C, p. 34.
Dis-tin′guish-er (*-ting′-gwish-*).
Dis-tin′guish-ing (*-ting′gwish-*).
Dis-tort′, 17.
Dis-tort′ed.
Dis-tort′ing.
Dis-tor′tion.
Dis-tract′, 10.
Dis-tract′ed.
Dis-tract′ing.
Dis-trac′tion.
Dis-trāin′.
Dis-trāin′a-ble, 164.
Dis-trāined′, 165.
Dis-trāin′or.
Dis-tress′, 15.
Dis-tressed′(*-trest′*),165.
Dis-tress′ful (*-fōōl*).
Dis-tress′ing.
Dis-trib′u-ta-ble, 164.
Dis-trib′u-ta-ry, 72.
Dis-trib′ute.
Dis-trib′ūt-er.
Dis-trib′ūt-ing.
Dis-tri-bu′tion.
Dis-trib′u-tīve.

Dis'trict (16) [*not* dĕs'-trikt, 127, 153.]
Dis'trict-ed.
Dis'trict-ing.
Dis-trust', 22.
Dis-trust'ed.
Dis-trust'ful (-*fōōl*).
Dis-trust'ing.
Dis-turb', 21.
Dis-turb'ance, 169.
Dis-turbed', 165.
Dis-turb'er.
Dis-turb'ing.
Dis-ūn'ion (-*ūn'yun*)(51) [so Sm. Wr. Wb. Gd.; *dis-u'nĭ-un*, Wk. 155.]
Dis-ūn'ion-ist (-*ūn'yŭn-ist*).
Dis-u-nite', 89.
Dis-u-nīt'ed, 183.
Dis-u-nīt'er.
Dis-u-nīt'ing.
Dis-u'ni-ty, 108, 169.
Dis-ūs'age (-*ūz'*-), 70.
Dis-use'(-*ūs'*), *n.* 26, 161.
Dis-use' (-*ūz'*), *v.* 161.
Dis-used'(-*ūzd'*),150,183.
Dis-ūs'ing (-*ūz'*-).
Ditch, 16, 44; Note D, p. 37.
Ditched (*dicht*), Note C, p. 34.
Ditch'er.
Ditch'ing.
Dī'the-ism (-*izm*), 136.
Dī'the-ist.
Dī-the-ist'ic, 109.
Dī the-ist'ic-al, 108.
Dith'y-ramb, 171.
Dith-y-ram'bic.
Dī'tone.
Dit'ri-glyph [so Sm. Wr.; *dī-trig'lif*, Gd. 155.]
Dī-tro'chee (-*ke*), 79.
Dit-tan'der.
Dit'ta-ny.
Dit'tīed (-*tid*), 99.
Dit'to, 170.
Dit'ty, 93, 170.
Di-u-ret'ic, 109.
Dī-ur'nal, 72, 79.
Dĭ-van', 121, 156.
Dī-văr'i-cate, 73, 170.
Dī-văr'i-cāt-ed.
Dī-văr'i-cāt-ing.
Dī-văr-i-ca'tion.
Dive, 25.
Dīved, 165, 183.
Dīv'er.
Dĭ-verge', 21, N.; 79, 156.
Dĭ-verged', 165.
Dĭ-verg'ence (-*verj'*-).
Dĭ-verg'ent (-*verj'*-)
Dĭ-verg'ing (-*verj'*-).
Di'vers (-*vurz*), *a.* 148.
Di'verse (-*vurs*), *a.* 148.
Di'verse-ly, 106.
Dĭ-ver'si-fīed, 186.
Dĭ-ver'si-form, 169.
Dĭ-ver'si-fȳ, 94.
Dĭ-ver'si-fȳ-ing.
Dĭ-ver'sion, 21, N.; 79.
Dĭ-ver'si-ty, 169.
Dĭ-vert', 21, 79.
Dĭ-vert'ed.
Dĭ-vert'er.
Dĭ-vert'ing.
Dĭ-ver'tīse-ment (-*tiz-mong*).

☞ Smart spells this word Divertizement, and says of it, "an old word in the language; but, as a modern word, revived with a half French pronunciation by making the last syllable nasal (-*mong*), to signify *a short ballet or other entertainment between the acts of longer pieces.*"

Dĭ-vert'īve, 84.
Dĭ-vest' (15, 79) [Devest, 203.—*See* Note under *Devest*.]
Dĭ-vest'ed.
Dĭ-vest'i-ble, 164, 169.
Dĭ-vest'ing.
Dĭ-vīd'a-ble, 164, 183.
Di'vi-di'vi (*de've-de've*).
Dĭ-vide', 25, 79.
Dĭ-vīd'ed, 183.
Div'i-dend, 169.
Dĭ-vīd'er.
Dĭ-vīd'ers (-*urz*), *n. pl.*
Dĭ-vīd'ing.
Div-ĭ-na'tion.
Dĭ-vine', *a. n.* & *v.* 25,79.
Dĭ-vīned', 165, 183.
Dĭ-vīn'er.
Dĭ-vīn'ing.
Dīv'ing, 183.
Dīv'ing-bell, 215.
Dĭ-vin'i-ty, 108, 169.
Dĭ-vis-i-bil'i-ty (-*viz*-).
Dĭ-vis'i-ble (-*viz'i-bl*), 164, 169.
Dĭ-vis'i-bly (-*viz'*-).
Dĭ-vĭ'sion (-*vizh'un*).
Dĭ-vī'sor (-*zur*), *n.* the number by which the dividend is divided. [*See* Deviser, 160.]
Dĭ-vōrce', 24, 79.
Dĭ-vōrced'(-*vōrst'*), 183.
Dĭ-vōrç'er.
Dĭ-vōrç'i-ble, 164.
Dĭ-vōrç'ing.
Dĭ-vōrç'īve.
Dĭ-vulge', 22, 45.
Dĭ-vulged', 165, 183.
Dĭ-vulg'er (-*vulj'*-).
Dĭ-vulg'ing (-*vulj'*-).
Dĭ-vul'sion.
Dĭ-vul'sīve, 84.
Diz'zi-ness, 169, 170.
Diz'zy, 93.
Do (*doo*), 19.
[Doat, 203.—*See* Dote]
Doç'i-ble (164) [so Wk. Sm. Wr.; *dō'si-bl*, or *dos'i-bl*, Gd. 155.]
Doç'ile (152) [so Wk. Sm. Wr.; *dō'sil*, or *dos'il*, Gd. 155], *a.* teachable. [*See* Dossil, 160.]
Do-cil'i-ty, 169.
Doç'i-ma-cy, 169.
Doç-i-mas'tic, 109.
Dock, 18, 181.
Dock'age, 169.
Dock'et.
Dock'et-ed.
Dock'et-ing.
Dock'-yard.
Doc'tor, 18, 88.
Doc'tored, 165.
Doc'tor-al.
Doc'tor-ate.
Doc'tor-ing.
Doc'trin-al.
Doc'trīne, 152.
Doc'u-ment.
Doc-u-ment'al.
Doc-u-ment'a-ry, 72.
Dod'der, 77.
Dod'dered (-*durd*), 165.
Do-dec'a-gon.
Do-dec-a-gyn'i-an (-*jin'*-).
Do-de-cag'y-noŭs (-*kaj'*-).
Do-dec-a-he'dral.
Do-dec-a-he'dron.
Do-de-can'dri-an.
Do-de-can'droŭs.
Dodge (*dŏj*), 18, 45.
Dodged (*dŏjd*), 150, 183.
Dodg'er.
Dodg'ing.
Dō'do, 24.
Dōe (*dō*), *n.* a she-deer. [*See* Dough, 160.]
Do'er (*doo'*-), 19, 77.
Does (*duz*) [*not* dooz, 153.]
Dōe'skin (*dō'*-), 206.
Doff, 18, 173.
Doffed (*doft*), Note C, [p. 34.

Doff′er, 170.
Doff′ing.
Dog, 18.
Dog′dāy, 206.
Dōge, 24, 45.
Dogged (*dogd*) (161), *v.* did dog; *a.* 138, 161.
Dog′ger-el (*-gur-el*) [D o g g r e l, 203.]
Dog′gish (*-ghish*).
Dog′ma, 72.
Dog-mat′ic, 109.
Dog-mat′ic-al.
Dog-mat′ics.
Dog′ma-tism (*-tizm*), 136
Dog′ma-tist.
Dog′ma-tize, 202.
Dog′ma-tīzed, 183.
Dog′ma-tīz-er.
Dog′ma-tīz-ing.
Dog′star, 206.
Dog′wŏŏd.
Doi′ly, 27, 93.
Do′ing (*doo′-*).
Doit, 27.
Do-lab′ri-form, 169.
Dole, 24.
Doled, 165.
Dole′ful (*-fŏŏl*).
Dōl′ing, 183.
Dole′some (*-sum*), 169.
Dŏll, 18, 172.
Dol′lar, 74, 170.
Dol′o-mīte.
Do′lor, 88.
Dol-o-rif′er-oŭs, 108.
Dol-o-rif′ic.
Dol′o-roŭs, 170.
Dol′phin, 18, 35.
Dōlt, 24.
Do-māin′, 23.
Dome, 24.
Do-mes′tic.
Do-mes′tic-ate.
Do-mes′tic-āt-ed.
Do-mes′tic-āt-ing.
Do-mes-tic-a′tion.
Dom′i-cīle, 152, 169.
Dom′i-cīled, 165.
Dom-i-cil′ia-ry (*-sil′ya-ry*) (72, 171) [so Wk. Sm. Wr.; *dom-i-sil′i-a ry*, Wb. Gd. 155.]
Dom-i-cil′i-ate, 73.
Dom-i-cil′i-āt-ed.
Dom-i-cil′i-āt-ing.
Dom-i-cil-i-a′tion.
Dom′i-cil-ing, 183.
Dom′i-nant, 169.
Dom′i-nate.
Dom′i-nāt-ed, 183.
Dom′i-nāt-ing.
Dom-i-na′tion.
Dom′i-nāt-ĭve [so Sm.; *dom′i-na-tiv*, Wr. Wb. Gd. 155.]
Dom′i-nāt-or.
Dom-i-neer′, 169.
Dom-i-neered′ (*-nērd′*).
Dom-i-neer′ing.
Do-min′i-cal, 72.
Do-min′i-can.
Do-min′ion (*-yun*).
Dom′i-nō [pl. Dom′i-nōs (*-nōz*), 192.]
Don, 18.
Do′nate.
Do′nāt-ed, 183.
Do′nāt-ing.
Do-na′tion.
Don′a-tĭve, 84.
Done (*dun*), *part.* from *Do* [*See* Dun, 160.]
Do-nee′, 118, 121.
[D o n j o n, 203.—*See* Dungeon.]
Don′key (*dong′ky*), 98.
Do′nor (*-nawr*), 17, 24.
Doom, 19.
Doomed, 165.
Doom′ing.
Dooms′day (*doomz′-*), 214.
Dōor (*dōr*), 24.
Dōor′-keep-er.
Dor [D o r r, 203.]
[D o r a, 203.—*See* Doura.]
Do-ree′, *or* Do′ree [so Wr.; *do-re′*, Wb. Gd.; *do′re*, Sm. 155.]
[D o r y, 203.]
Do′ri-an, 49, N.
Dŏr′ic, 170.
Dŏr′i-cism (*-sizm*), 136.
Dor′man-cy.
Dor′mant, 17, 72.
Dor′mer, 17, 77.
Dor′mi-tĭve, 84.
Dor′mi-to-ry, 86.
Dor′mouse, 206.
[D o r r, 203.—*See* Dor.]
Dor′sal, 17, 72, 148.
Dor′sel, 17, 76, 148.
Dor′ser, 17, 77.
Dor-sif′er-oŭs, 108.
Dor-sip′a-roŭs.
Do′ry (49, N.), *n.* a kind of fish. [D o r e e, 203.]
Do′ry, *n.* a kind of small boat.
Dose, 24.
Dos′sil (170), *n.* a lump of lint,—a term used in surgery. [*See* Docile, 160.]
Dost (*dust*) [*not* dōst, 153], *v.* the second person singular of the present tense indicative, from *Do.* [*See* Dust, 160.]
Dot, 18.
Do′tage, 24, 169.
Do′tal, 24, 72.
Do′tard.
Do-ta′tion.
Dote (24) [D o a t, 203.]
Dōt′ed, 183.
Dōt′er.
Dōt′ing.
Dot′tard, 170.
Dot′ted, 176.
Dot′ter-el.
Dot′ting.
Doŭb′le (*dub′l*), 164, 171.
Doŭb′led (*dub′ld*), 183.
Double-entendre (*doob′-l-ong-tong′dr.*)
Doŭb′let (*dub′-*), 22.
Doŭb′ling (*dub′-*).
Doŭb-loon′ (*dub-*), 121.
Doubt (*dout*), 28, 162.
Doubt′a-ble (*dout′a-bl*).
Doubt′ed (*dout′-*).
Doubt′er (*dout′-*).
Doubt′ful (*dout′fŏŏl*).
Doubt′ful-ly (*dout′fŏŏl-*).
Doubt′ing (*dout′-*).
Douceur (Fr.) (*doo sur′*)
Douche (Fr.) (*doosh*).
Dōugh (*dō*) (162), *n.* flour or meal moistened with water for making bread. [*See* Doe, 160.]
Dōugh′nut (*dō′-*), 162.
Dough′ti-ly (*dow′-*).
Dough′ti-ness (*dow′-*).
Dough′ty (*dow′-*), 162.
Dōugh′y (*dō′y*), 162.
Dou′ra (*doo′ra*) (Ar.) [D o r a, D h u r r a, D u r r a, 203.]
Douse, 28.
Doused (*dowst*).
Dous′ing.
Dove (*duv*), 22.
Dove′tāil (*duv′-*), 171.
Dove′tāiled (*duv′-*), 165.
Dove′tāil-ing (*duv′-*).
Dow′a-ble, 164, 169.
Dow′a-ger, 45.
Dow′dy.
Dow′el.
Dow′elled (*-eld*) [D o w-e l e d, Wb. Gd. 203.—*See* 177, and Note E, p. 70.]

Dow′el-ling [Dowel-ing, Wb. Gd. 203.]
Dow′er, 28, 77.
[Dowery, 203.—*See* Dowry.]
Down, 28.
Down′cast, 131, 206.
Down′fall.
Down′hâul.
Down′hill, *a.* & *n.*
Down′i-ness, 169.
Down′right (-*rīt*), 162.
Down′ward, 72.
Down′wards (-*wardz*).
Down′y.
Dow′ry [Dowery, 203.]
Dox-ol′o-gy, 108.
Doze, 24.
Dozed (*dozd*), 183.
Doz′en (*duz′n*) (149) [pl. Dozen, *rarely* Dozens.]
Dōz′i-ness, 171.
Dōz′ing.
Dōz′y.
Drab, 10.
Drab′ble, 164.
Drab′bled (*drab′ld*), 183.
Drab′bling.
Drachm (*dram*) (162, 171), *n.* a drachma;—a certain part of an ounce. [*See* Dram, 160.] [Dram (in the last sense), 203.]
Drach′ma (*drak′*-).
Draff (12, 131, 173) [Draugh, 203.]
Draft, *n.* a selection of men from a military body;—an order for the payment of money;—a drawing, or plan;—a written outline. [*See* Draught, 160.] [Draught, 203]

☞ The spelling *draught* is seldom used when this word has the first two senses above given. For the other senses, the form *draft* is less proper than *draught*.

Drâft, *v.* [Draught, 203.]

☞ When this word is used as a verb, the spelling *draught* is of rare occurrence.

[Draftsman, 203.—*See* Draughtsman.]
Drag, 10.
Dragged (*dragd*), 176.
Drag′ging (-*ghing*).
Drag′gle, 164.
Drag′gled (*drag′ld*), 183.
Drag′gling.
Drag′net, 206.
Drag′o-man [pl. Dragomans, 196.]
Drag′on, 170.
Drag′on-flȳ.
Drag′on's-blood (*drag′unz-blud*), 213.
Dra-goon′, *n.* & *v.*
Drag-oon-ade′.
Dra-gooned′, 165.
Dra-goon′ing.
Drāin, 23.
Drāin′a-ble, 164.
Drāin′age, 169.
Drāin′ing.
Drake, 23.
Dram (10), *n.* a certain part of an ounce;—the quantity of spirituous liquor that is drunk at once. [*See* Drachm, 160.] [Drachm (in the first sense), 203.]
Drā′ma, *or* Dram′a [so Wk. Wr.; *dram′a*, Sm.; *dra′ma*, or *drā′ma*, Gd. 155.]
Dra-mat′ic, 108.
Dra-mat′ic-al, 109.
Dra-mat′ic-al-ly.
Dram′a-tist.
Dram′a-tize, 202.
Dram′a-tized, 183.
Dram′a-tīz-ing.
Drank (*drangk*), 10, 54.
Drape, 23.
Draped (*drāpt*), 183.
Drāp′er.
Dra′per-y.
Drāp′ing.
Dras′tic.
[Draugh, 203.—*See* Draff.]
Drâught (*drâft*), *n.* act of drawing or pulling;—capability of being drawn;—that which is taken by drawing;—the act of drinking;—the liquor drunk,—a current of air;—a drawing, or plan;—a written outline;—a drain;—depth of water in which a ship floats;—bevel given to parts of a pattern;—a selection of men from a military body;—an order for the payment of money. [*See* Draft, 160.] [Draft, 203.]

☞ The spelling *draught* is more proper than *draft* for all the senses of this word except the last two.

Drâughts (*drâfts*), *n. pl.* a kind of game;—a mild vesicatory.
Drâughts′man (*drâfts′*-) [Draftsman, 203.]
Draw, 17.
Draw′back.
Draw′bridge, 206.
Draw-ee′ (118) [so Wr.; *draw′e*, Wb. Gd. 155.]
Draw′er, *n.* one who draws;—a box in a bureau, &c., to be drawn out.
Draw′ers (-*urz*) [*not* drawz, 153], *n. pl.* an under garment for the lower limbs.
Draw′ing.
Draw′ing-room.
Drawl, 17.
Drawled, 165.
Drawl′ing.
Drawn, 17.
Drāy, 23.
Drāy′age, 169.
Drāy′man.
Drĕad (*dred*), 15.
Drĕad′ed.
Drĕad′ful (-*fŏŏl*).
Drĕad′ing.
Drĕad′nâught (-*nawt*).
Drēam (*drēm*), 13.
Drēamed (*drēmd*), 165.
Drēam′er.
Drēam′ing.
Drĕamt, 165.
Drēam′y.
Drēar (*drēr*).
Drēar′i-ness, 169.
Drēar′y, 93.
Dredge, 15, 45.
Dredged (*drejd*), 165.
Dredg′er, 183.
Dredg′ing.
Dreg′gi-ness (-*ghĭ*-), 138.
Dreg′gy (-*ghy*).
Dregs (*dregz*), *n. pl.* 15.
Drench, 15, 44.
Drenched (*drencht*), Note C, p. 34.
Drench′ing.
Dress, 15, 174.

Dressed (*drest*) [Drest, 203.]
Dress'er.
Dress'ing.
Drib'ble, 164.
Drib'bled (*drib'ld*), 183.
Drib'bling.
Drib'let.
Drīed, 186.
Drī'er.
Drift, 16.
Drift'ed.
Drift'ing.
Drill, 16, 172.
Drilled, 165.
Drill'ing.
Drink (*dringk*), 16, 54.
Drink'a-ble, 164.
Drink'er.
Drink'ing.
Drip, 16.
Dripped (*dript*), Note C, p. 34; 176.
Drip'ping, 170.
Drīve, 25.
Driv'el (*driv'l*), 149.
Driv'elled (*driv'ld*) [Driveled, Wb. Gd. 203.—*See* 177, and Note E, p. 70.]
Driv'el-ler, [Driveler, Wb. Gd. 203.]
Driv'el-ling [Driveling, Wb. Gd. 203.]
Driv'en (*drĭv'n*), 149.
Drīv'er.
Drīv'ing.
Driz'zle, 164.
Driz'zled (*driz'ld*), 183.
Driz'zling.
Drōll, 24, 172.
Drōll'er-y.
Drom'e-da-ry (*drum'-*), 72, 171.
Drone, 24.
Drōned, 165, 183.
Drōn'ing.
Drōn'ish.
Droop (19), *v.* to hang down; to languish. [*See* Drupe, 160.]
Drooped (*droopt*), 165.
Droop'ing.
Drop, 18.
Dropped (*dropt*) (Note C, p. 34; 150, 176) [Dropt, 203.]
Drop'ping.
Drop'si-cal.
Drop'sy, 169.
[Dropt, 203.—*See* Dropped.]
Dross, 18, 174.
Dross'i-ness, 171, 186.
Dross'y.
Drought (*drowt*) (162) [Drouth, 203.]

☞ "This word is often pronounced as if written *drouth*, but improperly." *Walker.* "Our old authors, perhaps more correctly, write and pronounce *drouth*." *Smart.*

Drought'i-ness (*drowt'-*).
Drought'y (*drowt'y*).
Drouth [Drought, 203.]

☞ "This is usually written *drought*, after the Belgic dialect, but improperly." *Webster.* "This [*drouth*] was the original word, and it is still used in Scotland, and, to a considerable extent, in America." *Goodrich.*

Drove, 24.
Drōv'er.
Drown, 28.
Drowned, 165.
Drown'ing.
Drowse (*drowz*), *n.* & *v.*
Drowsed (*drowzd*), 183.
Drows'i-ly (*drowz'i-*).
Drows'i-ness (*drowz'i-*).
Drows'ing (*drowz'-*).
Drows'y (*drowz'y*).
Drub, 22.
Drubbed (*drubd*), 176.
Drub'bing.
Drudge, 22, 45.
Drudged, 165, 183.
Drudg'er.
Drudg'ing.
Drudg'er-y, 233, Exc.
Drug, 22.
Drugged (*drugd*), 176.
Drug'ging (*-ghing*), 138.
Drug'gist (*-ghist*).
Dru'id (*droo'id*), 19.
Dru-id'ic-al (*droo-*) 108.
Dru'id-ism (*droo'id-izm*), 136.
Drum, 22.
Drummed (*drumd*), 176.
Drum'mer.
Drum'ming.
Drunk (*drungk*), 23, 54.
Drunk'ard, 54, 72.
Drunk'en (*drungk'n*), 149.
Drunk'en-ness (*drungk'n-*), 170.
Dru-pa'ceous (*droo-pa'shus*).
Drupe (*droop*) (19), *n.* a fruit containing a nut or stone in which is the seed. [*See* Droop, 160.]
Druse (*droos*).
Drused (*droost*).
Dru'ses (*droo'zez*), *n. pl.*
Dru'sy (*droo'sy*).
Drȳ, 25.
Drȳ'ing.
Dry'-nurse, 206, Exc. 3.
Dry'-rot.
Du'al, 26, 72.
Du'al-ism (*-izm*), 136.
Du'al-ist, *n.* one who believes in the doctrine of dualism. [*See* Duellist, 148.]
Du-al-ist'ic.
Du-al'i-ty, 169.
Du'är-chy (*-ky*).
Dub, 22.
Dubbed (*dubd*), 176.
Dub'ber [Dupper, 203.]
Dub'bing.
Du'bi-ous, 78.
Du'bi-ta-ble, 164.
Du'cal, 26, 72.
Dūc'at [*not* du'kat, 153.]
Duch'ess.
Duch'y.
Duck, 22, 181.
Ducked (*dukt*), 165.
Duck'ing.
Duct, 22.
Duc'tĭle, 81, 152.
Duc-til'i-ty, 169.
Dudg'eon (*duj'un*).
Dūe (*du*), 26.
Du'el, 26, 76.
Du'el-ling [Dueling, Wb. Gd. 203.—*See* 177, and Note E, p. 70.]
Du'el-list, *n.* one who fights duels. [*See* Du-alist, 148.]
[Duelist, Wb. Gd. 203.]
Du-en'na, 170.
Du'et, 121.
Duf'fel [Duffle, 203.]
Dug, 22.
Du-gong', 121.
Dūke (26) [*not* dook, *nor* jook, 127, 134, 141, 153.]
Dūke'dom, 169.
Dul-ca-ma'ra, 72.
Dul'cet.
Dul-ci-fi-ca'tion.
Dul'ci-fīed, 186.
Dul'ci-fȳ, 78, 94.
Dul'ci-fȳ-ing.

Dul′ci-mer.
Du′li-a.
Dull, 22, 172.
Dull′ard.
Dul′ly, 66, N.; 178.
Dul′ness (178) [Dull-ness, Wb. Gd. 203.]
Dulse, 22; Note D, p. 37.
Du′ly, 26, 93.
Dumb (*dum*), 162.
Dum′found [Dumb-found, 203.]
Dum′found-ed.
Dum′found-ing.
Dump, 22.
Dump′ling.
Dum′py.
Dun (22), *a.* of a dark-brown color: — *v.* to solicit with importunity: — *n.* one who duns. [*See* Done, 160.]
Dunce, 22, 39.
Dunç′er-y.
Dun′der.
Dune, 26.
Dun′fish, 206.
Dung, 22, 54.
Dunged (*dungd*), 165.
Dun′geon (*-jun*) (171) [Donjon, 203.]
Dung′hill, 206.
Dung′ing.
Dung′y.
Dun′nage, 169, 170.
Dunned (*dund*), 176.
Dun′ner.
Dun′ning.
Dun′nish, 170.
Du-o-de-cen′ni-al, 170.
Du-o-deç′i-mal, 169.
Du-o-deç′im-fid, 171.
Du-o-deç′i-mō (169) [pl. Du-o-deç′i-mos (*-mōz*), 192.]
Du-o-dec′u-ple, 164.
Du-o-den′a-ry, 72.
Du-o-de′num.
Du-o-lit′er-al.
Dūp′a-ble, 164, 183.
Dupe, 26.
Dūped (*dūpt*), Note C, p. 34.
Dūp′er-y, 233, Exc.
Du′pli-cate, 73, 169.
Du′pli-căt-ed, 83.
Du′pli-căt-ing.
Du-pli-ca′tion, 112.
Du-pliç′i-ty, 108, 169.
Dup′per [Dubber, 203.]
Du-ra-bil′i-ty, 169.
Dū′ra-ble, 49, N.; 164.
Du′ra-bly.
Du′rance.
Du-ra′tion, 49, N.
Du′ress [so Wk. Sm. Wr.; *du-res′*, Wb. Gd. 155.] [Duresse, Sm. 203.]
Dūr′ing, 49, N.
[Durra, 203. — *See* Doura.]
Durst, 21.
[Duse, 203. — *See* Deuce.]
Dusk, 22.
Dusk′i-ly.
Dusk′i-ness, 169.
Dusk′y.
Dust (22), *n.* earthy or other matter in the state of a dry powder: — *v.* to free from dust. [*See* Dost, 160.]
Dust′ed.
Dust′er.
Dust′i-ness, 169.
Dust′ing.
Dust′y, 93.
Dutch, 22, 44.
Du′te-oŭs, 169.
Du′ti-a-ble, 164.
Du′ti-ful (*-fŏŏl*).
Du′ti-ful-ly (*-fŏŏl*).
Du′ty, 26, 93.
Du-um′vir (L.) [pl. *Du-um′vi-rī*, 198.]
Du-um′vi-ral.
Du-um′vi-rate, 73.
Dwale, 23.
Dwârf, 17, 171.
Dwârfed (*dworft*), Note C, p. 34.
Dwârf′ing.
Dwell, 15, 172.
Dwelled (*dweld*) (165) [Dwelt, 203.]

☞ *Dwelt* is now more commonly used than *dwelled*.

Dwell′er.
Dwell′ing.
Dwelt (165) [Dwelled, 203.]
Dwin′dle, 164.
Dwin′dled (*dwin′dld*), 183.
Dȳ-ad′ic.
Dye (*dī*) (25), *n.* a coloring liquor. [*See* Die, 160.]
Dȳed (*dīd*) (183), *part.* from *Dye.* [*See* Died, 160.]
Dȳe′ing (183), *part.* from *Dye.* [*See* Dying, 160.]
Dy′er (67, N.), *n.* one whose business it is to dye cloth, &c. [*See* Dire, 160.]
Dye′stuff, 206.
Dy′ing (184), *part.* from *Die* [*See* Dyeing, 160.]
Dȳ-nam′e-ter, 108.
Dyn-a-met′ric-al.
Dȳ-nam′ic, 109.
Dȳ-nam′ic-al, 108.
Dȳ-nam′ics.
Dyn-a-mom′e-ter, 108.
Dȳ-nas′tic.
Dyn′as-ty, *or* Dȳ′nas-ty [*din′as-ty*, Sm.; *dī′-nas-ty*, Wb. Gd.; *dī′-nas-ty*, or *din′as-ty*, Wk. Wr. 155.]

☞ Although Walker, in deference to the majority of orthoëpists, puts the pronunciation *di′nasty* first, he says that "analogy is clearly for the last" [*din′asty*.]

Dys′cra-sy, 169.
Dys-en-tĕr′ic.
Dys′en-ter-y, 171.
Dys-pep′si-a (L.).
Dys-pep′sy (107) [so Sm. Wb. Gd.; *dis′pep-sy*, Wk.; *dis′pep-sy*, or *dis-pep′sy*, Wr. 155.]
Dys-pep′tic, 109.
Dys-pep′tic-al, 108.
Dys′pha-gy.
Dys-pho′ri-a.
Dysp-nœ′a (*-nē′-*), 171.
Dysp-thet′ic.
Dys′u-ry [so Sm. Wb. Gd.; *dizh′u-ry*, Wk.; *dizh′u-ry*, or *dis′u-ry*, Wr. 155.]

E.

Each, 13, 44.
Ea′ger (*ē′gur*), *a.* ardent, earnest. [*See* Ea′gre, 160.]
Ea′gle (*ē′gl*), 164, 171.
Ea′gle-eyed (*ē′gl-īd*), 206, Exc. 2, 5.
Ea′glet.
Ea′gre (*ē′gur*) (164), *n.* a tide swelling above another tide. [*See* Eager, 160.] [Eger, 203.]
Ear (*ēr*), 13.
Eared (*ērd*), 165.

Ēar′ing.
Earl (*erl*), 21, N.
Ear′li-ness (*er′-*), 171.
Ear′ly (*er′-*), 21, N.
Earn (*ern*) (21, N.), *v.* to gain or to deserve by labor. [*See* Urn, 160.]
Earned (*ernd*), 165.
Ear′nest (*er′-*).
Earn′ing (*ern′-*).
Ēar′-ring, 206, Exc. 1.
Earth (*erth*), 21, N.
Earthed (*ertht*), Note C, p. 34.
Earth′en (*erth′n*), 149.
Earth′i-ness (*erth′-*), 169, 186.
Earth′ing (*erth′-*).
Earth′quake (*erth′-*).
Earth′worm (*erth′-wurm*), 206.
Earth′y (*erth′y*).
Ēar′wig.
Ēase (*ēz*), 13, 47.
Ēased (*ēzd*), 165, 183.
Ēa′sel (*ē′zl*) (149) [so Sm. Wr.; *ēz′el*, Wb. Gd. 155.]
Ēase′ment (*ēz′-*).
Ēas′i-ly (*ēz′-*), 169.
Ēas′i-ness (*ēz′-*).
Ēast, 13.
Ēast′er, 77.
Ēast′ern.
Ēast′ing.
Ēast′ward [*not* ēst′ard, 142, 153.]
Ēas′y (*ēz′y*), 13, 136.
Ēat (*ēt*), 13.
Ēat (*et*), past tense and past participle from *Eat*.

☞ "The preterite [of *eat*] is now seldom spelled *ate*; and *eaten* for the participle, which some years ago was the only sanctioned form, is giving way to *ēat* [et]." *Smart.*

Ēat′a-ble, 164.
Ēat′en (*ēt′n*), 149.
Ēat′er.
Ēat′ing.
Eau de Cologne (Fr.) (*ō′duh-ko-lōn′*).
Eau de vie (Fr.) (*ō′duh-vē′*).
Ēaves (*ēvz*), *n. pl.* 171.
Ēaves′drop-per (*ēvz′-*).
Ebb, 15, 175.
Ebbed (*ebd*), 150.
Ebb′ing.
Ebb′-tīde.
Eb′on, 15, 86.
Eb′on-y.
E-brac′te-ate, 73.
E-bri′e-ty, 75, 169.
E′bri-oŭs.
E-bŭll′ien-cy (*-yen-*), 51, 171.
E-bŭll′ient (*-yent*).
Eb-ul-lĭ′tion (*-lish′un*).
E-bur′ne-an, 110, 169.
Ec′ba-sis.
Ec-bat′ic.
Ec′bo-le (Gr.), 163.
Ec-cen′tric [Excentric, 203.]
Ec-cen′tric-al.
Ec-cen-triç′i-ty, 108, 169.
Ec-chy-mo′sis (*-kĭ-*), 198.
Ec-cle-si-as′tes (*-kle-zi-as′tēz*), 171.
Ec-clē-si-as′tic (*-kle-zi-as′tik*) [so Sm. Wb. Gd. Wr.; *ek-kle-zhĭ-as′tik*, Wk. 155.]
Ec-cle-si-as′tic-al (*-kle-zi-as′tik-*), 108.
Ec-cle-si-o-log′ic-al (*kle-zi-o-loj′ik-*).
Ec-cle-si-ol′o-gist (*-zĭ-*).
Ec-cle-si-ol′o-gy (*-zĭ-*).
Ec-co-prot′ic.
Échelon (Fr.) (*esh′e-lon*).
Ech′i-nate (*ek′-*) [so Sm. Wb. Gd.; *ek′i-nāt*, or *e-ki′nāt*, Wr. 155.]
E-chi′nus (L.) (*-ki′-*) [pl. *E-chi′nī* (*-ki′-*), 198.]
Ech′o (*ek′ō*) (52, 171) [pl. Ech′oes (*ek′ōz*), 192.]
Ech′oed (*ek′ōd*), 188.
E-chom′e-ter (*-kom′-*), 108.
E-chom′e-try (*-kom′-*).
Eclaircissement (Fr.) (*ek-lêr′sis-mäng*) [so Gd.; *ek-lêr′sis-mŏng*, Sm.; *ek-lêr′siz-ment*, Wk.; *e-klêr′sis-mäng′*, or *e-klêr′siz-ment*, Wr. 154, 155.]
Ec-lamp′sy.
E-clat′ (Fr.) (*ā-klä′*, or *e-klä′*) [*ā-klä′*, Sm.; *e-klä′*, Wr. Wb. Gd.; *e-klaw′*, Wk. 154, 155.]
Ec-lec′tic.
Ec-lec′ti-cism (*-sizm*).
Ec′legm (*-lem*), 162.
E-clipse′, 75, 171.
E-clipsed′ (*-klipst′*), 183.
E-clips′ing.
E-clip′tic.
Ec′lŏgue (*-log*), 87; Note D, p. 37.
Ec-o-nom′ic, *or* Ē-co-nom′ic.
Ec-o-nom′ic-al, *or* Ē-co-nom′ic-al [so Wr.; *ek-o-nom′i-cal*, Wk. Sm.; *ē-ko-nom′i-cal*, Wb. Gd. 155.]
Ec-o-nom′ic-al-ly, *or* Ē-co-nom′ic-al-ly.
E-con′o-mist.
E-con′o-mize.
E-con′o-mized, 183.
E-con′o-mīz-ing.
E-con′o-my, 108, 170.
Ec-pho-ne′sis (Gr).
Ec′sta-sy (169, 171) [Ecstacy, Extasy, 203.]
Ec-stat′ic [Extatic, 203.]
Ec-stat′ic-al.
Ec′ta-sis.
Ec-thlip′sis.
Ec′ty-pal.
Ec-u-men′ic-al [Œcumenical, 203.]
E-da′cious (*-shus*), 169.
E-daç′i-ty.
Ed′da, 170.
Ed′dĭed (*-did*), 99, 186
Ed′dy, 170.
Ed′dy-ing, 186.
E-dem′a-tose.
E-dem′a-toŭs.
E′den, 149.
E-den′tate.
E-den′tāt-ed.
Edge, 15, 45.
Edged (*ejd*), 150.
Edge′-rāil.
Edge′-tool.
Edge′wīse (*-wīz*)
Edg′ing, 183.
Ed′i-ble, 164, 169.
E′dict, 13, 16.
Ed-i-fi-ca′tion.
Ed′i-fīce (*-fis*), 169.
Ed′i-fīed, 99, 186.
Ed′i-fȳ, 94.
Ed′i-fȳ-ing.
E′dīle (152) [Ædile, 203.]
Ed′it, 13, 16.
Ed′it-ed.
Ed′it-ing.
E-dĭ′tion (*-dish′un*), 171.
Ed′it-or, 88, 228.
Ed-it-o′ri al.
Ed′u-cate, 45, N.; 73, 89.

Ed'u-cāt-ed, 183.
Ed'u-cāt-ing.
Ed-u-ca'tion, 169.
Ed-u-ca'tion-al.
Ed'u-cāt-or, 89, 228.
E-duce', 26, 75.
E-duced' (*-dūst'*).
E-dūç'ing.
E-duc'tion.
E-duc'tor.
E-dul'co-rate.
E-dul'co-rāt-ed, 183.
E-dul'co-rāt-ing.
E-dul-co-ra'tion.
E-dul'co-rāt-ive [so Sm. Wr.; *e-dul'ko-ra-tiv*, Wb. Gd. 155.]
E-dul'co-rāt-or.
Eel (*ēl*), 13.
Ef-face', 23.
Ef-face'a-ble, 164, 183.
Ef-faced' (*-fāst'*), 183.
Ef-fāç'ing.
Ef-fect', *n. & v.*
Ef-fect'ive.
Ef-fect'or, 88, 228.
Ef-fect'u-al, 169.
Ef-fect'u-al-ly.
Ef-fect'u-ate.
Ef-fect'u-āt-ed, 183.
Ef-fect'u-āt-ing.
Ef-fem'i-na-cy, 169.
Ef-fem'i-uate, *a. & v.* 73.
Ef-fem'i-nāt-ed, 183.
Ef-fem'i-nāt-ing.
Ef-fer-vesce' (*-ves'*), 171.
Ef-fer-vesced' (*-vest'*).
Ef-fer-ves'cence, 171.
Ef-fer-ves'cent.
Ef-fer-ves'ci-ble, 164.
Ef-fete', 121.
Ef-fi-ca'cious (*-shus*), 112, 169.
Ef'fi-ca-cy, 169.
Ef-fī'cience (*-fish'ens*).
Ef-fī'cien-cy (*-fish'en-sy*) [so Wb. Gd.; *ef-fish'ī-en-sy*, Sm. (*See* § 26); *ef-fish'yen-sy*, Wk. Wr. 155.]
Ef-fī'cient (*-fish'ent*).
Ef-fig'i-es (L.) (*-fij'i-ēz*), 144.
Ef'fi-gy, 170.
Ef-flo-resce' (*-res'*), 171.
Ef-flo-resced' (*-rest'*).
Ef-flo-res'cence.
Ef-flo-res'cen-cy.
Ef-flo-res'cent, 171.
Ef-flo-res'cing, 183.
Ef'flu-ence, 105, 169.
Ef'flu-ent.
Ef-flu'vi-um (L.) [pl. Ef-flu'vi-a, 198.]
Ef'flux.
Ef-flux'ion (*-fluk'shun*), 46, Note 1.
Ef'fōrt, 135.
Ef-front'er-y (*-frunt'-*), 233, Exc.
Ef-ful'gence.
Ef-ful'gent.
Ef-fuse' (*-fūz'*).
Ef-fused' (*-fūzd'*), 183.
Ef-fūs'ing (*-fūz'-*).
Ef-fu'sion (*-zhun*).
Ef-fu'sīve, 84.
Eft, 15.
E'ger (*-gur*) [E a g r e, 203. — *See* Eagre.]
E-gest'ion (*-yun*), 51.
Egg, 15, 175.
Eg'lan-tīne, *or* Eg'lan-tīne [so Wr. Gd.; *eg'-lan-tīn*, Sm.; *eg'lan-tīn*, Wk. 155.]
E'go-ism (*-izm*), 133.
E'go-ist.
E'go-tism, *or* Eg'o-tism (*-tizm*) [so Wr.; *e'go-tizm*, Wk. Wb. Gd.; *eg'o-tizm*, Sm.]

☞ Though Walker, in deference to all the authorities of his time, pronounces this word *e'go-tizm*, he says, that, by analogy, it ought to be pronounced *eg'otizm*.

E'go-tist, *or* Eg'o-tist.
Ē-go-tist'ic, *or* Eg-o-tist'ic, 109.
Ē-go-tist'ic-al, *or* Eg-o-tist'ic-al, 108.
E-gre'gioŭs (*e-gre'jus*) [so Wr. Wb. Gd.; *e-gre'ji-us*, Wk. Sm. 155.]
E'gress, 76.
E'gret.
E-gyp'tian (*-jip'shan*).
Eī'der-down (*ī'dur-*).
Eī'der-duck (*ī'dur-*).
Eight (*āt*) (162), *a. & n.* twice four. [*See* Ate, 160.]
Eigh'teen (*ā'tēn*).

☞ "When we are counting, *thir'teen, four'-teen, fif'teen*, &c., the former syllable will be accented; but, in using one of the words separately, either the last syllable will be accented, or each syllable will be pronounced as a distinct word." *Smart.*

Eigh'teenth (*a'tēnth*).
Eight'fōld (*āt'-*), 162.
Eighth (*ātth*).

☞ In this word, the *t* presents the singular anomaly of serving both as the last letter in *eight*, and as the first letter in the digraph *th*.

Eigh'ti-eth (*ā'ti-*), 171.
Eight'score (*āt'-*), 206.
Eigh'ty (*ā'ty*), 171.
Eigne (*ā'nē*, or *ān*) [so Wr.; *ā'nē*, Sm.; *ān*, Wb. Gd. 155.]
Ei'ther (*ē'thur*) [so Wk. Sm. Wr.; *ē'thur*, or *ī'thur*, Gd. 155.]

☞ With regard to the pronunciation of the words *either* and *neither*, Walker remarks: "Analogy, without hesitation, gives the diphthong the sound of long open e rather than that of *i*;" and Smart says: "Usage, as well as regularity, favors the sound *ē* in these two words."

E-jac'u-late, 73, 89.
E-jac'u-lāt-ed, 183.
E-jac'u-lāt-ing.
E-jac-u-la'tion.
E-jac'u-la-to-ry, 86.
E-ject', 15, 75.
E-ject'ed.
E-ject'ing.
E-jec'tion.
E-ject'ment.
E-ject'or, 88, 228.
Eke, *v.*
Eked (*ēkt*), Note C, p. 34.
Ēk'ing, 183.
E-lab'o-rate, *a. & v.* 73.
E-lab'o-rāt-ed, 183.
E-lab'o-rāt-ing.
E-lab-o-ra'tion.
E-lab'o-rāt-or.
E-la'in [so Sm. Gd.; *e-lān'*, or *e-lā'in*, Wr. 155.]
E-lapse', 10.
E-lapsed' (*-lapst'*).
E-laps'ing, 183.
E-las'tic.
E-las-tiç'i-ty, 169.
E-late', 23.
E-lāt'ed, 183.
E-lāt'er.
E-lāt'ing.

E-la′tion.
El′bōw, 15, 24.
El′bōwed (-*bōd*), 188.
El′bōw-ing.
El′der, *a.* & *n.*
El′dest.
El-Do-rä′do [so Sm. Wr.; *el-do-rā′do*, Gd. 155.]
El-e-cam-pāne′, 122.
E-lect′, *a.* & *n.*
E-lect′ed.
E-lect′ing.
E-lec′tion.
E-lec-tion-eer′, 169.
E-lec-tion-eered′ (-*ērd′*), 165.
E-lec-tion-eer′ing.
E-lect′ïve.
E-lect′or, 88, 228.
E-lect′o-ral.
E-lect′o-rate.
E-lect-o′ri-al.
E-lec′tric, 109.
E-lec′tric-al, 108.
E-lec′tric-al-ly.
E-lec-trĭ′cian (-*trish′-an*).
E-lec-triç′i-ty, 171.
E-lec′tri-fī-a-ble, 164.
E-lec-tri-fĭ-ca′tion.
E-lec′tri-fīed, 99, 186.
E-lec′tri-fȳ, 94, 169.
E-lec′tri-fȳ-ing.
E-lec′tro-chem′is-try (-*kem′*-, or -*kim′*-), 224.
E-lec′tro-dȳ-nam′ics.
E-lec-trol′y-sis.
E-lec′tro-lyte.
E-lec-tro-lyt′ic.
E-lec′tro-lȳz-a-ble, 164.
E-lec′tro-lyze, 171.
E-lec′tro-lyzed, 183.
E-lec′tro-lȳz-ing.
E-lec′tro-mag′net, 224.
E-lec′tro-mag-net′ic.
E-lec′tro-mag′net-ism (-*izm*).
E-lec-trom′e-ter, 108.
E-lec′tro-mo tïve.
E-lec′tro-mo′tor.
E-lec′tro-neg′a-tïve.
E-lec-troph′o-rus [pl. E-lec-troph′o-rī, 198.]
E-lec′tro-plāt′ing.
E lec′tro-po′lar.
E-lec′tro-pos′i tïve (-*poz′*-).
E-lec′tro-scope.
E-lec′tro-type, *n.* & *v.*
E-lec′tro-typed (-*tīpt*).
E-lec′tro-tȳp-ing, 183.
E-lect′u-a-ry, 72, 89.

El-ee-mos′y-na-ry (*el-ē-moz′*-), 72, 171.
El′e-gance, 169.
El′e-gant.
El-e-gi′ac, *or* E-le′gi-ac (108) [*el-e-jī′ak*, Wk. Sm. Wr.; *e-le′ji-ak*, Wb. Gd. 155.]

☞ "*El-e-gi′ac* is another exception [to the rule in § 108] from the undue weight of classical authority." *Smart.* — "*E-le′gi-ac* is the general pronunciation of this country [U. S.]." *Goodrich.*

El′e-gist, 45.
El′e-gy, 169, 170.
El′e-ment, 169.
El-e-ment′al.
El-e-ment′al-ly, 170.
El-e-ment′a-ry, 72.
El′e-mī.
E-lench′ (-*lengk′*) [so Sm.; *e-lenk′*, Wb. Gd.; *e-lengk′*, or *e-lench′*, Wr. 155.]
E-lench′ic-al (-*lengk′*-).
El′e-phant, 169.
El-e-phan-ti′a-sis.
El-e-phant′īne, 152.
El′e-phant-oid [so Wr.; *el-e-phan-toid′*, Wb. Gd. 155.]
El-e-phant-oid′al.
El-eu-sin′i-an (-*u-sin′*-).
El′e-vate, 73.
El′e-vāt-ed, 183.
El′e-vāt-ing.
El-e-va′tion.
El′e-vāt-or, 88, 228.
El′e-vāt-o-ry, 86.
E-lev′en (*e-lev′n*) (149) [*not* lev′n, 153.]
E-lev′enth (*e-lev′nth*).
Elf (15) [pl. Elves (*elvz*), 193.]
Elf′in.
Elf′ish.
E-liç′it, 171.
E-liç′it-ed.
E-liç′it-ing.
E-lide′.
E-līd′ed, 183.
E-līd′ing.
El-i-gi-bil′i-ty, 171.
El′i-gi-ble, 108, 164.
El′i-gi-bly.
E-lim′i-nate.
E-lim′i-nāt-ed, 183.
E-lim′i-nāt-ing.
E-lim-i-na′tion.
El-i-qua′tion.
E-lĭ′sion (-*lizh′un*).

*É*lite (Fr.) (*a-lēt′*).
E-lix′ir, 85.
E-liz′a-beth-an [so Sm. Wr.; *e-liz-a-beth′an*, Wb. Gd. 155.] [*not* e-liz-a-be′than, 153.]
Elk, 15.
Ell, 15, 172.
El-lipse′, 171.
El-lip′sis (L.) [pl. El-lip′sēs (-*sēz*), 198.]
El-lip′soid.
El-lip-soid′al.
El-lip′tic, 109.
El-lip′tic-al, 108.
El-lip′tic-al-ly.
El-lip-tiç′i-ty, 171.
Elm, 15, 133.
El′men.
Elm′y, 15, 93.
El-o-cu′tion (119, 170) [*See* Allocution, 148.]
El-o-cu′tion-a-ry, 72.
El-o-cu′tion-ist.
É-loge (Fr.) (*a-lōzh′*).
E-lon′gate (-*long′*-), 54.
E-lon′gāt-ed (-*long′*-).
E-lon′gāt-ing (-*long′*-).
E-lon-ga′tion (*e-long-ga′shun*) [so Sm. Wb. Gd.; *el-ong-ga′shun*, Wk. Wr. 155.]
E-lope′, 24.
Eloped′ (-*lōpt′*), Note C, p. 34.
E-lōp′ing, 183.
E-lope′ment, 185.
E′lops.
El′o-quence, 170.
El′o-quent, 34.
Else (*els*), Note D, p. 37.
Else′whêre (*els′whêr*).
E-lu′ci-date.
E-lu′ci-dāt-ed, 183.
E-lu′ci-dāt-ing.
E-lu-ci-da′tion, 112.
E-lu′ci-dāt-ïve, 84.
E-lu′ci-dāt-or.
E-lu′ci-dāt-o-ry, 86.
E-lude′, 26.
E-lūd′ed, 183.
E-lūd′i-ble, 164, 169.
E-lūd′ing.
E-lu′sion (-*zhun*), *n.* act of eluding. [*See* Illusion, 148.]
E-lu′sïve.
E-lu′so-ri-ness.
E-lu′so-ry.
E-lu′tri-ate, 73.
E-lu′tri-āt-ed, 183.
E-lu′tri-āt-ing.

E-lu-tri-a'tion.
Elves (*elvz*), pl. of *Elf.*
E-lȳ'si-an (*e-lizh'i-an*) [so Wk. Sm. Wr.; *e-lizh'yan*, Gd. 155.]
E-lȳ'si-um (*e-lizh'i-um*) [so Wk. Sm. Wr.; *e-lizh'yum*, Gd. 155.] [L. pl. *E-ly'si-a* (*e-lizh'i-a*); Eng. pl. E-lȳ'si-ums (*e-lizh'i-umz*), 198.]
E-lyt'ri-form, 169.
El'y-tron [pl. El'y-tra, 198.]
El'y-trum, *or* E-ly'-trum [so Wr.; *el'i-trum*, Gd.; *e-lī'trum*, Sm.] [pl. El'y-tra, *or* E-ly'tra, 198.]
El'ze-vir.
E-ma'ci-ate (*-shĭ-āt*) [so Wk. Sm. Wr.; *e-ma'-shāt*, Wb. Gd. 155.]
E-ma'ci-āt-ed (*-shĭ-āt-*).
E-ma'ci-āt-ing(*-shĭ-āt-*).
E-mā-ci-a'tion (*-shĭ-*).
Em'a-nant (169), *a.* flowing from. [*See* Eminent, 148.]
Em'a-nate, 169, 171.
Em'a-nāt-ed, 183.
Em'a-nāt-ing.
Em-a-na'tion.
Em'a-nāt-ĭve [so Sm. Wr. Wb. Gd.; *em'a-na-tĭv*, Wk. 155.]
E-man'ci-pate, 73.
E-man'ci-pāt-ed, 183.
E-man'ci-pāt-ing.
E-man-ci-pa'tion.
E-man'ci-pāt-or.
E-mar'gi-nate, *v.* & *a.*
E mar'gi-nāt-ed.
E-mar'gi-nāt-ing.
E-mar-gi-na'tion, 112.
E-mas'cu-late.
E-mas'cu-lāt-ed.
E-mas'cu-lāt-ing.
E-mas-cu-la'tion.
Em-bale'.
Em-baled', 165, 183.
Em-bāl'ing.
Em-bälm' (*-bäm'*), 162.
Em-bälmed' (*-bamd'*).
Em-bälm'er (*-bäm'-*).
Em-bälm'ing (*-bäm'-*).
Em-bank'ment (*em-bangk'-*) [Imbankment, 203.]
[Embarcation, 203. — *See* Embarkation.]
Em-bar'go, *n.* & *v.* [pl. of *n.* Em-bar'goes (*-gōz*), 192.] [Imbargo, 203.]
Em-bar'gōed (*-gōd*), 188.
Em-bar'go-ing.
Em-bark' [Imbark, 203.]
Em-barked' (*-barkt'*).
Em-bark'ing.
Em-bark-a'tion [Embarcation, 203.]
Em-băr'rass, 170.
Em-băr'rassed (*-rast*).
Em-băr'rass-ing.
Em-băr'rass-ment.
Em-bas'sa-dor [Ambassador, 203.—*See* Note under Ambassador.]
Em'bas-sy.
Em-bat'tle, 164.
Em-bat'tled (*-bat'ld*), 183.
Em-bat'tling.
Em-bed' [Imbed, 203.]
Em-bed'ded, 176.
Em-bed'ding.
Em-bel'lish, 170.
Em-bel'lished (*-lisht*).
Em-bel'lish-ing.
Em-bel'lish-ment.
Em'bers (*-burz*), *n. pl.*
Em'ber-week.
Em-bez'zle, 164.
Em-bez'zled (*-bez'ld*), 183.
Em-bez'zle-ment.
Em-bez'zler.
Em-bez'zling.
[Embitter, 203. — *See* Imbitter.]
Em-blaze'.
Em-blāzed', 183.
Em-blāz'ing.
Em-bla'zon (*-bla'zn*), 149.
Em-bla'zoned (*-bla'znd*)
Em-bla'zon-er (*-bla'zn-*)
Em-bla'zon-ing (*-bla'-zn*).
Em-bla'zon-ry(*-bla'zn-*)
Em'blem, 15, 76.
Em-blem-at'ic, 109.
Em-blem-at'ic-al, 108.
Em-blem-at'ic-al-ly.
Em'ble-ments (*em'bl-*), *n. pl.*
Em-bod'ĭed (*-id*), 99.
Em-bod'i-er.
Em-bod'i-ment, 169.
Em-bod'y, 93.
Em-bod'y-ing. [149.
Em-bōld'en (*-bōld'n*),
Em-bōld'ened(*-bōld'nd*)
Em-bōld'en-ing (*bōld'-n-*).
Em'bo-lism (*-lizm*), 136.
Em-bo-lis'mal (*-liz'-*).
Em-bo-lis'mic (*-liz'-*).
Em'bo-lus [pl. Em'bo-lī, 198.]
Embonpoint' (Fr.) (*ăng-bong-pwăng'*).
[Emborder, 203.—*See* Imborder.]
[Embosom, 203.—*See* Imbosom.]
Em-boss', 18, 171.
Em-bossed' (*-bost'*), 165; Note C, p. 34.
Em-boss'ing.
Em-boss'ment.
Embouchure' (Fr.) (*ăng-boo-shoor'*).
Em-bow'el [Imbowel, 203.]
Em-bow'elled(*-eld*)(150) [Emboweled, Wb. Gd. 203. — *See* 177, and Note E, p. 70.]
Em-bow'el-ler [Emboweler, Wb. Gd. 203.]
Em-bow'el-ling [Emboweling, Wb. Gd. 203.]
Em-bow'el-ment.
Em-brace', 23.
Em-brāced'(*-brāst'*),165.
Em-brāç'er, 183.
Em-brāç'er-y.
Em-brāç'ing.
Em-bra'sure (*-zhūr*, or *zhur*) [*em-bra'zhūr*, Wk. Gd.; *em-bra-zūr'*, Sm.; *em-bra-zhoor'*, or *em-bra'zhur*, Wr. 155.]
Em'bro-cate, 73.
Em'bro-cāt-ed, 183.
Em'bro-cāt-ing.
Em-bro-ca'tion.
Em-broid'er.
Em-broid'ered (*-urd*), 150, 165.
Em-broid'er-er, 77.
Em-broid'er-ing.
Em-broid'er-y, 171.
Em-broil', 27.
Em-broiled', 165.
Em-broil'ing.
Em-broil'ment.
Em'bry-ō, 160, 171 [pl. Em'bry-ōs (*-ōz*), 192.]
Em-bry-og'ra-phy, 108.
Em-bry-ol'o-gy, 108.

Em'bry-o-nate, *a.*
Em'bry-o-nāt-ed.
Em-bry-on'ic, 109.
Em-bry-ot'ic.
Em-bry-ot'o-my, 108.
[Emeer, 203. — *See* Emir.]
E-mend', 15.
E-mend'als (*-alz*), *n. pl.*
Em-en-da'tion.
Em'en-dāt-or.
E-mend'a-to-ry, 86.
E-mend'ed.
E-mend'ing.
Em'er-ald, 170, 171.
E-merge', 21, N.
E-merged', 165.
E-merg'ence (*-merj'-*).
E-merg'en-cy (*-merj'-*), 169, 183.
E-merg'ent (*-merj'-*).
E-merg'ing (*-merj'-*).
E-mĕr'it-ed.
E-mĕr'i-tus (L.), *a.* & *n.* [pl. of *n.* *E-mĕr'i-tī*, 198.]
Em'er-ods (*-odz*).
Em'er-oids.

☞ The two preceding words are corrupted from *Hemorrhoids.*

E-mer'sion (21, N.), *n.* act of emerging. [*See* Immersion, 148.]
Em'er-y, 93, 170.
E-met'ic.
E-met'ic-al.
E-met'ic-al-ly.
Em'e-tĭne (152) [Emetin, 203.]
E'meū (*-mū*) [Emew, Emu, 203.]
Émeute (Fr.) (*ā-mūt'*).
Em'i-cant.
Em'i-grant, 169.
Em'i-grāte, 73.
Em'i-grāt-ed, 183.
Em'i-grāt-ing.
Em-i-gra'tion.
Em'i-nence, 169.
Em'i-nen-cy.
Em'i-nent, *a.* conspicuous. [*See* Emanant, 148.]
E'mir [Emeer (*e-mēr'*), 203.]
Em'is-sa-ry, 72, 170.
E-mis'sion (*-mish'un*).
E-mis'sĭve, 84.
E-mit', 16.
E-mit'ted, 176.
E-mit'tent.
E-mit'ting.
Em'met, 170.
Em-ol-les'cence, 171.
E-mol'liate (*-mol'yāt*) [so Sm.; *e-mol'yi-āt*, Wr.; *e-mol'li-āt*, Wb. Gd. 155.]
E-mol'liāt-ed (*-mol'yāt-*)
E-mol'liāt-ing (*-mol'-yāt-*).
E-mol'lient (*-mol'yent*) [so Wk. Sm. Wr.; *e-mol'li-ent*, Wb. Gd. 155.]
E-mol'u-ment, 89.
E-mol-u-ment'al.
E-mo'tion.
E-mo'tion-al.
E-mo'tĭve, 84.
Em-pale', 23.
Em-pāled', 183.
Em-pale'ment.
Em-pāl'ing.
Em-pan'el [Empannel, Impanel, Impannel, 201, 203.]
Em-pan'elled (*-eld*) [Empanneled, Wb. Gd. 203.—*See* 177, and Note E, p. 70.]
Em-pan'el-ling [Empanneling, Wb. Gd. 203.]
Em-pasm' (*-pazm'*), 136.
Em'per-or, 171.
Em'pha-sis [pl. Em'pha-sēs (*-sēz*), 198.]
Em'pha-size, 202.
Em'pha-sized, 183.
Em'pha-sīz-ing.
Em-phat'ic, 109.
Em-phat'ic-al.
Em phy-se'ma.
Em phy-sem'a-toŭs.
Em'pire.
Em-pĭr'ic, *or* Em'pĭr-ic, *n.* [so Wr.; *em-pĭr'-ik*, Sm.; *em'pĭr-ik*, or *em-pĭr'ik*, Wk. Gd. 155.]
Em-pĭr'ic, *a.* 109.
Em-pir'ic-al, *a.* unwarranted by science. [*See* Empyrical, 160.]
Em-pĭr'i-cism (*-sizm*).
Em-pĭr'i-cist.
Em-plas'tic.
Em-ploy', 27.
Employé (Fr.)(*ong-ploi-a'*, or *em-ploi-a'*), 154.
Em-ployed', 165, 187.
Em-ploy'er.
Em-ploy'ing.
Em-ploy'ment.
Em po'ri-um (L.) [L. pl. *Em-po'ri-a*; Eng. pl. Em-po'ri-ums (*-umz*), 198.]
Em-pov'er-ish [Impoverish, 203.]
Em-pov'er-ished (*-isht*).
Em-pov'er-ish-er.
Em-pov'er-ish-ing.
Em-pov'er-ish-ment.
Em-pow'er [Impower, 203.]
Em-pow'ered(*-urd*),150.
Em-pow'er-ing.
Em'press.
Emp'tĭed (*em'tid*), 162.
Emp'ti-ness (*em'-*).
Emp'ty (*em'ty*), 93, 162.
Emp'ty-ing (*em'ty-*).
Emp'ty-ings (*em'ty-ingz*), *n. pl.* [*not* em'-tings, 153.]
Em-pur'ple, 164.
Em-pur'pled (*-pur'pld*).
Em-pur'pling.
Em-py-e'ma.
Em-pўr'e-al.
Em-py-re'an, *or* Em-pўr'e-an (110) [so Wk. Wr.; *em-py-re'an*,Sm. Wb. Gd. 155.]
Em-py-reu'ma (*-roo'-*).
Em-py-reu-mat'ic (*-roo-*).
Em-py-reu-mat'ic-al (*-roo-*).
Em-pўr'ic-al, *a.* pertaining to combustion. [*See* Empirical, 160.]
[Emu, 203. — *See* Emeu.]
Em'u-late, 73, 89.
Em'u-lāt-ed.
Em'u-lāt-ing.
Em-u-la'tion, 112.
Em'u-lāt-ĭve [so Wr.; *em'u-la-tiv*, Wb. Gd. 155.]
Em'u-lāt-or.
E-mul'gent.
Em'u-loŭs, 108.
E-mul'sion.
E-mul'sĭve, 84, 109.
E-munc'to-ry(*-mungk'-*)
En-a'ble, 164.
En-a'bled (*-a'bld*).
En-a'bling, 183.
En-act', 10.
En-act'ed.
En-act'ing.
En-act'ment.
En-act'or, 88, 228.

E-nal'la-ge (L.) (163) [so Sm. Wb. Gd.; *en-al'la-je*, Wk. Wr. 155.]
En-am'el.
En-am'el-lar, *a.* resembling enamel. [*See* Enameller, 160.] [Enamelar, Wb. Gd. 203.]
En-am'elled (*-eld*) [Enameled, Wb. Gd. 203. — *See* 177, and Note E, p. 70.]
En-am'el-ler, *n.* one who enamels. [*See* Enamelar, 160.] [Enameler, Wb. Gd. 203.]
En-am'el-ling [Enameling, Wb. Gd. 203.]
En-am'or [Enamour, Sm. 199.]
En-am'ored (*-urd*), 150.
En-am'or-ing.
En-an-the'sis.
En-armed' (*-armd'*), *a.*
En-ar-thro'sis.
En-cage' (23) [Incage, 201, 203.]
En-caged', 183.
En-căg'ing (*-kāj'-*).
En-camp', 10.
En-camped' (*-kampt'*).
En-camp'ing.
En-camp'ment.
[Encase, 201, 203. — *See* Incase.]
En-câu'ma.
En-câus'tic.
En-cave'.
En-căved', 183.
En-căv'ing.
En-ceinte (Fr.) (*ăng-sănt'*).
En-ce-phal'ic.
En-chafe'.
En-chăfed' (*-chăft'*).
En-chăf'ing, 183.
En-chăin', 23.
En-chăined', 165.
En-chăin'ing.
En-chȧnt', 131.
En-chȧnt'ed.
En-chȧnt'er.
En-chȧnt'ing.
En-chȧnt'ment.
En-chȧnt'ress.
En-chase' (23) [Inchase, 201, 203.]
En-chased' (*-chăst'*).
En-chăs'ing.
En-chi-rid'i-on (*en-kī-*) (171) [so Wr. Wb. Gd.; *eng-ki-rid'i-on*, Sm. 155.]
En-cho'ri-al (*-kō'-*), 171.
En-cir'cle (154) [Incircle, 201, 203.]
En-cir'cled (*-sir'kld*).
En-cir'cling.
[Enclasp, 201, 203. — *See* Inclasp.]
En-clit'ic, 109.
En-clit'ic-al, 108.
En-clit'ic-al-ly.
En-close' (*-klōz'*) [Inclose, 201, 203.]

☞ Both forms *enclose* and *inclose* are in good use. Walker, Smart, and Worcester, prefer the first; Webster and Goodrich the last.

En-clōsed' (*-klōzd'*), 183.
En-clōs'ing (*-klōz'-*).
En-clōs'ure (*-klōz'yur*) [Inclosure, 201, 203.]
En-co'mi-ast, 169.
En-co-mi-ast'ic, 109.
En-co-mi-ast'ic-al, 108.
En-co'mi-um (L.) (169) [L. pl. *En-co'mi-a*; Eng. pl. En-co'mi-ums (*-umz*), 198.]
En-com'pass (*-kum'-*), 171.
En-com'passed (*-kum'past*).
En-com'pass-ing (*-kum'-*).
Encore (Fr.) (*ăng-kōr'*), *n.* & *v.*
En-cored' (*-ăng-kōrd'*).
En-cōr'ing (*ang-kōr'-*).
En-coun'ter.
En-coun'tered, 150.
En-coun'ter-ing.
En-coŭr'age, 70.
En-coŭr'aged, 165.
En-coŭr'age-ment.
En-coŭr'a-ger, 183.
En-coŭr'a-ging.
En-cri'nal, 72.
En-cri'nic, 109.
En-crin'it-al.
En'cri-nīte, 152, 169.
En-crōach' (24, 44) [Incroach, 203.]
En-crōached' (*-krōcht'*), 165.
En-crōach'ing.
En-crōach'ment.
[Encrust, 201, 203. — *See* Incrust.]
En-cum'ber.
En-cum'bered (*-burd*), 150.
En-cum'ber-ing.
En-cum'brance (169) [Incumbrance, 203.]
En-cyc'lic-al, 171.
En-cȳ-clo-pæ'di-a, En-cȳ-clo-pe'di-a.

☞ Both modes of spelling this word are in good use. The former is preferred by Worcester; the latter by Walker, Smart, Webster, and Goodrich.

En-cȳ-clo-pe'di-an.
En-cȳ-clo-ped'ic.
En-cȳ-clo-ped'ic-al.
En-cȳ-clo-pe'dist.
En-cyst'ed, 171.
End, 15.
En-dăn'ger.
En-dăn'gered (*-jurd*), 150.
En-dăn'ger-ing.
En-dēar', 13.
En-dēared', 165.
En-dēar'ing.
En-dēar'ment.
En-dĕav'or (*-dev'ur*) [Endeavour, Sm. 199, 203.]
En-dĕav'ored (*dev'urd*).
En-dĕav'or-ing (*-dev'ur-*).
En-dec'a-gon.
End'ed.
En-deic'tic (*-dīk'-*), 171.
En-dem'ic, 109, 170.
En-dem'ic-al, 108.
[Endict, 201, 203. — *See* Indict.]
End'ing.
[Endite, 201, 203. — *See* Indite.]
En'dīve (84) [*not* en'dīv, 153.]
En'do-gen.
En-dog'en-oŭs (*-doj'-*).
En-do-phyl'loŭs, *or* En-doph'yl-loŭs [*See* Adenophyllous.]
En-dorse' [Indorse, 201, 203.]

☞ The two forms *endorse* and *indorse*, and their corresponding derivatives, are in good use. Walker gives only *endorse*, and Smart only *indorse*. Webster and Goodrich prefer *indorse*. Worcester has both forms; but he indicates no preference for either.

En-dorsed' (*-dorst'*), 183.

En-dors′er [Indorser, 201, 203.]
En-dors′ing.
En-dorse′ment [Indorsement, 203.]
En′dos-mose [so Sm. Gd.; ĕn-dos-mōs′, Wr. 155.]
En′do-sperm.
En′do-stome.
En-dow′, 28.
En-dowed′, 165.
En-dow′er.
En-dow′ment.
En-dūe′, 26.
En-dūed′, 165, 183.
En-du′ing.
En-dūr′a-ble, 164.
En-dūr′ance, 183.
En-dure′.
En-dūred′, 183.
En-dūr′ing.
E-ne′id, *or* E′ne-id [so Wr.; *e-ne′id*, Sm. Gd. 155.] [Æneid, 203.]
E-ne′ma [so Sm. Wb. Gd.; *en′e-ma*, Wr. 155.]

☞ "The customary pronunciation is as given [*e-ne′ma*]: Greek quantity would require *en′e-ma*." *Smart.*

En′e-my, 170.
En-er-get′ic, 45, 109.
En-er-get′ic-al, 108.
En-er-get′ic-al-ly.
En′er-gize.
En′er-gized, 183.
En′er-gīz-ing.
En′er-gy, 170.
E-nerv′ate (21, N.) [*not* en′er-vāt, 153.]
E-nerv′āt-ed, 183.
E-nerv′āt-ing.
En-er-va′tion.
En-fee′ble, 164.
En-fee′bled (*-fe′bld*), 183.
En-fee′bling.
En-fēoff′ (*-fĕf′*), 171.

☞ Walker's pronunciation is *en-fēf′*; but, under *feoff*, he says that it ought to have been *en-fĕf′*.

En-fēoffed′ (*-fĕft′*).
En-fēoff′ing (*-fĕf′-*).
En-fēoff′ment (*-fĕf′-*).
En-fi-lade′, *n.* & *v.* [so Wk. Wr. Wb. Gd.; *ong-fi-lād′*, Sm. 155.]
En-fi-lād′ed, 183.
En-fi-lād′ing.
[Enfold, 203. — *See* Infold.]
En-fōrce′, 24.
En-fōrced′ (*fōrst′*), 150, 183. Note C, p. 34.
En-fōrce′ment, 185.
En-fōrç′er.
En-fōrç′ing.
En-fran′chīse (*-chĭz*) (156) [Infranchise, 201, 203.]
En-fran′chīsed (*-chĭzd*).
En-fran′chīse-ment.
En-fran′chīs-ing (*-chĭz-*)
En-gage′, 23.
En-gaged′, 183.
En-gage′ment.
En-gāg′ing (*-gāj′-*).
En-gen′der. [150.
En-gen′dered (*-durd*),
En-gen′der-ing.
En′gīne (*-jĭn*) (82, 152) [*not* en′jīn, 153.]
En-gi-neer′, 122, 169.
En-gi-neer′ing.
En′gīne-ry [*not* en′jin-er-y, 145, 153.]
En-gird′ (*-ghird′*), 138.
En-gird′ed (*-ghird′-*).
En-gird′ing (*-ghird′-*).
En-girt′ (*-ghirt′*), 138.
En′glish (*ĭng′-*), 54.
En-gorge′ [Ingorge, 201, 203.]
En-gorged′, 165, 183.
En-gorge′ment, 185.
En-gor′ging.
[Engraft, 201, 203. — *See* Ingraft.]
En-grāil′, 23.
En-grāiled′, 165.
En-grāil′ing.
En-grāil′ment.
En-grāin′ [Ingrain, 201, 203.]
En-grāined′, 165.
En-grāin′ing.
En-grave′, 23.
En-graved′, 165, 183.
En-grāv′er.
En-grāv′ing.
En-grŏss′, 24.
En-grŏssed′ (*-grōst′*).
En-grŏss′ing.
En-grŏss′ment.
[Engulf, 201, 203. — *See* Ingulf.]
En-hànce′, 131.
En-hànced′ (*-hànst′*).
En-hance′ment.
En-hanç′ing.
En-har-mon′ic.
En-har-mon′ic-al.
E-nig′ma, 72.
E-nig-mat′ic, 109.
E-nig-mat′ic-al, 108.
E-nig′ma-tist.
En-join′ (27) [Injoin, 201, 203.]
En-joined′, 165.
En-join′ing.
En-joy′, 27.
En-joy′a-ble, 164.
En-joyed′, 165, 188
En-joy′ing.
En-joy′ment.
En-kin′dle, 164. [183.
En-kin′dled (*-kin′dld*),
En-kin′dling.
En-lard′ (11) [Inlard, 201, 203.]
En-lard′ed.
En-lard′ing.
En-large′ (11) [Inlarge, 201, 203.]
En-larged′, 165, 183.
En-large′ment, 185.
En-larg′ing (*-larj′-*).
En-līght′en (*-līt′n*), 149, 162.
En-līght′ened (*-līt′nd*).
En-līght′en-ing (*-līt′n-*).
En-list′ (16) [Inlist, 203.]
En-list′ed.
En-list′ing.
En-list′ment.
En-līv′en (*-līv′n*), 149.
En-līv′ened (*-līv′nd*).
En-līv′en-ing (*-līv′n-*).
En masse (Fr.) (*äng-mäs′*).
En′mi-ty, 93, 169.
En-ne-a-con-ta-he′dral.
En-ne′a-gon, *or* En′ne-a-gon [so Wr.; *en-ne′-a-gon*, Sm.; *en′ne-a-gon*, Wb. Gd. 155.]
En-ne-an′dri-an, 169.
En-ne-an′droŭs.
En-ne-a-pet′a-loŭs.
En-no′ble, 164.
En-no′bled (*-no′bld*), 183.
En-no′bling.
En-nui′ (Fr.) (*än-wē′*).
E-nor′mi-ty, 169.
E-nor′moŭs.
E-noŭgh′ (*-nŭf′*), 35, 171.
En-quire′ [Inquire, 201, 203.]

☞ Both forms, *enquire* and *inquire*, are used, but the preference is given to *inquire* in most of the dictionaries. See *Inquire*, and its derivatives.

En-rage′, 23.
En-rāged′, 165, 183.

En-răg'ing (-rāj'-).
En-rapt'ure, 91.
En-rapt'ured (-yurd).
En-rapt'ur-ing (-yur-), 91.
En-rav'ish.
En-rav'ished (-isht).
En-rav'ish-ing.
En-rich', 16, 44.
En-riched' (-richt'), 55, Note C, p. 34.
En-rich'ing.
En-rich'ment.
En-robe', 24.
En-robed', 165, 183.
En-rōb'ing.
En-rōll' [Enrol, Sm. 179, 203.]
En-rōlled' (-rōld'), 165.
En-rōll'ing.
En-rōl'ment [Enrollment, Wb. Gd. 178, 203.]
En-root', 19.
En-root'ed.
En-root'ing.
En-san'guīne (-sang'-gwin), 54, 171.
En-san'guīned (-sang'-gwind).
En-san'guīn-ing (sang'-gwin-).
En-sconce', 171.
En-sconced' (-skonst').
En-sconç'ing, 183.
En-shrine' (141) [Inshrine, 203.]
En-shrīned', 165, 183.
En-shrīn'ing.
En'si-form, 108, 169.
En'sīgn (-sīn), 162.
En-slave', 23.
En-slaved', 165.
En-slāv'er.
En-slāv'ing.
En-snare' (-snêr') (14) [Insnare, 201, 203.]

☞ Both forms, *ensnare* and *insnare*, are in good use. Smart prefers *ensnare*; Webster and Goodrich *insnare*. Worcester allows either.

En-snared' (-snêrd'), 165.
En-snar'er (-snêr'-).
En-snar'ing (-snêr'-).
En-sphere', 13, 35.
En-sphered', 165, 183.
En-sphēr'ing.
En-stamp', 10.
En-stamped' (-stampt').
En-stamp'ing.
En-sūe', 26.
En-sūed', 165, 183.
En-su'ing.
[Ensurance, 203. — See Insurance.]
En-sure' (-shoor') [Insure, 201, 203.]

☞ This word, according to Smart, should be spelled *ensure* when it is used in the general sense *to make certain*, and *insure* when it is used in the technical sense *to guarantee against loss*.

En-sured' (-shoord').
En-sur'er (-shoor'-).
En-sur'ing (-shoor'-).
En-tab'la-ture, 171.
En-tāil', *n.* & *v.* 23.
En-tāiled', 165.
En-tāil'ing.
En-tāil'ment.
En-tan'gle (-tang'gl), 54, 164.
En-tan'gled (-tang'gld), 183.
En-tan'gle-ment (-tang'-gl-).
En-tan'gling.
En'ta-sis (Gr.).
En-tas'tic.
En-tel'e-chy (-kĭ).
En'ter, 15, 77.
En'tered, 150.
En'ter-ing.
En-tĕr'o-cele.
En-ter-og'ra-phy, 108.
En-ter-ol'o-gy, 108.
En-ter-om'pha-lŏs [Enteromphalus, 203]
[Enterplead, 203. — See Interplead.]
En'ter-prise (-prīz), 136.
En'ter-prised (-prīzd).
En'ter-prīs-ing (-prīz-).
En-ter-tāin'.
En-ter-tāined', 165.
En-ter-tāin'ing.
En-ter-tāin'ment.
En-the-as'tic.
[Enthrall, 201, 203. — See Inthrall.]
En-throne', 24.
En-throned', 183.
En-thrōn'ing.
En-thu'si-asm (-zĭ-azm) (136, 171) [so Sm. Wr. Wb. Gd.; *en-thu'zhĭ-azm*, Wk. 155.]
En-thu'si-ast (-zĭ-).
En-thu-si-ast'ic (-zĭ-).
En-thu-si-ast'ic-al (-zĭ-).
En-thȳ-me-mat'ic.
En-thȳ-me-mat'ic-al.
En'thy-meme.
En-tice', 25.
En-tīced' (-tīst'), 183.
En-tīç'er.
En-tīç'ing.
En-tire' (25) [Intire, 201, 203.]
En-tire'ty.
En-ti'tle (164) [Intitle, 201, 203.]
En-ti'tled (-ti'tld), 183.
En-ti'tling.
En'ti-ty, 93, 169.
En-tomb' (-toom') (162) [Intomb, 201, 203.]
En-tombed' (-toomd').
En-tomb'ing (-toom'-).
En-tomb'ment (-toom'-)
En-tom'ic, 109.
En-tom'ic-al, 108.
En'to-moid.
En-to-mo-log'ic-al (-loj'-).
En-to-mol'o-gist, 108.
En-to-mol'o-gy, 108.
En-to-moph'a-goŭs.
En-to-mos'tra-can.
En-to-mos'tra-coŭs.
En-ton'ic.
En-to-zo'on [pl. En-to-zo'a, 198.]
En'trāils (-trālz), *n. pl.*
En'trance, *n.* 161.
En-trance', *v.* (131, 161) [Intrance, 203.]
En-tranced' (-trânst').
En-trânç'ing, 183.
En-trap', 10.
En-trapped' (-trapt'), 165, Note C, p. 34.
En-trēat', 13.
En-trēat'ed.
En-trēat'ing.
En-trēat'y.
Entrée (Fr.) (*äng trā'*).
Entremets (Fr.) (*ång-truh-ma'*), *n. pl.*
Entrepot (Fr.) (*äng-truh-po'*).
Entresol (Fr.) (*ång-truh-sol'*).
En'try (15, 93) [pl. En'-tries (-triz), 99, 190.]
[Entwine, 201, 203.— See Intwine.]
E-nu'cle-ate, 73, 179.
E-nu'cle-āt-ed.
E-nu'cle-āt-ing.
E-nu-cle-a'tion.
E-nu'mer-ate, 73.
E-nu'mer-āt-ed, 183.
E-nu'mer-āt-ing.
E-nu-mer-a'tion.

E-nu'mer-āt-ĭve [so Sm.; *e-nu'mer-a-tiv*, Wr. Wb. Gd. 155.]
E-nun'ci-ate (*-shĭ-at*) (171) [so Wk. Sm. Wr.; *e-nun'shāt*, Wb. Gd. 155.]
E-nun'ci-āt-ed (*-shĭ-*).
E-nun'ci-āt-ing (*-shĭ-*).
E-nun-ci-a'tion (*-shĭ-*).
E-nun'ci-āt-ĭve (*-shĭ-āt-*) [so Sm.; *e-nun'shĭ-a-tiv*, Wr.; *e-nun'sha-tiv*, Wb. Gd. 155.]
E-nun'ci-a-to-ry (*-shĭ-*).
En-vel'op, *v.* (170) [Envelope, 203.]
En-vel-ōpe' (Fr.) (*äng-vel-ōp'*, or *on-vel-ōp'*), *n.* [*ang-vel-ōp'*, Gd.; *on-ve-lōp'*, Wk.; *ŏngv'-lŏp*, Sm.; *äng-ve-lōp'*, or *ĕn-ve-lōp'*, Wr. 154, 155.] [Envelop, 203.]

☞ The French form of this word as a noun, *envelope*, is more in use than the English form, *envelop*. When the last is used it should be pronounced *en-vel op*, like the verb. Walker, who gives only the French form, and pronounces it *en-ve-lōp'*, remarks, however, that "it ought to be pronounced like the verb to *envelop*."

En-vel'oped (*-opt*), 150.
En-vel'op-ing.
En-vel'op-ment.
En-ven'om, 169.
En-ven'omed (*-umd*), 150
En-ven'om-ing.
En'vi-a-ble, 104, 169.
En'vĭed, 99, 186.
En'vi-er.
En'vi-oŭs.
En-vi'ron, 49, N.; 104.
En-vi'roned (*-rund*), 150.
En-vi'ron-ment.
En-vi'rons, *or* En'vi-rons (*-ronz*) [so Wr. Gd.; *en'vi-ronz*, Sm.; *on'vi-rōnz*, or *en-vi'-ronz*, Wk. 155.]

☞ Though Walker puts the pronunciation *on'-vi-rons* first, he says: "This word is in general use, and ought to be pronounced like the English verb to *environ*."

En'voy, 15, 27.
En'vy, 15, 93.
En'vy-ing.
[Enwrap, 201, 203.—*See* Inwrap.]
E'o-cene, 171.
E-o'li-an [Æolian, 203.]
E-ol'ic [Æolic, 203.]
E-ol'i-pile (81) [Æolipile, 203.]
E'on [Æon, 203.]
E'pact, 10, 13, 70.
Ep'arch (*-ark*), 52.
Ep'arch-y (*-ark-*).
E-pâule'ment [Epaulment, 203.]
Ep'âu-let (171) [Epaulette, 203.]
E-pen'the-sis (Gr.) [pl. E-pen'the-sēs (*-sēz*), 198.]
Épergne (Fr.) (*ā-pêrn'*).
E'pha (*e'fa*) (72) [Ephah, 203.]
E-phem'er-a, *n. sing.* & *pl.*

☞ *Ephemera* is singular in the sense of *a fever that continues only one day*, and plural in the sense of *insects that live but a day.*

E-phem'er-al, 171.
E-phem'er an.
E-phem'er-ic, 109.
E-phem'er-is (L.) (233, Exc.) [pl. Eph-e-mĕr'-i-dēs (*-dēz*), 198.]
E-phem'er-ist.
E-phem'er-on [pl. E-phem'er-a, 198.]
E-phe'sian (*-zhan*).
Eph-i-al'tēs (*-tēz*), *n. sing.*
Eph'od (*ef'od*) [so Sm. Wr. Wb. Gd.; *ef'od*, or *e'fod*, Wk. 155.]
Ep'ic, 170.
Ep'i-carp.
Ep-i-ce'di-al, 169.
Ep-i-ce'di-an.
Ep-i-ce'di-um.
Ep'i-cene, 171.
Ep-i-ce-ras'tic, 108.
Ep-i-chi-re'ma (*-kĭ-*) (Gr.) [pl. Ep-i-chi-re'-ma-ta, 198.]
Ep-ic-te'tian (*-shan*).
Ep'i-cure, 169, 170.
Ep-i-cu-re'an (110) [so Wk. Sm. Wr.; *ep-i-ku're-an*, or *e-pi-ku-re'an*, Wb. Gd. 110, 155.]
Ep-i-cu're-an-ism (*-izm*) (136) [so Sm. Wb. Gd.; *ep-i-ku-re'an-izm*, or *ep-i-ku're-an-ism*, Wr. 155.]
Ep'i-cūr-ism (*-izm*), 49, N.; 136.
Ep'i-cȳ cle, 78, 164.
Ep-i-cy'cloid.
Ep-i-cȳ-cloid'al [so Gd.; *ep-i-sĭ-cloid'al*, Wr. 155.]
Ep-i-dem'ic, 231.
Ep-i-dem'ic-al.
Ep'i-dem-y.
Ep-i-der'mal.
Ep-i-der'mic, 109.
Ep-i-der'mic-al, 108.
Ep-i-der'mi-dal.
Ep-i-der'mis (L.) [pl. Ep-i-der'mi-dēs (*-dēz*) 198.]
Ep'i-dote, 170.
Ep-i-gas'tric, 109.
Ep-i-gas'tro-cele.
Ep-i-ge'al.
Ep-i-glot'tic.
Ep-i-glot'tis, 170.
Ep'i-gram, 169, 170.
Ep-i-gram-mat'ic, 170.
Ep-i-gram-mat'ic-al.
Ep-i-gram'ma-tist.
Ep'i-grăph, 127.
E-pig'y-noŭs (*-pij'-*).
Ep'i-lep-sy, 169.
Ep-i-lep'tic, 109.
Ep-i-lep'tic-al, 108.
E-pil'o-gism (*-jizm*), 136.
E-pil-o-gist'ic.
Ep'i-lŏgue (*-log*), 87, 168, 171.
Ep-i-nĭ'cion (*-nish'un*) [so Sm. Wb. Gd.; *ep-i-nĭsh'i-un*, Wk. Wr. 155.]
E-piph'a-ny (*pif'-*), 171.
Ep-i-pho-ne'ma [so Wk. Wr. Wb. Gd.; *e-pif-o-ne'ma*, Sm. 155.]
E-piph'o-ra (*-e-pif'-*)
Ep-i-phyl'loŭs, *or* E-piph'yl-loŭs [*See* Adenophyllous.]
Ep-i-phys'e-al.
E-piph'y-sis (*-pif'-*), 171.
Ep'i-phȳte.
E-piph'y-tal (*-pif'-*) [so Wb. Gd., *ep-i-fī'tal*, Wr. 155.]
Ep-i-phyt'ic.
E-pip'lo-ce, 163.
E-pip'lo-cele.
E-pip'lo-ic [so Wr.; *ep-i-plo'ic*, Gd. 155.]

E-pip'lo-on.
E-pis'co-pa-cy, 169, 171.
E-pis'co-pal.
E-pis-co-pa'li-an.
E-pis-co-pa'li-an-ism (-*izm*), 136.
E-pis'co-pate.
Ep'i-sode, 78, 169.
Ep-i-so'di-al.
Ep-i-sod'ic.
Ep-i-sod'ic-al.
Ep-i-spas'tic.
Ep'i-sperm.
E-pis'tle (-*pis'l*), 162, 171.
E-pis'to-la-ry, 72.
Ep-is-tol'ic.
Ep-is-tol'ic-al.
E-pis-to-lo-graph'ic.
E-pis-to-log'ra-phy.
E-pis'tro-phe, 163.
Ep'i-style.
Ep'i-tăph (-*tăf*), [*not* ep'i-täf, 127, 153.]
Ep-i-ta'phi-an.
Ep-i-taph'ic.
E-pit'a-sis.
Ep-i-tha-la'mi-um.
Ep'i-thet, 78, 169.
Ep-i-thet'ic.
E-pit'o-me (163) [pl. E-pit'o-mes (-*mez*).]
E-pit'o-mist.
E-pit'o-mize, 202.
E-pit'o-mized, 183.
E-pit'o-mīz-er.
E-pit'o-mīz-ing.
Ep'i-trite.
E-pit'ro-pe, 163.
Ep-i-zo'an.
Ep-i-zo-ot'ic.
Ep'och (*ep'ok*) [so Sm. Wb. Gd.; *ep'ok*, or *ē'pok*, Wk. Wr. 155.]
Ep'o-cha (-*ka*).
Ep'ode [so Sm. Wb. Gd., *ep'ōd*, or *ē'pōd*, Wk. 155.]
Ep-od'ic [so Gd.; *e-pod'-ik*, Wr. 155.]
Ep-o-pee', 122.
Eprouvette (Fr.) (*ā-proo-vet'*).
Ep-u-lot'ic.
Ep-u-ra'tion.
E-qua-bil'i-ty (*ē-kwa-*), *or* Eq-ua-bil'i-ty (*ĕk-wa-*), 171.
E'qua-ble (*ē'kwa-bl*), or Eq'ua-ble (*ek'wa-bl*) (34, 164) [*e'kwa-bl*, Wk. Wr. Wb. Gd., *ek'wa-bl*, Sm. 155.]
E'qua-bly (*e'kwa-*), *or* Eq'ua-bly (*ek'wa-*).
E'qual, 34, 52.
[E q u a l e d, 203. — *See* Equalled.]
[E q u a l i n g, 203. — *See* Equalling.]
E-qual'i-ty (-*kwol'*-), 169.
E-qual-i-za'tion.
E'qual-ize, 202.
E'qual-ized, 183.
E'qual-īz-ing.
E'qualled (*e'kwald*) [E q u a l e d, Wb. Gd. 203. — *See* 177, and Note E, p. 70.]
E'qual-ling [E q u a l-i n g, Wb. Gd. 203.]
E'qual-ly, 93, 170.
[E q u a n g u l a r, 203. — *See* Equiangular.]
E-qua-nim'i-ty, 169, 171.
E-qua'tion, 34, 52.
E-qua'tor, 171.
E-qua-to'ri-al [so Wk. Wr. Wb. Gd., *ek-wa-to'rĭ-al*, Sm. 155.]
Eq'uer-ry (*ek'wer-y*, or *e-kwer'y*) (171, 190) [so Wr.; *ek'wer-y*, Sm.; *e-kwer'y*, Wk. Gd. 155.] [E q u e r y, 203.]
E-ques'tri-an.
E-ques'tri-an-ism (-*izm*).
E-qui-an'gu-lar (-*ang'*-) [so Wr. Wb. Gd.; *ek-wi-ang'gu-lar*, Sm. 155.]
E-qui-dis'tant [so Wk. Wr. Wb. Gd.; *ek-wi-dis'tant*, Sm. 155.]
E-qui-lat'er-al [so Wk. Wr. Wb. Gd.; *ek-wi-lat'er-al*, Sm. 155.]
E-qui-li'brate [so Wk. Wr. Wb. Gd.; *ek-wi-li'brāt*, Sm. 155.]
E-qui-li'brāt-ed.
E-qui-li'brāt-ing.
E-qui-li-bra'tion.
E-quil'i-brist, 169.
E-qui-lib'ri-um (171) [so Wk. Wr. Wb. Gd.; *ek-wi-lib'ri-um*, Sm. 155.]
E-qui-mul'ti-ple (164) [so Wr. Wb. Gd.; *ek-wi-mul'ti-pl*, Sm. 155.]
E-qui'nal.
E'quine, 34, 52.
E-qui-noc'tial (-*shal*) [so Wk. Wr. Wb. Gd.; *ek-wi-nok'shal*, Sm. 155.]
E'qui-nox [so Wk. Wr. Wb. Gd., *ek'wi-noks*, Sm. 155.]
E-quip', 16, 34, 52.
Eq'ui-page (*ek'wĭ-*), 171. [*not* e-kwip'āj, 153.]
E-quip'ment.
E'qui-poise (-*poiz*) (171) [so Wk. Wr. Wb. Gd.; *ek'wi-poiz*, Sm. 155.]
E-qui-pol'lence (169, 170) [so Wk. Wr. Wb. Gd., *ek-wĭ-pol'lens*, Sm. 155.]
E-qui-pol'len-cy.
E-qui-pol'lent [so Wk. Wr. Wb. Gd.; *ek-wĭ-pol'lent*, Sm. 155.]
E-qui-pon'der-ance [so Wk. Wr. Wb. Gd., *ek-wĭ-pon'der-ans*, Sm. 155.]
E-qui-pon'der-ant.
E-quipped' (-*kwipt*), 165, 176; Note C, p. 34.
E-quip'ping.
Eq-ui-se'tum (*ek-wĭ-*).
E-quis'o-nance [so Wr. Wb. Gd.; *ek-wĭ-so'-nans*, Sm. 155.]
Eq'ui-ta-ble (*ek'wi-ta-bl*), 122, 164, 171.
Eq'ui-ta-bly (*ek'wi-*).
Eq'ui-tant (*ek'wi-*).
Eq-ui-ta'tion (*ek-wi-*).
Eq'ui-ty (*ek'wi-ty*).
E-quiv'a-lence, 169.
E-quiv'a-len-cy.
E-quiv'a-lent.
E-quiv'o-cal, 171.
E-quiv'o-cal-ly.
E-quiv'o-cate, 73.
E-quiv'o-cāt-ed, 183.
E-quiv'o-cāt-ing.
E-quiv-o-ca'tion.
E-quiv'o-cāt-or.
E-quiv'o-ca-to-ry.
Eq'ui-voke (*ek'wĭ*).
E-qui-voque' (Fr.) (*ā-ke-vōk'*).
E-quiv'o-roŭs.
E'ra, 13, 49, N.; 72.
E-rad'i-ca-ble, 164.
E-rad'i-cate, 73, 169.
E-rad'i-cāt-ed, 183.

E-rad′i-căt-ing.
E-rad-i-ca′tion, 112.
E-rad′i-căt-ĭve (84) [so Sm.; *e-rad′i-ka-tiv*, Wr. Wb. Gd. 155.]
E-răs′a-ble, 164, 183.
E-rase′, 23.
E-rased′ (*-răst′*), 183.
E-răs′er.
E-răs′ing.
E-ra′sion (*-zhun*).
E-ră′sure (*-zhur*), 171.
Ere (*êr*), *ad.* & *prep.* before. [*See* Air, Heir, 160.]
E-rect′, 15.
E-rect′a-ble, 164.
E-rect′ed.
E-rect′ĭle, 152.
E-rect′ing.
E-rec′tion.
Ĕr′e-mite.
Ĕr-e-mit′ic.
Ĕr-e-mit′ic-al.
Ĕr′e-thism (*-thizm*), 136.
Ĕr-e-this′tic.
Er′got, 21, N.
Er′got-ism (*-izm*).
Ĕr-i-om′e-ter (108) [so Sm. Wr.; *ē-ri-om′e-tur*, Gd. 155.]
Er′mĭne (152) [Er-min, 203.]
Er′mĭned (*-mĭnd*), 150, 171, 183.
E-rode′, 24.
E-rōd′ed, 183.
E-rōd′ent.
E-rōd′ing.
E-rose′ (*-rōs′*), 121.
E-ro′sion (*-zhun*).
E-ro′sĭve, 84.
E-rot′ic, 109.
E-rot′ic-al, 108.
Ĕr-o-to-ma′ni-a.
Ĕr-o-tom′a-ny.
[Erpetology, 203. — *See* Herpetology.]
Err, 21, N.; 171, 175.
Ĕr′rand (170) [so Sm. Wr. Wb. Gd.; *ăr′-rand*, Wk. 155.]

☞ Though Walker pronounces this word *ar′-rand*, he says, that it "might, perhaps, without pedantry, be more properly pronounced as it is written."

Ĕr′rant.
Ĕr′rant-ry.
Ĕr-ra′ta (L.), *n. pl.* [*See* Erratum.]
Ĕr-rat′ic, 109.
Ĕr-rat′ic-al, 108.
Ĕr-ra′tum (L.) [pl. Er-ra′ta, 198.]
Ĕr′rhīne (*-rīn*), 162, 171.
Erred (*erd*), 21, N.; 171.
Err′ing.
Ĕr-ro′ne-oŭs.
Ĕr′ror, 15, 66, N.; 88.
Erse, 21, N.; 171.
Ĕr-u-bes′cence, 89.
Ĕr-u-bes′cen-cy, 89, 169.
Ĕr-u-bes′cent, 89.
E-ruc-ta′tion.
Ĕr′u-dīte (89) [so Sm. Wb. Gd.; *ĕr-u-dīt′*, Wk.; *ĕr′u-dīt*, or *ĕr′-u-dīt*, Wr. 155.]
Ĕr-u-dĭ′tion (*-dish′un*).
E-ru′gi-noŭs (*-roo′-*) [Æruginous, 203.]
E-rupt′ed.
E-rup′tion.
E-rup′tĭve, 84.
Ĕr-y-sip′e-las, 169, 171.
Ĕr-y-si-pel′a-toŭs, 116.
Ĕr-y-the′ma.
Ĕr-y-the-mat′ic.
Ĕr-y-them′a-toŭs.
Es-ca-lade′, *n.* & *v.* 122.
Es-ca-lād′ed.
Es-ca-lād′ing.
Escal′op (*skol′up*) [so Wk. Gd.; *skol′lop*, or *es-kol′up*, Wr. 155. [Scallop, Scollop, 203.]

☞ The more common form of spelling this word, at the present time, is *scallop*.

Es-ca-pade′, 122.
Es-cape′ (23) [so Wr. Wb. Gd.; *e-skāp′*, Wk. Sm. 155.]
Es-căped′ (*es-kāpt′*), 165, 183; Note C, p. 34.
Es-cape′ment.
Es-căp′ing.
Es-carp′, *n.* & *v.*
Es-carped′ (*-karpt′*), 165.
Es-carp′ing.
Es-carp′ment.
Esch′a-lot′ (*esh-a-lot′*) [so Sm. Gd.; *sha-lot′*, Wk.; *esh-a-lot′*, or *sha-lot′*, Wr. 155.] [Shallot, 203.]
Es′char (*-kar*), 52, 171.
Es-cha-rot′ic (*-ka-*), 109.
Es-cha-tol′o-gy (*-ka-*).
Es-chēat′, *n.* & *v.*
Es-chēat′a-ble, 164.
Es-chēat′age.
Es-chēat′ed.
Es-chēat′ing.
Es-chēat′or.
Es-chew′ (*-choo′*), 19, 26.
Es-chewed′ (*-chood′*), 165.
Es-chew′ing (*-choo′-*)
Es′cort, *n.* 103, 161.
Es-cort′, *v.* 103, 161.
Es-cort′ed.
Es-cort′ing.
Es-cri-toir′ (*es-kre-twor′*) [so Wb. Gd.; *es-kru-tōr′*, Wk. 145.]
Escritoire (Fr.) (*es-kre-twor′*) [so Wr.; *es-kre-twar′*, Sm. 154, 155.]

☞ Walker, Webster, and Goodrich give only the Anglicized form of this word (*escritoir*). Smart and Worcester give only the French form (*escritoire*).

Es-cri-to′ri-al.
Es-cu-la′pi-an, 169.
Es′cu-lent.
Es-cu′ri-al, 169.
Es-cutch′eon (*-kuch′-un*), 171.
Es-cutch′eoned (*-kuch′-und*).
[Esophagus, 203. — *See* Œsophagus.]
Es-o-tĕr′ic, 109.
Es-o-tĕr′ic-al, 108.
Es-o-tĕr′i-cism (*-sizm*).
Es-pal′ier (*-yur*), 171.
Es-pĕ′cial (*-pesh′al*), 231.
Es-pĕ′cial-ly (*-pesh′al-*), 171.
Es-pied′, 99, 186.
Es′pi-o-nage (*es′pi-o-nāj*, or *es′pi-o-nazh*) [so Wr. Gd.; *es′pĭ-o-nazh*, Sm. 155.]
Es-pla-nade′, 122.
Es-pou′sal (*-zal*), 171.
Es-pou′sals (*-zalz*).
Es-pouse′ (*-pouz′*).
Es-poused′ (*-pouzd′*), 183.
Es-pous′er (*-pouz′-*).
Es-pous′ing (*-pouz′-*).
Es-prit de corps (Fr.) (*es-pre′duh-kōr′*).
Es-py′, 25.
Es-py′ing.

Es'qui-mau (*es'kĭ-mō*) [pl. Es'qui-maux (*-mō*, or *-mōz*), 198.]
Es-quire' (*-kwīr'*).
Es'sāy, *n.* 161.
Es-sāy', *v.* 161.
Es-sāyed' (*-sād'*), 187.
Es-sāy'ing.
Es'sāy-ist, *or* Es-sāy'-ist [so Wr.; *es'sā-ist*, Sm.; *es-sā'ist*, Wk. Wb. Gd. 155.]
Es'sence, 170, 171.
Es'senced (*-senst*), 183.
Es-senç'ing.
Es-sen'tial (*-shal*).
Es-sen-ti-al'i-ty (*-shĭ-*).
Es-sen'tial-ly (*-shal-*), 170.
Es-tab'lish, 104.
Es-tab'lished (*-lisht*).
Es-tab'lish-ing.
Es-tab'lish-ment.
Es-ta-fet'.
Es-ta-fette' (Fr.).

☞ Smart gives only the English form of this word (*estafet*), Worcester only the French form (*estafette*). Goodrich gives both forms.

Es-tate', 23.
Es-teem', 13.
Es-teem'a-ble, 164.
Es-teemed' (*-tēmd'*), 165.
Es-teem'ing.
[Esthetic, 203.—*See* Æsthetic.]
Es'ti-ma-ble, 164, 171.
Es'ti-mate, *n.* & *v.* 73.
Es'ti-māt-ed, 183.
Es'ti-māt-ing.
Es-ti-ma'tion, 112.
Es'ti-māt-ĭve, 84.
Es'ti-māt-or, 183.
Es'ti-val, 78.
Es-ti-va'tion [Æstivation, 203.]
Es-top'.
Es-topped' (*-topt'*).
Es-top'pel [Estopple, Estopel, 203.]
Es-to'vers (*-vurz*), *n. pl.*
Es-träde' (Fr.) (*es-träd'*) [so Sm. Wr.; *es-trād'*, Wb. Gd. 154, 155.]
Es-trānge', 23, 45.
Es-trānged', 165.
Es-trānge'ment, 185.
Es-trāng'ing, (*-tranj'-*).
Es-tra-pade', 122.
Es-trāy', 23.
Es-trēat'.
Es-trēat'ed.
Es-trēat'ing.
Es-trepe'ment.
Est'u-a-ry, 72.
Étagère (Fr.) (*ā-tä-zhêr'*).
Etch (*ech*), 15, 44; Note D, p. 37.
Etched (*echt*), Note C, p. 34.
Etch'er (*ech'-*), 77.
Etch'ing (*ech'-*).
E-ter'nal, 21, Note.
E-ter'nal-ly, 170.
E-ter'ni-ty, 78, 93, 169.
E-ter'nize, 202.
E-ter'nized, 183.
E-ter'nīz-ing.
E-te'si-an (*-zhĭ-an*) [so Sm. Wr.; *e-te'zhan*, Wb. Gd. 155.]
E'ther, 13, 37, 77.
E-the're-al, 49, N.; 169.
E-the're-al-ize, 202.
E-the're-al-ized, 183.
E-the're-al-īz-ing.
E-thĕr-i-fĭ-ca'tion.
E-thĕr'i-form, 169.
E-ther-ĭ-za'tion.
E'ther-ize, 202.
E'ther-ized, 183.
E'ther-īz-ing.
Eth'ic, 15, 37.
Eth'ic-al, 108.
Eth'ics.
E-thi-o'pi-an, 169.
E-thi-op'ic.
Eth'moid.
Eth-moid'al.
Eth'nic.
Eth'nic-al, 108.
Eth-nog'ra-pher, 108.
Eth-no-graph'ic.
Eth-no-graph'ic-al.
Eth-nog'ra-phy, 108.
Eth-no-log'ic (*-loj'-*).
Eth-nol'o-gist, 108.
Eth-nol'o-gy.
E'ti-o-late, 73, 122.
E'ti-o-lāt-ed, 183.
E'ti-o-lāt-ing.
E-ti-o-la'tion, 112.
E-ti-o-log'ic-al (*-loj'-*).
E-ti-ol'o-gy, 108.
Et-i-quette' (*-ket'*), 122.
Et-ne'an, 110.
E-trus'can.
Étui (Fr.) (*et-wē'*) [so Wk. Sm. Wb. Gd.; *ā-twē'*, Wr. 154, 155.]

☞ Webster and Goodrich, besides this French form of the word, give also the Anglicized form Etwee.

Et-y-mo-log'ic (*-loj'-*).
Et-y-mo-log'ic-al(*-loj'-*).
Et-y-mo-log'ic-al-ly (*-loj'-*).
Et-y-mol'o-gist, 108.
Et-y-mol'o-gy, 108, 170.
Et'y-mon [Gr. & L. pl. Et'y-ma; Eng. pl. Et'-y-mons (*-monz*), 198.]
Eū'cha-rist (*u'ka-*), 171.
Eu-cha-rist'ic (*u-ka-*).
Eū-cha-rist'ic-al (*u-ka-*).
Eū'chy-my (*u'ky-*).
Eū'cra-sy, 169.
Eū'cre (*u'kur*), 164, 171.
Eū-di-om'e-ter, 108.
Eū-di-o-met'ric.
Eū-di-o-met'ric-al.
Eū-di-om'e-try, 108.
Eū'lo-gist, 108.
Eū-lo-gist'ic, 169.
Eū-lo-gist'ic-al, 108.
Eū-lo'gi-um, 169.
Eū'lo gize, 202.
Eū'lo-gized, 183.
Eū'lo-gīz-ing.
Eū'lo-gy, 26, 93.
Eū'no-my.
Eū'nuch (*-nuk*).
Eū'pa-to-ry, 86.
Eū-pep'sy [so Sm. Wb. Gd.; *u'pep-sy*, Wk.; *u'pep-sy*, or *u-pep'sy*, Wr. 155.]
Eū-pep'tic.
Eū'phe-mism (*-mizm*), 136, 169.
Eū'phe-mist.
Eū-phe-mist'ic.
Eū-phe-mist'ic-al.
Eū-phon'ic, 109.
Eū-phon'ic-al, 108.
Eū-pho'ni-oŭs, 169.
Eū'pho-nism (*-nizm*).
Eū'pho-ny, 86, 93.
Eū'phra-sy, 169.
Eū'phu-ism (*-izm*).
Eū'phu-ist.
Eū-phu-ist'ic.
Eū-plas'tic, 109.
Eū-ri'pus, *or* Eū'ri-pus [so Wr.; *u-ri'pus*, Wk. Gd.; *u'rĭ-pus*, Sm. 155.]
Eū-roc'ly-don.
Eū'rope, 171.
Eū-ro-pe'an (110) [*not* u-ro'pe-an, 153.]

Eū′ryth-my [so Wr. Wb. Gd.; *u-rith′my*, Sm. 155 [Eurith-my, Sm. 203.]
Eū-sta′chi-an (*-kĭ-*).
Eū′style.
Eū-ter′pe-an, 110, 169.
Eū-tha-na′si-a (*-zhĭ-a*).
Eū′than-ā-sy (*-zy*) *or* Eū-than′a-sy [*u′than-ā-zy*, Sm.; *u-than′a-sy*, Wk.; *u-than′a-sy*, or *u′than-ā-zy*, Wr.; *u′tha-nā-sy*, or *u-than′a-sy*, Gd. 155.]
E-vac′u-ant.
E-vac′u-ate, 73, 89.
E-vac′u-āt-ed, 183.
E-vac′u-āt-ing.
E-vac-u-a′tion, 112.
E-vac′u-āt-ĭve [so Sm.; *e-vak′u-a-tiv*, Wr. Wb. Gd. 155.]
E-vac′u-āt-or.
E-vade′, 23.
E-vād′ed, 188.
E-vād′ing.
Ev-a-nes′cence, 171.
Ev-a-nes′cent.
E-van-gel′ic.
E-van-gel′ic-al, *or* Ev-an-gel′ic-al [so Wr.; *e-van-jel′ik-al*, Wb. Gd.; *ev-an-jel′ik-al*, Wk. Sm. 155.]
E-van-gel′ic-al-ly.
E-van-gel′i-cism(*-sizm*).
E-van′gel-ism (*-izm*).
E-van′gel-ist.
E-van′gel-ize.
E-van′gel-ized, 183.
E-van′gel-īz-ing.
E-vap′o-ra-ble, 164.
E-vap′o-rate, 73.
E-vap′o-rāt-ed.
E-vap′o-rāt-ing.
E-vap-o-ra′tion.
E-vap′o-ra-tĭve.
E-va′sion (*-zhun*).
E-va′sĭve, 84.
Eve, 13.
E-vec′tion.
E′ven (*e′vn*), 149.
E′vened (*e′vnd*), 150.
E′ven-ing (*e′vn-*).
E′ven-ness (*e′vn-*), 66, N.
E-vent′, 15.
E-vent′ful (*-fŏŏl*).
E-ven-tra′tion.
E-vent′u-al.
E-vent-u-al′i-ty.
E-vent′u-al-ly.

Ev′er, 15, 77.
Ev′er-glade.
Ev′er-green.
Ev-er-last′ing.
Ev′er-liv′ing.
Ev-er-more′.
E-ver′sion.
E-ver′sĭve, 21, N.
Ev′er-y, 132, 233, Exc.
Ev′er-y-whêre.
E-vict′.
E-vict′ed.
E-vict′ing.
E-vic′tion.
Ev′i-dence, 169.
Ev′i-denced (*-denst*).
Ev′i-denç-ing.
Ev′i-dent, 169.
E′vil (*e′vl*), 149.
E′vil-do′er (*e′vl-doo′-*).
E-vince′, 16.
E-vinced′ (*-vinst′*).
E-vinç′i-ble, 164.
E-vinç′ing.
E-vis′cer-ate, 73.
E-vis′cer-āt-ed.
E-vis′cer-āt-ing.
E-vis-cer-a′tion.
E-voke′, 24.
E-voked′ (*-vōkt′*).
Ev-o-lat′ic, 109.
Ev-o-la′tion.
Ev′o-lute, 170.
Ev-o-lu′tion.
E-volve′ (*-volv′*), 18.
E-volved′ (*-volvd′*), 183.
E-volv′ing.
E-vul′sion.
Ewe (*yoo*) (171), *n.* a female sheep. [*See* You, 160.] [pl. Ewes. — *See* Use, 160.]
Ewer (*yoor*) (171), *n.* a kind of pitcher. [*See* Your, 160.]
Ew′ry (*yoo′ry*), 49, N.
Ex-aç′er-bate (*egz-as′-*) (137) [so Wk. Sm. Wr.; *eks-a-ser′bāt*, Wb. Gd. 155.]
Ex-aç′er-bāt-ed (*egz-*).
Ex-aç′er-bāt-ing (*egz-*).
Ex-aç-er-ba′tion (*egz-*).
Ex-act′ (*egz-*), 40, 137.
Ex-act′ed (*egz-*).
Ex-act′er (*egz-*) [Ex-actor, 203.]
Ex-act′ing (*egz-*).
Ex-ac′tion (*egz-*).
Ex-act′or (*egz-*) [Ex-acter, 203.]
Ex-ag′ger-ate (*egz-aj′-*), 45, 171.

Ex-ag′ger-āt-ed (*egz-aj′-*), 183.
Ex-ag′ger-āt-ing (*egz-aj′-*).
Ex-ag-ger-a′tion (*egz-aj-*).
Ex-âlt′ (*egz-*), 17, 137.
Ex-âlt-a′tion (*egz-*).
Ex-âlt′ed (*egz-*).
Ex-am′in-a-ble (*egz-*), 164.
Ex-am-in-a′tion (*egz-*).
Ex-am′ĭne (*egz*), 152.
Ex-am′ĭned (*egz-*), 165.
Ex-am′in-er (*egz-*), 183.
Ex-am′in-ing (*egz-*).
Ex-am′ple (*egz-am′pl*) (137, 164) [so Wk. Sm. Wb. Gd.; *egz-ȧm′pl*, Wr. 155.]
Ex-an′them (*egz-*).
Ex-an-thē′ma (Gr.) [pl. *Ex-an-them′a-ta*, 198.]
Ex-an-them′a-toŭs.
Ex-an-the′sis, 125.
Ex′arch (*-ark*).
Ex′arch-āte (*-ark-*) [so Wr.; *eks-ark′āt*, Wb. Gd. 155.]
Ex-as′per-ate (*egz-*).
Ex-as′per-āt-ed (*egz-*).
Ex-as′per-āt-ing (*egz-*).
Ex-as-per-a′tion (*egz-*).
Ex-can-des′cence, 171.
Ex-can-des′cent.
Ex-car′nate, *a.* & *v.*
Ex-car′nāt-ed, 183.
Ex-car′nāt-ing.
Ex-car-na′tion.
Ex-car-ni-fĭ-ca′tion.
Ex ca-the′dra (L.).

☞ "The Latin will allow of *cath′e-dra* or *ca-the′dra*, but the latter is most common in English." *Goodrich.*

Ex′ca-vate (137) [so Sm. Wb. Gd.; *eks-kā′vāt*, Wk.; *eks′ka-vāt*, or *eks-kā′vāt*, Wr. 155.]
Ex′ca-vāt-ed, 183.
Ex′ca-vāt-ing.
Ex-ca-va′tion, 112.
Ex′ca-vāt-or.
Ex-ceed′, 13, 137, 169.
Ex-ceed′ed.
Ex-ceed′ing.
Ex-cel′, 15, 137.
Ex-celled′, 165, 176.
Ex′cel-lence, 170, 177.
Ex′cel-len-cy, 169.

Ex′cel-lent.
Ex-cel′ling.
[Excentric, 203.—*See* Eccentric.]
Ex-cept′, 15.
Ex-cept′ed.
Ex-cept′ing.
Ex-cep′tion.
Ex-cep′tion-a-ble, 164.
Ex-cep′tion-al.
Ex-cept′ĭve, 84.
Ex-cept′or.
Ex-cerpt′ [so Sm. Wb. Gd.; *eks-serpt′*, or *eks′serpt*, Wr. 155.]
Ex-cerp′ta (L.), *n. pl.*
Ex-cess′, 121, 137, 171.
Ex-ces′sĭve, 84.
Ex-chānge′, 23.
Ex-chānge-a-bil′i-ty.
Ex-chānge′a-ble, 183.
Ex-chāng′er (*-chānj′-*).
Ex-cheq′uer (*-chek′ur*), 171.
Ex-cīs′a-ble (*-sīz′-*), 164.
Ex-cise′ (*-sīz′*), *n. & v.*
Ex-cised′ (*-sīzd′*), 150.
Ex-cise′man (*-sīz′-*), 196.
Ex-cīs′ing (*-sīz′-*).
Ex-cĭ′sion (*-sizh′un*).
Ex-cīt-a-bil′i-ty, 169.
Ex-cīt′a-ble, 164, 183.
Ex-cīt′ant, *or* Ex′ci-tant [so Wr.; *eks-sīt′-ant*, Wb. Gd.; *eks′sĭ-tant*, Sm. 155.]
Ex-ci-ta′tion.
Ex-cīt′a-tĭve, 84.
Ex-cīt′a-to-ry, 86.
Ex-cite′, 25, 137.
Ex-cīt′ed, 183.
Ex-cite′ment, 185.
Ex-cīt′er.
Ex-cīt′ing.
Ex-clāim′, 23.
Ex-clāimed′, 165.
Ex-clāim′ing.
Ex-cla-ma′tion, 171.
Ex-clam′a-tĭve.
Ex-clam′a-to-ry, 86.
Ex-clude′, 26.
Ex-clūd′ed, 183.
Ex-clūd′ing.
Ex-clu′sion (*-zhun*).
Ex-clu′sion-ist (*-zhun-*).
Ex-clu′sĭve, 84.
Ex-cog′i-tate (*-koj′-*).
Ex-cog′i-tāt-ed (*-koj′-*).
Ex-cog′i-tāt-ing (*-koj′-*).
Ex-cog-i-ta′tion (*-koj-*).
Ex-com-mu′ni-ca-ble, 164.
Ex-com-mu′ni-cate.
Ex-com-mu′ni-cāt-ed.
Ex-com-mu′ni-cāt-ing.
Ex-com-mu-ni-cā′tion.
Ex-co′ri-ate, 49, N.
Ex-co′ri-āt-ed, 183.
Ex-co′ri-āt-ing.
Ex-co-ri-a′tion.
Ex-cor-ti-ca′tion.
Ex′cre-ment.
Ex-cre-ment′al.
Ex-cre-men-tĭ′tious (*-tish′us*).
Ex-cres′cence, 171.
Ex-cres′cent.
Ex-crete′, 13, 137.
Ex-crēt′ed, 183.
Ex-crēt′ing.
Ex-cre′tion.
Ex-crēt′ĭve, *or* Ex′cre-tĭve [*eks-krēt′iv*, Sm.; *eks′kre-tiv*, Wk. Wb. Gd.; *eks′kre-tiv*, or *eks-krēt′iv*, Wr. 155.]
Ex-crēt′o-ry, *or* Ex′-cre-to-ry [*eks-krēt′o-ry*, Sm.; *eks′kre-to-ry*, Wk. Wb. Gd.; *eks′kre-to-ry*, or *eks-krēt′o-ry*, Wr. 155.]
Ex-cru′ci-ate (*-kroo′shi-āt*) [so Wk. Sm. Wr.; *eks-krū′shāt*, Wb. Gd. 155.]
Ex-cru′ci-āt-ed (*-kroo′-shĭ-*).
Ex-cru′ci-āt-ing (*-kroo′-shĭ-*).
Ex-cru-ci-a′tion (*-kroo′-shĭ-*).
Ex-cul′pate, 73, 137.
Ex-cul′pāt-ed, 183.
Ex-cul′pāt-ing.
Ex-cul-pa′tion, 112.
Ex-cul′pa-to-ry, 86.
Ex-cŭr′rent, 170.
Ex-cur′sion.
Ex-cur′sĭve.
Ex-cūs′a-ble (*-kūz′-*), 183.
Ex-cūs′a-to-ry (*kūz′-*).
Ex-cūse, *n.* 26, 161.
Ex-cuse′ (*-kūz′*), *v.* 136, 137, 161.
Ex-cūsed′ (*-kūzd′*), 183.
Ex-cūs′ing (*-kūz′-*).
Ex′e-cra-ble, 164.
Ex′e-cra-bly, 93.
Ex′e-crate, 137, 169.
Ex′e-crāt-ed.
Ex′e-crāt-ing.
Ex-e-cra′tion.
Ex′e-cra-to-ry (86) [so Wr. Wb. Gd.; *eks′e-crāt-o-ry*, Sm. 155.]
Ex′e-cute, 169.
Ex′e-cūt-ed, 183.
Ex′e-cūt-er [Executor, 203.]
Ex′e-cūt-ing.
Ex-e-cu′tion, 112.
Ex-e-cu′tion-er.
Ex-ec′u-tive (*egz-*), 40, N.; 84, 137.
Ex-ec′u-tor (*egz-*) [Executer, 203.]
Ex-ec-u-to′ri-al (*egz-*).
Ex-ec′u-to-ry (*egz-*).
Ex-ec′u-trix (*egz-*).
Ex-e-ge′sis (Gr.), 113.
Ex′e-gēte.
Ex-e-get′ic, 109.
Ex-e-get′ic-al, 108.
Ex-em′plar (*egz-*), 137.
Ex′em-pla-ry (*egz′-*), 107, 137.

☞ This word, as pronounced by all the orthoepists, is an exception to the general rule by which *x* at the end of an accented syllable has the sound of *ks*. It is sounded as *gz* in *exemplary*, because it has that sound in the primitive *exemplar*.

Ex-em-pli-fĭ-ca′tion (*egz-*), 112, 116.
Ex-em′pli-fīed (*egz-*), 99.
Ex-em′pli-fȳ (*egz-*), 94.
Ex-em′pli-fȳ-ing (*egz-*).
Ex-empt′ (*egz-emt′*), 137, 162.
Ex-emp′tion (*egz-em′-*).
Ex-e-qua′tur (L.).
Ex-e′qui-al.
Ex′e-quīes (*-kwiz*), *n.* pl. 171.
Ex′er-cise (*-sīz*), 137, 171.
Ex′er-cised (*-sīzd*), 183.
Ex-er-cīs′a-ble (*-sīz′-*), 164.
Ex-ergue′ (*egz-erg′*), 171.
Ex-ert′ (*egz-*), 21, N.; 137.
Ex-ert′ed (*egz-*).
Ex-ert′ing (*egz-*).
Ex-er′tion (*egz-*).
Ex-fo′li-ate.
Ex-fo′li-āt-ed, 183.
Ex-fo′li-āt-ing.
Ex-fo-li-a′tion.
Ex-fo′li-a-tĭve.

Ex-hāl'a-ble (*egz-*), 137, 164.
Ex-hāl'ant (*egz-*), 183.
Ex-ha-la'tion (*egz-*).
Ex-hale' (*egz-*), 23, 137, 139.
Ex-hāled' (*egz-*), 183.
Ex-hāl'ing (*egz-*).
Ex-hâust' (*egz-*), 17, 137, 139.
Ex-hâust'ed (*egz-*).
Ex-hâust'i-ble (*egz-*), 164, 169, 171.
Ex-hâust'ing (*egz-*).
Ex-hâust'ion (*egz-hawst'yun*), 171.
Ex-hâust'ĭve (*egz-*), 84.
Ex-hib'it (*egz-*), 137, 139.
Ex-hib'it-ed (*egz-*).
Ex-hib'it-er (*egz-*).
Ex-hib'it-ing (*egz-*).
Ex-hi-bĭ'tion (*-bish'un*), 171, 231, Exc.
Ex-hib'it-ĭve (*egz-*), 84.
Ex-hib'it-o-ry (*egz-*).
Ex-hil'a-rant (*egz-*).
Ex-hil'a-rate (*egz-*), 139.
Ex-hil'a-rāt-ed (*egz-*).
Ex-hil'a-rāt-ing (*egz-*).
Ex-hil-a-ra'tion (*egz-*).
Ex-hort' (*egz-*), 17, 137, 139.
Ex-hor-ta'tion (*eks-*).
Ex-hort'a-tĭve (*egz-*).
Ex-hort'a-to-ry (*egz-*).
Ex-hort'er (*egz-*).
Ex-hu-ma'tion (*eks-*).
Ex-hume' (*egz-*), 26, 137, 139.
Ex-humed' (*egz-hūmd'*), 183.
Ex-hūm'ing (*egz-*).
[Exiccate, 203.—*See* Exsiccate.]
Ex'i-gence, 137, 169.
Ex'i-gen-cy, 169.
Ex'i-gent.
Ex-i-gu'i-ty, 169.
Ex-ig'u-oŭs.
Ex'īle (*eks'īl*), *n.* 81, 137.
Ex'īle (*eks'īl*), *v.* [so Sm. Gd.; *eg-zīl'*, Wk.; *eg-zīl'*, or *eks'-īl*, Wr. 155.]
Ex-īle' (*eg-zīl'*), *a.* [so Wk. Sm. Wr.; *eks'īl*, Gd. 155.]

☞ "Authority is certainly on the side of the ultimate accent; but it may be questioned whether it is not contrary to analogy." *Walker.*

Ex'īled, 183.
Ex'īl-ing.
Ex-il'i-ty (*egz-*).
Ex-ist' (*egz-*), 137.
Ex-ist'ed (*egz-*).
Ex-ist'ence (*egz-*), 169.
Ex-ist'ent (*egz-*).
Ex-ist'ing (*egz-*).
Ex'it, 137.
Ex-mayor (*-ma'ur*, or *-mêr'*), 222, N.
Ex'ode.
Ex'o-dus.
Ex of-fĭ'ci-o (L.) (*eks-of-fish'ĭ-o*).
Ex'o-gen.
Ex-og'en-oŭs (*-oj'-*).
Ex-on'er-ate (*egz-*), 137.
Ex-on'er-āt-ed (*egz-*), 183.
Ex-on'er-āt-ing (*egz-*).
Ex-on-er-a'tion (*egz-*).
Ex-on'er-āt-ĭve (*egz-*) [so Sm.; *egz-on'ur-a-tiv*, Wr. Wb. Gd. 155.]
Ex-o-phy̆l'loŭs, *or* Ex-oph'y̆l-lous. [*See* Adenophyllous.]
Ex'o-ra-ble, 164.
Ex-or'bi-tance (*egz-*).
Ex-or'bi-tan-cy (*egz-*), 169.
Ex-or'bi-tant (*egz-*).
Ex'or-cise (*-awr-sīz*) (202) [*not* eks-or'siz, 135.]
Ex'or-cīsed (*-sīzd*), 183.
Ex'or-cīs-er (*-sīz-*).
Ex'or-cīs-ing (*-sīz-*).
Ex'or-cism (*-sizm*), 136.
Ex'or-cist.
Ex-or'di-al (*egz-*).
Ex'os-mose [so Sm. Gd.; *eks-os-mōs'*, Wr. 155.]
Ex-os'se-oŭs [so Wr. Wb. Gd.; *eks-osh''us*, Sm. (*See* § 26): *eks-osh'e-us*, Wk. 155.]
Ex-os-to'sis, 109, 125.
Ex-o-tĕr'ic, 109.
Ex-o-tĕr'ic-al, 108.
Ex-ot'ic.
Ex-ot'ic-al.
Ex-ot'i-cism (*-sizm*).
Ex-pand', 10, 137.
Ex-pand'ed.
Ex-pand'ing.
Ex-panse', 10, 137.
Ex-pan-si-bil'i-ty.
Ex-pan'si-ble, 164.
Ex-pan'sion.
Ex-pan'sĭve, 84.

Ex-pe-dĭ'tious (*-dish'us*).
Ex-pa'ti-ate (*-shĭ āt*) [so Wk. Sm. Wr.; *eks-pa'shāt*, Wb. Gd. 155.]
Ex-pa'ti-āt-ed (*-shĭ-*).
Ex-pa'ti-āt-ing (*-shĭ-*).
Ex-pa-ti-a'tion (*-shĭ-*).
Ex-pa'ti-āt-or (*-shĭ-*).
Ex-pa'ti-a-to-ry (*-shĭ-*).
Ex-pa'tri-ate.
Ex-pa'tri-āt-ed, 183.
Ex-pa'tri-āt-ing.
Ex-pa-tri-a'tion.
Ex-pect', 15, 137.
Ex-pect'ance, 169.
Ex-pect'an-cy, 169.
Ex-pect'ant.
Ex-pect-a'tion.
Ex-pect'ed, 150.
Ex-pect'er.
Ex-pect'ing.
Ex-pec'to-rant.
Ex-pec'to-rate, 73.
Ex-pec'to-rāt-ed.
Ex-pec'to-rāt-ing.
Ex-pec-to-ra'tion.
Ex-pec'to-rāt-ĭve (84) [so Sm.; *eks-pek'to-ra-tiv*, Wr. Wb. Gd. 155.]
Ex-pe'di-ence.
Ex-pe'di-en-cy, 169.
Ex-pe'di-ent [so Sm. Wr. Wb. Gd.; *eks-pe'di-ent*, or *eks-pe'ji-ent*, Wk. 155.]
Ex'pe-dite.
Ex'pe-dīt-ed, 183.
Ex'pe-dīt-ing.
Ex-pe-dĭ'tion (*-dish'un*), 231, Exc.
Ex-pe-dĭ'tion-a-ry (*-dish'un-*), 72.
Ex-pe-dĭ'tious (*-dish'us*).
Ex-pel', 15, 137.
Ex-pel'la-ble, 164, 176.
Ex-pelled' (*-peld'*), 165.
Ex-pel'ler, 176.
Ex-pel'ling.
Ex-pend', 15, 137.
Ex-pend'ed.
Ex-pend'ing.
Ex-pend'i-ture, 169.
Ex-pense', 15, 137.
Ex-pen'sĭve, 84.
Ex-pe'ri-ence, 169.
Ex-pe'ri-enced (*-enst*).
Ex-pe'ri-enç-ing, 183.
Ex-pĕr'i-ment, 169.
Ex-pĕr-i-ment'al.
Ex-pĕr-i-ment'al-ist.

Ex-ten′si-ble, 164.
Ex-ten′sïle, 152.
Ex-ten′sion.
Ex-ten′sïve, 84.
Ex-ten′sor.
Ex-tent′, 15, 137.
Ex-ten′u-ate, 73, 89.
Ex-ten′u-āt-ed, 183.
Ex-ten′u-āt-ing.
Ex-ten-u-a′tion.
Ex-ten′u-āt-or.
Ex-te′ri-or, 49, N.; 118.
Ex-te-ri-ŏr′i-ty, 169.
Ex-ter′mi-nate, 21, N.
Ex-ter′mi-nāt-ed, 183.
Ex-ter′mi-nāt-ing.
Ex-ter-mi-na′tion
Ex-ter′mi-nāt-or.
Ex-ter′mi-na-to-ry (86) [so Wr. Wb. Gd.; *eks-ter′mi-nāt-o-ry*, Sm. 155.]
Ex-tern′, 21, N.
Ex-ter′nal.
Ex-ter-nal′i-ty, 169.
Ex-ter-ra′ne-oŭs.
Ex-ter′sion.
Ex-tinct′ (*-tingkt′*), 16, 54.
Ex-tinc′tion.
Ex-tin′guish (*-ting′-gwish*), 104.
Ex-tin′guish-a-ble (*-ting′gwish-a-bl*), 164, 171.
Ex-tin′guished (*-ting′-gwisht*), Note C, p. 34.
Ex-tin′guish-er (*-ting′-gwish-*).
Ex-tin′guish-ing (*-ting′-gwish-*).
Ex-tin′guish-ment (*-ting′gwish-*).
Ex-tir′pa-ble, 164.
Ex-tir′pate, 21, N.
Ex-tir′pāt-ed, 183.
Ex-tir′pāt-ing.
Ex-tir-pa′tion.
Ex-tir′pāt-or, *or* Ex′-tir-pāt-or [so Wr.; *eks-tir′pāt-or*, Wk. Sm.; *eks′tir-pāt-or*, Wb. Gd. 155.]
Ex-tol′ [*not* eks-tōl′, 153.]
Ex-tolled′ (*-tŏld′*), 176.
Ex-tol′ler.
Ex-tol′ling.
Ex-tor′sïve, 84.
Ex-tort′, 17, 137.
Ex-tort′ed.
Ex-tort′ing.
Ex-tor′tion.
Ex-tor′tion-a-ry, 72.
Ex-tor′tion-ate, 73.
Ex-tor′tion-er.
Ex′tra (72) [*not* eks′trā, 153.]
Ex′tract, *n.* 103, 161.
Ex-tract′, *v.* 103, 161.
Ex-tract′ed.
Ex-tract′ing.
Ex-trac′tion.
Ex-tract′ïve, 84.
Ex-tract′or, 88.
Ex-tra-dï′tion (*-dish′-un*).
Ex-tra′dos.
Ex-tra-do′tal, 222.
Ex-tra-ju-dï′cial (*-dish′-al*), 222.
Ex-tra′ne-oŭs, 108, 169.
Ex-traor′di-na-rï-ly (*-tror′-*), 72.
Ex-traor′di-na-ry (*-tror′-*) (17, 72, 171) [so Wk. Sm. Wb. Gd.; *eks-tror′di-na-ry*, or *eks-tra-or′di-na-ry*, Wr. 155.]
Ex-trav′a-gance, 169.
Ex-trav′a-gant.
Ex-trav-a-gan′za.
Ex-trav′a-sate.
Ex-trav′a-sāt-ed, 183.
Ex-trav′a-sāt-ing.
Ex-trav-a-sa′tion.
Ex-treme′, 13.
Ex-trēm′ist.
Ex-trĕm′i-ty.
Ex′tri-ca-ble, 164.
Ex′tri-cate.
Ex′tri-cāt-ed.
Ex-tri-ca′tion.
Ex-trin′sic, 109.
Ex-trin′sic-al, 108.
Ex-trin′sic-al-ly.
Ex-trude′ (*-trood′*), 26.
Ex-trud′ed (*-trood′-*), 183.
Ex-trud′ing (*-trood′-*).
Ex-tru′sion (*-troo′-zhun*).
Ex-tu′ber-ance.
Ex-tu′ber-ant.
Ex-u′ber-ance (*egz-*), 137, 169.
Ex-u′ber-ant (*egz-*).
[Exuccous, 203.—*See* Exsuccous.]
Ex-u-da′tion.
Ex-ude′ (*eks-*), 26.

☞ This word is an exception to the general rule, (§ 137), by which *x* is sounded as *gz* at the end of a syllable, when the next syllable is accented, and begins with a vowel.

Ex-ūd′ed, 183.
Ex-ūd′ing.
Ex-ul′cer-ate (*egz-*), 137.
Ex-ul′cer-āt-ed (*egz-*), 183.
Ex-ul′cer-āt-ing (*egz-*).
Ex-ul-cer-a′tion (*egz-*).
Ex-ult′ (*egz-*), 22, 137.
Ex-ult′ant (*egz-*), 169.
Ex-ult-a′tion (*egz-*).
Ex-u′vi-æ (L.) (*egz-u′-vi-ē*), *n. pl.*
Eye (*ī*), 25, 171.
Eye′ball (*ī′-*), 206.
Eye′bright (*ī′brīt*), 162.
Eye′brow (*ī′-*), 206.
Eyed (*īd*), 150, 183.
Eye′-glass, 209.
Ey′ing (*ī′-*), 183.
Eye′lash (*ī′-*).
Eye′let (*ī′-*).
Eye′lid (*ī′-*).
Ey′er (*ī′-*) (67, 183), *n.* one who eyes. [*See* Ire, 148.]
Eye′-ser-vant (*ī′-*).
Eye′sïght (*ī′sīt*), 162, 206.
Eye′sore (*ī′-*).
Eye′-stōne (*ī′-*), 24, 156.
Eye′-tooth (*ī′-*).
Eye′-wâ-ter (*ī′-*).
Eye′-wit-ness (*ī′-*).
Eyre (*âr*), *n.* a journey; a court of justices itinerant. [*See* Air, Ere, Heir, 160.]
Ey′ry (*e′ry*), *or* Eyr′y, (*âr′y*) [*e′ry*, Sm.; *âr′y*, Wk. Wr. Gd. 155.] [Aerie, 203.]

F.

Fa-ba′ceous (*-shus*), 169.
Fā′bi-an, 78.
Fa′ble, 23, 164, 230.
Fa′bled (*fa′bld*), 183.
Fa′bler, 77.
Fa′bling.
Fab′ric [so Wr. Wb. Gd.; *fab′rik*, or *fa′-brik*, Wk.; *fa′brik*, Sm. 155.]
Fab′ric-ate, 73, 228.
Fab′ric-āt-ed, 183.
Fab′ric-āt-ing.
Fab-ric-a′tion.

Fab′ric-āt-or.
Fab′u-list, 89.
Fab′u-loŭs, 108.
Fa-çäde′ (Fr.) (*fa-säd′*) [so Sm. Wr.; *fa-sād′*, Gd. 155.]
Face, 23.
Faced (*fāst*), Note C, p. 34.
Faç′et (*fas′et*) (171), *n.* a small surface or face. [*See* Faucet, 148.]
Faç′et-ed (*fas′-*).
Fa-ce′ti-æ (L.) (*fa-se′-shĭ-ē*), *n. pl.*
Fa-ce′tioŭs (*-shus*), 169.
Fa′cial (*-shal*), 169.
Faç′ĭle (*fas′il*), 171.
Fa-cil′i-tate, 73, 169.
Fa-cil′i-tāt-ed, 183.
Fa-cil′i-tāt-ing.
Fa-cil-i-ta′tion, 112.
Fa-cil′i-ty, 78, 169.
Faç′ing.
Fac-sim′i-lē.
Fact, 10.
Fac′tion.
Fac′tion-ist.
Fac′tioŭs (*-shus*), 169.
Fac-tĭ′tious (*-tish′us*).
Fac′tor, 88.
Fac-to′ri-al.
Fac′to-ry, 86, 93.
Fac-to′tum.
Fac′ul-ty, 170.
Fade (23), *v.* to vanish; to decay. [*See* Fayed, 160.]
Fād′ed, 183.
Fād′ing.
[F æ c a l, 203 — *See* Fecal.]
Fæ′cēs (L.) (*fē′sēz*), *n. pl.* [F e c e s, 203.]
[F æ c u l a, 203. — *See* Fecula.]
[F a e r y, 203. — *See* Fairy.]
Fag, 10.
Fag-end′, 206, Exc. 3.
Fagged (*fagd*), 165, 176.
Fag′ging (*-ghing*), 138.
Fag′ot, 170.
Fähr′en-heĭt (*fär′en-ĭt*) (171) [so Gd.; *fä′-ren-hīt*, Wr. 155.]
Fa-ience′ (Fr.) (*fa-yans′*).
Fāil, 23.
Fāiled (*fāld*), 165.
Fāil′ing.
Fāil′ure, 91.
Fāin, *a.* glad: — *ad.* gladly. [*See* Fane, Feign, 160.]
Fāint, *a.* weak, swooning: — *v.* to grow weak; to swoon. [*See* Feint, 160.]
Fāint′ed.
Fāint-heärt′ed (206, Exc. 5) [so Wk. Sm. Wb. Gd.; *fānt′hart-ed*, Wr. 155.]
Fāint′ing.
Fair (*fêr*) (14), *a.* free from blemish: — *n.* a meeting for traffic. [*See* Fare, 160.]
Fair′y (*fêr′y*), *n.* & *a.* 49, N. [F a e r y, 203.]
Fair′y-land (*fêr′-*).
Fāith, 23, 37.
Fāith′ful (*-fŏŏl*), 180.
Fa′kir [so Sm. Gd.; *fa-kēr′*, or *fā′kur*, Wr. 155.] [F a q u i r, F a q u e e r, 203.]

☞ Goodrich pronounces this word *fa-keer′*, when it is spelled *Faquir*.

Fal-cade′, 121.
Fal′cate.
Fal′cāt-ed.
Fal-ca′tion.
Fâl′chion (*fawl′chun*) [so Sm. Wb. Gd.; *fawl′shun*, Wk.; *fawl′chun*, or *fawl′-shun*, Wr. 155.] [*not* făl′chun, 153.] [F a u l c h i o n, 203.]
Fâl′con (*faw′kn*) (149, 162) [so Wk. Sm. Wr.; *faw′kn*, or *fal-kon*, Gd. 155.]
Fâl′con-er (*faw′kn-ur*) [so Wk. Sm. Wr.; *faw′kn-ur*, or *fal′kon-ur*, Gd. 155.]
Făl′co-net [so Sm. Wb. Gd.; *fawl′ko-net*, Wk.; *fal′ko-net*, or *fawl′ko-net*, Wr. 155.]
Fâl′con-ry (*faw′kn-ry*) [so Sm. Wr.; *faw′-kn-ry*, or *fal′kon-ry*, Gd. 155.]
Fa-ler′ni-an, 21, N., 169.
Fâll, 17, 172.
Fal-la′cious (*-shus*), 169.
Fal′la-cy, 169, 170.
Fâllen (*fawln*).
Fal-li-bil′i-ty, 169.
Fal′li-ble, 78, 164, 170.
Fâll′ing.
Fal-lo′pi-an.
Fal′lōw, 10, 101.
Fal′lōw-deer.
Fal′lōwed (*-lōd*), 187.
Fal′lōw-ing.
Fâlse, 17.
Fâlse-heärt′ed, 206, Exc. 5.
Fâlse′hŏŏd, 171.
Fal-set′to (It.).
Fâl′si-fī-a-ble, 164.
Fâl-si-fĭ-ca′tion, 112.
Fâl′si-fīed, 99, 186.
Fâl′si-fī-er.
Fâl′si-fȳ, 94.
Fâl′si-ty, 78, 93.
Fâl′ter, 17, 77.
Fâl′tered, 150.
Fâl′ter-ing.
Fame, 23.
Famed (*fāmd*), 183.
Fa-mil′iar (*-yur*), 51, 171.
Fa-mil-iăr′i-ty (*-yăr′ĭ-ty*) [so Wb. Gd.; *fa-mil-i-ăr′i-ty*, Sm.; *fa-mil-yi-ăr′i-ty*, Wk. Wr. 155.]
Fa-mil′iar-ize (*-yur-*).
Fa-mil′iar-ized (*-yur-*).
Fa-mil′iar-īz-ing (*-yur-*).
Fam′i-ly, 78, 93.
Fam′ĭne, 10, 82, 152.
Fam′ish, 10.
Fam′ished (*-isht*).
Fam′ish-ing.
Fa′moŭs, 100, 169.
Fan, 10.
Fa-nat′ic, 109.
Fa-nat′ic-al, 108.
Fa-nat′i-cĭsm (*-sizm*).
Fan′cīed, 99, 186.
Fan′ci-er.
Fan′ci-ful (*-fŏŏl*).
Fan′cy, 10, 169.
Fan-dan′go (*-dang′-*).
Fane (23), *n.* a temple. [*See* Feign, 160.]
Fan′fāre (Fr.) (*-far*), 154.
Fan′fa-ron [so Sm. Wb. Gd.; *fan′fa-rōn*, Wk.; *fan′fa-ron*, or *fan′fa-rōn*, Wr. 155.]
Fan-fa-ron-ade′, 122.
Fang, 10, 54.
Fanged (*fangd*), 165.
Fan′got (*fang′-*).
Fan′ion (*-yun*).
Fanned (*fand*), 165, 176.

Fan′ner.
Fan′ning.
Fan-ta′si-a (It.) (-*zĭ*-).
[Fantasm, 203. — *See* Phantasm.]
Fan-tas′tic, 109.
Fan-tas′tic-al.
Fantoccini (It.) (*fan-to-chē′ne*).
[Fantom, 203. — *See* Phantom.]
[Faqueer, Faquir, 203. — *See* Fakir.]
Far, 11.
Farce (*färs*), 11, 39.
Far′ci-cal, 72, 78.
Far′cin.
Far′cy, 169.
Fare (*fêr*) (14), *n.* price of a passage: — *v.* to travel; to be treated. [*See* Fair, 160.]
Fare-well′ (*fêr-wel′*), *int.* [so Sm. Gd.; *fêr-wel′*, or *fêr′wel*, Wr.; *fêr′wel*, or *fêr-wel′*, *fär′wel* or *fär-wel′*, Wk. 155.]

☞ "When it is used as an interjection ... the accent is either on the first or second syllable, as the rhythm of pronunciation seems to require." *Walker.*

Fare′well (*fêr′wel*), *n.* [so Sm. Wr.; *fêr′wel*, or *fêr-wel′*, *fär′wel*, or *fär-wel′*, Wk.; *fêr-wel′*, Gd. 155.]

☞ "When it is used as a substantive, without an adjective before it, the accent is generally on the first syllable." *Walker.* — "It may be met with in poetry accented as the parent word [fare-well′, *int.*]; ... otherwise the proper accent is the one assigned [fare′well]." *Smart.*

Fare′well (*fêr′wel*), *a.* [so Sm. Wr.; *fêr′wel*, or *fär′wel*, Wk. 155.]

☞ Webster and Goodrich do not give this word as an adjective. Walker remarks: "When it is used as an adjective, the accent is always on the first syllable: as, 'A *fare′well* sermon.'" The words of Smart, as quoted under the noun, apply also to the adjective.

Far-fetched′ (*fecht′*), 206, Exc. 5.
Fa-ri′na.
Făr-i-na′ceous (-*shus*), 112.
Făr′i-nose.
Farm, 11, 135.
Farm′a-ble, 164, 169.
Farmed (*farmd*), 165.
Farm′er.
Farm′er-y, 233, Exc.
Farm′ing.
Far′o (*fêr′o*).
Făr-ra′go.
Făr′ri-er.
Făr′ri-er-y, 171.
Făr′rōw, 66, 101.
Far′ther, *ad.* to a greater distance: — *a.* more remote. [*See* Father, 148.] [Further, 203.]

☞ "The latter [*further*] is the genuine Saxon word; the former [*farther*] takes precedence in modern use." *Smart.* "Both are in good use." *Worcester.*

Far′ther-mōst [Furthermost, 203.]
Far′thest [Furthest, 203.]
Far′thing, 11, 38, 54.
Far′thin-gale (-*thing-găl*) [so Sm. Gd.; *far′-tuin-găl*, Wr.; *far′-thing-gāl*, Wk. 155.]
Fas′cēs (L.) (-*sēz*), *n. pl.*
Fas′ci-a (*fash′i-a*).
Fas′cial (*fash′yal*) (171) [so Sm. Wr.; *fash′i-al*, Gd. 155.]
Fas′ci-ate (*fash′i-āt*).
Fas′ci-āt-ed (*fash′i-āt*-).
Fas-ci-a′tion (*fash′ĭ*-).
Fas′ci-cle, 164.
Fas′ci-cled (-*kld*), 183.
Fas-cic′u-lar, 108.
Fas-cic′u-late, 108.
Fas-cic′u-lāt-ed.
Fas-cic′u-lus (L.) [pl. *Fas-cic′u-lī*, 198.]
Fas′ci-nate, 169.
Fas′ci-nāt-ed, 183.
Fas′ci-nāt-ing.
Fas-ci-na′tion, 112.
Fas-cine′ (-*sēn′*), 121.
Fash′ion (*fash′un*), 171.
Fash′ion-a-ble (*fash′-un-a-bl*), 164, 169.
Fash′ioned (*fash′und*), 165.
Fash′ion-er (*fash′un*-).
Fash′ion-ing (*fash′-un*-).
Fȧst, 12, 131.
Fȧst-dāy.
Fȧst′en (*fȧs′n*), 149, 162.
Fȧst′ened (*fȧs′nd*), 150.
Fȧst′en-ing (*fȧs′n*-).
Fas-tid′i-oŭs (169) [so Sm. Wr. Wb. Gd.; *fas-tid′i-us*, or *fas-tid′ji-us*, Wk. 155.]
Făs-tig′i-ate (-*tij′*-).
Făs-tig′i-āt-ed (-*tij′*-).
Fȧst′ing.
Fat, 10.
Fa′tal, 23, 72.
Fa′tal-ism (-*izm*), 136.
Fa′tal-ist.
Fa-tal′i-ty, 169.
Fate (23), *n.* destiny. [*See* Fête, 160.]
Fāt′ed.
Fä′ther (11, 38), *n.* a male parent. [*See* Farther, 148.]
Fä′thered (-*thurd*), 150.
Fä′ther-hōōd.
Fä′ther-ing.
Fä′ther-in-law.
Fä′ther-li-ness, 169.
Fä′ther-ly, 93.
Fath′om, 169.
Fath′om-a-ble, 164.
Fath′omed (-*umd*), 150.
Fa-tid′ic-al, 108.
Fa-tif′er-oŭs, 108.
Fa-tigue′ (-*tēg′*), 171.
Fa-tigued′ (-*tēgd′*), 183.
Fa-tigu′ing (-*tēg′*-).
Fa-til′o-quist.
Fa-tis′cence, 171.
Fat′ling.
[Fatner, 203. — *See* Fattener.]
Fat′ted, 176.
Fat′ten (*fat′n*), 149.
Fat′tened (*fat′nd*), 183.
Fat′ten-er (*fat′n-ur*) [Fatner, 203.]
Fat′ti-ness, 169.
Fat′ting, 176.
Fat′ty, 169, 170.
Fa-tu′i-toŭs.
Fa-tu′i-ty.
Fat′u-oŭs, 89, 100.
Fau′bourg (Fr.) (*fo′-boorg*).
Fau′ces (L.) (-*sēz*), *n. pl.*
Fau′cet (171), *n.* a spout with a spigot for drawing liquor from

a cask. [*See* Facet, 148.]
Fâult, 17, 156.
Fâult'i-ness, 169.
Fâult'y, 93.
Fâun (17), *n.* a rural deity. [*See* Fawn.]
Fâu'na, 72.
Fâun'ist.
Faux pas (Fr.) (*fo'pä*).
Fa-ve'o-late [so Wr.; *fa've-o-lāt*, Gd. 155.]
Fa-vil'loŭs, 170.
Fa'vor, 23, 88.
[Favour, Sm. 199, 203.]

☞ Smart inserts the *u* in all the derivatives of this word.

Fa'vor-a-ble, 164.
Fa'vored (*-vurd*), 150.
Fa'vor-er.
Fa'vor-ing.
Fa'vor-ĭte, 83, 152.
Fa'vor-it-ism (*-izm*).
Fa-vose'.
Fawn (17), *n.* the young of the fallow deer: — *v.* to court favor. [*See* Faun, 160.]
Fawned (*fawnd*), 150.
Fawn'er, 11, 77.
Fawn'ing.
Fāy, *n.* & *v.* 23.
Fāyed (*fād*) (187), *v.* did fay. [*See* Fade, 160.]
Fāy'ing.
Fe'al-ty, 144.
Fēar, 13, 67.
Fēared (*fērd*), 165.
Fēar'ful (*-fŏŏl*) (180) [so Sm. Wr. Wb. Gd.; *fēr'fŏŏl*, or *fĕr'fŏŏl*, Wk. 155.]
Fēar'ful-ly (*-fŏŏl-*), 170.
Fēar'nâught (*-nawt*) (162) [Fear-nought, 203.]
[Fease, 203. — *See* Feaze.]
Fēa-si-bil'i-ty (*-zĭ-*).
Fēa'si-ble (*-zĭ-bl*), 164.
Fēa'si-bly (*-zĭ-*).
Fēast, 13.
Fēast'ed.
Fēast'er, 77.
Fēast'ing.
Fēat, *n.* an exploit. [*See* Feet, 160.]
Fĕath'er, 15, 38, 77.
Fĕath'ered, 150, 171.
Fĕath'er-ing.
Fĕath'er-y.
Fēat'ure, 13, 91.
Fēat'ured (*-yurd*), 183.
Fēaze (13) [Fease, Pheese, 203.]
Fēazed, 165, 183.
Fēaz'ing.
Feb-ri-fa'cient (*-shent*).
Fe-brif'er-oŭs, 108.
Fe-brif'ic, 109.
Fe-brif'u-gal [so Wr.; *feb-ri-fu'gal*, Wb. Gd. 155.]
Feb'ri-fuge, 169.
Fe'brĭle, *or* Feb'rĭle (152) [so Wr. Wb. Gd.; *fĕb'ril*, Wk. Sm. 155.]
Feb'ru-a-ry (*-roo-*) (72, 171) [*not* feb'u-a-ry, 142, 153.]
Fe'cal [Fæcal, 203.]
[Feces, 203. — *See* Fæces.]
Fe'cial (*-shal*).
Fe'cit (L.).
Fec'u-la (108) [Fæcula, 203.]
Fec'u-lence, 169.
Fec'u-len-cy.
Fec'u-lent.
Fec'und [so Wk. Sm. Wr.; *fe'kund*, Wb. Gd. 155.]
Fec'un-date [so Sm.; *fe'kun-dāt*, Wb. Gd.; *fē-kun'dāt*, or *fek'un-dāt*, Wr. 155.]
Fec-un-da'tion, 112.
Fe-cund'i-ty, 169.
Fed, 15.
Fed'er-al, 233, Exc.
Fed'er-al-ism, 133, 136.
Fed'er-al-ist.
Fed'er-al-ize, 202.
Fed'er-al-ized, 183.
Fed'er-al-īz-ing.
Fed'er-ate, 73.
Fed-er-a'tion.
Fed'er-āt-ĭve [so Sm. *fed'er-a-tiv*, Wr. Wb. Gd. 155.]
Fee, 13.
Fee'ble, 164.
Fee'bly, 93.
Feed (188), *part.* from *Fee.*
Feed, *v.* to supply with food; to take food.
Feed'er, 77.
Feed'ing.
Fee'ing.
Feel, 13.
Feel'er.
Feel'ing.
Fee'-sim'ple, 164, 205.
Feet, *n.* plural of *Foot.* [*See* Feat, 160].
Fee'-tāil', 205.
Feign (*fān*) (23, 162), *v.* to dissemble. [*See* Fane, 160.]
Feigned (*fānd*), 162, 171.
Feign'ing (*fān'-*).
Feint (*fānt*) (23), *n.* a false appearance. [*See* Faint, 160.]
[Felanders, 203. — *See* Filanders.]
[Feldspar, 203. — *See* Felspar.]
Fe-liç'i-tate, 73, 169.
Fe-liç'i-tāt-ed, 183.
Fe-liç'i-tāt-ing.
Fe-liç-i-ta'tion.
Fe-liç'i-toŭs, 171.
Fe-liç'i-ty, 169.
Fe'line, 152.
Fell, *a.* & *v.* 15, 172.
Fell'a-ble, 164, 169.
Felled (*feld*), 165.
Fell'er, 77.
Fell'ing.
Fel'lōe, *n.* the rim of a wheel. [*See* Fellow, 160.] [Felly, 203.]
Fel'lōw (101), *n.* a companion. [*See* Felloe, 160.]
Fel'low-crēat'ure, 205.
Fel'ly, *ad.* 66, N.
Fel'ly, *n.* (66) [Felloe, 203.]

☞ *Felly* is now the more usual spelling of this word.

Fel'on, 86, 170.
Fe-lo'ni-oŭs, 78, 100.
Fel'on-y, 93.
Fel'spar [Feldspar, 203.]

☞ Smart gives only the form *felspar*, and Worcester prefers it. Webster and Goodrich prefer *feldspar*, and give also the forms feldspath and felspath.

Fel-spath'ic, 109.
Felt, *n.* & *v.* 15.
Felt'ed.
Felt'ing.
Fe-luc'ca, 170.
Fel'wort (*-wurt*).

Fe'male.
Feme-covert (Fr.) (*fĕm-ko-vert'*) [so Sm.; *fām-ko-vert'*, or *fĕm-kuv'urt*, Wr.; *fĕm-kuv'urt*, Wb. Gd. 154, 155.]
Feme-sole (Fr.) (*fĕm-sōl'*) [so Sm.; *fĕm-sōl'*, Gd., *fām-sōl'*, Wr. 154, 155.]
Fem'i-nal.
Fem-i-nal'i-ty, 169.
Fem'i-nīne, 152, 171.
Fem'o-ral, 72.
Fe'mur (L.) [pl. *Fem'o-ra*, 198.]
Fen, 15.
Fence, 15, 39.
Fenced (*fenst*) (165, 183); Note C, p. 34.
Fenç'er, 77, 183.
Fenç'i-ble, *a.* 164.
Fenç'i-bles (*-blz*), *n. pl.*
Fenç'ing.
Fend, 15.
Fend'ed.
Fend'er, 77.
Fend'ing.
Fe-nes'tral, 72.
Fe-nes'trate, *a.* 73.
Fen-es-tra'tion.
Fen'nec, 170.
Fen'nel, 66, 170.
Fen'ny, 176.
[Feod, 203.—*See* Feud.]
Fĕoff (*fef*), 171.
Fĕoff'ee, *or* Fĕoff-ee' (118) [so Wr.; *fef'ee*, Wk. Sm.; *fef-ee'*, Wb. Gd. 155.]
Fĕoff'er, *or* Fĕoff'or, 118.
Fĕoff'ment.
Fe'ri-al, 72, 78.
Fe'rīne, 152.
Fer-ment', *v.* 103, 161.
Fer'ment, *n.* 21, N.; 161.
Fer-ment-a-bil'i-ty.
Fer-ment'a-ble, 164, 169.
Fer-ment-a'tion.
Fer-ment'a-tīve.
Fer-ment'ed.
Fer-ment'ing.
Fern, 21, N.
Fern'y, 93, 169.
Fe-ro'cious (*-shus*), 169.
Fe-roç'i-ty, 169, 171.
Fĕr-ra-rese' (*-rēz'*).
Fĕr're-oŭs, 100, 170.
Fĕr'ret, *n.* & *v.* 66, 170.
Fĕr'ret-ed.
Fĕr'ret-er.
Fĕr'ret-ing.
Fĕr'ri-age, 70, 171.
Fĕr'rīed, 99.
Fĕr-rif'er-ous, 108.
Fĕr-ro-cy'an-ate.
Fĕr-ro-cȳ-an'ic, 109.
Fĕr-ro-cy'an-īde [Ferrocyanid, 203.]
Fĕr-ro-cȳ-an'o-gen.
Fĕr-ro-prus'si-ate (*-prush'ĭ-*), 46, 73.
Fĕr-ro-prus'sic.
Fĕr-ru'gi-nāt-ed.
Fer-ru'gi-noŭs, 169.
Fĕr'rule (*fĕr'ril*) (90, 171) [so Wk. Sm.; *fĕr'ril*, or *fer'rul*, Wr.; *fĕr'ril*, or *fĕr'rūl*, Gd. 155], *n.* a ring put round any thing to keep it from splitting. [*See* Ferule, 148.]
Fĕr'ry, 66, 170.
Fĕr'ry-bōat, 209.
Fer'tīle, 21, N.; 152.
Fer-til'i-ty, 169.
Fer-til-ī-za'tion.
Fer'til-ize, 202.
Fer'til-ized, 183.
Fer'til-īz-er.
Fer'til-īz-ing.
Fĕr-u-la'ceoŭs (*-shus*), 89, 169.
Fĕr'ule (*fĕr'ril*, or *fĕr'rūl*) [so Gd.; *fĕr'ul*, Wr. 155], *n.* a ruler or similar instrument used in schools to punish children by striking the palm of the hand: —*v.* to punish with the ferule. [*See* Ferrule, 148.]
Fĕr'uled (*fĕr'ild*, or *fĕr'rūld*), 165, 183.
Fĕr'ul-ing (*fĕr'ril-*, or *fĕr'rūl-*).
Fer'ven-cy, 169.
Fer'vent, 21, N.
Fer'vid, 169.
Fer'vor, 88.
Fes'cūe, 171.
Fes'cūed (*-kūd*), 183.
Fes'cu-ing.
Fes'cls (*-elz*), *n. pl.*
Fesse (*fes*).
Fes'tal, 15, 72.
Fes'ter, 15, 77.
Fes'tered, 150.
Fes'ter-ing.
Fes'ti-val, 72, 169.
Fes'tīve, 84.
Fes-tiv'i-ty, 169.
Fes-toon', 121.
Fes-tooned' (*-toond'*).
Fes'tu-cīne, 152.
Fes'tu-coŭs [so Sm. Wb. Gd.; *fes-tu'kus*, Wk. Wr. 155.]
Fe'tal.
Fetch, 15, 44.
Fetched (*fecht*), 165; Note C, p. 34.
Fetch'ing.
Fête (Fr.) (*fāt*), *n.* a festival. [*See* Fate, 160.]
Fête-champêtre (Fr.) (*fāt-sham-pātr'*).
Fe'tich (*-tish*), 171.
Fet'ich-ism (*-ish-izm*), *or* Fet'i-cism (*-sĭzm*), 133, 136.
Fet'id [*not* fe'tid, 153.]
Fe-tif'er-oŭs, 108.
Fet'lock.
Fe'tor (*-tawr*), 88.
Fet'ter, 170.
Fet'tered, 150.
Fet'ter-ing.
Fe'tus [pl. Fe'tus-es (*-ĕz*) [Fœtus, 203.]
Feūd (*fūd*) (26) [Feod, 203.]
Feūd'al, 72.
Feūd'al-ism (*-izm*), 136.
Feū-dal'i-ty, 169.
Feū-dal-ī-za'tion.
Feū'dal-ize, 202.
Feū'dal-ized, 183.
Feū'dal-īz-ing.
Feū'da-ry, 72.
Feū'da-to-ry, *a.* & *n.* [Feudatary, 203.]
Feu de joie (Fr.) (*foo' duh zhwa'*), 154.
Feūd'ist.
Feuillemorte (Fr.) (*foo'-il-mort*), 154.

☞ "It is Anglicized into *fil'e-mot*." *Smart.*

Feuilleton (Fr.) (*foo'il-tōng*), 154.
Fe'ver, 13, 77.
Fe'ver-few (*-fu*).
Few (*fu*), 26.
Fiacre (Fr.) (*fe-ä'kr*).
Fi'at.
Fib, 16.
Fibbed (*fibd*), 176.

Fib′ber.
Fib′bing.
Fi′bre (164) [Fiber, Wb. Gd. 203. — *See* Note E, p. 70.]
Fi′bril [*not* fib′ril, 153.]
Fī-bril′loŭs [so Gd.; *fī-bril′lus*, or *fib′ril-lus*, Wr. 155.]
Fi′brĭne (152) [*not* fib′-rin, 153.] [Fibrin, 203.]
Fi′brin-oŭs [so Gd.; *fib′-rin-us*, Wr. 155.]
Fi′broŭs, 25, 100, 169.
Fib′u-la (L.) [pl. Fib′u-læ, 198.]
Fic′kle (*fik′l*), 164.
Fick′ly.
Fic′tĭle, 152.
Fic′tion, 16, 46.
Fic′tion-al.
Fic′tion-ist.
Fic-tĭ′tious (*-tish′us*).
Fic′tor (*-tawr*), 88.
Fid, 16.
Fid′dle, 164.
Fid′dled (*fid′ld*).
Fid′dler, 183.
Fid′dling.
Fī-del′i-ty (79, 169) [*not* fĭ-del′i-ty, 153.]
Fidg′et.
Fidg′et-ed, 176.
Fidg′et-i-ness, 169.
Fidg′et-ing.
Fidg′et-y, 93.
Fī-du′cial (*-shal*), 79.
Fī-du′ci-a-ry (*-shĭ-a-ry*) [so Wk. Wr.; *fī-du′-sha-ry*, Sm. Wb. Gd. 155.] [203.]
Fīe (*fī*), *int.* (25) [Fy,
Fiēf (*fēf*), 13.
Fiēld (*fēld*), 13.
Fiēld′fare (*fēld′fêr*) [so Wr Wb. Gd.; *fēld′-fêr*, coll. *fĕl′fêr*, Sm. 155.]
Fiēnd (*fēnd*) [*not* fĕnd, 127, 153.]
Fiēnd′like, 206, Exc. 5.
Fiērce (*fērs*) [so Sm. Wr. Wb. Gd.; *fērs*, or *fĕrs*, Wk. 155.]

☞ "The first mode of pronouncing this word [*fērs*] is the most general; the second [*fĕrs*], is heard [1806] chiefly on the stage." *Walker*.

Fi′e-rī Fa′ci-as (L.) (*fī′-e-rī fa′shĭ-as*).
Fi′er-i-ly, 169.
Fi′er-i-ness, 171.
Fi′er-y, 93.
Fīfe, 25.
Fīfed (*fīft*), 183.
Fīf′er, 77.
Fīf′ing.
Fif′teen [*See* Eighteen.]
Fif′teenth.
Fifth, 16, 37.
Fif′ti-eth.
Fif′ty, 93.
Fig, 16.
Fīght (*fīt*), 25, 162.
Fīght′er (*fīt′-*).
Fīght′ing (*fīt′-*).
Fig′ment.
Fig′-tree, 206, Exc. 4.
Fig-u-ra-bil′i-ty, 169.
Fig′u-ra-ble, 164.
Fig′u-ral.
Fig′u-rănt (Fr.), *n. mas.* [so Gd.; *fig′u-rănt*, Wr.; *fig-u-rŏng′*, Sm. 155.]
Fig′u-rănte (Fr.), *n. fem.* [so Gd.; *fig-u-rănt′*, Wr.; *fig-u-rŏngt′*, Sm. 155.]
Fig′u-rate.
Fig′u-rāt-ed.
Fig-u-ra′tion.
Fig′u-ra-tĭve, 84.
Fig′ure, 91.
Fig′ured (*-yurd*).
Fig′ur-ing (*-yur-*).
Fī-la′ceous (*-shus*), 79.
Fil′a-cer.
Fil′a-ment.
Fil-a-ment′oŭs.
Fil′an-ders (*-durz*), *n. pl.* [Felanders, 203.]
Fil′a-to-ry.
Fil′a-ture.
Fil′bert.
Filch, 16, 44, N. 2.
Filched (*filcht*), 165; Note C, p. 34.
Filch′er.
Filch′ing.
File (25), *n.* a thread; a list; an instrument for abrading: — *v.* to string upon a thread; to place upon file; to abrade with a file. [*See* Phyle, 160.]
Filed, 183.
Fil′e-mot [*See* Feuille-morte.]
Fil′er.
Fil′ial (*-yal*), 16, 51.
Fil-i-a′tion.
Fil-i-bus′ter.
Fil-i-bus′ter-ing.
Fil-i-bus′ter-ism (*-izm*).
Fī-liç′i-form, 108.
Fil′i-coid.
Fil′i-form, 108.
Fil′i-grane.
Fil′i-gree, 169.
Fil′i-greed, 188.
Fīl′ing.
Fīl′ings (*-ingz*), *n. pl.*
Fill, 16.
Filled (*fild*), 165.
Fill′er.
Fil′let, 66, 170.
Fil′let-ed.
Fil′let-ing.
Fil′li-beg [Philibeg, 203.]
Fill′ing.
Fil′lip.
Fil′liped (*-lipt*), 165.
Fil′li-peen [Philopena, 203.]
Fil′ly, 170.
Film, 133.
Film′i-ness, 169.
Film′y.
Fī-lose′ [so Sm. Wr.; *fi′lōs*, Gd. 155.]
Fil′ter, *n.* a strainer: — *v.* to strain. [*See* Philter, 160.]
Fil′tered, 150.
Fil′ter-ing.
Filth, 16, 37.
Filth′i-ly.
Filth′i-ness, 169.
Filth′y, 93.
Fil′trate, 73.
Fil′trāt-ed, 183.
Fil′trāt-ing.
Fil-tra′tion, 112.
Fim′ble, 164.
Fim′bri-ate.
Fim′bri-āt-ed, 183.
Fim′bri-āt-ing.
Fin (16), *n.* a membranous organ projecting from the body of fishes; — a native of Finland. [Finn (in the last sense), 203.]
Fīn′a-ble, 164.
Fi′nal, 25, 72.
Fi-nä′le (It.) (*fe-nä′le*).
Fī-nal′i-ty, 169.
Fi′nal-ly, 66, N.
Fī-nance′ (121) [*not* fī′-nans, 153.]
Fī-nan′cial (*-shal*).
Fin-an-ciēr′ (*-sēr′*) (122,

169) [*not* fī-nan-sēr′, 153.]
Finch, 16, 44.
Fīnd (25), *v.* to discover. [*See* Fined, 160.]
Fīnd′er, 77.
Fīnd′ing.
Fine, 25.
Fined (*fīnd*) (183),*part.* from *Fine.* [*See* Find, 160.]
Fine′draw.
Fine′draw-er.
Fine′draw-ing.
Fine′drawn.
Fine′ness, 66, N.
Fīn′er.
Fīn′er-y.
Fi-nesse′ (Fr.) (*fe-nes′*), 114, 171.
Fī-nessed′ (*-nest′*).
Fī-ness′ing.
Fin′ger (*fing′gur*), 54, Note 2; 138.
Fin′gered (*fing′gurd*).
Fin′ger-ing (*fing′gur-*).
Fin′ger-ring (*fing′-gur-*), 206, Exc. 1.
Fin′i-al, 169.
Fin′i-cal, 72, 169.
Fīn′ing.
Fin′ish, 104.
Fin′ished (*-isht*).
Fin′ish-er.
Fin′ish-ing.
Fī′nīte, 152.
Fin′i-tude, 169.
Finn, *n.* a native of Finland. [Fin, 203.]
Finned (*fĭnd*), 176.
Fin′ny, 170.
Fī-no′chi-o [so Wb.Gd.; *fin′ŏch-o*, Sm.; *fe-no′-she-o*,Wk.Wr.154,155]
Fin′-tōed, 206, Exc. 5.
Fi-ord′ (*fe-ord′*).
Fir (21, N.), *n.* a kind of tree. [*See* Fur, 160.]
Fire, 25.
Fire′-arms (*-armz*).
Fire′brand, 206.
Fire′-brick.
Fire′-clāy.
Fired, 183.
Fire′-en′gīne, 205.
Fire′flaire(*-flêr*) [Fire-flair, 203.]
Fire′-flȳ.
Fire′lock.
Fire′man, 196.
Fire′place.
Fire′-plug.
Fire′-proof.
Fire′side.
Fire′wŏŏd.
Fire′works (*-wurks*), *n. pl.*
Fir′ing, 49, N.
Fir′kin, 21 N.; 169.
Firm, 21, N.
Firm′a-ment, 171.
Firm-a-ment′al.
Fir′man (21, N.; 169) [pl. Fir′mans (*-manz*), 196.]
First, 21, N.
First′-fruits (*-froots*), *n. pl.* 171.
First′ling.
First′-rate.
Firth, 21, N.
Fir′-tree, 206, Exc. 4.
Fisc, 181.
Fisc′al, 72.
Fish, 16, 46.
Fished (*fisht*), 165; Note C, p. 34.
Fish′er, 77.
Fish′er-man, 196.
Fish′er-y.
Fish′gig (*-ghig*) [Fizgig, 203.]
Fish′-hŏŏk, 206, Exc. 1.
Fish′ing.
Fish′ing-line, 215.
Fish′-shop, 66, N.; 206, Exc. 1.
Fish′y, 93, 169.
Fis′sīle, 152.
Fis-sil′i-ty, 169.
Fis′sion (*fish′un*).
Fis-sip′a-rism (*-rizm*).
Fis-sip′a-roŭs, 170.
Fis′si-ped.
Fis-si-ros′tral.
Fis′sure (*fish′yur*).
Fis′sured (*fish′yurd*).
Fist, 16.
Fist′i-cuffs, *n. pl.*
Fis′ti-nut.
Fis′tu-la (L.) [pl. Fis′-tu-læ, 198.]
Fis′tu-lar, 74.
Fis′tu-la-ry, 72.
Fis-tu′li-form (108) [so Wr.; *fis′tu-li-form*, Gd. 155.]
Fis′tu-loŭs, 89, 169.
Fit, 16.
Fitch, 16, 44.
Fitch′et.
Fitch′ew (*-oo*).
Fit′ful (*-fŏŏl*).
Fit′ted, 176.
Fit′ter.
Fit′ting.
Five, 25.
Five′-fōld, 206, Exc. 5.
Fix, 16, 39, N.
Fix′a-ble, 164.
Fix-a′tion.
Fixed (*fikst*), 165.
Fix′ed-ness, 150.
Fix′ing.
Fix′i-ty, 169.
Fixt′ure, 91.
Fiz′gig (*-ghig*) [Fish-gig (in the sense of *a harpoon*), 203.]
Fiz′zle, 164.
Fiz′zled (*fiz′ld*), 183.
Fiz′zling.
Flab′bi-ness, 169.
Flab′by, 93.
Fla-bel′late, 170.
Flab-el-la′tion.
Fla-bel′li-form, 108.
Flac′cid (*flak′sid*).
Flac-cid′i-ty, 171.
Flag, 10.
Flag′el-late (*flaj′-*), 170.
Flag′el-lāt-ed (*flaj′-*).
Flag′el-lāt-ing (*flaj′-*).
Flag-el-la′tion (*flaj-*).
Fla-gel′li-form, 108.
Flag′eo-let (*flaj′o-*)(171) [*not* flaj′e-o-let, 145, 153.]
Flagged (*flagd*), 176.
Flag′gi-ness (*-ghĭ-*).
Flag′ging (*-ghing*), 138.
Flag′gy (*-ghy*).
Fla-gĭ′tioŭs (*-jish′us*), 171, 231.
Flag′on, 170.
Fla′grance.
Fla′gran-cy, 169.
Fla′grant, 72.
Flāil, 23.
Flaire, *n.* a fish of the ray kind. [*See* Flare, 160.]
Flake, 23.
Flaked (*flākt*),183; Note C, p. 34.
Flāk′i-ness.
Flāk′y.
Flam′beau (Fr.) (*flam′-bo*) [Fr. pl. Flam′-beaux (*-bōz*), Eng. pl. Flam′beaus(*-bōz*),198]
Flam-boy′ant.
Flame, 23.
Flamed (*flāmd*), 183.
Fla′men (L.) [L. pl. *Flam′i-nēs* (*-nēz*); Eng. pl. Fla′mens (*-menz*), 198.]
Flām′ing.

Fla-min'go (*-ming'-*) (54) [pl. Fla-min'goes (*-ming'gōz*), 192.]
Fla-min'ic-al, 108.
Flam-ma-bil'i-ty, 169.
Flam'ma-ble, 164.
Flăm'y, 93.
Flanch [Flange, 203.]
Flănge [Flanch, 203.]
Flank (*flangk*), 10, 54.
Flanked (*flangkt*), 165.
Flank'er, *n.* & *v.*
Flank'ered, 150.
Flank'er-ing.
Flank'ing.
Flan'nel, 66, 170.
Flap, 10.
Flap'drag-on.
Flap'jack, 206.
Flapped (*flapt*), 176.
Flare (*flêr*) (14), *v.* to waver; to glitter; to spread outward. [*See* Flaire, 160.]
Flared (*flêrd*), 183.
Flar'ing (*flêr'-*).
Flash, 10, 46.
Flashed (*flasht*), 165.
Flash'i-ly.
Flash'i-ness, 169.
Flash'ing.
Flash'y, 93, 169.
Flȧsk, 12, 131.
Flȧsk'et.
Flat, 10.
Flat'fish, 206.
Flat'-ī-ron (*-ī-urn*).
Flat'ted, 176.
Flat'ten (*flat'n*), 149.
Flat'tened (*flat'nd*), 150.
Flat'ten-ing (*flat'n-*).
Flat'ter, 170.
Flat'tered, 150.
Flat'ter-ing.
Flat'ter-y, 171.
Flat'ting, 186.
Flat'u-lence.
Flat'u-len-cy, 169.
Flat'u-lent, 89.
Flӓunt (*flӓnt*) (11) [*not* flawnt, 153.]
Flӓunt'ed.
Flӓunt'er.
Flӓunt'ing.
Flâu'tist.
Fla'vor [Flavour, Sm. 199, 203.]
Fla'vored (*-vurd*) (150) [Flavoured, Sm. 199, 203.]
Fla'vor-ing [Flavouring, Sm. 199, 203.]
Fla'vor-oŭs.
Flaw, 17.
Flawed (*flawd*), 165.
Flaw'ing.
Flaw'y, 93.
Flax, 10, 39, N.
Flax'en (*flak'sn*), 149.
Flax'seed, 66 N.; 206.
Flax'y, 93, 169.
Flāy, 23.
Flāyed (*flād*), 187
Flāy'er.
Flāy'ing.
Flēa (13), *n.* a small insect of the genus *Pulex*. [*See* Flee, 160.]
Flēa'bane, 206.
Flēam (13) [Phleme, 203.]
Flēa'wort (*-wurt*).
Fleck, 15, 181.
Flecked (*flekt*), 165.
Flec'tion.
Flec'tor (*-tawr*), 88.
Fled, 15.
Fledge, 15, 45.
Fledged (*flejd*), 165.
Fledg'ing, 183.
Fledge'ling.
Flee (13), *v.* to run, as from danger. [*See* Flea, 160.]
Fleece, 13, 39.
Fleeced (*flēst*), 165, 183; Note C, p. 34.
Fleeç'er.
Fleeç'ing.
Fleeç'y, 93.
Fle'er (67, N.), *n.* one who flees.
Fleer (13, 67, N.), *v.* to mock; to gibe: — *n.* a gibe; a sneer.
Fleered (*flērd*), 165.
Fleer'er.
Fleer'ing.
Fleet, 13.
Fleet'ed.
Fleet'ing.
Fle'men.
Flem'ing, 170.
Flem'ish.
Flense (*flenz*), 136.
Flensed (*flenzd*).
Flens'ing (*flenz'-*).
Flesh, 15, 46.
Fleshed (*flesht*), 165.
Flesh'i-ness, 169.
Flesh'ing.
Flesh'li-ness, 169.
Flesh'ly, 93.
Flesh'-mon'ger [3. (*-mung'gur*), 205, Exc.
Flesh'y.
Fle-tif'er-oŭs, 108.
Fletz.
Fleur de lis (Fr.) (*flur-duh-le'*).
Flew (*flu*) (26) [*not* floo, 153], *part.* from *Fly*. [*See* Flue, 160.]
Flex-i-bil'i-ty, 169.
Flex'i-ble, 164.
Flex'i-bly, 93.
Flex'ĭle, 152.
Flex'ion (*flek'shun*), 46, Note 1.
Flex'or (*-awr*), 88.
Flex'u-ōse.
Flex'u-oŭs.
Flex'ure, 91.
Flick'er.
Flick'ered, 150.
Flick'er-ing.
Fli'er [Flyer, 203.]
Flight (*flīt*), 25, 162.
Flight'i-ness (*flīt'-*).
Flight'y, 93.
Flim'si-ly (*-zĭ-*), 136.
Flim'si-ness (*-zĭ-*).
Flim'sy (*-zy*), 136.
Flinch, 16, 44, Note 2.
Flinched (*flincht*), 165.
Flinch'ing.
Fling, 16, 54.
Fling'er.
Fling'ing.
Flint, 16.
Flint'i-ness, 169.
Flint'y, 93, 169.
Flip, 16.
Flip'-flap.
Flip'pan-cy, 169.
Flip'pant, 170.
Flip'per, 77, 170.
Flirt, 21, N.
Flirt-a'tion.
Flirt'ed.
Flirt'ing.
Flit, 16.
Flitch, 16, 44.
Flit'ted, 176.
Flit'ter.
Flit'tern.
Flit'ting.
Flōat, 24.
Flōat'ed.
Flōat'age [Flotage, 203.]
Flōat'ing.
[Floatsam, 203.—*See* Flotsam.]
Flōat'y.
Floc-cil-la'tion, 170.
Floc'cu-lence, 169.
Floc'cu-lent.
Flock (18, 181), *n.* a col-

lection of small animals, as sheep or fowls; a lock of wool or hair. [pl. Flocks. — *See* Phlox, 160.]
Flocked (*flŏkt*), 165.
Flock'ing.
Flock'y, 93.
Flōe, *n.* a mass of floating ice. [*See* Flow, 160.]
Flog, 18. [176.
Flogged (*flogd*), 165,
Flog'ging (*-ghing*), 138.
Flood (*flud*), 22.
Flood'ed (*flud'-*).
Flood'gate (*flud'-*).
Flood'ing (*flud'-*).
Flook'ing.
Flōor (*flōr*), 24.
Flōored (*flōrd*), 165.
Flōor'ing.
Flo'ra, 72.
Flo'ral, 49, N.
Flŏr'en-tīne, *or* Flŏr'en-tĭne [so Wr.; *flŏr'en-tin*, Wb. Gd. 155.]
Flo-res'cence, 171.
Flo'ret, 49, N.
Flŏr-i-cult'ure, 91.
Flŏr'id, 18, 48.
Flŏr'i-form, 108.
Flŏr'in [*not* flo'rin,153.]
Flo'rist, 49, N.
Flos'cu-lar.
Flos'cule.
Flos'cu-loŭs.
Floss.
Flōt'age [Floatage, 203.]
Flo-ta'tion.
Flo-til'la, 170.
Flot'sam [Flotson, Floatsam, 203.]
Flounce, 28, 39.
Flounced (*flounst*).
Flounc'ing.
Floun'der, 28, 77.
Floun'dered (*-durd*),150
Flour (67), *n.* the edible part of grain pulverized. [*See* Flower, 160.]
Floured (*flourd*), 165.
Flour'ing.
Flour'ish (*flŭr'-*), 22.
Flour'ished (*flur'isht*).
Flour'ish-er.
Flour'ish-ing.
Flout, 28.
Flout'ed.
Flout'er.
Flout'ing.
Flōw, *v.* to run or move as a fluid. [*See* Floe, 160.]
Flōwed (*flōd*), 188.
Flōw'age.
Flower (28, 67), *n.* that part of a plant by which the seed is produced; a blossom. [*See* Flour, 160.]
Flower'-de-luce.
Flowered, 28, 150.
Flower'i-ness, 171.
Flower'ing.
Flower'y.
Flōw'ing.
Flōwn, 24.
Flu'ate.
Fluc'tu-ate, 73, 89.
Fluc'tu-āt-ed, 183.
Fluc'tu-āt-ing.
Fluc-tu-a'tion, 112.
Flud'der [Fluder, 203.]
Flūe, *n.* a passage for smoke, as in a chimney. [*See* Flew, 160.]
Flu'en-cy, 169.
Flu'ent.
Fluf'fy, 170.
Flu'gel-man(*flu'gl-*),196
Flu'id, 23, 80.
Flu-id'i-ty, 169.
Fluke, 26.
Flum'mer-y, 170.
Flung, 22.
Flunk'y.
Flunk'y-ism (*-izm*).
Flu'or-īde [Fluorid, 203.]
Flu'or-īne.
Flu'or-spar.
Flŭr'rĭed, 186.
Flŭr'ry, 21, 22.
Flŭr'ry-ing.
Flush, 22.
Flushed (*flusht*), 165.
Flush'er.
Flush'ing.
Flus'ter.
Flus'tered. 150.
Flus'ter-ing.
Flute, 26.
Flūt'ed, 183.
Flūt'er.
Flūt'ing.
Flūt'ist.
Flut'ter, 170.
Flut'tered, 150.
Flut'ter-ing.
Flūt'y.
Flu'vi-al, 72, 169.
Flu'vi-al-ist.
Flu'vi-a-tĭle.
Flux, 22, 39. N.
Fluxed (*flukst*), 165.
Flux'ing. [N. 2.
Flux'ion(*fluk'shun*), 46,
Flux'ion-al (*fluk'shun-*)
Flux'ion-a-ry (*fluk'-shun-*), 72, 171.
Flux'ion-ist (*fluk'-shun-*).
Fly, 25.
Fly'catch-er, 206.
[Flyer, 203.—*See* Flier.]
Fly'ing.
Fly'ing-fish.
Fly'-trap.
Fly'-wheel.
Fōal, 24.
Fōaled (*fōld*), *v.* did foal. [*See* Fold, 160.]
Fōal'ing.
Fōam, 24.
Fōamed (*fōmd*), 165.
Fōam'ing.
Fōam'y.
Fob, 18.
Fobbed (*fobd*), 176.
Fob'bing.
Fo'cal, 72.
Fo'cĭle, 152.
Fo'cus (L.) [pl. Fo'cī, 198.]
Fod'der, 170.
Fod'dered, 150.
Fod'der-ing.
Fōe (*fō*), 24.
Fōe'man, 196.
Fœt'i-cide (*fet'-*).
Fœ'tus (13) [Fetus, 203.]
Fog, 18.
Fog'gy (*-ghy*), 138.
Fo'gy (*-ghy*) (138, 190) [Fogey, Fogie, 203.]
Fōh, *int.* [so Sm. Gd.; *fŏh*, Wk. Wr. 155.]
Foi'ble, 27, 164.
Foil, 27.
Foiled, 165.
Foil'er, 77.
Foil'ing.
Foist, 27.
Foist'ed.
Foist'er.
Foist'ing.
Fōld, *n.* an enclosure for sheep;—a flock of sheep;—a plait:—*v.* to lay in folds; to double. [*See* Foaled, 160.]

Fōld′age.
Fōld′ed.
Fōld′er.
Fōld′ing.
Fo-li-a′ceous (*-shus*).
Fo′li-age, 70.
Fo′li-ate.
Fo′li-āt-ed, 183.
Fo′li-āt-ing.
Fo-li-a′tion.
Fo′li-a-ture.
Fo′li-er.
Fo-lif′er-oŭs.
Fo′li-o [so Wk. Sm. Wb. Gd.; *fo′li-o*, or *fōl′yo*, Wr. 155.] [pl. Fo′li-ōs (*-ōz*), 192.]
Fo′li-o-mort.
Fo′li-oŭs.
Fōlk (*fōk*), 162, 171.
Fōlk′land (*fōk′-*), 162.
Fol′li-cle, 164, 170.
Fol-lic′u-lāt-ed.
Fol-lic′u-loŭs.
Fol′lōw, 18, 101, 170.
Fol′lōwed, 165, 188.
Fol′low-er.
Fol′low-ing.
Fol′ly, 66, 170.
Fo′mal-hâut.
Fo-ment′, 15, 103.
Fo-ment-a′tion, 112.
Fo-ment′ed.
Fo-ment′ing.
Fond, 18.
Fon′dle, 164.
Fon′dled (*fon′dld*).
Fon′dler, 183.
Fon′dling.
Fond′ly, 93.
Font, 18.
Font′al, 72.
Font′a-nel, 169.
Food, 19.
Fool, 19.
Fooled (*foold*), 165.
Fool′er-y.
Fool′hard-i-ness, 169.
Fool′hard-y.
Fool′ing.
Fools′cap (*foolz′-*).
Fŏŏt (20) [pl. Feet, 195.]
Fŏŏt′bâll, 206.
Fŏŏt′boy.
Fŏŏt′bridge.
Fŏŏt′ed.
Fŏŏt′fâll, 206.
Fŏŏt′guards (*-gardz*), *n. pl.*
Fŏŏt′hâlt.
Fŏŏt′hōld.
Fŏŏt′ing.
Fŏŏt′man, 196.
Fŏŏt′mark.
Fŏŏt′muff.
Fŏŏt′pace.
Fŏŏt′pad, 206.
Fŏŏt′pȧth.
Fŏŏt′print.
Fŏŏt′rope.
Fŏŏt′rot.
Fŏŏt′-sore, 216.
Fŏŏt′-sōl′dier (*-sōl′jur*), 206, Exc. 3.
Fŏŏt′stâlk (*-stawk*), 162.
Fŏŏt′stâll.
Fŏŏt′step.
Fŏŏt′stool.
Fŏŏt′way.
Fop, 18.
Fop′ling.
Fop′per-y, 170.
Fop′pish, 176.
For, 17, 135.
Fŏr′age, 18, 70.
Fŏr′aged, 165.
Fŏr′a-ger.
Fŏr′a-ging.
Fo-ra′men (L.) [pl. Fo-ram′i-na, 198.]
Fo-ram′i-nāt-ed.
Fo-ram-in′i-fer [so Gd.; *fŏr-a-min′i fur*, Wr. 155.]
Fo-ram-i-nif′er-oŭs.
For-as-much′ (*-az-*).
Fo-rāy′, *or* Fŏr′āy [so Wr.; *fo′rā*, Wb. Gd. 155] [F o r r a y, 203.]
For-băde′, 163, 171.
For-bear′ (*-bêr*), 14.
For-bear′ance (*-bêr′-*), 169.
For-bear′ing(*-bêr′-*),115.
For-bid′, 16.
For-bid′den(*-bid′n*),149.
For-bid′ding, 176.
For-bore′, 24.
For-bōrne′.
Fōrce, 24.
Fōrced (*fōrst*), 165, 183; Note C, p. 34.
Fōrce′ful (*-fŏŏl*), 180.
Fōrce′mēat, 206.
Fōrce′pump.
Fōrç′er, 183.
Fōrç′i-ble, 164.
Fōrç′i-bly.
Fōrç′ing.
For′ci-pāt-ed.
For-ci-pa′tion.
Fōrd, 24.
Fōrd′a-ble, 164.
Fōrd′ed.
Fōrd′ing.
Fore (24), *a.* anterior: — *ad.* anteriorly. [*See* Four, 160.]
Fore-bode′, 24, 103.
Fore-bōd′ed, 183.
Fore-bōd′er.
Fore-bōd′ing.
Fore′brace, 206.
Fore′cȧst.
Fore′cȧst-ing.
Fore′cas-tle (*-kas-l*), 162, 171. [*n. pl.*
Fore-chāins′ (*-chānz′*),
Fore-close′ (*-klōz′*).
Fore-closed′ (*-klōzd′*).
Fore-clōs′ing (*-klōz′-*).
Fore-clōs′ure (*-klōz′-*), [91.
Fore-date′.
Fore-dāt′ed, 183.
Fore-dāt′ing.
Fore′deck.
Fore′fä-ther, *or* Fore-fä′ther [so Wr. *fōr′-fä-thur*, Sm.; *fōr-fa′-thur*, Wk. Wb. Gd. 155.]
Fore-go′, 24, 103.
Fore-go′ing.
Fore-gŏne′, 18, N.
Fore′ground, 216.
Fore′hand-ed.
Forė′head (*fŏr′ed*, or *fōr′hed*) [so Wr.; *fŏr′hed*, coll. *fŏr′ed*, Sm.; *fŏr′ed*, or *fŏr′-hed*, Wb. Gd. 155.]
Fŏr′eign (*-in*), 97, 162.
Fŏr′eign-er (*-in-*), 162, 171.
Fore-knew′ (*-nu′*), 162.
Fore-knōw′ (*-no′*), 162.
Fore-knōw′er (*-no′-*).
Fore-knōw′ing (*-no′-*).
Fore-knŏwl′edge (*-nol′-ej*), 143, 162, 171.
Fore′lock.
Fore′man, 196.
Fore′mast, 72.
Fore′mōst.
Fore′name.
Fore-named′ (*-nāmd*) [so Wk. Wr.; *fōr′-nāmd*, Gd. 155.]
Fore′noon.
Fo-ren′sic.
Fore-or-dāin′, 223.
Fore-or-dāined′, 165.
Fore-or-dāin′ing.
Fore-or-di-na′tion.
Fore′part.
Fore′plane.
Fore-ran′.
Fore-run′.
Fore-run′ner, 176.

Fore-run′ning.
Fore′said (-*sed*).
Fore′sāil.
Fore-saw′.
Fore-see′.
Fore-see′ing.
Fore-seen′.
Fore-se′er, 183.
Fore-shad′ōw.
Fore-shad′ōwed, 188.
Fore-shad′ōw-ing.
Fore-short′en(-*short′n*), 149. [*nd*).
Fore-short′ened(-*short′*-
Fore-short′en-ing (-*short′n*-).
Fore-show′.
Fore-shōwed′, 188.
Fore-shōw′er.
Fore-shōw′ing.
Fore′side.
Fore′sight (-*sīt*), 162.
Fore′skin.
Fŏr′est, 170.
Fore′staff, 193.
Fore-stâll′[Forestal, Sm. 179, 203.]
Fore-tell′er.
Fore-tell′ing. [162.
Fore′thought (-*thawt*),
Fore-to′ken (-*to′kn*).
Fore-to′kened (-*to′knd*).
Fore-tōld′.
Fore′top.
For-ev′er.

☞ *For* and *ever* are generally written separate by English authors, and they are not given as forming a compound word in the Dictionaries of Walker and Smart. "It is the prevailing usage with American writers," says Worcester, "to form the two parts into one word, *forever*." Wilson says: "The words [*for* and *ever*] every where occur in the common version of the Bible as a phrase; and, the eye being thus accustomed to their separation, it would probably be better to retain this form."

Fore-wârn′.
Fore-wârned′, 165.
Fore-wârn′ing.
Fore-went′.
For′feĭt (-*fit*), 70, 97, 171.
For′feĭt-ure (-*fit*), 91.
For′fex.
For-gave′.
Fōrge, *n.* & *v.* (24) [*not* fawrj, 153.]
Fōrged, 165, 183.
Fōrg′er (*fōrj′*-), 24, 77.
Fōrg′er-y (*fōrj′*-) [*not* fawj′er-y, 153.]
For-get′ (-*ghet′*).
For-get′ful (-*ghet′fŏŏl*).
For-get′-me-not (-*ghet′*), 221.
For-get′ter (-*ghet′*-),176.
Fōrg′ing (*fōrj′*-).
For-gīve′, 163.
For-giv′er, 183.
For-giv′ing.
For-got′.
For-got′ten (-*got′n*).
Fo-ris-fa-mil′i-ate [so Sm. Wr.; *fo-ris-fa-mil′yāt*, Wb. Gd. 155.]
Fo-ris-fa-mil′i-āt-ed.
Fo-ris-fa-mil′i-āt-ing.
Fo-ris-fa-mil-i-a′tion.
Fork, 17.
Forked (*forkt*), 165.
Fork′y, 93.
For-lorn′, 17.
Form, 17, 135.

☞ When this word has the sense of *a long seat*, or of *a class of students*, the English pronunciation is *fōrm*.

Form′al.
Form′al-ism (-*izm*), 136.
Form′al-ist.
For-mal′i-ty, 169.
For′mal-ize, 202.
For′mal-ized, 183.
For′mal-īz-ing.
Form′al-ly, 66, N.
Form-a′tion.
Form′a-tīve, 84.
Formed (*formd*), 165.
Form′er (228), *n.* one who forms.
For′mer, *a.* anterior.
For′mic.
For′mi-cate, 73.
For-mi-ca′tion.
For′mi-da-ble (164) [*not* for-mid′a-ble, 153.]
For′mi-da-bly.
For′mu-la (L.) [L. pl. *For′mu-læ*; Eng. pl. For′mu-las, 198.]
Form′u-la-ry, 72.
For′ni-cate, *a.* & *v.*
For′ni-cāt-ed.
For′ni-cāt-ing.
For-ni-ca′tion.
For′ni-cāt-or.
For′ni-cāt-ress.
For-rāy′, *or* For′rāy [so Wr.; *for-ra′*, Sm. Gd. 155.] [Foray, 203.]
For-sake′, 23.
For-sāk′en (-*sāk′n*), 149.
For-sāk′er.
For-sāk′ing.
For-sŏŏk′, 20.
For-sooth′, 19.
For-swêar′ (-*swêr′*), 171.
For-swêar′er.
For-swore′.
Fōrt (24, 160), *n.* a small fortified place.
Fōrte (Fr.) (24, 160), *n.* that in which one excels.
For′te (It.) (*for′tā*),161.
Fōrth, *ad.* forward in time or in place. [*See* Fourth, 160.]
Fōrth′-com-ing(-*kum*-), 206, Exc. 5.
Fōrth-with′, 37.
For′ti-eth.
For′ti-fī-a-ble, 164.
For-ti-fĭ-ca′tion.
For′ti-fīed, 99.
For′ti-fī-er.
For′ti-fȳ, 94.
For-tis′si-mo (It.).
For′ti-tude, 169.
Fort′night (-*nīt*) (162) [so Wk. Sm. Gd.; *fort′nīt*, or *fort′nit*, Wr. 155.]
For′tress.
For-tu′i-toŭs, 169.
For-tu′i-ty, 108.
Fort′u-nate, 73, 89.
Fort′une [so Wr. Gd.; *for′tūn*, coll. *fort′-sh′oon* (*See* § 26); *for′-chūn*, Wk. (*See* § 44, N. 1), 155.]
Fort′une-tell′er, 205.
For′ty, 93.
Fo′rum (L.) [L. pl. *Fo′-ra*; Eng. pl. Fo′rums (-*rumz*), 198.]
For′ward.
For′ward-ed.
For′ward-er.
For′ward-ing.
For′wards (-*wardz*).
For-zan′do (It.) (*fort-san′do*).
Fosse (*fos*).
Fosse′wāy, 206.
Fos′sil, 66, 170.
Fos-sil-if′er-ous, 108.
Fos′sil-ist.
Fos-sil-ĭ-za′tion.
Fos′sil-ize, 202.
Fos′sil-ized, 183.
Fos′sil-īz-ing.

Fos-sil'o-gy, 108.
Fos-so'ri-al, 49, N.
Fos'ter, 77.
Fos'ter-child.
Fos'tered, 150.
Fos'ter-er.
Fos'ter-ing.
Fos'ter-ling.
Foth'er.
Foth'ered, 150.
Foth'er-ing.
Fought (*fawt*), 162.
Foul (28), *a.* not clean; not clear; shameful: — *v.* to soil. [*See* Fowl, 160.]
Fouled, 28, 165.
Foul'ing.
Foul'ly, 66, N.
Fou'mart (*foo'-*).
Found, 28.
Foun-da'tion.
Found'ed.
Found'er (228, N.), *n.* one who founds.
Foun'der, *v.* to fill with water, and sink; — to cause to be lame or sore, as the feet of a horse.
Foun'dered (*-durd*), 150.
Found'er-ous.
Found'er-y [Found-ry, 203.]

☞ The forms *foundery* and *foundry* are both in good use. Walker gives only *foundry*. Smart says *foundery* or *foundry*. Worcester and Goodrich give both, but prefer *foundery*.

Found'ing.
Found'ling.
Found'ry [Found-ery, 203.]
Fount, 28.
Fount'ain (*-in*), 70, 96, 171.
Fōur (*fōr*) (24), *a.* & *n.* twice two. [*See* Fore, 160.]
Fōur'fōld, 24, 217.
Fou'ri-er-ism (*foo'ri-er-ism*) [so Gd.; *foo'-rē-er-izm*, Wr. 155.]
Fōur'score.
Fōur'teen [*See* Eighteen.]
Fōur'teenth.
Fōurth.
Fo've-ate.
Fo-ve'o-late [so Wr.; *fo've-o-lāt*, Gd. 155.]
Fo-vil'la.
Fowl (28), *n.* a bird. [*See* Foul, 160.]
Fowl'er.
Fowl'ing.
Fox, 18.
Foxed (*fokst*), 165.
Fox'glove (*-gluv*).
Fox'like, 206, Exc. 5.
Fox'tāil.
Fra'cas (Fr.) [so Wb. Gd.; *frä-ka'*, Sm.; *fra'kas*, or *frä-ka'*, Wr. 154, 155.]
Frac'tion.
Frac'tion-al, 72.
Frac'tious (*-shus*), 169.
Fract'ure, 91.
Fract'ured (*-yurd*).
Fract'ur-ing (*-yur*).
Frag'ile (*fraj'-*), 152.
Fra-gil'i-ty, 108, 169.
Frag'ment, 10, 15.
Frag'ment-a-ry, 72.
Frag'ment-ed.
Fra'grance.
Fra'gran-cy, 169.
Fra'grant, 72.
Frāil, 23.
Frāil'ty.
Frām'a-ble, 164.
Frame, 23.
Frāmed, 165.
Frām'er, 183.
Frāme'work (*-wurk*).
Frām'ing.
Franc (*frangk*), *n.* a French silver coin. [*See* Frank, 160.]
Fran'chise (*-chiz*) (171) [*not* fran'chīz, 153.]
Fran-cis'can.
Fran'co-lin (*frang'-*), 54.
Fran-gi-bil'i-ty, 169.
Fran'gi-ble, 164.
Frank (*frangk*) (54), *a.* ingenuous; sincere. [*See* Franc, 160.]
Franked (*frangkt*).
Frank'in-cense (*frangk'-*) [so Wk. Sm. Wr.; *frank-in'-sens*, or *frank'in-sens*, Gd. 155.]
Frank'ing (*frangk'-*).
Frank'lin (*frangk'-*).
Frank'pledge, 206.
Fran'tic.
Frap, 10.
Frapped (*frapt*).
Frap'ping, 176.
Fra-ter'nal, 21, N.; 72.
Fra-ter'ni-ty, 108, 169.
Fra-ter-nī-za'tion [so Sm.; *frat-er-nī-za'-shun*, Wr. Gd. 155.]
Fra-ter'nize, 21, N.; 202 [*not* fra'tur-nīz, 153.]
Fra-ter'nized, 183.
Fra-ter'nīz-er.
Fra-ter'nīz-ing.
Frat-ri-cid'al, 183.
Frat'ri-cide, 169.
Frâud, 17.
Frâud'u-lent, 89.
Frâught (*frawt*), 162.
Frāy (23), *n.* a chafe in cloth; a fight; a quarrel: — *v.* to rub; to frighten. [pl. of *n.* Frays (*frāz*). — *See* Phrase, 160.]
Frāyed (*frād*), 187.
Frāy'ing.
Frēak, 13.
Frec'kle, 164.
Frec'kled (*frek'ld*), 150.
Frec'kling.
Free, 13.
Free'bench [so Sm. Wr.; *frē-bench'*, Wb. Gd. 155.]
Free'boot-er.
Free'boot-ing.
Free'born.
Freed, 188.
Free'man, 196.
Free'dom, 169.
Free'hōld, 206.
Free'hōld-er.
Free'ing.
Free'man, 196.
Free'mā-son (*-mā-sn*), 149.
Free'mā-son-ry (*-mā-sn-*).
Fre'er, 183, 188.
Free'stōne, 130.
Free'think-er (*-thingk-*) [so Sm. Wb. Gd.; *frē-thingk'ur*, Wk. 155.]
Free'think-ing.
Free-will', *n.* (161) [so Wk. Sm. Wb. Gd.; *frē'wil*, Wr. 155.]
Free'will, *a.* 161.
Freeze (13, 47), *v.* to be congealed with cold. [*See* Frieze, 160.]
Freez'ing, 183.

Freight (*frāt*), 162.
Freight'ed (*frāt'-*)
Freight'er (*frāt'-*).
Freight'ing (*frāt'-*).
French, 15, 44.
French'i-fīed, 186.
French'i-fȳ, 94.
French'i-fȳ-ing.
French'man, 196.
Fre-net'ic [Phrenetic, 203.]
Fren'zīed, 99.
Fren'zy, 169.
Fre'quen-cy, 169.
Fre'quent, *a.* 103, 161.
Fre-quent', *v.* 103, 161.
Fre-quent'a-tīve.
Fre-quent'ed.
Fre-quent'er.
Fre-quent'ing.
Fres'co (It.), *n.* [pl. Fres'cos (*-kōz*), 192.]
Fresh, 15, 46.
Fresh'en (*fresh'n*), 149.
Fresh'ened (*fresh'nd*), 150.
Fresh'en-ing (*fresh'n-*).
Fresh'et, 76.
Fresh'man, 196.
Fret, 15.
Fret'ful (*-fŏŏl*), 180.
Fret'ted, 176.
Fret'ter.
Fret'ting.
Fret'ty, 93.
Fret'work (*-wurk*).
Frī-a-bil'i-ty, 108.
Frī'a-ble, 164.
Frī'ar (74), *n.* a brother or member of any religious order. [*See* Frier, 160.]
Frī'ar-y.
Frib'ble, 164.
Frib'bled (*frib'ld*).
Frib'bler.
Frib'bling.
Fric-an-deau', (Fr.) (*frik-an-do'*) [Fricando, 203.]
Fric-as-see', 122, 171.
Fric-as-seed', 188.
Fric-as-see'ing.
Fric'tion.
Fric'tion-al, 72.
Frī'day (*-dy*).
Fried (*frīd*), 186.
Friĕnd (*frend*), 15.
Friĕnd'li-ness.
Friĕnd'ly, 93, 169.
Frī'er, *n.* one who fries. [*See* Friar, 160.]
Friēs'ic (*frēz'-*).

Friēze (*frēz*) (13), *n.* a coarse woollen cloth, with a nap on one side; — the part of an entablature between the architrave and the cornice. [*See* Freeze, 160.]
Frig'ate, 170.
Fright (*frīt*), 162.
Fright'en (*frīt'n*), 149, 162.
Fright'ened (*frīt'nd*), 150.
Fright'en-ing (*frīt'n-*).
Fright'ful (*-fŏŏl*).
Frig'id (*frij'-*), 16, 45.
Frĭ-gid'i-ty, 160.
Frill, 16, 172.
Frilled (*frild*), 165.
Frill'ing.
Fringe, 16, 45.
Fringed (*frinjd*), 183.
Fring'ing (*frinj'-*).
Fring'y (*frinj'-*).
Frip'per.
Frip'per-er.
Frip'per-y, 170.
Fri-seur' (Fr.) (*fre-zur'*).
Frisk, 16.
Frisked (*friskt*), 165; Note C, p. 34.
Frisk'er.
Frisk'et.
Frisk'ful (*-fŏŏl*).
Frisk'i-ly.
Frisk'i-ness, 169, 186.
Frisk'ing.
Frisk'y, 93, 169.
Frit, 16.
Frith, 16, 37.
Frit'ter, 170.
Frit'tered, 150.
Frit'ter-ing.
Frĭ-vol'i-ty, 108, 169.
Friv'o-loŭs.
Friz'zle, 164.
Friz'zled (*friz'ld*), 183.
Friz'zler.
Friz'zling.
Fro, 24.
Frock, 18, 181.
Frock'-cōat, 206, Exc. 1.
Frocked (*frokt*).
Frog, 18.
Frog'hop-per, 206.
Frol'ic, 18, 170.
Frol'icked (*-ikt*), 182.
Frol'ick-ing.
Frol'ic-some (*-sum*).
From, 18.

Frond, 18.
Fron-des'cence, 171.
Fron'doŭs.
Front (*frunt*) (22) [so Sm. Wr. Wb. Gd.; *frunt* or *front*, Wk. 155.]

☞ "Mr. Sheridan marks this word in the second manner only [*front*]; but I am much mistaken if custom does not almost universally adopt the first [*frunt*]." *Walker.*

Front'age (*frunt'-*), 70.
Frŏnt'al, 72.
Frŏnt'ā-ted.
Front'ed (*frunt'-*).
Frŏnt-iēr' (121, 169) [so Sm. Wr. Gd.; *fron'-chēr*, or *front'yēr*, Wk. 155.]
Frŏnt-iēred' (*-ērd'*), 165.
Front'ing (*frunt'-*).
Frŏnt'is-piēce, 171.
Front'let (*frunt'-*).
Frost (*frŏst*, or *frawst*) (18, N.) [so Wr. Gd.; *frŏst*, Wk. Sm. 155.]
Frost'ed.
Frost'i-ly.
Frost'i-ness, 169.
Frost'ing.
Frost'work (*-wurk*), 206.
Frost'wort (*-wurt*).
Frost'y, 93.
Froth (*frŏth*, or *frawth*) (18, N.) [so Wr. Gd.; *frŏth*, Wk. Sm. 155.]
Froth'i-ly.
Froth'i-ness, 169.
Froth'y, 93.
Frounce, 28.
Frounced (*frownst*).
Frounç'ing.
Fro'ward, 24, 72.
Frown, 28.
Frowned (*frownd*).
Frown'ing.
Froze, 24.
Frōz'en (*frōz'n*), 149.
Fruc-tes'cence, 171.
Fruc-tif'er-oŭs, 108.
Fruc-ti-fĭ-ca'tion.
Fruc'ti-fīed, 99.
Fruc'ti-fȳ, 94.
Fruc'ti-fȳ-ing.
Fru'gal (*froo'-*), 19, 72.
Fru-gal'i-ty (*froo-*), 108.

Fru′gal-ly (*froo′-*), 66, N.
Fru-gif′er-oŭs (*froo-*),
Fru-giv′o-roŭs (*froo-jiv′-*), 108.
Fruit (*froot*), 19.
Fruit′age (*froot′-*), 70.
Fruit′er-er (*froot′-*), 77.
Fruit′er-y (*froot′-*).
Fruit′ful (*froot′fo͝ol*), 19, 20.
Fruit′ing (*froot′-*).
Fru-ĭ′tion (*froo-ish′un*), 171.
Fru-men-ta′ceous (*froo-men-ta′shus*), 169, 171.
Fru′men-ty (*froo′-*).
Frush, 22.
Frus′trate.
Frus′trăt-ed, 183.
Frus-tra′tion.
Frus′tum (L.) [pl. Frus′ta, 198.]
Fru-tes′cent (*froo-*).
Fru′ti-cose (*froo′-*) [so Gd.; *froo-ti-kōs′*, Wr. 155.]
Fru′tĭ-coŭs (*froo′-*).
Fru-tic′u-lose.
Frȳ, 25.
Frȳ′ing.
Frȳ′ing-pan, 215.
Fu′cate.
Fu′căt-ed.
Fu′coid, 26, 27.
Fu-coid′al.
Fu′cus (L.) [pl. Fu′cī, 198.]
Fud′dle, 164.
Fud′dled (*fud′ld*), 183.
Fud′dler.
Fud′dling.
Fudge, 22, 45.
Fu′el, 26, 76.
Fu′elled (*-eld*) [Fueled, Wb. Gd. 203. — *See* 177, and Note E, p. 70.]
Fu′el-ler [Fueler, Wb. Gd. 203.]
Fu′el-ling [Fueling, Wb. Gd. 203.]
Fu-ga′cious, 169.
Fu-gaç′i-ty, 108.
Fu′gi-tĭve, 84, 171.
Fu′gle-man, 164, 196.
Fugue (*fūg*) (171; Note D, p. 37) [*not* fūj, 153.]
Fugu′ist (*fūg′-*)
Fŭl′crate.
Fŭl′crum (L.) [L. pl. *Ful′cra*; Eng. pl. Ful′crums (*-krumz*), 198.]
Ful-fil′ (*fo͝ol-*) (179, 180) [Fulfill, Wb. Gd. — *See* Note E, p. 70.]
Ful-filled′ (*fo͝ol-fild′*).
Ful-fil′ler (*fo͝ol-*), 176.
Ful-fil′ling (*fo͝ol-*).
Ful-fil′ment (*fo͝ol-*) [Fulfillment, Wb. Gd. 203.]
Fŭl′gen-cy.
Fŭl′gent.
Fŭl-gu-ra′tion.
Fŭl′gu-rīte, 152.
Fu-lig′i-noŭs (*-lij′-*).
Full (*fo͝ol*), 20, 172.
Full′-aged (*fo͝ol′-āgd*), 206, Exc. 5.
Full′-blōwn (*fo͝ol′-*).
Fulled (*fo͝old*), 20, 165.
Full′er (*fo͝ol′-*), 77.
Full′er-y (*fo͝ol′-*).
Full′ing (*fo͝ol′-*).
Full′y (*fo͝ol′y*), 178.
Fŭl′mar.
Fŭl′mi-nate, 73, 169.
Fŭl′mi-năt-ed, 183.
Fŭl′mi-năt-ing.
Fŭl-mi-na′tion.
Fŭl′mi-năt-o-ry [so Wk. Sm.; *fŭl′mi-na-to-ry*, Wr. Wb. Gd. 155.]
Ful′ness (*fo͝ol′-*) (178) [Fullness, Wb. Gd. 203.]
Fŭl′some (*fŭl′sum*) [*not* fo͝ol′sum, 153.]
Fŭl′vid.
Fŭl′voŭs, 169.
Fu-ma′do.
Fu′ma-to-ry [Fumitory, 203.]
Fum′ble, 164.
Fum′bled (*fum′bld*), 183.
Fum′bler, 77.
Fum′bling.
Fume, 26.
Fumed (*fūmd*), 165.
Fu-mif′er-oŭs, 108.
Fu′mi-gate, 73.
Fu′mi-găt-ed, 183.
Fu′mi-găt-ing.
Fu-mi-ga′tion, 112.
Fūm′ing.
Fu′mi-to-ry [Fumatory, 203.]
Fūm′oŭs.
Fūm′y, 93.
Fun, 22.
Fu-nam′bu-late.
Fu-nam′bu-lăt-ed.
Fu-nam′bu-lăt-ing.
Fu-nam-bu-la′tion.
Fu-nam′bu-lăt-o-ry [so Sm.; *fu-nam′bu-la-to-ry*, Wr. Wb. Gd.; 155.]
Func′tion (*fungk′-shun*), 54.
Func′tion-al, 72.
Func′tion-a-ry, 72.
Fund, 22.
Fun-da-ment′al, 72.
Fun-da-ment′al-ly.
Fund′ed.
Fund′ing.
Fu′ner-al, 26, 72.
Fu-ne′re-al, 49, N.; 169.
Fun′gi-form, 108.
Fun′goid (*fung′-*).
Fun-gos′i-ty (*fung-*).
Fun′goŭs (*fung′-*) (160), *a.* like a fungus; spongy.
Fun′gus (L.) (*fung′-*) (160) [L. pl. *Fun′gī*; Eng. pl. Fun′gus-es (*-ez*), 198], *n.* one of a class of cellular, flowerless plants; — a spongy excrescence.
Fu′ni-cle, 164.
Fu-nic′u-lar, 74.
Fun′nel, 66, 170.
Fun′ny, 169.
Fur (21), *n.* the finer, soft hair on certain animals; — a coating: — *v.* to cover with fur, or a coating. [*See* Fir, 148.] [pl. Furs (*furz*). — *See* Furze, 160.]
Fur′be-lōw, 169.
Fur′be-lōwed (*-lōd*), 188.
Fur′be-lōw-ing.
Fur′bish, 21, 104.
Fur′bished (*-bisht*).
Fur′bish-er.
Fur′bish-ing.
Fur′cate.
Fur′căt-ed.
Fur-ca′tion.
Fur′fur, 21, 169.
Fur-fu-ra′ceous (*-shus*).
Fu′ri-oŭs, 49, N.; 78.
Furl, 21, 135.
Furled (*furld*), 165.
Furl′ing.
Fur′long, 169.
Fur′lōugh (*-lō*), 162.
Fur′nace, 169.
Fur′nish, 21, 104.

Fur′nished (*-nisht*).
Fur′nish-er.
Fur′nish-ing.
Fur′ni-ture [so Wr. Wb. Gd.; *fur′ni-tūr*, coll. *fur′ni-ch'oor*, Sm. (*See* § 26); *fur′-ni-chūr*, Wk. 155.]
Furred (*furd*), 165, 176.
Fur′ri-er, 169.
Fur′ri-er-y.
Fur′ring.
Fŭr′rōw, 22, 101.
Fŭr′rōwed, 188.
Fur′ry, 21, 170.
Fur′ther, *a.* & *ad.* [Farther, 203.]
Fur′ther, *v.*
Fur′ther-ance.
Fur′thered (*-thurd*), 150.
Fur′ther-er.
Fur′ther-ing.
Fur′ther-more.
Fur′ther-mōst [Farthermost, 203.]
Fur′thest [Farthest, 203.]
Fur′tĭve, 84, 169.
Fu-run′cle (*-rung′kl*), 54, 164.
Fu′ry, 49, N.
Furze (*furz*) (21), *n.* a thorny shrub of the genus *Ulex.* [*See* Furs, pl. of Fur, 160.]
Furz′y, 93, 169.
Fus-ca′tion.
Fus′coŭs, 100, 169.
Fuse (*fūz*), *v.* 26, 136.
Fuse (*fūz*) *n.* [Fuze, 203.]
Fused (*fūzd*), 183.
Fu-see′ (*-ze′*), 121, 171.
Fūs-i-bil′i-ty (*fūz-*)
Fūs′i-ble (*fūz′-*) (164, 169) [so Sm. Wr. Wb. Gd.; *fu′si-bl*, Wk. 155.]
Fu′si-form, 108.
Fu′sil (*-zil*) (136), *a.* capable of being fused.
Fu′sil (*-zil*) [so Sm. Wb. Gd.; *fu-ze′*, Wk.; *fu′zil*, or *fu-ze′*, Wr. 155], *n.* a small musket.
Fu-sil-eer′ (*-zil-*), 122, 169.
Fūs′ing (*fūz′-*).
Fu′sion (*-zhun*).
Fuss, 22, 174.
Fussed (*fust*), *v.* did fuss. [*See* Fust, 160.]
Fuss′ing.
Fuss′y, 93.
Fust, *n.* a musty smell; mustiness. [*See* Fussed, 160.]
Fust′ian (*-yan*), 22, 51.
Fus′tic, 200.
Fus-ti-ga′tion.
Fust′i-ness, 169.
Fust′y, 93.
Fu′tĭle, 152.
Fu′tĭle-ly, 66, N.
Fu-til′i-ty, 108, 169.
Fut′tocks, *n. pl.*
Fūt′ure, 91.
Fu-tu′ri-ty, 89, 169.
Fūze, *n.* [Fuse, 203.]
Fuzz, 22, 175.
Fuzz′y, 93.
Fȳ, *int.* [Fie, 203.]

G.

Gab-ar-dine′ (*-dēn′*) (122) [Gaberdine, 203.]
Gab′ble, 164.
Gab′bled (*gab′ld*), 183.
Gab′bler, 77.
Gab′bling.
Ga′bi-on, 78, 86.
Gā-bi-on-nade′, 122.
Ga′ble, 164.
Ga′blet.
Gad, 10.
Gad′ded, 176.
Gad′der.
Gad′ding.
Gad′flȳ, 206.
Ga′doid [so Wr. Gd.; *gad′oid*, Sm. 155.]
Gael (*gāl*), *n. sing.* & *pl.*
Gael′ic (*gāl′ik*) (171) [so Wr. Wb. Gd.; *ga′cl-ik*, Sm. 155.]
Gaff (10) [*not* gaft, 153.]
Gaf′fer.
Gaf′fle, 164.
Gag, 10.
Gage (23, 45, 160), *n.* a pledge; — a challenge; — a kind of plum; — an instrument for measuring; — the number of feet which a ship sinks in water; — the position of one ship as regards another. [Gauge (in the last three senses), 203.]
Gage, *v.* to give as a pledge; — to bind by a pledge. [*See* Gauge, *v.* 160.]
Gaged, 165.
Gāg′er (*gāj′-*), *n.* one who gives a pledge. [*See* Gauger, 160.]
Gāg′ing (*gāj′-*), *part.* giving a pledge. [*See* Gauging, 160.]
Gagged (*gagd*), 176.
Gag′ger (*-gur*), 138.
Gag′gle, 164.
Gag′gled (*gag′ld*), 183.
Gag′gling.
[Gaiety, 203. — *See* Gayety.]
[Gaily, 203. — *See* Gayly.]
Gāin, 23.
Gāined (*gānd*), 165.
Gāin′er.
Gāin′ful (*-fool*), 180.
Gāin-said′ (*gān-sed′*), *or* Gāin′said (*gān′sed*) [Gainsayed, Wb. Gd. 203.]
Gāin-sāy′, *or* Gāin′sāy [so Wr. Gd.; *gān-sā′*, Wk.; *gān′sā*, Sm. 155.]
Gāin-sāy′er, *or* Gāin′-sāy-er.
Gāin-sāy′ing, *or* Gāin′-sāy-ing.
Gair′ish (*ghêr′-*) [Garish, 203.]

☞ Of the two forms of this word, Walker, Smart, Webster, and Goodrich prefer the first (*gairish*). Worcester prefers the last (*garish*).

Gāit (23), *n.* manner of walking. [*See* Gate, 160.]
Gāit′er.
Gāit′ered (*-urd*), 150.
Gāit′er-ing.
Ga′la, 72.
Ga-lac′tic, 109.
Gal-ac-tom′e-ter, 108.
Gal-ac-toph′a-gist (*-tof′-*).
Gal-ac-toph′a-goŭs (*-tof′-*).
Gal-ac-toph′o-roŭs (*-tof′-*), 108.
Ga-lac-to-poi-et′ic.
Ga-lan′gal (*-lang′-*), 54.

Gal′an-tīne, 152.
Ga-la′tians (*-shanz*), *n. pl.* 112.
Gal′ax-y, 93, 170.
Gal′ba-num.
Gale, 23.
Gal′e-as [so Sm. Wb. Gd.; *gal′yas*, Wk.; *gal′yas*, or *ga′le-as*, Wr. 155.]
Ga′le-ate, *a.* 73.
Ga′le-āt-ed.
Ga-lee′to.
Ga-le′na, 72.
Ga-len′ic, 109.
Ga-len′ic-al, 108.
Ga′len-ism (*-izm*), 136.
Ga′len-ist.
Ga-lī′cian (*-lish′un*).
Gal-i-le′an, 110.
Gal′i-lee (170), *n.* a porch or chapel.
Gal′i-ot [so Sm. Gd.; *gal′yut*, Wk.; *gal′yot*, Wr. 155.] [G a l l i o t, 203.]
Gal′i-pot (170), *n.* a kind of white resin. [*See* Gallipot, 160.]
Gall, 17.
Gal′lant (161), *a.* brave, high-spirited.
Gal-lȧnt′ [so Sm. Wr.; *gal-lănt′*, Wk. Wb. Gd. 155.] (161), *a.* attentive to ladies.
Gal-lȧnt′ [so Wk. Sm. Wr.; *gal-lănt′*, Wb. Gd. 155], *n.* one who is attentive to ladies: — *v.* to wait on or be attentive to, as ladies.
Gal-lȧnt′ed.
Gal-lȧnt′ing.
Gal′lant-ly (161), *ad.* bravely.
Gal-lȧnt′ly (161), *ad.* in the manner of a gallant.
Gal′lant-ry, 170.
Gal′late [so Wr. Wb. Gd.; *gawl′āt*, Sm. 155.]
Gâlled (*gawld*), 165.
Gal′le-on, 170.
Gal′ler-y, 171.
Gâl′less, 66, N.; 178.
Gal′ley (98) [pl. Gal′leys, 190.]
Gâll′flȳ, 206.
Gal′lic [so Wb. Gd.; *gawl′ik*, Sm. Wr. 155], *a.* denoting an acid obtained from gall-nuts.
Gal′lic, *a.* belonging to Gaul, or France.
Gal′lic-an.
Gal′li-cism (*-sizm*).
Gal′li-mâu-fry.
Gal-li-na′cean (*-shan*).
Gal-li-na′ceous (*-shus*), 169, 170, 171.
Gal′li-nip-per, 170.
Gal′li-nule.
[G a l l i o t, 203. — *See* Galiot.]
Gal′li-pot (170), *n.* a small glazed pot, used by apothecaries. [*See* Galipot, 160.]
Gâll′-nut.
Gal′lon, 10, 86, 170.
Gal-loon′, 121.
Gal′lop, 86, 170.
Gal-lop-äde′, 122.
Gal′loped (*-lupt*), 165.
Gal′lop-er.
Gal′lop-ing.
Gal′lo-wāy.
Gal′lows (*-lus*) [pl. Gal-lowses (*-lus-ez*), 189.]

☞ Some writers have regarded *gallows* as both singular and plural, but the best modern authorities regard it as singular only, with the regular plural *gallowses*.

Ga-loche′ (Fr.) (*ga lŏsh′*, or *ga-lōsh′*) [*ga-lŏsh′*, Sm.; *ga-lŏsh′*, Wk. Wr. Wb. Gd. 154, 155.]
[G a l t, 203. — *See* Gault.]
Gal-van′ic, 109, 170.
Gal′van-ism (*-izm*).
Gal′van-ist.
Gal′van-ize, 202.
Gal′van-ized, 183.
Gal′van-īz-ing.
Gal-va-nog′ra-phy.
Gal-va-nol′o-gist.
Gal-va-nol′o-gy, 108.
Gal-va-nom′e-ter.
Gal-van′o-scope.
Gam-ba′do [pl. Gam-ba′does (*-dōz*), 192.]
Gam′bit.
Gam′ble, 164.
Gam′bled (*gam′bld*).
Gam′bler.
Gam′bling.
Gam-boge′ (*-booj′*) (121) [so Wk. Sm. Wr.; *gam-bōj′*, Wb. Gd. 155.]
Gam-bo′gi-an.
Gam′bol, 10, 86.
Gam′bolled (*-bold*) (165) [G a m b o l e d, Wb. Gd. 203. — *See* 177, and Note E, p. 70.]
Gam′bol-ling [G a m b o l i n g, Wb. Gd. 203.]
Gam′brel [C a m b r e l, C h a m b r e l, 203.]
Game, 23.
Gamed, 165.
Game′ful (*-fŏŏl*).
Game′some (*-sum*).
Game′ster, 77.
Gām′ing.
Gam′mer.
Gam′mon, 170.
Gam′moned (*-mund*).
Gam′mon-ing.
Gam-o-pet′al-oŭs.
Gam-o-phyl′loŭs, *or* Ga-moph′yl-loŭs [*See* Adenophyllous.]
Gam-o-sep′al-oŭs.
Gam′ut, 170.
Ganch, 10, 44.
Ganched (*gancht*).
Ganch′ing.
Gan′der, 10, 77.
Gang (10, 54), *n.* a band; a crew. [*See* Gangue, 160.]
Gan′gli-ac (*gang′-*), 54.
Gan′gli-form (*gang′-*).
Gan′gli-o-form (*gang′-*).
Gan′gli-on (*gang′-*), 54.
Gan′gli-o-na-ry (*gang′-*), 72, 171.
Gan-gli-on′ic (*gang′-*),
Gan′gre-nate (*gang′-*).
Gan′gre-nāt-ed (*gang′-*).
Gan′gre-nāt-ing (*gang′-*).
Gan′grene (*gang′-*), 171.
Gan′grened (*gang′-*), 165.
Gan′grēn-ing (*gang′-*).
Gan-gre-nes′cent (*gang-*), 171.
Gan′gre-noŭs (*gang′-*).
Gangue (*gang*), *n.* the matrix of an ore. [*See* Gang, 160.]
Gang′wāy, 206.
Gan′net, 170.
Ga′noid [so Gd.; *gan′oid*, Sm. Wr. 155.]

Ga-noid′al.
Ga-noid′i-an.
Gănt′let, *n.* a military punishment inflicted by making the offender run between two rows of men, each of whom gives him a stroke with a switch or a whip. [*See* Gauntlet, 148.]
Gan′za.
Gāol (*jāl*) (158) [Jail, 203.]

☞ The form *gaol*, though heretofore common, and sanctioned by good authorities, is not now so generally used as *jail*.

Gaol′er (*jāl′-*) [Jailer, 203.]
Gap, 10.
Gape (*gäp*, or *gāp*) [so Wr.; *gäp*, Wk. Wb. Gd.; *gāp*, Sm. 155.]

☞ "The expressive but irregular pronunciation of this word with the Italian *a* [*gäp*] is no longer prevalent." *Smart.* "This pronunciation [*gäp*], however, is well supported by authorities, and it is common in the U. S." *Worcester.*

Gaped (*gäpt*, or *gāpt*).
Gap′er (*gäp′-*, or *gāp′-*).
Gap′ing (*gap′-*, or *gāp′-*).
Găr′a-gāy.
Găr′an-cine (*-sēn*) [so Sm. Wr.; *găr′an-sin*, Gd. 155.]
Garb, 11, 135.
Gar′bage, 70.
Gar′baged.
Gar′ble, 165.
Gar′bled (*gar′bld*), 183.
Gar′bler.
Gar′bles (*gar′blz*), *n. pl.*
Gar′bling.
Gar′bōard.
Gar′den (*gar′dn*) (53, 149) [so Gd.; *g′ar′dn*, Sm. (*See* § 26), *gar′dn*, or *gar′den*, Wr. 155.]
Gar′dened (*gar′dnd*).
Gar′den-er (*gar′dn-*).
Gar′den-ing (*gar′dn-*).
Gar′fish, 206.
Gar′gan-cy, 98, 169.
Gar′ga-rism (*-rizm*).
Gar′get (*-ghet*), 138.
Gar′gil (*-ghil*), 138.
Gar′gle, 164.
Gar′gled (*gar′gld*), 183.
Gar′gling.
Gar′gol.
Gar′ish (*ghêr′-*) [Gairish, 203.] [*See* Note under Gairish.]
Gar′land, 11, 72.
Gar′lic, 11, 200.
Gar′lick-y, 182.
Gar′ment.
Gar′ner, 11, 77.
Gar′nered (*-nurd*), 150.
Gar′ner-ing.
Gar′net, 11, 76.
Gar′nish, 104.
Gar′nished (*-nisht*).
Gar-nish-ee′, 122.
Gar′nish-er.
Gar′nish-ing.
Gar′nish-ment.
Gar′ni-ture, 169.
Gar′pike.
Ga′roŭs [so Wk. Wr. Wb. Gd.; *găr′us*, Sm. 155.]
Găr′ret, 11, N.
Găr′ret-ed.
Găr-ret-eer′, 122.
Găr′ret-ing.
Găr′ri-son (*-sn*), 149.
Găr′ri-soned (*-snd*), 165.
Găr-rōte′ (Sp.).
Gar-rōt′ed, 183.
Gar-rōt′ing.
Găr-ru′li-ty (*-roo′-*), 169.
Găr′ru-loŭs, (*-roo-*).
Gar′ter, 11, 77.
Gar′tered, 150.
Gar′ter-ing.
Ga′rum.
Găs (10, 174) [*not* gäs, *nor* găz, 153.]
Gas′con.
Gas-con-ade′, 122.
Gas-con-ăd′ed, 183.
Gas-con-ăd′ing.
Gas-con-ăd′er.
Gas′e-ous (*gaz′-*) (136, 171, 176) [so Sm. Gd.; *gaz′e-us*, or *ga′se-us*, Wr. 155.]
Gash, 10, 46.
Gashed (*gasht*), 165; Note C, p. 34.
Gash′ing.
Gas′-hōld-er, 206, Exc. 3.
Gas-i-fī-ca′tion.
Gas′i-fīed, 186.
Gas′i-form, 108.
Gas′i-fȳ, 94, 176.
Gas′i-fȳ-ing.
Gas′ket.
Gas′kins (*-kinz*), *n. pl.*
Gas′-me-ter, 206, Exc. 3.
Ga som′e-ter (*-zom′-*) (108) [so Sm. Wr.; *gaz-om′e-tur*, Gd. 155.]
Ga-som′e-try (*-zom′-*) [so Wr.; *gaz-om′e-try*, Gd. 155.]
Gȧsp, 12, 131.
Gȧsped (*gaspt*), 165.
Gȧsp′ing.
Gas′sing.
Gas′sy, 93, 170.
Gas′ter-o-pod [Gastropod, 203.]
Gas-ter-op′o-doŭs [Gastropodous, 203.]
Gas′tric, 200.
Gas-tril′o-quist.
Gas-tril′o-quy, 171.
Gas-tri′tis.
Gas′tro-cele.
Gas-trol′o-gy, 108.
Gas′tro-man-cy, 169.
Gas′tro-nome.
Gas-tron′o-mer.
Gas-tro-nom′ic, 109.
Gas-tron′o-mist.
Gas-tron′o-my.
Gas′tro-pod [Gasteropod, 203.]
Gas-trop′o-doŭs [Gasteropodous, 203.]
Gas-trŏr′a-phy.
Gas-tros′co-py.
Gas-trot′o-my.
Gate (23), *n.* a frame for closing a passage; — an avenue. [*See* Gait, 160.]
Gate′wāy, 206.
Gath′er, 10, 38, 77.
Gath′ered, 150.
Gath′er-er.
Gath′er-ing.
Gâud′i-ly.
Gâud′i-ness, 169.
Gâud′y.
Gâuf′fer-ing.
Gāuge (*gāj*) (23, 160), *n.* an instrument for measuring; — the number of feet which a ship sinks in the water; — the position of a ship as regards another; — the breadth of a railway.

[Gage (in the first three senses), 203.]
Gāuge (*gāj*), *v.* to measure. [*See* Gage, *v.* 160.]
Gāuge'a-ble (*gāj'*-), 164, 183.
Gāuged (*gājd*), 183.
Gāug'er (*gāj'*-), *n.* one who gauges, or measures. [*See* Gager, 160.]
Gāug'ing (*gāj'*-), *part.* & *n.* measuring. [*See* Gaging, 160.]
Gâul, 17.
Gâult [Galt, Golt, 203.]
Gäunt (*gänt*) [*not* gawnt, 153.]
Gäunt'let (*gant'*-), *n.* a large iron glove. [*See* Gantlet, 160.]
Gäunt'let-ed.
Gâuze, 17, 40.
Gâuz'y.
Gave, 23.
Gav'el, 170.
Gav'el-kind.
Ga-vot' [so Sm.; *gav'-ot*, Wr. Wb. Gd. 155.]
Gawk, 17.
Gawk'y, 93.
Gāy, 23.
Gāy'e-ty (171) [Gaiety, 203.]
Gāy'ly [Gaily, 203.]
Gaze, 23.
Gazed, 183.
Ga-zelle', 121, 171.
Gāz'er.
Ga-zette', 121, 171.
Ga-zet'ted, 171.
Gaz-et-teer', 122, 169.
Gāz'ing, 183.
Gēar (*ghēr*), 13, 138.
Gēared (*ghērd*), 165.
Gēar'ing (*ghēr'*-).
Gēat (*jēt*).
Geck'o (*ghek'o*) [so Wr.; *jek'o*, Gd. 155.]
Gee, 13, 45.
Geed, 188.
Gee'ing.
Geese (*ghēs*), *n. pl.* (138) [*See* Goose, 195.]
Ge-hen'na (*ghe*-), 138.
Ge'ĭne, 152.
Gel'a-ble, 164, 169.
Ge-lat'i-nate.
Ge-lat'i-nāt-ed.
Ge-lat'i-nāt-ing.
Ge-lat-i-na'tion.
Gel'a-tĭne (45,152)[Gelatin, 203.]
Gel-a-tin'i-fôrm (108)[so Wr.; *je-lat'i-ni-form*, Wb. Gd. 155.]
Ge-lat'i-nize, 202.
Ge-lat'i-nized, 183.
Ge-lat'i-nīz-ing.
Ge-lat'i-noŭs.
Geld (*gheld*).
Geld'ed (*gheld'*-).
Geld'er (*gheld'*-).
Geld'ing (*gheld'*-).
Gel'ly [Jelly, 203.]

☞ Both forms of this word are found in most of the Dictionaries. Smart and Worcester indicate a preference for *jelly*, and this form is now the more common.

Gelt (*ghelt*).
Gem, 15, 45.
Ge-mä'ra (*ghe*-), 138.
Ge-mär'ic (*ghe*-).
Gem'el.
Gem'i-nī (L.), *n. pl.*
Gem'i-noŭs.
Gem'ma-ry, 72, 170.
Gem'mate.
Gem'māt-ed.
Gem-ma'tion.
Gemmed (*jemd*), 176.
Gem'me-oŭs, 169.
Gem-mif'er-ous, 108.
Gem'ming, 176.
Gem-mip'a-roŭs.
Gem'mule, 170.
Gem-mu-lif'er-oŭs.
Gem'my, 170.
Gems'boc (*jemz'bŏŏk*) [Gemsbok, 203.]
Gen-darme' (*zhän-därm'*) [pl. Gen-darmes', *or* Gens d'armes(*zhän-darm'*).

☞ The plural form, *gens d'armes* (armed men), is the French expression, from which the word *gendarme* is formed.

Gen-darm'er-y.
Gen'der, 15, 45, 77.
Gen-e-a-log'ic-al, *or* Ge-ne-a-log'ic-al (*-loj'*-) [*jen-e-a-loj'ik-al*, Wr. Wb. Gd.; *jē-ne-a-loj'-ik-al*, Wk. Sm. 155.]
Gen-e-al'o-gist, *or* Ge-ne-al'o-gist.
Gen-e-al'o-gy, *or* Ge-ne-al'o-gy (108) [*jen-e-al'-o-jy*, Wr. Wb. Gd.; *jē-ne-al'o-jy*, Wk. Sm. 155.]
Gen'e-ra, *n. pl.* [*See* Genus.]
Gen'er-al, 108, 233, Exc.
Gen-er-al-is'si-mo, 169, 170.
Gen-er-al'i-ty, 108, 169.
Gen-er-al-ĭ-za'tion.
Gen'er-al-ize, 202.
Gen'er-al-ized, 183.
Gen'er-al-īz-ing.
Gen'er-al-ly, 170.
Gen'er-ant.
Gen'er-ate, 45, 72.
Gen'er-āt-ed, 183.
Gen'er-āt-ing.
Gen-er-a'tion, 45, 112.
Gen'er-āt-ĭve [so Sm.; *gen'er-a-tiv*, Wk. Wr. Wb. Gd. 155.]
Gen'er-āt-or, 228.
Gen'er-āt-rix.
Ge-nĕr'ic, 109.
Ge-nĕr'ic-al, 108.
Gen-er-os'i-ty, 169.
Gen'er-oŭs, 108, 169.
Gen'e-sis, 45, 169.
Gen'et, *n.* a small-sized Spanish horse; — an animal of the weasel kind. [*See* Genette, 148.] [Genette, 203.]
Ge-neth'li-ac.
Gen-eth-li'ac-al.
Ge-neth-lĭ-al'o-gy.
Ge-net'ic.
Ge-nette' (*-net'*), *n.* a cat skin made into a muff or a tippet; — a small-sized Spanish horse; — an animal of the weasel kind. [Genet (in the last two senses), 203.]
Ge-ne'van.
Ge-ne'van-ism (*-izm*).
Gen-e-vese' (*-vēz'*), *n. sing.* & *pl.*
Ge'ni-al, 72, 78, 156.
Ge-ni-al'i-ty, 169.
Ge'ni-al-ly, 66, N.
Ge-nic'u-late.
Ge-nic'u-lāt-ed.
Ge-nic-u-la'tion.
Gen'i-tal.
Gen'i-ting [Jenneting, 203.]
Gen'i-tiv-al.
Gen'i-tĭve, 84, 108.
Gēn'ius (*jēn'yus*), *or* Ge'ni-us [so Wr.; *jēn'yus*, Gd.; *jē'ni-us*,

Wk. Sm. 155] [pl. Geniuses], *n.* extraordinary mental power.
Ge'ni-us (L.) [pl. *Ge'-ni-ī*, 198], *n.* a tutelary deity.
Gen-o-ese' (*-ēz'*), *n. sing.* & *pl.*
Gen-teel', 45, 121.
Gen-teel'ly, 66, N.; 170.
Gen'tian (*-shan*).
Gen'til.
Gen'tile (81,152) [so Sm. Wr. Gd.; *jen'tīl*, or *jen'tīl*, Wk. 155.]

☞ Though Walker prefers *jen'tīl*, he says of *jen'tīl*, "This pronunciation [*jen'tīl*] is most agreeable to general usage."

Gen'til-ism (*-izm*), 143.
Gen-ti-lĭ'tial (*-lish'al*).
Gen-ti-lĭ'tioŭs (*-lish'us*).
Gen-til'i-ty, 169.
Gen'tle, 164.
Gen'tle-folk (*-fōk*) [pl. Gen'tle-folks (*-fōks*).]

☞ Though *gentlefolk* is a collective noun, writers who make use of the word generally give it the plural form.

Gen'tle-man (*jen'tl-*)(72, 164) [pl. Gen'tle-men (*jĕn'tl-men*), 156, 196.]

☞ The plural is often mispronounced *jen'tl-mun.*

Gen'tle-wom-an (*jen'-tl-wŏŏm-*).
Gen-too', 121.
Gen'try, 15, 93.
Gen-u-flec'tion [so Sm.; *jē-nu-flek'shun*, Wr. Wb. Gd. 155.]
Gen'u-ĭne, 152, 171.
Ge'nus (L.) [pl. Gen'-ĕr-a, 198.]
Ge-o-cen'tric, 109.
Ge-o-cen'tric-al, 108.
Ge'ode, 13, 24.
Ge-o-des'ic, 109.
Ge-o-des'ic-al, 108.
Ge-od'e-sy (105) [so Wr. Wb. Gd.; *je'o-des-y*, Sm. 155.]
Ge-o-det'ic, 109.
Ge-o-det'ic-al, 108.
Ge-o-dif'er-oŭs, 108.
Ge'og-nŏst.
Ge-og-nŏst'ic, 109.
Ge-og-nŏst'ic-al, 108.
Ge-og'no-sy, 105.
Ge-o-gon'ic.
Ge-og'o-ny, 105.
Ge-og'ra-pher, 45, 108.
Ge-o-graph'ic, 109.
Ge-o-graph'ic-al, 108.
Ge-og'ra-phy, 45, 108.
Ge-ol'o-ger, 45, 77.
Ge-o-lo'gi-an.
Ge-o-log'ic-al (*-loj'-*).
Ge-ol'o-gist, 45, 108.
Ge-ol'o-gy, 45, 108.
Ge'o-man-cer.
Ge'o-man-cy, 169.
Ge-o-man'tic.
Ge-om'e-ter, 108.
Ge-o-met'ric, 109.
Ge-o-met'ric-al, 108.
Ge-om-e-trĭ'cian (*-trish'an*), 112, 171.
Ge-om'e-try, 45, 108.
Ge-o-pon'ic, 109.
Ge-o-pon'ic-al, 108.
Ge-o-pon'ics.
Ge-o-ra'ma [so Wr.; *je-o-ra'ma*, Gd. 155.]
Geor'gi-an (*jor'-*).
Geor'gic (*jor'jik*), 45, 171; Note D, p. 37.
Geor'gic-al (*jor'jik-*).
Geor'gics (*jor'jiks*), *n. [pl.*
Ge-os'co-py, 105.
Ge-ra'ni-um, 169.
Ger'fâl-con (*jer'faw-kn*) (171) [Gyrfalcon, Jerfalcon, 203.]
Germ, 21, N.; 45.
Ger'man [pl. Ger'mans (*-manz*), 196.]
Ger'man-der, *or* Ger-man'der [so Wr.; *jer'-man-der*, Sm.; *jer-man'dur*, Wk. Wb. Gd. [155.]
Ger-mane', 121.
Ger-man'ic.
Ger'man-ism (*-izm*).
Germ'i-nal, 72, 78.
Germ'i-nant.
Germ'i-nate, 73.
Germ'i-năt-ed, 183.
Germ'i-năt-ing.
Germ-i-na'tion.
Ge-roc'o-my.
Gĕr'und, 15, 45.
Ge-rund'i-al.
Ge-rund'ĭve, 84.
Ges-ta'tion.
Ges'tic.
Ges-tic'u-late, 89.
Ges-tic'u-lāt-ed, 183.
Ges-tic'u-lāt-ing.
Ges-tic-u-la'tion, 112.
Ges-tic'u-lāt-or.
Ges-tic'u-lāt-o-ry [so Sm.; *jes-tik'u-la-to-ry*, Wr. Wb. Gd. 155.]
Gest'ure, 45, 91.
Gest'ured (*-yurd*), 165.
Gest'ur-ing (*-yur*).
Get (*ghet*) (138) [*not* ghit, 153.]
Gew'gaw (*gu'-*), 138, 171.
Geȳ'ser (*ghī'sur*) (138, 171) [so Wr. Gd.; *ghē'sur*, Sm. 155.]
Ghȧst'li-ness, 162, 186.
Ghȧst'ly, 12, 93, 162.
Ghee, 138. [D, p. 37.
Gher'kin, 21, N.; Note
Ghib'el-lĭne, 152, 162.
Ghōst, 24.

☞ "*Host, post, most, ghost*, &c., . . . instead of having the regular short sound as heard in *cost, frost, tost, lost*, are pronounced with *o* in its long or alphabetical sound; perhaps because they were once pronounced in two syllables, in correspondence with their old spelling, *ho-ste, po-ste*, &c." *Smart.*

Ghōst'like, 206, Exc. 5.
Ghōst'li-ness, 186.
Ghōst'ly, 93, 169.
Ghoul (*gool*), 19, 171.
Gial-lo-li'no (*jal-lo-le'-no*) [so Gd.; *jī-al-lo-le'no*, Wr. 155.]
Gi'ant, 25, 72.
Giaour (*jour*) (Turkish), 171.
Gib'ber-ing (*ghib'-*), 138.
Gib'ber-ish (*ghib'-*), 138
Gib'bet, 16, 45, 170.
Gib'bet-ed.
Gib'bet-ing.
Gib'bon (*ghib'-*), 138.
[Gib-boom, 203.—*See* Jib-boom.]
Gib-bose' (*ghib-*), 138.
Gib-bos'i-ty (*ghib-*), 169.
Gib'boŭs(*ghib'-*), 138, 171
Gib'cat (*ghib'-*), 138.
Gibe (25, 45), *n.* a sneer: —*v.* to sneer. [*See* Gybe, 160.]
Gibed, 165, 183.
Gīb'er.
Gīb'ing.
Gib'let, *a.*
Gib'lets, *n. pl.*
Gib'stȧff (*jib'stȧf*, or *ghib'stȧf*) [so Wr.; *jib'stȧf*, Wb. Gd.; *ghib'stȧf*, Sm. 155.]
Gid'di-ly (*ghid'-*).

Gid′di-ness (*ghid′-*).
Gid′dy (*ghid′-*), 138.
Gĭr′ēa-gle (*jĕr′ē-gl*),164.
Gift (*ghift*), 16, 138.
Gift′ed.
Gig (*ghig*), 16, 138.
Gī-gan-te′an, 110.
Gī-gan-tesque′ (*-tesk′*).
Gī-gan′tic, 79, 109.
Gī-gan-tol′o-gy, 108.
Gig′gle (*ghig′l*), 138,164.
Gig′gled (*ghig′ld*), 183.
Gig′gler (*ghig′-*).
Gig′gling (*ghig′-*).
Gild (*ghild*), 16, 138.
Gild′ed (*ghild′-*).
Gild′er (*ghild′ur*), *n.* one who gilds. [*See* Guilder, 160.]
Gild′ing (*ghild′-*).
Gill (*ghil*) (138, 161), *n.* the organ of respiration in fishes.
Gill (*jil*) (46, 161), *n.* the fourth part of a pint.
Gil′ly-flow-er, 206.
Gilt (*ghilt*), *part.* from Gild. [*See* Guilt, 160.]
Gim′bal, 16, 45, 72.
Gim′crack, 16, 45.
Gim′let (*ghim′-*) (138) [*not* ghim′blet, 153.]
Gim′let-ed (*ghim′-*).
Gim′let-ing (*ghim′-*).
Gimp (*ghimp*), 16, 138.
Gin, 16, 45.
Gin′ger, 16, 45, 77.
Gin′ger•brĕad, 206.
Ging′ham (*ghing′am*), 138, 162, 171.
Gin′ging (*jin′jing*), 45.
Gin′gi-val, 45, 78.
Ging′ko (45, 54), [Gin-ko, 203.]
Gin′gle, 45, 164.
Gin′gled (*jing′gld*), 183.
Gin′gler.
Gin′gling.
Gin′gly-moid (*ghing′-*), 53, 54, 171.
Gin′gly-mus (*ghing′-*) [pl. Gin′gly-mī, 198.]
[Ginko, 203.—*See* Gingko.]
Ginned (*jind*), 176.
Gin′net, 16, 45, 80.
Gin′ning, 176.
Gin′seng, 16, 45.
Gip, 16, 45.
Gipped (*jipt*).
Gip′ping, 176.
Gip′sy (45, 169) [Gypsy, 203.]

☞ Of the two modes of spelling this word, Walker, Webster, and Goodrich prefer the first (*gipsy*): Smart and Worcester prefer the last (*gypsy*).

Gip′sy-ism(*-izm*)[Gypsyism, 203.]
Gī-raffe′ (121, 171) [so Wr. Wb. Gd.; *zhĭ-raf′*, Sm. 155.]
Gi′ran-dole (*zhe′ran-dōl*) [so Sm.; *jĭr′an-dōl*, Wr. Wb. Gd. 155.]
Gĭr′a-sole, 16, 45.
Gird (*ghird*), 21, N.; 138.
Gird′ed (*ghird′-*).
Gird′er (*ghird′-*), 171.
Gird′ing (*ghird′-*).
Gir′dle (*ghir′dl*), 138,164
Gir′dled (*ghir′dld*).
Gir′dler (*ghir′-*).
Gir′dling (*ghir′-*).
[Gire, 203.—*See* Gyre.]
Girl (*ghirl*), 21, N.; 138, 146.
Gironde (Fr.) (*zhē-rōnd′*).
Gi-rōnd′ist (*je-rōnd′ist*) [so Wr.; *jĭ-rŏnd′ist*, Gd. 155.]
Girt (*ghirt*), 21, N.; 138.
Girth (*ghirth*), 37, 138.
Gist, 16, 45.
Gith (*ghith*), 16, 138.
Git′tern (*ghit′-*), 138.
Giusto (It.) (*jōō′s′to*).
Give (*ghiv*), 16, 138, 163.
Giv′en (*ghiv′n*), 149.
Giv′er (*ghiv′-*), 183.
[Gives, 203.—*See* Gyves.]
Giv′ing (*ghiv′-*).
Giz′zard (*ghiz′-*), 171.
Gla′broŭs.
Gla′ci-al (*-shĭ-al*) [so Wk. Sm. Wr.; *gla′-shal*, Wb. Gd. 155.]
Glaç′i-er (*glăs′i-ur*) [so Sm. Wr.; *gla′sēr*, Wb. Gd. 154, 155.]
Gla′cis (*gla′sis*, or *gla-sēs′*) [so Wk. Wr.; *gla′sis*, Wb. Gd.; *gla-sēs′*, Sm. 154, 155.]
Glad, 10.
Glad′den (*glad′n*), 149.
Glad′dened (*glad′nd*).
Glad′den-ing (*glad′n-*).
Glad′i-ate, 78.
Glad′i-āt-or [so Sm. Wr. Gd.; *glad-ĭ-āt′ur*, Wk. 155.]
Glad-i-a-to′ri-al.

Glad′i-a-to-ry [so Wr. Wb. Gd.; *glad′i-āt-o-ry*, Sm. 155.]
Glad′i-ole.
Glad′some (*-sum*).
Glair (*glêr*), *n.* the white of an egg; — any viscous, transparent matter: — *v.* to smear with glair. [*See* Glare, 160.]
Glaired (*glêrd*), 165.
Glair′ing (*glêr′-*).
Glair′y (*glêr′y*), 171.
Glânce, 12, 131.
Glânced (*glânst*), 165, 183; Note C, p. 34.
Glânç′ing.
Gland, 10.
Gland′ered (*-urd*).
Gland′ers (*-urz*), *n. pl.*
Gland-if′er-oŭs, 108.
Gland′i-form, 108.
Gland′u-lar, 108.
Gland-u-la′tion.
Gland′ule, 10, 90.
Gland-u-lif′er-oŭs, 108.
Gland-u-los′i-ty, 169.
Gland′u-loŭs.
Glare (*glêr*) (14), *n.* a dazzling light: — *v.* to shine with a dazzling light. [*See* Glair, 160.]
Glar′e-oŭs (*glêr′-*).
Glar′i-ness (*glêr′-*).
Glâss, 12, 131, 174.
Glâss′house, 206.
Glâss′i-ness, 186.
Glâss′works (*-wurks*), *n. pl.*
Glâss′wort (*-wurt*).
Glâss′y, 93, 169.
Glâu-ces′cent, 171.
Glâu′cĭne, 152.
Glâu-co′ma, 17, 72.
Glâu-co′ma-toŭs [so Gd.; *glaw-kom′a-tus*, Wr. 155.]
Glâu-co′sis, 109.
Glâu′coŭs, 17, 100, 169.
[Glāymore, 203.—*See* Claymore.]
Glaze, 23.
Glazed, 165, 183.
Glāz′er.
Glā′zier (*-zhur*), 47, N.
Glāz′ing.
Glēam, 13.
Glēamed (*glēmd*), 165.
Glēam′ing.
Glēam′y, 93.
Glēan, 13.

Glēaned (*glēnd*), 165.
Glēan'er, 77.
Glēan'ing.
Glebe, 13.
Glēb'y, 93, 169.
Glee, 13.
Gleet.
Gleet'y.
Glen, 15.
Gle'ne [so Wr. Gd.; *glēn*, Sm. 155.]
Gle'noid.
Glib, 16.
Glide, 25.
Glīd'ed, 183.
Glīd'er.
Glīd'ing.
Glim'mer, 66, 170.
Glim'mered (*-murd*), 150, 171.
Glim'mer-ing.
Glimpse (*glimps*) (16) [so Wk. Sm. Wr.; *glims*, Wb. Gd. 155.]
Glis'sa.
Glis'ten (*glis'n*), 149, 162.
Glis'tened (*glis'nd*), 165.
Glis'ten-ing (*glis'n-*).
Glis'ter.
Glis'tered, 150, 165.
Glis'ter-ing.
Glit'ter, 16, 77.
Glit'tered, 150, 165.
Glit'ter-ing.
Glōam'ing.
Glōat, 24.
Glōat'ed.
Glōat'ing.
Glo'bard.
Glo'bate.
Glo'bāt-ed.
Globe, 24.
Glo-bose'.
Glo-bos'i-ty, 108, 169.
Glo'boŭs.
Glob'u-lar, 108.
Glob'ule, 90.
Glob'u-līne (152) [Globulin, 203.]
Glob'u-loŭs.
Glome, 24.
Glom'er-ate, *a.* & *v.* 73.
Glom'er-āt-ed.
Glom'er-āt-ing.
Glom-er-a'tion.
Gloom (19) [*not* dloom, 141, 153.]
Gloomed, 165.
Gloom'i-ly, 186.
Gloom'i-ness, 169.
Gloom'ing.
Gloom'y.
Glo'rīed, 49, N.; 99.
Glo-ri-fī-ca'tion.
Glo'ri-fied.
Glo'ri-fȳ, 49, N.; 94.
Glo'ri-fȳ-ing.
Glo'ri-oŭs.
Glo'ry, 49, N.; 93.
Glo'ry-ing.
[Glose, 203.—*See* Gloze.]
Gloss, 18, 174.
Glos-sa'ri-al.
Gloss'a-rist, 170.
Gloss'a-ry, 72.
Glossed (*glost*), 165; Note C, p. 34.
Gloss'er.
Gloss'i-ly, 186.
Gloss'i-ness, 169.
Gloss'ing.
Gloss-og'ra-pher, 108.
Gloss-o-graph'ic-al.
Gloss-og'ra-phy, 108.
Gloss-o-log'ic-al (*-loj'-*).
Gloss-ol'o-gist.
Gloss-ol'o-gy, 108.
Gloss'y.
Glot'tal, 72, 170.
Glot'tis, 66, 170.
Glot-tol'o-gy, 108.
Glove (*gluv*), 22, 163.
Gloved (*gluvd*), 183.
Glov'er (*gluv'-*).
Glōw, 24.
Glōwed, 165.
Glōw'ing.
Glōw'worm (*-wurm*).
Gloze (24) [Glose, 203.]
Glozed, 165, 183.
Glōz'er.
Glōz'ing.
Glu'cic, 26, 39, 52.
Glu-ci'na.
Glu'cīne, 152.
Glu-cin'i-um.
Glu-ci'num.
Glu'cose.
Glūe, 26.
Glūed (*glūd*), 165, 183.
Glu'er.
Glu'ey, 98, 169.
Glu'ing, 183.
Glum, 22.
Glu-ma'ceous (*-shus*), 169.
Glume, 26.
Glūm'oŭs, 100.
Glut, 22.
Glu'te-al, 169.
Glu'ten, 26, 76, 149.
Glu'ti-nate.
Glu'ti-nāt-ed, 183.
Glu'ti-nāt-ing.
Glu'ti-noŭs.
Glut'ted, 176.
Glut'ting.
Glut'ton (*glut'n*), 149.
Glut'ton-oŭs (*glut'n-*).
Glut'ton-y (*glut'n-y*) [so Sm. Wr. Wb. Gd.; *glut'tun-y*, Wk. 155.]
Glyc'er-īne (152) [Glycerin, 203.]
Gly-co'ni-an.
Gly-con'ic.
Gly-cȳr'rhi-zīne [Glycyrrhizin, 203.]
Glyph (*glif*), 16, 35.
Glyph'ic.
Glyph'o-grăph.
Gly-phog'ra-pher, 108.
Glyph-o-graph'ic, 109.
Gly-phog'ra-phy, 108.
Glyp'tic.
Glyp-to-graph'ic.
Glyp-tog'ra-phy.
Glyp-to-the'ca.
Gnarl (*narl*), 11, 162.
Gnarled (*narld*) (161), *v.* did gnarl.
Gnarled (161), *a.* knotty.
Gnarl'ing (*narl'-*).
Gnarl'y (*narl'y*), *a.* knotty.
Gnash (*nash*), 10, 162.
Gnashed (*nasht*), 165.
Gnash'ing (*nash'-*).
Gnat (*nat*), 10, 162.
Gnaw (*naw*), 17, 162.
Gnawed (*nawd*), 165.
Gnaw'er (*naw'-*).
Gnaw'ing (*naw'-*).
Gneiss (*nīs*) (162, 171), *n.* a primary rock resembling granite in its composition, but of a slaty structure. [*See* Nice, 160.]
Gneis'soid.
Gneis'sose.
Gnome (*nōm*), 24, 162.
Gnom'ic (*nom'-*), 162.
Gnom'ic-al (*nom'-*).
Gnom-o-log'ic (*nom-o-loj'-*), 109.
Gnom-o-log'ic-al (*nom-o-loj'-*), 108.
Gno-mol'o-gy (*no-*), 108.
Gno'mon (*no'-*), 162, 171.
Gno-mon'ic (*no-*).
Gno-mon'ic-al (*no-*).
Gno-mon'ics (*no-*).

Gno'mon-ist (*no'-*).
Gno-mon-ol'o-gy (*no-*).
Gnos'tic (*nos'-*), 162, 171.
Gnos'ti-cism (*nos'ti-sizm*).
Gnu (*nū*), *n.* a species of antelope inhabiting Southern Africa. [*See* Knew, 160.]
Go, 24, 53.
Gōad, 24.
Gōad'ed.
Gōad'ing.
Gōal, 24.
Gōat, 24.
Gōat'herd, 206.
Gōat'suck-er.
Gob'bet, 170.
Gob'bing, *n.*
Gob'ble, 164.
Gob'bled (*gob'ld*).
Gob'bler, 183.
Gob'bling.
Gob'e-lin, *a.* denoting a fine kind of French tapestry. [*See* Goblin, 148.]
Gob'let, 18, 76.
Gob'lin, *n.* an evil spirit. [*See* Gobelin, 148.]
Go'by, 93.
Go'-cart, 206, Exc. 3.
God, 18.
God'chīld, 206.
God'-dâugh-ter (*-daw'-*), 66, N.; 162, 205, Exc. 1.
God'dess, 66, 170.
God'fä-ther, 206.
God'hĕad.
God'like, 206, Exc. 5.
God'li-ness, 186.
God'ly, 93.
God'moth-er (*muth'-*).
God'send.
God'son (*-sun*).
God'ward.
God'wit.
Go'er, (24, 67, 77) [*See* Gore, 148.]
Gog'gle, 164.
Gog'gled (*gog'ld*).
Gog'gle-eyed (*gog'l-īd*), 206, Exc. 5.
Gog'gles (*gog'lz*), *n. pl.* 171.
Go'ing.
Goi'tre (*-tur*) (27, 164) [Goiter, Wb. Gd. 203.— *See* Note E, p. 70.]
Goi'tred (*-terd*) [Goitered, Wb. Gd. 203.]
Goi'troŭs, 27.
Gōld [so Sm. Wr Wb. Gd.; *gōld*, or *goold*, Wk. 155.]

☞ Though Walker, in deference to the very general usage in his time, allows the pronunciation *goold*, he condemns it as a corruption, and "an unmeaning deviation from the general rule" for the sound of *o* in words of this class.

Gōld'en (*gold'n*).
Gōld'finch, 206.
Gōld'fish.
Gōld'ham-mer.
Gōld'ney, 98.
Gōld'smith, 206.
Gōld'stick.
Gōld'y-locks.
Golf, 18.
[Golt, 203.— *See* Gault.]
Gom-phi'a-sis.
Gom-pho'sis, 109.
Go-mu'tĭ.
Gon'do-la, (72, 86) [*not* gun'da-lo, 153.]
Gon-do-liēr', 114, 169.
Gŏne (18, N.; 163) [so Wk. Sm.; *gŏn*, or *gawn*, Wr.; "pronounced nearly *gawn*," Wb. Gd. 155.]
Gong, 18, 54.
Go-ni-om'e-ter (108) [so Wr. Wb. Gd.; *gon-i-om'e-tur*, Sm. 155.]
Go-ni-o-met'ric.
Go-ni-o-met'ric-al.
Go-ni-om'e-try, 108.
Gŏŏd, 20.
Gŏŏd'-by', 205.
Gŏŏd'li-er, 186.
Gŏŏd'li-est.
Gŏŏd'li-ness, 186.
Gŏŏd'ly, 20, 93.
Gŏŏds (*gŏŏdz*), *n. pl.*
Gŏŏd'y, 93, 169.
Goog'ings (*gooj'ingz*), *n. pl.*
Goos'an-der [so Wb. Gd.; *goos-an'dur*, Wr. 155.]
Goose (19) [pl. Geese (*ghēs*), 195.]
Goose'bĕr-ry (*gooz'-bĕr-y*) (190) [so Wk. Sm. Wr.; *goos'bĕr-ry*, Wb. Gd. 155.]
Goose'neck, 206.
Goos'er-y, 233, Exc.
Go'pher, 24, 35.
Gor'cock, 206.
Gor'crōw.
Gor'di-an, 78.
Gore, (24, 67) [*See* Goer, 148.]
Gored (183), *v.* did gore. [*See* Gourd, 160.]
Gorge, 17, 45.
Gorged, 183.
Gor'geoŭs (*-jus*), 169.
Gor'get (*-jet*), 156.
Gorg'ing (*gorj'-*), 183.
Gor'gon.
Gor-go-ne'ia (*-ne'ya*), *n. pl.* 51, 171.
Gor-go'ni-an [Gorgonean, 203.]
Gor'hen, 206.
Gōr'ing.
Gor'mand [Gourmand, 203.]

☞ *Gourmand* is the French form of this word, and is more generally used than *gormand*, the Anglicized form.

Gor'mand-ism (*-izm*).
Gor'mand-ize, 202.
Gor'mand-ized, 183.
Gor'mand-īz-er.
Gor'mand-īz-ing.
Gorse, 17; Note D, p. 37.
Gōr'y, 49, N.
Gos'hawk.
Gos'ling (*goz'-*).
Gos'pel, 18, 76.
Gos'pelled (165) [Gospeled, Wb. Gd. 203.— *See* 177, and Note E, p. 70.]
Gos'pel-ler [Gospeler, Wb. Gd. 203.]
Gos'pel-ling [Gospeling, Wb. Gd. 203.]
Gos'sa-mer, 170.
Gos'sa-mer-y.
Gos'sip, 66, 170.
Gos'siped (*-sipt*), 165.
Gos'sip-ing.
Got, 18.
Goth, 18, 37.
Goth'ic.
Goth'i-cism (*-sizm*), 136.
Goth'i-cize, 202.
Goth'i-cized, 183.

Goth'i-cīz-ing.
Got'ten (*got'n*), 149.
Gouge (*gowj*, or *gooj*) [so Wr.; *gowj*, Wb. Gd.; *gooj*, Wk. Sm. 155.]
Gouged (*gowjd*, or *goojd*), 183.
Goug'ing (*gowj'-*, or *gooj'-*).
Gōurd (*gōrd*) [so Sm. Wb. Gd.; *gōrd*, or *goord*, Wk. Wr. 155.]

☞ Though Walker allows *goord*, he says: "The first [*gōrd*] is, in my opinion, the most agreeable to English analogy."

Gōurd'i-ness, 186.
Gōurd'y, 93.
Gour'mänd (Fr.) (*goor'-mand*) [G o r m a n d, 203. — *See* Note under *Gormand.*]
[G o u r n e t, 203. — *See* Gurnet.]
Gout (28, 161), *n.* an inflammation of the joints, particularly those of the great toe.
Gout (Fr.) (*goo*) (19, 161), *n.* taste; relish.
Gout'i-ness, 28, 186.
Gout'y, 28, 93.
Gov'ern (*guv'urn*), 22, 171.
Gov'ern-a-ble (*guv'-*), 164.
Gov'ern-ante (*guv'urn-ănt*) [so Sm. Gd.; *guv-urn-ănt'*, Wr.; *go-vur-nănt'*, Wk. 155.]
Gov'erned (*guv'urnd*).
Gov'ern-ess (*guv'-*).
Gov'ern-ing (*guv'-*).
Gov'ern-ment (*guv'-*), 171.
Gov-ern-ment'al (*guv-*).
Gov'ern-or (*guv'-*), 88, 171.
Gov'ern-or-gen'er-al, 205, 216.
Gow'an.
Gown, 28.
Gowned (*gownd*), 165.
Gown'man, 196.
Gowns'man (*gownz'-*), 215.
Grab, 10.
Grabbed (*grabd*), 176.
Grab'bing.
Grace, 23, 39.
Graced (*grāst*), 165, 183; Note C, p. 34.
Grace'ful (*-fŏŏl*), 180.
Grā'çes (*-ez*), *n. pl.*
Grā'çing.
Gra'cious (*-shus*), 169.
Grac'kle (*grak'l*), 164.
Gra-da'tion.
Grad'a-to-ry, 86.
Grade, 23.
Grād'ed, 183.
Grād'i-ent.
Grād'ing.
Grad'u-al, 89, 92.
Grad'u-al-ly, 170.
Grad'u-ate, 73.
Grad'u-āt-ed, 183.
Grad'u-āt-ing.
Grad-u-a'tion, 112.
Grad'u-āt-or, 228.
Gradus (L.).
Graff, 10, 173.
Graf'fer, 170.
Graft, 12, 131.
Graft'ed.
Graft'er.
Graft'ing.
Grāil, 23.
Grāin, 23.
Grāined, 183.
Grāin'er.
Grāin'ing.
Grāin'y, 93, 169.
Gral-la-to'ri-al, 49, N.
Gral'la-to-ry.
Gral'lic.
Gram, *n.* the unity of the French system of weights. [G r a m m e, 203.]
Gra-min'e-al.
Gra-min'e-oŭs.
Gram-i-ni-fo'li-oŭs.
Gram-i-niv'o-roŭs.
Gram'mar, 66, 170.
Gram-ma'ri-an, 49, N.
Gram-mat'ic, 109.
Gram-mat'ic-al, 108.
Gram'ma-tist.
Gramme (Fr.) (*gram*) [G r a m, 203.]
[G r a n a d e, 203. — *See* Grenade.]
[G r a n a d o, 203. — *See* Grenade.]
Grăn'a-ry (72, 123, 169) [*not* grān'a-ry, 153.]
Grand, 10.
Gran'dam.
Grand'chīld, 206.
Grand'-dâugh-ter (*-daw-*), 206, Exc. 1.
Gran-dee', 121.
Grand'eur (*-yur*) (45, N.) [so Sm. Wr. Gd.; *gran'jur*, Wk. 155.]
Grand'fä-ther.
Gran-dil'o-quence.
Gran-dil'o-quent.
Gran-dil'o-quoŭs.
Gran'di ose.
Grand'moth-er (*-muth-*).
Grand'par-ent (*-pêr-*).
Grand'sire.
Grand'son.
Grānge, 23, 45.
Gra-nif'er-oŭs, 108.
Gran'i-form, 108.
Gran'ĭte, 152.
Gra-nit'ic, 109.
Gra-nit-i-fĭ-ca'tion.
Gra-nit'i-form, 108.
Gran'i-toid.
Gra-niv'o-roŭs, 100.
Grant, 12, 131.
Grant'a-ble, 164, 169.
Grant'ed.
Grant-ee', 118, 121.
Grant'er, 160.
Grant-or', *or* Grant'or (118, 160) [Law term, correlative of *Grantee.*]
Gran'u-lar, 72, 89.
Gran'u-la-ry.
Gran'u-late, 73.
Gran'u-lāt-ed.
Gran'u-lāt-ing.
Gran-u-la'tion.
Gran'ule, 90.
Gran'u-līte, 152.
Gran'u-loŭs.
Grape, 23.
Grāp'er-y, 233, Exc.
Graph'ic, 10, 35, 200.
Graph'ic-al, 108.
Graph'ic-al-ly.
Graph'īte, 70, 152.
Graph'o-līte, 152.
Graph-om'e-ter, 108.
Graph-o-met'ric-al.
Grap'nel (10, 76) [C r a p n e l, 203.]
Grap'ple, 164.
Grap'pled (*grap'ld*), 183.
Grap'pling.
Grap'to-līte, 152.
Grāp'y, 93, 169.
Grasp, 12, 131.
Grasp'a-ble, 164.
Grasped (*graspt*), 165; Note C, p. 34.

Gràsp′er.
Gràsp′ing.
Gràss, 12, 131, 174.
Gràssed (*gràst*), 165.
Gràss′hop-per, 171.
Gràss′i-ness, 169, 186.
Gràss′ing.
Gràss′y.
Grate (23), *n.* a frame of bars: — *v.* to rub; — to fret. [*See* Great, 160.]
Grāt′ed, 183.
Grate′ful (*-fōōl*), 180.
Grate′ful-ly (*-fōōl*).
Grāt′er (183), *n.* an instrument for grating. [*See* Greater, 160.]
Gra-tic-u-la′tion.
Grat-i-fĭ-ca′tion.
Grat′i-fīed, 186.
Grat′i-fī-er.
Grat′i-fȳ, 94, 169.
Grat′i-fȳ-ing.
Grāt′ing, 183.
Gra′tis, 23, 169.
Grat′i-tude, 108, 169.
Gra-tu′i-tous, 78, 100.
Gra-tu′i-ty, 169.
Grat′u-lant.
Grat′u-late, 73, 89.
Grat′u-lāt-ed.
Grat′u-lāt-ing.
Grat-u-la′tion.
Grat′u-la-to-ry [so Wk. Wr. Wb. Gd.; *grat′-u-lāt-o-ry*, Sm. 155.]
[Grauwacke, 203.— *See* Graywacke.]
Gra-va′men.
Grave, 23.
Graved, 165, 183.
Grav′el, 10, 76.
Grav′elled (*-eld*) (165) [Graveled, Wb. Gd. 203.— *See* 177, and Note E, p. 70.]
Grav′el-ling [Graveling, Wb. Gd. 203.]
Grav′el-ly.
Grāv′en (*grāv′n*), 149.
Grāv′er.
Grave′stōne, 206.
Grave′yard.
Gra-vim′e-ter, 108.
Grāv′ing.
Grav′i-tate, 73, 169.
Grav′i-tāt-ed.
Grav′i-tāt-ing.
Grav-i-ta′tion.
Grav′i-ty, 108, 169.
Gra′vy, 23, 93.
Grāy [Grey, 203.]

☞ "More properly and commonly written *gray*." *Worcester.*

[Grayhound, 203.— *See* Greyhound.]
Grāy′ling.
Grāy′wack-e [so Wr.; *gra′wak*, Wb. Gd. 155.] [Grauwacke, 203.]
Graze, 23, 40.
Grazed, 165.
Grāz′er, 183.
Gra′zier (*-zhur*), 47, N.
Grāz′ing. [161.
Grēase (*grēs*), *n.* 136,
Grease (*grēz*), *v.* 136, 161.
Grēased (*grēzd*), 165.
Grēas′i-ly (*grēz′-*).
Grēas′i-ness (*grēz′-*).
Grēas′ing (*grēz′-*).
Grēas′y (*grēz′y*) [*not* grēs′y, 153.]
Greāt (*grāt*) (23), *a.* large; grand. [*See* Grate, 160.]
Greāt′er, *a.* more great. [*See* Grater, 160.]
Grēave (*grēv*) (13), *n.* armor for the legs; — generally used in the plural. [*See* Grieve, 160.]
Grebe, 13.
Gre′cian (*-shan*).
Gre′cism (*-sizm*), 136.
Greed, 13.
Greed′i-ly, 186.
Greed′i-ness, 169.
Greed′y, 93.
Greek, 13.
Green, 13.
Green′finch, 206.
Green′house.
Green′ness, 66, N.
Green′room.
Greens (*grēnz*), *n. pl.*
Green′stōne, 130, 206.
Green′sward.
Greet, 13.
Greet′ed.
Greet′er.
Greet′ing.
Gre-ga′ri-ous, 49, N.
Gre-go′ri-an.
Gre-nade′ (121) [Granade, Granado, 203.]
Gren-a-dīēr′, 122, 169.
Gre-nat′i-form, 108.
Gren′a-tīte, 152.
Gres-so′ri-al, 169.
Greut (*groot*), 19.
Grew (*groo*), 19.
[Grey, 203.— *See* Gray.]
Grey′hound (*gra′-*) [Grayhound, 203.]

☞ Smart gives only the form *greyhound*, and remarks: "This is not a compound of *gray*, the color." It is derived from the Anglo-Saxon *grig-hund*, in which the first part (*grig*) does not appear to have the meaning of *gray*. No definition of it is given in the Anglo-Saxon Dictionaries of Bosworth and Lye, and the Anglo-Saxon origin of *gray* is there stated to be *græg*.

Grid′dle, 164.
Grid′e-lin.
Grid′i-ron (*-ī′urn*), 171.
Grīēf, 13, 169, N.
Grīēv′ance, 183.
Grīēve (13, 169, N.), *v.* to wound the feelings of; — to mourn. [*See* Greave, 160.]
Grīēved, 183.
Grīēv′er.
Grīēv′ing.
Grīēv′ous, 13, 169.
Grif′fin, *or* Grif′fon, 66, 170.
Grig, 16.
Grill, 16, 172.
Gril-lade′, 121.
Gril′lage.
Grilled (*grild*), 165.
Grill′ing.
Grim, 16.
Grĭ-mace′, 121, 171.
Grĭ-maced′ (*-māst′*).
Grĭ-maç′ing.
Grĭ-mal′kin.
Grime, 25.
Grimed, 183.
Grīm′ing.
Grīm′y, 93.
Grin, 16.
Grīnd, 25.
Grīnd′er.
Grīnd′ing.
Grīnd′stōne (130, 206) [so Wk. Wb. Gd.; *grīnd′stōne*, coll. *grĭn′stun*, Sm.; *grīnd′stōn*, or *grīnd′-stōn*, Wr. 155.]
Grinned (*grĭnd*), 176.
Grin′ner, 228, N.
Gripe, 25.
Griped (*grīpt*), 183.
Grīp′er.

Grĭp′ing.
Grisette (Fr.) (*gre-zet′.*)
Gris′li-ness (*griz′-*),186.
Gris′ly (*griz′ly*), *a.* horrible; frightful. [*See* Grizzly, 160.]
Gri′sons (*gre′zunz*), *n. pl.* [so Wr. Gd.; *gre′-zōnz*, Sm. 155.]
Grist, 16.
Gris′tle (*gris′l*), 162,164.
Grist′ly (*gris′ly*), 162.
Grit, 16.
Grit′stōne, 130, 206.
Grit′ti-ness, 186.
Grit′ty, 170, 176.
Griz′zle, 164.
Griz′zled (*griz′ld*), 183.
Griz′zly, *a.* somewhat gray. [*See* Grisly, 160.]
Grōan, *v.* to utter a mournful sound, as in pain: — *n.* a mournful sound uttered in distress. [*See* Grown, 160.]
Grōaned (*grōnd*), 165.
Grōan′ing.
Groat (*grawt*), 17, 171.
Groats (*grawts*), *n. pl.*
Groats′worth (*grawts′-wurth*), 171, 206.
Gro′cer (24, 39), *n.* a trader in goods required for the table. [*See* Grosser, 160.]
Gro′cer-y, 171.
Grog, 18.
Grog′ger-y (*-gur-*), 138.
Grog′ram [Grogeram, Grogran, 203.]
Grog′shop, 206.
Groin, 27.
Groined (*groind*), 165.
Grom′ill [Gromwell, 203.]
Grom′met, 170.

☞ Seamen usually pronounce this word *grum′et*; and hence it is sometimes incorrectly spelled Grummet.

Grom′well [Gromill, 203.]
Groom (19), *n.* a servant; — a bridegroom. [*See* Grume, 160.]
Groomed (*groomd*), 165.
Groom′ing.
Grooms′man (*groomz′-*), 196, 214.
Groove, 19.
Grooved, 183.
Groov′er.
Groov′ing.
Grope, 24.
Groped (*grōpt*), 165, 183; Note C, p. 34.
Grōs′bēak [Grossbeak, 203.]
Grōss, 24, 174.
Grōss′bēak (206) [Grosbeak, 203.]
Gros′su-lar, 72, 170.
Grot, 18. [171.
Gro-tesque′ (*-tesk′*), 121,
Grot′to (66, 170) [pl. Grot′tōs (*-tōz*), 192.]
Ground, 28.
Ground′age.
Ground′ed.
Ground′ing.
Ground′ling.
Ground′-nut.
Ground′sel, *n.* a plant of the genus *Senecio.*
Ground′sill, *or* Ground′-sel, *n.* the horizontal timber of a building lying next to the ground; sill.
Ground′work (*-wurk*).
Group (*groop*), 19.
Grouped (*groopt*), 183.
Group′ing (*groop′-*).
Grouse (*grous*), *n. sing.* & *pl.* 28.
Grout, 28.
Grout′ing.
Grove, 24.
Grov′el (*grov′l*), 149.
Grov′elled (*grov′ld*) [Groveled, Wb. Gd. 203. — *See* 177, and Note E, p. 70.]
Grov′el-ler (*grov′l-*) [Groveler, Wb. Gd. 203.]
Grov′el-ling (*grov′l-*), [Groveling, Wb. Gd. 203.]
Grōw, 24.
Grōw′er.
Grōw′ing.
Growl, 28.
Growled (*grould*), 165.
Growl′er, 28, 77.
Growl′ing.
Grōwn, *part.* from *Grow.* [*See* Groan, 160.]
Grōwth, 24.
Grub, 22.
Grubbed (*grubd*), 176.
Grub′bing.
Grudge, 22, 45.
Grudged (*grujd*), 165.
Grudg′er, 183.
Grudg′ing.
Gru′el (*groo′el*), 19, 26, 76.
Gruff, 22, 173.
Gruff′ly, 178.
Grum, 22.
Grum′ble, 164.
Grum′bled (*-bld*), 183.
Grum′bler.
Grum′bling.
Grume (*groom*), *n.* a clot, as of blood. [*See* Groom, 160.]
[Grummet, 203.— *See* Grommet.]
Gru′mous (*groo′-*), 19, 100.
Grunt, 22.
Grunt′ed.
Grunt′er.
Grunt′ing.
Gua-chä′ro (*gwa-*).
Gua′ia-cum (*gwa′ya-kum*), 34, 51, 171.
Guän (*gwän*).
Guä′na (*gwä′-*).
Gua-nä′co (*gwa-*) [pl. Gua-nä′cōs, 192.]
Gua-nif′er-ous (*gwa-*).
Guä′no (*gwä′no*).
Guä′ra (*gwä′-*).
Guăr-an-tee′ (*găr-*), *n.* & *v.* (122) [Guaranty, 203.]

☞ *Guarantee* is now more commonly used than *guaranty.*

Guăr-an-teed′ (188) [Guarantied, (*găr′an-tĭd*), 203.]
Guăr-an-tee′ing [Guarantying (*găr′an-ty-ing*), 203.]
Guăr′an-tor, 118.

☞ When this word is used as the correlative of *guarantee* (in the sense of *one to whom surety is given*), it is properly accented on the last syllable (*guar-an-tor′*).

Guăr′an-ty, *n.* & *v.* [Guarantee, 203. — *See* Note under *Guarantee.*]
Guăr′an-ty-ing [Guaranteeing, 203.]
Guard (*gard*) (11, 52, 53, 146) [so Wr. Wb. Gd.;

g'ard, Sm. (*See* § 26); *gyard*, Wk. 155.]
Guard'ed (*gard'-*).
Guard'er (*gard'-*).
Guard'i-an (*gard'i-an*) [so Wb. Gd.; *g'ard'-yan*, Sm. (*See* § 26); *gard'i-an*, or *gard'-yan*, Wr.; *gyard'i-an*, or *gyar'ji-an*, Wk. 155.]
Guä'va (*gwä'va*) [so Wr. Wb. Gd.; *gwā'-va*, Sm. 155.]
Gu-ber-na-to'ri-al.
Gud'geon (*-jun*), 22, 45.
Gue'bers, *or* Gue'bres (*ghe'burz*), *n. pl.*
Guelfs (*gwelfs*), *n. pl.* [Guelphs, 203.]
Guer'don (*gher'dun*) (21, N.) [so Wk. Wr. Wb. Gd.; *gh'er'dun*, Sm. (*See* § 26), 155.]
Gue-ril'la (*ghe-ril'la*) [so Wr.] [Guerrilla (*gwer-ril'la*), Gd. 155, 203.] [174.
Guess (*ghes*), 15, 171,
Guessed (*ghest*), *v.* did guess. [*See* Guest, 160.]
Guess'er (*ghes'-*).
Guess'ing (*ghes'-*).
Guess'work (*ghes'-wurk*).
Guest (*ghest*) (15, 174; Note D, p. 37), *n.* one entertained in the house or at the table of another. [*See* Guessed, 160.]
Guhr (*gur*), 21.
Guīd'a-ble (*ghīd'-*), 164.
Guīd'ance (*ghīd'-*), 169.
Guīde (*ghīd*), 25, 52, 53; Note D, p. 37.
Guīd'ed (*ghīd'-*).
Guīd'ing (*ghīd'-*).
Guild (*ghild*) (171), *n.* a fraternity, or association. [*See* Gild, 160.]
Guild'er (*ghild'-*), *n.* a Dutch coin. [*See* Gilder, 160.] [Gilder, 203.]
Guild'hâll (*ghild'-*).
Guīle (*ghīl*) [so Wr. Wb. Gd.; *gyīl*, Wk.; *gh'īl*, Sm. (*See* § 26), 52, 53, 155.]
Guīle'less (*ghīl'-*), 66, N.
Guil'le-mot (*ghil'-*).
Guil'le-vat (*ghil'-*).
Guil-lo-tine' (*ghil-lo-tēn'*) (122, 171) [so Wr.; *ghil-yo-tēn'*, Sm.; *ghil'lo-tēn*, Gd. 155.]
Guil-lo-tined' (*-tēnd'*).
Guil-lo-tin'ing (*-tēn'-*).
Guilt (*ghilt*) (16, 171), *n.* criminality. [*See* Gilt, 160.]
Guilt'i-ness (*ghilt'-*), 186.
Guilt'y (*ghilt'y*).
Guim'bard (*ghim'-*).
Guin'ea (*ghin'y*), 171.
Guin'iad (*gwin'yad*) [Gwiniad, 203.]
Gui-pure' (*ghe-pūr'*) [so Wr.; *ghe'pūr*, Gd. 154, 155.]
Guīse (*ghīz*), 25, 40.
Gu'lâund [so Gd.; *gu'-länd*, Wr. 155.]
Gules (*gūlz*).
Gulf, 22.
Gull, 22, 172.
Gulled (*guld*), 165.
Gul'let, 66, 170.
Gul'līed.
Gull'ing.
Gul'ly, 93, 170.
Gul'ly-ing.
Gulp, 22.
Gulped (*gulpt*), 165.
Gulp'ing.
Gum, 22.
Gum-Ăr'a-bic (216) [*not* gum-a-rab'ik, *nor* gum-a-ra'bik, 153.]
Gum'boil, 206.
Gum-e-las'tic, 205, 206.
Gum-mif'er-oŭs, 108.
Gum'mi-ness, 186.
Gum'moŭs.
Gum'my, 93, 170.
Gump'tion (*gum'shun*) [so Sm. Wr.; *gump'-shun*, Wb. Gd. 155.]
Gum-res'in (*-rez'in*) [so Sm. Wb. Gd.; *gum'-rez-in*, Wr. 155.]
Gum-sen'e-gal.
Gum-trag'a-canth.
Gum'-tree, 206, Exc. 4.
Gun, 22.
Gun'-băr-rel, 209.
[Gunnel, 203. — *See* Gunwale.]
Gun'nel, *n.* a small spotted fish. [*See* Gunwale, 160.]
Gun'ner, 77, 170.
Gun'ner-y, 171.
Gun'ning.
Gun'ny, 93, 169.
Gun'pow-der, 206.
Gun'room.
Gun'shot.
Gun'smith.
Gun'stick.
Gun'stock.
Gun'wale (*gun'el*) (171) [Gunnel, 203.]
Gur'gle, 164.
Gur'gled (*-gld*), 183.
Gur'gling.
Gur'nard.
Gur'net [Gournet, 203.]
Gŭr'rah, 72.
Gush, 22.
Gushed (*gusht*), 165; Note C, p. 34.
Gush'ing.
Gus'set, 66, 170.
Gust, 22.
Gust'a-to-ry.
Gus'to.
Gust'y, 93, 169.
Gut, 22.
Gut'ta per'cha [*not* gut'-ta per'ka, 153.]
Gut'ta se-re'na (L.).
Gut'tāt-ed.
Gut'ted, 176.
Gut'ter, 170.
Gut'tered, 165.
Gut'ter-ing.
Gut'ti-fer, 77, 78.
Gut-tif'er-oŭs, 108.
Gut'ting.
Gut'tur-al, 21, 22, 72.
Gut'ty.
Guȳ (*ghī*), 25, 171.
Guz'zle, 164.
Guz'zled (*-zld*), 183.
Guz'zler.
[Gwiniad, 203. — *See* Guiniad.]
Gy'âll (*ghī'-*).
Gybe (*jīb*) (25), *v.* to shift from one side of the vessel to the other, as the boom of a fore-and-aft sail. [*See* Gibe, 160.]
Gybed (*jībd*), 183.
Gȳb'ing (*jīb'-*).
Gym-na'si-arch (*jim-na'zi-ark*), 171.
Gym-na'si-um (*jim-na'-zhi-um*) [so Wr.; *jim-na'zi-um*, Gd.; *jim-näz'i-um*, coll. *jim-näzh'yum*, Sm. 155.] [L. pl. *Gym-na'si-a*

(*-zhĭ-a*); Eng. pl. Gym-na'si-ums (*-zhĭ-umz*), 198.]
Gym'nast (*jim'-*), 45.
Gym-nas'tic, 171.
Gym-nas'tics, *n. pl.*
Gym-nos'o-phist.
Gym'no-sperm.
Gym-no-sperm'oŭs.
Gym'note, 45.
Gym-no'tus.
Gȳ-nan'der (*jȳ-*), 45.
Gȳ-nan'dri-an.
Gȳ-nan'droŭs.
Gyn'ar-chy (*jin'ar-ky*).
Gyn-e'cian (*jin-e'shan*).
Gyn-e-coc'ra-cy, 169.
Gyp'se-oŭs.
Gyp-sif'er-oŭs, 108.
Gyp'sum (*jip'-*), 45, 169.
Gyp'sy [Gipsy, 203. —*See* Note under *Gipsy*.]
Gyp'sy-ism (*-izm*) [Gipsyism, 203.]
Gy'rate, *a.* & *v.* 73.
Gy'rāt-ed, 183.
Gy'rāt-ing.
Gy-ra'tion, 112.
Gy'ra-to-ry, 49, N.; 86.
Gyre (25, 45) [Gire, 203.]
[Gyrfalcon, 203. — *See* Gerfalcon.]
Gy'ro-man-cy, 169.
Gy'ro-scope, 49, N.
Gy'rose [so Gd.; *jī-rōs'*, Wr. 155.]
Gyve (*jīv*), *n.* & *v.* (25, 45) [Give, 203.]

☞ The plural, *gyves* (*jīvz*) is more commonly used than the singular.

Gyved (*jīvd*), 183.
Gȳv'ing.

H.

Hä (11, 29) [Hah, 203.]
Ha-ar'kīes (*-kiz*).
Ha'be-as cor'pus (L.).
Hab'er-dash-er, 171.
Hab'er-dash-er-y.
Hab'er-dīne [so Sm.; *hab'ur-dēn*, Gd.; *hab-ur-dēn'*, Wk. Wr. 155.]
Ha-ber'ge-on [so Wk. Wr. Gd.; *hab'ur-jun*, Sm. 155.]
Ha-bil'i-ment, 169.
Hab'it, 10, 16, 231.
Hab-it-a-bil'i-ty, 108.
Hab'it-a-ble, 164.
Hab'it-an-cy, 169.
Hab'i-tat, 78.
Hab-i-ta'tion.
Hab'it-ed.
Hab'it-ing.
Ha-bit'u-al, 72, 89.
Ha-bit'u-al-ly.
Ha-bit'u-ate.
Ha-bit'u-āt-ed, 183.
Ha-bit'u-āt-ing.
Ha-bit-u-a'tion.
Hab'i-tude, 78.
Hacienda (Sp.) (*hä-the-en'da*), 171.
Hack, 10.
Hack'bĕr-ry.
Hacked (*hakt*).
Hack'ing.
Hac'kle (164) [Heckle, Hatchel, 203.]
Hac'kled (*-kld*), 183.
Hac'kler.
Hac'kling.
Hack'ly, 93.
Hack'ma-tack, 171.
Hack'ney (10, 98), *n.*, *a.* & *v.* [pl. of *n.* Hack-neys (*-niz*), 190.]
Hack'neyed (*-nid*), 171.
Hack'ney-ing.
Had, 10.
Had'dock, 10, 86, 170.
Ha'dēs (*-dēz*).
Hadj (Ar.)
Hadj'ī (Ar.) [Hadjee, 203.]
Hæc-ce'i-ty, 171.
Hæ'mal (*he'-*), 13, 72.
Hæm-a-stat'ics (*hem-*).
[Hæmatite, 203. — *See* Hematite.]
[Hæmatology, 203. — *See* Hematology.]
[Hæmatosine, 203. — *See* Hematosine.]
Hæ-ma-to'sis (*he-*) (109) [so Sm.; *hem-a-to'sis*, Wr. 155.] [Hematosis, 203.]

☞ "Words of this class generally change the diphthong *æ* into *e*." *Smart.*

[Hæmorrhage, 203. — *See* Hemorrhage.]
[Hæmorrhoid, 203. — *See* Hemorrhoid.]
Hȧft, 12, 131.
Hȧft'ed.
Hȧft'ing.
Hag, 10.
Hag'gard, 10, 72.
Hag'ged (*-ghed*), 138.
Hag'gess (*-ghes*), *or* Hag'gis (*-ghis*).
Hag'gish (*-ghish*).
Hag'gle, 164.
Hag'gled (*-gld*), 183.
Hag'gler.
Hag'gling.
Ha'gi-ar-chy (*-ky*).
Ha'gi-o-grăph.
Ha-gi-og'ra-pha, *n. pl.*
Ha-gi-og'ra-phal.
Ha-gi-og'ra-pher, 108.
Ha-gi-og'ra-phy.
Ha-gi-ol'o-gist.
Ha-gi-ol'o-gy, 108.
Hăgue'but (*hag'but*) [so Wr., Wb. Gd.; *hag'-e-but*, Sm. 155.]
Häh (11, 29) [Ha, 203.]
Hä-hä', *n.* [Haw-haw, 203.]
Hāik (23), *n.* an under garment worn by an Arab. [*See* Hake, 160.] [Hyke, 203.]
Hāil (23), *n.* frozen drops of rain: — *v.* to pour down frozen drops of rain: — *int.* a term of salutation. [*See* Hale, 160.]
Hāiled (*hāld*), 165.
Hāil'ing.
Hāil'stōne, 24.
Hāil'y, 23, 93.
Hair (*hêr*) (14), *n.* a filament, or a collection of filaments, growing from the skin of an animal. [*See* Hare, 160.]
[Hairbell, 203. — *See* Harebell.]
Hair'cloth (*hêr'kloth*, or *hêr'klawth*), 18, N.
Haired (*hêrd*), *a.*
Hair'i-ness (*hêr'-*), 186.
Hair'y (*hêr'y*), 93.
Hake (23), *n.* a fish allied to the cod. [*See* Haik, 160.]
Hal'berd [so Sm. Wb. Gd.; *hawl'burd*, Wk.; *hawl'burd*, or *hal'burd*, Wr. 155.]
Hal-berd-ier', 122.
Hal'cȳ-on [so Sm. Wb. Gd.; *hal'she-un*, Wk.; *hal'shi-un*, or *hal'si-un*, Wr. 155.]

Hale (23), *a.* healthy. [*See* Hail, 160.]
Hale (*hāl*, or *hawl*), *v.* [so Wk. Wr. Gd.; *hāl*, Sm. 155.]

☞ "This word, in familiar language, is corrupted, beyond recovery, into *haul*; but solemn speaking still requires the regular sound, rhyming with *pale*; the other sound would, in this case, be gross and vulgar." *Walker.*

Haled (*hāld*, or *hawld*).
Hälf (*häf*) (162) [pl. Hälves (*hävz*), 193.]
Half′-pen-ny (*ha′pen-ny*) [so Wk. Sm.; *ha′-pen-ny*, *hap′en-ny*, or *haf′pen-ny*, Wr.; *hap′-en-ny*, or *ha′pen-ny*, Wb. Gd. 155.] [pl. Half′-pen-nies, *or* Half′pence, 194.]
Hal′i-but (*hol′i-but*) [so Wk. Wb. Gd.; *hăl′i-but*, Sm. 155.]
Hăl′i-mas (180) [so Sm. Wr. Wb. Gd.; *hol′i-mas*, Wk. 155.] [Halimass, 203.]
Hal′ing (*hāl′-*, or *hawl′-*)
Hal-i-og′ra-pher, 108.
Hal-i-og′ra-phy.
Hâll (17, 172), *n.* a large room at the entrance of a house, or for a public assembly. [*See* Haul, 160.]
Hal-le-lu′jah (*-lu′ya*) (51, 171) [so Wb. Gd.; *hal-le-l′oo′ya*, Sm. (*See* § 26); *hal-le-loo′ya*, Wr. 155.] [Allelujah, Alleluia, 203.]
Hal′liard (*hal′yard*) [Halyard, 203.]

☞ Of these two forms Smart gives only *halliard*; and this is preferred by Webster and Goodrich. Worcester prefers *halyard*.

Hal-loo′, *int.* & *v.*
Hal-looed′ (*-lood′*), 188.
Hal-loo′ing.
Hal′lōw.
Hal′lōwed, 165, 188.
Hal-lōw-een′ [so Wr.; *hal′lo-ēn*, Gd. 155.]
Hal′lōw-mas, 180.
Hal-lu-ci na′tion.
Hal-lu′ci-na-to-ry.
[Halm, 203. — *See* Haum.]
Ha′lo [pl. Ha′lōs (*-lōz*), 192.]
Ha′lōed, 188.
Hal′o-gen, 170.
Ha-log′e-noŭs (*-loj′-*).
Ha′loid.
Hâls′er (*haws′er*) [Hawser, 203.]
Hâlt, 17.
Hâlt′ed.
Hâlt′er.
Hâlt′ing.
Hälve (*häv*), 162.
Hälved (*hävd*).
Hälves (*havz*), *n. pl.*
Hal′yard [Halliard, 203. — *See* Note under *Halliard.*]
Ham, 10.
Ham′a-dry̆-ad [L. pl. *Ham-a-dry̆′a-dēs* (*-dēz*); Eng. pl. Ham′-a-dry̆-ads (*-adz*), 198.]
Ha′mate.
Ha′māt-ed.
Hāmes (*hāmz*), *n. pl.*
Ham′let, 10, 76.
Ham′let-ed.
Ham′mer, 66, 170.
Ham′mer-a-ble, 164, 169.
Ham′mered (*-murd*), 150
Ham′mer-er.
Ham′mer-ing.
Ham′mock, 170.
Ha′moŭs, 100, 169.
Ham′per, 10, 77.
Ham′pered (*-purd*), 150.
Ham′per-ing.
Ham′ster.
Ham′string, 206.
Ham′string-ing.
Ham′strung.
Han′a-per.
Han′ces (*-sez*), *n. pl.* [Hanches, 203.]
Hand, 10.
Hand′bill, 206.
Hand′bŏŏk.
Hand′brĕadth.
Hand′cart.
Hand′cuff.
Hand′cuffed (*-kuft*).
Hand′cuff-ing.
Hand′ed.
Hand′ful (*-fŏŏl*) (142) [pl. Hand′fuls (*-fŏŏlz*), 197.]
Hand′i-craft, 169.
Hand′i-crafts-man, 196.
Hand′i-ly, 186.
Hand′i-ness.
Hand′i-work (*-wurk*).
Hand′ker-chief (*hang′-kur-chif*), 171.
Han′dle, 164.
Han′dle-a-ble, 164.
Han′dled (*-dld*), 183.
Han′dler.
Han′dling.
Hand′māid, 206.
Hand′māid-en (*-mād-n*).
Hand′rāil.
Hand′saw.
Hand′screw (*-skroo*).
Hand′sel.
Hand′selled (*-seld*) [Handseled, Wb. Gd. 203.—*See* 177, and Note E, p. 70.]
Hand′sel-ling [Handseling, Wb. Gd. 203.]
Hand′some (*hand′sum*) [so Sm. Wb. Gd.; *han′sum*, Wk. Wr. 155], *a.* ample; — noble, — beautiful. [*See* Hansom, 148.]
Hand′spike.
Hand′wrīt-ing (*-rīt-*), 162.
Hand′y, 10, 93, 169.
Hang, 10, 54.
Hang′bird, 266.
Hang′dog.
Hang′er, 77.
Hang′er-on.
Hang′ing.
Hang′man, 196.
Hang′nāil.
Hank (*hangk*), 10, 54.
Hank′er.
Hank′ered (*-urd*), 150.
Hank′er-ing.
Han-o-ve′ri-an, 169.
Han′sard.
Hans, 10.
Han-se-at′ic.
Han′som, *n.* a low kind of travelling vehicle. [*See* Handsome, 148.]
Hap-haz′ard.
Hap′less.
Hap′ly, 10, 93.
Hap′pen (*hap′n*), 149.
Hap′pened (*hap′nd*), 165.
Hap′pen-ing.
Hap′pi-ly.
Hap′pi-ness, 106, 186.
Hap′py, 66, 170.
Ha-rangue′ (*-rang′*), 168.
Ha-rangued′ (*-rangd′*), 165.
Ha-rangu′er (*-ur*).

Ha-rangu'ing(*-ing*),171.
Hăr'ass, 10, 171.
Hăr'assed (*-ast*).
Hăr'ass-ing.
Har'bin-ger, 45, 171.
Har'bor (11, 88) [Harbour, Sm. 199, 203.]
Har'bored (*-bord*) (165) [Harboured, Sm. 199, 203.]
Har'bor-er [Harbourer, Sm.199,203.]
Har'bor-ing [Harbouring, Sm. 199, 203.]
Hard, 11.
Hard'bēam.
Hard'en (*hard'n*), 149.
Hard'ened (*hard'nd*), 150.
Hard'en-er (*hard'n-*).
Hard'en-ing (*hard'n-*).
Hard'-fought (*-fawt*), 206, Exc. 5.
Hard'hack.
Hard'hĕad.
Hard'i-hŏŏd, 169.
Hard'i-ly.
Hard'i-ness, 186.
Hard'y, 93, 169.
Hare (*hêr*), *n.* a small quadruped of the genus *Lepus.* [*See* Hair, 160.]
Hare'bell (*hêr'-*)[Hairbell, 203.]
Hair'-brāined (*hêr'-brānd*), 206, Exc. 5.
Hare'lip.
Hare'lipped (*-lipt*).
Ha'rem, 49, N.
Ha-ren'gi-form, 108.
Hăr'i-cot (Fr.) (*hăr'e-ko*).
[Harier, 203.—*See* Harrier.]
Hark, 11, 135.
Harl, 11.
Har'le-quin (*-kin*), 171.
Har'lock.
Har'lot.
Har'lot-ry.
Harm, 11, 135.
Har-mat'tan, 170.
Harmed (*harmd*), 165.
Harm'ful (*-fŏŏl*), 180.
Har-mon'ic.
Har-mon'ic-al.
Har-mon'i-ca.
Har-mon'ics, *n. pl.*
Har-mo'ni-oŭs, 78, 100.
Har-mon'i-phon.
Har'mon-ist.
Har'mon-ize, 202.
Har'mon-ized, 183.
Har'mon-īz-er.
Har'mon-īz-ing.
Har-mo-nom'e-ter, 108.
Har'mo-ny, 93.
Har'mŏst, 86.
Har'mo-tōme.
Har'ness.
Har'nessed (*-nest*).
Har'ness-er.
Har'ness-ing.
Harp, 11.
Harped (*harpt*), 165, Note C, p. 34.
Harp'er.
Harp'ing.
Harp'ings (*-ingz*), *n. pl.*
Harp'ist.
Har-po-neer' [Harpooneer, 203.]
Har-poon', 11, 19, 121.
Har-pooned' (*-poond'*).
Har-poon-eer' [Harponeer, 203.]
Har-poon'er.
Har-poon'ing.
Harp'sēal.
Harp'si-chord (*-kord*), 171.
Har'py, 11, 93, 190.
Hăr'rīed, 186.
Hăr'ri-er (77, 78, 171) [Harier, 203.]

☞ "The original spelling, *harier*, is disused." *Smart.*

Hăr'rōw, 101.
Hăr'rōwed, 165, 188.
Hăr'rōw-er.
Hăr'rōw-ing.
Hăr'ry.
Hăr'ry-ing.
Harsh, 11, 46, 135.
Hars'let (11, 76) [Haslet, 203.]

☞ Of these two forms Walker and Smart prefer *haslet*; Goodrich prefers *harslet*. Worcester gives both forms without indicating any preference.

Hart (11), *n.* the male of the red deer. [*See* Heart, 160.]
Harts'horn, 214.
Ha-rus'pice [Aruspice, 203.]
Ha-rus'pi-cy [Aruspicy, 203.]
Har'vest, 11, 76.
Har'vest-ed.
Har'vest-er.
Har'vest-ing.
Has (*haz*), 10, 174.
Hash, 10, 46.
Hashed (*hasht*), 165.
Hash'ish [Haschisch, Hasheesh, 203.]
Has'let [so Sm. Wb. Gd.; *hā'slet*, Wk.; *ha'slet*, or *has'let*, Wr. 155.] [Harslet, 203. —*See* Note under *Harslet*.]
Hȧsp, 12, 131.
Hȧsped (*hȧspt*).
Has'sock.
Hast, 10.
Has'tate.
Has'tāt-ed.
Hāste, 23.
Hāst'ed.
Hāst'en (*hās'n*), 149,162.
Hāst'ened (*hās'nd*).
Hāst'en er (*hās'n-*).
Hāst'en-ing (*hās'n-*).
Hāst'i-ly, 186.
Hāst'i-ness, 169.
Hāst'ing.
Hāst'y, 93, 169.
Hāst'y-pud'ding (*-pŏŏd'-*), 205.
Hat, 10.
Hăt'a-ble 164, 169.
Hatch, 10, 44.
Hatched (*hacht*).
Hatch'el [so Sm. Wb. Gd.; *hak'l*, Wk.; *hach'el*, or *hak'l*, Wr. 155.] [Hackle, 203.]
Hatch'elled (*-eld*) [Hatcheled, Wb. Gd. 203.—*See* 177, and Note E, p. 70.]
Hatch'el-ler [Hatcheler, Wb. Gd. 203.]
Hatch'el-ling [Hatcheling, Wb. Gd. 203.]
Hatch'er.
Hatch'et, 76.
Hatch'ing.
Hatch'ment.
Hatch'wāy.
Hate, 23.
Hāt'ed, 183.
Hate'ful (*-fŏŏl*), 180.
Hate'ful-ly (*-fŏŏl-*).
Hāt'er, 77.
Ha'tred.
Hat'ted, 176.
Hat'ti-shĕr'if, *or* Hat'-ti-schĕr'if.
Hâugh'ti-ly (*haw'-*),162.

Hâugh'ti-ness (*haw'-*), 171.
Hâugh'ty (*haw'-*), 162, 171.
Hâul, *v.* to pull; to draw. [*See* Hall, 160.]
Hâul'age.
Hâuled (*hawld*), 165.
Hâul'ing.
Hâum [Haulm, Halm, Hawm, 203.]
Häunch (*hänch*) (11) [*not* hawnch, 153.]
Häunched (*hăncht*).
Häunt (*hänt*) (11) [*not* hawnt, 153.]
Häunt'ed.
Häunt'er.
Häunt'ing.
Hâus'tel-late.
Haut'boy (*ho'-*), 171.
Hau-teur' (*ho-tur'*) [so Sm.; *ho-tur'*, or *ho-toor'*, Wr.; *ho-tŭr'*, or *ho-tâur'*, Gd. 154, 155.]
Haut gout (Fr.) (*ho-goo'*).
Hăve (*hav*), 10, 163.
Ha'ven (*ha'vn*), 149.
Hav'er-sack.
Hav'ing, 183.
Hav'oc, 10, 86.
Haw, 17.
Hawed, 165.
Haw-haw' [Haha, 203.]
Haw'ing.
Hawk, 17.
Hawked (*hawkt*), 165.
Hawk'er.
Haw'key, 17, 98, 169.
Hawk'ing.
Hawk'weed, 206.
Hawse (*hawz*) [so Sm. Wb. Gd.; *haws*, Wk. Wr. 155.]
[Hawm, 203.—*See* Haum.]
Haws'er [Halser, 203.]
Haw'thorn, 135.
Hāy, *n.* grass cut and dried for fodder. [*See* Hey, 160.]
Haz'ard, 10, 72.
Haz'ard-ed.
Haz'ard-ing.
Haz'ard-oŭs.
Haze, 23.
Hazed, 165, 183.
Ha'zel (*ha'zl*), 149.
Hā'z'i-ness, 186.
Hāz'ing, 183.
Hāz'y, 93.
He, 13, 29.
Hĕad, 15.
Hĕad'ache (*-āk*), 171.
Hĕad'-dress, 66, N.; 206, Exc. 1.
Hĕad'ed.
Hĕad'er.
Hĕad'făst, 206.
Hĕad'-first', 205.
Hĕad'i-ly, 186.
Hĕad'i-ness, 169.
Hĕad'ing.
Hĕad'land.
Hĕad'long.
Hĕad'man, 196.
Hĕad'mōst.
Heads'man (*hedz'-*), 214.
Hĕad'stâll.
Hĕad'stōne, 206.
Hĕad'strong.
Hĕad'wāy.
Hĕad'y, 15, 93.
Hēal, *v.* to cure. [*See* Heel, 160.]
Hēal'a-ble, 164.
Hēalds (*hēldz*), *n. pl.*
Hēaled (*hēld*), 165.
Hēal'er.
Hēal'ing.
Hĕalth, 15, 37.
Hĕalth'ful (*-fōōl*), 180.
Hĕalth'i-ly, 186.
Hĕalth'i-ness, 169.
Hĕalth'y.
Hēap, 13.
Hēaped (*hēpt*), 165; Note C, p. 34.
Hēap'er.
Hēap'ing.
Hēap'y, 93.
Hēar (13), *v.* to perceive by the ear. [*See* Here, 160.]
Heard (*herd*) [*not* hērd, 153] (21, N.), *v.* did hear. [*See* Herd, 160.]
Hēar'er.
Hēar'ing.
Heärk'en (*hark'n*), 149.
Heärk'ened (*hark'nd*).
Heärk'en-er (*hark'n-*).
Heärk'en-ing (*hark'n-*).
Hēar'sāy, 206.
Hearse (*hers*) (21, N.), *n.* a carriage for conveying the dead. [*See* Herse, 160.]
Heärt (*hart*) (11), *n.* the muscular organ by the alternate contraction and dilatation of which the blood is made to circulate in the body of an animal. [*See* Hart, 160.]
Heärt'-brōk'en (*hart'-brōk-n*), 206, Exc. 5.
Heärt'burn.
Heärth (*härth*) (11) [*not* hurth, 153.]
Heärt'i-ly, 186.
Heärt'i-ness, 169.
Heärt's'-ēase(*hartz'ēz*), 213.
Heärt'-sick, 206, Exc. 5.
Heärt'y (*hart'y*), 93.
Hēat, 13.
Hēat'ed.
Hēat'er.
Hēath, 13, 37.
Hēa'then (*he'thn*) (149) [pl. Hēa'then (*-thn*), *or* Hēa'thens (*-thnz*).]
Hēa'then-īze (*he'thn-*), 202.
Hēa'then-ized (*he'thn-*).
Hēa'then-īz-ing (*he'-thn-*).
Hēath'er (13, 37) [so Sm. Wr.; *hĕth'ur*, Gd. 155.]

☞ "This [*heth'ur*] is the only pronunciation in Scotland." *Goodrich.*

Hēath'er-y [so Wr.; *heth'ur-y*, Gd. 155.]
Hēath'y, 13, 93.
Hēat'ing.
Hēave (*hēv*), 13.
Hēaved (*hēvd*), 183.
Hĕav'en (*hev'n*), 149, 167.
Hĕav'en-ward (*hev'n-*).
Hēav'er, 183.
Hēaves (*hēvz*), *n. pl.*
Hĕav'i-ly, 186.
Hĕav'i-ness, 169, 171.
Hēav'ing.
Hĕav'y (*hev'y*), 15, 93.
Hĕav'y-lăd'en (*-lăd'n*), 205.
Heb-dom'a-dal, 72.
Heb-dom'a-da-ry, 72.
Heb'e-tate, 73.
Heb'e-tāt-ed, 183.
Heb'e-tāt-ing.
Heb-e-ta'tion, 112.
Heb'e-tude.
He'bra-ism (*-izm*) (133, 136) [so Sm. Wb. Gd.; *heb'ra-ism*, Wk.; *he'-bra-izm*, or *heb'ra-izm*, Wr. 155.]

He′bra-ist [so Sm. Wb. Gd.; *heb′ra-ist*, Wk.; *he′bra-ist*, or *heb′ra-ist*, Wr. 155.]
He-bra-ist′ic, 109.
He′bra-ize, 202.
He′bra-ized, 183.
He′bra-īz-ing.
He′brew (*-broo*), 13, 19.
He-brid′i-an.
Hec′a-tomb (*-toom*, or *tom*) [*hek′a-toom*, Wk. Wr. Wb. Gd.; *hek′a-tom*, Sm. 155.]
[Heckle, 203. — *See* Hackle.]
Hec′türe (Fr.), 154.
Hec′tic, 200.
Hec′tic-al, 108.
Hec′to-gramme (Fr.) (154) [Hectogram, 203.]
Hectolitre (Fr.) (*hek′to-le′tr*) (154) [Hectoliter (*hek-tol′i-tur*), Wb. Gd. 203.]
Hectomètre (Fr.) *hek′to-ma′tr*) (154) [Hectometer (*hek-tom′e-tur*), Wb. Gd. 203.]
Hec′tor, 15, 88.
Hec′tored, 150, 165.
Hec′tor-ing.
Hec-to′re-an, 110.
Hec′tor-ism (*-izm*), 136.
Hectostère (Fr.) (*hek′to-stēr*), 154.
Hed′dle, 164.
Hed-er-a′ceous (*-shus*).
Hed′er-al, 233, Exc.
Hed-er-if′er-oŭs, 108.
Hedge (*hej*), 15, 45.
Hedged (*hejd*), 183.
Hedge′hog, 206.
Hedg′er, 183.
Hedge′-rōw, 206, Exc.3.
Hedg′ing, 171, 183.
He-don′ic, 109, 200.
Hed′o-nism (*-nizm*).
Heed, 13.
Heed′ed.
Heed′ful (*-fo͝ol*), 180.
Heed′ing.
Heel (13), *n.* the hind part of the foot: — *v.* to put a heel to; — to incline. [*See* Heal, 160.]
Heel′er.
Heel′ing.
Heel′tap, 206.
He-gi′ra, *or* Heg′i-ra (*hej′-*) [so Wk. Wr.; *he-ji′ra*, Wb. Gd.; *hej′i-ra*, Sm. 155.]
Hĕif′er (*hef′ur*), 15, 171.
Heīgh′-hō (*hi′hō*), 162.
Heīght (*hīt*) (25, 162) [Hight, Wb. Gd. 203. — *See* Note E, p. 70.]
Heīght′en (*hīt′n*) (149, 162). [Highten, Wb. Gd. 203.]
Heīght′ened (*hīt′nd*).
Heīght′en-ing (*hīt′n-*).
Hei′noŭs (*ha′nus*) [*not* hān′yus, *nor* he′nus, 153.]
Heir (*êr*) (14, 139), *n.* one who inherits. [*See* Air, Ere, Eyre, 160.]
Heir-ap-par′ent (*êr-ap-pêr′ent*), 216.
Heir′ess (*êr′-*), 171.
Heir′loom (*êr′-*).
Hel′a-mys.
Held, 15.
He′li-ac.
He-li′ac-al, 108.
He-li′ac-al-ly.
Hel′i-cal, 72, 78.
Hel′i-cīne, 152.
Hel′i-cīte, 152.
Hel′i-coid.
Hel-i-co′ni-an.
He-li-o-cen′tric.
He-li-o-cen′tric-al.
He′li-o-chrome (*-krōm*).
He-li-o-chrom′ic (*-krom′-*).
He-li-och′ro-my (*-ok′-*) [so Wr.; *he′li-o-kro-my*, Gd. 155.]
He′li-o-grăph.
He-li-o-grăph′ic, 109.
He-li-og′ra-phy, 108.
He-li-ol′a-ter.
He-li-ol′a-try.
He-li-om′e-ter, 108.
He′li-o-scope.
He′li-o-stat.
He′li-o-trope.
Hel-i-sphĕr′ic.
Hel-i-sphĕr′ic-al.
He′lix [so Wk. Wr. Wb. Gd.; *hel′iks*, Sm. 155.] [pl. Hel′i-cēs (*-sēz*), 198.]
Hell, 15, 172.
Hel′le-bore.
Hel-le′ni-an.
Hel-le′nic, *or* Hel-len′ic (109) [*hel-le′nik*, Sm.; *hel-le′nik*, Wb. Gd.; *hel′le-nik*, or *hel-len′ik*, Wr. 155.]
Hel′le-nism (*-nizm*), 136.
Hel′le-nist.
Hel-le-nist′ic, 109.
Hel′le-nize, 202.
Hel′le-nized, 183.
Hel′le-nīz-ing.
Hel-les-pont′īne, 152.
Hell′ward.
Helm, 15, 133.
Helmed (*helmd*).
Hel′met, 15, 76.
Hel′met-ed.
Hel-min′thic.
Hel-min-tho-log′ic (*-loj′-*).
Hel-min-tho-log′ic-al (*-loj′-*).
Hel-min-thol′o-gist.
Hel-min-thol′o-gy, 108.
Helm′wīnd.
Hel′ot [so Sm. Wr.; *he′lot*, Wb. Gd. 155.]
Hel′ot-ism (*-izm*).
Help, 15.
Helped (*helpt*), 165.
Help′er.
Help′ful (*-fo͝ol*), 180.
Help′mate, 206.
Help′meet.
Hel′ter-skel′ter.
Helve (*helv*), 15, 171.
Helved (*helvd*), 165.
Hel-vet′ic.
Hel′vīne (152) [Helvin, 203.]
Helv′ing, 183.
Hem, 15.
Hem′a-chate (*-kāt*).
Hem-as-tat′ic-al.
Hem′a-tīne (152) [Hematin, 203.]
Hem′a-tīte (152) [Hæmatite, 203.]
Hem-a-tit′ic.
He-mat′o-cele [so Sm. Wr.; *hem′a-to-sēl*, Wb. Gd. 155.] [Hæmatocele, 203.]
Hem-a-tol′o-gy (108) [Hæmatology, 203.]
He-mat′o-sīne (152) [so Wr.; *hem-a-to′sin*, Gd. 155.] [Hematosin, 203.]
[Hematosis, 203. — *See* Hæmatosis.]
Hem′i-crā-ny.
Hem′i-cȳ-cle, 164, 171.
Hem-i-he′dral.

Hem′i-na.
Hem′i-op-sy.
Hem-i-pleg′ic (*-plej′-*).
Hem′i-pleg-y (*-plej-*) [so Wk. Sm. Wr.; *hem′i-ple-jy*, Wb. Gd. 155.]
He-mip′ter-al.
He-mip′ter-oŭs.
Hem′i-sphere, 78, 169.
Hem-i-sphĕr′ic, 109.
Hem-i-sphĕr′ic-al, 108.
Hem′is-tich (*-tik*) [so Sm. Wb. Gd.; *he-mis′tik*, Wk.; *hem′is-tik*, or *he-mis′tik*, Wr. 155.]
Hem-is′tich-al (*-tik-*) [so Sm.; *he-mis′tik-al*, Wr. Gd. 155.]
He-mit′ro-pal.
Hem′i-trope.
He-mit′ro-poŭs.
Hem′lock, 15, 18.
Hemmed (*hemd*), 176.
Hem′ming.
Hem′or-rhage (*-rāj*) (162, 171) [Hæmorrhage, 203.]
Hem-or-rhag′ic (*-raj′-*).
Hem-or-rhoid′al (*-roid′-*), 162.
Hem′or-rhoids (*-roidz*), *n. pl.* 162, 171.
Hemp, 15.
Hemp′en (*hemp′n*), 149.
Hem′stitch.
Hen, 15.
Hen′bane, 206.
Hence, 15, 39.
Hence-fōrth′ [so Sm. Gd.; *hens′fōrth*, Wk.; *hens′fōrth*, or *hens-fōrth′*, Wr. 155.]
Hence-for′ward.
Hen-dec′a-gon.
Hen-dec-a-syl-lab′ic.
Hen-dec-a-syl′la-ble, 164.
Hen-di′a-dys.
Hen′ner-y, 170.
[Hep, 203.—*See* Hip.]
He-pat′ic, 109.
He-pat′ic-al, 108.
Hep′a-tīte, 152.
Hep-a-tī-za′tion.
Hep′a-tize, 202.
Hep′a-tized, 183.
Hep′a-tīz-ing.
He-pat′o-cele, 171.
He-pat-o-gas′tric.
Hep-a-tog′ra-phy, 108.
Hep-a-tol′o-gy.
Hep-a-tos′co-py.
Hep′ta-chord (*-kord*).
Hep′ta-gon, 169.
Hep′ta-glot.
Hep-tag′o-nal.
Hep-ta-gyn′i-a (*-jin′-*).
Hep-ta-gyn′i-an.
Hep-tag′y-noŭs (*-taj′-*).
Hep-ta-he′dron [pl. Hep-ta-he′dra, 198.]
Hep-ta-hex-a-he′dral.
Hep-tam′e-rede.
Hep-tan′dri-a.
Hep-tan′dri-an, 169.
Hep-tan′droŭs.
Hep-tan′gu-lar (*-tang′-*).
Hep-ta-pet′al-oŭs.
Hep-ta-phyl′loŭs, *or* Hep-taph′yll-oŭs. [*See* Adenophyllous.]
Hep′tarch (*-tark*).
Hep-tarch′ic (*-tark′-*).
Hep′tarch-y (*-ky*), 171.
Hep-ta-sperm′oŭs.
Hep′ta-teŭch (*-tūk*).
Her, 21, N.
Hĕr′ald, 15, 72.
Hĕr′ald-ed.
He-ral′dic [so Wk. Sm. Wr.; *hĕr-al′dik*, Wb. Gd. 155.]
Hĕr′ald-ry, 93, 171.
Herb (*erb*, or *herb*) (21, N.; 139) [*erb*, Wk. Wr. Wb. Gd.; *herb*, Sm. 155.]
Herb′age (*erb′-*, or *herb′-*) [so Wr. Gd.; *erb′ij*, Wk.; *her′bāj*, Sm. 155.]
Herb′aged, 165, 183.
Herb′al (*herb′-*), 139.
Herb′al-ism (*herb′al-izm*), 136, 139.
Herb′al-ist (*herb′-*).
Her-ba′ri-um (*her-*) [L. pl. *Her-ba′ri-a*; Eng. pl. Her-ba′ri-ums (*-umz*), 198.]
Herb′a-ry, 72.
Herb-es′cent, 171.
Herb-if′er-oŭs, 108.
Herb′ist.
Herb-iv′o-ra, *n. pl.*
Herb-iv′o-roŭs.
Herb′let.
Her-bo-rī-za′tion.
Her′bo-rize, 202.
Her′bo-rized, 183.
Her′bo-rīz-ing.
Herb′oŭs.
Herb′y (*erb′y*, or *herb′-y*), 139.
Her-cu′le-an, 110.
Her-cyn′i-an.
Herd (21, N.), *n.* a number of beasts feeding together: — *v.* to associate, as beasts. [*See* Heard, 160.]
Herd′ed.
Herd′er.
Herd′ing.
Herds′grȧss (*herdz′-*), 171, 214.
Herds′man, 196, 214.
Here (13), *ad.* in this place. [*See* Hear, 160.]
Here′a-bout.
Here′a-bouts.
Here-ȧf′ter.
Here-by′.
He-red-i-ta-bil′i-ty, 108.
He-red′i-ta-ble, 164.
Hĕr-e-dit′a-ment.

☞ This word is sometimes pronounced *he-red′-i-ta-ment*, as sanctioned by Sheridan and some other orthoëpists: but Walker, Smart, Worcester, Webster, and Goodrich agree in pronouncing it *her-e-dit′a-ment*. Walker remarks of this accentuation, that it "is not only most agreeable to the best usage, and the most grateful to the ear, but it seems to accord better with the secondary accent of the later Latin *Hæreditamenta*."

He-red′i-ta-ry, 72, 171.
Here in′.
Here-of′ (*hēr-of′*) [so Wk. Sm. Gd.; *hēr-of′*, or *hēr-ov′*, Wr. 155.]
Here-on′.
He-re′si-arch (*-zĭ-ark*), *or* Hĕr′e-si-arch (*zĭ-ark*) [*he-re′zi-ark*, Wr.; *her′e-zi-ark*, Sm.; *hĕr′e-si-ark*, or *he-re′zi-ark*, Gd.; *he-re′zhi-ark*, Wk. 155.]
Hĕr-e-si-og′ra-pher.
Hĕr-e-si-og′ra-phy, 108.
Hĕr′e-sy, 169.
Hĕr′e-tic, 109.
He-ret′ic-al.
Here-to-fore′.
Here′up-on′, 205, Exc. 2.
Here-with′ [*not* hēr-with′, 153.]
Hĕr′ĭ-ot, 170.
Hĕr′i-ot-a-ble, 164.
Hĕr′is-son [so Wb.

Gd.; *he-ris'son*, Wr. 155.]
Hĕr'i-ta-ble, 164, 171.
Hĕr'i-tage, 169, 171.
Her-maph'ro-dīte, 152.
Her-maph-ro-dit'ic.
Her-maph-ro-dit'ic-al.
Her-me-neū'tic, 109.
Her-me-neū'tic-al, 108.
Her-me-neū'tics.
Her-met'ic, 109.
Her-met'ic-al, 108.
Her-met'ic-al-ly.
Her'mit, 21, N.
Her'mit-age, 169.
Her'mit-a-ry, 72.
Her-mit'ic-al.
Her-mo-dac'tyl [so Wr. Wb. Gd.; *her'mo-dak-til*, Sm. 155.] [Hermodactyle, Wr. 203.]
Hern [contracted from *Heron*.]
Her'ni-a, 21, N.
Her-ni-ot'o-my, 108.
He'ro, 13, 24, 49, N.
He-ro'ic, 109.
He-ro'ic-al, 108.
He-ro'ic-al-ly.
He-ro-i-com'ic [so Wr. Wb. Gd., *hĕr-o-ī-kom'ik*, Sm. 155.]
Hĕr'o-ĭne (82, 143) [so Wk. Sm. Wb. Gd.; *hĕr'o-in*, or *he'ro-in*, Wr. 155.]
Hĕr'o-ism (*-izm*) (136, 143) [so Wk. Sm. Wb. Gd.; *hĕr'o-izm*, or *he'ro-ism*, Wr. 155.]
Hĕr'on, 170.
Hĕr'on-ry.
Hĕr'on-shaw.
He-ro-ol'o-gist, 108.
He'ro-wor'ship (*-wur'-*).
Her'pēs (*-pēz*).
Her-pet'ic.
Her-pet-o-log'ic (*-loj'-*).
Her-pet-o-log'ic-al (*-loj'-*).
Her-pe-tol'o-gist, 108.
Her-pe-tol'o-gy (108) [Erpetology, 203.]
Hĕr'ring, 66, 170.
Hers (*herz*), 21, N.
Her'schel (*-shel*), 21, N.; 171.
Herse (*hers*), *n.* a lattice or portcullis set with spikes; — a kind of candlestick used in churches. [*See* Hearse, 160.]
Her-self'.
Her'sil-lon [so Sm. Wb. Gd.; *her-sil'lon*, Wr. 155.]
Hes'i-tan-cy (*hez'-*), 169.
Hes'i-tant (*hez'-*).
Hes'i-tate (*hez'-*).
Hes'i-tāt-ed (*hez'-*), 183.
Hes'i-tāt-ing (*hez'-*).
Hes-i-ta'tion (*hez-*).
Hes'i-tāt-ĭve (*hez'-*).
Hes'per.
Hes-pe'ri-an, 49, N.
Hes'pe-rus.
Hes'sian (*hesh'an*), 171.
Het-er-o-car'poŭs.
Het-er-o-ceph'a-loŭs.
Het-er-o-cer'cal.
Het-er-o-chro'moŭs (*-kro'-*) [so Wr.; *het-er-ok'ro-mus*, Sm. 155.]
Het'er-o-clīte, 152.
Het-er-o-clit'ic.
Het-er-o-clit'ic-al.
Het'er-o-dox, 122, 171.
Het'er-o-dox-y.
Het-er-og'a-moŭs.
Het-er-o-ge'ne-al.
Het-er-o-ge-ne'i-ty, 108.
Het-er-o-ge'ne-oŭs.
Het-er-o-mor'phoŭs.
Het-er-on'y-moŭs.
Het-er-o-path'ic.
Het-er-op'a-thy, 108.
Het-er-o-phyl'loŭs, *or* Het-er-oph'yl-loŭs [*See* Adenophyllous.]
Het'er-o-pod, 171.
Het-er-op'o-doŭs.
Het-er-os'cian (*-osh'an*).
Het-er-ot'ro-poŭs.
Het-er-ot'ro-pal.
Hew (*hū*) (26, 51, N.), *v.* to cut with an axe or other edged tool, so as to make an even surface. [*See* Hue, 160.]
Hewed (*hūd*), 165.
Hew'er (*hū'-*), 26, 77.
Hewn (*hūn*).
Hex'a-chord (*-kord*).
Hex-a-dac'tyl-oŭs.
Hex'ade.
Hex'a-gon, 169.
Hex-ag'o-nal.
Hex-a-gyn'i-an (*-jin'-*).
Hex-a-gyn'i-a (*-jin'-*).
Hex-ag'y-noŭs (*-aj'-*).
Hex-a-he'dral.
Hex-a-he'dron [pl. Hex-a-he'dra, 189.]
Hex-a-he'mer-on.
Hex-am'er-oŭs.
Hex-am'e-ter, 169.
Hex-a-met'ric.
Hex-a-met'ric-al.
Hex-an'dri-a.
Hex-an'dri-an.
Hex-an'droŭs.
Hex-an'gu-lar (*-ang'-*), 54, 108.
Hex-a-pet'al-oŭs.
Hex-a-phyl'loŭs, *or* Hex-aph'yl-loŭs [*See* Adenophyllous.]
Hex'a-pla.
Hex'a-plar, 135.
Hex'a-pod.
Hex-ap'ter-oŭs.
Hex'ă-stich (*-stik*).
Hex'a-style.
Hex-oc-ta-he'dron.
Hey (*hā*), *int.* an exclamation of joy or of exhortation. [*See* Hay, 160.]
Hey'dāy (*hā'dā*).
Hi-a'tus [L. pl. *Hi-a'-tus*; Eng. pl. Hi-a-tus-es (*-ez*), 198.]
Hī-ber'na-cle, 21, N.; 164.
Hī-ber'nal, 79.
Hi'ber-nate (73) [Hybernate, 203.]
Hi'ber-nāt-ed, 183.
Hi'ber-nāt-ing.
Hī-ber-na'tion, 112.
Hī-ber'ni-an, 21, N.; 79.
Hī-ber'ni-an-ism (*-izm*).
Hī-ber'ni-cism (*-sizm*).
Hic'cough (*hik'up*) (30) [so Wb. Gd.; *hik'-kup*, or *hik'kof*, Wk. Wr.; *hik'kof*, Sm. 155.] [Hiccup, Hickup, 203.]

☞ "Though *hiccough* is the most general orthography, *hick'up* is the most usual pronunciation." — *Walker*. Smart remarks that *hic'cup* is "preferable, in familiar use, both in spelling and sound."

Hic'coughed (*hik'upt*).
Hic'cough-ing (*hik'up-*).
[Hiccup, 203. — *See* Hiccough.]
Hick'o-ry, 86, 171.
[Hickup, 203. — *See* Hiccough.]
Hick'wâll.
Hick'wāy.

Hid, 16.
Hĭd'age.
Hi-dal'go (Sp.) (*he-dal'-go*), 154.
Hĭd'den (*hid'n*), 149.
Hide, 25.
Hide'bound, 206.
Hid'e-ous (134) [so Sm. Wr. Wb. Gd.; *hid'e-us*, or *hid'je-us*, Wk. 155.]
Hīd'er, 183.
Hīd'ing.
Hie, *v.* to hasten. [*See* High, 160.]
Hi'e-rarch (*-rark*), 169.
Hi'e-rarch-al (*-rark-*).
Hi-e-rarch'ic-al (*-rark'-*).
Hi'e-rarch-y (*-rark-*), 171.
Hī-e-rat'ic, 109.
Hī-e-roc'ra-cy, 169.
Hi'e-ro-glyph.
Hī-e-ro-glyph'ic.
Hī-e-ro-glyph'ic-al.
Hī-e-ro-glyph'ic-al-ly.
Hī-e-rog'ly-phist (108) [so Wr.; *hī-e-ro-glif'-ist*, Wb. Gd. 155.]
Hi'e-ro-gram.
Hī-e-ro-gram-mat'ic.
Hī-e-ro-gram'ma-tist.
Hī-e-rog'ra-pher, 108.
Hī-e-ro-graph'ic.
Hī-e-ro-graph'ic-al.
Hī-e-rog'ra-phy, 108.
Hī-e-rol'o-gist.
Hī-e-rol'o-gy, 108.
Hi'e-ro-man-cy.
Hī-e-rom-ne'mon.
Hi'e-ro-phant, *or* Hī-ĕr'o-phant [so Gd.; *hi'e-ro-fant*, Sm.; *hī-ĕr'o-fant*, Wk.; *hī-ĕr'o-fant*, or *hi'e-ro-fant*, Wr. 155.]
Hī-e-ro-phant'ic.
Hī-e-ros'co-py.
Hig'gle, 16, 164.
Hig'gled (*hig'ld*), 183.
Hig'gler.
Hig'gling.
High (*hī*) (25, 162), *a.* elevated; exalted. [*See* Hie, 160.]
High'er (*hi'ur*) (67), *a.* more high. [*See* Hire, 148.]
High'land (*hi'-*), 162.
High'-mīnd-ed.
[High, *n.* Wb. Gd. 203.—*See* Height.]
High-wāy' (*hi-wa'*) (162) [so Wk. Sm. Wr.; *hi'wā*, Gd. 155.]
High'wāy-man (*hi'-*), 162, 196.
Hī-la'ri-oŭs, 79, 100.
Hī-lăr'i-ty, *or* Hī-lăr'i-ty [*hī-lăr'i-ty*, Wk. Sm.; *hī-lăr'i-ty*, Wr. Gd. 155.]
Hil'a-ry.
Hill, 16, 172.
Hilled (*hild*), 165.
Hill'ing.
Hill'ock, 86.
Hill'-side.
Hill'y, 93.
Hilt, 16.
Hilt'ed.
Hi'lum.
Him, 16.
Him-a-lāy'an, 171.
Him-self'.
Hind, 25.
Hīnd'bĕr-ry.
Hīnd'er, *v.* 147, 161.
Hīnd'er, *a.* 147, 161.
Hin'der-ance [Hindrance, 203.]

☞ Both forms of this word are in good use, but the contracted form (*hindrance*), according to Smart, prevails.

Hin'dered (*-durd*), 150.
Hin'der-er, 77.
Hin'der-ing.
Hīnd'mōst.
Hin-doo' [so Sm. Wr.; *hin'doo*, Wb. Gd. 155.] [pl. Hin-doos' (*-dooz'*).]
Hin-doo'ism (*-izm*).
Hin-dos-tan'ee [Hindoostanee, 203.]
Hin'drance [Hinderance, 203.—*See* Note under *Hinderance.*]
Hinge, 16, 45.
Hinged (*hinjd*), 183.
Hing'ing (*hinj'-*).
Hin'ny, 66, 170.
Hint, 16.
Hint'ing.
Hint'ed.
Hip (16), *n.* & *v.* [Hep (in the sense of *the fruit of the wild brier*), Hyp (in the sense of *to make melancholy*), 203.]
Hipped (*hipt*) (165).
[Hypped (in the sense of dispirited), 203.]
Hip'po-camp.
Hip-po-cen'tâur.
Hip'po-cras.
Hip-po-crat'ic.
Hip'po-drome, 170.
Hip'po-griff.
Hip'po-mane.
Hip-po-pa-thol'o-gy.
Hip-poph'a-goŭs.
Hip-po-pot'a-mus [*not* hip-po-po-ta'mus, 153] [L. pl. *Hip-po-pot'a-mī*; Eng. pl. Hip-po-pot'a-mus-es (*-ez*), 198.]
Hip-pu'ric.
Hire, (25, 67), *v.* to procure temporarily for a price:—*n.* recompense. [*See* Higher, 148.]
Hired, 165, 183.
Hire'ling.
Hir'er.
Hir'ing.
Hir-sute', 121.
His (*hiz*), 16, 174.
His'pid.
Hiss, 16, 174.
Hissed (*hist*), *v.* did hiss. [*See* Hist, 160.]
Hiss'ing.
Hist, *int.* commanding silence. [*See* Hissed, 160.]
His-tog-e-net'ic (*-toj-*).
His-tog'e-ny (*-toj'-*).
His-tog'ra-phy.
His-to-log'ic (*-loj'-*).
His-to-log'ic-al (*-loj'-*).
His-tol'o-gist.
His-tol'o-gy, 108.
His-to'ri-an, 49, N.
His-tŏr'ic, 109.
His-tŏr'ic-al, 108.
His-to-ri-ette' (Fr.), 154.
His-to-ri-og'ra-pher.
His-to-ri-og'ra-phy, 108.
His'to-ry, 132.
His-tri-on'ic.
His-tri-on'ic-al.
His'tri-on-ism (*-izm*).
Hit, 16.
Hitch, 16, 44.
Hitched (*hicht*), 165.
Hitch'ing.
Hith'er, 16, 140.
Hith'er-to (*-too*).
Hith'er-ward.
Hit'ter, 176.
Hit'ting.

[Hity-tity, 203.— *See* Hoity-toity.]
Hive, 25.
Hived, 165, 183.
Hives (*hīvz*), *n. pl.*
Hiv'ing.
Ho, *int.* calling attention. [*See* Hoe, 160.] [Hoa (*ho*), 203.]
Hōar, 24.
Hōard (24), *v.* to store secretly; to accumulate. [*See* Horde, 160.
Hōard'ed.
Hōard'er.
Hōard'ing.
Hōar'frost, 206.
Hōar'hound [Hore-hound, 203.]

☞ The two forms of this word are both in use. Walker gives only *hoar-hound*, and Smart, as well as Webster and Goodrich, prefers it. Worcester prefers *horehound*.

Hōar'i-ness, 186.
Hōarse, 24.
Hōar'stone, 24.
Hōar'y, 93, 169.
Hōax.
Hōaxed (*hōkst*).
Hob, 18.
Hob'ble, 164.
Hob'bled (*hob'ld*).
Hob'bler, 183.
Hob'bling.
Hob'by, 93, 169.
Hob-gob'lin.
Hob'nāil, 206.
Hob'nāiled.
Hob'nob.
Hock, *n.* a white Rhenish wine; — in quadrupeds, the joint at the lower extremity of the tibia: — *v.* to disable in this joint. [Hough (in the last two senses), 203.]
Hocked (*hokt*) [Houghed, 203.]
Hock'ing [Hough-ing, 203.]
Hod, 18.
Hod'den-grāy (*hod'n-*).
Hodge'podge [Hotch-pot, Hotch-potch, 203.]
Hod'man, 196.
Hod'man-dod.
Hōe (24), *n.* a tool used in gardening, and shaped like an adze: — *v.* to dig or cut with a hoe. [*See* Ho, 160] [pl. Hōes (*hōz*)] [*See* Hose, 160.]
Hōed, 165, 183.
Hōe'ing, 183, Exc.
Hog, 18.
Hogged (*hogd*), 176.
Hog'ging (*-ghing*), 138.
Hog'gish (*-ghish*).
Hogs'hĕad (*hogz'-*).
Hoi'den (*hoi'dn*), 149.
Hoi'dened (*hoi'dnd*).
Hoi'den-ing (*hoi'dn-*).
Hoist, 27.
Hoist'ed.
Hoist'ing.
Hoi'ty-toi'ty, *a.* & *int.* [Hity-tity, 203.]
Hōld (24), *v.* to have or grasp in the hand. [*See* Holed, 160.]
Hōld'back, 206.
Hōld'er.
Hōld'ing.
Hole (24), *n.* a cavity: — to drive or to go into a hole. [*See* Hole, 160.]
Holed, *v.* did drive or go into a hole. [*See* Hold, 160.]
[Holibut, 203.— *See* Halibut.]
Hol'i-dāy [Holiday, 203.— *See* Note under *Holyday*.]
Ho'li-ly, 186.
Ho'li-ness, 169.
Hōl'ing.
Hol'la, *n. v.* & *int.* [so Sm. Wb. Gd.; *hol-lä'*, Wr.; *hol-lo'*, Wk. 155.] [Holloa, Hollo, Hollow, Halloo, 203.]
Hol'läed, 188.
Hol'la-ing.
Hol'land-er.
Hol-lo', *or* Hol-lōa', *int.* [*See* Holla.]
Hol'lo, *v.* [so Wb. Gd.; *hol-lo'*, Wr. 155.] [*See* Holla.]
Hol'lōed.
Hol'lo-ing.
Hol'lōw, *a.* having a void space within: — *n.* a cavity: — *v.* to excavate.
Hol'lōw [so Sm.; *hol'lo*, or *hol-lo'*, Wr. Gd. 155], *v.* to shout. [*See* Holla.]
Hol'lōwed, 188.
Hol'lōw-ing.
Hol'ly, 170.
Hol'ly-hock.
Hōlm [so Wr. Wb. Gd.; *hōlm*, Sm. 155.]
Hol'o-cāust.
Hol-o-he'dral.
Hōl'ster, 24, 77.
Hōl'stered (*-sturd*), 150.
Ho'ly, *a.* free from sin; — sacred. [*See* Wholly, 160.]
Hol'y-dāy [so Wk. Wr.; *ho'ly-da*, Gd. 155.] [Holiday, 203.]

☞ This word is now usually written *holiday*; but when it is used in the sense of *a day devoted to religious services*, it is properly written and pronounced, as Worcester remarks, *ho'ly-day*.

Ho'ly-rood.

☞ "As applied to the palace in Edinburgh, it is pronounced *hol'y-rood*." *Smart.*

Ho'ly-stone.
Hom'age, 70, 170.
Hom'age-a-ble, 164.
Home, 24, 130.
Home'li-ness, 169, 186.
Home'ly, 24.
[Homeopathy, 203. — *See* Homœopathy.]
Ho-mĕr'ic, 109.
Ho-mĕr'ic-al.
Home'sick, 206.
Home'spun, 24.
Home'stĕad.
Home'ward, *or* Home'wards (*-wardz*).
Hom-i-cīd'al.
Hom'i-cīde, 108.
Hom-i-let'ic.
Hom-i-let'ic-al.
Hom-i-let'ics.
Hom'i-list.
Hom'i-ly, 78, 93.
Hom'i-ny (169) [Homony, 203.]
[Hommock, 203.— *See* Hummock.]
Ho-mo-cen'tric [so Sm. Wr.; *hom-o-sen'trik*, Wb. Gd. 155.]
Ho-mo-cer'cal.
Ho-moch'ro-moŭs (*-mok'-*) [so Sm.; *ho-mok'ro-mus*, or *ho-mo-kro'mus*, Wr. 155.]
Ho-mœ-o-path'ic (*-me-*).

Ho-mœ-op'a-thy (-me-) (108, 171) [*not* ho'me-o-path-y, 153.]
Ho-mog'a-moŭs.
Ho-mo-ge'ne-al.
Ho-mo-ge-ne'i-ty, 108.
Ho-mo-ge'ne-oŭs, 169.
Ho-moi-op'to-ton [so Wr., *hom-oi-op'to-ton*, Gd. 155.]
Ho-moi-ou'si-an (*-ow'-zi-an*) (171) [so Sm.; *ho-moi-ow'si-an*, Gd.; *ho-moi-ow'shan*, Wr. 155.]
Ho-mol'o-gate.
Ho-mol'o-gāt-ed.
Ho-mol'o-gāt-ing.
Ho-mol-o-ga'tion.
Ho-mo-log'ic-al (*-loj'-*).
Ho-mol'o-goŭs, 170.
Hom'o-lŏgue (*-log*), 168.
Ho-mol'o-gy, 108.
[Homony, 203. — *See* Hominy.]
Hom'o-nȳme, *or* Hom'-o-nym, 203.
Hom-o-nym'ic, 109.
Hom-o-nym'ic-al, 108.
Ho-mon'y-moŭs.
Ho-mon'y-my, 171.
Ho-mo-ou'si-an (*-ow'zi-an*) [so Sm.; *ho-mo-ow'si-an*, Gd.; *ho-mo-ow'shan*, Wr. 155.]
Hom'o-phone, 35, 171.
Ho-moph'o-noŭs.
Ho-moph'o-ny, 171.
Ho-mop'ter-an.
Ho-mop'ter-oŭs.
Ho-mot'ro-pal.
Ho-mot'ro-poŭs.
Hom'o-type.
Hone, 24.
Honed, 165, 183.
Hon'est (*on'-*), 139, 171.
Hon'est-y (*on'-*).
Hone'wort (*-wurt*).
Hon'ey (*hun'y*), 98, 169.
Hon'ey-cōmb (*hun'y-kōm*), 162, 171.
Hon'eyed (*hun'id*).
Hon'ey-suc-kle(*hun'y-*), 164, 171.
Hong, 18, 54.
Hōn'ing.
Hon'or (*on'ur*) (138, 199) [Honour, Sm. 203.]

☞ Smart inserts the *u* in all the derivatives of this word except *honorary*.

Hon'or-a-ble (*on'-*), 164.
Hon'or-a-bly (*on'-*).
Hon'o-ra-ry (*on'-*), 72.
Hon'ored (*on'urd*), 138.
Hon'or-er (*on'-*), 77, 88.
Hon'or-ing (*on'-*).
Hŏŏd, 20.
Hŏŏd'ed.
Hŏŏd'ing.
Hŏŏd'wink (*-wingk*), 54.
Hŏŏd'winked (*-wingkt*).
Hŏŏd'wink-ing (*-wingk-*).
Hŏŏf, 20.
Hŏŏfed (*hŏŏft*), 171; Note C, p. 34.
Hŏŏk (20) [*See* Book.]
Hoo'kah, 72.
Hŏŏked (*hŏŏkt*), 165.
Hŏŏk'er.
Hŏŏk'y, 93.
Hoop (*hoop*, or *hŏŏp*)[so Wr.; *hoop*, Wk. Sm.; *hŏŏp*, Wb. Gd. 155], *n.* a band of wood or of metal used to bind together the parts of a cask, &c.; — a ring: — *v.* to bind with hoops; — to encircle.
Hoop (19), *n.* a shout: — *v.* to shout. [Whoop, 203.]
Hooped (*hoopt*, or *hŏŏpt*), *v.* did bind with hoops.
Hooped (*hoopt*), *v.* did shout. [Whooped, 203.]
Hoop'ing (*hoop'ing*, or *hŏŏp'ing*), *part.* binding with hoops.
Hoop'ing, *part.* shouting. [Whooping, 203.]
Hoop'ing-cough (*-kŏf*), 18, N. [Whooping-cough, 203.]
Hoo'poo, *or* Hoo'poe (*-poo*).

☞ Both forms of this word are given by Worcester and Goodrich, and the latter (*hoopoe*) is pronounced by them *hoo'po*; but Smart gives only this form, and pronounces it *hoo'poo*.

Hoot, 19.
Hoot'ed.
Hoot'ing.
Hoove (*hoov*).
Hop, 18.

Hop'-bīnd.
Hope, 24.
Hoped (*hōpt*), 183.
Hope'ful (*-fŏŏl*).
Hope'ful-ly (*-fŏŏl-*).
Hōp'er, 183.
Hōp'ing.
Hopped (*hopt*), 176.
Hop'per.
Hop'ping.
Hop'ple (164) [Hobble, 203.]
Hop'pled (*hop'ld*), 183.
Hop'ples (*hop'lz*), *n. pl.*
Hop'pling.
Ho'ral, 49, N.
Ho'ra-ry (49, N.; 72) [so Wk. Wr. Wb. Gd.; *hŏr'a-ry*, Sm. 155.]
Hōrde (*hōrd*) (24), *n.* a migratory body of men. [*See* Hoard, 160.]
Hor'de-īne (152) [Hordein, 203.]
Hore'hound [Hoarhound, 203. — *See* Note under *Hoarhound*.]
Ho-ri'zon (86, 111) [*not* hŏr'i-zon, 153.]
Hŏr-i-zon'tal, 72, 171.
Hŏr-i-zon'tal-ly.
Horn, 17.
Horn'bēam.
Horn'bill, 206.
Horn'blende, 171.
Horn-blend'ic, 109, 186.
Horn'-bŏŏk, 206, Exc. 4.
Horned (*hornd*), 165.
Horn'er.
Horn'et, 17, 76.
Horn'ing.
Hor'ni-to.
Horn'pipe, 206.
Horn'pout.
Horn'stone, 24.
Horn'work (*-wurk*).
Horn'wort (*-wurt*).
Horn'y, 93, 169.
Ho-rog'ra-phy, 108.
Hŏr'o-loge (*hŏr'o-lōj*) [so Sm. Gd.; *hŏr'o-lŏj*, Wk. Wr. 155.]
Ho-rol'o-ger.
Hŏr-o-log'ic (*-loj'-*).
Hŏr-o-log'ic-al (*-loj'-*).
Hŏr-o-lo-gi-og'ra-pher.
Hŏr-o-lo-gi-o-graph'ic.
Hŏr-o-lo-gi-og'ra-phy.
Ho-rol'o-gist.
Ho-rol'o-gy (108) [so Wk. Wr. Wb. Gd.; *hŏr'o-lō-jy*, Sm. 155.]

Ho-rom′e-ter, 108.
Ho-rom′e-try, 169.
Hŏr′o-scope.
Ho-ros′co-py, 108.
Hŏr′rent, 170.
Hŏr′ri-ble, 164, 170.
Hŏr′ri-bly, 93.
Hŏr′rid, 66, 170.
Hŏr-rif′ic, 109.
Hŏr′ri-fīed, 186.
Hŏr′ri-fȳ, 94.
Hŏr′ri-fȳ-ing.
Hŏr-rip-i-la′tion.
Hŏr′ror, 18, 88.
Hors de combat (Fr.) (*hŏr duh com-ba′*), 154.
Horse, 17.
Horse′back, 206.
Horse′fo͝ot.
Horse′-jock-ey, 98.
Horse′man, 196, 206.
Horse′shoe (*-shoo*), 171.
Horse′tāil.
Horse′whip.
Horse′whipped (*-whipt*)
Horse′whip-ping.
Hor′ta-tĭve, 84.
Hor′ta-to-ry, 86.
Hor′ti-cul-tor.
Hor-ti-cult′ur-al(*-yur-*).
Hor′ti-cult-ure, 91, 171.
Hor-ti-cult′ur-ist(*-yur-*)
Hor′tu-lan.
Hor′tus sic′cus (L.).
Ho-san′na (*-zan′-*), 170.
Hose, *n. sing.* & *pl.* stockings ; — a flexible tube for conducting water to extinguish fires, &c. [*See* Hoes, pl. of Hoe, 160.]
Ho′sier (*-zhur*) (171) [so Wk. Wr. Wb. Gd. ; *ho′zh′ur*, Sm. (*See* § 26), 155.]
Ho′sier-y (*-zhur-*).
Hos′pice (*-pēs*), 156.
Hos′pi-ta-ble (164, 171) [*not* hos-pit′a-bl, 153.]
Hos′pi-ta-bly.
Hos′pi-tal, 78, 139.
Hos-pi-tal′i-ty.
Hos′pi-tal-ler [H o s p i t a l e r, Wb. Gd. 203. — *See* 177, and Note E, p. 70.]
Hos′po-där.
Hŏst, (24) [*See* Ghost.]
Hŏst′age, 139.
Hŏst′ess.
Hos′tĭle, 81, 152.
Hos′tĭle-ly, 66, N.
Hos-til′i-ty, 108, 169.

Hos′tler (*os′lur*) (139, 162) [so Wk. Sm. Wr.; *hos′lur*, or *os′lur*, Gd. 155.]
Hot, 18.
Hot′bed, 206.
Hotch′pot, *or* Hotch′potch [H o d g e - p o d g e , 203.]
Ho-tel′.
Hotel de ville (Fr.) (*o-tel′ duh vēl*).
Hotel Dieu (Fr.) (*o-tel′ de-uh′*).
Hot′-house, 206, Exc. 3.
Hot′press.
Hot′pressed (*-prest*).
Hot′press-ing.
Hot′spur.
Hot′spurred (*-spurd*).
Hot′ten-tot (*hot′n-*),171.
Hou′dah (72) [H o w - d a h , 203.]
Hough (*hok*) (171), *n.* in quadrupeds, the joint at the lower extremity of the tibia : — *v.* to hamstring. [H o c k, 203.]
Houghed (*hokt*) H o c k e d , 203.]
Hough′ing (*hok′-*) [H o c k i n g , 203.]
[H o u l e t, 203. — *See* Howlet.]
Hound, 28.
Hour (*our*) (139), *n.* the twenty-fourth part of a day. [*See* Our, 160.]
Hour′glȧss (*our′-*).
Hour′ī (*howr′y*) [pl. Hour′ies (*-iz*).]
House, *n.* 28, 161.
House (*howz*), *v.*136,161.
Housed (*howzd*), 183.
House′hōld, 206.
House′leek.
House′wife (*hŭz′wĭf*, or *hous′wīf*) [so Wr. ; *huz′wĭf*, Wk. Sm. ; *hous′wīf*,Wb. Gd.155.] [H u s w i f e , 203.]

☞ In the sense of *a little case for pins, needles*, &c., this word, according to Smart, "is colloquially pronounced *huz′zif*."

House′wife-ry (*huz′wĭf-ry*, or *hous′wīf-ry*) [so Wr.; *huz′wĭf-ry*, Wk.; *hous′wīf-ry*, Wb. Gd.; *huz′wĭf-er-y*, Sm.155.]
House′wright (*-rīt*),162.
Hous′ing (*howz′-*).

Hove, 24.
Hov′el, 18, 76, 149.
Hov′elled (*-eld*) [H o v - e l e d, Wb. Gd. 203. — *See* 177, and Note E, p. 70.]
Hov′el-ling [H o v e l - i n g, Wb. Gd. 203.]
Hov′er (*huv′ur*),22, 171.
Hov′ered (*huv′urd*),150.
Hov′er-ing (*huv′-*).
How, 28.
How′dah (72) [H o u - d a h , 203.]
How-ev′er.
How′itz-er (*-its-*), 171.
How′ker.
Howl, 28.
Howled (*howld*), 165.
How′let [H o u l e t, 203]
Howl′ing.
How-so-ev′er.
Hoy, 27.
Hub (22) [H o b , 203.]
Hub′bub, 22.
Huck′a-back.
Huc′kle-backed (*huk′-l-bakt*), 164, 171.
Huc′kle-bĕr-ry (*huk′l-*), 164, 171.
Huck′ster, 22, 77.
Huck′stered (*-sturd*), 150, 165.
Huck′ster-ing.
Hud′dle, 164.
Hud′dled (*hud′ld*), 183.
Hud′dler.
Hud′dling.
Hu-di-bras′tic, 109.
Hūe, 26, 51, N.
Huff, 22, 173.
Huffed (*huft*).
Huff′er.
Huf′fi-ness, 186.
Huff′y, 93.
Hug, 22.
Huge, 26, 45.
Hugged (*hugd*), 176.
Hug′ging (*-ghing*), 138.
Hu′gue-not (*-ghe-*), 171.
Hu′gue-not-ism (*-ghe-not-izm*).
Hulk, 22.
Hull, 22, 172.
Hulled (*huld*), 165.
Hull′ing.
Hull′y.
Hul′ver.
Hum, 22.
Hu′man, 26, 72.
Hu-mane′, 23, 89.
Hu′man-ism (*-izm*), 136.
Hu′man-ist.
Hu-man-i-ta′ri-an, 49,N.

Hu-man-i-ta'ri-an-ism (*-izm*), 133, 136.
Hu-man'i-ty, 108, 169.
Hu-man-ĭ-za'tion.
Hu'man-ize, 202.
Hu'man-ized, 183.
Hu'man-īz-er.
Hu'man-īz-ing.
Hum'bird, 206.
Hum'ble (*hum'bl*, or *um-bl*) (139, 164, 171) [so Wr.; *hum'bl*, Wb. Gd., *um'bl*, Wk. Sm. 155.]
Hum'ble-bee (*hum'bl-*, or *um'bl-*).
Hum'bled (*hum'bld*, or *um'bld*), 165, 183.
Hum'bler (*hum'-*, or *um'-*).
Hum'bling (*hum'-*, or *um'-*).
Hum'bly (*hum'-*, or *um'-*).
Hum'drum, 22.
Hu'mer-al.
Hu'mic.
Hu'mid, 51, N.
Hu-mid'i-ty, 108, 169.
Hu-mil'i-ate, 169.
Hu-mil'i āt-ed, 183.
Hu-mil'i-āt-ing.
Hu-mil-i-a'tion.
Hu-mil'i-ty, 108, 169.
Hu'mīne [H u m i n, 203]
Hummed (*humd*), 176.
Hum'mel, 170.
Hum'melled (*-meld*) (165) [H u m m e l e d, Wb. Gd. 203.— *See* 177, and Note E, p. 70.]
Hum'mel-ler [H u m - m e l e r, Wb. Gd. 203.]
Hum'mel-ling [H u m - m e l i n g, Wb. Gd. 203.]
Hum'mer, 176.
Hum'ming.
Hum'ming-bird, 215.
Hum'mock (66, 170) [H o m m o c k, 203.]
Hum'mock-y, 93.
Hu'mor (*u'mur*, or *hu'-mur*) (51, N.; 88) [so Wr.; *u'mur*, Wk.; *hu'mur* (in the sense of *moisture or fluid of the animal body*), *u'-mur* (in other senses), Sm.; *hu'mur*, Wb. Gd.155.] [H u m o u r, 199, 203.]

☞ Smart omits the *u* in the last syllable of this word when it means *moisture*, as also in the derivatives having reference to this sense, but he inserts the *u* in all other cases.

Hu'mored (*u'murd*, or *hu'mord*), 150, 171.
Hu'mor-al (*u'-*, or *hu'-*).
Hu'mor-al-ism (*u'mur-al-izm*, or *hu'mur-al-izm*), 136.
Hu'mor-al-ist (*u'-*, or *hu'-*).
Hu'mor-ing(*u'-*, or *hu'-*)
Hu'mor-ism (*u'mur-izm*, or *hu'mur-izm*), 136.
Hu'mor-ist (*u'-*, or *hu'-*)
Hu'mor-oŭs(*u'-*,or *hu'-*)
Hu'mor-some (*u'mur-sum*, or *hu'mur-sum*), 171.
Hump, 22.
Hump'back, 206.
Hump'-backed (*-bakt*), 206, Exc. 5.
Humped (*humpt*), 165.
Hu'mus.
Hunch, 22, 44.
Hunch'back, 206.
Hunch'backed (*-bakt*).
Hun'dred [so Sm. Wr. Wb. Gd.; *hun'dred*, or *hun'durd*, Wk. 155.]
Hun'dred-er.
Hun'dredth.
Hung, 22, 54.
Hun-ga'ri-an, 49, N.
Hun'ger (*hung'gur*), 54, 138.
Hun'gered(*hung'gurd*), 150.
Hun'ger-ing (*hung'gur*)
Hun'gri-ly (*hung'-*),186.
Hun'gry (*hung'-*).
Hunks (*hungks*),*n.sing.*
Hunt, 22.
Hunt'ed.
Hunt'er.
Hunt'ing.
Hunts'man, 196.
Hur'dle, 104, 164.
Hur'dled (*hur'dld*), 183.
Hur'dling.
Hur'dy-gur'dy, 205.
Hurl, 21.
Hurl'bat.
Hurl'bone.
Hurled (*hurld*), 165.
Hurl'er.
Hurl'ing.
Hur'ly-bur'ly.
Hur-rah' [H u r r a, 203.]
Hŭr'ri-cane, 170, 171.
Hŭr'rĭed, 136.
Hŭr'ri-er.
Hŭr'ry, 21, 48, 66.
Hur'ry-ing.
Hurt, 21.
Hurt'er.
Hurt'ful (*-fŏŏl*), 180.
Hur'tle-bĕr-ry (*hur'tl-*).
Hus'band (*huz'-*).
Hus'band-ed (*huz'-*).
Hus'band-ing (*huz'-*).
Hus'band-man (*huz'-*).
Hus'band-ry (*huz'-*).
Hush, 22.
Hushed (*husht*).
Hush'ing.
Husk, 22.
Husked (*huskt*).
Husk'i-ness, 169, 186.
Husk'ing.
Husk'y, 93.
Hus-sar'(*hŏŏz-zar'*)(171) [so Wk. Sm.; *hooz-zar'*, Wr.; *huz-zar'*, Wb. Gd. 155], *n.* originally, a Hungarian or Polish horse-soldier. [*See* Huzza, 148.]
Hus'sy (*huz'zy*).
Hust'ings (*-ingz*), *n. pl.*
Hus'tle (*hus'l*), 162, 164.
Hus'tled (*hus'ld*), 162, 165.
Hus'tling (*hus'ling*).
Hus'wife (*huz'zif*, or *huz'wif*) [so Wr.; *huz'zif*, Wk. Gd.; *huz'wif*, Sm. 155.] [H o u s e w i f e, 203.]
Hus'wife-ry (*huz'zif-ry*, or *huz'wif-ry*) [H o u s e w i f e r y, 203.]
Hut, 22.
Hutch, 22, 44.
Hutched (*hucht*).
Hutch'ing.
Hut'ted, 176.
Hut'ting.
Hut-to'ni-an, 169.
Huz-zä' (*hŏŏz-zä'*) [so Sm. Gd.; *hooz-zä'*, Wr.; *hŏŏz-zä'*, Wk. 155], *int.* an exclamation of joy. [*See* Hussar, 148.]
Huz-zäed' (*hŏŏz-zäd'*), 188.
Huz-zä'ing (*hŏŏz-*).
Hy'a-cinth, 171.

Hy-a-cin'thĭne, 152.
Hy'a-dēs (-*dēz*), *n. pl.*
Hy'ads (-*adz*), *n. pl.*
Hy-a-les'cence, 171.
Hy'a-lĭne, 152.
Hy'a-loid.
Hy-al'o-type.
[Hybernate, 203.—*See* Hibernate.]
Hy'brid [so Sm.; *hi'-brid*, or *hib'rid*, Wr. Gd. 155.]
Hy'brid-ism (-*izm*).
Hy-brid'i-ty, 108.
Hy'brid-oŭs [so Sm.; *hib'rid-oŭs*, Wk. Wr. Wb. Gd. 155.]
Hy'da-tid [so Sm.; *hid'-a-tid*, Gd.; *hi'da-tid*, or *hid'a-tid*, Wr. 155.]
Hy'da-tis [so Sm. Wr.; *hid'a-tis*, Gd. 155.] [pl. Hy-dat'i-dēs (-*dēz*), 198.]
Hy'da-toid.
Hy'dra [L. pl. *Hy'dræ*; Eng. pl. Hy'dras (-*draz*), 198.]
Hy-draç'id.
Hy'dra-gŏgue (-*gog*), 87, 168, 171.
Hȳ-dran'ge-a.
Hy'drant, 25, 72.
Hȳ-drar'gy-rum.
Hy'drate, 25, 73.
Hȳ-drâu'lic, 109.
Hȳ-drâu'lic-al.
Hȳ-drâu'lic-on.
Hȳ-drâu'lics.
Hy'dri-ad.
Hy'dri-o-date [so Sm. Wr.; *hid'ri-o-dāt*, Wb. Gd. 155.]
Hȳ-dri-od'ic [so Sm. Wr.; *hid-ri-od'ik*, Wb. Gd. 155.]
Hȳ-dro-car'bon.
Hȳ-dro-car'bon-ate.
Hȳ-dro-car'bu-ret.
Hy'dro-cele.
Hȳ-dro-ceph'a-lus.
Hȳ-dro chlo'rate (-*klo'*-)
Hȳ-dro-chlo'ric (-*klo'*-).
Hȳ-dro-cy'a-nate.
Hȳ-dro-cȳ-an'ic.
Hȳ-dro-dy-nam'ics.
Hy'dro-gen, 25, 45, 171.
Hy'dro-gen-ate.
Hy'dro-gen-āt-ed.
Hy'dro-gen-āt-ing.
Hy'dro-gen-ize.
Hy'dro-gen-ized.
Hy'dro-gen-iz-ing.
Hȳ-drog'e-noŭs (-*droj'*-)
Hȳ-drog'ra-pher, 108.
Hȳ-dro-grăph'ic.
Hȳ-dro-grăph'ic-al.
Hȳ-drog'ra-phy, 108.
Hȳ-drog'u-ret.
Hȳ-dro-log'ic-al (-*loj'*-).
Hȳ-drol'o-gist.
Hȳ-drol'o-gy, 108.
Hy'dro-man-cy, 169.
Hȳ-dro-man'tic.
Hy'dro-mel.
Hȳ-drom'e-ter, 108.
Hȳ-dro-met'ric.
Hȳ-dro-met'ric-al.
Hȳ-drom'e-try.
Hȳ-dro-path'ic, 109.
Hȳ-dro-path'ic-al, 108.
Hȳ-drop'a-thist.
Hȳ-drop'a-thy (108)[*not* hy'dro-path-y, 153.]
Hy'dro-phane.
Hȳ-droph'a-noŭs.
Hy'dro-phid.
Hȳ-dro-pho'bi-a (171) [Hydrophoby, (*hy'dro-pho-by*), 203.]
Hȳ-dro-phob'ic.
Hȳ-droph-thal'my.
Hy'dro-phȳte.
Hȳ-drop'ic.
Hȳ-drop'ic-al.
Hȳ-dro-pneu-mat'ic (-*nu'*-).
Hy'dro-sâlt.
Hy'dro-scope.
Hy-dro-stat'ic.
Hȳ-dro-stat'ic-al.
Hy-dro-stat'ics.
Hȳ-dro-sul'phate.
Hȳ-dro-sul'phīte, 152.
Hȳ-dro-sul'phu-ret.
Hȳ-dro-sul'phu-ret-ted [Hydrosulphureted, Wb. Gd. 203.]
Hȳ-dro-sul-phu'ric.
Hȳ-drot'ic, 109.
Hy'droŭs, 25, 100.
Hȳ-e'mal [so Wk. Sm. Wb. Gd.; *hī-e'mal*, or *hi'e-mal*, Wr. 155.]
Hȳ-e'na, 72.
Hy'e-to-grăph.
Hȳ-e-to-grăph'ic.
Hȳ-e-tom'e-ter.
Hȳ-ge'ian (-*yan*), 51, 171.
Hy'gi-ene (-*jĭ-ēn*) [*hi'-ji-ēn*, or *hi'jēn*, Wr.; *hī-ji-ēn'*, Gd. 155.]
Hȳ-gi-en'ic, 109.
Hȳ-gol'o-gy, 108.
Hȳ-grom'e-ter, 108.
Hȳ-gro-met'ric.
Hȳ-gro-met'ric-al.
Hȳ-grom'e-try, 93, 169.
Hy'gro-scope.
Hȳ-gro-scop'ic.
Hyke [Haik, 203.]
Hȳ-læ-o-sâu'rus (-*le*-).
Hy'lo-bate.
Hy'lo-ist.
Hȳ-lop'a-thism(-*thizm*).
Hy'lo-the-ism (-*izm*) [so Sm. Gd.; *hī-loth'-e-izm*, or *hī-lo-the'izm*, Wr. 155.]
Hȳ-lo-zo'ic.
Hȳ-lo-zo'ism (-*izm*).
Hȳ-lo-zo'ist.
Hy'men.
Hȳ-me-ne'al.
Hȳ-me ne'an, 110.
Hȳ-men-op'ter.
Hȳ-men-op'ter-al.
Hȳ-men-op'ter-an.
Hȳ-men-op'ter-oŭs
Hymn (*him*) (162), *n.* a song for a religious service. [*See* Him, 160.]
Hymn'-bŏŏk (*him'*-), 206, Exc. 4.
Hymned (*himd*), *or* Hym'ned [so Wr.; *himd*, Gd. 155.]

☞ "The participles *hymning* and *hymned* are colloquially pronounced *him'ing* and *himd*, but with solemnity *him'ning* and *him'ned*." *Smart.*

Hym'nic.
Hymn'ing (*him'ing*), *or* Hym'ning [so Wr.; *him'ning*, Wk.; *him'-ning*, coll. *him'ing*, Sm.; *him'ing*, Wb. Gd. 155.]
Hym-nol'o-gist.
Hym-nol'o-gy, 108.
Hy'oid, 25, 27.
Hyp (16) [Hip, 203.]
Hȳ-pæ'thral (-*pe'*-) (171) [so Wr. Gd.; *hip-e'-thral*, Sm. 155.]
Hȳ-pal'la-ge, 163, 170.
Hȳ-pas'pist.
Hȳ-per-bat'ic, 109.
Hȳ-per'ba-ton.
Hȳ-per'bo-la, 21, N.; 171.
Hȳ-per'bo-le, 163.
Hȳ-per-bol'ic, 109.
Hȳ-per-bol'ic-al, 108.
Hȳ-per-bol'ic-al-ly.
Hȳ-per-bol'i-form, 108.

Hȳ-per′bo-lism (*-lizm*).
Hȳ-per′bo-list, 21, N.
Hȳ-per′bo-loid.
Hȳ-per-bo′re-an, 49, N.
Hȳ-per-car′bu-ret-ted [Hypercarbureted, Wb. Gd. 203.]
Hȳ-per-cat-a-lec′tic.
Hȳ-per-crit′ic, 109.
Hȳ-per-crit′ic-al, 108.
Hȳ-per-crit′i-cism (*-sizm*).
Hȳ-per-du′li-ȧ.
Hȳ-per′me-ter, 21, N.; 108.
Hȳ-per-met′ric-al.
Hȳ′per-sthene [Hyperstene, 203.]
Hȳ-per-sthen′ic, 109.
Hȳ-per-troph′ic, 109.
Hȳ-per-troph′ic-al, 108.
Hȳ-per′tro-phy, 21, N.
Hȳ′phen, 25, 35.
Hyp-nol′o-gist, 108.
Hyp-nol′o-gy.
Hyp-not′ic.
Hyp′no-tism (*-tizm*).
Hȳ-pob′o-le [so Sm. Wr.; *hī-pob′o-le*, Gd. 155.]
Hyp′o-câust.
Hyp-o-chon′dres (*-kon′-durz*), *n. pl.* [so Wk. Wr. Gd.; *hip-o-kon′-drēz*, Sm. 155.]
Hyp-o-chon′dri-a (*-kon′-*), *n. pl.*
Hyp-o-chon′dri-ac (*-kon′-*), 52, 171.
Hyp-o-chon-dri′ac-al (*-kon-*), 108.
Hyp-o-chon-dri′a-cism *-kon-dri′a-sizm*), 136, 171.
Hyp-o-chon-dri′a-sis (*-kon-*).
Hyp′o-cist.
Hyp-o-cra-tĕr′i-form (108) [so Sm. Wr.; *hī-po-kra-tĕr′i-form*, Gd. 155.]
Hȳ-poc′ri-sy (169, 171) [*not* hī-pok′ri-sy,153.]
Hyp′o-crīte, 152, 171.
Hyp-o-crit′ic, 109.
Hyp-o-crit′ic-al, 108.
Hyp-o-gæ′oŭs (*-jē′-*).
Hyp-o-gas′tric [so Wk. Sm. Wr.; *hī-po-gas′-trik*, Wb. Gd. 155.]
Hyp-o-gas′tro-cele [so Sm. Wr.; *hī-po-gas′-tro-sēl*, Wb. Gd. 155.]
Hyp′o-gene.
Hyp-o-ge′um [so Wk. Sm. Wr.; *hī-po-je′um*, Wb. Gd. 155.] [pl. Hyp-o-ge′a, 198.]
Hyp-o-glos′sal.
Hyp′o-gyn (*-jin*), 45.
Hȳ-pog′y-noŭs (*-poj′-*) [so Sm. Wr.; *hī-poj′-i-nus*, Wb. Gd. 155.]
Hȳ-po′pi-um [so Wr. Wb. Gd.; *hip-o′pi-um*, Sm. 155.]
Hȳ-pos′ta-sis [so Wk. Wr. Wb. Gd.; *hip-os′ta-sis*, Sm. 155.]
Hȳ-po-stat′ic, 109.
Hȳ-po-stat′ic-al [so Wk. Wr. Wb. Gd.; *hip-o-stat′ik-al*, Sm. 155.]
Hȳ-pot′e-nuse [so Wk. Wr. Wb. Gd.; *hip-ot′e-nūs*, Sm. 155.] [Hypothenuse, 203.]

☞ Walker, Smart, and Webster give only the form *hypotenuse*, and Goodrich prefers this form; but Worcester prefers *hypothenuse*.

Hȳ-poth′e-cate [so Wr. Wb. Gd.; *hip-oth′e-kāt*, Sm. 155.]
Hȳ-poth′e-cāt-ed, 183.
Hȳ-poth′e-cāt-ing.
Hȳ-poth-e-ca′tion.
Hȳ-poth′e-cāt-or.
Hȳ-poth′e-nuse [Hypotenuse, 203.— *See* Note under *Hypotenuse*.]
Hȳ-poth′e-sis [so Wr. Wb. Gd.; *hip-oth′e-sis*, or *hī poth′e-sis*, Wk.; *hip-oth′e-sis*, Sm. 155.]
Hȳ-po-thet′ic [so Wk. Wr. Wb. Gd.; *hip-o-thet′ik*, Sm. 155.]
Hȳ-po-thet′ic-al.
Hypped (*hipt*) (176) [Hipped, 203.]
Hyp′ping [Hipping, 203.]
Hyp′pish [Hippish, 203.]
Hyp-so-met′ric.
Hyp-som′e-try.
Hȳrse, 16, *n.* millet. [*See* Hearse, and Herse, 160.]
Hy′son, 25, 86.
Hys′sop (*his′sup*) [so Sm.; *hiz′zup*, or *hī′-sup*, Wk.; *hī′zup*, or *his′sup*, Gd. 155.]

☞ Though Walker allows *hī′zup*, he says: "To pronounce the *y* long before double *s* is contrary to every rule of orthoëpy; and, therefore, as the first mode is undoubtedly the best, the other ought to be relinquished."

Hys-te′ri-a.
Hys-tĕr′ic, 109.
Hys-tĕr′ic-al, 108.
Hys-tĕr′ics.
Hys-tĕr′o-cele.
Hys-ter-ot′o-my, 108.

I.

Ī-am′bic, 109.
Ī-am′bus [L. pl. *Ī-am′-bī*; Eng. pl. Ī-am′-bus-es (*-ez*), 198.]
I′bex, 15, 25.
I′bis, 16, 25.
Ī-ca′ri-an, 49, N.; 169.
Ice, 25, 39.
Ice′berg, 206.
Ice′bōat.
Ice′crēam.
Iced (*īst*), 183; Note C, p. 34.
Ice′house.
Ice′land-er.
Ice-land′ic, 109.
Ich-neu′mon (*ik-nu′-*), 171.
Ich-no-grăph′ic (*ik-*).
Ich-no-grăph′ic-al (*ik-*).
Ich-nog′ra-phy (*ik-*).
Ich-no-log′ic-al (*ik-no-loj′-*).
Ich-nol′o-gy (*ik-*), 108.
I′chor (*-kawr*), 171.
I′chor-oŭs.
Ich′thy-o-col (*ik′-*).
Ich-thy-o-col′la (*ik-*).
Ich-thy-og′ra-phy (*ik-*).
Ich′thy-o-līte (*ik′-*), 152.
Ich-thy-o-log′ic-al (*ik-thy-o-loj′ik-al*), 108.
Ich-thy-ol′o-gist (*ik-*).
Ich-thy-ol′o-gy (*ik-*).
Ich′thy-o-man-cy (*ik′-*).
Ich-thy-oph′a-gist (*ik-*).
Ich-thy-oph′a-goŭs (*ik-*).
Ich-thy-oph′a-gy (*ik-*).
Ich-thy-o-sâu′rus (*ik-*).

Ich-thy-o′sis (*ik-*), 109.
I′ci-cle (*i′sik-l*), 164, 171.
I′ci-ness, 169, 186.
Ī¢′ing, 183.
Ī-con′o-clasm (*-klazm*).
Ī-con′o-clăst.
Ī-con-o-clăst′ic, 109.
Ī-con-o-grăph′ic.
Ī-con-og′ra-phy, 108.
Ī-con-ol′a-ter.
Ī-con-ol′o-gy, 108.
Ī-co-sa-he′dral.
Ī-co-sa-he′dron [pl. Ī-co-sa-he′dra, 198.]
Ī-co-san′dri-a, *n. pl.*
Ī-co-san′dri-an.
Ī-co-san′droŭs.
Ic-tĕr′ic, 109.
Ic-tĕr′ic-al, 108.
Ic-ter-i′tious (*-ish′us*).
Ī¢′y, 93, 183.
Ī-de′a, 72, 79.
Ī-de′al, 72.
Ī-de′al-ism (*-izm*), 136.
Ī-de′al-ist.
Ī-de-al′i-ty, 108, 169.
Ī-de-al-ĭ-za′tion.
Ī-de′al-ize, 202.
Ī-de′al-ized, 183.
Ī-de′al-īz-ing.
I′dem (L.).
Ī-den′tic-al, 108.
Ī-den′tic-al-ly, 170.
Ī-den-ti-fĭ-ca′tion.
Ī-den′ti-fīed, 186.
Ī-den′ti-fȳ, 94.
Ī-den′ti-fȳ-ing.
Ī-den′ti-ty, 108, 169.
Ī-de-o-grăph′ic [so Sm. Wr.; *id-e-ogrăf′ik*, Gd. 155.]
Ī-de-o-grăph′ic-al.
Ī-de-og′ra-phy, 108.
Ī-de-o-log′ic-al (*-loj′-*) [so Wr.; *id-e-o-loj′ik-al*, Gd. 155.]
Ī-de-ol′o-gist [*ī-de-ol′o-gist*, or *id-e-ol′o-gist*, Wr.; *id-e-ol′o-gist*, Gd. 155.]
Ī-de-ol′o-gy (108) [so Sm.; *ī-de-ol′o-jy*, or *id-e-ol′o-jy*, Wr.; *id-e-ol′o-jy*, Gd. 155.]
Ides (*īdz*), *n. pl.*
Id-i-oc′ra-sy, 169.
Id-i-o-crat′ic, 109.
Id-i-o-crat′ic-al, 108.
Id′i-o-cy, 169, 171.
Id′i-om, 86, 169.
Id-i-o-mat′ic.
Id-i-o-mat′ic-al.
Id-i-o-mat′ic-al-ly.
Id-i-o-path′ic, 109.
Id-i-op′a-thy.
Id-i-o-syn′cra-sy, 171.
Id-i-o-syn-crat′ic.
Id′i-ot, 86, 169.
Id-i-ot′ic, 109.
Id-i-ot′ic-al, 108.
Id-i-ot′i-con.
Id′i-ot-ism (*-izm*).
I′dle (*i′dl*), 164.
I′dled (*i′dld*) 183.
I′dler.
I′dling.
I′dly, 93.
Id′o-crase [so Wr. Wb. Gd.; *i′do-krās*, Sm. 155.]
I′dol, 25, 86.
Ī-dol′a-ter, 169.
Ī-dol′a-tress.
Ī-dol′a-trize, 202.
Ī-dol′a-trized, 183.
Ī-dol′a-trīz-ing.
Ī-dol′a-troŭs.
Ī-dol′a-try, 171.
I′dol-ize, 202.
I′dol-ized, 183.
I′dol-īz-er.
I′dol-īz-ing.
I′dyl, 171.

☞ Walker quotes several authorities for pronouncing the *i* long in the first syllable of *idyl*, because, as he says, "there is sometimes an erroneous pronunciation of this word by making the *i* short, as in the first syllable of *idiot*."

Ī-dyl′lic.
If, 16, 35.
Ig′ne-oŭs, 100, 169.
Ig-nip′o tent.
Ig′nis Fat′u-us (L.) [pl. *Ig′nēs* (*-nēz*) *Fat′u-ī*, 198.]
Ig-nite′, 25, 103.
Ig-nīt′ed.
Ig-nīt′a-ble, 164, 169.
Ig-nĭ′tion (*-nish′un*).
Ig-niv′o-moŭs.
Ig-no′ble, 164.
Ig-no′bly.
Ig-no-min′i-oŭs [so Wr. Wb. Gd.; *ig-no-min′yus*, Wk. Sm. 155.]
Ig′no-min-y, 156.
Ig-no-ra′mus.
Ig′no-rance, 105, 169.
Ig′no-rant.
Ig-nore′, 24, 103.
Ig-nored′, 183.
Ig-nōr′ing.
Ĭ-guä′na (*-gwä′-*) [so Wr. Wb. Gd.; *ig-u-ā′na*, Sm. 155.]
Ĭ-guä′no-don (*-gwä′*) [so Wb. Gd.; *ĭ-gwan′o-don*, Wr.; *ig-u-an′o-don*, Sm. 155.]
Il′e-um.
Il′e-us.
I′lex.
Il′i-ac, 169.
Il′i-ad, 72, 169.
Ill, 16, 172.
Il-lapse′.
Il-la′tion.
Il′la-tĭve (84) [*not* il-la′-tiv, 153.]
Il-lâud′a-ble, 164.
Ill′-bred, 206, Exc. 5.
Il-le′gal, 72.
Il-le-gal′i-ty, 108, 169.
Il-le′gal-ly, 170.
Il-leg-i-bil′i-ty (*-lej-*).
Il-leg′i-ble (*-lej′-*), 164, 171.
Il-leg′i-bly (*-lej′-*).
Il-le-git′i-ma-cy, 169.
Il-le-git′i-mate.
Il-le-git′i-māt-ed.
Il-le-git′i-māt-ing.
Il-le-git-i-ma′tion.
Il-lev′i-a-ble, 164.
Il-lib′er-al, 233, Exc.
Il-lib-er-al′i-ty, 171.
Il-liç′it, 170.
Il-lim′it-a-ble, 164, 169.
Il-li-nĭ′tion (*-nish′un.*)
Il-li-qua′tion, 171.
Il-lĭ′sion (*-lizh′un*).
Il-lit′er-a-cy, 169.
Il-lit′er-al.
Il-lit′er-ate, 170.
Il-log′ic-al (*-loj′-*).
Il-lude′, 26, 103.
Il-lūd′ed, 183.
Il-lūd′ing.
Il-lume′, 26, 103.
Il-lumed′, 183.
Il-lūm′ing.
Il-lu′min-a-ble, 164.
Il-lu′min-ant.
Il-lu′min-ate, 73.
Il-lu′min-āt-ed.
Il-lu-mi-na′tī, *n. pl.*
Il-lu′min-āt-ing.
Il-lu-min-a′tion.
Il-lu′min-āt-ĭve (84) [so Sm.; *il-lu′min-a-tĭv*, Wr. Wb. Gd. 155.]
Il-lu′min-āt-or.
Il-lu′mĭne, 152.
Il-lu′mĭned (*-mĭnd*).
Il-lu-min-ee′, 122.
Il-lu′min-er.

Il-lu′min-ing, 183.
Il-lu′min-ism (*-izm*).
Il-lu′sion (*-zhun*), *n.* deception. [*See* Elusion, 148.]
Il-lu′sion-ist (*-zhun*).
Il-lu′sive, 84.
Il-lu′so-ry, 86.
Il-lus′trate.
Il-lus′trāt-ed, 183.
Il-lus′trāt-ing.
Il-lus-tra′tion, 112.
Il-lus′tra-tive, 84.
Il-lus′trāt-or.
Il-lus′tra-to-ry, 86.
Il-lus′tri-oŭs.
Im′age, 16, 70.
Im′age-a-ble, 164, 169.
Im′a-ger-y [so Wk. Sm.; *im′āj-ry*, Wb. Gd.; *im′a-jer-y*, or *im′āj-ry*, Wr. 155.]
Im-ag′i-na-ble (*-aj′-*), 164.
Im-ag′i-na-ry (*-aj′-*), 72.
Im-ag-i-na′tion (*-aj-*).
Im-ag′i-na-tive (*-aj′-*).
Im-ag′ine (*-aj′-*), 152.
Im-ag′ined (*-aj′ind*).
Im-ag′in-er (*-aj′-*), 183.
Im-ag′in-ing (*-aj′-*).
I′man, I-mäm′, *or* I-mâum′.
[Imbankment, 203. — *See* Embankment.]
[Imbargo, 203. — *See* Embargo.]
[Imbark, 203. — *See* Embark.]
Im-bāthe′.
Im-bāthed′, 165.
Im-bāth′ing.
Im′be-cile, *or* Im-be-cile′ (*-sēl′*) [so Gd.; *im-be-sēl′*, Sm.; *im-bes′il*, or *im-be-sēl′*, Wk. Wr. 155.]
Im-be-cil′i-ty, 169.
[Imbed, 203. — *See* Embed.]
Im-bibe′, 25, 103.
Im-bibed′, 183.
Im-bib′er.
Im-bib′ing.
Im-bit′ter [Embitter, 203.]
Im-bit′tered, 150.
Im-bit′ter-er, 77.
Im-bit′ter-ing.
Im-bor′der [Emborder, 203.]
Im-bor′dered (*-durd*).
Im-bor′der-ing.
Im-bo′som (*-bŏŏ′zum*) [Embosom, 203.]
Im-bo′somed (*-bŏŏ′-zumd*), 165, 171.
Im-bo′som-ing (*-bŏŏ′-zum-*).
[Imbowel, 203. — *See* Embowel.]
Im′bri-cate.
Im′bri-cāt-ed.
Im-bri-ca′tion.
Imbroglio (It.) (*im-brōl′yo*).
Im-brown′.
Im-browned′ (*-brownd′*).
Im-brown′ing.
Im-brue′ (*-broo′*), 19.
Im-brued′ (*-brood′*), 183.
Im-bru′ing (*-broo′-*).
Im-bru′ment (*-broo′-*).
Im-brute′ (*-broot′*), 19.
Im-brūt′ed (*-broot′-*).
Im-brūt′ing (*-broot′-*).
Im-bue′, 26.
Im-bued′, 183.
Im-bu′ing.
Im-i-ta-bil′i-ty, 169.
Im′i-ta-ble, 164.
Im′i-tate, 169.
Im′i-tāt-ed, 183.
Im′i-tāt-ing.
Im-i-ta′tion.
Im′i-tāt-ive, 84.
Im′i-tāt-or, 183.
Im-mac′u-late, 170.
Im′ma-nen-cy.
Im′ma-nent (169), *a.* inherent. [*See* Imminent, 148.]
Im-ma-te′ri-al, 49, N.
Im-ma-te′ri-al-ism (*-izm*).
Im-ma-te′ri-al-ist.
Im-ma-te-ri-al′i-ty.
Im-ma-ture′, 170.
Im-ma-tured′.
Im-ma-tu′ri-ty, 49, N.
Im-mĕas′ur-a-ble (*-mezh′ur-a-bl*) (171) [so Wb. Gd.; *im-mezh′u-ra-bl*, Wk. Wr.; *im-mezh′oo-ra-bl*, Sm. 155.]
Im-me′di-ate (73) [so Sm. Wr. Wb. Gd.; *im-me′di-at*, or *im-me′ji-āt*, Wk. 155.]
Im-med′i-ca-ble, 164.
Im-me-lo′di-oŭs.
Im-mem′o-ra-ble, 164.
Im-me-mo′ri-al, 49, N.
Im-mense′, 15, 39.
Im-men′si-ty, 169, 171.
Im-men′su-ra-ble (*-men′shoo-ra-bl*) [*im-men′sh′oo-ra-bl*, Sm. (*See* § 26); *im-men′shu-ra-bl*, Wk.; *im-men′su-ra-bl*, Gd. 155.]
Im-merge′, 21, N.
Im-merged′, 183.
Im-merg′ing (*-merj′-*).
Im-merse′, 21, N.
Im-mersed′ (*-merst′*).
Im-mers′ing.
Im-mer′sion, *n.* act of immersing or state of being immersed. [*See* Emersion, 148.]
Im-mer′sion-ist.
Im-mesh′, 15, 46.
Im-meshed′ (*-mesht′*).
Im-mesh′ing.
Im-me-thod′ic-al, 108.
Im′mi-grant, 66, 170.
Im′mi-grate, 73, 78.
Im′mi-grāt-ed, 183.
Im′mi-grāt-ing.
Im-mi-gra′tion, 112.
Im′mi-nent (169), *a.* threatening closely. [*See* Immanent, 148.]
Im-min′gle (*-ming′gl*).
Im-min′gled (*-ming′-gld*).
Im-min′gling (*-ming′-*).
Im-mis-ci-bil′i-ty.
Im-mis′ci-ble, 164, 171.
Im-mis′sion (*-mish′-un*).
Im-mit′i-ga-ble, 164.
Im-mo-bil′i-ty, 108, 169.
Im-mod′er-ate, 170.
Im-mod-er-a′tion.
Im-mod′est, 170.
Im-mod′es-ty.
Im′mo-late, 73, 170.
Im′mo-lāt-ed, 183.
Im′mo-lāt-ing.
Im-mo-la′tion.
Im-mo-lāt′or.
Im-mŏr′al, 66, N.
Im-mo-ral′i-ty, 169.
Im-mŏr′al-ly, 66, N.
Im-mor′tal, 72.
Im-mor-tal′i-ty, 171.
Im-mor-tal-i-za′tion.
Im-mor′tal-ize, 202.
Im-mor′tal-ized, 183.
Im-mor′tal-iz-ing.
Im-mov′a-ble, 164, 183.
Im-mu′ni-ty, 170.

Im-mure′, 26.
Im-mured′, 183.
Im-mūr′ing.
Im-mu-ta-bil′i-ty, 108.
Im-mu′ta-ble, 164.
Im-mu′ta-bly.
Imp, 16.
Im-pact′, *v.* 103, 161.
Im′pact, *n.* 103, 161.
Im-pact′ed.
Im-pact′ing.
Im-pair′ (*-pêr′*), 14.
Im-paired′ (*-pêrd′*), 165.
Im-pair′er (*-pêr′-*).
Im-pair′ing (*-pêr′-*).
Im-pal-pa-bil′i-ty, 169.
Im-pal′pa-ble, 164.
Im-pal′sied (*-pol′zid*).
Im-pal′sy (*-pol′zy*), 169.
Im-pal′sy-ing (*-pol′-zy-*).
Im-pa-na′tion.
Im-pan′el [Impanel, Empanel, Empannel, 203.]
Im-pan′elled (*-eld*) (165) [Impanneled, Wb. Gd. 203.] [*See* 177, and Note E, p. 70.]
Im-pan′el-ling [Impanneling, Wb. Gd. 203.]
Im-păr′a-dise.
Im-păr′a-dised (*-dīst*).
Im-păr′a-dīs-ing, 183.
Im-păr-i-syl-lab′ic.
Im-păr′i-ty, 108.
Im-parl′, 11.
Im-parl′ance, 169.
Im-parled′, 165.
Im-parl′ing.
Im-par-son-ee′, 122.
Im-part′, 11.
Im-part′ance.
Im-part′ed.
Im-part′er.
Im-part′ing.
Im-par′tial (*-shal*).
Im-par-ti-al′i-ty (*-shĭ-al′i-ty*) [so Wk. Sm. Wr.; *im-par-shal′i-ty*, Wb. Gd. 155.]
Im-part-i-bil′i-ty.
Im-part′i-ble, 164.
Im-pàss′a-ble, 164.
Im-păs-si-bil′i-ty, 169.
Im-păs′si-ble, 164.
Im-pas′sioned (*-pash′-und*), 171.
Im-păs′sĭve, 84.
Im-pas-siv′i-ty, 108.
Im-pas-ta′tion.
Im-pāste′, 23.
Im-păst′ed, 183.
Im-păst′ing.
Im-pa′tience (*-shens*).
Im-pa′tient (*-shent*), 171.
Im-pawn′, 17.
Im-pawned′, 165.
Im-pawn′ing.
Im-pēach′, 13, 44.
Im-pēach′a-ble, 164.
Im-pēached′ (*-pēcht′*).
Im-pēach′er.
Im-pēach′ment.
Im-pearl′ (*-perl′*), 21, N.
Im-pearled′ (*-perld′*).
Im-pearl′ing (*-perl′-*).
Im-pec-ca-bil′i-ty, 169.
Im-pec′ca-ble, 164.
Im-pec′can-cy.
Im-pec′cant.
Im-pe-cu-ni-os′i-ty.
Im-pede′, 13.
Im-pēd′ed.
Im-pēd′i-ble (164) [so Gd.; *im-pĕd′i-bl*, Wr. 155.]
Im-ped′i-ment, 169.
Im-pēd′ing, 183.
Im-ped′i-tĭve, 84.
Im-pel′, 15.
Im-pelled′ (*-peld′*), 165.
Im-pel′lent, 169, 170.
Im-pel′ler, 176.
Im-pel′ling.
Im-pen′.
Im-pend′ (15, 103), *v.* to hang over; to threaten. [*See* Impend, 160.]
Im-pend′ed.
Im-pend′ence.
Im-pend′en-cy.
Im-pend′ent, 169.
Im-pend′ing.
Im-pen-e-tra-bil′i-ty.
Im-pen′e-tra-ble, 164, 171.
Im-pen′i-tence.
Im-pen′i-ten-cy, 169
Im-pen′i-tent.
Im-pen′nate, 170.
Im-penned′ (*-pend′*), *v.* did impen. [*See* Impend, 160.]
Im-pen′ning, 176.
Im-pen′noŭs.
Im-pĕr′a-tĭve, 84.
Im-per-cep-ti-bil′i-ty.
Im-per-cep′ti-ble, 164.
Im-per′fect, 21, N.
Im-per-fec′tion.
Im-per′fo-ra-ble, 164.
Im-per′fo-rate, 21, N.
Im-per′fo-rāt-ed.
Im-per-fo-ra′tion.
Im-pe′ri-al, 49, N.
Im-pe′ri-al-ism (*-izm*).
Im-pe′ri-al-ist.
Im-pe-ri-al′i-ty, 108.
Im-pe′ri-al-ly.
Im-pĕr′il.
Im-pĕr′illed [Imperiled, Wb. Gd. 203. —*See* 177, and Note E, p. 70.]
Im-pĕr′il-ling [Imperiling, Wb. Gd. 203.]
Im-pe′ri-oŭs, 49, N.
Im-pĕr′ish-a-ble, 164.
Im-per′ma-nence, 21, N.
Im-per′ma-nen-cy.
Im-per′ma-nent.
Im-per-me-a-bil′i-ty.
Im-per′me-a-ble, 164.
Im-per′so-nal, 21, N.
Im-per-so-nal′i-ty.
Im-per′so-nal-ly.
Im-per′so-nate.
Im-per′so-nāt-ed.
Im-per-so-na′tion.
Im-per-sua′si-ble (*-swa′si-bl*), 164, 171.
Im-per′ti-nence, 21, N.
Im-per′ti-nen-cy.
Im-per′ti-nent, 169.
Im-per-tur-ba-bil′i-ty.
Im-per-tur′ba-ble, 164.
Im-per-tur-ba′tion.
Im-per-vi-a-bil′i-ty.
Im-per′vi-a-ble, 164.
Im-per′vi-oŭs.
Im-pe-tig′i-noŭs (*-tij′-*).
Im-pe-ti′go (L.).
Im-pet-u-os′i-ty, 108.
Im-pet′u-oŭs.
Im′pe-tus.
Im-piērce′, 13.
Im-piērce′a-ble, 183.
Im-piērced′ (*-pērst′*).
Im-piērç′ing.
Im-pi′e-ty, 169.
Im-pinge′, 16, 45.
Im-pinged′ (*-pinjd′*).
Im-pinge′ment.
Im-ping′ing (*-pinj′-*).
Im′pi-oŭs, 78, 169.
Im-plā-ca-bil′i-ty.
Im-pla′ca-ble, 164.
Im-pla′ca-bly, 93.
Im-plant′, 10, 103.
Im-plant-a′tion.
Im-plant′ed.
Im-plant′ing.

Im-plâu-si-bil′i-ty (-*zĭ*-), 108, 169.
Im-plâu′si-ble (-*zĭ-bl*).
Im-plēad′.
Im-plēad′ed.
Im-plēad′er.
Im-plēad′ing.
Im′ple-ment, 169, 171.
Im-ple′tion.
Im′plex.
Im′pli-cate, 73, 169.
Im′pli-căt-ed.
Im′pli-căt-ing.
Im-pli-ca′tion.
Im′pli-căt-ĭve [so Sm. Wr.; *im′pli-ka-tiv*, Wb. Gd. 155.]
Im-pliç′it.
Im-plīed′, 186.
Im-plī′ed-ly.
Im-plo-ra′tion.
Im-plore′, 24, 103.
Im-plored′, 165.
Im-plōr′er.
Im-plōr′ing.
Im-plumed′ (-*plūmd′*).
Im-ply′, 25.
Im-ply′ing.
Im-pol′i-cy, 169.
Im-po-līte′, 152.
Im-pol′i-tic, 109, Exc.
Im-pon-der-a-bil′i-ty.
Im-pon′der-a-ble, 164.
Im-pon′der-oŭs.
Im-po-ros′i-ty.
Im-po′roŭs, 49, N.
Im-pōrt′, *v.* 24, 49, 161.

☞ When this verb has the sense of *to signify*, Smart pronounces it *im-pawrt′*.

Im′pōrt, *n.* 16, 161.

☞ When this noun has the sense of *signification*, Smart pronounces it *im′-pawrt*.

Im-pōrt′a-ble, 164, 169.
Im-por′tance, 169.
Im-por′tant [so Sm. Wr. Wb. Gd.; *im-por′tant*, or *im-pōr′-tant*, Wk. 155.]

☞ "The best usage," says Walker, of the two modes which he gives, "is on the side of the first pronunciation [*im-por′tant*]."

Im-pōrt-a′tion.
Im-pōrt′ed.
Im-pōrt′er.
Im-pōrt′ing.
Im-port′u-nate (44, N. 1) [so Sm. Wr. Wb. Gd.; *im-por′chu-năt*, Wk. 155.]
Im-por-tune′, 122.
Im-por-tuned′, 183.
Im-por-tūn′er.
Im-por-tūn′ing.
Im-por-tu′ni-ty, 169.
Im-pōs′a-ble (-*pōz′*-), 164.
Im-pose′ (-*pōz′*), 24, 40.
Im-posed′ (-*pōzd′*).
Im-pōs′er (-*pōz′*-).
Im-pōs′ing (-*pōz′*-).
Im-po-sĭ′tion (-*zish′-un*).
Im-pos-si-bil′i-ty, 171.
Im-pos′si-ble, 164, 170.
Im′pōst, 16, 24.
Im-pŏst′hu-mate [so Sm. Wr.; *im-pos′tu-măt*, Wb. Gd.; *im-pos′chu-măt*, Wk. 155.]
Im-pŏst′hu-măt-ed.
Im-pŏst′hu-măt-ing.
Im-pŏst-hu-ma′tion.
Im-pŏst′hume [so Sm.; *im-pos′tūm*, Wr. Wb. Gd.; *im-pos′chūm*, Wk. 155.]
Im-pos′tor, 88.
Im-pŏst′ure (-*yur*) (91) [so Wr.; *im-pos′iūr*, coll. *im-pos′ch′oor*, Sm. (*See* § 26); *im-pos′chūr*, Wk. 155.]
Im′po-tence.
Im′po-ten-cy, 169.
Im′po-tent, 105.
Im-pound′, 28.
Im-pound′ed.
Im-pound′ing.
Im-pov′er-ish [Empoverish, 203.]
Im-pov′er-ished (-*isht*).
Im-pov′er-ish-er.
Im-pov′er ish-ing.
Im-pov′er-ish-ment.
[Impower, 203.—*See* Empower.]
Im-prac-ti-ca-bil′i-ty.
Im-prac′ti-ca-ble, 164.
Im′pre-cate, 73, 169.
Im′pre-căt-ed.
Im′pre-căt-ing.
Im′pre-căt-o-ry, 86.
Im-prēgn′ (-*prēn′*), 162.
Im-preg-na-bil′i-ty.
Im-preg′na-ble, 164
Im-preg′nate.
Im-preg′năt-ed.
Im-preg′năt-ing.
Im-preg-na′tion.
Im-prēgned′ (-*prēnd′*), 162.
Im-prēgn′ing (-*prēn′*-), 162.
Im-pre-scrip-ti-bil′i-ty.
Im-pre-scrip′ti-ble, 164.
Im-press′, *v.* 103, 161.
Im′press, *n.* 103, 161.
Im-pressed′ (-*prest′*), 165; Note C, p. 34.
Im-press-i-bil′i-ty, 108.
Im-press′i-ble, 164.
Im-press′ing.
Im-pres′sion (-*presh′-un*).
Im-press′ĭve, 84.
Im-press′ment.
Im-pri-ma′tur (L.).
Im-pri′mis (L.).
Im-print′, *v.* 16, 103, 161.
Im′print, *n.* 103, 161.
Im-pris′on (-*priz′n*), 149.
Im-pris′oned (-*priz′-nd*), 165.
Im-pris′on-er (-*priz′-n*-).
Im-pris′on-ing (-*priz′-n*-).
Im-pris′on-ment (-*priz′-n*-).
Im-prob-a-bil′i-ty, 169.
Im-prob′a-ble, 164.
Im-prob′i-ty.
Im-promp′tu [so Sm. Wr. Wb. Gd.; *im-prom′tu*, Wk. 155.]
Im-prop′er.
Im-pro′pri-ate.
Im-pro′pri-ăt-ed.
Im-pro′pri-ăt-ing.
Im-pro-pri-a′tion.
Im-pro′pri-ăt-or [so Sm. Wr. Wb. Gd.; *im-pro-pri-ăt′or*, Wk. 155.]
Im-pro-pri′e-ty, 169.
Im-prov-a-bil′i-ty (-*proov*-).
Im-prove′ (-*proov′*-), 19.
Im-proved′ (-*proovd′*).
Im-prov′er (-*proov′*-).
Im-prov′ing (-*proov′*-).
Im-prove′ment (-*proov′*-).
Im-prov′i-dence.
Im-prov′i-dent.
Im-prov′ing (-*proov′*-).
Im-prov-i-sa′tion.

Im-pro-vis′a-tize (-*viz′*-), 202.
Im-pro-vis′a-tized (-*viz′*-), 183.
Im-pro-vis′a-tīz-ing (-*viz′*-).
Im-pro-vis′a-tor (-*viz′*-).
Im-pro-vise′ (-*vīz′*), 202.
Im-pro-vised′ (-*vīzd′*).
Im-pro-vīs′er (-*vīz′*-).
Im-pro-vīs′ing (-*vīz′*-).
Im-prov-vi-sa-to′re (It.) [pl. *Im-prov-vi-sa-to′-ri* (-*re*), 198.]
Im-prov-vi-sa-tri′ce (It.) (*im-prov-ve-sa-tre′-chā*).

☞ Goodrich remarks of the two preceding words, that they are "usually spelled with but one *v* by the English and French."

Im-pru′dence (-*proo′*-).
Im pru′dent (-*proo′*-).
Im′pu-dence, 169.
Im′pu-dent.
Im-pu-diç′i-ty, 169, 171.
Im-pūgn′ (-*pūn*), 162.
Im-pūgned′ (-*pūnd′*).
Im-pūgn′er (-*pūn′*-).
Im-pu′is-sant, 169, 170.
Im′pulse (-*puls*), 171.
Im-pul′sion, 118.
Im-pul′sive.
Im-pu′ni-ty, 108, 169.
Im-pure′.
Im-pū′ri-ty, 49, N. [*See* Purify.]
Im-pur′ple, 104, 164.
Im-pur′pled (-*pur′pld*).
Im-pur′pling.
Im-pūt′a-ble, 164.
Im-pu-ta′tion.
Im-pūt′a-tĭve, 84.
Im-pute′, 26.
Im-pūt′ed, 183.
Im-pūt′ing.
In, *prep.* & *ad.* within. [*See* Inn, 160.]
In-a-bil′i-ty, 108, 169.
In-ac-ces-si-bil′i-ty.
In-ac-ces′si-ble, 164.
In-ac′cu-ra-cy, 169.
In-ac′cu-rate.
In-ac′tion.
In-ac′tĭve, 84.
In-ac-tiv′i-ty.
In-ad′e-qua-cy, 171.
In-ad′e-quate.
In-ad-mis-si-bil′i-ty.
In-ad-mis′si-ble, 164.
In-ad-ver′tence, 21, N.
In-ad-ver′ten-cy.
In-ad-ver′tent.
In-āl′ien-a-ble (-*yen*-), 164.
In-am-o-rä′ta, *n. fem.*
In-am-o-rä′to, *n. mas.* [so Wr. Gd.; *in-am-o-ra′to*, Sm. 155.]
In-ane′, 23.
In-an′i-mate, 169.
In-an′i-māt-ed.
In-a-nĭ′tion, 112.
In-an′i-ty, 108, 169.
In-ap pli-ca-bil′i-ty.
In-ap′pli-ca-ble, 164.
In-ap-pre′ci-a-ble (-*pre′-shi-a-bl*), 164.
In-ap-pro′pri-ate.
In-apt′.
In-apt′i-tude, 108.
In-ar-tic′u-late, 73, 89.
In-ar-ti-fĭ′cial (-*fish′al*).
In-at-ten′tion.
In-at-ten′tĭve, 84.
In-âu′di-ble, 164.
In-âu′gu-ral, 72.
In-âu′gu-rate.
In-âu′gu-rāt-ed, 183
In-âu-gu-ra′tion.
In-âu′gu-rāt-or.
In-âu-spĭ′cious (-*spish′-us*), 112, 171.
In′born, 135.
In′bred.
In′ca (*ing′ka*) [so Sm.; *in′ka*, Wr. Wb. Gd. 155.]
In-cage′ (23, 45) [Encage, 203.]
In-caged′, 165.
In-cāg′ing (-*kāj′*-).
In-cal′cu-la-ble, 164.
In-ca-les′cence, 39, 171.
In-ca-les′cen-cy, 169.
In-ca-les′cent.
In-can-des′cence, 39.
In-can-des′cent.
In-can-ta′tion.
In-can′ta-to-ry, 86.
In-ca-pa-bil′i-ty, 108.
In-ca′pa-ble, 164.
In-ca-paç′i-tate.
In-ca-paç′i-tāt-ed.
In-ca-paç′i-tāt-ing.
In-ca-paç′i-ty.
In-car′cer-ate, 73.
In-car′cer-āt-ed.
In-car′cer-āt-ing.
In-car-cer-a′tion.
In-car′nate, *a.* & *v.* 73.
In-car′nāt-ed, 183.
In-car′nāt-ing.
In-car-na′tion.
In-car′na-tĭve, 84.
In-case′ [Encase, 203.]
In-cased′ (-*kāst′*).
In-cās′ing.
In-câu′tious (-*shus*), 169.
In-cend′i-a-rism (-*rizm*).
In-cend′i-a-ry (72, 169) [so Wr. Wb. Gd.; *in-send′yur-y*, Sm.; *in-cen′di-a-ry*, or *in-sen′-ji-a-ry*, Wk. 155.]
In-cense′ (161), *v.* to inflame with anger; to provoke.
In′cense [so Wk. Sm. Wb. Gd.; *in′sens*, or *in-sens′*, Wr. 155], *v.* to burn; — to perfume with incense.
In′cense, *n.* 161.
In-cen′sĭve.
In-cen′sor, 88.
In′cen-so-ry, *or* In-cen′-so-ry [so Wr.; *in′-sen-sur-y*, Wk. Sm.; *in-sen′so-ry*, Wb. Gd. 155.]
In-cen′tĭve, 84.
In-cep′tion.
In-cep′tĭve, 84.
In-cep′tor.
In-cer′ti-tude, 21, N. 108.
In-ces′san-cy.
In-ces′sant.
In′cest.
In-cest′u-oŭs.
Inch, 16, 44.
[Inchase, 201, 203. — *See* Enchase.]
In-cho′a-tĭve (-*ko′*-) [so Wk. Wr. Wb. Gd.; *ing′ko-a-tiv*, Sm. 155.]
In′ci-dence, 39, 169.
In′ci-dent, 127.
In-ci-dent′al.
In-ci-dent′al-ly.
In-cin′er-ate.
In-cin′er-āt-ed.
In-cin′er-āt-ing.
In-cin-er-a′tion.
In-cip′i-ence.
In-cip′i-en-cy, 169.
In-cip′i-ent.
In-cise′ (-*sīz′*-), 202.
In-cised′ (-*sīzd′*).
In-cīs′ing (-*sīz′*-).
In-cĭ′sion (-*sizh′un*).
In-ci′sĭve, 84.
In-ci′sor.
In-cīt′ant.
In-cĭ-ta′tion.
In-cite′, 25.
In-cīt′ed, 183.

In-cite′ment.
In-cīt′er.
In-cīt′ing.
In-cĭ-vil′i-ty.
In-clăsp′, 12, 131.
In-clăsped′ (-*klăspt′*).
In-clăsp′ing.
In-clem′en-cy, 169.
In-clem′ent.
In-clin′a-ble, 164.
In-cli-na′tion.
In-clin′a-to-ry (86) [so Sm. Wb. Gd.; *ĭn-klĭn′a-to-ry*, Wk. Wr. 155.]

☞ "The termination *atory* has a tendency to shorten the preceding vowel, as is evident in *declamatory*, *predatory*, &c." *Walker.*

In-cline′, 25.
In-clined′, 165, 183.
In-clīn′er.
In-clīn′ing.
In-close′ (-*klōz′*) [E n c l o s e, 201, 203.— *See* Note under *Enclose.*]
In-closed′ (-*klōzd′*), 183.
In-clōs′ing (-*klōz′*-).
In-clōs′ure (-*klōz′yur*) [E n c l o s u r e, 201, 203.]
In-clude′, 26.
In-clūd′ed.
In-clūd′ing.
In-clu′sion (-*zhun*).
In-clu′sĭve, 84.
In-cog′.
In-cog′ni-to.
In-cog′ni-za-ble, 164.
In-cog′ni-zance.
In-cog′ni-zant, 169.
In-co-he′rence, 49, N.
In-co-he′ren-cy.
In-co-he′rent.
In-com-bus-ti-bil′i-ty.
In-com-bus′ti-ble, 164.
In′come (-*kum*).
In-com-men-su-ra-bil′i-ty (-*shoo*-), 26, 46, Note 2.
In-com-men′su-ra-ble (-*shoo*-), 164, 171.
In-com-men′su-rate (-*shoo*-) 46, Note 2, 171.
In-com-mode′, 66, 170.
In-com-mōd′ed, 183.
In-com-mōd′ing.
In-com-mo′di-oŭs [so Sm. Wr. Wb. Gd.; *in-kom-mo′di-us*, or *in-kom-mo′ji-us*, Wk. 155.]
In-com-mu-ni-ca-bil′i-ty.
In-com-mu′ni-ca-ble, 164
In-com′par-a-ble (164) [*not* in-kom-pêr′a-ble, 153.]
In-com-pat-i-bil′i-ty.
In-com-pat′i-ble, 164.
In-com′pe-tence.
In-com′pe-ten-cy, 169.
In-com′pe-tent.
In-com-plete′.
In-com-pos′ĭte (-*pŏz′*-) (152) [so Sm. Wr.; *in-kom-poz′it*, or *in-kom′po-zit*, Gd. 155.]
In-com-pre-hen-si-bil′i-ty, 116.
In-com-pre-hen′si-ble, 164.
In-com-press-i-bil′i-ty.
In-com-press′i-ble, 164.
In-con-ceiv′a-ble, 164, 169.
In-con-clu′sĭve.
In-con′dĭte [so Sm. Wb. Gd.; *in′kon-dĭt*, Wk; *in′kon-dĭt*, or *in-kon′dit*, Wr. 155.]
In-con-gru′i-ty (-*groo′*-).
In-con′gru-oŭs (-*kong′-groo*-), 19, 54, 169.
In-con′se-quence.
In-con′se-quent.
In-con-se-quen′tial (-*shal*).
In-con-sid′er-a-ble, 164.
In-con-sid′er-ate, 73.
In-con-sist′en-cy, 169.
In-con-sist′ent.
In-con-sōl′a-ble, 164.
In-con-spic′u-oŭs.
In-con′stan-cy, 169.
In-con′stant.
In-con-test′a-ble, 164.
In-con′ti-nence.
In-con′ti-nent.
In-con-tro-vert-i-bil′i-ty
In-con-tro-vert′i-ble.
In-con-vēn′ience (-*yens*) [so Gd.; *in-kon-vēn′yens*, or *in-kon-ve′ni-ens*, Wr.; *in-kon-ve′ni-ens*, Wk. Sm. 155.]
In-cor′po-rate, 73.
In-cor′po-rāt-ed.
In-cor′po-rāt-ing.
In-cor-po-ra′tion.
In-cor-po′re-al, 49, N.
In-cor-po-re′i-ty, 169.
In-cor-rect′, 66, 170.
In-cor-ri-gi-bil′i-ty.
In-cor′ri-gi-ble, 164.
In-cor-rupt′.
In-cor-rupt-i-bil′i-ty.
In-cor-rupt′i-ble, 164.
In-cor-rup′tion.
In-cras′sate, 73.
In-cras′sāt-ed.
In-cras′sāt-ing.
In-cras-sa′tion.
In-cras′sa-tĭve.
In-crēase′, *v.* 103, 161.
In′crēase, *or* In-crēase′ *n.* [so Wr.; *in′krēs*, Wk. Sm.; *in-krēs′*, or *in′krēs*, Gd. 155.]
In-crēased′, 165.
In-crēas′er.
In-crēas′ing.
In-cred-i-bil′i-ty.
In-cred′i-ble, 164.
In-cre-du′li-ty, 108, 169.
In-cred′u-loŭs (45, N.) [so Sm. Wr. Wb. Gd.; *in-kred′u-lus*, or *in-kred′ju-lus*, Wk. 155.]
In′cre-ment (54) [so Sm. Wb. Gd.; *ing′kre-ment*, Wk. Wr. 155.]
[I n c r o a c h, 203.— *See* Encroach.]
In-crust′ [E n c r u s t, 203.]
In-crust-a′tion, 112.
In-crust′ed.
In-crust′ing.
In′cu-bate (54), [so Sm. Wb. Gd.; *ing′ku-bāt*, Wk. Wr. 155.]
In′cu-bāt-ed.
In′cu-bāt-ing.
In-cu-ba′tion, 112.
In′cu-bus (54) [so Sm. Wb. Gd.; *ing′ku-bus*, Wk. Wr. 155.] [L. pl. *in′cu-bī*; Eng. pl. In′cu-bus-es (-*ez*), 198.]
In-cul′cate, 73.
In-cul′cāt-ed, 183.
In-cul′cāt-ing.
In-cul-ca′tion.
In-cul′cāt-or.
In-cul′pate, 73.
In-cul′pāt-ed, 183.
In-cul′pāt-ing.
In-cul-pa′tion.
In-cul′pa-to-ry.
In-cum′ben-cy, 169.
In-cum′bent.
[I n c u m b r a n c e, 203. — *See* Encumbrance.]
In-cur′, 21.
In-cūr-a-bil′i-ty, 108.

In-cūr′a-ble, 164.
In-cu′ri-oŭs, 49, N.
In-curred′ (-*kurd′*), 165.
In-cur′rence, 169.
In-cur′ring, 21.
In-cur′sion.
In-cur′sĭve, 84.
In-curv′ate.
In-curv′āt-ed, 183.
In-curv′āt-ing.
In-curv-a′tion.
In-debt′ed (-*det′*-), 162.
In-de′cen-cy, 169.
In-de′cent.
In-de-cĭ′sion (-*sizh′un*).
In-de-clīn′a-ble, 164.
In-de-co′roŭs, *or* In-dec′o-roŭs (108) [so Wk. Wr. Gd.; *in-de-ko′rus*, Sm. 155.]
In-de-co′rum.
In-deed′.
In-de-fat-i-ga-bil′i-ty.
In-de-fat′i-ga-ble, 164.
In-de-fat′i-ga-bly.
In-de-fēa-si-bil′i-ty (-*zĭ*-).
In-de-fēa′si-ble (-*zĭ-bl*-).
In-de-fen-si-bil′i-ty.
In-de-fen′si-ble, 164.
In-de-fīn′a-ble, 164.
In-def′i-nĭte, 152, 169.
In-de-his′cence, 39, 171.
In-de-his′cent.
In-del-i-bil′i-ty, 108.
In-del′i-ble, 164, 169.
In-del′i-ca-cy, 72, 169.
In-del′i-cate, 73.
In-dem-ni-fĭ-ca′tion.
In-dem′ni-fīed, 186.
In-dem′ni-fȳ.
In-dem′ni-fȳ-ing.
In-dem′ni-ty, 108, 169.
In-dent′, *n.* & *v.* 15.
In-dent-a′tion.
In-dent′ed.
In-dent′ing.
In-dent′ure, 91.
In-de-pend′ence, 169.
In-de-pen′den-cy.
In-de-pen′dent.
In-de-scrīb′a-ble, 164.
In-de-struct-i-bil′i-ty.
In-de-struct′i-ble, 164.
In-de-ter′mi-nate.
In′dex, *n.* & *v.* [pl. of *n.* In′dex-es (-*ez*), *or* (in the sense of *exponents of quantities*) In′di-cēs (-*sēz*).]
In′dexed (-*dekst*).
In-dex′ic-al.
In′dex-ing.
Ind′ian (-*yan*) (45, N.; 51) [so Sm. Wr. Wb. Gd.; *in′di-an*, *in′ji-an*, or *ind′yan*, Wk. 155.]
Ind′ia-rub′ber (*ind′ya*-) (171, 205) [so Sm. Wb. Gd.; *in-ja-rub′ber*, Wr. 155.]
In′di-cant.
In′di-cate, 73, 78.
In′di-cāt-ed.
In′di-cāt-ing.
In-di-ca′tion.
In-dic′a-tĭve [so Wk. Wr. Wb. Gd.; *in′di-cāt-iv*, (in the general sense of *showing*, or *pointing out*), *in-dik′-a-tiv* (as applied to note the mode of a verb), Sm. 155.]
In′di-cāt-or.
In′di-ca-to-ry (86) [so Wr. Wb. Gd.; *in′di-kā-tur-y*, Sm. 155.]
In′di-cēs (-*sēz*), *n. pl.* [*See* Index.]
In-dīct′ (-*dīt′*) (162), *v.* to accuse. [*See* Indite, 160.] [Endict, 201, 203.]
In-dīct′a-ble (-*dīt′*-), 164.
In-dīct′ed (-*dīt′*-).
In-dīct′er (-*dīt′*-), *n.* one who accuses. [*See* Inditer, 160.]
In-dīct′ing (-*dīt′*-).
In-dic′tion.
In-dīct′ment (-*dīt′*-) (162), *n.* an accusation. [*See* Inditement, 160.]
In-dif′fer-ence, 169, 170.
In-dif′fer-ent.
In′di-gence, 39, 45.
In′di-gene.
In-dig′e-noŭs (-*dij′*-), 169, 171.
In′di-gent.
In-di-gest-i-bil′i-ty.
In-di-gest′i-ble, 108.
In-di-gest′ion (-*yun*).
In-dig′nant.
In-dig-na′tion.
In-dig′ni-ty, 108, 169.
In′di-go.
In-di-gom′e-ter, 108.
In′di-go-tĭne, 152.
In-dĭ-rect′.
In-dis-cern′i-ble (-*diz-zern′i-bl*), 164, 171.
In-dis-creet′ (160), *a.* imprudent.
In-dis-crete′ (160), *a.* not separated.
In-dis-crĕ′tion (-*kresh′-un*).
In-dis-crim′i-nate, 73, 169
In-dis-pen′sa-ble, 164, 171.
In-dis-pose′ (-*pōz′*).
In-dis-posed′ (-*pōzd′*).
In-dis-po-sĭ′tion (-*zish′-un*).
In-dis′pu-ta-ble (164) [so Sm. Wr. Wb. Gd.; *in-dis′pu-ta-bl*, or *in-dis-pu′ta-bl*, Wk. 155.]

☞ Though Walker, in deference to the authority of Johnson, Ash, and others, allows the pronunciation *in-dis-pu′ta-bl*, he says of the other mode (*in-dis′pu-ta-bl*): "My experience and recollection grossly fail me, if this is not the general pronunciation of polite and lettered speakers."

In-dis-so-lu-bil′i-ty.
In-dis′so-lu-ble, 164.
In-dis-tinct′.
In-dis-tin′guish-a-ble (-*ting′gwish*-), 164, 171.
In-dite′ (25), *v.* to compose, or write. [*See* Indict, 160.]
In-dite′ment, *n.* act of one who composes, or writes. [*See* Indictment, 160.]
In-dit′er, *n.* one who composes or writes. [*See* Indicter, 160.]
In-di-vid′u-al (45, N.) [so Sm. Wr. Wb. Gd.; *in-di-vid′u-al*, or *in-di-vid′ju-al*, Wk. 155.]
In-di-vid′u-al-ism (-*izm*), 136.
In-di-vid-u-al′i-ty, 108.
In-di-vid-u-al-ĭ-za′tion.
In-di-vid′u-al-ize, 202.
In-di-vid′u-al-ized.
In-di-vid′u-al-iz-ing.
In-di-vis-i-bil′i-ty (-*viz*-)
In-di-vis′i-ble (-*viz′*-), 164
In-doç′i-ble [so Wk. Sm. Wr.; *in-do′si-bl*, or *in-dos′i-bl*, Gd. 155.]
In-doç′ĭle (152) [so Wk. Sm. Wr.; *in-do′sil*, or *in-dos′il*, Gd. 155.]
In-do-cil′i-ty.
In-doc′trin-ate, 73.

In-doc'trin-āt-ed.
In-doc'trin-āt-ing.
In-doc-trin-ā'tion.
In'do-lence.
In'do-lent, 169.
In-dom'i-ta-ble, 164.
In-dorse' [Endorse, 201, 203. — *See* Note under *Endorse.*]
In-dorsed' (-*dorst'*).
In-dorse'ment [Endorsement, 203.]
In-dors'er, 183.
In-dors'ing.
In'drī, 191.
In-du'bi-ta-ble, 164.
In-duce'.
In-duced' (-*dūst'*).
In-duce'ment.
In-duç'ing, 183.
In-duct'.
In-duct'ed.
In-duct'ing.
In-duc'tion.
In-duct'īve.
In-duct'or.
In-duct'ric, 109.
In-duct'ric-al, 108.
In-dūe' [Endue, 203.]
In-dūed', 165, 183.
In-du'ing.
In-dulge', 22, 45.
In-dulged' (-*duljd'*), 183.
In-dulg'ence (-*dulj'*-).
In-dulg'ent (*dulj'*-).
In-dulg'er (-*dulj'*-).
In'du-rate, 73.
In'du-rāt-ed.
In'du-rāt-ing.
In-du-ra'tion.
In-du'si-al (-*zhi-al*) [so Sm.; *in-du'shal*, Wr. Gd. 155.]
In-du'si-um (-*zhi-um*) [so Sm. Wr.; *in-du'shi-um*, Gd. 155.]
In-dus'tri-al.
In-dus'tri-oŭs, 169.
In'dus-try (105) [*not* in-dus'try, 153.]
In-e'bri-ant.
In-e'bri-ate, 73, 78.
In-e'bri-āt-ed, 183.
In-e'bri-āt-ing.
In-e-bri-a'tion.
In-e-bri'e-ty, 169.
In-ef'fa-ble, 164, 170.
In-ef-face'a-ble, 183.
In-ef-fect'īve, 84.
In-ef-fect'u-al, 72, 89.
In-ef-fi-ca'cious (-*shus*).
In-ef'fi-ca-cy, 169.
In-ef-fī'cien-cy (-*fish'en-sy*), 171.
In-ef-fī'cient (-*fish'ent*).
In-el'e-gance, 169.
In-el'e-gant.
In-el-i-gi-bil'i-ty, 108.
In-el'i-gi-ble, 108, 164.
In-ept'.
In-ept'i-tude, 108, 169.
In-e-qual'i-ty (-*kwol'*-).
In-eq'ui-ta-ble (-*ek'wi-ta-bl*), 164, 171.
In-ert', 21, N.
In-er'ti-a (-*shĭ-a*) [so Sm. Wr.; *in-er'sha*, Wb. Gd.]
In-es'ti-ma-ble, 164.
In-ev'i-ta-ble, 164.
In-ex-act'.
In-ex-cūs'a-ble (-*kūz'*-), 164.
In-ex-hâust'i-ble, 164, 169.
In-ex'o-ra-ble, 164, 171.
In-ex-pe'di-ent.
In-ex-pe'ri-ence, 48, N.
In-ex-pe'ri-enced (-*enst*).
In-ex-pert', 21, N.
In-ex'pi-a-ble, 164, 169.
In-ex'pli-ca-ble, 164.
In-ex-press'i-ble, 164.
In-ex-pug'na-ble, 164.
In-ex-tin'guish-a-ble (-*ting'gwish-a-bl*), 164, 171.
In-ex'tri-ca-ble, 164, 169.
In-fal-li-bil'i-ty, 108.
In-fal'li-ble, 164, 170.
In'fa-moŭs, 100, 169.
In'fa-my, 93.
In'fan-cy, 169.
In'fant, 16, 72.
In-fan'ta (Sp.), *n. fem.*
In-fan'te (Sp.) (-*tā*), *n. mas.*
In-fant'i-cide, 169.
In'fant-īle, *or* In'fant-īle [so Wr.; *in'fant-īl*, Wk. Gd.; *in'fant-īl*, Sm. 155.]
In'fant-īne, *or* In'fant-īne [so Wr.; *in'fant-īn*, Wk. Gd.; *in'fant-īn*, Sm. 155.]
In'fant-ry, 93, 105.
In-fat'u-ate, 73, 89.
In-fat'u-āt-ed, 183.
In-fat'u-āt-ing.
In-fat-u-a'tion.
In-fect', 15, 103.
In-fect'ed.
In-fect'ing.
In-fec'tion.
In-fec'tioŭs (-*shus*).
In-fec'und [so Wk. Sm. Wr.; *in-fe'kund*, Wb. Gd. 155.]
In-fe-cund'i-ty.
In-fe-liç'i-toŭs, 171.
In-fe-liç'i-ty.
In-fer', 21, N.
In-fer'a-ble (164) [Inferrible, 203.]

☞ Smart says of this word: "It is better to spell it *Inferrible.*"

In'fer-ence, 176.
In-fer-en'tial (-*shal*).
In-fe'ri-or, 49, N.
In-fe-ri-or'i-ty, 108.
In-fer'nal, 21, N.
In-ferred' (-*ferd'*), 176.
In-fer'ri-ble (164) [Inferable, 203. — *See* Note under *Inferable.*]
In-fer'ring, 176.
In-fest', 15, 103.
In-fest-a'tion.
In-fest'ed.
In-fest'er.
In-fest'ing.
In'fi-del, 76, 78.
In-fi-del'i-ty, 108, 169.
In-fil'trate, 73.
In-fil'trāt-ed, 183.
In-fil'trāt-ing.
In-fil-tra'tion.
In'fi-nīte, 152.
In-fin-i-tes'i-mal, 116.
In-fin'i-tīve, 84.
In-fin'i-tude, 108.
In-fin'i-ty, 108, 169.
In-firm', 21, N.
In-firm'a-ry, 72.
In-firm'i-ty, 169.
In-fix', 16, 39, N.
In-fixed' (-*fĭkst'*), 165; Note C, p. 34.
In-fix'ing.
In-flame', 23.
In-flamed', 183.
In-flām'er.
In-flām'ing.
In-flam-ma-bil'i-ty.
In-flam'ma-ble, 164, 170.
In-flam-ma'tion, 112.
In-flam'ma-to-ry, 86.
In-flate', 23.
In-flāt'ed, 183.
In-flāt'ing.
In-fla'tion.
In-flect', 15.

In-flect′ed.
In-flec′tion.
In-flec′tion-al.
In-flexed′ (-*flekst′*).
In-flex-i-bil′i-ty, 108.
In-flex′i-ble, 164.
In-flict′, 16, 103.
In-flict′ed.
In-flict′er.
In-flict′ing.
In-flic′tion.
In-flict′ive, 84.
In-flo-res′cence, 171.
In′flu-ence, 169.
In′flu-enced (-*enst*).
In′flu-enç-ing.
In-flu-en′tial (-*shal*).
In-flu-en′za.
In′flux.
In-fōld′ [Enfold, 203.]
In-fōld′ed.
In-fōld′ing.
In-form′, 17.
In-form′al.
In-for-mal′i-ty, 108.
In-for′mal-ly.
In-form′ant.
In-form-a′tion.
In-formed′ (-*formd′*), 165.
In-form′er.
In-frac′tion.
[Infranchise, 201, 203. — *See* Enfranchise.]
In-fran′gi-ble, 164.
In-fre′quen-cy, 169.
In-fre′quent.
In-fringe′, 16, 45.
In-fringed′ (-*frinjd′*), 183.
In-fringe′ment, 185.
In-fring′er (-*frinj′*-).
In-fring′ing (-*frinj′*-).
In-fun-dib′u-lar, 108.
In-fun-dib′u-li-form.

☞ This word is an exception to the general rule (§ 108), by which words ending in *i-form* take the primary accent on the antepenult.

In-fu′ri-ate, 49, N.
In-fu′ri-āt-ed, 183.
In-fu′ri-āt-ing.
In-fus′cate.
In-fus′cāt-ed, 183.
In-fus′cāt-ing.
In-fus-ca′tion, 112.
In-fuse′, 26, 136.
In-fused′ (-*fūzd′*), 183.
In-fūs-i-bil′i-ty (-*fūz*-).
In-fus′i-ble (-*fūz*-), 164.
In-fūs′ing (-*fūz′*-).
In-fu′sion (-*zhun*).
In-fu′sīve, 84.
In-fu-so′ri-a, *n. pl.*
In-fu-so′ri-al.
In-fu′so-ry, 190.
In′gath-er-ing [so Wk. Sm. Wr.; *in-gath′ur-ing*, Wb. Gd. 155.]
In-gel′a-ble, 45, 164, 169.
In-gēn′ioŭs (-*jēn′yus*), *or* In-ge′ni-ous (-*je′-ni-us*) [so Wr.; *in-jēn′yus*, Gd.; *in-je′ni-us*, Wk. Sm. 155.]
In-gen′ĭte (152) [so Sm. Wb. Gd.; *in′jen-it*, Wk.; *in-jen′it*, or *in′-jen-it*, Wr. 155.]
In-ge-nu′i-ty, 108.
In-gen′u-oŭs, 89, 100.
In-glo′ri-oŭs, 49, N.
In-glu′vi-ēs (-*ēz*).
[Ingorge, 201, 203. — *See* Engorge.]
In′got, 16, 86.

☞ This word is an exception to the general rule (§ 54), by which *n* is sounded as *ng* at the end of an accented syllable (unless this syllable is one of the prefixes *in*, *non*, or *un*) before the sound of *k* or of hard *g* at the beginning of the next syllable.

In-grȧft′ (12, 131) [Engraft, 203.]
In-grȧft′ed.
In-grȧft′ing.
In-grāin′ [Engrain, 201, 203.]
In-grāined′, 165.
In-grāin′ing.
In′grate, *a.* [so Sm. Wb. Gd.; *in-grāt′*, Wk.; *in-grāt′*, or *in′grāt*, Wr. 155.]
In′grate, *n.* [so Sm. Wb. Gd.; *in-grāt′*, Wr. 155.]
In-gra′ti-ate (-*shĭ-āt*) [so Wk. Sm. Wr.; *in-gra′shāt*, Wb. Gd. 155.]
In-gra′ti-āt-ed (-*shĭ-āt*-).
In-gra′ti-āt-ing (-*shĭ-āt*-).
In-grat′i-tude, 108, 169.
In-gre′di-ent [so Sm. Wr. Wb. Gd.; *in-gre′jent*, Wk. 134. 155.]
In′gress.
In′gui-nal (*ing′gwi*-), 34, 54, 171.
In-gulf′ (22) [Engulf, 201, 203.]
In-gulfed′ (-*gulft′*).
In-gulf′ing.
In-gulf′ment.
In-gur′gi-tate, 73.
In-gur′gi-tāt-ed.
In-gur′gi-tāt-ing.
In-gur-gi-ta′tion.
In-hab′it.
In-hab′it-a-ble, 164, 169.
In-hab′i-tan-cy.
In-hab′i-tant.
In-hab-i-ta′tion.
In-hab′it-a-tīve-ness.
In-hab′it-ed.
In-hab′it-er.
In-hab′it-ing.
In-ha-la′tion, 171.
In-hale′, 23.
In-haled′, 183.
In-hāl′er.
In-hāl′ing.
In-here′, 13.
In-hered′, 165, 183.
In-hēr′ence.
In-hēr′en-cy.
In-hēr′ent.
In-hĕr′it.
In-hĕr′i-ta-ble, 164.
In-hĕr′i-tance, 169.
In-hĕr′it-ed.
In-hĕr′it-ing.
In-hĕr′it-or.
In-hib′it.
In-hib′it-ed.
In-hib′it-ing.
In-hi-bĭ′tion (-*bish′un*).
In-hib′it-o-ry, 86.
In-hos′pi-ta-ble, 164, 171.
In-hos-pi-tal′i-ty.
In-hu′man.
In-hu-man′i-ty.
In-hu-ma′tion.
In-hume′, 26.
In-humed′, 183.
In-hūm′ing.
In-im′ic-al [so Wb. Gd.; *in-i-mĭ′kal*, Sm.; *in-im′ik-al*, or *in-i-mi′kal*, Wk. Wr. 155.]

☞ Though Walker allows the pronunciation *in-i-mi′kal*, he condemns it as contrary to analogy. Ellis says: "We have never heard any other pronunciation but *in-im′ic-al* in actual use."

In-im'i-ta-ble, 164.
In-iq'ui-toŭs (*-ik'wi-*).
In-iq'ui-ty (*-ik'wi-*), 171.
In-ĭ'tial (*-ish'al*).
In-ĭ'ti-ate (*-ish'i-*) (171) [so Wk. Sm. Wr.; *in-ish'ate*, Wb. Gd. 155.]
In-ĭ'ti-āt-ed (*-ish'i-*).
In-ĭ'ti-āt-ing (*-ish'i-*).
In-ĭ-ti-a'tion (*-ish-i-*).
In-ĭ'ti-a-tĭve (*-ish'i-*).
In-ĭ'ti-a-to-ry (*-ish'i-*).
In-ject', 15.
In-ject'ed.
In-ject'ing.
In-jec'tion.
[I n j o i n, 201, 203. — *See* Enjoin.]
In-ju-dĭ'cioŭs (*-dish'-us*).
In-junc'tion.
In'jure, 91.
In'jured (*-jurd*), 183.
In'jur-er.
In'jur-ing.
In-ju'ri-oŭs, 49, N.
In'ju-ry, 89, 93.
In-jus'tĭce (*-tis*), 115, 169.
Ink (*ingk*), 16, 54.
Ink'horn (*ingk'-*), 206.
Ink'ling (*ingk'-*).
Ink'stand (*ingk'-*), 206.
Ink'y (*ingk'y*).
In-lace', 23.
In-laced' (*-lāst'*).
In-lāç'ing.
In-lāid', 187.
In'land.
In-lāy', 23.
In-lāy'er, 187.
In-lāy'ing.
In'let.
[I n l i s t, 201, 203. — *See* Enlist.]
In'mate.
In'mōst.
Inn (16, 175), *n.* a house of entertainment for travellers; a tavern. [*See* In, 160.]
In-nate' (66, 170) [so Wk. Sm. Wr.; *in'-nāt*, or *in-nāt'*, Gd. 155.]
In-nav'i-ga-ble, 164.
In'ner, 170.
In-nerv-a'tion.
In-nerve', 21, N.
In-nerved' (*-nervd'*), 183.
In-nerv'ing.
Inn'hōld-er.
Inn'ing.
Inn'keep-er.
In'no-cence, 170.
In'no-cent.
In-noc'u-oŭs.
In'no-vate, 105, 170.
In'no-vāt-ed, 183.
In'no-vāt-ing.
In-no-va'tion.
In'no-vāt-or, 88.
In-nox'ioŭs (*-nok'-shus*), 46, Note 1.
In-nu-en'do (170, 171) [pl. In-nu-en'does (*-dōz*), 192.]
In-nu'mer-a-ble, 164.
In-oc'u-late, 73, 89.
In-oc'u-lāt-ed, 183.
In-oc'u-lāt-ing.
In-oc-u-la'tion, 112.
In-oc'u-lāt-or.
In-o'dor-oŭs.
In-or'di-nate, 73, 78.
In-os'cu-late.
In-os'cu-lāt-ed, 183.
In-os'cu-lāt-ing.
In-os-cu-la'tion.
In'quest, 34.
In-qui'e-tude, 169.
In-quīr'a-ble, 164, 183.
In-quire' [E n q u i r e, 201, 203.]
In-quired', 165, 183.
In-quīr'er.
In-quīr'ing.
In-qui-sĭ'tion (*-zish'-un*), 171, 231, Exc.
In-quis'i-tĭve (*-kwiz'-*).
In-quis'i-tor (*-kwiz'-*).
In-quis-i-to'ri-al (*-kwiz-*).
In'rōad.
In-san'a-ble, 164.
In-sane', 23.
In-san'i-ty, 108, 169.
In-sā-ti-a-bil'i-ty (*-sā-shĭ-*), 169, 171.
In-sa'ti-a-ble (*-sa'shĭ-*) (164) [so Wk. Sm. Wr.; *in-sa'sha-bl*, Wb. Gd. 155.]
In-sa'ti-a-bly (*-sa'shĭ-*).
In-sa'ti-ate (*-sa'shĭ-*) [so Wk. Sm. Wr.; *in-sa'-shāt*, Wb. Gd. 155.]
In-sat'u-ra-ble, 164.
In-scrīb'a-ble, 164, 169.
In-scribe', 25.
In-scribed', 183.
In-scrīb'er.
In-scrīb'ing.
In-scrip'tion.
In-scrip'tĭve, 84.
In-scrōll' [I n s c r o l Sm. 179, 203.]
In-scrōlled' (*-skrōld'*), 165.
In-scrōll'ing.
In-scru'ta-ble (*-skroo'-*), 164.
In'sect, 16, 76.
In-sect'ĭle, 152.
In-sect-iv'o-roŭs, 108.
In-se-cure'.
In-se-cu'ri-ty, 49, N.
In-sen'sate, 73.
In-sen-si-bil'i-ty, 108.
In-sen'si-ble, 164.
In-sen'tient (*-sen'-shent*), 46, 171.
In-sep-a-ra-bil'i-ty, 169.
In-sep'a-ra-ble, 164.
In-sert', 21, N.
In-sert'ed.
In-sert'ing.
In-ser'tion.
In-ses-so'rēs (*-rēz,*) *n. pl.*
In-ses-so'ri-al, 49, N.
In-shore'.
[I n s h r i n e, 201, 203. — *See* Enshrine.]
In-sic-ca'tion.
In'side.
In-sid'i-oŭs [so Sm. Wr. Wb. Gd.; *in-sid'i-us*, or *in-sid'ji-us*, Wk. 155.]
In'sight (*-sīt*), 162.
In-sig'ni-a (L.), *n. pl.*
In-sig-nif'i-cance, 169.
In-sig-nif'i-can-cy.
In-sig-nif'i-cant.
In-sig-nif'i-ca-tĭve.
In-sin-cere'.
In-sin-cĕr'i-ty.
In-sin'u-ate, 73.
In-sin'u-āt-ed.
In-sin'u-āt-ing.
In-sin-u-a'tion.
In-sin'u-a-tĭve, 84.
In-sin'u-āt-or [so Wk. Wr. Gd.; *in-sin'u-a-tor*, Sm. 155.]
In-sip'id, 170.
In-si-pid'i-ty, 108.
In-sist', 16.
In-sist'ed.
In-sist'ing.
In-sĭ'tion (*-sish'un*) [so Wk. Sm. Wb. Gd.; *in-sizh'un*, or *in-sish'-un*, Wr. 155.]
In sĭ'tu (L.).
In-snare' (*-snêr'*) (14) [E n s n a r e, 201, 203.]

In-snared′(*-snêrd′*), 183.
In-snar′er (*-snêr′-*).
In-snar′ing (*-snêr′-*).
In′so-late, *v.* to dry by the heat of the sun; to expose to the rays of the sun. [*See* Insulate, 148.]
In′so-lāt-ed.
In′so-lāt-ing.
In-so-la′tion.
In′so-lence.
In′so-len-cy, 169.
In′so-lent.
In-sol-u-bil′i-ty, 108.
In-sol′u-ble, 164.
In-solv′a-ble, 164.
In-solv′en-cy.
In-solv′ent.
In-som′ni-oŭs.
In-spect′, 15, 103.
In-spect′ed.
In-spect′ing.
In-spec′tion.
In-spect′ĭve, 84.
In-spect′or, 88, 169.
In-spīr′a-ble, 164.
In-spi-ra′tion.
In′spi-ra-to-ry, *or* In-spīr′a-to-ry (86) [so Wr.; *in-spīr′a-to-ry*, or *in′spi-ra-to-ry*, Gd. 155.]
In-spīre′, 25.
In-spīred′, 183.
In-spīr′er.
In-spīr′ing.
In-spĭr′it.
In-spĭr′it-ed.
In-spĭr′it-ing.
In-spis′sate, 170.
In-spis′sāt-ed, 183.
In-spis′sāt-ing.
In-spis-sa′tion.
In-sta-bil′i-ty, 108.
In-sta′ble, 164.
In-stâll′ (17) [Instal, 203.]
In-stall-a′tion, 171.
In-stâlled′ (*-stawld′*).
In-stâll′ing.
In-stâl′ment (178) [Installment, Wb. Gd. 203.]
In′stance.
In′stanced (*-stanst*).
In′stanç-ing.
In′stant.
In-stant-a′ne-oŭs, 169.
In stā′tu quo (L.) [*not* in stat′yoo kwo, 153.]
In-stĕad′ (*-sted′*) [*not* in-stid′, 153.]

In′step.
In′sti-gate, 73, 78.
In′sti-gāt-ed, 183.
In′sti-gāt-ing.
In-sti-ga′tion, 112.
In′sti-gāt-or, 88.
In-stil′ (179, 180) [Instill, Wb. Gd. 203.]
In-stil-la′tion.
In-stilled′ (*-stild′*), 165.
In-stil′ler, 176.
In-stil′ling.
In-stil′ment [Instillment, Wb. Gd. 203.]
In′stinct (*-stingkt*) (54, 161), *n.* natural impulse as distinguished from reason or deliberation.
In-stinct′ (*-stingkt′*) (54, 161), *a.* moved; animated.
In-stinct′ĭve(*-stingkt′-*).
In′sti-tute, 26, 127.
In′sti-tūt-ed, 183.
In′sti-tūt-ing.
In-sti-tu′tion.
In-sti-tu′tion-al.
In-sti-tu′tion-a-ry, 72.
In′sti-tūt-ist, 183.
In′sti-tūt-or, 88.
In-struct′, 22.
In-struct′ed.
[Instructer, 203.—*See* Instructor.]
In-struct′ing.
In-struc′tion.
In-struct′ĭve, 84.
In-struct′or [Instructer, 203.]
In-struct′ress.
In′stru-ment (*-stroo-*).
In-stru-ment′al (*-stroo-*)
In-stru-ment-al′i-ty (*-stroo-*), 108, 169.
In-stru-ment-a′tion (*-stroo-*).
In-sub-or′di-nate.
In-sub-or-di-na′tion.
In-suf′fer-a-ble, 164.
In-suf-fĭ′cien-cy (*-fish′en-*).
In-suf-fĭ′cient(*-fish′ent*)
In′su-lar (72) [so Sm. Wr. Wb. Gd.; *in′shu-lar*, Wk. 155.]
In-su-lăr′i-ty, 108.
In′su-late (73), *v.* to detach; to isolate. [*See* Insolate, 148.]
In′su-lāt-ed, 183.
In′su-lāt-ing.
In-su-la′tion.

In′su-lāt-or, 88
In′sult, *n.* 103, 161.
In-sult′, *v.* 103, 161.
In-sult′ed.
In-sult′er.
In-sult′ing.
In-su-per-a-bil′i-ty, 108.
In-su′per-a-ble, 164.
In-sup-pōrt′a-ble, 164.
In-sur′a-ble (*-shoor′-*), 164.
In-sur′ance (*-shoor′-*) (46, 183) [Ensurance, 201, 203.]
In-sure′ (*-shoor′*) (19, 46) [Ensure, 201, 203.—*See* Note under *Ensure.*]
In-sured′ (*-shoord′*).
In-sur′er (*-shoor′-*).
In-sur′ing (*-shoor′-*).
In-sur′gent.
In-sur-mount′a-ble, 164.
In-sur-rec′tion, 170.
In-sur-rec′tion-al.
In-sur-rec′tion-a-ry, 72.
In-sur-rec′tion-ist.
In-tact′.
In tagl′io (It.) (*-tal′yo*).
In-tan-gi-bil′i-ty, 108.
In-tan′gi-ble, 164.
In′te-ger, 45, 105.
In′te-gral, 72.
In′te-grant.
In′te-grate, 73, 169.
In′te-grāt-ed.
In′te-grāt-ing.
In-te-gra′tion.
In-teg′ri-ty, 108, 169.
In-teg′u-ment, 89.
In-teg-u-ment′a-ry, 72.
In′tel-lect, 66, 170.
In-tel-lec′tion.
In-tel-lect′ĭve, 84.
In-tel-lect′u-al, 72, 170.
In-tel-lect′u-al-ist.
In-tel′li-gence, 170.
In-tel′li-genç-er, 183.
In-tel′li-gent, 169, 170.
In-tel-li-gen′tial (*-shal*).
In-tel′li-gi-ble, 108, 164, 171.
In-tem′per-ance, 169.
In-tem′per-ate, 73.
In-tend′, 15.
In-tend′an-cy, 169.
In-tend′ant.
In-tend′ed.
In-tend′ing.
In-tend′ment.
In-tense′, 15.
In-ten′si-fīed, 186.
In-ten′si-fȳ, 94.

In-ten′si-fȳ-ing.
In-ten′sion, *n.* act of making intense. [*See* Intention, 160.]
In-ten′si-ty, 108, 169.
In-ten′sĭve, 84.
In-tent′, *a.* & *n.* 15.
In-ten′tion, *n.* design; purpose. [*See* Intension, 160.]
In-ten′tion-al.
In-ten′tioned (*-shund*).
In-ter′, 21, N.
In-ter′ca-lar.
In-ter′ca-la-ry (72) [so Sm. Wr. Wb. Gd.; *in-ter-kal′a-ry*, Wk. 155.]
In-ter′ca-late, 21, N.; 73.
In-ter′ca-lāt-ed, 183.
In-ter′ca-lāt-ing.
In-ter-ca-la′tion.
In-ter-cede′, 169.
In-ter-cēd′ed, 183.
In-ter-cēd′ent
In-ter-cēd′er.
In-ter-cēd′ing.
In-ter-cept′.
In-ter-cept′ed.
In-ter-cept′er.
In-ter-cept′ing.
In-ter-cep′tion.
In-ter-ces′sion (*-sesh′-un*), 46, 171.
In-ter-ces′sion-al(*-sesh′-un-*).
In-ter-ces′sor, 88.
In-ter-ces′so-ry, 86.
In′ter-chānge, *n.* 161.
In-ter-chānge′, *v.* 161.
In-ter-chānge-a-bil′i-ty.
In-ter-chānge′a-ble, 164.
In-ter-chānge′a-bly.
In-ter-chānged′, 183.
In-ter-cip′i-ent.
In-ter-clude′.
In-ter-clūd′ed.
In-ter-clūd′ing.
In-ter-clu′sion (*-zhun*).
In-ter-co-lum-ni-a′tion.
In-ter-cos′tal, 72.
In′ter-cōurse (*-kōrs*).
In′ter-dict, *n.* 161.
In-ter-dict′, *v.* 161.
In-ter-dict′ed.
In-ter-dict′ing.
In-ter-dic′tion.
In-ter-dict′ĭve, 84.
In-ter-dict′o-ry, 86.
In′ter-est, *n.* & *v.*
In′ter-est-ed.
In′ter-est-ing [*not* in-ter-est′ing, 126, 153.]
In-ter-fa′cial (*-shal*).
In-ter-fēre′, 171.
In-ter-fēred′, 183.
In-ter-fēr′ence.
In-ter-fēr′er.
In-ter-fēr′ing.
In′ter-im.
In-te′ri-or, 49, N.
In-ter-ject′.
In-ter-ject′ed.
In-ter-ject′ing.
In-ter-jec′tion.
In-ter-jec′tion-al.
In-ter-lace′.
In-ter-laced′ (*-lāst′*).
In-ter-lā̧ç′ing, 183.
In-ter-lard′.
In-ter-lard′ed.
In-ter-lard′ing.
In′ter-lēaf [pl. In′ter-lēaves (*-lēvz*), 193.]
In-ter-lēave′.
In-ter-lēaved′, 183.
In-ter-lēav′ing.
In-ter-line′.
In-ter-lin′e-al.
In-ter-lin′e-ar, 72, 169.
In-ter-lin-e-a′tion.
In-ter-lined′, 183.
In-ter-līn′ing.
In-ter-loc′u-tor [so Sm. Wb. Gd.; *in-ter-lok′-u-tur*, or *in-ter-lo-ku′-tur*, Wr.; *in-ter-lo-ku′tur*, or *in-ter-lok′-u-tur*, Wk. 155.]
In-ter-loc′u-to-ry, 86.
In-ter-lope′.
In-ter-loped′ (*-lōpt′*).
In-ter-lōp′er, 183.
In-ter-lōp′ing.
In′ter-lude.
In-ter-lūd′ed.
In-ter-lu′nar.
In-ter-lu′na-ry, 72.
In-ter-măr′riage (*-rij*), 171.
In-ter-măr′rĭed.
In-ter-măr′ry.
In-ter-măr′ry-ing.
In-ter-med′dle, 164.
In-ter-med′dled (*-med′-ld*).
In-ter-med′dler.
In-ter-med′dling.
In-ter-me′di-al [so Sm. Wr. Wb. Gd.; *in-ter-me′di-al*, or *in-ter-me′-ji-al*, Wk. 155.]
In-ter-me′di-a-ry, 72.
In-ter-me′di-ate, 73.
In-ter′mi-na-ble, 21, N.; 164, 169.
In-ter-min′gle (*-ming′-gl*), 164.
In-ter-min′gled (*-ming′-gld*), 183.
In-ter-min′gling (*-ming′-*).
In-ter-mis′sion (*-mish′-un*).
In-ter-mis′sĭve, 84.
In-ter-mit′.
In-ter-mit′ted, 176.
In-ter-mit′tent.
In-ter-mit′ting.
In-ter-mix′.
In-ter-mixed′ (*-mikst′*).
In-ter-mix′ing.
In-ter-mixt′ure, 91.
In-ter′nal, 21, N.
In-ter′nal-ly, 170.
In-ter-nă′tion-al (*-nash′un-al*) [so Sm. Wr.; *in-ter-na′shun-al*, Wb. Gd. 155.]
In-ter-ne′cĭne, 152.
In-ter-pel-la′tion.
In-ter-plēad′ [Enter-plead, 201, 203.]
In-ter-plēad′ed.
In-ter-plēad′er.
In-ter-plēad′ing.
In-ter′po-late (21, N.; 105) [so Wk. Sm. Wr.; *in′ter-po-lāt*, or *in-ter′po-lāt*, Gd. 155.]
In-ter′po-lāt-ed.
In-ter′po-lāt-ing.
In-ter-po-la′tion.
In-ter′po-lāt-or.
In-ter-pose′ (*-pōz′*).
In-ter-posed′ (*-pōzd′*).
In-ter-pōs′er (*-pōz′-*), 183.
In-ter-pōs′ing (*pōz′-*).
In-ter-po-sĭ′tion (*-zish′-un*).
In-ter′pret, 21, N.
In-ter′pret-a-ble, 164.
In-ter-pre-ta′tion.
In-ter′pre-tāt-ĭve [so Wk. Sm. Wr.; *in-ter′-pre-ta-tiv*, Wb. Gd. 155.]
In-ter-ra′di-al, 224.
In-terred′ (*-terd′*), 21, N.
In-ter-reg′num (L.).
In-ter′ring, 176.
In-tĕr′ro-gate, 73, 170.
In-tĕr′ro gāt-ed.
In-tĕr-ro-ga′tion.
In-ter-rog′a-tĭve.
In-tĕr′ro-gāt-or.
In-ter-rog′a-to-ry, 86.
In-ter-rupt′.

In-ter-rupt'ed.
In-ter-rupt'er.
In-ter-rupt'ing.
In-ter-rup'tion.
In-ter-sect'.
In-ter-sect'ed.
In-ter-sect'ing.
In-ter-sec'tion.
In-ter-sperse', 21, N.
In-ter-spersed' (*-sperst'*)
In-ter-spers'ing.
In-ter-sper'sion.
In-ter-stel'lar, 170.
In-ter-stel'la-ry, 72.
In'ter-stĭce, *or* In-ter'-stĭce (*-stis*) (169) [so Wk Wr. Gd., *in-ter'-stis*, Sm. 155.]
In-ter-stĭ'tial (*-stish'al*).
In-ter-text'ure, 91.
In-ter-trop'ic-al, 108.
In-ter-twine'.
In-ter-twined', 183.
In-ter-twīn'ing.
In-ter-twist'.
In-ter-twist'ed.
In-ter-twist'ing.
In'ter-val, 72.
In-ter-vene'.
In-ter-vened', 183.
In-ter-vēn'er.
In-ter-vēn'ing.
In-ter-ven'tion.
In'ter-view (*-vū*).
In-ter-wēave'.
In-ter-wēaved', 183.
In-ter-wēav'ing.
In-ter-wove'.
In-ter-wōv'en (*-wōv'n*).
In-test'a-ble, 164.
In-test'a-cy, 169.
In-test'ate, 73.
In-tes'tin-al.
In-tes'tĭne, 152.
In-thrâll' (179) [In-thral, Sm. — En-thrall, 201, 203.]
In-thrâlled' (*-thrawld'*).
In-thrâll'ing.
In-thrâl'ment (178) [In-thrallment, Wb. Gd. 203.]
In'ti-ma-cy, 169.
In'ti-mate, *a.* & *v.* 73.
In'ti-māt-ed, 183.
In'ti-māt-ing.
In-ti-ma'tion.
In-tim'i-date, 169.
In-tim'i-dāt-ed.
In-tim'i-dāt-ing.
In-tim-i-da'tion.
[Intire, 201, 203. — *See* Entire.]

[Intitle, 201, 203. — *See* Entitle.]
In'to (*-too*), 16, 19.
In-tol'er-a-ble, 164.
In-tol'er-ance, 169.
In-tol'er-ant.
In'to-nate.
In'to-nāt-ed.
In'to-nāt-ing.
In-to-na'tion.
In-tox'i-cate, 169.
In-tox'i-cāt-ed, 183.
In-tox'i-cāt-ing.
In-tox-i-ca'tion.
In-trac-ta-bil'i-ty.
In-trac'ta-ble, 164, 169.
In-tra'dos.
[Intrance', 203.—*See* Entrance'.]
In-tran'si-tĭve, 84.
In-trench', 15, 44.
In-trenched' (*-trencht'*), 165; Note C, p 34.
In-trench'ing.
In-trench'ment.
In-trep'id, 170.
In-tre-pid'i-ty.
In'tri-ca-cy, 169.
In'tri-cate, 73, 78.
In-trigue' (*-trēg'*), 168.
In-trigued' (*-trēgd'*).
In-trigu'er (*-trēg'-*).
In-trigu'ing (*-trēg'-*).
In-trin'sic, 109.
In-trin'sic-al, 108.
In-tro-ces'sion (*-sesh'-un*).
In-tro-duce'.
In-tro-duced' (*-dūst'*).
In-tro-dūç'er.
In-tro-dūç'ing.
In-tro-duc'tion.
In-tro-duc'tĭve, 84.
In-tro-duc'to-ry, 86.
In-tro'it [so Sm. Wr.; *in-troit'*, Wb. Gd. 155.]
In-tro-mis'sion (*-mish'-un*).
In-tro-mit'.
In-tro-mit'ted, 176.
In-tro-mit'ting.
In-trorse'.
In-tro-spec'tion.
In-tro-spec'tĭve.
In-tro-sus-cep'tion.
In-tro-ver'sion.
In-tro-vert', 21, N.
In-tro-vert'ed.
In-tro-vert'ing.
In-trude' (*-trood'*).
In-trud'ed (*-trood'-*).
In-trud'er (*-trood'-*).
In-trud'ing (*-trood'-*).

In-tru'sion (*-troo'zhun*).
In-tru'sĭve (*-troo'-*).
In-trust', 22.
In-trust'ed.
In-trust'ing.
In-tu-ĭ'tion (*-ish'un*).
In-tu'i-tĭve, 84, 169.
In-tu-mesce' (*-mes'*), 171.
In-tu-mesced' (*-mest'*).
In-tu-mes'cing, 183.
In-tu-mes'cence, 171.
In-tus-sus-cep'tion.
In-twine' [Entwine, 201, 203.]
In-twined', 183.
In-twīn'ing.
In-um'brate.
In-um'brāt-ed, 183.
In-um'brāt-ing.
In-un'date.
In-un'dāt ed.
In-un'dāt-ing.
In-un-da'tion.
In-ure', 26.
In-ured', 165, 183.
In-ūr'ing.
In-ure'ment.
In-urn', 21.
In-urned' (*-urnd'*).
In-urn'ing.
In-u-til'i-ty, 108, 169.
In-vade' (23), *v.* to enter with a hostile army. [*See* Inveighed, 160.]
In-vād'ed, 183.
In-vād'er.
In-vād'ing.
In-vag-i-na'tion (*-vaj-*).
In-val'id (161), *a.* of no force; weak.
In'va-lid, *or* In-va-lid' (*-lēd*) [*in'va-lid*, Wb. Gd.; *in-va-lēd'*, Wk. Sm. Wr. 155] (161), *n.* one who is weak, or infirm.
In-val'i-date, 73, 169.
In-val'i-dāt-ed, 183.
In-val'i-dāt-ing.
In-val-i-da'tion.
In-va-lid'i-ty, 108.
In-val'u-a-ble, 164.
In-vā-ri-a-bil'i-ty.
In-va'ri-a-ble, 49, N.; 164.
In-va'sion (*-zhun*).
In-va'sĭve, 84.
In-vec'tĭve.
In-veigh' (*-va'*), 162.
In-veighed' (*-vād'*), *v.* did inveigh, or rail. [*See* Invade, 160.]
In-veigh'er (*-va'-*).

In-veigh'ing (*-va'-*).
In-vēi'gle (*-ve'gl*), 164, 169.
In-vēi'gled (*-ve'gld*).
In-vēi'gler.
In-vēi'gling.
In-vent', 15.
In-vent'ed.
[In-vent-er, 203.—*See* Inventor.]
In-vent'ing.
In-ven'tion.
In-vent'ĭve, 84.
In-vent'or (88) [In-vent-er, 203.]
In'ven-to-ry (86) [*not* in-ven'to-ry.]
In-verse', 21, N.
In-ver'sion.
In-vert', 21, N.
In-ver'te-brate, 72.
In-ver'te-brāt-ed.
In-vert'ed.
In-vert'ing.
In-vest', 15.
In-vest'ed.
In-ves'ti-ga-ble, 164.
In-ves'ti-gate, 169.
In-ves'ti-gāt-ed, 183.
In-ves'ti-gāt-ing.
In-ves-ti-ga'tion.
In-ves'ti-gāt-or.
In-vest'ing.
In-vest'i-ture.
In-vest'ment.
In-vet'er-a-cy, 169.
In-vet'er-ate, 73.
In-vid'i-oŭs (169) [so Sm. Wr. Wb. Gd.; *in-vid'i-us*, or *in-vid'-ji-us*, Wk. 155.]
In-vig'o-rate.
In-vig'o-rāt-ed.
In-vig'o-rāt-ing.
In-vig-o-ra'tion.
In-vin-ci-bil'i-ty, 108.
In-vin'ci-ble, 164.
In-vi-o-la-bil'i-ty.
In-vi'o-la-ble, 164.
In-vi'o-late, 73.
In-vis-i-bil'i-ty (*-viz-*), 169.
In-vis'i-ble (*-viz'-*), 164.
In-vi-ta'tion.
In-vīt'a-to-ry, 86.
In-vite', 25.
In-vīt'ed, 183.
In-vīt'er.
In-vīt'ing.
In-vit'ri-fī-a-ble (164) [so Wr. Wb. Gd.; *in-vit-ri-fī'a-bl*, Sm. 155.]
In-vo-ca'tion.
In'voice.
In'voiced (*-voist*).
In'voiç-ing.
In-voke', 24.
In-voked' (*-vōkt'*).
In-vōk'ing, 183.
In-vol'u-cel [so Wb. Gd.; *in'vo-lu-sel*, Wr. 155.]
In-vo-lu'cel-late.
In-vo-lu'cral.
In-vo-lu'crate.
In-vo-lu'cre (*-kur*) (164) [so Wb. Gd.; *in'vo-lu-kur*, Wr. 155.]
In-vo-lu'cred (*-kurd*),
In-vo-lu'cret. [171.
In-vo-lu'crum.
In-vol'un-ta-ry, 72.
In'vo-lute.
In-vo-lūt-ed.
In-vo-lu'tion.
In-volve', 18.
In-volved' (*-volvd'*), 165.
In-volv'ing, 183.
In-vul-ner-a-bil'i-ty.
In-vul'ner-a-ble, 164.
In'ward, *ad.* & *n.*
In'wards (*-wardz*), *ad.* & *n. pl.*
In-wrap' (*-rap'*) (162) [En-wrap, 203.]
In-wrapped' (*-rapt'*), 176
In-wrap'ping.
I'o-date.
Ī-od'ic, 109.
I'o-dīde [Iodid, 203.]
I'o-dīne, 152.
I'o-dize, 202.
I'o-dized, 183.
I'o-dīz-ing.
I'o-doŭs.
Ī-od'u-ret, 79, 89.
I'o-līte, 152.
I'on.
Ī-o'ni-an, 169.
Ī-on'ic, 79, 109.
Ī-o'ta, 72.
Ip-e-cac-u-an'ha (116, 171) [so Sm. Wr. Wb. Gd.; *ip-e-kak-u-a'na*, Wk. 155.]

☞ This word is often abridged, in common discourse, to *ip'e-cac*.

Ī-ras-ci-bil'i-ty, 108, 169.
Ī-ras'ci-ble, 164, 171.
Ire (*īr*), 25, 163.
Ire'ful (*-fŏŏl*).
I'ren-arch (*-ark*).
Ī-ren'ic-al.
I'ri-an, 169.
I'ri-dal, 72, 78.
Ĭr-i-des'cence, 39, 171.
Ĭr-i-des'cent [so Wr. Wb. Gd.; *ī-ri-des'sent*, Sm. 155.]
Ī-rid'i-um, 169.
I'ris (49, N.) [L. pl. *Ĭr'-i-dēs* (*-dēz*); Eng. pl. I'ris-es (*-ez*), 198.]
I'ri-sāt-ed.
I'ri-scope.
I'rised (*-rist*).
I'rish, 49, N.
I'rish-ism (*-izm*).
Ĭr'ish-ry.
Irk'some (*-sum*), 21, N.
I'ron (*i'urn*), 171.
I'roned (*i'urnd*).
I'ron-er (*i'urn-*).
Ī-ron'ic, 109.
Ī-ron'ic-al, 108.
I'ron-ing (*i'urn-*).
I'ron-mon'ger (*i'urn-mung'gur*), 205, Exc. 3.
I'ron-mon-ger-y (*i'urn-mung-gur-y*), 171.
I'ron-y (*i'urn-y*) (161), *a.* made of iron;—resembling iron.
I'ron-y (*i'run-y*) (161), *n.* a species of ridicule in which what is said is contrary to what is meant.
Ĭr-ra'di-ance.
Ĭr-ra'di-an-cy.
Ĭr-ra'di-ant.
Ĭr-ra'di-ate, 169.
Ĭr-ra'di-āt-ed, 183.
Ĭr-ra'di-āt-ing.
Ĭr-ra-di-a'tion.
Ĭr-ra'tion-al (*-rash'un-al*) [so Sm. Wr.; *ĭr-rash'o-nal*, Wk.; *ĭr-ra'shun-al*, or *ĭr-rash'un-al*, Gd. 155.]
Ĭr-ră-tion-al'i-ty (*-rash-un-*), 108, 169, 171.
Ĭr-re-clāim'a-ble, 164.
Ĭr-rec-on-cīl'a-ble, 164.
Ĭr-rec'on-ciled.
Ĭr-re-cov'er-a-ble (*-kuv'-ur-a-bl*), 164, 169.
Ĭr-re-deem'a-ble, 164.
Ĭr-re-dūç'i-ble, 164, 169.
Ĭr-ref-ra-ga-bil'i-ty.
Ĭr-ref'ra-ga-ble (164) [so Sm. Wr., *ĭr-ref'ra-ga-bl*, or *ĭr-re-frag'a-bl*, Wk., *ĭr-re-fra'-ga-bl*, or *ĭr-ref'ra-ga-bl*, Gd. 155.]

☞ Walker remarks of the first pronunciation which he gives (*ir-ref′ra-ga-bl*): "If I am not much mistaken, it has not only the best usage on its side, but the clearest analogy to support it."

Ĭr-re-fūt′a-ble, *or* Ir-ref′-u-ta-ble (164) [so Wr.; *ĭr-re-fūt′a-bl*, Wk. Sm.; *ĭr-ref′u-ta-bl*, or *ĭr-re-fūt′a-bl*, Gd. 155.]

☞ Though Walker, in deference to all the authorities that preceded him, adopts the pronunciation *ir-re-fut′a-bl*, he says that analogy is in favor of *ir-ref′u-ta-bl*.

Ĭr-reg′u-lar, 72, 89.
Ĭr-reg-u-lăr′i-ty, 108.
Ĭr-rel′a-tĭve, 84.
Ĭr-rel′e-vant.
Ĭr-re-lig′ion (*-lij′un*).
Ĭr-re-lig′ioŭs (*-lij′us*).
Ĭr-re′me-a-ble, 164.
Ĭr-re-me′di-a-ble, 164.
Ĭr-re-mis′si-ble, 164.
Ĭr-re-mis′sĭve.
Ĭr-re-mov′a-ble (*moov′-a-bl*), 164.
Ĭr-re-mu′ner-a-ble, 164.
Ĭr-rep-a-ra-bil′i-ty, 169.
Ĭr-rep′a-ra-ble (164, 169) [*not* ir-re-pêr′a-bl, 153.]
Ĭr-rep′a-ra-bly.
Ĭr-re-pēal-a-bil′i-ty.
Ĭr-re-pēal′a-ble, 164, 169.
Ĭr-re-plev′i-a-ble, 164.
Ĭr-re-plev′i-sa-ble, 164.
Ĭr-rep-re-hen′si-ble, 164.
Ĭr-re-press′i-ble, 164, 169.
Ĭr-re-prōach′a-ble, 164.
Ĭr-re-prov′a-ble (*-proov′-a-bl*), 164.
Ĭr-re-sist-i-bil′i-ty (*-zist-*), 108, 169.
Ĭr-re-sist′i-ble (*-zist′-*), 164.
Ĭr-res′o-lu-ble (*-rez′-*), 164.
Ĭr-res′o-lute (*-rez′-*).
Ĭr-res-o-lu′tion (*-rez-*).
Ĭr-re-solv-a-bil′i-ty (*-zolv-*), 108, 169.
Ĭr-re-solv′a-ble (*-zolv′-*), 164.
Ĭr-re-spect′ĭve, 84.
Ĭr-res′pi-ra-ble, 164.
Ĭr-re-spon-si-bil′i-ty.
Ĭr-re-spon′si-ble, 164.
Ĭr-re-triēv′a-ble, 164.
Ĭr-rev′er-ence, 169.
Ĭr-rev′er-ent.
Ĭr-re-vers′i-ble, 164.
Ĭr-rev-o-ca-bil′i-ty.
Ĭr-rev′o-ca-ble.
Ĭr′ri-gate, 78, 169.
Ĭr′ri-gāt-ed.
Ĭr′ri-gāt-ing.
Ĭr-ri-ga′tion.
Ĭr-rig′u-oŭs, 108.
Ĭr-ris′i-ble (*-riz′-*), 164.
Ĭr-rĭ′sion (*-rizh′un*).
Ĭr-ri-ta-bil′i-ty.
Ĭr′ri-ta-ble, 164, 169.
Ĭr′ri-tant.
Ĭr′ri-tate, 78, 169.
Ĭr′ri-tāt-ed, 183.
Ĭr′ri-tāt-ing.
Ĭr-ri-ta′tion.
Ĭr′ri-tāt-ĭve [so Sm. Wr.; *ĭr′ri-ta-tiv*, Wb. Gd. 155.]
Ĭr′ri-ta-to-ry (72) [so Wr. Wb. Gd.; *ĭr′ri-tāt-o-ry*, Sm. 155.]
Ĭr-ro-ra′tion.
Ĭr-rupt′ed.
Ĭr-rup′tion.
Ĭr-rup′tĭve, 84.
Is (*iz*), 174.
Ī-sa-gog′ic (*goj′-*), 109.
Ī-sa-gog′ic-al (*goj′-*), 108.
Ī′sa-gon.
Is-chi-ad′ic (*-kĭ-*), 52, 109.
Is-chi-ag′ra (*-kĭ-*).
Is-chu-ret′ic (*-ku-*).
Is-chu′ri-a (*-ku′-*).
Is′chu-ry (*-ku-*).
I′sin-glass (*-zing-* (171) [Isingglass, Sm. 203.]
Is′lam (*iz′-*), 171.
Is′lam-ism (*iz′lam-izm*).
Is-lam-it′ic (*iz-*), 109.
Is′land (*i′land*), 162, 171.
Is′land-er (*i′land-*).
Isle (*īl*), 162, 171.
Isl′et (*īl′et*).
I′so-bare (*-bêr*).
Ī-so-băr-o-met′ric.
Ī-so-chi′mal (*-kĭ′-*) [Isocheimal, Wb. Gd. 203.]
Ī-so-chi′men-al (*-kĭ′-*) [so Gd.; *ī-so-kim′e-nal*, Wr. 155.]
Ī-so-chi′mene (*-kĭ′-*).
Ī-soch′ro-nal (*-sok′-*).
Ī-soch′ro-nism (*-sok′ro-nizm*), 136, 171.
Ī-soch′ro-noŭs (*-sok′-*).
Ī-so-cli′nal [so Wr.; *ī-sok′li-nal*, Gd. 155.]
Ī-sod′o-mon.
Ī-so-dȳ-nam′ic, 109.
Ī-so-ge-o-ther′mal.
Ī-so-gon′ic.
Ī-sog′ra-phy, 108.
Ī-so-hy′e-tose.
Is′o-late (*iz′o-lāt*) [so Wk. Sm. Wr.; *is′o-lāt*, Wb. Gd. 155.] [*not* i′so-lāt, 153.]
Is′o-lāt-ed (*iz′-*).
Is′o-lāt-ing (*iz′-*).
Is-o-la′tion (*iz-*).
Ī-sol′o-goŭs.
Ī-so-mĕr′ic.
Ī-som′er-ism (*-izm*), 136.
Ī-so-met′ric, 109.
Ī-so-met′ric-al, 108.
Ī-so-mor′phĭsm (*-fizm*)
Ī-so-mor′phoŭs.
Ī-son′o-my, 108.
Ī-so-pĕr-i-met′ric-al.
Ī-so-pe-rim′e-try, 169
I′so-pod.
Ī-sop′o-doŭs.
I′so-pyre.
Ī-sos′ce-lēs (*-lēz*), 171.
Ī-so-stem′o-nous.
Ī-soth′er-al.
I′so-thēre.
I′so-therm.
Ī-so-therm′al, 21, N.
Ī-soth-e-rom′brose.
Ī-so-ton′ic.
Is′rā-el-īte (*iz′rā-*) (72) [so Sm.; *iz′ra-el-īt*, Wr. Wb. Gd. 155.]
Is-rā-el-īt′ic (*iz-*), 72, 109.
Is-rā-el-īt′ish (*iz-*).
Is′su-a-ble (*ish′shoo-a-bl*), 169, 183.
Is′sue (*ish′shoo*) (171) [*ish′oo*, Sm. (*See* § 26); *ish′shu*, Wr. Wb. Gd. 155.]
Is′sued (*ish′shood*), 183.
Is′su-er (*ish′shoo-*).
Is′su-ing (*ish′shoo-*).
Isth′mi-an (*ist′-*), 171.
Isth′mus (*ist′-*), 41, 171.
It, 16, 41.
Ī-tal′ian (*-yan*) (51, 79) [*not* ī-tal′yan, 153.]
Ī-tal′ic (170) [*not* ī-tal′-ic, 153.]
Ī-tal′i-cize, 202.
Ī-tal′i-cized, 183.
Ī-tal′i-cīz-ing.
Itch, 16, 44.
Itched (*icht*), Note C, p. 34.
Itch′ing.
Itch′y.

I'tem.
It'er-ate.
It'er-āt-ed, 183.
It'er-āt-ing.
It'er-a-tion.
It'er-āt-ĭve (84) [so Sm.; *it'er-a-tiv*, Wr. Wb. Gd. 155.]
Ī-tin'er-an-cy, 169.
Ī-tin'er-ant.
Ī-tin'er-a-ry, 72.
Ī-tin'er-ate.
Ī-tin'er-āt-ed.
Ī-tin'er-āt-ing.
Its, 16, 39, 41.
It-self'.
[I t t r i a, 293.—*See* Yttria.]
[I t t r i u m, 203.—*See* Yttrium.]
Ī-u'li-dan [so Wr.; *yoo'-li-dan*, Sm. 155.]
I'vĭed [I v y e d, 203.]
I'vo-ry, 93.
I'vy, 169.
[I v y e d, 203.—*See* Ivied.]
I'vy-man'tled (*-tld*), 205.]

J.

Jab'ber, 66, 170.
Jab'bered (*-burd*), 150.
Jab'ber-er, 77.
Jab'ber-ing.
Jab'i-ru (*-roo*).
Jac'a-mar.
Ja'cent.
Ja'cinth.
Jack, 181.
Jack-a-dan'dy.
Jack'āl [so Sm. Wr. Wb. Gd.; *jak-āl'*, Wk. 155.]
Jack'a-lent.
Jack'an-ape, *or* Jack'an-apes.
Jack'ăss, 12, 131.
Jack'block, 206.
Jack'boots, *n. pl.* [so Sm. Wr. Wb. Gd.; *jak-boots'*, Wk. 155.]
Jack'daw.
Jack'et, 76.
Jack'et-ed.
Jack'-knife (*-nīf*), 162, 206, Exc. 1.
Jack'plane, 206.
Jack'-screw (*-skroo*), 206, Exc. 3.
Jack'straw.
Jac'o-bin.
Jac-o-bin'ic, 109.
Jac-o-bin'ic-al, 108.
Jac'o-bin-ism (*-izm*), 136.
Jac'o-bīte, 152.
Jac-o-bit'ic-al, 108.
Jac'o-bit-ism (*-izm*).
Jā'cob's-lad'der, 205, 213.
Jac'o-net.
Jac-quard' (*-kard'*).
Jac-ta'tion.
Jac-ti-ta'tion.
Jac-u-la'tion.
Jac'u-lāt-or.
Jac'u-la-to-ry (86) [so Wr. Wb. Gd.; *jak'u-lāt-o-ry*, Sm. 155.]
Jade, 23.
Jād'ed, 183.
Jād'ing.
Jād'ish.
Jag (10) [J a g g, 203.]
Jagged (*jagd*) (161, 165), *v.* did jag, or notch.
Jag'ged (*jag'ghed*) (161, 165), *a.* notched, uneven.
Jag'ger (*-gur*), 138.
Jag'gher-y [J a g g e r y, 203.]
Jag'gy (*-ghy*), 138, 170.
Jag'hire (*-hēr*).
Jag-hire-dar' (*-hēr-*).
Jag-u-ar' (122) [*not* jag'-war, *nor* ja'gwar, 153.]
Jäh, 72.
Jāil (23) [G a o l, 203.—*See* Note under *Gaol.*]
Jāil'er [G a o l e r, 203.]
Jal'ap [*not* jol'up, 153.]
Jam (10), *n.* a conserve of fruit;—a thick bed of stone in a lead mine:—*v.* to squeeze tight; to press. [*See* Jamb, 160.] [J a m b (in the second sense of the noun), 203.]
Jamb (*jam*) (10, 162), *n.* the side piece of a door, fireplace, &c.;—a thick bed of stone in a lead mine. [*See* Jam, 160.] [J a m (in the second sense), 203.]
Jammed (*jamd*), 176.
Jam'ming.
[J a n e, 203.—*See* Jean.]
Jan'gle (*jang'gl*), 54, 164.
Jan'gled (*jang'gld*), 183.
Jan'gler (*jang'-*).
Jan'gling (*jang'-*).
[J a n i s s a r y, 203.—*See* Janizary.]
Jan'i-tor, 88, 169.
Jan-i-za'ri-an.
Jan'i-za-ry (72, 171) [J a n i s s a r y, 203.]
Jan'sen-ism (*-izm*).
Jan'sen-ist.
[J a n t, 203.—*See* Jaunt.]
Jänt'i-ly.
Jänt'i-ness.
Jänt'y [J a u n t y, 203.]
Jan'u-a-ry (72) [*not* jen'u-a-ry, 127, 153.]
Ja-pan'.
Jap-an-ese' (*-ēz'*), *a.* & *n. sing.* & *pl.* 122, 171.
Ja-panned' (*-pand'*), 176.
Ja-pan'ner.
Ja-pan'ning.
Ja-phet'ic, 109.
Jar, 11, 49, 135.
Jăr-a-rac'a.
Jardes (*jardz*), *n. pl.* [so Wr. Wb. Gd., *zhardz*, Sm. 155.]
Jar'gon, 11, 86.
Jar-go-nelle' (*-nel'*), 114.
Jarred (*jard*), 165, 176.
Jar'ring.
Ja'sey (*-zy*), 169.
Jas'hawk.
Jas'mĭne (*jaz'min*, or *jas'min*) (152) [so Wr.; *jaz'min*, Wk. Sm.; *jas'min*, Wb. Gd. 155.] [J e s s a-m i n e, 203.]
Jas'per, 10, 77.
Jas'per-āt-ed.
Jas'per-y, 93.
Jas-pid'e-an, 110.
Jäun'dĭce (*-dis*), 169, 171.
Jäun'diced (*-dist*).
Jäunt (11) [J a n t, 203.]
Jäunt'ed.
Jäunt'ing.
[J a u n t y, 203.—*See* Janty.]
Jav-a-nese' (*-nēz'*), *a.*
Jăve'lin, 145, 171.
Jaw, 17, 45.

Jaw′bone, 206.
Jawed (*jawd*), *a.*
Jaw′y.
Jāy, 23.
Jaz′er-ant.
Jĕal′oŭs, 15, 100.
Jĕal′oŭs-y.
Jēan (23) [so Wb. Gd.; *jĕn*, Wr. 155.] [Jane, 203.]
Jēars (*jērz*), *n. pl.* [Jeers, 203.]
Jeer, 13.
Jeered (*jērd*), 165.
Jeer′er.
Jeer′ing.
Jeers (*jērz*), *n. pl.* [Jears, 203.]
Je-ho′vah, 72.
Je-ho′vist.
Je-june′ (*-joon′*) [so Wk. Wr.; *je-jūn′*, Wb. Gd.; *jed′joon*, Sm. 155.]
Jel′lied, 170, 171.
Jel′ly (93, 170) [Gelly, 203. — *See* Note under *Gelly*.]
Jen′net-ing [Geniting, 203.]
Jen′ny, 66, 170.
Jĕof′āil (*jef′al*) [so Sm. Gd.; *jef′al*, Wr. 155.]
Jĕop′ard (*jep′ard*), 15.
Jĕop′ard-ed.
Jĕop′ard-ing.
Jĕop′ard-ize, 202.
Jĕop′ard-ized, 183.
Jĕop′ard-īz-ing.
Jĕop′ard-y, 171.
Jer′bo-a, 21, N.
Jer-e-mi′ade, 171.
[Jerfalcon, 203. — *See* Gerfalcon.]
Jerk, 21, N.
Jerked (*jerkt*), 165; Note C. p. 34.
Jer′kin (148), *n.* a jacket.
Jerk′ing (141, 148), *part.* from *Jerk*.
Jer′sey (*-zy*), 21, N.
Jess, 15, 174.
Jes′sa-mīne [Jasmine, 203.]
Jes′se.
Jessed (*jest*) (160), *a.* having jesses on.
Jest (15, 160), *n.* a joke: — *v.* to joke.
Jest′ed.
Jest′er.
Jest′ing.
Jes′u-it (*jez′-*).
Jes-u-it′ic (*jez-*), 109.
Jes-u-it′ic-al (*jez-*), 108.
Jes′u-it-ism (*jez′u-it-izm*), 136.
Jet, 15.
Jet-d′eau (Fr.) (*zhā-do′*) [pl. *Jets-d′eau* (*zhā-do′*, 198).]
Jet′sam [Jetson, Jettison, 203.]
Jet′tee, *n.* a projection in a building; — a kind of pier. [Jetty (in the second sense), Jutty (in both senses), 203.]
Jet′ty, *n.* a kind of pier; a mole. [Jettee, 203.]
Jet′ty (176), *a.* made of jet; black as jet.
Jeu d′esprit (Fr.) (*zhoo des-prē′*).
Jew (*ju*) (26, 171) [so Wk. Wb. Gd.; *j′oo*, Sm. (*See* § 26); *ju*, or *joo*, Wr. 155.]
Jew′el (*ju′-*).
Jew′elled (*ju′eld*) [Jeweled, Wb. Gd. 203. — *See* 177, and Note E, p. 70.]
Jew′el-ler (*ju′-*) [Jeweler, Wb. Gd. 203.]
[Jewellery, 203. — *See* Jewelry.]
Jew′el-ling (*ju′-*) [Jeweling, Wb. Gd. 203.]
Jew′el-ly (*ju′-*).
Jew′el-ry (*ju′-*) [Jewellery, 203.]

☞ "*Jewellery* is the more regularly formed word; but *jewelry* is perhaps the more common." *Worcester.* — *Jewelry* is the only form given by Smart, Webster, and Goodrich.

Jew′ess (*ju′-*).
Jew′ish (*ju′-*).
Jew′ry (*ju′-*).
Jew′s-harp (*jūz′-*), 213.
Jez′e-bel.
Jib, 16.
Jibbed (*jibd*), 176.
Jib′bing.
Jib′-boom (206, Exc. 1) [Gib-boom, 203.]
Jif′fy, 66, 170.
Jig, 16.
Jig′ger (*-gur*) (138) [Chigre, Chigger (in the sense of *a kind of insect*), 203. — *See* Chigre.]
Jilt, 16.
Jilt′ed.
Jilt′ing.
Jim′my, 170.
Jin′gle (*jing′gl*) (54, 164) [Gingle, 203.]
Jin′gled (*jing′gld*), 183.
Jin′gling (*jing′-*).
Jip′po.
Job, 18.
Jobbed (*jobd*), 176.
Job′ber.
Job′bing.
Jock′ey, 169.
Jock′eyed (*-id*), 171.
Jock′ey-ing.
Jock′ey-ism (*-izm*).
Jo-cose′, 121.
Joc′u-lar, 72, 89.
Joc-u-lăr′i-ty, 108, 169.
Joc′und.
Jo-cund′i-ty.
Jog, 18.
Jogged (*jogd*), 165, 176.
Jog′ger (*-gur*), 138.
Jog′ging (*-ghing*).
Jog′gle, 164.
Jog′gled (*jog′ld*), 183.
Jog′gling.
Join, 27.
Join′der.
Joined, 165.
Join′er.
Join′er-y.
Join′ing.
Joint, 27.
Joint′ed.
Joint′er.
Joint′ing.
Joint′ress [Jointuress, 203.]
Joint′ure, 91.
Joint′ured (*-yurd*).
Joint′ur-ing (*-yur-*).
Joint′ur-ess [Jointress, 203.]
Joist, 27.
Joist′ed.
Joist′ing.
Joke, 24.
Joked (*jōkt*), 165.
Jōk′er.
Jōk′ing.
Jole (24) [Jowl, 206.]
Jol′li-ty, 108, 169.
Jol′ly, 66, 170.
Jōlt, 24.
Jōlt′ed.
Jōlt′er.

Jōlt′ing.
Jon′quille, *or* Jon′quil (*jon′kwil*) [so Wr. Wb. Gd.; *jun′kwil*, Wk.; *jung′kwil*, Sm. 155.]

☞ Walker and Smart give only the French form of this word (*jonquille*); Webster and Goodrich give only the Anglicized form (*jonquil*); Worcester gives both, but prefers *jonquille*.

Jos′tle (*jos′l*), 162.
Jos′tled (*jos′ld*), 183.
Jos′tling (*jos′ling*).
Jot, 18.
Jot′ted, 176.
Jot′ting.
Jounce, 28.
Jounced (*jounst*), 165.
Jounç′ing.
Jour′nal (*jur′-*), 21, 72.
Jour′nal-ism (*jur′nal-izm*), 133, 136.
Jour′nal-ist (*jur′-*).
Jour′nal-ize (*jur′-*), 202.
Jour′nal-ized (*jur′-*).
Jour′nal-īz-ing (*jur′-*).
Jour′ney (*jur′ny*), 98, 169.
Jour′neyed (*jur′nid*).
Jour′ney-er (*jur′-*).
Jour′ney-ing (*jur′-*).
Jour′ney-man (*jur′-*).
Joŭst (*just*), *n.* & *v.* [*not* joost, 153.] [Just, 203.]

☞ Walker and Smart prefer *joust*; Webster and Goodrich *just*. Worcester prefers *just* for the noun.

Joŭst′ed.
Joŭst′er.
Joŭst′ing.
Jo′vi-al, 72, 78.
Jo-vi-al′i-ty, 108, 169.
Jōwl [so Sm. Wr.; *joul*, Wb. Gd. 155] [Jole, Choule, 203.]
Jowl′er (*joul′ur*) [so Sm. Wb. Gd.; *jōl′ur*, Wk.; *jōl′ur*, or *joul′ur*, Wr. 155.]
Joy, 27.
Joyed (*joid*), 165.
Joy′ful (*-fŏŏl*), 180.
Joy′ful-ly (*-fŏŏl-*).
Joy′ing.
Joy′oŭs.
Ju′bi-lant.
Ju-bi-la′te (L.) (163) [so Sm. Wr.; *ju-bi-lā′te*, Wb. Gd. 155.]
Ju-bi-la′tion.
Ju′bi-lee.
Ju-da′ic, 109.
Ju-da′ic-al, 108.
Ju′dā-ism (*-izm*) (72) [so Wk. Sm.; *ju′da-izm*, Wr. Wb. Gd. 155.]
Ju′dā-ist.
Ju-dā-ist′ic.
Ju-dā-ī-za′tion.
Ju′dā-ize, 72, 202.
Ju′dā-ized, 183.
Ju′dā-iz-er.
Ju′dā-iz-ing.
Judge (*juj*), 22, 45.
Judged (*jujd*), 165, 183.
[Judgement, 203.—*See* Judgment.]
Judg′er.
Judg′ing.
Judg′ment (185) [Judgement, Sm. 203.]
Ju′di-ca-to-ry [so Wr. Wb. Gd.; *ju′di-cā-tur-y*, Wk. Sm. 155.]
Ju′di-ca-ture (*-tūr*) [so Wr. Wb. Gd.; *ju′di-cā-tūr*, Wk. Sm. 155.]
Ju-dĭ′cial (*-dish′al*).
Ju-dĭ′ci-a-ry (*-dish′i-a-ry*) [so Wr.; *ju-dish′-′ar-y* (*See* § 26), Sm.; *ju-dish′a-ry*, Wk. Wb. Gd. 155.]
Ju-dĭ′cioŭs (*-dish′us*).
Jug, 22.
Ju′gāt-ed.
Jug′gle, 164.
Jug′gled (*jug′ld*), 183.
Jug′gler.
Jug′gler-y.
Jug′gling.
Ju′gu-lar, 72, 89, 108.
Jūice (*jūs*), 26, 39.
Jūi′ci-ness, 186.
Jūi′cy, 93.
Ju′jube, 26.
Ju′lep, 26, 76.
Jūl′ian (*-yan*), 51.
Ju′lus.
Ju-ly′.
Ju′mart.
Jum′ble, 164.
Jum′bled (*jum bld*).
Jum′bler.
Jum′bling.
Jump, 22.
Jumped (*jumpt*), 165.
Jump′er.
Jump′ing.
[Juncate, 203.—*See* Junket.]
Junc′tion (*jungk′-*).
Junc′ture (*junkt′yur*), 44, N. 1; 91, 171.
June, 26.
Jun′gle (*jung′gl*), 164.
Jun′gly (*jung′-*).
Jūn′ior (*jūn′yur*) [so Wb. Gd.; *jūn′yur*, or *ju′ni-ur*, Wr.; *ju′ni-ur*, Wk.; *j′oo′ni-ur* (*See* § 26), Sm. 155.]
Jūn-iŏr′i-ty (*-yŏr′-*), 108.
Ju′ni-per, 77, 78.
Junk (*jungk*), 22, 54.
Junk′et (*jungk′-*), *n.* & *v.* [Juncate, *n.* 203.]
Junk′et-ed.
Junk′et-ing.
Ju′no, 26, 127.
Jun′ta (Sp.), 154.
Jun′to (Sp.) (154) [pl. Jun′tōs (*-tōz*), 192.]
Ju′pi-ter, 77, 78.
Jup-pon′ [so Sm. Wb. Gd.; *jup-pon′*, or *jup′pon*, Wr. 155.]
Ju′rat.
Ju′ra-to-ry, 86.
Ju-rid′ic-al, 108.
Ju-rid′ic-al-ly.
Ju-ris-con′sult [so Wk. Wr. Wb. Gd.; *ju′ris-kon-sult*, Sm. 155.]
Ju-ris-dic′tion.
Ju-ris-dic′tion-al.
Ju-ris-dic′tĭve.
Ju-ris-pru′dence (*-proo′-*).
Ju-ris-pru′dent (*-proo′-*).
Ju′rist, 49, N.
Ju′ror, 88.
Ju′ry, 49, N.
Ju′ry-man, 196.
Ju′ry-mȧst, 206.
Just, *a.* & *ad.* (22) [*not* jest, 127, 153.]
Just, *n.* & *v.* [Joust, 203.—*See* Note under *Joust*.]
Just′ed.
Just′ing.
Juste milieu (Fr.) (*zhoost mil-yoo′*), 154.
Jus′tĭce (*-tis*), 169.
Jus-tĭ′ci-a-ry (*-tish′i-a-*

ry) [so Wk. Wr.; *jus-tish'ar-y* (*See* § 26), Sm.; *jus-tish'a-ry*, Wb. Gd. 155.]
Just'i-fī-a-ble, 164.
Just-i-fī-ca'tion.
Just'if-i-cā-tīve [so Sm.; *just-if'i-ka-tiv*, Wk. Wr. Wb. Gd. 155.]
Just'if-i-ca-to-ry [so Sm.; *just-if'i-ka-to-ry*, Wr. Wb. Gd. 155.]
Just'i-fīed, 186.
Just'i-fi-er.
Just'i-fȳ, 94.
Just'i-fȳ-ing.
Jus'tle (*jus'l*), 162).
Jus'tled (*jus'ld*), 183.
Jus'tling (*jus'ling*).
Jut, 22.
Jute, 26.
Jut'ted, 176.
Jut'ting.
Jut'ty [Jettee, 203.]
Ju-ve-nes'cence.
Ju-ve-nes'cent.
Ju've-nīle, 152.
Ju-ve-nil'i-ty, 108, 169.
Jux-ta-po-sī'tion (*-zish'un*), 171, 231.

K.

[Kaffre, Kafir, 203. — *See* Caffre.]
Kale (23), *n.* a kind of cabbage. [*See* Kayle, 160.] [Kail, 203.]
Ka-leid'o-scope, 171.
Ka'lī.
[Kalif, 203. — *See* Caliph.]
Kal'so-mīne, 152.
Kam'a-chi (*-kī*).
Kam'sin [Khamsin, 203.]
[Kan, 203. — *See* Khan.]
Kan-ga-roo' (*kang-*).
Kant'i-an.
Kant'ism (*-izm*), 136.
Kant'ist.
Ka'o-lin [Kaoline, 203.]
Ka'ty-did.
[Kaun, 203. — *See* Khan.]
Kāyle (*kāl*), *n.* a nine-pin; — a kind of game in Scotland. [*See* Kale, 160.]
Keb'lah, 72.
Kec'kle, 164.
Kec'kled (*kek'ld*), 183.
Kec'kling.
Keck'sy, 169.
Keck'y.
Kedge, 15, 45.
Kedged (*kejd*), 165.
Kedg'er, 183.
Kedg'ing.
Keel, 13.
Keel'age.
Keeled (*kēld*), 165.
Keel'er.
Keel'hâul [Keelhale, 203.]
Keel'hâuled, 165.
Keel'hâul-ing.
Keel'ing.
Kĕel'son (*kĕl'sun*) [so Sm. Wb. Gd.; *kēl'son*, Wk.; *kēl'son*, or *kĕl'son*, Wr. 155.]
Keen, 13.
Keen'ness, 66, N.
Keep, 13.
Keep'er, 77.
Keep'ing.
Keg (15) [Cag, 203.]
Kelp, 15.
[Kelt, 203. — *See* Kilt.]
Ken'nel, 66, 170.
Ken'nelled (*-neld*) [Kenneled, Wb. Gd. 203. — *See* 177, and Note E, p. 70.]
Ken'nel-ling [Kenneling, Wb. Gd. 203.]
Ken'tle (164) [Quintal, 203.]
Kent'ledge.
Kept, 15, 142.
Ker'chĭef (*-chif*), 21, N.; 52, 146.
Ker'chĭefed (*-chift*).
Kerf, 21, N.
Kēr-i-che'tib (*-ke'-*) [so Sm.; *kĕr-i-ke'tib*, Wr. 155.]
Ker'mēs (*-mēz*).
Kern, 21, N.
Ker'nel, 21, N.
Ker'nelled (*-neld*) [Kerneled, Wb. Gd. 203. — *See* 177, and Note E, p. 70.]
Ker'nel-ly.
Kĕr'o-sene, 171.
Ker'sey (*-zy*), 21, N.; 169.
Ker'sey-mere (*-zy-*) [Cassimere, 203.]
Kes'trel [Castrel, 203.]
Ketch, 15, 44.
[Ketchup, 203. — *See* Catchup.]
Ket'tle, 164.
Kev'el.
Kex, 15, 39, N.
Kēy (*kē*) (13, 190), *n.* an instrument for fastening and unfastening a lock; — a guide, &c. [*See* Quay, 160.]
Kēy'-bōard, 209.
Kēy'-stone, 24.
[Khamsin, 203. — *See* Kamsin.]
Khan (*kawn*, or *kăn*) [so Wr.; *kawn*, Sm. Wb. Gd. 155.], *n.* in Persia, a governor; in Tartary, a prince. [*See* Can, 160.] [Kan, Kaun, 203.]
Khan'ate (*kawn-*, or *kan-*).
Kibe, 25.
Kibed (*kībd*).
Kib'y, 93, 169.
Kick, 16, 181.
Kicked (*kikt*), 165; Note C, p. 34.
Kick'er.
Kick'ing.
Kick'shaw.
Kid, 16.
Kid'dle (164) [*not* kit'l, *nor* ket'l, 153.]
Kid'dōw, 101.
Kid'ling.
Kid'nap, 10, 16.
Kid'napped (*-napt*), 177.
Kid'nap-per.
Kid'nap-ping.
Kid'ney (98, 169) [pl. Kid'neys (*-niz*), 190.]
Kil'der-kin.
Kill (16, 172), *v.* to put to death. [*See* Kiln, 160.]
Kill'dee, *or* Kill'deer.
Killed (*kild*), 165.
Kill'er.
Kill'ing.
Kiln (*kil*) (162, 171), *n.* a kind of oven for heating or drying any thing. [*See* Kill, 160.]
Kiln'-drīed (*kil'-*), 162.
Kiln'-drȳ (*kil'-*), 162.
Kiln'-drȳ-ing (*kil'-*), 162.
Kil'o-gram (Eng.), *or* *Kil'o-gramme* (Fr.), 203.

Kil'o-li-tre (Fr.) (*-le-tr*) [Kiloliter, 203.]
Kil-ol'i-ter [so Wb. Gd.; *kil'o-lī-tur*, Sm. 155.]
Kil'o-me-tre (Fr.) (*-me'-tr*) (154) [Kilometer, 203.]
Kil-om'e-ter [so Wb. Gd.; *kil'o-mē-tur*, Sm. 155.]
Kilt [Kelt, 203.]
Kilt'ed.
Kim'bo.
Kin, 16.
Kīnd (52, 146) [so Sm. Wr. Wb. Gd.; *kyīnd*, Wk. 155.]
Kīnd-heärt'ed, 206, Exc. 5.
Kin'dle, 164.
Kin'dled (*kin'dld*), 183.
Kin'dler.
Kīnd'li-ness, 186.
Kin'dling.
Kīnd'ly.
Kin'dred, *a.* & *n. sing.* & *pl.*
Kine (*kīn*) (25, 52) [so Wr. Wb. Gd.; *k'īn*, Sm. (*See* § 26), *kyīn*, Wk. 155.]
☞ This word is the old plural of *cow*, and is now obsolete, except in poetry.
Kī-ne-mat'ic, 109.
Kī-ne-mat'ic-al, 108.
Kī-ne-mat'ics.
Kī-ne-sip'a-thist.
Kī-ne-sip'a-thy, 108.
Kī-net'ics.
King, 16, 54.
King'bird, 205.
King'crȧft.
King'cup.
King'dom, 86, 169.
King'fish-er.
King'like, 206.
King'li-ness, 186.
King'ly, 93.
King'pōst, 205.
Kink (*kingk*), 16, 54.
Kin'ka-jou (*king'ka-joo*)
Ki'no.
Kins'man (*kinz'-*), 196.
Kins'wom-an (*kinz'-wŏŏm-an*), 214.
Ki-osk' (*ke-*) (Turkish).
Kip, 16.
Kirsch'was-ser (Ger.) (*kērsh'väs-sur*) [so Wr.; *kērsh'was-sur*, Gd. 154, 155.]
Kir'tle, 21, N.; 164.
Kir'tled (*kir'tld*), 183.
Kiss, 16, 174.
Kissed (*kist*), 165; Note C, p. 34.
Kiss'er.
Kiss'ing.
Kit, 16.
Kit'cat, 52.
Kitch'en, 149.
Kite, 25.
Kit'ling.
Kit'ten (*kit'n*), 149.
Klop-e-ma'ni-a.
Knab (*nab*), 10, 162.
Knabbed (*nabd*), 162, 165.
Knab'bing (*nab'-*), 162, 176.
Knack (*nak*), 10, 162, 182.
Knack'er (*nak'ur*), 162.
Knag (*nag*), 10, 162.
Knagged (*nagd*), 165.
Knag'gi-ness (*nag'ghi-*).
Knag'gy (*nag'ghy*), 138.
Knap'sack (*nap'-*), 162.
Knap'weed (*nap'-*), 162.
[Knarled (*narld*), 203. — *See* Gnarled.]
Knave (*nāv*) (23, 162), *n.* a villain; — the card next below the queen. [*See* Nave, 160.]
Knāv'er-y (*nāv'-*), 162.
Knāv'ish (*nāv'-*), 162.
Knaw'el (*naw'-*), 162.
Knēad (*nēd*) (13, 162), *v.* to work or press together, as dough or clay. [*See* Kneed, *and* Need, 160.]
Knēad'ed (*nēd'-*), 162.
Knēad'er (*nēd'-*), 162.
Knēad'ing (*nēd'-*), 162.
Knee (*nē*), 13, 162.
Kneed (*nēd*), *a.* having knees. [*See* Knead, *and* Need, 160.]
Knee'-deep (*nē'-*), 162, 206, Exc. 5.
Kneel (*nēl*), 162.
Kneeled (*nēld*), 162, 165.
Kneel'er (*nēl'-*), 162.
Kneel'ing (*nēl'-*), 162.
Knee'pan (*nē'-*), 162.
Knell (*nel*), 15, 162, 172.
Knelt (*nelt*), 15, 162.
Knew (*nū*), *v.* did know. [*See* Gnu, *and* New, 160.]
Knick'-knack (*nik'-nak*), 162, 206, Exc. 1.
Knife (*nīf*) (162) [pl. Knīves (*nīvz*), 193.]
Knight (*nīt*) (162), *n.* one admitted to a certain military rank by appropriate ceremonies; — a piece in chess. [*See* Night, 160.]
Knight'age (*nīt'-*), 162.
Knight'ed (*nīt'-*), 162.
Knight'-ĕr'rant (*nīt'-*), 162, 205.
Knight'-ĕr'rant-ry (*nīt'-*), 162.
Knight'hŏŏd (*nīt'-*), 162.
Knight'li-ness (*nīt'-*), 186.
Knight'ly (*nīt'ly*) (162), *a.* becoming a knight: — *ad.* in a manner suitable to a knight. [*See* Nightly, 160.]
Knit (*nit*) (16, 162), *v.* to weave by the hand with needles; — to unite. [*See* Nit, 160.]
Knit'ta-ble (*nit'-*), 164.
Knit'ter (*nit'-*), 176.
Knit'ting (*nit'-*).
Knit'tle (*nit'l*), 162, 164.
Knīves (*nīvz*), *n. pl.* 162. [*See* Knife.]
Knob (*nob*), 18, 162.
Knobbed (*nobd*), 165.
Knob'bi-ness (*nob'-*), 186.
Knob'by (*nob'-*).
Knock (*nok*), 18, 162.
Knocked (*nokt*), 165.
Knock'er (*nok'-*)
Knock'ing (*nok'-*).
Knōll (*nōl*), 162.
Knōlled (*nōld*), 165.
Knōll'ing (*nōl'-*), 162.
Knop'pern (*nop'-*), 162.
Knot (*not*) (162), *n.* a part that is complicated or tied in a cord; — a part in a tree where a branch shoots; — a cluster; — a division of a log-line: — *v.* to complicate in knots, — to unite. [*See* Not, 160.]
Knot'bĕr-ry (*not'-*), 206.
Knot'grȧss (*not'*).
Knot'ted (*not'-*), 162, 176.
Knot'ti-ness (*not'-*), 186.
Knot'ting (*not'-*).
Knot'ty (*not'-*), 66, 170.
Knot'weed (*not'-*).
Knot'wort (*not'wurt*), 171.
Knout (*nowt*), 28.

Knōw (*nō*) (162), *v.* to perceive intellectually; — to be informed. [*See* No, 160.]
Knōw'a-ble (*nō'-*), 164
Knōw'er (*nō'ur*), 77.
Knōw'ing (*nō'-*).
Knŏwl'edge (*nol'ej*)(162, 171) [so Sm. Wr. Wb. Gd.; *nol'ej*, or *no'lej*, Wk. 155.]

☞ Though Walker, in deference to the opinion of a few orthoëpists, allows *no'lej*, he remarks upon the greater consistency of the first pronunciation [*nol'ej*] with analogy.

Knōwn (*nōn*), 162.
Knuc'kle (*nuk'l*), 162, 164.
Knuc'kled (*nuk'ld*), 183.
Knuc'kling (*nuk'-*).
Knurl (*nurl*), 21, 162.
Knurled (*nurld*), 165.
Knurl'y (*nurl'y*), 171.
Ko-ä'la.
Ko'ba.
Kōh, 24.
Kōhl'-ra'bi.
Ko'kob.
Koo'doo, 19.
Ko'peck.
Ko'ran, 49, N.
Ko'ret.
Kou'miss (*koo'-*) [Kumiss, 203.]
Krâal (*krawl*) [*krā'al*, Sm. Wr. Wb. Gd. 155], *n.* a Hottentot village, or collection of huts.

☞ The pronunciation assigned to this word is that given to it by a resident of Cape Colony who recently visited one of the compilers of this volume.

Kra'ken.
Krem'lin.
[Krout, 203. — *See* Crout.]
Kru'ka (*kroo'-*)
Krul'ler (*krool'-*).
Ku'fic.
[Kumiss, 203. — *See* Koumiss.]
Ku'ril.
Ky'a-nize, 202.
Ky'a-nized, 183.
Ky'a-nīz-ing.
Kȳr'i-e.
Kȳr-i-o-log'ic (*-loj'-*).
Kȳr-i-o-log'ic-al (*-loj'-*).

L.

Lä (11, 161), the name of the sixth sound in the ascending diatonic scale.
Lâ (17, 161), *int.* behold. [*See* Law, 160.]
Lab'a-dist, 105.
Lab'a-rum, 113, 233.
La'bel, 76.
La'belled (*-beld*) [Labeled, Wb. Gd. 203. — *See* 177, and Note E, p. 70.]
La'bel-ling [Labeling, Wb. Gd. 203.]
La'bent.
La'bi-al, 72, 78.
La'bi-ate, 73.
La-bi-o-dent'al, 228.
La'bor (88) [Labour, Sm., 199, 203.]
Lab'o-ra-to-ry, 86.
La'bored (*-burd*) (165) [Laboured, Sm. 199, 203.]
La'bor-er [Labourer, Sm. 199, 203.]
La'bor-ing [Labouring, Sm. 199, 203.]
La-bo'ri-oŭs, 49, N.; 100, 169.
La'bor-some (*-sum*), 22.
Lab'ra-dōr-īte, 83.
La'brose, *or* La-brose' [*la'brōs*, Wb. Gd.; *la-brōs'*, or *lā'brōs*, Wr. 155.]
La-bur'num, 169.
Lab'y-rinth, 93.
Lab-y-rinth'al, 72.
Lab-y-rinth'i-an, 169.
Lab-y-rinth'ic, 109.
Lab-y-rinth'ic-al, 108.
Lab-y-rinth'i-form, 108.
Lab-y-rinth'ïne, 82, 152.
Lac (181), *n.* a resinous substance. [*See* Lack, 160.]
Lac'cic (*lak'sik*), 39, 52, 200.
Lac'cïne, 82, 152.
Lace, 163.
Laced (*lāst*), Note C, p. [34.
Laç'er-a-ble, 164, 169.
Laç'er-ate, 169.
Laç'er-āt-ed.
Laç'er-āt-ing.
Laç-er-a'tion, 112.
Laç'er-āt-ïve, 84, 106.

La-cer'ta (L.), 21, Note.
La-cer'tian (*-shan*), 112.
La-cer'tïne, 82, 152.
Lăche, *n. sing.*, *or* Lach'es (*-ez*), *n. pl.* negligence. [Law term.]
Lach'ry-mal (*lak'-*), 52, 72.
Lach'ry-ma-ry (*lak'-*), 52, 72.
Lach'ry-ma-to-ry (*lak'-*), 86.
Lach'ry-mose (*lak'-*), [so Wb. Gd.; *lak-ri-mōs'*, Wr. 155.]
Lāç'ing, 183.
La-cin'i-āte.
La-cin'i-āt-ed.
Lack (181), *n* deficiency, want: — *v.* to be in want of. [*See* Lac, 160.]
Lack-a-dāi'sic-al (*-zik-*), 116, 171.
Lack-a-dāi'sy (*-zy*), 169.
Lacked (*lakt*). Note C, p. 34.
[Lacker. — *See* Lacquer, 203.]
Lack'ey (*lak'y*), *n.* & *v.* (98, 169) [pl. of *n.* Lack'eys (*-iz*), 190.]
Lack'eyed (*-id*), 165.
Lack'ey-ing (*-ĭ-ing*).
Lack'ing.
Lack'-lus-tre (*-tur*) (164) [*See* Lustre.]
La-con'ic, 109.
La-con'ic-al, 72, 108.
La-con'ic-al-ly, 170.
La-con'i-cism (*-sizm*), 133, 136.
Lac'on-ism (*-izm*) [so Wk. Sm. Wr.; *la'kon-izm*, Wb. Gd. 155.]
Lac'quer (*-kur*) [Lacker, 203.]
Lac'quered (*-kurd*), 155.
Lac'quer-ing (*-kur-*).
Lac'ta-rene, 171.
Lac'ta-ry, *n.* 72.
Lac'tate.
Lac-ta'tion, 112, 169.
Lac'te-al (72) [so Sm. Wr. Wb. Gd.; *lak'te-al*, or *lak'che-al*, Wk. 155.]
Lac-tes'cence, 39, 171.
Lac-tes'cent.
Lac'tic.
Lac-tif'er-oŭs, 100, 108.
Lac-tom'e-ter, 108.
Lac-u-nose', 89, 122.

La-cus′tral, 122.
La-cus′trīne [so Wr. Wb. Gd.; la′kus-trin, Sm. 155.]
Lad, 10.
Lad′a-num, 169.
Lad′der, 66, 170.
Lade, *v.* to load. [*See* Laid, 160.]
Lăd′ed, 183.
Lăd′en (*lăd′n*), 149.
Lăd′ing, 183.
La′dle (*-dl*), 164.
La′dle-ful (*la′dl-fo͝ol*), 180, 197.
La′dy, 93, 190.
La′dy-dāy (209) [so Wr. Wb. Gd.; *lā-dy-dā′*, Wk. Sm. 155.]
La′dy's-bed′straw (*-dĭz-*), 213.
La′dy-love (*-lŭv*).
La-dy's-fin′ger (*la′diz-fing′gur*), 213.
La′dy's-slip′per (*-diz-*).
[L æ m m e r g e y e r, 203. — *See* Lammergeir.]
Lag, 10, 50, 53.
Lä′ger-beer (*-gur-*), 205.
Lag′gard, 66, 72.
Lagged (*lagd*), 165, 176.
Lag′ger (*-gur*), 138.
Lag′ging (*-ghing*), 141.
Lag′o-mys.
La-goon′ [L a g u n e, 203.]
La′ic, 109.
La′ic-al, 72, 108.
Lāid (23,187), *v.* did lay. [*See* Lade, 160.]
Lāin (187), *part.* from *Lie.* [*See* Lane, 160.]
Lair (*lêr*) (14, 67), *n.* the couch of a wild beast. [*See* Layer, 148.]
Laird (*lêrd*), 14, 49.
La′i-ty, 93, 108, 169.
Lake, 23.
Lake′let, 76.
Lāk′er.
Lal-la′tion, 66, 170.
Lā′ma [*not* lä′ma, 153.] [L l a m a (in the sense of a wool-bearing quadruped of South America), 203.]
La′ma-ism (*-izm*), 133,
La′ma-ist. [188.
La′ma-īte, 83.
La-man′tīne (152) [L a m a n t i n, L a m e n t i n, 203.]

Lamb (*lam*), 162.
Lam′ba-tīve, 84.
Lamb′da-cism (*lam′da-sizm*), 162.
Lamb-doid′al (*lam-*) (162) [L a m d o i d a l, 203.]
Lam′bent, 76.
Lamb′kin (*lam′-*).
Lamb's′-wool (*lamz′-wo͝ol*) (213), *n.* a kind of beverage.
Lame, 23.
Lamed, 165, 183.
Lam′el, 170.
La-mel′la (L.) [pl. *La-mel′læ* (*-le*), 198.]
Lam′el-lar, 169, 170.
Lam′el-late, 73.
Lam′el-lāt-ed.
Lam-el-lif′er-oŭs, 108.
La-mel′li-form, 108.
La-ment′, *v.* & *n.* 121.
Lam′ent-a-ble, 123.
Lam′ent-a-bly, 93.
Lam-ent-a′tion.
La-ment′ed.
La-ment′er, 77, 169.
La-ment′ing.
Lam′i-na, (L.) [pl. *Lam′i-næ* (*-ne*) 198.]
Lam-in-a-bil′i-ty, 108, 169.
Lam′in-a-ble, 164, 169.
Lam′in-ar, 169.
Lam′in-a-ry, 72.
Lam′in-āt-ed.
Lam-in-a′tion.
Lām′ing.
Lam′mas, 180.
Lam′mer-geīr (*-ghīr*), *or* Lam′mer-geȳ-er (*-ghī-ur*) [L æ m m e r g e y e r, 203.]
Lamp, 10.
Lam′pass, 171.
Lamp′black, 142.
Lam′per-eel, 206, Exc. 3.
Lamp′ic.
Lamp′light (*-līt*), 206.
Lam-poon′, *n.* & *v.* 121.
Lam-pooned′, 165.
Lam-poon′er.
Lam-poon′ing.
Lam-poon′ry.
Lam′prey, 98, 169.
La′na-ry, 233.
La′nate.
La′nāt-ed.
Lȧnce, 12.
Lȧnced (*lȧnst*), 183; Note C, p. 34.

Lăn′ce-o-lar, 74.
Lăn′ce-o-late.
Lăn′ce-o-lāt-ed.
Lȧnç′er, 131.
Lăn′çet, 76, 156.
Lȧnch (13, 44), *v.* to throw, as a lance from the hand. [*See* Launch, 160.]
Lȧnched (*lȧncht*).
Lȧnch′ing.
Lăn′ci-form, 108.
Lăn′ci-nate, 169.
Lăn-ci-na′tion.
Lȧnç′ing.
Land, 10.
Land′am-man, 196.
Lan′dau [so Sm. Wb. Gd.; *lan-daw′*, Wk. Wr. 155.] [L a n-d a w (*lan′daw*, Wr.), 203.]
Lan-dau-let′, 122.
Land′ed.
Land′grave.
Land-grāv′i-ate, 123,171.
Land′gra-vine (*-vēn*).
Land′hōld-er.
Land′ing.
Land′lā-dy (206) [so Sm. Wr. Wb. Gd.; *lan′lā-dy*, Wk. 155.]
Land′lock, 206.
Land′locked (*-lokt*).
Land′lock-ing.
Land′lō-per.
Land′lord.
Land′lub-ber, 206.
Land′mark.
Land′reeve.
Land′scape, 142.
Land′slide.
Land′slip.
Lands′man (*landz′-man*), 214.
Lane, *n.* a narrow way or passage. [*See* Lain, 160.]
Lan′grage (*lang′grāj*), 54.]
Lan′grel (*lang′-*).
Läng-sȳne′, 156.
Lan′guage (*lang′gwāj*), 34, 54.
Lan′guid (*lang′gwid*), 141.
Lan′guish (*lang′gwish*), 104.
Lan′guished (*lan′-gwisht*), 165; Note C. p. 34.
Lan′guish-er (*lang′-gwish-er*), 77.

Lan′guish-ing (*lan′-gwish-ing*).
Lan′guish-ment (*lang′-gwish-*).
Lan′guor (*lang′gwur*) [*not* lang′gur, 153.]
[Laniard, 203.—*See* Lanyard.]
La′ni-a-ry, *or* Lan′ia-ry (*-ya-*) [so Wr.; *la′ni-a-ry*, Gd.; *lan′-yăr-y*, Sm. 155.]
La′ni-ate, *or* Lan′i-ate (169) [so Wr.; *la′ni-āt*, Wk. Gd.; *lan′i-āt*, Sm. 155.]
La-nif′er-oŭs, 108.
La-nig′er-oŭs (*-nij′-*).
Lank (*langk*), 10, 54.
Lank′y (*langk′y*), 169.
Lan′ner, 170.
Lan′ner-et.
Lans′que-net (*-ke-*), 52.
Lan′tern [Lanthorn, 203.]
Lan′tha-num, *or* Lan-tha′ni-um.
La-nu′gi-nose, 2, 465.
La-nu′gi-noŭs, 100.
Lan′yard [Laniard, 203.]
Lā-od-i-ce′an, 72, 110.
Lap, *n.* & *v.* (10) [pl. of *n.* Laps.—*See* Lapse, 160.]
Lap′dog, 206.
La-pel′, 121.
Lap′ful (*-fo͝ol*), 180, 197.
Lap-i-da′ri-an, 49, N.
Lap′i-da-ry, 72, 169.
Lap-i-des′cence, 39, 171.
Lap-i-des′cent.
Lap-i-dif′ic, 170.
Lap-i-dif′ic-al.
La-pid-i-fĭ-ca′tion, 112.
La-pid′i-fīed.
La-pid′i-fȳ, 94, 108.
La-pid′i-fȳ-ing.
La′pis laz′u-lī [so Sm. Wr. Wb. Gd.; *lazh′-ū-lī*, Wk. 155.]
Lapped (*lapt*), 163; Note C, p. 34.
Lap′per, 77.
Lap′pet.
Lap′ping, 176.
Laps′a-ble, 169.
Lapse, *n.* & *v.* (10) [*See* Laps, pl. of Lap, 160.]
Lapsed (*lapst*).
Lap′sīd-ed.
Laps′ing, 183.
Lap′stōne, 206.

Lap′sus lin′guæ (L.) (*ling′gwe*).
Lap′wing.
Lar (L.) [pl. *La′res* (*-rēz*), 198.]
Lar′bōard.
Lar′ce-ny, 93, 169.
Larch, 135.
Lard, 49.
Lar-da′ceous (*-shus*), 112.
Lard′ed.
Lard′er.
Lard′ing.
La′res (*-rēz*), *n. pl.* [*See* Lar.]
Large.
Lar′gess (*-jes*), 45.
Lăr′i-at, 48, 66.
Lark, 135.
Lark′spur, 206.
Lar′mi-er, 49.
Lăr′um (169) [so Wk. Sm. Gd.; *lăr′um*, or *la′rum*, Wr. 155.]
Lar′va (135) [pl. Lar′-væ (*-ve*), 198.]
Lar′val.
Lar′vāt-ed.
Larve, 189.
La-ryn′ge-al (*-je-*) [so Wr. Gd.; *la-ring′ghe-al*, Sm. 155.]
La-ryn′ge-an (*-je-*), 110.
Lăr-yn-gi′tis.
Lăr-yn-got′o-my, 108, 116, 233.
Lăr′ynx (*lăr′ingks*) (16, 48, 52, N.; 54) [so Sm. Wb. Gd.; *lā′ringks*, Wk.; *lăr′ingks*, or *lā′ringks*, Wr. 155.]
Las-car′, *or* Las′car [so Wr.; *las-kar′*, Sm.; *las′kar*, Wb. Gd. 155.]
Las-civ′i-oŭs, 39, 100.
Lash, 46.
Lashed (*lasht*), 165; Note C, p. 34.
Lash′er, 169.
Lash′ing.
Làss, 12, 174.
Las′si-tude, 108, 127, 170.
Las′so (86) [pl. Las′sos (*-sōz*), 192.]
Làst, 131.
Làst′ed.
Làst′ing.
Latch, 44; Note D, p. 37.
Latched (*lacht*), 34.
Latch′et.
Latch′ing, 141.
Late, 163.

La-teen′, 121.
La′tent.
Lat′er-al, 233, Exc.
Lat′er-al-ly, 170.
Lat′er-an, 72. [171.
Lat-er-i-fo′li-oŭs, 116,
Lat-er-ĭ′tious (*-ish′us*).
Làth, *n.* & *v.* (14) [*not* Làth, 153] [pl. of *n.* Làths (*làthz*).]
Lāthe, 38, 163.
Làthed (*làtht*), 131, 140.
Lăth′er, *n.* & *v.* 77.
Lăth′ered (*-urd*), 150, 165, 171.
Lăth′er-ing.
Làth′ing, 140.
Làth′y, 169.
La′tian (*-shan*).
La-tib′u-lize, 202.
La-tib′u-lized, 183.
La-tib′u-līz-ing.
Lat′i-clave.
Lat-i-cos′tate, 116.
Lat-i-den′tate.
Lat-i-fo′li-ate.
Lat-i-fo′li-oŭs, 171.
Lat′ĭn (149) [*not* lat′n, 153.]
Lat′ĭn-ism (*-izm*), 133.
Lat′ĭn-ist, 170.
La-tin′i-tas-ter.
La-tin′i-ty, 108.
Lat-ĭn-ĭ-za′tion, 112, 116.
Lat′ĭn-ize, 202.
Lat′ĭn-ized.
Lat′ĭn-īz-ing.
Lat-i-ros′troŭs [so Sm. Wb. Gd. Wr.; *lā-ti-ros′trus*, Wk. 155.]
Lāt′ish, 183.
Lat′i-tat (L.).
Lat′i-tude, 26, 108, 170.
Lat-i-tūd′in-al, 26, 72.
Lat-i-tūd-in-a′ri-an, 49, N.; 116.
Lat-i-tūd-in-a′ri-an-ism (*-izm*), 133, 136.
Lat-i-tūd′in-oŭs, 108.
La′trant.
La-trī′a, *or* La′tri-a [*la-trī′a*, Sm. Wb. Gd.; *la′tri-a*, Wk. Wr. 155.]
Lat′ro-bite, 152.
Lat′ten, 66, 132, 149.
Lat′ter, 170.
Lat′tĭce, 66, 169.
Lat′ticed (*-tist*), 183; Note C, p. 34.
Lat′tiç-ing, 183.
Lâud (17), *n.* praise. [*See* Lord, 148.]

Laud′a-ble, 164, 169.
Laud′a-bly.
Laud′a-num (*lawd′a-num*, or *lŏd′a-num*) [so Wr.; *lawd′a-num*, Wb. Gd.; *lŏd′-a-num*, Wk. Sm. 155.]
Lâud-a′tion.
Lâud′a-to-ry, 86.
Lâud′ed.
Lâud′er.
Lâud′ing.
Laugh (*läf*) (11, 35) [*not* lăf, 153.]
Laugh′a-ble (*läf′*-), 169.
Laughed (*läft*), 165; Note C, p. 34.
Laugh′er (*läf′*-).
Laugh′ing (*läf′*-), 141.
Laugh′ter (*läf′*-).
Läunce.
Läunch (11, 44), *v.* to cause to slide into the water, as a vessel: — *n.* the act of launching a vessel; — a kind of long-boat. [*See* Lanch.]
Läunched (*läncht*).
Läunch′ing.
Läun′der, 11, 156.
Läun′dress [*not* lawn′-dress, 153.]
Läun′dry, 127.
Lâu′re-ate, *a.* & *v.* 73, 169.
Lâu′re-āt-ed.
Lâu′re-āt-ing.
Lâu-re-a′tion.
Lau′rel (*lŏr′el*, or *law′-rel*) [so Wr.; *lŏr′ĭl*, Wk.; *lŏr′ĕl*, Sm.; *law′rel*, Wb. Gd. 155.]
Lau′relled (*lŏr′eld*, or *law′reld*) (177) [Laureled, Wb. Gd. 203. — *See* 177, and Note E, p. 70.]
Lâu′res-tīne, 152, 171.
Lā′va [so Wk. Sm. Gd.; *lā′va*, or *lä′va*, Wr. 155.]
Lav′a-to-ry, 86.
Lave, 36.
Laved, 183.
Lav′en-der, 170.
La′ver.
Lāv′ing, 228, N.
Lav′ish, 66, 104.
Lav′ished (*-isht*).
Lav′ish-er, 169.
Lav′ish-ing.
Law (17, 125), *n.* an established rule. [*See* La, 160.]
Law′ful (*-fool*), 180.
Law′ful-ly (*-fool*-).
Law′giv-er (*ghiv*-), 206.
Lawn, 17.
Law′sūit, 26, 206.
Law′yer, 112.
Lax, 10, 39, N.
Lax-a′tion.
Lax′a-tĭve, 84.
Lax′i-ty, 108.
Lāy, 23, 50.
Lāy′er (67), *n.* a stratum. [*See* Lair, 148.]
Lāy′er-ing.
Lāy′ing.
Lāy′man, 196, 206.
La′zar, 74, 169.
Laz-a-ret′, 122.
Laz-a-ret′to, 170.
Laz′a-rist, 105.
[Lazaroni, 203. — *See* Lazzaroni.]
Laze, 40.
La′zi-ly, 186.
La′zi-ness. [uli.]
Laz′u-lī [*See* Lapis laz-
La′zy, 169.
Laz-za-ro′nĭ [Lazaroni, 203.]
Lēa (13), *n.* a meadow. [*See* Lee, 160.]
Lēach, *v.* to wash by percolation, as ashes. [*See* Leech, 160.] [Letch, 203.]
Lēached (*lēcht*).
Lēach′ing.
Lĕad (161), *n.* a metal. [*See* Led, 160.]
Lēad (161), *v.* to guide or conduct.
Lĕad′ed.
Lĕad′en (*led′n*), 149.
Lēad′er.
Lēad′ing.
Lēaf, *n.* & *v.* [pl. of *n.* Leaves (*lēvz*), 193.] [*See* Lief, 160.]
Lēafed (*lēft*) (165; Note C, p. 34). [*See* Leaved.]
Lēaf′i-ness, 186.
Lēaf′ing.
Lēaf′let, 76.
Lēaf′y, 93, 169.
Lēague (*lēg*), 168.
Lēagued (*lēgd*).
Lēagu′er (*lēg′*-).
Lēagu′ing (*lēg′*-).
Lēak (13), *n.* a fissure or crack that lets a fluid in or out: — *v.* to trickle or run in or out. [*See* Leek, 160.]
Lēak′age, 183.
Lēaked (*lēkt*), 165; Note C, p. 34.
Lēak′ing.
Lēak′y, 169.
Lēal [so Wr. Gd.; *le′al*, Sm. 155.]
Lēan, 43, 50.
Lēaned, 165.
Lēan′ing.
Lēan′ness, 66, N.
Lĕant, *v.* did lean; — used colloquially for *Leaned.* [*See* Lent, 160.]
Lēan′-to (*-too*), 206, Exc. 4.
Lēap, *n.* & *v.*
Leaped (*lĕpt*, or *lēpt*) [so Wr.; *lĕpt*, Sm.; *lēpt*, or *lĕpt*, Gd. 155.]
Lēap′er.
Lēap′frog, 206.
Lēap′ing.
Lēap′yēar.
Learn (*lern*), 21, N.
Learned (*lernd*), *part.* 150.
Learn′ed (*lern′ed*), *a.* 144, 150.
Learn′er (*lern′*-).
Learn′ing (*lern′*-), 141.
Learnt (*lernt*).
Lēase, 136.
Lēased (*lēst*).
Lēash, 46.
Lēashed (*lēsht*), 165.
Lēash′ing.
Lēast.
Lĕath′er, 15, 38.
Lĕath′ern, 135.
Lĕath′er-y, 169.
Lēave, 13.
Lēaved (165), *part.* having leaves or foliage.

☞ Of *leaved* and *leafed*, Smart says, "*Leaved* is most in use."

Lĕav′en (*lev′n*) [so Wr. Gd.; *lev′ĕn*, Wk. Sm. 155.]
Lĕav′ened (*lev′nd*).
Lĕav′en-ing (*lev′n-ing*).
Lēav′ing, 183.
Lech′er.
Lech′er-oŭs.
Lech′er-y.
Lec′tion, 169.
Lec′tion-a-ry, 72.

Lect'ure, 26, 91.
Lect'ured (*-yurd*), 183.
Lect'ur-er (*-yur-*), 91.
Lect'ur-ing (*-yur-*), 91.
Led, *v.* did lead. [*See* Lĕad, 160.]
Ledge, 15, 45.
Ledg'er [Leger, 203.]

☞ "Usually and properly written *ledger*." *Webster.*

[Ledger-line, 203. — *See* Leger-line.]
Lee (13), *n.* the side of any thing opposite to that from which the wind blows. [*See* Lea, 160.]
Leech (13), *n.* an aquatic worm, a blood-sucker; — *v.* to apply leeches to. [*See* Leach, 160.]
Leeched (*lēcht*), 165; Note C, p. 34.
Leech'ing.
Leek (13), *n.* a plant allied to the onion. [*See* Leak, 160.]
Leer, 13, 49.
Leered, 165.
Leer'ing.
Lees (*lēz*), *n. sing. & pl.*
Leet, 13, 41.
Lee'ward (*lē'wurd*, or *lū'urd*) (26) [so Wr.; *lē'wurd*, Wk. Gd.; *lē'-wurd*, coll. *l'oo'urd*, Sm. (*See* § 26), 155.]
Lee'wāy.
Left'-hand'ed, 205.
Left'-off, 206, Exc. 4.
Leg, 15.
Leg'a-cy, 105, 169.
Le'gal, 72.
Le'gal-ism (*-izm*), 133.
Le'gal-ist.
Le-gal'i-ty, 108, 233.
Le-gal-ĭ-za'tion, 112.
Le'gal-ize, 202.
Le'gal-ized, 165.
Le'gal-īz-ing, 183.
Le'gal-ly, 93, 170.
Leg'ate (73) [*not* le'gāt, 153.]
Leg-a-tee', 122.
Leg'a-tīne, 82, 152.
Le-ga'tion, 75, 112.
Leg-a-tor', 122.
Le'gend (*le'jend*), *or* Leg'end (*lej'end*) [so Wr. Gd.; *le'jend*, Wk.; *lej'end*, Sm. 155.]
Leg'end-a-ry (*lej'-*), 72.
[Leger, 203. — *See* Ledger.]
Leg-er-de-māin' (*lej-*), 114.
Leg'er-līne (*lej'-*) [Ledger-line, 203.]
Leg'ging (*-ghing*) (66, 189) [Leggin, 203.]
Leg'horn.
Leg-i-bil'i-ty (*lej-*), 108.
Leg'i-ble (*lej'-*), 164, 169.
Leg'i-bly (*lej'-*), 93.
Le'gion (*-jun*).
Le'gion-a-ry (*-jun-*), 72.
Leg'is-late (*lej'-*), 73.
Leg'is-lāt-ed (*lej'-*).
Leg'is-lāt-ing (*lej'-*).
Leg'is-lāt-ive (*lej'-*)(116) [*not* leg-is-lāt'iv, lē'-jis-lāt-iv, *nor* le-jĭs'la-tiv, 153.]
Leg'is-lāt-or (*lej'-*).
Leg'is-lāt-ure (*lej'is-lāt-yur*) (26, 91, 122) [*not* le-jis'la-tūr, 153.]
Le-git'i-ma-cy, 72, 169.
Le-git'i-mate, *a.* & *v.* 73.
Le-git'i-māt-ed.
Le-git'i-māt-ing, 183.
Le-git-i-ma'tion, 116.
Le-git'i-ma-tist.
Le-git'i-mist, 105.
Leg'ume (26, 90) [*not* le'gūm, 153.]
Le-gu'men (L.) [L. pl. *Le-gu'mi-na*; Eng. pl. Le-gu'mens (*-menz*), 198.]
Le-gu'min-oŭs, 228.
Lēi'sure (*lē'zhur*)(13, 47, 91, 169, N.) [so Wr.; *lē'zhūr*, Wk.; *lē'-zh'oor* (*See* § 26), Sm.; *lē'zhur*, or *lĕzh'yur*, Gd. 155.]

☞ "I acknowledge that between *ēi'ther* and *eī'ther*, *lēi'sure* and *lĕis'ure*, *haunt* with the Italian *a*, and *haunt* with the broad *a*. — and the instances might be multiplied to a very considerable extent, — there is little in point of good usage to choose; but I have always thought it best to exhibit only one of the modes in such cases, lest the inspector, after consulting the Dictionary to fix his practice, should still be left in a state of doubt." *Smart.*

Lem'ma, 72.
Lem'ming, 66, 170.
Lem-nis'cate.
Lem'on, 86, 170.
Lem-on-ade', 114, 122.
Le'mur, 92, 169.
Lend, 15.
Lend'er, 77.
Lend'ing.
Le'ne, 144, 163.
Length, 15, 64.
Length'en (*length'n*), 149.
Length'ened (*length'-nd*).
Length'en-ing (*length'-n-ing*).
Length'i-ly, 93.
Length'i-ness, 186.
Length'wise (*-wīz*).
Length'y.
Le'ni-ence, 169.
Le'ni-en-cy, 169.
Le'ni-ent (78) [*not* len'-ĭ-ent, 155.]
Len'i-fied, 186.
Len'i-fȳ, 94.
Len'i-fȳ-ing, 186.
Len'i-tive, 84, 108.
Len'i-ty, 108.
Lens (*lenz*), 15; Note C, p. 34.
Lent, *n.* a fast of forty days observed by some churches. [*See* Lĕant, 160.]
Lent'en (*lent'n*), 149, 167.
Len-tic'u-lar, 108.
Len'ti-form, 108.
Len-tig'i-noŭs (*-tij'-*).
Len-tī'go (L.).
Len'til, 171.
L'en'voy (Fr.) (*läng'-vwaw*).
Le'o (L.).
Le'o-nīne, 105, 152.
Lĕop'ard, 15, 170, 171.
Lep'er, 77, 170.
Lep'er-oŭs, 100.
Lep'i-do-līte, *or* Le-pid'-o-līte (152) [so Wr.; *lep'i-do-līt*, Wb. Gd.; *le-pid'o-līt*, Sm. 155.]
Lep-i-dop'ter-al, 72.
Lep-i-dop'ter-oŭs, 108.
Lep-i-do'sis, 109.
Lep'i-dote.
Lep'o-rīne, *or* Lep'o-rīne (82, 152) [so Wr. Gd.; *lep'o-rĭn*, Wk. Sm. 155.]
Lep'ro-sy, 169.
Lep'roŭs, 100.
Lep-to-dac'tyl.

Lep-to-dac'tyl-ous.
Les'bi-an, 78, 169.
Le'sion (*-zhun*), 47, 86.
Less, 15, 174.
Les-see', 121.
Less'en (*les'n*) (104,149), *v*. to make less. [*See* Lesson, 160.]
Less'ened (*les'nd*), 165.
Less'en-ing (*les'n-*).
Less'er.
Les'son (*les'n*) (104,149), *n*. a portion of a book required to be learned and recited by a pupil. [*See* Lessen, 160.]
Les'sor, 66, 118.

☞ It is pronounced *les-sor'* when contrasted with *les-see'*.

Lĕst [so Sm. Wb. Gd. Wr.; *lĕst*, or *lēst*, Wk. 155.]

☞ Though Walker allows *lēst* (1806), he condemns it as contrary to analogy.

Let, 15.
[Letch, 203. — *See* Leach.]
Le'thal, 72.
Le-thar'gic, 75, 200.
Le-thar'gic-al.
Leth'ar-gy.
Le'the, 163.
Le-the'an, 110.
Let'ter, 66, 170.
Let'tered, 150, 165.
Let'ter-ing, 141.
Let'ter-pa'per, 205.
Let'ter-press.
Let'ting. [171.
Let'tuce (*let'tis*), 90, 156,
Leū-co'ma.
Le'vant, *or* Lev'ant, *a*. [*le'vant*, Wk. Wb. Gd.; *lev'ant*, Sm.; *le'vant*, or *le-vant'*, Wr. 155.]
Le-vant', *n*. & *v*., 121.
Le-vant'er.
Le-vant'ine, *or* Lev'ant-ine [so Wr. Gd.; *le-van'tĭn*, Sm. 155.]
Lev'ee, *n*. a ceremonious morning reception of visitors; — an embankment on the margin of a river. [*See* Levy, 160.]

☞ When used to signify an evening party or assembly, it is often pronounced, in the United States, *le-ve'*.

Lev'el (Note F, p. 79) [*not* lev'l, 155.]
Lev'elled (*-eld*) [Leveled, Wb. Gd. 203. — *See* 177, and Note E, p. 70.]
Lev'el-ler [Leveler, Wb. Gd. 203.]
Lev'el-ling [Leveling, Wb. Gd. 203.]
Le'ver [so Wk. Sm. Wr.; *lev'er*, Wb. Gd. 155.]
Lev'er-age, 70.
Lev'er-et.
Lev'i-a-ble, 186.
Le-vi'a-than.
Lev'ĭed, 99, 186.
Lev'i-gate, 169.
Lev'i-gāt-ed.
Lev'i-gāt-ing, 183.
Lev-i-ga'tion, 112.
Lev'i-rate [so Wr.; *le-vi'rate*, Gd. 155.]
Lev-i-ra'tion.
Lev-i-ta'tion.
Le'vite, 83, 163.
Le-vit'ic-al, 108.
Le-vit'i-cus, 171.
Lev'i-ty, 108.
Lev'y (93, 169), *n*. the act of raising or collecting money or men; — the quantity, amount, or number raised: — *v*. to raise, as taxes. [*See* Levee, 160.]
Lev'y-ing, 186.
Lewd (*lūd*), 26, 128.
Lew'is (*lū'is*) (26) [so Gd.; *loo'is*, Wr.; *l'oo'is*, Sm. 155.]
Lex (L.), 52, N.
Lex'ic-al, 72, 108.
Lex-i-cog'ra-pher, 108.
Lex-i-co-graph'ic, 109.
Lex-i-co-graph'ic-al.
Lex-i-cog'ra-phy, 108.
Lex-i-col'o-gy, 108.
Lex'i-con.
Lex-i-graph'ic.
Lex-i-graph'ic-al.
Lex-ig'ra-phy, 93.
[Ley, 203. — *See* Lye.]
Ley'den (*lā'dn*, or *lī'dn*) (149) [*lā'dn*, Sm.; *lī'dn*, Gd. Wr. 155.]
Lī-a-bĭl'i-ty, 108.
Lī'a-ble, 164, 169.
Lī'a-ble-ness, 185.
Liaison (Fr.) (*lē-ā-zōng'*).
Lī'ar (67, 169), *n*. one who lies, or falsifies. [*See* Lyre, 148, *and* Lier, 160.]
Lī'as, 72.
Lī-as'sic, 109, 170.
Lī-ba'tion.
Lī'bel, 76.
Lī'bel-lant [Libelant, Wb. Gd. 203.]
Lī'belled (*-beld*) [Libeled, Wb. Gd. 203. — *See* 177, *and* Note E, p. 70.]
Lī'bel-ler [Libeler, Wb. Gd. 203.]
Lī'bel-ling [Libeling, Wb. Gd. 203.]
Lī'bel-lous [Libelous, Wb. Gd. 203.]
Lī'ber (L.).
Lib'er-al, 66, 233.
Lib'er-al-ism (*-izm*), 133.
Lib'er-al-ist.
Lib-er-al'i-ty, 108, 169.
Lib'er-al-ize, 202.
Lib'er-al-ized, 165.
Lib'er-al-īz-ing.
Lib'er-al-ly, 170.
Lib'er-al-mind'ed, 205.
Lib'er-ate.
Lib'er-āt-ed, 183.
Lib'er-āt-ing.
Lib-er-a'tion, 112.
Lib'er-āt-or, 88, 169.
Lib-er-ta'ri-an, 49, N.
Lib'er-ti-cide, 103.

☞ So pronounced by all the orthoëpists, though *li-ber'ti-cide* would be more analogical, and has the authority of Shelley (Adonais, st. iv.) to support it. Compare *infanticide*, *parenticide*, *sororicide*, and *tyrannicide*.

Lib'er-tĭne, 82, 152.
Lib'er-tin-ism (*-izm*).
Lib'er-ty, 93, 105.
Lī-bid'in-oŭs, 108.
Lī'bra (L.), 72.
Lī-bra'ri-an, 49, N.
Lī'bra-ry, 72, 105.
Lī'brate.
Lī'brāt-ed.
Lī'brāt-ing.
Lī-bra'tion.
Lī'bra-to-ry, 86.
Lĭ-bret'to (It.).
Lice (195), *n. pl.* [*See* Louse.]
Lī'cense [Licence, Sm. 203.]
Lī'censed (*-senst*), 165, 183; Note C, p. 34.

Li-cens-ee′, 122.
Li′cens-er.
Li′cens-ing.
Lī-cen′ti-ate (*-shĭ-āt*) (73) [so Wk. Sm. Wr.; *lī-sen′shāt*, Wb. Gd. 155.]
Lī-cen′tious (*-shus*), 169.
Li′chen (*lī′ken*, or *lich′-en*) (52, 149) [so Wr. Gd.; *lich′en* (as the name of a tetter, or ringworm, *li′ken*), Sm. 155.]
Lich-en-og′ra-phy (*lik-*).
Lick, 16, 181.
Licked (*likt*), 165; Note C, p. 34.
Lick′er, *n.* one who licks. [*See* Liquor, 160.]
Lick′er-ish, 171.
Lick′ing.
Lick′spit-tle, 164.
Lic′o-rice (169) [Liquorice, 203.]
Lic′tor.
Lid, 16, 42, 50.
Līe, 25.
Liēf (13), *ad.* willingly. [*See* Leaf, 160.] [Lieve, 203.]
Liēge, 13, 45.
Li′en (*lē′en*, or *lī′en*) [so Wr. Gd.; *lī′en*, Sm. 155.] [*not* lēn, 153.]
Lī-en-tĕr′ic, 109.
Lī′en-tĕr-y, 116, 122.
Lī′er (67, 169), *n.* one who lies down. [*See* Lyre, 148, *and* Liar, 160.]
Lieū (*lū*), 26.
Lieū-ten′an-cy (*lū-ten′-*, or *lev-ten′-*).
Lieū-ten′ant (*lū-ten′ant*, or *lev-ten′ant*) [*lev-ten′ant*, Wk. Sm.; *lū-ten′ant*, or *lef-ten′-ant*, Gd.; *lev-ten′ant*, or *lū-ten′ant*, Wr. 155.]

☞ "The irregularity in sounding *lieutenant* may be accounted for by the practice, common when the word was first introduced from the French, of confounding the letters *v* and *u*: the word was written *lievtenant*, and sounded *leevtenant*, which naturally shortened into *levtenant*." *Smart.*

[Lieve, 203. — *See* Lief.]
Life, *n.* (163) [pl. Lives, 193.]
Life′blood (*-blud*), 206.
Life′bōat.
Life′-giv-ing, 206, Exc. 5
Life′guard (*-gard*).
Life′-in-sur′ance (*-shoor′-*), 205.
Life′like, 206, Exc. 5.
Life′-long, 206, Exc. 5.
Life′time, 206.
Lift, 16.
Lift′ed.
Lift′er, 77.
Lift′ing, 141.
Lig′a-ment, 105, 169.
Lig-a-ment′al, 72, 123.
Lig-a-ment′oŭs.
Lig′an, 72.
Lī-ga′tion, 112, 151.
Lig′a-ture, 90.
Light (*līt*), 162.
Light′ed (*līt′-*).
Light′en (*līt′n*), 149, 162.
Light′ened (*līt′nd*).
Light′en-ing (*līt′n-ing*).
Light′er (*līt′-*).
Light′-hĕad-ed (*līt′-*), 206, Exc. 5.
Light′-house (*līt′-*), 206, Exc. 3.
Light′-in′fant-ry (*līt′-*), 205.
Light′ing (*līt′-*), 162.
Light′ning (*līt′-*), 171.
Līghts (*lītz*), *n. pl.*
Light′some (*līt′sum*), 162, 169.
Lig-nal′oes (*lig-nal′ōz*, or *līn-al′ōz*) [so Gd.; *lig-nal′ōz*, Sm.; *līn-al′ōz*, or *lig-nal′ōz*, Wr. 155.]
Lig′ne-oŭs, 169.
Lig-ni-fĭ-ca′tion, 116.
Lig′ni-form, 169.
Lig′ni-fȳ, 94, 169.
Lig′ni-fȳ-ing.
Lig′nīne (82, 152) [Lignin, 203.]
Lig′nīte, 83, 152.
Lig′num vi′tæ (L.) (*vī′te*).
Lig′u-la.
Like, 25.
Liked (*līkt*), 183; Note C, p. 34.
Like′li-hŏŏd, 186.
Like′ly, 93, 185.
Līk′en (*līk′n*), 149.
Līk′ened (*līk′nd*).
Līk′en-ing (*līk′n-*).
Like′wise (*-wīz*).
Līk′ing, 183.
Li′lac, 72.

☞ "This word, without any reason for it, is often spelled Lilach; and is often corruptly pronounced *la′lok*." *Smart.*

Lil-i-a′ceous (*-shus*), 112.
Lil′ĭed, 186.
Lil-i-pu′tian (*-shan*), 171.
Lil-lĭ-bul-e′ro [*lil-ĭ-bul′-e-ro*, Gd. 155.]
Lil′y, 169, 170, 190.
Lī-ma′ceous (*-shus*).
Li′ma-ture.
Limb (*lim*) (162), *n.* one of the extremities of the body: — *v.* to dismember. [*See* Limn, 160.]
Lim′bate.
Limbed (*limd*), 162, 165.
Lim′ber, 77.
Limb′ing (*lim′-*), 162.
Lim′bo (86) [pl. Lim′bos (*-bōz*), 192.]
Lim′bus, 169.
Limo, 163.
Limed, 165.
Līm′ing 183.
Lime′kiln (*-kil*), 162, 206.
Lime′stone.
Lim′it, 66, 170.
Lim′it-a-ble, 164, 169.
Lim′it-a-ry, 72.
Lim-it-a′tion.
Lim′it-ed.
Lim′it-ing.
Limn (*lim*) (162), *v.* to draw or paint. [*See* Limb, 160.]
Lim′ner.
Lim′ning.
Limp, 16.
Limped (*limpt*), 165.
Lim′pet, 76.
Lim′pid.
Lim-pid′i-ty, 108, 169.
Limp′ing.
Līm′y, 169, 183.
Lin′a-ment (169), *n.* lint; a tent for a wound. [*See* Lineament, *and* Liniment, 148.]
Linch, 16, 44.
Linch′pin.
Lin′den, 149.
Line, 25.
Lin′e-age, 169.
Lin′e-al, 72.
Lin′e-al-ly, 170.
Lin′e-a-ment (169), *n.* a

feature. [*See* Linament, *and* Liniment, 148.]
Lin'e-ar, 74, 169.
Lined, 183.
Lin'en, 66, 170.
Lin'er.
Ling, 16, 54.
Lin'ger (*ling'gur*), 54.
Lin'gered (*ling'gurd*).
Lin'ger-ing (*ling'gur-*).
Lin'go (*ling'go*), 86.
Lin-gua-dent'al (*ling-gwa-*), 34.
Lin'gual (*ling'gwal*), 72.
Lin'gui-fôrm (*ling'-gwĭ-*), 169.
Lin'guist (*lin'gwist*).
Lin-guist'ic (*ling-gwist'ik*), 109.
Lin-guist'ic-al (*ling-gwist'ik-al*), 108.
Li-nig'er-oŭs (*-nij'-*).
Lin'i-ment (169), *n.* a semi-fluid ointment. [*See* Linament, *and* Lineament, 148.]
Lin'ing.
Link (*lingk*, 54), *n.* & *v.* [pl. of *n.* Links.—*See* Lynx, 160.]
Linked (*lingkt*).
Link'ing.
Lin-næ'an (13, 72) [*not* lin'e-an, 153] [Linnean, 203.]
Lin'net, 66, 170.
Lin'seed.
Lin'sey-wŏŏl'sey (*lin'-zy-wŏŏl'zy*) [so Sm.; *lin'sy wŏŏl'sy*, Wk. Wr. Wb. Gd. 155.]
Lin'stock [Lintstock, 203.]
Lint, 16.
Lin'tel, 76.
Li'on, 25, 86.
Li'on-ess.
Li'on-ize, 202.
Li'on-ized, 183.
Li'on-īz-ing.
Lip, 16, 30.
Lip'o-gram, *or* Li'po-gram [*lip'o-gram*, Wr. Wb. Gd.; *li'po-gram*, Sm. 155.]
Lip-o-gram-mat'ic, *or* Li-po-gram-mat'ic.
Lip-o-gram'ma-tist, *or* Li-po-gram'ma-tist.
Li-poth'y-my (151, 171) [so Wk. Sm. Gd.; *lĭ-poth'i-my*, Wr. 155.]
Lipped (*lipt*), 176.
Lip'pi-tude, 127, 170.
Liq'ua-ble (*lik'wa-bl*), 164.
Li-qua'tion.
Liq-ue-fa'cient (*lik-we-fa'shent*), 112.
Liq-ue-fac'tion (*-we-*).
Liq-ue-fi'a-ble (*-we-*), 164, 169, 171.
Liq'ue-fīed (*-we-*).
Liq'ue-fȳ (*-we-*), 34, 169.
Liq'ue-fȳ-ing.
Lī-ques'cen-cy, 151, 171.
Lī-ques'cent, 34, 39, 52.
Li-queur' (Fr.) (*lē-kur'*) [so Sm.; *lē-kŭr'*, Wk. Wr. Wb. Gd. 155.]
Liq'uid (*lik'wid*), 171.
Liq'uid-ate (*-wid-*).
Liq'uid-āt-ed (*-wid-*).
Liq'uid-āt-ing (*-wid-*).
Liq-uid-a'tion (*-wid-*).
Liq'uid-āt-or (*-wid-*), 169.
Lĭ-quid'i-ty (*-kwid'-*), 108, 169, 232.
Liq'uid-ize (*-wid-*) 202.
Liq'uid-ized (*-wid-*).
Liq'uid-īz-ing (*-wid-*).
Liq'uor (*lik'ur*) (171), a liquid substance. [*See* Licker, 160.]
[Liquorice 203.—*See* Licorice.]
Lis'bon (*liz'-*), 86, 136.
Lisp, 16.
Lisped (*lispt*).
Lisp'er, 77.
Lisp'ing.
List, 16.
List'ed.
List'el.
List'en (*lis'n*), 149, 162.
List'ened (*lis'nd*), 165.
List'en-er (*lis'n-*).
List'en-ing (*lis'n-*).
List'ing.
List'less.
Lit, 16.
Lit'a-ny, 66, 170.
[Liter, 203. *See* Litre.]
Lit'er-al, *a.* pertaining to, or consisting of, letters; according to the exact words or their strict meaning. [*See* Littoral, 148.]
Lit'er-al-ism (*-izm*), 136.
Lit'er-al-ist, 171.
Lit'er-al-ly, 170.
Lit'er-a-ry, 72, 169.
Lit'er-ate, *n.* & *a.* 73.
Lit-er-a'ti (L.), *n. pl.*
Lit-er-a'tim (L.).
Lit'er-a-ture, 26, 90.
Lith'arge.
Lithe, 140.
Lithe'some (*līth'sum*) [so Sm. Wr. Wb.Gd.; *lith'sum*, Wk. 155.]
Lith'i-a, 169.
Lith'ic.
Lith'i-um, 169.
Lith'o-dome.
Lĭ-thod'o-mī, *n. pl.*
Lĭ-thod'o-moŭs.
Lith'o-glyph, 171.
Lith'o-grăph, 127.
Lith'o-grăphed (*-grăft*), 171; Note C, p. 34.
Li-thog'ra-pher.
Lith-o-graph'ic, 109.
Lith-o-graph'ic-al, 108.
Lith'o-graph-ing.
Li-thog'ra-phy, 108, 169.
Lith-oid'al.
Lith-o-log'ic (*-loj'-*).
Lith-o-log'ic-al (*-loj'-*).
Li-thol'o-gy, 108.
Lith'o-man-cy.
Lith-on-trip'tic [Lithontryptic, 203.]
Lith-on-trip'tist [so Wr.; *lith'on-trip-tist*, Sm. 155.]
Lith-on-trip'tor [so Wr.; *lith'on-trip-tor*, Sm. Gd. 155.]
Lĭ-thoph'a-goŭs, 171.
Lith'o-tint.
Lith'o-tome.
Lĭ-thot'o-mist, 151.
Lĭ-thot'o-my, 108, 231.
Lith'o-trip-sy, 169.
Lĭ-thot'ri-ty, *or* Lith'o-trī-ty [so Wr.; *li-thot'ri-ty*, Gd.; *lith'-o-trī-ty*, Sm. 155.]
Lith'o-type.
Lit'i-gant, 72.
Lit'i-gate, 73, 169.
Lit'i-gāt-ed.
Lit'i-gāt-ing.
Lit-i-ga'tion, 112.
Lit'i-gāt-or, 169.
Li-tig'ioŭs (*lĭ-tij'us*), 145.
Lit'mus, 169.
Lĭ-to'tes (*-tēz*).
Lĭ-tram'e-ter, 108.
Li'tre (*li'tur*, or *le'tur*) [*li'tur*, Sm.; *le'tur*, Wr.Gd.155.] [Līter, preferred by Gd. *See* Note E, p. 70.]

Lit′ter, 170.
Lit′tered, 150.
Lit′ter-ing.
Lit′tle (*lit′l*), 66, 162.
Lit′to-ral (230), *a.* pertaining to, or growing on, the shore. [*See* Literal, 148.]
Lĭ-tur′gic.
Lĭ-tur′gic-al, 72.
Lit′ur-gy.
Lĭve, *v.* 161, 163.
Līve, *a.* 161, 163.
Lĭved (*lĭvd*) (161), *v.* did live.
Līved (*līvd*) (161), *a.* having life.
Līve′li-hŏŏd, 186.
Līve′li-ness. [153.]
Līve′long [*not* lĭv′long,
Līve′ly, 93.
Liv′er.
Liv′er-ĭed (*-id*).
Liv′er-wort (*-wurt*), 206.
Liv′er-y, 105.
Liv′er-y-man, 196.
Līves (*līvz*) (161, 193), *n. pl.* [*See* Life.]
Lĭves (*lĭvz*) (161), *v.* does live.
Liv′id, 170.
Liv′ing.
Livraison (Fr.) (*lēv-rā-zōng′*).
Li′vre (*li′vur*, or *le′vur*), [so Wr. Gd.; *li′vur*, Wk. Sm. 155.]
Lix-iv′i-al, 232, Exc.
Lix-iv′i-ate, *a.* & *v.* 73.
Lix-iv′i-āt-ed.
Lix-iv′i-āt-ing.
Lix-iv-i-a′tion.
Lix-iv′i-um, 169.
Liz′ard, 72.
Lla′ma (171) [Lama, 203.]
Lo (24), *int.* look; behold. [*See* Low, 160.]
Lōach, 24, 44.
Lōad (24), *n.* a burden: — *v.* to freight; to burden. [*See* Lowed, 160.] [Lode (in the sense of *a mineral vein*), 203.]
Lōad′ed.
Lōad′ing.
Lōad′star [Lodestar, 203.]
Lōad′stone [Lodestone, 203.]
Lōaf (24), *n.* [pl. Lōaves (*lōvz*, 166), 193.]
Lōaf′er.
Lōam, 24, 153, 156.

☞ "Vulgarly *loom*." *Walker.*

Lōam′y, 169.
Lōan (24), *v.* to lend. [*See* Lone, 160.]
Lōaned (*lōnd*), 165.
Lōan′ing.
Lōath, *a.* (24, 37) [Loth, 203.]
Lōathe, *v.* 140, 163.
Lōathed, 165.
Lōath′ing.
Lōath′some (*loth′sum*).
Lōaves (*lōvz*) (193), *n. pl.* [*See* Loaf.]
Lo′bate, 73.
Lo′bāt-ed.
Lob′by, 66, 170.
Lobe, 24, 163.
Lo-be′li-a, 72, 78.
Lob′lol-ly.
Lob′scouse.
Lob′ster, 18, 77.
Lob′ule, 90.
Lo′cal, 72.
Lo-câle′ (Fr.).
Lo′cal-ism (*-izm*), 133.
Lo-cal′i-ty, 108, 169.
Lo-cal-ĭ-za′tion.
Lo′cal-ize, 202.
Lo′cal-ized, 183.
Lo′cal-īz-ing.
Lo′cate.
Lo′cāt-ed, 228, N.
Lo′cāt-ing, 183.
Lo-ca′tion.
Loch (18, 52), *n.* a lake. [*See* Lock, 160.] [Lough, 203.]
Lo-cha′ber-ăxe (*-ka′-*), 156, 171.
Lock (18, 52, 181), *n.* a fastening for a door, &c.: — *v.* to fasten close. [*See* Loch *and* Lough, 160.]
Lock′age, 70.
Locked (*lokt*), 165; Note C, p. 34.
Lock′er, 77.
Lock′et, 76.
Lock′ing.
Lock′ist.
Lock′jaw, 206.
Lock′smith.
Lock′-up, 206, Exc. 4.
Lo′co-fo′co, 24.
Lo-co-mo′tion.
Lo-co-mo′tĭve (84, 86) [so Wk. Wr. Wb. Gd.; *lo′ko-mo-tiv*, Sm. 155.]
Loc′u-la-ment.
Loc′u-lous.
Lo′cust.
Lode [Load, 203.]
[Lodestar, 203. — *See* Loadstar.]
[Lodestone, 203. — *See* Loadstone.]
Lodge, 45, 171.
Lodged (*lojd*).
Lodge′ment (185) [Lodgment, Wb. Gd. 203.]
Lodg′er, 45.
Lodg′ing.
Loft, 18, N.
Loft′i-ly, 186.
Loft′i-ness.
Loft′y.
Log, 18, 53.
Log′a-rithm, 133, 140.
Log-a-rith′mic, 109.
Log-a-rith′mic-al, 108.
Log′-book, 206, Exc. 4.
Logged (*logd*), 165, 176.
Log′ger-hĕad (*-gur-*).
Log′ging (*-ghing*), 138, 170, 176.
Log′ic (*loj′-*), 45, 200, 235.
Log′ic-al (*-loj′-*), 72, 108.
Log′ic-al-ly (*loj′-*).
Lo-gi′cian (*-jish′an*), 46, 234.
Lo-gis′tic (*-jis′-*).
Lo-gis′tic-al (*-jis′-*).
Lo-gom′a-chist (*-kist*), 52
Lo-gom′a-chy (*-ky*), 108.
Log-o-met′ric.
Log′o-type, 170.
Log′wood, 206.
Loin, 27, 156.
Loi′ter, 77, 104.
Loi′tered, 150.
Loi′ter-er.
Loi′ter-ing. [153.
Lŏll, (18, 172) [*not* lōl,
Lol′lard, 72.
Lolled (*lold*), 165.
Lol′li-pop, 170.
Lŏll′ing.
Lom′bard (*lum′burd*, or *lom′burd*) [*lum′burd*, Sm.; *lom′burd*, Wr. Gd. 155.]
Lom-bard′ic (*lum-*, or *lom-*).
Lo′ment, 103.
Lon′don-er (*lun′-*), 22.
Lone (24), *a.* solitary. [*See* Loan, 160.]
Lone′li-ness, 186.

Lone'ly, 93. [171.
Lone'some (-*sum*), 22,
Long, 18, N.
Longe (*lunj*) [Lunge, 203.]
Longed (*longd*), 165.
Long'er (161), *n.* one who longs.
Lon'ger (*long'gur*)(161), *a.* more long.
Lon-ge'val (-*je'*-).
Lon-gev'i-ty, 108.
Lon-ge'voŭs, 100.
Long'-hĕad-ed.
Long'ing.
Long'ish.
Lon'gi-tūde, 26, 169.
Lon-gi-tūd'in-al.
Long'-līved, 206, Exc. 5.
Loo, 19, 50.
Loof [so Wk. Sm. Wb. Gd.; *lŭf*, Wr. 155], *n.* the after part of a ship's bow. [Commonly written Luff, 203.]
Loof (*loof*, or *lŭf*) [*loof*, Sm.; *luf*, Wk.; *lŭf*, or *loof*, Wr. 155], *v.* to bring nearer the wind, as the head of a ship. [Luff, 203.]
Lo͝ok (20) [so Sm. Wr. Wb. Gd.; *look*, Wk. 155.] [*See* Note under *Book.*]
Lo͝oked (*lo͝okt*), 165; Note C, p. 34.
Lo͝ok'er.
Lo͝ok'ing.
Lo͝ok'ing-glȧss (131, 206, Exc. 4) [so Sm. Wr. Wb. Gd.; *look'-in-glȧs*, Wk. 155.]
Lo͝ok'-out, 206, Exc. 4.
Loom, 19.
Loomed, 165.
Loom'ing.
Loon, 19, 43.
Loop, 19, 30.
Looped (*loopt*).
Loop'-hole, 206, Exc. 3.
Loop'ing.
Loose, *a.* & *v.*
Loosed (*loost*), Note C, p. 34.
Loos'en (*loos'n*), 167.
Loos'ened (*loos'nd*), 165.
Loose'ness, 185.
Loose'strife, 66, N.; 216.
Loos'ing.
Lop, 18.
Lopped (*lopt*), 176.
Lop'per.
Lop'ping.
Lo-qua'cious (-*kwa'-shus*), 46, 112, 171.
Lo-quaç'i-ty (-*kwas'*-), 169, 235.
Lo'rate, 49, N.
Lord (17, 135) [*not* law'-urd, 153.]
Lord'ed.
Lord'ing.
Lord'li-ness, 186.
Lord'ly, 93.
Lore (49, 67), *n.* learning. [*See* Lower, 148.]
Lorgnette (Fr.) (*lorn-yet'*).
Lŏr'i-cate, 108, 169.
Lŏr'i-cāt-ed.
Lŏr-i-ca'tion.
Lŏr'i-keet, 48, 171.
Lŏr'i-ot.
Lorn, 17.
Lo'ry, 49, Note; 190.
Lose (*looz*), 19, 136.
Los'er (*looz'*-).
Los'ing (*looz'*).
Loss, 18, N.; 174.
Lost, 18.
Lot, 18.
Lote'-tree, 206, Exc. 4.
[Loth, 203.—*See* Loath.]

☞ "The common orthography is *loath*, pronounced with *o* long, but both the orthography and pronunciation originally followed the analogy of *cloth*." *Webster*.

Lo'tion.
Lo'tos (86) [Lotus, 203.]
Lot'ter-y, 169, 170.
Lo'tus [Lotos, 203.]
Loud, 28.
Lough (*lok*) (52, 156), *n.* a lake. [*See* Lock, 160.] [Loch, 203.]
Louis-d'or (Fr.) (*loo-e-dŏr'*).
Lounge, 28, 45.
Lounged, 165.
Loung'er (*lounj'*-).
Loung'ing (*lounj'*-).
Louse [pl. Lice, 195.]
Lou'sy (-*zy*), 136, 169.
Lout, 28.
Lou'ver (*loo'*-), 19, 77.
Lov'a-ble (*luv'*-), 164.
Lov'age (*luv'*-), 70, 169.
Love (*luv*), 22, 163.
Love'-ap-ple (*luv'*-), 206, Exc. 2.
Love'let-ter (*luv'*-).
Love'-lies-bleed'ing (*luv'līz*-), 221.
Love'li-ness (*luv'*-).
Love'lock (*luv'*-).
Love'lorn (*luv'*-).
Love'ly (*luv'*-), 93, 185.
Lov'er (*luv'*-).
Love'-sick (*luv'*-), 206, Exc. 5.
Lov'ing (*luv'*-).
Lov'ing-kind'ness (*luv'*-), 205.
Lōw (24), *a.* not high or elevated. [*See* Lo, 160.]
Lōw [so Sm. Wr. Wb. Gd.; *lo*, or *low*, Wk. 155], *v.* to bellow, as a cow.
Lōw'-bred, 206, Exc. 5.
Lōwed, *v.* did low. [*See* Load, 160.]
Lōw'er (161), *v.* to take or bring down. [*See* Lore, 148.]
Lower (*lour*) (28, 161), *v.* to appear dark or gloomy.
Lōw'ered, 150, 161.
Lowered (*lourd*), 150, 161.
Lōw'er-ing, 161.
Lower'ing (*lour'*-), 161.
Lōw'er-mōst.
Lower'y (*lour'y*), 169.
Lōw'ing.
Lōw'land, 216.
Lōw'li-ness, 186.
Lōw'ly.
Lōw'-spir'it-ed, 205.
Lox-o-drom'ic, 109, 170.
Loy'al [*not* law'yal, 153.]
Loy'al-ist.
Loy'al-ly.
Loy'al-ty.
Loz'enge, 156.
Lub'ber, 66, 170.
Lū'bric, 26.
Lu'bric-al.
Lu'bri-cant, 72.
Lu'bri-cate, 78, 169
Lu'bri-cāt-ed.
Lu'bri-cāt-ing.
Lu-bri-ca'tion, 112.
Lu-briç'i-ty, 169, 235.
Luce, 26, 127.
Lu'cent, 76.
Lu'cern (26), *n.* a sort of hunting dog;—a species of trefoil. [*See* Lusern, 160.]

Lu-cern'al.
Lu'cid [*not* loo'sid, 127, 153.]
Lu'ci-fer, 26, 78.
Lu-cif'er-oŭs, 108, 169.
Lu-cif'ic, 109.
Lu'ci-form, 171.
Luck, 22, 181.
Luck'i-ly, 186.
Luck'y, 93, 169.
Lu'cra-tĭve, 72, 84.
Lu'cre (*-kur*), 164; Note E, p. 70.
Lu'cu-brate, 26, 89.
Lū-cu-bra'tion, 112.
Lu'cu-lent, 89, 156.
Lu'di-croŭs, 78, 171.
Luff (22, 173) [Loof, 203.]
Luffed (*luft*), 165; Note [C, p. 34.
Luff'ing.
Lug, 22.
Lug'gage, 176.
Lugged (*lugd*), 165.
Lug'ger (*-gur*).
Lug'ging (*-ghing*), 138.
Lu-gu'bri-oŭs, 169.
Lūke'wârm, 26, 127
Lull, 22, 172.
Lull'a-bȳ.
Lulled (*luld*), 165.
Lull'ing.
Lu'ma-chel (*-kel*) [so Wb. Gd.; *l'oo'ma-kel*, Sm. (*See* § 26); *lu'ma-chel*, Wr. 155.]
Lu-ma-chel'la (*-kel'-*).
Lum-bag'in-oŭs (*-baj'-*).
Lum-ba'go, 122.
Lum'bar (70, 169), *a.* pertaining to the loins. [*See* Lumber, 160.]
Lum'ber (70, 169), *n.* any thing useless and cumbersome; — sawed or split timber: — *v.* to heap in disorder. [*See* Lumbar, 160.]
Lum'bered (*-burd*), 150.
Lum'ber-er, 77.
Lum'ber-ing.
Lum'bric-al.
Lu'min-a-ry, 26, 72, 169.
Lu-min-if'er-ous, 108.
Lu-min-os'i-ty, 108.
Lu'min-oŭs, 26, 100.
Lump, 22, 64.
Lumped (*lumpt*).
Lump'ing.
Lump'ish, 80.
Lump'suck-er.
Lump'y, 169.
Lu'na (L.), 26.
Lu'na-cy, 169.
Lu'nar, 74, 127.
Lu-na'ri-an, 49, N.
Lu'nate.
Lu'nāt-ed.
Lu'na-tic, 26, 109.
Lu-na'tion, 89.
Lunch, 22, 44.
Lunched (*luncht*).
Lunch'eon (*lunch'un*) (171) [so Sm. Wr. Wb. Gd.; *lun'shun*, Wk. 155.]
Lunch'ing.
Lune, 127.
Lu-nette' (Fr.), 154.
Lung, 22, 54.
[Lunge, 203. — *See* Longe.]
Lung'wort (*-wurt*).
Lu'ni-form, 108, 169.
Lu-ni-so'lar, 122.
Lu'nu-lar, 108.
Lu'nu-late, 108.
Lu'nu-lāt-ed.
Lu-per'cal [so Sm. Wr.; *lu'per-kal*, Wb. Gd. 155.]

☞ Shakespeare accents the first syllable (*lu'per-cal*).

Lu'pĭne, 26, 82, 152.
Lurch, 21, 44.
Lurched (*lurcht*), 165; Note C, p. 34.
Lurch'er.
Lurch'ing.
Lure, 26, 49.
Lured, 165.
Lu'rid, 26, 49, N.
Lūr'ing, 49, Note; 235.
Lurk, 21.
Lurked (*lurkt*).
Lurk'er, 228.
Lurk'ing.
Lurk'ing-place, 206, Exc. 4.
Lus'cious (*lush'us*), 171.
Lu'sern (26), *n.* the lynx. [*See* Lucern, 160.]
Lu'si-ad (*-zĭ-*) [so Wb. Gd.; *lu'si-ad*, Wr. 155.]
Lust, 22.
Lust'ed.
Lust'ful (*-fŏŏl*).
Lust'i-ly, 186.
Lust'i-ness.
Lust'ing.
Lus'tral, 230.
Lus-tra'tion, 112.
Lus'tre (169) [Luster, Wb. Gd. 203. — *See* Note E, p. 70.]
Lus'tring [so Wk. Sm. Wb. Gd.; *lus'tring*, or *lūt'string*, Wr. 155], *n.* a lustrous silk. [Lutestring, 203. — *See* Note under *Lutestring*.]
Lus'troŭs, 100.
Lus'trum (L.) [pl. *Lus'tra*, 198.]
Lust'y, 169.
Lu'sus Na-tu'ræ (L.).
Lu'tan-ist.
Lu-ta'ri-oŭs, 49, N.
Lu-ta'tion.
Lute, 26, 163.
Lūt'ed, 183.
Lu'te-oŭs, 169.
Lute'string, *n.* the string of a lute.

☞ "By misapprehension of its etymology, the word *lustring* is also often spelled thus [*lutestring*]: but however presenting this form to the eye, it has long since regained its true character to the ear [*lus'tring*]." *Smart.*

Lu'ther-an, 26, 72.
Lu'ther-an-ism (*-izm*), 127, 133.
Lu'thern, 26.
Lūt'ing, 183.
Lu'tose.
Lux'ate.
Lux'āt-ed.
Lux'āt-ing.
Lux-a'tion, 232, Exc.
Lux-u'ri-ance (*lugz-*), 40, Note; 49, N.; 137.
Lux-u'ri-an-cy (*lugz-*).
Lux-u'ri-ant (*lugz-u'rĭ-ant*) (40, 49, N.) [so Wr.; *lug-zū'rĭ-ant*, Wk. Sm.; *luks-ū'ri-ant*, Wb. Gd. 155.]
Lux-u'ri-ate (*lugz-*), 49, N.
Lux-u'ri-āt-ed (*lugz-*).
Lux-u'ri-āt-ing (*lugz-*).
Lux-u'ri-oŭs (*lugz-*) (137, 232, Exc.) [so Wr.; *lug-zu'ri-us* (49, N.), Wk. Sm.; *luks'-ū'ri-us*, Wb. Gd. 155.]
Lux'u-ry (89) [so Wb. Gd.; *luk'shu-ry*, Wk.

Wr.; *luks'u-ry*, coll. *luk'sh'oo-ry* (*See* § 26), Sm. 155.]
Lȳ-can'thro-py (105) [so Wk. Sm. Wb. Gd.; *lĭ-kan'thro-py*, Wr. 155.]
Lȳ-ce'um (111, 125) [L. pl. *Lȳ-ce'a*; Eng. pl. Ly-ce'ums (*-umz*), 198] [*not* li'se-um, 153.]
Lyd'i-an, 171.
Lye (25), *n.* water impregnated with alkaline salt imbibed from the ashes of wood. [*See* Lie, 160.] [Ley, 203.]
Ly'ing, 184.
Lymph (*limf*), 16
Lym-phat'ic, 109.
Lynch, 16, 44, Note 2.
Lynched (*lincht*), 165; Note C, p. 34.
Lynch'ing.
Lynx (*lingks*) (16, 54), *n.* a quadruped of the cat kind. [*See* Link, 160.]
Lynx'-eyed (*lingks'īd*), 206, Exc. 5.
Ly'ra, 49, N.
Ly'rate.
Ly'răt-ed.
Lyre (25, 49) [*See* Liar, *and* Lier, 148.]
Lȳr'ic.
Lȳr'ic-al, 108.
Lȳr'i-cism (*-sizm*), 133.
Ly'rist, 49, N.
Lȳ-te'ri-an, 49, N.

M.

Mab, 10, 31, 32.
Mac-ad-am-ī-za'tion.
Mac-ad'am-ize, 202.
Mac-ad'am-īzed, 183.
Mac-ad'am-īz-ing.
Mac-a-ro'nĭ, 170.
Mac-a-ron'ic.
Mac-a-roon', 122.
Ma-caw', 121.
Mac'co-boy, 105.
Mace, 23.
Maç-e-do'ni-an.
Maç'er-ate, 171, 233, Exc.
Maç'er-ăt-ed, 183.
Maç'er-ăt-ing.
Maç-er-a'tion, 112.
Mach-i-a-vĕl'ian (*mak-i-a-vĕl'yan*) [so Wr. Wb. Gd.; *mak-i-a-ve'li-an*, Sm. 155.]
Mach'i-a-vel-ism (*mak'-i-a-vel-izm*), 133, 136.
Ma-chic'o-lăt-ed.
Mach-i-co-la'tion (*mach-*, or *mash-*) [*mach-i-ko-la'shun*, Wr. Gd.; *mash-i-kō-la'shun*, Sm. 155.]
Mach'in-al (*mak'-*), *or* Ma-chin'al (*ma-shēn'-*) [so Wr.; *mak'in-al*, Wk. Wb. Gd.; *ma-shē'nal*, Sm. 155.]
Mach'in-ate (*mak'-*).
Mach'in-ăt-ed (*mak'-*).
Mach'in-ăt-ing (*mak'-*).
Mach-in-a'tion (*mak-*).
Ma-chine' (*-shēn'*), 114.
Ma-chin'er-y (*-shēn'-*).
Ma-chin'ist (*-shēn'-*).
Mack'er-el, Note D, p. 37.
Mack'in-tosh, 171.
Mack'le (*mak'l*), *n.* a blur in printing. [*See* Macle, 160.]
Mac'le (*mak'l*) [so Sm. Wb. Gd.; *ma'kl*, Wr. 155], *n.* a tessellated appearance in crystals. [*See* Mackle, 160.]
Ma'cro-cosm (*-kozm*) (133) [so Wk. Sm. Wr.; *mak'ro-kozm*, Wb. Gd. 155.]
Ma-crom'e-ter, 108.
Ma'cron.
Mac-ro-phyl'loŭs, *or* Ma-croph'yl-loŭs. — [*See* Adenophyllous.]
Ma-crou'ran, *or* Ma-cru'ran (*-kroo'-*), 203.
Ma-crou'roŭs, *or* Ma-cru'roŭs (*-kroo'-*), 203.
Mac'u-la (L.) [pl. *Mac'-u-læ* (*-le*), 198.]
Mac'u-late, *v.* & *a.*
Mac'u-lăt-ed.
Mac'u-lăt-ing.
Mac-u-la'tion.
Mad, 10, 42.
Mad'am, 72, 170.
Ma-dăme' (Fr.) [pl. *Mesdames* (*mā-dăm'*), 198.]
Mad'cap, 206.
Mad'ded.
Mad'den (*mad'n*), 149.
Mad'dened (*mad'nd*), 165, 167.
Mad'den-ing (*mad'n-*).
Mad'der, 66, 170.
Mad'ding, 176.
Made, *v.* did make. [*See* Maid, 160.]
Ma-dei'ra (*ma-de'ra*, or *ma-da'ra*) (49, N.) [*ma-de'ra*, Wr.; *ma-dēr'ra*, Sm.; *ma-da'ra*, Wb. Gd. 155.]
Mad-em-oi-selle' (*mad-mwä-zel'*) [so Sm. Gd.; *mad-em-wä-zel'*, Wr. 155.]
Mad'house, 216.
Mad'măn, 196.
Ma-don'na, 66, 170.
Mad're-pore, 105, 171.
Mad'ri-er, *or* Ma-driēr' [so Wr.; *mad'ri-er*, Sm.; *mad-rēr'*, Gd. 155.]
Mad'ri-gal, 72.
Mä-es-to'so (It.) (*-zo*).
Mag-a-zine' (*-zēn'*), 122.
Mag'da-len, 105.
Mag-el-lan'ic (*maj-*) [so Wr. Gd.; *mag-el-lan'-ik*, Sm. 155.]
Mag'got, 170.
Mag'got-y, 169, 176.
Ma'gī (*-jī*), *n. pl.*
Ma'gi-an, 78, 171.
Mag'ic (*maj'-*), 200, 235.
Mag'ic-al (*maj'-*), 228.
Ma-gi'cian (*-jish'an*).
Ma-gilp' (*-ghilp'*), 121.
Mag-is-te'ri-al (*maj-*), 49, N.
Mag'is-tra-cy (*maj'-*).
Mag'is-trate (*maj'-*).
Mag'ma, 72.
Mag'na Char'ta (L.), (*kar'-*), 156.
Mag-na-nim'i-ty, 169.
Mag-nan'i-moŭs.
Mag'nate.
Mag-ne'si-a (*-zhĭ-a*) [so Wr.; *mag-ne'si-a*, coll. *mag-ne'shi-a*, Sm.; *mag-ne'zha*, Gd. 155.]
Mag-ne'si-an (*-zhĭ-an*).
Mag'net, 76.
Mag-net'ic, 109.
Mag-net'ic-al, 108.
Mag'net-ism (*-izm*), 136.
Mag'net-ize, 202.
Mag'net-ized, 165.
Mag'net-īz-er.
Mag'net-īz-ing.
Mag'net-o-e-lec'tric, 224
Mag'net-o-e-lec-triç'i-ty [so Sm. Wr.; *mag-*

ne'to-e-lek-tris'i-ty, Gd. 155.]
Mag-net-om'e-ter, 108.
Mag'net-o-mo'tor [Magneto-moter, 203.]
Mag-nif'ic, 109.
Mag-nif'ic-al, 108.
Mag-nif'i-cence, 171.
Mag-nif'i-cent, 127.
Mag'ni-fīed.
Mag'ni-fī-er, 186.
Mag'ni-fȳ, 94.
Mag'ni-fȳ-ing, 186.
Mag-nil'o-quence (*-kwens*).
Mag-nil'o-quent (*-kwent*).
Mag'ni-tude, 169.
Mag-no'li-a, 156.
Mag'pīe.
Mag'uey (*magh'y*), Note D, p. 37; 169.
Mag'yar (*mad'yar*).
Ma-hă-ba-rä'ta, *or* Ma-hab-a-ra'ta [*ma-hab-a-rä'ta*, Sm.; *mä-ha-bä'ra-tȧ*, Wr. 155.]
Ma-hog'a-ny, 171.
Ma-hom'et-an [Mahomedan, Mohammedan, 203.]
Ma-hom'et-an-ism (*-izm*).
Māid, *n.* a virgin. [*See* Made, 160.]
Māid'en (*mād'n*), 149.
Māid'en-hŏŏd (*mād'n-*).
Māid-ma'ri-an [so Wr. Gd.; *mād-mêr'yan*, Wk.; *mād-mêr'i-an*, Sm. 155.]
Māil, *n.* defensive armor;—postal conveyance: — *v.* to send by post. [*See* Male, 160.]
Māil'a-ble, 164, 169.
Māiled, 165.
Māil'ing.
Māim, 23, 32.
Māimed, 165.
Māim'ing.
Māin, *a.* principal, chief: — *n.* the ocean, the continent. [*See* Mane, 160.]
Māin'mȧst, 206, 216.
Māin'prise (*-prīz*) [Mainprize, 203.]
Māin'sāil.
Main-tāin' (*men-tān'*) [so Wk. Wb. Gd.; *man-tān'*, or *mān-tān'*, Wr.; *mān-tān'*, Sm. 155.]
Main-tāin'a-ble (*men-*), 169.
Main-tāined' (*men-*), 165.
Main-tāin'er (*men-*), *n.* one who maintains or supports. [*See* Maintainor, 160.]
Main-tāin'ing (*men-*).
Main-tāin'or (*men-*), *n.* one who maintains a suit between others by furnishing money. [Law term. — *See* Maintainer, 160.]
Māin'ten-ance (169, 171) [so Sm. Wr. Wb. Gd.; *men'ten-ans*, Wk. 155.]
Māize (23, 40), *n.* Indian corn. [*See* Maze, 160.]
Ma-jes'tic, 109.
Ma-jes'tic-al, 228.
Ma-jes'tic-al-ly.
Maj'es-ty, 105.
Ma'jor, 88, 169.
Ma'jor-do'mo.
Ma'jor-gen'er-al, 205.
Ma-jor'i-ty, 169.
Ma-jus'cule.
Make, 23, 52.
Māk'er.
Make'-shift, 206, Exc. 4.
Make'-weight (*-wāt*).
Māk'ing, 141.
Mal'a-chite (*-kīt*), 52.
Mal-a-col'o-gy, 108.
Mal-a-cop-te-ryg'i-oŭs (*-rij'i-us*), 116, 171.
Mal-a-cos'tra-can.
Mal-a-cos'tra-coŭs.
[Maladministration, 203. *See* Maleadministration.]
Mal-a-droit', 122.
Mal'a-dy, 105.
Mal'a-ga, 72.
Mal'an-ders (*-durz*).
Mal'a-pert, 21, N.
Mal-ap-ro-pos' (Fr.) (*-po'*).
Ma'lar.
Ma-la'ri-a (49, N.) [so Wb. Gd.; *mal-a'ri-a*, Wr.; *mal-ä're-a*, Sm. 155.]
Ma-la'ri-oŭs, 100.
Ma'late.
Ma-lāy' (121, 156), *n.* a native or an inhabitant of Malacca. [*See* Mêlée, 160.]
Ma-lāy'an.
[Malconformation, 203.—*See* Maleconformation.]
[Malcontent.—*See* Malecontent.]
Māle, *a.* of the sex that begets young: — *n.* a he-animal. [*See* Mail, 160.]
Măle, a prefix signifying *ill*.

☞ As a prefix, *male* is pronounced *măl* by Smart, Worcester, and most other orthoepists, but by Walker *māl*; and the *e*, which is sunk in the pronunciation, is often omitted in the orthography. Worcester remarks: "There are words in which *male* has the same origin and meaning [ill]; but the letters are not so separable as to have the character of a prefix; as, *malefactor*."

Măle-ad-min-is-tra'tion [Maladministration, 203.]
Măle-con-form-a'tion [Malconformation, 203.]
Măle-con-tent' [Malcontent, 203.]
Mal-e-dic'tion, 144.
Mal-e-fac'tor, *or* Mal'e-fac-tor (88, 116) [*mal-e-fak'tur*, Wk. Wr. Wb. Gd.; *mal'e-fak-tur*, Sm. 155.]
Măle-fēa'sance (*mal-fe'-zans*) [so Wr. Gd.; *mal-fa'zans*, Sm. 155.] [Malfeasance, 203.]
[Maleformation, 203.— *See* Malformation.]
Măle-prac'tice (171) [Malpractice, 203.]
[Maletreat, 203. — *See* Maltreat.]
Ma-lev'o-lence, 169.
Ma-lev'o-lent.
[Malfeasance, 203. — *See* Malefeasance.]
Mal-form-a'tion [Maleformation, 203.]
Ma'lic, 200.
Mal'īce, 169, 170.
Ma-lī'cious (*-lish'us*), 112, 169.
Ma-līgn' (*-līn'*), *a.* & *v.* 103, 121, 162.
Ma-lig'nan-cy, 169.

Ma-lig′nant, 72.
Ma-ligned′ (-*līnd′*), 162.
Ma-lign′er (-*līn′*-).
Ma-lign′ing (-*līn′*-).
Ma-lig′ni-ty, 169.
Ma-lin′ger (*ma-ling′-gur*) (54, 138) [so Gd. Sm.; *ma-lin′jur*, Wr. 155.]
Ma-lin′gered (-*ling′-gurd*), 165.
Ma-lin′ger-er (-*ling′-gur*-).
Ma-lin′ger-ing (-*ling′-gur*).
Mal′i-son (-*zn*), 136, 149.
Mâl′kin (*maw′kin*), 162, 171.
Mâll [so Wr. Wb. Gd.; *mal*, Wk. Sm. 155], *n.* a heavy wooden hammer or beetle. [Maul, 203.]
Măll [so Sm. Wr. Wb. Gd.; *mel*, Wk. 155], *n.* a public walk.
Mâll, *v.* to beat with a mall. [Maul, 203.—*See* Mall.]
Mal′lard, 72.
Mal-le-a-bil′i-ty, 169.
Mal′le-a-ble, 164, 229.
Mal′le-ate, 170.
Mal′le-āt-ed, 183.
Mal′le-āt-ing.
Mal-le-a′tion, 112.
Mâlled, 165.
Mal′le-o-lar.
Mal′let, 66, 76, 170.
Mâll′ing.
Mal′lōw [pl. Mal′lōws (-*lōz*), 189.]

☞ "Seldom used but in the plural form."—*Worcester.*

Mälm′sey (*mäm′zy*), 162, 169.
[Malpractice, 203. —*See* Malepractice.]
Mâlt, 17.
Mâlt′ed.
Mâl-tese′ (-*tēz′*) (121) [so Wr.; *mawl-tēs′*, Gd. 155.]
Mal′tha, 72.
Mal-thu′sian (-*zhan*) (112, 127) [*mal-thu′-shan*, Wr.; *mal-thu′-si-an*, Gd. 155.]
Mâlt′ing.
Mal-trēat′ [Maletreat, 203.]
Mal-trēat′ed.
Mal-trēat′ing.
Mal-trēat′ment.
Mâlt′ster, 77.
Ma′lum in se (L.).
Mal-va′ceous (-*shus*).
Mal-ver-sa′tion.
Mam′e-lūke, 26.
Mam-mä′, 171.
Mam′mal, 72, 170.
Mam-ma′li-a, *n. pl.*
Mam-ma′li-an.
Mam-mal′o-gist, 45.
Mam-mal′o-gy, 108.
Mam′ma-ry, 72.
Mam′mi-fer, 78.
Mam-mif′er-ous, 108.
Mam′mi-form, 108.
Mam′mil-la-ry, 170.
Mam′mil-lāt-ed.
Mam′mon, 66, 86, 170.
Mam′mon-ist.
Mam′moth, 86, 170.
Man, *n.* & *v.* (10, 43) [pl. of *n.* men, 195.]
Man′a-cle, 104, 164.
Man′a-cled (-*kld*), 183.
Man′a-cling.
Man′age, 169, 170.
Man′age-a-ble, 164, 183.
Man′aged.
Man′age-ment, 185.
Man′a-ger.
Man′a-ging.
Man′a-kin, 169.
Man-a-tee′, 122.
Manch-i-neel′, 122, 171.
Man-ci-pa′tion.
Man′ci-ple, 164.
Man-dā′mus (L.).
Man-da-rin′ (-*rēn′*), 122.
Man′da-ta-ry, 72.
Man′date.
Man′da-to-ry, 86.
Man′di-ble, 164, 169.
Man-dib′u-lar, 74, 108.
Man-dib′u-late, 89.
Man-dib′u-lāt-ed.
Man-di-bu′li-form, 108.
Man′drake, 103.
Man′drel (76), *n.* an instrument for holding the work in a turner's lathe. [*See* Mandrill, 148.]
Man′drill, *n.* a large and powerful species of baboon. [*See* Mandrel, 148.]
Mane (23), *n.* the long hair on the neck of certain animals. [*See* Main, 160.]
Ma-nege′ (*ma-nāzh′*) [so Wr.; *măn-āzh′*, Sm.; *ma-nāzh′*, or *man′ej*, Gd. 155.]
Ma′nes (L.) (-*nēz*), *n. pl.*
Man′ful (-*fōōl*), 178.
Man′ful-ly (-*fōōl*-).
[Maneuver, Wb. Gd. 203.—*See* Manœuvre.]
[Maneuverer, Wb. Gd. 203. — *See* Manœuvrer.]
[Maneuvering, Wb. Gd. 203. — *See* Manœuvring.]
Man′ga-by (*mang′*-), 54.
Man-ga-nese′ (*mang-ga-nēz′*) (122) [so Sm. Wr.; *mang-ga-nēs′*, Gd. 155.]
Man-ga-ne′sian (*mang-ga-ne′zhi-an*) [so Wr.; *mang-ga-ne′-shan*, Gd. 155.]
Mānge, 23, 127.
Man′gel-wur′zel (*mang′gl-wur′zl*).
Mān′ger, 45.
Mān′gi-ness, 186.
Man′gle (*mang′gl*), 54, 164.
Man′gled (*mang′gld*).
Man′gler (*mang′*-).
Man′gling (*mang′*-).
Man′go (*mang′*-).
Mangoose, 203.—*See* Mongoose, 203.]
Man′go-stan (*mang′*-), *or* Man′go-steen (*mang′*-).
Man′grove (*mang′*-) [so Wr. Gd.; *man′grōv*, Sm. 155.]
Mān′gy, 93, 156.
[Manhaden, 203.—*See* Menhaden.]
Man′hŏŏd.
Ma′ni-a.
Ma′ni-a ā po′tu (L.).
Ma′ni-ac, 108.
Ma-ni′ac-al, 108.
Man-i-che′an (-*ke′*-).
Man′i-chee (-*ke*-) [so Sm. Gd.; *man-i-ke′*, Wr. 155.]
Man-i-chee′ism (-*ke′-izm*) [so Sm. Wr.; *man′i-ke-izm*, Gd. 155.]
Man′i-chord (-*kord*).
Man′i-fest.
[Manifestable,

203.—*See* Manifestible.]
Man-i-fest-a'tion.
Man'i-fest-ed.
Man'i-fest-i-ble (164) [Manifestable, 203.]
Man'i-fest-ing.
Man'i-fest-ly, 126.
Man-i-fest'o, *n.* [pl. Man-i-fest'oes (-ōz), 192.]
Man'i-fōld.
Man'i-kin, 169, 170.
Ma'ni-oc.
Man'i-ple, 164.
Ma-nip'u-lar, 108.
Ma-nip'u-late.
Ma-nip'u-lāt-ed.
Ma-nip'u-lāt-ing.
Ma-nip-u-la'tion.
Ma'nis.
Man'i-tou (*-too*).
Man-kīnd' (52, 146) [so Wr. Wb. Gd.; *man-k'īnd'*, Sm. (*See* § 26); *man-kyīnd'*, Wk. 155.]

☞ When used antithetically with respect to *womankind*, the accent is on the first syllable.

[Manks, 203.—*See* Manx.]
Man'like, 206, Exc. 5.
Man'li-ness, 78, 186.
Man'ly, 93.
Man'-mid'wīfe [so Wr.; *man-mid'wīf*, Sm. 155.]
Man'-mil'li-ner.
Man'na, 66, 72.
Man'na-drop'ping, 205.
Man'naed, 165, 188.
Manned, 165, 176.
Man'ner (70, 170), *n.* mode, method. [*See* Manor, 160.]
Man'nered (*-nurd*).
Man'ner-ism (*-izm*), 133.
Man'ner-ist.
Man'ner-lĭ-ness.
Man'ner-ly.
Man'ning.
Man'nish, 176.
Ma-nœu'vre (*-noo'vūr*) (169, 171) [so Wk. Sm. Wr.; *ma-nū'vur*, Wb. Gd. 155] [Maneuver, preferred by Gd. 203.]
Ma-nœu'vred (*-noo'vurd*) [Maneuvered, 203.]
Ma-nœu'vrer (*-noo'-*) [Maneuverer, 203.]
Ma-nœu'vring (*-noo'-*) [Maneuvering, 203.]
Man-of-wâr', 221.
Ma-nom'e-ter, 108.
Man-o-met'ric-al.
Man'or (66, 70, 170), *n.* a nobleman's estate in lands. [*See* Manner, 160.]
Ma-no'ri-al, 49, N.
Manse, Note D, p. 37.
Man'sion, 112, 234.
Man'slaugh-ter(*-slaw-*), 206.
Man'sue-tude(*-swe-*),169
Man'tel (*man'tl*) (149), *n.* the work in front of a chimney over the jambs of a fireplace.

☞ "This spelling is now prevalent instead of *mantle*, in order to distinguish between this word and *mantle*, a garment." *Goodrich.*

Man'tel-et (*man'tl-et*) [so Sm., *man'tel-et*, Wb. Gd.; *man-te-let'*, Wk. Wr. 155.]
Man'ti-ger (*-gur*), *or* Man'tĭ-ger (*-gur*) [*man'tĭ-gur*, Wr. Wb. Gd.; *man'tī-gur*, Sm.; *man-tī'gur*, Wk. 155.]
Man'tle (*-tl*), 164.

☞ When this word means *the work in front of a chimney, over the jambs of a fireplace*, it is now more commonly written *mantel.*—*See* Note under *Mantel.*

Man'tled (*-tld*), 164, 165.
Man'tling, 183.
Man'tua (*man'tu*, or *man'tu-a*) [*man'tu*, Sm., *man'chu-a*, Wk.; *man'tu-a*, or *man'tu*, Wr. Gd. 155.]

☞ '*Manteau* . . . is the original word, and suggests the usual pronunciation: the word has no relationship to the Italian city, and may therefore properly differ from it in sound." *Smart.*

Man'tua-māk-er (*-tu-*), 205.
Man'u-al, 72, 89.
Man-u-duc'tion, 112.
Man-u-fact'o-ry, 89.
Man-u-fact'ure, *n.* & *v.* 89, 91.
Man-u-fact'ured, 165.
Man-u-fact'ur-er(*-yur-*), 91, 171, 183.
Man-u-fact'ur-ing.
Man-u-mis'sion (*-mish'un*), 112, 169.
Man-u-mit' (122)[so Wk. Wr. Gd.; *man'u-mit*, Sm. 155.]
Man-u-mit'ted, 176.
Man-u-mit'ting.
Man-u-mit'tor, 169.
Ma-nūr'a-ble, 49, N.; 169.
Ma-nure', 103, 121.
Ma-nured', 165.
Ma-nūr'er, 183.
Ma-nūr'ing.
Man'u-script, 89.
Manx (*mangks*), 52, 54. [Manks, 203.]
Man'y (*men'y*), 170, 171.

☞ "*Ma'ny* and *a'ny*, as they were originally pronounced, have been shortened, by their frequent occurrence in discourse, into *menny* and *enny*." *Smart.*

Map, 10, 30, 32.
Ma'ple, 164.
Mapped (*mapt*), 176.
Map'ping.
Mar, 11, 49, 135.
Măr'a-bou (*-boo*), 105 [so Gd.; *măr-a-boo'*, Wr. 155.]
Măr'a-bout (*-boot*) [so Gd.; *măr-a-boot'*, Wr. 155.]
Măr-a-nä'tha (Heb.) (156) [so Sm. Gd.; *măr-a-nath'a*, Wk. Wr. 155.]
Mar-as-chi'no (*-ke'-*).
Ma-ras'mus (*-raz'-*),136.
Ma-râud', 17, 103.
Ma-râud'ed.
Ma-râud'er [so Sm. Wr. Wb. Gd.; *ma-ro'dur*, Wk. 155.]
Ma-râud'ing.
Mar-a-ve'dĭ, 153.
Mar'ble, 135, 164.
Mar'bled (*-bld*), 165.
Mar'bler, 183.
Mar'bling.
Marc(11,52,181),*n.* refuse matter remaining after the pressure of fruit. [*See* Mark, *and* Marque, 160.]

Mar′ca-sīte.
Mar-ces′cent, 122.
March, 11, 44, 49, 135.
Marched (*marcht*), 165; Note C, p. 34.
March′er.
March′es (-*ĕz*), 76.
March′ing.
Mar′chion-ess (-*shun*), 141, 156.
March′pane.
Mar′cid, 80.
Mar-cid′i-ty, 108, 169.
Mare (*mêr*) (14), *n.* the female of the horse. [*See* Mayor, 160.]
Mare′schal (*mar′shal*) [so Wk. Wr. Wb. Gd.; *măr′esh-al*, by contraction *mar′shal*, Sm.] [Marshal (the common orthography), 203.]
Mar′ga-rate.
Mar-găr′ic.
Mar′ga-rīne (152) [Margarin, 203.]
Marge, 11, 45, 49.
Mar′gin, 11, 45.
Mar′gin-al, 72, 106
Mar′gin-ate.
Mar′gin-āt-ed.
Mar′grave, 103.
Mar-grăv′i-ate, 123.
Mar′gra-vine (-*vēn*), 183.
Măr′i-gōld, 48, 105.
Ma-rine′ (-*rēn′*), 121.
Măr′i-ner, 105.
Ma-ri-ol′a-try.
Măr′ish [so Sm. Wb. Gd.; *mär′ish*, Wk., *mêr′ish*, Wr. 155.]
Măr′i-tal [so Wk. Wr. Wb. Gd.; *ma-rī′tal*, Sm. 155.]
Măr′i-tīme [*not* măr′a-tīm, 127, 153.]
Mar′jo-ram, 72, 105.
Mark (11, 135), *n.* a trace or impression: — *v.* to trace or impress. [*See* Marc, *and* Marque, 160.]
Marked (*markt*), 165; Note C, p. 34.
Mark′er, 228.
Mar′ket, 11, 76.
Mar′ket-a-ble, 106, 169.
Mar′ket-dāy′, 205.
Mar′ket-ed.
Mar′ket-ing.
Mar′ket-man.
Mar′ket-place.
Mar′ket-wom′an (-*wŏŏm′*-), 205.
Mark′ing.
Marks′man, 214.
Marl, 11, 135.
Marled (*marld*), 165.
Mar′līne, 82, 152.
Marl′ing.
Marl′y, 93, 169.
Mar′ma-lade, 105.
Mar-mo-ra′ceoŭs (-*shus*), 112.
Mar-mo′re-an, 49, N.; 110
Mar-mo-set′ (-*zet′*) (122) [so Wk. Wr.; *mar′-mo-zet*, Sm.; *mar′mo-set*, Gd. 155.]
Mar′mot, *or* Mar-mot′ [so Wr.; *mar′mot*, Wb. Gd.; *mar-mot′*, Sm.; *mar′moot*, Wk. 155.]
[Marone, 203. — *See* Marroon.]
Măr′on-īte.
Ma-roon′ (121), *n.* a free negro living on the mountains in the West Indies. [*See* Marroon, 148.]
Mar′plot, 205.
Marque (*mark*), *n.* permission to pass the frontier of a country in order to make reprisals. [*See* Marc, *and* Mark, 160.]
Mar-quee′ (-*kē′*), 114.
Mar′quess (-*kwes*) (171) [Marquis, 203.]

☞ "Till of late, *marquis* was the usual form, . . . but this is now in a great degree discontinued, or used only with reference to the foreign title." *Smart.*

Mar′quet-ry (-*ket*-).
Mar′quis [Marquess, 203.]
Mar′quis-ate (-*kwiz*-) [so Wk. Sm. Wr.; *mar′kwis-āt*, Wb. Gd. 155.]
Marred (*mard*), 165.
Măr′riage (-*rij*), 70, 169.
Măr′riage-a-ble (-*rij*-), 183.
Măr′rīed, 99.
Măr′ri-er, 186.
Măr-roon′ (121), *n.* a very deep red color with a brownish cast. [*See* Maroon, 148.]

☞ "It is generally though wrongly spelled *maroon* or *marone*." *Smart*

Măr′rōw, 48, 101.
Măr′rōw-bone.
Măr′rōw-făt.
Măr′rōw-y, 93.
Măr′ry, 48, 93, 104.
Măr′ry-ing, 186.
Mars (*marz*), 11, 40.
Marsh, 11, 46, 64.
Mar′shal (230), *n.* a civil or a military officer of high rank. [*See* Martial, 160.] [Mareschal, 203.]
Mar′shalled (165) [Marshaled, Wb. Gd. 203. — *See* 177, and Note E, p. 70.]
Mar′shal-ler (177) [Marshaler, Wb. Gd. 203.]
Mar′shal-ling (177) [Marshaling, Wb. Gd. 203.]
Mar′shal-sēa.
Marsh′-mal′lōw, 205.
Marsh′-măr′i-gōld.
Marsh′y, 169.
Mar-su′pi-al, 127.
Mar-su′pi-um, 169.
Mart, 11, 41, 49.
Mar-tel′lo, 85, 170.
Mar′tĕn (149), *n.* a large kind of weasel: — a kind of swallow.

☞ In the last sense, the more usual orthography is Martin.

Mar′tial (-*shal*), *a.* pertaining to war or battle. [*See* Marshal, 160.]
Mar′tĭn (149), *n.* a sort of swallow that builds in the eaves of houses. [*See* Marten, 148.] [Marten, 203. — *See* Note under *Marten*.]
Mar′tin-et (122) [so Sm. Wb. Gd.; *mar-ti-net′*, Wr.; *mar-tin-et′*, in the sense of *a rigid disciplinarian*—*mar′-tin-ĕt*, in the sense of *a martin*, Wk. 155.]
Mar′tin-gale (105) [Martingal, 203.]
Mar′tin-mas, 72, 180.
Mart′let, 230.
Mar′tyr, 95, 169.

Mar′tyr-dom (-*dum*′ 169.
Mar′tyred, 150, 165.
Mar′tyr-ing, 176.
Mar-tyr-o-log′ic (-*loj*′-).
Mar-tyr-o-log′ic-al (-*loj*′-).
Mar-tyr-ol′o-gist.
Mar-tyr-ol′o-gy.
Mar′vel, 149.
Mar-velled [Mar-veled, Wb. Gd. 203. — *See* 177, and Note E, p. 70.]
Mar′vel-ling [Marvel-ing, Wb. Gd. 203.]
Mar′vel-lous (169, 177) [Marvelous, Wb. Gd. 203.]
Mas′cle (*mas′kl*) [so Sm. Wr.; *mas′kl*, or *mas′l*, Gd. 155.]
Mas′cu-līne, 89, 152.
Mash, 10, 46.
Mashed (*masht*), 165; Note C, p. 34.
Mash′ing.
Mash′y, 93, 169.
Måsk, 12, 131.
Måsked (*måskt*), 165.
Måsk′er, 77.
Måsk′ing.
Mas′lin (*maz′lin*) [Mastlin, Meslin, Mislin, 203.]
Ma′son (*ma′sn*), 149.
Ma-son′ic, 109, 123.
Ma′son-ry (-*sn*-), 106.
Mas′o-rah [Masora, Massora, 203.]
Mas-o-ret′ic.
Mas-o-ret′ic-al.
Mas′o-rīte, 152.
[Masque, 203. — *See* Mask.]
Mas-quer-ade′ (-*kur*-), 122.
Mas-quer-ād′ed (-*kur*-).
Mas-quer-ād′er (-*kur*-).
Mas-quer-ād′ing (*kur*-).
Måss, 12, 174.
Măs′sa-cre (-*kur*-), 171; Note E, p. 70.
Măs′sa-cred (-*kurd*), 171.
Măs′sa-crer (-*krur*).
Măs′sa-crĭng.
Mass′-book, 206, Exc. 4.
Mas′si-cot.
Mas′si-ness, 186.
Mas′sīve, 84.
Måss′-meet-ing.
Måss′y, 66, 169.
Måst, 12, 131.
Måst′ed.
Mås′ter (12) [*See* Mister.]
Mås′ter-build′er, 205.
Mås′ter-ing.
Mås′ter-ly.
Mås′ter-piēce.
Mås′ter-ship.
Mås′ter-stroke.
Mås′ter-work′man (-*wurk*′-), 205.
Mas′ter-y, 93, 169.
Mast′-hĕad, 206, Exc. 3.
Mas′tic [Mastich, 203.]
Mas′ti-ca-ble, 164.
Mas′ti-cate, 73, 169.
Mas′ti-cāt-ed, 183.
Mas′ti-cāt-ing.
Mas-ti-ca′tion, 112, 169.
Mas′ti-cāt-o-ry, 86.
Mås′tiff, 103.

☞ "The plural is regular: Johnson gives *mastives*, which is out of use." *Smart.*

[Mastlin (*maz′lin*) [so Sm. Wr.; *mes′-lin*, Wk.; *măst′lin*, Wb. Gd. 155). — *See* Maslin, 203.]
Mas′to-don (105) [so Wr. Wb. Gd.; *mast-o′don*, Sm. 155.]
Mas′toid.
Mat, 10, 41.
Mat′a-co, 156, 170.
Mat′a-dōre [so Sm. Wb. Gd.; *mat-a-dōr′*, Wk. Wr. 155.]
Match, 10, 44.
Match′a-ble, 164, 169.
Matched (*macht*), 165; Note C, p. 34.
Match′er, 77.
Match′ing.
Match′lock, 206.
Mate (23, 161), *n.* a companion; — a subordinate officer of a ship: — *v.* to match.
Ma′te (Sp.) (*mä′tā*) (161) [*mä′te*, Wr.; *ma-tā′*, Gd. 155], *n.* Paraguay tea, — being the dried leaf of the Brazilian holly.
Māt′ed, 183.
Ma-te′ri-al, 49, N.; 72.
Ma-te′ri-al-ism (-*izm*).
Ma-te′ri-al-ist, 106.
Ma-te-ri-al-ist′ic.
Ma-te-ri-al-ist′ic-al.
Ma-te-ri-al′i-ty, 169.
Ma-te′ri-al-ize, 202.
Ma-te′ri-al-ized, 183.
Ma-te′ri-al-īz-ing.
Ma-te′ri-al-ly, 170.
Ma-te′ri-a med′i-ca (L.).
Matériel (Fr.) (*ma-tā′-re-ēl*).
Ma-ter′nal, 21, N.; 72.
Ma-ter′nal-ly, 170.
Ma-ter′ni-ty, 169.
Math-e-mat′ic, 109.
Math-e-mat′ic-al, 108.
Math-e-mat′ic-al-ly.
Math-e-mat′ics, 109.
Ma-the′sis, 122.
Mat′īn, 149, 170.
Māt′ing, 183.
Mat′ins (-*inz*), *n. pl.*
Mat′rass, *n.* a chemical vessel used in sublimations. [*See* Mattress, 148.]
[Matress, 203. — *See* Mattress.]
Ma′trīce (-*tris*) (161, 169), *n.* the cavity in which any thing is formed; the womb; matrix.
Mat′rīce (-*ris*) (161, 169), *n.* a mould, — particularly for type, or for coin; — in dyeing, the five simple colors, black, white, blue, red, and yellow.
Mat′ri-cī-dal (106) [so Sm. Wb. Gd.; *mat-ri-sī′dal*, Wr. 155.]
Mat′ri-cide, 170, 230.
Ma-tric′u-late, 89.
Ma-tric′u-lāt-ed, 183.
Ma-tric′u-lāt-ing.
Ma-tric-u-la′tion, 112.
Mat-ri-mo′ni-al, 72.
Mat-ri-mo′ni-al ly.
Mat′ri-mo-ny, 86, 126.
Ma′trix (L.).
Ma′tron (86) [so Wk. Sm. Wr.; *mat′ron*, Wb. Gd. 155.]
Mat′ron-age, 70.
Ma′tron-al (72) [so Sm.; *mat′ron-al*, or *ma′-tron-al*, Wr.; *mat′-run-al*, or *ma-tro′nal*, Wk.; *mat′ron-al*, Wb. Gd. 155.]
Mat′ron-ize, 202.
Mat′ron-ized, 183.
Mat′ron-īz-ing.
Ma′tron-ly [so Wk. Sm.

Wr.; *mat'ron-ly*, Wb. Gd. 155.]
Ma-tross', 121.
Mat'ted, 176.
Mat'ter, 66, 170.
Mat'ter-of-fact, *a.* 220.
Mat ting.
Mat'tock, 171.
Mat'tress (170) [*not* ma-tras', 153], *n.* a quilted bed, stuffed with hair, moss, husks, wool, or other soft material, instead of feathers. [*See* Matrass, 148.] [Matress, 203.]
Mat'u-rate.
Mat'u-răt-ed, 183.
Mat'u-răt-ing.
Mat-u-ra'tion, 112.
Mat'u-ra-tive (84) [so Wr. Wb. Gd., *mat'u-rā-tiv*, Sm.; *mach'u-ra-tiv*, Wk. 155.]
Ma-ture', 26, 127.
Ma-tured', 165.
Ma-ture'ly, 185.
Mat-u-res'cent, 171.
Ma-tūr'ing, 183.
Ma-tu'ri-ty, 49, N.; 169.
Mat'u-ti-nal [*not* ma-tu'ti-nal, 153.]
Mâud'lin, 17, 171.
Mâu'gre (*-gur*) (164) [Mauger, preferred by Gd. — *See* Note E, p. 70.]
[Maukin, 203. — *See* Malkin.]
Mâul (17) [Mall, 203.]

☞ As a noun, meaning *a heavy wooden hammer or beetle*, this word is commonly written *mall*: as a verb, in the literal sense, *to strike with a mall*, it follows the spelling of the noun; in the derivative sense, *to beat and bruise in a coarse manner*, it is oftener spelled *maul*.

Mâuled, 165.
Mâul'ing.
Mâul'stick, 206.
Mäund (12) [so Wk. Sm. Wr.; *mând*, or *mawnd*, Gd. 155.]
Mâun'dy-Thurs'day (*-thurz'-*).
Mâu-so-le'an, 110.
Mâu-so-le'um, *n.* (111, 156) [L. pl. *Mâu-so-le'a*; Eng. pl. Mau-so-le'ums (*-umz*), 198.]
Ma'vis, 156.
Maw, 17, 32.
Mawk'ish.
Maw'-worm (*-wurm*), 206, Exc. 1.
Max'il-lar [so Sm. Wb. Gd.; *mag-zil'lar*, Wk.; *max'il-lar*, or *max-il'lar*, Wr. 155.]
Max'il-la-ry, 72.
Max-il'li-form, 108.
Max'im, 10, 80.
Max'i-mum (L.) [pl. *Max'i-ma*, 198.]
Māy, 23, 32.
Māy'be, 206.
Māy'dāy.
Māy'flower (*-flour*).
Māy'hap [so Gd.; *mā-hap'*, Wr. 155.]
Māy'hem, (*ma'hem*, or *mām*) [so Wr.; *ma'-hem*, Wb. Gd.; *mām*, Sm. 155.] [Law term. — *See* Maim.]
Māy'ing.
Māy'or, *or* Mayor (*mêr*) (23, 67) [*ma'ur*, Wk. Wr. Wb. Gd.; *mêr*, Sm. 155], *n.* the chief magistrate of a city. [*See* Mare, 160.]
Māy'or-al-ty.
Māy'or-ess.
Māy'pole, 206.
Maz'ard, 72, 170.
Maz-a-rine' (*-rēn'*), 122.
Maze (23, 40), *n.* a labyrinth. [*See* Maize, 160.]
Ma-zol'o-gy, 108.
Māz'y, 169.
Me, 13, 32.
Mēad, *n.* a kind of beverage, — a meadow. [*See* Meed, 160.]
Mĕad'ōw, 101.
Mĕad'ōw-y, 93.
Mēa'gre (*-gur*) [Meager, 203; Note E, p. 70.]

☞ "In Johnson's Dictionary, it is spelt *meager*; in the English Dictionaries which preceded that of Johnson, generally *meagre*; and in most of those published since, *meager*." *Worcester*. "*Meager*, however justifiable and desirable, is quite disused." *Smart*.

Mēa'gre-ly (*-gur-*).
Mēa'gre-ness (*-gur-*).
Mēal, 13, 50.
Mēal'i-ness, 186.
Mēal'time, 206.
Mēal'y, 228.
Mēal'y-mouthed, 165, 206, Exc. 5.
Mēan, *a.* wanting dignity or worth: — *n.* medium: — *v.* to intend; to signify. [*See* Mien, 160.]
Me-an'der, 77, 122.
Me-an'dered(*-durd*),165.
Me-an'der-ing.
Mēan'ing.
Mēan'ing-less.
Mēan'ing-ly, 93.
Mēan'ness, 66, N.
Mēans (*mēnz*), *n. sing. & pl.*
Mĕant.
Mēan'time, 206.
Mēan'while.
Mēase (*mēs*, or *mēz*) [*mēs*, Wk. Wr. Wb. Gd., *mēz*, Sm. 155.]
Mēa'sled (*me'zld*).
Mēa'sles (*me'zlz*), 171.
Mēa'sly (*me'zly*).
Mĕas'ur-a-ble (*mezh'ur-a-bl*), 47, 164.
Mĕas'ur-a-bly (*mezh'-ur-*).
Mĕas'ure (*mezh'ur*), 47, N., 91, 156.
Mĕas'ured (*mezh'urd*), 165.
Mĕas'ure-ment (*mezh'-ur-*).
Mĕas'ur-ing (*mezh'ur-*), 91.
Mēat, *n.* food, — particularly flesh used for food. [*See* Meet, *and* Mete, 160.]
Me-chan'ic (*-kan'-*), 109.
Me-chan'ic-al (*-kan'-*), 108.
Me-chan'ic-al-ly (*-kan'-*)
Mech-a-nĭ'cian (*mek-a-nish'an*), 112.
Me-chan'ic-o-chem'ic-al (*-kan'ik-o-kem'-*), 224.
Me-chan'ics (*-kan'-*).
Mech'an-ism (*mek'an-izm*), 52, 133, 136.
Mech'an-ist (*mek'-*).
Mech-an-og'raph-ist (*mek-*).
Mech an-og'ra-phy (*mek-*), 108.
Mech'lin (*mek'-*).
Me-cho'a-can (*-ko'-*, or

-cho'-) [so Wr.; *me-ko'a-kan*, Sm.; *me-cho'a-kan*, or *me-ko'a-kan*, Gd. 155.]
Me-co'ni-um, 169.
Med'al (72) [*See* Meddle, 148.]
Me-dal'lic, 170.
Me-dal'lion (*me-dal'-yun*), 51, 170.
Med'al-list [Medalist, Wb. Gd. 203. — *See* 177, and Note E, p.70.]
Med'al-lur-gy [Medalurgy, Wb. Gd. 203.]
Med'dle (104, 164, 170) [*See* Medal, 148.]
Med'dled (*med'ld*).
Med'dler (70), *n.* one who meddles. [*See* Medlar, 160.]
Med'dle-some (*med'l-sum*), 171.
Med'dling, 66, 170.
Me'di-a (L.), *n. pl.* [*See* Medium.]
Me-dĭ-æ'val (13, 72) [so Sm. Wb. Gd.; *med-i-e'val*, Wr. 155.] [Medieval, 203.]
Me'di-al, 78, 171.
Me'di-an, 72.
Me'di-ant, 72.
Me-di-as'tĭne, 82, 152.
Me-di-as-ti'num.
Me'di-ate, *a.* & *v.* 73.
Me'di-āt-ed, 183.
Me'di-ate-ly, 185.
Me'di-āt-ing.
Me-di-a'tion, 112.
Me-di-at-ĭ-za'tion, 116.
Me'di-a-tize, 202.
Me'di-a-tized.
Me'di-a-tĭz-ing.
Me'di-āt-or, 126, 169.
Me-di-a-to'ri-al, 49, N.
Me'di-āt-rix [so Sm. Wr.; *me-di-a'trix*, Wk. Gd. 155.]
Med'ic-a-ble, 126, 164.
Med'ic-al, 108.
Med'ic-al-ly, 170.
Med'ic-a-ment, 169.

☞ Walker, Smart, Worcester, Webster, and Goodrich, agree in pronouncing this word with the accent on the first syllable: but Walker remarks: "My judgment much fails me if the true pronunciation ought not to be with the accent on the second, as in *predicament*."

Med'i-cate, 169.
Med'i-cāt-ed.
Med'i-cāt-ing.
Med-i-ca'tion.
Med'i-ca-tĭve, 106.
Med-i-ce'an, 110.
Me-diç'in-al [so Sm. Wr. Wb. Gd.; *me-dis'i-nal*, or *med-i-si'nal*, Wk. 155.]

☞ "In poetry it will sometimes be necessary to accent the penultimate." *Smart.*

Med'i-cĭne (156) [so Wk. Wr. Wb. Gd.; *med'i-sin*, coll. *med'-sin*, Sm. 155.]

☞ "Vulgarly and improperly pronounced *med'-sn*." *Webster.*

Med'i-co-le'gal, 224.
[Medieval, 203. — *See* Mediæval.]
Me'di-o-cral, 72.
Me'di-o-cre (*-kur*), 126, 156.
Me'di-o-crist.
Me-di-oc'ri-ty (169) [so Sm. Wr. Wb. Gd.; *me-di-ok'ri-ty*, or *me-ji-ok'ri-ty*, Wk. 134, 155.]
Med'i-tate, 169.
Med'i-tāt-ed.
Med'-i-tāt-ing.
Med-i-ta'tion.
Med'i-tāt-ĭve.
Med-i-ter-ra'ne-an, 110, 171.
Me'di-um (169) [so Sm. Wr. Wb. Gd.; *me'di-um*, or *me'ji-um*, Wk. 134, 155.] [L. pl. *Me'di-a*; Eng. pl. Me'di-ums (*-umz*), 198.]
Med'lar (70), *n.* a kind of tree and its fruit. [*See* Meddler, 160.]
Med'ley, 98, 169.
Me-dul'lar, 74, 170.
Med'ul-la-ry, 72.
Me-dul'lĭne (152) [Medullin, 203.]
Me-du'sa (L.) (26) [pl. Me-du'sæ (*-se-*), 198.]
Meech'ing.
Meed (13, 42), *n.* a reward. [*See* Mead, 160.]
Meek, 13, 52.
Meek'en (*mēk'n*), 104.
Meek'ened (*mēk'nd*).
Meek'en-ing (*mēk'n-*).
Meer'schaum (*-shawm*, or *-shoum*), 154, 156.

☞ This word is pronounced by all the orthoepists *mēr'shoum*, but the current, if not universal pronunciation, in the United States, is *mēr'shawm*.

Meet (13), *a.* fit, proper: —*v.* to encounter. [*See* Meat, 166.]
Meet'ing, *n.* an interview; an assembly. [*See* Meting, 160.]
Meet'ing-house, 206, Exc. 4; 215.
Meg'a-cosm (*-kozm*), 136. [112.
Meg-a-le'sian (*-zhan*),
Meg-a-lo'nyx (122) [so Sm. Wr.; *meg-a-lon'-iks*, Gd. 155.]
Meg-a-lo-sâu'rus.
Me-ga'ri-an, 49, N.
Me-găr'ic, 109.
Meg'a-scope.
Meg-a-the'ri-um, 49, N.
Me'grim [*not* me-grim', 153.]
Meĭ-bo'mi-an, 25, 169.
[Meiocene, 203. — *See* Miocene.]
Meĭ-o'sis [*mī-o'sis*, Wr. Wb. Gd.; *mī'o-sis*, Sm. 155.]
Mel-an-chol'ic (*-kol'-*).
Mel'an-chol-y (*-kol-y*).
Mélange (Fr.) (*mā-länzh'*) [so Wr. Wb. Gd.; *mā'longzh*, Sm. 154.]
Mel'an-īte, 152.
[Melasses, 203. — *See* Molasses.]
Mel-chis-e-di'cian (*-kiz-e-dish'an*), 171.
Mêlée (Fr.) (*mā-lā'*), *n.* a confused fight. [*See* Malay, 160.]
Me-lic'ra-to-ry, 86.
Mel'i-lot, 170.
Mēl'io-rate (*-yo-*) (51) [so Sm. Wr.; *me'li-o-rāt*, Wk.; *mēl'yor-āt*, Wb. Gd. 155.]
Mēl-io-ra'tion (*-yo-*).
Mel-lif'er-oŭs, 108.
Mel-lif'ic, 109.
Mel-li-fĭ-ca'tion.

Mel-lif'lu-ence, 169.
Mel-lif'lu-ent, 108.
Mel-lif'lu-oŭs, 100.
Mel-lig'e-noŭs (*-lij'-*).
Mel'li-lite, 152.
Mel-liph'a-gan, 105.
Mel'lit.
Mel'lite, 152, 170.
Mel'lon (170), *n.* a yellow powder composed of carbon and nitrogen. [*See* Melon, 160.]
Mel'lōw (101) [*not* mel'lur, 153.]
Mel'lōwed, 165, 188.
Mel'lōw-ing.
Mel-o-co-ton' (*-toon'*) (122) [so Wr. Gd.; *mel-o-ko'ton*, Sm. 155.]
Me-lo'de-on, *or* Mel-o-de'on (154, 169) [so Wr.; *me-lo'de-on*, Gd. 155.]
Me-lo'di-oŭs (169) [so Wr. Wb. Gd.; *mel-o'di-us*, Sm.; *me-lo'di-us*, or *me-lo'ji-us*, Wk. 134, 155.]
Mel'o-dist.
Mel'o-dize, 202.
Mel'o-dized, 165.
Mel-o-dīz'ing, 183.
Mel-o-dra'ma [*See* Drama.]
Mel-o-dra-mat'ic, 109.
Mel-o-dra-mat'ic-al, 108.
Mel-o-dram'a-tist.
Mel'o-drame [so Wr. Wb. Gd.; *me'lo-drăm*, Sm. 155.]
Mel'o-dy, 170.
Mel'on (170), *n.* a trailing plant, and its fruit of several varieties. [*See* Mellon, 160.]
Melt, 15, 64.
Melt'ed, 228.
Melt'er, 77.
Melt'ing.
Mem'ber, 70, 103.
Mem'bered (*-burd*), 77, 165.
Mem-bra-na'ceoŭs (*-shus*), 171.
Mem'brane.
Mem-bra'ne-oŭs, 169.
Mem-bra-nif'er-oŭs, 108.
Mem-bra'ni-form, 108.
Mem-bra-nol'o-gy, 108.
Mem'bra-noŭs, 126.
Me-men'to (86, 122) [pl. Me-men'tōs (*-tōz*), 192.]
Mem'oir (*mem'wor*) (56) [so Sm. Wb. Gd.; *me-moir'*, or *mem'wor*, Wk. Wr. 155.]
Mem-o-ra-bil'i-a (L.), *n. pl.*
Mem-o-ra-bil'i-ty, 108.
Mem'o-ra-ble, 164.
Mem'o-ra-bly, 72.
Mem-o-ran'dum, *n.* [L. pl. *Mem-o-ran'da*; Eng. pl. Mem-o-ran'dums (*-dumz*), 198.]
Me-mo'ri-al, 49, N.; 169.
Me-mo'ri-al-ist.
Me-mo'ri-al-ize, 202.
Me-mo'ri-al-ized.
Me-mo'ri-al-īz-ing.
Me-mo'ri-a tech'ni-ca (L.) (*tek'-*).
Me-mŏr'i-ter (L.).
Mem'o-rize.
Mem'o-rized, 183.
Mem'o-rīz-ing.
Mem'o-ry, 86, 233.
Mem'phi-an, 35, 169.
Men (15, 43), *n. pl.* [*See* Man.]
Men'ace, 70.
Men'aced, 165, 183.
Men'a-cer.
Men'a-cing.
Men-ăge' (*men-ăzh'*).
Men-ăg'er-ie (*men-azh'-ur-e*) [so Sm. Wr. Gd.; *men-azh-ur-e'*, Wk. 155.] [Menagery (*men-a'jer-y*;—so Wr.; *men'a-jer-y*, Wb. Gd.), 203.]
Mend, 15.
Mend'a-ble, 164, 169.
Men-da'cious (*-shus*).
Men-daç'i-ty, 169.
Mend'ed.
Mend'er.
Men'di-can-cy.
Men'di cant, 169.
Men-diç'i-ty, 108.
Mend'ing.
Men-gre'tian (*-shan*).
Men-ha'den [Manhaden, 203.]
Me'ni-al, 72, 169.
Me-nin'ge-al (*-je-*), 169.
Me-nin'gēs (*-jēz*), *n. pl.*
Me-nis'cal, 72.
Me-nis'coid, 122.
Me-nis'cus.
Men'i-ver, *or* Me'ni-ver [*men'i-vur*, Wr. Wb. Gd.; *me'ni-vur*, Sm. 155.] [Minever, 203.]
Men'non-ite, 170.
Men'sa et tho'ro (L.).
Men'sal, 230.
Men'sēs (*-sēz*), *n. pl.*
Men'stru-al (*-stroo-*).
Men'stru-ate (*-stroo-*).
Men'stru-āt-ed (*-stroo-*).
Men'stru-āt-ing (*-stroo-*)
Men-stru-a'tion (*-stroo-*)
Men'stru-oŭs (*-stroo-*).
Men'stru-um (*-stroo-*), *n.* (L.) [pl. *Men'stru-a* (*-stroo-*), 198.]
Men-su-ra-bil'i-ty (*-shoo-*).
Men'su-ra-ble (*men'-shoo-ra-bl*) (164) [*men'-sh'oo-ra-bl*, Sm. (*See* § 26); *men'shu-ra-bl*, Wk. Gd.; *mens'yoo-ra-bl*, Wr. 155.]
Men'su-ral (*-shoo-*).
Men-su-ra'tion (*-shoo-*)
Men'tal, 72, 230.
Men'tal-ly, 170.
Men'tion.
Men'tion-a-ble, 164.
Men'tioned (*-shund*), 165
Men'tion-ing.
Men'tor, 88.
Men-to'ri-al, 49, N.
Me-phit'ic, 109.
Me-phit'ic-al, 108.
Me-phi'tis [so Wr. Gd.; *mef'i-tis*, Sm. 155] [pl. *Meph'i-tēs* (*-tēz*), 198.]
Meph'i-tism (*-tizm*).
Mer'can-tīle (81, 105) [so Wk. Wr. Gd.; *mer'-kan-tĭl*, Sm. 155] [*not* mer-kan'til, *nor* mer-kan-tēl', 153.]
Mer-cap'tan.
Mer'ce-na-ri-ly, 72.
Mer'ce-na-ry, 169.
Mer'cer, 21, N.; 77.
Mer'chan-dise (*-dīz*), 202
Mer'chant, 21, N.; 72, 169.
Mer'chant-a-ble, 164.
Mer'chant-man, 206.
Mer'chant-ry.
Mer'ci-ful (*-fŏŏl*), 186.
Mer'ci-ful-ly (*-fŏŏl-*).
Mer'ci-less.
Mer-cu'ri-al, 72, 169.
Mer-cu'ri-al-ist.
Mer-cu'ri-al-ize, 202.
Mer-cu'ri-al-ized.

Mer-cu′ri-al-īz-ing.
Mer-cu′ri-fȳ, 94.
Mer′cu-ry, 21, N.; 89.
Mer′cy, 129, 169.
Mer′cy-sēat.
Mere, 13, 67.
Mere′ly, 185.
Mĕr-e-trĭ′cious (*-trish′-us*), 46, 112.
Mer-gan′ser [so Wr. Wb. Gd.; *mer′gan-ser*, Sm. 155.]
Merge, 21, N.
Merged, 165.
Merg′er (*merj′-*).
Merg′ing (*merj′-*).
Mĕr′i-carp, 169.
Me-rid′i-an (169) [so Sm. Wr. Wb. Gd.; *me-rid′i-an*, or *me-rid′ji-an*, Wk. 134, 155.]
Me-rid′i-on-al [so Wk. Wr. Wb. Gd.; *me-rid′jun-al*, Sm. 155.]
Me-ri′no (*-rē′-*) (13, 122) [pl. Me-ri′noes (*-rē′-nōz*), 192.]
Mĕr-is-mat′ic (*-iz-*) [so Gd.; *mĕr-is-mat′ik*, Wr. 155.]
Mĕr′it, 48, 170.
Mĕr′it-ed.
Mĕr′it-ing, 176.
Mĕr-it-o′ri-oŭs, 49, N.
Mĕr′i-tot, 105.
Mer′lin, 169.
Mer′ling, 129.
Mer′lon, 21, N.
Mer′māid, 169.
Mer′man, 196.
Me′ro-cele.
Me-rop′i-dan.
Mĕr′ri-ly, 170.
Mĕr′ri-ment, 169, 186.
Mĕr′ry, 15, 48, 66.
Mĕr′ry-An′drew (*-droo*).
Mĕr′ry-māk′ing.
Mĕr′ry-thought (*-thawt*), 206.
Mer′sion, 169.
Me-ru′li-dan (*-roo′-*).
Me-seems′ (*-sēmz′*).
Mes-en-tĕr′ic (*mez-*).
Mes′en-tĕr-y (*mez′-*) [so Wk. Sm. Wr.; *mes′-en-tĕr-y*, Wb. Gd. 155.]
Mesh, 15, 46.
Meshed (*mesht*), 165; Note C, p. 34.
Mesh′ing.
Mesh′y, 169.
Mes′i-al (*mez′i-al*, or *mezh′i-al*) [so Sm.; *mez′i-al*, Wr.; *me′zhal*, Gd. 155.]
[Meslin (*mez′lin*), 203. — *See* Mastlin.]
Mes-mer-ee′ (*mez-*), 122.
Mes-mĕr′ic (*mez-*), 109.
Mes-mĕr′ic-al (*mez-*).
Mes′mer-ism (*mez′mur-izm*), 136, 156.
Mes′mer-ist (*mez′-*).
Mes-mer-ĭ-za′tion (*mez-*), 112.
Mes′mer-ize (*mez′-*), 202.
Mes′mer-ized (*mez′-*).
Mes′mer-īz-er (*mez′-*).
Mes′mer-īz-ing (*mez′-*).
Mesne (*mēn*) (162), *a.* in law, intervening. [*See* Mean, Mien, 160.]
Mes′o-carp (*mes′-*, or *mez′-*).
Mes′o-co-lon (*mes′-*, or *mez′-*) [*mes′o-ko-lon*, Wb. Gd.; *mez′o-ko-lun*, Sm.; *mes-o-ko′-lun*, Wr. 155.]
Mes′o-labe (*mes′-*, or *mez′-*) [*mes′o-lāb*, Wr. Wb. Gd.; *mez′o-lāb*, Sm. 155.]
Mes′o-sperm (*mes′-*, or *mez′-*).
Mes′o-tho-rax (*mes′-*, or *mez′-*) [*mes′o-tho-rax*, Wb. Gd.; *mez′o-tho-rax*, Sm.; *mes-o-tho′-rax*, Wr. 155.]
Mes′o-type (*mes′-*, or *mez′-*).
Mess, 15, 174.
Mes′sage, 70, 170.
Messed (*mest*), Note C, p. 34.
Mes′sen-ger.
Mes-si′ad, 122.
Mes-si′ah, 72.
Mes-si-an′ic.
Mes′sieurs (*mes′yurz*) [so Sm.; *mesh′shoorz*, or *mesh-shoorz′*, Wk.; *mesh′yurz*, Gd.; *mesh′urz*, or *mes′-yurz*, Wr. 155.]
Mess′ing, 228.
Mess′mate, 180, 206.
Mes′suage (*-swāj*), 66.
Mes-tee′ [Mustee, 203.]
Mes-ti′zo (*-te′-*) (13, 86) [pl. Mes-ti′zōs (*-te′-zōs*), 192.]
Met, 15, 41.
Me-tab′a-sis (Gr.).
Met-a-bo′li-an, 169.
Met-a-car′pal, 72.
Met-a-car′pus, 169.
Me-tach′ro-nism (*-tak′-ro-nizm*), 136.
Met′a-cism, 136.
Me′tage, 70.
Met-a-gram′ma-tism (*-tizm*), 133, 136.
Met′al (72) [so Sm.; *met′l*, Wk. Wb. Gd.; *met′l*, or *met′al*, Wr. 155.]

☞ Walker says of the pronunciation *met′l*, "The impropriety is so striking as to encourage an accurate speaker to restore the *a* to its sound as heard in *medal*."

Met-a-lep′sis (Gr.) [pl. *Met-a-lep′sēs* (*-sēz*), 198.]
Met′a-lep-sy, 169.
Met-a-lep′tic, 109.
Met-a-lep′tic-al, 108.
Me-tal′lic, 170.

☞ In this word, as well as in other derivatives of *metal*, as *metalline*, *metallurgy*, &c., the *l* is doubled, contrary to the general rule (§ 176), on account of the two *l*'s in the original Latin, *metallum*.

Met-al-lif′er-oŭs, 108.
Me-tal′li-form, 108.
Met′al-līne (105, 152) [so Wk. Wr. Wb. Gd.; *met′al-lin*, Sm. 155.]
Met′al-list.
Met-al-lĭ-za′tion, 112.
Met′al-līze, 202.
Met′al-lized, 165.
Met′al-līz-ing, 183.
Me-tal′lo-chrome (*-krōm*).
Met-al-loch′ro-my (*-lok′-*), 105.
Met-al-log′ra-phist.
Met-al-log′ra-phy, 108.
Met′al-loid.
Met-al-loid′al, 72.
Met-al-lur′gic.
Met-al-lur′gic-al.
Met′al-lur-gist [*not* met-al-lur′gist, 123, 153.]
Met′al-lur-gy, 122.
Met′al-măn, 196, 206.
Met-a-mĕr′ic.
Met-a-mor′phic.
Met-a-mor′phism (*-fizm*).

Met-a-mor'phist.
Met-a-mor'phose (-*fos*), 136.
Met-a-mor'phosed (-*fost*), 165.
Met-a-mor'phos-er.
Met-a-mor'phos-ic.
Met-a mor'phos-ing.
Met-a mor'pho-sis (105, 109, 153) [pl. Met-a-mor'pho-ses (-*sēz*), 198.]
Met'a-phor, 171.
Met-a phŏr'ic, 108.
Met-a-phŏr'ic-al.
Met-a-phŏr'ic-al-ly.
Met'a-phŏr-ist [so Sm. Wr.; *met'a-for-ist*, Wb. Gd. 155.]
Met'a-phrase (-*frāz*).
Met'a-phrast.
Met-a-phrast'ic.
Met-a-phrast'ic-al.
Met-a-phys'ic (-*fiz'*-).
Met-a-phys'ic-al (-*fiz'*-).
Met-a-phys'ic-al-ly (-*fiz'*-), 170.
Met-a phy-sĭ'cian (-*zish'an*), 46, 171.
Met-a-phys'ic-o-the-o-log'ic-al (-*fiz'ik-o-the-o-loj'*-), 224.
Met-a-phys'ics (-*fiz'*-), 109.
Met'a-plasm (-*plazm*), 136.
Me-tas'ta-sis, 156.
Met-a-stat'ic, 109.
Met-a-tar'sal.
Met-a-tar'sus, 169.
Me-tath'e-sis (L.) [pl. Me-tath'e-sēs (*sēz*), 198.]
Met-a-thet'ic, 109.
Met-a-thet'ic-al, 108.
Met-a-tho'rax, 122.
Mete, *v.* to measure: — *n.* a boundary. [*See* Meat, *and* Meet, 160.]
Mēt'ed, 183.
Me-temp-sy-cho'sis (-*ko'*-), 109, 171.
Met-emp-to'sis.
Me'te-or (88, 169) [so Sm. Wr. Wb. Gd.; *me'te-ur*, or *me'che-ur*, Wk. 155.]
Me-te-ŏr'ic, 109.
Me-te-ŏr'ic-al, 108.
Me'te-or-īte, 152.
Me-te-or-og'ra-phy, 108.
Me'te-ŏr-o-līte, *or* Me-te-ŏr'o-līte (152) [*me'-te-ŏr-o-līt*, Sm.; *me-te-ŏr'o-līt*, Wr. Gd. 155.]
Me-te-ŏr-o-log'ic (-*loj'*-).
Me-te-or-o-log'ic-al (-*loj'*-), 108.
Me-te-or-ol'o-gist, 108.
Me-te-or-ol'o-gy, 108.
Me-te-ŏr'o-man-cy.
Me'te-ŏr-o-scope, *or* Me-te-or'o-scope [*me'te-ŏr-o-skōp*, Sm.; *me-te-or'o-skōp*, Gd.; *me-te'o-ro-skōp*, Wk.; *me-te-or'o-skōp*, or *me-te'o-ro-skōp*, Wr. 155.]
Me-te-or-os'co-py, 108.
Me'ter, *n.* one who metes, or measures. [*See* Metre, 160.]
[Meter, 203. — *See* Metre.]
Me-theg'lin.
Me-thinks', 64.
Meth'od, 86.
Me-thod'ic, 109.
Me-thod'ic-al, 108.
Me-thod'ic-al-ly.
Meth'od-ism (-*izm*).
Meth'od-ist.
Meth-od-ist'ic.
Meth-od-ist'ic-al.
Meth-od-ist'ic-al-ly.
Meth-od-ĭ-za'tion, 112.
Meth'od-ize, 202.
Meth'od-ized.
Meth'od-īz-er.
Meth'od-īz-ing.
Meth-od-ol'o-gy, 108.
Me-thought' (-*thawt'*), 162.
Met'ic (156) [so Sm. Gd.; *me'tik*, Wr. 155.]
Mēt'ing, *part.* from *Mete.* [*See* Meeting, 160.]
Me-ton'ic, 109.
Met-o-nym'ic.
Met-o-nym'ic-al, 108.
Met'o-nym-y, *or* Me-ton'y-my (171) [so Gd.; *met'o-nim-y*, Sm.; *me-ton'i-my*, or *met'o-nim-y*, Wk. Wr. 155.]
Met'o-pe, 163.
Met-o-po-scop'ic-al.
Met-o-pos'co-pist.
Met-o-pos'co-py, 108.
Me'tre (*me'tur*) (164), *n.* measure. [*See* Meter, 160.] [Meter, preferred by Gd. — *See* Note E, p. 70.]
Met'ric-al, 72.
Met'ric-al-ly, 170.
Met'ro-chrome (-*krōm*).
Met'ro-grăph.
Me-trol'o-gy.
Met'ro-nome.
Me-tron'o-my, 108.
Me-trop'o-lis.
Met-ro-pol'i-tan [so Wk. Wr. Wb. Gd.; *me-tro-pol'i-tan*, Sm. 155.]
Met'tle (*met'l*), 164.
Met'tled (*met'ld*).
Met'tle-some (*met'l-sum*), 171.
Mew (*mu*), *n.* & *v.* [pl. of *n.* Mews (*mūz*), stables. — *See* Muse, 160.]
Mewed (*mūd*).
Mew'ing (*mu'*-).
Mewl, *v.* to cry, as an infant. [*See* Mule, 160.]
Mewled (*mūld*).
Mewl'er (*mūl'*-).
Mewl'ing.
Mex'i-can.
Me-ze're-on, 49, Note; 169.
Mez'za-nine (-*nēn*) [so Sm. Gd.; *mez'za-nīn*, Wr. 155.]
Mez'zo-ri-liē'vo (It.) (*med'zo*-).
Mez'zo-tint (*med'zo*-).
Mez-zo-tin'to (*med-zo*-) [*med-zo-tin'to*, or *met-zo-tin'to*, Wr.; *mez-zo-tint'o*, or *med-zo-tint'o*, Gd.; *met-so-tin'to*, Wk.; *met-zo-tin'to*, Sm. 155.]
Mi'asm (*mi'azm*), 133, 136.
Mī-as'ma (-*az'*-) (L.) (151) [pl. *Mī-as'ma-ta* (-*az'*-), 198.]
Mī-as'mal (-*az'*-), 72.
Mī-as-mat'ic (-*az*-).
Mī-as-mat'ic-al (-*az*-).
Mī-as'ma-tist (-*az'*-).
Mi'ca, 25, 72.
Mī-ca'ceous (-*shus*), 112.
Mice (26), *n. pl.* [*See* Mouse.]
Mich'ael-mas (*mik'el*-), 171, 180.
Mick'le (*mik'l*), 164.

Mi′cro-cosm (*-kozm*).
Mī-cro-cos′mic (*-koz′-*).
Mī-cro-cos′mic-al (*koz′-*).
Mī-cro-cous′tic, 28, 109.
Mī-cro-graph′ic, 109.
Mī-crog′ra-phy, 108, 169.
Mī-crol′o-gy, 108.
Mī-crom′e-ter, 108.
Mī-cro-met′ric, 109.
Mī-cro-met′ric-al.
Mi′cro-phone.
Mī-cro-phon′ics.
Mī-croph′o-noŭs, 100.
Mī-croph′thal-my (*-krof′-*, or *-krop′-*)[*mi-krof′thal-my*, Wr.; *mi-krop′thal-my*, Sm. 155.]
Mī-cro-phyl′loŭs, *or* Mī-croph′yl-loŭs [*See* Adenophyllous.]
Mi′cro-pyle.
Mi′cro-scope, 156.
Mī-cro-scop′ic, 109.
Mī-cro-scop′ic-al, 108.
Mi′cro-scŏp-ist, 106.
Mī-cros′co-py, 108.
Mic-tu-ri′tion (*-rish′-un*), 112.
Mid, 16, 42.
Mi′das′s-ēar (*-das-ez-ēr*), 213.
Mid′-day, 66, N.
Mid′dle (*mid′l*), 164, 170.
Mid′dle-aged (*mid′l-ājd*).
Mid′dle-man (*mid′l-*), 206.
Mid′dle-mōst (*mid′l-*).
Mid′dling, 66, 170.
Midge, 16, 45.
Midg′et (*mij′-*).
Mid′land, 206.
Mid′mōst, 206.
Mid′nīght (*-nīt*).
Mid′rib.
Mid′riff, 189.
Mid′ship.
Mid′ship-man, 72, 196, 206
Mid′ships.
Midst, 16, 64.
Mid′sum-mer, 216.
Mid′wāy.
Mid′wife, 189.
Mid′wīfe-ry [so Wk. Sm. Wr.; *mid′wīf-ry*, Wb. Gd. 155.]
Mid′win-ter, 216.
Miēn (13), *n.* external appearance and carriage. [*See* Mean, Mesne, 160.]
Miff, 16, 173.
Miffed (*mift*), 165; Note C, p. 34.
Miff′ing.
Might (*mīt*), 162.
Might′i-ly (*mīt′-*), 186.
Might′i-ness (*mīt′-*).
Might′y (*mīt′-*) (169), *a.* powerful. [*See* Mity, 160.]
Mign-on-ette′ (*min-yun-et′*), 162, 171.
Mi′grate, 72.
Mi′grāt-ed, 183.
Mi′grāt-ing.
Mi-gra′tion, 112.
Mi′gra-to-ry, 86.
Mil-an-ese′ (*-ēz′*), *n. sing. & pl.*
Milch, 16, 44, Note 2.
Mīld, 25.
Mil′dew (*-du*).
Mil′dewed (*-dūd*).
Mil′dew-ing (*-du-*).
Mile, 25, 163.
Mile′age, 183.
Mile′stone, 206.
Mil′foil, 103.
Mil′ia-ry (*-ya-*) (145), *a.* resembling a millet-seed; granulated. [*See* Miliary, 148.]
Mil′i-tant.
Mil′i-ta-ry, 72.
Mil′i-tate, 169.
Mil′i-tāt-ed, 183.
Mil′i-tāt-ing.
Mi-li′tia (*mĭ-lish′a*) [so Wb. Gd.; *mĭ-lish′yȧ*, Wk.; *mĭ-lish′ya*, Wr.; *mĭ-lish′ā*, Sm. (*See* § 26), 155.]
Milk, 16, 50, 52.
Milked (*milkt*), 165; Note C, p. 34; 64.
Milk′er, 77.
Milk′ing.
Milk′i-ness, 186.
Milk′māid, 206.
Milk′man, 196.
Milk′pāil.
Milk′păn.
Milk′sop.
Milk′tooth.
Milk′wârm.
Milk′white.
Milk′wort (*-wurt*).
Milk′y, 169.
Mill, 16, 172.
Mill′dăm, 206.
Milled, 165.
Mil-le-na′ri-an, 49, N.; 169.
Mil-le-na′ri-an-ism, (*-izm*).
Mil′le-na-ry (72, 169), *n.* the space of a thousand years. [*See* Millinery, 148.]
Mil-len′ni-al, 169.
Mil-len′ni-al-ist.
Mil-len′ni-um, 169, 170.
Mil′le-ped, 189.

☞ So spelled and pronounced by Worcester, Webster, and Goodrich; by Smart, *mil′le-pede*; and by Walker, who gives only the plural form, *mil′le-pedes* (*-pēdz*), or *mil-lep′e-des* (*-dēz*).

Mil′le-pore, 170.
Mill′er, 169.
Mill′er-īte, 152.
Mill′er′s-thumb (*mil′-erz-thum*), 162, 213.
Mil-les′i-mal, 72, 169.
Mil′let, 66, 76.
Mill′hĕad, 206.
Mil′li-a-ry (169), *a.* pertaining to, or denoting, a mile. [*See* Miliary, 148.]
Mil′li-gram (Eng.), or *Mil′li-gramme* (Fr.).
Mil′li-li-ter [so Sm.; *mil-lil′i-tur*, Gd. 155.]
Mil′li-li-tre (Fr.) (*mil′-le-le-tur*).
Mil′li-me-ter (Eng.), or *Mil′li-me-tre* (Fr.) (*mil′le-mā-tur*).
Mil′li-ner, 77, 170.
Mil′li-ner-y (169, 171), *n.* the work or the goods of a milliner. [*See* Millenary, 148.]
Mil-li-net′, 171.
Mill′ing.
Mill′ion (*-yun*), 51, 86.
Mill′ion-a-ry (*-yun-*), 169.
Mill′ion-aire (*-yun-ȇr*) (Eng.), or *Mill-ion-naire′* (*-yun-ȇr′*) (Fr.).
Mill′ionth (*-yunth*).
Mill′pŏnd.
Mill′race.
Mill′rēa, *or* Mill′ree, 203.
Mill′stōne, 24.
Mill′wheel.
Mill′wright (*-rīt*), 162.
Milt, 16.
Mil-ton′ic, 170.
Milt′wort (*-wurt*), 206.

Mil'vīne (152) [so Sm.; *mil'vin*, Wr. 155.]
Mime, 25, 163.
Mī-met'ic [so Sm.; *mĭ-met'ik*, Wk. Wr. Gd. 155.]
Mī-met'ic-al.
Mim'ic, 200.
Mim'ic-al.
Mim'icked (*-ikt*), 200.
Mim'ick-ing.
Mim'ic-ry.
Mi-mog'ra-pher, 108.
Mī-mo'sa, *or* Mĭ-mo'sa (*-za*) [*mī-mo'sa*, Gd.; *mĭ-mo'za*, Sm.; *mĭ-mo'sa*, Wr. 155.]
Mĭ-na'cioŭs (*-shus*), 112.
Mĭ-naç'i-ty, 169.
Min'a-ret, 76.
Min'a-to-ry, 86.
Mince, 16, 39.
Minced (*minst*), 165; Note C, p. 34.
Mince'mēat, *or* Minced'-mēat(*minst'*)
Mince'pīe, *or* Minced'-pīe (*minst'-*).
Minç'ing.
Mīnd, 25.
Mīnd'ed.
Mīnd'ful (*-fo͝ol*), 180.
Mīnd'ful-ly (*-fo͝ol-*), 170.
Mīnd'ing.
Mīne, 163.

☞ "When this word is used adjectively before a word beginning with a vowel or *h* mute, as in saying, 'On *mine* honor,' the complete absence of accentual force, and a style quite colloquial, will permit the shortening of the sound into *min*." *Smart.*

Mīned, 165.
Min'er (170), *n.* one who mines. [*See* Minor, 160.]
Min'er-al, 233, Exc.
Min'er-al-ist, 106.
Min-er-al-ĭ-za'tion.
Min'er-al-ize, 202.
Min'er-al-ized, 165.
Min'er-al-iz-er, 228, N.
Min'er-al-īz-ing.
Min-er-al-og'ic (*-oj'-*).
Min-er-al-og'ic-al (*-oj'-*).
Min-er-al'o-gist, 108.
Min-er-al'o-gy [*not* min-ur-ol'o-jy, 127, 153.]
Min'e-ver [M e n i v e r, 203.]
Min'gle (*ming'gl*), 54.
Min'gled (*ming'gld*), 183.
Min'gler (*ming'-*).
Min'gling (*ming'-*).
Min'i-ate, *v.* & *a.* 73, 169.
Min'i-āt-ed, 183.
Min'i-āt-ing.
Min'ia-ture (*min'i-tūr*), *or* Min'i-a-ture [so Gd. Wr.; *min'i-tūr*, Wk. Sm. 155.]
Min'ia-tūr-ist (*min'i-*), *or* Min'i-a-tūr-ist.
Min'i-bus, 170.
Min'ic-ri'fle (*-fl*) (205) [so Wr.; *min-e'-ri'fl*, Gd. 155.]
Min'i-kin, 66, 169.
Min'im, 103.
Min'i-mum (L.) [pl. *Min'i-ma*, 198.]
Mīn'ing, 183.
Min'ion (*-yun*), 51, 86.
Min'is-ter, 230.
Min'is-tered, 150.
Min-is-te'ri-al, 49, N.; 169.
Min-is-te'ri-al-ly, 93.
Min'is-ter-ing.
Min'is-trant.
Min-is-tra'tion, 112.
Min'is-trāt-ĭve.
Min'is-tress.
Min'is-try.
Min'i-um (169) [so Sm. Wb. Gd.; *min'yum*, Wk.; *min'i-um*, or *min'yum*, Wr. 155.]
Mink (*mingk*), 16, 54.
Min'ne-sing-er, 171.
Min'nōw, 101, 170.
Mī'nor (70, 169), *a.* smaller: — *n.* one under age. [*See* Miner, 160.]
Mĭ-nŏr'i-ty, 169.
Min'o-tâur [*not* mī'no-tâur, 153.]
Min'ster, 77.
Min'strel, 230.
Min'strel-sy, 169.
Mint, 16.
Mint'age, 228.
Mint'ed.
Mint'ing.
Min'u-end, 89.
Min'u-et, 89, 156.
Mī'nus (L.), 169.
Mĭ-nus'cule.
Mĭ-nute', *a.* (121, 161) [so Wk. Sm. Wb. Gd.; *mĭ-nūt'*, or *mī-nut'*, Wr. 155.]

☞ "If we wish to be very *minute*, we pronounce the *i* in the first syllable long." *Walker.*

Min'ute, *n.* (*min'it*) (90, 160) [so Wb. Gd.; *min'ūt*, or *min'it*, Wr.; *min'ūt*, coll. *min'it*, Wk. Sm. 155.]
Min'ut-ed (*min'it-*).
Min'ute-gun' (*min'it-*), 205.
Min'ute-ly (*min'it-ly*), 161.
Mĭ-nute'ly, 161.
Min'ute-man (*-it-*), 196.
Mĭ-nute'ness, 185.
Min'ut-ing (*-it-*), 183.
Mĭ-nu'ti-æ (L.) (*-shĭ-ē*).
Minx (*mingks*), 16, 54.
Min'y, 169, 183.
Mi'o-cene [M e i o c e n e, 203.]
Miq'ue-let (*-we-*).
Mi-rab'i-le dic'tu (L.).
Mi'rach (*-rak*), 49, N.
Mĭr'a-cle (*-kl*) (164) [*not* mĕr'a-kl, 153.]
Mĭr'a-cle-mon'ger (*-kl-mung'gur*), 205, Exc. 3.
Mĭ-rac'u-loŭs, 100, 108.
Mirage'(Fr.)(*me-räzh'*), 171.
Mire, 25, 49.
Mired, 165, 183.
Mĭ-rif'ic, 109.
Mĭ-rif'ic-al, 108.
Mīr'i-ness, 49, N.; 186.
[M i r k y (21, N.), 203. — *See* Murky.]
Mĭr'ror, 48, 66, 170.
Mirth, 21, N.
Mirth'ful (*-fo͝ol*), 180.
Mirth'ful-ly (*-fo͝ol-*).
Mīr'y, 49, N.; 235.
Mir'za, *n.* the common title of honor in Persia. [*See* Murza, 160.]
Mis-ad-vent'ure, 91.
Mis-ad-vent'ur-oŭs (*-yur-us*), 91, 171.
Mis-al-li'ance.
Mis-al-lied'.
Mis'an-thrope (105) [*not* mis-an'thrŏp, 153.]
Mis-an-throp'ic, 109.
Mis-an-throp'ic-al, 108.
Mis-an'thro-pist.
Mis-an'thro-py, 105, 156.
Mis-ap-pli-ca'tion.
Mis-ap-plīed', 186.
Mis-ap-ply'.
Mis-ap-ply'ing, 186.

Mis-ap-pre-hend′, 116.
Mis-ap-pre-hend′ed.
Mis-ap-pre-hend′ing.
Mis-ap-pre-hen′sion.
Mis-ap-pro-pri-a′tion.
Mis-be-came′ (-kām′).
Mis-be-come′ (-kum′).
Mis-be-com′ing (kum′-).
Mis-be-have′, 116.
Mis-be-haved′, 183.
Mis-be-hāv′ing.
Mis-be-hāv′ior (-yur), 51, 171.
Mis-be-lief′.
Mis-be-liēve′, 169.
Mis-be-liēved′, 183.
Mis-be-liēv′er.
Mis-be-liēv′ing.
Mis-cal′cu-late.
Mis-cal′cu-lāt-ed.
Mis-cal′cu-lāt-ing.
Mis-cal-cu-la′tion.
Mis-câll′ [Miscal, 203.]
Mis-câlled′.
Mis-câll′ing.
Mis-car′riage (-rij), 70.
Mis-car′rïed, 99.
Mis-căr′ry, 66, 170.
Mis-căr′ry-ing.
Mis-càst′, 131.
Mis-càst′ing.
Mis-cel-la-na′ri-an, 49, N.; 169.
Mis-cel-la′ne-a (L.), *n. pl.*
Mis-cel-la′ne-oŭs, 169, 171.
Mis-cel′la-nist, 105.
Mis′cel-la-ny, 72, 156, 171.
Mis-chànce′.
Mis-charge′.
Mis′chĭef (-chĭf), 171.
Mis′chĭef-māk′er, 205.
Mis′chĭev-oŭs (103, 156, 171) [*not* mis-chēv′us, 153.]

☞ "Some old authors, and the vulgar still, accent the second syllable." *Smart*

[Mischna, 203.— *See* Mishna.]
Mis-con-cēive′, 169.
Mis-con-cēived′, 165.
Mis-con-cēiv′ing.
Mis-con-cep′tion, 112.
Mis-con′duct, *n.* 161.
Mis-con-duct′, *v.* 161.
Mis-con-struc′tion.
Mis-con′strue (-*stroo*) (156) [*See* Note under *Construe.*]
Mis-con′strued (-*strood*).
Mis-con′stru-ing (-*stroo*-).
Mis′cre-ant, 144, 169.
Mis-date′.
Mis-dāt′ed.
Mis-dāt′ing.
Mis-deed′.
Mis-de-mean′or, 199.
Mis-dĭ-rect′, 151.
Mis-dĭ-rect′ed.
Mis-dĭ-rect′ing.
Mis-dĭ-rec′tion, 112.
Mis-do′ (-*doo*′), 19.
Mis-do′er (-*doo*′-), 77.
Mis-do′ing (-*doo*′-).
Mis-done′ (-*dun*′).
Mis-em-ploy′.
Mis-em-ployed′, 187.
Mis-em-ploy′ing.
Mis-em-ploy′ment.
Mis-en′try, 93.
Mi′ser (-*zur*), 136.
Mis′er-a-ble (*miz′ur-a-bl*), 164, 169.
Mis′er-a-bly (*miz*′-).
Mis-e-re′re (L.), 49, N.
Mi′ser-ly (-*zur*-).
Mis′er-y (*miz*′-), 169, 233, Exc.
Mis-fēa′sance (-*zans*) [so Wr. Wb. Gd.; *mis-fa′zans*, Sm. 155.]
Mis-form′, 17.
Mis-formed′.
Mis-form′ing.
Mis-fort′une (90) [*See* Fortune.]
Mis-gave′.
Mis-give′ (-*ghiv*′).
Mis-giv′en (-*ghiv′n*), 149.
Mis-giv′ing (-*ghiv*′-).
Mis-got′ten (-*got′n*), 149.
Mis-gov′ern (-*guv*′-).
Mis-gov′erned (-*guv′-urnd*), 165.
Mis-gov′ern-ing (-*guv*′-).
Mis-gov′ern-ment (-*guv*′-).
Mis-guīd′ance, 53, 183.
Mis-guide′.
Mis-guīd′ed.
Mis-guīd′ing.
Mis-hap′.
Mish′mash.
Mish′na [Mischna, 203.]
Mis-in-form′.
Mis-in-form-a′tion, 112.
Mis-in-formed′, 165.
Mis-in-form′er.
Mis-in-form′ing.
Mis-in-ter′pret.
Mis-in-ter-pret-a′tion.
Mis-in-ter′pret-ed.
Mis-in-ter′pret-er.
Mis-in-ter′pret-ing.
Mis-join′, 27.
Mis-join′der, 77.
Mis-joined′, 165.
Mis-join′ing.
Mis-judge′, 45.
Mis-judged′, 183.
Mis-judg′ing (-*juj*′-).
Mis-judg′ment (185) [Misjudgement, Sm. 203.— *See* Note under *Abridgment.*]
Mis-lāid′.
Mis-lāy′.
Mis-lāy′ing.
Mis′le(*miz′l*)(164)[Mizzle, 203.]
Mis-lēad′.
Mis-lēad′er.
Mis-lēad′ing.
Mis′led (*miz′ld*) (161), *v.* did misle, or rain in very fine drops. [Mizzled, 203.]
Mis-led′(161), *v.* did mislead.
[Misletoe, 203.— *See* Mistletoe.]
Mis-man′age.
Mis-man′aged, 183.
Mis-man′age-ment.
Mis-man′a-ger.
Mis-man′a-ging.
Mis-mark′.
Mis-marked′ (-*markt*′).
Mis-mark′ing.
Mis-match′.
Mis-matched′ (-*măcht*′).
Mis-match′ing.
Mis-mēas′ure (-*mezh′-ur*).
Mis-mēas′ured (-*mezh′-urd*).
Mis-mēas′ur-ing (-*mezh′ur*-).
Mis-name′.
Mis-named′, 183.
Mis-nām′ing.
Mis-no′mer, 122.
Mĭ-sog′a-mist, 151.
Mĭ-sog′a-my, 169.
Mĭ-sog′y-nist (-*soj*′-), 151, 156, 171.
Mĭ-sog′y-ny (-*soj*′-), 93.
[Mispell, 203.— *See* Misspell.]

[Mispend, 203.—*See* Misspend.]
Mis-pick'el (*-pik'l*) (167) [so Gd.; *mis-pik'el*, Wr. 155.]
Mis-place'.
Mis-placed' (*-plāst'*), 165, Note C, p. 34.
Mis-place'ment, 185.
Mis-plāç'ing, 183.
Mis-plēad'.
Mis-plēad'ed.
Mis-plēad'ing.
Mis-point', 27.
Mis-point'ed.
Mis-point'ing.
Mis-print'.
Mis-print'ed.
Mis-print'ing.
Mis-pris'ion (*-prizh'un*) [*not* mis-priz'n, 153.]
Mis-prize'.
Mis-prized'.
Mis-prīz'ing, 183.
Mis-pro-nounce'.
Mis-pro-nounced' (*-nounst'*), Note C, p. 34.
Mis-pro-nounç'ing.
Mis-pro-nun-çi-a'tion (*-shĭ-a'-*, or *sĭ-a'-*) (116) [*See* Pronunciation.]
Mis-pro-pōr'tion.
Mis-pro-pōr'tioned, 165.
Mis-pro-pōr'tion-ing.
Mis-quo-ta'tion, 112.
Mis-quote'.
Mis-quōt'ed, 183.
Mis-quōt'ing. [149.
Mis-reck'on (*-rek'n*),
Mis-reck'oned (*-rek'nd*).
Mis-reck'on-ing (*-rek'n*).
Mis-re-mem'ber.
Mis-re-mem'bered, 165.
Mis-re-mem'ber-ing.
Mis-ren'der.
Mis-ren'dered (*-durd*).
Mis-ren'der-ing.
Mis-re-pōrt'.
Mis-re-pōrt'ed.
Mis-re-pōrt'ing.
Mis-rep-re-sent' (*-zent'*).
Mis-rep-re-sent'ed (*-zent'-*).
Mis-rep-re-sent'ing (*-zent'-*).
Mis-rep-re-sent-a'tion (*-zent-*).
Mis-rule', 26, 128.
Miss, *n.* & *v.* (16, 174) [pl. of *n.* Miss'es, 189.]
Mis'sal (72), *n.* the Roman Catholic mass-book. [*See* Missile, 148.]
Missed (*mist*), (Note C, p. 34), *v.* did miss. [*See* Mist, 160.]
Mis'sel-thrush (*miz'-zel-*).
[Misseltoe, 203.—*See* Mistletoe.]
Mis-send', 66, N.
Mis-send'ing.
Mis-sent'.
Mis-serve', 21, N.
Mis-served', 165.
Mis-serv'ing.
Mis-shape'.
Mis-shaped' (*-shāpt'*).
Mis-shāp'en (*-shāp'n*), 149.
Mis'sĭle (81), *n.* a weapon to be thrown. [*See* Missal, 148.]
Miss'ing.
Mis'sion (*mish'un*), 46, Note 2; 171.
Mis'sion-a-ry (*mish'-un-*), 72, 169.
Mis'sis.

☞ This form of spelling represents the *pronunciation* of the common title of married women of all classes. It is a corruption of *mistress*, and is always abbreviated, in writing, to *Mrs.*

Mis'sĭve, 66, 84.
Mis-spell' (66, N.) [Mispell, 203.]

☞ Smart, following Johnson, gives Misspel.

Mis-spelled', 165.
Mis-spell'ing.
Mis-spelt', 165.
Mis-spend' (64) [Mispend, 203.]
Mis-spend'ing.
Mis-spent'.
Mis-state', 66, N.
Mis-stāt'ed.
Mis-state'ment, 185.
Mis-stāt'ing.
Mis-step'.
Mist (16), *n.* rain in the form of fine and almost imperceptible drops. [*See* Missed, 160.]
Mis-tāk'a-ble, 164, 183.
Mis-take'.
Mis-tāk'en (*-tāk'n*), 149.
Mis-tāk'ing, 183.
Mis-tâught' (*-tawt'*), 162.
Mis-tēach'.
Mis-tēach'ing.
Mis'ter.

☞ This form of spelling represents the *pronunciation* of the common title of men of all ranks. It is never used except in connection with a proper name, the word *sir* taking its place in addressing a person. It is always abbreviated in writing to *Mr.* "This form of the word *master*," says Smart, "seems to have been adopted, or at least promoted, for the sake of analogy with *mistress*; for *mistress* among our old writers often had the form *mastress*, in order to suit with *master*, which was then used where we now find *mister*."

Mis-time'.
Mis-timed', 165.
Mis-tīm'ing, 183.
Mist'i-ness, 186.
[Mistle, 203.—*See* Mizzle.]
Mis'tle-tōe (*miz'l-tō*) (156, 162) [Misletoe, Misseltoe, 203.]
Mist'lĭke, 206, Exc. 5.
Mis-tŏŏk'.
Mis'tral, 72, 103.
Mis-trans-late', 116.
Mis-trans-lāt'ed, 228, N.
Mis-trans-lāt'ing.
Mis-trans-la'tion, 112.
Mis'tress (76) [*See* Note under *Missis.*]
Mis-trust'.
Mis-trust'ed.
Mis-trust'ful (*-fŏŏl*).
Mis-trust'ing.
Mis-tune', 26, 127.
Mis-tuned', 165, 183.
Mis-tūn'ing.
Mist'y, 169.
Mis-un-der-stand'.
Mis-un-der-stand'ing.
Mis-un-der-stŏŏd'.
Mis-us'age (*-yooz'-*), 136.
Mis-use' (*-yooz'*), *v.* 161.
Mis-use', *n.* 161.
Mis-used' (*-yoozd'*).
Mis-us'er (*-yooz'-*).
Mis-ūs'ing (*-yooz'-*).
Mis-wed'.
Mis-wed'ded, 176.
Mis-wed'ding.
Mis-write' (*-rīt'*), 162.
Mis-wrīt'ing (*-rīt'-*).

Mis-writ′ten (*-rit′n*).
Mis-wrote′ (*-rōt′*), 24.
Mis-wrought′ (*-rawt′*), 162.
Mis-yoke′.
Mis-yoked′ (*-yōkt′*).
Mitch′ell, 171.
Mite (25), *n.* a very minute animal or particle. [*See* Might, 160.]
[Miter, 203.—*See* Mitre.]
Mit′i-ga-ble, 164.
Mit′i-gant, 72.
Mit′i-gate, 73, 169.
Mit′i-gāt-ed, 183.
Mit′i-gāt-ing.
Mit-i-ga′tion, 112.
Mit′i-gāt-ĭve, 84.
Mit′i-gāt-or, 169.
Mi′tral, 72.
Mi′tre (*-tur*) (164) [Miter, preferred by Wb. and Gd.— *See* Note E, p. 70.]
Mi′tred (*mi′turd*).
Mit′ri-form, 169.
Mit′ten [*not* mit′n, 149, 153.]
Mit′ti-mus (L.), 169.
Mitts, *n. pl.*
Mit′y (169), *n.* having mites. [*See* Mighty, 160.]
Mix, 16, 39, N.
Mix′a-ble, 164, 169.
Mixed (*mikst*) (66, Note C, p. 34) [Mixt, 203.]

☞ "This being necessarily pronounced, if in one syllable, as if written *mixt*, is quite unnecessarily made irregular by being so written." *Smart.*

Mix′ed-ly, *or* Mixed′ly (*mikst′ly*) [so Wr.; *miks′ed-ly*, Gd.; *mikst′ly*, or *miks′ed-ly*, Sm. 155.] [Mixtly, 203.]
Mix′er.
Mix′ing.
Mix-ti-lin′e-al.
Mix-ti-lin′e-ar, 169.
Mixt′ion (*-yun*), 86.
Mixt′ure, 91.
Miz′zen (*miz′n*), 149.
Miz′zen-mȧst (*miz′n-*).
Miz′zle (164) [Misle, Mistle, 203.]

☞ "The former spelling [*misle*] is sanctioned by etymology; the latter [*mistle*] is more analogical; the most usual spelling is, however, that which conforms to the pronunciation, namely, *mizzle*."—*Smart.*

Miz′zled (*-zld*), 165.
Miz′zling.
Miz′zly, 170.
Mne-mon′ic (*ne-*), 162.
Mne-mon′ic-al (*ne-*).
Mnem-o-nĭ′cian (*nem-o-nish′an*), 46, 162.
Mne-mon′ics (*ne-*), 109, 171.
Mnem′o-tech-ny (*nem′-o-tek-ny*), 162.
Mōan (24, 43), *v.* to bewail. [*See* Mown, 160.]
Mōaned, 165.
Mōan′ing, *part.* from *Moan.* [*See* Moning, 160.]
Mōat (24, 41), *n.* a ditch round a castle, filled with water. [*See* Mote, 160.]
Mob, 18, 31.
Mobbed, 165, 176.
Mob′bing.
Mob′bish.
Mob′ĭle (81) [so Sm.; *mo-bēl′*, Wk.; *mo′-bil*, Wb. Gd.; *mo-bēl′*, or *mob′il*, Wr. 155.]
Mo-bil′i-ty, 169.
Mob-i-lĭ-za′tion, 112.
Mob′il-ize, 202.
Mob′il-ized, 183.
Mob′il-īz-ing.
Mob′le (*mob′l*) (164) [so Sm. Wb. Gd.; *mo′bl*, Wk.; *mob′l*, or *mo′-bl*, Wr. 155.]
Mob′led (*mob′ld*) [*not* mob′led, 156.]
Mob′ling.
Mŏb-oc′ra-cy (169) [so Gd.; *mo-bok′ra-sy*, Wr. 155.]
Moc′ca-son (*-sn*) (167) [Moccasin, Moggason, 203.]

☞ "Often written *moccasin*, and also often written and pronounced *moggason*." *Worcester.*

Mo′cha (*-ka*), 52, 72.
Mock, 18, 181.
Mocked (*mokt*), 165; Note C, p. 34.
Mock′er, 77.
Mock′er-y, 169.
Mock′ing.
Mock′ing-bird, 206, Exc. 5.
Mock′-he-ro′ic.
Mock′-or′ange.
Mock′-tur′tle, 164.
Mo′co (86) [pl. Mo′cōs (*-kōz*), 192.]
Mo′dal, 72.
Mo′dal-ist, 106.
Mo-dal′i-ty, 108, 169.
Mode (163), *n.* manner. [*See* Mowed, 160.]
Mod′el, *n.* & *v.* (76) [*not* mod′l, 149.]
Mod′elled (*-eld*) (165) [Modeled, Wb. and Gd. 203.—*See* 177 and Note E, p. 70.]
Mod′el-ler [Modeler, Wb. and Gd. 203.]
Mod′el-ling [Modeling, Wb. and Gd. 203.]
Mo-de′na.
Mod′er-ate, *a.* & *v.* 73, 108, 233, Exc.
Mod′er-āt-ed.
Mod′er-ate-ly, 185.
Mod′er-āt-ing.
Mod-er-a′tion, 112.
Mod′er-āt-ism (*-izm*).
Mod-e-rä′to (It.), 154.
Mod′er-āt-or, 88.
Mod′er-āt-rix.
Mod′ern.
Mod′ern-ism (*-izm*), 133
Mod′ern-ist.
Mod-ern-ĭ-za′tion, 112.
Mod′ern-īze, 202.
Mod′ern-īzed, 165.
Mod′ern-īz-er.
Mod′ern-īz-ing.
Mod′ern-ness, 66, N.
Mod′est, 76, 103.
Mod′est-y, 93, 169.
Mod′i-cum. [186.
Mod-i-fī′a-ble, 164, 169,
Mod-i-fĭ-ca′tion, 233.
Mod′i-fīed, 99.
Mod′i-fī-er, 186.
Mod′i-fȳ, 94.
Mod′i-fȳ-ing, 186.
Mo-dil′lion (*-dil′yun*).
Mo-di′o-lar, *or* Mo′di-o-lar [*mo-di′o-lar*, Wr.; *mo′di-o-lar*, Sm. Gd. 155.]
Mōd′ish, 156.
Mōd′ist, 183.
Mod′ū-late (89) [so Sm. Wr. Wb. Gd.; *mod′-*

ū-lāt, or *mod'jū-lāt*, Wk. 134, 155.]
Mod'ū-lāt-ed, 183.
Mod'ū-lāt-ing.
Mod-ū-la'tion, 112.
Mod'ū-lāt-or.
Mod'ule (90) [so Sm. Wr. Wb. Gd.; *mod'-ūl*, or *mod'jūl*, Wk. 134, 155.]
Mod'ū-lus (L.) (89) [pl. *Mod'u-lī*, 198.]
Mo'dus (L.) [L. pl. *Mo'-dī*; Eng. pl. Mo'dus-es (*-ez*), 198.]
Mod'wâll.
Mœ'so-Goth'ic(*me'so-*), 13, 224.
[Moggason, 203. — *See* Moccason.]
Mo-gul', 121.
Mo'hair (*-hêr*).
Mo-ham'med-an(72,170) [Mahometan, Mahomedan, 203.]
Mo-ham'med-an-ism (*-izm*), 133, 136.
Mo-ham'med-an-ize, 202.
Mo-ham'med-an-ized.
Mo-ham'med-an-iz-ing.
Mo'hâwk [Mohock, 203.]
Mo-ho'lī, 191.
Mōhr (*mōr*) (162), *n.* a species of antelope inhabiting Africa. [*See* Mohur, 148; *and* More, 160.]
Mo'hur, *n.* an East Indian gold coin, worth about $6.67. [*See* Mohr, *and* More, 148; *and* Mower, 160.]
Moi'dore (171) [so Wr. Wb. Gd.; *maw'i-dōr*, Sm.; *moi-dōr'*, Wk. 155.]
Moi'e-ty (*moi'-*, or *maw'-*) [*moi'e-ty*, Wk. Wr. Wb. Gd.; *maw'-e-ty*, Sm. 155.]
Moil, 27.
Moiled, 165.
Moil'ing.
Moi'neau(Fr.) (*-no*), 154.
Moire'-an-tique' (Fr.) (*mwor'an-tēk'*).
Moist, 27.
Moist'en (*mois'n*), 149, 162, 167.
Moist'ened (*mois'nd*).
Moist'en-ing (*mois'n-*).
Moist'ure, 91.
Mo'lar, 74.
Mo'lar-y, 169.
Mo-lăs'ses (*-lăs'ez*) (76) [*mo-lăs'ez*, Wb. Gd.; *mo-lăs'ez*, Wr.; *mo-lăs'iz*, Wk.; *mo-lăs'-es*, Sm. 155.][Melasses, 203.]

☞ "Commonly called *molasses*... properly *melasses*." *Smart.* — "*Melasses*... is more accordant with etymology." — *Goodrich.*

[Mold, Wb. Gd. 203. — *See* Mould.]
[Molder, Wb. Gd. 203. — *See* Moulder.]
[Moldy, Wb. Gd. 203. — *See* Mouldy.]
Mole, 24.
Mo-lec'u-lar (89) [*not* mōl'cu-lar, 144, 153.]
Mo-lec-u-lăr'i-ty, 169.
Mol'e-cule [*not* mōl'-kūl, 144, 153.]
Mole'hill, 206.
Mo-lest', 103.
Mol-est-a'tion, 112, 143.
Mo-lest'ed.
Mo-lest'er.
Mo-lest'ing.
Mo'lin-ism (*-izm*), 133.
Mo'lin-ist.
Mŏll, 18, 172.
Mol'lah (72) [Moollah, 203.]
Mol'lient (*mol'yent*), *or* Mol'li-ent [so Wr.; *mol'yent*, Wk. Sm.; *mol'i-ent*, Wb. Gd. 155.] [186.
Mol'li-fī-a-ble, 164, 169,
Mol-li-fī-ca'tion, 233.
Mol'li-fīed, 99.
Mol'li-fȳ, 94, 170.
Mol'li-fȳ-ing, 186.
Mol-lus'ca (L.), *n. pl.*
Mol-lus'can, 72.
Mol-lus'coŭs, 100.
Mol'lusk, 66, 170.
Mo'loch (*-lok*), 52.
Mo-losse' (*-los'*), 121.
Mo-los'sus, 170.
[Molt, Wb. Gd. 203. — *See* Moult.]
Mōlt'en (*mōlt'n*), 24, 149, 167.
Mol-yb-de'na, 122.
Mo-lyb'de-noŭs.
Mol-yb-de'num (171) [*not* mo-lib'de-num, 153.]
Mo'ment, 24, 76.
Mo'ment-a-ri-ly, 126, 186.
Mo'ment-a-ry, 72, 169.
Mo-ment'oŭs, 100.
Mo-men'tum (L.) [L. pl. *Mo-men'ta*; Eng. pl. Mo-men'tums (*-tumz*), rare, 198.]
Mom'i-er (*mum'-*), 22.
Mo'mŏt.
Mo'mus, 169.
Mon'a-chal (*-kal*), 52, 72.
Mon'a-chism (*-kizm*), 133.
Mon'ăd (103) [so Sm. Wr. Wb. Gd.; *mon'-ad*, or *mo'nad*, Wk. 155.]
Mon'a-delph.
Mon-a-delph'i-an, 169.
Mon-a-delph'oŭs.
Mo-nad'ic, 109.
Mo-nad'ic-al, 108.
Mo-nan'der.
Mo-nan'dri-an, 169.
Mo-nan'droŭs, 100.
Mo-nan'thoŭs.
Mon'arch (*-ark*), 52, 72.
Mo-narch'i-al (*-nark'-*), 169.
Mo-narch'ic (*-nark'-*).
Mo-narch'ic-al(*-nark'-*).
Mon'arch-ist (*-ark-*).
Mon'arch-ize (*-ark-*).
Mon'arch-ized (*-ark-*).
Mon'arch-īz-ing (*-ark-*).
Mon'arch-y (*-ark-*), 169.
Mon-as-te'ri-al, 49, N.
Mon'as-tĕr-y (116, 122) [so Wr. Wb. Gd.; *mon'as-try*, or *mon'-as-tĕr-y*, Wk.; *mon'-as-tĕr-y*, coll. *mon'as-try*, Sm. 155.]
Mo-nas'tic, 109.
Mo-nas'tic-al, 108.
Mo-nas'tic-al-ly, 170.
Mo-nas'ti-cism (*-sizm*).
Mo-nas'ti-con.
Mo'nâul, 156.
Mon'day (*mun'dy*), 22.
Mŏnde (Fr.) (154) [so Sm. Wb. Gd.; *mŏnd*, Wr. 155.]
Mon'e-ta-ry (*mun'-*) (72) [so Sm. Wb. Gd.; *mon'e-ta-ry*, or *mun'e-ta-ry*, Wr. 155], *a.* pertaining to money. [*See* Monitory, 148.]
Mon'ey (*mun'y*) (98,

169, 190) [pl. Moneys, 171, 187.]
Mon′ey-age (*mun′-*).
Mon′ey-bro′ker (*mun′-*), 205.
Mon′eyed (*mun′id*), 171.
Mon′ey-er (*mun′-*).
Mon′ey-mak′er (*mun′-*), 205.
Mon′ger (*mung′gur*), 54, 138, 171.
Mon′gol (*mong′-*), 86.
Mon-go′li-an, 169.
Mon′goose (*mong′-*) [Mangoose, Mongooz′, 203.]
Mon′grel (*mung′-*), 22, 54, 141, 171.
Mo-nil′i-form, 108.
Mo′ning, *n.* a fine kind of black tea. [*See* Moaning, 160.]
Mo-nĭ′tion (*-nish′un*).
Mon′i-tĭve, 84.
Mon′i-tor, 169.
Mon-i-to′ri-al, 49, N.
Mon′i-to-ry (86), *a.* giving admonition. [*See* Monetary, 148.]
Mon′i-tress.
Monk (*mungk*), 22, 54.
Monk′er-y (*mungk′-*).
Mon′key (*mung′ky*), 22, 54, 169.
Mon′key-jack′et (*mung′-*), 205.
Monk′hŏŏd (*mungk′-*).
Monk′ish (*mungk′-*).
Monk′s′hŏŏd (*mungks′-*), 213.
Mon-o-ba′sic, 109.
Mon-o-car′di-an.
Mon-o-car′poŭs, 100.
Mon-o-ceph′a-loŭs.
Mon-o-chla-myd′e-oŭs (*-kla-*), 108, 169.
Mon′o-chord (*-kord*).
Mon-o-chro-mat′ic (*-kro′-*).
Mon′o-chrome (*-krōm*).
Mon-o-chron′ic (*-kron′-*), 52.
Mon-o-cli′noŭs, 122.
Mon-o-co-tyl-e′don [so Gd.; *mon-o-kot-y-le′-don*, Sm. Wr. 155.—*See* Cotyledon.]
Mon-o-co-tyl-e′don-oŭs, 143.
Mo-noc′ra-cy, 108.
Mo-noc′u-lar, 108.
Mon′o-cule.
Mo-noc′u-loŭs, 108.
Mon-o-dac′tyl-oŭs.
Mon′o-delph.
Mon′o-dist.
Mon′o-don.
Mon-o-dra-mat′ic, 109.
Mon′o-drame, 105.
Mon′o-dy.
Mo-nœ′cian (*-ne′shan*), 13, 46, 169.
Mo-nœ′cioŭs (*-ne′-shus*).
Mo-nog′a-mist.
Mo-nog′a-moŭs.
Mo-nog′a-my, 93.
Mon-o-gas′tric, 230.
Mon′o-gram, 105.
Mon-o-gram′mic, 109.
Mon′o-gram-mal, 72.
Mon-o-gram-mat′ic, 170.
Mon′o-gram-moŭs.
Mon′o-grăph, 127.
Mo-nog′ra-pher, 108.
Mon-o-graph′ic.
Mon-o-graph′ic-al.
Mo-nog′ra-phist.
Mo-nog′ra-phy, 108.
Mon′o-gyn (*-jin*).
Mon-o-gyn′i-an (*-jin′-*).
Mo-nog′y-noŭs (*-noj′-*).
Mon′o-lith.
Mon′o-lith-al, 106.
Mon-o-lith′ic, 109.
Mo-nol′o-gist, 108.
Mon′o-lŏgue (*-log*), 87.
Mo-nom′a-chy (*-ky*), 108.
Mon-o-ma′ni-a.
Mon-o-ma′ni-ac, 108.
Mon′ome [so Sm. Gd.; *mon′o-me*, Wr. 155.]
Mo-nom′e-ter, 108.
Mon-o-met′ric.
Mo-no′mi-al, 169.
Mon-o-mor′phoŭs.
Mon-o-ou′si-an (*-ow′zi-an*) [*mon-o-ow′si-an*, Gd.; *mon-o-ow′shan*, Wr. 155.—*See* Homoousian.]
Mo-nop′a-thy, 108.
Mon-o-per′so-nal.
Mon-o-pet′al-oŭs.
Mo-noph′a-noŭs.
Mo-noph′thong (*-nop′-*), *or* Mon′oph-thong (*-of-*) [*mo-nop′-thong*, Sm.; *mon′of-thong*, Wb. Gd.; *mo-nof′thong*, or *mon′of-thong*, Wr. 155.]
Mon-oph-thon′gal (*-op-thong′-*), 54, 72.
Mon-o-phyl′loŭs, *or* Mo-noph′yl-loŭs. [*See* Adenophyllous.]
Mon-o-phy′o-dont.
Mo-noph′y-sĭte, 152.
Mo-noph-y-sit′ic-al.
Mo-nop′o-dy, 105.
Mo-nop′o-list.
Mo-nop′o-lize, 202.
Mo-nop′o-lized, 183.
Mo nop′o-lĭz-er, 183.
Mo-nop′o-lĭz-ing.
Mo-nop′o-ly.
Mon-o-pol′y-lŏgue, 87.
Mo-nop′ter-al, 72.
Mon′op-tote, *or* Mo-nop′tote [so Wk.; *mon′op-tōt*, Sm. Wr.; *mo-nop′tōt*, Wb. Gd. 155.]
Mon′o-rhyme (*-rīm*), 162.
Mon-o-sep′a-loŭs.
Mon-o-sperm′oŭs.
Mon-o-sphĕr′ic-al.
Mon′o-stich (*-stik*), 141.
Mon-o-stroph′ic.
Mon-o-syl-lab′ic.
Mon-o-syl-lab′ic-al.
Mon′o-syl-la-ble, 164.
Mon-o-thal′a-moŭs.
Mon′o-the-ism (*-izm*), 133, 136.
Mon′o-the-ist.
Mon-o-the-ist′ic, 109.
Mo-noth′e-lĭte, 152, 169.
Mon′o-tone, 156.
Mo-not′o-noŭs, 100.
Mo-not′o-ny, 105.
Mon′o-treme.
Mon-o-tri′glyph, 122.
Monseigneur (Fr.) (*mōng-sĕn′yur*) [pl. *Messeigneurs*, (*mā-sĕn′yurz*), 154.]
Monsieur (Fr.) (*mos-sĕr′*, or *mos-yur′*) [*mos-sĕr′*, Gd.; *mōngs-yoor′*, or nearly *mŏs′yur′*, Sm.; *mŏs′yur′*, or *mon-sĕr′*, Wr. 155] [pl. *Messieurs*, 198.—*See* Messieurs.]
Mon-soon′, 121.
Mon′ster, 77, 230.
Mon′strance, 64.
Mon-stros′i-ty, 169.
Mon′stroŭs, 100, 169.
Mon-tan′ic, 109.
Mon′ta-nism (*-nizm*), 136.
Mon′ta-nist.

Mon-ta-nist'ic.
Mon-ta-nist'ic-al.
Mon'tant, 72.
Mont de piété (Fr.) (*mōngd'pē-ā-tā'*).
Mon'te (*-tā*) (Sp.).
Mon-te-fī-as'co.
Mon'tem.
Mon-teth', *or* Mon'teth [*mon-teth'*, Wb. Gd.; *mon'teth*, Sm.; *mon'-teth*, or *mon-teth'*, Wr. 155.]
Month (*munth*), 22.
Month'ly (*munth'-*).
Mon-tic'u-late, 89.
Mont-mar'tri e, 152.
Mon-toir' (*mōng-twor'*) [so Sm.; *mon'twor*, Gd.; *mon-twor'*, Wr. 155.]
Mon'u-ment, 89.
Mon-u-ment'al.
Moo, 19, 32.
Mood (19), *n.* state of mind; — the form of a verb. [*See* Mooed, 160.]
Mooed (165, 188), *v.* did moo. [*See* Mood, 160.]
Moo'ing.
Mood'i-ly, 186.
Mood'i-ness.
Mood'y, 169.
[Moollah, 203. — *See* Mollah.]
Moon, 19, 32, 43.
Moon'bēam, 206.
Moon'calf (*-käf*).
Mooned, 165.
Moon'-eyed (*-īd*), 206, Exc. 5.
Moon'ish.
Moon'light (*-līt*).
Moon'lit.
Moon'shee.
Moon'shine, 206.
Moon'shīn-y, 169.
Moon'stone.
Moon'-struck.
Moon'wort (*-wurt*).
Moon'y, 93.
Moor, 19, 49.
Moor'age, 70.
Moor'-cock.
Moored, 165.
Moor'-fowl.
Moor'-game.
Moor'-grȧss.
Moor'-hen.
Moor'ing.
Moor'ish.
Moor'land, 206.
Moor'-stone.
Moor'y, 169.
Moose.
Moose'wŏŏd.
Moot, 19.
Moot'a-ble, 164, 169.
Moot'ed.
Moot'er.
Moot'ing.
Mop, 18, 30.
Mope, 163.
Moped (*mōpt*), 183; Note C, p. 34.
Mōp'ing, 183.
Mōp'ish.
Mopped (*mopt*), 176.
Mop'pet, 66, 170.
Mop'ping, 176.
Mop'sey, 98, 169.
Mo-rāine'.
Mŏr'al, 48, 66, 170.
Mō-rāle' (Fr.).
Mŏr'al-ist.
Mo-ral'i-ty, 108, 169.
Mŏr-al ĭ-za'tion, 112.
Mŏr'al-ize, 202.
Mŏr'al-ized, 165.
Mŏr'al-īz-er.
Mŏr'al-īz-ing.
Mŏr'al-ly, 170.
Mŏr'als (*-alz*), *n. pl.*
Mo-rȧss', 121.
Mo-rȧss'y, 93, 169.
Mo-ra'vi-an, 169.
Mo-ra'vi-an-ism (*-izm*), 136.
Mor'bid, 135.
Mor-bid'i-ty, 108.
Mor-bif'ic, 170.
Mor-bif'ic-al, 228.
Mor-bil'loŭs, 171.
Mor-bose', 121.
Mor-ceau' (Fr.) (*mor-so'*) [pl. *Mor-ceaux'* (*mor-so'*).]
Mor-da'cioŭs (*-shus*), 46.
Mor-daç'i-ty, 169.
Mor'dant, 72.
More (135), *a.* greater in degree, quantity, or amount. [*See* Mohur, *and* Mower, 148; *and* Mohr, 160.]
Mo-reen', 121.
Mo-rel' (121) [Moril (in the sense of *a kind of mushroom*), 203.]
More'land, 72.
More-o'ver.
Mo-resque' (*-resk'*), 114.
Mor-ga-nat'ic, 109.
Mor'gāy.
Morgue (Fr.) (*morg*).
Mŏr'i-bund.
Mŏr'il [Morel, 203.]
Mo-ril'lon, 170.
Mŏr'i-nel, 48.
Mo'ri-on, 49, N.
Mo-ris'co, 86.
Mor'mon, 86.
Mor'mon-īte.
Morn, 17, 135.
Morn'ing, 141.
Morn'ing-glo'ry, 205.
Mo-roc'co, 66, N.
Mo-rone'.
Mo-rose', 121.
Mo-rose'ly, 185.
Mor'pheŭs [so Wr.; *mor'fe-us*, Wk. Sm. Gd. 155.]

☞ "The termination *eus* in proper names which in Greek end in εύς, as *Orpheus*, *Prometheus*, is to be pronounced as one syllable, the *eu* being a diphthong. Walker, following Labbe, generally separates the vowels in pronunciation. But the diphthong is never resolved in Greek; and very rarely, if ever in Latin poetry of the golden or silver age. . . . The usage of the English poets, of modern classical scholars, and of the best speakers generally, also favors, it is believed, the pronunciation which the analogy of the original languages requires, and which is supported by the authority of the best Latin grammarians from Priscian to the present time." *Worcester.*

Mor'phew (*-fū*), 26.
Mor'phi-a.
Mor'phīne, 82, 152.
Mor-pho-log'ic (*-loj'-*).
Mor-pho-log'ic-al (*-loj'-*)
Mor-phol'o-gy (*-jy*), 108.
Mŏr'ris (170) [Morrice, 203.]
Mŏr'ris-dȧnce.
Mŏr'rōw, 66, 101.
Mors (L.) (*morz*).
Morse, Note D, p. 37.
Mor'sel, 149.
Mort, 49.
Mor'tal, 72.
Mor-tal'i-ty, 108, 169.
Mor'tal-ly, 170.
Mor'tar, 74, 169.
Mort'gage (*mor'-*), 162.
Mort'gaged (*mor'gājd*).

Mort-ga-gee′ (*mor-ga-jē′*).
Mort-gage-or′ (*mor-gāj-or′*) (Note D, p. 37) [so Wr. Gd.; *mor′ga-jor*, Sm. 155.] [Law term, — correlative of *mortgagee*.] [**Mortgagor**, 203.]

☞ "*Mortgagor* is an orthography that should have no countenance." *Webster.*

Mort′ga-ger (*mor′ga-jur*).
Mor-tif′er-oŭs.
Mor-ti-fĭ-ca′tion, 112.
Mor′ti-fīed, 99.
Mor′ti-fȳ, 108.
Mor′ti-fȳ ing, 186.
Mor′tĭse, 136, 169.
Mor′tĭsed (*-tist*), 165.
Mor′tis-ing, 183.
Mort′māin.
Mort′u-a-ry, 72, 89.
Mo-sa′ic (*-za′-*).
Mo-sa′ic-al (*-za′-*).
Mos′cha-tel (*-ka-*).
Mo-selle′ (*-zel′*), 121.
Mos′lem (*moz′-*) (136) [so Sm. Gd.; *mos′lem*, Wr. 155.]
Mosque(*mosk*) [**Mosk**, 203.]
Mos-qui′to (*-ke′-*) (171) [pl. **Mos-qui′tōes,** (*-ke′tōz*), 192.]

☞ "This word has been spelled in various ways, but *musquito* and *mosquito* are most prevalent." *Goodrich.* — "*Moschetto, musqueto*, and other forms yield in frequent occurrence to the one given [*mosquito*], which may be considered as the established one in our language." *Smart.*

Moss, 18, N.; 174.
Moss′-clad, 206, Exc. 5.
Moss′i-ness, 186.
Moss′-troop-er.
Moss′y, 169.
Mōst (24) [*See* Ghost.]
Mos′tick [**Mostic**, 203.]

☞ "A corruption of *maul-stick*." *Worcester.*

Mōst′ly, 93.
Mŏt, 18.
Mote (24, 163), *n.* a small particle. [*See* Moat, 160.]
Moth (18, N.; 156) [pl. **Moths** (*mothz*), 140. — *See* Note C, p. 34.]
Moth′-ēat′en (*-ēt′n*).
Moth′er (*muth′ur*).
Moth′er-hood (*muth′-*).
Moth′er-ing (*muth′-*).
Moth′er-in-lâw.
Moth′er-less (*muth′-*).
Moth′er-li-ness (*muth′-*), 186.
Moth′er-ly (*muth′-*).
Moth′er-of-pearl′ (*muth′ur-ov-perl′*),221
Moth′er-of-thyme′ (*muth′ur-ov-tīm′*).
Moth′er-wort (*muth′ur-wurt*).
Moth′er-y (*muth′-*), 169.
Moth′y, 18, N.; 93.
Mo-tif′ic, 66, 170.
Mo′tĭle, 81, 152.
Mo-til′i-ty, 108, 169.
Mo′tion.
Mo′tioned (*-shund*), 165.
Mo′tion-ing.
Mo′tĭve, 84.
Mo-tiv′i-ty.
Mot′ley, 169.
Mot′mot.
Mo′tor, 88, 169.
Mo-to′ri-al, 49, N.
Mo′to-ry, 86.
Mot′tle (*mot′l*), 164.
Mot′tled (*-ld*), 165.
Mot′to (86, 153) [pl. **Mot′tōes** (*-tōz*), 192.]
Mouf′flon (*moof′-*), 170.
Mōuld (24) [**Mold**, Wb. Gd. 203. — *See* Note E, p. 70.]

☞ "This word, before Dr. Johnson wrote his Dictionary, was frequently written *mold*, which was perfectly agreeable to its Saxon derivation, and was less liable to mispronunciation than the present spelling." *Walker.*

Mōuld′a-ble, 164.
Mōuld′ed [**Molded**, Wb. Gd. 203.]
Mōuld′er [**Molder**, Wb. Gd. 203.]
Mōuld′ered (165) [**Moldered**, Wb. Gd. 203.]
Mōuld′er-ing [**Moldering**, Wb. Gd. 203.]
Mōuld′i-ness (186) [**Moldiness**, Wb. Gd. 203.]
Mōuld′ing [**Molding**, Wb. Gd. 203.]
Mōuld′wârp [**Moldwarp**, Wb. Gd. 203.]
Mōuld′y (169) [**Moldy**, Wb. Gd. 203.]
Mōult (24) [**Molt**, Wb. Gd. 203. — *See* Note E, p. 70.]
Mōult′ed [**Molted**, Wb. Gd. 203.]
Mōult′ing [**Molting**, Wb. Gd. 203.]
Mound, 28.
Mount, 28.
Mount′a-ble, 164, 169.
Mount′aĭn (*-in*), 96.
Mount′aĭn-ash.
Mount-aĭn-eer′, 169.
Mount′aĭn-oŭs, 145.
Mount′e-bank, 144.
Mount′ed.
Mount′ing.
Mōurn, 24, 135.
Mōurned, 165.
Mōurn′er.
Mōurn′ful (*-fŏŏl*), 180.
Mōurn′ful-ly (*-fŏŏl*).
Mōurn′ing.
Mōurn′ing-ring, 206, Exc. 4.
Mouse, *n.* (28, 161) [pl. **Mice,** 195.]
Mouse (*mouz*), *v.* 161.
Moused (*mouzd*), 165.
Mouse′-ēar, 206, Exc. 2.
Mous′er (*mouz′-*).
Mouse′tāil, 206.
Mouse′trap.
Mous′ing (*mouz′-*), 183.
[**Moustache** (Fr.) (*moos-tăsh′*), 203. — *See* Mustache.]
Mouth, *n.* (28, 37, 161) [pl. **Mouths** (*mouthz*), 38, 140; Note C, p. 34.]
Mouth, *v.* 38, 161.
Mouthed, 165.
Mouth′er.
Mouth′ful (*-fŏŏl*), 197.
Mouth′ing.
Mouth′piēce, 206.
Mov′a-ble (*moov′a-bl*) (164, 169, 171, 183) [**Moveable**, 203.]
Mov′a-bly (*moov′-*).
Move (*moov*), 19.
Moved (*moovd*).
Move′ment(*moov′-*),185.
Mov′er (*moov′-*), 77.
Mov′ing (*-moov′-*), 183.
Mow (*mou*), *n.* 161.

Mow (*mou*) (161), *v.* to put into a mow.
Mōw (161), *v.* to cut with a scythe, as grass.
Mowed (*moud*) (161), *v.* did mow, or put into a mow.
Mowed (*mōd*) (161), *v.* did mōw, or cut with a scythe. [*See* Mode, 160.]
Mōw'er, *n.* (67), one who mōws. [*See* More, 148; *and* Mohur, 160.]
Mow'ing (*mou'ing*) (161), *part.* putting into a mow.
Mōw'ing (161), *part.* cutting with a scythe.
Mōwn (24), *part.* from *Mōw.* [*See* Moan, 160.]
Mox'a, 231.
Mox-i-bus'tion (*-bust'-yun*).
Mr. [*See* Mister.]
Mrs. [*See* Missis.]
Much, 22, 44.
Mu-cif'ic, 109.
Mu'ci-form, 108.
Mu'ci-lage, 169.
Mu-ci-lag'in-oŭs (*-laj'-*), 108, 116.
Mu-cip'a-roŭs, 108.
Muck, 22, 181.
Muck'worm (*-wurm*).
Muck'y, 169.
Mu'co-cele.
Mu'co-pu'ru-lent, 224.
Mu-cos'i-ty, 108, 169.
Mu-co'so-sac'cha-rīne (*-ka-*), 224.
Mu'coŭs (100), *a.* pertaining to mucus; slimy. [*See* Mucus, 160.]
Mu'cro-nate, 105.
Mu'cro-nāt-ed.
Mu'cu-lent, 89.
Mu'cus (169), *n.* a viscid fluid secreted by the membrane lining the cavities of the body. [*See* Mucous, 160.]
Mud, *n.* & *v.* 22, 42.
Mud'ded (176), *v.* did mud. [*See* Muddied, 148.]
Mud'dīed (99), *v.* did make muddy. [*See* Mudded, 148.]
Mud'di-ly, 186.
Mud'di-ness.
Mud'ding, 176.
Mud'dle, 66, 164, 170.
Mud'dled (*mud'ld*), 183.
Mud'dling.
Mud'dy, 176.
Mud'dy-ing, 186.
Mu-ez'zin, 66, 170.
Muff, 22, 173.
Muf'fin.
Muf'fle (*muf'l*), 66, 164.
Muf'fled (*muf'ld*), 183.
Muf'fler.
Muf'fling.
Muf'tĭ, 127, 191.
Mug, 22, 53.
Mug'gent (*-ghent*) (138) [so Wb. Gd.; *mug'-jent*, Wr. 155.]
Mug'get (*-ghet*), 76, 138.
Mug-gle-to'ni-an (*mug-l-*), 169.
Mug'gy (*-ghy*).
Mu-lat'to (170) [pl. Mu-lat'tōes (*-tōz*), 192.]
Mu-lat'tress.
Mul'ber-ry, 170.
Mulch, 22, 44.
Mulched (*mulcht*), 165; Note C, p. 34.
Mulch'ing.
Mulct, 22, 52, 64.
Mulct'ed.
Mulct'ing.
Mulct'u-a-ry, 72, 89.
Mule (26), *n.* a mongrel animal or plant. [*See* Mewl, 160.]
Mu-let-eer', 144, 169.
Mu-li-eb'ri-ty, 108.
Mūl'ish, 183.
Mull, 22, 172.
Mul'la, 189.
Mul-la-ga-taw'ny, 171.
Mulled (*muld*), 165.
Mul'leĭn (*-lin*) (97, 170, 171) [Mullen, 203.]
Mul'let, 170.
Mull'ing.
Mull ion (*mul'yun*), 170.
Mult-an'gu-lar (*-ang'-*).
Mul-ti-ar-tic'u-late.
Mul-ti-cap'su-lar.
Mul-ti-căr'i-nate, 108.
Mul-ti-cus'pi-date.
Mul-ti-den'tate.
Mul-ti-fa'ri-oŭs, 49, N.; 169.
Mul'ti-fid.
Mul'ti-flo-roŭs, *or* Mul-tif'lo-roŭs [*mul'ti-flo-rus*, Sm.; *mul-tif'lo-rus*, Wb. Gd.; *mul-ti-flo'rus*, Wr. 155.]
Mul'ti-foil.
Mul'ti-fōld.
Mul'ti-form, 108.
Mul-ti-form'i-ty, 108.
Mul-ti-gen'er-ous (*-jen'-*).
Mul-ti-gran'u-late.
Mul-tij'u-goŭs [so Sm. Wr.; *mul-ti-ju'gus*, Wb. Gd. 155.]
Mul-ti-lat'er-al.
Mul-ti-lin'e-al, 169.
Mul-ti-loc'u-lar, 108.
Mul-til'o-quence.
Mul-til'o-quent, 169.
Mul-til'o-quoŭs.
Mul-ti-no'date.
Mul-ti-no'doŭs.
Mul-ti-no'mi-al, 72, 169.
Mul-tip'a-roŭs, 108.
Mul-tip'ar-tīte, 152, 156.
Mul'ti-ped [Multipede, 203.]
Mul'ti-ple, 164.
Mul'ti-plex, 76, 78.
Mul-ti-pli'a-ble, 164.
Mul-ti-plĭ-cand' (122) [*not* mul'ti-plĭ-kand, 153.]
Mul'ti-plĭ-cate, *or* Mul-tip'li-cate [*mul'ti-plĭ-kāt*, Sm. Wb. Gd.; *mul-tip'li-kāt*, Wk.; *mul-tip'li-kāt*, or *mul'-ti-plĭ-kāt*, Wr. 155.]
Mul-ti-plĭ-ca'tion, 112.
Mul'ti-pli-cāt-ĭve.
Mul'ti-pli-cāt-or [so Sm. Wr.; *mul-ti-pli-ka'-tur*, Wk. Wb. Gd. 155.]
Mul-ti-pliç'i-ty, 108, 169.
Mul'ti-plīed, 99, 186.
Mul'ti-plī-er.
Mul'ti-plȳ, 94.
Mul'ti-plȳ-ing, 186.
Mul-tip'o-tent.
Mul-ti-pres'ence (*-prez'-*).
Mul-ti-ra'di-ate, 169.
Mul-ti-se'ri-al, 49, N.
Mul-tis'o-noŭs, 156.
Mul-ti-spi'ral, 49, N.
Mul-ti-stri'ate.
Mul-ti-sul'cate.
Mul'ti-tude (26, 169) [*not* mul'ti-tood, 127, 153.]
Mul-ti-tu'din-a-ry, 72.
Mul-ti-tu'din-oŭs, 108.
Mul'ti-valve.
Mul-ti-valv'u-lar, 108.
Mul-to'ca.

Mult-oc′u-lar, 169.
Mul′tum in par′vo (L.).
Mult-un′gu-late (*-ung′-*)
Mul′ture, 91.
Mum (22, 32), *a.* silent. [*See* Mumm, 160.]
Mum′ble, 164.
Mum′bled, 165, 183.
Mum′bler.
Mum′bling.
Mumm (175), *v.* to mask one's self. [*See* Mum, 160.]
Mum′ma-chog [Mummychog, 203.]
Mummed (*mumd*), 165.
Mum′mer, 170.
Mum′mer-y, 169.
Mum-mi-fĭ-ca′tion.
Mum′mi-fied, 99.
Mum′mi-form, 108, 186.
Mum′mi-fȳ, 94.
Mum′mi-fȳ-ing, 186.
Mum′ming, 170.
Mum′my, 66, 170.
Mump, 22, 64.
Mumped (*mumpt*), 165.
Mump′er.
Mump′ing.
Mump′ish.
Mumps, 22.
Munch, 22, 44.
Munched (*muncht*), 165; Note C, p. 34.
Munch′ing.
Mun′dane, 103.
Mun-di-fĭ-ca′tion.
Mun-dif′i-ca-tĭve.
Mun-dun′gus (*-dung′-*), 54, 169.
Mu-niç′i-pal, 72.
Mu-niç-i-pal′i-ty, 108.
Mu-nif′i-cence, 105.
Mu-nif′i-cent, 171.
Mu′ni-ment, 169.
Mu-nĭ′tion (*-nish′un*).
Mun-jeet′, 121.
Mun′nion (*mun′yun*).
Mu′ral, 49, N.; 72.
Mur′der, 77.
Mur′dered, 150.
Mur′der-er, 135.
Mur′der-ess.
Mur′der-ing.
Mur′der-oŭs.
Mur′dress, 169.
Mu′ri-ate, 49, N.; 108, 169.
Mu′ri-āt-ed.
Mu-ri-at′ic, 109.
Mu′ri-cate, 108.
Mu′ri-cāt-ed.
Mu-ri-ca′to-his′pid, 224.
Mu′ri-form, 108.
Mu′rīne, 49, N.; 152.
Murk, 21.
Murk′i-ly, 186.
Murk′y (169) [Mirky, 203.]
Mur′mur, 92, 169.
Mur′mured, 150, 165.
Mur′mur-er, 135.
Mur′mur-ing.
Mur′mur-oŭs, 100.
Mŭr′raĭn (*-rin*), 96, 171.
Mŭr′rhīne (*-rĭn*) (171) [so Sm.; *mŭr′in*, Wr. Wb. Gd. 155.]
Mur′za, *n.* an hereditary nobleman among the Tartars. [*See* Mirza, 160.]
Mu-sa′ceous (*-za′shus*), 46, 112.
Mu-sa-rab′ic (*-za-*).
Mus′ca-del, 105.
Mus′ca-dīne, *or* Mus′ca-dīne [so Wr.; *mus′ka-dīn*, Wk. Gd.; *mus′ka-din*, Sm. 155.]
Mus′car-dīne, 152.
Mus-căr′i-form, 108.
Mus′cat.
Mus′ca-tel.
Musch′el-kalk (*mōōsh′-*) [so Sm.; *mush′el-kalk*, Wb. Gd.; *moosh′el-kalk*, Wr. 155.]
Mus′cle (*mus′l*) (162, 164). [*See* Mussel.]
Mus′cled (*mus′ld*).
Mus′cling (*mus′ling*).
Mus′coid.
Mus-col′o-gy, 108.
Mus-cos′i-ty, 108, 169.
Mus-co-va′do [*not* mus-ko-vä′do, 153.]

☞ This word is from the Spanish *mas-ca-bä′do* (uncleyed sugar), in which *a* of the third syllable has properly the Italian sound, or that of *a* in *far*; but the best authorities give to *a* its long sound in the Anglicized form *Muscovado.*

Mus′co-vīte, 105.
Mus′co-vy.
Mus′cu-lar, 89, 108.
Mus-cu-lăr′i-ty.
Mus′cu-loŭs, 100.
Muse (*mūz*), *n.* one of the nine sister goddesses who presided over the liberal arts: — *v.* to meditate. [*See* Mews, 160.]
Mused (*mūzd*), 183.
Muse′ful (*mūz′fōōl*), 180.
Mūs′er (*mūz′-*).
Mu-se′um (*-ze′-*) (111, 113, 125) [*not* mu′ze-um, 153.]
Mush, 22.
Mush′room.
Mu′sic (*-zik*), 200.
Mu′sic-al (*-zik-*), 72.
Mu′sic-al-ly (*-zik-*), 170.
Mu-si′cian (*-zish′an*).
Mu′sic-mȧs′ter (*-zik-*), 205, 209.
Mu′sic-o-ma′ni-a (*-zik-*), 224.
Mu′sic-stool (*-zik-*).
Mūs′ing (*mūz′-*), 183.
Musk, 22.
Mus′ket (76) [Musquet, 203.]
Mus-ket-eer′, 122, 169.
Mus-ket-oon′, 122.
Mus′ket-ry, 93.
Musk′i-ness, 186.
Musk′rat, 206.
Musk′y, 169.
Mus′lin (*muz′-*).
Mus′lin-de-lāine (*muz′-*), 171.
Mus′lin-et (*muz′-*).
Mus′mon, *or* Mus′i-mon
Mu-so-ma′ni-a (*-zo-*), 169.
Mus′quash (*-kwosh*).
[Musquet, 203. — *See* Musket.]
[Musquito, 203. — *See* Mosquito.]
Mus′rōl (*mus′-*, or *muz′-*) [*mus′rōl*, Sm.; *muz′rōl*, Wr. Wb. Gd. 155.] [Musrole, Wb. Gd. 203.]
Muss, 22, 174.
Mus′sel (*mus′l*), *n.* a kind of bivalve mollusk. [Muscle, 203.]
Mus′sul-man (171) [pl. Mus′sul-mans (*-manz*) 196.]
Mus-sul-man′ic, 170.
Mus′sul-man-ish.
Must, 22.
Mus-tăche′ (*-tăsh′*) (189) [so Sm. Gd.; *mus-tāsh′*, Wk.; *mus-tȧsh′*, or *mus-tāsh′*, Wr. 155.] [Moustache, 203.]
Mus-tăch′io (*-tăsh′o*) [pl. Mus-tach′ios (*mus-tăsh′ōz*), 192.]
Mus-tăch′ioed (*-tăsh′ōd*) (188) [so Wb. Gd.;

mus-tä'shĭ-ōd, Wr. 155.]
Mus'tang, 103.
Mus'tard.
Mus-tee' [Mestee, 203.]
Mus'te-line, 152.
Mus'ter, 77.
Mus'tered, 150, 165.
Mus'ter-ing.
Mus'ti-ly, 186.
Mus'ti-ness.
Mus'ty, 93.
Mu-ta-bil'i-ty, 108.
Mu'ta-ble, 164.
Mu'ta-bly.
Mu'tage.
Mu-ta'tion.
Mu'ta-to-ry, 86.
Mute, 26.
Mute'ly, 185.
Mute'ness.
Mu'ti-late, 169.
Mu'ti-lăt-ed, 183.
Mu'ti-lăt-ing.
Mu-ti-la'tion, 112.
Mu'ti-lăt-or.
Mu-ti-neer', 122, 169.
Mu'ti-nīed, 99, 186.
Mu'ti-noŭs, 100, 108.
Mu'ti-ny, 169.
Mu'ti-ny-ing, 186.
Mut'ter, 66, 170.
Mut'tered, 150, 165.
Mut'ter-er.
Mut'ter-ing.
Mut'ton (*mut'n*), 149.
Mū'tu-al (*mūt'yoo-al*) (89) [so Sm. Wr. Gd.; *mu'chū-al*, Wk. 134, 155.]
Mu-tu-al'i-ty, 108, 169.
Mu'tu-al-ly, 170.
Mu'tu-a-ry, 72, 89.
Mu'tule (*mūt'ūl*), 26.
Muz'zle, 66, 164.
Muz'zled (*muz'ld*), 165.
Muz'zling.
Mȳ (often *mĭ*) [so Sm.; *mĭ*, or *mĭ*, Wk. Wr. 155.]

☞ "The word *my*, when used without emphasis, takes its regular short sound in England, and to some extent in this country; as, 'I took down *mȳ* hat.' This sound, however, should not be given in serious or solemn discourse, nor should the *y* ever be turned into long *e*, after the Irish fashion, 'I took down *mee* hat.'" *Goodrich.*

Mȳ-co-log'ic (*-loj'-*), 109.
Mȳ-co-log'ic-al (*-loj'-*), 108.
Mȳ-col'o-gy, 108.
Myl'o-don.
Mȳn-heer' [*not* mīn-hĕr', 153.]
Mȳ-o-dȳ-nam'ics, 109.
Mȳ-o-dȳ-nam-i-om'e-ter, 108, 116, 171.
Mȳ-o-graph'ic.
Mȳ-o-graph'ic-al.
Mȳ-og'ra-phist.
My-og'ra-phy, 108.
Mȳ-o-log'ic (*-loj'-*).
Mȳ-o-log'ic-al (*-loj'-*).
Mȳ-ol'o-gy, 108.
My'ope, 189.
My-op'ic.
My'op-sy, 169.
My'o-py, 93.
Mȳ-o'sis, 109.
Mȳ-o-sit'ic.
Mȳ-o-til'i-ty, 108.
Mȳ-ot'o-my, 108.
Mȳr'i-ad.
Mȳr'i-a-gram [Myriagramme, 203.]
Myr'i-a-gramme' (Fr.) [so Wr.; *mir'i-a-gram*, Gd. 155.]
Mȳr-i-a-li'ter [*mĭr-i-al'-i-tur*, Gd. 155] [Myrioliter, (*mĭr-i-o-li'-tur*), Sm.; Myrialitre, 203.]
Myr-i-a-li'tre (Fr.) (*-le'-tur*) [so Wr.; *mĭr'i-a-le-tur*, Gd. 155.]
Mȳr-i-am'e-ter (108) [so Gd.; *mĭr-i-a-me'tur*, Sm. 155.] [Myriametre, 203.]
Myr-i-a-me'tre (Fr.) (*-ma'tur*) [so Wr.; *mĭr'i-a-mā-tur*, Gd. 155.]
Mȳr'i-a-pod.
Mȳr'i-arch (*-ärk*).
Myr'i-are (Fr.) (*-êr*).
Mȳr'i-cīne (82) [Myricin, 203.]
Mȳr'i-o-lŏgue (*-log*), 87.
Mȳr-i-o-phyl'loŭs, *or* Mȳr-i-oph'yl-loŭs [*See* Adenophyllous.]
Mȳr-i-o-rā'ma, *or* Mȳr-i-o-rā'ma [*mĭr-i-o-ra'-ma*, Gd.; *mĭr-i-o-rā'-ma*, Wr. 155.]
Myr'mi-don, 169, 171.
Myr-mi-do'ni-an.
My-rob'a-lan.

My-rop'o-list.
Myrrh, 21, N.; 49, 162, 171.
Mȳr'rhīne (*-rin*), 152.
Myr'ti-form, 108, 169.
Myr'tle, 21, N.; 164, 169.
My-self' (*mĭ-self'*, or *mī-self'*) [so Wr.; *mĭ-self'*, Wk. Sm.; *mī-self'*, Wb. Gd. 155] [*See* Note under *My*.]
Mys-ta-gog'ic (*-goj'-*).
Mys-ta-gog'ic-al (*-goj'-*).
Mys'ta-gŏgue (*-gog*), 87.
Mys-te'ri-arch (*-ärk*), 49, N.; 169.
Mys-te'ri-oŭs, 171.
Mys'ter-y, 169, 223, Exc.
Mys'tic.
Mys'tic-al.
Mys'tic-al-ly, 170.
Mys'ti-cism (*-sizm*), 133.
Mys-ti-fī-ca'tion, 112.
Mys'ti-fi-că-tor.
Mys'ti-fīed, 99.
Mys'ti-fȳ, 94.
Mys'ti-fȳ-ing, 186.
Myth (16, 37) [Mythe, 203.]
Myth'ic.
Myth'ic-al.
Mȳ-thog'ra-pher, 108.
Mȳ-thol'o-ger, 108.
Myth-o-log'ic (*-loj'-*).
Myth-o-log'ic-al (*-loj'-*).
Myth-o-log'ic-al-ly (*-loj'-*), 170.
Mȳ-thol'o-gist, 108.
Mȳ-thol'o-gize, 202.
Mȳ-thol'o-gized, 165.
Mȳ-thol'o-gīz-ing.
Myth'o-lŏgue (*-log*), 87.
Mȳ-thol'o-gy.

N.

Nab, 10, 31.
Nabbed, 165, 176.
Nab'bing.
Na'bob, 103.

☞ "This is the proper pronunciation adopted and established by us: though *na-bob'* is said to be nearer the native mode of sounding it." *Smart.*

Nac'a-rat, 105.
Na'cre (*-kur*), 164.

Na′cre-oŭs, 169.
Na′crīte, 152.
Na′dir, 70, 169.
Nag, 10, 53.
Nä′gel-fluh (Ger.) (*nah′-gl-floo*).
Na′iad (*na′yad*), *or* Nāi′-ad (*na′ad*) [*na′yad*, Wr. Wb. Gd.; *na′ad*, Wk. Sm. 155.] [Eng. pl. Naiads; L. pl. *Na′ia-des* (*na′ya-dēz*), 198.]
Nāil, 23, 50.
Nāiled, 165.
Nāil′er, 169.
Nāil′er-y, 233, Exc.
Nāil′ing.
Na′ive (Fr.) (-*ēv*), 154.
Nä′ive-ly (-*ēv*-) [so Gd.; *na′ēv-ly*, or *nāv′ly*, Wr. 155.]
Naiveté (Fr.) (*nah′ēv-tā*).
Na′ked, 127.
Na′kir, 169.
Nām′a-ble, 164, 183.
Nam′by-pam′by, 205.
Name, 23, 163.
Named, 165.
Name′less, 185.
Name′ly, 93.
Nām′er.
Name′sake, 206.
Nām′ing.
Nan-keen′ (121) [N a n - k i n, 203.]
Nap (10, 30), *n.* a short sleep; — woolly or downy fibres on cloth: — *v.* to take a short sleep. [*See* Nappe, 160.]
Na-pæ′an (-*pe′*-), 13.
Nape (23) [*not* nap, 148, 153.]
Naph′tha (*nap′*-), 30, 141.
Naph-thal′ic (*nap*-), 122.
Naph′tha-līne (*nap′*-) (152) [N a p h t h a l i n, 203.]
Na′pi-er′s-bones (*na′-pi-urz-bōnz*), 213.
Na′pi-form [so Sm. Wb. Gd.; *nap′i-form*, Wr. 155.]
Nap′kin, 230.
Na-po′le-on, 171.
Nappe (*nap*), *n.* one of the two parts of a conic surface which meet at the vertex. [*See* Nap, 160.]
Nap′pi-ness, 186.
Nap′py, 66, 170.
Nar-cis′sus, 170.
Nar-cot′ic, 109.
Nar-cot′ic-al, 108.
Nar-cot′ic-o-ac′rid, 224.
Nar′co-tīne (82, 152) [N a r c o t i n, 203.]
Nar′co-tism (-*tizm*), 133.
Nar′co-tize, 202.
Nar′co-tīzed.
Nar′co-tīz-ing.
Nard, 11, 135.
Nard′īne, 152.
Na′rēs (L.) (-*rēz*), *n. pl.*
Năr′rate, *or* Năr-rate′ [so Wr. Gd.; *năr′-rāt*, Wk.; *năr-rāt′*, Sm. 155.]
Năr′rāt-ed, *or* Năr-rāt′-ed.
Năr′rāt-ing, *or* Năr-rāt′-ing.
Năr-ra′tion, 46, Note 2; 112.
Năr′ra-tīve, 84.
Năr-rāt′or, 169.
Năr′rōw, 101, 153.
Năr′rōwed (-*rōd*), 188.
Năr′rōw-er.
Năr′rōw-ing.
Năr′rōw-mīnd′ed, 205.
Năr′rōws (-*rōz*), *n. pl.*
Nar′whal (135) [N a r - w a l, N a r w h a l e, N a r v a l, 203.]
Na′sal (-*zal*), 72, 136.
Na-sal′i-ty (-*zal′*-), 156, 169.
Na-sal-ĭ-za′tion (-*zal*-).
Na′sal-ize (-*zal*-), 202.
Na′sal-ized (-*zal*-), 183.
Na′sal-īz-ing (-*zal*-).
Na′sal-ly (-*zal*-), 170.
Nas′cen-cy, 169.
Nas′cent, 39, 76.
Nase′ber-ry (*nāz′*-).
Nas-i-cor′noŭs (*naz*-).
Nas′i-form (*naz′*-), 136.
Na-sol′o-gy, 108.
Nȧs′ti-ly, 12, 186.
Nȧs′ti-ness.
Nas-tur′tion.
Nas-tur′ti-um (-*shĭ*-).
Nȧs′ty, 12, 131.
Na′tal, 72.
Na-tal-ĭ′tial (-*ish′al*).
Na-tal-ĭ′tious (-*ish′us*), 112.
Na′tant, 156.
Na-ta′tion, 112.
Nā-ta-to′ri-al, 49, N.
Na′ta-to-ry, 86.
Natch, 10, 44; Note D, p. 37.
Na′tion, 234.
Nă′tion-al (*nash′un-al*) (143) [so Wk. Sm. Wr.; *na′shun-al*, or *nash′un-al*, Gd. 155.]
Nă′tion-al-ism (*nash′-un-al-izm*), 133, 136.
Nă′tion-al-ist (*nash′-un*-).
Nă-tion-al′i-ty (*nash-un*-), 108, 169.
Nă-tion-al-ĭ-za′tion (*nash-un*-), 112.
Nă′tion-al-ize (*nash′-un*-), 202.
Nă′tion-al-ized (*nash′-un*-), 165.
Nă′tion-al-īz-ing (*nash′-un*-), 183.
Nă′tion-al-ly (*nash′un*-), 171.
Na′tīve, 84, 156.
Na′tiv-ism (-*izm*), 183.
Na-tiv′i-ty, 108.
Na′tro-līte [so Sm. Wb. Gd.; *nat′ro-līt*, Wr. 155.]
Na′tron, 86.
Nat′ter-jack.
Nat′ty, 66, 170.
Nat′u-ral (44, Note 1; 89, 108) [so Wr. Wb. Gd.; *nat′chū-ral*, Wk.; *nat′ch′oo-ral*, Sm. (*See* § 26), 155.]
Nat′u-ral-ism (-*izm*), 136.
Nat′u-ral-ist, 106.
Nat-u-ral-ĭ-za′tion.
Nat′u-ral-ize, 202.
Nat′u-ral-ized, 165.
Nat′u-ral-īz-ing, 183.
Nat′u-ral-ly, 170.
Na′ture (*nāt′yur*) (44, Note 1; 91, 156) [so Wr. Wb. Gd.; *na′-chūr*, Wk.; *na′tūr*, coll. *na′ch′oor* (*See* § 26), Sm. 155.]
Nȧught (*nawt*) (17, 162), *n.* & *a.*

☞ The noun is often written N o u g h t, to distinguish it from *naught*, *a.* — *See* Note under *Nought*.

Nȧught′i-ly (*nawt′*-) 186.
Nȧught′i-ness (*nawt′*-).
Nȧught′y (*nawt′*-), 169.
Nȧu′ma-chy (-*ky*), 52, 108.
Nȧus′co-py, 108.

Nâu′se-a (*-she-*), 144, 171.
Nâu′se-ant (*-she-*), 72.
Nâu′se-ate (*-she-*).
Nâu′se-āt-ed (*-she-*).
Nâu′se-āt-ing (*-she-*).
Nâu-se-a′tion (*-she-*), 112
Nau′seous (*-shus*), 46, Note 2; 171.
Nâu′tic.
Nâu′tic-al, 108.
Nâu′ti-līte, 152.
Nâu′ti-lus (169) [L. pl. *Nâu′ti-lī*; Eng. pl. Nâu′ti-lus-es (*-ez*), 198.]
Na′val (72), *a.* pertaining to ships. [*See* Navel, 148.]
Na′varch (*-vark*).
Na′varch-y (*-vark-*), 169.
Nave, 23, 163.
Na′vel (*-na′vl*) (149), *n.* the round cicatrix in the middle of the abdomen. [*See* Naval, 148.]
Na′vew (*-vu*), 26.
Na-vic′u-lar, 108.
Nav-i-ga-bil′i-ty, 108, 169.
Nav′i-ga-ble, 164.
Nav′i-ga-bly.
Nav′i-gate, 108, 169.
Nav′i-gāt-ed, 183.
Nav′i-gāt-ing.
Nav-i-ga′tion, 112.
Nav′i-gāt-or.
Nav′vy, 66, 170.
Na′vy, 93, 169.
Nāy (23, 56, Rem.), *ad.* a word of negation; no. [*See* Neigh, 160.]
Naz-a-rene′, 122, 171.
Naz′a-rīte, 152.
Naz′a-rit-ism (*-izm*) [so Wb. Gd.; *naz′a-rīt-izm*, Wr. 155.]
Naze, 23, 40.
Nēap, 13, 30.
Nēaped (*nēpt*), 165; Note C, p. 34.
Ne-a-pol′i-tan.
Nēar, 13, 49.
Nēared, 165.
Nēar′ing.
Nēar′-sight-ed (*-sīt-*), 162.
Nēat, 13, 41.
Nēat′-herd, 206, Exc. 3.
Neb, 15.
Neb′u-la (L.) (89, 108) [pl. Neb′u-læ, 198.]
Neb′u-lar, 108.
Neb′ule, 90.
Neb-u-los′i-ty, 108, 169.
Neb′u-loŭs, 108, 169.
Neç-es-sa′ri-an, 49, N.
Neç′es-sa-rīes (*-riz*), *n. pl.*
Neç′es-sa-ri-ly, 72, 106, 126, 171.
Neç′es-sa-ri-ness, 186.
Neç′es-sa-ry, 72, 171.
Ne-ces-si-ta′ri-an, 49, N.
Ne-ces′si-tate, 169.
Ne-ces′si-tāt-ed, 183.
Ne-ces′si-tāt-ing.
Ne-ces-si-ta′tion, 112.
Ne-ces′si-toŭs, 100.
Ne-ces′si-ty, 169.
Neck, 15, 181.
Neck′cloth, 66, N.
Neck′er-chīef (*-chif*).
Neck′-hand′ker-chīef (*-hang′-*), 205.
Neck′lace, 206.
Neck′tie.
Neck′verse.
Nec-ro-log′ic (*-loj′-*).
Nec-ro-log′ic-al (*-loj′-*).
Nec-rol′o-gist, 108.
Nec-rol′o-gy, 108.
Nec′ro-man-cer.
Nec′ro-man-cy, 169.
Nec-ro-man′tic (109) [so Sm. Wb. Gd.; *nek′-ro-man-tik*, Wr. 155.]
Nec-ro-man′tic-al, 108.
Nec′ro-nīte, 152.
Nec-roph′a-gan, 105.
Nec-roph′a-goŭs, 169.
Ne-crop′o-lis (105) [so Sm. Wr.; *nek-rop′o-lis*, Wb. Gd. 155.]
Nec-ro-scop′ic.
Nec-ro-scop′ic-al.
Ne-cro′sis, 109, 113.
Nec′tar, 74, 169.
Nec-ta′re-al, 169.
Nec-ta′re-an, 49, N.
Nec-ta′re-oŭs, 169.
Nec-tar-if′er-oŭs, 108.
Nec′tar-īne, 82, 152.
Nec′tar-oŭs, 100.
Nec′ta-ry, 72.
Née (Fr.)(*na*), *part. fem.*
Need (13, 42), *n.* necessity: — *v.* to be in want of. [*See* Knead, 160.]
Need′ed.
Need′er.
Need′ful (*-fŏŏl*), 180.
Need′i-ly, 186.
Need′i-ness.
Need′ing.
Nee′dle, 164.
Nee′dle-book, 206, Exc. 4.
Nee′dle-ful (*-fŏŏl*), 180, 197.
Nee′dle-shaped (*-shāpt*)
Nee′dle-wom′an (*-wŏŏm′-*), 205.
Nee′dle-work (*-wurk*).
Need′y, 93, 169.
Nê′er (*nêr*) (14) [*not* nēr, 153.]
Ne ex′e-at (L.).
Ne-fan′doŭs.
Ne-fa′ri-oŭs, 49, N.
Ne-ga′tion.
Neg′a-tīve, *a.* & *n.*
Neg′a-tīve, *v.* [so Wr. Wb. Gd.; *neg′a-tīv*, Sm. 155.]
Neg′a-tīved, 165.
Neg′a-tīve ly, 185.
Neg′a-tiv-ing, 183.
Neg-a-tiv′i-ty, 169.
Neg-lect′.
Neg-lect′ed.
Neg-lect′er.
Neg-lect′ful (*-fŏŏl*), 180.
Neg-lect′ing.
Négligée (Fr.) (*neg-le-zhā′*).
Neg′li-gence, 169.
Neg′li-gent.
Ne-go-ti-a-bil′i-ty (*-shĭ-*), 108.
Ne-go′ti-a-ble (*shĭ-a-bl*), 164.
Ne-go′ti-ate (*-shĭ-*) (108) [so Wk. Sm. Wr.; *ne-go′shāt*, Wb. Gd. 155.] [Negociate, 203.]
Ne-go′ti-āt-ed (*-shĭ-*).
Ne-go′ti-āt-ing (*-shĭ-*).
Ne-go-ti-a′tion (*-shĭ-*), 112.
Ne-go′ti-āt-or (*-shĭ-*), 106
Ne go′ti-a-to-ry (*-shĭ-*), 86, 171.
Ne′gress, 76.
Ne′gro (86) [*not* nig′ro, 153], [pl. Ne′groes (*-grōz*), 192.]
Ne′gro-loid.
Ne′gus, 169.
Neigh (*nā*) (23, 162), *n.* the cry of a horse: — *v.* to whinny, or cry as a horse. [*See* Nay, 160.]
Neigh′bor (*na′bur*) [Neighbour, Sm. 199, 203.]
Neigh′bored (*na′burd*)

[Neighboured, Sm. 203.]
Neigh'bor-hŏŏd [Neighbourhood, Sm. 203.]
Neigh'bor-ing (*nā'*-) [Neighbouring, Sm. 203.]
Neigh'bor-li-ness(-*na'*-) [Neighbourliness, Sm. 203.]
Neigh'bor-ly (*na'*-) [Neighbourly, Sm. 203.]
Neighed (*nād*), 162, 165.
Neigh'ing (*nā'*-).
Nēi'ther (169, N.) [so Wk. Sm. Wr.; *nē'thur*, or *nī'thur*, Gd. 155.]

☞ "The former [*ne'thur*] is given in most Dictionaries, and still prevails in America. The latter [*ni'ther*] is now common in England." *Goodrich.* — *See* Note under *Either*.

Ne'me-an (110) [so Wr.; *ne-me'an*, Sm. Wb. Gd. 155.]

☞ "Often incorrectly spelt and pronounced *Nemœ'an.*" *Worcester.*

Nem'e-sis, 156.
Nen'u-phar, 105.
Ne-od'a-mode.
Ne-og'a-mist.
Ne-og'ra-phy, 108.
Ne-o-lo'gi-an.
Ne-o-log'ic (-*loj'*-), 109.
Ne-o-log'ic-al (-*loj'*-).
Ne-ol'o-gism (-*jizm*).
Ne-ol'o-gist, 108.
Ne-ol-o-gist'ic.
Ne-ol-o-gist'ic-al.
Ne-ol'o-gy, 108.
Ne-o-no'mi-an.
Ne'o-phi-los'o-pher, 224.
Ne'o-phyte, 171.
Ne'o-pla-ton'ic.
Ne'o-pla-to-nĭ'cian (-*nish'an*).
Ne'o-pla'to-nism, 136.
Ne'o-pla'to-nist, 224.
Ne-o-ra'ma, 156.
Ne o-tĕr'ic, 109, 122.
Ne-o-tĕr'ic-al, 108.
Ne-o-zo'ic.
Ne-pen'the, 163.
Neph'e-līne (82, 152) [so Wr. Wb. Gd.; *nef'-e-lĭn*, Sm. 155] [Nephelin, 203.]
Neph-el-o-coc-cyg'i-a (-*sij'*-).
Neph'ew (*nev'yoo*, or *nef'yoo*) [so Wr.; *nev'yoo*, Wk. Sm.; *nef'yoo*, Wb. Gd. 155.]

☞ "This word is uniformly pronounced *nev'yoo* by the English orthoëpists; but in the United States it is often pronounced *nef'-yoo.*" *Worcester.*

Ne-phral'gi-a.
Ne-phral'gy.
Ne'phrite, *or* Neph'-rite [*ne'frīt*, Sm.; *nef'rīt*, Wr. Wb. Gd. 155.]
Ne-phrit'ic.
Ne-phrit'ic-al.
Ne-phri'tis (L.).
Ne-phrog'ra-phy, 108.
Neph-ro-lith'ic.
Ne-phrol'o-gy, 108.
Ne-phrot'o-my, 108.
Ne plus ultra (L.).
Nep'o-tal, 72.
Nep'o-tism (-*tizm*) (136) [*not* ne'po-tizm, 153.]
Nep'o-tist.
Nep'tune.
Nep-tu'ni-an.
Nep'tu-nist.
Ne quid ni'mis (L.).
Ne're-id, 49, N.
Ne-re-id'i-an, 169.
Ne'rīte, 152.
Nĕr'o-lĭ, *or* Ne-ro'lĭ [*nĕr'o-lĭ*, Wr. Wb. Gd.; *ne-ro'lĭ*, Sm. 155.]
Nerve, 21, N.; 135.
Nerved (*nervd*), *v.* & *part.*
Nerved (*nervd*) (150) [so Sm. Wb. Gd.; *nerv'ed*, or *nervd*, Wr. 155], *a.*
Nerv-i-mo'tion.
Nerv'īne, 152.
Nerv'ing.
Nerv-ose' [so Wr.; *nerv'ōs*, Wb. Gd. 155.]
Nerv'oŭs, 100.
Ner'vūre, 21, N.
Nes'ci-ence (*nesh'ĭ-ens*) [so Wk. Wr.; *nesh'-ens*, Sm. (*See* § 26); *nesh'ens*, Wb. Gd. 155.]
Nest, 15.
Nest'ed.
Nest'ing.
Nes'tle (*nes'l*), 162.
Nes'tled (*nes'ld*), 183.
Nes'tling (*nes'ling*).
Nes-to'ri-an, 169.
Nes-to'ri-an-ism (-*izm*).
Net, 15.
Neth'er.
Neth'er-mōst, 130.
Net'ted, 66, 176.
Net'ting, 170.
Net'tle (*net'l*), 66, 164.
Net'tled (*net'ld*), 183.
Net'tler (*net'lur*).
Net'tling (*net'ling*).
Net'work (-*wurk*).
Neū'ral, 26, 72.
Neū-ral'gi-a.
Neū-ral'gic, 45.
Neū-ral'gy, 145.
Neu'rīne, 82, 152.
Neū-rog'ra-phy, 108.
Neū-ro-log'ic-al (-*loj'*-).
Neū-rol'o-gist, 108.
Neū-rol'o-gy, 108.
Neū rop'ter.
Neū-rop'ter-a (L.).
Neū-rop'ter-al.
Neū-rop'ter-an.
Neū-rop'ter-oŭs.
Neū-rot'ic.
Neū-ro-tom'ic-al.
Neū'ro-tome.
Neū-rot'o-my, 108.
Neū-ryp-nol'o-gist.
Neū-ryp-nol'o-gy, 108.
Neū'ter [*not* noo'tur, 127, 153.]
Neū'tral, 72.
Neū-tral'i-ty, 108, 169.
Neū-tral-ĭ-za'tion.
Neū'tral-ize, 202.
Neū'tral-ized, 165.
Neū'tral-īz-er, 183.
Neū'tral-īz-ing.
Neū'tral-ly, 170.
Neū-vāines' (Fr.) (*nu-vānz'*), *n. pl.*
Nev'er, 66, 77.
Nev'er-the-less', 205, Exc. 2.
New (*nu*) (26) [*not* noo, 127, 153], *a.* of recent origin. [*See* Gnu, *and* Knew, 160.]
New'el (*nu'*-).
New-fan'gled (*nu-fang'gld*), 206, Exc. 5.
New-fash'ioned (*nu-fash'und*).
New'ish (*nu'*-).

New'ly (*nu'*-).
New'-made (*nu'*-).
New'ness (*nu'*-).
News (*nūz*).
News'boy (*nūz'*-), 206.
News'man (*nūz'*-), 196.
News'mon'ger (*nūz'-mung'gur*).
News'pa-per (*nūz'*-).
News-pa-pe'ri-al (*nūz*-), *or* News-pa-pō'ri-al (*nūz*-), 203.

☞ The former spelling of this colloquial word is the more analogical, but the latter is perhaps the more common.

News'room (*nūz'*-).
Newt (*nūt*).
New-to'ni-an, 169.
New'-yēar, *a.* 212.
Nex'īle, 152.
Next, 15, 39, N.
Nib, 16.
Nibbed, 165, 176.
Nib'ble (*nib'l*), 66, 164.
Nib'bled (*nib'ld*), 183.
Nib'bler, 170.
Nib'bling.
Nice (25, 163), *a.* delicate; exact; requiring scrupulous care. [*See* Gneiss, 160.]
Nice'ly, 185.
Ni'cene, *or* Nī-cene' [*ni'sēn*, Wr. Wb. Gd.; *nī-sēn'*, Sm. 155.]
Nice'ness.
Ni'ce-ty, 233.

☞ "In this word of our own composition from *nice*, we have unaccountably run into the pronunciation of the mute *e*." *Walker.*

Nīche, 16, 163.
Niched (*nicht*) (Note C, p. 34) [so Wb. Gd.; *nich'ed*, or *nicht*, Wr. 155.]
Nick, 16, 181.
Nick'ar-tree, *or* Nick'er-tree, 206, Exc. 4.
Nicked (*nikt*), 165; Note C, p. 34.
Nick'el, 149.
Nick-el'ic (109) [so Sm. Wr.; *nik'el-ik*, Wb. Gd. 155.]
Nick-el-if'er-oŭs, 108.
Nick'ing.
[Nicknack, 203. — *See* Knickknack.]
Nick'name, *n.* & *v.*
Nick'named, 183.
Nick'nām-ing.
Nic-o-la'i-tan [so Gd. Wr.; *nik-o-la'tan*, Sm. 155.]
Ni-co'tian (-*shan*) [so Wr. Wb. Gd.; *nī-ko'shī-an*, Sm. 155.]
Ni-co'ti-a-nīne (-*shī*-) [so Sm. Wr.; *nī-ko'sha-nin*, Wb. Gd. 155.]
Nic'o-tīne (82, 152) [Nicotin, 203.]
Nic'tate.
Nic'tāt-ed.
Nic'tāt-ing.
Nic-tā'tion.
Nic'ti-tate.
Nic'ti-tāt-ed, 183.
Nic'ti-tāt-ing.
Nic-ti-ta'tion, 112.
Nid-a-ment'al, 109.
Nide, 25.
Nid'get (*nij'et*).
Nid'i-fī-cate, 169.
Nid-i-fī-ca'tion, 112.
Nid'u-lant.
Nid-u-la'tion.
Ni'dus (L.).
Niēce, 169, N.; 171.
Nī-el'lo (It.), 170.
Nig'gard, 66, 72.
Nig'gard-li-ness, 106.
Nig'gard-ly.
Nigh (*nī*), 162.
Night (*nīt*) (162), *n.* the time between sunset and sunrise. [*See* Knight, 160.]
Night'-bloom-ing (*nīt'*-), 206, Exc. 5.
Night'cap (*nīt'*-), 206.
Night'fąll (*nīt'*-).
Night'gown (*nīt'*-).
Night'-hawk (*nīt'*-), 206, Exc. 3.
Night'in-gale (*nīt'*-).
Night'jar (*nīt'*-).
Night'ly (*nīt'*-).
Night'mare (*nīt'mêr*).
Night'shade (*nīt'*-).
Night'-time (*nīt'*-), 66, N.; 206, Exc. 1.
Night'-walk-er (*nīt'-wawk*-).
Night'-walk-ing (*nīt'-wawk*-).
Night'-watch (*nīt'*-).
Nī-gres'cent, 171.
Nig-ri-fī-ca'tion [so Wr.; *nī-grĭ-fī-ka'shun*, Sm. 155.]
Ni'grīne [Nigrin, 203.]
Nig'ri-tude, 108.
Ni'hil de'bet, or *Nil de'bet* (L.).
Ni'hil di'cit, or *Nil di'cit* (L.).
Ni'hil ha'bet, or *Nil ha'bet* (L.).
Ni'hil-ism (-*izm*), 136.
Nī-hil-ist'ic, 109.
Nī-hil'i-ty, 108, 169.
Nil (L.), *n.* nothing, — a term in book-keeping to denote an entry that is cancelled. [*See* Nill, 160.]
Nill (172), *v.* to be unwilling. [*See* Nil, 160.]
Nī-lom'e-ter, 108.
Ni'lo-scope.
Nī-lot'ic, 109.
Nim-bif'er-oŭs, 108, 169.
Nim'ble, 61, 164.
Nim'bly.
Nim'bus (L.), 169.
Nīne, 25.
Nine'fōld, 217.
Nine'pence (217) [pl. Nine'pen-ces (-*sez*).]
Nine'pins (-*pinz*), *n. pl.*
Nine'teen. [*See* Eighteen.]
Nine'teenth.
Nine'ti-eth, 186.
Nine'ty, 93.
Nin'ny, 66, 170.
Nin'sin.
Nīnth, 25, 37.
Nip, 16, 30.
Nipped (*nipt*), 165; Note C, p. 34.
Nip'per, 176.
Nip'per-ing.
Nip'pers (-*purz*), *n. pl.*
Nip'ping.
Nip'ple, 164.
Ni'san.
Ni'sī pri'us (L.) [so Wr.; *ni'sī pri'us*, Wk. Sm. Wb. Gd. 155.]
Nit (16), *n.* the egg of any small insect. [*See* Knit, 160.]
[Niter, 203. — *See* Nitre.]
Nit'id, 66, 170, 156.
Ni'trate.
Ni'tre (-*tur*) (164) [Niter, 203.]
Ni'tric, 200.
Nī-tri-fī-ca'tion.
Ni'tri-fīed, 99.

Ni′tri-fȳ, 94.
Ni′trīte, 70, 152.
Ni′tro-a-e′ri-al, 224.
Ni′tro-gen.
Nī-tro-ge′ne-oŭs.
Ni′tro-gen-ize (103, 202) [so Wr.; nĭ-troj′e-nīz, Gd. 155.]
Nī-trom′e-ter, 108.
Ni′tro-mu-ri-at′ic.
Ni′trose.
Ni′troŭs, 100, 169.
Ni′try, 93, 169.
Nit′ty, 173.
Niv′e-oŭs, 169.
Ni-vette′ (Fr.).
Nix, 16, 39, N.
Nī-zam′.
No (24), *ad.* a word of denial or refusal: — *a.* not any: — *n.* a vote in the negative. [*See* Know, 160.]
No-a′chi-an (-*kĭ*-) (52) [so Wb. Gd.; *no-ak′-ĭ-an*, Wr. 155.]
Nob, 18, 31, 43.
No-bil′i-ty, 108, 169.
No′ble, 164.
No′ble-man, 72, 164, 196.
No-bless′, *or* No′bless [*no-bles′*, Wk. Wr. Wb. Gd.; *no′bles*, Sm. 155.] [Noblesse (Fr.), 203.]
No′bly, 93.
No′bod-y, 221, 227.
No′cent, 76.
Noc-tam-bu-la′tion.
Noc-tam′bu-lism (-*lizm*), 133, 136.
Noc-tam′bu-list.
Noc-til′u-coŭs.
Noc-tiv′a-gant, 156.
Noc-tiv-a-ga′tion.
Noc-tiv′a-goŭs.
Noc′to-grăph.
Noc′tu-a-ry, 72, 89.
Noc′tule.
Noc′turn.
Noc-turn′al, 72.
Noc′u-oŭs.
Nod, 18.
No′dal, 72.
No′dāt-ed.
No-da′tion, 112.
Nod′ded, 176.
Nod′ding, 170.
Nod′dle, 164.
Nod′dy, 66, 93.
Node, 24, 163.
No-dose′.
No-dos′i-ty, 108, 169.
No′doŭs, 100, 169.
Nod′u-lar, 108, 169.
Nod′ule (45, N.; 90) [so Sm. Wr. Wb. Gd.; *noj′ūl*, Wk. 134, 155.]
Nod′u-lose.
No-et′ic, 109.
No-et′ic-al, 108.
Nog, 18.
Nog′gin (-*ghin*) (66, 170), *n.* a small cup; a gill. [*See* Nogging, 148.]
Nog′ging (-*ghing*), *n.* a partition of scantlings filled with bricks. [*See* Noggin, 148.]
Noise (*noiz*), 27.
Noised (*noizd*), 165.
Nois′i-ly (*noiz′*-), 186.
Nois′i-ness (*noiz′*-).
Nois′ing (*noiz′*-), 183.
Noi′some (-*sum*), 169.
Noi′sy (-*zy*), 169.
No′lens vo′lens (L.) (*no′-lenz vo′lenz*).
No′lī me tan′ge-re (L.).
Nol′le pros′e-quī (L.).
Nom′ad (66) [so Sm. Wr.; *no′mad*, Wb. Gd. 155] [Nomade, 203.]
No-ma′di-an, 169.
No-mad′ic, 109.
Nom′ad-ism (-*izm*), 133.
Nom′ad-ize, 202.
Nom′ad-ized.
Nom′ad-īz-ing.
No′man-cy, 169.
Nom′arch (-*ark*), 52.
Nom′bles (*num′blz*), *n. pl.* [Numbles, 203.]
Nom′bril.
Nom de guerre′ (-*ghêr′*) (Fr.), 154.
Nom de plume′ (Fr.).
Nome, 24, 163.
No′men-clā-tor [so Wr. Wb. Gd.; *no-men-kla′tur*, Sm.; *nom-en-kla′tur*, Wk. 155.]
No′men-clā-tress.
No-men-clā′tur-al (-*klāt′yur*-), 91, 108.
No′men-clā-ture (-*klāt′-yur*) (44, Note 1, 91) [so Wr. Gd.; *no′men-kla-tūr*, Sm.; *nom′en-kla-tūr*, Wk. 155.]
No-men-clā′tur-ist (-*klāt′yur*-), 91, 171.
No′mi-al, 72.
Nom′i-nal, 72, 78.
Nom′i-nal-ism (-*izm*).
Nom′i-nal-ist.
Nom-i-nal-ist′ic, 109.
Nom′i-nal-ly, 170.
Nom′i-nate, 169.
Nom′i-nāt-ed, 183.
Nom′i-nāt-ing, 228, N.
Nom-i-na′tion, 112.
Nom′i-na-tĭve, 132.
Nom-i-nee′.
Nom-i-nor′, 122.
No-mog′ra-phy, 108.
No-mol′o-gy, 108.
Nom′o-thete, 105.
Nom-o-thet′ic, 109.
Nom-o-thet′ic-al, 108.
Non (L.).

☞ This Latin adverb is used in English only as a prefix, and is employed to give a negative sense to words. The compounds thus formed are printed with or without a hyphen after the prefix, according as they more or less frequently occur. When the primary accent is on any other syllable, the prefix takes a secondary accent.

Non-a-bil′i-ty.
Non-ac-cept′ance.
Non′age, 70.
Non-a-ge-na′ri-an, 49, N.; 169.
Non-a-ges′i-mal.
Non′a-gon, 170.
Non-ap-pēar′ance.
Non as-sump′sit (L.).
Non-at-tend′ance.
Nonce, 18; Note D, p. 37.
Nonchalance (Fr.) (*non-sha-lans′*, or *nōng′-shal′ongs′*), 154.
Nonchalant (Fr.) (*non-sha-lang′*, or *nong′-shal-ong′*), 154.
Non-com-mis′sioned (-*mish′und*), 171.
Non-com-mit′tal.
Non com′pos men′tis (L.).
Non-con-cur′.
Non-con-duct′or.
Non-con-form′ist.
Non-con-form′i-ty.
Non-con-tent′.
Non′de-script.
Non det′i-net (L.).
None (*nun*) (163) [so Wk. Sm. Wr.; *nōn*, or *nun*, Gd. 155], *a.* & *pron.* not one. [*See* Nun, 160.]
Non-e-lect′.
Non-en′ti-ty, 169.

Nōnes (*nōnz*), *n. pl.* 24, 136.
None'-so-pret'ty (*nun'so-prit'ty*), 221.
Non-es-sen'tial (*-shal*).
Non est fac'tum (L.).
Non est in-ven'tus (L.).
None'such (*nun'-*).
Non-ex-ist'ence (*-egz-*).
Non-ill'ion (*-il'yun*) (170) [so Sm.; *no-nil'-yun*, Wr. Wb. Gd. 155.]
Non'ju-ring (49, N.) [so Sm.; *non-jūr'ing*, Wr. Wb. Gd. 155.]
Non'ju-ror (49, N.) [so Wk. Sm.; *non-ju'ror*, Wb. Gd.; *non'ju-ror*, or *non-ju'ror*, Wr. 155.]
Non-nat'u-ral, 66, N.
Non-ob-serv'ance (*-zerv'-*), 169.
Non ob-stan'te (L.).
Non-o-ge-na'ri-an.
Non-pa-rĕil', 156, 171.
Non-per-form'ance.
Non'plus.
Non'plussed (*-plust*), 165; Note C, p. 34.
Non'plus-sing.
Non'-pros.
Non'-prossed (*-prost*).
Non-res'i-dent (*-rez'-*).
Non-re-sist'ance (*-zist'-*), 169.
Non'sense.
Non-sens'ic-al, 72.
Non-sens'ic-al-ly, 170.
Non seq'ui-tur (*sek'wĭ-*) (L.).
Non'sūit.
Non'sūit-ed.
Non'sūit-ing.
Non-ūs'er (*-yooz'-*).
Noo'dle, 164.
Nŏŏk (20) [so Sm. Wb. Gd.; *nook*, Wk.; *nook*, or *nŏŏk*, Wr. 155. — *See* Book.]
No-o-log'ic-al (*-loj'-*).
No-ol'o-gist, 108.
No-ol'o-gy, 108.
Noon, 19, 127.
Noon'dāy.
Noon'ing.
Noon'tide.
Noose (*nooz*, or *noos*), *n.* [so Wr.; *nooz*, Sm. Wb. Gd.; *noos*, Wk. 155.]
Noose (*nooz*), *v.*
Noosed (*noozd*).
Noos'ing (*nooz'-*).
No'pal, 72.
Nor, 17, 135.
Norm, 49.
Norm'al, 72, 228.
Nor'man, 72.
Nŏr'roy.
Norse, 135.
North.
North-ēast', 140.
North-ēast'er-ly.
North-ēast'ern.
North'er-li-ness, 186.
North'er-ly.
North'ern, 135.
North'ern-er.
North'ern-mōst.
North'ing, 142.
North'man (72, 140) [pl. Northmen, 196.]
North-um'bri-an.
North'ward, *or* North'-wards (*-wardz*).
North'ward-ly, 93.
North-west'.

☞ "Colloquially *nŏr-west'*." *Smart.*

North-west'er-ly.
Nor-we'gi-an, 169.
Nose (*nōz*), *n.* & *v.* 24, 40.
Nose'band (*nōz'-*), 206.
Nose'bleed (*nōz'-*).
Nosed (*nōzd*), 165.
Nose'gāy (*nōz'-*).
Nose'smart (*nōz'-*).
Nōs'ing (*nōz'-*).
[Nosle, 203. — *See* Nozzle.]
No-sog'ra-phy, 108.
Nos-o-log'ic-al (*-loj'-*).
No-sol'o-gist, 108.
No-sol'o-gy (108) [so Sm. Wb. Gd.; *no-zol'o-jy*, Wk.; *no-sol'-o-jy*, or *no-zol'o-jy*, Wr. 155.]
Nos-tal'gi-a.
Nos-tal'gic, 109.
Nos'toc.
Nos'tril, 80.
Nos'trum, 169, 189.
Not (18, 41), *ad.* the negative particle. [*See* Knot, 160.]
No'ta be'ne (L.), 156.
No-ta-bil'i-ty, 108.
Nōt'a-ble (161, 164), *a.* worthy of notice; remarkable.
Not'a-ble (161, 164), *a.* careful, thrifty, and bustling.
Nōt'a-bly (161), *ad.* remarkably.
Not'a-bly (161), *ad.* with bustling activity and thrift.
No'tal, 72.
No-tan'da (L.), *n. pl.*
No-ta'ri-al, 49, N.
No'ta-ry, 72, 93.
No'tate.
No-ta'tion, 112.
Notch, 18, 44; Note D, p. 37.
Notched (*nocht*), 165; Note C, p. 34.
Note, 24, 163.
Note'-bŏŏk, 203, Exc. 4.
Nōt'ed, 183.
Note'-pa-per.
Note'-wor-thy (*-wur-*).
Noth'ing (*nuth'ing*) [so Wk. Sm. Wr.; *nŏth'-ing*, or *nuth'ing*, Gd. 155.]
No'tīce, 169.
No'tīce-a-ble, 164, 183.
No'tīce-a-bly.
No'tīced (*-tist*), 165; Note C, p. 34.
No'tiç-ing.
No-ti-fī-ca'tion.
No'ti-fīed, 99.
No'ti-fȳ, 94.
No'ti-fȳ-ing, 186.
Nōt'ing, 228.
No'tion.
No'tion-al, 72.
No-to-ri'e-ty, 169.
No-to'ri-oŭs, 49, N.; 169.
Not-with-stand'ing.
[Nought, *n.* — *See* Naught, 203.]

☞ Johnson remarks that this word should be written *naught*, according to analogy, as it corresponds to *aught*; "but a custom," he adds, "has irreversibly prevailed of using *naught* for *bad*, and *nought* for *nothing*." — "Commonly, though improperly, written *nought*." *Walker.* — "This word should not be written *nought*." *Webster.* — "More properly written *naught*." *Worcester.* — "*Nought* is the proper spelling, when the word is used in the sense of *nothing*." *Smart.*

Noun, 28, 43.

Noŭr′ish, 48, 104, 171.
Noŭr′ish-a-ble, 164.
Noŭr′ished (*-isht*).
Noŭr′ish-er.
Noŭr′ish-ing.
Noŭr′ish-ment.
No-vac′u-lite (152) [so Wr. Wb. Gd.; *no-va′-kū-lĭt*, Sm. 155.]
No-va′tian (*-shan*), 169.
Nov′el, 149.
Nov-el-ette′, 114.
Nov′el-ist.
Nov′el-ty.
No-vem′ber, 126.
Nov′en-a-ry (72) [so Wk. Wr.; *nov′en-ăr-y*, Sm.; *no′ven-a-ry*, Wb. Gd. 155.]
No-ven′ni-al, 170.
No-ver′cal, 21, N.
Nov′ice, 169.
Nov′i-lu-nar [so Wr.; *no-vi-lu′nar*, Wb. Gd. 155.]
No-vi′ti-ate (*-vish′ĭ-āt*) [so Wk. Sm. Wr.; *no-vish′āt*, Wb. Gd. 155] [N o v i c i a t e, 203.]
Now, 28.
Now′-a-days (*-dāz*).
No′wāy, *or* No′ways (*-wāz*).
Now′el [so Wr.; *no′el*, Gd. 155.]
No′whêre.
No′wise (*-wīz*).
Nox′ioŭs (*nok′shus*), 46, Note 1; 171.
Noyades (Fr.) (*nwä-yäd′*), *n. pl.*
Noyau (Fr.) (*no′yo*).
Noz′zle (*noz′l*) [N o z l e, N o s l e, 203.]
Nu′bĭle, 81.
Nu-ca-men-ta′ceous (*-shus*), 112.
Nu-ca-ment′oŭs.
Nu′ci-form, 108.
Nu′cle-ar, 74.
Nu′cle-āt-ed.
Nu-cle′i-form.
Nu′cle-us, 169.
Nu′cule.
Nude, 26, 127.
Nudge, 22, 45; Note D, p. 37.
Nudged (*nujd*), 183.
Nudg′ing (*nuj′-*).
Nu-di-bran′chi-ate (*-brang′kĭ-*), 52, 54.
Nu-di-fĭ-ca′tion.
Nu′di-ty, 108, 156.
Nu′dum pac′tum (L.).
Nu-gaç′i-ty, 169.
Nu′gæ (*-jē*) (L.).
Nu′ga-to-ry, 86, 126.
Nug′get (*-ghet*), 138, 170.
Nū′sance, 171.
Null, 22, 172.
Nul-li-fĭ-ca′tion.
Nul-li-fid′i-an, 169.
Nul′li-fīed.
Nul′li-fȳ, 78, 94.
Nul′li-fȳ-ing.
Nul′li-ty, 169.
Numb (*num*), 162.
Numbed (*numbd*), 165.
Numb′er (*num′er*) (161), *a.* more numb.
Num′ber (161), *n.* a collection of things of the same kind; — a numeral character, &c.: — *v.* to count; to designate by a number.
Num′bered (*-burd*), 150.
Num′ber-ing.
Numb′ing (*num′-*), 162.
Nu′mer-a-ble, 164.
Nu′mer-al, 233, Exc.
Nu′mer-a-ry, 72.
Nu′mer-ate, 26.
Nu′mer-āt-ed, 183.
Nu′mer-āt-ing.
Nu-mer-a′tion.
Nu′mer-āt-or.
Nu-mer′ic-al.
Nu′mer-oŭs, 169.
Nu-mis-mat′ic (*-miz-*), 109.
Nu-mis-mat′ic-al (*-miz-*), 108.
Nu-mis-mat′ics (*-miz-*).
Nu-mis′ma-tist (*-miz′-*).
Nu-mis-ma-tol′o-gist (*-miz-*), 108.
Nu-mis-ma-tol′o-gy (*-miz-*).
Num′ma-ry, 72.
Num′mu-lar, 108, 169.
Num′mu-la-ry, 72.
Num′skull, 171.
Nun, 22, 43.
Nun′ci-o (*-shĭ-o*) (192) [so Wk. Sm. Wr.; *nun′sho*, Wb. Gd. 155.]
Nun′cu-pā-tĭve, *or* Nun-cu′pa-tĭve [*nun′ku-pā-tiv*, Sm.; *nun-ku′-pa-tiv*, Wk. Wr. Wb. Gd. 155.]
Nun′cu-pa-to-ry, *or* Nun-cu′pa-to-ry [*nun′-ku-pāt-ŭr-y*, Sm.; *nun-ku′pa-to-ry*, Wk. Wr. Wb. Gd. 155.]
Nun′di-nal, 72.
Nun′ner-y, 66, 170.
Nup′tial (*-shal*) [*not* nup′chal, 153.]
Nup′tials (*-shalz*).
Nurse, 21, 135; Note D, p. 37.
Nursed (*nurst*), 165, 183; Note C, p. 34.
Nurs′er-y, 169.
Nurs′ing, 183.
Nurs′ling, 183.
Nur′ture (*nurt′yur*), 44, Note 1; 91.
Nur′tured (*nurt′yurd*), 165, 183.
Nur′tur-ing (*nurt′yur-*), 91, 171.
Nut, 22.
Nu′tant, 72.
Nu-ta′tion.
Nut′-brown, 206, Exc. 5.
Nut′-crack-er.
Nut′gâll.
Nut′-hatch, 206, Exc. 3.
Nut′-hŏŏk.
Nut′meg, 76.
Nut′megged (*-megd*).
Nu′tri-ent, 78.
Nu′tri-ment (108) [*not* noo′tri-ment, 127, 153.]
Nu-tri-ment′al.
Nu-trĭ′tial (*-trish′al*).
Nu-trĭ′tion (*-trish′un*).
Nu trĭ′tious (*-trish′us*).
Nu′tri-tĭve, 26, 78, 84.
Nut′shell.
Nut′ted, 176.
Nut′ting, 170.
Nut′-tree, 66, N.; 206, Exc. 1, 4.
Nux vom′i-ca (L.).
Nuz′zle (*nuz′l*), 164.
Nuz′zled (*nuz′ld*), 183.
Nuz′zling.
Nyc-ta-lo′pi-a.
Nyc′ta-lo-py.
Nyc′ta-lops.
Nyl′ghâu [so Sm. Wb. Gd.; *nil-gaw′*, Wr. 155] [N i l g h a u, N y l g a u, 203.]
Nymph (*nimf*), 16, 35.
Nym′pha (L.) [pl. *Nym′-phæ* (*-fe*), 198.]
Nymph-e′an, 110.
Nymph′ic.
Nymph′ic-al.
Nymph-ip′a-roŭs, 108.
Nymph′like, 206, Exc. 5.
Nymph-o-lep′sy, 169.

O.

O (24), an interjection used to denote a calling to, or exclamation; also to express a wish, emotion, or earnestness. [*See* Oh, *and* Owe, 160.]

☞ "*O* and *oh* are often used indiscriminately; but *oh* is expressive of a wish, emotion, or earnestness." *Worcester.*

Ōaf, 24, 35.
Ōak, 24, 52.
Ōak'en (*ōk'n*), 149.
Ōak'um, 169.
Ōak'y, 93.
Ōar (24, 135), *n.* an instrument by which boats are rowed. [*See* O'er, *and* Ore, 160.]
Oars'man (*ōrz'-*).
O'a-sis [*not* o-a'sis, 153.]
Ōat, 24, 41.
Ōat'en (*ōt'n*), 61, 149.
Ōath (24, 37) [pl. Ōaths (*ōthz*), 38, 140.]
Ōat'mēal (205) [so Sm. Wr. Wb. Gd.; *ŏt'mĕl*, or *ōt'mĕl*, Wk. 155.]
Ob-cla'vate.
Ob-com-pressed' (*-prest'*).
Ob-con'ic, 109.
Ob-con'ic-al, 108.
Ob-cor'date.
Ob'du-ra-cy, *or* Ob-du'ra-cy (49, N.; 169) [so Wr. Gd.; *ob'dū-rā-sy*, Sm.; *ob'jū-ra-sy*, or *ob-du'ra-sy*, Wk. 134, 155.]
Ob'du-rate, *or* Ob-du'rate.
O'be-ah (72) [so Gd.; *o-be'ah*, Wr. 155.]
O-be'di-ence (78) [so Sm. Wr. Wb. Gd.; *o-be'jĭ-ens*, Wk. 134, 155.]
O-be'di-ent.
O-bei'sance (*-ba'-*, or *-be'-*) (136) [so Wr.; *o-ba'sans*, Wk. Sm.; *o-be'sans*, or *o-ba'sans*, Gd. 155.]
O-bei'sant (*-ba'-*, or *-be'-*).
Ob'e-lisk, 169.
Ob'e-lize, 202.
Ob'e-lized.
Ob'e-liz-ing.
Ob'e-lus (L.) [pl. *Ob'e-li*, 198.]
O-bese' (121) [*not* o-bēz', 136, 153.]
O-bes'i-ty, 108, 169.
O-bey' (*-ba'*), 23, 86.
O-beyed' (*-bād'*), 187.
O-bey'er (*-ba'-*).
O-bey'ing (*-ba'-*).
Ob-fus'cate, *a.* & *v.* (73) [Offuscate, 203.]
Ob-fus'cāt-ed, 183.
Ob-fus'cāt-ing.
Ob-fus-ca'tion [Offuscation, 203.]
O'bit, *or* Ob'it [so Wr.; *o'bit*, Wk. Sm.; *ob'it*, Wb. Gd. 155.]
Ob'i-ter (L.).
O-bit'u-al, 89.
O-bit'u-a-ry, 72.
Ob'ject, *n.* 103, 161.
Ob-ject', *v.* 103, 161.
Ob-ject'ed.
Ob-ject'i-fīed, 99.
Ob-ject'i-fȳ, 94.
Ob-ject'i-fȳ-ing.
Ob-ject'ing.
Ob-jec'tion, 234.
Ob-jec'tion-a-ble, 164.
Ob-ject'ĭve, 84.
Ob-ject'ĭve-ly, 185.
Ob-ject-iv'i-ty.
Ob-ject'or, 169.
Ob-ju-ra'tion.
Ob-jur'gate, 122.
Ob-jur'gāt-ed.
Ob-jur'gāt-ing.
Ob-jur-ga'tion.
Ob-jur'ga-to-ry, 86.
Ob-lan'ce-o-late.
Ob-late', 121.
Ob-la'tion, 112.
Ob'li-gate, 169.
Ob'li-gāt-ed, 183.
Ob'li-gāt-ing.
Ob-li-ga'tion.
Ob'li-ga-to-ri-ly, 126, 171, 186.
Ob'li-ga-to-ri-ness.
Ob'li-ga-to-ry (72, 86) [so Wk. Wr. Wb. Gd.; *ob'li-gā-tur-y*, Sm. 155] [*not* o-blig'a-to-ry, 153.]
O-blige' (103) [so Sm. Wr. Wb. Gd.; *o-blīj'*, or *o-blēj'*, Wk. 155.]
O-bliged' (*-blījd'*), 165.
Ob-li-gee' (*-jee'*), 122.
O-blīg'ing (*-blīj'-*), 183.
Ob-li-gor'.
Ob-lig'u-late, 108.
Ob-lique' (*ob-lēk'*, or *ob-līk'*) [so Wr.; *ob-lēk'*, Sm.; *ob-līk'*, Wk.; *ob-līk'*, or *ob-lēk'*, Gd. 155] [Oblike, 203.]

☞ "When it becomes a custom to *write* this word in the English form *oblike'*, it will be consistent to give up the French pronunciation; but not till then." *Smart.*

Ob-liq'ui-ty (*-lik'wĭ-*), 143, 171.
Ob-lit'er-ate.
Ob-lit'er-āt-ed, 183.
Ob-lit'er-āt-ing.
Ob-lit-er-a'tion.
Ob-lit'er-a-tĭve, 84.
Ob-liv'i-on, 169.
Ob-liv'i-oŭs, 100.
Ob'long.
Ob'long-ish.
Ob'lo-quy (*-kwy̆*).
Ob-mu-tes'cence.
Ob-nox'ious (*-nok'shus*), 46, Note 2.
O'bo-e, 144.
Ob'ole [Obol, 203.]
Ob'o-lus (L.) [pl. *Ob'o-lī*, 198.]
Ob-o'val, 72.
Ob-o'vate.
Ob-rep'tion.
Ob-rep-tĭ'tious (*-tish'us*), 171.
Ob-scene', 121.
Ob-scen'i-ty, 143, 169.
Ob-scu'rant, 49, N.; 72.
Ob-scu-ra'tion.
Ob-scure', *a.* & *v.*
Ob-scured', 165.
Ob-scure'ly, 93, 185.
Ob-scūr'ing, 183.
Ob-scu'ri-ty, 108.
Ob-se-cra'tion.
Ob'se-quĭes (*-kwiz*), *n. pl.* 171.

☞ The singular, *Ob'se-quy*, is rarely used.

Ob-se'qui-oŭs, 171.
Ob-serv'a-ble (*-zerv'a-bl*), 21, N.
Ob-serv'a-bly (*-zerv'-*).
Ob-serv'ance (*-zerv'-*).
Ob-ser-van'da (L.) (*-zer-*).
Ob-serv'ant (*-zerv'-*).
Ob-serv-a'tion (*-zerv-*).

Ob-serv-a'tion-al (*-zerv-*).
Ob-serv'a-tive (*-zerv'-*).
Ob'serv-ā-tor (*-zerv-*).
Ob-serv'a-to-ry(*-zerv'-*), 86, 171.
Ob-serve' (*-zerv'-*), 103.
Ob-served' (*-zervd'*), 165.
Ob-serv'er (*-zerv'-*).
Ob-serv'ing (*-zerv'-*).
Ob-sess'ion (*-sesh'un*).
Ob-sid'i-an (169) [so Wr. Wb. Gd. ; *ob-sid'yan*, Sm. 155.]
Ob-sid'i-on-al [so Wr. Wb. Gd. ; *ob-sid'yun-al*, Sm. ; *ob-sid'i-un-al*, or *ob-sij'i-un-al*, Wk. 134, 155.]
Ob-so-les'cence, 39, 171.
Ob-so-les'cent, 127.
Ob'so-lete [*not* ob-so-lēt', 153.]
Ob'sta-cle, 164.
Ob-stet'ric.
Ob-stet'ric-al, 72.
Ob-stet-rī'cian (*-rish'-an*).
Ob-stet'rics, 109.
Ob'sti-na-cy, 72, 169.
Ob'sti-nate, 73.
Ob-sti-pa'tion.
Ob-strep'er-oŭs, 100, 233, Exc.
Ob-stric'tion.
Ob-struct'.
Ob-struct'ed.
Ob-struct'er.
Ob-struct'ing.
Ob-struc'tion.
Ob-struct'ĭve, 84.
Ob'stru-ent (*-stroo-*).
Ob-tāin', 23.
Ob-tain'a-ble, 164.
Ob-tāined', 165.
Ob-tāin'er.
Ob-tāin'ing.
Ob-test'.
Ob-test-a'tion.
Ob-test'ed.
Ob-test'ing.
Ob-trude' (*-trood'*).
Ob-trud'ed (*-trood'-*).
Ob-trud'er (*-trood'-*).
Ob-trud'ing (*-trood'-*).
Ob-tru'sion (*-troo'-zhun*).
Ob-tru'sĭve (*-troo'-*)[*not* ob-troo'ziv, 136, 153.]
Ob-tund'.
Ob-tund'ed.
Ob-tund'ent, 127.
Ob-tund'ing.
Ob-tŭs-an'gu-lar (*-ang'-*).
Ob-tuse', 26.
Ob-tuse'-an'gled (*-ang'-gld*).
Ob-tuse'ness, 185.
Ob-tu'sion (*-zhun*).
Ob'verse, *n.* 135, 161.
Ob-verse', *a.* 161.
Ob-vert'.
Ob-vert'ed.
Ob-vert'ing.
Ob'vi-ate, 169.
Ob'vi-āt-ed, 183.
Ob'vi-āt-ing.
Ob-vi-a'tion.
Ob'vi-oŭs, 100.
Ob'vo-lute.
Oc'ca-my, 170.
Oc-ca'sion (*-zhun*).
Oc-ca'sion-al (*-zhun-*).
Oc-ca'sion-al-ism (*-zhun-al-izm*), 133, 136.
Oc-ca-sion-al'i-ty (*-zhun-*).
Oc-ca'sion-al-ly (*-zhun-*), 170.
Oc-ca'sioned (*-zhund*).
Oc-ca'sion-ing (*-zhun-*).
Oc-ca'sĭve, 84, 136.
Oc'ci-dent.
Oc-ci-dent'al, 109.
Oc-cip'it-al, 72.
Oc'ci-put, 171.
Oc-clu'sion (*-zhun*) (47, N.) [so Wk. Wr. Wb. Gd. ; *ok-loo'zhun*, Sm. 155.]
Oc-cult', 121.
Oc-cult-a'tion.
Oc-cult'ing.
Oc'cu-pan-cy, 169.
Oc'cu-pant, 89.
Oc-cu-pa'tion, 112.
Oc'cu-pīed, 99.
Oc'cu-pī-er.
Oc'cu-pȳ, 94.
Oc'cu-pȳ-ing, 186.
Oc-cur', 21.
Oc-curred', 165, 176.
Oc-cŭr'rence, 21, 66.
Oc-cŭr'rent, 76.
Oc-cur'ring, 21, 49.
O'cean (*-shan*), 46, Note 2 ; 234.
O-ce-an'ic (*-she-*), 156.
O-cel'la-ted [so Sm. Wr. ; *o-sel'ā-ted*, Wk. ; *o'sel-ā-ted*, Wb. Gd. 155.]
O'ce-lot, 171.
[O c h e r, 203.—*See* Ochre.]
[O c h e r o u s, 203.—*See* Ochreous.]
[O c h e r y, 203.—*See* Ochrey.]
Och'i-my (*ok'-*), 52.
Och-loc'ra-cy (*ok-*), 108.
Och-lo-crat'ic (*ok-*).
Och-lo-crat'ic-al (*ok-*).
[O c h r a, 203.—*See* Okra.]
O-chra'ceous (*-kra'-shus*).
O'chre (*o'kur*) (52, 164) [O c h e r, Wb. Gd. 203.]
O'chre-a (L.) (*-kre-*) [pl. *O'chre-æ* (*-kre-e*), 198.]
O'chre ate (*-kre-*), 171.
O'chre-oŭs (*-kre-*) [O c h e r o u s, Wb. Gd. 303.]
O'chrey (*-kry*) (169) [O c h r y, O c h e r y, Wb. Gd. 203.]
O-chro-leū'coŭs (*-kro-*).
O'cre-āt-ed.
Oc'ta-chord (*-kord*).
Oc'ta-gon, 72.
Oc-tag'o-nal, 108.
Oc-ta-he'dral [O c t a-e d r a l, 203.]
Oc-ta-he'dron [O c t a-e d r o n, 203.]
Oc-tam'er-oŭs.
Oc-tan'dri-a.
Oc-tan'dri-an, 169.
Oc-tan'droŭs.
Oc-tan'gu-lar (*-tang'-*), 108.
Oc'tant, 72.
Oc'tar-chy (*-ky*).
Oc'tave, 230.
Oc-ta'vo (86) [pl. Oc-ta'vos (*-vōz*), 192.]
Oc-ten'ni-al, 171.
Oc-till'ion (*-til'yun*), 171.
Oc-to'ber.
Oc-to-deç'i-mo [pl. Oc-to-deç'i-mos (*-mōz*), 192.]
Oc-to-den'tate.
Oc'to-fid.
Oc-to-ge-na'ri-an, 49, N. ; 169.
Oc-tog'e-na-ry (*-toj'-*), *or* Oc'to-ge-na-ry (72) [so Wr. ; *ok-toj'e-na-ry*, Wk. Sm. ; *ok'to-ge-na-ry*, Wb. Gd. 155.]

Oc-tog′y-noŭs (-*toj′*-).
Oc-to-loc′u-lar, 108.
Oc′to-na-ry, 72.
Oc-to-noc′u-lar, 169.
Oc-to-pet′al-oŭs.
Oc′to-pod.
Oc-to-sperm′oŭs.
Oc′to-style.
Oc-to-syl-lab′ic.
Oc-to-syl-lab′ic-al.
Oc-to-syl′la-ble, 164.
Oc-troi′ (Fr.) (-*trwaw′*), 154.
Oc′tu-ple, 164.
Oc′u-lar, 89, 108.
Oc′u-late.
Oc′u-li-form.

☞ This word is an exception to the general rule (§ 108) by which words ending in *i-form* are accented on the antepenult.

Oc′u-list.
Od, *or* Ŏd.
O′da-lisk,*or* O′da-lisque [Odalik, Odalique, 203.]

☞ "Properly *o-dah′-lic*." *Goodrich*. — Spelled and pronounced by Smart, *o′dal-ique* (-*ēk*).

Odd, 18, 175.
Odd′-fel-lōw.
Odd′i-ty, 108. [34.
Odds (*odz*), Note C, p.
Ode (24, 163), *n.* a short song or poem. [*See* Owed, 160.]
O-de′on (125) [*not* o′de-on, 153.]
Od′ic, *or* Ŏd′ic.
O′din.
O-din′ic.
O′di-oŭs (169) [so Wb. Gd.; *o′di-us*, or *o′ji-us*, Wk.; *o′di-us*, or *ōd′yus*, Sm.; *ōd′yus*, or *o′di-us*, Wr. 134, 155.]
O′di-um, 108, 169.
O′dize.
O′dized.
O′dīz-ing.
O-dom′e-ter, 108.
O-do-met′ric-al.
O-dom′e-try.
Od-on-tal′gic, *or* O-don-tal′gic [so Wr.; *od-on-tal′jik*, Sm.; *o-don-tal′jik*, Wb. Gd. 155.]
Od-on-tal′gi-a.
Od-on-tal′gy.

Od-on-tog′e-ny (-*toj′*-).
O-don′to-grăph, 127.
Od-on-tog′ra-phy, 108.
O-don′toid.
O-don′to-līte, 152.
Od-on-tol′o-gy, 108.
O′dor (70, 88) [Odour, Sm. 199.]
O′dor-ant.
O-dor-if′er-oŭs, 108.
O′dor-oŭs, 100.
O′dȳle, 156, 171.
O-dyl′lic, 170.
Od′ys-sey (98, 169, 171) [*not* o-dis′y, 153.]
[Œconomics, 203. — *See* Economics.]

☞ "The digraph *œ* is to be esteemed a mere equivalent for [the] letter *e*, and subject, like *e*, to be shortened [*See* § 56]; hence, it is now usual to employ *e* alone, instead of *œ*, in this and many other words." *Smart.*

[Œcumenical, 203. — *See* Ecumenical.]
Œ-de′ma (*e-de′ma*).
Œ-il′iad (*e-il′yad*, or *īl′-yad*) [so Wr.; *e-il′-yad*, Wk. Wb. Gd.; *īl′yad*, Sm. 155.]
Œ-nan′thic (*ē*-).
Œ-nom′e-ter (*ē*-), 108.
Ō′er (*ōr*), *prep.* & *adv.* a poetical contraction of *over*. [*See* Oar, *and* Ore, 160.]
Œs-o-pha′ge-al(*ĕs*-),169.
Œ-soph-o-got′o-my (*ē-sof*-), 108.
Œ-soph′a-gus (*ē-sof′*-) (169) [pl. *Œ-soph′a-gī*, 198.]
Œs′trum (*es′*-), 15, 169.
Of (*ov*), 36, 173.
Off (18, N. 173) [so Wk. Sm. Gd.; *ŏf*, or *awf*, Wr. 155.]
Of′fal.
Of-fence′ [Offense, Wb. Gd. 203. — *See* Note E, p. 70.]
Of-fend′, 66.
Of-fend′ed.
Of-fend′er.
Of-fend′ing.
[Offense. — *See* Offence.]
Of-fen′sīve, 84.
Of′fer, 77, 104.
Of′fered (-*furd*), 150,165.
Of′fer-ing.

Of′fer-to-ry, 86.
Off′-hand.
Of′fice, 169.
Of′fi-cer.
Of′fi-cered (-*surd*), 150.
Of′fi-cer-ing.
Of-fĭ′cial (-*fish′al*), 46, Note 2.
Of-fĭ′cial-ly (-*fish′al*-).
Of-fĭ′cial-ty (-*fish′al*-), 145.
Of-fĭ′ci-a-ry (-*fish′ĭ*-),72.
Of-fĭ′ci-ate (-*fish′ĭ*-) [so Wk. Sm. Wr.; *of-fish′-āt*, Wb. Gd. 155.]
Of-fĭ′ci-āt-ed (-*fish′ĭ*-).
Of-fĭ′ci-āt-ing (-*fish′ĭ*-).
Of-fĭ′ci-āt-or (-*fish′ĭ*-).
Of-fĭ-ci′nal, *or* Of-fiç′i-nal [so Wr.; *of-i-si′-nal*, Sm.; *of-fis′ĭ-nal*, Wb. Gd. 155.]
Of-fĭ′cious (-*fish′us*).
Off′ing, 66, 170.
Off′scour-ing.
Off′scum.
Off′set, *n.*
Off-set′, *or* Off′set, *v.* [*of-set′*, Sm.; *of′set*, Wr. Wb. Gd. 155.]
Off-set′ting, *or* Off′set-ting.
Off′shoot.
Off′skip.
Off′spring.
[Offuscate, 203. — *See* Obfuscate.]
[Offuscation, 203. — *See* Obfuscation.]
Off′ward.
Oft (18, N.) [so Wk. Sm. Wb. Gd.; *oft*, or *awft*, Wr. 155.]
Of′ten (*of′n*) (18, N.; 149, 162) [so Wk. Sm. Wb. Gd.; *of′n*, or *awf′n*, Wr. 155] [*not* of′ten, 153.]
Of′ten-times (*of′n-tīmz*)
Oft′times (-*tīmz*).
Og′do-ad.
Og-do-as′tich (-*tik*).
O-gee′ (*o-je′*).
Og′ham.
O′gīve (-*jīv*), *or* O-give′ (-*jīv′*) [*o′jīv*, Wb. Gd.; *o-jīv′*, Sm. Wr. 155.]
O′gle (*o′gl*), 164 [*not* og′l, 127, 153.]
O′gled (*o′gld*), 165, 183.
O′gling.
[Oglio (*ō′li-o*), 203. — *See* Olio.]

O'gre (*o'gur*), 164.
O'gress, 76.
O-gyg'i-an (*-jĭ'-*).
Oh (24), an exclamation of pain, sorrow, surprise, or anxiety. [*See* O *and* Owe, 160.]
Oil (27) [*not* īl, 153.]
Oiled, 165.
Oil'cloth, 206.
Oil'er-y.
Oil'i-ness, 186.
Oil'man, 196.
Oil'-tree, 206, Exc. 4.
Oil'y, 93.
Oint, 27.
Oint'ed.
Oint'ing.
Oint'ment.
O'kra [Ochra, Okro, 203.]
Ōld, 24.
Ōld'en (*ōld'n*), 149.
Ōld'-fash'ioned (*-und*).
Ōld'ish.
Old'wife [pl. Old'wīves (*-wīvz*), 193.]
O-le-ag'in-oŭs (*-aj'-*),169
O-le-an'der, 126.
O-le-as'ter, 126.
O'le-fī-ant [so Sm. Gd.; *o-lef'i-ant*, or *o'le-fī-ant*, Wr. 155.]
O'le-ic.

☞ "This word, which might undoubtedly be accented on the penultimate [*See* § 109], seems, in practice, to yield to the more general principle." [*See* § 105.] *Smart.*

O-le-if'er-oŭs, 108.
O'le-īne [Olein, 203.]
O-le-om'e-ter, 108.
O'le-o-res'in (*-rez'-*).
O'le-ose, *or* O-le-ose' [*o'le-ōs*, Sm. Wb. Gd.; *o-le-ōs'*, Wk. Wr. 155.]
O'le-oŭs.
Ol-er-a'ceous (*-shus*).
Ol-fac'tion.
Ol-fac'to-ry, 86.
O-lib'a-num, *or* Ol-i-ba'num (169) [*o-lib'a-num*, Wr. Wb. Gd.; *ol-i-ba'num*, Sm. 155.]
Ol'id, 170.
Ol'id-oŭs.
Ol'i-garch (*-gark*).
Ol'i-garch-al (*-gark-*).
Ol-i-garch'ic (*-gark'-*).
Ol-i-garch'ic-al (*-gark'-*)
Ol'i-garch-y (*-gark-*).
Ol'i-gist.
Ol-i-gist'ic, 109.
O'li-o, *or* Ōl'io (*ōl'yo*) [so Wr.; *o'li-o*, Wk. Sm. Wb. Gd. 155.]
Ol'i-to-ry, 86.
Ol-i-va'ceous (*-shus*),112.
Ol-i-vas'ter.
Ol'ĭve, 84, 170.
Ol'i-vīne [so Wr. Wb. Gd.; *ol'ĭ-vīn*, Sm. 155] [Olivin, 203.]
Ol'la po-dri'da (Sp.) (*-dre'-*).
O-lym'pi-ad, 169.
O-lym'pi-an, 72.
O-lym'pic, 109.
Om'bre (*ōm'bur*, or *ŏm'-bur*) [*ōm'bur*, Wk. Sm. Wr.; *ŏm'bur*, Wb. Gd. 155.]
Om-brom'e-ter, 108.
O-me'ga, *or* O-meg'a [*o-me'ga*, Wk. Wb. Gd. Wr.; *o-meg'a*, Sm. 155.]
Om'e-let, *or* Ŏme'let [*om'e-let*, Wb. Gd.; *om'let*, Wk. Wr.; *om'-e-let*, coll. *om'let*, Sm. 155.]
O'men, 76.
O-men'tum.
O'mer.
Om'in-oŭs (108) [*not* o'-min-ous, 153.]
O-mis'si-ble, 164.
O-mis'sion (*-mish'un*), 112.
O-mis'sĭve, 84.
O-mit', 103.
O-mit'ted, 176.
O-mit'ting.
Om'ni-bus, 169.
Om-ni-fa'ri-oŭs, 49, N.
Om-nif'er-oŭs, 108.
Om-nif'ic, 109.
Om'ni-form, 108.
Om-ni-form'i-ty, 108.
Om-nig'e-noŭs (*-nij'-*).
Om'ni-grăph, 127.
Om-ni-pa'ri-ent.
Om-ni-păr'i-ty, 170.
Om-nip'a-roŭs, 108.
Om-nip'o-tence.
Om-nip'o-ten-cy, 169.
Om-nip'o-tent.
Om-ni-pres'ence (*-prez'-*).
Om-ni-pres'ent (*-prez'-*).
Om-nĭ'sci-ence (*om-nish'ĭ-ens*), *or* Om-nĭ'science (*om-nish'-ens*) [so Wr.; *om-nish'-ĭ-ens*, Wk. Sm.; *om-nish'ens*, Wb. Gd. 155.]
Om-nĭ'sci-en-cy (*om-n sh'ĭ-en-sy*), *or* Om-nĭ'scien-cy (*om-nish'-e-sy*).
Om-nĭ'sci-ent (*-nish'ĭ-ent*), *or* Om-nĭ'scient (*-nish'ent*), 171.
Om'ni-um, 169.
Om'ni-um gath'er-um.
Om-niv'a-gant.
Om-niv'o-roŭs, 108.
O-mog'ra-phy, 108.
Om'o-plate.
Om'pha-cīne, 152.
Om-phal'ic, 109.
Om-pha-lop'ter.
Om-pha-lop'tic.
Om-pha-lot'o-my, 108.
On, 18, 43.
On'a-ger.
Once (*wuns*), 171.
On-cot'o-my.
On dit (Fr.) (*on de*).
One (*wun*) (163), *a.* single: —*pron.* & *n.* a single person or a single thing. [*See* Won, 160.]
One'-eyed (*wun'-īd*), 206, Exc. 5.
O-neī-ro-crit'ic, 49.
O-neī-ro-crit'ic-al.
O-neī-ro-crit'ics.
O-neī-rol'o-gist, 108.
O-neī-rol'o-gy, 108.
O-neī'ro-man-cy, 169.
O-neī-ros'co-pist.
O-neī-ros'co-py, 108.
One'ness (*wun'nes*), 66, N.; 171.
On'er-a-ry (72), *a.* pertaining to burdens; burdensome. [*See* Honorary, 160.]
On'er-oŭs [*not* o'nur-us, 127, 153.]
One'-sīd-ed, 206, Exc. 5.
On'ion (*un'yun*), 22, 51, 171.
On'-lŏŏk-er.
Ōn'ly, 24.
On'o-man-cy, 169.
On-o-man'tic.
On-o-man'tic-al.
On-o-mas'tic.
On-o-mas'ti-con (Gr.) [pl. *On-o-mas'ti-ca*, 198.]
On-o-ma-tech'ny (*-tek'-*).

On-o-ma-tol′o-gist [so Wb. Gd.; *o-nom-a-tol′o-jist*, Wr. 155.]
On-o-ma-tol′o-gy, 108.
On′o-ma-tope.
On-o-mat′o-py.
On-o-mat-o-pœ′ia (*-pe′-ya*), 171.
O-nom-a-to-po-et′ic.
On′set, 18, 76.
On′slâught (*-slawt*), 162, 171.
On-to-log′ic (*-loj′-*).
On-to-log′ic-al (*-loj′-*).
On-tol′o-gist.
On-tol′o-gy.
O′nus pro-ban′dī (L.).
On′ward, 72.
On′wards (*-wardz*).
On′y-cha (*on′ĭ-ka*), *or* O′ny-cha (*o′nĭ-ka*) [*on′i-ka*, so Wk. Wr. Wb. Gd.; *o′ni-ka*, Sm. 155.]
O-nych′o-man-cy (*-nik′-*), 52, 171.
O′nyx, 93, 171.
O′o-līte, 152, 229.
O-o-lit′ic, 109.
O-ol′o-gist.
O-ol′o-gy, 108.
Oo-long′ [so Wr.; *oo′-long*, Gd. 155] [Ou-long, 203.]
Ooze, 19, 40.
Oozed, 165, 183.
Ooz′ing.
Ooz′y, 93, 169.
O-paç′i-ty, 169.
O-pa′coŭs, 100.
O′pah, 72.
[Opake, 203.—*See* Opaque.]
O′pal (72) [so Wk. Wr. Wb. Gd.]

☞ Smart marks the *a* in this word as having a sound intermediate between that of *o* in *orb* and that of *o* in *on*. *See* § 18, N.

O-pal-esce′, 39.
O-pal-esced′ (*-est′*).
O-pal-es′cence, 171.
O-pal-es′cent.
O-pal-es′cing.
O′pal-ĭne, 82, 152.
O′pal-ize, 202.
O′pal-īzed.
O′pal-īz-ing, 183.
O′pal-oid.
O-pāque′ (168, 171; Note D, p. 37) [Opake, 203.]
Ope, 24, 163.
O′pen (*o′pn*), 24, 149.
O′pened (*o′pnd*), 150.
O′pen-ing (*-pn-*), 142.
O′pen-ness (*o′pn-nes*), 66, N.
Op′er-a, 72, 189.
Op-er-am′e-ter, 108.
Op′er-ant. [Exc.
Op′er-ate, 73, 170, 233,
Op′er-āt-ed, 183.
Op-er-at′ic.
Op-er-at′ic-al, 228.
Op′er-āt-ing.
Op-er-a′tion.
Op′er-a-tĭve, 84.
Op′er-āt-or.
O-per′cu-lar, 108.
O-per′cu-late.
O-per′cu-lāt-ed.
Op-er-cu′li-form (108) [so Sm. Wr.; *o-per′-ku-li-form*, Wb. Gd. 155.]
O-per′cu-lum (L.) [pl. *O-per′cu-la*, 198.]
Op-er-et′ta, 171.
Op′er-ose, *or* Op-er-ose′ [*op′ur-ōs*, Sm. Wb. Gd.; *op-ur-ōs′*, Wk. Wr. 155.]
Oph′i-cleīde (*-klīd*), 156.
O-phid′i-an, 169.
O-phid′i-oŭs.
Oph-i-o-log′ic (*-loj′-*).
Oph-i-o-log′ic-al (*-loj′-*).
Oph-i-ol′o-gist.
Oph-i-ol′o-gy, 45.
Oph′i-o-man-cy, 169.
Oph-i-o-mor′phoŭs.
Oph-i-sâu′rus.
O′phīte, 152.
Oph-i-u′chus (*-kus*).
Oph-thal′mi-a.
Oph-thal′mic (*op-thal′-mik*, or *of-thal′mik*) [so Wr.; *op-thal′mik*, Wk. Sm.; *of-thal′-mik*, Wb. Gd. 155.]
Oph-thal-mog′ra-phy (*op-*, or *of-*), 108.
Oph-thal-mol′o-gist (*op-*, or *of-*).
Oph-thal-mol′o-gy (*op-*, or *of-*), 108.
Oph-thal-mom′e-ter (*op-*, or *of-*), 108.
Oph-thal′mo-scope (*op-*, or *of-*).
Oph-thal-mos′co-py (*op-*, or *of-*), 108.
Oph-thal-mo-tol′o-gist (*op-*, or *of-*).
Oph-thal-mo-tol′o-gy (*op-*, or *of-*).
Oph-thal-mot′o-my (*op-*, or *of-*), 108.
Oph′thal-my (*op′-*, or *of′-*).
O′pi-ate, 73, 78.
O-pif′er-oŭs, 108.
O-pine′, 25, 103.
O-pined′, 165.
O-pīn′ing.
O-pin′ion (*-yun*), 51.
O-pin′ion-āt-ed (*-yun-*).
O-pin′ion-a-tĭve (*-yun-*).
O′pi-um, 78, 169.
Op-o-bâl′sam [so Sm. Wr.; *o-po-bawl′sam*, Wb. Gd. 155.]
Op-o-del′doc (171) [so Sm. Wr.; *o-po-del′-dok*, Wb. Gd.; 155] [*not* o-po-dil′dok, 127, 153.]
O-pos′sum, 169, 170.
Op′pi-dan.
Op-po′nen-cy.
Op-po′nent (122) [*not* op′o-nent, 153.]
Op-por-tune′, 122.
Op-por-tune′ly, 185.
Op-por-tune′ness, 66, N.
Op-por-tu′ni-ty (26, 108) [*not* op-por-too′-ni-ty, 127, 153.]
Op-pōs′a-ble (*-pōz′a-bl*), 164, 169.
Op-pose′ (*-pōz′*).
Op-posed′ (*-pōzed′*).
Op-pōs′ing (*-pōz′-*).
Op′po-sĭte (*-zit*), 152.
Op-po-sĭ′tion (*-zish′un*).
Op-po-sĭ′tion-ist (*-zish′-un-*).
Op-pos′i-tĭve (*-poz′-*).
Op-press′, 15, 103.
Op-pressed′ (*-prest′*).
Op-press′ing.
Op-pres′sion (*-presh′-un*), 112.
Op-pres′sĭve, 84.
Op-press′or, 88, 169.
Op-pro′bri-oŭs, 100.
Op-pro′bri-um, 169.
Op-pugn′ (*-pūn′*), 162.
Op-pugned′ (*-pūnd′*).
Op-pugn′er (*-pūn′-*).
Op-pugn′ing (*-pūn′-*).
Op-si-om′e-ter, 108.
Op′ta-tĭve, 84.
Op′tic.
Op′tic-al, 108.
Op-tĭ′cian (*-tish′an*).
Op′tics.

Op′ti-grăph, 127.
Op′ti-ma-cy, 169.
Op′ti-mate.
Op′ti-me (L.).
Op′ti-mism (*-mizm*).
Op′ti-mist.
Op′tion.
Op′tion-al.
Op-tom′e-ter, 108.
Op′u-lence, 105.
Op′u-lent, 108.
O-pus′cu-lum (L.) [pl. *O-pus′cu-la*, 198.]
O′pus op-e-ra′tum (L.).
Or, 17, 49.
Ŏr′ach (44, 156) [Or-rach, 203.]
Ŏr′a-cle, 164.
O-rac′u-lar, 108.
O-rac′u-loŭs, 108.
O′ral, 49, N.; 72.
O′ral-ly, 170.
Ŏr′ange (*ŏr′inj*) [so Wk.; *ŏr′ănj*, or *ŏr′-enj*, Sm.; *ŏr′anj*, Wr. Wb. Gd. 155.]
Ŏr-ange-ade′ (*-inj′-*).
Or-an-geat′ (Fr.). (*-zhat′*).
Ŏr′an-ger-y (*-jer-*) (169) [so Sm. Wr. Wb. Gd.; *o-rawn′zhur-y*, Wk. 155.]
O-rang′-ou-tang′ (*o-rang′-oo-tang′*) [so Sm.; *o-rang′-ow-tang′*, Gd.; *o-rang′-oo-tang′*, or *o′rang-oo′tang*, Wr. 155.]
O-ra′tion.
Ŏr′a-tor, 88, 113, 169.
Ŏr-a-to′ri-al, 49, N.
Ŏr-a-tŏr′ic-al, 108.
Ŏr-a-to′ri-o, 192.
Ŏr′a-to-ry, 86.
Orb, 17, 135.
Orbed (*orbd*), *v.*
Orbed (*orbd*), *a.* (150) [so Wb. Gd.; *or′bed*, or *orbd*, Wk. Wr.; *or′-bed*, Sm. 155.]
Orb′ic.
Orb′ic-al, 72.
Or-bic′u-lar, 108.
Or-bic′u-late.
Orb′ing.
Orb′it, 80.
Orb′it-al.
Orb′y, 169.
Orc (17, 181) [Ork, 203.]
[Orchal, 203. — *See* Orchil.]
Or′chard, 135.
Or′chard-ing.
Or′chard-ist.
[Orchel, 203. — *See* Orchil.]
Or′ches-tra (*-kes-*), *or* Or-ches′tra (*-kes′-*) [so Wr.; *or′kes-tra*, Wb. Gd.; *or-kes′tra*, Wk. Sm. 155.]

☞ Walker says: "Notwithstanding the numbers against me, the very general rule is on my side; which is, that, when we adopt a word whole from the Latin or Greek, it ought to have the same accent as in those languages." *See* § 113.

Or′ches-tral (*-kes-*).
Or-ches-tra′tion (*-kes-*).
Or′ches-tre (*-kes-tur*) (164) [Orchester, preferred by Wb. and Gd. 203. — *See* Note E, p. 70.]
Or-ches′tric (*-kes′-*), 109.
Or′chid (*-kid*), 49, 52.
Or-chid-a′ceous (*or-kid-a′shus*), 112.
Or-chid′e-oŭs (*-kid′-*), 169.
Or′chil (44, 141) [Archil, Orchal, Orchel, 203.]
Or′chi-o-cele (*-kĭ-*).
Or′chis (*-kis*), 169, 171.
Or′cine, 152.
Or-dāin′, 103.
Or-dāined′, 165.
Or-dāin′ing.
Or′de-al (169) [so Sm. Wr. Wb. Gd.; *or′de-al*, or *or′je-al*, 134, 155] [*not* or-de′al, 153.]
Or′der, 104, 135.
Or′dered (*-durd*), 150.
Or′der-ing, 142.
Or′der-li-ness, 186.
Or′der-ly.
Or′di-nal, 78.
Or′di-nance (169), *n.* a law. [*See* Ordnance *and* Ordonnance, 148.]
Or′di-nand.
Or′di-nant.
Or′di-na-ri-ly, 72, 126.
Or′di-na-ry (72), *a.* [so Sm. Wr. Wb. Gd.; *or′-di-na-ry*, or *ord′na-ry*, Wk. 155.]
Or′di-na-ry, *n.* [so Sm. Wb. Gd.; *ord′na-ry*, Wk.; *or′di-na-ry*, or *ord′na-ry*, Wr. 155.]
Or′di-nate.
Or-di-na′tion.
Ord′nance (169), *n.* cannon. [*See* Ordinance *and* Ordonnance, 148.]
Or′don-nance (Fr.) [so Wk. Wr. Wb. Gd.; *or-don′ans*, Sm. 155], *n.* the proper disposition of the parts in a work of art. [*See* Ordinance, *and* Ordnance, 148.]
Ord′ure, 91.
Ore (24, 49), *n.* a metal combined with some mineralizing substance. [*See* Oar, *and* O'er, 160.]
O′re-ad, 49, N.; 189.
Or′gan, 72.
Or-gan′ic, 109.
Or-gan′ic-al, 108.
Or′gan-ism (*-izm*), 136.
Or′gan-ist.
Or-gan-īz-a-bil′i-ty, 116, 169.
Or′gan-īz-a-ble, 164.
Or-gan-ĭ-za′tion.
Or′gan-ize, 202.
Or′gan-ized, 165.
Or′gan-īz-ing, 183.
Or-gan-o-graph′ic.
Or-gan-og′ra-phist.
Or-gan-og′ra-phy, 108.
Or-gan-ol′o-gy.
Or-gan-os′co-py, 108.
Or′gan-zine (*-zēn*), *or* Or-gan-zine′ (*-zēn′*) [*or′gan-zēn*, Wr. Wb. Gd.; *or-gan-zēn′*, Sm. 155.]
Or′gasm (*-gazm*), 133.
Or′geat (Fr.) (*or′zhat*) [*not* or′je-at, 145, 153.]
Or′gies (*-jiz*), *n. pl.* [*See* Orgy.]
Orgues (*orgz*), *n. pl.* 171.
Or′gy (*or′jy*) [pl. Or′-gies (*-jiz*), 190.]

☞ This word is rarely used in the singular.

Ŏr′i-chalch (*-kalk*), 52.
O′ri-el, 49, N.
O′ri-ent.
O-ri-ent′al, 109.
O-ri-ent′al-ism (*-izm*).
O-ri-ent′al-ist.
O-ri-ent′al-ize, 202.
O-ri-ent′al-ized.

O-ri-ent'al-īz-ing.
O-ri-ent-a'tion, 116.
O'ri-ent-ā-tor.
Ŏr'i-fīce, 169.
Or'i-flamme [Ori-flamb, 203.]
Ŏr'i-gan, 170.
O-rig'a-num.
Ŏr'i-gen-ism (*-jen-izm*), 133.
Ŏr'i-gen-ist (*-jen-*).
Ŏr'i-gin, 78.
O-rig'i-na-ble(*-rij'-*),164, 169.
O-rig'in-al (*-rij'-*).
O-rig-in-al'i-ty (*-rij-*).
O-rig'in-ate (*-rij'-*).
O-rig'in-āt-ed (*-rij'-*).
O-rig'in-āt-ing (*-rij'-*).
O-rig-in-a'tion (*-rij-*).
O-rig'in-a-tīve (*-rij'-*).
O-rig'in-āt-or (*-rij'-*).
O-ril'lon, 170.
O'ri-ole, 49, N.
O-ri'on, 122.
O-ris-mo-log'ic-al(*-loj'*).
O-ris-mol'o-gy (108) [so Wb. Gd.; *or-is-mol'-o-jy*, Wr. 155.]
Ŏr'i-son (*-zun*), 149.
[Ork, 203.—*See* Orc.]
Orle (*orl*).
Or'le-ans (*-anz*).
Or'let.
Or'lo.
Or'lop, 86.
Or-mo-lū' [so Wb. Gd.; *or-mo-l'oo'*, Sm. (*See* § 23); *or'mo-loo*, Wr. 155.]
Or'na-ment, 169.
Or-na-ment'al, 109.
Or-na-ment-a'tion.
Or'na-ment-ed.
Or'na-ment-ing.
Or'nate [*not* or-nāt', 153.]
Or-nith'ic.
Or-nith-ich'nite (*-ik'-*).
Or-nith-ich-nol'o-gy (*-ik-*), 108.
Or-nith'o-līte, 152.
Or-nith-o-log'ic-al (*loj'-*)
Or-nith-ol'o-gist, 108.
Or-nith'o-man-cy, 169.
Or-nith-o-rhyn'chus (*-ring'kus*), 54.
Ŏr-o-graph'ic.
Ŏr-o-graph'ic-al.
O-rog'ra-phy, 108.
Ŏr-o-log'ic-al.
O-rol'o-gy, 108.
O'ro-tund (105) [so Gd.; *o-ro-tund'*, Wr. 155.] [*not* ŏr'o-tund, 127, 153.]
Or'phan, 72.
Or'phan-age, 70.
Or'phaned (*-fand*).
Or-phe'an (110) [so Sm. Wr.; *or'fe-an*, Wb. Gd. 155.]
Or'phic.
Or'pi-ment, 169.
Or'pīne (82, 152) [Orpin, 203.]
Ŏr'rer-y, 233, Exc.
Ŏr'ris, 169.
Orse'dew (*-dū-*) [Orsedue, 203.]
Ort (17), *n.* a fragment; — refuse.
Or'tho-clase.
Or'tho-dox, 156.
Or'tho-dox-y, 169.
Or-tho-drom'ic.
Or-tho-drom'ics, 109.
Or'tho-drom-y [so Sm. Wr.; *or'tho-dro-my*, Wb. Gd. 155.]
Or-tho-ep'ic, 109.
Or-tho-ep'ic-al, 108.
Or'tho-e-pist.
Or'tho-e-py (122, 229) [*not* or-tho'e-py, 153.]
Or'tho-gon.
Or-thog'o-nal, 108.
Or-thog'ra-pher.
Or-thog'ra-phy, 108.
Or-tho-graph'ic, 109.
Or-tho-graph'ic-al, 108.
Or-thog'ra-phist.
Or-thog'ra-phy, 108; Note F, p. 79.
Or-thol'o-gy.
Or-tho-met'ric.
Or-thom'e-try.
Or-tho-ped'ic.
Or-tho-ped'ic-al.
Or-thop'e-dist.
Or-thop'e-dy.
Or-thoph'o-ny.
Or-thop-nœ'a (*-ne'-*).
Or-thop'ny.
Or-thop'ter-an.
Or-thop'ter-oŭs.
Or'tho-style.
Or-thot'ro-pal, 105.
Or-thot'ro-poŭs.
Or'tīve, 84.
Or'to-lan, 72.
Orts, *n. pl.* (17) [*See* Ort.]
Or'val, 72.
O-ryc'ter-ope.
Ŏr-yc-tog-nos'tic.
Ŏr-yc-tog'no-sy, 105.
Ŏr-yc-tog'ra-phy.
Ŏr-yc-to-log'ic-al (*-loj'-*).
Ŏr-yc-tol'o-gy, 93.
O'ryx [so Gd.; *ŏr'ix*, Wr. 155.]
Os'che-o-cele (*-ke-*).
Os'cil-lan-cy, 169.
Os'cil-late, 105, 170.
Os'cil-lāt-ed, 183.
Os'cil-lāt-ing.
Os-cil-la'tion, 112.
Os'cil-la-to-ry (86) [so Wb. Gd.; *os'il-ā-tŭr-y*, Sm.; *os-il'a-tŭr-y*, Wk.; *os'il-a-to-ry*, or *os-il'a-to-ry*, Wr. 155.]
Os'ci-tan-cy, 169.
Os'ci-tant, 78.
Os-ci-ta'tion.
Os'cu-lant, 89.
Os'cu-late.
Os'cu-lāt-ed.
Os'cu-lāt-ing, 183.
Os-cu-la'tion.
Os'cu-la-to-ry, 86.
Os'cu-lāt-rix.
Os'cule.
O'sier (*-zhur*), 47, N.
O'siered (*-zhurd*), 165.
Os'man-li, 191.
Os'ma-zome (*oz'-*).
Os'mi-um (*oz'-*), 169.
Os'mose (*oz'-*).
Os-mot'ic (*oz-*), 109.
Os'na-burg (*oz'-*).
Os'prāy (23) [Osprey, 203.]

☞ "The more common orthography of this word in the Dictionaries is *ospray*, as it is found in the Bible; but the orthography of the ornithologists is *osprey*." *Worcester.*

Os'se-let.
Os'se-oŭs (*os'e-us*, coll. *osh'us*) [so Sm.; *os'-e-us*, Wb. Gd.; *os'e-us*, or *osh'e-us*, Wr. 155.]
Os'si-cle, 164.
Os-sif'er-oŭs, 108.
Os-sif'ic.
Os-si-fī-ca'tion, 170.
Os'si-fīed, 99.
Os'si-frage.
Os'si-fȳ, 94.
Os'si-fȳ-ing, 186.
Os-siv'o-roŭs, 108.
Os'su-a-ry (*osh'u-a-ry*, or *os'u-a-ry*) [so Wr.;

osh'u-a-ry, Wb. Gd.; *os'u-ăr-y*, Sm. 155.]
Os'te-ĭne.
Os-ten-si-bil'i-ty.
Os-ten'si-ble, 164.
Os-ten'si-bly.
Os-ten'sĭve, 84.
Os-tent' [so Wk. Sm. Wr.; *os'tent*, Wb. Gd. 155.]
Os-tent-a'tion.
Os-tent-a'tioŭs, 171.
Os'te-o-cele.
Os'te-o-cope [so Wk. Sm. Wb. Gd.; *os'te-o-kōp*, or *os-te'o-kōp*, Wr. 155.]
Os-te-o-den'tĭne.
Os-te-og'e-ny (*-oj'-*), 169.
Os-te-og'ra-phy.
Os-te-ol'o-ger, 108.
Os-te-o-log'ic (*-loj'-*).
Os-te-o-log'ic-al (*-loj'-*).
Os-te-ol'o-gist.
Os-te-ol'o-gy.
Os'te-o-plas-ty.
Os-te-ot'o-my, 108.
Os'ti-a-ry, *or* Ost'ia-ry (*ost'yar-y*) [so Wr.; *os'ti-a-ry*, Wb. Gd.; *ost'yŭr-y*, Sm. 155.]
[Ostler, 203.— *See* Hostler.]
Os'tra-cism (*-sizm*), 136.
Os'tra-cize, 202.
Os'tra-cized.
Os'tra-cīz-ing, 183.
Os-tre-a'ceous (*-shus*), 234.
Os'trich [*not* os'trij, 153.]
Os'tro-goth.
Ot-a-cous'tic [so Wk. Wr. Wb. Gd.; *o-ta-kows'tik*, Sm. 155.]
O-tal'gi-a, 72.
O-tal'gic, 45.
O-tal'gy, *or* O'tal-gy [*o-tal'jy*, Wr. Wb. Gd.; *o'tal-jy*, Sm. 155.]
Oth'er (*uth'ur*), 38, 77.
Oth'er-wise (*uth'ur-wīz*) [so Sm. Wr. Wb. Gd.; *uth'ur wīz*, or *uth'ur-wīz*, Wk. 155.]
O-ti-ose' (*-shī-*) [so Wr.; *o'shōs*, Gd. 155.]
O'ti-um cum dig-ni-ta'-te (L.) (*o'shi um*).
O-tog'ra-phy, 108.
O-tol'o-gy.
O-top'a-thy, 108.
O-tot'o-my, 108.
Ot'tar (66, 74), *n.* the essential oil of roses. [*See* Otter, 160] [Attar, Otto, 203.]
Ot'ter (66, 77), *n.* an aquatic quadruped of the weasel kind. [*See* Ottar, 160.]
Ot'to, 86.

☞ This is another spelling of *ottar*: both forms are in good use. Smart gives *otto* only, in his Dictionary, but says: "some persons have lately chosen to spell it *ottar*."

Ot'to-man, 196.
Ou-bli-ette' (Fr.) (*oo-*).
Ouch, 28, 44.
Ought (*awt*) (162), *v.* was obliged; should. [*See* Aught, 160.]
Oui-dire (Fr.) (*oo-e-dēr'*)
[Oulong, 203.— *See* Oolong.]
Ounce, 28.
Our (28, 49), *pron.* or *a.* belonging to us. [*See* Hour, 160.]
Ou-ran-og'ra-phist.
Ou-ran-og'ra-phy, 108.
Ou-ret'ic.
Ou-rol'o-gy.
Ou-ros'co-py.
Ours (*owrz*), 28.
Our-self'.
Our-selves' (*-selvz'*).
[Ousel, 203.— *See* Ouzel.]
Oust (28) [*not* oost, 153.]
Oust'ed.
Oust'er, 77.
Oust'ing.
Out, 28, 41.
Out'blōwn [so Sm.; *out-blōn'*, Wb. Gd. Wr. 155.]
Out'cȧst, 131.
Out'crop, *n.* 103, 161.
Out-crop', *v.* 103, 161.
Out'crȳ, *n.*
Out-cry', *v.*
Out-do' (*-doo'*), 142.
Out'dōor, 206.
Out'er, 77, 169.
Out'er-mōst, 130.
Out'fit.
Out'go-ing [so Sm.; *out-go'ing*, Wb. Gd. Wr. 155.]
Out'-house, 206, Exc. 3.
Out-land'ish, 126.
Out'law.
Out'lawed, 188.
Out'law-ing.
Out'law-ry.
Out'lāy.
Out'let.
Out'līne, 206.
Out'lȳ-ing [so Wk. Wr.; *out-lī'ing*, Sm. Wb. Gd. 155.]
Out'-of-door', *a.* 220.
Out'pōst.
Out'pōur-ing [so Sm. Wb. Gd.; *out-pōr'-ing*, Wr. 155.]
Out'rage, 70.
Out'raged.
Out-ra'geoŭs (*-jus*), 169.
Out'rāg-ing (*-rāj-*).
Outré (Fr.) (*oo-trā'*).
Out'rīd-er, 126.
Out'rig-ger (*-gur*), 138.
Out-rīght' (*-rīt'*) (162) [so Wk. Sm. Wr.; *out'rīt*, Wb. Gd. 155.]
Out'side.
Out-sīd'er, 126.
Out-stretch'.
Out-stretched'. (*-stretcht'*), 150; Note C, p. 34.
Out-stretch'ing.
Out-talk' (*-tawk'*), 66, N.
Out-tell'.
Out'ward.
Out'wards (*-wardz*).
Out'work (*-wurk*), *n.* 103, 161.
Out-work' (*-wurk'*), *v.* 103, 161.
Ou'zel (*oo'zl*) (19, 149) [Ousel, 203.]
O'val, 72.
O-val-bu'men, 156.
O-val'i-form, 108.
O-va'ri-al, 49, N.
O-va'ri-an, 169.
O-va'ri-oŭs, 100.
O-va'ri-um (L.) [pl. *O-va'ri-a*, 198.]
O'va-ry.
O'vate.
O'vate-ob'long.
O-va'tion, 112.
Ov'en (*uv'n*), 22, 149.
O'ver, 77, 205, Exc. 1.
O'ver-ȧlls (*-awlz*), *n. pl.*
O-ver-bal'ance, *v.* 161.
O'ver-bal-ance, *n.* (161) [so Wk. Sm. Wr.; *o-vur-bal'ans*, Wb. Gd. 155.— *See* Note under *Counterbalance*.]

O′ver-bōard.
O-ver-came′.
O-ver-cȧst′, *v.* 131, 161.
O′ver-cȧst, *a.* 131, 161.
O-ver-charge′, *v.* 161.
O′ver-charge, *n.* 161.
O-ver-come′ (*-kum′*).
O-ver-com′ing (*-kum′-*).
O-ver-flōw′, *v.* 161.
O′ver-flōw, *n.* 161.
O-ver-flōwed′, 165.
O-ver-flōw′ing.
O-ver-hâul′.
O-ver-hâuled′.
O-ver-hâul′ing.
O′ver-land.
O′ver-lāy-ing, *n.* [so Sm.; *o-vur-lā′ing*, Wr. Gd. 155.]
O-ver-lŏŏk′.
O-ver-lŏŏked′ (*-lŏŏkt′*).
O-ver-lŏŏk′ing.
O-ver-match′, *v.* 161.
O′ver-match, *n.* 161.
O-ver-matched′ (*macht′-*).
O-ver-match′ing.
O-ver-much′.
O′ver-plus.
O-ver-rate′, 206, Exc. 1.
O-ver-rāt′ed.
O-ver-rāt′ing.
O-ver-rēach′.
O-ver-reached′(*-rēcht′*).
O-ver-reach′ing.
O′ver-right′eous (*ri′-chus*), 205, Exc. 1.
O′ver-rig′id (*-rij′-*).
O-ver-rule′.
O-ver-ruled′.
O-ver-rūl′ing.
O-ver-ran′.
O-ver-rŭn′.
O-ver-run′ning, 176.
O′ver-sight (*-sīt*).
O′vert (*-vurt*).
O-ver-threw′ (*-throo′*).
O-ver-thrōw′, *v.* 161.
O′ver-thrōw, *n.* 161.
O-ver-thrōw′ing.
O-ver-thrōwn′.
O′ver-tūre, 26.
O-ver-turn′, *v.* 161.
O′ver-turn, *n.* 161.
O-ver-turned′, 165.
O-ver-turn′ing.
O-ver-ween′.
O-ver-weened′, 165.
O-ver-ween′ing.
O-ver-whelm′.
O-ver-whelmed′, 165.
O-ver-whelm′ing.
O-vi-cap′sule.
O-vic′u-lar, 108.
O-vid′i-an, 169.
O′vi-duct.
O-vif′er-ous, 108.
O′vi-form.
O-vig′er-ous (*-vij′-*).
O′vine, 82, 152.
O-vip′a-roŭs, 108.
O-vi-pos′it (*-poz′-*).
O-vi-pos′it-or (*-poz′-*).
O′vi-sac.
O′void.
O-void′al.
O′vo-lo [*not* o-vo′lo, 153.]
O-vol′o-gy, 108.
O-vo-vī-vip′a-roŭs, 108.
O-vu-la′tion.
O′vule, 90.
O′vum (L.) [pl. *O′va*, 198.]
Ōwe (*ō*) (24), *v.* to be indebted to. [*See* O, *and* Oh, 160.]
Owed (*ōd*), *v.* was indebted to. [*See* Ode, 160.]
Ow′el-ty, 28.
Ōw′ing, 183.
Owl, 28, 50.
Owl′er (*owl′ur* or *ŏŏl′-ur*) [*owl′ur*, Wk. Wr. Wb. Gd.; *ŏŏl′ur*, Sm. 155.— *See* Owling.]
Owl′et, 76.
Owl′ing (*owl′ing*, or *ŏŏl′ing*) [*owl′ing*, Wk. Wr. Wb. Gd.; *ŏŏl′ing*, Sm. 155.]

☞ "Blackstone considers the word as related to *owl*, because the offence of transporting wool or sheep is generally committed at night: such relationship, if real, would require a correspondent pronunciation of the word." *Smart.*

Owl′ish, 176.
Owl′-līke, 206, Exc. 1.
Ōwn, 24, 43.
Ōwned (*ōnd*), 165.
Ōwn′er.
Ōwn′er-ship.
Ox (18, 52, N.) [pl. Ox′-en (*oks′n*), 195.]
Ox-al′ic, 109.
Ox′bird, 206.
Ox′en (*oks′n*), *n. pl.* (149) [*See* Ox.]
Ox′eȳe, 206.
Ox′-eȳed (*-īd*), 206, Exc. 5.
Ox′flȳ.
Ox-id-a-bil′i-ty (108) [Oxydability, Wb. Gd. 203.]
Ox′id-a-ble (164) [Oxydable, Wb. Gd. 203.]
Ox′id-ate [Oxydate, Wb. Gd. 203.]
Ox′id-āt-ed [Oxydated, Wb. Gd. 203.]
Ox′id-āt-ing [Oxydating, Wb. Gd. 203.]
Ox-id-a′tion (112) [Oxydation, Wb. Gd. 203.]
Ox′id-āt-or [Oxydator, Wb. Gd. 203.]
Ox′īde (163) [Oxyde, Oxyd, 203.]

☞ "The true orthography of this word is *oxyd*, as originally written by Lavoisier and his associates. No analogy in the language is better established than the uniform translation of the Greek *υ* into the English *y*, as in Latin, and it is very absurd to preserve this analogy in *oxygen*, *oxymuriate*, and *hydrogen*, and depart from it in *oxyd*." *Webster.*— "*Oxyde* is etymologically correct; but the other form (*oxide*), &c., exhibits the scientific termination by which compounds are distinguished that possess no sensible properties of acids, and are supporters of combustion." *Smart.*— "The orthography of *oxide*, *oxidate*, &c., is that of the English scientific dictionaries, encyclopædias, &c., and seems to be established by common usage, especially in chemical and scientific books." *Worcester.*

Ox-id-īz′a-ble (164)(Oxydizable, Wb. Gd. 203.]
Ox′id-ize (202) [Oxydize, Wb. Gd. 203.]
Ox′id-īzed [Oxydized, Wb. Gd. 203.]
Ox′id-ize-ment (185) [Oxydizement, Wb. Gd. 203.]
Ox′id-īz-ing (183) [Oxydizing, Wb. Gd. 203.]
Ox′lip, 206.
Ox-o′ni-an, 108, 169.
Ox′peck-er.
Ox′tongue (*-tung*).

Ox′y-gen, 45.
Ox′y-gen-ate, 106, 122.
Ox′y-gen-āt-ed.
Ox′y-gen-āt-ing.
Ox-y-gen-a′tion, 126.
Ox′y-gen-āt-or.
Ox′y-gen-īz-a-ble, 106.
Ox′y-gen-ize, 202.
Ox′y-gen-ized, 165.
Ox′y-gen-ize-ment.
Ox′y-gen-īz-ing, 183.
Ox-yg′en-oŭs (*-ij′-*),100.
Ox′y-gon.
Ox-yg′on-al, 108.
Ox-y-hy′dro-gen.
Ox′y-mel.
Ox-y-mo′ron.
Ox-y-mu′ri-ate, 49, N.
Ox-y-mu-ri-at′ic, 109.
Ox′y-ō-py.
Ox-yph′o-ny, 108.
Ox′y-sâlt.
Ox′y-sel.
Ox′y-tone (105) [Oxyton, 203.]
Ō′yer [*not* oy′er, 153.]
O-yes′ [so Sm. Wr.; *o-yis′*, Wk. 155] [Oyez, 203.]
Oys′ter.
Oys′ter-catch′er, 205.
Oys′ter-wom′an (*-wŏŏm′-*).
Oz-o-ce′rīte, (49, N.) [so Wr.; *oz-o-sēr′īt*, Sm.; *o-zo-ke′rīt*, Gd. 155.]
Oz-o-na′tion.
O′zone.
O-zo-ni-fĭ-ca′tion.
Oz′o-nize (202) [so Wr.; *o′zo-nīz*, Gd. 155.]
Oz′o-nized.
Oz′o-nīz-ing.
Oz-o-nom′e-ter, 108.
Oz-o-no-met′ric.
Oz-o-nom′e-try.

P.

Pab′u-lar, 108.
Pab-u-la′tion.
Pab′u-loŭs.
Pab′u-lum (L.).
Pā′ca, 189.
Pace, 23, 163.
Paced (*pāst*), 165; Note C, p. 34.
Pāç′er, 228.
Pa-châ′ (*pa-shaw′*) (121) [Pasha, Pashaw, 203.]
Pa-châ′lic (*-shaw′-*), 122.
Pach-y-dac′tyl-oŭs (*pak-*).
Pach′y-derm (*pak′-*).
Pach-y-derm′al (*pak-*).
Pach-y-derm′a-ta (*pak-*)
Pach-y-derm′a-toŭs (*pak-*).
Pach-y-derm′oid (*pak-*).
Pa-cif′ic.
Paç-i-fĭ-ca′tion, *or* Pa-cif-ĭ-ca′tion [so Wr.; *pas-ĭ-fĭ-ka′shun*, Wk.; *pa-sif-i-ka′shun*, Sm. Wb. Gd. 155.]
Paç-i-fĭ-ca′tor, *or* Pa-cif-i-ca′tor.
Pa-cif′ĭ-ca-to-ry, 86.
Paç′i-fīed.
Paç′i-fī-er.
Paç′i-fȳ, 235.
Paç′i-fȳ-ing, 186.
Pāç′ing, 183.
Pack, 10, 181.
Pack′age, 70.
Packed (*pakt*), 165; Note C, p. 34.
Pack′er.
Pack′et.
Pack′et-ed.
Pack′et-ing.
Pack′et-ship.
Pack′fong [Pakfong, 203.]
Pack′horse, 206.
Pack′ing.
Pack′thrĕad.
Pack′wax [Paxwax, 203.]
Pa′co, *n.* a species of llama. [pl. Pa′cōs (*pa′kōz*), 161, 192.]
Pa′cos (161), *n.* a kind of mineral.
Pact, 10.
Pac′tion.
Pac′tion-al, 72.
Pac-tĭ′tious (*-tish′us*).
Pac-to′li-an.
Pad, 10, 30, 42.
Pad′ded, 176.
Pad′ding.
Pad′dle, 164, 170.
Pad′dled (*pad′ld*), 165.
Pad′dling.
Pad′dock, 66.
Pad′dy.
Pȧ-di-shah′ [Padisha, 203.]
Pad′lock.
Pad-u-a-soy′ (*pad-u-a-soy′*, coll. *pad-u-soy′*) (89) [so Sm.; *pad-u-a-soy′*, Wb. Gd.; *pad-u-soy′*, Wr. 155.]
Pæ′an (13, 72) [*See* Pæon, *and* Peon, 148.]
[Pædobaptism. — *See* Pedobaptism, 203.]
[Pædotrophy, 203. — *See* Pedotrophy.]
Pæ′on, *n.* a foot consisting of one long syllable and three short syllables. [*See* Pæan, 148; *and* Peon, 160.]
[Pæony, 203. — *See* Peony.]
Pa′gan.
Pa-gan′ic, 109.
Pa-gan′ic-al, 108.
Pa′gan-ish.
Pa′gan-ism (*-izm*).
Pa′gan-ize, 202.
Pa′gan-ized.
Pa′gan-īz-ing.
Page, 23, 163.
Pag′eant (*paj′ent*), *or* Pa′geant (*pa′jent*) [so Wr.; *paj′unt*, Wk. Sm.; *pa′jent*, or *paj′ent*, Gd. 155.]
Pag′eant-ry (*paj′ent-*).
Paged, 165.
Pag′i-nal (*paj′-*).
Pag-i-na′tion (*paj-*).
Pāg′ing (*pāj′-*).
Pa-go′da.
Pa-gu′ri-an, 169.
Pāid, 23, 171, 187.
Pāil (23), *n.* a vessel with a bail, used for carrying liquids. [*See* Pale, 160.]
Pāil′ful (*-fŏŏl*), 197.
Pāin (23), *n.* a sensation of uneasiness. [*See* Pane, 160.]
Pāined, 165.
Pāin′ful (*-fŏŏl*), 180.
Pāi′nim [Paynim, 203.]
Pāin′ing.
Pāins (*pānz*).
Pains′tāk-er (*pānz′-*).
Pains′tāk-ing (*pānz′-*).
Pāint, 23.
Pāint′ed.
Pāint′er.
Pāint′ing.
Pāint′strake.
Pair (*pêr*) (67), *n.* two things of the same kind, which go together, or suit each

other. [*See* Payer, 148; *and* Pare, Pear, 160.]
Paired (*pêrd*), 165.
Pair'ing (*pêr'*-).
Päix'han.
[Pakfong, 203.—*See* Packfong.]
Pâl [Pall, 203.]
Pal'ace (70, 170) (coll. *pal'is*, in the U. S.; *pal'ăs*, or *pal'us*, in Eng.)

☞ "In ... *palace* ... although the *a* in the last syllable may be marked *ā* [*ā* unaccented], yet the shortening of this sound brings it to *ĕ*, and this again easily slides into ... *ă*, so that for common pronunciation the word ... might be marked ... *pal'lăs* [*pal'as*, or *pal'us*]." *Smart.*

Pal'a-din.
[Palæo- (initial syllables).—*See* Paleo-, 203.]
Pa-læs'tra (*-les'-*) (L.) [pl. *Pa-læs'træ* (*-les'-tre*), 198.]
Pa-læ-ti-ol'o-gy (*-le-shĭ-*), 108.
Pal-an-quin' (*-kēn'*) [so Wk. Wr. Wb. Gd.; *pal-ang-kēn'*, Sm. 155] [Palankeen, 203.]
Pal'a-ta-ble, 164.
Pal'a-tal, 72.
Pal'ate (170), *n.* the roof of the mouth. [*See* Palette, *and* Pallet, 148.]
Pa-la'tial (*-shal*).
Pa-lat'ic, *or* Pal'a-tic [*pa-lat'ik*, Wk. Wr.; *pal'a-tik*, Sm.; *pal'a-tik*, or *pa-lat'ik*, Gd. 155.]
Pa-lat'in-ate.
Pal'a-tīne, 82, 152.
Pa-lä'ver.
Pa-lä'vered (*-vurd*).
Pa-lä'ver-ing.
Pale, *a.* wan; pallid:—*n.* a stake; a district:—*v.* to enclose;—to make pale. [*See* Pail, 160.]
Paled, 165.
Pā-le-a'ceous (*-shus*), 46.
Pā'le-o-grăph.
Pā-le-og'ra-pher, 108.
Pā-le-o-graph'ic, 109.
Pā-le-o-graph'ic-al.
Pā-le-og'ra-phist.
Pā-le-og'ra-phy, 108.
Pā-le-ol'o-gist, 45.
Pā-le-ol'o-gy, 108.
Pā-le-on-to-graph'ic-al.
Pā-le-on-tog'ra-phy.
Pā-le-on-to-log'ic-al (*-loj'-*), 108.
Pā-le-on-tol'o-gy, 127.
Pā-le-o-the'ri-um.
Pal-es-tin'e-an, 110, 169.
Pa-les'tric.
Pa-les'tric-al.
Paletot (Fr.) (*pal'to*).
Pal'ette, *n.* a painter's board. [*See* Palate, 148; *and* Pallet, 160.] [Pallet, 203.]
Pâl'frey, *or* Pal'frey (169) [so Wk. Wr.; *pawl'fry*, Wb. Gd.; *pal'fry*, Sm. 155.]
Pal-i-fī-ca'tion [so Wr. Wb. Gd.; *pa-lĭ-fĭ-ka'shun*, Sm. 155.]
Pa-lil'o-gy, 108.
Pal'imp-sest [*not* pa-limp'sest, 153.]
Pal'in-drome.
Pal-in-drom'ic.
Pal-in-drom'ic-al.
Pāl'ing.
Pal-in-ge-ne'si-a (Gr.) (*-zhĭ-*).
Pal-in-gen'e-sy, 169.
Pal'in-ode.
Pal-in-ōd'i-al.
Pal-i-sade'.
Pal-i-săd'ed.
Pal-i-săd'ing.
Pal-i-sā'do [pl. Pal-i-sā'does (*-dōz*), 192.]
Pāl'ish, 183.
Pâll (17) [*See* Pawl.]
Pal'la (L.).
Pal-la'di-um (169) [L. pl. *Pal-la'di-a*; Eng. pl. Pal-la'di-ums (*-umz*), 198.]
Pal'lah, 72.
Pal'las.
Pal'let, *n.* a small, rude bed;—a particular part of the mechanism of a clock or a watch. [*See* Palate, 148; *and* Palette, 160.] [Pallat (in the latter sense), 202.]
Pal'li-al.
Pal'li-ate, 170.
Pal'li-āt-ed, 183.
Pal'li-āt-ing.
Pal-li-a'tion.
Pal'li-a-tīve, 126.
Pal'li-a-to-ry, 86.
Pal'lid, 66, 170.
Pal'li-er.
Pâll'ing.
Pal'li-o-bran'chi-ate (*-brang'kĭ-*).
Pal'li-um (L.) [pl. *Pal'li-a.*]
Pall-Mall' (*pel-mel'*) (156), *n.* a game formerly practised in England;—a street in London, so named from this game. [*See* Pellmell, 160.]
Pal'lor (*-lawr*), 88.
Palm (*pahm*), 162.
Pal'mar.
Pal-ma'ceoŭs (*-shus*).
Pal'ma-ry (72) [so Wr. Wb. Gd.; *pahm'ŭr-y*, Sm. 155.]
Pal'mate.
Pal'māt-ed.
Pal-mat'i-fid.
Palmed (*pahmd*), 162.
Palm'er (*pahm'-*).
Pal-met'to (86) [pl. Pal-met'tōes (*-tōz*), 192.]
Pal'mi-grade.
Pal'mīne, 82, 152.
Palm'ing (*pahm'-*).
Pal'mi-ped [Palmipede, 203.]
Pal'mis-ter.
Pal'mis-try, 156.
Palm'-tree (*pahm'-*), 206, Exc. 4.
Palm'y (169) (*pahm'y*).
Palp, 10, 30, 50.
Pal-pa-bil'i-ty, 108.
Pal'pa-ble, 164.
Pal-pa'tion.
Pal'pe-bral, 72, 169.
Pal'pe-broŭs, 100.
Palp'i-form, 108.
Palp-ig'er-oŭs (*-ij'-*).
Pal'pi-tate.
Pal'pi-tāt-ed, 183.
Pal'pi-tāt-ing.
Pal-pi-ta'tion.
Pâls'grave (*pawlz'-*).
Pâls-gra-vine' (*pawlz-gra-vēn'*), 156.
Pâl'sied (*-zid*).
Pâl'sy (*-zy*), 169.
Pâl'sy-ing (*-zy-*).
Pâl'ter, 17.
Pâl'tered, 150, 165.

Pâl′ter-ing.
Pâl′tri-ness, 186.
Pâl′try, 169.
Pa-lu′dal.
Pa-lu′di-noŭs.
Păl′y, 169.
Pam′pas (-*paz*), *n. pl.*
Pam′per (77), *v.* to feed luxuriously. [*See* Pampre, 160.]
Pam′pered (-*purd*).
Pam′per-ing.
Pam′phlet, 230.
Pam-phlet-eer′, 169.
Pam-phlet-eer′ing.
Pam-pin′i-form.
Pam′pre (-*pur*), *n.* an ornament for columns, consisting of vine-leaves and clusters of grapes. [*See* Pamper, 160.]
Pan, 10, 30, 43.
Pan-a-ce′a [L. pl. *Pan-a-ce′æ*; Eng. pl. Pan-a-ce′as (-*az*), 198.]
Pan-a-ce′an, 110.
Panache (Fr.) (*pan-ăsh′*). [203.
Pa-na′da, *or* Pa-na′do,
Pan′cake, 206.
Pan′carte [so Gd.; *pan-kart′*, Wr. 155.]
Pan-cra′tian (-*shan*).
Pan-cra′ti-ast.
Pan′cra-tist.
Pan-cra′ti-um (L.) (-*shĭ*-).
Pan′cre-as (*pang′*-) (54) [so Wk. Sm. Wr.; *pan′kre-as*, Wb. Gd. 155.]
Pan-cre-at′ic (*pang*-) [so Wk. Sm.; *pan-kre-at′ik*, Wr. Wb. Gd. 155.]
Pan-da-na′ceous (-*shus*).
Pan-de′an (110) [so Gd.; *pan′de-an*, Wr. 155.]
Pan′dect.
Pan-dem′ic.
Pan-de-mo′ni-um, 169.
Pan′der.
Pan′dered (-*durd*), 150.
Pan′der-ing.
Pan′der-ism (-*izm*).
Pan-dic-u-la′tion.
[Pandit, 203.—*See* Pundit.]
Pan-do′ra, 49, N.
Pan-dore′ [so Sm. Wr.; *pan′dōr*, Wb. Gd. 155] [Bandore, 203.]
Pan′dour (-*door*) [so Sm.; *pan-door′*, Wr. 155] [Bandoor, 203.]
Pan-dow′dy.
Pan′dress.
Pan′du-rate, 105.
Pan-du′ri-form, 108.
Pane (23, 163), *n.* a square of glass. [*See* Pain, 160.]
Paned, 165.
Pan-e-gy̆r′ic (-*jĭr′*-), *a.*& *n.* [so Wr. Wb. Gd.; *pan-e-jĕr′ik*, Wk. Sm. 155.]

☞ In the United States, this word is pronounced by most speakers with the regular short sound of *i*, in the penultimate syllable: in England, it is commonly pronounced with the sound of short *e*, in the same syllable. Smart says: "The irregular sound of *i* and *y*, in *squirrel* and *panegyric*, we may hope in time to hear reclaimed; a correspondent reformation having taken place in *spirit* and *miracle*."

Pan-e-gy̆r′ic-al.
Pan-e-gy̆r′ist, 45, 126.
Pan′e-gyr-ize, 202.
Pan′e-gyr-ized.
Pan′e-gyr-īz-ing.
Pan′el (66, 170), *n.* a square of wainscot; —a schedule of jurors' names. [*See* Pannel, 160.]
Pan′elled (-*eld*) [Paneled, Wb. Gd. 203. —*See* 177, and Note E, p. 70.]
Pan′el-ling (177) [Paneling, Wb. Gd. 203.]
Pang, 10, 30, 54.
Pan′go-lin (*pang′*-), 54.
Pan-hel-len′ic.
Pan-hel′len-ism (-*izm*).
Pan-hel′len-ist.
Pan′ic, 170.
Pan′i-cle, 164.
Pan′i-cled (-*kld*).
Pa-niv′o-roŭs, 108.
Pan-nade′ [*not* pan-näd′, 153.]
Pan′nel (66, 170), *n.* a kind of rustic saddle; —a hawk's stomach. [*See* Panel, 160.]
Pan′nier (*pan′yur*), *or* Pan′ni-er [so Wr.; *pan′yur*, Wk. Wb. Gd.; *pan′ni-ur*, Sm. 155.]
Pan′o-plīed (-*plid*).
Pan′o-ply, 93.
Pan-op′ti-con.
Pan-o-ra′ma, *or* Pan-o-rä′ma [so Wr.; *pan-o-ra′ma*, Sm.; *pan-o-rä′ma*, Wb. Gd. 155.]
Pan-o-ram′ic.
Pan-o-ram′ic-al.
Pan-phar′ma-con.
Pan-soph′ic-al.
Pan′so-phy.
Pan-ste-o-ra′ma, *or* Pan-ste-o-rä′ma [*pan-ste-o-ra′ma*, Sm. Wr.; *pan-ste-o-rä′ma*, Gd. 155.]
Pan′sy (-*zy*), 169.
Pȧnt, 12, 131.
Pan′ta-cosm (-*kozm*).
Pan′ta-grăph (127) [Pantograph, Pentagraph, 203.]
Pan-ta-let′, 122.
Pan-ta-loon′ (122) [pl. Pan-ta-loons′ (-*loonz′*), 189] [*not* pan′ta-loonz, 153.]
Pan-ta-morph′ic.
Pan-tech′ni-con (-*tek′*-).
Pȧnt′ed, 131.
Pȧnt′er.
Pan′the-ism (-*izm*), 136.
Pan′the-ist.
Pan-the-ist′ic.
Pan-the-ist′ic-al.
Pan-the-ol′o-gist.
Pan-the-ol′o-gy.
Pan-the′on.

☞ As a classical word, it is pronounced *pan′the-on*, by Walker, Smart, and Goodrich; but, as an English word, they pronounce it *pan-the′on*. Worcester's pronunciation is *pan-the′on*, in both cases.

Pan′ther.
Pan′ther-īne, 82, 152.
Pan′tīle [Pentile, 203.]
Pȧnt′ing.
Pant′ler.
Pan-to-chro-nom′e-ter (-*kro*-), 108.
Pan-to′fle (-*too′fl*), 156.
Pan′to-grăph (127) [Pantagraph, Pentagraph, 203.]
Pan-to-graph′ic.
Pan-to-graph′ic-al.

Pan-tog′ra-phy, 108.
Pan-to-log′ic (-loj′-).
Pan-to-log′ic-al (-loj′-).
Pan-tol′o-gist.
Pan-tol′o-gy.
Pan-tom′e-ter, 108.
Pan-tom′e-try.
Pan′to-mīme, 141.
Pan-to-mim′ic.
Pan-to-mim′ic-al.
Pan′to-mīm-ist.
Pan′ton.
Pan-toph′a-gist.
Pan-toph′a-goŭs, 105.
Pan-toph′a-gy, 45.
Pan′try, 93.
Pap, 10, 30.
Pa-pä′, 11, 72.
Pa′pa-cy, 169.
Pa′pal, 72.
Pa′par-chy (-ky), 52.
Pa-pa′ver (L.).
Pa-pav-er-a′ceoŭs (-shus), 112.
Pa-pav′er-oŭs.
Pa-paw′ (121) [Paw-paw, 203.]
Pa′per, 231.
Pa′per-cut′ter, 205.
Pa′pered (-purd).
Pa′per-māk′er.
Pa′per-y, 169.
Pa-pes′cent.
Pa′phi-an, 78.
Papier-maché (Fr.) (*pap-yā-mah′shā*).
Pa-pil-io-na′ceous (-yo-na′shus), 112.
Pa-pil′la (L.) [pl. *Pa-pil′læ* (-le), 198.]
Pap′il-la-ry, 72, 122.
Pa-pil′late.
Pa-pil′li-form.
Pap-il-lose′ [so Wr.; *pap′il-lōs*, Wb. Gd. 155.]
Pa-pil′loŭs, *or* Pap′il-loŭs [so Wr.; *pa-pil′-lus*, Wk.; *pap′il-lus*, Sm. Wb. Gd. 155.]
Pa′pist.
Pa-pist′ic.
Pa-pist′ic-al.
Pa′pist-ry, 156.
Pap-poose′ (148, 171), *n.* [Papoose, 203.]
Pap-pose′, *a.* 148.
Pap′poŭs (160), *a.* pertaining to, or consisting of, pappus.
Pap′pus (160), *n.* the soft, downy substance that grows on the seeds of certain plants.
Pap′py, 167, 176.
Pap′u-a, 89.
Pap′u-an.
Pap′u-la (L.) [pl. *Pap′-u-læ* (-le), 198.]
Pap′u-lar, 108.
Pap-u-lose′ [so Wr.; *pap′u-lōs*, Wb. Gd. 155.]
Pap′u-loŭs, 100.
Pap-y-ra′ceous (-shus), 93.
Pa-pȳr′e-an, 110.
Pap-y-rog′ra-phy, 108.
Pa-py′rus (113) (L.) [pl. *Pa-py′rī*, 198.]
Par (11), *n.* equal value; — a small fish. [Parr (in the latter sense), 203.]
Păr′a-ble, 164.
Pa-rab′o-la, 72, 189.
Păr-a-bol′ic, 109.
Păr-a-bol′ic-al, 108.
Păr-a-bol′i-form, 108.
Pa-rab′o-list.
Pa-rab′o-loid.
Păr-a-bo-loid′al, 126.
Păr-a-cel′sian (-shan), 112.
Păr-a-cel′sist.
Păr-a-cen′tric.
Păr-a-cen′tric-al.
Pa-rach′ro-nism (-rak′-ro-nizm), 133.
Păr-a-chute′ (-shoot′) (26, 114) [so Sm.; *par-a-shūt′*, Wr.; *par′a-shūt*, Wb. Gd. 155.]
Păr′a-clete, 171.
Păr-ac-mas′tic.
Păr-a-cros′tic, 109.
Pa-rade′.
Pa-răd′ed, 183.
Păr′a-digm (-dim), 162.
Păr-a-dig-mat′ic.
Păr-a-dig-mat′ic-al.
Pa-răd′ing.
Păr-a-di′sal.
Păr′a-dīse, 136.
Păr-a-dī-si′ac-al, 108, 171.
Păr′a-dos.
Păr′a-dox, 171.
Păr-a-dox′ic-al.
Păr′af-fīne, *or* Păr′af-fīne [*par′af-fīn*, Sm. Wb. Gd.; *par′af-fīn*, Wr. 155.]
Păr-a-gen′ic (-jen′-).
Păr-a-go′ge (-je) (Gr.) (113, 163) [so Wk. Wr. Wb. Gd.; *par′a-gō-jē*, Sm. 155.]
Păr-a-gog′ic (-goj′-).
Păr-a-gog′ic-al (-goj′-).
Păr′a-gŏn.
Păr′a-gram.
Păr-a-gram′ma-tist.
Păr′a-grăph, 127.
Păr-a-graph′ic.
Păr-a-graph′ic-al.
Păr-a-leip′sis [Paralipsis, Paralepsis, Paralepsy, 203.]
Pa-ra′li-an.
Păr-a-lī-pom′e-na (Gr.) *n. pl.*
Păr-al-lac′tic.
Păr-al-lac′tic-al.
Păr′al-lax, 170.
Păr′al-lel, 171.
Păr′al-leled (-leld), 177.
[Parallelepiped, 203. — *See* Parallelopiped.]
Păr′al-lel-ism, 133, 136.
Păr-al-lel′o-gram, 170.
Păr-al-lel-o-gram′mic.
Păr-al-lel-o-gram′mic-al
Păr-al-lel-o-gram-mat′-ic, 109, 116.
Păr-al-lel-o-pī′ped (171) [so Wk. Wr. Wb. Gd.; *par-al-lel-o-pip′ed*, Sm. 155] [Parallelepiped, 203.]
Păr-al-lel-o-pip′e-don.
Pa-ral′o-gism (-jizm).
Pa-ral′o-gize, 202.
Pa-ral′o-gized.
Pa-ral′o-gīz-ing.
Pa-ral′o-gy, 108.
Pa-ral′y-sis, 93, 171.
Păr-a-lyt′ic, 171.
Păr-a-lyt′ic-al.
Păr-al-ȳ-za′tion [so Wr.; *păr-a-lī-za′shun*, Gd. 155.]
Păr′a-lyze, 171.
Păr′a-lyzed, 183.
Păr′a-lȳz-ing.
Păr-a-mag-net′ic.
Păr-a-mag′net-ism (-izm).
Par′a-ment.
Pa-ram′e-ter, 108.
Păr′a-mount (105) [so Sm. Wr. Wb. Gd.; *par-a-mount′*, Wk. 155.]
Păr′a-mour (-moor).
Păr′a-nymph.
Păr′a-pegm (-pem), 162.
Păr′a-pet, 48.

Păr′a-pet-ed.
Pär′aph.
Păr-a-pher′nal.
Pár-a-pher-na′li-a, 144.
Păr′a-phrase (*-frāz*).
Pár′a-phrased (*-frāzd*).
Pár′a-phras-ing(*-frāz-*).
Pár′a-phrast.
Păr-a-phrast′ic.
Pár-a-phrast′ic-al.
Pár-a-phre-ni′tis.
Păr-a-ple′gi-a.
Păr′a-pleg-y (*-plej-*).
Pár-ap′o-plex-y.
Păr′a-sang.
Păr-a-scene′ (*-sēn′*).
Păr-a-sce′ni-um (L.).
Păr-a-se-le′ne (Gr.),163.
Pár′a-sīte, 83, 152.
Pár-a-sit′ic.
Păr-a-sit′ic-al.
Pár′a-sit-ism (*-izm*).
Pár′a-sol [so Wb. Gd.; *păr′a-sōl*, Wk.; *păr-a-sōl′*, Sm.; *păr′a-sol*, or *păr′a-sōl*, Wr. 155.]
Păr-a-sol-ette′, 14, 156.
[Parasyllabic, 203. — *See* Parisyllabic.]
Par-a-ther′mic, 109.
Pa-rath′e-sis.
Păr-a-ton-nêrre′ (Fr.).
Păr-a-vāil′.
Par′boil.
Par′boiled, 165.
Par′boil-ing.
Par′buc-kle (*-kl*).
Par′buc-kled (*-buk-kld*).
Par′buc-kling.
Par′cel, 149.
Par′celled (165) [Parceled, Wb. Gd. 203. — *See* 177, and Note E, p. 70.]
Par′cel-ling (177)[Parceling, Wb. Gd. 203.]
Par′ce-na-ry, 72.
Par′ce-ner.
Parch, 11, 135.
Parched (*parcht*), .165; Note C, p. 34.
Parch′ing.
Parch′ment.
Pard, 11, 49, 142.
Par′don (*-dn*) [so Wk. Wr.Wb.Gd.;*par′dun*, coll. *par′dn*, Sm. 155.]
Par′don-a-ble (*par′dn-a-bl*), 164, 169.
Par′doned (*-dnd*).
Par′don-er (*-dn-*).
Par′don-ing (*-dn-*).

Pare (*pêr*) (14, 67), *v.* to cut off the surface of. [*See* Payer, 148; *and* Pair, Pear, 160.]
Pared (*pêrd*).
Pa-reg′me-non.
Pár-e-gŏr′ic, 48.
Pa-rel′con.
Pa-rem′bo-le (Gr.), 163.
Pa-ren′chy-ma (*-reng′-kĭ-*) (52, 54) [so Sm.; *pa-ren′kĭ-ma*, Wk. Wr. Wb. Gd. 155.]
Pa-ren-chym′a-toŭs (*-kim′-*).
Pa-ren′chy-moŭs (*-reng′kĭ-*).
Pa-ren′e-sis [so Wk. Wr. Wb. Gd.; *păr-e′ne-sis*, Sm. 155.]
Păr-e-net′ic.
Pár-e-net′ic-al.
Par′ent (*pêr′rent*) (14, 49, N.) [so Sm. Wr. Wb. Gd.; *pa′rent*, Wk. 155.] [*not* pa′rent *nor* păr′ent, 153.]

☞ Though Walker divides this word *pa′rent*, as if the *a* were to have its long sound (No. 14, § 23), and the *r* its rough or trilled sound merely (No. 39, § 48), it is well ascertained that his own pronunciation was *pêr′rent*. In reference to words like the present, Smart says: "The first syllables of *va′ry*, *se′ri-ous*, *wi′ry*, *po′rous*, *cu′rate*, and the like . . . in all Dictionaries previously to 'Walker Remodelled' [Smart's edition of Walker's Dictionary. *See* p. xvii.], are wrongly referred to the same mode of pronunciation as the first syllables of *va′cant*, *se′cret*, *wi′ly*, *po′tent*, *cu′bic*, and the like."

Par′ent-age (*pêr′-*), or Păr′ent-age [so Wr.; *pêr′rent-āj*, Sm. Wb. Gd.; *păr′ent-āj*, Wk. 155.]
Pa-rent′al.
Pa-ren′the-sis (Gr.) [pl. Pa-ren′the-sēs (*-sēz*), 198.]
Păr-en-thet′ic.
Păr-en-thet′ic-al.
Pa-rent′i-cide.
Par′er (*pêr′rur*).
Par′gas-īte, 152.
Par′get (*-jet*), 45.

Par′get-ing (*-jet-*), 176.
Par-hel′ic, 109.
Par-he′li-on, *or* Par-hēl′ion (*-yun*) [so Wr.; *par-he′li un*, Wk. Sm.; *par-hēl′-yun*, Wb. Gd. 155.]
Pa′ri-ah, *or* Pár′i-ah [*pa′ri-a*, Wb. Gd.; *păr′ĭ-a*, Sm.; *pah′ri-ah*, Wr. 155] [*not* pa-ri′a, 153.]
Pa-ri′al, 122.
Pa′ri-an, 49, N.; 169.
Păr-i-dig′i-tate (*-dij′-*).
Pa-ri′e-tal (105) [*not* păr-i-e′tal, 153.]
Pa-ri′e-ta-ry, 72.
Pa-ri′e-tēs (L.) (*-tēz*), *n pl.*
Par′ing (*pêr′ring*).
Pa′rī pas′su (L.).
Păr-i-pin′nate.
Păr′ish, 11, N.
Pa-rish′ion-er (*-un-*).
Pa-ris′ian (*-riz′yan*) [so Wb. Gd.; *pa-riz′yan*, coll. *pa-rizh′′an*, Sm. (*See* § 26); *pa-rizh′ĭ-an*, Wr. 155.]
Păr-i-sol′o-gy, 108.
Pár-i-syl-lab′ic [Parasyllabic, 203.]
Păr-i-syl-lab′ic-al.
Păr′i-ty, 48, 169.
Park, 11, 49, 135.
Par′lance, 72.
Par′ley, 98, 169.
Par′leyed (*-lid*), 171.
Par′ley-ing.
Par′lĭa-ment (*-lĭ-*), 145, 171.
Par-lĭa-ment-a′ri-an (*-lĭ-*), 49, N.; 169.
Par-lĭa-ment′a-ry (*-lĭ-*), 72, 156.
Par′lor (88) [Parlour, 203.]
Par′loŭs.
Par-me-san′ (*-zan′*) [*not* Par-me′san, 153.]
Par-nas′si-an (*-nash′ĭ-an*), 171.
Pa-ro′chi-al(*-kĭ-*),52,153.
Pa-rod′ic.
Pa-rod′ic-al.
Păr′o-dĭed (*-did*), 99.
Păr′o-dist.
Păr′o-dy, 93.
Păr′o-dy̆-ing.
Păr′ol, *a.* & *n.* [Law term] (170) [so Sm. Wr.; *pa-rōl′*, Wb.

Gd. 155] [Parole, 203.]
Pa-role′, *n.* [Military term.]
Păr-o-mol′o-gy, 108.
Păr-o-no-ma′si-a (*-ma′-zhĭ-a*) [so Wk. Sm. Wr.; *păr-o-no-ma′-zha*, Wb. Gd. 155.]
Păr-o-no-mas′tic.
Păr-o-no-mas′tic-al.
Păr-o-nom′a-sy.
Păr′o-nÿme, 171.
Pa-ron′y-moŭs, 93.
Pa-ron′y-my.
Păr-o-quet′ (*-ket′*) [so Sm.; *păr′o-ket*, Wk. Wr. Wb. Gd. 155] [Paroket, Parrakeet, 203.]
Pa-rot′id, 156.
Păr-o-ti′tis.
Păr′ox-ysm (*-izm*), 136, 171.
Păr-ox-ys′mal (*-iz′-*).
Par-quet′ (Fr.)(*par-ka′*) [so Wr.; *par-ket′*, Gd. 155] [Parquette, 203.]
Par′quet-ry (*-ket-*).
Parr (11, 171), *n.* a small fish. [Par, 203.]
[Parrakeet, 203. — *See* Paroquet.]
Păr′ral, *or* Păr′rel, 203.
Par-rhe′si-a (*-re′zi-a*) [so Wr.; *par-re′zha*, Gd. 155.]
Păr-ri-ci′dal.
Păr′ri-cide, 170.
Par′rïed, 99, 186.
Păr′rot, 48, 66, 86.
Păr′ry.
Păr′ry-ing, 186.
Parse, 11, 49, 135.
Parsed (*parst*), 165; Note C, p. 34.
Par′see [so Wr. Wb. Gd.; *par-see′*, Sm. 155.]
Pars′er.
Par-si-mo′ni-oŭs, 169.
Par′si-mo-ny, 86.
Pars′ing, 183.
Pars′ley, 98, 169.
Pars′nip [Parsnep, 203.]
Par′sŏn (*par′sn*) (149, 167) [so Wk. Wr. Wb. Gd.; *par′sun*, coll. *par′sn*, Sm. 155.]
Par′son-age (*par′sn-*).
Part, 11, 49, 142.
Par-take′.
Par-tāk′en (*-tāk′n*).
Par-tāk′er.
Par-tāk′ing.
Part′ed.
Part′er.
Par-têrre′ (Fr.), 114, 171.
Par-then′ic (109) [so Wb. Gd.; *par′the-nik*, Wr. 155.]
Par′the-non.
Par-then′o-pe, 163.
Par-the-no′pi-an, 169.
Par′tial (*-shal*), 234.
Par′tial-ism (*-shal-izm*).
Par′tial-ist (*-shal-*).
Par-ti-al′i-ty (*-shĭ-al′-*) (108, 169) [so Wk. Sm. Wr.; *par-shal′i-ty*, Wb. Gd. 155.]
Part-i-bil′i-ty.
Part′i-ble, 164, 169.
Par′ti-ceps crim′i-nis (L.).
Par-tiç′i-pa-ble, 164.
Par-tiç′i-pant, 72.
Par-tiç′i-pate.
Par-tiç′i-pāt-ed, 183.
Par-tiç′i-pāt-ing.
Par-tiç-i-pa′tion, 116.
Par-tiç′i-pāt-ĭve [so Sm.; *par-tis′i-pa-tiv*, Wr. Wb. Gd. 155.]
Par-tiç′i-pāt-or.
Par-ti-cip′i-al (189) [so Wk. Wr. Wb. Gd.; *par-ti-sip′yal*, Sm. 155]
Par′ti-ci-ple, 164.
Par′ti-cle, 164.
Par-tic′u-lar, 89, 108.
Par-tic′u-lar-ism (*-izm*).
Par-tic′u-lar-ist.
Par-tic-u-lăr′i-ty.
Par-tic′u-lar-ize, 202.
Par-tic′u-lar-ized, 165.
Par-tic′u-lar-īz-ing, 183.
Par-tic′u-lar-ly, 156.
Part′ing.
Par′ti-san (*-zan*) [*not* par-ti-zan′, 153] [Partizan, 203.]
Par′tīte, 152.
Par-tĭ′tion (*-tish′un*).
Par-tĭ′tion-al (*-tish′un-*).
Par-tĭ′tioned (*-tish′und*)
Par-tĭ′tion-ing (*-tish′-un-*).
Par′ti-tĭve, 84.
Part′let.
Part′ner, 77.
Par-tŏŏk′ [so Sm. Wr. Wb. Gd.; *par-took′*, Wk. 155. — *See* Book.]
Par′tridge (11, 49) [*not* pat′rij, 153.]
Par-tu′ri-ent, 49, N.
Par-tu-ri-fa′cient (*-shent*).
Par-tu-rĭ′tion (*-rish′-un*), 89.
Par′ty, 11, 49, 135.
Par′ty-col′ored (*-kul′-urd*), 205.
Par-ve-nu′ (Fr.) (*-noo′*).
Pas (Fr.) (*pah*).
Pas′chal (*-kal*), 52, 72, 171.
[Pasch-flower, 203. — *See* Pasque-flower.]
[Pasha, 203. — *See* Pacha.]
[Pashaw, 203. — *See* Pacha.]
Pas-i-graph′ic.
Pas-i-graph′ic-al.
Pa-sig′ra-phy, 108.
Pas′i-lā-ly.
Pasque′-flower (*-flour*) [Pasch-flower, 203.]
Pas′quin (*-kwin*).
Pas-quin-ade′ (*-kwin-*).
Pȧss, 12, 174.
Pȧss′a-ble, 164, 169.
Pas-sāde′.
Pas-sa′do, *or* Pas-sä′do [*pas-sa′do*, Wk. Wr. Wb. Gd.; *pas-sa′do*, Sm. 155.]
Pas′sage, 70, 170.
Pas′sant.
Pȧss′-bŏŏk, 206, Exc. 4.
Pasée (Fr.) (*păs-sā′*).
Pȧssed (*pȧst*), *v.* & *part.* [165; Note C, p. 34] [*See* Past, 160.]

☞ "*Pass* is a regular verb; and *past*, for *passed*, is a correct pronunciation, but a wrong orthography for the *proper participle* [and imperfect tense]." *Worcester.*

Pas′sen-ger, 45.
Pȧsse-par-tout′ (Fr.) (*-too′*).
Pȧss′er.
Pas′ser-ĭne, 152.
Pas-si-bil′i-ty.
Pas′si-ble, 164.
Pas-si-flo-ra′ceous (*-shus*).
Pas′sim (L.).
Pȧss′ing.
Pȧss′ing-bell, 206, Exc. 4

fall; ê *as in* there; ŏŏ *as in* foot; ç *as in* facile; gh *as* g *in* go; t̲h̲ *as in* this.

Pas'sion (*pash'un*).
Pas'sion-al.
Pas'sion-ate, 73.
Pas'sion-ist.
Pas'sĭve, 84.
Pas-siv'i-ty, 108, 169.
Pȧss'o-ver, 206.
Pȧss-pa-role'.
Pȧss'pōrt.
Pȧss'word (*-wurd*).
Pȧst, *n. a.* & *prep.* [*See* Passed, 160.]
Paste, 23, 163.
Paste'bōard.
Pāst'ed.
Pas'tel.
Pas'tern.
Pasticcio (It.) (*pas-tich'yo*).
Pas'til.
Pastille (Fr.) (*pas-tēl'*).
Pȧs'tīme [*not* pas'tim, 153.]
Pāst'ing.
Pȧs'tor, 88.
Pȧs'tor-age.
Pȧs'tor-al.
Păs-to-rä'le (It.).
Pȧs'tor-ate.
Pās'try, 93, 169.
Pȧs'tur-a-ble (*păst'yur-a-bl*), 91, 164. [91.
Pȧs'tur-age (*pȧst'yur-*),
Pȧs'ture (*pȧst'yur*), 91.
Pȧs'tured (*pȧst'yurd*).
Pȧs'tur-ing (*pȧst'yur-*).
Pās'ty, *or* Pas'ty (161) [*pās'ty*, Sm. Wb. Gd.; *păs'ty*, Wk.; *pās'ty*, or *păs'ty*, Wr. 155], *n.* a kind of pie.
Pāst'y (161), *a.* resembling paste.
Pat, 10, 30, 41.
Pat-a-coon', 122.
Pat-a-go'ni-an.
Pat-a-re'mo.
Pat-a-vin'i-ty, 108, 169.
Patch, 10, 44.
Patched (*pacht*).
Patch'er.
Patch'ing.
Pat-chou'ly (*pa-choo'-*).
Patch'work (*-wurk*).
Patch'y, 169.
Pate (23, 161), *n.* the head.
Paté (Fr.) (*pä-tā'*) (161), *n.* a kind of platform. [A term in fortification.]
[P a t e e, 203.—*See* Pattee.]
Pat-e-fac'tion.
Pa-tel'la (L.) [L. pl. *Pa-tel'læ*, 198; Eng. pl. Pa-tel'las (*-laz*), 189.]
Pa-tel'li-form, 108.
Pat'en (149), *n.* the vessel on which the consecrated bread is placed. [*See* Patten, 160] [P a t i n, P a-t i n e, 203.]
Pat'ent, *or* Pa'tent, *n. a.* & *v.* [so Wk. Wr.; *pat'ent*, Sm. Wb. Gd. 155.]
Pat'ent-a-ble, *or* Pa'-tent-a-ble, 164.
Pat'ent-ed, *or* Pa'tent-ed.
Pat-ent-ee', *or* Pa-tent-ee'.
Pat'ent-ing, *or* Pa'tent-ing.
Pa-ter'nal, 21, N.
Pa-ter'ni-ty.
Pa'ter Nos'ter (L.) [so Wr. Wb. Gd.; *pat'ur nos'tur*, Sm. 155.]
Päth (11, 37) [pl. Päths (*pä'thz*), 140, 189.]
Pa-thet'ic.
Pa-thet'ic-al.
Päth'less.
Pa-thog'e-ny (*-thoj'-*).
Pa-thog-no-mon'ic.
Pa-thog'no-my, 103.
Path-o-log'ic (*-loj'-*).
Path-o-log'ic-al, (*-loj'-*).
Pa-thol'o-gist.
Pa-thol'o-gy.
Path-o-pœ'ia (*-pe'ya*).
Pa'thŏs.
Päth'wāy, 206.
Pa'tience (*-shens*).
Pa'tient (*-shent*).
Pat'in [P a t e n, 203.]
Pat'ĭne [P a t e n, 203.]
Pa-ti'na (It.) (*-te'-*) [so Gd.; *pat'i-na*, Wr. 155.]
Patois (Fr.) (*pat-waw'*).
Pa'trēs Con-scrip'tī (L.) (*pa'trēz-*).
Pa'tri-al.
Pa'tri-arch (*-ark*).
Pa-tri-arch'al (*-ark'-*).
Pa-tri-arch'ate (*-ark'-*).
Pa-tri-arch'ic (*-ark'-*).
Pa'tri-arch-y (*-ark-*).
Pa-trĭ'cian (*-trish'an*), 46, 171.
Pat-rĭ-cīd'al.
Pat'ri-cide, 78.
Pat-rĭ-mo'ni-al.
Pat'ri-mo-ny, 86.
Pa'tri-ot, *or* Pat'ri-ot [so Gd.; *pa'tri-ot*, Wk. Sm. Wr. 155.]
Pa-tri-ot'ic, *or* Pat-ri-ot'ic.
Pa'tri-ot-ism, *or* Pat'ri-ot-ism (*-izm*), 136.
Pă-trĭ-pas'sian (*-pash'-an*).
Pa-tris'tic.
Pa-tris'tic-al.
Pa-trōl', *n.* & *v.*
Pa-trōlled', 165, 176.
Pa-trōl'ling.
Pa'tron, *or* Pat'ron (86) [so Gd.; *pa'trun*, Wk. Sm. Wr. 155.]
Pa'tron-age, *or* Pat'-ron-age [*pa'trun-āj*, Sm.; *pat'run-āj*, Wk. Wr. Wb. Gd. 155.]
Pa'tron-al, *or* Pat'ron-al [*pa'trun-al*, Sm.; *pat'run-al*, Wk. Wr. Wb. Gd. 155.]
Pa'tron-ess, *or* Pat'ron-ess [so Gd.; *pa'trun-es*, Wk. Sm. Wr. 155.]
Pa'tron-ize, *or* Pat'ron-ize (202) [*pa'trun-īz*, Sm.; *pat'run-īz*, Wk. Wr. Wb. Gd. 155] [P a t r o n i s e, Sm. 203.]
Pa'tron-ized, *or* Pat'-ron-ized, 164.
Pa'tron-īz-ing, *or* Pat'-ron-īz-ing.
Pat-ro-nym'ic, 171.
Pat-ro-nym'ic-al.
Pa-troon', 121.
Pat-tee' [P a t e e, 203.]
Pat'ten (149), *n.* a kind of wooden shoe. [*See* Paten, 160.]
Pat'ter, 66, 170.
Pat'tered, 150.
Pat'ter-ing.
Pat'tern, 170.
Pat'terned (*-turnd*).
Pat'tern-ing.
Pat'ty.
Pat'u-loŭs, 108.
Pâu'ci-ty, 169.
Pâu'gĭe (*-ghĭ*) [P o r-g e e, P o r g y, P o-g y, P o g g y, 203.]
Pâu-hâu'gen (*-ghen*) [P o h a g e n, 203.]
[P a u l, 203.—*See* Pawl.]

Pâu'li-an-ist.
Pâu-lĭ'ci-an (*-lish'i-an*).
Pâul'īne, 152.
Päunch, *or* Pâunch (44, N. 2) [so Wr.; *panch*, Sm.; *pänsh*, Wk.; *pawnch*, Wb. Gd. 155.]
Pâu'per.
Pâu'per-ism (*-izm*), 136.
Pâu'per-ize.
Pâu'per-ized.
Pâu'per-īz-ing.
Pâuse (*pawz*) (17, 40), *n.* a cessation: — *v.* to cease. [*See* Paws (pl. of Paw), 160.]
Pâused (*pawzd*), 165.
Paus'er (*pawz'-*), 183.
Paus'ing (*pawz'-*).
Pāv'age.
Pav'an [Pavane, Paven, Pavin, 203.]
Pave (23, 161), *v.* to floor with stone, brick, or other material.
Pavé (Fr.) (*pa-vā'*), *n.* the pavement.
Paved, 165, 183.
Pave'ment, 185.
[Paven, 203. — *See* Pavan.]
Pāv'er [Pavier, Pavior, 203.]
Pav-e-säde', 114.
Pa'vi-age.
Pāv'ier (*-yur*) [Paver, 203.]
Pa-vil'ion (*-vil'yun*), 171.
[Pavin, 203. — *See* Pavan.]
Pāv'ing, 183.
Pāv'ior (*-yur*) [Paver, Pavier, 203.]
Pav'o-nīne, 82, 152.
Paw (17, 30) [pl. Paws (*pawz*), 189. — *See* Pause, 160.]
Pawed, 165.
Paw'ing.
Pawl (17), *n.* a detent or click to stop the backward revolution of a ratchet wheel, a windlass, &c. [*See* Pall, 160] [Paul, 203.]
Pawn, 17.
Pawn'bro-ker.
Pawned (*pawnd*), 165.
Pawn-ee' (118, 121) [Law term, — correlative of *Pawnor*.]
Pawn'er.
Pawn-or' (118, 121) [Law term, — correlative of *Pawnee*.]
[Pawpaw, 203. — *See* Papaw.]
Pax, 10, 39, N.
Pax-il-lose' [so Sm.; *pax'il-lōs*, Wr. 155.]
[Paxwax, 203. — *See* Packwax.]
Pāy, 23, 30.
Pāy'a-ble, 164, 169.
Pāy'dāy.
Pāy-ee' (118, 121) [Law term, — correlative of *Payor*.]
Pāy'er (67) [*See* Pair, Pare, *and* Pear, 148.]
Pāy'ing.
Pāy'mas-ter.
Pāy'nim [Painim, 203.]
Pāy-or' (118, 121) [Law term, — correlative of *Payee*.]
Paz-a-ree', 122.
Pēa (13) [pl. Peas (*pēz*), for the individual seeds; Pease (*pēz*), for the fruit taken collectively, 194.]
Pēace (13, 39), *n.* freedom from commotion or disturbance. [*See* Piece, 160.]
Pēace'a-ble, 169, 183.
Pēace'a-bly, 93.
Pēace'fụl (*-fool*), 180.
Pēace'fụl-ly (*-fool-*), 170.
Peace'māk-er.
Pēach, 13, 44.
Pēa'chick.
Pēach'-tree, 206, Exc. 4.
Pēach'y.
Pēa'cock.
Pēa'fowl.
Pēa'hen.
Pēa'-jack-et.
Pēak (13), *n.* the pointed top of any thing. [*See* Peek, *and* Pique, 160.]
Pēak'ed, *a.* (150) [so Wr.; *pēkt*, Gd. 155.]
Pēak'ish.
Pēal (13), *n.* a loud, continued sound: — *v.* to utter a loud, prolonged sound. [*See* Peel, 160.]
Pēaled, 165.
Pēal'ing.
[Pean, 203. — *See* Pæan.]
Pēa'nut, 206.
Pêar (14, 48, 67), *n.* a well-known fruit of many varieties. [*See* Payer, 148; *and* Pair, Pare, 160.]
Pearl (*perl*) (21, N.), *n.* a hard, smooth, lustrous, silvery-white substance, found in the shells of many species of mollusks. [*See* Purl, 148.]
Pearl'ash (*perl'-*).
Pearled (*perld*), 165.
Pearl'y (*perl'-*), 169.
Pêar-māin' [so Wk. Sm. Wr.; *pêr'mān*, Gd. 155.]
Pêar'-shaped (*-shāpt*), 206, Exc. 5.
Pêar'-tree, 206, Exc. 4.
Pĕas'ant (*pez'-*).
Pĕas'ant-ry (*pez'-*).
Pēas'cod (*pēz'-*) (214) [so Sm. Gd.; *pēs'kod*, Wk.; *pēz'kod*, or *pēs'kod*, Wr. 155.]
Pēase (*pēz*), (13, 194), *n. pl.* [*See* Pea.]
Pēat, 13, 30, 41.
Pe'ba.
Peb'ble, 164, 170.
Peb'bled (*peb'ld*), 183.
Peb'bly.
[Pecal, 203. — *See* Pecul.]
Pe-can', 121.
Pe-că'na [so Gd.; *pe-kan'a*, Wr. 155.]
[Pecary, 203. — *See* Peccary.]
Pec-ca-bil'i-ty, 170.
Pec'ca-ble, 164.
Pec-ca-dil'lo (170) [pl. Pec-ca-dil'loes (*-lōz*), 192.]
Pec'can-cy, 169.
Pec'cant, 72.
Pec'ca-ry (72, 93) [Pecary, Peccory, 203.]
Pec-ca'vī (L.) [so Wr. Gd.; *pek-ka'vī*, Sm. 155.]
[Pechblende, 203. — *See* Pitchblende.]
Peck, 15, 181.
Pecked (*pekt*), 165; Note C, p. 34.
Peck'ing.

Pec'ten.
Pec'tic.
Pec'ti-nal, 78.
Pec'ti-nate, 169.
Pec'ti-nāt-ed.
Pec-ti-na'tion.
Pec'tīne (82, 152) [Pectin, 203.]
Pec'to-līte, 152.
Pec'to-ral, 72.
Pec-to-rĭ-lo'qui-al.
Pec-to-ril'o-quism (-*kwizm*), 136.
Pec-to-ril'o-quoŭs.
Pec-to-ril'o-quy, 93.
Pec'ul [so Gd.; *pe'kul*, Wr. 155.] [Pecal, Picul, 203.]
Pec'u-late, 108.
Pec'u-lat-ed, 183.
Pec'u-lat-ing.
Pec-u-la'tion.
Pec'u-lat-or.
Pe-cūl'iar (-*yar*), *or* Pe-cu'li-ar [so Wr.; *pe-kūl'yar*, Wb. Gd.; *pe-ku'li-ar*, Wk. Sm. 155.]
Pe-cu-li-ăr'i-ty [so Wk. Sm.; *pe-kūl-yăr'i-ty*, Wb. Gd.; *pe-kūl-yi-ăr'i-ty*, Wr. 155.]
Pe-cūl'iar-ize (-*yar*-).
Pe-cūn'ia-ri-ly (-*ya*-), *or* Pe-cu'ni-a-ri-ly, 171.
Pe-cūn'ia-ry (-*ya*-), *or* Pe-cu'ni-a-ry [so Wr.; *pe-kun'ya-ry*, Gd.; *pe-ku'ni-ăr-y*, Wk. Sm. 155.]
Ped-a-gog'ic (-*goj'*-).
Ped-a-gog'ic-al (-*goj'*-).
Ped'a-gog-ism (-*izm*) (171) [so Sm. Gd.; *ped'a-go-jizm*, Wr 155.]
Ped'a-gŏgue (-*gog*), 87, 168, 171.
Ped'a-go-gy [so Wb. Gd.; *ped'a-goj-y*, Wr. 155.]
Pe'dal (161), *a.* [so Wk. Wr. Wb. Gd.; *ped'al*, Sm. 155.]
Ped'al (161), *n.* [so Sm. Wr. Wb. Gd.; *ped'al*, or *pe'dal*, Wk. 155.]
Pe-da'li-an, 169.
Pe-dal'i-ty.
Ped'ant, 66, 170.
Pe-dant'ic.
Pe-dant'ic-al.
Ped'ant-ry.
Pe-da'ri-an, 49, N.
Ped'ate.
Pe-dat'i-fid.
Ped'dle (*ped'l*), 164.
Ped'dled (*ped'ld*), 165.
[Peddler, 203.—*See* Pedler.]
[Peddlery, 203.—*See* Pedlery.]
Ped'dling.
Ped'es-tal (105) [*not* pe-des'tal, 153.]
Pe-des'tri-al.
Pe-des'tri-an.
Pe-des'trian-ism (-*izm*).
Pe-des'tri-an-ize, 202.
Pe'di-al, 169.
Ped'i-cel, 171.
Ped'i-cĕl-late.

☞ So pronounced by Worcester, as an adjective or a botanical term, meaning *furnished with a pedicel*, but *pe-dic'el-late* (-*dis'*-), as a noun, or the name of *one of an order of echinoderms*. Smart's pronunciation of the word, for both senses, is *ped'i-cel-late*. Webster and Goodrich give the word only as an adjective and pronounce it *ped'i-cel-late*.

Ped'i-celled (-*seld*).
Ped'i-cle, 164.
Pe-dic'u-lar, 108.
Pe-dic-u-la'tion.
Pe-dic'u-loŭs.
Pe-dig'er-oŭs (-*dij'*-).
Ped'i-gree, 78.
Pe-dim'a-noŭs.
Ped'i-mane.
Ped'i-ment, 108, 169.
Ped'i-palp.
Ped'ler [Peddler, *formerly* Pedlar, 203.]

☞ This word is spelled *pedler*, by Johnson, Walker, Smart, Worcester, and most other English lexicographers, but *peddler* by Webster and Goodrich. Worcester says: "If regularly formed, as a verbal noun, from the verb to *peddle*, the proper orthography would be *peddler*: but the noun *pedler*, or *pedlar*, appears to have been in use much longer than the verb to *peddle*: and this fact accounts for the apparent inconsistency in the orthography;—*peddle* not being found in the English Dictionaries which were published before that of Johnson." Walker remarks that "there is the same impropriety in spelling this word with one *d* only, as there would be in spelling *saddler* and *fiddler* in the same manner," and the reason he assigns is, that the vowel in the first syllable is liable to be wrongly pronounced with its long sound.

Ped'ler-y.
Pe-do-bap'tism (-*tizm*) [so Sm. Wr. Wb. Gd.; *ped-o-bap'tizm*, Wk. 155.]
Pe-do-bap'tist.
Ped'o-man-cy, 169.
Pe-dom'e-ter, 108.
Ped-o-met'ric.
Ped-o-met'ric-al.
Pe-dot'ro-phy [Pædotrophy, 203.]
Pe-dun'cle (*dung'kl*), 54, 164.
Pe-dun'cled (-*dung'kld*).
Pe-dun'cu-lar (-*dung'*-).
Pe-dun'cu-late (-*dung'*-)
Pe-dun'cu-lāt-ed (-*dung'*-).
Peek (13), *v.* to look slyly. [*See* Peak, *and* Pique, 160.]
Peel (13), *n.* skin, bark, or rind;—a wooden shovel used by bakers:—*v.* to strip off, as skin, &c. [*See* Peal, 160.]
Peeled (*pēld*), 165.
Peel'er.
Peel'ing.
Peep, 13, 30.
Peeped (*pēpt*), 165.
Peep'er.
Peep'ing.
Peer (13, 49), *n.* an equal; a nobleman:—*v.* to look narrowly. [*See* Pier, 160.]
Peer'age (49, N.), *n.* the body of peers; the nobility. [*See* Pierage, 160.]
Peered, 165.
Peer'ess.
Peer'ing.
Peer'less.
Pee'vish.
Peg, 15, 30, 53.
Pe-gā'se-an, 110.
Peg'a-sus.
Pegged, 176.
Peg'ger (-*gur*), 138.

Peg′ging (*-ghing*).
Peg′o-man-cy.
Peĭ-ram′e-ter.
Peĭ-ras′tic.
Pek′ōe [so Gd.; *pe′ko*, or *pek′o*, Wr. 155.]
Pel′age, 70, 170.
Pe-la′gi-an.
Pe-la′gi-an-ism (*-izm*).
Pe-lag′ic (*-laj′-*).
[Pelecan, 203. — *See* Pelican.]
Pel′e-coid [Pelicoid, 203.]
Pel′e-rĭne, 82, 152.
Pelf, 15, 64.
Pel′i-can (66, 72) [Pelecan, 203.]
[Pelicoid, 203. — *See* Pelecoid.]
Pel′i-om [so Wr.; *pe′li-om*, Wb. Gd. 155.]
Pe-lisse′ (*-lēs′*), 114, 171.
Pell, 15, 172.
Pel′lage.
Pel′let, 170.
Pel′li-cle, 78, 164.
Pel-lic′u-lar, 108.
Pel′li-to-ry, 85.
Pell-mell′, *ad.* confusedly. [*See* Pall-Mall, 160.]
Pel-lu′cid (26) [*not* pel-loo′sid, 153.]
Pel-lu-cid′i-ty, 89.
Pel-o-pon ne′sian (*-shan*) (171) [so Gd.; *pel-o-pon-ne′shĭ-an*, Wr. 155.]
Pelt, 15.
Pel′tate.
Pel′tāt-ed.
Pelt′ed.
Pel′ti-form, 108.
Pel′ti-nerved, 165.
Pelt′ing.
Pel′try, 93, 169.
Pel′vic.
Pel′vis.
Pem′mi-can [Pemican, 203.]
Pen, 15.
Pe′nal, 72.
Pen′al-ty, 93.
Pen′ance, 170.
Pe-na′tēs (L.) (*-tēz*), *n. pl.*
Penchant (Fr.) (*pong-shong′*), 154.
Pen′cil, *n.* a small brush of hair; an instrument for writing or drawing without ink: — *v.* to paint or draw. [*See* Pensile, 160.]
Pen′cilled (*-sild*) [Penciled, Wb. Gd. 203. — *See* 177, and Note E, p. 70.]
Pen′cil-ling [Penciling, Wb. Gd. 203.]
Pen′dant, *n.* any thing hanging, particularly by way of ornament. [*See* Pendent, 148.]
Pen′dence, 171.
Pen′den-cy, 169.
Pen′dent, *a.* hanging. [*See* Pendant, 148.]
Pen-den′te li′te (L.).
Pen-den′tĭve, 84.
Pend′ing.
Pend′u-loŭs, 45, N.
Pend′u-lum, 169, 189.
Pen-e-tra-bil′i-ty, 108.
Pen′e-tra-ble, 126, 164.
Pen-e-tra′li-a (L.), *n. pl.*
Pen′e-trate, 169.
Pen′e-trāt-ed, 183.
Pen′e-trāt-ing.
Pen-e-tra′tion.
Pen′e-trāt-ĭve [so Sm. Wr.; *pen′e-tra-tiv*, Wb. Gd. 155.]
Pen′guin (*-gwin*), 171.
Pen′hōld-er.
Pen′i-cil.
Pen-i-cil′late.
Pen-i-cil′lāt-ed. [108.
Pen-in′su-la, 46, Note 2;
Pen-in′su-lar, 108.
Pen-in′su-late.
Pen-in′su-lāt-ed.
Pen-in′su-lāt-ing.
Pen′i-tence, 169.
Pen′i-ten-cy.
Pen′i-tent, 171.
Pen-i-ten′tial (*-shal*).
Pen-i-ten′tia-ry (*-sha-*).
Pen′knife (*pen′īf*) (162) [pl. Pen′knives (*pen′-īvz*), 193.]

☞ This word is an exception to the remark contained in the last part of the note under § 66, the consonant sound of *n* not being dwelt upon in the pronunciation.

Pen′man, 196, 206.
Pen′nant, 170.
Pen′nate.
Pen′nāt-ed.
Penned, 165, 176.
Pen′ni-form, 66.
Pen-nig′er-oŭs (*-nij′-*).
Pen′ni-nerved, 165.
Pen′ning, 176.
Pen-nip′o-tent.
Pen′non, 86, 170.
Pen′ny [pl. Pen′nies (*-niz*), for the individual coins; Pence, for an aggregate sum, 194.]
Pen′ny-a-lĭn′er.
Pen-ny-roy′al.
Pen′ny-weight (*-wāt*), 162, 171.
Pen-ny-wise′ (*-wīz′*) (206, Exc. 5) [so Sm.; *pen′ny-wīz*, Wk. Wr. Wb. Gd. 155.]
Pen′ny-worth (*-wurth*) [so Wk. Wr. Wb. Gd.; *pen′ny-wurth*, coll. *pen′nurth*, Sm. 155.]

☞ "This word is commonly and without vulgarity contracted [in speaking] into *pennurth*." *Walker.*

[Penology, 203. — *See* Pœnology.]
Pen′sĭle (81, 152), *a.* hanging, pendulous. [*See* Pencil, 160.]
Pen′sion, 169.
Pen′sion-a-ry, 72.
Pen′sioned (*-shund*).
Pen′sion-er.
Pen′sion-ing.
Pen′sĭve, 84.
Pen′sĭve-ly, 185.
Pent, 15.
Pen-ta-cap′su-lar, 108.
Pen′ta-chord (*-kord*).
Pen′ta-cle, 164.
Pen′ta-coc-coŭs [so Sm.; *pen-ta-kok′kus*, Wr. Gd. 155.]
Pen-tac′ri-nīte, 152.
Pen-ta-cros′tic.
Pen′ta-dac-tyl.
Pen′ta-gŏn.
Pen-tag′o-nal, 108.
Pen-tag′o-noŭs.
Pen′ta-gram.
[Pentagraph, 203. — *See* Pantograph.]
Pen-ta-gyn′i-a (*-jin′-*).
Pen-ta-gyn′i-an (*-jin′-*).
Pen-tag′yn-oŭs (*-taj′-*)
Pen-ta-he′dral [Pentaedral, 203.]
Pen-ta-hed′ric-al [Pentaedrical, 203.]
Pen-ta-he′dron [Pentaedron, 203.]

Pen-ta-he′droŭs, 100.
Pen-ta-hex-a-he′dral, 116.
Pen-ta-me′ran.
Pen-tam′er-oŭs, 108.
Pen-tam′e-ter, 108.
Pen-tam′y-ron.
Pen-tan′der.
Pen-tan′dri-a.
Pen-tan′droŭs.
Pen-tan′gle (*-tang′gl*).
Pen-tan′gu-lar (*-tang′-*).
Pen-ta-pet′al-oŭs.
Pen-ta-phyl′loŭs, *or* Pen-taph′yl-loŭs. [*See* Adenophyllous.]
Pen-tap′o-dy.
Pen′tap-tote.
Pen′tar-chy (*-kȳ*), 52.
Pen′ta-spast.
Pen-ta-sperm′oŭs.
Pen′ta-stich (*-stik*).
Pen′ta-style.
Pen′ta-teŭch (*-tūk*), 171.
Pen-ta-teŭch′al (*-tūk′-*).
Pen′te-con-ter.
Pen′te-cŏst [so Sm. Wr. Wb. Gd.; *pen′te-kōst*, Wk. 155.]
Pen-te-cost′al.
Pen′te-cos-ter.
Pen-tel′ic.
Pen-tel′ic-an.
Pent′-house, 205, Exc.3.
Pen′tīle [Pantile, 203.]
Pe-nult′, *or* Pe′nult [*pe-nult′*, Sm.; *pe′-nult*, Gd.; *pe′nult*, or *pe-nult′*, Wr. 155.]
Pe-nult′i-ma.
Pe-nult′i-mate.
Pe-num′bra, 72.
Pe-num′bral.
Pe-nu′ri-oŭs, 49, N.
Pen′u-ry, 89.
Pe′on (86), *n.* in Mexico, a bondman for debt; in India, a native constable. [*See* Pæan, 148; *and* Pæon, 160.]
Pe′on-age.
Pe′o-ny [Pæony, Piony, 203.]
Pēo′ple (*pe′pl*), 13, 164.

☞ This word sometimes takes the plural form, but only when it is used in the sense of *nation.*

Pēo′pled (*pe′pld*), 183.
Pēo′pling.
Pe-pas′tic.
Pep′per, 170.
Pep′pered (*-purd*), 150.
Pep′per-grass.
Pep′per-idge, 169, 171.
Pep′per-ing.
Pep′per-mint.
Pep′per-sâuce.
Pep′per-y, 169.
Pep′sin.
Pep′tic.
Per, 21, N.
Pĕr-ad-vent′ure (91) [*not* pur-ad-vent′yur, 153.]
Per-am′bu-late, 127.
Per-am′bu-lāt-ed.
Per-am′bu-lāt-ing.
Per-am-bu-la′tion.
Per-am′bu-lāt-or.
Per an′num (L.).
Per-bī-sul′phate [so Sm.; *pur-bī-sul′fāt*, Wr. 155.]
Per cap′i-ta (L.).
Per-cēiv′a-ble, 164, 183.
Per-cēive′, 169, N.
Per-cēived′, 183.
Per-cēiv′er.
Per-cēiv′ing.
Per-cent′age, 169.
Per cen′tum (L.).

☞ Commonly abbreviated to *per cent.*

Per′cept.
Per-cep-ti-bil′i-ty.
Per-cep′ti-ble, 164.
Per-cep′tion, 169.
Per-cep′tīve, 84.
Per-cep-tiv′i-ty, 108, 169.
Perch, 21, N.
Per-chânce′.
Perched (*percht*), 165; Note C, p. 34.
Perch′er.
Perch′ing.
Per-chlo′rate (*-klo′-*).
Per-chlo′ric (*-klo′-*).
Per-chlo′rīde (*-klo′-*).
Per-cip′i-ence.
Per-cip′i-ent, 169.
Per′coid.
Per′co-late.
Per′co-lāt-ed, 183.
Per′co-lāt-ing.
Per-co-lā′tion.
Per′co-lāt-or.
Per-cuss′.
Per-cussed′ (*-kust′*).
Per-cuss′ing.
Per-cus′sion (*-kush′un*).
Per-cus′sion-cap.
Per-cus′sīve, 84.
Per-cu′tient (*-shent*), 112.
Per di′em (L.).
Per-di′tion (*-dish′un*).
Per-du′, *or* Per-dūe′, 203.
Pĕr′e-gri-nate.

☞ This word is an exception to the general rule (§ 108), by which words ending in *i-nate* are accented on the antepenult.

Pĕr-e-gri-na′tion.
Pĕr′e-gri-nāt-or.
Pĕr′e-grīne, 82. 152.
Pĕr′emp-to-ri-ly (*-em-*), 86, 126, 162.
Pĕr′emp-to-ri-ness (*-em-*).
Pĕr′emp-to-ry (*-em-*) (86, 122, 162) [so Sm. Wr. Wb. Gd.; *per′-em-tŭr-y*, or *pe-rem′-to-ry*, Wk. 155.]

☞ Though Walker gives two modes of pronouncing this word, he says: "I am much mistaken, if the first [*per′em-tur-y*] has not obtained a complete victory."

Pĕr-en′ni-al, 170.
Pĕr-en-nī-bran′chi-ate (*-brang′kī-*).
Per′fect, *a.* & *v.* 21, N.; 169.

☞ The verb is sometimes erroneously accented on the last syllable.

Per′fect-ed.
Per-fect-i-bil′i-ty.
Per-fect′i-ble, 164, 169.
Per′fect-ing, 156.
Per-fec′tion, 169.
Per-fec′tion-ism (*-izm*).
Per-fec′tion-ist.
Per-fect′īve, 84. [112.
Per-fi′cient (*-fish′ent*),
Per-fid′i-oŭs, *or* Per-fid′-ious (*-yus*) [so Wr.; *pur-fid′i-us*, Wb. Gd.; *per-fid′yus*, Wk. Sm. 155.]
Per′fi-dy, 21, N.; 169.
Per-fo′li-ate.
Per-fo′li-āt-ed.
Per′fo-rate.
Per′fo-rāt-ed.
Per′fo-rāt-ing.
Per-fo-ra′tion.
Per′fo-ra-tīve.
Per′fo-rāt-or, 169.
Per-fōrce′.
Per-form′ (17) [so Sm. Wr. Wb. Gd.; *per-*

form', or *per-fōrm'*, Wk. 155.]

☞ Walker characterizes the second mode of pronunciation which he assigns to this word, as "a wanton deviation from rule," and says that "it seems chiefly confined to the stage, where it probably originated."

Per-form'a-ble, 164.
Per-form'ance.
Per-formed', 165.
Per-form'er.
Per-form'ing.
Per'fume, *or* Per-fume', (161), *n.* [so Wr.; *per'-fūm*, Wk.; *per-fum'*, or *per'fūm*, Sm. Gd. 155.]

☞ "The analogy of dissyllable nouns and verbs seems now to have fixed the accent of the substantive on the first, and that of the verb on the last [syllable]." *Walker.*—"The poets frequently accent both the verb and the noun on the former syllable, the noun so frequently that it is difficult to decide whether its predicament is the one here assigned, or Prin. 83 [corresponding to that in § 103 of this Manual], under which it is also placed: what is conceived to be the seat of accent in present colloquial use, has here determined the preference." *Smart.*

Per-fume', *v.* 161.
Per-fumed', 165.
Per-fūm'er.
Per-fūm'er-y.
Per'func-to-ri-ly, *or* Per-func'to-ri-ly.
Per'func-to-ri-ness, *or* Per-func'to-ri-ness.
Per'func-tō-ry, *or* Per-func'to-ry (86) [*per'-funk-tō-ry*, Sm.; *pur-funk'to-ry*, Wk. Wb. Gd.; *pur-funk'to-ry*, or *pur'funk-to-ry*, Wr. 155.]

☞ "The original of this word is a Latin adverb [or a Latin adjective, meaning *carelessly done*], of which the verb, participle, and the other related words, have just the contrary meaning, so that if it had been derived from them, instead of the adverb, it would have signified *completely done, thoroughly performed*, in which case its accentuation would have been *perfunc'tory*; but formed as it is by abbreviation from *per''-func-to ri-e*, its proper accentuation is deemed to be that assigned to it above [*per'func-to-ry*]." *Smart.*

Per-fuse' (*-fūz'*), 121.
Per-fu'sĭve.
Per-ga-me'ne-oŭs [Pergamenious, 203.]
Per-haps', 132, 139.
Pe'rī, 49, N.; 191.
Pĕr'i-ănth.
Pĕr-i-car'di-ac.
Pĕr-i-car'di-al.
Pĕr-i-car'di-an.
Pĕr-i-car'dic.
Per-i-car-di'tis.
Pĕr-i-car'di-um, 169.
Pĕr'i-carp.
Pĕr-i-carp'i-al, 169.
Pĕr-i-carp'ic.
Pĕr'i-chæth (*-keth*).
Pĕr-i-chæ'tial (*-ke'shal*).
Pĕr'i-chete (*-kēt*).
Pĕr'i-clase.
Pe-ric'o-pe, 163.
Pĕr-i-cra'ni-um.
Pĕr-i-do-dec-a-he'dral.
Pĕr'i-dot.
Pĕr'i-drome.
Pĕr-i-e'sian (*-shan*).
Pĕr-i-er'gy.
Pĕr-i-ge'an, 45.
Pĕr'i-gee (*-je*), 138.
Pĕr'i-gōne [so Wr.; *pĕr-ig'o-ne*, Sm. 155.]
Pĕr'i-grăph.
Pĕr-i-gyn'i-um, 45.
Pe-rig'y-noŭs (*-rij'-*), 171.
Pĕr-i-he'li-on (Gr.) [pl. *Pĕr-i-he'li-a*, 198.]
Pĕr-i-hex-a-he'dral.
Pĕr'il, 48, 170.
Pĕr'illed (165) [Periled, Wb. Gd. 203.—*See* 177, and Note E, p. 70.]
Pĕr'il-ling (177) [Periling, Wb. Gd. 203.]
Pĕr'il-ous, 169, 171.

☞ "Not *perillous*, though the usual practice of the language is to double *l* in situations where other consonants are not doubled." *Smart. See* § 177.

Pĕr'i-lymph.
Pe-rim'e-ter, 108.
Pĕr-i-oc-ta-he'dral.
Pe'ri-od, 49, N.
Pe-ri-od'ic.
Pe-ri-od'ic-al.
Pe-ri-od'ic-al-ly, 170.
Pe-ri-od-iç'i-ty.
Pĕr-i-œ'cī (*e'sī*), 13.
Pĕr-i-œ'cian (*-e'shan*) [so Wb. Gd.; *pĕr-ĭ-e'-sh'an*, Sm. (*See* § 26); *pĕr-ĭ-e'sĭ-an*, Wr. 155.]
Pĕr-i-os'te-um, 111, 169.
Pĕr-i-os-ti'tis.
Pĕr-i-pa-tet'ic.
Pĕr-i-pa-tet'ic-al.
Pĕr-i-pa-tet'i-cism (*-sizm*), 136.
Pĕr-i-pet'al-oŭs.
Pe-riph'er-al, 106.
Pĕr-i-phĕr'ic, 109.
Pĕr-i-phĕr'ic-al.
Pe-riph'er-y, 171.
Pĕr'i-phrase (*frāz*).
Pe-riph'ra-sis (L.) [pl. Pe-riph'ra-sēs (*-sēz*), 198.]
Pĕr-i-phras'tic.
Pĕr-i-phras'tic-al.
Pĕr-ip-neū-mo'ni-a (L.).
Pĕr-ip-neū-mon'ic.
Pĕr-ip-neū-mon'ic-al.
Pĕr-ip-neū'mo-ny.
Pe-rip'ter-al.
Pe-rip'ter-oŭs.
Pe-rip'ter-y.
Pe-ris'cian (*-rish'an*).
Pe-ris'ci-ī (*-rish'ĭ-ī*).
Pĕr'i-scope.
Pĕr-i-scop'ic.
Pĕr-i-scop'ic-al.
Pĕr'ish, 104.
Pĕr'ish-a-ble, 164, 169.
Pĕr'ish-a-bly.
Pĕr'ished (*-isht*).
Pĕr'i-sperm.
Pĕr-i-sphĕr'ic.
Pĕr-i-sphĕr'ic-al.
Pĕr-is-so-log'ic-al (*-loj'-*).
Pĕr-is-sol'o-gy, 93.
Pĕr-i-stal'tic.
Pĕr'i-stome.
Pĕr-i-streph'ic.
Pĕr'i-style.
Pĕr-i-sys'to-le, 163.
Pe-rit'o-moŭs.
Pĕr-i-to-næ'um (L.) [Peritoneum, 203.]
Pĕr-i-to-ni'tis.
Pe-rit'ro-pal.
Pĕr'i-wig, 169.

Pĕr'i-win-kle (-*wing-kl*) (54, 164) [so Wr. Wb. Gd.; *pĕr'ĭ-win-kl*, Wk.; *pĕr-ĭ-wing'kl*, Sm. 155.]
Per'jure (-*jur*), 91.
Per'jured (-*jurd*).
Per'jur-er.
Per'jur-ing.
Per'ju-ry, 21, N.; 169.
Perk, 21, N.
Perked (*perkt*), 165.
Per'kin-ism (-*izm*).
Per'kin-ist.
Perk'y, 169.
Per-la'ceous (-*shus*), 112, 169.
Per'ma-nence.
Per'ma-nen-cy.
Per'ma-nent.
Per-man-gan'ic.
Per-me-a-bil'i-ty.
Per'me-a-ble, 164.
Per'me-ate, 169.
Per'me-āt-ed, 183.
Per'me-āt-ing.
Per-me-a'tion, 112.
Per'mi-an.
Per-mis-si-bil'i-ty.
Per-mis'si-ble, 164.
Per-mis'sion (-*mish'un*).
Per-mis'sĭve, 84.
Per-mis'sĭve-ly, 185.
Per-mit', *or* Per'mit, *n.* [so Gd.; *per'mit*, Wk. Sm.; *per'mit*, or *pur-mit'*, Wr. 155.]
Per-mit', *v.*
Per-mit'ted, 176.
Per-mit-tee'.
Per-mit'ter.
Per-mit'ting.
Per-mixt'ion (-*yun*).
Per-mu-ta'tion.
Per'nan-cy.
Per-nĭ'cious (-*nish'us*).
Per-noc-ta'li-an.
Per-noc-ta'tion.
Pĕr'o-nate.
Pĕr'o-ne, 163.
Pĕr-o-ne'al.
Pĕr-o-ra'tion.
Per-ox'ĭde (21, N.) [Peroxyd, Wb. Gd. 203.]
Per-pen-dic'u-lar, 108.
Per-pen-dic-u-lar'i-ty.
Per'pe-trate, 169.
Per'pe-trāt-ed, 183.
Per'pe-trāt-ing.
Per-pe-tra'tion.
Per'pe-trāt-or.
Per-pet'u-al, 108.
Per-pet'u-ate, 73, 89.
Per-pet'u-āt-ed, 183.
Per-pet'u-āt-ing.
Per-pet-u-a'tion.
Per-pe-tu'i-ty.
Per-plex', 103.
Per-plexed' (-*plekst'*), 165; Note C, p. 34.
Per-plex'ing.
Per-plex'i-ty.
Per'qui-sĭte (-*zit*), 152.
Per-qui-sĭ'tion (-*kwĭ-zĭsh'un*).
Pĕr'ron.
[Perroquet, 203.—*See* Paroquet.]
Pĕr'ry, 48, 66.
Per sal'tum (L.).
Per-scru-ta'tion (-*skroo*-).
Per se (L.).
Per'se-cute, 169.
Per'se-cūt-ed, 183.
Per'se-cūt-ing.
Per-se-cu'tion, 112.
Per'se-cūt-or, 228.
Per'se-cūt-rix.
Per-se-pol'i-tan.
Per'seūs [*See* Note under *Morpheus*.]
Per-se-vēr'ance, 169.
Per-se-vere'.
Per-se-vered'.
Per-se-vēr'ing.
Per'sian (-*shan*), 169.
Per'sic, 200.
Per'si-cot (Fr.) [so Gd.; *pêr-se-ko'*, Wr. 154, 155.]
Persiflage (Fr.) (*pêr-se-fläzh'*).
Per-sist', 136.
Per-sist'ed.
Per-sist'ence, 169.
Per-sist'en-cy.
Per-sist'ent, 228.
Per-sist'ĭve, 84.
Per'son (*per'sn*) (149, 169) [so Wk. Wr. Wb. Gd.; *per'sun*, coll. *per'sn*, Sm 155.]

☞ Walker remarks that he has "not the least objection" to the preservation of the sound of the *o* in this word, "on solemn occasions."

Per'son-a-ble, 164, 169.
Per'son-age.
Per'son-al, 72.
Per-son-al'i-ty, 108.
Per'son-al-ty, 145.
Per'son-ate, 73.
Per'son-āt-ed, 183.
Per'son-āt-ing.
Per-son-a'tion.
Per'son-āt-or.
Per-sŏn-i-fĭ-ca'tion, 116.
Per-son'i-fĭed, 99.
Per-son'i-fȳ, 94.
Per-son'i-fȳ-ing.
Personnel (Fr.) (*pêr-so-nel'*).
Per-spec'tĭve [*not* per'-spek-tiv, 153.]

☞ "In the poets, this word often has the accent on the first syllable." *Smart*

Per-spec'to-grăph.
Per-spec-tog'ra-phy, 108.
Per-spi-ca'cious (-*shus*), 112, 169.
Per-spi-caç'i-ty.
Per-spi-cu'i-ty.
Per-spic'u-oŭs, 108.
Per-spir-a-bil'i-ty.
Per-spīr'a-ble (49, N.; 164, 169) [*not* per'spi-ra-bl, 153.]
Per-spi-ra'tion.
Per-spīr'a-tĭve, 156.
Per-spīr'a-to-ry, 86.
Per-spire', 135.
Per-spired', 165.
Per-spīr'ing, 183.
Per-suād'a-ble (-*swād'a-bl*), 164.
Per-suade' (-*swād'*), 34.
Per-suād'ed (-*swād'*-).
Per-suād'ing (-*swād'*-).
Per-sua'si-ble (-*swa'sĭ-bl*) [so Sm. Wr. Wb. Gd.; *per-swa'zĭ-bl*, Wk. 155.]
Per-sua'sion (-*swa'-zhun*), 47, N.
Per-sua'sĭve (-*swa'*-).
Per-sua'sĭve-ly (-*swa'*-), 185.
Per-sua'so-ry (-*swa'*-), 86, 171.
Per-sul'phate, 21, N.; 117.
Per-sul-ta'tion.
Pert, 21, N.; 135.
Per-tāin'.
Per-tāined' (-*tānd'*).
Per-tāin'ing.
Per-ti-na'cious (-*shus*), 46, 112.
Per-ti-naç'i-ty.
Per'ti-nence, 169.
Per'ti-nen-cy.
Per'ti-nent, 108, 171.
Per-turb', 103.

Per-turb'ance, 169.
Per-turb-a'tion.
Per-turbed', 164.
Per-turb'ing.
Per-tu'sion (*-zhun*).
Pĕr'uke (*-ōōk*) [*not* pe-rook', 153.]
Pĕr'ule (*-ool*).
Pe-rus'al (*-rooz'-*), 19.
Pe-ruse'(*-rooz'*), 128, 136.
Pe-rused' (*-roozd'*).
Pe-rus'er (*-rooz'-*).
Pe-rus'ing (*-rooz'-*).
Pe-ru'vi-an (*-roo'*).
Per-vade' (103, 169), to be in all parts. [*See* Purveyed, 160.]
Per-văd'ed, 183.
Per-văd'ing.
Per-va'sion (*-zhun*).
Per-va'sĭve, 84.
Per-verse', 21, N.
Per-ver'sion.
Per-ver'si-ty.
Per-ver'sĭve.
Per'vert, *n.* 103, 161.
Per-vert', *v.* 103, 161.
Per-vert'ed.
Per-vert'er.
Per-vert'i-ble, 169.
Per-vert'ing.
Per'vi-oŭs, 21, N.; 169.
Pe-sade' (*-zăd'*) [so Sm.; *pe-săd'*, Gd.; *pe-săd'*, Wr. 155.]
Pes'sa-ry, 72.
Pes'si-mism (*-mizm*).
Pes'si-mist.
Pes'so-man-cy, 169.
Pest, 15.
Pes'ter, 77.
Pes'tered, 150, 165.
Pes'ter-er.
Pes'ter-ing.
Pest'-house, 206, Exc. 3.
Pest-if'er-oŭs, 108.
Pes'ti-lence, 169.
Pes'ti-lent.
Pes-ti-len'tial(*-shal*), 169
Pes'tle (*pes'l*) (162) [so Sm. Wb. Gd.; *pes'tl*, Wk.; *pes'l*, or *pes'tl*, Wr. 155.]
Pet, 15.
Pet'al [so Sm.; *pet'al*, or *pe'tal*, Wr. Gd.; *pe'tal*, or *pet'al*, Wk. 155.]

☞ "However right the long sound of *e* may be by analogy, I am apprehensive that .... the short sound is in more general use." *Walker.*

Pet-al-if'er-oŭs.
Pe-tal'i-form, 108.
Pet'al-īne, 152.
Pet'al-ism (*-izm*).
Pet'al-īte, 152.
Pet'al-oid.
Pet'al-oŭs.
Pe-tard', 121.
Pet-ard-eer' (169) [Pet-ardier, 203.]
Pet'a-sus (L.).
Pe-tâu'rist [so Wr. Wb. Gd.; *pet-a-u'rist*, Sm. 155.]
Pe-te'chi-al (*-kĭ-*), *or* Pe-tech'i-al (*-tek'-*) [*pe-te'ki-al*, Wk. Wr.; *pe-tek'i-al*, Sm. Wb. Gd. 155] [Petecchial, Wb. Gd. 203.]
[Peterel, 203.—*See* Petrel.]
Pe'ter-pence, *n. pl.*
Pe'ter-wort (*-wurt*).
Pet'i-o-lar.
Pet'i-o-la-ry, 72.
Pet'i-o-late.
Pet'i-o-lăt-ed.
Pet-i-ol'u-late, 89.
Pet'i-o-lule, 26.
Petit (Fr.) (*pet-ēt'*, meaning *little in figure*; in other senses, *pet'y*) [so Sm.; *pet'y*, Wb. Gd.; *pet'y*, or *pet'it*, Wr. 155.]
Pe-tĭ'tion (*-tish'un*).
Pe-tĭ'tion-a-ry (*-tish'-un-*), 72.
Pe-tĭ'tioned (*-tish'und*).
Pe-ti-tion-ee' (*-tish-un-*), 118, 122.
Pe-ti'tion-er (*-tish'un-*).
Pe-tĭ'tion-ing(*-tish'un-*)
Pe-ti'ti-o prin-cip'i-ī (L.) (*pe-tish'ĭ-o*).
Petit-maitre(Fr.)(*pet'y-ma'tr*).
Pet'i-to-ry, 86.
Pe-tong'.
Pe tra'ry, 49, N.
Pe-tre'an, 110.
Pet'rel [so Wb. Gd.; *pet'rel*, or *pe'trel*, Wr. 155] [Peterel, 203.]
Pe-tres'cence, 169.
Pe-tres'cent, 171.
Pet-ri-fac'tion.
Pet-ri-fac'tĭve, 84.
Pe-trif'ic, 109.
Pet-ri-fĭ-ca'tion.
Pet'ri-fīed.
Pet'ri-fȳ, 94.

Pet'ri-fȳ-ing.
Pe'trine (82, 152) [so Wr.; *pe'trīn*, Gd. 155.]
Pet-ro-graph'ic.
Pet-ro-graph'ic-al.
Pe-trog'ra-phy.
Pe-trŏl' [so Sm.; *pe'-trol*, Wk.; *pe'trol*, or *pe-trŏl'*, Wr. 155.]
Pe-tro'le-um, 111, 169.
Pet'ro-līne, 152.
Pe-trol'o-gy.
Pet'ro-sal.
Pet-ro-si'lex, *or* Pe-tro-si'lex [so Wr.; *pet-ro-si'lex*, Gd.; *pe-tro-sil'ex*, Sm. 155.]
Pet-ro-sĭ-lĭ'cious (*-lish'-us*).
Pe'troŭs.
Pet'ted, 176.
Pet'ti-cōat, 24.
Pet'ti-fog-ger (*-gur*).
Pet'ti-fog-ger-y (*-gur-*).
Pet'ti-fog-ging (*-ghing*).
Pet'ti-ly, 186.
Pet'ti-ness.
Pet'ting.
Pet'tish.
Pet'ti-toes (*-tōz*), *n. pl.*
Pet'to.
Pet'ty, 66, 170.
Pet'ty-chaps (*-chops*) [so Wr. Gd.; *pet'ty-chaps*, Sm. 155.]
Pet'u-lance, 89, 169.
Pet'u-lan-cy.
Pet'u-lant.
Pe-tu'ni-a.
Pe-tunse' [Petunce, Petuntse, Petuntze, 203.]
Pet'worth (*-wurth*).
Pew (*pu*), 26, 30.
Pe'wit, *or* Pe'wet (203) [*not* pu'it, pu'et, pe-wit', *nor* pe-wet', 153.]
Pew'ter (*pu'-*), 26, 77.
Pew'ter-er (*pu'-*).
Pew'ter-y (*pu'-*), 169.
Pez'i-zoid.
Pfen'nig (*fen'-*), 162.
Pha'coid.
Phæ-nog'a-moŭs [Phenogamous, 203.]
[Phœnomenon, 203.—*See* Phenomenon.]
Pha'e-ton [*not* phæ'ton (*fe'tun*), 144, 153.]
Phag-e-de'na (*faj-*) [so Wr. Gd.; *fagh-e-de'-na*, Sm. 155.]
Phag-e-den'ic (*faj'-*).
Phag-e-de'noŭs (*faj-*).

Pha-lan'gal (*-lang'-*).
Pha-lan'ge-al, 45, 169.
Pha-lan'ge-an, 110.
Pha-lan'ger (*-jur*).
Pha-lan'gi-an, 169.
Pha-lan'gi-oŭs.
Pha-lan'gīte (*-jīt*).
Phal-an-ste'ri-an.
Phal-an-ste'ri-an-ism (*-izm*), 136.
Pha-lan'ster-ism (*-izm*).
Pha-lan'ster-y.
Phal'anx (*-angks*) (54) [so Sm. Wb. Gd.; *fa'langks*, or *fal'-angks*, Wk. Wr. 155.] [L. pl. *Pha-lan'gēs* (*-jēz*); Eng. pl. Phal'-anx-es(*-angk-ez*),198.]

☞ "The second manner of pronouncing this word [*fal'angks*] is more general; but the first [*fa'-langks*] is more analogical." *Walker.*

Phal'a-rope [Phalerope, Sm. 203.]
Pha-le'cian (*-shan*).
Phal'lic, 170.
Phan-er-o-ga'mi-an.
Phan-er-o-gam'ic.
Phan-er-og'a-moŭs.
Phan'ta-scope.
Phan'tasm (*-tazm*) (133, 136)[Fantasm,203.]
Phan-tas'ma (*-taz'-*).
Phan-tas-ma-go'ri-a (*-taz-*), 116, 171.
Phan-tas-ma-go'ri-al (*-taz-*).
Phan-tas-ma-gŏr'ic (*-taz-*).
Phan-tas'ma-go-ry (*-taz'-*), 86, 136.
Phan-tas'mal (*-taz'-*).
Phan-tas'ma-scope (*-taz'-*). [(*-taz-*).
Phan-tas-ma-tog'ra-phy
[Phantastic, 203.—*See* Fantastic.]
[Phantasy, 203. — *See* Fantasy.]
Phan'tom (35, 86) [Fantom, 203.]
Phā-rā-on'ic (72) [so Sm.; *făr-a-on'ik*, Wr. Gd. 155.]
Phăr-i-sa'ic, 109.
Phăr-i-sa'ic-al, 108.
Phăr'i-sā-ism (*-izm*).
Phăr'i-see (11, N.; 171) [*not* făr'i-ze, 153.]
Phăr'i-see-ism (*-izm*).
Phar-ma-çeū'tic, 171.
Phar-ma-çeū'tic-al.
Phar-ma-çeū'tics, 109.
Phar-ma-çeū'tist.
Phar'ma-cist.
Phar-mac'o-līte, 152.
Phar-ma-col'o-gist.
Phar-ma-col'o-gy, 108.
Phar-ma-co-pœ'ia (*-pe'-ya*), 171, 189.
Phar'ma-cy, 169.
[Pharo, 203. — *See* Faro.]
Pha'rŏs, 49, N.
Pha-ryn'ge-al (*-je-*).
Phăr-yn-gi'tis.
Pha-ryn'go-glos'sal (*-ring'-*), 224.
Phăr-yn-gog'ra-phy, 108.
Phăr-yn-gol'o-gy.
Phăr-yn-got'o-my.
Phăr'ynx (*-ingks*) (54, 93) [so Sm. Wr. Wb. Gd.; *fa'ringks*, Wk. 155.]
Phas'co-lome.
Phase (*fāz*) (23, 35, 40) [pl. Phas'es (*fāz'ez*), 189.]
Pha'sis (Gr.) [pl. Pha'-sēs (*-zēz*), 198.]
Phĕas'ant (*fez'-*), 72.
Phĕas'ant-ry (*fez'-*).
Phĕas'ant's-eye (*fez'-*), 213.
[Pheese, 203. — *See* Feaze.]
Phen'a-cite.
Phen-a-kis'to-scope.
Phen'gite (*-jīt*).
[Phenician, 203. — *See* Phœnician.]
Phen'i-cīne [Phenicin, 203.]
Phen'i-cop-ter [so Wr. Wb. Gd.; *fe-ni-kop'-tur*, Wk. 155.]
[Phenix, 203. — *See* Phœnix.]
Phen'o-gam.
Phe-no-ga'mi-an.
Phen-o-gam'ic.
Phe-nog'a-moŭs.
Phe-nom'e-nal.
Phe-nom-e-nol'o-gy.
Phe-nom'e-nŏn (L.) [pl. Phe-nom'e-na,*or* Phe-nom'e-nons (*-nonz*), 198.]

☞ "This word has a regular plural, as having been long adopted in our language; but the classical plural, *phenomena*, is more common in works of science." *Smart.*

Phi'al [Vial, 203.]
Phī-ga'li-an.
Phil-a-del'phi-an.
Phil-an-throp'ic.
Phil-an-throp'ic-al.
Phil-an-throp'i-nism (*-nizm*) [so Wr.; *fil-an-thro'pi-nizm*, Sm. 155.]
Phil-an-throp'i-nist.
Phĭ-lan'thro-pist.
Phĭ-lan'thro-py [*not* fī-lan'thro-py, 153.]
Phil-har-mon'ic.
Phil-hel'lene.

☞ Smart gives only the plural of this word, and he pronounces it as a classical word, *phil-hel-le'nēs* (*nēz*).

Phil-hel-len'ic.
Phil-hel'len-ism (*-izm*).
Phil-hel'len-ist.
[Philibeg, 203.—*See* Fillibeg.]
Phi-lip'pi-an, 170.
Phi-lip'pic, 171.
[Philippine, 203.—*See* Philopena.]
Phĭ-lis'ter.
Phĭ-lis'tīne, 82, 152.
Phĭ-lis'tin-ism (*-izm*).
Phil-o-hel-le'ni-an.
Phĭ-lol'o-ger.
Phil-o-log'ic (*-loj'-*).
Phil-o-log'ic-al (*-loj'-*).
Phĭ-lol'o-gist.
Phĭ-lol'o-gy [*not* fī-lol'-o-jy, 153.]
Phil'o-math [so Sm. Wr.; *fī'lo-math*, Wb. Gd. 155.]
Phil-o-math'ic.
Phil-o-math'ic-al.
Phĭ-lom'a-thy, 108.
Phil'o-mel [so Wk. Sm. Wr.; *fī'lo-mel*, Wb. Gd. 155.]
Phil-o-me'la.
Phil'o-mot.
Phil-o-pe'na [Fillipeen, Philippine, 203.]
Phī-lo-po-lem'ic.
Phī-lo-po-lem'ic-al.
Phī-lo-pro-gen'i-tĭve-ness.
Phĭ-los'o-pher.
Phil-o-soph'ic (*-sof'-*, or

-*zof'*-) [*fil-o-sof'ik*, Wb. Gd.; *fil-o-zof'ik*, Wk. Sm.; *fil-o-zof'ik*, or *fil-o-sof'ik*, Wr. 155.]
Phil-o-soph'ic-al (-*sof'*-, or -*zof'*-).
Phĭ-los'o-phism (-*fizm*).
Phĭ-los'o-phist.
Phĭ-los-o-phist'ic.
Phĭ-los-o-phist'ic-al.
Phĭ-los'o-phize, 202.
Phĭ-los'o-phized.
Phĭ-los'o-phīz-ing.
Phĭ-los'o-phy (169) [*not* fi-los'o-fy, 153.]
Phil-o-stor'gy.
Phil-o-tech'nic (-*tek'*-).
Phil-o-tech'nic-al(-*tek'*-)
Phil'ter, *n.* a love-potion. [*See* Filter, 160] [Philtre, 203.]
Phiz, 16, 35, 40.
Phle-bog'ra-phy, 108.
Phleb'o-līte, 152.
Phle-bol'o gy.
Phle-bop'ter-oŭs.
Phleb'or-rhage (-*rāj*), 162, 171.
Phleb-or-rha'gi-a (-*ra'*-).
Phle-bot'o-mist.
Phle-bot'o-my, 108.
Phlegm (*flem*), 162, 171.
Phleg'ma-gŏgue, 87.
Phleg-mat'ic [so Sm. Wb. Gd.; *fleg'ma-tik*, Wk.; *fleg-mat'ik*, or *fleg'ma-tik*, Wr. 155.]

☞ "*Phlegmatic*, . . . though more frequently heard with the accent on the antepenultimate syllable, ought, if possible, to be reduced to regularity." *Walker*. — "This word is often heard with the accent on the first syllable, and some of the poets so use it, particularly in the figurative sense." *Smart*.

Phleg-mat'ic-al.
Phleg'mon-oid.
Phleg'mon-oŭs.
Phle-græ'an, 171.
[Phleme, 203. — *See* Fleam.]
Phlo-gis'tic, 45.
Phlo-gis'ti-cate.
Phlo-gis'ti-cāt-ed.
Phlo-gis'ti-cāt-ing.
Phlo-gis-ti-ca'tion.
Phlo-gis'ton (-*jis'*-) [so Sm. Wr. Wb. Gd.; *flo-jis'ton*, or *flo-ghis'ton*, Wk. 155.]

☞ Walker considered *flo-ghis'ton* to be the pronunciation in established use among the scientific men of his day; yet he says: "Those who are not chemists ought, in my opinion, to protest against the irregular sound of the *g* in this and similar words [from the Greek]. Pronouncing the *g* soft would only hurt the pride of the professor; but pronouncing it hard would hurt the genius of the language." *Walker*.

Phlox (*floks*) (171), *n.* the name of an American plant, or genus of plants. [*See* Flock, 160.]
Pho'ca (L.) [pl. *Pho'cæ* (-*se*), 198.]
Pho-ca'cean (-*shan*) (112) [so Wr.; *fo-ka'she-an*, Sm. 155.]
Pho'cal.
Pho'cīne, 82, 152.
Phœ'bus (-*fe'*-).
Phœ-nĭ'cian (*fe-nish'an*) [Phenician, 203.]
Phœ-nĭ'ceous(-*nish'us*). [Phenicеous, 203.]
Phœ'nix (13) [Phenix, 203.]
Pho-la'de-an.
Pho-li-doph'er-oŭs.
Phon-as-cet'ic.
Pho-na'tion.
Pho-net'ic.
Pho-net'ic-al.
Pho-net'ics.
Pho-net-ĭ-za'tion.
Phon'ic.
Phon'ic-al.
Phon'ics.
Pho'no-grăph, 127.
Pho-nog'ra-pher.
Pho-no-graph'ic.
Pho-no-graph'ic-al.
Pho-nog'ra-phist.
Pho-nog'ra-phy, 108.
Pho'no-līte, 152.
Pho-nol'o-ger.
Pho-no-log'ic (-*loj'*-).
Pho-no-log'ic-al (-*loj'*-).
Pho-nol'o-gist, 108.
Pho-nol'o-gy.
Pho'no-type.
Pho-no-typ'ic.
Pho-no-typ'ic-al.
Pho-not'y-pist.
Pho-not'y-py [so Wr.; *fo'no-typ-y*, Gd. 155.]
Phos'phate.
Phos-phat'ic.
Phos'phīte.
Phos'pho-līte.
Phos'phor, 35.
Phos'phor-ate.
Phos'phor-āt-ed, 228.
Phos'phor-āt-ing.
Phos-phor-esce', 171.
Phos-phor-esced' (-*est'*).
Phos-phor-es'cence.
Phos-phor-es'cent.
Phos-phor-es'cing.
Phos-phŏr'ic, 109.
Phos-phŏr'ic-al, 108.
Phos'phor-oŭs, *a.* pertaining to phosphorus; — denoting an acid formed of one equivalent of phosphorus and three equivalents of oxygen. [*See* Phosphorus, 160.]
Phos'phor-us, *n.* the morning star; — an inflammable, poisonous substance, luminous in the dark. [*See* Phosphorous, 160.]
Phos'phu-rĕt.
Phos'phu-rĕt-ted [Phosphureted, Wb. Gd. 203.]
Pho-to-chem'ic-al (-*kĕm'*-).
Pho-to-gen'ic.
Pho-tog'e-ny (-*toj'*-).
Pho'to-grăph.
Pho-tog'ra-pher, 108.
Pho-to-graph'ic.
Pho-to-graph'ic-al.
Pho-tog'ra-phist.
Pho-tog-ra-phom'e-ter.
Pho-tog'ra-phy.
Pho-to-log'ic (-*loj'*-).
Pho-to-log'ic-al (-*loj'*-).
Pho-tol'o-gy, 108.
Pho-tom'e-ter.
Pho-to-met'ric.
Pho-to-met'ric-al.
Pho-tom'e-try.
Pho-to-pho'bi-a.
Pho-top'si-a.
Pho-top'sy.
Phrag'ma-cone.
Phrase (-*frāz*), *n.* an expression forming part of a sentence, and not making complete

sense by itself :— *v.* to express in words. [*See* Fraise, 160.]
Phrased (*frāzd*), 165.
Phrā-se-o-log′ic (*-ze-o-loj′-*).
Phrā-se-o-log′ic-al (*-ze-o-loj′-*).
Phrā-se-ol′o-gist (*-ze-*).
Phrā-se-ol′o-gy (*-ze-*).
Phrās′ing (*frāz′-*).
Phra′try.
Phre-net′ic [Frenetic, 203.]
Phren′ic, 156.
Phre-ni′tis, 113.
Phre-nol′o-ger, 108.
Phren-o-log′ic (*-loj′-*) [so Sm. Wr.; *fre-no-loj′ik*, Wb. Gd. 155.]
Phren-o-log′ic-al(*-loj′-*).
Phre-nol′o-gist.
Phre-nol′o-gy.
Phren-o-mag′net-ism (*-izm*), 224.
[Phrensy, 203.— *See* Frenzy.]
Phryg′i-an (*-frij′-*).
Phthis′ic (*tiz′ik*), 156, 162, 171.

☞ "As to the letters *phth* meeting in the same syllable, who can wonder that an English eye, affrighted by such an assemblage, should close its lid on the first two letters, and consider only how the second two are to be pronounced?" *Smart.*

Phthis′ic-al (*tiz′-*).
Phthis′ick-y (*tiz′-*).
Phthis-i-ol′o-gy (*tiz-*).
Phthi′sis (*thi′sis*, or *ti′sis*) [so Wr.; *thi′sis*, Wk. Wb. Gd.; *ti′sis*, Sm. 155.]
Phthon-gom′e-ter (*thong-*), 162.
Phy̆-lac′ter-y, 171.
Phy′larch (*-lark*).
Phy′larch-y (*-lark-*).
Phyle (*fīl*), *n.* a tribe in ancient Athens. [*See* File, 160.]
Phyl′lode.
Phyl-lo-nyc′ter-an.
Phyl-loph′a-gan, 169.
Phyl-loph′o-roŭs.
Phyl′lo-pod.
Phyl′lo-stome.
Phyl-lo-tac′tic.
Phyl′lo-tax-y.
Phy̆-se′ter [so Wr.; *fis′-e-tur*, Wb. Gd. 155.]
Phys-i-an′thro-py (*fiz′-*)
Phys′ic (*fiz′-*), 200.
Phys′ic-al (*fiz′-*), 72.
Phy-sĭ′cian (*-zish′an*), 46, 171, 234.
Phys′i-cist (*fiz′-*).
Phys′icked (*fiz′ikt*),200.
Phys′ick-ing (*fiz′-*).
Phys′ic-o-log′ic-al (*fiz′-ik-o-loj′-*), 224.
Phys′ic-o-the-ol′o-gy (*fiz′-*).
Phys′ics (*fiz′-*), *n. pl.*
Phys-i-og-nom′ic (*fiz-*).
Phys-i-og-nom′ic-al (*fiz-*).
Phys-i-og-nom′ics(*fiz-*), 109.
Phys-i-og′no-mist(*fiz-*).
Phys-i-og′no-my (*fiz-*) [so Sm. Wr. Wb. Gd.; *fizh-ĭ-og′no-my*, Wk. 155] [*not* fiz-ĭ-on′o-my, 153.]

☞ Walker attempts to justify his pronunciation of *s* as *zh*, in words like *physiognomy*, by an appeal to analogy; but he acknowledges that "this is far from being the most general pronunciation."

Phys-i-og′o-ny (*fiz-*).
Phys-i-o-graph′ic-al (*fiz-*).
Phys-i-og′ra-phy (*fiz-*).
Phys-i-ol′o-ger (*fiz-*), 108.
Phys-i-o-log′ic (*fiz-i-o-loj′ik*).
Phys-i-o-log′ic-al (*fiz-i-o-loj′ik-al*).
Phys-i-ol′o-gist (*fiz-*).
Phys-i-ol′o-gy (*fiz-*) [so Sm. Wr. Wb. Gd.; *fizh-ĭ-ol′o-jy*, Wk. 155] [*See* Note under *Physiognomy*.]
Physique (Fr.) (*fē-zēk′*).
Phys′o-cele (*fiz′-*).
Phys′o-grade (*fiz′-*).
Phy̆-tiph′a-gan.
Phy̆-tiv′o-roŭs (108) [so Wk. Sm. Wb. Gd.; *fĭ-tiv′o rus*, Wr. 155.]
Phy̆-to-chem′is-try (*-kem′-*).
Phy̆-toch′i-my (*-tok′-*).
Phy̆-tog′e-ny (*-toj′-*).
Phy̆-to-ge-og′ra-phy.
Phy̆-to-graph′ic-al.
Phy̆-tog′ra-phy, 108.
Phy̆-to-li-thol′o-gy.
Phy̆-to-log′ic-al (*-loj′-*).
Phy̆-tol′o-gist, 45.
Phy̆-tol′o-gy.
Phy′ton.
Phy̆-ton′o-my [Phytonymy, 203.]
Phy̆-toph′a-goŭs, 100
Phy̆-tot′o-mist, 108.
Phy̆-tot′o-my.
Phy̆-to-zo′on [so Gd.; *fĭ-toz′o-on*, Sm.; *fĭ-toz′o-ŏn*, Wr. 155] [pl. Phy-to-zo′a, 198.]
Pī, *n.* a confused mass of types. [Pie, 203.]
Pī-ac′u-lar, 108.
Pī′a ma′ter (L.).
Pī-ä′nist [*not* pī′a-nist, pe′a-nist, *nor* pī-an′-ist, 153.]
Pi-ä′no (*pe-*) (It.) (161) *a.* soft.
Pī-an′o [*pĭ-ä′no*, or *pĭ-ăn′o*, Wr. 155], *n.* a musical stringed instrument with keys.
Pī-an′o-for′te (163) [so Sm.; *pĭ-ä-no-fōr′tā*, Gd.; *pĭ-a′no-fōr′te*, or *pĭ-an′o-for′te*; often *pĭ-an′o-fōrt*, Wr. 155.]

☞ The pronunciation *pi-an′o-fōrt* is not countenanced by any good orthoëpist except Worcester.

Pī′a-rist.
Pī-as′ter.
Pī-az′za, 170, 189.
Pib′corn.
Pi′broch (*pe′brok*) [so Sm.; *pī′brok*, Wr. Wb. Gd. 155.] [Pibrach, 203.]

☞ Smart says: "Without difference of sound, it is also spelled *pibrach*;" but Worcester pronounces this form of the word *pī′-brăk*.

Pi′ca, 25, 72.
Pic-a-dōr′ (Sp.).
Pic′a-mar.
Pic′ard.
Pic-a-roon′, 122.
Pic-a-yune′, 26, 122.
Pic-ca-dil′ly [so Sm.; *pik′a-dil-ly*, Wr. Gd. 155.]
Pic′ca-lil-lĭ.

Pic'co-lo (It.).
Piç'e-oŭs.
Pick, 16, 181.
Pick'a-nin-ny.
Pick'äxe [Pickax, 203.]
Picked (*pikt*) (Note C, p. 34), *v.* did pick. [*See* Pict, 160.]
Pick'ed (150), *a.* pointed; sharp.
Pick'er.
Pick'er-el, 76, 77.
Pick'et.
Pick'et-ed.
Pick'et-ing.
Pick'ing.
Pic'kle (*pik'l*), 104, 164.
Pic'kled (*pik'ld*), 183.
Pic'kling.
Pick'lock, 206.
Pick'pock-et.
Pick-wick'i-an.
Pic'nic, 171.
Pic-o-tee', 122.
Pic'ro-līte, 152.
Pic'ro-mel, 105.
Pic-ro-phar'ma-co-līte.
Pic'ro-phyll.
Pic-ro-phyl'līte, *or* Pic-roph'yl-līte, 152.
Pic-ros'mīne (*-roz'-*) (152) [so Gd.; *pik'-ros-min*, Wr. 155.]
Pic-ro-tox'īne [Picrotoxin, 203.]
Pict (16, 52), *n.* one of a tribe of Scythians or Germans who settled in Scotland. [*See* Picked, 160.]
Pict'ish, 228.
Pic-to'ri-al, 49, N.; 169.
Pic'ture (*pikt'yur*), 91.
Pic'ture-bŏŏk, 206, Exc. 4.
Pic'tured (*pikt'yurd*).
Pic-tur-esque' (*pikt-yur-esk'*), 122, 171.
Pic'tur-ing (*pikt'yur-*).
Pic'ul [Pecal, Pecul, 203.]
Pic'u-let, 89.
Pid'dle, 164.
Pid'dled (*pid'ld*).
Pid'dler.
Pid'dling.
Pie, 25.

☞ Written also Pi, in the sense of *types thrown confusedly together*; and, in the sense of *a Roman Catholic service-book*, it is sometimes written Pye.

Pīe'bâld, 171.
Piēce (13, 169), *n.* a part, or portion. [*See* Peace, 160.]
Piēced (*pēst*), 165, 183; Note C, p. 34.
Piēce'mēal.
Piēce'ner.
Piēç'er.
Piēç'ing, 183.
Pīed, 25.
Piē droit (Fr.) (*pe drwä*).
Pie'pow-der [Piepoudre, 203. [Law term.]
Piēr (13), *n.* the mass of masonry supporting an arch; — a mole or jetty. [*See* Peer, 160.]
Piēr'age, *n.* toll paid for the use of a pier. [*See* Peerage, 160.]
Piērce [so Sm. Wb. Gd.; *pērs*, or *pers*, Wk. Wr. 155.]
Piērced (*pērst*), 165, 183.
Piēr'cel.
Piērç'er.
Piērç'ing.
Pī-e'ri-an, 49, N.
Piēr'-tā-ble, 164, 206, Exc. 3.
Pi'e-tism (*-tizm*), 136.
Pi'e-tist.
Pī-e-tist'ic.
Pī-e-tist'ic-al.
Pi'e-ty, 169.
Pī-e-zom'e-ter, 108.
Pig, 16, 30, 53.
Pig'eon (*pij'un*) [so Sm. Wb. Gd.; *pij'in*, Wk.; *pij'un*, or *pij'in*, Wr. 155.]
Pig'eon-hole (*pij'un-*).
Pig'eon-liv'ered (*pij'-un-liv'urd*), 205.
Pig'eon-ry (*pij'un-*).
Pig'ger-y (*-gur-*), 169.
Pig'gin (*-ghin*).
Pig'gish (*-ghish*), 138.
Pig'-hĕad-ed.
Pig'-i-ron (*-ī-urn*).
Pig'-lĕad.
[Pigmean, 203. — *See* Pygmean.]
Pig'ment.
Pig-ment'al, 72.
Pig'ment-a-ry, 72.
[Pigmy, 203. — *See* Pygmy.]
Pig-no-ra'tion.

Pig'no-ra-tīve.
Pig'nut, 206.
Pig'ot-īte.
Pig'pen, 206.
Pig'stȳ.
Pig'tāil.
Pig'wid-geon (*-jun*).
Pike, 25.
Pik'ed [so Wk. Wr.; *pīkt*, Sm. Gd. 155.]
Pike'stâff.
Pī-las'ter (122) [*not* pi'-las-tur, 153.]
Pī-las'tered, 150, 165.
[Pilau, 203. — *See Pil-lau.*]
Pilch, 16, 44, Note 2.
Pilch'ard, 135.
Pile, 25.
Pi'le-ate.
Pi'le-āt-ed [so Sm.; *pil'-e-āt-ed*, Wr. Wb. Gd. 155.]
Piled, 165.
Pile'-drīv-er, 209.
Pi'le-oŭs, 100, 169.
Pīl'er, 183.
Piles (*pīlz*), *n. pl.*
Pi'le-us (L.)
Pile'wort (*-wurt*).
Pil'fer, 104.
Pil'fered, 150, 165.
Pil'fer-er.
Pil'fer-ing.
Pil-gar'lic [Pilled-garlic, 203.]
Pil'grim, 80.
Pil'grim-age, 70.
Pī-lif'er-oŭs [so Gd.; *pī-lif'er-us*, Wr. 155.]
Pi'li-form [*pil'i-form*, Wr. 155.]
Pī-lig'er-oŭs (*-lij'-*).
Pīl'ing, 183.
Pill, 16, 172.
Pil'lage, 70.
Pil'laged, 165.
Pil'la-ger.
Pil'la-ging.
Pil'lar, 70, 148, 170.
Pil'lared (*-lurd*).
Pil'lar-ist.
Pil-lâu' (Turkish) [Pilau, 203.]
Pilled-gar'lic [Pilgarlic, 203.]
Pill'ion (*pil'yun*), 170.
Pil'lo-rīed.
Pil'lo-ry.
Pil'lōw (101) [*not* pil'-lur, 148, 153.]
Pil'lōw-case.
Pil'lōwed, 165, 188.

Pil'lōw-ing.
Pil'lōw-y, 93.
Pill'wort (*-wurt*).
Pi-lose' [so Sm. Gd.; *pī-lōs'*, Wr. 155.]
Pi-los'i-ty [so Sm. Gd.; *pī-los'i-ty*, Wk. Wr. 155.]
Pi'lot, 86.
Pi'lot-age.
Pi'lot-ed, 176.
Pi'lot-fish.
Pi'lot-ing.
Pi'loŭs, 100, 169.
Pil'u-lar, 108.
Pim'el-īte, 152.
Pī-men'ta, *or* Pī-men'to, 203.
Pimp, 16.
Pimped (*pimpt*), 64.
Pim'per-nel [Pimpinel, 203.]
Pimp'ing.
Pim'ple, 164.
Pim'pled (*-pld*), 183.
Pim'ply, 93.
Pin, 16.
Pin'a-fore.
Pī-nas'ter.
Pin'case, 206.
Pin'cers (*-surz*), *n. pl.* [Pinchers, 203.]
Pinch, 16, 44, Note 2.
Pinch'beck [*not* pinch'bak, 127, 153.]
Pinched (*pincht*), 41.
Pinch'ers (*-urz*), *n. pl.*

☞ "Commonly spelled *pincers*, in which case it certainly ought not to be pronounced as *pinchers*; yet the identical meaning of the words generally produces this effect: — why not always write the word as coming from the verb?" *Smart.*

Pinch'ing.
Pin'cush-ion (*-kŏŏsh-un*).
Pin-där'ic.
Pin'dar-ism (*-izm*).
Pin'dar-ist.
Pine, 25, 30, 43.
Pin'e-al (169) [so Wk. Wr. Wb. Gd.; *pī'ne-al*, Sm. 155.]
Pine'-ap-ple, 164, 206, Exc. 2.
Pined, 165, 183.
Pine'-mar-ten.
Pīn'er-y.
Pine'-tree, 206, Exc. 4.
Pīn'ey, *n.* a kind of resin. [*See* Piny, 160.]
Pin'fōld.
Pi'nic.
Pīn'ing, 183.
Pin'ion (*-yun*), *n.* & *v.*
Pin'ioned (*-yund*).
Pin'ion-ing (*-yun-*).
Pin'ite, *or* Pī'nite [*pin'īt*, Wr. Wb. Gd.; *pī'nīt*, Sm. 155.]
Pink (*pingk*), 16, 54.
Pinked (*pingkt*), 165.
Pink'er (*-pingk'-*).
Pink'ing (*pingk'-*).
Pin'-mon-ey (*-mun-*).
Pin'nace, 170.
Pin'na-cle, 164, 169.
Pin'nate.
Pin'nāt-ed.
Pin-nat'i-fid, *or* Pin'na-ti-fid [so Wr.; *pin-nat'i-fid*, Gd.; *pin'na-ti-fid*, Sm. 155.]
Pin-nat'i-ped, *or* Pin'na-ti-ped.
Pinned, 165.
Pin'ner, 176.
Pin'ni-form, 108.
Pin'ni-grade.
Pin'ning, 176.
Pin'ni-ped.
Pin'nock, 170.
Pin'non-ade.
Pin'nu-late, 108.
Pin'nule, 26.
Pint, 25.
Pin'tāil.
Pin'tle, 164.
Pīn'y, *a.* abounding with pines; — belonging to the pine. [*See* Piney, 160.]
Pī-o-neer', 122.
Pī-o-neered', 165.
Pī-o-neer'ing.
[Piony, 203.— *See* Peony.]
Pi'oŭs, 100, 169.
Pip, 16, 30.
Pipe, 25, 163.
Piped (*pīpt*), 165; Note C, p. 34.
Pipe'fish.
Pīp'er.
Pip-er-a'ceous (*-shus*).
Pip'er-īne (152) [Piperin, 203.]
Pī-pette' (Fr.) [so Wr.; *pī-pet'*, Gd. 155.]
Pipe'wort (*-wurt*).
Pīp'ing, 183.
Pī-pis'trel.
Pip'it, 66.
Pip'kin.
Pip'pin, 170.
Pi'quan-cy (*pe'kan-sy*) (169) [*See* Piquant.]
Pi'quant (*pe'kant*) [so Sm.; *pik'ant*, Wk. Wr. Wb. Gd. 155.]
Pique (*pēk*), *n.* slight and sudden anger: — *v.* to offend; — to pride. [*See* Peak *and* Peek, 160.]
Piqued (*pēkt*), 165, 183; Note C, p. 34.
Pī-quet' (*pī-ket'*) (121) [Picket, Picquet, 203.]
Piqu'ing (*pēk'ing*).
Pi'ra-cy, 169.
Pī-ra'gua (Sp.) (*pī-rä'gwa*) [so Wr.; *pī-rag'u-a*, Sm.; *pī-raw'ga*, Gd. 155] [Pirogue, 203.]
Pī-ram'e-ter, 108.
Pi'rate, 49, N.
Pi'ra-ted, 183.
Pī-rat'ic, 109.
Pī-rat'ic-al, 108.
Pi'ra-ting.
Pirn, 21, N.
Pi-rōgue' [Piragua, 203.]
Pīr-ou-ette' (*-oo-*), 114.
Pi'san (*pe'zan*).
[Pisasphalt, 203.— *See* Pissasphalt.]
Pis'ca-ry, 72.
Pis-ca-to'ri-al.
Pis'ca-to-ry, 86.
Pis'cēs (L.) (*-sēz*), *n. pl.*
Pis'ci-cult-ure, 91.
Pis'ci-cult-ur-ist (*-yur-*).
Pis'ci-form, 108.
Pis'ci-nal.
Pis'cīne [so Sm.; *pis'sin*, Wr. Wb. Gd. 155.]
Pis-civ'o-roŭs.
Pisé (Fr.) (*pe'zā*).
Pish, 16, 46.
Pi'si-form.
Pis'mire (*piz'-*) [so Wk. Sm.; *pis'mīr*, Wb. Gd.; *piz'mīr*, or *pis'mīr*, Wr. 155.]
Pi'so-līte, 152.
Pis'sas-phalt [Pisasphalt, Pissaphalt, 203.]
Pis'so-phane.
Pis-ta'chio (*-sho*) [so Wk. Wr. Wb. Gd.;

pis-ta'ch'o, Sm. (*See* § 26), 155.]
Pis-ta-reen', 122.
Pis'til, 80.
Pis-til-la'ceous (*-shus*).
Pis'til-late, 73.
Pis til-lif'er-oŭs, 108.
Pis'tol, 86.
Pis-tol-ade'.
Pis-tole', 121.
Pis-tol-et', 122.
Pis'ton, 86.
Pit, 16.
Pit-a-hā'ya.
Pit'a-pat, *n.* & *adv.* [so Sm. Wb. Gd.]

☞ Worcester pronounces the noun with the accent on the first syllable, and the adverb with the accent on the last syllable.

Pitch, 16, 44; Note D, p. 37.
Pitch'blende.
Pitched (*picht*), 41.
Pitch'er.
Pitch'er-plănt.
Pitch'fork.
Pitch'ing.
Pitch'pine.
Pitch'pipe.
Pitch'y, 169.
Pit'e-oŭs (169) [so Sm. Wr. Wb. Gd.; *pich'e-us*, Wk. 134, 155.]
Pit'fall.
Pith (16, 37) [*not* peth, 153.]
Pith'i-ly, 186.
Pith'i-ness.
Pith'y.
Pit'i-a-ble, 164.
Pit'i-a-bly.
Pit'ied, 99.
Pit'i-er.
Pit'i-ful (*-fōōl*).
Pit'i-less.
Pit'man, 196.
Pit'ta-căl, *or* Pit'ta-câl, 203.
Pit'tance, 66, 72.
Pit'ted, 176.
Pit'ting.
Pĭ-tu'i-ta-ry, 72.
Pit'u-ĭte, 152.
Pĭ-tu'i-toŭs.
Pit'y, 93, 170.
Pit'y-ing.
Pit-y-ri'a-sis.
Pit'y-roid.
Pi'u (It.) (*pe'oo*).
Piv'ot, 86.
Piv'ot-al.
Pix [Pyx, 203.]
Pix'ing.
Pix'y.
Plā-ca-bil'i-ty.
Pla'ca-ble (164) [*not* plak'a-bl, 153.]
Pla-card' (121), *n.* & *v.* [*not* plak'ard, 153.]
Pla-card'ed.
Pla-card'ing.
Pla'cate.
Pla'căt-ed.
Pla'căt-ing.
Place, *n.* a particular portion of space: — *v.* to put or set. [*See* Plaice, 160.]
Pla-ce'bo (L.).
Placed (*plāst*), 183.
Place'man, 196.
Pla-cen'ta (L.) [pl. *Pla-cen'tæ* (*-te*), 198.]
Pla-cen'tal.
Pla-cen'ta-ry, 72.
Plaç-en-ta'tion, 143.
Plaç-en-tif'er oŭs, 108.
Pla-cen'ti-form.
Plăç'er (161), *n.* one who places.
Plă'cer, *or* Pla'cer (Sp.) [so Gd.; the Spanish pronunciation is *plah-thĕr'*] (161), *n.* a place where gold is found.
Plaç'id.
Pla-cid'i-ty, 108, 169.
Plăç'ing, 183.
Plaç'i-to-ry, 86.
Plac'oid.
Pla-coid'i-an [Placoidean, 203.]
Pla-fond', 121.
Pla'gal.
Pla'gi-a-rism (*-rizm*) [so Wr. Wb. Gd.; *pla'ja-rizm*, Wk.; *pla'j'a-rizm*, Sm. (*See* § 26) [155.]
Pla'gi-a-rist.
Pla'gi-a-rize.
Pla'gi-a-rized.
Pla'gi-a-riz-ing.
Pla'gi-a-ry [so Wb. Gd.; *pla'ja-ry*, Wk.; *pla'j'a-ry*, Sm. (*See* § 26); *pla'ji-a-ry*, or *pla'ja-ry*, Wr. 155.]
Pla-gi-he'dral.
Pla'gi-os-tome.
Plāgue (*plāg*)(168; Note D, p. 37) [*not* pleg, 127, 153.]
Plāgued (*plāgd*), 165.
Plāgu'er (*plāg'-*), 183.
Plāgu'i-ly, 186.
Plāgu'ing.
Plāgu'y, 171.
Plāice (23), *n.* a species of flat fish. [*See* Place, 160.] [Plaise, 203.]
Plāid (*plăd*), 10.

☞ The Scottish pronunciation is *plăd*, which is current to some extent in England.

Plāid'ing.
Plāin, *n.* level ground: — *a.* smooth; free from difficulty, obscurity, ornament, or disguise. [*See* Plane, 160.]
Plāin'-dēal-ing.
Plāin'ly, 93.
Plāin'ness, 66, N.
Plāin'-spōk-en (*-spōk-n*)
Plāint, 23.
Plāin'tiff [*not* plan'tif, 127, 153.]
Plāin'tĭve, 84.
Plāit (127), *n.* a fold, as of cloth; — *v.* to fold. [*See* Plate, 160.]

☞ "Often wrongly pronounced *plĕt*." *Smart.*

Plāit'ed.
Plāit'ing.
Plan, 10.
Pla-na'ri-an.
Pla-na'ri-oid.
Plan-ceer', 169.
Plan'cher.
Plan'chet.
Plane, *n.* a level superficies; a carpenter's or joiner's tool; the sycamore-tree: — *a.* having an even or flat surface: — *v.* to make smooth. [*See* Plain, 160.]
Planed, 165.
Plān'er.
Plan'et, 66, 170.
Plan-et-a'ri-um, 169.
Plan'et-a-ry, 72.
Plan'et-oid.
Plan-et-oid'al.
Plane'-tree, 206, Exc. 4.
Plan'et-ule.
Plan'et-wheel.
Plan'gent, 45.
Plan-i-fo'li-oŭs [so Sm. Wr.; *pla-nĭ-fo'li-us*, Gd. 155.]

Pla-nim'e-ter.
Plan-i-met'ric.
Plan-i-met'ric-al.
Pla-nim'e-try.
Plăn'ing.
Plăn'ing-mill, 206, Exc. 4.
Plan-i-pen'nate.
Plan-i-pet'al-oŭs [so Sm. Wr.; *plăn-ĭ-pet'-al-us*, Gd. 155.]
Plan'ish, 170.
Plan'ished (*-isht*).
Plan'ish-er.
Plan'ish-ing.
Plan'i-sphere.
Plank (*plangk*), 10, 54.
Planked (*plangkt*).
Plank'ing.
Plank'y.
Planned, 165, 176.
Plan'ner, 170.
Plan'ning.
Pla'no-con'cave (*-kong'-*).
Pla'no-con'ic-al.
Pla'no-con'vex, 224.
Plănt, *n.* & *v.* 10.

☞ "There is a coarse pronunciation of this word, chiefly among the vulgar, which rhymes it with *aunt*." *Walker*.

Plan'taĭn, 96.
Plan'tar, 74.
Plănt-a'tion.
Plănt'ed.
Plănt'er.
Plan'ti-cle, 164.
Plan'ti-grade.
Plănt'ing.
Plănt'like, 206.
Plănt'ule.
Plash.
Plashed (*plasht*).
Plash'ing.
Plash'y.
Plasm (*plazm*), 133, 136.
Plas'ma (*plaz'-*).
Plas-mat'ic (*plaz-*).
Plȧs'ter, *n.* & *v.* [Plaister, 203.]
Plȧs'tered, 150, 165.
Plȧs'ter-er, 77.
Plȧs'ter-ing.
Plăs'tic.
Plas-tiç'i-ty, 169.
Plas-tog'ra-phy.
Plas'tron.
Plat, 10.
Plat'ane [*not* pla'tăn, 127, 153.]
Plat'a-nist.
Plat'band.
Plate, *n.* a shallow table dish: — *v.* to cover with a coating of metal. [*See* Plait, 160.]
Plă-teau' (Fr.) (*-to'*) [*not* plat'o, 153] [Fr. pl. *Plă-teaux'* (*plă-to'*); Eng. pl. Plă-teaus' (*-tōz'*), 198.]
Plăt'ed.
Plate'ful (*-fool*), 197.
Plat'en, 149.
Plăt'er.
Plat-er-esque' (*-esk'*), 122.
Plat'form.
Plat'i-na, 78, 154.

☞ This word is from the Spanish, and is often pronounced, as in that language, *pla-te'na*; but the English, as well as the American orthoëpists, are unanimous in Anglicizing the pronunciation by accenting the first syllable.

Plăt'ing.
Pla-tin'ic.
Plat-i-nif'er-oŭs.
Plat'i-nize, 202.
Plat'i-nized, 183.
Plat'i-nīz-ing.
Plat'i-node.
Plat'i-noid.
Plat'i-noŭs.
Plat'i-num (154, 169) [*See* Note under *Platina*.]
Plat'i-tude, 26, 108.
Pla-tom'e-ter.
Pla-ton'ic.
Pla-ton'ic-al.
Pla'to-nism (*-nizm*).
Pla'to nist [so Sm. Wr. Wb. Gd.; *plat'o-nist*, Wk. 155.]
Pla'to-nize, 202.
Pla'to-nized.
Pla'to-nīz-ing.
Pla-toon', 121.
Plat'ted, 176.
Plat'ter, 170.
Plat'ting.
Plat-y-ceph'a-loŭs.
Plat-y-cri'nite.
Plat'y-pod.
Pla-typ'ter.
Plat'y-pus, 169.
Plat'y-rhine (*-rīn*).
Plat'y-some (*-sōm*).
Plâu'dit.
Plâu'dit-o-ry, 86.
Plâus-i-bil'i-ty (*plawz'-*), 119, 169.
Plâus'i-ble (*plawz'-*), 164, 169.
Plâus'i-bly (*plawz'-*).
Plâu'sĭve, 84.
Plāy, 23, 56, Rem.
Plāy'bill, 206.
Plāyed, 165.
Plāy'er.
Plāy'fel-lōw.
Plāy'ful (*-fool*), 180.
Plāy'house.
Plāy'ing.
Plāy'mate.
Plāy'thing.
Plēa (13) [pl. Pleas (*plēz*), 189. — *See* Please, 160.]
Plēad, 13.

☞ "It is a regular verb: yet the Scotch use *pled*, or *plead*, for the imperfect tense and past participle, instead of *pleaded*; as also do many Americans, especially in conversation." *Worcester*.

Plēad'a-ble, 164, 169.
Plēad'ed.
Plēad'er.
Plēad'ing.
Plĕas'ant (*plez'-*), 15.
Plĕas'ant-ry (*plez'-*)
Plēase (*plēz*), *v.* to gratify. [*See* Pleas (pl. of Plea), 160.]
Plēased (*plēzd*), 183.
Plēas'er (*plēz'-*).
Plēas'ing (*plēz'-*).
Plĕas'ur-a-ble (*plezh'-ur-a-bl*), 164, 171.
Plĕas'ur-a-bly (*plezh'-*).
Plĕas'ure (*plezh'ur*), 47, N.; 91.
Plĕas'ur-ing (*plezh'-*).
Ple-be'ian (*-yan*) (112) [*not* ple'be-an, 153.]
Ple-be'ian-ism (*-yan-izm*), 106, 136.
Ple-be'ian-ize (*-yan-*).
Ple-be'ian-ized (*-yan-*).
Ple-be'ian-īz-ing (*-yan-*).
Ple-bis'o-list.
Ple-bis'cit.
Plec'tog-nāthe [Plectognath, 203.]
Plec-tog-nath'ic.
Plec-tog'na-thoŭs.
Plec'tro-pome.
Plec'trum (L.).
[Pled. — *See* Plead.]
Pledge (*plej*), 15, 45.

Pledged (*plejd*), 183.
Pledg-ee′ (*plej-*) (118) [Law term,—correlative of *Pledgeor*.]
Pledge-or′ (183) [Law term,—correlative of *Pledgee*.]
Pledg′er (*plej′-*).
Pledg′er-y (*plej′-*).
Pledg′et (*plej′-*).
Pledg′ing (*plej′-*), 183.
Ple′iad (*-yad*) (51) [*not* pli′ad, 153.]
Ple′ia-dēs (*-ya-dēz*) (L.), *n. pl.* [*not* pli′a-dēz, 153.]
[Pleiocene, 203.—*See* Pliocene.]
Pleis′to-cene.
Ple′na-ri-ly [*See* Plenary.]
Plen′ar-ty.
Ple′na-ry [so Sm. Wb. Gd.; *plen′a-ry*, or *ple′na-ry*, Wk. Wr. 155.]
Plen′i-corn.
Plen-i-lu′nar.
Ple-nip′o-tence.
Ple-nip′o-ten-cy.
Ple-nip′o-tent.
Plen-i-po-ten′tia-ry (*-sha-*) (72, 171) [so Wk. Wb. Gd.; *plen-i-po-ten′sh′ŭr-y*, Sm. (*See* § 26); *plen-i-po-ten′shi-a-ry*, Wr. 155.]
Ple′nist.
Plen′i-tude (26, 108) [*not* plen′i-tood, 153.]
Plen-i-tūd-i-na′ri-an, 49, N.
Plen-i-tūd′i-na-ry, 72.
Plen′te-oŭs [so Sm. Wr. Wb. Gd.; *plen′che-us*, Wk. 134, 155.]
Plen′ti-ful (*-fŏŏl*), 180, 186.
Plen′ty.
Ple′num (L.).
Ple-och′ro-ic (*-ok′-*).
Ple-och′ro-ism (*-ok′ro-izm*) [so Wr. *ple′o-kro-izm*, Gd. 155.]
Ple-o-chro′ma-tism (*-kro′ma-tizm*).
Ple-o-chro-mat′ic (*-kro-*) [*ple-o-kro′-ma-tik*, Gd. 155.]
Ple-och′ro-oŭs (*-ok′-*).
Ple-o-mor′phism(*-fizm*).
Ple-o-mor′phoŭs.
Ple′o-nasm (*-nazm*),133.
Ple-o-nas′tic, 109.
Ple-o-nas′tic-al, 108.
Ple-si-o-mor′phism (*-fizm*).
Ple-si-o-mor′phoŭs.
Ple′si-o-sâur.
Ple-si-o-sâu′rus [pl. Ple-si-o-sâu′rī, 198.]
Pleth′o-ra [*not* ple′tho-ra, *nor* ple-tho′ra,153.]
Ple-thŏr′ic (109) [so Wk. Sm.; *pleth′o-rik*, Wb. Gd.; *ple-thŏr′ik*, or *pleth′o-rik*, Wr. 155.]
Ple-thŏr′ic-al.
Pleū′ra, 26, 72.
Pleū′ral.
Pleū′ri-sy (169) [Plurisy, 203.—*See* Note under *Plurisy*.]
Pleū-rit′ic.
Pleū-rit′ic-al.
Pleū-ro-pĕr-ip-neū′mo-ny, 116.
Pleū-ro-pneū-mo′ni-a (*-nū-*), 162.
Plex′i-form, 108.
Plex-im′e-ter, *or* Plex-om′e-ter, 108, 203.
Plex′ure, 91.
Plex′us, 169.
Plī-a-bil′i-ty.
Plī′a-ble, 164.
Plī′a-bly.
Plī′an-cy, 169.
Plī′ant, 72.
Plī′cate.
Plī′cāt-ed.
Plic′a-tūre,44,Note 1; 90.
Pliç-i-den′tīne.
Plied, 186.
Plī′ers (*-urz*), *n. pl.* [Plyers, 203.]
Plī′form.
Plight (*plīt*), 162.
Plight′ed (*plīt′-*).
Plight′er (*plīt′-*).
Plight′ing (*plīt′-*).
Plinth, 16, 37.
Plī′o-cene [Pleiocene, 203.]

☞ "The word in both ways of spelling has the same pronunciation. Mr. Lyell, the author of the word, . . . spells, in the more English way, *Pliocene*; and correspondently, *Miocene*." — *Smart*.

Plod, 18.
Plod′ded, 176.
Plod′der.
Plod′ding.
Plot, 18.
Plo-ti′nist [*plot′i-nist*, Wr. 155.]

☞ This word is derived from the proper name *Plo-ti′nus*, in which the accent is on the second syllable.

Plot′ted, 176.
Plot′ter.
Plot′ting.
Plough (*plou*), *n.* & *v.* (28, 162) [Plow, 203.]

☞ Goodrich gives both forms of this word, but he prefers *plow*. "Plow," he remarks, "is the spelling of the English Bible, and is preferable as more nearly representing the sound."

Plough′a-ble (*plou′-*), 164.
Plough′boy (*plou′-*).
Ploughed (*ploud*), 165.
Plough′er (*plou′-*).
Plough′ing (*plou′-*).
Plough′man (*plou′-*), 196.
Plough′share (*plou′-shêr*).
Plough′tāil (*plou′-*).
Plov′er (*pluv′-*), 22, 156.
[Plow, 203.—*See* Plough.]
Pluck, 22, 181.
Plucked (*plukt*), 156.
Pluck′i-ly.
Pluck′ing.
Pluck′y.
Plug, 22, 53.
Plugged (*plugd*), 165, 176.
Plug′ging (*-ghing*), 138.
Plum (22), *n.* a fruit of many varieties. [*See* Plumb, 160.]
Plu′mage, 70.
Plumb (162), *n.* a plummet:—*a.* perpendicular to the horizon:—*v.* to adjust by a plumb-line. [*See* Plum, 160.]
Plum-ba′gīne [Plumbagin, 203.]
Plum-bag′i-noŭs (*-baj′-*).
Plum-ba′go, 122.
Plum′be-an, 110.
Plum′be-oŭs.
Plumb′er (*plum′-*), 162.
Plumb′er-y (*plum′-*).
Plum′bic.
Plum-bif′er-oŭs, 108.

Plumb′ing (*plum′*-).
Plumb′-line (*plum′*-), 206, Exc. 3.
Plume, 26.
Plumed, 165.
Plume′let, 185.
Plūm′er-y, 233, Exc.
Plu-mig′er-oŭs (-*mij′*-).
Plu-mil′i-form, 108.
Plūm′ing, 183.
Plu′mi-ped [Plumipede, 203.]
Plum′met, 170.
Plum′ming.
Plu-mose′ [so Wr.; *plu′mōs*, Wb. Gd. 155.]
Plu′moŭs, 100.
Plump, 22, 64.
Plump′er.
Plum′-tree, 206, Exc. 4.
Plu′mule, 26.
Plu′mu-lose.
Plūm′y, 169.
Plun′der, 77.
Plun′der-age.
Plun′dered (-*durd*).
Plun′der-er, 77.
Plun′der-ing.
Plunge, 22, 45; Note D, p. 37.
Plunged, 165, 183.
Plung′er (*plunj′*-).
Plung′ing (*plunj′*-).
Plu′per-fect [so Wr.; *plu-per′fekt*, Gd. 155.]
Plu′ral, 26, 49, N.
Plu′ral-ism (-*izm*), 136.
Plu′ral-ist.
Plu-ral′i-ty, 108, 169.
Plu′ral-ize, 202.
Plu′ral-ized, 183.
Plu′ral-iz-ing.
Plu-ri-fa′ri-oŭs.
Plu-ri-fo′li-ate.
Plu-ri-lit′er-al.
Plu-ri-loc′u-lar, 108.
Plu-ri-pres′ence (-*prez′*-).
Plu′ri-sy.

☞ "A word used by our old dramatists to signify superabundance, and being pronounced exactly as *pleurisy*, the disease, liable to be alluded to also as a disease." *Smart.*

Plus (L.), 22.
Plush, 22, 46.
Plush′er.
Plu-to′ni-an, 78, 169.
Plu-ton′ic, 109.
Plu′to-nism (-*nizm*).
Plu′to-nist.
Plu′vi-al, 72, 78.
Plu-vi-am′e-ter [Pluviometer, 203.]
Plu-vi-a-met′ric.
Plu-vi-a-met′ric-al.
Plu′vi-oŭs, 78.
Plȳ, 25, 64.
[Plyers, 203. — *See* Pliers.]
Ply′ing.
Pneū-mat′ic (*nu*-), 162, 171.
Pneū-mat′ic-al (*nu*-).
Pneū-mat′ics (*nu*-), 162.
Pneū-mat′o-cele (*nu*-).
Pneū-ma-to-log′ic-al (*nu-ma-to-loj′*-).
Pneū-ma-tol′o-gist (*nu*-), 108.
Pneū-ma-tol′o-gy (*nu*-.)
Pneū-ma-tom′e-ter (*nu*-).
Pneū-mo-bran′chi-ate (*nu-mo-brang′ki-āt*), 171.
Pneū-mo-gas′tric (*nu*-).
Pneū-mog′ra-phy (*nu*-).
Pneū-mol′o-gy (*nu*-), 108.
Pneū-mom′e-ter (*nu*-).
Pneū-mom′e-try (*nu*-).
Pneū-mo′ni-a (*nu*-), 162.
Pneū-mon′ic (*nu*-).
Pneū-mo-nit′ic (*nu*-).
Pneu-mo-ni′tis (*nu*-).
Pneū′mo-ny (*nu′*-).
Pnyx (Gr.) (*niks*), 162.
Pōach, 24, 44.
Pōach′ard [Pochard, 203.]
Pōached (*pōcht*), 165; Note C, p. 34.
Pōach′er.
Pōach′ing.
Pōach′y.
Poc-coon′, 121.
Pōch′ard [Poachard, 203.]
Pock, 18, 181.
Pock′et, 76.
Pock′et-bŏŏk, 206, Exc. 4.
Pock′et-com′pass (-*kum′*-), 205.
Pock′et-ed, 176.
Pock′et-hand′ker-chief (-*hang′kur-chif*), 205.
Pock′et-ing.
Pock′-fret′ten (-*tn*).
Pock′mark.
Pock′y.
Po′co (It.).
Poc′u-li-form.

☞ This word is an exception to the general rule by which words ending in *i-form* are accented on the antepenult.

Pod′a-gra [*pod′a-gra*, or *po-dag′ra*, Wr. 155]
Pod′a-gral.
Po-dag′ric, 109.
Po-dag′ric-al.
Pod′a-groŭs.
Po-des′ta (It.).
Po′di-um (L.).
Pod′o-gyn (-*jin*).
Po-dol′o-gy.
Pod-oph-thal′mic.
Pod′o-sperm.
Po′e-bird.
Pœ′cil-īte (*pe′*-) [Poikilite, 203.]
Pœ-cil-it′ic (*pe*-) [so Sm. Gd.; *pes-i-lit′ik*, Wr. 155] [Poikilitic, 203.]
Pœ-cil′o-pod (*pe*-).
Po′em, 76, 144.
Pœ-nol′o-gy [Penology, 203.]
Po′e-sy, 169.
Po′et, 24, 76.
Po′et-as-ter.
Po′et-ess.
Po-et′ic.
Po-et′ic-al.
Po-et′ic-al-ly.
Po-et′ics, 109.
Po′et-ry, 93.
[Poggy, Pogy, 203. — *See* Paugie.]
Pōh, 24, 139.
[Pohagen, 203. — *See* Pauhaugen.]
Poig′nan-cy (*poi′*-), 162.
Poig′nant (*poi′*-), 156, 171.
[Poikilite, 203. — *See* Pœcilite.]
[Poikilitic, 203. — *See* Pœcilitic.]
Point, 27.
Point′blank, *n. a.* & *ad.* [so Gd.; *point-blangk′*, n. *point′blangk*, a. & ad. Wr. 155.]
Point d'appui (Fr.) (*pwang-dap′pwe*), 154.
Point′ed.
Point′er.
Point′ing.
Points′man, 214.
Poise (*poiz*), 27, 40.
Poised (*poizd*), 183.
Pois′ing (*poiz′*-).

Poi′son (*poi′zn*), 149.
Poi′soned (*-znd*).
Poi′son-er (*-zn-*).
Poi′son-ing (*-zn-*).
Poi′son-oŭs (*-zn-*).
Poke, 24, 163.
Poked (*pōkt*), 165, 183; Note C, p. 34.
Pōk′er.
Pōke′weed.
Pōk′ing, 183.
Po-lac′ca (170), *n.* a kind of vessel with three masts, common in the Mediterranean; — a Polish air and dance. [Polacre (in the first sense), 203.]
Po-lä′cre (164) [*not* po′-la-kur, *nor* po-la′kur, 153] [Polacca, 203.]
Po′lar, *a.* pertaining to the pole or poles. [*See* Poller, 160.]
Po-lar-im′e-ter, 108.
Po-lar-im′e-try.
Po-lăr′is-cope.
Po-lăr′i-ty, 108, 169.
Po′lar-īz-a-ble, 164.
Po-lar-īz-a′tion.
Po′lar-ized.
Po′lar-īz-er.
Po′lar-īz-ing.
Po′lar-y.
Pōl′der.
Pole (24, 163), *n.* one of the extremities of an axis; — a native or an inhabitant of Poland: — *v.* to furnish with poles; — to carry on poles. [*See* Poll, 160.]
Pole′-ăxe (206, Exc. 2). [Pole-ax, 203.]
Pole′cat.
Poled (165), *v.* did pole. [*See* Polled, 160.]
Pol′e-march (*-mark*).
Po-lem′ic.
Po-lem′ic-al.
Po-lem′ics.
Pol′e-mist.
Po-lem′o-scope.
Pole′star, 206.
Po-lice′ (*-lēs′*), 121, 171.
Po-lice′man (*-lēs′-*), 196.
Pol′i-cied (*-sid*).
Pol′i-cy, 169.
Pōl′ing (183), *part.* from *Pole.* [*See* Polling, 160.]
Pol′ish (104, 161, 170), *v.* to smooth and brighten, as by friction: — *n.* gloss produced by friction.
Po′lish (161), *a.* pertaining to Poland, or its inhabitants.
Pol′ish-a-ble, 164.
Pol′ished (*-isht*).
Pol′ish-er.
Pol′ish-ing.
Po-lite′, 121.
Po-lite′ness, 185.
Pol-i-tesse′ (Fr.).
Pol′i-tic, 109, 170.
Po-lit′ic-al.
Po-lit′ic-al-ly.
Pol-i-tĭ′cian (*-tish′an*).
Pol′i-tic-ly.
Pol′i-tics, 109.
Pol′i-ty, 78, 93.
Pōl′ka, 72, 130.
Pōll (161), *n.* a head; an election: — *v.* to cut or clip off; — to register, as a vote. [*See* Pole, 160.]
Pŏll (161), *n.* the familiar name for a parrot; — one who, at Cambridge University, Eng., does not try for honors, but is contented to obtain a degree merely.

☞ In the latter sense, pronounced *pōll* by Worcester, but *pŏll* by Smart. The word, in this use of it, is an abbreviation of *οἱ πολλοί* (*hoy pol′-loy*), the multitude.

Pol′lard, 72.
Pōll′-book.
Pōlled, *v.* did poll. [*See* Poled, 160.]
Pol′len, 66, 170.
Pōll′er, *n.* one who polls. [*See* Polar, 160.]
Pol-liç-i-ta′tion.
Pōll′ing, *part.* from *Poll.* [*See* Poling, 160.]
Pol-li-nif′er-oŭs, 108.
Pol′li-nose.
Pol′li-wig.

☞ Worcester says of this word, that it is provincial in England; and that it is "vulgarly called, in the United States, *polliwog*."

Pōll′-tax.
Pol-lute′, 103.
Pol-lūt′ed, 183.
Pol-lūt′er.
Pol-lūt′ing.
Pol-lu′tion.
Pol′lux.
Polonaise (Fr.) (*po-lo-nāz′*).
Po-lo-nese′ (*-nēz′*).
Po-lo′ny [so Gd.; *pol′-o-ny*, Wr. 155], *n.* a dried sausage.

☞ "Probably abridged from *Bologna-sausage*." *Goodrich.*

Pōlt.
Pol-troon′, 121.
Pol-troon′er-y.
Pol′ver-īne, 152.
Pol′y- [A prefix in words of Greek origin.]
Pol-y-a-cous′tic (28) [so Sm. Wr. Wb. Gd.; *po-ly-a-kous′tik*, Wk. 155.]
Pol-y-a-del′phi-a.
Pol-y-a-del′phi-an.
Pol-y-a-del′phoŭs.
Pol-y-an′dri-a.
Pol-y-an′dri-an.
Pol-y-an′droŭs.
Pol-y-an′dry.
Pol-y-an′thus [so Sm. Wr. Wb. Gd.; *po-lȳ-an′thus*, Wk. 155] [Polyanthos, Wk. 203.]
Pol′y-ärch-ist (*-ärk-*).
Pol′y-arch-y (*-ark*), 52.
Pol-y-ba′sic.
Po-lyb′a-sīte, 152.
Pol-y-car′poŭs.
Pol′y-chord (*-kord*).
Pol′y-chrest (*-krest*).
Pol′y-chro-īte (*-kro-*).
Pol-y-chro-mat′ic (*-kro-*), 108.
Pol′y-chro-my (*-kro-*).
Pol-y-chro′ni-oŭs (*-kro′-*) [so Wr.; *pol-i-krŏn′i-us*, Sm. 155.]
Pol-y-co-tyl-e′don, 122.
Pol-y-co-tyl-e′don-oŭs [*See* Cotyledonous.]
Po-lyc′ra-cy, 169.
[Polyedron, 203. — *See* Polyhedron.]
Pol-y-em-bry′o-nate.
Pol-y-em-brȳ-on′ic.
Pol-y-em′bry-o-ny, 93.
Pol′y-foil.
Pol-y-ga′mi-a.
Pol-y-ga′mi-an.
Po-lyg′a-mist.

Po-lyg'a-moŭs.
Po-lyg'a-my, 171.
Pol-y-gas'tri-an.
Pol-y-gas'tric.
Po-lyg'e-noŭs (-*lij'*-).
Pol'y-glŏt, 171.
Pol'y-gon.
Po-lyg'o-nal, 108.
Pol-y-gon-om'e-try.
Po-lyg'o-noŭs.
Po-lyg'o-ny.
Pol'y-gram.
Pol'y-grăph, 127.
Pol-y-graph'ic.
Pol-y-graph'ic-al.
Po-lyg'ra-phy.
Pol'y-gyn (-*jin*).
Pol-y-gyn'i-a (-*jin'*-).
Pol-y-gyn'i-an, 45.
Po-lyg'y-noŭs (-*lij'*-).
Po-lyg'y-ny (-*lij'*-).
Pol-y-he'dral.
Pol-y-hed'ric-al.
Pol-y-he'droŭs.
Pol-y-he'dron [*pl.* Pol-y-he'dra, 198] [Polyedron, 203.]
Pol-y-hy'drīte, 152.
Pol-y-hym'ni-a [Polymnia, 203.]
Pol-y-math'ic.
Po-lym'a-thy, 108.
Po-lym'er-ism (-*izm*).
Po-lym'er-oŭs.
Pol-y-mig'nīte, 152.
Po-lym'ni-a [Polyhymnia, 203.]
Pol'y-morph.
Pol-y-morph'ic.
Pol-y-morph'ism(-*izm*), 136.
Pol-y-morph'oŭs.
Pol'y-morph-y.
Pol'y-neme.
Pol-y-ne'si-a (-*ne'zhĭ-a*) [so Wr.; *pol-y-ne'zi-a*, or *pol-y-nēz'ya*, Sm.; *pol-y-ne'zha*, Wb. Gd. 155.]
Pol-y-ne'si-an (-*ne'zhĭ-an*).
Pol-y-no'mi-al, 171.
Pol-y-om'ma-toŭs, 170.
Pol-y-on'o-moŭs.
Pol-y-on'o-my.
Pol-y-op'tron.
Pol-y-o-rä'ma [so Gd.; *pol-y-o-rā'ma*, Wr. 155.]
Pol'yp [Polype, 203.]
Po-lyp'a-roŭs.
Po-lyp'a-ry, 72.
Pol'ȳpe, *or* Pol'y-pe [*pol'i-pe*, Sm.; *pol'i-pe*, or *pol'ip*, Wr. 155] [Polyp, 203.]
Pol-y-pe'an, 110.
Pol-y-pet'al-oŭs, 100.
Po-lyph'a-goŭs.
Pol-y-phar'ma-cy, 169.
Pol-y-phon'ic, 109.
Po-lyph'o-nism (-*nizm*).
Po-lyph'o-nist.
Po-lyph'o-ny.
Pol'y-phore.
Pol-y-phyl'loŭs, *or* Po-lyph'yl-loŭs. [*See* Adenophyllous.]
Pol'yp-īde [Polypid, 203.]
Po-lyp'i-dom, 169.
Pol-yp-if'er-ous.
Pol-yp-ip'a-roŭs.
Pol'yp-ode.
Po-lyp'o-dy.
Pol'yp-oid.
Po-lyp'o-rīte, 152.
Po-lyp'o-roŭs.
Pol'y-poŭs, *a.* pertaining to, or resembling, a polypus. [*See* Polypus, 160.]
Pol-y-prag-mat'ic.
Pol-y-prag-mat'ic-al.
Pol-y-pris-mat'ic (-*priz*-).
Po-lyp'to-ton (L.).
Pol'y-pus (169), *n.* a polype; — a tumor in a mucous membrane, as in that of the nose. [*See* Polypous, 160] [L. pl. *Pol'y-pī*; Eng. pl. Pol'y-pus-es (-*ez*), 198.]
Pol-y-sche'ma-tist (-*ske*-).
Pol'y-scope.
Pol-y-sep'a-loŭs.
Pol'y-sperm.
Pol-y-sperm'oŭs.
Pol-y-spo'roŭs.
Pol'y-style.
Pol-y-syl-lab'ic, 116.
Pol-y-syl-lab'ic-al.
Pol-y-syl-lab'i-cism (-*sizm*), 171.
Pol-y-syl'la-bism (-*bizm*).
Pol'y-syl-la-ble, 126,164.
Pol-y-syn'de-ton.
Pol-y-syn-thet'ic.
Pol-y-syn-thet'ic-al.
Pol-y-tech'nic (-*tek'*-).
Pol-y-tech'nic-al(-*tek'*-).
Pol-y-thal'a-moŭs.
Pol'y-the-ism (-*izm*).
Pol'y-the-ist.
Pol-y-the-ist'ic.
Pol-y-the-ist'ic-al.
Po-lyt'o-moŭs.
Pol-y-zo'a, *n. pl.* [*See* Polyzoon.]
Pol-y-zo'an.
Pol-y-zo'a-ry.
Pol-y-zo'nal.
Pol-y-zo'on [so Wr.; *po-liz'o-on*, Sm. 155.] [pl. Pol-y-zo'a, 198.]
Pom'ace (*pum'*-), *n.* the substance of apples after the juice is expressed. [*See* Pumice, 148] [Pommace, 203.]
Po-ma'ceous (-*shus*), 112.
Po-made' [*not* po-mäd', 127, 153.]
Po-man'der.
Po-ma'tum, 169.
Pome, 24.
Pome-gran'ate (*pum*-), 122, 171.
[Pomelion, 203. — *See* Pommelion.]
Pŏm'ey, 98, 169.
Pŏm'fret.
Po-mif'er-oŭs.
Pom'mage (*pum'*-), 170.
Pom'mel (*pum'*-) (22, 170) [Pummel, 203.]
Pom-me'li-on, *or* Pom-mel'ion (-*yun*) [*pom-me'lĭ-on*, Sm.; *pom-mĕl'yun*, Gd. 155] [Pomelion (*po-mĕl'yun*), Wr. 203.]
Pom'melled (*pum'-meld*) [Pommeled, Wb. Gd. 203. — *See* 177, and Note E, p. 70.]
Pom'mel-ling (*pum'*-) (177) [Pommeling, Wb. Gd. 203.]
Pŏm-o-log'ic-al (-*loj'*-) [so Wr.; *po-mo-loj'ik-al*, Gd. 155.]
Po-mol'o-gist.
Po-mol'o-gy, 108.
Po-mo'na.
Pomp, 18, 64.
Pom'pet, 76, 230.
Pom'pho-lyx.
[Pompion (*pump'-yun*) [so Sm.; *pum'-pi-un*, Wr. Gd. 155], 203. — *See* Pumpkin.]
Pomp-os'i-ty, 108, 169.

Pomp′oŭs, 100, 228.
Pomp′tĭne (152) [Pontine, 203.]
Pon′cho.
Pond, 18.
Pon′der, 77.
Pon-der-a-bil′i-ty.
Pon′der-a-ble, 164, 169.
Pon′der-ance.
Pon′dered (*-durd*), 150.
Pon′der-er, 77.
Pon′der-ing.
Pon-der-os′i-ty.
Pon′der-oŭs, 100.
Pond′weed.
Pone, 24.
Po′nent, 76, 127.
[Poney, 203. — *See* Pony.]
Pon-gee′, 45.
Pon′go (*pong′-*), 54, 86.
Pon′iard (*-yurd*) (51) [*not* pun′yurd, *nor* poin′yurd, 153.]
Pons as-i-no′rum (L.) (*ponz*).
Pon′tac.
Pon′tage, 169.
Pon-tee′ [so Sm. Wb. Gd.; *pon′tee,* Wr. 155.]
Pon′tic, 200.
Pon′tiff, 171.
Pon-tif′ic, 178.
Pon-tif′ic-al.
Pon-tif′i-cate.
Pon′tĭne (152) [Pomptine, 203.]
Pon-to-niēr′, *or* Ponton-niēr′, 114, 122, 203.
Pon-toon′, 121.
Pont-vo-lant′.
Po′ny [Poney, 203.]
Poo′dle, 164.
Pooh, 19, 139.
Pool, 19.
Pool′er.
Pool′ing.
Pool′snipe.
Poop, 19, 30.
Pooped (*poopt*), *v.*
Poop′ed, *or* Pooped (*poopt*) [so Wr.; *poop′ed,* coll. *poopt,* Sm.; *poopt,* Gd. 155], *a.*
Poop′ing.
Poor, 19, 49, 135.
Poor′house, 216.
Poor′jŏhn (*-jon*) [so Sm. Wb. Gd.; *poor-jon′*, Wk. Wr. 155.]
Poor′law, 221.
Poor′-rate, 206, Exc. 1.
Pop, 18, 30.
Pope, 24, 163.
Pope′dom, 169, 185.
Pope′jōan [so Sm.; *pōp-jōn′*, Wk. Gd. Wr. 155.]
Pōp′er-y, 169.
Pop′gun.
Pop′in-jāy.
Pōp′ish, 183.
Pop′lar, 72.
Pop′lin, 80.
Pop-lit′e-al.
Pop-lit′ic.
Popped (*popt*), 165, 176; Note C, p. 34.
Pop′pet.
Pop′ping, 176.
Pop′py, 93, 170.
Pop′u-lace, 89.
Pop′u-lar, 108, 169.
Pop-u-lăr′i-ty.
Pop-u-lăr-ĭ-za′tion.
Pop′u-lar-ize, 106, 202.
Pop′u-lar-ized.
Pop′u-lar-īz-er.
Pop′u-lar-īz-ing, 183.
Pop′u-lar-ly.
Pop′u-late.
Pop′u-lāt-ed, 183.
Pop′u-lāt-ing.
Pop u-la′tion.
Pop′u-lĭne [Populin, 203.]
Pop′u-loŭs.
Por′cate.
Por′cāt-ed.
Por′ce-laĭn (17, 96) [so Gd.; *pors′lān,* Sm.; *por′se-lan,* or *pōr′se-lān,* Wr.; *pōr′se-lān,* Wk. 155.]
Por-cel-la′ne-ous (171) [so spelled by Sm. Wb. Gd. — Porcelaneous, Wr. 203.]

☞ "The *l* is doubled as from the Italian form of the word." *Smart.*

Pōrch, 24, 49, 135.
Por′cīne (152) [so Sm. Gd.; *por′sĭn,* Wr. 155.]
Por′cu-pīne, 89.
Pore (24, 49), *n.* a minute opening or passage in the skin or other substances: — *v.* to examine any thing with steady attention. [*See* Pour, 160.]
Pored, 165.
[Porgee, Porgy, 203. — *See* Paugie.]
Po-rif′er-an.
Po′ri-form, 49, N.; 108.
Pōr′i-ness.
Pōr′ing.
Po′rism (*-rizm*), 49, N.
Po-ris-mat′ic (*-riz-*).
Po-ris-mat′ic-al (*-riz-*).
Po-ris′tic.
Po-ris′tic-al.
Po′rīte, 152.
Pōrk, 24, 49, 135.
Pōrk′er.
Po-ros′i-ty.
Po-rot′ic.
Po′roŭs, 169.
[Porpess, Porpesse, 203. — *See* Porpoise.]
Por-phy-ra′ceous (*-shus*), 112.
Por-phy-rit′ic, 109.
Por-phy-rit′ic-al, 108.
Por′phy-ry, 93, 135.
Por′poise (*-pus*) (171) [Porpess, Porpesse, Porpus, 203.]
Por-ra′ceous(*-shus*),112.
Por-rect′.
Por-rect′ed.
Pŏr′ridge, 48, 66, 169.
Pŏr′rin-ger, 170.
Pōrt (24), *n.* a harbor; — the left side of a ship; — bearing; — a kind of wine. [*See* Porte, 160.]
Pōrt-a-bil′i-ty.
Pōrt′a-ble, 164, 169.
Pōrt′age, 70.
Pōr′tal, 72.
Pōr′tate.
Port′-crāy′on (205) [*pōrt′krā-un,* Wr. Gd.; *pōrt-kra′un,* Sm. 155.]
Pōrt-cul′lis.
Pōrte (24), *n.* the Turkish court or government. [*See* Port, 160.]
Pōrte-feuille (Fr.) (*-fōōl′ye*), 154.
Pōrte-mon-nāie′ (Fr.).
Por-tend′, 103.
Por-tend′ed.
Por-tend′ing.
Por-tent′, *n.* 121.
Por-tent′ĭve.
Por-tent′oŭs.
Pōr′ter, 77.
Pōr′ter-age, 70, 169.

Pŏr′ter-ess [Portress, 203.]
Pōrt-fōl′io (-yo) [so Sm. Wb. Gd.; pōrt-fo′li-o, Wk.; port-fo′li-o, or pōrt-fōl′yo, Wr. 155] [pl. Pōrt-fōl′iōs (-yōz), 192.]
Pōrt′-hole, 206, Exc. 3.
Pōr′ti-co (78, 86) [so Sm. Wr. Wb. Gd.; por′ti-ko, Wk. 155] [pl. Pōr′ti-cōs (-kōz), 192.]
Pōr′tion, 169.
Pōr′tioned (-shund), 165.
Pōr′tion-er.
Pōr′tion-ing.
Pōr′tion-ist.
Pōrt′li-ness, 186.
Pōrt′ly, 93.
Pōrt-man′teau (-to), 189.
Pōr′trāit [not por′trāt, 153.]
Pōr′trāit-ūre, 90.
Pōr-trāy′, 56, Rem.
Pōr-trāy′al, 72.
Pōr-trāyed′, 187.
Pōr-trāy′er.
Pōr-trāy′ing.
Pōr′tress [Porteress, 203.]
Pōrt′so-ken (-so-kn), 149.
Pōrt′-tōll, 206, Exc. 1.
Pōrt′-town, 66, N.
Pōr′tu-guese (-ghēz), 171
Por-tu-lac′ca [so Gd.— Portulaca (pōr-tu-la′ka), Wr. 203]
Pōrt-wâr′den (-wor′dn).
Pōr′y, 49, N.
Pose (pōz), 24, 40.
Posed (pōzd), 165.
Pōs′er (pōz′-), 183.
Pōs′ing (pōz′-).
Pos′it-ed (poz′-).
Po-sĭ′tion (-zish′un).
Pos′i-tĭve (poz′-), 84.
Pos′i-tiv-ism (poz′i-tiv-izm), 183.
Pos′i-tiv-ist (poz′-).
Pos-o-log′ic (-loj′-).
Pos-o-log′ic-al (-loj′-).
Po-sol′o-gy [so Wr. Gd.; po-zol′o-jy, Sm. 155.]
Pos′po-līte, 152.
Pos′se (L.).
Pos′se-com-i-ta′tus (L.).
Pos-sess′ (poz-zes′) [so Wk. Sm. Wr.; pos-ses′, Wb. Gd. 155.]

☞ "*Possess* is, by the English orthoëpists, pronounced *pozzess*; but why not, then, pronounce *assess, assist, assassin, concession, obsession*, with the sound of *z*? Can any good reason be assigned for making *possess* an exception to the pronunciation of this class of words?" *Webster*. — Dr. Webster seems to have supposed that *possess* is the only exception to the general rule that *s*, when doubled, preserves its aspirate sound; but such is not the fact. In *dissolve, hussar, hussy, scissors*, and, according to some orthoëpists, in *hyssop*, the *s*, though doubled, is vocal, or has the sound of *z*. All these words, except the last, are correctly but inconsistently pronounced by Webster and Goodrich with the sound of *z* instead of *s*.

Pos-sessed′ (poz-zest′), 165, 171.
Pos-sess′ing (poz-zes′-).
Pos-ses′sion (poz-zesh′un), 171.
Pos-ses′sion-a-ry (poz-zesh′un-) [so Wr.; pos-sesh′un-a-ry, or poz-zesh′un-a-ry, Gd. 155] [*See* Possess.]
Pos-sess′ĭve (poz-zes′-) [so Wk. Sm. Wr.; pos-ses′iv, Wb. Gd. 155] [*See* Possess, *and* Possessionary.]
Pos-sess′or (poz-zes′-), 169.
Pos-sess′o-ry (poz-zes′-) [so Sm.; poz′zes-sŭr-y, Wk.; pos′ses-so-ry, Wb. Gd.; poz-zes′so-ry, or poz′zes-so-ry, Wr. 155.]

☞ Walker considers it more agreeable to analogy to place the accent on the first syllable, rather than on the second. He says, however: "Most of our ... orthoëpists accent the second syllable."

Pos′set, 76, 170.
Pos-si-bil′i-ty, 108.
Pos′si-ble, 164, 169.
Pos′si-bly, 66.
Pōst (24) [*See* Note under *Ghost*.]
Pōst′a-ble, 164.
Pōst′age, 70.
Pōst′al, 72.
Pōst′boy.
Pōst′-cap′taĭn [so Gd.; post-kap′tin, Sm.; pōst′kap-tin, Wr. 155.]
Pōst′-chāise (-shāz).
Pōst′date.
Pōst′dāt-ed, 183.
Pōst′dāt-ing.
Pōst-dĭ-lu′vi-al.
Pōst-dĭ-lu′vi-an.
Pōst′e-a (L.).
Pōst′ed.
Pōst′-en-try.
Pōst′er.
Pŏs-te′ri-or, 49, N.
Pŏs-te-ri-ŏr′i-ty, 169.
Pŏs-te′ri-or-ly.
Pŏs-tĕr′i-ty.
Pŏs′tern [not pŏs′turn, 127, 153.]
Pōst′fix, *n*.
Pōst-fix′, *v*. [so Wb. Gd.; pōst′fix, Wr. 155.]
Pōst-fixed′ (-fikst′).
Pōst-fix′ing.
Pōst′-hāste′ [so Sm.; pōst′hāst, Wb. Gd.; pōst-hāst′, Wr. 155.]
Pŏs-thet′o-mist.
Pŏs-thet′o-my, 108.
Pŏs-thĭ-o-plas′tic.
Pōst′-horn, 206, Exc. 3.
Pōst′-horse.
Pŏst′hu-moŭs (105) [not pōst′hu-mus, 153] [Postumous, 203.]
Pos′til.
Pŏs-til′lion (-yun) (5') [so Sm. Wr. Wb. Gd.; pŏs-til′yun, Wk. 155] [Postillion, 203.]
Pōst′ing.
Pos′tique (-tēk) [so Sm. Gd.; pos-tēk′, Wr. 155.]
Pōst-li-min′i-ar.
Pōst-li-min′i-oŭs.
Pōst-li-min′i-um (L.).
Pōst-lim′i-ny.
Pōst′mark, *n*. & *v*.
Pōst′marked (-markt).
Pōst′mark-ing.
Pōst′mȧs-ter.
Pōst-me-rid′i-an.
Pōst-mor′tem (L.), *a*.
Pōst′-note.
Pōst-nup′tial (-shal).
Pōst-o′bit [so Sm. Wr.; pōst-ob′it, Wb. Gd. 155.]
Pōst′-of-fĭce.
Pōst′pāid.
Pōst-pone′, 163.
Pōst-poned′, 183.
Pōst-pone′ment, 185.

Pōst-pōn′ing, 183.
Pōst-po-sĭ′tion (*-zish′-un*).
Pōst-pos′i-tĭve (*-poz′-*).
Pōst-pran′di-al.
Pōst-sce′ni-um (L.).
Pōst′script, 141.
Pōst′-town, 66, N.; 206, Exc. 2.
Pŏst′u-late, 89, 108.
Pŏst′u-lāt-ed, 183.
Pŏst′u-lāt-ing.
Pŏst-u-la′tion, 112.
Pŏst′u-la-to-ry, 86.
[P o s t u m o u s , 203. — *See* Posthumous.]
Pos′ture (*pŏst′yur*), 91.
Pos′ture-mȧs′ter, 205.
Pōst-ven′tion-al.
Po′sy (*-zy*), 169.
Pot, 18.
Po′ta-ble, 164.
Pot-a-mog′ra-phy.
Pot-a-mol′o-gy.
Po′tance.
Pot′ash.
Po-tas′sa, 170.
Po-tas′si-um (169) [so Sm. Wb. Gd.; *po-tash′ĭ-um*, Wr. 155.]
Po-ta′tion, 169.
Po-ta′to [pl. Po-ta′toes (*-tōz*), 192.]
Po-teen′ [P o t t e e n, 203.]
Po′te-lot.
Po′ten-cy, 169.
Po′tent, 76, 127.
Po′ten-tate [*not* pot′en-tāt, 153.]
Po-ten′tial (*-shal*), 112, 169.
Po-ten-ti-al′i-ty (*-shĭ-*) [so Wk. Sm. Wr.; *po-ten-shal′i-ty*, Wb. Gd. 155.]
Po-ten′tial-ly.
Poth′er [so Sm. Wb. Gd.; *puth′ur*, Wk. 155.]
Pot′-herb (*-erb*), 206, Exc. 3.
Poth′ered (*-urd*).
Poth′er-ing.
Pot′-hŏŏk.
Pot′-house.
Po-ti-cho-ma′ni-e (Fr.) (*po-te-shoo-*), 154.
Po′tion.
Pot′luck.
Pot′-pour′ri (Fr.) (*-poor′re*), 154.
Pot′sherd.
Pot′stōne.
Pot′tage, 70, 170.
Pot′ted, 176.
[P o t t e e n, 203. — *See* Poteen.]
Pot′ter, 66.
Pot′tered, 150, 165.
Pot′ter-ing.
Pot′ter-y, 233, Exc.
Pot′ting.
Pot′tle, 164.
Pot-wal′lop-er (*-wol′-*).
Pot-wal′lop-ing (*-wol′-*).
Pouch, 28, 44.
Pouched (*poucht*).
Pouch′ing.
Pou-chong′ (*poo-shong′*).
Poudrette (Fr.) (*poo-dret′*).
[P o u l d r o n, 203. — *See* Powldron.]
Poulp (*poolp*) [so Gd.; *powlp*, Wr. 155.]
Pōul′ter-er.
Pōul′tĭce (*-tis*), 24, 169.
Pōul′ticed (*-tist*).
Pōul′tiç-ing.
Pōul′try, 93, 130.
Pounce, 28, 39.
Pounce′-box.
Pounced (*pounst*), 165.
Poun′cet-box.
Pounç′ing, 183.
Pound, 28.
Pound′age.
Pound′ed.
Pound′er.
Pound′ing.
Pōur (24, 49), *v.* to let out, as a liquid, in large quantities. [*See* Pore, 160.]
Pōured, 165.
Pōur′ing.
Pour′par-ty (*poor′-*) [P u r p a r t y, 203.]
Pour-prest′ure (*poor-prest′yur*), 91. [P u r-p r e s t u r e, 203.]
[P o u r s u i v a n t, 203. — *See* Pursuivant.]
Pout, 28.
Pout′ed.
Pout′er, *n.* one who pouts; — a kind of pigeon. [P o w t e r (in the last sense), 203.]
Pout′ing.
Pov′er-ty.
Pow′der, 28.
Pow′dered (*-durd*).
Pow′der-flȧsk.
Pow′der-horn.
Pow′der-ing.
Pow′der-mill.
Pow′der-y, 233, Exc.
Power (*pour*), 28, 67, N.
Power′ful (*-fŏŏl*).
Power′ful-ly (*-fŏŏl-*).
Powl′dron (28, 86) [P o u l d r o n, 203.]

☞ Smart pronounces *powldron* as here given, with the sound of *ou* in *ounce* (§ 28), but *pouldron* with the sound of *o* in *old* (§ 24).

Pow′ter [P o u t e r, 203. — *See* Pouter.]
Pow′wow.
Pox, 18, 52, N.
Poy, 27, 56, Rem.
Poy′al.
Poynt′ell.
Poy′ou (*-oo*).
Poz-zu-o-lä′na [P o z-z o l a n a, P u z z o l a-n a, P u z z o l a n o, 203.]
Prac-ti-ca-bil′i-ty.
Prac′ti-ca-ble, 164.
Prac′ti-ca-bly.
Prac′ti-cal, 78.
Prac-ti-cal′i-ty, 108.
Prac′ti-cal-ly.
Prac′tĭce, *n.* 160.
Prac′tĭse (*-tĭs*), *v.* (160) [P r a c t i c e, Wb. Gd. 203. — *See* Note E, p. 70.]
Prac′tised (*-tist*), 165.
Prac′tis-er, 183.
Prac′tis-ing.
Prac-tĭ′tion-er (*-tish′-un-*).
[P r æ, 203. — *See* Pre.]
Præç′i-pe (L.) (*pres′i-pe*)
[P r æ c o r d i a l, 203. — *See* Precordial.]
[P r æ d i a l, 203. — *See* Predial.]
[P r æ f l o r a t i o n, 203. — *See* Prefloration.]
[P r æ f o l i a t i o n, 203. — *See* Prefoliation.]
[P r æ m o r s e, 203. — *See* Premorse.]
Præm-u-ni′re (*prem-*) [P r e m u n i r e, 203.]
Præ-no′men (L.).
Præ-tex′ta (L.).
[P r æ t o r, 203. — *See* Pretor.]
Præ-to′ri-um (L.) [pl. *Præ-to′ri-a*, 198.]

Prag-mat′ic.
Prag-mat′ic-al.
Prāi′rĭe, 59, N.; 171.
Prāise (*prāz*) (23, 40), *n.* commendation:— *v.* to commend. [*See* Prase, Prays, *and* Preys, 160.]
Prāised (*prāzd*).
Prāis′er (*prāz′-*).
Praise′wor-thi-ness (*prāz′wur-*).
Prāise′wor-thy (*prāz′-wur-*).
Prȧnce, 12, 131.
Prȧnced (*prȧnst*), Note C, p. 34.
Prȧnç′ing, 228.
Prank (*prangk*), 54.
Pranked (*prangkt*).
Prank′ing (*prangk′-*).
Prank′ish (*prangk′-*).
Prase (*prāz*) (23, 40), *n.* a leek-green variety of massive quartz. [*See* Praise, Prays, *and* Preys, 160.]
Pras′i-noŭs (*praz′-*).
Prās′oid (*prāz′-*), 183.
Prate, 23, 163.
Prāt′ed, 183.
Prāt′er.
Prăt′ic [Pratique, 203.]
Pra′tin-cole.
Prāt′ing.
Prăt′ique (Fr.) (*prat′-ēk*) [so Gd.; *prat′ik*, Wr. 155] [Pratic, 203.]
Prat′tle, 164.
Prat′tled (*prat′ld*)
Prat′tler.
Prat′tling.
Prav′i-ty.
Prawn, 17.
Prax′e-an.
Prax′is (Gr.).
Prāy (23), *v.* to supplicate. [*See* Prey, 160.]
Prāyed (*prād*), *v.* did pray. [*See* Preyed, 160.]
Prayer (*prêr*) (14, 67, N.; 161), *n.* supplication.
Prāy′er (23, 67, N.; 161), *n.* one who prays, or supplicates. [*See* Preyer, 160.]
Prayer′-bŏŏk (*prêr′-*).
Prayer′ful (*prêr′fŏŏl*).
Prāy′ing, *part.* from *Pray.* [*See* Preying, 160.]
Prāys (*prāz*) (23, 40), *v.* does pray. [*See* Praise, Prase, *and* Preys, 160.]
Pre, a prefix from the Latin, denoting priority. [Præ, 203.]

☞ "The Latin form *præ* is still retained in some words scarcely naturalized." *Worcester.*

Prēach, 13, 44.
Prēached (*prēcht*), *v.* 165; Note C, p. 34.
Prēach′ed, *a.* 150.
Prēach′er.
Prēach′ing.
Prēach′ment.
Pre-ac-quāint′, 223.
Pre-ac-quāint′ance.
Pre-ac-quāint′ed.
Pre-ac-quāint′ing.
Pre-Ad-am′ic.
Pre-Ad′am-ite.
Pre-Ad-am-it′ic.
Pre-ad-mon′ish.
Pre-ad-mon′ished (*-isht*).
Pre-ad-mo-nĭ′tion (*-nish′un*).
Pre′am-ble, 164.
Pre-an-te-pe-nult′i-mate.
Pre-as-sur′ance (*-shoor′-*).
Pre-âu′di-ence.
Preb′end (170) [*not* pre′-bend, 153.]
Pre-bend′al, 123.
Preb′end-a-ry, 72, 106.
Pre-ca′ri-oŭs, 49, N.
Prec′a-to-ry.
Pre-câu′tion.
Pre-câu′tion-a-ry, 72.
Pre-câu′tioned (*-shund*).
Pre-câu′tion-ing.
Pre-câu′tioŭs (*-shus*), 112
Pre-cede′, 118, 171.
Pre-cēd′ed, 183.
Pre-cēd′ence, 169.
Pre-cēd′en-cy.
Pre-cēd′ent, *a.* 161.
Preç′e-dent, *n.* 161.
Preç′e-dent-ed.
Pre-cēd′ent-ly.
Pre-cēd′ing.
Pre-cen′tor.
Pre′cept [*not* pres′ept, 153.]
Pre-cep′tĭve.
Pre-cep′tor.
Pre-cep-to′ri-al, 49, N.
Pre′cep-to-ry (86) [so Sm.; *pres′ep-tŭr-y*, Wk. Wr.; *pre-sep′-to-ry*, Wb. Gd. 155.]
Pre-cep′tress.
Pre-ces′sion (*-sesh′un*).
Pre′cinct (*-singkt*) (54) [so Sm. Wr. Wb. Gd.; *pre-singkt′*, Wk. 155.]
Prĕ′cious (*presh′us*), 234.
[Precipe, 203.—*See* Præcipe, 203.]
Preç′i-pĭce, 169, 171.
Pre-cip′i-ent.
Pre-cip-i-ta-bil′i-ty.
Pre-cip′i-ta-ble, 164.
Pre-cip′i-tance, 169.
Pre-cip′i-tan-cy.
Pre-cip′i-tant.
Pre-cip′i-tate, 170.
Pre-cip′i-tāt-ed.
Pre-cip′i-tāt-ing, 183.
Pre-cip-i-ta′tion.
Pre-cip′i-tāt-or, 169.
Pre-cip′i-toŭs.
Pre-cise′.
Pre-cise′ly, 136, 156.
Pre-cise′ness, 39.
Pre-cĭ′sian (*-sizh′an*) (72), *n.* one who is very precise or rigorous. [*See* Precision, 160.]
Pre-cĭ′sian-ism (*-sizh′-an-izm*).
Pre-cĭ′sian-ist (*-sizh′-an-*).
Pre-cĭ′sion (*-sizh′un*), *n.* the state of being precise. [*See* Precisian, 160.]
Pre-clude′, 26.
Pre-clūd′ed, 183.
Pre-clūd′ing.
Pre-clu′sion (*-zhun*), 47, N.
Pre-clu′sĭve, 84.
Pre-co′cioŭs (*-shus*).
Pre-coç′i-ty, 171.
Pre-cog′i-tate (*-koj′-*).
Pre-cog′i-tāt-ed (*-koj′-*).
Pre-cog′i-tāt-ing (*-koj′-*)
Pre-cog-i-ta′tion (*-koj-*).
Pre-cog-nĭ′tion (*-nish′-un*).
Pre-con-cēit′.
Pre-con-cēive′, 169.
Pre-con-cēived′.
Pre-con-cēiv′ing.
Pre-con-cep′tion.
Pre-con-cert′, *v.* 161.
Pre-con′cert, *n.* 161.

Pre-con-cert'ed.
Pre-con-cert'ing.
Pre-con'tract, *n.* 161.
Pre-con-tract', *v.* 161.
Pre-con-tract'ed.
Pre-con-tract'ing.
Pre-cor'di-al [Præ cor-dial, 203.]
Pre-cur'sĭve, 84.
Pre-cur'sor.
Pre-da'cean (*-shan*), 112.
Pre-da'ceoŭs (*-shus*), 169
Pred'a-to-ri ly, 186.
Pred'a-to-ry, 86.
Pred-e-ces'sor [*not* pre-de-ses'sur, pre'de-ses-sur, *nor* pred'e-ses-sur, 126, 153.]
Pre-des-ti-na'ri-an.
Pre-des'ti-nate, 108.
Pre-des'ti-nāt-ed, 183.
Pre-des'ti-nāt-ing.
Pre-des-ti-na'tion.
Pre-des'ti-nāt-ĭve.
Pre-des'ti-nāt-or.
Pre-des'tĭne, 82, 152.
Pre-des'tĭned, 150.
Pre-des'tin-ing.
Pre-de-ter'min-ate.
Pre-de-ter-min-a'tion.
Pre-de-ter'mĭne.
Pre-de-ter'mĭned.
Pre-de-ter'min-ing.
Pre'di-al, 169.
Pred-i-ca-bil'i-ty.
Pred'i-ca-ble.
Pre-dic'a-ment, 169.
Pred'i-cant.
Pred'i-cate.
Pred'i-cāt-ed, 183.
Pred'i-cāt-ing.
Pred-i-ca'tion.
Pre-dic'a-tĭve, 84.
Pred'i-ca-to-ry, 86.
Pre-dict', 103.
Pre-dict'ed.
Pre-dict'ing.
Pre-dic'tion, 169.
Pre-dict'ĭve.
Pre-dict'or.
Pre-di-lec'tion [*not* pred-i-lek'shun, *nor* pre-di-lik'shun, 153.]
Pre-dis-po'nent.
Pre-dis-pose' (*-pōz'*).
Pre-dis-posed' (*-pōzd'*).
Pre-dis-pōs'ing (*-pōz'-*).
Pre-dis-po-sĭ'tion (*-zish'un*).
Pre-dom'i-nance.
Pre-dom'i-nan-cy, 169.
Pre-dom'i-nant.
Pre-dom'i-nate.
Pre-dom'i-nāt-ed.
Pre-dom'i-nāt-ing.
Pre-dom-i-na'tion.
Pre-dor'sal.
Pre'dy.
Pre-e-lect', 223.
Pre-e-lect'ed.
Pre-e-lect'ing.
Pre-e-lec'tion.
Pre-em'i-nence.
Pre-em'i-nent.
Pre-empt' (*-emt'*), 162.
Pre-empt'ed (*-emt'-*).
Pre-empt'ing (*-emt'-*).
Pre-emp'tion (*-em'-*), 162, 171.
Pre-emp'tĭve (*-em'-*).
Pre-emp'tor (*-em'-*).
Preen, 13.
Preened, 165.
Pre-en-gage'.
Pre-en-gaged' (*-gājd'*).
Pre-en-gage'ment.
Pre-en-gāg'ing (*-gāj'-*).
Preen'ing.
Pre-es-tab'lish.
Pre-es-tab'lished (*-lisht*)
Pre-es-tab'lish-ing
Pre-es-tab'lish-ment.
Pre-ex-am-in-a'tion (*-egz-*).
Pre-ex-am'ĭne (*-egz-*).
Pre-ex-am'ĭned (*-egz-*).
Pre-ex-am'in-ing (*-egz-*)
Pre-ex-ist' (*-egz-*).
Pre-ex-ist'ed (*-egz-*).
Pre-ex-ist'ence (*-egz-*).
Pre-ex-ist'ent (*-egz-*).
Pre-ex-ist'ing (*-egz-*).
Pref'ace, *n.* & *v.*
Pref'aced (*-āst*).
Pref'a-cer.
Pref'a-cing.
Pref-a-to'ri-al.
Pref'a-to-ry, 86.
Pre'fect (76) [*not* pref'-ekt, 153.]
Pre'fect-ure (90) [so Sm. Wb. Gd.; *pref'ekt-yoor*, Wk. Wr. 155.]
Pre-fer', 21, N.
Pref'er-a-ble, 169.
Pref'er-a-bly.
Pref'er-ence, 169.
Pref-er-en'tial (*-shal*).
Pre-fer'ment [*not* pref'-ur-ment, 153.]
Pre-ferred' (*-ferd'*).
Pre-fer'rer, 21, N.
Pre-fer'ring.
Pre-fig-ur-a'tion (*-yur-*), 91.
Pre-fig'ur-a-tĭve (*-yur-*).
Pre-fig'ure, 91.
Pre-fig'ured (*-yurd*).
Pre-fig'ure-ment.
Pre-fig'ur-ing (*-yur-*).
Pre-fix', *v.* 103, 161.
Pre'fix, *n.* 103, 161.
Pre-fixed' (*-fikst'*).
Pre-fix'ing.
Pre-flo-ra'tion [Præ-floration, 203.]
Pre-fo-li-a'tion [Præ-foliation, 203.]
Preg'nan-cy, 169.
Preg'nant, 72.
Pre-gus-ta'tion.
Pre-hen'si-ble, 164, 169.
Pre-hen'sĭle, 81, 152.
Pre-hen'sion, 112.
Pre-hen'so-ry, 86.
Pre-his-tŏr'ic, 109.
Prehn'ite (*prĕn'īt*).
Pre-judge' (*-juj'*).
Pre-judged' (*-jujd'*).
Pre-judg'ing (*-juj'-*).
Pre-judg'ment (*-juj'-*) [Prejudgement, 185, 203.]
Pre-ju'di-cate.
Pre-ju'di-cāt-ed.
Pre-ju'di-cāt-ing.
Pre-ju-di-ca'tion.
Pre-ju'di-ca-tĭve.
Prej'u-dĭce, 169.
Prej'u-dĭced (*-dist*).
Prej-u-dĭ'cial (*-dish'al*).
Prej'u-diç-ing.
Prel'a-cy [so Wk. Sm. Wr.; *prel'a-sy*, or *pre'la-sy*, Gd. 155.]
Prel'ate.
Pre-lat'ic.
Pre-lat'ic-al.
Prel'a-tist.
Pre-lec'tion.
Pre-lec'tor.
Pre-lī-ba'tion.
Pre-lim'i-na-ri ly.
Pre-lim'i-na-ry, 72.
Prel'ude, *n.* (103, 161) [so Wk. Sm. Wr.; *pre'-lūd*, or *prel'ūd*, Gd. 155.]
Pre-lude', *v. active* (103, 161) [so Wk. Wr. Gd.; *prel'ūd*, Sm. 155.]
Pre-lude', *v. neuter* [so Sm. Gd.; *pre-lūd'*, or *prel'ūd*, Wr. 155.]
Pre-lūd'ed, 183.
Pre-lūd'er, *or* Prel'ūd-er [so Wr.; *pre-lūd'er*, Gd.; *prel'u-der*, Sm. 155.]

Pre-lūd'ing.
Pre-lum'bar, 74.
Pre-lu'sĭve.
Pre-lu'sĭve-ly.
Pre-lu'so-ry, 86.
Pre-ma-ture', 122.
Pre-ma-tu'ri-ty.
Pre-med'i-tate.
Pre-med'i-tāt-ed.
Pre-med'i-tāt-ing.
Pre-med-i-ta'tion.
Pre'mi-er [so Sm.; *prĕm'yur*, Wk.; *prĕm'-yur*, Wb. Gd.; *prĕm'-yur*, or *pre'mĭ-ur*, Wr. 155.]
Pre-mise' (-*mīz'*), *v.* 103, 161.
Prem'ĭse, *n.* (161, 169) [pl. Prem'is-es (-*ez*), 189. — *See* Pre-mi'ses, 160.] [Premiss, 203.]
Pre-mised' (-*mīzd'*).
Pre-mi'ses (-*zez*), *v.* does premise. [*See* Prem'is-es (pl. of Premise), 160.]
Pre'mi-um, 169.
Pre-mon'ish, 170.
Pre-mon'ished (-*isht*).
Pre-mon'ish-ing.
Pre-mon'ish-ment.
Pre-mo-nĭ'tion (-*nish'-un*).
Pre-mon'i-tor, 169.
Pre-mon'i-to-ri-ly, 171.
Pre-mon'i-to-ry, 86.
Pre-mon'strant.
Pre-mon'strā-tor.
Pre-morse' (121) [Præmorse, 203.]
Pre-morsed' (-*morst'*).
[Premunire, 203. — *See* Præmunire.]
Pre-mu'ni-to-ry.
Pren'der.
[Prenomen, 203. — *See* Prænomen.]
Pre-nom-i-na'tion.
Pren'tĭce.

☞ A colloquial contraction of *apprentice*.

Pre-oc'cu-pan-cy.
Pre-oc-cu-pa'tion.
Pre-oc'cu-pīed.
Pre-oc'cu-pȳ, 223.
Pre-oc'cu-pȳ-ing.
Pre-or-dāin'.
Pre-or-dāined', 165.
Pre-or-dāin'ing.
Pre-or-di-na'tion.
Pre-pāid', 187.
Pre-par'a-ble (-*pêr'a-bl*).
Prep-a-ra'tion.
Pre-păr'a-tĭve.
Pre-păr'a-to-ry, 86.
Pre-pare' (-*pêr'*).
Pre-pared' (-*pêrd'*).
Pre-par'ed-ly (-*pêr'*-).
Pre-par'er (-*pêr'*-).
Pre-par'ing (-*pêr'*-).
Pre-pāy'.
Pre-pāy'ing.
Pre-pāy'ment.
Pre-pense'.
Pre-pol'lence.
Pre-pol'len-cy.
Pre-pol'lent.
Pre-pon'der-ance.
Pre-pon'der-an-cy.
Pre-pon'der-ant, 169.
Pre-pon'der-ate.
Pre-pon'der-āt-ed.
Pre-pon'der-āt-ing.
Pre-pon-der-a'tion.
Prep-o-sĭ'tion (-*zish'-un*), 119.
Prep-o-sĭ'tion-al (-*zish'-un*-).
Pre-pos'i-tĭve (-*poz'*-).
Pre-pos'i-tor (-*poz'*-).
Pre-pos'i-ture (-*poz'*-).
Pre-pos-sess' (-*poz-zes'*) [*See* Possess.]
Pre-pos-sessed' (-*poz-zest'*).
Pre-pos-sess'ing (-*poz-zes'*-).
Pre-pos-ses'sion (-*poz-zesh'un*).
Pre-pos-sess'or (-*poz-zes'*-).
Pre-pos'ter-oŭs.
Pre-pos'ter-oŭs-ly.
Pre-Răph'a-el-ism (-*izm*).
Pre-Răph'a-el-īte [so Wr.; *pre-rah'fa-el-īt*, Gd. 155.]
Pre-req'ui-sĭte (-*wĭ-zit*), 171.
Pre-rog'a-tĭve, 84.
Pre-sage', *v.* 103, 161.
Pres'age, *n.* (103, 161) [so Wk. Sm. Wr.; *pre'sāj*, or *pres'āj*, Gd. 155.]
Pre-saged', 165.
Pre-sāg'ing (-*sāj'*-).
Pres'by-ope (*prez'*-) [*See* Presbyopy.]
Pres-by-o'pi-a (*prez*-).
Pres'by-o-py (*prez'*-) [so Sm.; *pres'bĭ-o-py*, Wr. Gd. 155.]
Pres-by-op'ic (*prez*-).
Pres'bȳte (*prez'*-).
Pres'by-ter (*prez'*-) (136, 171) [so Wk. Sm. Wr.; *pres'bĭ-tur*, Wb. Gd. 155.]
Pres-byt'er-al (*prez*-).
Pres-byt'er-ate (*prez*-).
Pres-by-te'ri-an (*prez*-), 49, N.; 169.
Pres-by-te'ri-an-ism (*prez-by-te'ri-an-izm*), 133, 136.
Pres'by-tĕr-y (*prez'*-) [*not* pres-bit'er-y, 153.]
Pre'sci-ence (*pre'shĭ-ens* [*not* pre'shens, *nor* pre'sĭ-ens, 153.]
Pre'sci-ent (*pre'shĭ-ent*), 171.
Pre-scribe'.
Pre-scribed', 165.
Pre-scrīb'er.
Pre-scrīb'ing.
Pre'script.
Pre-script-i-bil'i-ty.
Pre-script'i-ble, 164, 169.
Pre-scrip'tion.
Pre-script'ĭve, 84.
Pres'ence (*prez'*-).
Pres'ence-chām'ber (*prez'*-), 205.
Pres'ent (*prez'*-), *a.* & *n.* 103, 161.
Pre-sent' (-*zent'*), *v.* 103, 161.
Pre-sent'a-ble (-*zent'a-bl*), 169.
Pres-ent-a'tion (*prez*-) [*not* prē-zen-tā'shun, 143, 153.]
Pre-sent'a-tĭve (-*zent'*-), 84.
Pre-sent'ed (-*zent'*-).
Pres-ent-ee' (*prez*-).
Pre-sent'er (-*zent'*-).
Pre-sen'ti-ent (-*sen'-shĭ*-), 171.
Pre-sent'i-ment [*not* pre-zent'i-ment, 136, 153.]
Pre-sent'ing (-*zent'*-).
Pres'ent-ly (*prez'*-).
Pre-sent'ment (-*zent'*-).
Pre-serv'a-ble (-*zerv'a-bl*), 183.
Pres-er-va'tion (*prez*-).
Pre-serv'a-tĭve (-*zerv'*-).
Pre-serv'a-to-ry (-*zerv'*-), 86.
Pre-serve' (-*zerv'*), 21, N.

Pre-served′ (*-zervd′*).
Pre-serv′er (*-zerv′-*).
Pre-serv′ing (*-zerv′-*).
Pre-side′ (*-zīd′*), 136.
Pre-sid′ed (*-zīd′-*).
Pres′i-dence (*prez′-*).
Pres′i-den-cy (*prez′-*).
Pres′i-dent (*prez′-*), 136.
Pres-i-den′tial (*prez-i-den′shal*), 169.
Pre-sīd′er (*-zīd′-*).
Pre-sid′i-al (39, 136) [so Wb. Gd. Wr.; *pre-sid′yal*, Sm.; *pre-sij′ĭ-al*, Wk. 155.]
Pre-sid′i-a-ry (72) [so Wr. Wb. Gd.; *pre-sid′yŭr-y*, Sm. 155.]
Pre-sid′ing (*-zīd′-*).
Pre-sig-ni-fĭ-ca′tion.
Pre-sig′ni-fīed.
Pre-sig′ni-fȳ.
Pre-sig′ni-fȳ-ing.
Press, 15, 174.
Pressed (*prest*).
Press′er.
Press′-gang.
Press′ing, 228.
Pres′sion (*presh′un*).
Pres si-ros′ter, 126.
Pres-si-ros′tral.
Press′man, 196.
Press′ure (*presh′ur*), 46, Note 2; 91.
Press′work (*-wurk*).
Pres′ter [so Wr. Wb. Gd.; *pre′stur*, Sm. 155.]
Pres′tige (*pres′tēzh*) [so Sm.; *pres′tij*, Gd.; *pres-tēj′*, or *pres′tij*, Wr. 155.]

☞ This word was formerly used in the plural to signify *illusions*, or *impostures*, and in this form is pronounced *pres′ti-ges* (*-jez*), by Smart and Worcester. In its present acceptation of *moral influence created by past successes*, it hardly admits of being pluralized. Webster and Goodrich give the word only in the former sense, which is now obsolete.

Pres′ti-mo-ny, 86.
Pres-tis′si-mo (It.).
Pres′to.
Pre-sūm′a-ble (*-zūm′a-bl*), 164, 169.
Pre-sume′ (*-zūm′*), 26.
Pre-sumed′ (*-zūmd′*).
Pre-sūm′er (*-zūm′-*).
Pre-sūm′ing (*-zūm′-*).
Pre-sump′tion (*-zum′-*), 162, 171.
Pre-sump-tĭve (*-zum′-*).
Pre-sumpt′u-oŭs (*-zumt′-*) (89, 100) [*not* pre-zum′shus, 153.]
Pre-sup-pose′ (*-pōz′*).
Pre-sup-posed′ (*-pōzd′*).
Pre-sup-pōs′ing (*-pōz′-*).
Pre-sup-po-sĭ′tion (*-zish′un*).
Pre-tence′ (121) [Pretense, Wb. Gd. 203. — *See* Note E, p. 70.]
Pre-tend′, 103.
Pre-tend′ed.
Pre-tend′er, 77.
Pre-tend′ing.
[Pretense, 203. — *See* Pretence.]
Pre-tensed′ (*-tenst′*), Note C, p. 34.
Pre-ten′sion, 112, 169.
Pre-ten′tioŭs (*-shus*).
Pre-tĕr′i-ent [so Gd.; *pre-te′ri-ent*, Wr. 155.]
Pre′ter-im-per′fect.
Pret′er-it, *or* Pret′er-ĭte (203) [*pret′ur-it*, Sm.; *pre′tur-it*, Wk. Wb. Gd.; *pret′ur-it*, or *pre′tur-it*, Wr. 155]

☞ Of the two forms of spelling this word, Walker, Smart, Webster, and Goodrich, give only *preterit*; Worcester gives both, but prefers *preterite*.

Pret-er-ĭ′tion (*-ish′un*).
Pre-tĕr′i-tĭve [so Gd.; *pret′ur-it-iv*, Wr. 155.]
Pre-ter-mis′sion (*-mish′un*).
Pre-ter mit′.
Pre-ter-mit′ted, 176.
Pre-ter-mit′ting.
Pre-ter-nat′u-ral.
Pre′ter-per′fect.
Pre′ter-plu′per-fect.
Pre-text′, *or* Pre′text [so Wr. Gd.; *pre-tekst′*, Wk. Sm. 155] [*See* Note under *Prolix.*]
[*Pretexta*, 203. — *See Prœtexta.*]
Pre′tor (*-tawr*) (88) [Prætor, 203.]
Pre-to′ri al, 169.
Pre-to′ri-an, 49, N.
Pret′ti-ly (*prit′-*).
Pret′ti-ness (*prit′-*).
Pret′ty (*prit′y*) (66, 170) [*not* prĕt′y, *nor* pŏŏt′y, 153.]
Preux-chev-a-liēr′ (Fr.) (*proo-shev-a-lēr′*).
Pre-vāil′.
Pre-vāiled′, 165.
Pre-vāil′ing.
Prev′a-lence, 169.
Prev′a-len-cy.
Prev′a-lent.
Pre-văr′i-cate [so Wk. Wb. Gd. Wr.; *pre-vêr′rĭ-kāt*, Sm. 155.]
Pre-văr′i-cāt-ed.
Pre-văr′i-cāt-ing.
Pre-văr-i-ca′tion.
Pre-văr′i-cāt-or.
Pre-ve′ni-ent.
Pre-vent′.
Pre-vent′a-ble, 164.
Pre-vent′ed.
Pre-vent′er.
Pre-vent′ing.
Pre-ven′tion.
Pre-vent′ĭve.

☞ Sometimes incorrectly written *preventative*.

Pre′vi-oŭs, 78.
Pre-vĭ′sion (*-vizh′un*).
Prey (*prā*) (23), *n.* goods taken in war, or food seized to be devoured: — *v.* to plunder; — to feed by violence. [*See* Pray, 160.]
Preyed (*prād*), *v.* did prey. [*See* Prayed, 160.]
Prey′er (*prā′-*) (67), one who preys, or plunders. [*See* Prāy′-er, 160.]
Preys (*prāz*), *v.* does prey. [*See* Praise, Prase, *and* Prays, 160.]
Pri-a-pe′an, 110.
Price, 25, 39.
Price-cŭr′rent [so Wb. Gd.; *prīs′kŭr-rent*, Wr. 155.]
Priced (*prīst*), 165, 183; Note C, p. 34.
Price′less, 185.
Priç′ing, 183.
Prick, 16, 181.
Pricked (*prikt*).
Prick′er.
Prick′ing.

Pric'kle (*prik'l*), 164.
Pric'kle-back (*prik'l-*).
Prick'li-ness, 186.
Prick'ly.
Prick'wŏŏd.
Pride, *n.* inordinate self-esteem : — *v.* to plume ; to value. [*See* Pried, 160.]
Prīd'ed, 183.
Prīd'ing.
Prīed, *v.* did pry. [*See* Pride, 160.]
Prī'er, *n.* one who pries. [*See* Prior, 160.]
Prīes, *v.* does pry. [*See* Prize, 160.]
Priēst, 13.
Priēst'crȧft, 206.
Priēst'ess.
Priēst'hŏŏd.
Priēst'like, 206, Exc. 5.
Priēst'li-ness.
Priēst'-rid-den (*-rid'n*).
Prig, 16, 64.
Prig'ger-y (*-gur-*), 138.
Prig'gish (*-ghish*), 138.
Prig'gism (*-ghizm*).
Prill, 16, 172.
Prim, 16, 32.
Prī'ma-cy, 72, 169.
Prī'ma don'na (It.) (*pre'-*).
Prī'ma fa'ci-e (L.) (*-fa'-shĭ-ē*).
Prī'mage, 70.
Prī'mal, 72.
Prī'ma-ri-ly, 126.
Prī'ma-ry (72) [*not* prī'-mĕr-y, 126, 153.]
Prī'mate, 73.
Prī-ma'tial (*-shal*) [so Gd. ; *prĭ-ma'shal*, Wr. 155.]
Prī-mat'ic-al [so Sm. Gd. ; *prĭ-mat'ik-al*, Wr. 155.]
Prime, 25, 163.
Primed, 165, 183.
Prĭm'er (170), an elementary book in which children are taught to read ; — a kind of type. [*See* Primmer, 160.]
Prī-me'val.
[Primigenial, 203. — *See* Primogenial.]
Prī-mig'e-noŭs (*-mij'-*), 169, 171.
Prī'mĭne.
Prīm'ing, 183.
Prī-mip'i-lar.
Prī-mĭ'ti-æ (L.) (*prī-mish'e-e*).
Prim'i-tĭve, 84.
Primmed (*primd*), 165, 176.
Prim'mer, *a.* more prim. [*See* Primer, 160.]
Prim'ming, 176.
Pri-mo-ge'ni-al. [Primigenial, 203.]

☞ "This is the usual form ; but old writers more correctly use *primigenial*." *Smart.*

Pri-mo-gen'i-tor, 169.
Pri-mo-gen'i-ture, 90, 171.
Prī-mor'di-al [so Sm. Wr. Gd. ; *prī-mor'di-al*, or *prī-mor'ji-al*, Wk. 134, 155.]
Prim'rose (*-rōz*).
Prī'mum mob'i-le (L.).
Prince, 16, 39.
Prince'dom, 169.
Prince'ly, 185.
Prin'ce's-fĕath'er (*-sez-*), 213.
Prin'ce's-met'al (*-sez-*), 213.
Prin'cess, 106.

☞ In England sometimes pronounced *prin-cess'*. Walker speaks of this pronunciation as a "glaring absurdity, which prevails [1806] even in the first circles."

Prin'ci-pal, *a.* chief. [*See* Principle, 148.]
Prin-ci-pal'i-ty, 108, 169.
Prin-cip'i-a (L.). *n. pl.*
Prin'ci-ple (164, 171), *n.* a fundamental truth ; a rule of action ; — an element. [*See* Principal, 160.]
Prin'ci-pled (*-pld*).
Prink, 16, 54.
Prinked (*pringkt*).
Prink'ing.
Print.
Print'ed.
Print'er.
Print'ing.
Print'ing-of'fĭce.
Prī'or (88), *n.* the superior of a priory : — *a.* preceding in time. [*See* Prier, 160.]
Prī'or-ate.
Prī'or-ess.
Prī-ŏr'i-ty.
Prī'or-y, 169.
Prī'sage (*prī'zăj*) [so Wr. Gd. ; *prī'săj*, Sm. 155], *n.* a right belonging to the English crown of taking two tuns of wine from every ship importing twenty tuns or more, — afterwards exchanged into a duty of two shillings for every tun imported, and called *butlerage.*

☞ Smart pronounces this word *prī'săj*, because, as he supposes, it is derived from *price*, and in order to distinguish it from another word of the same spelling, derived, according to him, from *prize*, and meaning, *the share of merchandise taken as lawful prize at sea, which belongs to the king or admiral.* This derivative from *prize* he pronounces *prī'zăj*. But Worcester and Goodrich give the word only in the sense of the royal right now called *butlerage*, and derive it from the French *prise* (*prēz*).

Pris-cill'ian-ist (*-yan-*).
[Prise, 203. — *See* Prize.]
Prism (*prizm*), 61, 136.
Pris-mat'ic (*priz-*).
Pris-mat'ic-al (*priz-*).
Pris-ma-toid'al (*priz-*).
Pris'moid (*priz'-*).
Pris-moid'al (*priz-*).
Pris'on (*priz'n*) (149) [so Wk. Wr. Wb. Gd. ; *priz'un*, coll. *priz'n*, Sm. 155.]
Pris'on-base (*priz'n-*) [Prison-bars, 203.]
Pris'on-er (*priz'n-*).
Pris'tĭne, 82, 152.
Prith'ee (140) [*not* prith'-ee, 153.]
Prī'va-cy (169) [so Sm. Wr. Wb. Gd. ; *prī'va-sy*, or *priv'a-sy*, Wk. 155.]

☞ "My ear and observation greatly fail me, if the first mode of pronouncing this word [*prī'va-sy*] is not the most agreeable to polite as well as general usage." *Walker.*

Prī'vate, 73.

Pri-va-teer′, 122, 169.
Pri-va-teer′ing.
Pri-va-teers′man (-*tērz′*-).
Pri-va′tion, 112, 169.
Priv′a-tive, 156.
Priv′et.
Priv′i-lĕge (-*lej*), 171.
Priv′i-leged (-*lejd*), 183.
Priv′i-leg-ing (-*lej*-).
Priv′i-ly, 186.
Priv′i-ty.
Priv′y.
Prize (25, 46), *n.* a reward gained by competition; — money drawn by a lottery ticket; — goods or a vessel taken from an enemy at sea; — a lever: — *v.* to value; — to move with a lever. [*See* Pries, 160.]

☞ As a noun, in the sense of *a lever*, and as a verb, in a corresponding sense, this word is generally written, in the United States, Pry. In England it is sometimes written Prise.

Prized, 165.
Prize′-fight (-*fīt*).
Prīz′ing.
Pro (L.).

☞ The phrase *pro and con* (that is, *pro* and *contra*, for and against) is sometimes used in a plural form, *pros* (*prōz*) *and cons* (*konz*).

Pro′a, 72, 189.
Prob′a-bil-ism (-*izm*).
Prob′a-bil-ist.
Prob-a-bil′i-ty, 119.
Prob′a-ble, 164, 169.
Prob′a-bly.
Pro′bang.
Pro′bate.
Pro-ba′tion.
Pro-ba′tion-al.
Pro-ba′tion-a-ry, 72.
Pro-ba′tion-er.
Pro′ba-tive, 84.
Pro′ba-to-ry(86)[so Sm. Wr. Wb. Gd.; *prob′-a-tŭr-y*, Wk. 155.]
Pro-ba′tum est (L.).
Probe, 24, 163.
Probed, 165.
Prōb′ing, 183.
Prob′i-ty, 170.
Prob′lem, 76.
Prob-lem-at′ic.
Prob-lem-at′ic-al.
Prob-lem-at′ic-al-ly.
Pro-bos′ci-date.
Pro-bos-cid′i-al.
Pro-bos-cid′i-an (169) [so Sm. Gd.; *prob-o-sid′ĭ-an*, Wr. 155.]
Pro-bos-cid′i-form, 108.
Pro-bos′cis, 171.
Pro-cat-arc′tic.
Pro-ce-den′do (L.).
Pro-cēd′ure, 91, 171.
Pro-ceed′, 118, 169.
Pro-ceed′ed.
Pro-ceed′ing.
Pro′ceeds (*pro′sēdz*), *or* Proç′eeds (*pros′ēdz*) [*pro′sēdz*, or *pro-sēdz′*, Wr.; *pros′ēdz*, Sm.; *pro-sēdz′*, Wk.; *pro-sēdz′*, or *pro′sēdz*, Gd. 155.]
Proç-e-leŭs-mat′ic.
Pro-cel-la′ri-an.
Proç′ess [*not* pro′ses, 153.]
Pro-ces′sion (-*sesh′un*).
Pro-ces′sion-al (-*sesh′-un*-).
Pro-ces′sion-a-ry(-*sesh′-un*-).
Pro-ces′sive.
Procès verbal (Fr.) (*pro′sā vĕr′bal*) (154) [so Gd.; *pros′sā vĕr-băl′*, Wr. 155.]
Pro′chein (-*shen*).
Pro′chro-nism (-*kro-nizm*) [so Gd.; *pro′-kron-izm*, Wr. 155.]
Proç′i-dence, *or* Pro′ci-dence [so Wr.; *pros′-i-dens*, Sm.; *pro′si-dens*, Wb. Gd. 155.]
Pro-cid′u-oŭs.
Pro-clāim′, 23, 103.
Pro-clāimed′, 165.
Pro-clāim′er.
Pro-clāim′ing.
Proc-la-ma′tion.
Pro-cliv′i-ty, 108, 169.
Pro-cœ′li-an (-*se′*-), 171.
Pro-con′sul.
Pro-con′su-lar, 108.
Pro-con′su-la-ry.
Pro-con′sul-ate.
Pro-cras′ti-nate, 108.
Pro-cras′ti-nāt-ed.
Pro-cras′ti-nāt-ing, 183.
Pro-cras-ti-na′tion.
Pro-crăs′ti-nāt-or.
Pro-cras′ti-na-to-ry, 86.
Pro′cre-ant.
Pro′cre-ate, 169.
Pro′cre-āt-ed.
Pro′cre-āt-ing.
Pro-cre-a′tion.
Pro′cre-āt-ive, 84.
Pro′cre-āt-or.
Pro-crus′te-an (110) [so Wr.; *pro-krus-te′an*, Sm. 155.]
Proc′to-cele.
Proc′tor, 88, 169.
Proc-to′ri-al.
Pro-cum′bent.
Pro-cūr′a-ble, 164.
Proc-u-ra′tion.
Proc′u-rā-tor, 88.
Pro-cure′.
Pro-cured′, 165.
Pro-cure′ment, 185.
Pro-cūr′er, 49, N.
Pro-cūr′ess.
Pro-cūr′ing, 183.
Pro′cy-on, 93.
Prod′i-gal, 72.
Prod-i-gal′i-ty.
Prod′i-gal-ly.
Pro-dig′ioŭs (-*dij′us*).
Prod′i-gy, 45, 93.
Prod′i-to-ry, 86.
Pro-duce′, *v.* 103, 161.
Prod′uce, *n.* (103, 161) [*not* pro′dūs, 153.]
Pro-duced′ (-*dūst′*).
Pro-dūç′ent.
Pro-dūç′er.
Pro-du′ci-ble, 164.
Pro-dūç′ing.
Prod′uct [*not* pro′dukt, 153.]
Pro-duc′tile, 81, 152.
Pro-duc′tion.
Pro-duc′tive, 84.
Pro-duc′tress.
Pro-e-gu′mi-nal.
Pro′em, 76.
Pro-emp-to′sis (-*em*-), 109, 162.
Prof-a-na′tion.
Pro-fane′, *a.* & *v.*
Pro-faned′, 165.
Pro-fane′ly, 185.
Pro-fane′ness, 66, N.
Pro-fān′er, 169.
Pro-fān′ing.
Pro-fan′i-ty, 78, 93.
Pro-fec-ti′tious (-*tish′-us*).
Pro-fess′.
Pro-fessed′ (-*fest′*).
Pro-fess′ed-ly, 150.
Pro-fess′ing.
Pro-fes′sion (-*fesh′un*), 169, 234.

Pro-fes'sion-al (*-fesh'-un-*).
Pro-fes'sion-al-ly (*-fesh'un-*).
Pro-fess'or, 88.
Pro-fes-so'ri-al, 49, N.
Pro-fess'or-ship.
Prof'fer, 170.
Prof'fered, 150, 165.
Prof'fer-er, 77.
Prof'fer-ing.
Pro-fĭ'cience (*-fish'ens*).
Pro-fĭ'cien-cy (*-fish'-en-*), 171.
Pro-fĭ'cient (*-fish'ent*).
Pro'file (*-fēl*) [so Sm.; *pro-fēl'*, Wk.; *pro'fil*, *pro'fēl*, Gd.; *pro'fēl*, *pro-fēl'*, or *pro'fīl*, Wr. 155.]
Pro'fil-ist, *or* Pro-fil'ist (*-fēl'-*) [*pro'fil-ist*, Wb. Gd.; *pro-fēl'ist*, Sm. Wr. 155.]
Prof'it (66, 170), *n.* advantage, gain: — *v.* to benefit. [*See* Prophet, 148.]
Prof'it-a-ble, 164.
Prof'it-a-bly.
Prof'it-ed.
Prof'it-ing.
Prof'li-ga-cy, 169.
Prof'li-gate, 169.
Prof'lu-ent.
Pro for'ma (L.).
Pro-found'.
Pro-fun'di-ty.
Pro-fuse', 121, 136.
Pro-fu'sion (*-zhun*).
Pro-gen'i-tor, 78, 88.
Prog'e-ny (*proj'-*).
Prog-na'thoŭs.
Prog-no'sis, 109.
Prog-nos'tic.
Prog-nos'tic-a-ble.
Prog-nos'tic-ate.
Prog-nos'tic-āt-ed.
Prog-nos'tic-āt-ing.
Prog-nos-tic-a'tion.
Prog-nos'tic-āt-or.
Pro'gramme (*-gram*) (171) [Program, 203.]
Prog'ress (103, 161), *n.* [*not* pro'gres, 153.]
Pro-gress', *v.* 103, 161.
Pro-gressed' (*-grest'*), 165; Note C, p. 34.
Pro-gress'ing. [*un*).
Pro-gres'sion (*-gresh'-*
Pro-gres'sion-al (*-gresh'un-*).
Pro-gres'sion-ist (*-gresh'un-*).
Pro-gres'sĭve, 84.
Pro-hib'it.
Pro-hib'it-ed.
Pro-hib'it-er.
Pro-hib'it-ing.
Pro-hi-bĭ'tion (*-bish'-un*).
Pro-hi-bĭ'tion-ist (*-bish'un-*).
Pro-hib'i-tĭve, 84.
Pro-hib'i-to-ry, 86.
Pro-ject', *v.* 124.
Proj'ect, *n.* (124) [*not* pro'jekt, 153.]
Pro-ject'ed.
Pro-ject'ĭle, 81, 152.
Pro-ject'ing.
Pro-jec'tion.
Pro-ject'or.
Pro-ject'ure, 91.
Projet (Fr.) (*pro'zhā*).
Pro-lap'sus (L.).
Pro-lap'tion.
Pro'late [so Wr. Wb. Gd.; *prol'āt*, Wk.; *pro-lāt'*, Sm. 155.]
Pro-la'tion.
Pro'leg.
Prol-e-gom'e-na, *n. pl.* [so Wk. Sm. Wr.; *pro-le-gom'e-na*, Wb. Gd. 155.]
Prol-e-gom'e-na-ry, 72.
Pro-lep'sis.
Pro-lep'tic.
Pro-lep'tic-al.
Pro-lep'tics, 109.
Prolétaire (Fr.) (*pro-le-têr'*).
Pro-le-ta'ri-an (49, N.) [so Sm. Wb. Gd.; *prol-e-ta'ri-an*, Wr. 155.]
Pro-le-ta'ri-an-ism (*-izm*), 136.
Pro'le-ta-ry, 72.
Prol'i-cide.
Pro-lif'er-oŭs.
Pro-lif'ic, 170.
Pro-lif'ic-al.
Pro-lif-ic-a'tion.
Pro-lix', 121.

☞ "*Pro'lix* and *pre'text* (for *pro-lix'* and *pre-text'*) are widely prevalent, especially the former." *Goodrich.*

Pro-lix'i-ty.
Prol'o-cu-tor [so Sm.; *prol-o-ku'tur*, Wk.; *pro-lo-ku'tur*, Gd.; *prol'o-ku-tur*, or *pro-lok'u-tur*, Wr. 155.]
Prol'ogue, *or* Pro'lŏgue [*prol'og*, Wk. Sm. Wr.; *pro'log*, Wb. Gd. 155.]
Pro-long', 18, N.
Pro-lon-ga'tion (*-long-*) [so Sm. Gd.; *prol-ong ga'shun*, Wk.; *pro-lon-ga'shun*, Wr. 155.]
Pro-longed' (*-longd'*).
Pro-long'er.
Pro-long'ing.
Pro-lu'sion (*-zhun*).
Prom-e-näde', *or* Prom-e-nāde', *n.* & *v.* (122) [so Wr.; *prom-e-näd'*, Sm.; *prom-e-nād'*, Wb. Gd. 155.]
Prom-e-näd'ed, *or* Prom-e-nād'ed.
Prom-e-näd'er, *or* Prom-e-nād'er.
Prom-e-näd'ing, *or* Prom-e-nād'ing.
Pro-me'the-an, 110.
Prom'i-nence.
Prom'i-nen-cy, 169.
Prom'i-nent.
Pro-mis'cu-oŭs.
Prom'ĭse, *n.* (169) [so Sm. Wr. Wb. Gd.; *prom'iz*, Wk. 155.]
Prom'ĭse, *v.* [so Wr. Wb. Gd.; *prom'iz*, Wk. Sm. 155.]
Prom'ised (*-ist*).
Prom-is-ee' [so Wr. Wb. Gd.; *prom-i-zee'*, Sm. 155.]
Prom'is-er, 106.
Prom'is-ing.
Prom'is-or, *or* Prom-is-or' (118) [Law term.]
Prom'is-so-ri-ly.
Prom'is-so-ry, 86, 106.
Prom'on-to-ry, 122, 126.
Pro-mote', 103.
Pro-mōt'ed.
Pro-mōt'er.
Pro-mōt'ing.
Pro-mo'tion.
Pro-mōt'ĭve.
Prompt (*promt*), 162.
Prompt'ed (*promt'-*).
Prompt'er (*promt'-*).
Prompt'ing (*promt'-*).
Prompt'i-tude (*promt'-*)
Prompt'u-a-ry (*promt'-*)
Pro-mul'gate (122) [*not* prom'ul-gāt, 153.]

Pro-mul′gāt-ed.
Pro-mul′gāt-ing.
Prom-ul-ga′tion, *or* Pro-mul-ga′tion, (112) [*prom-ul-ga′shun*, Wk. Sm. Wr.; *pro-mul-ga′shun*, Wb. Gd. 155.]
Prom′ul-gāt-or, *or* Pro-mul-gāt′or [*prom′ul-gā-tur*, Sm.; *pro-mul-ga′tur*, Gd.; *prom-ul-ga′tur*, Wk.; *prom′-ul-gā-tur*, or *prom-ul-ga′tur*, Wr. 155.]
Pro-mulge′.
Pro-mulged′ (*-muljd′*).
Pro-mulg′er (*-mulj′-*).
Pro-mulg′ing (*-mulj′-*).
Pro-na′os.
Pro′nate.
Pro-na′tion.
Pro-na′tor.
Prone, 24.
Prone′ly, 93.
Prone′ness, 66, N.
Prong, 18, N.
Prong′-buck.
Pro-nom′i-nal.
Pro′noun.
Pro-nounce′. [185.
Pro-nounce′a-ble, 164.
Pro-nounced′ (*-nounst′*)
Pro-nounç′ing.
Pro-nun′cial (*-shal*).
Pro-nun-ci-a-men′to.
Pro-nun-ci-a′tion (*-shĭ-a′shun*, or *-sĭ-a′shun*) [*pro-nun-shĭ-a′shun*, Wk. Wr.; *pro-nun-sĭ-a′shun*, Sm. Wb. Gd. 155.]

☞ "The word *pronunciation* is regularly pronounced *pro-nun-shi-a′-shun*, and by all speakers would probably be so sounded, if it were related to any such verb as to *pronunciate*, in the same way that *association* and *enunciation* are related to *associate* and *enunciate*. In the absence of any such related verb, most speakers say *pro-nun-si-a′shun*, and so avoid the double occurrence of the sound of *sh* in the same word." *Smart.*

Pro-nun′ci-a-tĭve (*-shĭ-*) [so Wk. Sm. Wr.; *pro-nun′sha-tiv*, Wb. Gd. 155.]
Pro-nun′ci-a-to-ry (*-shĭ-*), 86.
Proof, 19.
Proof′-sheet.
Proof′-text.
Prop, 18, 64.
Pro-pæ-deū′tic (*-pe-du′-*), 171.
Pro-pæ-deū′tic-al.
Pro-pæ-deū′tics.
Prop′a-ga-ble, 164.
Prop-a-gan′da.
Prop-a-gan′dism (*-dizm-*).
Prop-a-gan′dist.
Prop′a-gate, 169.
Prop′a-gāt-ed, 183.
Prop′a-gāt-ing.
Prop-a-ga′tion.
Prop′a-gāt-ĭve.
Prop′a-gāt-or.
Pro-pel′.
Pro-pelled′, 165.
Pro-pel′ler.
Pro-pel′ling, 176.
Pro-pend′en-cy.
Pro-pend′ent, 169.
Pro-pense′, 171.
Pro-pen′sion, 169.
Pro-pen′si-ty.
Prop′er, 170.
Prop′er-ly.
Prop′er-ty, 135.
Proph′e-cy (171), *n.* [*See* Prophesy, 148.]
Proph′e-sīed.
Proph′e-sī-er.
Proph′e-sȳ (94, 171), *v.* [*See* Prophecy, 148.]
Proph′e-sȳ-ing, 186.
Proph′et (76; Note F, p. 79), one who foretells future events. [*See* Profit, 148.]
Proph′et-ess.
Pro-phet′ic.
Pro-phet′ic-al.
Pro-phet′ic-al-ly.
Proph-y-lac′tic.
Proph-y-lac′tic-al.
Pro-pin′qui-ty (*-ping′-kwĭ-*), 54, 171.
Pro-pĭ′ti-a-ble (*-pish′i-a-bl*), 164.
Pro-pĭ′ti-ate (*-pish′ĭ-*) [so Wk. Sm. Wr.; *pro-pish′āt*, Wb. Gd. 155.]
Pro-pĭ′ti-āt-ed(*-pish′ĭ-*).
Pro-pĭ′ti-āt-ing(*-pish′ĭ-*)
Pro-pĭ-ti-a′tion (*-pish-ĭ-ā′shun*).
Pro-pĭ′ti-at-or (*-pish′ĭ-*).
Pro-pĭ′ti-a-to-ri-ly (*-pish′ĭ-*).
Pro-pĭ′ti-a-to-ry (*-pish′-ĭ-*), 86.
Pro-pĭ′tioŭs (*-pish′us*).
Pro-pĭ′tioŭs-ly (*-pish′-us-*).
Pro′plasm, 136.
Pro-plas′tic.
Pro′po-lis.
Pro-po′nent, 122.
Pro-pōr′tion.
Pro-pōr′tion-a-ble, 164.
Pro-pōr′tion-a-bly.
Pro-pōr′tion-al.
Pro-pōr-tion-al′i-ty.
Pro-pōr′tion-al-ly.
Pro-pōr′tion-ate.
Pro-pōr′tion-āt-ed.
Pro-pōr′tion-āt-ing.
Pro-pōr′tion-ate-ly.
Pro-pōr′tioned (*-shund*)
Pro-pōr′tion-ing.
Pro-pōr′tion-ment.
Pro-pōs′al (*-poz′-*), 40, 72.
Pro-pose′ (*-pōz′*).
Pro-posed′ (*-pōzd′*).
Pro-pōs′er (*-pōz′-*).
Pro-pōs′ing (*-pōz′-*).
Prop-o-sĭ′tion (*-zish′-un*), 119.
Prop-o-sĭ′tion-al (*-zish′-un-*).
Pro-pound′, 103.
Pro-pound′ed.
Pro-pound′er.
Pro-pound′ing.
Propped (*propt*) (Note C, p. 34) [Propt, 203]
Prop′ping, 176.
Pro-pre′tor (*-tawr*) (88) [Propraetor, 203.]
Pro-pri′e-ta-ry, 72.
Pro pri′e-tor.
Pro-pri′e-ty, 169.
Pro-proc′tor.
[Propt, 203.—*See* Propped.]
Pro-pugn′ (*-pūn′*), 162.
Pro-pugn′er (*-pūn′-*).
Pro-pul′sion.
Pro-pul′sĭve.
Prop-y-læ′um (L.)(*-le′-*) [pl. *Prop-y-læ′a*, 198.]
Pro ra′ta (L.).
Prore, 24.
Pro-rec′tor.
Pro-rec′tor-ate.
Pro-rep′tion.
Pro-ro-ga′tion.
Pro-rōgue′, 168; Note D, p. 37.
Pro rōgued′ (*-rōgd′*).
Pro-rōgu′ing (*-rōg′-*).

Pro-rup′tion.
Pro-sa′ic (*-za′-*).
Pro-sa′ic-al (*-za′-*).
Pro-sa′ism (*-za′izm*).
Pro-sa′ist (*-za′-*) [so Sm. Wr.; *pro′zā-ist*, Gd. 155.]
Pro-sce′ni-um, 169.
Pro-scribe′.
Pro-scribed′, 165.
Pro-scrīb′ing, 183.
Pro-scrip′tion.
Pro-scrip′tĭve, 84.
Prose (*prōz*), 24, 40.
Pro-sec′tor.
Pros′e-cute.
Pros′e-cūt-ed, 183.
Pros′e-cūt-ing.
Pros-e-cu′tion.
Pros′e-cūt-or, 228.
Pros′e-cūt-rix.
Prosed (*prōzd*), 165.
Pros′e-lyte, 171.
Pros′e-lȳt-ed.
Pros′e-lȳt-ing.
Pros′e-lȳt-ism (*-izm*).
Pros′e-lȳt-ize, 202.
Pros′e-lȳt-ized.
Pros′e-lȳt-īz-ing.
Prŏs-en-ne-a-he′dral.
Prōs′er (*prōz′-*).
Pro-sil′i-en-cy.
Prōs′i-ly (*prōz′-*).
Prōs′i-ness (*prōz′-*)
Prōs′ing (*prōz′-*),
Pro-slāv′er-y.
Pros-o-di′ac-al, 108.
Pro-so′di-al, 169.
Pro-so′di-an.
Pro-sod′ic-al.
Pros′o-dist, 141.
Pros′o-dy [*not* proz′o-dy, 153.]
Pros-o-pog′ra-phy.
Pros-o-po-lep′sy, 169.
Pros-o-po-pœ′ia (*-pe′-ya*), 113, 171.
Pros′pect.
Pro-spec′tion.
Pro-spect′ĭve, 84.
Pro-spect′ĭve-ly.
Pro-spect′us, 169, 189.
Pros′per.
Pros′pered, 150, 165.
Pros′per-ing.
Pros-pĕr′i-ty, 108, 169.
Pros′per-oŭs, 100.
Pros′tate.
Pros-tat′ic.
Pros′the-sis.
Pros-thet′ic, 109.
Pros′ti-tute, 26, 169.
Pros′ti-tūt-ed.
Pros′ti-tūt-ing.
Pros-ti-tu′tion.
Pros′ti-tūt-or.
Pros′trate.
Pros′trāt-ed, 183.
Pros′trāt-ing.
Pros-tra′tion.
Pro′style.
Prōs′y (*prōz′-*), 169.
Pro-syl′lo-gism (*-jizm*).
Pro-tag′o-nist.
Prot′a-sis.
Pro-tat′ic.
Pro′te-an, *or* Pro-te′an (110) [*pro′te-an*, Wr. Wb. Gd.; *pro-te′an*, Sm. 155.]
Pro-tect′.
Pro-tect′ed.
Pro-tect′ing.
Pro-tec′tion.
Pro-tec′tion-ist.
Pro-tect′ĭve, 228.
Pro-tect′or, 169.
Pro-tect′or-al.
Pro-tect′or-ate.
Pro-tect-o′ri-al.
Pro-tect′ress.
Pro-tect′rix.
Protégé (Fr.) (*pro-tā-zhā′*), *n. mas.* 163.
Protégée (Fr.) (*pro-tā-zhā′*), *n. fem.*
Pro-te-in-a′ceoŭs(*-shus*)
Pro-te′in-oŭs.
Pro′te-ĭne (152) [Protein, 203.]
Pro tem′po-re (L.).
Pro-ter-an′thoŭs.
Pro-test′, *v.* 103, 161.
Pro′test, *or* Prot′est, *n.* (103, 161) [so Wr.; *pro′test*, Wb. Gd.; *pro′test*, Sm.; *pro-test′*, or *prot′est*, Wk. 155.]
Prot′est-ant, 169.
Prot′est-ant-ism (*-izm*), 133, 136.
Prot-est-a′tion [*not* prō-tĕst-a′shun, 143, 153.]
Pro-test′ed.
Pro-test′er.
Pro-test′ing.
Pro′teŭs, *or* Pro′te-us [so Wr.; *pro′te-us*, Sm. Wb. Gd. 155.] [*See* Note under *Morpheus*.]
Proth′e-sis.
Pro-thon′o-ta-ry (72) [*not* pro-tho-no′ta-ry, 153.]
Prō-tho′rax [so Wr. Gd.; *pro′tho-raks*, Sm. 155.]
Pro′to-cōl, 171.
Pro′to-cōl-ist.
Pro′to-gĭne (*-jin*) [so Gd. Wr.; *pro′to-jīn*, Sm. 155.]
Pro′to-mar′tyr, 224.
Pro′to-phyte.
Pro-to-phȳ-tol′o-gy.
Pro′to-plasm (*-plazm*).
Pro-to-plas′mic (*-plaz′-*)
Pro′to-plast.
Pro-to-plas′tic.
Pro′to-sâlt.
Pro′to-type.
Pro-tox′ĭde. [*See* Note under *Oxide*.]
Pro-tox′id-ize.
Pro-tox′id-ized.
Pro-tox′id-īz-ing.
Pro-to-zo′a, *n. pl.*
Pro-to-zo′ic.
Pro-tract′.
Pro-tract′ed.
Pro-tract′ing.
Pro-tract′ĭle, 152.
Pro-trac′tion.
Pro-tract′ĭve, 84.
Pro-tract′or.
Pro-trude′ (*-trood′*), 19.
Pro-trud′ed (*-trood′-*).
Pro-trud′ing (*-trood′-*).
Pro-tru′sĭle (*-troo′-*).
Pro-tru′sion (*-troo′-zhun*).
Pro-tru′sĭve (*-troo′-*).
Pro-tu′ber-ance.
Pro-tu′ber-an-cy.
Pro-tu′ber-ant, 169.
Pro-tu′ber-ate.
Pro-tu′ber-āt-ed.
Pro-tu′ber-āt-ing.
Pro-tu-ber-a′tion.
Proud, 28.
Proud′ly, 93.
Prov′a-ble (*proov′a-bl*), 164, 171.
Prove (*proov*), 19.
Proved (*proovd*), 183.
Pro-ved′i-tor.
Prov′e-dore [so Gd.; *prov-e-dōr′*, Wr. 155.]
Prov′en (*proov′n*), 149.

☞ This participle from *prove* is distinctively a term of Scottish law; but it is occasionally used by English and American writers instead of *proved*.

Pro-ven′cial (*-shal*), *a.* of, or belonging to,

Provence, in France. [*See* Provincial, 148.]
Prov′en-der.
Prov′er (*proov′-*), 183.
Prov′erb, 135.
Pro-verb′i-al.
Pro-verb′i-al-ism (*-izm*).
Pro-verb′i-al-ist.
Pro-verb′i-al-ly.
Pro-vide′.
Pro-vīd′ed, 183.
Prov′i-dence.
Prov′i-dent, 76.
Prov-i-den′tial (*-shal*), 169.
Pro-vīd′er.
Pro-vīd′ing.
Prov′ince.
Pro-vin′cial (*-shal*)(112), *a.* pertaining to a province. [*See* Provencial, 148.]
Pro-vin′cial-ism (*-shal-izm*), 136.
Pro-vin′cial-ist (*-shal-*).
Pro-vin-cĭ-al′i-ty (*-shĭ-*).
Pro-vine′.
Pro-vined′.
Pro-vīn′ing.
Prov′ing (*proov′-*), 183.
Pro-vĭ′sion (*-vizh′un*).
Pro-vĭ′sion-al (*-vizh′-un-*).
Pro-vĭ′sion-al-ly (*-vizh′-un-*).
Pro-vĭ′sion-a-ry (*vizh′-un-*), 72.
Pro-vĭ′sioned (*-vizh′-und*).
Pro-vĭ′sion-ing (*-vizh′-un-*).
Pro-vi′so (*-zo*) [pl. Pro-vi′sos (*-zōz*), 192.]
Pro-vi′sor (*-zur*).
Pro-vi′so-ry (*-zo-*), 86.
Prov-o-ca′tion.
Pro-vo′ca-tĭve [so Wk. Wr. Wb. Gd.; *pro-vok′a-tiv*, Sm. 155.]
Pro-vōk′a-ble, 164, 169.
Pro-voke′.
Pro-voked′ (*-vōkt′*).
Pro-vōk′er.
Pro-vōk′ing.
Prov′ost (86) (*prov′ust*) [so Wk. Sm. Wr. Gd.], *n.* the chief or head of any body, as of a college.
Prov′ost (*prov′ust*) [so Sm.; *pro-vo′*, Wk. Gd.; *pro-vo′*, or *prov′ust*, Wr. 155], *n.* an executioner, or a superintendent of executions.
Prow (28) [so Wb. Gd.; *prou*, or *pro*, Wk. Wr.; *pro*, Sm. 155.]

☞ Though Walker, in deference to the authorities whom he cites, gives *pro* as an alternative pronunciation of this word, he says: "Analogy . . . is clearly for the first pronunciation."

Prow′ess (28, 76) [so Sm. Wr. Wb. Gd.; *prou′es*, or *pro′is*, Wk. 155.]

☞ Walker remarks that "analogy must decide" for the pronunciation *prou′es* in preference to *pro′es*.

Prowl (28) [so Sm. Wr. Wb. Gd.; *proul*, or *prōl*, Wk. 155.]

☞ "The former [*proul*] is more agreeable to analogy." *Walker.*

Prowled (*prould*).
Prowl′er.
Prowl′ing.
Prox′ene, 171.
Prox′i-mal.
Prox′i-mate, 73.
Prox-im′i-ty.
Prox′i-mo.
Prox′y, 169.
Prude (*prood*), 19.
Pru′dence (*proo′-*), 169.
Pru′dent (*proo′-*).
Pru-den′tial (*proo-den′-shal*), 112.
Pru′dent-ly (*proo′-*).
Prud′er-y (*prood′-*).
Prud′homme (Fr.) (*proo-dom′*).
Prud′ish (*prood′-*).
Pru′i-nate (*proo′-*).
Pru′i-nose (*proo′-*).
Prune (*proon*), 19.
Pruned (*proond*), 183.
Pru-nel′la (*proo-*) [Prunello (in the sense of *a kind of woollen cloth*), 203.]
Pru-nel′lo [Prunella, 203.]
Prun′er (*proon′-*).
Pru-nif′er-oŭs (*proo-*).
Prun′ing (*proon′-*), 183.
Prun′ing-hŏŏk (*proon′-*), 206, Exc. 4.
Pru′ri-ence (*proo′-*), 49, N.
Pru′ri-en-cy (*proo′-*).
Pru′ri-ent (*proo′-*).
Pru-rig′i-nous (*proo-rij′-*).
Prus′sian (*prush′an*) [so Sm.; *pru′shan*, Wb. Gd.; *prush′an*, or *proo′shun*, Wr. 155.]

☞ "The old name for Prussia was *Pruce*: hence the present word, with its relations, was for a long time subject to a similar sound of the *u*, which in the metropolis [London] is now deemed a vulgarism." *Smart.*

Prus′si-ate [so Sm.; *prŭsh′āt*, Wb. Gd.; *prŭs′sĭ āt*, or *proo′sĭ-āt*, Wr. 155.]
Prus′sic [so Sm.; *prŭs′-sik*, Wb. Gd.; *prus′-sik*, or *proos′sik*, Wr. 155.]
Pru-ten′ic (*proo-*).
Pry (25, 30, 48) [*See* Prize.]
Pry′ing.
Pryt-a-ne′um (L.) (122) [so Gd. Wr.; *prī-ta-ne′um*, Sm. 155.]
Pryt′a-nis (L.) [pl. *Pryt′a-nes* (*-nēz*), 198.]
Pryt′a-ny.
Psalm (*säm*), 11, 162.
Psalm′ist (*säm′ist*) [so Sm. Gd.; *sal′mist*, Wk.; *sal′mist*, or *säm′ist*, Wr. 155.]
Psalm′ist-ry (*säm′ist-ry*) [*sal′mist-ry*, Wr. 155.]
Psal-mod′ic (*sal-*).

☞ "This word and the following are pronounced not as formatives from *psalm*, but with reference to Greek formatives." *Smart.*

Psal-mod′ic-al (*sal-*).
Psal′mo-dist (*sal′-*).
Psal′mo-dy (*sal′-*) (162) [so Wk. Sm. Wr.; *säm′o-dy*, or *sal′mo-dy*, Gd. 155.]
Psal-mog′ra-phy (*sal-*).
Psal′ter (*sawl′tur*, or *sal′tur*) (162) [*sawl′-tur*, Wk. Wr. Gd.; *sal′tur*, Sm. 155.]

☞ "Such [*sal′tur*] is the present pronunciation

of this word, with reference to the original Greek [ψαλτήρ], and not to the intervening Saxon [*psaltere*]." *Smart.*

Psal'ter-y (*sawl'tur-y*, or *sal'tur-y*).
Pse'phism (*se'fizm*).
Pseū-de-pig'ra-phy (*su-*).
Pseū'do- (*su'do*) (162), a prefix from the Greek signifying *false*.
Pseū'do-dip'ter-al (*su'-*), 224.
Pseū'do-grăph (*su'-*).
Pseū-dog'ra-phy (*su-*).
Pseū-dol'o-gist (*su-*).
Pseū-dol'o-gy (*su-*).
Pseū'do-mar'tyr (*sū'-*).
Pseū'do-morph (*su'-*).
Pseū-do-morph'oŭs (*su-*), 171.
Pseū'do-nȳme, *or* Pseū'do-nym, 203.
Pseū-don'y-moŭs (*su-*).
Pseū'do-phi-los'o-pher (*su'-*).
Pseū'do-scope (*su'-*).
Pseū-do-sperm'ic (*su-*).
Pshaw (*shaw*), 162.
Psī-lan'thro-pism (*sī-lan'thro-pizm*), 136, 162.
Psī-lan'thro-pist (*sī-*).
Psit-ta'ceoŭs (*sit-ta'-shus*), 171.
Pso'ra (*so'-*), 162.
Pso'ric (*so'-*).
Psȳ-chi'a-ter (*sī-ki'-*).
Psȳ-chi'a-try (*sī-ki'-*).
Psy'chic (*si'kik*), 171.
Psy'chic-al (*si'kik-*).
Psy'chism (*si'kizm*), 133, 136.
Psȳ-cho-log'ic (*sī-ko-loj'ik*), 109, 171.
Psȳ-cho-log'ic-al (*sī-ko-loj'-*), 108.
Psȳ-chol'o-gist (*sī-kol'-*).
Psȳ-chol'o-gy (*sī-kol'-*), 162.
Psȳ-chom'a-chy (*sī-kom'a-ky*), 171.
Psy'cho-man-cy (*si'ko-*).
Psȳ-cho-pan'ny-chism (*sī-ko-pan'nī-kizm*), 136, 171.
Psȳ-chrom'e-ter (*sī-krom'-*), 108.
Psȳ-chrom'e-try (*sī-krom'-*), 171.
Psy-chro-pho'bi-a (*sī-kro-*).
Psych'tic (*sik'-*).
Ptar'mic (*tar'-*).
Ptar'mi-gan (*tar'-*), 162.
Ptĕr-i-ple-gis'tic (*tĕr-*).
Ptĕr-o-dac'tyl (*tĕr-*).
Ptĕr'o-pod (*tĕr'-*).
Ptĕr-op'od-oŭs (*tĕr-*).
Pter-yg'i-an (*tĕr-rij'-*), 171.
Ptĕr'y-goid (*tĕr'-*).
Ptis'an (*tiz'an*) [so Sm. Wb. Gd.; *tī-zan'*, Wk.; *tī-zan'*, or *tiz'-an*, Wr. 155.]
Ptol-e-ma'ic (*tol'-*), 171.
Pty'a-līne (*tī'-*), 152.
Pty'a-lism (*tī'a-lizm*), 133, 136.
Ptȳ-al'o-gŏgue (*tī-*), 87, 162.
Ptys'ma-gŏgue (*tiz'-*), 87, 171.
Pu'ber-al.
Pu'ber-ty, 93.
Pu-bĕr'u-lent, 89.
Pu-bes'cence, 171.
Pu-bes'cent.
Pu'bic.
Pub'lic, 200.
Pub'li-can, 72, 78.
Pub-li-ca'tion, 112.
Pub'li-cist.
Pub-liç'i-ty, 169, 171.
Pub'lic-ly.
Pub'lic-spĭr'it-ed.
Pub'lish.
Pub'lish-a-ble, 164, 169.
Pub'lished (*-lisht*).
Pub'lish-er.
Pub'lish-ing.
Pub'lish-ment.
Puc-coon', 121.
Puce, 26, 39.
Puck, 22, 181.
Puck'er, 104.
Puck'ered, 150.
Puck'er-ing.
Puck'er-y.
Pud'den-ing (*pŏŏd'n-*).
Pud'der.
Pud'dered, 150.
Pud'der-ing.
Pud'ding (*pŏŏd'-*), 20, 66, 170.
Pud'ding-stone (*pŏŏd'-*).
Pud'dle (*pud'l*), *n.* & *v.*
Pud'dled (*-dld*).
Pud'dler.
Pud'dling.
Pu-diç'i-ty.
Pu'er-īle, 81, 152.
Pu-er-il'i-ty.
Pu-er'per-al, 21, N.
Pu-er'per-oŭs.
Puff, 22, 173.
Puff'bâll.
Puffed (*puft*), 165; Note C, p. 34.
Puff'er.
Puff'er-y.
Puf'fin, 170.
Puff'i-ness, 186.
Puff'ing.
Puff'y, 169.
Pug, 22, 30, 53.
Pug'ging (*-ghing*), 138.
Pugh (*poo*), 162.
Pu'gil, 26, 45.
Pu'gil-ism (*-izm*).
Pu'gil-ist.
Pu-gil-ist'ic.
Pug-na'cioŭs (*-shus*), 46, Note 2.
Pug-naç'i-ty.
Pug'-nosed (*-nōzd*), 206, Exc. 5.
Puis'ne (*pu'ne*), *a.* inferior in rank; subordinate. [Law term.] [*See* Puny, 160.]
Pu'is-sance (169) [so Sm. Wr. Wb. Gd.; *pu'is-sans*, or *pu-is'-sans*, Wk. 155.]
Pu'is-sant.
Puke, 26, 163.
Puked (*pūkt*), 165.
Pūk'ing, 183.
Pul'chri-tude (*-krī-*).
Pule, 26, 163.
Puled, 165.
Pūl'er.
Pu'lic.
Pu'li-cene, 171.
Pūl'ing.
Pull (*pŏŏl*), 20, 172.
Pull'-back (*pŏŏl'-*), 215.
Pulled (*pŏŏld*), 165.
Pull'er (*pŏŏl'-*).
Pul'let (*pŏŏl'-*).
Pul'ley (*pŏŏl'y*) (169) [pl. Pul'leys (*pŏŏl'iz*), 190.]
Pŭl'li-cat [so spelled by Wb. Gd. — Pullicate (*pŏŏl'i-kāt*), Wr. 203.]
Pŭl'lu-late.
Pŭl'lu-lāt-ed.
Pŭl'lu-lāt-ing.
Pŭl-mo-bran'chi-ate (*-brang'kī-*), 54, 171.
Pŭl'mo-grade.

Pŭl'mo-na-ry, 72.
Pŭl'mo-nate.
Pŭl-mon'ic.
Pŭl-mon'ic-al.
Pŭl-mo-nif'er-oŭs.
Pŭlp, 22, 64.
Pŭlped (*pulpt*), 165.
Pŭlp'i-ness.
Pŭlp'ing.
Pul'pit (*pŏŏl'*-).
Pŭlp'oŭs, 100.
Pŭlp'y, 169.
Pulque (Sp.) (*pŏŏl'kā*) [so Wr.; *pul'kā*, Gd. 155.]
Pŭl'sate.
Pŭl'sāt-ed.
Pŭl'sa-tīle, 152.
Pŭl'sāt-ing.
Pŭl-sa'tion.
Pŭl'sa-tĭve, 84.
Pŭl'sa-to-ry, 86.
Pŭlse, 22, 189.

☞ As a noun in the sense of *leguminous plants*, it does not take the plural form.

Pŭlsed (*pulst*), 165.
Pŭlse'-glȧss.
Pŭl-sif'ic.
Pŭl-sim'e-ter, 108.
Pŭls'ing, 183.
Pŭl-ta'ceoŭs (*-shŭs*).
Pu'lu.
Pŭl'ver-a-ble, 164.
Pŭl-ver-a'ceoŭs (*-shus*).
Pŭl'ver-īne (152) [Pulverin, 203.]
Pŭl'ver-īz-a-ble, 164.
Pŭl-ver-īz-a'tion.
Pŭl'ver-ize.
Pŭl'ver-ized.
Pŭl'ver-īz-er.
Pŭl'ver-īz-ing.
Pŭl'ver-oŭs.
Pŭl-vĕr'u-lence.
Pŭl-vĕr'u-lent, 108.
Pŭl-vi'nar.
Pŭl'vi-nate.
Pŭl'vi-nāt-ed.
Pu'ma, 72.
Pu'mīce, *or* Pum'īce (169) [so Wr.; *pu'mis*, Wk. Sm.; *pum'is*, Wb. Gd. 155.]
Pu-mĭ'ceoŭs (*-mish'us*).
[Pummace, 203.—*See* Pomace.]
[Pummel, 203.—*See* Pommel.]
Pump, 22, 64.
Pumped (*pumpt*), 165; Note C, p. 34.
Pump'er.
Pump'er-nick'el.
Pump'ing.
[Pumpion (*pump'yun*), 203.—*See* Pumpkin.]
Pump'kin (80) [Pumpion, Pompion, 203.]

☞ *Pumpkin*, though a corrupted form of *pumpion*, or *pompion*, is now the common orthography.

Pun, 22.
Punch, 22, 44, Note 2.
Punched (*puncht*).
Punch'eon (*-un*), 171.
Punch'er.
Pun-chi-nel'lo.
Punch'ing.
Punc'tate (*pungk'*-)
Punc'tāt-ed.
Punc'ti-form, 108.
Punc-til'io (*pungk-til'yo*) (54) [so Wk. Wr. Wb. Gd.; *pungk-til'i-o*, Sm. 155.] [pl. Punc-til'iōs (*-yōz*), 192.]
Punc-til'ious (*pungk-til'yus*), 51, 54.
Punc'tion (*pungk'*-).
Punct'u-al (*pungkt'*-), 89.
Punct'u-al-ist.
Punct-u-al'i-ty.
Punct'u-al-ly, 170.
Punct'u-ate, 73, 89.
Punct'u-āt-ed.
Punct'u-āt-ing.
Punct-u-a'tion, 112.
Punct'u-āt-or.
Punct'u-ist, 89.
Punct'ure (*pungkt'yur*), 91, 171.
Punct'ured (*-yurd*).
Punct'ur-ing (*-yur*-).
Pun'dit [Pandit, 203.]
Pung, 22, 54.
Pun'gence, 45.
Pun'gen-cy, 169.
Pun'gent.
Pu'nic, 26, 80.
Pu'ni-ca fi'des (L.) (*-dēz*)
Pu'ni-ness, 186.
Pun'ish, 104.
Pun'ish-a-ble, 164, 169.
Pun'ished (*-isht*).
Pun'ish-er, 77.
Pun'ish-ing.
Pun'ish-ment.
Pu'ni-tĭve, 84.
Punk (*pungk*), 22, 54.
Pun'ka (*pung'ka*) [so Wr.; *pun'ka*, Gd. 155.]
Punned, 165, 176.
Pun'ner.
Pun'net, 66, 170.
Pun'ning.
Pun'ster.
Punt, 22.
Punt'er.
Punt'ing.
Pun'to.
Pu'ny, *a.* inferior; small; weak. [*See* Puisne, 160.]
Pup, 22.
Pu'pa (L.) [pl. *Pu'pæ* (*-pe*), 198.]
Pupe.
Pu'pil, 26, 80.
Pu'pil-age, 171.
Pu-pil-lăr'i-ty.
Pu'pil-la-ry [*not* pu-pil'la-ry, 153] [Pupilary, 203.]

☞ Johnson, Smart, Webster, and Goodrich, spell this word with one *l*, as if derived from our own word *pu'pil*; Walker and Worcester spell it with two *l's*, in accordance with its Latin original, *pupillaris*.

Pu'pi-pare (*-pêr*).
Pu-pip'a-roŭs, 108.
Pu'pi-vore.
Pu-piv'o-roŭs, 108.
Pupped (*pupt*), 176.
Pup'pet, 230.
Pup'ping, 176.
Pup'py, 66, 170.
Pup'py-ism (*-izm*), 136.
Pur (21, 49) [Purr, 203.]
Pu-rä'na [so Wr. Gd.; *pū-rā'na*, Sm. 155.]
Pu-ran'ic, 109.
Pur'blīnd, 169.
Pur'chas-a-ble, 164.
Pur'chase, *n.* & *v.*
Pur'chased (*-chăst*).
Pur'chase-mon'ey (*-mun'*-), 205.
Pur'chas-er.
Pur'chas-ing.
Pure, 26, 49.
Pur'fled (*-fld*).
Pur-ga'tion, 169.
Pur'ga-tĭve, 84.
Pur-ga-to'ri-al, 49, N.
Pur-ga-to'ri-an.
Pur'ga-to-ry, 86, 169.
Purge, 21, 135.
Purged (*purjd*).
Purg'er (*purj'*-).

Purg′ing (*purj′*-).
Pu-ri-fĭ-ca′tion. [*See* Note under *Purify*.]
Pu-rif′i-ca-tĭve.
Pu′ri-fi-cā-tor.
Pu-rif′i-ca-to-ry, 86.
Pu′ri-fīed. [*See* Purify.]
Pu′ri-fī-er. [*See* Purify.]
Pu′ri-form, 108.
Pu′ri-fy, 169.

☞ We should naturally expect *purify*, *purity*, and other English derivatives from *pure*, to be pronounced *pūr′ri-fy*, *pūr′ri-ty*, &c.; but the general, if not universal practice, in the United States, is to say *pu′ri-fy*, *pu′ri-ty*, &c.; and this is the mode adopted in the Dictionaries of Webster, Goodrich, and Worcester. *See* § 49, N.

Pu′ri-fȳ-ing.
Pu′rim, 49, N.
Pu′rism (-*rizm*) (136) [*See* Purify.]
Pu′rist. [*See* Purify.]
Pu′ri-tan. [*See* Purify.]
Pu-ri-tan′ic (170) [*See* Purify.]
Pu-ri-tan′ic-al.
Pu′ri-tan-ism (-*izm*) (136) [*See* Purify.]
Pu′ri-ty (169) [*See* Purify.]
Purl (21, 49), *n.* a kind of border; — a circle made by a flowing liquid; — two rounds in knitting: — *v.* to flow with a gentle noise; — to move in waves. [*See* Pearl, 148.]
Purled, 165.
Pur′lieū (-*lu*), 169, 171.
Pur′lin [P u r l i n e, 203.]
Purl′ing.
Pur-loin′, 103.
Pur-loined′, 165.
Pur-loin′ing.
Pur′par-ty [P o u r p a r t y, 203.]
Pur′ple, 164.
Pur′pled (*pur′pld*).
Pur′pling.
Pur′plish.
Pur′pōrt, *n.* & *v.* 121.
Pur′pōrt-ed.
Pur′pōrt-ing.
Pur′pose (*pur′pus*).
Pur′posed (-*pust*).
Pur′pose-ly (-*pus*-).
Pur′pos-er (-*pus*-).
Pur′pos-ing (-*pus*-), 183.
Pur-prest′ure (91) [P o u r p r e s t u r e, 203.]
Pur′prise (-*prīz*).
Pur′pure.
Pur-pu′re-al.
Purr, *n.* & *v.* (21, 175) [P u r, 203.]
Purred, 165.
Pŭr′ree.
Purr′ing.
Purse, 21, 49, 135; Note D, p. 37.
Pursed (*purst*).
Purse′net, 206. [5.
Purse′-proud, 206, Exc.
Purs′er.
Pur′si-ness, 186.
Purs′ing.
Purs′laīn (96) [P u r s l a n e, 203.]
Pur-su′a-ble, 164.
Pur-su′al.
Pur-su′ance, 72.
Pur-su′ant.
Pur-sūe′, 169.
Pur-sūed′.
Pur-su′er.
Pur-su′ing, 183.
Pur-sūit′, 171. [171.
Pur′sui-vant (-*swĭ*-), 169,
Pur′sy, 93, 169.
Pur′te-nance.
Pu′ru-lence (-*roo*-).
Pu′ru-len-cy (-*roo*-).
Pu′ru-lent (-*roo*-) [*not* pŭr′oo-lent, 153.]
Pur-vey′ (-*va′*).
Pur-vey′ance (-*va′*-).
Pur-veyed′ (-*vād′*) (187), *v.* did purvey. [*See* Pervade, 160.]
Pur-vey′ing (-*va′*-).
Pur-vey′or (-*va′*-), 169.
Pur′view (-*vu*), 171.
Pus, 22, 174.
Pu′sey-ism (-*zĭ-ism*) [*not* pu′sĭ-izm, 153.]
Pu′sey-ist (-*zĭ*-).
Pu′sey-īte (-*zĭ*-), 152.
Push (*poosh*), 20, 46.
Pushed (*poosht*), 165; Note C, p. 34.
Push′er (*poosh′*-).
Push′ing (*poosh′*-).
Pu-sil-la-nim′i-ty, 171.
Pu-sil-lan′i-moŭs.
Puss (*poos*), 20, 174.
Pus′sy (*poos′*-).
Pŭs′tu-lar, 89, 108.
Pŭs′tu-late.
Pŭs′tu-lāt-ed.
Pŭs-tu-la′tion.
Pŭs′tule (26, 44, Note 1) [so Sm.; *pus′chūl*, Wk.; *pus′l*, or *pust′-yūl*, Wb. Gd.; *pus′-tūl*, or *pust′yūl*, Wr. 155.]

☞ Webster says that *pus′l*, "is the usual pronunciation in America;" but this pronunciation is not supported by analogy, and it is now heard, for the most part, only among uneducated speakers. It should be carefully avoided as a vulgarism.

Pŭs′tu-loŭs.
Put (*poot*), *v.* 161.

☞ As a neuter or intransitive verb, Walker pronounces it *poot*, or *put*.

Put (*poot*), *n.* [so Sm. Wb. Gd.; *pŭt*, Wk. Wr. 155], *n.* an action of distress.
Pŭt (161), *n.* a clown; a game at cards.
Pu′ta-tĭve.
Pŭt-chock′ [so Gd.] [P u t c h u c k (*pŭch′-uk*), Wr. 203.]
Pu′te-al.
Put′log (*poot′*-) [so Sm. Gd.; *put′log*, Wk. Wr. 155.]
Put′-off (*poot′*-), 18, N.; 206, Exc. 4.
Pu-tred′i-noŭs, 108.
Pu-tre-fac′tion, 171.
Pu-tre-fac′tĭve, 84.
Pu′tre-fīed.
Pu′tre-fȳ, 94, 169.
Pu′tre-fȳ-ing.
Pu-tres′cence, 171.
Pu-tres′cent.
Pu-tres′ci-ble, 164.
Pu′trid, 26, 80.
Pu-trid′i-ty, 108.
Pu′tri-lage.
Put′ter (*poot′*-), 176.
Pŭt′tĭed.
Put′ting (*poot′*-).
Pŭt′ty, 22, 170.
Pŭt′ty-ing.
Pŭz′zle, 104, 164.
Pŭz′zled (-*zld*), 183.
Pŭz′zler.
Pŭz′zling.
[P u z z o l a n, P u z z o l a n a, P u z z o l a n o, 203. — *See* Pozzuolana.]
Pyc′nīte, 152.

Pyc'no-dont.
Pyc'no-style, 171.
[Pye, 203. — *See* Pie.]
Py'garg.
Pyg-me'an (110) [Pigmean, 203.]
Pyg'my [Pigmy, 203.]
Pyl'a-gore.
Pȳ-lŏr'ic, 109.
Pȳ-lo'rus (L.) [pl. Pȳ-lo'rī, 198.]
Pȳ-o-gen'ic.
Pȳr'a-canth.
Pȳr-al'lo-līte, 152.
Pȳr'a-mid, 105, 171.
Pȳ-ram'i-dal [*not* pȳr-a-mi'dal, 153.]
Py-ram'i-dal-ly.
Pȳr-a-mid'ic.
Pȳr-a-mid'ic-al.
Pȳ-ram'i-doid.
Pȳ-rar'gil-līte, 152.
Pȳre, 25, 171.
Pȳ-rene', 171.
Pȳr-e-ne'an, 110.
Pȳ-ret'ics, 109.
Pȳr-e-tol'o-gy.
Pȳ-rex'i-al [so Wr.; *pȳ-reks'i-al*, Gd. 155.]
Pȳ-rex'ic-al.
Pȳr-he-li-om'e-ter.
Pȳr'i-form, 108.
Pȳr-i-ta'ceoŭs (*-shus*).
Pȳr'īte, 16, 152.

☞ Smart says of this modern Anglicized form of *pyrites*: "The plural is *pyrites*, which may be considered the regular English plural, and pronounced accordingly [*pĭr'its*]; or the classical plural, and pronounced in three syllables, *pĭr-ī'tēs*: the latter practice is more common, the noun singular [*pyrite*] being unusual."

Pȳ-rī'tēs (*-tēz*) (L.), *n. sing.* & *pl.* [so Sm. Wr. Gd.; *pĭ-rī'tēz*, or *pĭr'ĭ-tēz*, Wk. 155] [*See* Note under *Pyrite*.]
Pȳ-rit'ic.
Pȳ-rit'ic-al.
Pȳr'i-toid.
Pȳr-i-to-he'dral.
Pȳr-i-to-he'dron.
Pȳr'i-toŭs.
Py'ro-a-cet'ic, *or* Py'ro-a-ce'tic [*pī-ro-a-se'tik*, Gd.; *pĭr-o-a-set'ik*, Sm. Wr. 155.]
Py'ro-aç'id.
Pȳr'o-chlore (*-klōr*).
Py-ro-cit'ric.
Py'ro-e-lec'tric.
Pȳ-rog'e-noŭs (*-roj'-*).
Pȳ-rol'a-try.
Pȳ-ro-lig'ne-oŭs.
Pȳ-ro-lig'nic.
Pȳ-ro-lig'nīte, 152.
Pȳ-ro-lig'noŭs.
Pȳ-ro-lith'ic.
Pȳ-rol'o-gist, 45.
Pȳ-rol'o-gy.
Pȳ-ro-lu'site, 152.
Pȳr'o-man-cy.
Pȳ-ro-man'tic [so Gd.; *pĭr'o-man-tik*, Wr. 155], *n.*
Pȳ-ro-man'tic [so Gd.; *pĭr-o-man'tik*, Wr. 155], *a.*
Pȳ-rom'e-ter, 108.
Pȳ-ro-met'ric.
Pȳ-ro-met'ric-al.
Py-rom'e-try.
Pȳ-ro-mor'phīte, 152.
Pȳ-ro-mor'phoŭs.
Pȳ-ro-nom'ics, 109.
Pȳr'ope, 16, 24.
Pȳ-roph'a-noŭs.
Pȳ-ro-phŏr'ic.
Pȳ-roph'o-roŭs, *a.* 160.
Pȳ-roph'o-rus, *n.* 160.
Pȳ-ro-phyl'līte, *or* Pȳ-roph'yl-līte, 152.
Pȳ-ror'thīte, 152.
Pȳr'o-scope.
Pȳ-ro'sis, 109.
Pȳ-ros'ma-līte, 152.
Pȳr'o-some.
Pȳr-o-tech'nic (*-tek'-*).
Pȳr-o-tech'nic-al (*-tek'-*)
Pȳr-o-tech'nics (*-tek'-*), 171.
Pȳr-o-tech'nist (*-tek'-*).
Pȳr'o-tech-ny (*-tek-*).
Py-rot'ic.
Pyr'ox-ene.
Pȳ-rox-en'ic.
Pȳ-rox-yl'lic.
Pȳ-rox'y-līne, 152.
Pȳr'rhic (*-rik*), 171.
Pȳr'rhi-cist (*-rĭ-*), 171.
Pȳr'rhīte (*-rīt*), 152.
Pȳr-rho-ne'an.
Pȳr-rhon'ic (*-ron'-*).
Pȳr'rho-nism (*pĭr'o-nizm*), 136.
Pȳr'rho-nist (*-ro-*).
Pȳr'rho-tīne (*-ro-*).
Pȳ-thag-o-re'an (110) [so Wk. Sm. Wr.; *pith-a-go're-an*, or *pi-thag-o-re'an*, Gd. 155.]
Pȳ-thag'o-rism (*-rizm*).
Pyth'i-ad.
Pyth'i-an, 169.
Py'thon.
Pyth'o-ness.
Pȳ-thon'ic.
Pyth'o-nism (*-nizm*) (133) [so Wr.; *pi'thon-izm*, Gd. 203.]
Pyth'o-nist.
Pȳ-ul'con.
Pyx (16, 171) [Pix, 203.]
Pyx-id'i-um.
Pyx'is.

Q.

Quab (*kwob*), 18, 34, 52.
Qua-chil'to.
Quack, 10, 34, 181.
Quacked (*kwakt*), 165; Note C, p. 34.
Quack'er-y, 233, Exc.
Quack'ing.
Quack'ish.
Quack'ism, 133, 136.
Quack'sal-ver (*kwak'-sal-vur*, or *kwak'sä-vur*) [*kwak'sal-vur*, Wk. Wr. Wb. Gd.; *kwak'sä-vur*, Sm. 155.]
Quad'ra (*kwod'-*) (L.) [pl. *Quad'ræ* (*kwod'-rē*), 198.]
Quad'ra-gene (*kwod'-*).
Quad-ra-ges'i-ma (*kwod-*), 116.
Quad-ra-ges'i-mal (*kwod-*).
Quad'ran-gle (*kwod'-rang-gl*), 54, 164, 171.
Quad-ran'gu-lar (*kwod-rang'-*), 108.
Quad'rans (*kwod'ranz*).
Quad'rant (*kwod'-*) (18, 72) [so Sm. Wr. Wb. Gd.; *kwaw'drant*, Wk. 155.]
Quad-rant'al (*kwod-*).
Quad'rat (*kwod'-*).
Quad'rate (*kwod'-*).
Quad-rat'ic (*kwod-*) (109) [so Sm. Wb. Gd.; *kwa-drat'ik*, Wk. Wr. 155.]
Quad-ra'trix (*kwod-*).
Quad'ra-ture (*kwod'-*), 90.
Quad'rel (*kwod'-*).
Quad-ren'ni-al (*kwod-*), 169, 170.

Quad'ri-ble (*kwod'ri-bl*), 164.
Quad ri-cap'su-lar (*kwod-*).
Quad'ri corn (*kwod'-*).
Quad-ri-corn'oŭs (*kwod-*).
Quad-ri-deç'i-mal (*kwod-*).
Quad-ri-den'tate (*kwod-*).
Quad-ri-fa'ri-oŭs (*kwod-*), 49, N.
Quad'ri-fid (*kwod'-*).
Quad'ri-foil (*kwod'-*).
Quad-ri-fo'li-ate (*kwod-*).
Quad'ri-fur-cāt-ed (*kwod'-*).
Quad-ri'ga (*kwod-*) (L.) [pl. *Quad-ri'gæ* (*kwod-ri'jē*), 198.]
Quad-ri-ge-na'ri-oŭs (*kwod-*).
Quad-ri-ju'gate (*kwod-*), *or* Quad-rij'u-gate (*kwod-*).
Quad-ri-ju'goŭs (*kwod-*), *or* Quad-rij'u-goŭs (*kwod-*) [so Wr.; *kwod-ri-ju'gus*, Sm.; *kwod-rij'u-gus*, Wb. Gd. 155.]
Quad-ri-lat'er-al (*kwod-*).
Quad-ri-lit'er-al (*kwod-*), 171.
Qua-drille' (*ka-dril'*, or *kwa-dril'*) [*ka-dril'*, Wk. Sm. Wr.; *kwa-dril'*, or *ka-dril'*, Wb. Gd. 155.]
Quad-rill'ion (*kwod-ril'-yun*), 51, 171.
Quad-ri-lo'bate (*kwod-*).
Quad'ri-lobed (*kwod'-*), 165.
Quad-ri-loc'u-lar (*kwod-*), 108.
Quad-ri-mem'bral (*kwod-*).
Quad-ri-no'mi-al (*kwod-*), 169.
Quad-ri-nom'ic-al (*kwod-*).
Quad-rip'ar-tīte (*kwod-*) (152, 156) [so Sm. Wb. Gd.; *kwa-drip'ar-tīt*, Wk. Wr. 155.]
Quad-ri-pen'nate (*kwod-*).
Quad-ri-phyl'loŭs (*kwod-*), *or* Quad-riph'yl-loŭs (*kwod-*) [*See* Adenophyllous.]
Quad'ri-reme (*kwod'-*).
Quad-ri-sec'tion (*kwod-*).
Quad ri-sul'cate (*kwod-*).
Quad-ri-syl-lab'ic (*kwod-*).
Quad-ri-syl-lab'ic-al (*kwod-*).
Quad-ri-syl'la-ble (*kwod-*), 164.
Quad'ri-valve (*kwod'-*).
Quad-ri-valv'u-lar (*kwod-*).
Quad-riv'i-al (*kwod-*).
Quad-roon' (*kwod-*) (122, 171), *n.* the offspring of a mulatto and a white person. [*See* Quadrune, 148.]
Quad-ru'ma-na (L.) (*kwod-roo'-*), *n. pl.*
Quad'ru-mane (*kwod'-*) [Quadruman, 203.]
Quad-ru'ma-noŭs (*kwod-roo'-*) [so Wr.; *kwod-rū'ma-nus*, Wb. Gd.; *kwod'roo-măn-us*, Sm. 155.]
Quad'rune (*kwod'roon*), *n.* a kind of gritstone. [*See* Quadroon, 148.]
Quad'ru-ped (*kwod'-roo-*).
Quad-ru'pe-dal (*kwod-roo'-*) [so Gd.; *kwod'-roo-pē-dal*, Sm.; *kwod-roo-pe'dal*, or *kwod-roo'pe-dal*, Wr. 155.]
Quad'ru-ple (*kwod'roo-pl*), 164.
Quad'ru-pled (*kwod'-roo-pld*), 183.
Quad-ru'pli-cate (*kwod-roo'-*), 73.
Quad-ru'pli-cāt-ed (*kwod-roo'-*), 183.
Quad-ru'pli-cāt-ing (*kwod-roo'-*).
Quad-ru-pli-ca'tion (*kwod-roo-*), 112.
Quad'ru-pling (*kwod'-roo-*).
Quad'ru-ply (*kwod'-roo-*).
Quæ're (L.) (*kwe're*), 163.
[Quæstor, 203. — *See* Questor.]
Quaff, 12, 131, 173.
Quaffed (*kwaft*), 165; Note C, p. 34.
Quaff'ing, 228.
Quăg, 10, 34.
Quăg'ga, 66, 127.
Quăg'gy (*-ghy*), 138.
Quăg'mire (10) [*not* kwog'mīr), 153.
Quâ'haug (*kwaw'hog*) [so Wb. Gd.; *kwaw-hawg'*, Wr. 155] [Quahog, 203.]
Quāil, 23, 34.
Quāiled, 165.
Quāil'ing.
Quāint, 23, 34, 52.
Quake, 23, 163.
Quaked (*kwākt*), 165, 183; Note C, p. 34.
Quāk'er.
Quāk'er-ish.
Quāk'er-ism (*-izm*).
Quāk'ing, 183.
Qual'i-fī-a-ble (*kwol'-*), 164, 186.
Qual-i-fĭ-ca'tion (*kwol'-*), 112.
Qual'i-fi-cā-tive (*kwol'-*), 84.
Qual'i-fi-cā-tor (*kwol'-*).
Qual'i-fīed (*kwol'-*), 99.
Qual'i-fī-er (*kwol'-*), 186.
Qual'i-fȳ (*kwol'-*), 94.
Qual'i-fȳ-ing (*kwol'-*), 186.
Qual'i-tā-tĭve (*kwol'-*).
Qual'i-ty (*kwol'-*) (169) [*not* kwăl'i-ty, 127, 153.]
Qualm (*kwahm*) (162) [so Sm. Wb. Gd.; *kwawm*, Wk.; *kwahm*, or *kwawm*, Wr. 155.]
Qualm'ish (*kwahm'-*).
Quam'ash (*kwom'-*), 18.
Quăm'o-clit, 105.
Quan-da'ry (*kwon-*), *or* Quan'da-ry (*kwon'-*) (105) [so Wr.; *kwon-da'ry*, Wk.; *kwon-dêr'y*, Sm.; *kwon'da-ry*, Wb. Gd. 155.]

☞ "*Quan'dary* (for *quanda'ry*), in accordance with *bound'ary*, and nearly every other word in *-ary*, is our prevailing pronunciation." *Goodrich.*

Quănt [so Gd.]

☞ Worcester does not indicate the pronunciation of this word.

Quan'ti-ta-tĭve (*kwon'-*).

Quan'ti-ty (*kwon'-*) (108) [*not* kwan'ti-ty, 127, 153.]
Quan'tum (*kwon'-*).
Quăn'tum mĕr'u-it (L.).
Quăn'tum suf'fi-cit (L.).
Quan'tum va-le'bat (L.).
Quā-qua-ver'sal, 21, N.
Quar'an-tine (*kwŏr'an-tēn*) (161) [so Sm. Wb. Gd.; *kwŏr-an-tēn'*, Wk. Wr. 155], *n.*
Quar-an-tine' (*kwŏr-an-tēn'*), *v.* 161.
Quar'rel (*kwŏr'-*), 48, 171.
Quar'relled (*kwŏr'reld*) (165) [Quarreled, Wb. Gd. 203. — *See* 171, and Note E, p. 70.]
Quar'rel-ler (*kwŏr'-*) [Quarreler, Wb. Gd. 203.]
Quar'rel-ling (*kwŏr'-*) [Quarreling, Wb. Gd. 203.]
Quar'rel-some (*kwŏr'-rel-sum*), 169.
Quar'rĭed (*kwŏr'-*), 99
Quar'ri-er (*kwŏr'-*).
Quar'ry (*kwŏr'-*).
Quar'ry-ing (*kwŏr'-*).
Quârt, *n.* two pints. [pl. Quarts. — *See* Quartz, 160.]
Quâr'tan, 72.
Quâr-ta'tion, 112.
Quâr'ter.
Quâr'ter-age.
Quâr'ter-dāy.
Quâr'ter-deck.
Quâr'tered, 165.
Quâr'ter-ing.
Quâr'ter-ly, 93.
Quâr'ter-mȧs'ter, 205.
Quâr'tern.
Quar'ter-on.
Quâr-ter-oon', 122.
Quâr'ter-ses'sions (*-sesh'unz*), 205.
Quâr'ter-stȧff.
Quâr-tet', *or* Quâr-tette', 203.
Quâr'tīle, 152.
Quâr'tīne, 82, 152.
Quâr'to (86) [pl. Quâr'-tōs (*-tōz*), *or* Quâr'-tōes (*-tōz*), 192], *n.* a book of which each sheet is folded so as to make four leaves. [*See* Quartoze, 160.]
Quâr'toze, *n.* a name given to the four aces in piquet. [*See* Quartos, pl. of Quarto, 160.]
Quârtz (*kworts*) (17; Note C, p. 34), *n.* a silicious mineral. [*See* Quarts (pl. of Quart), 160.]
Quârt-zif'er-oŭs, 108.
Quârtz'ose (*kworts'-*) [so Wb. Gd.; *kwort-zōs'*, Sm. *kwort'zōs*, Wr. 155.]
Quârtz'-sin-ter (*kworts'-*), 66, N.
Quârtz'y (*kworts'-*), 169.
Quăs, *or* Quăss, 203.
Quash (*kwosh*), 18, 46.
Quashed (*kwosht*), 165; Note C, p. 34.
Quash'ee (*kwosh'-*).
Quash'ing (*kwosh'-*).
Qua'sī (L.).
Quăs-i-mo'do [so Wr. Wb. Gd.; *kwā-zim'o-do*, Sm. 155.]
Quas-sa'tion.
Quas'si-a (*kwosh'ĭ-a*) [so Wr.; *kwosh'yä*, Gd.; *kwozh'ĭ-a*, Sm. 155] [*not* kwosh'y, 153.]
Quas'sīne (*kwos'-*), 152.
Quas'sīte (*kwos'-*), 152.
Qua'ter-cous'ins (*ka'-tur-kuz'nz*), 171.
Qua-ter'na-ry, 72.
Qua-ter'nate, 21, N.
Qua-ter'ni-on.
Qua-ter'ni-ty, 108.
Qua'ter-on.
Quat'rāin (*kwot'-*) [so Sm. Gd.; *kwaw'trin*, Wk. Wr. 155.]
Qua'ver, 34, 77.
Qua'vered (*-vurd*), 165.
Qua'ver-ing.
Quay (*ke*), 13, 156, 171.
Quay'age (*ke'-*).
Quēach'y, 169.
Quēan, *n.* a worthless or lewd woman. [*See* Queen, 160.]
Quēa'si-ness (*-zĭ-*), 186.
Quēa'sy (*kwe'zy*), 169.
Queen, *n.* the wife of a king; a female who is the ruler of a kingdom. [*See* Quean, 160.]
Queened, 165.
Queen'ing.
Queen'like, 206, Exc. 5.
Queen'ly, 93.
Queen'pōst.
Queen's-met'al (*kweenz'-*), 213.
Queer, 13, 49.
Queer'ish.
Quell, 15, 34, 172.
Quelled, 165.
Quell'er.
Quell'ing.
Quelque-chose (Fr.) (*kek'shōz*), 154.
Quench, 15, 44.
Quench'a-ble, 164, 169.
Quenched (*kwencht*).
Quench'er.
Quench'ing.
Quer'cit-ron (105) [so Wb. Gd.; *kwer'sĭ-trun*, Sm.; *kwer-sit'-ron*, Wr. 155.]
Que'rĭed, 99.
Quer-i-mo'ni-oŭs, 100.
Que'rist, 80.
Quern, 21, N.
[Querpo, 203. — *See* Cuerpo.]
Quer'que-dule.
Quer'u-loŭs, 89.
Que'ry, 49, N.
Que'ry-ing.
Quest, 15, 34.
Quest'ion (*kwest'yun*), 44, Note 1.
Quest'ion-a-ble (*kwest'-yun-*), 164, 169.
Quest'ion-a-ry (*kwest'-yun-*), 72, 169.
Quest'ioned (*kwest'-yund*).
Quest'ion-er (*kwest'-yun-*).
Quest'ion-ing (*kwest'-yun-*).
Quest'ion-ist (*kwest'-yun-*).
Quest'man, 196.
Ques'tor, 127.
[Queue (*kū*), 203. — *See* Cue.]
Quib'ble, 164.
Quib'bled, 165.
Quib'bler.
Quib'bling, 183.
Quick, 16, 34, 181.
Quick'en (*kwik'n*), 149.
Quick'ened (*kwik'nd*), 150.
Quick'en-er (*kwik'n-*).
Quick'en-ing (*kwik'n-*).
Quick'en-tree (*kwik'n-*), 206, Exc. 4.
Quick'grȧss, 216
Quick'lime, 206.
Quick'match.

Quick′sand.
Quick′set.
Quick′sil-ver.
Quick′step.
Quick′-wit-ted, 206, Exc. 4.
Quid, 16, 34, 52.
Quid′di-ty (169, 170) [Quidity, 203.]
Quid′dle, 164.
Quid′dled, 165.
Quid′dler.
Quid′dling, 183.
Quid′nunc.
Quid pro quo (L.).
Quī-esce′ (*-es′*), 171.
Quī-esced′ (*-est′*).
Quī-es′cence.
Quī-es′cen-cy, 169.
Quī-es′cent.
Quī-es′cing.
Qui′et, 76.
Qui′et-ed, 176.
Qui′et-er.
Qui′et-ing.
Qui′et-ism (*-izm*), 136.
Qui′et-ist.
Qui-et-ist′ic.
Qui′e-tude, 26, 108, 169.
Quī-e′tus, 156.
Quill, 16, 34, 172.
Quilled, 165.
Quil′let, 66, 170.
Quill′ing, 228.
Quill′wort (*-wurt*).
Quilt (*kwilt*), 16, 64.
Quilt′ed, 176.
Quilt′er.
Quilt′ing.
Qui′na-ry, 72.
Qui′nate.
Quince, 16, 39; Note D, p. 37.
Quince′-tree, 206, Exc. 4.
Quin-cun′cial(*-shal*),112.
Quin′cunx (*kwing′-kungks*) (54) [so Wk. Sm.; *kwin′kungks*, Wb. Gd. Wr. 155.]

☞ "As the accent is on the first syllable of this word, it is under the same predicament as the first syllable of *congregate*." *Walker*.

Quin-dec′a-gon.
Quin-de-cem′vir [L. pl. *Quin-de-cem′vi-rī*; Eng. pl. Quin-de-cem′-virs (*-vurz*), 198.]
Quin-de-cem′vi-rate, 73.
Quin′i-a, 72, 78.
Quĭ-nīne′, *or* Quī′nīne [*kwĭ-nīn′*, Sm.; *kwī′-nīn*, Wb. Gd.; *kwĭ-nīn′*, or *kwin′īn*, Wr. 155.]
Quin-qua-ges′i-ma.
Quin-quan′gu-lar (*-kwang′-*), 108.
Quin-que-an′gled(*-ang′-gld*).
Quin-que-cap′su-lar.
Quin-que-den′tate.
Quin-que-den′tāt-ed.
Quin-que-fa′ri-oŭs.
Quin′que-fid, 169.
Quin-que-fo′li-ate.
Quin-que-fo′li-āt-ed.
Quin-que-lit′er-al.
Quin-que-lo′bate.
Quin′que-lobed, 165.
Quin-que-loc′u-lar.
Quin′que-nerved, 165.
Quin-quen′ni-al, 170.
Quin-quep′ar-tīte, 105, 152.
Quin′que-reme, 171.
Quin-que-syl′la-ble, 164.
Quin′que-valve, 169.
Quin-que-valv′u-lar.
Quin′que-vir [L. pl. *Quin-quev′i-rī*; Eng. pl. Quin′que-virs (*-vurz*), 198.]
Quin-qui′na.
Quin′sy (*-zy*), 169.
Quĭnt (*kwint*) [so Wr. Wb. Gd.; *kint*, Wk.; *kăngt*, Sm. 155.]

☞ Although Walker respells this word *kint*, he remarks that it is "a term at cards, pronounced *kent*."

Quin′taĭn (96), *n.* a figure set up for tilters to run at. [*See* Quintine, 160.]
Quin′tal (72) [Kentle, 203.]
Quin′tan.
Quin′ter-on.
Quin-tes′sence (107) [so Wk. Sm. Wb. Gd.; *kwin-tes′sens*, or *kwin′tes-sens*, Wr. 155.]

☞ "My opinion is, that it may have the accent either on the first or second [syllable], as the rhythm of the phrase requires." *Walker*. — "The accent on the first syllable is very unnatural." *Goodrich*.

Quin-tes-sen′tial (*-shal*).
Quin-tet′ [so Gd.; *kwin′-tet*, Wr. 155], *or* Quintette′, 203.
Quin′tĭle, 81, 152.
Quin-till′ion (*-yun*), 51, 171.
Quin′tĭne (82, 152), *n.* the fifth and innermost ovule in some plants. [*See* Quintain, 160.]
Quint-roon′ [so Wr.; *kwin′troon*, Gd. 155.]
Quin′tu-ple, 89, 164.
Quin′tu-pled, 165.
Quin′tu-pling.
Quin′zāine [Quinzain (*kwin′zen*), Sm. 203.]
Quip, 16, 34, 52.
Qui′po (Sp.) (*ke′po*) [pl. Qui′pōs (*ke′pōz*), 189] [Quippo, Quippa, Quippu, 203.]
Quire (*kwīr*) (25, 34, 52), *n.* twenty-four sheets of paper. [*See* Choir, 160.]
[Quire, 203. — *See* Choir.]
Quĭr′is-ter.
Quĭr′īte, 152.
Qui-ri′tēs (L.) (*-tēz*), *n. pl.*
Quirk, 21, N.; 135.
Quirked (*kwirkt*), 165: Note C, p. 34.
Quirk′ish.
Quit, 16, 34, 52.
Quī tam (L.).
Quit′clāim, *n.* & *v.*
Quit′clāimed, 165.
Quit′clāim-ing.
Quite, 25, 34, 52.
Quit′rent.
Quits, *int.*
Quit′ta-ble, 164, 169.
Quit′tance, 72, 176.
Quit′ted.
Quit′ter.
Quit′ting, 141.
Quiv′er, 77.
Quiv′ered (*-urd*), 150.
Quiv′er-ing.
Qui vive (Fr.) (*ke vēv′*).
Quix-ot′ic, 109.
Quix′ot-ism (*-izm*), 133.
Quix′ot-ry, 169.
Quiz, 16, 34, 40.
Quizzed, 165.
Quiz′zer, 176.
Quiz′zic-al.
Quiz′zing.

Quiz'zing-glȧss, 215.
Quo'ad hoc (L.).
Quo an'i-mo (L.).
Quod'li-bet (L.), 156.
[Quoif, 203.—*See* Coif.]
Quoin (*kwoin*, or *koin*) [so Wr. Gd.; *koin*, Sm. 155], *n.* a corner; — a wedge. [Coin, Coigne, 203.]
Quoit (*kwoit*), 27, 34, 52.
Quöll, 18, 172.
Quon'dam.
Quo'rum, 49, N.; 169.
Quo'ta.
Quōt'a-ble, 164, 169.
Quo-ta'tion.
Quote (*kwōt*) (24, 34) [*not* kōt, 153.]
Quōt'ed.
Quōt'er.
Quoth (*kwŏth*, or *kwuth*) (130) [so Wr. Gd.; *kwuth*, or *kwŏth*, Wk.; *kwuth*, Sm. 155.]
Quo-tid'i-an (169) [so Sm. Wr. Wb. Gd.; *kwo-tid'yĭ-an*, Wk. 155]
Quo'tient (-*shent*), 171.
Quōt'ing.
Quo war'ran-to (L.) (-*wŏr'*-).

R.

Rab'bet, *v.* to cut in a particular way, as boards, in order to join their edges: — *n.* a cut made in the edges of boards for the purpose of joining them. [*See* Rabbit, 148.]
Rab'bet-ed.
Rab'bet-ing.
Rab'bī, *or* Rab'bĭ [*rab'bē*, or *rab'bī*, Wk. Wr. Gd.; *rab'bī*, Sm. 155.] [pl. Rab'bies, 191.]

☞ "When pronounced in Scripture, [it] ought to have the last syllable like the verb *to buy*." *Walker.*

Rab'bin.
Rab-bin'ic, 170.
Rab-bin'ic-al, 108.
Rab'bin-ism (-*izm*), 136.
Rab'bin-ist.
Rab'bin-īte, 152.
Rab'bit (170), *n.* an animal of the genus *Lepus.* [*See* Rabbet, 148.]
Rab'ble (*rab'l*), 164.
Rab'ble-ment (*rab'l*-).
[Rabdology, 203.—*See* Rhabdology.]
[Rabdomancy, 203. — *See* Rhabdomancy.]
Rab'id, 66, 170.
Ra'bi-ēs (L.) (-*ēz*)
Rā'ca (Chaldee.)
Rac-coon' [Racoon, Rackoon, 203.]
Race, 23, 39.
Race'-cōurse.
Raced (*rāst*), 165, 183; Note C, p. 34.
Raç-e-ma'tion.
Ra-ceme', *or* Raç'eme [*ra-sēm'*, Wr. Gd.; *ras'ēm*, Sm. 155.]
Ra-cem'ic.
Raç-e-mif'er-oŭs [Racimiferous, 203.]
Raç-e-mose', *or* Ra-ce'-mose [*ras-e-mōs'*, Wr.; *ra-se'mōs*, Gd. 155.]
Raç'e-moŭs, *or* Ra-ce'-moŭs [so Wr. Gd.; *ra-se'mus*, Sm. 155.]
Ra-cem'u-lose.
Rāç'er, 183.
Ra-chil'la (-*kil'*-.)
Ra'chis (*ra'kis*) [Rhachis, 203.]
Ra-chit'ic (-*kit'*-.)
Ra-chi'tis (-*ki'*-).
Ra'ci-ness, 186.
Rāç'ing, 183.
Rack, 10, 181.
Racked (*rakt*), 165.
Rack'er.
Rack'et.
Rack'et-ed.
Rack'et-ing.
Rack'ing.
[Rackoon, 203.—*See* Raccoon.]
Rack'-rent.
[Racoon, 203. — *See* Raccoon.]
Ra-co'vi-an.
Ra'cy, 169.
Rad'dle, 164.
Ra-deau' (-*do'*).
Ra'di-al, 78.
Ra'di-ance, 169.
Ra'di-an-cy.
Ra'di-ant [so Sm. Wr. Wb. Gd.; *ra'dĭ-ant*, or *ra'jĭ-ant*, Wk. 134, 155.]
Ra'di-a-ry, 72.
Ra-di-a'ta (L.), *n. pl.*
Ra'di-ate (108) [so Sm. Wr. Wb. Gd.; *ra'dĭ-āt*, or *ra'jĭ-āt*, Wk. 134, 155.]
Ra'di-āt-ed, 183.
Ra'di-āt-ing.
Ra-di-a'tion.
Ra'di-āt-or, 169.
Rad'i-cal.
Rad'i-cal-ism (-*izm*), 136.
Rad-i-cal'i-ty.
Rad'i-cal-ly.
Rad'i-cant.
Rad-i-ca'tion.
Rad'i-cel, 76, 78.
Rad'i-cle, 164.
Rad'i-cule.
Ra'di-o-līte, 152.
Ra-di-om'e-ter.
Ra'di-oŭs, 100.
Rad'ish (66, 170) [*not* red'ish, 153.]
Ra'di-us (169) [so Sm. Wr. Wb. Gd.; *ra'dĭ-us*, or *ra'jĭ-us*, Wk. 134, 155] [L. pl. Ra'dĭ-ī; Eng. pl. Ra'di-us-es (-*ez*), 198.]

☞ The English plural, *radiuses*, is very rarely used.

Ra'di-us-vec'tor.
Ra'dix (L.) [pl. *Rad'i-cēs* (-*sēz*), 198.]
Ra-du'li-form.
Rȧff.
Raf'fle (*raf'l*).
Raf'fled (*raf'ld*), 183.
Raf'fler.
Raf'fling.
Rȧft, 12, 131.
Rȧft'er.
Rȧft'ered (-*urd*), 150.
Rȧft'ing.
Rȧfts'man, 214.
Rag, 10, 48, 53.
Rag-a-muf'fin, 171.
Rage, 23, 163.
Raged, 165, 183.
Rag'ged (-*ghed*), 138, 176.
Rāg'ing (*rāj'*-).
Rag'lan.
Rag'man.
Ragout (Fr.) (*ră-goo'*).
Ra-guled', 165.
Rag'weed, 206.
Rāid, *n.* a hostile incursion. [*See* Rayed, 160.]

Rāil, 23.
Rāiled, 165.
Rāil'er.
Rāil'ing.
Răil'ler-y (*ral'-*) (171) [*not* rāl'lur-y, 153.]
Rāil'rōad, 206.
Rāil'wāy.
Rāi'ment, 171.
Rāin, *n.* the water that falls in drops from the clouds: — *v.* to fall in drops from the clouds, as water. [*See* Reign, *and* Rein, 160.]
Rāin'bōw.
[Raindeer, 203. — *See* Reindeer.]
Rāin'drop, 206.
Rāined, 165.
Rāin'-gāuge, 171.
Rāin'i-ness, 186.
Rāin'ing, *part.* from *Rain.* [*See* Reining, 160.]
Rāin'-wâ-ter.
Rāin'y, 93, 169.
Rāis'a-ble (*rāz'a-bl*).
Rāise (*rāz*) (23, 40), *v.* to put, place, take, or set, up. [*See* Rays, *and* Raze, 160.]
Rāised (*rāzd*), 165.
Rāis'er (*rāz'-*) (70), *n.* one who raises. [*See* Razor, 160.]
Rāi'sin (*rā'zn*) (149, 167) [so Sm. Wr. Wb. Gd.; *re'zn*, Wk. 155.]

☞ Walker's pronunciation of this word, though agreeable to the current usage of his time, and though it may, as he remarks, "be traced as far back as the days of Queen Elizabeth," is now wholly obsolete.

Raisonné (Fr.) (*rā-zon-na'*) [so Sm. Wr.; *rā-zon'nā*, Gd. 155.]
Rā'jah, *or* Rä'jah [*rā'-ja*, Sm. Wb. Gd.; *rä'-ja*, or *rā'ja*, Wr. 155] [Raja (*ra'ja*, Gd.) 203.]
Räj-poot', 122.
Rake, 23.
Raked (*rākt*), 165, 183; Note C, p. 34.
Rake'hell.

☞ "Not originally a compound, though taken for one." *Smart.*

Rāk'er, 77, 228.
Rāk'ing, 183.
Rāk'ish.
Ral'līed (*-lid*), 99.
Ral'li-er.
Ral'ly, 170.
Ral'ly-ing.
Ram, 10.
Ram'a-dan [so Sm. Wb. Gd.; *ram-a-dan'*, Wr. 155] [Rhamadan, Ramadhan, Ramazan, 203.]
Ram-a-yā'na (Sanscrit) [so Sm.; *ram-a-ya'na*, Wr. 155.]
Ram'ble, 164.
Ram'bled, 165, 183.
Ram'bler.
Ram'bling.
Ra'me-al.
Ra'me-an, 110.
Ra-men'ta (L.) *n. pl.*
Ram-en-ta'ceoŭs (*-shus*).
Ra'me-oŭs.
Ram-i-fī-ca'tion.
Ram'i-fīed.
Ram'i-form.
Ram'i-fȳ, 94.
Ram'i-fȳ-ing.
Ra'mist.
Rammed (*ramd*), 165, 176.
Ram'mer.
Ram'ming.
Ram'mish.
Ra-moon'-tree.
Ra'mose [so Gd.; *ra-mōs'*, Wr. 155.]
Ra'moŭs.
Ramp, 10, 64.
Ramp'an-cy.
Ramp'ant, 72.
Ram'pärt.
Ramped (*rampt*), 165.
Ramp'ing.
Ram'pi-on.
Ram'rod, 206.
Ram'son (*-zun*), 86
Ram'u-lose, 136.
Ram'u-loŭs, 100.
Ran, 10.
Ra'na (L.).
Ra'nan-īte, 152.
Ran-ces'cent, 171.
Rănch [so Gd.; *rȧnch*, Wr. 155.]
Ran-che'ro (Sp.). (*-cha'-*).
Ran'cho (Sp.)
Ran'cid, 80.
Ran-cid'i-ty, 108, 169.

Ran'cor (*rang'-*) (54), *n.* deep malignity. [*See* Ranker, 160] [Rancour, Sm. 199, 203.]
Ran'cor-oŭs (*rang'-*).
Ran'dom, 86, 169.
[Ranedeer, 203. — *See* Reindeer.]
Rang, 10 54.
Rānge, 23; Note D, p. 37.
Rānged (*rānjd*), 183.
Rāng'er (*rānj'-*).
Rāng'ing (*rānj'-*).
Ra'nīne, 152.
Rank (*rangk*), 10, 54.
Ranked (*rangkt*), 165.
Rank'er, *a.* more rank. [*See* Rancor, 160.]
Rank'ing.
Ran'kle (*rang'kl*), 104.
Ran'kled (*rang'kld*).
Ran'kling (*rang'-*).
Rank'ly, 93.
Ran'nee (Hindostanee) [so Sm.][Ranee (*ra-ne'*, Gd.) Ranny, 203.]
Ran'sack.
Ran'sacked (*-sakt*).
Ran'sack-ing.
Ran'som, 86, 169.
Ran'somed (*-sumd*).
Ran'som-er.
Ran'som-ing.
Rant, 10.
Rant'ed.
Rant'er.
Ran'ter-ism (*-izm*), 133.
Rant'ing.
Ran'ti-pole.
Rant'ism (*-izm*), 136.
Ra-nun-cu-la'ceoŭs (*ra-nung-ku-la'shus*), 112.
Ra-nun'cu-lus (*-nung'-*) [L. pl. *Ra-nun'cu-lī* (*nung'-*); Eng. pl. Ra-nun'cu-lus-es (*nung'-ku-lus-ez*), 198.]
Ranz des vaches (Fr.) (*rŏngz dā vȧsh*).
Rap, *n.* a smart, quick blow: — *v.* to strike with a quick, smart blow. [*See* Wrap, 160.]
Ra-pa'cioŭs (*-shus*), 112, 169.
Ra-paç'i-ty, 108.
[Raparee, 203. — *See* Rapparee.]
Rape, 23.
Ra'phe (*ra'fe*) [*not* rāf, 153] [Rhaphe, 203.]

Răph'a-el-ism (*-izm*) [*ra'fa-el-izm*, Gd. 155.]
Răph'a-el-īte (152) [*See* Pre-raphaelite.]
Răph'i-dēs (*-dēz*) [so Wr. Gd.; *ra'fidz*, Sm. 155] [Rhaphides, 203.]
Răph'il-īte, 152.
Rap'id, 66.
Ra-pid'i-ty, 169.
Ra'pi-er, 63, 229.
Rap'il.
Ra-pil'lo, 170.
Rap'ine, 82, 171.
Rap-pa-ree' (122) [Raparee, 203.]
Rapped (*rapt*), *part.* struck with a quick, smart blow. [*See* Rapt, *and* Wrapped, 160.]
Rap-pee', 121.
Rap'pel, 170.
Rap'per (176), *n.* one who, or that which, raps; — the knocker of a door. [*See* Wrapper, 160.]
Rap'ping.
Rapt, *part.* & *a.* transported; ravished. [*See* Rapped, *and* Wrapped, 160.]

☞ This word is from the obsolete verb *rap*, meaning *to snatch or hurry away, to ravish.*

Rap'tor.
Rap-to'ri-al, 49, N.
Rap-to'ri-oŭs.
Rapt'ure, 44, Note 1; 91.
Rapt'ur-oŭs (*-yur-*), 91.
Ra'ra a'vis (L.).
Rare (*rêr*), 14, 48, 49.
Rar'ee-shōw (*rêr'-*).
Răr-e-fac'tion [*See* Rarefy.]
Răr'e-fī-a-ble, 164.
Răr'e-fīed.
Răr'e-fȳ (108, 169, 171) [so Wk. Wr. Wb. Gd.; *rêr'e-fȳ*, Sm. 155.]
Răr'e-fȳ-ing.
Rare'ly (*rêr'-*), 93.
Rar'i-ty (*răr'i-ty*, or *rêr'i-ty*), 169.

☞ In the sense of *uncommonness, infrequency,* and also in the sense of *a thing valued for its scarcity,* this word is pronounced by Walker and Worcester *rêr'i-ty*; while in the sense of *thin'ness, subtilty,* they pronounce it *rărĭty*. In all its senses, it is pronounced, by Smart, *rêr'-i-ty*, and by Webster and Goodrich *răr'i-ty*.

Ra'sant (*-zant*).
Ràs'cal, 12, 131.
Răs-cal'i-ty.
Răs-call'ion (*-kal'yun*) [Rascalion, 203.]
Ràs'cal-ly, 170.
[Rascolnik, 203. — — *See* Raskolnik.]
Rase (*rāz*) [so Sm. Wb. Gd.; *rāz*, or *rās*, Wk. Wr. 155], *v.* to touch superficially in passing; — to erase; — to destroy completely. [Raze (in the last sense), 203.]
Rash, 10, 46.
Rash'er.
Ras-kol'nik [Rascolnik, 203.]
Ra-so'ri-al (*-zo'-*) [so Sm. Gd.; *ra-so'ri-al*, Wr. 155.]
Ràsp, 12, 131.
Ràsp'a-to-ry, 86.
Rasp'ber-ry (*răz'-*) (162) [so Sm. Gd.; *ràs'ber-ry*, Wk.; *ràs'-ber-ry*, or *răs'ber-ry*, Wr. 155.]
Ràsped (*ràspt*).
Ràsp'er.
Ràsp'ing.
Răsse.
Ra'sure (*-zhur*) (47, 171) [Razure, 203.]
Rat, 10.
Rāt-a-bil'i-ty, 108.
Rāt'a-ble, 164.
Rāt'a-bly.
Rat-a-fi'a (*rat-a-fe'a*, coll. *rat-a-fe'*) [so Sm.; *rat-a-fe'a*, Wk. Wb. Gd.; *rat-a-fe'a*, or *rat-a-fe'*, Wr. 155] [Ratifia, Ratafee, 203.]
[Ratan, 203. — *See* Rattan.]
Rat'a-ny, *or* Rat'an-hy (93) [Rhatany, 203.]
Ratch, 10, 44.
Ratch'et.
Rate, 23, 163.
Rāt'ed.
Rāt'er.
Răth'er, *or* Răth'er [*răth'ur*, Wr. Wb. Gd.; *răth'ur*, Sm.; *răth'ur*, or *rā'thur*, Wk. 155.]

☞ Walker says: "When *rather* signifies *just preferable*, we lengthen the first vowel, and pronounce it long and slender, as if written *rayther.*" But he adds: "Usage seems to be clearly on the side of the other pronunciation."

Rath'off-īte, 83, 152.
[Ratifia, 203. — *See* Ratafia.]
Rat-i-fī-ca'tion.
Rat'i-fīed, 99.
Rat'i-fī-er.
Rat'i-fȳ, 169.
Rat'i-fȳ-ing.
Rāt'ing.
Ra'ti-o (*-shĭ-*) [pl. Ra'-ti-ōs (*-shĭ-ōz*), 192.]
Ră-ti-oç'i-nate (*rash-i-os'-*) [so Wk. Sm. Wr.; *rā-shos'ĭ-nāt*, Wb. Gd. 165.]
Ră-ti-oç-i-na'tion (*rash-i-os-*), 156, 171.
Ră-ti-oç'i-na-tive (*rash-i-os'-*).
Ra'tion, 169.
Ră'tion-al (*rash'un-*) [so Wk. Sm. Wr.; *ra'-shun-al*, or *rash'un-al*, Gd. 155.]
Ră-ti-o-na'le (*rā-shĭ-o-*), *or* Ră-ti-o-na'le (*rash-i-o-*) [*rā-shĭ-o-na'le*, Sm.; *rash-ĭ-o-na'le*, Wk. Wr.; *rā-shun-a'-le*, or *rash-un-a'le*, Gd. 155.]
Ră'tion-al-ism (*rash'un-al-izm*) [*See* Rational.]
Ră'tion-al-ist (*rash'un-*)
Ră-tion-al-ist'ic (*rash'-un-*).
Ră-tion-al-ist'ic-al (*rash-un-*).
Ră-tion-al'i-ty (*rash-un-*) [so Sm.; *rash-ĭ-o-nal'i-ty*, Wk. Wr.; *ra-shun-al'i-ty*, or *rash-un-al'i-ty*, Gd. 155.]
Ră'tion-al-ize (*rash'-un-*) [*See* Rational.]
Ră'tion-al-ized (*rash'-un-*), 165.

Ră′tion-al-īz-ing (*rash′-un-*).
Ră′tion-al-ly (*rash′un-*), 171.
Ră′tion-a-ry (*rash′un-*), 72.
Rat′lĭnes (*-linz*), *n. pl.* [Ratlings, 203.]
Ra-toon′, 121, 171.
Rats′bane, 214.
Rat′-tāils (*-tālz*), *n. pl.* 206, Exc. 1.
Rat-tan′ (121, 170) [Ratan, 203.
Rat′ted, 176.
Rat-teen′, 121.
Rat-ti-net′, 78, 122.
Rat′ting, 176.
Rat′tle (*rat′l*), 164.
Rat′tled (*rat′ld*).
Rat′tle-hĕad′ed.
Rat′tle-snake.
Rat′tling.
Râu′ci-ty, 17, 169.
Râu′cous, 100.
Rav′age, 70.
Rav′aged, 150.
Rav′a-ger.
Rav′a-ging.
Rave, 23, 163.
Raved, 165.
Rav′el (*rav′l*), 149, 167.
Rav′e-lin (coll. *rav′lin*) [so Sm.; *rav′lin*, Wk. Wr. Gd. 155.]
Rav′elled (*-eld*) (177) [Raveled, Wb. Gd. 203. — *See* Note E, p. 70.]
Rav′el-ling (177) [Raveling, Wb. Gd. 203.]
Ra′ven (*-vn*), *n.* 161.
Rav′en (*rav′n*), *v.* 149, 161.
Rav′ened (*-nd*), 149, 150.
Rav′en-er.
Rav′en-ing (*rav′n-*).
Rav′en-oŭs (*rav′n-*).
Rāv′er, 228.
Rav′in (*rav′n*), 149, 167.
Ra-vine′ (*-vēn′*), 121.
Rāv′ing.
Rav′ish, 104.
Rav′ished (*-isht*).
Rav′ish-er.
Rav′ish-ing.
Rav′ish-ment.
Rav′is-sant.
Raw, 17, 48.
Raw′-bōned, 206, Exc. 5.
Raw′hĕad, 206.
Rāy (23; Note D, p. 37) [pl. Rāys (*rāz*). — *See* Raise, *and* Raze, 160.]
Ra′yah, *or* Rä′yah (139) [*ra′ya*, Sm.; *rah′ya*, Gd. Wr. 155.]
Rāyed (150), *part. & a.* marked with rays, radiate. [*See* Raid, 160.]
Rāy′ing.
Rāy′less.
Rāy′on-nant.
Raze (23, 40), *v.* to destroy completely. [*See* Raise, *and* Rays (pl. of Ray), 160.] [Rase, 203.]
Razed, 165.
Ra-zee′, *n. & v.*
Ra-zeed′, 188.
Ra-zee′ing, 188.
Rāz′ing, 183.
Ra′zor (77), *n.* an instrument for shaving. [*See* Raiser, 160.]
Ra′zor-back.
Ra′zor-bill.
[Razure. 203. — *See* Rasure.]
Raz′zi-a (*rat′sĭ-a*).
Re-ab-sorb′, 223.
Rēach (13, 44) [*See* Note under *Retch*.]
Rēach′a-ble, 164, 169.
Rēached (*rēcht*), 165; Note C, p. 34.
Rēach′er.
Rēach′ing.
Re-act′, 223.
Re-ac′tion, 117.
Re-ac′tion-a-ry, 72.
Re-act′ĭve.
Rēad (13, 161), *v.* to peruse. [*See* Reed, 160.]
Rĕad (15, 161), *v.* did rēad. [*See* Red, 160.]
Rēad′a-ble, 164.
Rēad′er.
Rĕad′i-ly, 186.
Rĕad′i-ness.
Rēad′ing.
Rēad′ing-bŏŏk, 215.
Rēad′ing-room.
Re-ad-just′.
Re-ad-mis′sion (*-mish′-un*).
Rĕad′y, 169, 170.
Re-af-firm′, 21, N.
Re-a′gent, 223.
Re′al, 72.
Re-al′gar, 122.
Re′al-ism (*-izm*), 133.
Re′al-ist.
Re-al-ist′ic, 109.
Re-al′i-ty (169), *n.* state of being real; actual existence. [*See* Realty, 148.]
Re′al-īz-a-ble, 164.
Rē-al-ĭ-za′tion [*not* re-ăl-ĭ-za′shun, *nor* rē-al-īz-a′shun, 126, 153.]
Re′al-ize, 202.
Re′al-ized, 165.
Re′al-īz-er.
Re′al-īz-ing.
Re′al-ly, 144, 170.
Rĕalm, 15, 133.
Re′al-ty, *n.* quality, in certain kinds of property, of being real, or immovable. [Law term.] [*See* Reality, 148.]
Rēam, 13.
Re-an′i-mate, 223.
Re-an′i-māt-ed.
Re-an′i-māt-ing.
Rēap, 13.
Rēaped (*rēpt*), 165; Note C, p. 34.
Rēap′er.
Rēap′ing.
Rēap′ing-hŏŏk.
Rēar, *n. & a.* 13, 48, 49.
Rēar, *v.* [*not* rêr, 127, 153.]
Rēared, 165.
Rēar′er, 49, N.
Rēar′ing.
Rēar′mouse [Reermouse, 203.]
Rēar′ward.
Re-as-cend′, 223.
Rēa′son (*re′zn*), 104, 149.
Rēa′son-a-ble (*re′zn-a-bl*), 164.
Rēa′son-a-bly (*re′zn-*).
Rēa′soned (*re′znd*).
Rēa′son-er (*re′zn-*).
Rēa′son-ing (*re′zn-*).
Re-as-sert′, 21, N.
Rēave, 13, 36.
Rēav′er.
Rēav′ing.
Re-bate′, *n. & v.*
Re-bāt′ed.
Re-bate′ment, 185.
Re-bāt′ing, 183.
Re′bec [*not* reb′ek, 127, 153] [Rebeck, 203.]
Reb′el, *n.* 103, 161.
Re-bel′, *v.* 103, 161.
Re-belled′ (*-beld′*), 176.
Re-bel′ling.
Re-bell′ion (*-yun*), 51.
Re-bell′ioŭs (*-yus*), 112.
Re-bound′, *n. & v.*
Re-bound′ed.

Re-bound'ing.
Re-buff', *n.* & *v.*
Re-buffed' (*-buft'*).
Re-buff'ing.
Re-buke', *n.* & *v.* 26.
Re-buked' (*-bŭkt'*).
Re-bŭk'er.
Re-bŭk'ing.
Re'bus, 189.
Re-but', 22.
Re-but'ted, 176.
Re-but'ter.
Re-but'ting.
Re-cal'ci-trant.
Re-cal'ci-trate.
Re-cal'ci-trāt-ed.
Re-cal'ci-trāt-ing.
Re-cal-ci-tra'tion.
Re-câll' (17, 222) [Recal, Sm. 179, 203.]
Re-cănt'.
Re-cănt-a'tion.
Re-cănt'ed.
Re-cănt'er.
Re-cănt'ing.
Re-ca-pit'u-late.
Re-ca-pit'u-lāt-ed.
Re-ca-pit'u-lāt-ing.
Re-ca-pit-u-la'tion.
Re-ca-pit'u-la-to-ry, 86, 126, 233.
Re-cap'tion.
Re-capt'ure, 91.
Re-cȧst', 117.
Re-cede', 171.
Re-cēd'ed, 183.
Re-cēd'ing.
Re-cēipt' (*-sēt'*), *n.* & *v.* 162, 169, N.
Re-cēipt'-bŏŏk (*-sēt'-*), 206, Exc. 4.
Re-cēipt'ed (*-sēt'-*).
Re-cēipt'ing (*-sēt'-*).
Re-cēipt'or (*-sēt'-*), 88.
Re-cēiv-a-bil'i-ty.
Re-cēiv'a-ble, 164.
Re-cēive', 169, N.
Re-cēived', 150, 165.
Re-cēiv'er.
Re-cēiv'ing, 183.
Re'cen-cy, 169.
Re-cen'sion, 112, 169.
Re'cent.
Re-cep'ta-cle (107, 164) [so Sm. Wr. Wb. Gd.; *res'ep ta-kl*, or *re-sep'-ta-kl*, Wk. 155.]

☞ "The first of these pronunciations [*res'ep-ta-kl*] is by far the most fashionable, but the second [*re-sep'ta-kl*] most agreeable to analogy and the ear." *Walker*, 1806.—"This is one of the words over which fashion relaxes its sway in favor of the more consistent accentuation [*re-sep'ta-kl*]." *Smart*, 1836.

Reç-ep-tac'u-lar (108) [so Gd.; *re-sep-tak'-u-lar*, Wr. 155.]
Re-cep-ti-bil'i-ty.
Re-cep'ti-ble, 164, 169.
Re-cep'tion.
Re-cep'tĭve, 84.
Reç-ep-tiv'i-ty [so Wr.; *re-sep-tiv'i-ty*, Sm. Wb. Gd. 155.]
Re-cep'to-ry (86, 107) [so Sm. Wb. Gd.; *res'ep-tŭr-y*, Wk.; *res'ep-to-ry*, or *re-sep'to-ry*, Wr. 155.]
Re-cess' (121) [*not* re'-ses, 153.]
Re-cessed' (*-sest'*).
Re-ces'sion (*-sesh'un*), 234.
Re'chab-īte (*-kab-*) (152) [*not* rek'ab-īt, 153.]
Recherché (Fr.) (*ră-shĕr-shā'*).
Reç'i-pe, 163.
Re-cip'i-en-cy.
Re-cip'i-ent (169) [so Wk. Wr. Wb. Gd.; *re-sip'yent*, Sm. 155.]
Re-cip'ro-cal, 171.
Re-cip-ro-cal'i-ty.
Re-cip'ro-cal-ly.
Re-cip'ro-cate.
Re-cip'ro-cāt-ed.
Re-cip'ro-cāt-ing.
Re-cip-ro-ca'tion.
Reç-i-proç'i-ty [*not* re-si-pros'i-ty, 153.]
Re-cip-ro-corn'oŭs.
Re-cĭ'sion (*-sizh'un*).
Re-cīt'al, 72.
Reç-i-ta'tion.
Reç-i-ta-tive' (*-tēv'*) [*not* re-sīt'a-tiv, 153.]
Reç-i-ta-ti'vo (It.) (*-te'-*).
Re-cite'.
Re-cīt'ed, 183.
Re-cīt'er.
Re-cīt'ing.
Reck (15, 181), *v.* to heed. [*See* Wreck, 160.]
Recked (*rekt*), *v.* did reck. [*See* Wrecked, 160.]
Reck'ing, *part.* from *Reck.* [*See* Wrecking, 160.]
Reck'less.
Reck'on (*rek'n*), 104, 149, 167.
Reck'oned (*rek'nd*).
Reck'on-er (*rek'n-*).
Reck'on-ing (*rek'n-*).
Re-clāim'.
Re-clāim'a-ble, 164.
Re-clāimed', 165.
Re-clāim'ing.
Rec-la-ma'tion.
Rec'li-nate.
Rec-li-na'tion.
Re-cline'.
Re-clined'.
Re-clīn'er, 183.
Re-clīn'ing.
Re-clūse', 26, 121.
Re-clu'sion (*-zhun*), 112.
Re-clu'sĭve, 84.
Re-clu'so-ry, 86.
Rec-og-nĭ'tion (*-nish'-un*), 112.
Re-cog'ni-tor (*-tawr*).
Re-cog'ni-to-ry, 86.
Rec'og-nīz-a-ble (164) [so Sm.; *re-kog'nĭ-za-bl*, or *re-kon'ĭ-za-bl*, Gd.; *rek-og-nī'za-bl*, or *re-kog'nĭ-za-bl*, Wr. 155] [Recognisable, 203.]
Re-cog'ni-zance [so Wk. Sm. Wr.; *re-kog'nĭ-zans*, or *re-kon'i-zans*, Gd. 155] [Recognisance, 203.]

☞ "In the general sense, the *g* is sounded; in professional legal use, it is generally sunk." *Smart.*

Re-cog-ni-za'tion.
Rec'og-nize [so Wk. Sm. Wr.; *rek'og-nīz*, or *rek'o-nīz*, Gd. 155] [Recognise, 203.]

☞ "With respect to the orthography of this class of words, *recognize* or *recognise*, *recognizance* or *recognisance*, &c., good usage, as well as the Dictionaries, is much divided, and both modes may be said to be well authorized; but the greater part of the English Dictionaries seem to give the preference to the use of *s*." *Worcester.*

Rec'og-nized [Recognised, 203.]
Re-cog-ni-zee' [Recognisee, 203.]
Rec'og-nīz-er [Recogniser, 203.]

Rec′og-nīz-ing [Rec-ognising, 203.]
Re-cog-ni-zor′ (118) [Recognisor, 203.]
Re-coil′, *n.* & *v.* 121.
Re-coiled′, 165.
Re-coil′er.
Re-coil′ing.
Rec-ol-lect′ (161), *v.* to recall to mind. [*not* rē-kol-lekt′, 153.]
[Recollect, *n.* 203. — *See* Recollet.]
Rē-col-lect′ (161), *v.* to collect again.
Rec-ol-lect′ed, 161.
Rē-col-lect′ed, 161.
Rec-ol-lect′ing, 161.
Rē-col-lect′ing, 161.
Rec-ol-lec′tion, 161.
Rē-col-lec′tion, 161.
Rec-ol-lect′ĭve, 84.
Rec′ol-let [Recollect, 203.]
Rec-om-mend′, 171.
Rec-om-mend′a-ble, 164.
Rec-om-mend-a′tion.
Rec-om-mend′a-to-ry.
Rec-om-mend′ed.
Rec-om-mend′er.
Rec-om-mend′ing.
Rec′om-pense.
Rec′om-pensed (*-penst*).
Rec′om-pens-ing.
Rec-on-cīl′a-ble, 164.
Rec-on-cīl′a-bly.
Rec′on-cīle, 81, 152.
Rec′on-ciled, 165.
Rec′on-cile-ment.
Rec′on-cīl-er.
Rec-on-cil-i-a′tion.
Rec-on-cil′i-a-to-ry [so Wr. Wb. Gd.; *rek-on-sil′ya-tŭr-y*, Sm. 155.]
Rec′on-cīl-ing, 183.
Rec′on-dīte, *or* Re-con′dĭte [so Wr.; *rek′on-dīt*, Wk. Wb. Gd.; *re-kon′dĭt*, Sm. 155.]

☞ "I am much deceived if the analogy of pronunciation be not decidedly in favor of that accentuation which I have given [*rek′on-dīt*]. We have but few instances in the language, where we receive a word from the Latin by dropping a syllable, that we do not remove the accent higher than the original." *Walker.*

Re-con′noĭs-sănce (Fr.).
Rec-on-noi′tre (164, 171) [so Sm. Wr.; *re-kon-noi′tur*, Wb. Gd. 155] [Reconnoiter preferred by Gd. — *See* Note E, p. 70.]
Rec-on-noi′tred (*-terd*) [Reconnoitered, Gd. 203.]
Rec-on-noi′tring [Reconnoitering, Gd. 203.]
Re-con-sid′er, 222.
Re-con-struct′.
Re-cord′, *v.* 103, 161.
Rec′ord, *n.* (86, 103, 161) [so Sm. Wr. Wb. Gd.; *rek′ord*, or *re-kord′*, Wk. 155.]

☞ Though Walker, in deference to the current practice of his day, gives *re-kord′* as an alternative mode of pronouncing this word, yet he says that to pronounce it thus "is overturning one of the most settled analogies of our language in the pronunciation of dissyllable nouns and verbs of the same form." *See* § 103.

Re-cord′ed.
Re-cord′er.
Re-cord′ing.
Re-count′, 222.
Re-count′ed.
Re-count′ing.
Re-coup′ (*-koop′*), *v.* [Recoupe (*re-koop′*, Wr.; *re-koo′pa*, Gd. 155) 203.]
Recoupe (Fr.) (*re-koop′*), *n.*
Re-couped′ (*-koopt′*).
Re-coup′ing (*-koop′-*).
Re-coup′ment (*-koop′-*).
Re-cōurse′ (121), *n.* [*not* re′kōrs, 153.]
Re-cov′er (*-kuv′-*).
Re-cov′er-a-ble (*-kuv′-ur-a-bl*), 164.
Re-cov′er-ed(*-kuv′urd*).
Re-cov-er-ee′ (*-kuv-*) [Law term, correlative of *Recoveror*.]
Re-cov′er-er. (*-kuv′-*) [*See* Recoveror.]
Re-cov′er-ing (*-kuv′-*).
Re-cov-er-or′ (*-kuv-*) (118) [Law term, correlative of *Recoveree*.]
Re-cov′er-y (*-kuv′-*).
Rec′re-ant, 156.
Rec′re-ate (161, 228, N.), *v.* to refresh.
Re-cre-ate′ (161, 228, N.), *v.* to create again.
Rec′re-āt-ed, 161.
Re-cre-āt′ed, 161.
Rec′re-āt-ing, 161.
Re-cre-āt′ing, 161.
Rec-re-a′tion, 161.
Re-cre-a′tion, 161.
Rec′re-āt-ĭve, 84.
Rec′re-ment.
Rec-re-ment′al.
Rec-re-ment-ĭ′tial (*-ish′-al*), 112.
Rec-re-ment-ĭ′tious (*-ish′us*).
Re-crim′i-nate.
Re-crim-i-na′tion.
Re-cruit′ (*-kroot′*), *n.* & *v.* 19, 171.
Re-cruit′ed (*-kroot′-*).
Re-cruit′ing (*-kroot′-*).
Rec′tal.
Rect-an′gle (*-ang′gl*).
Rect-an′gled (*-ang′ld*).
Rect-an′gu-lar (*-ang′-*).
Rect-an-gu-lăr′i-ty (*-ang-*).
Rec′ti-fī-a-ble, 164.
Rec-ti-fĭ-ca′tion.
Rec′ti-fīed.
Rec′ti-fī-er.
Rec′ti-fȳ, 94.
Rec′ti-fȳ-ing.
Rec-ti-lin′e-al, 169.
Rec-ti-lin′e-ar.
Rec-ti-lin-e-ăr′i-ty.
Rec′tion, 169.
Rec′ti-tude, 78, 108.
Rec′tor, 88.
Rec′tor-ate.
Rec′tor-ess.
Rec-to′ri-al, 49, N.
Rec′to-ry, 86.
Rec′tum, 169.
Rec′tus in cu′ri-a (L.).
Rec-u-ba′tion, 112.
Re-cum′bence.
Re-cum′ben-cy, 169.
Re-cum′bent, 169.
Re-cu′per-ate.
Re-cu′per-āt-ed.
Re-cu′per-āt-ing.
Re-cu′per-āt-ĭve.
Re-cur′, 21.
Re-curred′ (*-kurd′*).
Re-cŭr′rence.
Re-cŭr′rent.
Re-cur′ring, 21.
Re-cur′sant.
Re-curv′ate.
Re-curv-a′tion.
Re-curv-i-ros′ter.
Re-curv′i-ty.

Re-curv'oŭs.
Rec'u-san-cy, *or* Re-cu'-san-cy (*-zan-*).
Rec'u-sant, *or* Re-cu'-sant (*-zant*) [*rek'u-zant*, Sm.; *re-ku'zant*, Wb. Gd.; *re-ku'zant*, or *rek'u-zant*, Wk. Wr. 155.]

☞ The accent is placed [on the first syllable] according to modern usage. *Smart.*

Rec-u-sa'tion (*-za'-*).
Re-cu'sa-tive (*-za-*).
Re-cus'sion (*-kush'un*).
Red, *a.* being of a color which resembles that of arterial blood: — *n.* a red color. [*See* Rĕad, 160.]
Re-dac'tion.
Re-dan' [so Sm. Wb. Gd.; *re-dan'*, or *re'-dan*, Wr. 155.]
Red'brĕast, 216.
Red'cap.
Red'cross.
Red'den (*red'n*), 149.
Red-den'dum (L.).
Red'dened (*red'nd*).
Red'den-ing (*red'n-*).
Red'dish, 176.
Red-dĭ'tion (*-dish'un*).
Red'di-tĭve, 84.
Re-deem'.
Re-deem'a-ble, 164.
Re-deemed', 165.
Re-deem'er.
Re-deem'ing.
Re-demp'ti-ble (*-dem'ti-bl*), 162, 164. [162.
Re-demp'tion (*-dem'-*),
Re-demp'tion-a-ry (*-dem'-*), 72.
Re-demp'tion-er(*-dem'-*)
Re-demp'tĭve (*-dem'-*).
Re-demp'to-rist(*-dem'-*)
Re-demp'to-ry (*-dem'-*), 86.
Red'eȳe (*-ī*), 216.
Red'gum.
Red'hĕad, 206.
Red-hi-bĭ'tion(*-bish'un*)
Red-hib'i-to-ry, 86.
Red'-hot', 205.
Re-din'te-grate, 169.
Re-din'te-grāt-ed.
Re-din'te-grāt-ing.
Re-din-te-gra'tion.
Red'o-lence.
Red'o-len-cy, 169.
Red'o-lent, 105.
Re-doŭb'le (*-dub'l*).
Re-doubt' (*-dowt'*) (121, 162) [Redout, 203.]
Re-doubt'a-ble (*-dowt'-a-bl*) (171) [Redoutable, 203.]
Re-doubt'ed (*-dowt'-*) [Redouted, 203.]
Re-dound', 28, 222.
Re-dound'ed.
Re-dound'ing.
Red'ow-a (*red'o-a*), 156.
Re-dress'.
Re-dressed' (*-drest'*).
Re-dress'i-ble, 164, 169.
Re-dress'ĭve, 84.
Red'root, 206.
Red'shank.
Red'start.
Red'strĕak.
Red'top.
Re-duce', 26, 127.
Re-duced' (*-dūst'*), 165; Note C, p. 34.
Re-dūç'ent.
Re-dūç'i-ble, 169.
Re-dūç'ing, 183.
Re-duct', *n.* 121.
Re-duc'ti-o ad ab-sur'-dum(L.)(*re-duk'shĭ-o*)
Re-duc'tion, 112, 169.
Re-duc'tĭve, 84.
Re-dun'dance.
Re-dun'dan-cy.
Re-dun'dant, 72.
Re-du'pli-cate.
Re-du'pli-cāt-ed.
Re-du'pli-cāt-ing.
Re-du-pli-ca'tion.
Re-du'pli-ca-tĭve.
Red'wing, 217.
Re-ech'o (*-ek'-*), 117, 223.
Reed (13), *n.* a plant having a hollow, jointed stem; — a musical tube or vibrating tongue; — an instrument used by weavers. [*See* Rĕad, 160.]
Reed'-bunt'ing.
Reed'en (*rēd'n*), 149.
Reed'ing.
Reed'y.
Reef, 13. [C, p. 34.
Reefed (*rēft*), 165; Note
Reef'ing.
Reef'y, 169.
Reek (13), *n.* exhalation: — *v.* to exhale. [*See* Wreak, 160.]
Reeked (*rēkt*), *v.* did reek. [*See* Wreaked, 160.]
Reek'ing, *part.* from *Reek.* [*See* Wreaking, 160.]
Reek'y, 93.
Reel, 13, 48, 50.
Re-e-lect', 223.
Re-e-lec'tion.
Reeled, 165.
Reel'ing.
Re-em-bark', 223.
Reem'ing.
Re-en-fōrce' [Re-inforce, 203.]
Re-en-fōrce'ment [Re-inforcement, 202.]
Re-en'ter.
Re-en'tered, 150, 165.
Re-en'ter-ing.
Re-en'try.
[Reermouse, 203. — *See* Rearmouse.]
Re-es-tab'lish, 223.
Reeve, 13.
Reeved, 165.
Reev'ing.
Re-ex-chānge'.
Re-fec'tion.
Re-fec'tĭve, 84.
Re-fec'to-ry (86, 107) [so Sm. Wr. Wb. Gd.; *re-fek'tŭr-y*, or *ref'ek-tŭr-y*, Wk. 155.]

☞ "I am decidedly in favor of the accentuation on the second syllable." *Walker.* — Smart says: "This is one of the words which of late years have taken a more consistent accentuation," though he states that it is "still often pronounced *ref'ecto-ry*," when used to denote *the eating-room in monasteries.*

Re-fer', 21, N.
Ref'er-a-ble (164, 176) [Referrible, 203. — *See* Note under *Referrible.*]
Ref-er-ee', 122.
Ref'er-ence, 176.
Ref-er-en'da-ry [Referendiary, 203.]
Ref-er-en'tial.
Re-ferred' (*-ferd'*), 176.
Re-fer'rer, 21, N.
Re-fer'ri-ble (21, N.; 164, 176) [Referable, 203.]

☞ "*Ref'erable*, which is to be met with, evidently violates the usual practice of deduction from the verb, and *refer'rable*, which would be regular, is destitute of the old authority on which the orthography as above given rests." *Smart.* — "*Referrible* is the form that seems to be the more countenanced by the Dictionaries." *Worcester.*

Re-fine′.
Re-fīned′, 165.
Re-fīn′ed-ly, 150.
Re-fine′ment, 185.
Re-fīn′er-y.
Re-fīn′ing, 183.
Rē-fit′, 222.
Re-fit′ted, 176.
Re-fit′ting.
Re-flect′.
Re-flect′ed.
Re-flect′ent.
Re-flect′i-ble, 164, 169.
Re-flect′ing.
Re-flec′tion (234) [Reflexion, 203.]
Re-flect′ĭve, 84, 228.
Re-flect′or.
Re′flex [*not* re-fleks′, 153.]
Re-flexed′ (*-flekst′*).
Re-flex-i-bil′i-ty, 169.
Re-flex′i-ble, 164.
Re-flex′ĭve, 84.
Ref′lu-ence.
Ref′lu-en-cy.
Ref′lu-ent, 169.
Re′flux, 156.
Re-form′ (161), *v.* to amend.
Rē-form′ (117, 161), *v.* to form anew.
Re-form′a-ble, 164.
Ref-or-ma′tion (161, 228, N.), *n.* amendment.
Rē-form-a′tion (161), *n.* a new formation.
Re-form′a-tĭve.
Re-form′a-to-ry, 86.
Re-formed′ (161), *v.* did reform, or amend.
Rē-formed′ (161), *v.* did reform, or make anew.
Re-form′er, 228.
Re-form′ing (161), *part.* amending.
Rē-form′ing (161), *part.* forming anew.
Re-fract′.
Re-fract′ed.
Re-fract′ing.
Re-frac′tion.
Re-fract′ĭve, 84.
Re-fract-om′e-ter.
Re-fract′o-ri-ly, 186.
Re-fract′o-ri-ness.
Re-fract′o-ry, 86.
Ref′ra-ga-ble (164) [*not* re-fra′ga-bl, *nor* re-frag′a-ble, 153.]
Re-frāin′, *n.* & *v.* 121.
Re-frāined′, 150, 165.
Re-frāin′ing.
Re-fran-gi-bil′i-ty.
Re-fran′gi-ble, 164, 171.
Re-fresh′.
Re-freshed′ (*-fresht′*), 165; Note C, p. 34.
Re-fresh′ing.
Re-fresh′ment.
Re-frig′er-ant (*-frij′-*).
Re-frig′er-ate (*-frij′-*).
Re-frig′er-āt-ed (*-frij′-*).
Re-frig′er-āt-ing (*-frij′-*).
Re-frig-er-a′tion (*-frij-*).
Re-frig′er-āt-ĭve (*-frij′-*).
Re-frig′er-āt-or (*-frij′-*).
Re-frig′er-a-to-ry (*-frij′-*).
Re-frin′gen-cy.
Re-frin′gent.
Reft, 15.
Ref′uge, 90.
Ref-u-gee′, 122.
Re-ful′gence.
Re-ful′gen-cy, 169.
Re-ful′gent.
Re-fund′.
Re-fund′ed.
Re-fund′ing.
Re-fūs′a-ble (*-fūz′a-bl*).
Re-fūs′al (*-fūz′-*).
Re-fuse′ (*-fūz′-*), *v.* 161.
Ref′use (39, 103, 161) [*not* ref′yooz, 153.]
Re-fused′ (*-fūzd′*),
Re-fūs′er (*-fūz′-*).
Re-fus′ing (*-fūz′-*).
Re-fūt′a-ble (164) [*not* ref′u-ta-bl, 153.]
Ref-u-ta′tion.
Re-fūt′a-to-ry, 86.
Re-fute′.
Re-fūt′ed.
Re-fūt′ing.
Re-gāin′, 222.
Re′gal, 72.
Re-gale′.
Re-galed′, 183.
Re-gale′ment.
Re-ga′li-a (L.), *n. pl.*
Re-gāl′ing.
Re-gal′i-ty, 108.
Re′gal-ly, 170.
Re-gard′, *n.* & *v.* 53, 146.
Re-gard′ant [Reguardant, 203.]
Re-gard′ed.
Re-gard′ful (*-fōōl*).
Re-gard′ing.
Re-gat′ta, 170.
Re′gel (*-ghel*) [Rigel, 203.]
Re′gen-cy, 169.
Re-gen′er-a-cy.
Re-gen′er-ate, 233, Exc.
Re-gen′er-āt-ed, 183.
Re-gen′er-āt-ing.
Re-gen-er-a′tion, 126.
Re-gen′er-āt-ĭve, 84.
Re-gen′er-a-to-ry.
Re′gent, 76.
Reg-i-cīd′al (*rej-*).
Reg′i-cide (*rej′-*) [*not* re′ji-sīd, 153.]
Régime (Fr.) (*rā-zhēm′*).
Reg′i-men (*rej′-*).
Reg′i-ment (*rej′-*).
Reg-i-ment′al (*rej-*).
Re-gim′i-nal.
Re′gion (*-jun*), 171; Note D, p. 37.
Reg′is-ter (*-rej′-*), *n.* & *v.* 104, 235.
Reg′is-tered (*rej′-*), 150.
Reg′is-ter-ing (*-rej′-*).
Reg′is-trar (*rej′-*).
Reg-is-tra′tion (*rej-*).
Reg′is-try (*rej′-*).
Re′gi-us (L.).
Reg′let.
Reg′ma, 72.
Reg′nan-cy, 169.
Reg′nant.
Re-gorge′.
Re-gorged′ (*-gorjd′*).
Re-gorg′ing (*-gorj′-*).
Re-grate′.
Re-grāt′ed.
Re-grāt′er [Regrator, 203.]
Re-grāt′ing.
Re-grāt′or. [Law term.]
Re′gress, *n.*
Re-gres′sion (*-gresh′un*)
Re-gress′ĭve.
Re-gret′.
Re-gret′ful (*-fōōl*), 180.
Re-gret′ted, 176.
Re-gret′ting.
[Reguardant, 203. — *See* Regardant.]
Reg′u-lar (108, 169) [*not* reg′ur-lur, 153.]
Reg-u-lăr′i-ty.
Reg′u-lar-ly, 156.
Reg′u-late, 73, 89.
Reg′u-lāt-ed, 183.
Reg′u-lāt-ing.

Reg-u-la′tion.
Reg′u-la-tĭve, 84.
Reg′u-lāt-or, 169.
Reg′u-līne.
Reg′u-lus [L. pl. *Reg′-u-lī*; Eng. pl. Reg′u-lus-es (*-ez*), 198.]
Re-gur′gi-tate.
Re-gur′gi-tāt-ed.
Re-gur′gi-tāt-ing.
Re-gur-gi-ta′tion.
Re-ha-bil′i-tate.
Re-ha-bil′i-tāt-ed.
Re-ha-bil′i-tāt-ing.
Re-ha-bil-i-ta′tion.
Re-hēar′.
Re-heard′ (*-herd′*),21,N.
Re-hēar′ing.
Re-hears′al (*-hers′-*), 21, Note.
Re-hearse′ (*-hers′*), 21, Note.
Re-hearsed′ (*-herst′*).
Re-hears′ing (*-hers′-*).
Rēi′gle, 13, 164.
Reign (*rān*) (23, 162), *n.* sovereign power; — the time a sovereign's authority lasts: — *v.* to exercise sovereign authority. [*See* Rain *and* Rein, 160.]
Reigned (*rānd*).
Reign′ing (*rān′-*).
Re-im-burse′, 223.
Re-im-bursed′ (*-burst′*).
Re-im-burse′ment.
Re-im-burs′ing.
Rein (*rān*) (23), *n.* the strap of a bridle by which a horse is guided: — *v.* to govern by reins. [*See* Rain, *and* Reign, 160.]
Rein′deer (*rān′-*) (171) [Raindeer, Ranedeer, 205.]

☞ "*Reindeer* .... is now the prevailing orthography in works of science and literature." *Worcester.*

Reined (*rānd*).
Re in-fec′ta (L.).
[Re-inforce, 203. — *See* Re-enforce.]
Rein′ing (*rān′-*), *part.* from *Rein.* [*See* Raining, 160.]
Reins (*rānz*) (23), *n. pl.*
Re-in-state′.
Re-in-sure′ (*-shoor′*).
Rēis ef-fen′dī (Turkish) (*rēz-*) [so Sm. Wr.; *rēs ef-fen′dī*, Gd. 155.]
Re-it′er-ate, 223.
Re-it′er-āt-ed.
Re-it′er-āt-ing.
Re-it-er-a′tion.
Re-it′er-a-tĭve.
Re-ject′.
Re-ject′a-ble, 164, 169.
Re-ject′ed.
Re-ject′ing.
Re-jec′tion, 112.
Re-ject′ive, 84.
Re-ject′ment.
Re-joice′, 27.
Re-joiced′ (*-joist′*).
Re-joiç′ing.
Re-join′, 222.
Re-join′der, 77.
Re-ju′ve-nate, 169.
Re-ju′ve-nāt-ed.
Re-ju′ve-nāt-ing.
Re-ju-ve-nes′cence.
Re-ju-ve-nes′cen-cy.
Re-ju-ve-nes′cent, 171.
Relais (Fr.) (*re-lā′*).
Re-lapse′, *n.* & *v.*
Re-lapsed′ (*-lapst′*), 165, 183; Note C, p. 34.
Re-laps′ing.
Re-late′.
Re-lāt′ed, 183.
Re-lāt′ing.
Re-la′tion.
Re-la′tion-al.
Rel′a-tĭve, 84, 170.
Rel′a-tĭve-ly, 186.
Re-lāt′or.
Re-lāt′rix.
Re-lax′.
Re-lax′ant.
Rel-ax-a′tion [so Wk. Sm. Wr.; *re-laks-a′-shun*, Wb. Gd. 155.]
Re-lax′a-tĭve.
Re-laxed′ (*-lakst′*).
Re-lax′ing.
Re-lāy′.
Re-lēas′a-ble, 164.
Re-lēase′, 39.
Re-lēased′ (*-lēst′*).
Re-lēas′ing.
Rel′e-gate, 66.
Rel′e-gāt-ed.
Rel′e-gāt-ing.
Rel-e-ga′tion.
Re-lent′, 103.
Re-lent′ed.
Re-lent′ing.
Rel′e-vance, 169.
Rel′e-van-cy.
Rel′e-vant, 105.
Re-lī-a-bil′i-ty.
Re-lī′a-ble, 164, 186.
Re-lī′ance, 171.
Re-lī′ant.
Rel′ic (148, 170, 200), *n.* that which is left.
Rel′ict (148, 170), *n.* a widow.
Re-lict′ed.
Re-lic′tion.
Re-līed′, 186.
Re-lief′, 169, N.
Re-lī′er.
Re-liēv′a-ble, 164.
Re-liēve′, 169, N.
Re-liēved′, 165.
Re-liēv′ing.
Re-liē′vo [Rilievo, 203.]
Re-lig′ion (*-lij′un*), 171.
Re-lig′ion-ism (*-lij′un-izm*), 133, 136.
Re-lig′ion-ist (*-lij′un-*).
Re-lig′ioŭs (*-lij′us*), 171.
Re-lig′ioŭs-ly (*-lij′us-*).
Re-lin′quent (*-ling′-*).
Re-lin′quish (*-ling′-*).
Re-lin′quished (*-ling′-kwisht*), 171.
Re-lin′quish-ment (*-ling′-*).
Rel′i-qua-ry, 72.
Re-liq′ui-æ (L.) (*-lik′-wi-e*).
Rel′ish.
Rel′ish-a-ble, 164.
Rel′ished (*-isht*), 165; Note C, p. 34.
Rel′ish-ing.
Re-lu′cent.
Re-luct′.
Re-luct′ance, 169.
Re-luct′an-cy.
Re-luc′tant.
Re-luct′ed.
Re-luct′ing.
Re-lume′.
Re-lumed′.
Re-lūm′ing.
Re-lu′mīne.
Re-lu′mined (*-mĭnd*).
Re-lu′min-ing.
Re-ly′.
Re-lȳ′ing.
Re-māin′.
Re-māin′der, 169.
Re-māined′.
Re-māin′ing.
Re-mănd′ [so Wk. Sm.; *re-mȧnd′*, Wb. Gd.; *re-mȧnd′*, Wr. 155.]
Re-mănd′ed.
Re-mănd′ing.

Re-mănd′ment.
Re-mark′, 135.
Re-mark′a-ble, 164.
Re-mark′a-bly.
Re-marked′ (*-markt′*).
Re-mark′ing.
Remblai (*rŏng′blā*) (Fr.) [so Sm.; *răm′blā*, Gd.; *răm-blā′*, Wr. 155.]
Re-me′di-a-ble, 164.
Re-me′di-a-bly.
Re-me′di-al, 169.
Rem′e-dĭed (*-did*).
Rem′e-di-less, *or* Re-med′i-less (105, 106) [so Wr.; *rem′e-di-les*, Wk. Sm.; *re-med′i-les*, Wb. Gd. 155.]
Rem′e-dȳ, 170.
Rem′e-dȳ-ing.
Re-mem′ber, 169.
Re-mem′bered, 150.
Re-mem′ber-ing.
Re-mem′brance, 72.
Re-mem′branç-er.
Rem′i-form.
Rem′i-grate [so Wk. Sm.; *rē-mī′grāt*, Wb. Gd.; *rem′i-grāt*, or *rē-mī′grāt*, Wr. 155.]
Re-mīnd′.
Re-mīnd′ed.
Re-mīnd′er.
Re-mīnd′ing.
Rem-i-nis′cence, 171.
Rem-i-nis′cent.
Rem-i-nis-cen′tial (*-shal*).
Rem′i-ped.
Re-mise′ (*-mīz′*), *n.* & *v.*
Re-mised′ (*-mīzd′*).
Re-mīs′ing (*-mīz′-*).
Re-miss′.
Re-miss-i-bil′i-ty.
Re-miss′i-ble, 164, 169.
Re-mis′sion (*-mish′un*).
Re-miss′ĭve, 84.
Re-miss′ness.
Re-miss′o-ry, 86.
Re-mit′.
Re-mit′tal, 176.
Re-mit′tance, 170.
Re-mit′ted.
Re-mit′tent, 169.
Re-mit′ter [Remittor, 203.]
Re-mit′ting.
Re-mit′tor [Law term.]
Rem′nant.
Re-moll′ient (*-mol′-yent*).
Re-mon′strance.
Re-mon′strant.
Re-mon′strate.
Re-mon′strāt-ed.
Re-mon′strāt-ing.
Re-mon′strāt-or.
Rem′o-ra.
Re-morse′ (17) [so Sm. Wr. Wb. Gd.; *re-mors′*, or *re-mōrs′*, Wk. 155.]

☞ Walker says of those who pronounce this word *re-mors′*, that they have "analogy and the best usage on their side. The final *e*," he adds, "does not lengthen the *o*, but serves only to keep the *s* from going into the sound of *z*." *See* Note D, p. 37.

Re-morse′ful (*-fo͝ol*).
Re-morse′less, 185.
Re-mote′.
Re-mote′ly.
Re-mount′, 222.
Re-mov-a-bil′i-ty (*-moov′-*), 108, 169.
Re-mov′a-ble (*-moov′-a-bl*), 164.
Re-mov′al (*-moov′-*).
Re-move′ (*-moov′*), 19.
Re-moved′ (*-moovd′*).
Re-mov′ing (*-moov′-*).
Rem′phan.
Re-mu-ner-a-bil′i-ty.
Re-mu′ner-a-ble, 164.
Re-mu′ner-ate.
Re-mu′ner-āt-ed.
Re-mu′ner-āt-ing.
Re-mu-ner-a′tion.
Re-mu′ner-a-tĭve.
Re-mu′ner-a-to-ry, 86.
Re-mur′mur, 92.
Re-nāis′sance.
Re′nal, 72.
Ren′ard [Reynard, 203.]
Re-nas′cence.
Re-nas′cen-cy.
Re-nas′cent, 171.
Ren-con′tre (Fr.) (*-tur*) [*răn-kon′tr*, Gd. 154.]
Ren-coun′ter [so Wk. Wr. Wb. Gd.; *ren′-koun-tur*, Sm. 155], *n.* & *v.*
Rend, 15.
Rend′er (161, 228, N.), *n.* one who rends.
Ren′der (161), *v.* to return.
Ren′dered, 150, 165.
Ren′der-ing.
Rendezvous (*ren′de-voo*) (161, 189) [so Sm. Gd.; *ren-de-vooz′*, Wk.; *ren′de-voo*, or *ren′de-vooz*, Wr. 155], *n.*
Rendezvous (*ren-de-voo′*) (161) [so Sm.; *ren′de-voo*, Gd.; *ren-de-vooz′*, Wk.; *ren-de-voo′*, or *ren-de-vooz′*, Wr. 155], *v.*
Rendezvoused (*ren-de-vood′*).
Rendezvousing (*ren-de-voo′ing*).
Rend′i-ble, 164, 169.
Rend′ing, 228.
Ren-dĭ′tion (*-dish′un*).
Ren′e-gade, 169.
Ren-e-ga′do [pl. Ren-e-ga′does (*-dōz*), 192.]
Re-new′ (*-nu′*), 26.
Re-new′a-ble (*-nu′a-bl*).
Re-new′al (*-nu′-*).
Re-newed′ (*-nūd′*).
Re-new′ing (*-nu′-*).
Ren′i-form (108) [so Wr. Wb. Gd.; *re′ni-form*, Sm. 155.]
Re-nĭ′tence.
Re-ni′ten-cy [so Wk. Sm. Wr.; *ren′i-ten-sy*, Wb. Gd. 155.]
Re-ni′tent.
Ren′net (66, 170) [Runnet, 203.]
Ren′net-ing.
Re-nounce′, 28.
Re-nounced′ (*-nounst′*).
Re-nounce′ment, 185.
Re-nounç′er.
Re-nounç′ing.
Ren′o-vate, 86.
Ren′o-vāt-ed, 183.
Ren′o-vāt-ing.
Ren-o-va′tion.
Re-nown′, 28.
Re-nowned′, 150.
Re-nown′ing.
Rent, 15.
Rent′a-ble, 164.
Rent′al, 72.
Rente (*rănt*) (Fr.).
Rent′ed.
Rent′er.
Ren-ti-er (Fr.) (*răn-te-ā′*).
Rent′ing.
Ren′u-ent, 169.
Re-nun-ci-a′tion (*-shĭ-a′-*) [so Wk. Sm. Wr.; *re-nun-sĭ-a′shun*, Wb. Gd. 155.]

Ren-verse', 21, N.
Re-oc'cu-py, 223.
[Reometer, 203.—See Rheometer.]
Re-or'gan-ize.
Re'o-trope [Rheotrope, 203.]
Re-pāid'.
Re-pair' (-pêr').
Re-paired' (-pêrd').
Re-pair'ing (-pêr'-).
Re-pand'.
Re-pand'oŭs.
Rep'a-ra-ble (164) [*not* re-pêr'a-ble, 153.]
Rep'a-ra-bly.
Rep-a-ra'tion.
Re-păr'a-tĭve, 84.
Rep-ar-tee', 122.
Re-par-tĭ-mĭ-en'to (Sp.).
Re-pȧss', 12, 131, 222.
Re-pȧssed' (-pȧst') (160), *v.* did repass.
Re-pȧss'ing.
Re-pȧst' (160), *n.* act of taking food; a meal.
Re-pāy'.
Re-pāy'a-ble, 164.
Re-pāy'ing.
Re-pāy'ment.
Re-pēal'.
Re-pēal-a-bil'i-ty.
Re-pēal'a-ble, 164.
Re-pēaled'.
Re-pēal'ing.
Re-pēat'.
Re-pēat'ed.
Re-pēat'er.
Re-pēat'ing.
Re-pel'.
Re-pelled', 165, 176.
Re-pel'lence.
Re-pel'len-cy.
Re-pel'lent, 169.
Re-pel'ler.
Re-pel'ling, 176.
Re-pent'.
Re-pent'ance, 169.
Re-pent'ant.
Re-pent'ed.
Re-pent'ing.
Re-per-cuss'.
Re-per-cussed' (-kust').
Re-per-cuss'ing.
Re-per-cus'sion (-kush'un).
Re-per-cuss'ĭve, 84.
Rep'er-to-ry (86) [*not* re-pur'to-ry, 153.]
Rep-e-tend', 122.
Rep-e-tĭ'tion (-tish'un), 228, N.
Rep-e-tĭ'tion-al (-tish'un-).
Rep-e-tĭ'tioŭs (-tish'us).
Re-pine'.
Re-pined', 165.
Re-pīn'ing.
Re-place'.
Re-placed' (-plāst').
Re-place'ment.
Re-plāç'ing.
Re-plen'ish, 66, 170.
Re-plen'ished (-isht).
Re-plen'ish-ing.
Re-plen'ish-ment.
Re-plete'.
Re-ple'tion, 112.
Re-plev'i-a-ble, 164.
Re-plev'ĭed (-id).
Re-plev'in, 171.
Re-plev'y.
Re-plev'y-ing.
Rep'li-cant, 72.
Rep'li-cate, 78.
Rep'li-cāt-ed.
Rep-li-ca'tion.
Re-plied'.
Rep'lum [so Gd.; *re'plum*, Wr. 155.]
Re-ply'.
Re-ply'ing.
Re-pōrt'.
Re-pōrt'ed.
Re-pōrt'er.
Re-pōrt'ing.
Re-por-to'ri-al.
Re-pōs'al (-pōz'-).
Re-pose' (-pōz').
Re-posed' (-pōzd').
Re-pōs'ing (-pōz'-).
Re-pos'it (-poz'-).
Re-pos'it-ed (-poz'-).
Re-pos'it-ing (-poz'-).
Rep-o-sĭ'tion (-zish'un).
Re-pos'it-o-ry (-poz'-), 86.
Rep-re-hend'.
Rep-re-hend'ed.
Rep-re-hend'ing.
Rep-re-hen'si-ble, 164.
Rep-re-hen'si-bly.
Rep-re-hen'sion.
Rep-re-hen'sĭve, 84.
Rep-re-hen'so-ry, 86.
Rep-re-sent' (-zent').
Rep-re-sent'a-ble (-zent'a-bl), 164.
Rep-re-sent'ant (-zent'-)
Rep-re-sent-a'tion (-zent-).
Rep-re-sent-a'tion-a-ry (-zent-), 72, 116.
Rep-re-sent'a-tĭve (-zent'-).
Rep-re-sent'ed (-zent'-).
Rep-re-sent'ing (-zent'-)
Re-press'.
Re-pressed' (-prest').
Re-press'ing.
Re-pres'sion (-presh'un)
Re-press'ĭve, 84.
Re-priēve', 13, 169, N.
Re-priēved', 165.
Re-priēv'ing.
Rep'ri-mănd, *v.* [so Sm. Gd.; *rep-ri-mănd'*, Wk.; *rep-ri-mȧnd'*, Wr. 155.]
Rep'ri-mănd, *n.* [so Sm. Gd.; *rep-ri-mand'*, Wk.; *rep'ri-mȧnd*, Wr. 155.]
Rep'ri-mănd-ed.
Rep'ri-mănd-ing.
Rē-print', *v.* 103, 161.
Re'print, *n.* 103, 161.
Rē-print'ed.
Rē-print'ing.
Re-prīs'al (-prīz'-).
Re-prise' (-prīz'), *n.*
Re-prōach', 24.
Re-prōach'a-ble, 164.
Re-prōached' (-prōcht'), 165; Note C, p. 34.
Re-prōach'ful (-fŏŏl).
Re-prōach'ful-ly (-fŏŏl-), 170.
Re-prōach'ing.
Rep'ro-bate, 105.
Rep'ro-bāt-ed.
Rep'ro-bāt-ing, 228, N.
Rep-ro-ba'tion, 112.
Rep'ro-bāt-ĭve.
Re-pro-duce', 222.
Re-pro-duc'tion.
Re-pro-duc'tĭve, 84.
Re-proof'.
Re-prov'a-ble (-proov'a-bl), 164.
Re-prov'al (-proov'-).
Re-prove' (-proov').
Re-proved' (-proovd').
Re-prov'ing (-proov'-).
Rep'-sil-ver.
Rep-ta'tion.
Rep'ta-to-ry, 86.
Rep'tĭle (81, 152) [*not* rep'tīl, 153.]
Rep-til'i-a (L.), *n. pl.*
Rep-til'i-an, 169.
Re-pub'lic, 75.
Re-pub'lic-an.
Re-pub'lic-an-ism (-izm)
Re-pub'lic-an-ize.
Re-pub'lic-an-ized.
Re-pub'lic-an-īz-ing.
Re-pub-li-ca'tion.

Re-pub'lish, 116, 222.
Re-pu'di-a-ble, 164.
Re-pu'di-ate.
Re-pu'di-āt-ed, 183.
Re-pu'di-āt-ing.
Re-pu-di-a'tion, 169.
Re-pu'di-āt-or.
Re-pug'nance, 169.
Re-pug'nan-cy.
Re-pug'nant, 169.
Re-pulse', *n.* & *v.*
Re-pulsed' (*-pulst'*).
Re-puls'ing, 183.
Re-pul'sion, 234.
Re-puls'ĭve.
Re-puls'ĭve-ly, 93, 185.
Re-puls'o-ry, 86.
Rep'u-ta-ble (164) [*not* re-pūt'a-bl, 153.]
Rep'u-ta-bly, 156.
Rep-u-ta'tion.
Re-pute', *n.* & *v.*
Re-pūt'ed, 183.
Re-pūt'ing.
Re-quest', *n.* & *v.* 34, 52.
Re-quest'ed.
Re-quest'ing.
Re'qui-em, *or* Req'ui-em [so Wr.; *re'kwi-em*, Wk. Wb. Gd.; *rek'wi-em*, Sm. 155.]
Re'quin.
Re-quīr'a-ble, 164.
Re-quire'.
Re-quired', 165.
Re-quire'ment.
Re-quīr'ing.
Req'ui-sĭte (*rek'wi-zit*), 171.
Req-ui-sĭ'tion (*rek-wi-zish'un*), 171.
Re-quis'i-tĭve (*-kwiz'-*).
Re-quis'i-tor (*-kwiz'-*).
Re-quīt'al.
Re-quite'.
Re-quīt'ed.
Ra-quīt'er.
Re-quīt'ing.
Re-re-solve' (*-zolv'*).
Re-scind', 39, 171.
Re-scind'a-ble.
Re-scind'ed.
Re-scind'ment.
Re-scind'ing.
Re-scis'sion (*-sizh'un*), 171.
Re-scis'so-ry (*-siz'zo-ry*).
Res'coŭs.
Re-scribe'.
Re-scribed'.
Re-scrīb'en-da-ry, 72.
Re-scrīb'ing.
Re'script [*not* res'kript, 153.]
Re-scrip'tion.
Re-scrip'tĭve-ly.
Res'cu-a-ble, 164, 183.
Res'cūe, 26.
Res'cūed, 183.
Res'cu-er.
Res'cu-ing.
Res-cus-see', 122.
Res'cus-sor, *or* Res-cus-sor' (118) [*res'kus-sor*, Sm.; *res-kus'sor*, or *res-kus-sor'*, Wr. 155] [Law term, correlative of *Rescussee.*]
Re-search' (*-serch'*), *n.* (21, N.) [*not* re'serch, 153.]
Re-sec'tion.
Re-sem'blance (*-zem'-*), 169.
Re-sem'ble (*-zem'bl*), 164, 171.
Re-sem'bled (*-zem'bld*).
Re-sem'bling (*-zem'-*).
Re-sent' (*-zent'*).
Re-sent'ed (*-zent'-*).
Re-sent'er (*-zent'-*).
Re-sent'ful (*-zent'fŏŏl*), 180.
Re-sent'ing (*-zent'-*).
Re-sent'ĭve (*-zent'-*).
Re-sent'ment (*-zent'-*).
Res-er-va'tion (*rez-*).
Re-serv'a-to-ry(*-zerv'-*), 86, 136.
Re-serve' (*-zerv'*), 21, N.
Re-served' (*-zervd'*).
Re-serv'ed-ly (*-zerv'-*), 150.
Re-serv'ed-ness(*-zerv'-*)
Rēs-er-vee' (*rez-*) (122) [Law term, correlative of *Reservor.*]
Re-serv'er (*-zerv'-*).
Re-serv'ing (*-zerv'*).
Res-er-voir' (*rez-er-vwor'*), 122, 141, 171.
Res-er-vor' (*rez-*) (118) [Law term, correlative of *Reservee.*]
Re-set', 222.
Re-set'ting, 176.
Re-side' (*-zīd'*).
Re-sīd'ed (*-zīd'-*), 183.
Res'i-dence (*rez'-*), 169.
Res'i-den-cy (*rez'-*).
Res'i-dent (*rez'-*), 169.
Res-i-den'tial (*rez-i-den'shal*), 112.
Res-i-den'tia-ry (*-sha-*) (72) [so Wk. Sm. Wb. Gd.; *rez-i-den'shĭ-a-ry*, Wr. 155.]
Re-sīd'er (*-zīd'-*).
Re-sīd'ing (*-zīd'-*).
Re-sid'u-al (*-zid'-*), 108.
Re-sid'u-a-ry (*-zid'-*),72.
Res'i-due (*rez'-*) (26) [*not* rez'i-doo, 153.]
Re-sid'u-um (*-zid'-*),169.
Re-sign' (*-zīn'*) (147, 162), *v.* to relinquish.
Rē-sign' (*-sīn'*) (147, 162), *v.* to sign again.
Res-ig-na'tion (*-rez-*) [*not* res-ig-na'shun, 136, 153.]
Re-signed' (*-zīnd'*), 147.
Rē-signed' (*-sīnd'*), 147.
Re-sign'ed-ly (*-zīn'-*), 150.
Res-ign-ee' (*rez-i-ne'*), 156, 171.
Re-sign'er (*-zīn'-*).
Re-sign'ing (*-zīn'-*).
Re-sile' (*-zīl'*).
Re-siled' (*-zīld'*).
Re-sil'i-ence (*-zil'-*).
Re-sil'i-en-cy (*-zil'-*).
Re-sil'i-ent (*-zil'-*), 169.
Re-sīl'ing (*-zīl'-*).
Res-i-lĭ'tion (*rez-i-lish'un*), 112.
Res'in (*rez'in*) (149) [*not* rez'n, 153] [*See* Note under *Rosin.*]
Res-in-a'ceoŭs (*rez-in-a'shus*).
Res-in-if'er-ous (*rez-*), 108.
Res'in-i-form (*rez'-*)106.
Res'in-o-cere (*rez'-*).
Res'in-o-e-lec'tric (*rez'-*), 224.
Res'in-oŭs (*rez'-*), 100.
Re-sist' (*-zist'*), 136.
Re-sist'ance (*-zist'-*).
Re-sist'ant (*-zist'-*).
Re-sist'ed (*-zist'-*).
Re-sist-i-bil'i-ty(*-zist'-*).
Re-sist'i-ble (*-zist'i-bl*), 164, 169.
Re-sist'ing (*-zist'-*).
Re-sist'less (*-zist'-*)
Res'o-lū-ble (*rez'-*) (164) [*not* re-sol'u-bl, 153.]
Res'o-lute (*rez'-*), 26.
Res'o-lute-ly (*rez'-*).
Res-o-lu'tion (*rez-*).
Re-solv-a-bil'i-ty (*-zolv-*), 108, 169.
Re-solv'a-ble (*-zolv'a-bl*), 164, 169.
Re-solve' (*-zolv'*), 136.

Re-solved′ (*-zolvd′*), 165.
Re-solv′ent (*-zolv′-*), 169.
Re-solv′ing (*-zolv′-*).
Res′o-nance (*rez′-*).
Res′o-nant (*rez′-*), 169.
Re-sorb′.
Re-sorbed′ (*-sorbd′*).
Re-sorb′ent, 169.
Re-sorb′ing.
Re-sorp′tion.
Re-sort′ (*-zort′*), *n.* & *v.*
Re-sort′ed (*-zort′-*).
Re-sort′ing (*-zort′-*).
Re-sound′ (*-zound′*), 28.
Re-sound′ed (*-zound′-*).
Re-sound′ing (*-zound′-*).
Re-sōurce′ (121) [*not* re′sōrs, 153.]
Re-spect′, *n.* & *v.*
Re-spect-a-bil′i-ty.
Re-spect′a-ble, 164.
Re-spect′a-bly.
Re-spect′ant.
Re-spect′ed.
Re-spect′er, 169.
Re-spect′ful (*-fŏŏl*), 180.
Re-spect′ful-ly (*-fŏŏl-*).
Re-spect′ing.
Re-spect′ive, 84.
Rē-spell′, 117, 222.
Re-spīr-a-bil′i-ty, 108.
Re-spīr′a-ble (164) [*not* res′pi-ra-bl, 153.]
Res-pi-ra′tion.
Res-pi-ra′tion-al.
Res′pi-rā-tor.
Re-spīr′a-to-ry, 49, N.; 86, 171.
Re-spire′.
Re-spired′, 165.
Re-spīr′ing, 183.
Res′pĭte, *n.* & *v.* 83, 152.
Res′pit-ed, 176.
Res′pit-ing.
Re-splen′dence, 169.
Re-splen′den-cy, 169.
Re-splen′dent.
Re-spond′.
Re-spond′ed.
Re-spond′ence, 169.
Re-spond′en-cy.
Re-spond′ent.
Re-spond′ing.
Re-sponse′.
Re-spon-si-bil′i-ty.
Re-spon′si-ble, 164, 169.
Re-spon′si-bly.
Re-spon′sion.
Re-spon′sĭve, 84.
Re-spon′sĭve-ly.
Re-spon′so-ry.

Rest (15), *n.* repose; — residue; — *v.* to cease from action or motion of any kind; to remain. [*See* Wrest, 160.]
Res′tant.
Restaurant (Fr.) (*res-to-rŏng′*, or *res′to-rŏng*).
Restaurateur (Fr.) (*res-to′ra-tur*), 154.
Rest′ed.
Res′tiff [Restive, Resty, 203. — *See* Note under *Restive.*]
Rest′ing.
Res-ti-tu′tion.
Res′tive [Restiff, Resty, 203.]

☞ "*Restive*, which has been discountenanced by some, has been long in use, and is now more common than *restiff*." *Worcester.*

Re-stōr′a-ble, 164, 183.
Res-to-ra′tion.
Res-to-ra′tion-er.
Res-to-ra′tion-ist.
Res-to-ra′tion-ism (*-izm*).
Re-stōr′a-tĭve, *a.* & *n.* (49, N.) [*not* res-tōr′a-tiv, 153.]
Res′to-rā-tor.
Re-store′.
Re-stored′, 165.
Re-stōr′er.
Re-stōr′ing, 183.
Re-strāin′.
Re-strāin′a-ble, 164.
Re-strāined′, 165.
Re-strāin′er.
Re-strāint′.
Re-strict′.
Re-strict′ed.
Re-strict′ing.
Re-stric′tion.
Re-stric′tion-a-ry, 72.
Re-strict′ĭve, 84.
Re-strict′ĭve-ly.
Re-stringe′.
Re-strin′gen-cy.
Re-strin′gent.
[Resty, 203. — *See* Restive.]
Re-sult′ (*-zult′*), *n.* & *v.*
Re-sult′ance (*-zult′-*).
Re-sult′ant (*-zult′-*), 169.
Re-sult′ed (*-zult′-*).
Re-sult′ing (*-zult′-*).
Re-sūm′a-ble (*-zūm′a-bl*).
Re-sume′ (*-zūm′*), *v.* 161.

Résumé (Fr.) (*rā-zoo-mā′*), *n.* 161.
Re-sumed′ (*-zūmd′*).
Re-sūm′ing (*-zūm′-*), 183.
Re-sump′tion (*-zum′-*), 162.
Re-sump′tĭve (*-zum′-*).
Re-su′pi-nate.
Re-su-pine′, 122.
Re-sur′gence.
Re-sur′gent.
Res-ur-rec′tion (*rez-*).
Res-ur-rec′tion-ist (*rez-*).
Re-sus′ci-ta-ble, 164.
Re-sus′ci-tant, 171.
Re-sus′ci-tate.
Re-sus′ci-tāt-ed.
Re-sus′ci-tāt-ing.
Re-sus-ci-ta′tion.
Re-sus′ci-tāt-or.
Re-sus′ci-tāt-ĭve.
Ret, 15, 41, 48.
Re-tāil′, *v.* 103, 161.
Re′tāil, *n.* 103, 161.
Re-tāiled′.
Re-tāil′er, *or* Re′tāil-er [so Wr. Wb. Gd.; *re-tāl′ur*, Wk. Sm. 155.]

☞ "This word, like the noun *retail*, is often, perhaps generally, accented on the first syllable in America." *Webster.*

Re-tāil′ing.
Re-tāin′, 23.
Re-tāin′a-ble, 164.
Re-tāined′, 165.
Re-tāin′er.
Re-tāin′ing.
Rē-take′, 117, 222.
Re-tal′i-ate, 169, 170.
Re-tal′i-āt-ed, 183.
Re-tal′i-āt-ing.
Re-tal-i-a′tion, 171.
Re-tal′i-āt-ĭve, 84.
Re-tal′i-a-to-ry, 86.
Re-tard′, 135.
Rē-tärd-a′tion [so Sm. Wb. Gd.; *ret-är-da′shun*, Wk. Wr. 155.]
Re-tard′a-tĭve.
Re-tard′ed.
Re-tard′ing.
Retch (*rĕch*, or *rēch*) [so Wk. Wr.; *rēch*, Sm.; *rĕch*, Wb. Gd. 155] [Reach, 160.]

☞ "This word is derived from the same Saxon original as the verb to *reach*. . . . The pronunciation of both is generally the same." *Walker.*

Retched (*rĕcht*, or *rĕcht*).
Rĕtch'ing, *or* Rĕtch'-ing.
Re'tē mu-co'sum (L.).
Re-ten'tion.
Re-ten'tĭve, 84.
Re-ten'tĭve-ly.
Re'ti-a-ry (*-shĭ-*), 72.
Ret'i-cence, 170.
Ret'i-cen-cy.
Ret'i-cent.
Re-tic'u-lar, 108.
Re-tic'u-late.
Re-tic'u-lāt-ed.
Re-tic-u-la'tion.
Ret'i-cule, 78, 90.
Ret'i-form, 108.
Ret'i-na (L.) [pl. Ret'i-næ, (*-ne*), 198.]
Ret'i-nal, 72.
Ret-in-as'phalt (107) [so Sm.; *ret-in-as-falt'*, Wb. Gd.; *ret'i-nas-falt*, Wr. 155.]
Ret-in-as-phalt'um.
Ret'i-nīte, 83, 152.
Ret'i-noid.
Ret'i-nūe [so Sm. Wr. Wb. Gd.; *ret'i-nu*, or *re-tin'u*, Wk. 155.]

☞ Though Walker, in deference to the divided usage of his day, gives two modes of pronouncing this word, he says that "analogy ought to decide for placing the accent on the first syllable." "*Retinue* and *revenue*," says Smart, "have long struggled against the tendency [to accent polysyllabic words on the antepenult], but the struggle will be in vain, and speakers will do well to yield them up to their natural antepenultimate accent."

Ret'i-ped.
Ret-i-răde' (Fr.).
Re-tire'.
Re-tired', 165.
Re-tire'ment, 185.
Re-tīr'er.
Re-tīr'ing, 183.
Re-tort', *n.* & *v.* 135.
Re-tort'ed.
Re-tort'ing.
Re-tor'tion [Retorsion, 203.]
Re-tose'.
Re-tŏŭch'.
Re-trace'.
Re-tract'.
Re-tract'a-ble [Retractible, 203.]
Re-tract'ed.
Re-tract'i-ble [Retractable, 203.]
Re-tract'ĭle, 81, 152.
Re-tract'ing.
Re-trac'tion.
Re-tract'ĭve.
Re-tract'or.
Re-trax'it (L.).
Re-trēat', *n.* & *v.*
Re-trēat'ed.
Re-trēat'ing.
Re-trench'.
Re-trenched'(*-trencht'*).
Re-trench'ing.
Re-trench'ment.
Re-trib'ute [*not* ret'ri-būt, 153.]
Re-trib'ūt-ed.
Re-trib'ūt-ing.
Ret-ri-bu'tion.
Re-trib'ūt-ĭve, 84.
Re-trib'u-to-ry, 86.
Re-triēv'a-ble, 164.
Re-triēv'a-bly.
Re-triēv'al.
Re-triēve', 169, N.
Re-triēved', 165.
Re-triēv'ing, 183.
Re-tro-act'ĭve [so Sm. Gd.; *re-tro-ak'tiv*, or *ret-ro-ak'tiv*, Wr. 155.]
Rē'tro-cede, *or* Ret'ro-cede (171) [so Wr.; *re'tro-sēd*, Sm.; *ret'-ro-sēd*, Wb. Gd. 155.]
Re'tro-cēd-ed, *or* Ret'-ro-cēd-ed.
Re-tro-cēd'ent, *or* Ret-ro-cēd'ent [so Wr.; *re-tro-sēd'ent*, Sm. Gd. 203.]
Re'tro-cēd-ing, *or* Ret'-ro-cēd-ing [*See* Retrocede.]
Re-tro-ces'sion, *or* Ret-ro-ces'sion (*-sesh'un*) [so Wr.; *re-tro-sesh'-un*, Sm. Gd.; *ret-ro-sesh'un*, Wk. 155.]
Re-tro-duc'tion.
Re'tro-flex, *or* Ret'ro-flex.
Re'tro-flexed, *or* Ret'-ro-flexed (*-flekst*).
Re-tro-fract'ed, *or* Ret-ro-fract'ed.
Re-tro-gra-da'tion, *or* Ret-ro-gra-da'tion [*re-tro-gra-da'shun*, Sm. Gd.; *ret-ro-gra-da'shun*, Wk. Wr. 155.]
Re'tro-grade, *or* Ret'ro-grade, *a.* & *v.* [*re'tro-grād*, Sm.; *ret'ro-grād*, Wk. Wr. Wb. Gd. 155.]
Re'tro-grād-ed, *or* Ret'-ro-grād-ed.
Re'tro-grād-ing, *or* Ret'ro-grād-ing.
Re-tro-gres'sion, *or* Ret-ro-gres'sion (*-gresh'un*) [*re-tro-gresh'un*, Sm. Gd.; *ret-ro-gresh'un*, Wk. Wr. 155.]
Re-tro-gres'sĭve, *or* Ret-ro-gres'sĭve.
Re-tro-pul'sĭve, *or* Ret-ro-pul'sĭve.
Re-trorse'ly.
Re'tro-spect, *or* Ret'ro-spect [*re'tro-spekt*, Sm.; *ret'ro-spekt*, Wk. Wr. Wb. Gd. 155.]
Re-tro-spec'tion, *or* Ret-ro-spec'tion [*re-tro-spek'shun*, Sm. Gd.; *ret-ro-spek'-shun*, Wk. Wr. 155.]
Re-tro-spect'ĭve, *or* Ret-ro-spect'ĭve.
Re-tro-ver'sion, *or* Ret-ro-ver'sion.
Re'tro-vert, *or* Ret'ro-vert [*re-tro-vert'*, Sm.; *ret'ro-vert*, Wr. Wb. Gd. 155.]
Re'tro-vert-ed, *or* Ret'-ro-vert-ed.
Re'tro-vert-ing, *or* Ret'-ro-vert-ing.
Re-trude' (*-trood'*).
Re-trud'ed (*-trood'-*).
Re-trud'ing (*-trood'-*).
Re-truse' (*-troos'*).
Ret'ted, 176.
Ret'ting.
Re-turn', *n.* & *v.* 135.
Re-turn'a-ble, 164.
Re-turned', 150.
Re-turn'ing.
Re-tuse', 26.
Re-ūn'ion (*-ūn'yun*)
Re-u-nite', 223.
Reuss'in (*roos'-*).
Reuss'īte (*roos'-*), 26, 152.
Re-vac'ci-nate.
Re-vac-ci-na'tion.

Re-vēal′, 13.
Re-vēal-a-bil′i-ty, 108.
Re-vēal′a-ble, 164.
Re-vēaled′.
Re-vēal′ing.
Reveille (Fr.) (*re-vāl′*, or *re-vāl′yā*) [so Wr.; *rā-vāl′*, Sm.; *re-vāl′-yā*, Gd. 154, 155.]

☞ Although Smart authorizes the pronunciation *rā-vāl′*, only, yet he says, in a note, "also pronounced *rā-vāl′yā*."

Rev′el (124, 149, 161), *n.* a carousal: — *v.* to carouse.
Re-vel′ (124, 161), *v.* to pull or draw back.
Rev-e-la′tion.
Rev′elled (*-eld*) (161, 177) [Reveled, Wb. Gd. 203. — *See* Note E, p. 70.]
Re-velled′ (*-veld′*), 161, 176.
Re-vel′lent, 176.
Rev′el-ler (177) [Reveler, Wb. Gd. 203.]
Rev′el-ling (161, 177) [Reveling, Wb. Gd. 203.]
Re-vel′ling, 161, 176.
Rev′el-ry [*not* rev′l-ry, 132, 153.]
Re-ven′di-cate.
Re-ven′di-cāt-ed.
Re-ven′di-cāt-ing.
Re-ven-di-ca′tion.
Re-venge′, *n.* & *v.* Note D, p. 37.
Re-venge′a-ble, 164, 183.
Re-venged′, 165.
Re-venge′ful (*-fŏŏl*), 180.
Re-veng′er (*-venj′-*).
Re-veng′ing (*-venj′-*).
Rev′e-nūe [so Sm. Wr. Wb. Gd.; *rev′e-nu*, or *re-ven′u*, Wk. 155. — *See* Note under *Retinue*.]
Re-ver′ber-ant, 72.
Re-ver′ber-ate.
Re-ver′ber-āt-ed, 183.
Re-ver′ber-āt-ing.
Re-ver-ber-a′tion, 112.
Re-ver′ber-a-to-ry, 86.
Re-vere′, 169.
Re-vered′.
Rev′er-ence, 169.
Rev′er-enced (*-enst*).
Rev′er-enç-ing, 183.
Rev′er-end.
Rev′er-ent.
Rev-er-en′tial (*-shal*).
Rev-er-iē′ [so Sm. Wr.; *rev′er-ē*, Wb. Gd. 155] [Revery, 203.]

☞ "Both the orthography and pronunciation of this word are unsettled, some good writers and speakers using one form, and some the other." *Worcester*. — "In present usage, this word is more frequently written *reverie*." *Goodrich*. *See* Note under *Revery*.

Re-vers′al, 21, N.
Re-verse′.
Re-versed′ (*-verst′*).
Re-verse′ly.
Re-vers′i-ble [Reversable, 203.]
Re-vers′ing.
Re-ver′sion, 169.
Re-ver′sion-a-ry, 72.
Re-ver′sion-er.
Re-ver′sis.
Re-vert′, 21, N.; 135.
Re-vert′ed.
Re-vert′ent, 169.
Re-vert′er, 77.
Re-vert′i-ble, 164, 169.
Re-vert′ing.
Re-vert′īve.
Rev′er-y [*not* rev-ur-e′, 153] [Reverie, 203.]

☞ "If we place the accent on the last [syllable] of *revery*, and pronounce the *y* like *e*, there arises an irregularity which forbids it: for *y* with the accent on it is never so pronounced." *Walker*. *See* Note under *Reverie*.

Re-vest′.
Revêtement (Fr.) (*rev-āt′mŏng*) [so Sm.; *re-vēt′ment*, Wr. 155] [Revetment (*re-vet′ment*), Wb. Gd. 203.]
Re-view′ (*-vu′*), 26.
Re-view′a-ble (*-vu′a-bl*).
Re-view′al (*-vu′-*), 72.
Re-viewed′ (*-vūd′*).
Re-view′er (*-vu′-*), 169.
Re-view′ing (*-vu′-*).
Re-vile′, 25, 163.
Re-viled′, 165.
Re-vīl′ing, 183.
Re-vīs′al (*-vīz′-*).
Re-vise′ (*-vīz′*), *n.* & *v.*
Re-vised′ (*-vīzd′*).
Re-vīs′er (*-vīz′-*).
Re-vīs′ing (*-vīz′-*).
Re-vĭ′sion (*-vizh′un*).
Re-vĭ′sion-al (*-vizh′un-*)
Re-vĭ′sion-a-ry (*-vizh′-un-*).
Rē-vis′it (*-viz′-*), 222.
Re-vīs′o-ry (*vīz′-*), 86.
Re-vīv′a-ble, 164.
Re-vīv′al, 72.
Re-vīv′al-ism (*-izm*), 136.
Re-vīv′al-ist.
Re-vive′, 25, 163.
Re-vived′, 165.
Re-vīv′er.
Re-viv-i-fĭ-ca′tion, 116.
Re-viv′i-fīed.
Re-viv′i-fȳ, 169.
Re-viv′i-fȳ-ing.
Re-vīv′ing.
Rev-i-vis′cence.
Rev-i-vis′cen-cy, 169.
Re-vīv′or [Law term.]
Rev-o-ca-bil′i-ty, 108.
Rev′o-ca-ble, 164.
Rev′o-ca-bly.
Rev-o-ca′tion, 112.
Rev′o-ca-to-ry, 86.
Re-voke′, 163.
Re-voked′ (*-vōkt′*), 165; Note C, p. 34.
Re-vōk′ing, 183.
Re-vōlt′, *or* Re-vŏlt′, *n.* & *v.* [so Wk. Wr.; *re-vōlt′*, Sm.; *re-vŏlt′*, Wb. Gd. 155.]

☞ Walker says of this word, "that pronunciation ... which rhymes it with *bolt*, *jolt*, &c. has ... a clear analogy, and, if I am not mistaken, the best usage on its side."

Re-vōlt′ed, *or* Re-vŏlt′-ed.
Re-vōlt′ing, *or* Re-vŏlt′-ing.
Rev′o-lu-ble, 164.
Rev′o-lute, 169.
Rev-o-lu′tion.
Rev-o-lu′tion-a-ry, 72.
Rev-o-lu′tion-ism (*-izm*)
Rev-o-lu′tion-ist.
Rev-o-lu′tion-ize, 202.
Rev-o-lu′tion-ized, 165.
Rev-o-lu′tion-īz-ing.
Re-volve′.
Re-volved′.
Re-volve′ment.
Re-volv′en-cy, 169.
Re-volv′er, 183.
Re-volv′ing.
Re-vul′sion.
Re-vul′sĭve, 84.

Re-wârd′, 17, 135.
Re-wârd′a-ble, 164, 169.
Re-wârd′ed.
Re-wârd′er, 77.
Re-wârd′ing.
Rey′nard (*ra′nard*, or *ren′ard*) [*ra′nard*, Gd.; *ren′ard*, or *ra′-nard*, Wr. 155] [Renard, 203.]
Rha-bar′ba-rate (*ra*-).
Rha-bar′ba-rīne (*ra*-), 152, 171.
Rhab-dol′o-gy (*rab′*-) (108) [Rabdology, 203.]
Rhab′do-man-cy (*rab′*-) [Rabdomancy, 203.]
Rha′chi-al-gy (*ra′ki*-), 171.
[Rhachis, 203.—*See* Rachis.]
[Rhamadan, 203.—*See* Ramadan.]
Rham-na′ceoŭs (*ram-na′shus*).
Rham-phas′toŭs(*ram*-).
[Rhaphe, 203.—*See* Raphe.]
Rha-pon′ti-cīne [Rhaponticin, 203.]
Rhap-sod′ic (-*rap*-).
Rhap-sod′ic-al (*rap*-).
Rhap′so-dist (*rap′*-).
Rhap′so-dize (*rap′*-), 202.
Rhap′so-dized (-*rap′*-).
Rhap′so-dīz-ing (*rap′*-).
Rhap′so-dy (*rap′*-), 171.
[Rhatany, 203.—*See* Ratany.]
Rhe′īne (*re′*-) (152) [Rhein, 203.]
Rhen′ish (*ren′*-), 171.
Rhe-om′e-ter (*re*-) [Reometer, 203.]
Rhe-o-met′ric (*re*-).
Rhe-om′e-try (*re*-).
Rhe′o-scope (*re′*-).
Rhe′o-stat (-*re′*-).
[Rheotrope, 203.—*See* Reotrope.]
Rhe′ti-an (*re′shĭ-an*).
Rhet′o-ric (*ret′*-), 109.
Rhe-tŏr′ic-al (*re*-).
Rhet-o-rĭ′cian (*ret-o-rish′an*).
Rheum (*room*) (26, 171), *n.* a thin, watery discharge from the mucous membranes. [*See* Room, 160.]
Rheum-at′ic (*room*-)
Rheum′a-tism (*room′-a-tizm*), 133, 136, 171.
Rheum′ic (*room′*-).
Rheum′y (*room′*-) (169), *a.* pertaining to, or affected by, rheum. [*See* Roomy, 160.]
Rhi′nal (*ri′*-).
Rhine′grave (*rīn*-).
Rhi′no (*ri′*-).
Rhi-no-ce′ri-al (*ri*-), 49, N.
Rhī-noç′er-ŏs (*rī-nos′*-), 79, 171.
Rhī-no-plas′tic (*rī*-).
Rhi′no-plas-ty (*ri′*-).
Rhī-pip′ter-an (*rī*-).
Rhī-zan-tha′ceoŭs (-*shus*), 112.
Rhĭz′o-dont.
Rhi-zo′ma (*rī*-).
Rhi′zome (*ri′*-).
Rhī-zoph′a-goŭs (*rī*-).
Rhī-zoph′o-roŭs (*rī*-).
Rhiz′o-pod (*riz′*-).
Rhī′zo-stome (*rī′*-).
Rhō′di-an, 169.
Rho′di-um (*ro′*-), 169.
Rhod′i-zīte (*rod′*-).
Rho-do-den′dron [so Sm. Wb. Gd.; *ro-do-den′dron*, or *rod-o-den′dron*, Wr. 155.]
[Rhodomontade, 203.—*See* Rodomontade.]
Rhomb (*romb*) (142) [so Sm. Wb. Gd.; *rumb*, Wk.; *rumb*, or *romb*, Wr. 155], *n.* an oblique-angled parallelogram, having equal sides. [*See* Rhumb, 148.]

☞ "In the mathematical term *rhomb*, the *b* is always heard." *Walker.*

Rhom′bic, 228.
Rhom-bo-he′dral.
Rhom-bo-he′dron.
Rhom′boid, *n.* 161.
Rhom-boid′, *a.* 161.
Rhom-boid′al.
Rhom′bus (*rom′*-) (169) [L. pl. *Rhom′bī*; Eng. pl. Rhom′bus-es (-*ez*), 198.]
Rhonch-is′o-nant (*rongk*-).
Rhon′cus (*rong′*-), 54.
Rhu′barb (*roo′*-) (19, 171) [*not* roo′bub, 135, 153.]
Rhumb (*rumb*) (142) [so Sm. Wr.; *rum*, Gd. 155], *n.* a vertical circle, making an angle with the meridian of any place; — the intersection of such a circle with the horizon; — the track of a ship sailing constantly toward the same point of the compass. [*See* Rhomb, 148.]
Rhyme (*rīm*) (171), *n.* correspondence of the sound of one word or syllable with that of another: — *v.* to accord in sound. [*See* Rime, 160.]
Rhymed (*rīmd*), 165.
Rhȳm′er (*rīm′*-), 77.
Rhyme′ster, 185.
Rhȳm′ic (*rīm′*-).
Rhȳm′ing, 183.
Rhȳm′ist.
Rhyn′cho-līte(*ring′ko*-)
Rhyn′cho-phore(*ring′*-)
Rhyn′chops (*ring′-kops*), 171.
Rhythm (*rithm*) (133, 171) [so Wk. Sm. Wb. Gd.; *rithm*, or *rithm*, Wr. 155.]
Rhyth′mic-al (*rith′*-).
Rhyth-mom′e-ter (*rith*-).
Rhyth′mus (*rith′*-).
[Rial (*re′al*), 203.—*See* Real.]
Ri′al, *n.* an English gold coin current in the reign of Henry IV., and in that of Elizabeth.
Riant (Fr.) (*re′ong*) [so Sm.; *re′äng*, Gd.; *re-an′*, Wr. 154, 155.]
Rib, 16, 31, 48.
Rib′ald, 72, 170.
Rib′ald-ry.
[Riband, 203.—*See* Ribband, *and* Ribbon.]
[Ribband, 203.—*See* Ribbon.]
Rib′-band (206, Exc. 1), *n.* a long, narrow, flexible piece of timber nailed horizontally to the outside of a

ship's ribs. [Rib-and, Ribbon, 203.]
Ribbed (*ribd*), 176.
Rib′bing.
Rib′bon (66, 149, 170), *n.* a woven strip of silk; — an ordinary which is the eighth part of a bend; — a flexible strip of timber nailed across the outside of a vessel's ribs: — *v.* to adorn with ribbons. [Riband, Rib-band, and (in the last sense of the noun) Rib-band, 203.]

☞ *Ribbon* is now the prevailing form of this word in the first two senses. "The orthography *riband* [or *ribband*] has nothing to plead in its favor, and is least used." *Smart.*

Rib′boned, 150, 165.
Rib′bon-ing.
Rib′rōast.
Rib′rōast-ed.
Rib′rōast-ing.
Rib′wort (*-wurt*).
Rice (25, 39), *n.* a kind of esculent grain. [*See* Rise, *n.* 160.]
Rice′-bird.
Rice′-pā-per.
Rich, 16, 44.
Rich′es (*-ez*).

☞ "This is in the singular number in fact, but treated as the plural." *Webster.* — It is derived from the French *richesse*, and was formerly written *richesse*, or *richess*.

Rich′ly, 93.
Rick, 16, 181.
Rick′ets, *n. pl.*
Rick′et-y, 169.
Ricochet (Fr.) (*rik′o-shā*, or *rik′o-shet*) [so Wr.; *rik′o-shā*, Sm.; *rik′o-shet*, or *rik′o-shā*, Gd. 155], *n.*

☞ "The verb *ricochet* having been naturalized as an English word, it is desirable that the noun should likewise have an English pronunciation." *Goodrich.*

Ric-o-chet′ (*-shet′*) [so Gd.; *rik′o-shet*, Wr. 155], *v.*
Ric-o-chet′ted (*-shet′-*).
Ric-o-chet′ting (*-shet′-*).
Rid (16, 42, 48) [*not* red, 127, 153.]
Rid′dance, 72, 176.
Rid′den (*rid′n*), 149.
Rid′der.
Rid′ding, 170.
Rid′dle (*rid′l*), 164.
Rid′dled (*rid′ld*).
Rid′dler.
Rid′dling, 183.
Ride, 25, 163.
Rideau (Fr.) (*re-do′*).
Rīd′er, 169.
Ridge, 16, 45.
Ridged (*rijd*), 165.
Ridg′ing (*rij′-*).
Rid′i-cule [*not* red′i-kūl, 137, 153.]
Rid′i-culed, 165.
Rid′i-cūl-ing.
Ri-dic′u-loŭs, 108.
Rīd′ing, 183.
Rīd′ing-màs′ter.
Rī-dot′to (It.) [pl. *Rī-dot′tos* (*-tōz*), 192.]
Riēt′boc, 171.
Rife, 25, 163.
Riff′raff, 171.
Ri′fle, 164.
Ri′fle-man, 196.
Ri′fled (*-fld*).
Ri′fler, 77, 183.
Ri′fling.
Rift, 16.
Rift′ed.
Rift′ing.
Rig, 16.
Rig-a-doon′, 122.
Ri′gel (*-ghel*), 138.
Rigged (*rigd*), 165, 176.
Rig′ger (*-gur*) (138), *n.* one who rigs. [*See* Rigor, 160.]
Rig′ging (*-ghing*), 138.
Right (*rīt*) (162), *a.* conformable to rule, fact, reason, truth, justice, or duty: — *adv.* directly; in a right manner: — *n.* rectitude; — prerogative; — side opposed to the left: — *v.* to restore to an upright position; — to do justice to. [*See* Rite, Wright, *and* Write, 160.]
Right′-an-gled (*rīt′-ang-gld*).
Right′ed (*rīt′-*).
Right′eous (*rī′chus*), (44, Note 1; 171) [so Wr. Wb. Gd.; *rīt′-yus*, Sm.; *rī′che-us*, Wk. 155.]
Right′eoŭs-ly (*-rī′chu-s*)
Right′eoŭs-ness (*rī′-chus-*).
Right′er (*rīt′-*), *n.* one who sets right. [*See* Writer, 160.]
Right′ful (*rīt′fŏŏl*), 180.
Right′-hand-ed.
Right′ing (*rīt′-*), *part.* from *Right.* [*See* Writing, 160.]
Right′-mind-ed (*rīt′-*).
Rig′id (*rij′-*), 45, 80.
Ri-gid′i-ty, 108.
Rig′ma-role, 171.
Rig′or (66, 88, 169), *n.* stiffness; — inflexibility in opinion or judgment; — in medicine, a sensation of cold, with an involuntary shuddering. [*See* Rigger, 160] [Rigour, (in the first two senses), Sm. 199, 202.]
Rig′or-ism (*-izm*), 136.
Rig′or-ist, 106.
Rig′or-oŭs, 100, 108.
[Rile, 203. — *See* Roil.]
[Rilievo (It.), 203. — *See* Relievo.]
Rill, 16, 172.
Rilled (*rild*), 165.
Rill′et, 228.
Rill′ing.
Rim, 16, 32, 48.
Rime (25), *n.* hoar frost. [*See* Rhyme, 160.]
Rimmed (*rimd*), 176.
Rim′ming.
Rī-mose′ [*rī-mōs′*, Wr.; *rī′mōs*, Wb. Gd. 155.]
Rī-mos′i-ty [so Gd.; *rī-mos′i-ty*, Wr. 155.]
Rī′moŭs.
Rim′ple, 164.
Rim′pled (*-pld*).
Rim′pling.
Rīm′y, 169.
Rīnd, 25, 142.
Rin-for-zan′do (It.) *rin-fort-san′do* [so Gd.; *rin-for-zan′do*, Wr. 155.]
Ring (16, 54), *n.* any thing in the form of a circle; — a sound, as of a bell: — *v.* to encircle; — to cause to sound, as a bell or

other sonorous body. [*See* Wring, 160.]
Ring′bone.
Ring′dove (*-duv*).
Ringed (*ringd*), *a.*
Rin′gent (*-jent*), 45.
Ring′er.
Ring′ing, *n.* & *part.* from *Ring.* [*See* Wringing, 160.]
Ring′lēad-er.
Ring′let, 76.
Ring′-shaped (*-shāpt*).
Ring′tāil.
Ring′worm (*-wurm*).
Rinse (Note D, p. 37) [*not* rens, 153.]
Rinsed (*rinst*), 165.
Rins′ing, 183.
Ri′o-līte, 152.
Ri′ot, *n.* a tumultuous disturbance of the peace: — *v.* to revel; — to be seditious. [*See* Ryot, 160.]
Ri′ot-ed.
Ri′ot-er.
Ri′ot-ing.
Ri′ot-oŭs, 100.
Rip, 16, 30, 48.
Rĭ-pa′ri-an, 49, N.; 79.
Ripe, 25, 163.
Rīp′en (*rīp′n*), 149, 167.
Rīp′ened (*rīp′nd*).
Ripe′ness, 185.
Rīp′en-ing (*rīp′n-*).
Rī-phe′an, 79, 110.
Rip-i-e′no (*-ā′-*) (It.) [so Gd.; *rip-i-e′no*, Wr. 154, 155.]
Ripped (*ript*), 156, 176; Note C, p. 34.
Rip′ping, 176.
Rip′ple, 164, 170.
Rip′pled (*rip′ld*).
Rip′pling.
Rip′rap.
Rīse (*rīz*), *v.* 161.
Rise (*rīs*) (161) [so Wk. Sm. Wr. Wb. Gd.] [*not* rīz, 153], *n.* the act of rising; ascent; — origin; — increase. [*See* Rice, 160.]

☞ Walker, after alluding to the fact that this noun is sometimes pronounced "with the *s* like *z*," remarks: "The pure *s*, however, is more agreeable to analogy, and ought to be scrupulously preserved . . . by all correct speakers."

Ris′en (*riz′n*).
Rīs′er (*rīz′-*), 169.
Ris-i-bil′i-ty (*riz-*).
Ris′i-ble (*riz′i-bl*) (164, 169) [so Wk. Sm. Wr.; *riz′i-bl*, or *ri′si-bl*, Gd. 155.]
Ris′i-bly (*riz′-*).
Rīs′ing (*rīz′-*).
Risk, 16.
Risked (*riskt*), 165.
Risk′ing.
Rĭ-so′ri-al, 49, N.
Rite (25), *n.* a religious or external observance. [*See* Right, Wright, *and* Write, 160.]
Ri-tor-nel′lo (It.) (*rē-*).
Rit′u-al, 108.
Rit′u-al-ism (*-izm*).
Rit′u-al-ist, 106.
Rit-u-al-ist′ic, 109.
Rit′u-al-ly.
Rī′val, 72.
Rī′valled (*-vald*) [Rivaled, Wb. Gd. 203. — *See* 177, and Note E, p. 70.]
Rī′val-ling [Rivaling, Wb. Gd. 203.]
Rī′val-ry, 93.
Rive, 25, 163.
Rived, 150, 165.
Riv′en (*riv′n*), 149, 167.
Riv′er.
Riv′er-horse.
Riv′et, 76.
Riv′et-ed.
Riv′et-ing.
Rīv′ing, 183.
Rĭ-vose′, 79.
Riv′u-let.
Rōach, 24.
Rōad (24), *n.* a public way for travelling. [*See* Rode, *and* Rowed, 160.]
Rōad′stēad.
Rōad′ster, 77.
Rōad′wāy.
Rōam, 24.
Rōamed, 165.
Roam′ing.
Rōan, 24.
Rōar (24, 48, 49, 67), *n.* a loud continuous cry, as of a lion, or a loud noise, as of the sea: — *v.* to bellow as a beast; — to make a noise like that of the sea. [*See* Rower, 148.]

Rōared, 150.
Rōar′er, 49, N.
Rōar′ing.
Rōast, 24.
Rōast′ed.
Rōast′ing.
Rob, 18.
Robbed (*robd*).
Rob′ber, 77, 176.
Rob′ber-y.
[Robbin, 203. — *See* Rope-band.]
Rob′bing.
Robe, 24, 163.
Robed, 165.
Robe de chambre (Fr.) (*rōb duh shäm′br*).
Rob′ert-īne, 152.
Rob′in, 66, 170.
Rob′in-et.
Rōb′ing, 183.
Rob′o-rant (72) [so Wr. Wb. Gd.; *ro′bo-rant*, Sm. 155.]
Ro-bust′, 121.
Ro-bust′ioŭs (*-yus*).
Roc, *n.* a monstrous bird of Arabian mythology. [*See* Rock, 160] [Rukh, 203.]
Ro-cä′ille (Fr.).
Roc′am-bole.
Ro-cel′lic, 170.
Roch′et (*rok′et*, or *roch′et*) [*rok′et*, Sm.; *roch′et*, Wb. Gd.; *roch′et*, or *rok′et*, Wr. 155], *n.* a linen habit, like a surplice, worn by bishops. [*See* Rocket, 160.]
Roch′et (44), *n.* the red gurnard.
Rock (18, 181), *n.* a large mass of stony matter: — *v.* to move backwards and forwards. [*See* Roc, 160.]
Rock′-bound, 206, Exc. 5
Rock′-crys′tal.
Rocked (*rokt*).
Rock′er.
Rock′et, *n.* a kind of projectile firework; — a cruciferous plant. [*See* Rochet, 160.]
Rock′i-ness, 186.
Rock′ing.
Rock′ing-chair.
Rock′ing-horse.
Rock′ling.
Rock′-rose (*-rōz*).

Rock′work (*-wurk*).
Rock′y, 169.
Ro-co′co.
Rod, 18, 42, 48.
Rōde (24), *v.* did ride. [*See* Road, *and* Rowed, 160.]
Ro′dent.
Ro-den′ti-a (*-shĭ-a*), *n. pl.* 171.
Rodge, 18, 45.
Rod′o-mel.
Rod-o-mont-ade′ (122) [Rhodomontade, 203.]
Rod-o-mont-ād′ing.
Rod-o-mont-ād′ist.
Rod-o-mont-ād′or, 169.
Rōe (24), *n.* a small species of deer; — the seed or spawn of fishes. [pl. Roes (*rōz*), 189. — *See* Rose, *and* Rows (pl. of Row), 160.]
Rōe′buck.
Rōe′stōne.
Ro-ga′tion.
Rōgue, 24, 168; Note D, p. 37.
Rōgu′er-y (*rōg′-*).
Rōgu′ish (*rōg′-*), 183.
Roil (27) [Rile, 203.]
Roiled, 165.
Roil′ing.
Roil′y.
Rois′ter-er [Roysterer, 203.]
Rôle (Fr.) (*rōl*), *n.* 160.
Rōll, *v.* & *n.* 24, 160, 172.
Rōll′a-ble, 164.
Rōlled, 150, 165.
Rōll′er.
Rol′lic (170) [Rollick, Sm. Gd. 200, 203.]
Rol′licked (*-likt*).
Rol′lick-ing, 182.
Rōll′ing.
Rōll′ing-pin, 215.
Ro-ma′ic, 109.
Ro-mâl′ [so Wb. Gd.; *ro′mal*, Wr. 155.]
Ro′man, 196.
Ro-mance′, *n.* & *v.* (121) [*not* ro′mance, 153.]
Ro-manced′ (*-manst′*).
Ro-manç′er.
Ro-manç′ing.
Ro-manç′ist.
Ro-man-esque′ (*-esk′*).
Ro-man′ic, 66, 170.
Ro′man-ish.
Ro′man-ism (*-izm*), 136.
Ro′man-ist.
Ro′man-ize, 202.
Ro′man-ized.
Ro′man-īz-ing.
Ro-mănsh′ [so Sm. Wb. Gd.; *ro-mănsh′*, Wr. 155] [Romansch, Wr.; Ruminsch, Rumonsch, 203.]
Ro-man′tic, 109.
Ro-man′tic-al-ly, 170.
Ro-man′ti-cism (*-sizm*).
Ro-man′ti-cist.
Rōm′ish, 183.
Rōm′ist.
Romp, 18, 64.
Romped (*rompt*), 165; Note C, p. 37.
Rom-pee′, 121.
Romp′ing.
Romp′ish.
Ron′deau (*-do*), *or* Ron-deau′ (*-do′*) (Fr.) [*ron′do*, Sm.; *ron-do′*, Wk. Wb. Wr. 155] [Fr. pl. *Ron-deaux′* (*-dō′*); Eng. pl. Ron-deaus (*ron′dōz*, or *ron-dōz′*), 198] [Rondo, 203.]
Ron′del.
Ron′ion (*run′yun*) (51) [Ronyon, 203.]
Rood (19), *n.* the fourth part of an acre; — a representation of the crucified Saviour, or of the Trinity. [*See* Rude, *and* Rued, 160.]
Roof (19) [*not* rŏŏf, *nor* ruf, 153.]
Roofed (*rooft*), 41.
Roof′ing.
Roof′y, 93.
Rŏŏk (20) [so Sm. Wr. Wb. Gd.; *rook*, Wk. 155] [*See* Note under *Book*.]
Rŏŏked (*rŏŏkt*), 41.
Rŏŏk′er-y.
Rŏŏk′y.
Room (19) [*not* rŏŏm, 153], *n.* space; — an apartment. [*See* Rheum, 160.]
Room′age, 169.
Room′ful (*room′fŏŏl*), 180, 197.
Room′i-ness, 186.
Room′y, *a.* having room; spacious. [*See* Rheumy, 160.]
Roost, 19.
Roost′ed.
Roost′er.
Roost′ing.
Root (19) [*not* rŏŏt, 153.]
Root′ed.
Root′-house, 206, Exc. 3.
Root′ing.
Root′let, 76.
Root′stock.
Root′y, 93, 169.
Ro-pal′ic.
Rope, 24, 163.
Rope′-band [Robbin, 203.]
Roped (*rōpt*), 165, 183; Note C, p. 34.
Rope′-pump, 66, N.
Rōp′er-y.
Rope′walk (*-wawk*), 162.
Rōp′i-ness, 186.
Rōp′y, 93, 183.
Roquelaure (Fr.) (*rok-e-lōr′*) [so Sm.; *rok-e-lōr′*, Wk. Wr.; *rok′-e-lōr*, Gd. 155.]
Ro-rif′er-oŭs, 108.
Ror′qual.
Ro′ru-lent, 108.
Ro-sa′ceoŭs (*-za′shus*), 112, 169.
Ros′am-bole (*roz′-*).
Ro′sa-ry (*-za-*).
Rose (*rōz*) (24), *n.* a well-known plant and its flower: — *v.* did rise. [*See* Roes (pl. of Roe), *and* Rows (pl. of Rōw), 160.]
Ro′se-ate (*ro′ze-āt*, or *ro′zhe-āt*) (169) [*ro′-ze-āt*, coll. *ro′zhe-āt*, Sm.; *ro′zhe-āt*, Wk. Gd.; *ro′zhe-āt*, or *ro′-ze-āt*, Wr. 155.]
Rose′bāy (*rōz′-*).
Rose′ma-ry (*rōz′-*), 72.
Ro-se′o-la (*-ze′-*).
Ro-sette′ (*-zet′*), 171.
Rose′wŏŏd (*rōz′-*).
Rŏs-i-cru′cian (*roz-i-kroo′shan*) (112) [*not* ro-zi-kroo′shan, 153.]
Rōs′ĭed (*rōz′id*).
Ros′in (*roz′in*), 149.

☞ *Rosin* is a different orthography of *resin*. The latter is the scientific term: the former is the commercial name of the commonest resin in use, being that which is left after distilling turpentine with water.

Ros'ined (*roz'ind*).
Ros'in-y (*roz'-*).
Ros'tel.
Ros'tel-late, 170.
Ros-tel'li-form, 108.
Ros'ter.
Ros'tral.
Ros'trate.
Ros'trāt-ed.
Ros'tri-form, 108.
Ros'trum (L.) [pl. *Ros'-tra*, 198.]
Ros'u-late (*roz'-*).
Rōs'y (*rōz'-*), 136.
Rot, 18.
Rot'a-cism (*-sizm*).
Ro'ta-ry, 72.
Ro'tate, *a.* & *v.*
Ro'tāt-ed, 183.
Ro'tāt-ing.
Ro-ta'tion, 169.
Ro'ta-tive, 84.
Ro-ta'to-plane, 224.
Ro-ta'tor.
Ro'ta-to-ry, 86, 126.
Rote (24), *n.* mechanical repetition;—the noise of surf upon the shore. [*See* Wrote, 160.]
Roth'er-nāil [so Sm. Wb. Gd.; *roth'ur-nāl*, Wr. 155.]
Ro'ti-fer [so Sm. Wb. Gd.; *rot'i-fur*, Wr. 155.]
Ro'ti-form.
Rot'ted, 176.
Rot'ten (*rot'n*), 149, 170.
Rot'ten-ness (*rot'n-*), 66, N.
Rot'ting.
Rot'u-lar, 108.
Ro-tund', 121.
Ro-tun'da [Rotundo, 203.]
Ro-tund-i-fo'li-oŭs.
Ro-tund'i-ty.
Ro-tun'do [Rotunda, 203.]
[Rouble, 203.—*See* Ruble.]
Rouche (Fr.) (*roosh*) [Ruche, 203.]
Roué (Fr.) (*roo-ā'*).
Rouge (*roozh*), 47.
Rouged (*roozhd*).
Rouge-et-noir (Fr.) (*roozh-ā-nwor'*).
Rough (*ruf*) (22, 35), *a.* having inequalities on the surface; harsh. [*See* Ruff, 160.]
Rough'cȧst (*ruf'-*), *n.* & *v.*
Rough'cȧst-ing (*ruf'-*).
Rough'drâw (*ruf'-*).
Rough'drâw-ing(*ruf'-*).
Rough'drâwn (*ruf'-*).
Rough'drew (*ruf'droo*).
Rough'en (*ruf'n*), 171.
Rough'ened (*ruf'nd*).
Rough'en-ing (*ruf'n-*).
Rough'-hew (*ruf'hu*) (206, Exc. 1) [so Sm. Wb. Gd.; *ruf-hū'*, Wk.; *ruf-hu'*, or *ruf'-hu*, Wr. 155.]
Rough'-hewed (*ruf'-hūd*).
Rough'-hew-ing (*ruf'-hu-ing*).
Rough'-hewn(*ruf'hūn*).
Rough'ish (*ruf'-*).
Rough'ly (*ruf'-*), 93.
Rough'ness (*ruf'-*).
Rough'-shod (*ruf'-*).
Rough'work (*ruf'-wurk*).
Rough'worked (*ruf'-wurkt*).
Rough'work-ing (*ruf'-wurk-*).
Rough'wrought (*ruf'-rawt*).
Roug'ing (*roozh'-*) (183) [Rougeing, Gd. 203.]
Roulade (Fr.) (*roo-läd'*).
Rouleau (Fr.) (*roo-lo'*) [pl. *Rouleaux* (*roo-lōz'*), 198.]
Rou-lette' (Fr.) (*roo-*).
Rounce, 28.
Roun'ce-val.
Round, 28.
Round'a-bout.
Round'ed.
Round'el.
Round'e-lāy.
Round'hĕad, 216.
Round'house.
Round'ing.
Round'ish.
Round'let.
Round'ly.
Rous'ant (*rouz'-*).
Rouse (*rouz*), 28.
Roused (*rouzd*), 165.
Rous'er (*rouz'-*).
Rous'ing (*rouz'-*).
Rout, *n.* & *v.* 28.
Route (*root*, or *rout*), *n.* [so Wr.; *root*, Sm.; *rout*, or *root*, Wk. Gd. 155.]
Rout'ed.
Rou-tine' (*roo-tēn'*), 114.
Rout'ing.
Rove, 24.
Roved, 150, 165.
Rōv'er.
Rōv'ing, 183.
Rōw (24, 161), *n.* a number arranged in a line:—*v.* to impel, as a boat, by oars. [pl. Rows (*rōz*), 189.—*See* Roes (pl. of Roe), *and* Rose, 160.]
Row (*rou*), 28, 161.
Rōw'a-ble, 164, 169.
Rōw'an-tree.
Row'dy (*rou'-*).
Rōwed, *v.* did row. [*See* Road, *and* Rode, 160.]
Row'el, 28.
Row'elled [Roweled, Wb. Gd. 203.—*See* 177, and Note E, p. 70.]
Row'el-ling [Roweling, Wb. Gd. 203.]
Row'en, 28.
Rōw'er (67), *n.* one who rows. [*See* Roar, 148.]
Rōw'ing.
Rōw'land.
Rōw'lock (*ro'lok*, coll. *rul'uk*) [so Sm.; *ro'-lok*, Gd.; *ro'lok*, or *rul'uk*, Wr. 155.]
Roy'al (27, 72) [*not* raw'yal, 153.]
Roy'al-ism (*-izm*), 136.
Roy'al-ist.
Roy'al-ty.
[Roysterer, 203. *See* Roisterer.]
Rub, 22, 31, 48.
Rubbed (*rubd*), 165, 176.
Rub'bing.
Rub'bish, 66, 170.
Rub'bish-y.
Rub'ble, 164.
Rub'bly, 93.
Ru-be-fa'cient (*roo-be-fa'shent*), 112.
Ru-be-fac'tion (*roo-*).
Ru'bel-līte (*roo'-*), 152.
Ru-be'o-la (*roo-*).
Ru-bes'cence (*roo-*), 39, 171.
Ru-bes'cent (*roo-*).
Ru'bi-can (*roo'-*), 78.
Ru-bic'a-tive (*roo-*).
Ru'bi-celle (*roo'-*), 171.
Ru'bi-cŏn (*roo'-*).

Ru′bi-cund (*roo′-*).
Ru-bi-cund′i-ty (*roo-*).
Ru′bĭed (*roo′bid*), 99.
Ru-bif′ic (*roo-*), 109.
Ru-bi-fi-ca′tion (*roo-*).
Ru′bi-fĭed (*roo′-*).
Ru′bi-form (*roo′-*), 108.
Ru′bi-fȳ (*roo′-*), 94.
Ru′bi-fȳ-ing (*roo′-*)
Ru-big′i-noŭs (*roo-bij′-*).
Ru-bi′go (L.) (*roo-*).
Ru′ble (*roo′bl*) (171) [Rouble, 203.]
Ru′bric (*roo′-*), 200.
Ru′bric-al (*roo′-*).
Ru′bric-ate (*roo′-*).
Ru-brĭ′cian (*roo-brish′-an*).
Ru′bri-cist (*roo′-*).
Ru′by (*roo′-*), 93.
[Ruche, 203. — *See* Rouche.]
Ruck, 22, 181.
Ruc-ta′tion, 112.
Rudd [Rud, 203.]
Rud′der, 170.
Rŭd′di-ness.
Rud′dle, 164.
Rud′dock, 66.
Rud′dy, 170.
Rude (*rood*) (19), *a.* rough, coarse. [*See* Rood, *and* Rued, 160.]
Rude′ly (*rood′-*).
Rude′ness (*rood′-*).
Ru′den-tūre (*roo′-*), 90.
Ru′di-ment (*roo′-*), 169.
Ru-di-ment′al (*roo-*).
Ru-di-ment′a-ry, (*roo-*), 72.
Rūd′ish (*rood′-*), 183.
Ru-dol′phĭne (*roo-*).
Rue (*roo*), 19.
Rued (*rood*), *v.* did rue. [*See* Rood, *and* Rude, 160.]
Rue′ful (*roo′fo͝ol*), 180.
Rue′ful-ly (*roo′fo͝ol-*).
Ru-fes′cent (*roo-*).
Ruff (22, 173), *n.* a plaited ornament of cloth worn about the neck; a kind of bird: — *v.* to ruffle. [*See* Rough, 160.]
Ruffed (*ruft*), 150.

☞ As a *participial adjective*, pronounced by Worcester, *ruff′ed*.

Ruf′fian (*ruf′yan*) [*not* ruf′i-an, *nor* ruf′in, 153.]
Ruf′fian-ish (*ruf′yan-*).
Ruf′fian-ism (*ruf′yan-izm*), 133, 136.
Ruf′fian-ly (*ruf′yan-*).
Ruff′ing.
Ruf′fle (*ruf′l*), 164.
Ruf′fled (*ruf′ld*).
Ruf′fling, 183.
Ru′foŭs, 156.
Rug, 22, 48, 53.
Ru′gate (*roo′-*).
Rug′ged (*-ghed*), 138.
Rug′ging (*-ghing*), 176.
Ru′gine (*roo′jēn*).
Ru-gose′ (*roo-*) (26) [so Wk. Sm. Wr.; *rū′gōs*, Wb. Gd. 155.]
Ru-gos′i-ty (*roo-*).
Ru′goŭs (*roo′-*).
Ru-gu-lose′ (*roo-*).
Ru′in (*-roo′-*), *n.* & *v.*
Ru-in-a′tion (*roo-*).
Ru′ined (*roo′ind*).
Ru′ing (*roo′-*), 183.
Ru′in-i-form (*roo′-*).
Ru′in-ing (*roo′-*).
Ru′in-oŭs (*roo′-*), 228.
[Rukh, 203. — *See* Roc.]
Rul′a-ble (*rool′-*), 164, 169.
Rule (*rool*), 19, 128.
Ruled (*roold*), 165.
Rul′er (*rool′-*), 169.
Rul′ing (*rool′-*), 183.
Rum, 22, 32, 48.
Rum′ble, 164.
Rum′bled (*-bld*).
Rum′bling, 183.
Ru′mi-nal (*roo′-*), 105.
Ru′mi-nant (*roo′-*).
Ru′mi-nate (*roo′-*), 108.
Ru′mi-nāt-ed (*roo′-*).
Ru′mi-nāt-ing (*roo′-*).
Ru-mi-na′tion (*roo-*).
Ru′mi-nāt-or (*roo′-*).
[Ruminsch (*roo′-minsh*), 203. — *See* Romansh.]
Rum′mage, 170.
Rum′maged.
Rum′ma-ging.
Ru′mor (*roo′-*) (88) [Rumour, Sm. 199, 203.]
Ru′mored (*roo′murd*) [Rumoured, Sm. 203.]
Ru′mor-er (*roo′-*) (77) [Rumourer, Sm. 203.]
Ru′mor-ing (*roo′-*) [Rumouring, Sm. 203.]
Rump, 22.
Rum′ple, 164.
Rum′pled (*-pld*).
Rum′pling, 183.
Run, 22, 43, 48.
Run′a-wāy.
Run′ci-nate.
Run′dle, 164.
Rund′let [Runlet, 203.]
Rune (*roon*), 189.
Ru′ner (*roo′-*).
Rung (22, 54), *v.* did ring. [*See* Wrung, 160.]
Ru′nic (*roo′-*).
Run′let [Rundlet, 203.]
Run′nel, 66, 170.
Run′ner, 176.
Run′net (170) [Rennet, 203.]
Run′ning.
Run′ning-fire.
Runt, 22.
Ru-pee′ (*roo-*), 121.
Rup′tion.
Rupt′ure, 91.
Rupt′ured (*-yurd*).
Rupt′ur-ing (*-yur-*), 91.
Ru′ral (*roo′-*), 49, N.
Ru′ral-ly (*roo′-*).
Ruse (Fr.) (*rooz*).
Ruse de guerre (Fr.) (*rooz-duh-ghêr′*).
Rush, 22, 46, 48.
Rushed (*rusht*), 165.
Rush′er.
Rush′i-ness, 186.
Rush′ing.
Rush′y, 93, 169.
Rusk, 22.
Russ, 22, 174.
Rus′set, 76, 170.
Rus′set-ing [Russetting, Wr. 203.]
Rus′set-y [Russetty, Wr. 203.]
Rus′sian (*rush′an*) [so Sm.; *rū′shan*, Gd.; *rush′an*, or *roo′shan*, Wr. 155.]
Rust, 22.
Rust′ed.
Rus′tic, 200.
Rus′tic-al, 109.
Rus′tic-ate, 108.
Rus′tic-āt-ed, 183.
Rus′tic-āt-ing.
Rus-tic-a′tion.
Rus-tiç′i-ty, 108, 169.
Rust′i-ness.
Rust′ing.

Rus′tle (*rus′l*), 162, 164.
Rus′tled (*rus′ld*).
Rus′tling (*rus′ling*).
Rust′y.
Rut, 22, 41, 48.
Ru′ta-ba′ga (*roo′-*).
Ru-ta′ceous (*roo-ta′-shus*).
Ruth (*rooth*) [so Wk. Wr.; *rŏŏth*, Sm.; *rŭth*, Wb. Gd. 155.]
Ru-the′ni-um (*roo-*).
Ruth′less (*rooth′-*).
Ru′tīle (*roo′-*), 81, 152.
Ru′ti-līne, 152.
Rut′ty.
Rȳe (25), *n.* a kind of esculent grain. [*See* Wry, 160.]
[Rynchops, 203. — *See* Rhynchops.]
Rȳnd, 16.
Ry′ot, *n.* a Hindoo peasant. [*See* Riot, 160.]

S.

Sa′ba, 23, 72.
Sab-a-dil′la.
Sab-a-dill′ia (*-ya*).
Sab-a-dil′līne, 152.
Sa-bæ′an [Sabean, Sabian, 203.]
Sa-bæ′an-ism (*-izm*).
Sa′ba-ism (*-izm*), 136.
Sa-ba′ŏth, *or* Sab′a-oth (72) [so Wr.; *sa-ba′-oth*, Sm.; *sab′a-oth*, Wk. Wb. Gd. 155.]
Sab-ba-ta′ri-an.
Sab-ba-ta′ri-an-ism (*-izm*), 133, 136.
Sab′bath, 66, 170.
Sab′bath-breāk′er, 205.
Sab-bat′ic, 109.
Sab-bat′ic-al, 108.
Sab′ba-tism (*-tizm*), 133.
Sa-be′an [Sabæan, Sabian, 203.]
Sa′be-ism (*-izm*), 136.
Sab-el-la′na.
Sa-bell′ian (*-bel′yan*), 51, 112.
Sa-bell′ian-ism (*-bel′-yan-izm*), 133, 136.
[Saber, Wb. Gd. 203. — *See* Sabre.]
Sa′bi-an (169) [Sabæan, Sabean, 203.]
Sa′bi-an-ism (*-izm*).
Sab′īne, *n.* a kind of plant or shrub; — a kind of small fish. [Savin (in the former sense), 203.]
Sa′ble, 164.
Sabot (Fr.) (*sa-bōt′*) [so Sm.; *sa-bo′*, Wr. Gd. 154, 155.]
Sa′bre (*-bur*) [Saber, Wb. Gd. 203. — *See* Note E, p. 70.]
Sac (10, 181), *n.* in natural history, a little pouch or receptacle for a liquid; — in law, the privilege of the lord of a manor to hold courts, try causes, and impose fines. [*See* Sack, 160.]
Sac-cade′, 121.
Sac′cate, 176.
Sac′căt-ed.
Sac′cha-rate (*-ka-*), 52.
Sac-chăr′ic (*-kăr′-*).
Sac-cha-rif′er-ous (*-ka-*), 108.
Sac-chăr′i-fīed (*-kăr′-*).
Sac-chăr′i-fȳ (*-kăr′-*), 108
Sac-chăr′i-fȳ-ing (*kăr′-*).
Sac-cha-ril′la (*-ka-*).
Sac-cha-rim′e-try (*-ka-*), 171.
Sac′cha-rīne (*-ka-rin*) (152, 171) [so Sm. Wb. Gd.; *sak′ka-rīn*, Wk.; *sak′ka-rīn*, or *sak′ka-rīn*, Wr. 155.]
Sac′cha-rīte (*-ka-*), 152.
Sac′cha-rize (*-ka-*), 202.
Sac′cha-rized (*-ka-*).
Sac′cha-rīz-ing.
Sac′cha-roid (*-ka-*).
Sac-cha-roid′al (*-ka-*).
Sac-cha-rom′e-ter (*-ka-*), 108, 171.
Sac-cho-lac′tate (*-ko-*).
Sac-cho-lac′tic (*-ko-*).
Sac′cho-late (*-ko-*).
Sac′ci-form (*sak′si-*), (108) [so Wr.; *sak′ki-form*, Gd. 155.]
Sac′cu-lar.
Sac′cule, 66, 90.
Sa-cel′lum, 170.
Saç-er-do′tal (*sas-*) [so Wk. Wr. Wb. Gd.; *sas′ur-dō-tal*, Sm. 155] [*not* sā-sur-do′tal, 153.]
Saç-er-do′tal-ism (*sas-ur-do′tal-izm*), 136.
Sa′chem (44) [*not* sa′-kem, 141, 153.]
Sack (10, 181), *n.* a bag or pouch, commonly of large size; — the measure of three bushels. [*See* Sac, 160.]
Sack′age, 70, 169.
Sack′but.
Sack′cloth, 66, N.
Sacked (*sakt*), 165; Note C, p. 34.
Sack′er.
Sack′ful (*-fŏŏl*), 197.
Sack′ing.
Sa′cral, 72.
Sac′ra-ment (169) [*not* sa′kra-ment, 153.]
Sac-ra-ment′al.
Sac-ra-ment-a′ri-an.
Sac-ra-ment′a-ry, 72.
Sa′cred, 230.
Sa-crif′ic.
Sa-crif′ic-al.
Sac′ri-fice (*-fīz*), *v.* 171.
Sac′ri-fice (*-fīz*, or *fīs*), *n.* [*sak′ri-fīz*, Wk. Wr. Wb. Gd.; *sak′ri-fīs*, Sm. 153.]

☞ Smart says that the principle of distinguishing "from each other nouns and verbs that are the same, or almost the same, in form," by giving "certain consonant letters a sharp, hissing sound in the noun, and a vocalized sound in the verb," has, in the verbs to *suffice* and to *sacrifice*, "been allowed to communicate a most irregular sound to the letter c." "This," he adds, "if not altered in the verb, certainly ought not to be adopted in the noun *sacrifice*; yet such is the practice of most speakers, and according to this practice is the word marked [*sak′-ri-fiz*] in all former pronouncing dictionaries."

Sac′ri-ficed (*-fīzd*).
Sac′ri-fīc-er (*-fīz-*).
Sac-ri-fī′cial (*-fish′al*).
Sac′ri-fīc-ing (*-fīz-*).
Sac′ri-lĕge (*-lĕj*), 156, 171.
Sac-ri-le′gioŭs (*-jus*) (Note D, p. 37) [*not* sak-ri-lij′us, 153.]
Sac′ri-le-gist, 126.
Sa′cring-bell.
Sa′crist.
Sac′ris-tan [*not* sa-kris′-tan, 153.]
Sac′ris-ty.

Sa'crum (L.).
Sad, 10, 39, 42.
Sad'den (*sad'n*), 149.
Sad'dle (*sad'l*), 164.
Sad'dle-bag (*-dl-*).
Sad'dled (*sad'ld*).
Sad'dler, 183.
Sad'dler-y.
Sad'dle-shaped (*sad'l-shāpt*), 206, Exc. 5.
Sad'dling, 170.
Sad-du-ce'an.
Sad'du-cee, 89, 171.
Sad-du-cee'ism (*-izm*), 136.
Sad'du-cism (*-sizm*).
Sad'du-cize, 202.
Sad'du-cized.
Sad'du-cīz-ing.
Sad'-i'ron (*-ī'urn*).
Safe, 23, 35.
Safe-con'duct.
Safe'guärd (*-gard*), 171.
Safe-keep'ing.
Safe'ty, 93.
Safe'ty-lamp.
Safe'ty-valve.
Saf'flower (*-flour*), 67.
Saf'fron (86) [so Sm. Wb. Gd.; *saf'furn*, Wk.; *saf'frun*, or *saf'furn*, Wr. 155.]
Saf'fron-y.
Sag, 10, 39, 53.
Sa'ga, 189.
Sa-ga'cioŭs (*-shus*), 169.
Sa-gaç'i-ty, 108, 171.
Sag'a-more, 105.
Sag'a-pen.
Sag-a-pe'num.
Sag'a-thy.
Sage, 23, 45.
Sag'e-nīte (*saj'-*), 152.
Sagged (*sagd*), 176.
Sag'ger (*-gur*).
Sag'ging (*-ghing*), 138.
Sa-git'ta (L.).
Sag'it-tal (*saj'-*) (170) [*not* sa-jit'tal, 153.]
Sag-it-ta'ri-us (L.) (*saj-*).
Sag'it-ta-ry (*saj'-*), 72.
Sag'it-tate (*saj'-*)
Sa'go, 86.
Sa-goin' [Sagouin, 203.]
Săg'y (*săj'-*), 183.
Sah'līte, 152.
Sa'ic [Saik, 206.]
Said (*sed*), 15, 187.
Sāil (23), *n.* a sheet of canvas by which the wind impels a ship: —*v.* to move with sails, as a ship, or in a ship. [*See* Sale, 160.]
Sāil'a-ble (164), *a.* navigable. [*See* Salable, 160.]
Sāiled, 165.
Sāil'er (77, 169), *n.* one that sails; — a sailing vessel. [*See* Sailor, 160.]
Sāil'ing.
Sāil'-lŏft, 18, N.; 206, Exc. 1.
Sāil'-măk-er.
Sāil'or (88, 169), *n.* a seaman; a mariner. [*See* Sailer, 160.]
Sāil'yard.
Sāin'foin [so Sm. Wb. Gd.; *san'foin*, Wk.; *săn'foin*, or *san'foin*, Wr. 155] [Saint-foin, 203.]
Sāint, 23.
Sāint'ed.
Sāint-John's'-wort (*-jonz'wurt*).
Sāint'like.
Sāint'li-ness, 186.
Sāint'ly, 93.
Sāint-Sī-mo'ni-an.
Sāint-Si'mon-ist.
Sāint-Si'mon-īte.
Sāint-Vi'tus's-dănce (*-vi'tus-ez*), 221.
Saith (*seth*), 187.
Sake, 23.
Sa'ker.
Sa'ker-et [so Sm.; *sak'-ur-et*, Wk. Wr. Wb. Gd. 155.]
Sa'kĭ, 191.
Sal (L.).
Săl'a-ble (164, 183), *a.* that may be sold; marketable. [*See* Sail-able, 160] [Sale-able, Wk. Sm. 203.]
Săl'a-bly [Saleably, 203.]
Sal'ad, 72, 170.

☞ "This word is often pronounced as if written *sal'let.*" *Walker*, 1806.

[Salæratus, 203. — *See* Saleratus.]
Săl-al-bĕr'ry [so Wr.; *sā-lal-bĕr'ry*, Gd. 155.]
Sal-a-lem'brŏth.
Sa-lām' (Persian) [Salaam, 203.]
Sal'a-man-der [so Wk. Wr. Wb. Gd.; *sal-a-man'dur*, Sm. 155.]
Sal-a-man'drīne, 152.
Sal-a-man'droid.
Sal'a-rĭed (*-rid*).
Sal'a-ry, 72, 169.
Sal'a-rȳ-ing.
Sale (23), *n.* act or opportunity of selling. [*See* Sail, 160.]
Sal'ep [so Gd.; *sa-lep'*, Wr. 155] [Saleb, Salop, Saloop, 203.]
Sal-e-ra'tus [Salæratus, 203.]
Sales'man (*sālz'-*), 196.
Sal'ic [*not* sa'lik, 153] [Salique, 203.]
Sal-i-ca'ceoŭs (*-shus*), 169
Sal-i-ci'loŭs.
Sal'i-cīne (82, 152) [Salicin, 203.]
Sa'li-ent, 169.
Sa-lif'er-oŭs, 233, Exc.
Sal'i-fī-a-ble, 164.
Sal-i-fī-ca'tion.
Sal'i-fīed.
Sal'i-fȳ, 94.
Sal'i-fȳ-ing.
Sal-i-na'tion.
Sa-līne', *or* Sa'līne [so Wk.; *sa-līn'*, Sm. Wr. Wb. Gd. 155], *a.* & *n.*

☞ "As this word is derived from the Latin *salinus* by dropping a syllable, the accent ought, according to the general rule of formation, to remove to the first [syllable]." *Walker*.

Sal-i-nif'er-oŭs, 108.
Sa-lin'i-form.
Sal-i-nom'e-ter.
Sa-li'no-tĕr-rene', 224.
[Salique, 203. — *See* Salic.]
Sa-li'va, 72.
Sa-li'val [so Sm. Wr. Wb. Gd.; *sal'i-val*, or *sa-li'val*, Wk. 155.]
Sal'i-vant.
Sal'i-va-ry, 72, 169.
Sal'i-vate, 73.
Sal'i-văt-ed, 183.
Sal'i-văt-ing.
Sal-i-va'tion, 169.
Sa-li'voŭs [so Sm. Wr. Wb. Gd.; *sa-li'vus*, or *sal'i-vus*, Wk. 155.]
Sal'let, *n.* a light kind of helmet. [*See* Note under *Salad*.]
Sal'lĭed (*-lid*).

Sal′lōw, 101, 127, 170.
Sal′ly, 93.
Sal′ly-ing.
Sal-ma-gun′dĭ, 78.
Salm′on (*sam′un*), 162.
Salm′on-et (*sam′un-*).
Sal′mon-oid.
Salm′on-trout (*sam′-*).
Sal′o-gen, 45, 105.
Salon (Fr.) (*sä-lŏng′*).
Sa-loon′, 121.
[Salop (*sal′up*; — so Gd.; *sa′lup*, Wr. 155), Saloop (*sa-loop′*), 203. — *See* Salep.]
Salp, 10.
Sal′pi-con [so Sm. Wb. Gd.; *sal′pi-kon*, or *sal-pe′kon*, Wr. 155.]
Sal′pinx (*-pingks*).
Sal′si-fy̆ [so Sm.; *sal′-si-fĭ*, Wr. Gd. 155] [Salsafy, 203.]
Sal-so-la′ceoŭs (*-shus*).
Sâlt, 17.

☞ Smart marks the *a* in this word as having a sound intermediate between that of *a* in *all* (or *o* in *orb*, No. 8, § 17) and that of *o* in *on* (No. 9, § 18).

Sal′tant.
Sal′tate.
Sal-ta′tion.
Sal-ta-to′ri-al.
Sal-ta-to′ri-oŭs.
Sal′ta-to-ry, 86.
Sâlt′-cel-lar.
Sâlt′ed.
Sâlt′er, *n.* one who salts. [*See* Psalter, 160.]
Sal′tiĕr [Saltire, 203.]
Sâlt′ing.
Sâlt′ish.
Sâlt-pe′tre (*-tur*) [Saltpeter, preferred by Wb. and Gd. 203.]
Sâlt-pe′troŭs.
Sâlt′-rheum (*-room*).
Sâlt′wort (*-wurt*).
Sa-lu′bri-oŭs.
Sa-lu′bri-ty, 108.
Sal′u-ta-ri-ly.
Sal′u-ta-ri-ness.
Sal′u-ta-ry, 72.
Sal-u-ta′tion.
Sa-lu-ta-to′ri-an.
Sa-lu′ta-to-ry, 86.
Sa-lute′, 26.
Sa-lūt′ed, 183.
Sa-lūt′er.
Sal-u-tif′er-oŭs.
Sa-lūt′ing.
Sal-va-bil′i-ty.
Sal′va-ble, 164.
Sal′vage, 70, 169.
Sal-va′tion.
Sal′va-to-ry, 86.
Salve (11, 162) [*säv*, Sm. Wb. Gd.; *sälv*, Wk.; *säv*, or *sälv*, Wr. 155.]
Salved (*sävd*), 165.
Sal′ver [*not* sä′vur, 153.]
Salv′ing (*säv′-*).
Sal′vo [pl. Sal′vōes, *or* Sal′vōs (*-vōz*), 192.]
Sal vo-lat′-i-le (L.).

☞ "Anglicized *sal vol′a-tile.*" *Worcester.*

Sal′vor.
Sam-a-ne′an.
Sa-ma′ra.
Sa-măr′i-tan, 169.
Sam′a-roid [so Wr. Gd.; *sa-ma′roid*, Sm. 155.]
Sam′bo.
Same, 23.
Same′ness, 185.
Sa′mi-an, 169.
Sa′mi-el, *or* Sä′mi-el [*sa′mi-el*, Wr. Wb. Gd.; *sä′mi-el*, Sm. 155.]
Sam′let, 76.
Sa′moid.
Sam-o-thra′cian (*-shan*).
Samp, 10.
Sam′păn [Sanpan, 203.]
Sam′phire (*sam′fur*) [so Wk. Sm. Wr.; *sam′-fīr*, Wb. Gd. 155] [*See* Note under *Sapphire.*]
Sam′ple (164) [*not* säm′-pl, 153.]
Sam′pler.
Sam′pling.
San-a-bil′i-ty, 108.
San′a-ble, 164.
San′a-tĭve, 84.
San′a-to-ry, 86.
Sanc-ti-fĭ-ca′tion, 54.
Sanc′ti-fīed, 186.
Sanc′ti-fī-er.
Sanc′ti-fȳ.
Sanc′ti-fȳ-ing.
Sanc-til′o-quent.
Sanc-ti-mo′ni-al.
Sanc-ti-mo′ni-oŭs.
Sanc′ti-mo-ny, 86.
Sanc′tion.
Sanc′tion-a-ry, 72.
Sanc′tioned (*-shund*).
Sanc′tion-ing.
Sanc′ti-tude, 108, 169.
Sanc′ti-ty, 108.
Sanc′tu-a-ry, 72, 89.
Sanc′tum sanc-to′rum (L.).
Sand, 10.
San′dal, 72.
San-dal′i-form, 108.
San′dal-wŏŏd.
San′da-rach (*-rak*) (171) [Sandarac, 203.]
Sand′ed.
San′der-ling.
San′ders (*-durz*) [Saunders, 203.]
San′de-ver [Sandiver, 203.]
Sand′hill.
Sand′i-ness, 186.
Sand′ing.
San′di-ver [Sandever, 203.]
Sand′stone, 206.
Sand′wich (*-wij*) [so Sm. Wr.; *sand′wich*, Wb. Gd. 155.]
Sand′wort (*-wurt*).
Sand′y, 93, 169.
Sane, 23.
Sane′ness, 66, N.
Sang, 10, 39, 54.
San-ga-ree′ (*sang-*), 122.
Sang froid (Fr.) (*song-frwah′*) (154) [*song-fro′â*, Sm.; *säng-frwah*, Gd.; *säng′-frwaw′*, Wr. 155.]
San′gi-ac [Sanjak, 203.]
San′gi-ac-ate.
San-guif′er-oŭs (*sang-*).
San-gui-fĭ-ca′tion (*sang-*), 112.
San′gui-fīed (*-sang′-*).
San-guif′lu-oŭs (*-sang-*).
San′gui-fȳ (*sang′-*), 94.
San′gui-fȳ-ing (*sang′-*).
San-guig′e-noŭs (*sang-gwij′-*), 171.
San′guin-a-ri-ly (*sang′-*)
San′guin-a-ri-ness (*sang′-*), 171, 186.
San′guin-a-ry (*sang′-*).
San′guĭne (*sang′gwin*), 152, 171.
San′guine-ness (*sang′-gwin-*), 66, N.
San-guin′e-oŭs (*sang-*), 169.
San-guin-iv′o-roŭs (*sang-*), 108.
San-guin′o-len-cy (*sang-*).

San-guin'o-lent (*sang-*).
San'gui-suge (*sang'-*).
San'he-drim [*not* san-he'drim, 153.]
San'i-cle, 164.
Sa'ni-ēs (L.) (*-ēz*).
Sa'ni-oŭs, 169.
San'i-ta-ry, 72.
San'i-ty, 66, 170.
San'jak [Sangiac, 203.]
Sank (*sangk*), 52, 54.
[Sanpan, 203. — *See* Sampan.]
Săns (*sănz*)[so Wk. Sm. Wr. Wb. Gd.]

☞ "By our old poets this French word was adopted and naturalized, but as an English word it is obsolete: hence, in order to be understood, modern reciters give it a French pronunciation, nearly as *song* before a consonant, and *songz* before a vowel." *Smart.*

San'scrit (230) [Sanskrit, 203.]
Sans culotte (Fr.) (*sŏng koo-lot'*) [*sŏng k'oo-lot'*, Sm. (*See* § 26); *săng ku-lot'*, Gd.; *sănz ku-lot'*, Wr. 154, 155.]
Sans-cu-lott'ism (*sănz-ku-lot'izm*) [*sănz-ku-lot'izm*, or *sănz-ku'-lot-izm*, Wr.; *sănz-ku'lot-izm*, Gd. 155.]
Sans souci (Fr.) (*sŏng-soo-se'*) [so Sm.; *săng-soo-se'*, Wr. Gd. 155.]
San'ta-līne (82, 152) [Santalin, 203.]
San'to-nīne (82, 152) [Santonin, 203.]
Sap, 10, 30, 39.
Sap'a-jou (*-joo*) [so Wr. Gd.; *sap'a-zhoo*, Sm. 155] [Sapajo (*sap'a-joo*; — so Gd.; *sap'a-jō*, Wr. 155), 203.]
Sa-pan'-wŏŏd [Sapan-wood, 203.]
Sap'id, 66, 170.
Sa-pid'i-ty.
Sa'pi-ence [*not* sap'i-ens, 153.]
Sa'pi-ent.
Sap-in-da'ceoŭs (*-shus*).
Sap'ling.
Sap-o-dil'la [Sappodilla, 203.]
Sap-o-na'ceoŭs (*-shus*).
Sap-o-naç'i-ty.
Sa-pon'i-fī-a-ble, 164.
Sa-pon-i-fĭ-ca'tion.
Sa-pon'i-fīed.
Sa-pon'i-fȳ, 108.
Sa-pon'i-fȳ-ing.
Sap'o-nīne (152) [Saponin, 203.]
Sap'o-nite, 152.
Sap'o-nule, 90.
Sa'por (*-pawr*), 88.
Sap-or-if'ic, 109.
Sap-or-os'i-ty, 108.
[Sappan-wood, 203. — *See* Sapan-wood.]
Sapped (*sapt*), 165; Note C, p. 34.
Sap'per, 176.
Sap'phic (*saf'ik*), 171.
Sap'phire (*saf'fur*) (171) [so Wk. Sm. Wr.; *saf'fīr*, or *saf'fur*, Gd. 155.]

☞ "*Ire* is pronounced *ur* in *sapphire* and in *satire*, not without the sanction of a principle; for the syllable being unaccented, the final *e* is dropped, as it is in many other similar cases, and the remaining letters *ir* are then necessarily sounded *ur*." *Smart.*

Sap'phir-īne(*saf'fur-in*) [so Sm. Wb. Gd.; *saf'fur-īn*, Wk. Wr. 155.]
Sap'pi-ness, 186.
Sap'ping, 176.
Sap-po-dil'la [Sapodilla, 203.]
Sap'py.
Sa-proph'a-gan.
Săr'a-ba-ite, 72, 152.
Săr'a-bănd.
Săr'a-cen, 169.
Săr-a-cen'ic, 170.
Sar-a-cen'ic-al, 108.
Sar'casm (*-kazm*), 133.
Sar-cas'tic, 109.
Sar-cas'tic-al, 108.
Sar'cel, 76.
Sarce'net (*sars'net*) [*not* sar'se-net, 145, 153.]
Sar'co-carp, 135.
Sar'co-cele.
Sar'co-col.
Sar'code.
Sar-co-derm'a.
Sar'coid.
Sar'co-līne, 82, 152.
Sar'co-līte, 152.
Sar-co-log'ic (*-loj'-*).
Sar-co-log'ic-al (*-loj'-*).
Sar-col'o-gist, 108.
Sar-col'o-gy.
Sar-co'ma.
Sar-com'a-toŭs.
Sar-coph'a-gan.
Sar-coph'a-goŭs (160), *a.* feeding on flesh.
Sar-coph'a-gus(160,169), *n.* a coffin made of stone. [L. pl. Sar-coph'a-gī; Eng. pl. Sar-coph'a-gus-es (*-ez*), 198.]

☞ "The former plural is the more common." *Worcester.*

Sar-coph'a-gy.
Sar-cot'ic.
Sard, 11, 49, 142.
Sard'a-chate (*-kăt*).
Sar'del, *n.* a kind of small fish; — a species of chalcedony. [Sardine (in both senses), 203.]
Sar'dīne (82, 152) [so Sm. Wb. Gd.; *sar'-dīn*, Wk.; *sar'dīn*, or *sar'dīn*, Wr. 155], *n.* a species of chalcedony. [Sardel, Sardoin, 203.]
Sar'dīne, *or* Sar-dine', (*-dēn'*) [so Wr.; *sar'-din*, Sm. Wb. Gd. 155], *n.* a small fish allied to the anchovy. [Sardin, Sardel, 203.]
Sar-din'i-an, 72, 78.
Sar'di-us [so Sm. Wr. Gd.; *sar'di-us*, or *sar'ji-us*, Wk. 134, 155.]
[Sardoin, 203. — *See* Sardine.]
Sar-don'ic, 109.
Sar'do-nyx (93) [*not* sar-do'niks, 153.]
Sar-gas'so, 170.
Sa-rigue' (Fr.) (*sa-rēg'*) [so Wr.; *săr'i-gu*, Gd. 155.]
Sark'ing.
Sar'lyk (93) [Sarlac, 203.]
Sar-ma'tian (*-shan*).
Sar-mat'ic, 109.
Sar'ment.
Sar-ment-a'ceoŭs (*-shus*), 112, 169.
Sar-ment-ose'.
Sar-ment'oŭs.
Sa'rŏs.

Sar'plar.
Săr'ra-sin, *or* Săr'ra-sīne [Sarasin, 203.]
Sar-sa-pa-ril'la (171) [*not* sas-a-pa-ril'la, 135, 153.]
Sar-to'ri-al.
Sash, 10, 39, 46.
Sashed (*sasht*), 41.
Sa'sin.
Sas'sa-fras, 72, 171.
Sas'sa-nage, 70, 169.
Sas'so-līne (152) [Sassolin, 203.]
[Sastra, 203. — *See* Shaster.]
Sat (10, 39, 41) [Sate, 203.]
Sa'tan [so Sm. Wr. Wb. Gd.; *sa'tan*, or *sat'-an*, Wk. 155.]

☞ Though Walker allows the pronunciation *sat'an*, he says that "making the first syllable long [*sa'tan*] is so agreeable to analogy that it ought to be indulged wherever custom will permit, and particularly in proper names."

Sa-tan'ic, 109.
Sa-tan'ic-al, 108.
Sa'tan-ism (*-izm*).
Satch'el, 149, 167.
Săte (*sat*) (160, 163), *v.* did sit. [Sat, 203.]
Sāte (160), *v.* to satiate.
Sāt'ed.
Sat'el-līte (83, 152) [pl. Sat'el-lītes(*-līts*),189.]

☞ "If [a] word should be an English adaptation of a Latin word,—e. g. *satellite* from the Latin *satelles*,—as the singular must be sounded according to common rules, so likewise must the plural; though the English word *satellites* happening to identify in spelling with the Latin plural, Pope has taken the liberty in one of his lines to pronounce it as a Latin word [*sa-tel'li-tes*]." *Smart.* — The line to which Smart refers, is in the following couplet:

"Or ask of yonder argent fields above
Why Jove's *satellites* are less than Jove."
Essay on Man.

Sat-el-lĭ'tioŭs (*-lish'us*).
Sa'ti-ate (*sa'shi-āt*) [so Wk. Sm. Wr.; *sa'-shāt*, Wb. Gd. 155.]
Sa-ti-a'tion (*sa-shi-a'-shun*), 112.
Sa-ti'e-ty, 169.
Sat'in, 149.
Sat-in-et' [so Sm. Wb. Gd.; *sat'i-net*, Wr. 155.]
Sāt'ing, 183.
Sat'in-y, 93.
Sat'ire (*sat'ur*, or *sat'īr*) [*sat'ur*, Sm.; *sat'īr*, Wb. Gd.; *sa'tur*, *sat'-ur*, *sa'tīr*, or *sat'ĕr*, Wk.; *sa'tur*, *sat'īr*, or *sat'ur*, Wr. 155] [*See* Note under *Sapphire*], *n.* an invective poem; — ridicule. [*See* Satyr, 148.]
Sa-tĭr'ic, *a.* pertaining to satire; sarcastic. [*See* Satyric, 160.]
Sa-tĭr'ic-al.
Sat'ir-ist.
Sat'ir-ize, 202.
Sat'ir-ized, 183.
Sat'ir-īz-ing.
Sat-is-fac'tion, 116, 169.
Sat-is-fac'to-ri-ly.
Sat-is-fac'to-ri-ness.
Sat-is-fac'to-ry, 86.
Sat'is-fī-a-ble, 164.
Sat'is-fīed, 186.
Sat'is-fī-er.
Sat'is-fȳ, 94.
Sat'is-fȳ-ing.
Sa'trap [so Sm. Wr.; *sa'trap*, or *sat'rap*, Gd. 155.]
Sa'trap-al [so Sm.; *sat'-rap-al*, Wr. Wb. Gd. 155.]
Sa'trap-ess.
Sa'trap-y, 93.
Sat'u-ra-ble, 164.
Sat'u-rant, 72.
Sat'u-rate, 89.
Sat'u-rāt-ed, 183.
Sat'u-rāt-ing.
Sat-u-ra'tion, 112.
Sat'ur-day (*-dy*).
Sat'urn [so Sm. Wr. Wb. Gd; *sa'turn*, or *sat'urn*, Wk. 155.]
Sat-ur-na'li-a (L.), *n.pl.*
Sat-ur-na'li-an.
Sa-tur'ni-an, 78.
Sat'ur-nīne, 82, 152.
Sat'urn-ist.
Sat'urn-īte, 152.
Sa'tyr, *or* Sat'yr (95) [so Wk. Wr.; *sa'tur*, Wb. Gd.; *sat'ur*, Sm. 155], *n.* in mythology, a sylvan deity. [*See* Satire, 148.]
Sa-tȳr'ic, *a.* relating to satyrs. [*See* Satiric, 160.]
Sâuce, 17, 39.

☞ "There is a corrupt pronunciation of this diphthong [*au*] among the vulgar, which is, giving the *au* in *daughter*, *sauce*, *saucer*, and *saucy*, the sound of the Italian *a* [*a* in *far*]; but this pronunciation cannot be too carefully avoided." *Walker.*

Sâuce'box, 205.
Sâuced (*sawst*), 165; Note C, p. 34.
Sâuce'pan.
Sâu'cer [*See* Note under *Sauce.*]
Sâu'ci-ly, 186.
Sâu'ci-ness.
Sâuç'ing, 183.
Saucisse (Fr.) (*saw-sēs'*) [so Sm.; *so-sēs'*, Wr.; *saw'sis*, Wb. Gd. 154, 155.]
Sâu'cis-son (Fr.) [so Sm. Wb. Gd.; *so'sē-sŏng'*, Wr. 154, 155.]
Sau'cy (169) [*See* Note under *Sauce.*]
Sauer'kraut (Ger.) (*sour'krout*) (28, 171) [Sourkrout, Sourcrout, 203.]
Sâul (17), *n.* a kind of timber used in India.
Sault (Fr.) (*sō*, or *soo*) [*sō*, Wr.; *soo*, Gd. 155.]
Säun'ders (*-durz*) [Sanders, 203.]
Säun'ter (*sän'*) [so Sm. Wb. Gd.; *sän'tur*, or *sawn'tur*, Wk. Wr. 155.]

☞ "The first mode of pronouncing this word [*sän'tur*] is the most agreeable to analogy, if not in the most general use." *Walker.* — Smart says that good usage at the present day is in favor of the pronunciation *sän'tur*, instead of *sawnter*.

Säun'tered, 150.
Säun'ter-er, 77.
Sâu'ri-an, 78.
Sâu'roid.
Sâu'sage (70, 169) [so

Wr. Wb. Gd.; *saw'sij*, or *săs'ij*, Wk. 155.]

☞ The *au* in this word is marked by Smart as having a sound intermediate between that of *a* in *all* (or *o* in *orb*, No. 8, § 17), and that of *o* in *on* (No. 9, § 18). *See* § 18, Note. — Walker remarks: "This word is pronounced in the first manner [*saw'sij*] by correct, and in the second [*sas'ij*] by vulgar speakers."

Sāv'a-ble, 164, 183.
Sav'age, 70, 169.
Sav'age-ly, 185.
Sav'age-ness.
Sav'age-ry, 145.
Sa-van'na [Savannah, 203.]
Savant (Fr.) (*sä-vŏng'*) [*sa-văng'*, Wr. Gd. 155] [pl. *Savans* (*sä-vŏngz'*), 198.]

☞ By English writers the plural is often incorrectly spelled *savants*.

Save, 23, 163.
Save'-âll, 206, Exc. 2.
Sav'e-loy, 169.
Saved, 165.
Sāv'er (77), *n.* one who saves. [*See* Savor, 160.]
Sav'in (149) [Savine, Sabine, 203.]
Sāv'ing, 183.
Sāv'iour, *or* Sāv'ior (*-yur*), 199, 203.

☞ This word is given in both forms of spelling by Worcester and by Goodrich. It is, perhaps, more commonly written *Savior* in the United States. Worcester remarks: "The omission of the *u* [in this word] is offensive to the eyes of many who are accustomed to see it inserted." And Goodrich says, in reference to the general rule which excludes the *u* from those words which formerly ended in *our*, that "*Saviour*, from the sacredness of its associations, may stand for a time as a solitary exception." The fact that this word is derived directly from the French *sauveur*, rather than from the Latin *salvator*, is sometimes urged in favor of retaining the *u*; and English writers generally retain the *u* in all words of this class that are of French rather than of Latin origin.

Sa'vor (70), *n.* a flavor or odor: — *v.* to have a particular taste or smell; to smack. [*See* Saver, 160.] [Savour, Sm. 203.]
Sa'vored (*-vurd*) [Savoured, Sm. 203.]
Sa'vor-i-ly (186) [Savourily, Sm. 203.]
Sa'vor-i-ness [Savouriness, Sm. 203.]
Sa'vor-ing [Savouring, Sm. 203.]
Sa'vor-y [Savoury, Sm. 203.]
Sa-voy', 121.
Sa-voy'ard.
Saw, 17, 39.
Saw'dust, 206.
Sawed, 150, 165.
Saw'er (77), *n.* one that saws. [Sawyer, 203.]
Saw'fish, 206.
Saw'ing.
Saw'mill.
Sawn, 17.
Saw'yer (77), *n.* one that saws: — a tree with its roots fastened in the bottom of a river, and its top moving up and down by the action of the current. [Sawer (in the first sense), 203.]

☞ *Sawyer*, though a corruption of *sawer*, is now the more common.

Sax'a-tĭle, 81, 152, 169.
Sax'-horn.
Sax-i-ca'voŭs.
Sax-if'ra-gant.
Sax'i-frage, 169.
Sax-if'ra-goŭs, 105.
Sax'on (*saks'n*) (149) [so Sm.; *saks'un*, Wr. Wb. Gd. 155.]
Sax'on-ism (*saks'n-izm*), 133, 136.
Sax'on-ist (*saks'n-*).
Sax'o-phone.
Sāy, 56, Rem.
Sāy'ing.
Says (*sez*), 15.
Scab, 10.
Scab'bard, 170.
Scabbed, *a.* (165, 176) [so Sm.; *skab'bed*, or *skabd*, Wk. Wr.; *skabd*, or *skab'bed*, Gd. 155.]
Scab'bi-ness, 186.
Scab'ble (164, 170) [Scapple, 203.]
Scab'bled (*skab'ld*).
Scab'bling.
Scab'by, 66, 93.
Sca'bi-ēs (L.) (*-ēz*).
Sca'bi-oŭs [*not* skab'i-us, 153.]
Sca'broŭs.
Scad, 10.
Scaf'fold, 66, 170.
Scaf'fold-ing.
Scaglia (It.) (*skal'ya*) [so Wr.; *skal'ye-a*, Gd. 155.]
Scagl-i-o'la (*skal-ye-o'la*) [so Wr. Gd.; *skal-e-o'la*, Sm. 155.]
Scāl'a-ble, 164, 183.
Sca-lade', 121.
Sca-lăr'i-form, 108.
Sca'la-ry [so Sm. Wr. Wb. Gd.; *skal'a-ry*, Wk. 155.]
Scâld (17, 161) [*not* skold, 153], *v.* to burn with hot liquid or hot vapor: — *n.* a burn caused by hot liquid or hot vapor.
Scâld, *a.* scurfy; scabby. [Scalled, 203.]
Scăld (10, 161) [so Sm.; *skawld*, or *skald*, Wr.; *skawld*, Gd. 155], *n.* an ancient Scandinavian bard. [Skald, 203.]
Scâld'ed.
Scăl'der [*See* Scăld.]
Scăl'dic.
Scâld'ing.
Scale, 23.
Scaled, 165, 183.
Sca-lene', 121, 171.
Sca-lēn-o-he'dron, 224.
Sca-lēn'oŭs.
Scāl'er.
Scāl'i-ness, 186.
Scāl'ing, 183.
Scâll, 17, 172.
[Scâlled, *a.* 203. — *See* Scald.]
Scăll'ion (*-yun*), 51.
Scal'lop (*skol'lup*), *n.* & *v.* (18, 86, 103, 104) Escalop, [Scollop, 203.]
Scăl'loped (*skol'lupt*).

Scal′lop-ing (*skol′lup-*).
Scălp, 10, 64.
Scălped (*skalpt*), 41.
Scăl′pel, 76.
Scălp′er, 77.
Scălp′ing.
Scălp′ing-knife (*-nīf*).
Scal′pri-form, 108.
Scăl′y, 93, 183.
Scam′ble, 164.
Scam′bled (*-bld*).
Scam′bling.
Scam′mo-ny, 170.
Scamp, 10, 64.
Scam′per, 77.
Scam′pered (*-purd*).
Scam′per-ing.
Scan, 10.
Scan′dal, 72.
Scan′dal-ize, 202.
Scan′dal-ized, 165.
Scan′dal-īz-ing.
Scan′dal-oŭs, 100.
Scan′da-lum mag-na′-tum (L.).
Scan′dent, 127.
Scan-di-na′vi-an.
Scanned (*skand*), 176.
Scan′ning.
Scan′sion.
Scan-so′res (L.) (*-rēz*), *n. pl.*
Scan-so′ri-al.
Scant, 10, 64.
Scant′ed.
Scant′i-ly, 186.
Scant′i-ness.
Scant′ing.
Scant′ling.
Scant′y, 93.
Scape, 23, 163.
Scape′gōat, 206.
Scape′grace.
Scape′ment.
Scăph′ism (*-izm*).
Scăph′īte [so Wr. Gd.; *ska′fīt*, Sm. 155.]
Scăph′oid [so Gd.; *ska′foid*, Sm. Wr. 155.]
Sca′pi-form [so Gd.; *skap′i-form*, Wr. 155.]
Scap′o-lite, 152.
[S c a p p l e, 203. — *See* Scabble.]
Scap′u-la (L.) (108) [pl. *Scap′u-læ*, 198.]
Scap′u-lar, 108.
Scap′u-la-ry, 72.
Scar, 11, 49.
Scăr′ab.
Scăr-a-bæ′i-dan (*-be′-*).
Scăr′a-bee, 169.
Scăr′a-mouch, 28.
Scar′bro-īte, 152.
Scarce (*skêrs*) [*not* skars, *nor* skurs, 127, 153.]
Scarce′ly (*skêrs′-*).
Scarce′ness (*skêrs′-*).
Scarç′i-ty (*skêrs′-*).
Scare (*skêr*), 14.
Scare′crōw (*skêr′-*).
Scared (*skêrd*).
Scarf, 11, 49, 135.
Scarfed (*skarft*), 165; Note C, p. 34.
Scarf′ing.
Scarf′skin.
Scăr-i-fī-ca′tion.
Scăr′i-fī-cā-tor.
Scăr′i-fīed.
Scăr′i-fī-er.
Scăr′i-fȳ.
Scăr′i-fȳ-ing.
Scar′ing (*-skêr′-*).
Sca′ri-ose [so Gd.; *skā-ri-ōs′*, Wr. 155.]
Sca′ri-oŭs.
Scar-la-ti′na (*-te′-*) [so Sm. Wr.; *skar-lat′i-na*, or *skar-la-te′na*, Gd. 155.]
Scar-lat′i-noŭs.
Scar′let, 76.
Scarp, 11, 49, 135.
Scarped (*skarpt*).
Scarred (*skard*).
Scăr′ring.
Scat, 10, 64.
Scăth (10, 37) [S c a t h e, 203.]
Scathed (*skatht*) [*not* skāthd, 153.]
Scath′ing (*skath′ing*) [*not* skāth′ing, 153.]
Scat′ter, 104, 170.
Scat′tered, 150.
Scat′ter-er, 77.
Scat′ter-ing.
Scâup, 17.
Scâup′-duck.
Scâup′er.
Scav′age, 70, 169.
Scav′en-ger, 45.
Scene (*sēn*), *n.* the stage of a theatre; — place represented by the stage; — division of an act of a play; — a view; — place where any thing is exhibited; — any remarkable exhibition. [*See* Seen, *and* Seine, 160.] [Exc.
Scēn′er-y (*sēn′-*), 39, 233,
Scen′ic [so Wk. Wr. Wb. Gd.; *se′nik*, Sm. 155.]
Scen′ic-al (*sen′-*) [so Wk. Sm. Wr. Wb. Gd.]
Scen-o-graph′ic.
Scen-o-graph′ic-al.
Sce-nog′ra-phy, 108.
Scent (*sent*), *n.* odor: — *v.* to smell. [*See* Cent, *and* Sent, 160.]
Scent′ed (*sent′-*), 39.
Scent′ing (*sent′-*).
Scep′tic (*skep′-*) (171) [*not* sep′tik, 153] [S k e p t i c, 203.]

☞ "In the word *sceptic*, the *c* is kept hard for the purpose of showing off a familiarity with the word in Greek, although no letter intervenes between the *c* and the *e*, and consistency requires that the *c* in *scene*, equally related to the Greek *k*, and the *c* in *sceptic*, should be sounded alike. As, however, on other occasions, so in this, we must give way to usage, or incur the effect of opposing it." *Smart.* — "The old orthography of this word was *sceptic*, and it is so printed in the old Dictionaries which preceded those of Dr. Johnson; . . . but Dr. Johnson introduced the orthography of *skeptic*. and in this he has been followed by a majority of succeeding lexicographers." *Worcester.* — Walker makes objection to the use of *k* instead of *c*, in this word, and remarks: "In this I think I am supported by the best authorities since the publication of Johnson's Dictionary." *Skeptic* is the orthography preferred by Webster and Goodrich: but *sceptic*, as Worcester remarks, "continues to be the prevailing and best usage."

Scep′tic-al (*skep′-*).
Scep′ti-cism (*skep′ti-sizm*), 136, 171.
Scep′tre (*sep′tur*) (39, 164, 171) [S c e p t e r preferred by Gd. 203. — *See* Note E, p. 70.]
Scep′tred (*sep′-*) (164, 165) [S c e p t e r e d preferred by Gd.]
Schaal′stein (Ger.) (*shäl′stīn*).
[S c h a h (*shah*), 203. — *See* Shah.]

Sche′dar (*ske′-*).
Sche′di-asm (*ske′di-azm*), 171.
Sched′ule (*sked′ūl*, or *shed′ūl*) (171) [*sked′-ūl*, Wb. Gd.; *shed′ūl*, Sm.; *sed′jūl*, or *sked′-jūl*, Wk.; *sked′ūl*, *shed′ūl*, or *sed′ūl*, Wr. 155.]

☞ "Nothing can be more evident than that, if the Greek χ is to be supplied in our orthography by *ch*, and if this, in default of the extra aspiration which our language allows not to a consonant, necessarily identifies with *k*, the words *schism* and *schedule* should have *sch* pronounced as they are in *scheme*: yet an unnecessary reference of *schedule* to its French denizenship [Old Fr. *schedule*; Fr. *cédule*], with some vague notion, perhaps, of the alliance of our English *sh* to the Teutonic *sch*, has drawn the word into the very irregular pronunciation *shed′ule*; while the other word, *schism*, from a notion, probably, that, as *h* is silent, the *c* should be soft before *i*, has taken the equally irregular sound *sizm*." *Smart.* — In the United States, the customary pronunciation of *schedule* is *sked′ūl*.

Scheel′e-tīne (*shēl′-*).
Scheel′īte (*shēl′-*).
[Scheik, 203. — *See* Sheik.]
Sche′ma-tism (*ske′ma-tizm*), 171.
Sche′ma-tist (*ske′-*).
Scheme (*skēm*), 13, 52.
Schemed (*skēmd*).
Schēm′er (*skēm′-*).
Schem′ing (*skēm′-*).
Schēm′ist (*skēm′-*).
Schene (*skēn*).
[Scherif (*shĕr′if*), 203. — *See* Sherif.]
Scherzando (It.) (*skĕr-tsän′do*).
Scherzo (It.) (*skĕr′tso*).
Sche′sis (*ske′-*) (Gr.) [pl. Sche′sēs (*ske′sēz*), 198.]
Schet′ic (*-sket′-*).
[Schiah, 203. — *See* Shiah.]
Schiē-dam′ (*skē-*), 121.
Schism (*sizm*) (162, 171) [*See* Note under Schedule.]
Schis-mat′ic (*siz-*), *a.* 109.
Schis′ma-tic (*siz′-*), *n.* [so Wk. Sm.; *siz-mat′ik*, Wb. Gd.; *siz′-ma-tik*, or *siz-mat′ik*, Wr. 155.]
Schis-mat′ic-al (*siz-*).
Schis-mat′ic-al-ly (*-siz-*).
Schist (*shist*) (16, 46) [Shist, 203.]
Schist′ose (*shist′-*) [so Wr. Gd.; *shis-tōs′*, Sm. 155.]
Schist′oŭs (*shist′-*).
Schiz′o-pod (*skiz′-*)(171) [so Wr. Gd.; *ski′zo-pod*, Sm. 155.]
Schi-zop′ter (*skī-*).
Schnapps (Ger.) (*shnaps*) [Schnaps, 203.]
Schol′ar (*skol′-*), 74, 171.
Schol′ar-ly (*skol′-*).
Schol′ar-ship (*skol′-*).
Scho-las′tic (*sko-*).
Scho-las′tic-al (*sko-*).
Scho-las′tic-al-ly (*sko-*).
Scho-las′ti-cism (*sko-*), 133, 136.
Scho′li-ast (*sko′-*), 169.
Scho-li-ast′ic (*sko-*).
Scho′li-um (*sko′-*) [L. pl. *Scho′li-a* (*sko′-*); Eng. pl. Scho′li-ums (*sko′li-umz*), 198.]
School (*skool*), 171.
School′-bŏŏk (*skool′-*), 206, Exc. 4.
School′-boy (*skool′-*).
Schooled (*skoold*).
School′-fel-low (*skool′-*)
School′-house (*skool′-*).
School′ing (*skool′-*).
School′man (*skool′-*), 196.
School′-mȧs-ter (*skool′-*).
School′-mate (*skool′-*).
School′-mis-tress (*skool′-*).
School′-tēach′er (*skool′-*).
School′-tēach′ing (*skool′-*).
Schoon′er (*skoon′-*) (19) [*not* skŏŏn′ur, 153.]
Schorl (*shorl*) [Shorl, 203.]
Schorl-a′ceoŭs (*shorl-a′shus*), 112, 171.
Schorl′īte (*shorl′-*).
Schorl′oŭs (*shorl′-*).
Schorl′y (*shorl′-*).
Schot′tische (Fr.)(*shot′-tēsh*), 154.
Schrode (*skrōd*) [Scrod, Scrode, 203.]
Sci′a-grăph (*si′-*).
Scī-a-graph′ic.
Scī-a-graph′ic-al.
Scī-ag′ra-phy (108) [Sciography, 203.]
Scī-am′a-chy (*-ky*) [Sciomachy, 203.]
Scī-a-thĕr′ic [Sciotheric, 203.]
Scī-a-thĕr′ic-al.
Scī-at′ic (*sī-*), 109.
Scī-at′ic-a.
Scī-at′ic-al, 108.
Sci′ence (*si′-*), 171.
Scī-en-tif′ic.
Scī-en-tif′ic-al.
Scī-en-tif′ic-al-ly, 170.
Sci′en-tist.
Scil′i-cet (L.) [abbreviated *sc.* or *ss.*]
Scil′li-tīne (82, 152) [Scillitin, 203.]
Scim′i-tar (*sim′-*) (169) [Cimeter, Scymitar, Simitar, 203.]
Scin′coid (*sing′-*), 54.
Scin-coid′i-an.
Scin-til′la (L.).
Scin′til-lant, 72.
Scin′til-late, 170.
Scin′til-lāt-ed, 183.
Scin′til-lāt-ing.
Scin-til-la′tion, 112.
Scī-og′ra-phy (*sī-*) [Sciagraphy, 203.]
Sci′o-lism (*si′o-lizm*), 133, 136.
Sci′o-list, 105, 171.
Scī-om′a-chy (*-ky*) [Sciamachy, 203.]
Sci′o-man-cy.
Sci′on [Cion, 203.]
Scī-op′tic, 200.
[Sciotheric, 203. — *See* Sciatheric.]
Sci′re fa′ci-as (L.)(*-fa′-shi-as*).
Scĭr′rhoid (*skĭr′roid*).
Scĭr-rhos′i-ty (*skĭr-ros′-*), 108, 169.
Scĭr′rhoŭs (*skĭr′rus*) (160, 162), *a.* pertaining to, or characterized by, scirrhus. [Skirrhous, 203.]
Scĭr′rhus (*skĭr′rus*)

(160, 162) [L. pl. *Scĭr′rhī* (*skĭr′rī*); Eng. pl. Scĭr′rhus-es (*skĭr′rus-ez*), 198], *n.* an indurated gland. [S k i r r h u s, 203.]

☞ "This word is sometimes, but improperly, written *schirrus*, with *h* in the first syllable instead of the last." *Walker.*

Scis′sel (*sis′l*) (149) [so Sm.; *sis′sel*, Wr. 155] [S i z e l, 203.]
Scis′sĭle (*sis′-*), 152, 171.
Scis′sion (*sizh′un*).
Scis′sors (*siz′zurz*), *n. pl.* 171.
Scit-a-min′e-oŭs (169) [so Wr. Gd.; *sī-ta-min′e-us*, Sm. 155.]
Sci-u′rĭne [so Sm.; *sī′-u-rīn*, Wr. Gd. 155.]
Scla-vo′ni-an [S l a v o-n i a n, 203.]
Scla-von′ic.
Scle′ro-derm [so Sm.; *sklĕr′o-derm*, Wr. Wb. Gd. 155.]
Scle′ro-gen, 45.
Scle-ro′ma.
Scle-ro′tal.
Scle-rot′ic, 109.
Scle′roŭs, 100.
Scob′i-form, 108.
Scobs (*skobz*), *n. sing.* & *pl.*; Note C, p. 34.
Scoff, 18, 173.
Scoffed (*skoft*), 165; Note C, p. 34.
Scoff′er, 228.
Scoff′ing.
Scoke, 24, 52.
Scōld, 24.
Scōld′ed.
Scōld′er, 77, 169.
Scōld′ing.
Scol′e-cite [S k o l e-c i t e, S k o l e z i t e, 203] [*See* Note under *Skolecite.*]
[S c o l l o p, 203. — *See* Scallop.]
Scom′ber-oid, 233, Exc.
Sconce (18, 39) [S k o n c e, 203.]
Scoop, 19.
Scooped (*skoopt*), 165.
Scoop′er.
Scoop′ing.
Scope, 24, 163.
Sco-pif′er-oŭs.
Scop′i-form, 108.
Scop′i-ped [so Sm.; *sko′pi-ped*, Wr. Wb. Gd. 155.]
Scor-bu′tic [*not* skor-but′ik, 127, 153.]
Scor-bu′tic-al.
Scorch, 17, 49, 135.
Scorched (*skorcht*).
Scorch′ing.
Score, 24, 49.
Scored, 165.
Sco′ri-a (49, N.) (L.) [pl. Sco′ri-æ, 198.]
Sco′ri-ac.
Sco-ri-a′ceoŭs (*-shus*).
Sco-ri-fĭ-ca′tion.
Sco′ri-fīed.
Sco′ri-form, 108.
Sco′ri-fȳ.
Sco′ri-fȳ-ing.
Scōr′ing, 49, N.
Sco′ri-oŭs.
Scorn, 17, 135.
Scorned, 165.
Scorn′er.
Scorn′ful (*-fŏŏl*), 180.
Scorn′ful-ly (*-fŏŏl-*).
Scorn′ing.
Scŏr′o-dite (152) [S k o r o d i t e, 203] [*See* Note under *Skorodite.*]
Scor′pi-oid.
Scor-pi-oid′al.
Scor′pi-on, 78, 86.
Scor′za.
Scot, 18, 52.
Scotch, Note D, p. 37.
Scotched (*skocht*), 165; Note C, p. 34.
Scotch′ing.
Scotch′man, 196.
Sco′ter.
Scot′-free (216) [S h o t-f r e e, 203.]
Sco′ti-a (*sko′shi-a*).
Sco′tist, 80.
Scot′o-grăph.
Scot′o-my.
Scots, *a.*
Scot′ti-cism, 136.
Scot′tish.
Scoun′drel, 28, 76.
Scoun′drel-ism (*-izm*).
Scour, 28, 49.
Scoured, 165.
Scour′er.
Scourge (*skurj*), 171.
Scourged (*skurjd*).
Scourg′er (*skurj′ur*).
Scourg′ing (*skurj′-*)
Scour′ing.
Scout, 28.
Scout′ed.
Scout′ing.
Scov′el (*skuv′l*), 149.
Scow (28) [S k o w, 203.]
Scowl, 28.
Scowled, 150, 165.
Scowl′ing.
Scrab′ble, 164.
Scrab′bled (*skrab′ld*).
Scrab′bling, 183.
Scrag, 10.
Scrag′ged (*-ghed*).
Scrag′gi-ly (*-ghĭ-*).
Scrag′gy (*-ghy*), 158.
Scram′ble, 164.
Scram′bled (*-bld*).
Scram′bler.
Scram′bling, 183.
Scran′nel, 66, 170.
Scrap, 10.
Scrap′-bŏŏk, 206, Exc. 4.
Scrape, 23.
Scraped (*skrāpt*).
Scrāp′er.
Scrāp′ing, 183.
Scratch, 10, 44.
Scratched (*skracht*).
Scratch′ing.
Scrawl, 17.
Scrawled, 165.
Scrawl′er.
Scrawl′ing.
Scrāy, 23.
Scrēam, 13.
Scrēamed, 165.
Scrēam′er.
Scrēam′ing.
Screech, 13.
Screeched (*skreecht*).
Screech′ing.
Screech′-owl.
Screed, 171.
Screen, 13.
Screened, 165.
Screen′ing.
Screw (*skroo*), 19.
Screw′-drīv-er (*skroo′-*).
Screwed (*skrood*).
Screw′ing (*skroo′-*).
Screw′-jack (*skroo′-*).
Screw′-pine (*skroo′-*).
Scrib′ble, 164.
Scrib′bled (*-bld*).
Scrib′bler.
Scrib′bling, 183.
Scribe, 25.
Scribed, 165.
Scrīb′ing, 183.
Scrip, 16.
Script.
Script′ur-al (*-yur-*).

Script′ur-al-ism (*-yur-al-izm*), 91, 136.
Script′ur-al-ist (*-yur-*).
Script′ur-al-ly (*-yur-*).
Script′ure, 91.
Script′ur-ist (*-yur-*).
Scri-vel′lo.
Scriv′en-er (*skriv′n-ur*) [so Sm.; *skriv′nur*, Wk. Wr. Gd. 155.]
Scro-bic′u-late, 108.
Scrod [S c r o d e, S c h r o d e, 203.]
Scrof′u-la, 72, 108.
Scrof′u-loŭs.
Scrōll, 24, 172.
Scrōlled, 165.
Scrub, 22.
Scrubbed (*skrubd*), *v.*
Scrub′bed, *a.* 150.
Scrub′bing, 176.
Scrub′by, 93.
Scru′ple (*skroo′pl*).
Scru′pled (*skroo′pld*).
Scru′pling (*skroo′-*).
Scru-pu-los′i-ty (*skroo-*), 108, 169.
Scru′pu-loŭs, 108.
Scru-ti-neer′ (*skroo-*), 122, 169. [202.
Scru′ti-nize (*skroo′-*),
Scru′ti-nized (*skroo′-*), 165, 183.
Scru′ti-nīz-er (*skroo′-*).
Scru′ti-nīz-ing (*skroo′-*).
Scru′ti-ny (*skroo′-*), 169.
Scru-toire′ (*skroo-twor′*) [so Wr. Gd.; *skroo-twär′*, Sm.; *skroo-tōr′*, Wk. 155.]
Scud, 22.
Scud′ded, 176.
Scud′ding.
Scu′do (It.) (*skoo′do*) [pl. *Scu′di* (*skoo′de*), 198.]
Scuf′fle, 164.
Scuf′fled (*skuf′ld*).
Scuf′fling.
[S c u l k, 203. — *See* Skulk.]
Scull, *n.* a kind of small boat; — one who rows such a boat; — a short oar; — an oar placed over the stern of a boat: — *v.* to impel, as a boat, by a single oar over the stern. [*See* Skull, 160.]
Sculled (*skuld*).
Scull′er.
Scul′ler-y.
Scull′ing.
Scull′ion (*-yun*).
Scul′pin.
Sculp′tor, 169, 230.
Sculp′tress.
Sculpt′ur-al (*-yur-*), 91.
Sculpt′ure, 91.
Sculpt′ured (*-yurd*).
Sculpt-ur-esque′ (*-yur-esk′*), 171.
Sculpt′ur-ing (*-yur-*).
Scum, 22.
Scum′bling.
Scummed (*skumd*), 165.
Scum′ming, 176.
Scup′per.
Scurf, 21, 49, 135.
Scurf′i-ness, 186.
Scurf′y, 169.
Scŭr′rīle, 48, 66, 82.
Scŭr-ril′i-ty, 169.
Scŭr′ril-oŭs, 170.
Scur′vi-ly, 186.
Scur′vi-ness.
Scur′vy, 93.
Sçut, 22.
Scu′tage, 70, 169.
Scu′tate.
Scutch, 22, 44.
Scutched (*skucht*), 165.
Scutch′eon (*-un*), 171.
Scutch′ing.
Scute, 26.
Scu′tel, 76.
Scu′tel-late [so Wr.; *sku-tel′lāt*, Gd. 155.]
Scu′tel-lāt-ed.
Scu-tel′li-form, 108.
Scu-tel′lum (L.).
Scu-ti-bran′chi-an (*-brang′ki-*), 171.
Scu-ti-bran′chi-ate (*-brang′ki-*).
Scu-tif′er-oŭs, 108.
Scu′ti-form, 108.
Scu′ti-ger.
Scu′ti-ped.
Scut′tle, 164.
Scut′tled (*skut′ld*).
Scut′tling, 183.
Scu′tum (L.).
Scyl-la′ri-an (*sĭl-*).
[S c y m i t a r, 203. — *See* Scimitar.]
Scy′phus (L.) (*sī′-*).
Scythe (*sīth*) (171) [S ī t h e, S y t h e, 203.]
Scythed (*sīthd*).
Scyth′i-an (*sĭth′-*).
Sēa (13, 39), *n.* the ocean; — a large body of salt water communicating with the ocean. [*See* See, *and* Si, 160] [pl. Sēas (*sēz*), 189. — *See* Sees, *and* Seize, 160.]
Sēa′bōard, 206.
Sēa′-cap-taĭn.
Sēa′-egg, 206, Exc. 2.
Sēa′-el′e-phant.
Sēa′-far-er (*-fêr-*).
Sēa′-far-ing (*-fêr-*).
Sēa′-green.
Sēa′-horse.
Sēa′-kāle.
Sēa′-king.
Sēal (13), *n.* a stamp for making an impression on some soft substance, as wax; — wax impressed with a seal; attestation; — a marine carnivorous quadruped: — *v.* to fasten or close with a seal; — to ratify; — to mark with a stamp. [*See* Ceil, *and* Seel, 160]
Sēa′-lĕop′ard.
Sēal′ing, *part.* from *Seal*: — *n.* act of one who seals. [*See* Ceiling, 160.]
Sēal′ing-wax.
Sēa′-lī-on.
Sēam (13), *n.* the line formed by sewing together two edges of cloth or other material; a line of juncture: — *v.* to join together by a seam; — to scar. [*See* Seem, 160.]
Sēa′man, 196.
Sēamed, 165.
Sēam′ing.
Sēa′-mouse.
Sēam′ster [S e m p s t e r, 203.]
Sēam′stress [so Sm. Gd.; *sem′stres*, Wk. Wr. 155] [S e m s t r e s s, S e m p s t r e s s, 203.]
Se′ance, 72.
[S e a n n a c h i e, S e a n n a c h y (*sen′naky*), 203. — *See* Sennachy.]
Sēa′pōrt, 206.
Sēar (13), *v.* to wither; — to cauterize: — *a.* dry; withered. [*See* Cere, *and* Seer, 160] [S e r e, 203.]

Search (*serch*), 21, N.
Search'a-ble (*serch'a-bl*), 164, 171, 183.
Searched (*sercht*), Note C, p. 34.
Search'er (*serch'-*).
Search'ing (*serch'-*)
Sēar'cloth.
Sēared (*sērd*), *v.*
Sēared (*sērd*) [so Wb. Gd.; *sēr'ed*, or *sērd*, Wr. 155], *a.*
Sēar'ing.
Sēa'-room.
Sēa'-rōv-er.
Sēa'-ser-pent.
Sēa'-shore.
Sēa-sick, 206, Exc. 5.
Sēa'-snāil.
Sēa'son (*se'zn*), 149.
Sēa'son-a-ble (*se'zn-a-bl*), 164, 171.
Sēa'son-a-bly (*se'zn-*).
Sēa'soned (*se'znd*).
Sēa'son-er (*se'zn-*).
Sēa'son-ing (*se'zn-*).
Sēat, 13.
Sēat'ed.
Sēa'-term.
Sēat'ing.
Sēa'-town.
Sēa'-ur'chin.
Sēa'-wâll.
Sēa'ward.
Sēa'-weed.
Sēa'-wor-thi-ness (*-wur-*).
Sēa'-wor-thy (*-wur-*).
Sēa'-wrack (*-rak*), 162.
Se-ba'ceoŭs (*-shus*), 112, 169.
Se-baç'ic, 109.
Se'bate.
Se-bif'er-oŭs.
Seb-un-dee', or *Seb'un-dy*, 203.
Se-ca'le (L.) [so Wr. Gd.; *se'kāl*, Sm. 155.]
Se'cant, 72, 231.
Se-cede', 169.
Se-cēd'ed, 183.
Se-cēd'er.
Se-cēd'ing.
Se-cern', 21, N.
Se-cerned', 165.
Se-cern'ent, 169.
Se-cern'ing.
Se-ces'sion (*-sesh'un*).
Seck'el (*sek'l*), 149.
Se-clude' [*not* se-klood', 127, 153.]
Se-clūd'ed, 183.
Se-clūd'ing.
Se-clu'sion (*-zhun*), 47, 112.
Se-clu'sĭve.
Sec'ond, 86.
Sec'ond-a-ri-ly.
Sec'ond-a-ry, 169.
Sec'ond-best.
Sec'ond-ed.
Sec'ond-hand.
Sec'ond-ing.
Sec'ond-rate.
Sec'ond-sight (*-sīt*).
Se'cre-cy, 169.
Se'cret.
Sec-re-ta'ri-at.
Sec're-ta-ry, 169.
Sec're-ta-ry-bird.
Se-crete'.
Se-crēt'ed, 183.
Se-crēt'ing.
Se-cre'tion, 169.
Se-cre-tĭ'tious (*-tish'us*) [so Sm. Wb. Gd.; *sek-re-tish'us*, Wk. Wr. 155.]
Se-crēt'ĭve, 84.
Se-crēt'o-ry, *or* Se'cre-to-ry [so Wr.; *se-krēt'ur-y*, Wk. Sm.; *se'kre-to-ry*, Wb. Gd. 155.]
Sect, 15.
Sect-a'ri-an, 169.
Sect-a'ri-an-ism (*-izm*), 133, 136.
Sect-a'ri-an-ize.
Sect'a-rist.
Sect'a-ry, 72.
Sec'tĭle, 83, 152.
Sec'tion.
Sec'tion-al.
Sec'tion-al-ism (*-izm*), 136.
Sec'tion-al-ly, 170.
Sect'or.
Sec-to'ri-al.
Sec'u-lar, 89, 108.
Sec'u-lar-ism, 136.
Sec-u-lăr'i-ty, 169.
Sec-u-lăr-ĭ-za'tion.
Sec'u-lar-ize, 202.
Sec'u-lar-ized.
Sec'u-lar-īz-ing, 183.
Sec'u-lar-ly.
Se'cund [so Wr. Wb. Gd.; *sek'und*, Sm. 155.]
Sec'un-dīne, 105, 189.

☞ Smart pronounces this word thus in his Dictionary, but *sek'un-din*, in the Supplement.

Se-cun'dum ar'tem (L.)
Se-cūr'a-ble, 164.
Se-cure', 26, 75.
Se-cured'.
Se-cure'ly, 185.
Se-cūr'er, 183.
Se-cu'ri-fer, 49, N.
Se-cu'ri-form.
Se-cūr'ing.
Se-cu'ri-palp.
Se-cu'ri-ty, 49, N.; 169.
Se-dan', 121.
Se-date'.
Se-date'ly.
Se-date'ness, 185.
Sed'a-tĭve, 84.
Se de-fen-den'do (L.).
Se'dent, 13, 76.
Sed'en-ta-ri-ly.
Sed'en-ta-ri-ness.
Sed'en-ta-ry (72) [*not* se'den-ta-ry, *nor* se-den'ta-ry, 153.]
Se-de'runt, (L.), 49, N.
Sedge, 15, 45.
Sedg'y, 169.
Sed'i-ment, 169.
Sed-i-ment'a-ry, 72.
Se-dĭ'tion (*-dish'un*).
Se-dĭ'tion-a-ry (*-dish'-un-*), 72.
Se-dĭ'tious (*-dish'us*).
Se-duce', 26, 75.
Se-duced' (*-dūst'*).
Se-dūç'er.
Se-dūç'i-ble, 164, 169.
Se-dūç'ing, 183.
Se-duc'tion.
Se-duc'tĭve, 84.
Se-du'li-ty, 108.
Sed'u-lous, 89.
See (13), *n.* a diocese: — *v.* to behold. [*See* Sea, *and* Si, 160.]
Seed (13), *n.* the substance, animal or vegetable, which nature provides for the reproduction of the species. [*See* Cede, *and* Seid, 160.]
Seed'ed.
Seed'-lac.
Seed'ling.
Seeds'man (*seedz'-*), 214.
Seed'-time.
Seed'-ves-sel.
Seed'y, 93.
See'ing, 188.
Seek, 13, 39, 52.
Seek'er.
Seek'ing.
Seel (13), *v.* to close the eyelids of, as those of

a hawk, by passing a fine thread through them. [*See* Ceil, *and* Seal, 160.]
Seeled, 165.
Seel′ing.
Seem (13), *v.* to appear. [*See* Seam, 160.]
Seemed, 150.
Seem′er.
Seem′ing.
Seem′li-ness, 186.
Seem′ly, 93.
Seen, *part.* from *See.* [*See* Scene, *and* Seine, 160.]
Se′er (67, 161), *n.* one who sees with the eye.
Seer (67, 161), *n.* a prophet; one who foresees. [*See* Cere, *and* Sear, 160.]

☞ The two preceding words are pronounced *se′-ur* by Smart and Worcester, but *sēr* by Walker, Webster, and Goodrich. The distinction here made is in conformity with the principle laid down in § 67, and accords, it is believed, with the best and most general usage." "It would be false policy," says Ellis, "when it can be so easily avoided (and *is* by many persons avoided), to confuse . . . *seer* (a prophet) with *se-er* (one who sees)."

Seer′suck-er, 171.
Sees (*sēz*) (13, 40), *v.* does see. [*See* Seas (pl. of Sea), *and* Seize, 160.]
See′saw.
See′sawed, 165.
See′saw-ing.
Seethe (163; Note D, p. 37) [Seeth, 203.]
Seethed, 165.
Seeth′er.
Seeth′ing.
Se-fa′tian (*-shan*), 112.
[Segar, 203. — *See* Cigar.]
Seg′gar, 66, 170.
Seg′ment, 127.
Seg-ment′al.
Seg-ment-a′tion.
Seg′re-gate (169) [*not* se′gre-gāt, 160.]
Seg′re-gāt-ed, 183.
Seg′re-gāt-ing.
Seg-re-ga′tion.
Seīd (13) [so Wr. Gd.; *se′id*, Sm. 155], *n.* a descendant of Mahomet. [*See* Cede, *and* Seed, 160.]
Sēign-eū′ri-al (*sēn-u′-*), 49, N.; 162.
Sēign′ior (*sēn′yur*), a lord of a manor; — in the South of Europe, a title of honor, equivalent to *Lord.* [*See* Senior, 160] [Signior, 203.]

☞ In the second sense, Smart pronounces this word *sēn-yor′.*

Sēign′ior-age (*sēn′yur-*).
Sēign-io′ri-al (*sēn-yo′-*).
Sēign′ior-y (*sēn′yur-*), 171.
Sēine (*sēn*) [*not* sān, 153] (13, 169, N.), *n.* a kind of large fishing-net. [*See* Scene, *and* Seen, 160.]
Sēin′er.
Sēis′in (*sēz′-*), *or* Sēiz′-in.

☞ In law-books, generally written *seisin.*

Seīs′mic.
Seīs-mom′e-ter, 108.
Sēiz′a-ble, 164.
Sēize (13, 169), *v.* to take possession of by force. [*See* Seas (pl. of Sea), *and* Sees, 160.]
Sēized, 165.
Sēiz′er.
Sēiz′in, *or* Sēis′in (*sēz′-*) [*See* Note under *Seisin.*]
Sēiz′ing, 183.
Sēiz′or. [Law term.]
Sēiz′ure (*sēzh′yur*).
Se-ju′goŭs [so Wb. Gd.; *se-j′oo′gus*, Sm. (*See* § 26); *se-ju′gus*, or *sej′u-gus*, Wr. 155.]
Se-la′cian (*-shan*), 169.
Se′lah (Heb.).
Sel′dom, 86, 169.
Se-lect′, 103.
Se-lect′ed.
Se-lect′ing.
Se-lec′tion.
Se-lect′ĭve, 84.
Se-lect′-măn, 196.
Se-lect′or, 169.
Se-le′ni-ate.
Se-len′ic.
Sel′e-nīde.
Sel-e-nif′er-oŭs, 108.
Se-le′ni-oŭs.
Sel′e-nīte, 169.
Sel-e-nit′ic.
Sel-e-nit′ic-al.
Se-le′ni-um.
Sel-e-ni′u-ret.
Sel-e-ni′u-ret-ted.
Se-le′no-cen′tric, 224.
Sel-e-nog′ra-pher.
Sel-e-no-graph′ic.
Sel-e-no-graph′ic-al.
Sel-e-nog′ra-phist.
Sel-e-nog′ra-phy, 108.
Self (15) [pl. Selves, 193.]

☞ *Self* is much used in composition, and the compounds thus formed have their parts separated by a hyphen; as, *self-control, self-evident, self-same, self-willed.*

Sell, 15, 172.
Sel′lan-ders, *or* Sel′len-ders (*-durz*), *n. pl.* 203.
Sell′er, 77.
Sell′ing, 228.
Sel′vage (70, 169) [Selvedge, 203.]
Sel′vaged, 150; Note D, p. 37.
Sel-va-gee′ [so Gd.; *sel′va-je*, Wr. 155.]
Selves (*selvz*) (15, 40) [pl. of *Self.*]
Sem′a-phore, 171.
Sem-a-phŏr′ic.
Sem-a-phŏr′ic-al.
Sem-a-tol′o-gy, 108.
Sem′blance, 169.
Sémé (Fr.) (*sā-mā′*).
Se-meī-og′ra-phy [Semiography, 203.]
Se-meī-o-log′ic-al (*-loj′-*), 108.
Se-meī-ol′o-gy (171) [Semiology, 203.]
Se-meī-ot′ic, 109.
Se-meī-ot′ics.
Se-mes′ter (Ger.).
Sem′i (L.), a prefix signifying half; — much used in composition.
Sem-ĭ-an′nu-al.
Sem-ĭ-A′ri-an.
Sem′ĭ-breve, 222.
Sem-ĭ-cir′cle, 164.
Sem-ĭ-cir′cu-lar.
Sem′ĭ-co-lon (86) [so Sm. Wb. Gd.; *sem-i-ko′lun*, Wk. Wr. 155.]

Sem-ĭ-cu′bic-al.
Sem-ĭ-cu′bi-um, *or* Sem-ĭ-cu′pi-um, 203.
Se-mid′a-līte, 152.
Sem-ĭ-dī-am′e-ter.
Sem′ĭ-nal, 72, 78.
Sem′ĭ-na-rist, 72.
Sem′ĭ-na-ry, 72.
Sem-ĭ-na′tion, 169.
Sem-ĭ-nif′er-oŭs.
Sem-ĭ-nif′ic, 109.
Sem-ĭ-nif′ic-al, 108.
Sem′ĭ-nymph.
[Semiography, 203. —*See* Semeiography.]
[Semiology, 203. — *See* Semeiology.]
Sem-ĭ-o′pal, 223.
Sem-ĭ-o′vate.
Sem-ĭ-pal′mate.
Sem′ĭ-ped, 78.
Sem-ĭ-pe′dal, *or* Se-mip′e-dal [so Wr.; *se-mip′e-dal*, Wk. Wb Gd.; *sem-ĭ-ped′al*, Sm. 155.]
Sem-ĭ-Pe-la′gi-an.
Sem′ĭ-quā-ver.
Se-mit′ic (170) [Shemitic, 203.]
Sem′ĭ-tone, 78.
Sem-ĭ-ton′ic.
Sem′ĭ-vow-el, 28.
Sem-o-lel′la (It.).
Sem-o-li′no (It.) (*-le′-*).
Sémoule (It.) (*sā-mool′*).
Sem-per-vi′rent, 49, N.
Sem′per-vīve.
Sem-pi-ter′nal, 21, N.
Sem-pi-ter′ni-ty.
Sempre (It.) (*sem′prā*).
[Sempster, 203. — *See* Seamster.]
[Sempstress, Semstress, 203. — *See* Seamstress.]
Sen′a-ry, *or* Se′na-ry [*sen′a-ry*, Wk. Wr. Wb. Gd.; *se′na-ry*, Sm. 155.]
Sen′ate, 66, 170.
Sen′ate-house.
Sen′a-tor, 88.
Sen-a-to′ri-al, 49, N.
Sen-a-to′ri-an.
Se-na′tus con-sul′tum (L.).
Send, 15.
Send′er, 228.
Sen′e-ga, *or* Sen′e-ka, 203.
Sen′e-gal.
Sen′e-gīne (45) [Senegin, 203.]
Se-nes′cence, 171.
Sen′esch-al (*-esh-*) (46) [so Sm. Wr. Wb. Gd.; *sen′es-kal*, Wk. 155.]

☞ Walker, in deference to most of the authorities of his day, pronounces this word *sen′es-kal*; but he says: "As the word does not come from the learned languages, if usage were equal, I should prefer Dr. Kenrick's pronunciation [*sen′esh-al*]."

Sen′green.
Se′nīle (81, 152) [*not* se′-nīl, 153.]
Se-nil′i-ty, 169.
Sēn′ior (*sēn′yur*) (51), *a.* elder;—*n.* one older than another, or having priority over him;—a member of the highest class in an American college or a professional school. [*See* Seignior, 160.]
Sēn-iŏr′i-ty (*-yor′-*).
Sen′nā (15, 72) [*not* se′-na, *nor* se′nā, 127, 153.]
Sen′na-chy (*-ky*) [Seannachie, Seannachy, 203.]
Sen′nĭght (*-nĭt*) (160, 162), *n.* the space of seven nights and days. [Sevennight, 203.]
Sen′nit (160), *n.* a sort of flat, braided cordage;—plaited straw or palm-leaves, &c.
Sen-oc′u-lar, 108.
Sen′sate.
Sen′sāt-ed.
Sen-sa′tion.
Sen-sa′tion-al.
Sen-sa′tion-al-ism (*-izm*), 136.
Sen-sa′tion-al-ist.
Sen-sa′tion-a-ry, 72.
Sense (15, 39), *n.* that capacity of the mind by which corporal impressions are felt;—understanding. [*See* Cense, 160.]
Sense′less, 185.
Sens-i-bil′i-ty, 171.
Sens′i-ble, 164, 169, 183.
Sens′i-bly.
Sens-if′er-oŭs, 108.
Sens-if′ic, 109.
Sens′ism (*-izm*), 133.
Sens′i-tĭve, 84.
Sens-i-tiv′i-ty, 169.
Sen′si-tize, 202.
Sen′si-tized, 150.
Sen′si-tīz-ing.
Sens-o′ri-al, 49, N.
Sen-so′ri-um (L.) [L. pl. *Sen-so′ri-a*, Eng. pl. Sen-so′ri-ums (*-umz*), 198.]
Sens′o-ry, 86.
Sens′u-al, 46, Note 2, 89.
Sens′u-al-ism (*-izm*).
Sens′u-al-ist, 106.
Sens-u-al′i-ty, 108.
Sens-u-al-ĭ-za′tion.
Sens′u-al-ize, 202.
Sens′u-al-ized, 165.
Sens′u-al-īz-ing.
Sens′u-al-ly, 170.
Sens′u-ism (*-izm*), 133, 136.
Sens′u-oŭs, 100.
Sent (15), *v.* did send. [*See* Cent, *and* Scent, 160.]
Sen′tence, 169.
Sen′tenced (*-tenst*), 165, 183; Note C, p. 34.
Sen′tenç-er.
Sen′tenç-ing.
Sen-ten′tial (*-shal*), 112.
Sen-ten′ti-a-ry (*-shĭ-*) (72) [so Wr.; *sen-ten′-sha-ry*, Wb. Gd. 155.]
Sen-ten′tioŭs (*-shus*).
Sen′ti-en-cy (*-shĭ-*) [so Gd.; *sen′shen-sy*, Wr. 155.]
Sen′ti-ent(*-shĭ-*)[so Wk. Wr.; *sen′sh′ent*, Sm. (*See* § 26); *sen′shent*, Wb. Gd. 155.]
Sen′ti-ment, 169.
Sen-ti-ment′al, 109.
Sen-ti-ment′al-ism (*-izm*), 133, 136.
Sen-ti-ment′al-ist.
Sen-ti-ment-al′i-ty.
Sen-ti-ment′al-ize.
Sen-ti-ment′al-ized.
Sen-ti-ment′al-īz-ing.
Sen-ti-ment′al-ly.
Sen′ti-nel, 76, 78.
Sen′ti-nelled (*-neld*) [Sentineled, Wb. Gd. 203.—*See* 177, and Note E, p. 70.]
Sen′try, 93, 169.

Se′pal (72) [*not* sep′al, 127, 153.]
Sep′al-ĭne (82, 152) [so Wr.; *sep′al-ĭn*, Gd. 155.]
Se′palled (*-pald*) [Sepaled, Wb. Gd. 203. — *See* 177, and Note E, p. 70.]
Sep′al-oid, 143.
Sep′al-oŭs, 228.
Sep-a-ra-bil′i-ty, 108.
Sep′a-ra-ble, 164, 169.
Sep′a-ra-bly.
Sep′a-rate, 73, 171.
Sep′a-răt-ed, 183.
Sep′a-rate ly, 185.
Sep′a-răt-ing.
Sep-a-ra′tion.
Sep′a-ra-tism(*-tizm*),136
Sep′a-ra-tist.
Sep-a-ra-tist′ic.
Sep′a-ra-tĭve.
Sep′a-răt-or, 169.
Sep′a-ra-to-ry, 72, 86.
Se′peck, 171.
Se′pi-a (L.), the generic name of the cuttle-fish; — a pigment prepared from the ink of the cuttle-fish. [pl. *Se′pi-æ*, 198.]

☞ Smart says that "as the name of a pigment, it is commonly pronounced *sep′i-a*"; but Webster, Goodrich, and Worcester, pronounce the word *se′-pi-a*, in both senses.

Sep-i-da′ceoŭs (*-shus*).
Se′poy.
Sept, 15.
Sept′an-gle (*-ang-gl*).
Sept-an′gu-lar (*-ang′-*).
Sep′tate.
Sep-tem′ber, 126.
Sep-tem′brist.
Sep-tem′vir (L.) [L. pl. *Sep-tem′vĭ-rī*; Eng. pl. (rarely) Sep-tem′-virs (*-vurz*), 198.]
Sep-tem′vĭ-ratê, 78.
Sep′ten-a-ry, 72.
Sep′ten-ate.
Sep-ten′ni-al, 66, 169.
Sep-ten′tri-al.
Sep-ten′tri-on.
Sep-ten′tri-on-al.
Sept′foil.
Sep′tic.
Sep′tic-al.
Sep-ti-ci′dal [so Wr. Gd.; *sep′ti-sī-dal*, Sm. 155.]
Sep-tiç′i-ty, 171.
Sep-ti-fa′ri-oŭs, 49, N.
Sep-tif′er-oŭs.
Sep-tif′ra-gal [so Wr. Gd.; *sep′ti-fră-gal*, Sm. 155.]
Sep-ti-lat′er-al.
Sep-tin′su-lar.
Sep-ti-syl′la-ble, 164.
Sep-tu-a-ge-na′ri-an, 116, 171.
Sep-tu-ag′e-na-ry (*-aj′-*), 72.
Sep-tu-a-ges′i-ma.
Sep-tu-a-ges′i-mal.
Sep′tu-a-gint, 171.
Sep′tu-a-ry, 72.
Sep′tu-late.
Sep′tum (L.) [pl. *Sep′-ta*, 198.]
Sep′tu-ple, 164.
Sep′tu-pled (*-pld*).
Se-pul′chral (*-kral*), 52.
Sep′ul-chre (*-kur*), *n.* 161, 171.

☞ Formerly pronounced *se-pul′kur*.

Se-pul′chre (*-kur*) (161) [so Wk. Sm. Wr.; *sep′ul-kur*, Wb. Gd. 155], *v.*
Se-pul′chred (*-kurd*).
Se-pul′chring (*-kring*).
Sep′ul-ture, 90.
Se-qua′cioŭs (*-shus*), 169.
Se′quel, 76.
Se′quence.
Se′quent.
Se-quen′tial (*-shal*).
Se-ques′ter, 104.
Se-ques′tered, 150.
Se-ques′ter-ing.
Se-ques′tra-ble, 164, 169.
Se-ques′trate.
Se-ques′trăt-ed, 183.
Se-ques′trăt-ing.
Seq-ues-tra′tion (*sek-wes-*) [so Wk. Sm. Wr.; *se-kwes-tra′-shun*, Wb. Gd. 155.]
Seq′ues-trăt-or (*sek′-wes-*) (169) [so Sm. Wr.; *sek-wes-tra′tur*, Wk.; *se-kwes-tra′tur*, Wb. Gd. 155.]
Se′quin [Cecchin, Chequin, Zechin, 203.]
Se-ragl′io (*-ral′yo*), 162, 171.
Sĕr-al-bu′men.
Sĕr′aph [Heb. pl. Sĕr′-a-phim; Eng. pl. Sĕr′-aphs, 198.]

☞ In the Common Version of the Bible, the plural form, *seraphims*, is also found; but this form is no longer in use.

Se-raph′ic, 109.
Se-raph′ic-al, 108.
Sĕr′a-phim, *n. pl.* [*See* Seraph.]
Sĕr′a-phine (*-fēn*).
Se-ras′kiēr [so Sm. Wb. Gd.; *se-ras′kēr*, or *sĕr-as-kēr′*, Wr. 155.]
[Sere, 203. — *See* Sear.]
Sĕr-e-nade′, 122.
Sĕr-e-năd′ed.
Sĕr-e-năd′ing,
Sĕr-e-nä′ta (It.).
Se-rene′, 13, 121.
Se-rene′ness, 66, N.
Se-ren′i-ty, 169.
Serf (21, N.), *n.* a slave attached to the soil. [*See* Surf, 148.]
Serf′age, 70, 169.
Serf′dom, 86, 169.
Serge (21, N.; 135), *n.* a kind of twilled cloth. [*See* Surge, 148.]
Ser′gean-cy (*sar′jan-sy*, or *ser′jan-sy*) [Serjeancy, 203] [*See* Note under *Serjeant.*]
Ser′geant (*sar′jant*, or *ser′jant*) (72; Note D, p. 37) [Serjeant, 203. — *See* Note under *Serjeant.*]
Ser′geant-ry (*sar′jant-ry*, or *ser′jant-ry*) [Serjeantry, 203.]
Ser′geant-y (*sar′jant-y*, or *ser′jant-y*) [Serjeanty, 203.]
Se′ri-al, 49, N.; 169.
Se′ri-ate.
Se-ri-a′tim (L.).
Se-rĭ′ceoŭs (*-rish′us*).
Sĕr-i-cult′ure, 91.
Se′ri-ēs (*-ēz*), *n. sing. & pl.* (49, N.; 144) [so Wk. Sm. Wr.; *se′rēz*, Wb. Gd. 155.]
Sĕr′in.
Se′ri-o-com′ic, 224.
Se′ri-o-com′ic-al.
Se′ri-oŭs, 49, N.
Ser′jeant (*sar′jant*, or *ser′jant*) (21, N.; 72)

[so Wr.; *sar'jant*, Wk. Sm.; *sar'jent*, Wb. Gd. 155] [Sergeant, 203.]

☞ This word is written *sergeant* by Johnson, Walker, Webster, Goodrich, and some other lexicographers; *serjeant* by Smart, and many others; *sergeant*, or *serjeant*, by Worcester, who remarks that both orthographies are well authorized. *Serjeant*, however, is the more common form in England, at the present day. In the United States, the prevalent pronunciation is *ser'jant*.

Ser'jeant-ry (*sar'jant-ry*, or *ser'jant-ry*) [Sergeantry, 203.]
Ser'jeant-y (*sar'jant-y*, or *ser'jant-y*) [Sergeanty, 203.]
Ser'mon, 86, 135.
Ser-mon'ic-al.
Ser'mon-ist, 106.
Ser'mon-ize, 202.
Ser'mon-ized, 165.
Ser'mon-īz-er.
Ser'mon-īz-ing.
Ser'mount-aĭn.
Se-ron' (*-roon'*) [so Gd.; *se-ron'*, Wr. 155], *or* Se-roon' [Ceroon, 203.]
Se-ros'i-ty, 233.
Sĕr'o-tīne, 82, 152.
Se-rot'i-noŭs.
Se'roŭs, 49, N.
Ser'pent, 21, N.; 127.
Ser-pent'i-form, 108.
Ser-pent-ig'e-noŭs (*-ij'-*), 171.
Ser'pent-īne, 82, 152.
Ser-pent'i-noŭs (108) [so Gd.; *ser-pen-ti'nus*, Wr. 155.]
Ser'pent-ry.
Ser'pent's-tongue (*-tung*), 213.
Ser-pig'i-noŭs (*-pij'-*).
Ser-pi'go, *or* Ser-pi'go (*-pe'-*) [so Wk. Wr.; *sur-pi'go*, Wb. Gd.; *ser-pe'go*, Sm. 155.]
Ser-pu'le-an, 110, 169.
Sĕr'rate, 48, 66.
Sĕr'răt ed, 183.
Sĕr'ra-ture, 90.
Sĕr'ri-căt-ed.
Sĕr'ri-corn, 48, 49.
Sĕr'rīed, 99.
Sĕr'ru-late, 89.
Sĕr-ru-la'tion.
Se'rum, 169.
Serv'a-ble, 164.
Serv'ant, 21, N.; 129.
Serve, 21, N.; 135.
Served, 150, 165.
Ser'vi-an.
Serv'ĭce, 169.
Serv'ĭce-a-ble, 164, 183.
Serv'ĭce-a-ble-ness, 106.
Serv'ĭce-a-bly.
Serv'ĭce-bĕr-ry.
Serv'ĭce-bŏŏk.
Serv'i-ent.
Serv'ĭle, 81, 152.
Serv'ĭle-ly, 66, N.
Serv-il'i-ty, 169.
Serv'ing, 183.
Serv'ing-măn.
Serv'i-tor, 88.
Serv'i-tude, 26, 169.
Ses'a-me, 144.
Ses'a-mum (L.).
Ses'a-moid [so Sm. Gd.; *ses-a-moid'*, Wr. 155.]
Ses-quĭ-ăl'ter.
Ses-quĭ-ăl'ter-al.
Ses-quĭ-ăl'ter-ate.
Ses-quĭ-ăl'ter-oŭs.
Ses-quĭ-bro'mīde.
Ses-quĭ-car'bon-ate.
Ses-quĭ-chlo'rīde (*-klo'-*), 49, N.
Ses-quĭ-cy'a-nīde.
Ses-quĭ-du'pli-cate.
Ses-quĭ'o-dīde.
Ses-quĭ-ox'īde [*See* Note under *Oxide*.]
Ses-quip'e-dal, *or* Ses'-quĭ-pē-dal [*ses-kwip'-e-dal*, Wk. Wr. Wb. Gd.; *ses'kwĭ-pē-dal*, Sm. 155.]
Ses-quĭ-pe-da'li-an.
Ses-quĭ-pe-dal'i-ty.
Ses-quip'li-cate [so Wr. Wb. Gd.; *ses'kwĭ-plī-kāt*, Sm. 155.]
Ses-quĭ-quad'rate (*-kwod'-*).
Ses-quĭ-quin'tīle, 152.
Ses'quĭ-sâlt.
Ses-quĭ-sul'phīde.
Ses-quĭ-sul'phu-ret.
Ses-quĭ-ter'tial (*-shal*).
Ses-quĭ-ter'tian (*-shan*).
Ses-quĭ-ter'tian-al. (*-shan-*).
Ses-quĭ-ter'tioŭs (*-shus*), 112, 169.
Ses'quĭ-tone.
Ses'sĭle, 82, 152.
Ses'sion (*sesh'un*), *n.* the sitting of a court, council, legislature, or other assembly. [*See* Cession, 160.]
Ses'sion-al (*sesh'un-*), 72.
[Sesspool, 203.—*See* Cesspool.]
Ses'terce, 189.
[Sestet, Sestett, Sestette, Sestetto, 203.—*See* Sextet.]
Ses'tīne, 82, 152.
Set, 15, 39, 41.

☞ As a noun meaning *a number of things of the same kind or suited to each other*, it is sometimes improperly written *sett*.

Se'ta (L.) [pl. *Se'tæ*, 198.]
Se-ta'ceoŭs (*-shus*), *a.* bristly; — bristle-shaped. [*See* Cetaceous, 160.]
Seth'i-an.
Seth'ic.
Se'ti-cer.
Se-tif'er-oŭs, 108.
Se'ti-form.
Se'ti-ger, 45.
Se-tig'er-oŭs (*-tij'-*).
Se'ti-reme [so Sm. Wb. Gd.; *set'i-rēm*, Wr. 155.]
Set'-off, 206, Exc. 4.; 215.
Se'ton (86) [so Sm. Wb. Gd.; *se'tn*, Wk. Wr. 155.]
Se'tose [so Gd.; *se-tōs'*, Wr. 155.]
Se'toŭs, 100.
Set-tee', 121, 170.
Set'ter, 176.
Set'ting.
Set'tle (*set'l*), 164.
Set'tled (*set'ld*), 171.
Set'tle-ment (*-tl-*).
Set'tler.
Set'tling, 183.
Set'-to (*-too*), 66, N.; 206, Exc. 4.
Se'tule.
Set'u-lose.
Set'wâll [Setwal, 203.]
Sev'en (*sev'n*), 61, 149.
Sev'en-fōld (*sev'n-*), 217.
Seven'nīght (*sen'nĭt*) [Sennight, 203.]

Sev′en-teen (*sev′n-*) [*See* Note under *Eighteen.*]
Sev′en-teenth (*sev′n-*).
Sev′enth(*sev′nth*),61,149
Sev′en-ti-eth (*sev′n-*).
Sev′en-ty (*sev′n-*).
Sev′er, 104.
Sev′er-al, 233, Exc.
Sev′er-al-ly, 170.
Sev′er-al-ty, 145.
Sev′er-ance, 169.
Se-vere′, 13, 75.
Sev′ered (*-urd*).
Se-vere′ly, 185.
Sev′er-er (77, 161), *n.* one who severs.
Se-vĕr′er (161), *a.* more severe.
Sev′er-ĭng.
Se-vĕr′i-ty, 169.
Sew (*so*) (24, 39), *v.* to join or fasten with a thread and needle. [*See* So, *and* Sōw, 160]
Sewed (*sōd*), *v.* did sew. [*See* Sowed, 160.]
Sew′er (*so′-*) (67, 161), *n.* one who sews. [*See* Sore, 148.]
Sewer (*soor*) (67, 161) [so Sm., *shōr*, Wk.; *su′ur*, Wb. Gd.; *soo′-ur*, or *shōr*, Wr. 155], *n.* an underground passage for conveying water. [*See* Suer, 148.]

☞ "*Sewer*, a drain, by those who wish to avoid the vulgarism of the common pronunciation [*shōr*], and yet not deviate into a sound wholly unlike it, will be...... pronounced *soor*." *Smart.*

Sewer′age (*soor′-*).
Sew′ing (*so′-*), *part.* from *Sew.* [*See* Sowing, 160.]
Sew′ing-silk (*so′-*).
Sewn (*sōn*), *part.* from *Sew.* [*See* Sown, 160.]

☞ This form of the participle from *sew* is rarely used instead of the regular form *sewed.*

Sex, 15, 52, N.
Sex-a-ge-na′ri-an, 49, N.; 171.
Sex-ag′e-na-ry (*-aj′-*)[so Wk. Sm. Wr., *seks′-a-jen-a-ry*, or *seks-aj′-en-a-ry*, Gd. 155.]
Sex-a-ges′i-ma, 45.
Sex-a-ges′i-mal.
Sex′an-gle (*-ang-gl*).
Sex′an-gled (*-ang-gld*).
Sex-an′gu-lar(*-ang′gu-*)
Sex-deç′i-mal.
Sex-dig′it-ism (*-dij′it-izm*), 136.
Sex-dig′it-ist (*-dij′-*).
Sex-du-o-deç′i-mal.
Sex′e-na-ry, 72.
Sex-en′ni-al, 66.
Sex′fid, *or* Sex′i-fid, 203.
Sex′i-syl-la-ble (164) [*seks-i-sil′la-bl*, Wr. 155.]
Sex-loc′u-lar, 108.
Sex′taĭn, 96.
Sex′tant, 72.
Sex′ta-ry, 72.
Sex′tet [Sestet, Sestett, Sestette, Sestetto, 203.]
Sex′tĭle, 81, 152.
Sex-till′ion (*-yun*), 112.
Sex′to, *n.* [pl. Sex′tōs (*-tōz*), 192.]
Sex′ton, 86.
Sex′tu-ple (*-pl*).
Sex′u-al, 89.
Sex′u-al-ist, 106.
Sex-u-al′i-ty, 108.
Sex′u-al-ly, 170.
Sfor-zan′do (It.), 154.
Sfor-zä′to (It.), 154.
Sfu-mä′to (It.) (*sfoo-*).
Sgraf′fĭ-to (It.).

☞ "In the doubled consonants [in Italian]... the tongue, by resting on the sound at the place of contact, must mark the difference between the articulation signified in this manner, and the same articulation signified by the single letter." *Smart.* — Compare § 66, N.

Shab, 10
Shab′bi-ly, 186.
Shab′bi-ness.
Shab′by, 66, 93.
Shab′rack.
Shack, 10.
Shac′kle (*shak′l*), 171.
Shac′kled (*shak′ld*), 150.
Shac′kling.
Shad (10) [Chad, Sm. 203.]
Shad′dock, 170.
Shade, 23, 163.
Shād′ed, 183.
Shād′i-ly, 171.
Shād′i-ness.
Shād′ing.
Shad′ōw, 101.
Shad′ōwed (*-ōd*), 171.
Shad′ōw-ing.
Shad′ōw-y.
Shād′y, 169.
Shȧft, 12, 131.
Shȧft′ed.
Shag, 10, 46, 53.
Shag′bark, 206.
Shag′-ēared, 165.
Shag′ged (*-ghed*), 138.
Shag′gi-ness (*-ghĭ-*).
Shag′gy (*-ghy*), 170.
Sha-green′, *n.* a dried animal skin, resembling parchment, but granulated. [*See* Chagrin, 160] [Chagreen, 203.]
Sha-greened′, 165.
Shah (11, 46) [Schah, 203.]
Shah Nameh (Persian) (*shä nä-mā′*) [Shanamah, Sm. 203.]
Shake, 23.
Shāk′en (*shāk′n*), 149.
Shāk′er.
Shake-spēar′i-an (49, N.) [*shāks-pe′ri-an*, Gd. Wr.] [Shakespearean, Shakspearian, Shakspearean, Shaksperean, Shaksperian, 203.]
Shāk′ing, 183.
Sha′ko.
Shāk′y, 93.
Shale, 23.
Shäll, 10, 172.
Shal′lĭ.
Shal-loon′, 121.
Shal′lop, 66, 86.
Shal′lōw, 153.
[Shalm (*shawm*), 203. — *See* Shawm.]
Shalt, 10.
Shāl′y, 183.
Sham, 10, 32, 46.
Shä′man (196) [so Sm.; *sham′an*, Wb. Gd.; *sha′man*, Wr. 155.]
Shä′man-ism (*-izm*).
Sham′ble, 164.
Sham′bled (*-bld*), 150.
Sham′bling.
Shame, 23, 163.
Shamed, 165.
Shame′faced (*-fāst*).

☞ This is a corruption of *shamefast* (made *fast*, or restrained, by *shame*), a

fall; ê *as in* there; ŏŏ *as in* foot; ç *as in* facile, gh *as* g *in* go; th *as in* this.

word found so written in old authors. "The source of the change is obviously from the effect of *shame*, in many cases, upon the *face*." *Richardson.*

Shame′ful (*-fo͝ol*), 180.
Shame′ful-ly (*-fo͝ol-*), 170.
Shame′less, 185.
Shăm′ing.
Shammed (*shamd*), 165, 176.
Sham′mel
Shăm′mer.
Sham′ming.
Sham′my [Chamois, Shamois, Shamoy, 263.]
Sha-moy′ing.
Sham-poo′ [Champoo, 203.]
Sham-pooed′, 188.
Sham-poo′er.
Sham-poo′ing.
Sham′rock.
Shank (*shangk*), 54.
Shanked (*shangkt*).
[Shanker, 203. — *See* Chancre.]
Shank′ing.
Shan′ny.
Sha'n't [contracted from *shall not*.]

☞ "The *a* in *can't* and *sha'n't* is broad [or has its Italian sound, No. 2, § 11] in consequence of lengthening the vowel to compensate for the omitted sounds." *Smart.*

Shan′ty [Shantee, 203.]
Shăp′a-ble, 164, 183.
Shape, 23.
Shaped (*shāpt*), 165; Note C, p. 34.
Shăp′ing, 183.
Shape′less, 185.
Shape′li-ness, 186.
Shape′ly, 93.
Shard [Sherd, 203.]
Share (*shêr*), 14, 46, 49.
Shared (*shêrd*).
Share′hōld-er (*shêr′-*), 206.
Shar′er (*shêr′rur*), 48, 49, N.
Shar′ing (*shêr′ring*).
Shark, 11, 49, 135.
Sharked (*sharkt*), 165.
Shark′er.
Shark′ing.
Sharp, 11, 49, 135.
Sharped (*sharpt*), 41.
Sharp′-edged (*-ejd*).
Sharp′en (*sharp′n*), 149
Sharp′ened (*-nd*).
Sharp′en-ing (*sharp′n-*).
Sharp′er, 77, 169.
Sharp′ing.
Sharp′-point-ed, 66, N.; 206, Exc. 1.
Sharp′-sīght-ed (*-sīt-*).
Shas′ter, *or* Shas′tra [Sastra, 203.]
Shat′ter, 66.
Shat′tered, 150, 165.
Shat′ter-ing.
Shat′ter-y, 93, 169.
Shave, 23.
Shaved (*shāvd*), 165.
Shave′ling.
Shāv′en (*shāv′n*).
Shāv′er.
Shāv′ing, 183.
Shāv′ing-brush.
Shawl, 17, 46.
Shawm [Shalm, 203.]
She, 13, 46.
Shēaf (13, 35) [pl. Shēaves (*shēvz*), 193.]
Shēaf′y.
Shēal′ings (*-ingz*), *n. pl.*
Shēar (13, 49), *v.* to cut or clip the wool or hair from. [*See* Sheer, *and* Shire, 160.]
Shēared (*shērd*), 165.
Shēar′er.
Shēar′-hulk [Sheer-hulk, 203.]
Shēar′ing.
Shēars (*shērz*), *n. pl.* large scissors; — an apparatus used for raising heavy weights. [Sheers (in the last sense), 203. — *See* Note under *Sheers*.]
Shēar′-steel.
Shēar′wâ-ter [Sheerwater, 203.]
Shēat′-fish.
Shēath (13, 37) [pl. Shēaths, 38, 140, 189.]
Shēath′bill.
Shēathe (Note D, p. 37) [Sheath, 203.]

☞ "Less properly spelled *Sheath*." *Smart.*

Shēathed, 165.
Shēath′er.
Shēath′ing.
Shēath′y, 37, 169.
Shēave (*shēv*), 13.
Shech′i-nah (*shek′-*), *or* She-chi′nah (*-ki′-*) [so Wr.; *shek′i-nä*, Wk. Sm.; *she-ki′na*, Wb. Gd. 155] [Shekinah, 203.]
Shed, 15.
Shed′der, 176.
Shed′ding.
Sheel′ing [Shieling, 203.]
Sheen, 13.
Sheen′y, 93.
Sheep, *n. sing. & pl.*
Sheep′cot.
Sheep′fōld.
Sheep′hook.
Sheep′ish.
Sheep′-pen, 66, N.
Sheep′run.
Sheep's′-eȳe, 221.
Sheep′-shēar-ing.
Sheep′skin.
Sheer (13, 67), *a.* pure and unmixed; — very thin, as muslin: — *v.* to turn aside from a direct course: — *n.* the longitudinal curve of a ship's deck or sides. [*See* Shear, *and* Shire, 160.]
Sheered, 165.
Sheer′-hulk [She hulk, 203.]
Sheer′ing.
Sheers (*shērz*), *n. pl.* two spars raised vertically, and crossing each other near the top, — used for raising great weights. [Shears, 203.]

☞ *Sheers* is the more common orthography.

Sheer′-strake.
Sheer′wâ-ter [Shear water, 203.]
Sheet, 13, 41, 46.
Sheet′-an-chor (*-ang-kur*).
Sheet′ing.
Shēik (13, 169, N.) [Scheik, 203.]
Shēil′ing (170) [Sheeling, 203.]
Shek′el (*shek′l*) (149, 167) [*not* she′kel, *nor* she′kl, 153.]
Shek′i-nah, *or* She-ki′nah [Shechinah, 203.]
Shel′drake (171) [Shield-drake, 203.]

Shel′duck.
Shelf [pl. Shelves (*shelvz*), 193.]
Shelf′y, 93.
Shell, 15, 172.
Shel′lac (66), *or* Shell′-lac, 66, N.; 203.
Shelled, 165.
Shell′-fish.
Shell′ing
Shell′work (*-wurk*).
Shell′y, 93.
Shel′ter, 77.
Shel′tered, 150, 165.
Shel′ter-ing.
Shel′ter-less, 106.
Shel′tĭe, 99.
Shelve, 15.
Shelved, 165.
Shelves (*shelvz*), *n. pl.* [*See* Shelf.]
Shelv′ing, 183.
Shelv′y.
She-mit′ic (109) [Se-mitic, 203.]
Shem′īte, 152.
Shem′i-tism (*-tizm*).
She′ōl (Heb.) [so Wr.; *she′ōl*, Gd. 155.]
Shep′herd (*shep′hurd*) (139, 171) [so Sm.; *shep′urd*, Wk. Wr. Gd. 155.]
Shep′herd-ess.
Shep′herd's-purse (*-hurdz-*).
Sher′bet [so Sm. Wb. Gd.; *shur-bet′*, Wk.; *sher′bet*, or *shur-bet′*, Wr. 155.]
[Sherd, 203. — *See* Shard.]
Shĕr′if (Ar.) [Shereef (*shĕr′ēf*, Gd.), Sheriffe (*shĕr-rēf′*, Sm.), Scherif, 203.]
Shĕr′iff, 171.
Shĕr′ry, 48, 66.
[Shew (*sho*), 203. — *See* Show.]
[Shewed (*shōd*), 203. — *See* Showed.]
[Shewing (*sho′ing*), 203. — *See* Showing.]
[Shewn (*shōn*), 203. — *See* Shown.]
Shi′ah (*she′-*) [so Wr. Gd.; *shī′a*, Sm. 155] [Schiah, 203.]
Shib′bo-leth, 170.
[Shie, 203 — *See* Shy.]
Shīed, 186.
Shiēld, 13.
[Shield-drake, 203. — *See* Sheldrake.]
Shiēld′ed.
Shiēld′ing.
Shiēld′-shāped (*-shāpt*), 206, Exc. 5.
Shift, 16.
Shift′ed.
Shift′er.
Shift′ing.
Shift′less, 142.
Shift′y.
Shi′īte (*she′-*), 156.
Shil-la′lah, *or* Shil-la′ly [Shillelah, Shillely, 203.]
Shil′ling, 66, 141.
Shil′lĭ-shal-lĭ [Shilly-shally, 203.]

☞ This is a corrupt reduplication of *shall I?*

Shi′loh, 139.
[Shily, 203.— *See* Shyly.]
Shim′mer, 104, 170.
Shim′mered, 165.
Shim′mer-ing.
Shin, 16, 43, 46.
Shine, 25, 163.
Shined (*shīnd*), 183.
Shīn′er.
[Shiness, 203. — *See* Shyness.]
Shin′gle (*shing′gl*).
Shin′gled (*shing′gld*).
Shin′gling (*shing′-*).
Shin′gly (*shing′-*).
Shīn′ing, 183.
Shin′ney, 169.
Shin′ty.
Shīn′y, 93, 228, N.
Ship, 16, 46.
Ship′bōard.
Ship′-buĭld-ing.
Ship′-car-pen-ter.
Ship′-mȧs-ter.
Ship′mate, 206.
Ship′ment.
Ship′-mon-ey (*-mun-*).
Ship′-ōwn-er.
Shipped (*shipt*), Note C, p. 34.
Ship′per.
Ship′ping, 176.
Ship′-shape.
Ship's-hus′band (*-huz′-*) (213) [so Gd.; *ships′-huz-band*, Wr. 155.]
Ship′wreck (*-rek*).
Ship′wrecked (*-rekt*), 171
Ship′wreck-ing.
Ship′yard, 206.
Shire (*shēr*) [so Wk. Sm.; *shīr*, or *shēr*, Gd.; *shēr*, or *shīr*, Wr. 155], *n.* a county. [*See* Shear, *and* Sheer 160.]

☞ Walker says that the pronunciation *shēr* is an irregularity "so fixed as to give the regular sound [*shīr*] a pedantic stiffness." He also observes that "this word, when unaccented at the end of words, as Nottingham*shire*, Wilt*shire*, &c., is always pronounced with the *i* like *ee*." But, according to Webster, "it is pronounced, in compound words, *shir*, as in Hamp*shire*, Berk*shire*."

Shire′-town (*shēr′town*)
Shirk, 21, N.; 49.
Shirked (*shirkt*), 165.
Shirk′ing.
Shirr, 171.
Shirred (*shird*).
Shirt, 21, N.; 135.
Shirt′ed.
Shirt′ing.
[Shist, 203. — *See* Schist.]
Shit′tah, *or* Shit′tim, 203
Shive, 25.
Shiv′er, 104.
Shiv′ered (*-urd*).
Shiv′er-ing.
Shiv′er-y, 228.
[Shoad, 203. — *See* Shode.]
Shōal, 24.
Shōal′y, 169.
[Shoar, 203. — *See* Shore.]
[Shoat, 203. — *See* Shote.]
Shock [Shough, (in the sense of *a shaggy dog*), 203.]
Shocked (*shokt*), 41.
Shock′-hĕad-ed.
Shock′ing.
Shod, 18.
Shod′dy, 170.
Shode [Shoad, 203.]
Shōd′ing.
Shoe (*shoo*) (19) [pl. Shoes (*shooz*), 189.]
Shoe′ing (*shoo′-*), 183.
Shoe′māk-er (*shoo′-*).
Shoe′māk-ing (*shoo′-*).
Sho′er (*shoo′-*) (67) [*See* Sure, 148.]
Shoe′string (*shoo′-*).
Shŏne, *or* Shōne [so Wr.; *shŏn*, Wk. Sm.; *shōn*, Wb. Gd. 155.]

☞ "This word is frequently pronounced so as to rhyme with *tone*; but the short sound of it is by far the most usual among those who may be styled polite speakers." *Walker.*

Shŏŏk (20) [*See* Book.]
Shoon, 19.

☞ This is the old plural of *shoe*, still used in the North of England.

Shoot, 19, 41, 46.
Shoot'ing.
Shoot'ing-star.
Shop, 18.
Shop'keep-er, 206.
Shop'lift-er.
Shop'man, 196.
Shop'ping, 176.
Shop'wom-an (*-wŏŏm-*).
Shore [S h o a r (in the sense of *a prop*, or *support*), 203.]
Shored, 165.
Shore'less, 185.
Shōr'ing, 183.
[S h o r l, 203. — *See* Schorl.]
Shōrn, 24, 127.
Short, 17, 49, 135.
Short'com-ing (*-kum-*).
Short'en (*short'n*), 149.
Short'ened (*-nd*), 171.
Short'en-er (*short'n-*).
Short'en-ing (*short'n-*).
Short'hand, 216.
Short'-līved, 165.
Short'-sight-ed (*-sīt-*).
Shot, 18.
Shote [S h o a t, 203.]

☞ This word is variously written in England. In the United States, according to Worcester, "the common form is *shote*."

[S h o t f r e e, 203. — *See* Scotfree.]
Shot'ten (*shot'n*), 149.
Shough (*shok*) (161), *n.* a shaggy dog. [S h o c k, 203.]
Shough (*shoo*) (161), an exclamation used in driving away fowls, &c.
Should (*shŏŏd*), 162.
Shōul'der.
Shōul'der-blade.
Shōul'dered, 150, 165.
Shōul'der-ing.
Shōul'der-knot (*-not*).
Shout, 28.
Shout'ed.
Shout'er.
Shout'ing.
Shove (*shuv*), 22, 163.
Shoved (*shuvd*).
Shov'el (*shuv'l*), 149, 167.
Shov'el-ful (*shuv'l-fŏŏl*), 180, 197.
Shov'elled (*shuv'ld*) [S h o v e l e d, Wb. Gd. 203. — *See* 177, and Note E, p. 70.]
Shov'el-ler (*shuv'l-*) (177) [S h o v e l e r, Wb. Gd. 203.]
Shov'el-ling (*shuv'l-*) (177) [S h o v e l i n g, Wb. Gd. 203.]
Show [S h e w, 203.]

☞ The form *shew*, according to Smart, is "almost obsolete." But Worcester remarks: "*Shew* maintains its ground by perhaps the prevailing usage of the best authors." *Worcester.*

Shōw'brĕad [S h e w - b r e a d (*sho'bred*), 203.]
Shōw'-case.
Shōwed (*shōd*). [S h e w e d, 203.]
Shōw'er (161), *n.* one who shows.
Shower (*shour*) (28, 67, 161), *n.* a fall of rain of short duration: — *v.* to wet with a shower, or with falling water.
Showered (*shourd*).
Shower'ing (*shour'-*).
Shower'y (*shour'-*).
Shōw'i-ly, 186.
Shōw'i-ness.
Shōw'ing (24) [S h e w - i n g, 203.]
Shōw'man, 196.
Shōwn (24) [S h e w n, 203.]
Shōw'y, 169.
Shrank, 10, 46, 48.

☞ "Nearly obsolete." *Webster.*

Shrap'nel.
Shred, 15, 48, 141.
Shred'ding, 176.
Shred'dy, 66, 170.
Shrew (*shroo*), 128.
Shrewd (*shrood*) [*not* srood, 141, 153.]
Shrew'ish (*shroo'ish*), 46, 48.
Shrew'-mole (*shroo'-*).
Shrew'-mouse(*shroo'-*), 195.
Shriēk (13, 169, N.) [*not* srēk, 141, 153.]
Shrieked (*shrēkt*), 165; Note C, p. 34.
Shriēk'ing.
Shriēv'al.
Shriēv'al-ty.
Shrike, 25, 163.
Shrill, 16, 46, 141, 172.
Shrill'ing.
Shrill'ness.
Shrill'y, 93.
Shrimp, 48, 141.
Shrimp'ing.
Shrine (25, 46) [*not* srīn, 141, 153.]
Shrink (*shringk*), 54, 141.
Shrink'age, 70, 169.
Shrink'ing.
Shrive, 25, 46.
Shrived, 165, 183.
Shriv'el (*shriv'l*), 149.
Shriv'elled (*-ld*). [S h r i v e l e d, Wb. Gd. 203. — *See* 177, and Note E, p. 70.]
Shriv'el-ling (*shriv'l-*) (177) [S h r i v e l i n g, Wb. Gd. 203.]
Shriv'en (*shriv'n*), 149.
Shrīv'ing, 183.
Shroff, 18, 173.
Shroff'age, 228.
Shroud, 28, 46, 141.
Shroud'ed.
Shroud'ing.
Shrove-Tues'day (*-tūz'dy*).
Shrub (22, 46) [*not* srub, 141, 153.]
Shrub'ber-y, 176.
Shrub'bi-ness.
Shrub'by.
Shrug, 22, 46, 156.
Shrugged (*shrugd*), 165, 176.
Shrug'ging(*-ghing*), 138.
Shrunk (*shrungk*), 54.
Shrunk'en (*shrungk'n*).
Shud'der, 104, 170.
Shud'dered (*-durd*).
Shud'der-ing.
Shuf'fle, 164, 170.
Shuf'fled (*shuf'ld*).
Shuf'fler, 77.
Shuf'fling.
[S h u m a c, 203. — *See* Sumach.]

Shun, 22, 43, 46.
Shunned (*shund*), 176.
Shun′ning.
Shunt, 22.
Shut, 22.
Shut′ter, 176.
Shut′ting.
Shut′tle, 164, 170.
Shut′tle-cock (*-tl-*).
Shwan′păn (Chinese) (*shwon′-*) [so Sm.; *shwawn′păn*, Wr. 155.]
Shy (25, 46) [Shie (as a verb, meaning *to sheer, or start aside*), 203.]
Shy′ing, 186.
Shy′ly [Shily, 203.]
Shy′ness (186) [Shiness, 203.]
Si (*se*) (13, 39), the syllabic name of the seventh tone of any major diatonic scale. [*See* Sea, *and* See, 160.]
Sī-al′a-gŏgue, 87, 168, 171.
Sī-am-ese′ (*-ēz′*) [so Wr.; *sī-am-ēs′*, Gd. 155.]
Sī-be′ri-an, 49, N.; 151.
Sī-be′rīte, *or* Sib′er-īte [*sī-be′rīt*, or *sib′e-rīt*, Wr.; *sib′ur-īt*, Wb. Gd. 155.]
Sib′i-lance.
Sib′i-lant, 72, 169.
Sib-i-la′tion, 112.
Sib′yl (171) [*not* si′bil, 127, 153.]
Sib′yl-līne, *or* Sib′yl-līne [*sib′il-līn*, Wr. Gd.; *sib′il-līn*, Sm. 155.]
Sib′yl-list, 170.
Sic′ca (Hindostanee).
Sic′ca-tīve, 84.
Sic′ci-ty (*sik′si-ty*).
Sice (*sīz*) (40, 156), *n.* the number six at dice. [*See* Size, 160.]
Sī-cil′i-an (169, 170) [so Sm. Wr.; *sī-sil′yan*, Wb. Gd. 155.]
Sick, 16, 52, 181.
Sick′-bed.
Sick′en (*sik′n*), 149.
Sick′ened (*-nd*).
Sick′en-ing (*sik′n-*).
Sick′ish.
Sic′kle (*sik′l*), 164.
Sic′kled (*sik′ld*).
Sic′kle-wort (*-kl-wurt*).
Sick′lied (*-līd*), 99.
Sick′li-ness, 186.
Sick′ly, 93.
Sick′ness.
Side (25), *n.* the broad or long part of any thing, as distinguished from the end; — one part placed in contradistinction or opposition to another: — *v.* to espouse a cause: — *a.* lateral. [*See* Sighed, 160.]
Side′bōard.
Sīd′ed.
Side′ling.
Side′long.
Sid′er-al [so Wk. Wr. Wb. Gd.; *sī′der-al*, Sm. 155.]
Sid-er-a′tion, 169.
Si-de′re-al (49, N.; 151) [so Sm. Wb. Gd.; *sī-de′ri-al*, Wr. 155.]
Sid′er-īte (152) [so Wr. Wb. Gd.; *sī-dēr′īt*, Sm. 155.]
Sid-er-o-cal′cīte [so Wr. Wb. Gd.; *sī-dē-ro-kal′sīt*, Sm. 155.]
Sid-er-o-graph′ic.
Sid-er-o-graph′ic-al.
Sid-er-og′ra-phist.
Sid-er-og′ra-phy, 108.
Sid′er-o-man-cy.
Sid-er-om′e-lane.
Sid′er-o-scope [so Wb. Gd.; *sī-de′ro-skōp*, Sm. (49, N.); *sid′e-ro-skōp*, or *sī-de′ro-skōp*, Wr. 155.]
Side′-sad-dle, 164.
Side′-ta-ble (*-bl*).
Side′walk (*-wawk*).
Side′wise (*-wīz*).
Sīd′ing, 183.
Sī′dle, 164.
Sī′dled (*sī′dld*).
Sī′dling.
Siēge, 13, 169, N.
Sī′e-nīte [Siennite, Syenite, 203] [*See* Note under *Syenite*.]
Sī-e-nit′ic.
Sī-ĕr′ra (Sp.).
Sī-es′ta (Sp.).
Sieve (*siv*), 16, 171.
Sift, 16.
Sift′ed.
Sift′er, 77.
Sift′ing.
Sigh (*sī*), 25, 162.

☞ According to Walker, this word is often pronounced *sith* in London; and Worcester states that this pronunciation "is more or less common in some parts of the United States." In Old English, the word was sometimes written *sithe*, or *sythe*.

Sighed (*sīd*), *v.* did sigh. [*See* Side, 160.]
Sigh′er (*sī′-*) (67, 162), *n.* one who sighs. [*See* Sire, 148.]
Sigh′ing (*sī′-*).
Sight (*sīt*) (25, 162), *n.* view; — the sense of seeing; — a spectacle: *v.* to bring in sight; — to take sight. [*See* Cite, *and* Site, 160.]
Sight′ed (*sīt′-*).
Sight′ing (*sīt′-*).
Sight′less (*sīt′-*).
Sight′li-ness (*sīt′-*).
Sight′ly (*sīt′-*).
Sight′-see-ing (*sīt′-*).
Sight′-se-er (*sīt′-*).
Sig′il (*sij′-*).
Sig-il-la′ri-a (L.) (*sij-*).
Sig′moid.
Sig-moid′al.
Sign (*sīn*) (25, 162), *n.* a token; — a symbol; — a portent; — a twelfth part of the ecliptic or zodiac: — *v.* to subscribe. [*See* Sine, 160.]
Sig′nal, 72, 230.
Sig′nal-ize, 202.
Sig′nal-ized, 165.
Sig′nal-īz-ing.
Sig′nal-ly.
Sig′na-tūre, 26, 90.
Signed (*sīnd*), 162.
Sign′er (*sīn′-*).
Sig′net, *n.* a seal, particularly a private seal of a sovereign. [*See* Cygnet, 169.]
Sig-nif′i-cance.
Sig-nif′i-can-cy.
Sig-nif′i-cant, 169.
Sig-nif′i-cate.
Sig-ni-fī-ca′tion.
Sig-nif′i-ca-tīve.
Sig-nif′i-cāt-or, 169.
Sig-nif′i-ca-to-ry, 72, 86.
Sig-ni-fi-ca′vit (L.).
Sig′ni-fīed, 186.
Sig′ni-fȳ, 94.
Sig′ni-fȳ-ing.
Sīgn′ing (*sīn′-*), 162.

[Signior, 203. — *See* Seignior.]
Sīgn′-man′u-al (*sīn′*-), 205.
Sīgn′post (*sīn′*-).
Si′lence.
Si′lenced (-*lenst*).
Si′lenç-ing.
Si′lent, 127.
Sī-le′si-a (-*shĭ*-) [so Sm. Wr.; *sī-le′sha*, Gd. 155.]
Sī-le′sian (-*shan*), 169.
Si′lex, 76.
Sil′hou-ette (*sil′oo-et*) [so Sm. Gd.; *sil-oo-et′*, Wr. 155.]
Sil′i-ca, 233.
Sil′i-cate.
Sil′i-căt-ed.
Sil′ice (-*is*), 169, 170.
Sī-liç′ic.
Sī-liç-i-cal-ca′re-oŭs (116) [so Wb. Gd.; *sil-ĭ-sĭ-kal-ka′re-us*, Wr. 155.]
Si-liç′i-calce [so Gd.; *sil-i-sĭ-kals′*, Wr. 155.]
Sil-i-cif′er-oŭs.
Sī-liç-i-fĭ-ca′tion.
Sī-liç′i-fīed.
Sī-liç′i-fȳ, 151.
Sī-liç′i-fȳ-ing.
Sī-lĭ′cioŭs (-*shus*), *a.* pertaining to silica, or partaking of its nature and qualities. [*See* Cilicious, 160] [Siliceous, 203.]

☞ The Latin adjective from which this word is derived, is spelled *silicius*, or *siliceus*. Worcester says: "The orthography of *silicious* is that which is found in nearly or quite all the common English dictionaries; but that of *siliceous* is more common in works of science."

Sil′i-cīte, 152.
Sī-liç′it-ed.
Sī-lĭ′ci-um (-*lish′ĭ*-) [so Wr.: *sĭ-lis′i-um*, coll. *sĭ-lish″um*, Sm. (*See* § 26); *sĭ-lish′um*, Gd. 155.]
Sī-liç′i-u-ret-ted.
Sil′i-cle, 164.
Sil′i-co-flu′ate, 224.
Sil-i-co-flu-ŏr′ic.
Sil′i-co-flu′or-īde.
Sil′i-cŏn, 78.
Sil′i-cule.
Sī-lic′u-lose [so Sm. Gd.; *sĭ-lik-u-lōs′*, Wr. 155.]
Sil′ique (-*ik*) (171) [so Sm. Wb. Gd.; *sĭ-lēk′*, Wr. 155.]
Sil-i-quel′la.
Sil′i-qui-form.

☞ This word is an exception to the general rule (§ 108), by which words ending in *i-form* are accented on the antepenult.

Sil′i-quose [so Wb. Gd.; *sil-i-kwōs′*, Sm. Wr. 155.]
Silk, 16.
Silk′en (*silk′n*), 149.
Silk′i-ness, 186.
Silk′weed.
Silk′worm (-*wurm*)
Silk′y, 93.
Sill, 16, 172.
Sil′la-bub [Syllabub, 203.]
Sil′li-ness, 186.
Sil′lon.
Sil′ly, 93, 170.
Silt, 16.
Silt′ed.
Silt′ing.
Silt′y, 228.
Sī-lu′ri-an (49, N.) [*sĭ-lūr′ri-an*, Sm.; *sĭ-lu′ri-an*, Wb. Gd. Wr. 155.]
Sī-lu′ri-dan.
Sil′van [Sylvan, 203.]
Sil′van-īte, 152.
Sil′ver, 77.
Sil′vered (-*vurd*).
Sil′ver-grāy, *a.*
Sil′ver-ing.
Sil′ver-ize, 202.
Sil′ver-ized.
Sil′ver-īz-ing.
Sil′ver-smith.
Sil′ver-stick, 221.
Sil′ver-tree, 206, Exc. 4.
Sil′ver-y, 93.
Sī-mar′ [Cymar, Simarre, 203.]
Sim-a-ru′ba (-*roo′*-).
Sim′i-lar (78, 169), *a.* like; resembling. [*See* Similor, 148.]
Sim-i-lăr′i-ty.
Sim′i-lar-ly, 106.
Sim′i-lē, 163.
Sĭ-mil′i-ter (L.).
Sī-mil′i-tude, 151.
Sim′i-lor (-*lawr*) (88), *n.* an alloy of copper and zinc. [*See* Similar, 148.]
Sim′i-oŭs, 169.
[Simitar, 203. — *See* Scimitar, *and* Cimeter.]
Sim′mer, 104, 170.
Sim′mered (-*murd*).
Sim′mer-ing.
Sī-mo′ni-ac.
Sim-o-ni′ac-al, 108.
Sī-mo′ni-an [so Sm. Wr.; *sĭ-mo′ni-an*, Wb. Gd. 155.]
Sim′on-ist.
Sim′o-ny [*not* si′mo-ny, 153.] [203.
Sī-moom′, *or* Sī-moon′, Si′moŭs.
Sim′per, 77.
Sim′pered (-*purd*).
Sim′per-er, 77.
Sim′per-ing.
Sim′ple, 164.
Sim′ple-mīnd′ed.
Sim′ple-ton (-*pl*-).
Sim-pliç′i-mane.
Sim-pliç′i-ty.
Sim-pli-fĭ-ca′tion.
Sim′pli-fīed.
Sim′pli-fȳ.
Sim′pli-fȳ-ing.
Sim′pling.
Sim′plist.
Sim-plist′ic.
Sim′ply, 93.
Sim′u-late, 89.
Sim′u-lāt-ed, 183.
Sim′u-lāt-ing.
Sim-u-la′tion, 112.
Sī-mul-ta′ne-oŭs, *or* Sim-ul-ta′ne-oŭs (169) [*sī-mul-ta′ne-us*, Wk. Wr. Wb. Gd.; *sim-ul-ta′ne-us*, Sm. 155.]
Sin, 16, 39, 43.
Sī-na-it′ic, 72.
Sin′a-pīne, 152.
Sin′a-pis-īne (152) [Sinapisin, 203.]
Sin′a-pism (-*pizm*), 133.
Sīnce (16, 39) [*not* sens, 127, 153.]
Sin-cere′, 171.
Sin-cere′ly.
Sin-cĕr′i-ty, 108, 169.
Sin-cip′i-tal.
Sin′ci-put, 171.
Sin′don.
Sine (25), *n.* a line drawn from one extremity of an arc perpendicularly to the

diameter drawn through the other extremity. [*See* Sign, 160.]
Si'ne-cūr-al.
Si'ne-cure [*not* sin'e-kūr, 153.]
Si'ne-cūr-ism (*-izm*).
Si'ne-cūr-ist.
Si'nē di'ē (L.).
Si'nē quā non (L.).
Sin'ew (*-ū*) (171) [*not* sin'oo, 153.]
Sin'ew-y (*-ū-*).
Sin'ful (*-fōōl*), 180.
Sin'ful-ly (*-fōōl-*).
Sin'ful-ness (*-fōōl-*).
Sing, 16, 54.
Singe (*sinj*) (16, 45), Note D, p. 37.
Singed (*sinjd*).
Singe'ing (*sinj'-*), 183.
Sin'ger (*-jur*) (161), *n.* one who singes.
Sing'er (161), *n.* one who sings.
Sin-gha-lese' (*sing-ga-lēz'*) (171) [Cingalese, 203.]
Sing'ing, 141.
Sing'ing-bōōk, 206, Exc. 4, 215.
Sing'ing-school (*-skool*)
Sin'gle (*sing'gl*), 54, 164.
Sin'gled (*sing'gld*).
Sin'gle-hand'ed (*sing'-gl-*), 205.
Sin'gle-heärt'ed (*sing'-gl-*).
Sin'gle-ness (*sing'gl-*).
Sin'gling (*sing'-*).
Sin'gly (*sing'-*), 93.
Sing'song.
Sin'gu-lar (*sing'-*), 108, 169.
Sin-gu-lăr'i-ty (*sing-*).
Sin'gu-lar-ly (*sing'-*).
Sin-gul'toŭs, 100.
Sin'ic-al, *a.* pertaining to a sine, or to sines. [*See* Cynical, 160.]
Sin'is-ter (meaning *dishonest, insidious*), Sĭ-nis'ter (meaning *left*) [so Sm.; *sin'is-tur*, Wk. Wb. Gd.; *sin'is-tur*, or *sĭ-nis'tur*, Wr. 155.]
Sĭ-nis'tral [*sin'is-tral*, Wr. Gd. 155. — *See* Sinister, *and* Sinistrous], *a.* on the left hand.
Sin-is-tral'i-ty.
Sin-is-tror'sal.
Sin'is-trorse.
Sin'is-trous (meaning *unfair, insidious*), *or* Sĭ-nis'trous (meaning *on the left hand*) [so Sm.; *sin'is-trus*, Wk. Wb. Gd.; *sin'is-trus*, or *sĭ-nis'trus*, Wr. 155.]
Sink (*singk*) (16, 54), *v.* to fall through any medium, as water; — to depress; — to dig; — to reduce: — *n.* a drain. [*See* Cinque, 160.]
Sink'ing.
Sink'ing-fund, 215.
Sinned (*sind*), 165, 176.
Sin'ner, 170.
Sin'ning.
Sin'o-pite.
Sin'o-ple, 164.
Sin'ter.
Sin'u-ate, 89.
Sin'u-āt-ed.
Sin'u-āt-ing.
Sin-u-a'tion, 112.
Sin'u-ose [so Gd.; *sin-u-ōse'*, Wr. 155.]
Sin-u-os'i-ty, 169.
Sin'u-oŭs.
Si'nus (L.) [L. pl. *Si'nus*; Eng. pl. Si'nus-es (*-ez*), 198.]
Sip, 16, 30, 39.
Si'phoid.
Si'phon (35, 86) [Syphon, 203.]
Si'phon-al.
Sī-phon'ic (109) [so Gd.; *sī-phon'ik*, Wr. 155.]
Sī-phon-ap'ter-an.
Sī-phon'i-fer.
Sī-phon-if'er-oŭs.
Sī-phon-o-bran'chi-ate (*-brang'kĭ-*).
Sī-phon'o-phore.
Sī-phon'os-tome [so Sm.; *sī-fo-nos'tōm*, Wr. 155.]
Sī-pho-rhin'ian (*-rin'-yan*), 112.
Si'phun-cle (*-fung-kl*) [Sipuncle, 203.]
Sī-phun'cu-lar (*-fung'-*) [*sī-fun'ku-lar*, Gd.; *sī-fung'ku-lur*, Wr. 155.]
Sī-phun'cu-lāt-ed (*-fung'-*).
Sipped (*sipt*), 165, 176.
Sip'ping, 176.
Si'pun-cle (*-pung'kl*) (164) [so Sm.; *sip'-ung-kl*, Wr. 155.]
Sī quis (L.).
Sir, 21, N.
Sire (25), *n.* a father; — a title used in addressing kings; — the male parent of a beast. [*See* Sigher, 148.]
Si'ren (49, N.) [Syren, 203.]
Sī-rene' (121) [so Sm.; *sī-rēn'*, Wr. Gd. 155.]
Sī-ri'a-sis (L.).
Sĭr'i-us, 171.
Sir'loin (21, N.; 104) [Surloin, 203.]

☞ This word, derived undoubtedly from the Fr. *surlonge* (*sur*, upon, or above, and *longe*, loin), is not found, according to Worcester, "in any English Dictionary previous to that of Johnson with the orthography of *sirloin*, the earlier orthography being *surloin*." To account for the form *sirloin*, a story is related that King James I., of England, in a fit of good humor, knighted a loin of beef, crying out, "Bring hither that *sirloin*, sirrah, for 'tis worthy of a more honorable post, being, as I may say, not *sur*-loin, but *sir*-loin, the noblest joint of all." *See* Surloin.

[Sirname, 203. — *See* Surname.]

☞ "*Sir'*name, which some interpret *sire'*name, or one's father's name, is really *sur'*name, that is, additional name." *Smart.*

Sĭ-roc'co [pl. Sĭ-roc'cōs (*kōz*), 192.]
Sir'rah (*sĕr'ra*, or *sĭr'-ra*) [*sĕr'ra*, Sm.; *sĭr'-ra*, Wb. Gd.; *săr'ra*, Wk.; *săr'ra*, or *sĭr'-ra*, Wr. 155.]

☞ Walker says of *sar'-ra*, that it is "a corruption of the first magnitude."

Sĭr'up (*sĭr'rup*, coll. *sŭr'rup*) (48) [so Sm.; *sĭr'rup*, Wb. Gd.; *sŭr'rup*, Wk.; *sĭr'-rup*, or *sŭr'rup*, Wr. 155.] [Syrup, 203.]

☞ "It is now perhaps more commonly written *syrup*." *Worcester.*

Sĭr'up-y (*sir'rup-y*, coll. *sŭr'rup-y*).
Sis'kin.
Sis'ki-wit.
Sis-soo' [so Gd.; *sis'-soo*, Wr. 155.]
Sis'ter.
Sis'ter-hōōd.
Sis'ter-in-lâw.
Sis'ter-ly.
Sis'trum (L.).
Sis-y-phe'an, 110.
Sit (16), *v.* to occupy a seat. [*See* Cit, 160.]
Site (163), *n.* situation. [*See* Cite, *and* Sight, 160.]
[Sithe, 203. — *See* Scythe.]
Sī-tol'o-gy.
Sit'ter, 176.
Sit'ting.
Sit'u-ate, 89.
Sit'u-āt-ed.
Sit-u-a'tion.
Si'va (*se'-*).
Six, 16, 39, N.
Six'fōld, 217.
Six'pence, 217.
Six'pen-ny.
Six'teen. [*See* Note under *Eighteen.*]
Six'teenth.
Sixth, 16, 39, N.; 37.
Six'ti-eth.
Six'ty, 93.
Sīz'a-ble, 164, 183.
Si'zar (169) [Sizer, 203.]
Size (25), *n.* magnitude; — a kind of glue: — *v.* to cover with glutinous matter. [*See* Sice, 160.]
Sized, 165.
[Sizel, 203. — *See* Scissel.]
[Sizer, 203. — *See* Sizar.]
Sīz'ing, 183.
Siz'zle, 164.
Siz'zled (*-zld*).
Siz'zling.
[Skald, 203. — *See* Scald.]
Skate, 23.
Skāt'ed, 183.
Skāt'er.
Skāt'ing.
Skeet, 13.
Skein (*skān*), 23.
Skel'e-tal.
Skel-e-tol'o-gy, 108.
Skel'e-ton, 170.
Skep'tic [Sceptic, 203.] [*See* Note under *Sceptic.*]
Sketch, 15, 44, 171.
Sketch'-bōōk, 206, Exc. 4.
Sketched (*sketcht*), 165; Note C, p. 34.
Sketch'er.
Sketch'i-ly.
Sketch'ing.
Sketch'y.
Skew'-back (*sku'-*).
Skew'er (*-sku'-*).
Skid, 16.
Skiff, 16, 173.
Skil'ful (*-fōōl*) (178) [Skillful, Wb. Gd. 203. — *See* Note E, p. 70.]
Skil'ful-ly (*-fōōl-*) [Skillfully, Wb. Gd. 203.]
Skil'ful-ness [Skillfulness, Wb. Gd. 203.]
Skill, 16, 172.
Skilled (*skild*), 165.
Skil'less, 178.
Skil'let, 66, 170.
Skil'ling.
Skim, 16.
Skimmed, 150, 176.
Skim'mer.
Skim'ming.
Skim'ming-ton [Skimmerton, 203.]
Skin, 16.
Skin'flint, 206.
Skin'ful (*-fōōl*), 197.
Skink (*skingk*), 54.
Skinned (*skind*), 176.
Skin'ner.
Skin'ning.
Skin'ni-ness, 186.
Skin'ny, 93, 176.
Skip, 16.
Skipped (*skipt*), 165.
Skip'per.
Skip'ping, 176.
Skir'mish, 21, N.
Skir'mished (*-misht*).
Skir'mish-er.
Skir'mish-ing.
Skir'ret (*skĭr'ret*, or *skĕr'ret*) [*skĭr'ret*, Wr. Wb. Gd.; *skĕr'-ret*, Wk. Sm. 155.]
Skirt, 21, N.
Skirt'ed.
Skirt'ing.
Skirt'ing-bōard.
Skit'tish.
Skit'tles (*skit'lz*), *n. pl.*
Ski'ver.
Skol'e-cīte, *or* Skōl'e-zīte [Scolecite, 203.]

☞ *Scolecite* is, etymologically, the proper spelling." *Goodrich.*

Skŏr'o-dīte [so Wr. Wb. Gd.; *skōr'o-dīt*, Sm. 155] [Scorodite, 203.]

☞ "*Scorodite* is, etymologically, the proper spelling." *Goodrich.*

[Skow, 203. — *See* Scow.]
Skreed.
Skulk [Sculk, 203.]

☞ Smart prefers *sculk* to *skulk*, but the latter is the prevailing orthography.

Skulked (*skulkt*), 165.
Skulk'ing.
Skull (172), *n.* the cranium. [*See* Scull, 160.]
Skull'cap.
Skunk (*skungk*), 54.
Skȳ (25, 39, 52) [so Wr. Wb. Gd.; *skēī*, Wk.; *sk'ī*, Sm. (*See* § 26), 155]
Sky'-blue.
Sky'ey, 98, 169.
Sky'ish.
Sky'lark.
Sky'lark-ing.
Sky'light (*-līt*).
Sky'sāil.
Slab, 10.
Slăb'ber (*slăb'bur*, coll. *slob'bur*) [so Sm.; *slab'bur*, Wr. Wb. Gd.; *slab'bur*, or *slob'bur*, Wk. 155] [Slobber, 203.]

☞ "The second sound of this word [*slob'bur*] is by much the more usual one; but as it is in direct opposition to the orthography, it ought to be discountenanced, and the *a* restored to its true sound." *Walker.*

Slab'bered (*slab'burd*; coll. *slob'burd*).
Slab'ber-er (*slab'bur-ur*; coll. *slob'bur-ur*).
Slab'ber-ing (*slab'bur-ing*; coll. *slob'bur-ing*).
Slab'bi-ness, 186.
Slab'by, 93, 170.

Slack, 10, 181.
Slacked (*slăkt*), 165; Note C, p. 34.
Slack'en (*slak'n*), 149.
Slack'ened (*-nd*), 171.
Slack'en-ing (*slak'n-*).
Slack'ing.
Slag, 10.
Slag'gy (*-ghy̆*), 138.
Slaie [S l e y, 203.]
Slāin, 23.
Slake, 23.
Slaked (*slākt*), 165.
Slāk'ing, 183.
Slam, 10.
Slammed (*slamd*), 165.
Slam'ming, 176.
Slăn'der [so Wk. Sm. Wb. Gd.; *slân'dur*, Wr. 155.]
Slăn'dered (*-durd*).
Slăn'der-er.
Slăn'der-ing.
Slăn'der-oŭs.
Slang, 10, 54.
Slan'goŭs (*slang'-*).
Slȧnt, 12, 131.
Slȧnt'ed.
Slȧnt'ing.
Slȧnt'wise (*-wīz*).
Slap, 10.
Slapped (*slapt*), 165.
Slap'ping, 176.
Slash, 10, 46.
Slashed (*slasht*), 41.
Slash'ing.
Slat (10) [S l o a t (in Eng.), 203.]
Slatch, 10, 44.
Slate, 23, 163.
Slāt'ed, 183.
Slāt'er.
Slāt'ing.
Slat'tern, 135, 170.
Slat'tern-li-ness, 171.
Slat'tern-ly.
Slāt'y, 183.
Slâugh'ter (*slaw'-*), 162.
Slâugh'tered (*slaw'-*), 150, 165.
Slâugh'ter-er (*slaw'-*).
Slâugh'ter-ing (*slaw'-*).
Slâugh'ter-oŭs (*slaw'-*).
Slave (23, 161), *n.* a bondman.
Slăve (11, 161), *n.* a native, or an inhabitant, of Slavonia.
Slaved (*slāvd*), 165.
Slave'hōld-er.
Slave'hōld-ing, 206, Exc. 5.
Slave'-ōwn-er.
Slāv'er (147, 161), *n.* a vessel in the slave-trade; — one who trades in slaves.
Slăv'er (147, 161), *n.* spittle running from the mouth: — *v.* to emit spittle; — to drivel.
Slăv'ered (*-urd*), 150.
Slăv'er-er, 77.
Slăv'er-ing.
Slāv'er-y, 183.
Slave'-ship.
Slave'-trade.
Slāv'ing, 183.
Slāv'ish.
Slāv'ism (*-izm*), 183.
Sla-von'ic (109) [S c l a - v o n i c, 203.]
Slaw, 17.
Slāy (23), *v.* to put to death. [*See* Sleigh, *and* Sley, 160.]
Slāy'er.
Slāy'ing.
Slēave, *n.* raw, untwisted silk. [*See* Sleeve, 160.]
Slēa'zi-ness.
Slēa'zy, 169.
Sled, 15.
Sled'ded, 176.
Sled'ding.
Sledge, 15, 45.
Sledge'-ham-mer.
Sleek, 13.
Sleeked (*slēkt*), 41.
Sleek'ing.
Sleep, 13.
Sleep'er.
Sleep'i-ly.
Sleep'i-ness, 186.
Sleep'ing.
Sleep'-walk-er (*wawk-*).
Sleep'-walk-ing (*-wawk-*).
Sleep'y, 93.
Sleet, 13.
Sleet'i-ness.
Sleet'y.
Sleeve (13), *n.* that part of a garment which covers the arm. [*See* Sleave, 160.]
Sleid (*slād*), 23, 171
Sleid'ed (*slād'-*).
Sleid'ing (*slād'-*).
Sleigh (*slā*) (162), *n.* a vehicle with runners for travelling on snow. [*See* Slay, *and* Sley, 160.]
Sleigh'-bell (*slā'-*).
Sleigh'ing (*slā'-*).
Sleight (*slīt*) (25, 162), *n.* a sly artifice; — adroitness. [*See* Slight, 160.]
Slen'der.
Slept (41) [*not* slep, 153.]
Slew (*slu*), *v.* did slay. [*See* Slue, 160.]
[S l e w, *v.* to turn, 203. — *See* Slue.]
Sley (*slā*), *n.* a weaver's reed: — *v.* to separate into threads, as weavers. [*See* Slay, *and* Sleigh, 160.] [S l a i e, 203.]
Slice, 25, 39.
Sliced (*slīst*), 183.
Slīç'er.
Slīç'ing, 183.
Slid, 16.
Slid'den (*slid'n*), 149.
Slide, 25, 163.
Slīd'er.
Slīd'ing.
Slīght (*slīt*) (162), *a.* of little account, importance, or strength: — *n.* contemptuous disregard: — *v.* to neglect intentionally. [*See* Sleight, 160.]
Slīght'ed (*slīt'-*).
Slīght'er (*slīt'-*).
Slīght'ing (*slīt'-*).
Slīght'ly (*slīt'-*).
[S l i l y, 186, 203. — *See* Slyly.]
Slim, 16.
Slime, 25.
Slīm'i-ness, 186.
Slīm'y, 93, 169.
[S l i n e s s, 186, 203. — *See* Slyness.]
Sling, 16, 54.
Sling'er, 77.
Sling'ing.
Slink (*slingk*), 54.
Slink'ing.
Slip, 16.
Slip'knot (*-not*), 162, 206.
Slipped (*slipt*), 165; Note C, p. 34.
Slip'per, 170.
Slip'per-i-ness, 171.
Slip'per-y.
Slip'ping, 176.
Slip'shod.
Slip'slop.
Slit, 16.

Slit'ted, 176.
Slit'ter, 228, N.
Slit'ting.
Sli'ver, *or* Sliv'er [so Wr.; *sli'vur*, Wk. Sm.; *sliv'ur*, Wb. Gd. 155.]
Slōam, 24.
Slōat [Slat (in the U. S.), 203.]
Slob'ber [Slabber, 203.]
Slob'bered (*-burd*) [Slabbered, 203.]
Slob'ber er [Slabberer, 203.]
Slob'ber-ing [Slabbering, 203.]
Slōe (24, 39, 50), *n.* the blackthorn. [*See* Slow, 160.]
Slo'gan.
Sloke, 24, 163.
Sloop, 19.
Slop, 18.
Slop'bōwl.
Slope, 24.
Sloped (*slōpt*), 41.
Slōp'ing, 183.
Slopped (*slŏpt*), 176.
Slop'pi-ness, 186.
Slop'ping.
Slop'py, 170.
Slōp'y, 183.
Slosh, 18.
Slosh'y, 93.
Slot, 18.
Slŏth [so Wk. Sm. Wr.; *slŏth*, or *slōth*, Gd. 155.]

☞ The best modern orthoëpists, with the exception of Goodrich, do not sanction the pronunciation *slŏth*.

Slōth'ful (*-fŏŏl*), 180.
Slōth'ful-ly (*-fŏŏl-*).
Slōth'ful-ness (*-fŏŏl-*).
Slouch, 28.
Slouched (*sloucht*).
Slouch'ing.
Slough (*slou*) (28, 161, 162), *n.* a deep, miry pit.
Slough (*sluf*) (22, 35, 161, 171), *n.* the cast skin of a serpent;—the dead part which separates from the living in mortification; a scab:—*v.* to separate from the sound flesh, as a scab.
Sloughed (*sluft*).
Slough'ing (*sluf'-*).
Slough'y (*slou'-*), 28, 161.
Slough'y (*sluf'-*), 161.
Slov'en (*sluv'en*), 149.
Slov'en-li-ness (*sluv'-en-*), 186.
Slov'en-ly.
Slōw (24), *a.* not swift or fast. [*See* Sloe, 160.]
Slōw'-worm (*-wurm*), 206, Exc. 1.
Slub, 22.
Sludge, 22, 45.
Slūe (26), *v.* to turn around, as a mast or boom lying on its side, by moving the ends while the centre remains stationary, or nearly so. [*See* Slew, 160] [Slew, 203.]
Slūed, 165.
Slug, 22.
Slug'gard, 72, 170.
Slug'gish (*-ghish*), 138.
Slūice, 26.
Slu'ing, 183.
Slum, 22.
Slum'ber, 104.
Slum'bered, 150, 165.
Slum'ber-er, 77.
Slum'ber-ing.
Slum'ber-oŭs, 100.
Slump, 22.
Slumped (*slumpt*), 165.
Slump'ing.
Slung, 22.
Slunk (*slungk*), 54.
Slur, 21, 49.
Slurred (*slurd*), 135.
Slur'ring, 49, N.
Slush, 22.
Slut, 22.
Slut'tish, 176.
Sly, 25, 39, 50.
Sly'ly (186) [Slily, 203]
Sly'ness (186) [Sliness, 203.]
Smack, 10, 181.
Smacked (*smakt*), 165; Note C, p. 34.
Smack'ing.
Smâll, 17, 172.
Smâll'age, 70, 169.
Smâll'clothes (*klothz*) [*See* Clothes.]
Small-pox' [so Wk. Wb. Gd.; *smawl'-poks*, Sm.; *smawl-poks'*, or *smawl'poks*, Wr. 155.]
Smâlt, 17.
Smâlt'īne, 82, 152.
Smăr'agd, 170.
Sma-rag'dīne, 82.
Sma-rag'dīte, 152.
Smart, 11, 49, 135.
Smart'ed.
Smart'ing.
Smart'-mon-ey (*-mun-*).
Smash, 10, 46.
Smashed (*smasht*), 165; Note C, p. 34.
Smash'er.
Smash'ing.
Smat'ter, 170.
Smat'tered, 150.
Smat'ter-er.
Smat'ter-ing.
Smēar, 13, 49.
Smēared, 165.
Smēar'ing, 49, N.
Smec'tīte, 83.
Smell, 15, 172.
Smelled (*smeld*), 165.
Smell'er, 228.
Smell'ing.
Smell'ing-bot'tle, 164, 205, 215.
Smelt, 15.
Smelt'ed.
Smelt'er.
Smelt'er-y.
Smelt'ing.
Smew (*smu*), 26.
Smift, 16.
Smil'a-cīne (82, 152) [Smilacin, 203.]
Smi'lax (L.).
Smile, 25.
Smiled, 165.
Smīl'ing, 183.
Smirch, 21, N. [171.
Smirched (*smircht*), 165, 171.
Smirch'ing.
Smirk, 21, N.; 49, 135.
Smirk'ing.
Smit (16), *v.* did smite. [*See* Smitt, 160.]
Smite, 25.
Smith, 16, 37.
Smith'er-y, 233, Exc.
Smith'ing.
Smith'y, 93, 140.
Smit'ing.
Smitt (16), *n.* fine clayey ore or ochre, used for marking sheep. [*See* Smit, 160.]
Smit'ten (*smit'n*), 149.
Smoke, 24, 130.
Smoked (*smōkt*), 165; Note C, p. 34.
Smōk'er.
Smōk'i-ly.
Smōk'i-ness.
Smōk'ing, 183.

Smōk′y, 130.
Smŏlt′, 18.
Smooth, *a.* & *v.* 171.
Smoothed, 165.
Smooth′er.
Smooth′-faced (*-fāst*), 206, Exc. 5.
Smooth′ing.
Smooth′ly.
Smooth′ness.
Smor-zan′do (It.), 154.
Smor-za′to (It.), 154.
Smote, 24, 163.
Smoth′er (*smuth′-*), 22, 104.
Smoth′ered (*smuth′-urd*), 150.
Smoth′er-ing (*smuth′-*).
Smōul′der (24). [Smolder, 203.]
Smōul′dered (*-durd*).
Smōul′der-ing.
Smug, 22.
Smug′gle, 164, 170.
Smug′gled (*smug′ld*), 165, 171, 183.
Smug′gler.
Smug′gling.
Smut, 22.
Smutch (Note D, p. 37) [*not* smooch, 127, 153.]
Smutched (*smucht*), 165, 171.
Smutch′ing.
Smut′ted, 176.
Smut′ti-ly, 186.
Smut′ti-ness.
Smut′ting.
Smut′ty.
Snack, 10, 52, 181.
Snaf′fle, 164.
Snaf′fled (*snaf′ld*), 170.
Snaf′fling, 183.
Snag, 10.
Snāil, 23, 64.
Snāil′-like, 206, Exc. 1.
Snake, 23.
Snake′root, 206.
Snake′stōne, 130.
Snake′wood.
Snāk′ish, 183.
Snāk′y, 93.
Snap, 10.
Snap′-drag-on.
Snap′hance.
Snapped (*snapt*) (Note C, p. 34) [Snapt, 203]
Snap′per, 176.
Snap′ping.
Snap′pish.
[Snapt, 203.—*See* Snapped.]
Snare (*snêr*), 14.
Snared (*snêrd*).
Snar′er (*snêr′rur*), 49, N.; 77.
Snar′ing (*snêr′-*).
Snarl, 11, 49, 135.
Snarled, 165.
Snarl′er, 49.
Snarl′ing.
Snar′y (*snêr′-*).
Snatch, 10, 44.
Snatched (*snacht*), 165.
Snatch′ing.
Snăth (10, 37), *n.* the handle of a scythe.

☞ So spelled in the United States. In England this word is variously written *snathe, sneathe, snead, sneed,* &c.

Snēak, 13.
Snēaked (*snēkt*).
Snēak′er.
Snēak′ing.
Sneer, 13.
Sneered, 165.
Sneer′er, 49, N.; 77.
Sneer′ing.
Sneeze, 13.
Sneezed, 165.
Sneez′ing, 183.
Snick′er [Snigger, 203.]
Snick′ered (*-urd*).
Snick′er-ing.
Sniff, 173.
Sniffed (*snift*), 171.
Snift′ing-valve, 215.
[Snigger, 203.—*See* Snicker.]
Snip, 16.
Snipe, 25, 163.
Snipped (*snipt*), 165.
Snip′per-snap′per.
Snip′ping, 176.
Snip′snap.
Sniv′el (*-sniv′l*), 149.
Sniv′elled (*sniv′ld*) [Sniveled, Wb. Gd. 203.—*See* 177, and Note E, p. 70.]
Sniv′el-ler (*sniv′l*) (177) [Sniveler, Wb. Gd. 303.]
Sniv′el-ling (*sniv′l*)(177) [Sniveling, Wb. Gd. 203.]
Snob, 18.
Snob′bish, 176.
Snob′bism (*-bizm*), 136.
Snood, 19.
Snooze, 19.
Snore, 24.
Snored, 150, 165.
Snōr′er, 49.
Snōr′ing, 183.
Snort, 17, 49, 135.
Snort′ed.
Snort′ing, 49.
Snout, 28.
Snōw, 24.
Snōw′ball.
Snōw′bĕr-ry.
Snōw′bird.
Snōw′blind, 206, Exc. 5.
Snōw′drift.
Snōw′drop.
Snōwed (*snōd*).
Snōw′flake.
Snōw′ing.
Snōw′shoe (*-shoo*).
Snōw′storm.
Snōw′-whīte, 206, Exc. 1.
Snōw′y, 93, 169.
Snub, 22.
Snubbed (*snubd*), 165.
Snub′bing, 176.
Snuff, 22, 173.
Snuff′box.
Snuffed (*snuft*), 165; Note C, p. 34.
Snuff′er, 77, 228.
Snuff′ing.
Snuf′fle, 164, 170.
Snuf′fled (*snuf′ld*).
Snuf′fles (*snuf′lz*), *n. pl.*
Snuf′fling.
Snuff′-tāk-ing.
Snuff′y.
Snug, 22.
Snugged (*snugd*), 171.
Snug′ger-y (*-gur-*).
Snug′ging (*-ghing*), 138.
Snug′gle, 164.
Snug′gled (*snug′ld*), 165.
Snug′gling.
So (24, 39), *adv.* thus;—in like manner;—therefore:—*conj.* provided that. [*See* Sew, *and* Sow, 160.]
Sōak (24), *v.* to steep. [*See* Soke, 160.]
Sōak′age, 70, 169.
Soaked (*sōkt*), 41.
Sōak′er.
Sōak′ing.
Sōap, 24, 130.
Sōap′-bub-ble, 164.
Sōap′stōne.
Sōap′wort (*-wurt*).
Sōar (24, 49, 135), *v.* to fly aloft. [*See* Sore, 160.]
Sōared (165), *v.* did soar. [*See* Sword, 160.]

Sōar'ing, 49, N.
Sob, 18.
Sobbed (*sobd*), 176.
Sob'bing.
So'ber.
So'bered (*-burd*).
So'ber-ing.
Sob-o-lif'er-oŭs.
So-bri'e-ty, 169.
Sobriquet (Fr.) (*sob-re-kā'*), 154.
Soc, 18.
Soc'age (70, 169) [Soc-cage, Sm. 203.]
So-ci-a-bil'i-ty (*-shĭ-*), 108, 169.
So'ci-a-ble (*so'shĭ-a-bl*) [so Wk. Sm. Wr.; *so'-sha-bl*, Wb. Gd. 155.]
So'ci-a-bly (*-shĭ-*).
So'cial (*-shal*), 169.
So'cial-ism (*-shal-*).
So'cial-ist (*-shal-*).
So-cial-ist'ic (*-shal-*).
So-ci-al'i-ty (*-shĭ-*) [so Sm. Wr.; *so-shal'i-ty*, Gd. 155.]
So'cial-ize (*-shal-*), 202.
So'cial-ized (*-shal-*).
So'cial-īz-ing (*-shal-*).
So'cial-ly (*-shal-*).
So-ci'e-ty, 169.
So-cin'i-an, 169, 170.
So-cin'i-an-ism (*-izm*).
So-ci-o-log'ic (*-loj'-*).
So-ci-o-log'ic-al (*-loj'-*).
So-ci-ol'o-gy (*-shĭ-*).
Sock, 18, 181.
Sock'et, 76.
Soc'le (*sok'l*), *or* So'cle (*so'kl*) [so Wr.; *sok'l*, Sm.; *so'kl*, Wk. Wb. Gd. 155] [Sokle, 203.]
Soc'man, 196.
Soc'o-trīne, 82, 152.
So-crat'ic, 109.
So-crat'ic-al, 108.
Soc'ra-tism (*-tizm*), 133, 136.
Soc'ra-tist.
Sod, 18, 39, 42.
So'da, 72
So'da-līte, 152.
So-dal'i-ty, 108, 169.
Sod'ded, 176.
Sod'den (*sod'n*), 149, 170.
Sod'ding.
Sod'dy, 93.
[Soder, 203.—*See* Solder.]
So'di-um, 169.
So-ev'er.
So'fa, 72, 189.
Sof'fit, 170.
So'fĭ (191) [Sophi, Sufi, 203.]
So'fism (*-fizm*), 136.
Soft, 18, N.
Soft'en (*sof'n*), 162.
Soft'ened (*sof'nd*), 171.
Soft'en-er (*sof'n-ur*) [Softner (*sof'nur*), 203.]
Soft'en-ing (*sof'n-*).
Soft'ness, 41, 142.
Sog'gy (*-ghy*), 138.
So-ho'.
Soi-disant (Fr.) (*swä-de-zŏng'*) [so Sm.; *swä-de-zang'*, Gd. Wr. 154, 155.]
Soil, 27, 39, 50.
Soiled, 165.
Soil'ing, 171.
Soirée (Fr.) (*swä-rā'*) (154) [so Gd.; *swaw'-rā*, Sm.; *swaw-rā'*, Wr. 155.]
So'journ (*-jurn*), *n.*

☞ "The poets often accent the last syllable." *Smart.*

So'journ (*-jurn*), *v.* [so Wk. Sm. Wr.; *so'-jurn*, or *so-jurn'*, Gd. 155.]
So'journed (*-jurnd*).
So'journ-er (*-jurn-*).
So'journ-ing (*-jurn-*).
Soke (24), *n.* a territorial division in England. [*See* Soak, 160.]
Sŏl (L.), *n.* the sun.
Sol (*sōl*, or *sŏl*) [*sōl*, Wb. Gd.; *sŏl*, Wr. 155], *n.* the note G of the musical scale;—the fifth tone of any major diatonic scale.
Sol'ace, 170.
Sol'aced (*-āst*).
Sol'a-cing.
Sol-a-na'ceoŭs (*-shus*) [so Wr. Gd.; *so-la-na'shus*, Sm. 155.]
So-lan'der, 77, 169.
So'land-goose, *or* So'-lan-goose, 203.
Sol'a-nīne, 152.
So-lä'no (It.).
Sol'a-noid.
So'lar, 74.
So-lar-ĭ-za'tion.
So'lar-ize, 202.
So'lar-ized.
So'lar-īz-ing.
Sōld, *v.* did sell. [*See* Soled, 160.]
Sŏl'dan (72) [so Sm. Wr. Wb. Gd.; *sōl'dan*, Wk. 155.]
Sol'der (*saw'dur*) [so Sm.; *sol'dur*, Wk. Wb. Gd.; *sol'dur*, or *saw'dur*, Wr. 155] [Soder, 205.]

☞ Sheridan pronounces this word *sod'ur*, and this mode, though sanctioned by no other orthoëpist, is a common, if not the prevailing, pronunciation in the United States.

Sol'dered (*saw'durd*).
Sol'der-er (*saw'dur-er*).
Sōl'dier (*sōl'jur*), 45, N.
Sōl'dier-ing (*sōl'jur-*).
Sōl'dier-ly (*sōl'jur-*).
Sōl'dier-y (*sōl'jur-*).
Sole (24), *a.* alone; single:—*n.* the under surface of the foot;—the flat bottom part of any thing;—a kind of flat fish:—*v.* to furnish with a sole, or with soles. [*See* Soul, 160.]
Sol'e-cism (*-sizm*), 133.
Sol'e-cist.
Sol-e-cist'ic.
Sol-e-cist'ic-al.
Soled (165), *v.* did sole. [*See* Sold, 160.]
Sole'ly, 66, N.
Solemn (*sol'em*), 127, 162.
Sol'em-ness, 171.
So-lem'ni-ty.
Sol-em-nĭ-za'tion, 112.
Sol'em-nize, 202.
Sol'em-nized.
Sol'em-nīz-ing.
Sol'emn-ly (*-em-*), 162.
So'len.
So-len-a'cean (*-shan*).
So-len-a'ceoŭs (*-shus*) [so Sm.; *sol-e-na'shus*, Wr. 155.]
So'len-īte, 152.
So'len-oid.
Sŏl'fä, *or* Sŏl'fä [*sōl-fä'*, Wb. Gd.; *sŏl'fä*, Sm., *sŏl-fa'*, Wr. 155.]
Sol-fa-nä'ri-a.
Sol-fa-tä'ra (It.).
Sol-fa-tär'īte
Solfeggiare (It.) (*sol-fed-jä'rā*).

Solfeggio (It.) (*sol-fed'-jo*).
So-liç'it, 235.
So-liç'it-ant.
So-liç-it-a'tion.
So-liç'it-ed.
So-liç'it-ing.
So-liç'it-or, 70, 169.
So-liç'it-or-gen'er-al, 205.
So-liç'it-oŭs, 228.
So-liç'i-tude, 108.
Sol'id, 170.
Sol-i-där'i-ty.
So-lĭd-i-fĭ-ca'tion, 112.
So-lid'i-fīed.
So-lid'i-fȳ, 94.
So-lid'i-fȳ-ing.
Sol'id-ism (*-izm*), 136.
Sol'id-ist, 106.
So-lid'i-ty, 132.
Sol-id-un'gu-lar (*-ung'-*), 54, 108.
Sol-id-un'gu-loŭs (*-ung'-*).
Sol-i-fid'i-an [so Wr. Wb. Gd.; *so-lĭ-fid'-yan*, Sm. 155.]
Sol-i-fid'i-an-ism (*-izm*).
So-lil'o-quize, 170.
So-lil'o-quīzed, 165.
So-lil'o-quīz-ing.
So-lil'o-quy, 171.
Sol'i-ped [Solipede, 203.]
So-lip'e-doŭs, 105.
Sol-i-taire' (*-têr'*), 171.
Sol-i-ta'ri-an.
Sol'i-ta-ri-ly, 171.
Sol'i-ta-ry, 72.
Sol'i-tude, 26, 108, 169.
So-liv'a-gant.
So-liv'a-goŭs.
Sol-mi-za'tion.
So'lo [pl. So'lōs (*-lōz*), 192.]
Sol'o-mon's-sēal (*-munz-*), 213.
Sol'stĭce, 169.
Sol-stĭ'tial (*-stish'al*).
Sol-u-bil'i-ty.
Sol'u-ble, 89, 164.
So'lus (L.).
So-lute', 26, 127.
So-lu'tion.
Sol'u-tĭve, 84.
Solv-a-bil'i-ty.
Solv'a-ble, 164, 169.
Solve (*solv*), 18.
Solved, 165.
Solv'en-cy, 169.
Solv'end.
Solv'ent, 76.
Solv'er, 77.
Solv'ing.
So-ma-tol'o-gy.
So-ma-tot'o-my, 108.
Sŏm'bre, *or* Sŏm'bre (164) [*sŏm'bur*, Sm. Wr.; *sŏm'bur*, Gd. 155] [Somber preferred by Wb. and Gd. 203.]
Sŏm'broŭs, *or* Sŏm'-broŭs [*sŏm'brus*, Sm.; *sŏm'brus*, Gd.; *sŏm'-brus*, or *sŏm'brus*, Wr. 155.]
Some (*sum*) (22, 163), *a.* more or less as to quantity or number; — one; an. [*See* Sum, 160.]
Some'bod-y (*sum'-*).
Some'how (*sum'hou*).
Som'er-sâult (*sum'-*) [Summersault, 203.]
Som'er-set (*sum'-*) [Summerset, 203.]
Som'er-vill-īte (*sum'-*), 152.
Some'thing (*sum'-*).
Some'times (*sum'tīmz*).
Some'what (*sum'whot*), 171.
Some'whêre (*sum'-*) [*not* sum'whêrz, 153.]
Som'mīte, 83, 152.
Som-nam-bu-la'tion.
Som-nam-bu-la'tor, 169.
Som-nam'bu-lic, 106.
Som-nam'bu-lism (*-lizm*), 133, 136.
Som-nam'bu-list.
Som-nam-bu-list'ic.
Som'ni-al, 169.
Som-nif'er-oŭs.
Som-nif'ic, 109.
Som-nil'o-quence.
Som-nil'o-quism (*-kwizm*).
Som-nil'o-quist.
Som-nil'o-quoŭs, 171.
Som-nil'o-quy (*-kwy̆*).
Som'no-lence.
Som'no-len-cy.
Som'no-lent.
Som-nop'a-thy.
Son (*sun*) (22, 39, 43), *n.* a male child. [*See* Sun, 160.]
So'nance, 72.
So-nä'ta (It.) [so Sm. Wr. Wb. Gd.; *so-nä'-ta*, Wk. 155.]
Song, 18, N.
Song'ster, 77.
Song'stress.
So-nif'er-oŭs.
Son'-in-lâw, 197.
Son'net, 171.
Son-net-eer', 122, 171.
Son'net-ing.
[Sonnite, 203. — *See* Sunnite.]
So-nom'e-ter, 108.
Son-o-rif'ic.
So-no'roŭs, 49, N.; 108.
Son'ship (*sun'-*).
Soo'der [Sudder, 203.]
Soo'dra [so Wr. Gd.; *sŏŏd'ra*, Sm. 155] [Sudra, 203.]
Soo'fee.
Soo'fee-ism (*-izm*).
Soon, 19, 127.

☞ "The quality of the [vowel] sound in *soon* should be the same as in *moon*, though the vowel is hardly prolonged so much in *quantity*, except in dignified utterance." *Goodrich.*

Soo'nee [Sunnie, 203.]
[Sooshong, 203. — *See* Souchong.]
Sŏŏt [so Sm. Wb. Gd.; *soot*, Wk.; *soot*, or *sŏŏt*, Wr. 155.]

☞ Smart says that, "though this word, probably from being confounded with those which are spelled with *u*, long exhibited the anomaly of being pronounced *sut*, it is now, by the best speakers, classed with" *book*, *foot*, *good*, &c.

Sŏŏt'ed.
Sooth, 19, 37.
Soothe (38) [Sooth, 203.]
Soothed, 165.
Sooth'ing, 183.
Sooth'sāy-er (37) [*not* sooth'sā-ur, 153.]
Sooth'sāy-ing.
Sŏŏt'i-ness. [*See* Soot.]
Sŏŏt'y. [*See* Soot.]
Sop, 18.
Soph, 18, 35.
So'phĭ (191) [Sofi, 203.]
Soph'ism (*-izm*), 136.
Soph'ist.
Soph'ist-er.
So-phist'ic, 109.
So-phist'ic-al, 108.
So-phist'ic-al-ly.

So-phist′ic-ate.
So-phist′ic-āt-ed.
So-phist′ic-āt-ing.
So-phist-ic-a′tion.
So-phist′ic-āt-or.
Soph′ist-ry, 93.
Soph′o-more, 86.
Soph-o-mŏr′ic.
Soph-o-mŏr′ic-al.
Sop-o-rif′er-oŭs.
Sop-o-rif′ic [*not* sō-por-if′ik, 153.]
Sop′o-rose [so Gd.; *sop-o-rōs′*, Wr. 155.]
Sop′o-roŭs [so Sm.Wr.; *so′po-rus*, Wb. Gd. 155.]
Sopped (*sopt*), 165; Note C, p. 34.
Sop′ping, 176.
So-prä′nist.
So-prä′no (It.) [pl. *So-prä′ni* (*-ne*), 198.]
Sorb, 17, 49.
Sor-be-fa′cient (*-shent*), 112, 171.
Sor-bon′ic-al.
Sor′bon-ist.
Sor-bonne′ (Fr.) (*sor-bon′*).
Sor′cer-er, 77.
Sor′cer-ess.
Sor′cer-oŭs, 100.
Sor′cer-y, 93.
Sor′did.
Sor′dīne (82, 152) [so Sm. Wb. Gd.; *sor-dēn′*, Wk. Wr. 155.]
Sore (24, 67), *n.* a tender and painful place on the body, resulting from inflammation or excoriation;—a hawk of the first year;—a buck of the third year:—*a.* tender and painful. [*See* Sewer, Sower, 148; *and* Soar, 160.]
Sŏr′el (66, 160, 170) [so Sm. Wr. Wb. Gd.; *so′ril*, Wk. 155], *n.* a buck of the third year;—a reddish color. [S o r r e l (in the latter sense), 203.]

☞ In the latter sense, the more common orthography is *sorrel*.

Sor′ghum (*-gum*), 53.
Sor′go.
So-ri′tēs (L.) (*-tēz*).
Sorn, 17, 49, 135.
Sorned (*sornd*).
Sorn′er.
Sorn′ing.
So-rŏr′i-cīde [so Wk. Wr. Wb. Gd.; *so-rŏr′-i-sīd*, Sm. 155.]
Sŏr′rel (66, 160, 170), *n.* a plant so named from its acid taste:—*a.* of a yellowish red or brown. [S o r e l, 203.—*See* Note under *Sorel*.]
Sŏr′ri-ly, 186.
Sŏr′rōw, 48, 66, 101.
Sŏr′rōwed, 165.
Sŏr′rōw-ful (*-fōōl*), 180.
Sŏr′rōw-ful-ly (*-fōōl*).
Sŏr′rōw-ing.
Sŏr′ry, 170.
Sort (17, 49, 135), *n.* kind; species:—*v.* to assort, to arrange. [*See* Sought, 148.]
Sort′a-ble, 164, 169.
Sort′ed.
Sort′er.
Sor′tiē [so Sm. Gd.; *sor-te′*, Wr. 155.]
Sor′ti-lēge, 156, 171.
Sor-ti-le′gioŭs (*-jus*), 169.
Sort′ing.
Sos-te-nu′to (It.) (*-tā-noo′-*).
Sot, 18.
So-te-ri-ol′o-gy, 108.
Soth′ic.
Sot′tish, 176.
Sot′to vo′ce (It.) (*vo′-chā*).
Sou (Fr.) (*soo*) [pl. Sous (*soo*;—so Sm. Gd.; *sooz*, Wr. 155), 198.]
Sou-brette′ (Fr.) (*soo-*).
Sou-chong′ (*soo-shong′*) [so Sm. Wr. Wb. Gd.; *sow-chong′*, Wk. 155] [S o o s h o n g, 203.]
Sough (*suf*) (22, 35, 39) [so Wr. Wb. Gd.; *sŏf*, Sm. 155.]
Sought (*sawt*) (162), *v.* did seek. [*See* Sort, 148.]
Sōul (24), *n.* the immaterial and immortal part of man. [*See* Sole, 160.]
Sōul′less, 66, N.
Sōul′-stir-ring.
Sound, 28.
Sound′bōard.
Sound′ed.
Sound′ing.
Sound′ing-bōard, 215.
Sound′ly, 93.
Soup (*soop*), 19.
Soupe maigre (Fr.) (*soop ma′gr*).
Sour, 28, 39, 49.
Sōurce [*not* soors, 153.]
[S o u r c r o u t, 203.—*See* Sauerkraut.]
Soured, 28, 165.
Sour′ing, 49, N.
Sour′ish.
[S o u r k r o u t, 203.—*See* Sauerkraut.]
Sous (*soo*) [so Sm. Wr. Gd.; *sous*, or *soo*, Wk. 155.]

☞ "Considered as a French word, it is the plural of *sou*." *Worcester.*—"In plain, vulgar English, we say *a sowse*." *Smart.*

Souse, 28, 39.
Soused (*sowst*), 165.
Sous′ing.
Sous′lik (*soos′-*).
South, 28, 37.
South-cott′i-an.
South-ēast′.
South-ēast′er-ly.
South-ēast′ern.
Soŭth′er-li-ness.
Soŭth′er-ly [so Wr. Wb. Gd.; *suth′er-ly*, or *sowth′er-ly*, Wk.; *sowth′ur-ly*, coll. *suth′ur-ly*, Sm. 155.]
Soŭth′ern [so Wr. Wb. Gd.; *sowth′urn*, or *suth′urn*, Wk.; *sowth′urn*, coll. *suth′-urn*, Sm. 155.]
Soŭth′ern-er.
South′ing, 28, 37, 140.
South′mōst.
Soŭth′ron, 86.
South′ward (coll. *suth′-urd*) [so Sm.; *sowth′-ward*, or *suth′urd*, Wk. Wr.; *suth′urd*, Wb. Gd. 155.]
South-west′.

☞ "Colloquially contracted to *sow-west*."—*Smart.*

South-west′er.
Souve′nir (Fr.) (*soov′-nēr*) [so Sm. Wr.; *soov′e-nēr*, Gd. 155.]
Sov′er-eign (*suv′ur-in*, or *sŏv′ur-in*) (162) [so

Wr.; *suv'ur-in*, Wk. Gd.; *sŏv'er-in*, Sm. 155] [Sovran, 203.]

☞ "There was a time when *sovereign* and *comrade* were always pronounced with the *o* as short *u*; but since the former word has been the name of a current coin, the regular sound of the *o* has been getting into use, and bids fair to be completely established."*Smart.*

Sov'er-eign-ty (*suv'ur-in-ty*, or *sov'ur-in-ty*).
Sow (28, 161), *n.* a female pig or swine; — a large trough for melted metal; — a mass of metal.
Sōw (24, 161), *v.* to propagate by seed; — to scatter seed into; — to disseminate. [*See* So, *and* Sew, 160.]
Sow'brĕad, 28, 206.
Sōwed, *v.* did sow. [*See* Sewed, 160.]
Sow'ens (*sou'enz*), *n. pl.* [Sowans, Sowins, 203.]
Sōw'er, *n.* one who sows. [*See* Sore, 148; *and* Sewer (one who sews), 160.]
Sōw'ing.
Sōwn (*sōn*), *part.* from *Sōw.* [*See* Sewn, 160.]
Soy, 27, 39.
Spa (*spä*, or *spaw*) [*spä*, Wb. Gd.; *spaw*, Sm. 155.]
Space, 23.
Spaced (*spāst*), 165; Note C, p. 34.
Spāç'ing.
Spa'cioŭs (*-shus*), 169.
Spa'cioŭs-ly (*-shus*).
Spa'cioŭs-ness (*-shus-*).
Spad'dle, 164.
Spade, 23.
Spade'ful (*-fŏŏl*), 180, 197.
Spa-dĭ'ceoŭs (*-dish'us*), 171.
Spa-dĭlle', 121.
Spa'dix.
Spa-droon', 121.
Spa-gy̆r'ic (*-jĭr'-*) [Spagiric, Sm. 203.]
Spa-gy̆r'ic-al.
Spah'ee [Spahi, 203.]
Spake, 23.
Spâll, 17.
Spâlt, 17.
Span, 10.
Span'drel, 76.
Span'gle (*spang'gl*), 54, 164.
Span'gled (*spang'gld*).
Span'gler (*spang'-*).
Span'gling (*spang'-*).
Span'iard (*-yard*), 51.
Span'iel (*-yel*) (142) [*not* span'el, 153.]
Span'ish, 170.
Spank (*spangk*), 10, 54.
Spanked (*spangkt*), 165; Note C, p. 34.
Spank'er (*spangk'-*).
Spank'ing.
Spanned (*spand*), 165.
Span'ner, 176.
Span'-new, 66, N.; 206, Exc. 1.
Span'ning.
Spar, 11, 49, 135.
Spare (*spêr*), 14.
Spared (*spêrd*).
Spar'er (*spêr'-*).
Spare'rib (*spêr'rib*), 48, 49, 171.
Spar-ge-fac'tion, 169.
Spar'ger, 45, 77.
Spar'ing (*spêr'ring*), 183.
Spark, 11, 49, 135.
Spark'le (*spark'l*), 164.
Spark'led (*spark'ld*).
Spark'ling.
Spa'roid [so Wr. Gd.; *spăr'oid*, Sm. 155.]
Sparred (*spard*), 165.
Spär'ring, 11, 48, 49.
Spăr'rōw, 49, N.; 66, 101.
Spăr'rōw-hawk.
Spăr'ry.
Sparse, 11; Note D, p. 37.
Sparse'ly, 185.
Spar'tan.
Spar'ter-iē.
Spasm (*spazm*), 133.
Spas-mod'ic (*spaz-*).
Spas-mod'ic-al (*spaz-*).
Spas-mol'o-gy (*spaz-*), 108.
Spas'tic.
Spas-tiç'i-ty.
Spat, 10.
Spa-tha'ceoŭs (*-shus*), 112.
Spa'thal.
Spathed (165) [*spātht*, Gd. 155.]
Spathe, 23, 38; Note D, p. 37.
Spath'ic, 143.
Spath'i-form, 108.
Spath'ose.
Spath'oŭs.
Spath'u-late, 108.
Spat'ter, 66, 104.
Spat'ter-dash-es (*ez*), *n. pl.*
Spat'tered, 150.
Spat'ter-ing.
Spat'u-la, 108.
Spat'u-late.
Spav'in, 149.
Spawn, 17.
Spawned, 165.
Spawn'ing.
Spāy, 23.
Spāyed (*spād*).
Spāy'ing.
Spēak, 13.
Spēak'a-ble, 164.
Spēak'er.
Spēak'ing, 141.
Spēak'ing-trum-pet.
Spēak'ing-tube, 206, Exc. 4; 215.
Spēar, 13, 49.
Spēared, 165.
Spēar'ing.
Spēar'mint.
Spēar'wort (*-wurt*).
Spĕ'cial (*spesh'al*).
Spĕ'cial-ist (*spesh'al-*).
Spĕ-ci-al'i-ty (*spesh-ĭ-*).
Spĕ-cial-ĭ-za'tion (*spesh-al-*). [202.
Spĕ'cial-ize (*spesh'al-*),
Spĕ'cial-ized (*spesh'al-*).
Spĕ'cial-īz-ing (*spesh'-al-*).
Spĕ'cial-ly (*spesh'al-*).
Spĕ'cial-ty (*spesh'al-*).
Spe'cie (*-shy*), 99.
Spe'cies (*spe'shez*) [so Wk. Wr.; *spe'sh'ēz*, Sm. (*See* § 26); *spe'-shēz*, Gd. 155], *n. sing. & pl.*
Spe-cif'ic, 109.
Spe-cif'ic-al, 108.
Spe-cif'ic-al-ly.
Speç-i-fĭ-ca'tion.
Speç'i-fīed, 99.
Speç'i-fȳ, 94.
Speç'i-fȳ-ing, 186.
Speç'i-men, 171.
Spe'cioŭs (*-shus*) [*not* spesh'us, 127, 153.]
Speck, 15, 181.
Specked (*spekt*), 165.
Speck'ing.
Speck'le (*spek'l*).
Speck'led (*spek'ld*).

Speck'ling.
Spec'ta-cle, 164, 171.
Spec'ta-cled (-*kld*).
Spec-tac'u-lar, 108.
Spec-ta'tor, 169.
Spec-ta-to'ri-al.
Spec-ta'tress.
Spec-ta'trix.
Spec'tral, 72.
Spec'tre (-*tur*) (164) [Specter preferred by Gd. 203.]
Spec'trum (L.) [pl. Spec'tra, 198.]
Spec'u-lar.
Spec'u-late, 72, 89.
Spec'u-lāt-ed.
Spec'u-lāt-ing, 183.
Spec-u-la'tion.
Spec'u-lāt-ist.
Spec'u-la-tĭve.
Spec'u-lāt-or, 169.
Spec'u-la-to-ry, 86.
Spec'u-lum (L.) [pl. *Spec'u-la*, 198.]
Sped, 15.
Speech, 13.
Speech'i-fīed, 186.
Speech'i-fȳ.
Speech'i-fȳ-ing.
Speed, 13.
Speed'i-ly.
Speed'ing.
Speed'well, 206.
Speed'y, 93.
Speiss (25, 174), *n.* arseniuret of nickel. [*See* Spice, 160.]
Spell, 15, 172.
Spell'-bound, 206, Exc. 5.
Spelled (165) [Spelt, 203.]
Spell'er.
Spell'ing.
Spell'ing-bŏŏk, 215.
Spelt (15), *v.* [Spelled, 203.]

☞ Smart characterizes *spelt* as "colloquial."

Spelt, 15, *n.*
Spel'ter.
Spen'cer, 171.
Spend, 15.
Spend'er.
Spend'ing.
Spend'thrift.
Sperm, 21, N.; 49.
Sperm-a-ce'tĭ [*not* sperm-a-sit'y, *nor* par-ma-sit'y, 153.]
Sperm-at'ic.
Sperm-at'ic-al.
Spew (*spu*) (26) [Spue, 203.]
Spewed (*spūd*).
Spew'er (*spu'-*).
Spew'ing (*spu'-*).
Sphaç'e-late.
Sphaç'e-lāt-ed.
Sphaç'e-lāt-ing.
Sphaç-e-la'tion.
Sphaç'e-lus.
Sphag'noŭs, 100.
Sphene (*sfēn*) [*not* sfe'-ne, 145, 153.]
Sphe'noid.
Sphe-noid'al.
Sphere, 13, 49, 135.
Sphered, 150.
Sphĕr'ic.
Sphĕr'ic-al, *a.* globular. [*See* Sphericle, 148.]
Sphe-riç'i-ty, 108.
Sphĕr'i-cle (164, 171), *n.* a small sphere. [*See* Spherical, 148.]
Sphĕr'ics.
Sphēr'ing.
Sphe'roid, *n.* (103) [so Wk. Wr. Gd.; *sfe-roid'*, Sm. 155.]
Sphe-roid'al.
Sphe-roid'ic, 228.
Sphe-roid'ic-al.
Sphe-roid'i-ty.
Sphe-rom'e-ter, 108.
Sphĕr-o-sid'er-īte.
Sphĕr'u-lāte.
Sphĕr'ule, 89, 90.
Sphĕr'u-līte, 152.
Sphēr'y.
[Sphigmometer, 203. — *See* Sphygmometer.]
Sphinc'ter (*sfingk'-*), 54.
Sphinx (*sfingks*), 171.
Sphrag'ide (*sfraj'id*) [Sphragid, Sm. 203.]
Sphra-gis'tics, 109.
Sphyg'mic, 171.
Sphyg'mo-grăph, 127.
Sphyg-mom'e-ter (108) [Sphigmometer, 203.]
Spi'cate.
Spi'căt-ed.
Spic-ca'to (It.) [*See* Note under *Sgraffito*.]
Spice (25), *n.* any pungent aromatic vegetable substance for seasoning food. [*See* Speiss, 160.]
Spiced (*spīst*), 165; Note C, p. 34.
Spīç'er.
Spīç'er-y.
Spīç'i-form (108) [so Wr.; *spi'si-form*, Gd. 155.]
Spīç'i-ly, 186.
Spīç'i-ness.
Spīç'ing.
Spick'nel [Spignel, 203.]
Spic'u-lar, 108.
Spic'u-late.
Spic'ule, 90.
Spic-ūl'i-form (109) [so Wr.; *spik'u-li-form*, Gd. 155.]
Spic-ūl-ig'e-noŭs (-*ij'-*).
Spīç'y, 93.
Spi'der, 77.
Spig'nel [Spicknel, 203.]
Spig'net.
Spig'ot, 66, 86, 170.
Spĭ-gur'nel.
Spike, 25.
Spiked (*spīkt*), 165; Note C, p. 34.
Spike'let.
Spīke'nard [so Wk. Sm. Wr.; *spīk'nard*, Wb. Gd. 155.]

☞ "Though I am well aware of the common idiom of our pronunciation to shorten the simple in the compound, yet I think this idiom ought not to be sought after, when not established by custom." *Walker.*

Spīk'ing, 183.
Spīk'y.
Spill, 16, 172.
Spilled (*spild*) [Spilt, 203.]
Spill'er, 170.
Spill'ing, 228.
Spilt [Spilled, 203.]

☞ *Spilt* is "colloquial," according to Smart.

Spin, 16.
Spĭ-na'ceoŭs (-*shus*), 112, 169.
Spin'ach (-*āj*) [so Sm. Gd.; *spin'ach*, Wr. 155], *or* Spin'age, 203.

☞ "*Spinach* is another example [of words in which *ch* is sounded as *j*]; but this word is often written as it is pronounced, *spinage*." *Smart.*

Spi'nal.
Spin'dle, 164.
Spin'dle-tree, 206, Exc. 4.
Spin'dling.
Spine, 25, 163.
Spīned, 165.
Spi nel, *or* Spin'el [*spi'-nel*, Wk. Wr. Wb. Gd.; *spin'el*, Sm. 155] [Spinelle (Fr.) (*spĭ-nel'*), 203.]
Spī-nes'cent, 171.
Spĭ-net', *or* Spin'et [*spĭ-net'*, Wk. Sm.; *spin'-et*, Wb. Gd.; *spin'et*, or *spĭ-net'*, Wr. 155.]
Spīn-if'er-ous.
Spīn-ig'er-oŭs (*-ij'-*).
Spīn'i-ness, 186.
Spin'ner, 176.
Spin'ner-et.
Spin'ner-y.
Spin'ney (169, 170) [Spinny, 203.]
Spin'ning, 176.
Spin'ning-jen'ny, 205.
Spin'ning-wheel.
Spi'nose [so Gd.; *spī'-nōs*, or *spī-nōs'*, Wr. 155.]
Spī-nos'i-ty, 108, 169.
Spi'noŭs.
Spi'no-zism (*-zism*) [so Sm. Wb. Gd.; *spin'o-zism*, Wr. 155.]
Spi'no-zist.
Spin'ster, 77.
Spin'thēre, 37, 171.
Spin'ule, 90.
Spin-u-les'cent.
Spin u-lose'.
Spin'u-loŭs.
Spīn'y, 93.
Spĭr'a-cle, *or* Spi'ra-cle (164) [so Wr. Gd.; *spĭr'a-kl*, Wk.; *spi'-ra-kl*, Sm. 155.]
Spi'ral [so Wk. Wr. Wb. Gd.; *spĭr'ral*, Sm. 155.]
Spi'ral-ly.
Spire, 25, 135.
Spĭr'it, 16, 48.

☞ "*Spirit*, sounded as if written *sper'it*, begins to grow vulgar." *Walker* [1806]. *See* Note under *Panegyric*.

Spĭr'it-ed.
Spĭr'it-ing.
Spĭr'it-ist, 106.
Spĭr-i-to'so (It.).
Spĭr'it-oŭs.
Spĭr'it-u-al, 108.
Spĭr'it-u-al-ism (*-izm*), 136.
Spĭr'it-u-al-ist.
Spĭr-it-u-al-ist'ic.
Spĭr-it-u-al'i-ty.
Spĭr-it-u-al-ĭ-za'tion.
Spĭr'it-u-al-ize, 202.
Spĭr'it-u-al-ized, 165.
Spĭr'it-u-al-īz-ing, 183.
Spĭr'it-u-al-ly, 170.
Spĭr'it-u-oŭs, 108.
Spir'ket-ing, 21, N.
Spī-rom'e-ter, 151.
Spirt (21, N.) [Spurt, 203. — *See* Note under *Spurt*.]
Spirt'ed.
Spirt'ing.
Spīr'y, 49, N.
Spis'săt-ed.
Spis'si-tude, 171.
Spit, 16.
Spitch'cock.
Spitch'cocked (*spich'-kokt*).
Spitch'cock-ing.
Spite, 25.
Spīt'ed.
Spite'ful (*-fŏŏl*), 180.
Spite'ful-ly (*-fŏŏl-*).
Spit'fire.
Spīt'ing, 183.
Spit'ted, 176.
Spit'ting.
Spit'tle, 164.
Spit-toon', 121.
Splanch'nic (*splangk'-*).
Splanch-nog'ra-phy (*splangk-*), 108.
Splanch-nol'o-gy (*splangk-*).
Splanch-not'o-my (*splangk-*).
Splash, 10, 46.
Splashed (*splasht*), 165.
Splash'er.
Splash'ing.
Splash'y, 93.
Splāy, 23.
Splāy'-fŏŏt.
Spleen, 13.
Spleen'ish.
Spleen'wort (*-wurt*).
Spleen'y, 93.
Splen'dent.
Splen'did.
Splen'dor, 88.
Splen'e-tic (109) [*not* sple-net'ik, 153.]
Sple-net'ic-al.
Splen'ic, 143.
Splen'ic-al.
Splen-ĭ-za'tion.
Splen'o-cele.
Sple-nog'ra-phy.
Sple-nol'o-gy.
Sple-not'o-my, 108.
Splice, 25.
Spliced (*splīst*), Note C, p. 34.
Spliç'ing.
Splint, 16.
Splint'er.
Splint'ered (*-urd*).
Splint'er-ing.
Splint'er-y.
Split, 16.
Split'ted, 176.
Split'ter.
Splut'ter.
Splut'tered, 150.
Splut'ter-ing.
Spod'o-man-cy.
Spod-o-man'tic, 109.
Spod'u-mene.
Spoff'ish.
Spoil, 27.
Spoiled (165) [Spoilt, 203.]
Spoil'er.
Spoil'ing.
Spoilt [Spoiled, 203.]
Spōke, *n.* & *v.* 24.
Spōk'en (*spōk'n*), 149.
Spoke'shave, 206.
Spo'li-a-ry, 72.
Spo'li-ate.
Spo'li-āt-ed.
Spo'li-āt-ing.
Spo-li-a'tion, 156.
Spo'li-a-tĭve.
Spo'li-āt-or, 183.
Spon-da'ic.
Spon-da'ic-al.
Spon'dee.
Spon'dyl [Spondyle, 203.]
Sponge (*spunj*) (22, 45) [Spunge, 203.]
Sponged (*spunjd*).
Sponge'let (*spunj'-*) [so Wr.; *spun'je-let*, Sm. 155.]
Spong'e-oŭs (*spunj'-*).
Spong'er (*spunj'-*).
Spong'i-form (*spunj'-*), 108.
Spong'i-ness (*spunj'-*).
Spong'ing (*spunj'-*).
Spong'ing-house (*spunj'-*), 215.
Spon'gi-ole (*spun'-*) [so Sm. Gd.; *spŏn'ji-ōl*, Wr. 155.]

Spon′gi-o-līte (*spun′-*), 152.
Spon′gi-ose (*spun′-*).
Spon′goid (*spung′goid*) [*spung′oid*, Wr. 155.]
Spong′y (*spunj′-*).
Spon′sal, 72.
Spon′sion, 169.
Spon′sor, 88.
Spon-so′ri-al, 49, N.
Spon-ta-ne′i-ty, 169.
Spon-ta′ne-oŭs, 169.
Spon-toon′, 121.
Spool, 19.
Spoon (19) [*not* spŏŏn, 153.]
Spoon′bill.
Spoon′drift.
Spoon′ey, 169.
Spoon′ful (*-fŏŏl*), 197.
Spo-ra′di-al, 169.
Spo-rad′ic, 170.
Spo-rad′ic-al.
Spore, 24.
Spŏr′ran, 66, 170.
Spōrt, 24, 49, 135.
Spōrt′al.
Spōrt′ed.
Spōrt′ful (*-fŏŏl*), 180.
Spōrt′ing.
Spōrt′ĭve, 84.
Sports′man, 196.
Spŏr′ule, 90.
Spŏr-u-lif′er-oŭs.
Spot, 18.
Spot′ted, 176.
Spot′ti-ness, 186.
Spot′ting.
Spot′ty, 93, 170.
Spous′al (*spowz′-*).
Spouse (*spowz*), 28, 40.
Spout, 28.
Spout′ed.
Spout′er.
Spout′ing.
Sprāin, 23.
Sprāined, 165.
Sprāin′ing.
Sprang, 10, 54.
Sprat, 10.
Sprawl, 17.
Sprawled, 150, 165.
Sprawl′ing.
Sprāy, 23, 56, Rem.
Sprĕad, 15.
Sprĕad′ing.
Spree, 13.
Sprig, 16.
Sprigged (*sprigd*), *v.*
Sprig′ged (*-ghed*), *a.*
Sprig′ging (*-ghing*).
Sprig′gy (*-ghy*), 138.
Sprīght (*sprīt*) (162) [Sprite, 203.—*See* Note under *Sprite.*]
Sprīght′li-ness (*sprīt′-*), 186.
Sprīght′ly (*sprīt′-*).
Spring, 16, 54.
Springe (*sprinj*), 16, 45.
Springed (*sprinjd*).
Springe′ing (*sprinj′-*), 183.
Spring′er.
Spring′i-ness, 186.
Spring′ing.
Spring′y [so Sm. Wr. Wb. Gd.; *spring′y*, or *sprin′jy*, Wk. 155], *a.* elastic;—full of springs, or fountains.

☞ Though Walker, in deference to a common usage at the time he wrote (1806), allowed the pronunciation *sprin′jy*, he says: "A most absurd custom has prevailed in pronouncing this adjective, as if it were formed from *springe*, a gin, rhyming with *fringe*."

Sprin′kle (*spring′kl*), 54, 164.
Sprin′kled (*spring′kld*).
Sprin′kler (*spring′-klur*).
Sprin′kling (*spring′-*).
Sprit, 16.
Sprite [Spright, 203.]

☞ In the only sense in which this word is now used, namely, that of *a spirit or apparition*, the usual orthography is *sprite*.

Sprit′sāil.
Sprout, 28.
Sprout′ed.
Sprout′ing.
Spruce (*sproos*), 19.
Spruced (*sproost*), Note C, p. 34.
Spruç′ing (*sproos′-*), 183.
Sprung, 22, 54.
Sprunt, 22.
Spry, 25.
Spud, 22.
[Spue, 203.—*See* Spew.]
Spume, 26.
Spumed, 150, 165.
Spu-mes′cence, 171.
Spu-mif′er-oŭs.
Spūm′i-ness, 186.
Spūm′ing.
Spūm′oŭs.
Spūm′y, 169.
Spun, 22.
[Spunge, 203.—*See* Sponge.]
Spunk (*spungk*).
Spur, 21, 49, 135.
Spurge, 21.
Spu′ri-oŭs, 49, N.
Spurn, 21.
Spurned, 165.
Spurn′er.
Spurn′ing.
Spurred (*spurd*), 176.
Spur′rer, 21.
Spŭr′rey (169) [Spurry, 203.]
Spur′ri-er, 21.
Spur′ring, 21.
Spur′-roy-al [so Wr.; *spur-roi′al*, Gd. 155] [Spur-rial, Spur-ryal, 203.]
[Spurry, 203.—*See* Spurrey.]
Spurt [Spīrt, 203.]

☞ Webster says that *spurt* is a "more correct orthography" than *spirt*; but Smart prefers the latter form.

Spurt′ed.
Spurt′ing.
Spu-ta′tion, 112.
Sput′ter, 170.
Sput′tered, 150.
Sput′ter-ing.
Spy, 25.
Spy′glȧss, 206.
Spy′ing, 186.
Squab (*skwob*), 18, 34.
Squab′ble (*skwob′bl*), 164.
Squab′bled (*skwob′bld*).
Squab′bler (*skwob′-*).
Squab′bling (*skwob′-*).
Squab′by (*skwob′-*), 176.
Squad (*skwod*), 18, 171.
Squad′ron (*skwod′-*), 86.
Squal′id (*skwol′-*) (170) [*not* skwăl′id, 127, 153.]
Squa-lid′i-ty.
Squâll, 17, 34, 172.
Squâlled, 165.
Squâll′er, 169.
Squâll′ing.
Squâll′y.
Squā′loid.
Squa′lor (L.) (*skwā′-lawr*) (88) [*not* skwol′-ur, 127, 153.]
Squa-ma′ceoŭs (*-shus*).
Squa′mate.
Squa′māt-ed.

Squa'mel-late, 170.
Squa'mi-form, 108.
Squa-mig'er-oŭs (*-mij'-*), 108.
Squam'i-pen.
Squa'moid.
Squa'mose [so Gd.; *skwa-mōs'*, Wr. 155.]
Squa'moŭs, 100.
Squa'mu-lōse [so Wr.; *skwam'u-lōs*, Gd. 155.]
Squan'der (*skwon'-*).
Squan'dered (*skwon'-durd*), 150, 171.
Squan'der-ing (*skwon'-*).
Square (*skwêr*), 14, 49.
Squared (*skwêrd*).
Squar'er (*skwêr'rur*), 48, 49.
Square'-rigged (*skwêr'-rigd*).
Squar'ish (*skwêr'rish*), 183.
Squăr-rose' [*skwar-rōs'*, Wr.; *skwăr'rōs*, Gd.; *skwŏr'rōs*, Sm. 155.]
Squăr'roŭs.
Squăr'ru-lose.
Squash (*skwosh*), 18, 34, 52.
Squashed (*skwosht*), 165; Note C, p. 34.
Squash'er (*skwosh'-*).
Squash'ing (*skwosh'-*).
Squash'y (*skwosh'-*), 169.
Squat (*skwot*), 18, 34.
Squat'ted (*skwot'-*), 176.
Squat'ter (*skwot'-*).
Squat'ting (*skwot'-*).
Squaw, 17, 34.
Squēak, 13, 34.
Squēaked (*skwēkt*), 41, 165.
Squēak'ing.
Squēal, 13.
Squēaled, 165.
Squēal'ing.
Squēam'ish.
Squeeze, 13, 34, 171.
Squeezed.
Squeez'ing.
Sque-teague' (*skwe-tēg'*), 168, 171.
Squib, 16, 34.
Squid, 16, 34.
Squill, 172.
Squint, 16, 34.
Squint'ed.
Squint'er, 77.
Squint'-eyed (*-īd*), 206, Exc. 5.
Squint'ing.
Squīr'arch-y (*-ark-*) [Squirearchy, 203.]
Squire, 25, 34.
Squir-een' [so Wr.; *skwīr'rēn*, Gd. 155.]
Squirm, 21, N.; 34.
Squir'rel (*skwĕr'rel*, or *skwŭr'rel*) [so Gd.; *skwĕr'rel*, Wk. Sm.; *skwĭr'rel*, *skwĕr'rel*, or *skwur'rel*, Wr. 155.]

☞ "The *i* in this word ought not, according to analogy, to be pronounced like *e*, but custom seems to have fixed it too firmly in that sound to be altered without the appearance of pedantry." *Walker*. *See* Note under *Panegyric*.

Squirt, 21, N.
Squirt'ed.
Squirt'ing.
Stab, 10.
Sta'bat ma'ter (L.).
Stabbed (*stabd*), 165, 176.
Stab'ber.
Stab'bing.
Sta-bil'i-ty, 108, 169.
Sta'ble, 164.
Sta'bled (*-bld*).
Sta'ble-keep'er, 205.
Sta'bling.
Sta'bly, 93.
Stac-cā'to (It.) [*See* Note under *Sgraffito*.]
Stack, 10, 181.
Stacked (*stakt*), 165.
Stack'ing.
Stac'te (163) [so Sm. Wr. Wb. Gd.; *stakt*, Wk. 155.]
Stad'dle, 164, 170.
Sta'di-um (L.) [so Wr. Wb. Gd.; *stad'i-um*, Sm. 155] [pl. *Sta'di-a*, 198.]
Stadt'hōld-er (*stat'-*) [so Wk. Wr. Gd.; *stad'hōld-ur*, Sm. 155.]
Stadt'hōld-er-ate (*stat'-*)
Stăff (12, 131, 173) [pl. Staffs (in the sense of *a body of officers assisting a commander in chief, or attached to any establishment*); Staves (in other senses), 193.—*See* Staves.]
Stag, 10.
Stage, 23, 45.
Stage'-cōach, 24.
Stāg'er (*stāj'-*).
Stag'ger (*-gur*), 138.
Stag'gered (*-gurd*).
Stag'ger-ing (*-gur-*).
Stāg'ing (*stāj'-*).
Stag'i-rite (*staj'-*), 171.
Stag'nan-cy.
Stag'nant.
Stag'nate, 73.
Stag'nāt-ed, 183.
Stag'nāt-ing, 228, N.
Stag-na'tion.
Stāhl'ian (*stäl'yan*).
Stāhl'ian-ism (*stäl'yan-izm*), 136.
Stāid, *v.* [Stayed, 187, 203.]
Stāid, *a.*
Stāin, 23.
Stāined, 165.
Stāin'ing.
Stair (*stêr*) (14, 49, 135), *n.* one of a series of steps. [*See* Stare, 160.]
Stair'case (*stêr'-*).
Stair'-rod, 206, Exc. 1.
Stair'wāy (*stêr'-*), 206.
Stāith, 23, 37.
Stake (23), *n.* a stick sharpened at one end for driving into the ground;—money, &c., pledged or wagered: —*v.* to mark off, as land, by driving stakes; — to wager. [*See* Steāk, 160.]
Staked (*stākt*).
Stāk'ing.
Sta-lac'tic.
Sta-lac'tic-al.
Sta-lac'ti-form, 108.
Sta-lac'tīte (152) [pl. Sta-lac'tītes (*-tīts*), 189.]

☞ Byron, by an unexampled poetical license, has pronounced the plural of this word in four syllables, accenting the second:

"Thus Nature played with
the *sta-lac'ti-tes*,
And built herself a chapel
of the seas."

This seems to have been in imitation of Pope's pronunciation of *satellites*; though it is to be observed that Pope might plead in his justification the fact that *satellites* is a Latin, as well as an English, plural. *See* Note under *Satellite*.

Stal-ac-tit'ic, 109.
Stal-ac-tit'ic-al, 108.
Stal-ac-tit'i-form.
Sta-lag'mīte, 83, 152.

Stal-ag-mit'ic, 122.
Stal-ag-mit'ic-al.
Stâl'der.
Stale, 23.
Stale'mate.
Stâlk (*stawk*), 17, 162.
Stâlked (*stawkt*).
Stâlk'er (*stawk'-*).
Stâlk'ing (*stawk'-*).
Stâlk'y (*stawk'-*).
Stâll, 17, 172.
Stâll'age, 70.
Stâlled (*stawld*).
Stâll'-fed, 206, Exc. 5.
Stâll'-feed, *v.*
Stâll'-feed-ing.
Stăll'ion (*-yun*).
Stâl'wart (*-wurt*), *or* Stâl'worth (*-wurth*), 203.

☞ "The form *stalwart* is getting ground. . . . It is in Scotland that the word has acquired this form." *Smart.*

Sta'men (L.) [L. pl. Stam'i-na; Eng. pl. Sta'mens (*-menz*), 198.]

☞ As a botanical term denoting *the fertilizing organ of a flower*, the word takes a regular English plural; in other senses, the Latin plural is retained.

Sta'mened (*-mend*), 150.
Stam'i-nal, 72.
Stam'i-nate, 108.
Sta-min'e-oŭs.
Stam-i-nif'er-oŭs, 116.
Stam'mer, 66, 170.
Stam'mered, 150.
Stam'mer-er, 77.
Stam'mer-ing.
Stămp, *v.* (10) [*not* stomp, 127, 153.]
Stămp, *n.* 10.
Stămped (*stampt*), 165; Note C, p. 34.
Stăm-pede', 171.
Stămp'er.
Stămp'ing.
Stănch, *v.* 44, Note 2.

☞ "The usual spelling not long since was *staunch*." *Smart.*

Stănch, *a.* [Staunch, 203.]

☞ Smart says that this word, as an adjective, still retains the *u*. Both forms, however, *staunch* and *stanch*, are in good use.

Stănched (*stăncht*).
Stănch'ing.
Stan'chion (*-shun*) [so Wk. Wr. Gd.; *stan'-chun*, Sm. 155.]
Stand, 10.
Stand'ard, 72.
Stand'ard-bêar'er.
Stand'er.
Stand'ing.
Stand'ish.
Stand'-point.
Stand'-still.
Stan'hope (coll. *stan'-up*).
Stank (*stangk*).
Stan'na-ry, 72.
Stan'nate, 170.
Stan'nic.
Stan-nif'er-oŭs.
Stan'nīne, 82, 152.
Stan'noŭs.
Stan'za, 72, 189.
Stan-za'ic, 109.
Sta-pe'di-al.
Sta'pēs (L.) (*-pēz*).
Staph'y-līne, 82, 152.
Staph-y-lo-plas'tic.
Staph-y-lŏr'a-phy.
Sta'ple, 164.
Sta'pled (*-pld*).
Star, 11, 49.
Star'bōard (coll. *star'-burd*).
Starch, 11, 49, 135.
Star'-chăm-ber.
Starched (*starcht*), 41, 165.
Starch'er, 49.
Starch'ing.
Starch'y, 93.
Stare (*stêr*) (14), *v.* to look fixedly with the eyes wide open: — *n.* the act of one who stares. [*See* Stair, 160.]
Stared (*stêrd*), 183.
Star'-fish.
Star'-flower (*-flour*), 28, 67.
Star'-găz-er.
Star'i-kĭ, 191.
Star'ing (*stêr'-*), 183.
Stark, 11, 49, 135.
Star'light (*-līt*), 206.
Star'like.
Star'ling.
Stăr'ost.
Stăr'ost-y.
Stärred (*stärd*), 165.
Stär'ri-ness.
Stär'ring, 11, N.; 176.
Stär'ry, 93.
Star'-span'gled(*spang'-gld*), 206, Exc. 5.
Start, 11, 49, 135.
Start'ed.
Start'ing.
Start'ing-point, 215.
Start'le (*start'l*), 164.
Start'led (*start'ld*).
Start'ling, 183.
Starv-a'tion.
Starve, 11, 49, 135.
Starved (*starvd*), 165.
Starve'ling, 145, 185.
Starv'ing, 183.
Star'wort (*-wurt*), 206.
Sta'tant.
State, 23, 163.
Stăt'ed.
State'house.
State'li-ness, 186.
State'ly.
State'ment, 183.
Stăt'er (228), *n.* one who states.
Sta'ter, *n.* a gold coin of ancient Greece.
State'room, 19.
Stātes'man, 196.
Stātes'man-like.
Stātes'man-ly, 93.
Stat'ic.
Stat'ic-al.
Stat'ics [*not* sta'tiks, 153.]
Stăt'ing.
Sta'tion.
Sta'tion-al.
Sta'tion-a-ri-ness.
Sta'tion-a-ry (72, 169), *a.* fixed; motionless. [*See* Stationery, 148.]
Sta'tioned (*-shund*).
Sta'tion-er.
Sta'tion-er-y (169), *n.* articles usually sold by a stationer, as paper, pens, ink, &c. [*See* Stationary, 148.]
Sta'tion-ing.
Sta'tist.
Sta tis'tic.
Sta-tis'tic-al.
Stat-is-tĭ'cian (*-tish'an*), 231.
Sta-tis'tics, 109.
Stat-is-tol'o-gy, 108.
Sta'tĭve, 84.
Stat'u-a-ry, 72, 89.
Stat'ūe, 26.
Stat'ūed.
Stat'u-esque (*-esk*), 168, 171.
Stat-u-ette', 114, 122.

Sta′tu quo (L.) [*not* stat′yoo kwo, 153.]
Stat′ure, 91.
Sta′tus (L.).
Stat′u-ta-ble, 72, 164.
Stat′u-ta-bly.
Stat′ute, 90.
Stat′ute-bŏŏk.
Stat′u-to-ry, 86.
Stäunch [Stanch, 203.] [*See* Note under *Stanch.*]
Stâu′ro-līte, 152.
Stâu′ro-tīde.
Stāve, *n.* & *v.*
Staved, 165.
Stāves (*stāvz*), *n. pl.* of *Stave.*
Staves (*stāvz*, or *stävz*) [so Gd.; *stāvz*, Wk. Sm.; *stävz*, or *stāvz*, Wr. 155], *n. pl.* of *Staff.*

☞ "Some people pronounce the plural of *staff* (*staves*) with the Italian *a*, but the practice is not general" *Smart.* — "It is often thus pronounced in the United States." *Worcester.*

Staves′ā-cre (*stāvz′ā-kur*), 171.
Stāv′ing, 183.
Stāy, 56, Rem.
Stāyed (*stād*)(187), *part.* from *Stay.* [Staid, 203.]
Stāy′er.
Stāy′ing.
Stāys (*stāz*), *n. pl.*
Stāy′sāil.
Stĕad, 15.
Stĕad′făst.
Stĕad′ĭed, 186.
Stĕad′i-ly.
Stĕad′i-ness, 171.
Stĕad′y [*not* stid′y, 127, 153.]
Stĕad′y-ing.
Steāk (23), *n.* a slice of meat for broiling or frying. [*See* Stake, 160.]
Stēal, *v.* to purloin. [*See* Steel, 160.]
Stēal′er.
Stēal′ing.
Stĕalth, 15.
Stĕalth′i-ly.
Stĕalth′i-ness, 186.
Stĕalth′y, 93.
Stēam, 13.
Stēam′bōat, 24.
Stēamed, 165.
Stēam′-en-gīne.
Stēam′er.
Stēam′-gāuge.
Stēam′ing.
Stēam′ship, 206.
Stēam′y, 169.
Ste′a-rate, 233.
Ste-ăr′ic.
Ste′a-rīne (82,152) [Stearin, 203.]
Ste′a-tīte, 152.
Ste-a-tit′ic, 109.
Ste-a-tom′a-toŭs [so Wr.; *ste-a-to′ma-tus*, Wb. Gd. 155.]
Steed, 13.
Steel (13), *n.* a carburet of iron. [*See* Steal, 160.]
Steeled, 165.
Steel′i-ness, 186.
Steel′ing.
Steel′-plăt-ed.
Steel′y, 93.
Steel′yard (coll. *stil′-yard*) (171) [so Wr.; *stēl′yard*, Wk. Wb. Gd.; *stēl′yard*, coll. *stĕl′yard*, Sm. 155.]

☞ "This word, in common usage among those who weigh heavy bodies, has contracted its double *e* into single *i*, and is pronounced as if written *stilyard*. This contraction is so common in compound words of this kind, as to become an idiom of pronunciation which cannot be easily counteracted without opposing the current of the language." *Walker.*

Steep, 13.
Steeped (*stēpt*), Note C, p. 34.
Steep′ing.
Stee′ple, 164.
Stee′ple-chase.
Steep′y, 93.
Steer, 13, 49, 135.
Steer′age, 70, 169.
Steered, 165.
Steer′ing.
Steers′man (*stērz′-*).
Steeve, 13.
Steeved, 165.
Steev′ing, 183.
Steg-a-nog′ra-phist, 108.
Steg-a-nog′ra-phy.
Ste-gan′o-pod, 105.
Steg-not′ic.
Steīn, 25.
Steīn′boc [Steinbock, 203.]
Ste′la (L.).
Stel′e-chīte (*-kīt*).
Stel′ene, 143.
Stel′lar, 74, 170.
Stel′la-ry, 72.
Stel′late, 170.
Stel′lāt-ed, 228.
Stel-lĕr′i-dan.
Stel-lif′er-oŭs.
Stel′li-form, 108.
Stell′ion (*-yun*) [so Wr. Wb. Gd.; *stĕl′li-un*, Sm. 155.]
Stell′ion-ate (*-yun-*).
Stel′līte, 83, 152.
Stel′lu-late.
Stel′lu-lar, 89, 108.
Stel′o-chite (*-kīt*).
Ste-log′ra-phy.
Stem, 15.
Stemmed (*stemd*), 165.
Stem′ming, 176.
Stem′ple, 164.
Stem′son, 86.
Stench, 44, Note 2.
Sten′cil, 80.
Sten′cilled (*-sild*), 177.
Sten′cil-ling [Stenciling, Gd. 203. — *See* Note E, p. 70.]
Ste-nog′ra-phy, 108.
Sten-o-graph′ic, 143.
Sten-o-graph′ic-al.
Ste-nog′ra-phist.
Ste-nog′ra-phy, 169.
Sten′tor, 88.
Sten-to′ri-an, 49 N.; 169.
Step, *n.* a pace; a stair; gait: — *v.* to walk. [*See* Steppe, 160.]
Step′-broth-er(*-bruth′-*)
Step′-chīld.
Step′-dame.
Step′-dâugh-ter(*-daw-*).
Step′-fä-ther.
Steph′an-īte.
Step′-moth-er (*-muth-*).
Steppe (*step*) [so Wr. Wb. Gd.; *step′pe*, Sm. 155], *n.* a vast, uncultivated plain, as in Russia. [*See* Step, 160.]
Stepped (*stept*)[Stept, 203.]
Step′ping, 176.
Step′ping-stone, 215.
Step′-sis-ter.
Step′-son (*-sun*).
[Stept, 203. — *See* Stepped.]

Ster-co-ra'ceoŭs (-*shus*), 21, N.; 169.
Ster-co-ra'ri-an.
Ster'co-ra-ry, 72.
Ster-co'ri-an-ism (-*izm*).
Stère (Fr.), 154.
Ste're-o-bate [*stĕr'e-o-bāt*, Wr. 155.]
Ste-re-och'ro-my (-*ok*-) [*stĕr-e-ok'ro-my*, Wr.; *ste're-o-krom-y*, Gd. 155.]
Ste-re-o-graph'ic.
Ste-re-o-graph'ic-al.
Ste-re-og'ra-phy (49, N.) [so Wb. Gd.; *stĕr're-og'ra-fy̆*, Sm.; *stĕr-e-og'ra-fy̆*, Wk. Wr. 155.]
Ste-re-o-e-lec'tric, 224.
Ste-re-om'e-ter, 108.
Ste-re-o-met'ric.
Ste-re-o-met'ric-al.
Ste-re-om'e-try, 169.
Ste-re-o-mon'o-scope.
Ste're-o-scope [so Sm. Gd.; *stĕr'e-o-skōp*, Wr. 155.]
Ste-re-o-scop'ic.
Ste-re-o-scop'ic-al.
Ste're-o-scōp-ist.
Ste-re-o-tom'ic.
Ste-re-o-tom'ic-al.
Ste-re-ot'o-my, 108.
Ste're-o-type [so Wk. Sm. Wb. Gd; *stĕr'e-o-tīp*, Wr. 155.]
Ste're-o-typed (-*tīpt*).
Ste're-o-tȳp-er.
Ste-re-o-typ'ic.
Ste're-o-tȳp-ing, 183.
Ste-re-o-ty̆-pog'ra-pher.
Ste-re-o-ty̆-pog'ra-phy.
Stĕr'ile, 48, 66, 152.
Ste-ril'i-ty, 169.
Ster'ling, 21, N.
Stern, 21, N.; 49, 135.
Stern'al.
Stern'bōard.
Stern'mōst, 24.
Stern'ness, 66, N.
Ster-no-cos'tal.
Stern'son, 86.
Ster'num.
Ster-nu-ta'tion, 161.
Ster-nu'ta-tĭve, 26.
Ster-nu'ta-to-ry, 86.
Ster-to'ri-oŭs.
Ster'to-roŭs, 21, N.
Ste-thom'e-ter.
Steth'o-scope, 105.
Steth-o-scop'ic.
Steth-o-scop'ic-al.
Ste've-dore, 171.
Stew (*stu*), 26.
Stew'ard (*stu'*-), 72.
Stew'ard-ess (*stu'*-).
Stewed (*stūd*).
Stew'ing (*stu'*-).
Sthen'ic.
Sti-ac-cia'to (It.) (*ste-ät-cha'to*).
Sti'an.
Stib'i-al, 66, 169.
Stib'i-ät-ed.
Stib'i-oŭs.
Stib'i-um, 169.
Stib'nīte, 152.
Stic-cä'do.
Stich (*stik*) (52), *n.* a line or verse in poetry. [*See* Stick, 160.]
Stich'ic (*stik'*-).
Stich'o-man-cy (*stik'*-).
Stich-om'e-try (*stik*-).
Stich'wort (-*wurt*). [Stitchwort, 203.]
Stick (181), *n.* a small or short piece of wood: — *v.* to pierce; to infix; — to attach. [*See* Stich, 160.]
Stick'i-ness.
Stick'ing.
Stick'le (*stik'l*), 164.
Stick'le-back (*stik'l*-).
Stick'led (*stik'ld*).
Stick'ler.
Stick'ling.
Stick'y.
Stiff, 16, 173.
Stiff'en (*stif'n*), 149.
Stiff'ened (-*nd*).
Stiff'en-ing (*stif'n*-).
Stiff'-necked (-*nekt*).
Sti'fle, 164.
Sti'fled (*sti'fld*), 171.
Sti'fling, 183.
Stig'ma (L.) [L. pl. *Stig'ma-ta*; Eng. pl. Stig'mas (-*maz*), 198.]
Stig-ma'ri-a.
Stig-mat'ic, 109.
Stig-mat'ic-al, 108.
Stig'ma-tize, 202.
Stig'ma-tized, 183.
Stig'ma-tīz-ing.
Stig'ma-tose.
Stig'o-no-man-cy.
[Stilar, 203. — *See* Stylar.]
Stil'bīte, 152.
Stile (25), *n.* a set of steps for passing over a fence or wall; — the vertical piece in framing or panelling. [*See* Style, 160.]
Stĭ-let'to [pl. Stĭ-let'toes (-*tōz*), 192.]
Still, 16, 172.
Stil-la'tim (L.).
Stil-la-tĭ'tious (-*tish'us*), 171.
Still'-born.
Still'burn.
Still'burned.
Still'burn-ing.
Stilled (*stild*), 165.
Still'er.
Stil'li-form.
Still'ing.
Still'ness, 178.
Stil'ly, 66, 170.
Stilp-no-sid'er-īte (233, Exc.) [so Wr. Wb. Gd.; *stilp-noz-ĭ-dĕr'-rit*, Sm. 155.]
Stilt, 16.
Stilt'ed.
Stilt'ing.
Stilt'y, 93.
Stim'u-lant, 89.
Stim'u-late, 108.
Stim'u-lāt-ed.
Stim'u-lāt-ing.
Stim-u-la'tion.
Stim'u-lāt-ĭve.
Stim'u-lāt-or, 169.
Stim'u-lus (L.) (169) [pl. Stim'u-lī, 198.]
Sting, 16, 54.
Stin'gi-ly, 45, 186.
Stin'gi-ness.
Sting'ing.
Stin'go (*sting'*-), 54.
Stin'gy (-*jy*).
Stink (*stingk*), 16, 54.
Stink'ard (*stingk'*-).
Stink'ing (*stingk'*-).
Stint, *n.* & *v.* 16.

☞ As a noun in the sense of *an allotted task* or *performance*, often mispronounced *stent*.

Stint'ed.
Stint'ing.
Stipe, 25, 163.
Sti'pel.
Stī-pel'late (170) [so Gd.; *stĭ-pel'lāt*, Wr. 155.]
Sti'pend.
Stī-pend-i-a'ri-an.
Stī-pend'i-a-ry (72, 151) [so Sm. Wr. Gd.; *stī-pen'di-a-ry*, or *stī-pen'ji-a-ry*, Wk. 134, 155.]
Stip'ple, 164.

Stip′pled (*stip′ld*).
Stip′pling, 183.
Stip-u-la′ceoŭs (*-shus*), 112, 169.
Stip′u-la-ry, 72.
Stip′u-late, 89.
Stip′u-lāt-ed.
Stip′u-lāt-ing.
Stip-u-la′tion.
Stip′u-lāt-or.
Stip′ule, 90.
Stip′uled, 165.
Stir, 21, N.; 135.
Stĭr′i-āt-ed.
Stirps (L.) [pl. *Stir′pēs* (*-pēz*), 198.]
Stirred (*stird*).
Stir′rer, 21, N.
Stir′ring, 176.
Stir′rup (*stĕr′rup*, or *stŭr′rup*) [*stĕr′rup*, Sm.; *stŭr′rup*, Wk.; *stŭr′rup*, or *stĕr′rup*, Gd.; *stĭr′rup*, or *stŭr′-rup*, Wr. 155.]
Stitch, 16, 44; Note D, p. 37.
Stitched (*sticht*), 41.
Stitch′ing.
Stitch′wort (*-wurt*) [Stichwort, 203.]
Stith′y, 37, 169.
Stive, 25.
Stived (*stīvd*).
Sti′ver.
Stīv′ing, 183.
Stōat, 24.
[Stoccade, 203.—*See* Stockade.]
Stoc-ca′do.
Stock, 18, 181.
Stock-ade′ [Stoccade, 203.]
Stock′dove (*-duv*), 206.
Stocked (*stokt*), Note C, p. 34.
Stock′fish.
Stock′hōld-er.
Stock′ing.
Stock′ish.
Stock′-job-ber.
Stock′-list.
Stock′-still, 206, Exc. 5.
Stock′y.
Sto′ic, 63, 229.
Sto′ic-al, 72.
Stoi-chi-o-met′ric-al (*-ki-*) [Stœchiometrical, (*stek-*), 203.]
Stoi-chi-om′e-try (*-kĭ-*) [Stœchiometry, (*stek-*), 203.]
Sto′i-cism (*-sizm*), 133, 136.
Sto′ker.
Stole, 24.
Stoled, 165.
Stolen (*stōln*), 149.
Stol′id, 66, 170.
Sto-lid′i-ty, 108, 169.
Sto′lon, 86.
Sto-lon-if′er-oŭs [so Sm.; *stol-o-nif′ur-us*, Wr. Gd. 155.]
Sto′ma (Gr.) [pl. *Stom′-a-ta*, 198.]
Stom′ach (*stum′ak*), 171.
Stom′ach-al (*stum′ak-*).
Stom′ached (*stum′akt*).
Stom′a-cher (*stum′a-chur*), 44, 141.
Sto-mach′ic (*-mak′-*) [*not* sto-mat′ik, 153.]
Sto-mach′ic-al (*-mak′-*).
Stom′a-pod [so Sm. Wr.; *sto′ma-pod*, Gd. 155.]
Stom′a-ta (Gr.), *n. pl.* [*See* Stoma.]
Sto′mate.
Sto-mat′ic, 170.
Sto-ma′to-gas′tric, 224.
Sto-ma′to-plas′tic.
Stōne, 24, 130.
Stone′-blīnd.
Stone′-cōld, 216.
Stone′-cut-ter.
Stoned, 165.
Stōn′er, 183.
Stōn′i-ness, 186.
Stōn′ing.
Stōn′y, 24, 130.
Stōn′y-heärt′ed.
Stŏŏd, 20.
Stŏŏk.
Stool, 19.
Stoop (19), *v.* to bend forward;—to condescend:—*n.* act of one who stoops;—a flagon. [*See* Stoup, 160.]
Stooped (*stoopt*), Note C, p. 34.
Stoop′ing.
Stop, 18.
Stop′cock, 206.
Stope, 24.
Stop′page, 70, 176.
Stopped (*stopt*).
Stop′per.
Stop′ping.
Stop′ple, 164.
Stōr′age, 70, 169.
Sto′rax, 49, N.
Store, 24.
Store′house.
Stored, 165.
Store′ship.
Stor′ge (Gr.) (*-je*) [so Gd.; *stor′ghe*, Sm.; *stor′je*, or *storj*, Wr. 155.]
Sto′rĭed, 49, N.
Stōr′ing, 228.
Stork, 17, 49, 135.
Stork's-bill, 213.
Storm, 17, 49, 135.
Stormed, 165.
Storm′i-ness, 186.
Storm′ing.
Storm′y, 93, 169.
Storth′ing (*stort′ing*), 41, 156.
Sto′ry, 49, N.
Sto′ry-bŏŏk, 206, Exc. 4.
Sto′ry-tel′ler.
Stoup (*stoop*) (19), *n.* a stone basin for holy water near the door of a church. [*See* Stoop, 160.]
Stour, 28.
Stout, 28.
Stove, 24, 163.
Stōw, 24.
Stōw′age, 70, 169.
Stōwed, 165.
Stōw′ing.
Stra′bism (*-bizm*), 136.
Stra-bis′mus (*-biz′-*) [so Gd.; *stra-bis′mus*, Wr. 155.]
Stra-bot′o-my, 108.
Strad′dle, 164.
Strad′dled (*strad′ld*).
Strad′dling, 183.
Strad-o-met′ric-al.
Strag′gle (*strag′l*), 164.
Strag′gled (*strag′ld*).
Strag′gler.
Strag′gling.
Strāhl′stein.
Strāight (*strāt*) (23, 162), *a.* not having a change of direction between any two points. [*See* Strait, 160.]
Strāight′en (*strāt′n*) (149, 160, 162), *v.* to make straight. [*See* Straiten, 160.]
Strāight′ened (*strāt′-nd*), 150, 171.
Strāight′en-er (*strāt′n-ur*).
Strāight′en-ing (*strāt′-n-ing*).

Strāight′for-ward (*strāt′-*).
Strāight′ly (*strāt′-*), *ad.* in a straight line. [*See* Straitly, 160.]
Strāight′wāy (*strāt′-*).
Strāin, 23.
Strāined, 165.
Strāin′er.
Strāin′ing.
Strāit (23), *a.* confined; narrow; — strict; rigorous: — *n.* a narrow passage of water between two seas; — distress; difficulty. [*See* Straight, 160.]
Strāit′en (*strāt′n*), *v.* to limit or confine; — to perplex; to distress. [*See* Straighten, 160.]
Strāit′-laced (*-lāst*), 206, Exc. 5.
Strāit′ly, *ad.* narrowly; closely. [*See* Straightly, 160.]
Strake, 23.
Stra-min′e-oŭs, 169.
Stram′o-nīne, 82, 152.
Stra-mo′ni-um, 169.
Stram′o-ny, 170.
Strand, 10.
Strand′ed.
Strand′ing.
Strānge, 23, 45; Note D, p. 37.
Strānge′ly, 185.
Strānge′ness.
Strāng′er (*strānj′-*).
Stran′gle (*strang′gl*), 54, 164.
Stran′gled (*strang′gld*).
Stran′gles (*strang′glz*), *n. pl.* 171.
Stran′gling (*strang′-*).
Stran′gu-lāt-ed (*strang′-*).
Stran-gu-la′tion (*strang-*), 112.
Stran′gu-ry (*strang′-*), 89.
Strap, 10.

☞ "When it means a slip of leather dressed and prepared for sharpening a razor, it is usually spelled *strop*." *Smart.*

Strap-pa′do [*not* strap-pä′do, 153.]
Strapped (*strapt*), 165.
Strap′per, 176.
Strap′ping, 141.
Strass, 10, 174.
Stra′ta, *n. pl.* [*See* Stratum.]
Strat′a-gem, 171.
Strat-a-rith′me-trȳ, 93.
Strat-e-get′ic (*-jet′-*), 171.
Strat-e-get′ic-al (*-jet′-*).
Strat-e-get′ics (*-jet′-*), 109.
Stra-te′gic [so Wb. Gd.; *stra-tej′ik*, Wr. 155.]
Stra-te′gic-al.
Strat′e-gist.
Strat′e-gy, 169.
Strath, 10, 37.
Strath′spey, 98, 169.
Strat-i-fī-ca′tion, 116.
Strat′i-fīed (*-fīd*), 186.
Strat′i-form, 108.
Strat′i-fȳ, 94.
Strat′i-fȳ-ing, 186.
Strat-i-graph′ic-al.
Stra-toc′ra-cy, 169.
Stra-tog′ra-phy, 169.
Stra-ton′ic, 170.
Stra′tum (L.) [L. pl. Stra′ta; Eng. pl. (rare) Stra′tums (*-tumz*), 198.]
Stra′tus (L.).
Straw, 189.

☞ "It has a plural with reference to single straws: but it is generally used collectively." *Smart.*

Straw′ber-ry, 126.
Straw′y, 93, 169.
Strāy, 23.
Strāyed (*strād*).
Strāy′er, 67.
Strāy′ing.
Strēak, 13.
Strēaked (*strēkt*), *v.*
Strēak′ed, *or* Strēaked (150) [so Wr.; *strēkt*, or *strēk′ed*, Gd.; *strēkt*, Sm. 155], *a.*
Strēak′ing.
Strēak′y, 93.
Strēam, 13.
Strēamed, 165.
Strēam′er, 77.
Strēam′ing.
Strēam′let.
Strēam′y.
Street, 13.
Strength [*not* strenth, 153.]
Strength′en (*strength′n*), 149.
Strength′ened (*strength′nd*).
Strength′en-er (*strength′n-*) [Strengthner, 203.]
Strength′en-ing (*strength′n-*).
Stren′u-oŭs, 89, 169.
Streps-ip′ter-oŭs.
Stress, 15, 174.
Stretch, 15, 44; Note D, p. 37.
Stretched (*strecht*), 165.
Stretch′er.
Stretch′ing.
Strew (*stroo*, or *stro*) [so Wr.; *strū*, or *stro*, Gd.; *stroo*, Sm.; *stro*, Wk. 155] [Strow, 203.]
Strewed (*strood*, or *strōd*). [*strō′-*).
Strew′ing (*stroo′-*, or
Stri′æ (L.), *n. pl.*
Stri′ate.
Stri′āt-ed.
Stri′a-ture, 90.
Strick′en (*strik′n*), 149.
Strick′le (*strik′l*), 164.
Strict, 16.
Strict′ure, 91.
Strict′ured (*-yurd*).
Strid, 16.
Strid′den (*strid′n*), 149.
Stride, 25, 163.
Stri′dent.
Strīd′ing.
Strife, 25.
Strig′il (*strij′-*).
Strig′il-lose (*strij′-*) [so Wr.; *strī-jil′lōs*, Gd. 155.]
Strī-gose′.
Stri′goŭs, 100.
Strike, 25.
Strīk′er, 183, 228, N.
Strīk′ing.
String, 16, 54.
Stringed (*stringd*), *v.*
Stringed (*stringd*), *or* String′ed [so Sm.; *stringd*, Wk. Wr. Gd. 155], *a.*
Strin′gent.
String′er.
String′i-ness, 186.
String′ing, 141.
String′y, 93.
Strip, 16.
Stripe, 25.
Strīped (*strīpt*), *v.*
Strīp′ed (150) [so Wr.; *strīpt*, Sm. Gd. 155], *a.*
Strīp′ing, 183.
Strip′ling.

Stripped (*strĭpt*) [S t r i p t, 203.]

☞ "This [*stripped*] is often spelled as pronounced, but improperly." *Smart.*

Strip′ping, 176.
[S t r i p t, 203. — *See* Stripped.]
Strive, 25.
Striv′en (*striv′n*), 149.
Strīv′er.
Strīv′ing, 183.
Strob-i-la′ceoŭs (-*shus*), 169.
Strob′īle (81, 152) [S t r o b i l, 203.]
Stro-bil′i-form, 108.
Strob′il-īne, 82, 152.
Strob′il-īte, 152.
Stro′cal, Stro′cle, *or* Stro′kal, 203.
Strode (*strŏd*), 18.
Stroke, 24.
Stroked (*strōkt*), 165.
Strōk′er.
Strokes′man, 196.
Strōk′ing.
Strōll, 24, 172.
Strōlled (*strōld*).
Strōll′er.
Strōll′ing.
Stro-mat′ic.
Strŏmb (*strŏm*), 162.
Strom′bite, 152.
Strom-bu′li-form.
Strom′eȳ-er-īte, 171.
Strong, 18, 54.
Stron′ger (*strong′gur*), 54, Note 2.
Stron′gest (*strong′-ghest*).
Strong′hōld, 217, 221.
Strong′ish.
Strong′-mīnd-ed.
Stron′ti-a (-*shĭ*-)[so Sm. Wr.; *stron′sha*, Gd. 155.]
Stron′ti-an (-*shĭ*-).
Stron′ti-an-īte (-*shĭ*-).
Stron-tit′ic, 109.
Stron′ti-um (-*shĭ*-).
Strop. [*See* Note under *Strap*.]
Stro′phe (163, 169) [so Wk. Wb. Gd. Wr.; *strof′e*, Sm. 155.]
Stro′phic[so Gd.; *strof′-ik*, Wr. 155.]
Stro′phi-o-late [so Sm. Gd.; *strof′i-o-lāt*, Wr. 155.]
Stro′phi-o-lāt-ed.
Stro′phi-ole.
Strove.
Strōw [S t r e w, 203.]
Strōwed (*strōd*).
Strōw′ing.
Strōwn, 24.
Struck, 181.
Struct′ur-al (-*yur*-).
Struct′ure, 91.
Struct′ur-ist, 91.
Strug′gle, 104, 164.
Strug′gled (*strug′ld*).
Strug′gling.
Strull, 172.
Stru′ma (L.) (*stroo′*-).
Stru-mose′ (*stroo*-), 121.
Stru′moŭs (*stroo′*-).
Strung, 22, 54.
Strut, 48.
Stru′thi-oŭs(*stroo′*-),19.
Strut′ted, 176.
Strut′ter.
Strut′ting.
Struv′īte (*stroov′*-), 152.
Strych′ni-a (*strik′*-),171.
Strych′nīne (*strik′*-), 82, 152, 171.
Stub, 22.
Stubbed (*stubd*), *v.*
Stub′bed, *a.* 150.
Stub′bing, 176.
Stub′ble, 164.
Stub′born, 86, 170.
Stub′born-ness, 66, N.
Stub′by, 93.
Stuc′co, 86.
Stuc′cōed, 188.
Stuc′co-er.
Stuc′co-ing.
Stuck, 22, 181.
Stud, 22.
Stud′ded, 176.
Stud′ding.
Stu′dent (26) [*not* stoo′-dent, 127, 153.]
Stud′ĭed (-*id*).
Stu′di-o, 192.
Stu′di-oŭs [so Sm. Wr. Wb. Gd.; *stu′di-us*, or *stu′ji-us*, Wk. 134, 155.]
Stud′y, 170.
Stud′y-ing.
Stu′fa (It.) (*stoo′*-).
Stuff, 22, 173.
Stuffed (*stuft*).
Stuff′ing.
Stuff′ing-box, 215.
Stul-ti-fī-ca′tion.
Stul′ti-fīed.
Stul′ti-fī-er, 186.
Stul′ti-fȳ, 94.
Stul′ti-fȳ-ing.
Stum, 22.
Stum′ble, 164.
Stum′bled (-*bld*).
Stum′bler.
Stum′bling.
Stum′bling-block.
Stummed (*stumd*).
Stum′ming.
Stump, 22.
Stumped (*stumpt*).
Stump′i-ness.
Stump′ing.
Stump′y, 93.
Stun, 22.
Stung, 22, 54.
Stunk (*stungk*), 54.
Stunned(*stund*),165,176.
Stun′ner.
Stun′ning.
Stunt, 22.
Stunt′ed.
Stunt′ing.
Stupe, 26, 163.
Stuped (*stūpt*).
Stu-pe-fa′cient (-*shent*), 112.
Stu-pe-fac′tion, 169.
Stu-pe-fac′tĭve, 84.
Stu′pe-fīed.
Stu′pe-fī-er.
Stu′pe-fȳ [S t u p i f y, 203.]

☞ This word, from the L. *stupefacio*, Fr. *stupéfier*, should obviously be spelled with *e* in the second syllable, as are the related words *stupefacient*, *stupefaction*, and *stupefactive*, and it is generally so spelled in the United States; but Johnson, Walker, Smart, and most other English lexicographers, give only the form *stupify*. According to Worcester, "the prevailing usage in England still appears to be to spell this word *stupify*."

Stu′pe-fȳ-ing.
Stu-pen′doŭs [*not* stu-pen′di-us, 153.]
Stu′pe-oŭs, 169.
Stu′pid [*not* stoo′pid, 127, 153.]
Stu-pid′i-ty, 170.
[S t u p i f y, 203. — *See* Note under *Stupefy*.]
Stūp′ing, 26.
Stu′por (-*pawr*), 88.
Stu-pose′ [so Sm. Wr.; *stu′pōs*, Gd. 155.]
Stu′pu-lose.
Stur′di-ly.
Stur′di-ness, 186.
Stur′dy, 135.

Stur′geon (-*jun*), 171; Note D, p. 37.
Stu-ri-o′ni-an.
Stut′ter, 77, 104.
Stut′tered, 150.
Stut′ter-er.
Stut′ter-ing.
Sty (25) [Stye, 203.]
[Styan, 203. — *See* Stian.]
Styg′i-an (*stij′*-), 171.
Sty-la-gal-ma′ic [so Wb. Gd.; *stil-a-gal′ma-ik*, Wr. 155] [Stylogalmaic, 203.]
Sty′lar [Stilar, 203.]
Style, *n.* a kind of pencil; — diction; — title; — manner; fashion; — a gnomon; — a filament of a pistil; — manner of reckoning time: — *v.* to denominate. [*See* Stile, 160.]
Styled, 165.
Styl′et.
Styl′i-form.
Styl′ing.
Styl′ish, 183.
Styl′ist.
Sty′lite, 83, 152.
Sty′lo-bate, 233.
[Stylogalmaic, 203. — *See* Stylagalmaic.]
Sty-lo-graph′ic.
Sty-lo-graph′ic-al.
Sty-log′ra-phy.
Sty′lo-hy′oid, 224.
Sty′loid, 27.
Sty′lo-mas′toid.
Sty-lom′e-ter, 108.
Sty′lus (L.).
Styp′tic.
Styp′tic-al.
Styp-tiç′i-ty, 169.
Styr′a-cine, 152.
Su-a-bil′i-ty.
Su′a-ble, 164, 183.
Sua′sion (*swa′zhun*), 47, 171.
Sua′sive (*swa′*-), 34, 39.
Sua′so-ry (*swa′*-).
Suav′i-fied (*suav′*-).
Suav′i-fy (*suav′*-).
Suav′i-fy-ing (*suav′*-).
Suav′i-ty (*swav′*-).
Sub-, a Latin prefix signifying *under*, *below*.
Sub-aç′e-tate.
Sub-aç′id.
Sub-ac′tion.
Sub-a′gent.
Su′bah [India.]
Su-bah-dar′ [so Sm.; *su′ba-dar*, Wr. Gd. 155.]
Sub′al-tern, *or* Sub-âl′tern [so Wr.; *sub′al-tern*, Wk. Sm.; *sub-awl′turn*, Gd. 155.]
Sub-al-ter′nate.
Sub-a′que-oŭs.
Sub-âu-dĭ′tion (-*dish′un*).
Sub-băss′ [so Wr.; *sub′băs*, Wb. Gd. 155] [Sub-base, 203.]
Sub-bra′chi-al (-*ki*-).
Sub-bra′chi-an (-*ki*-).
Sub-cla′vi-an.
Sub-com-mit′tee.
Sub-con′tra-ry, 72.
Sub-cor′date.
Sub-dĭ-vide′.
Sub-dĭ-vĭ′sion (-*vizh′un*).
Sub-dom′i-nant.
Sub-du′a-ble, 164, 169, 183.
Sub-du′al.
Sub-duce′, 103.
Sub-duced′ (-*düst′*).
Sub-duç′ing.
Sub-duct′.
Sub-duct′ed.
Sub-duct′ing.
Sub-duc′tion.
Sub-due′ (26) [*not* sub-doo′, 127, 153.]
Sub-dued′, 171.
Sub-du′er.
Sub-du′ing, 183.
Sub′du-ple, 164.
Su′ber-ate.
Su-bĕr′e-oŭs, 169.
Su-bĕr′ic (109) [so Sm. Wr.; *su′bur-ik*, Wb. Gd. 155.]
Su′ber-ine (152) [Suberin, 203.]
Su′ber-ose [so Sm. Wb. Gd.; *su-bur-ōs′*, Wr. 155.]
Su′ber-oŭs.
Sub-fam′i-ly.
Sub-ge′nus.
Sub-has-ta′tion.
Sub-i′o-dide.
Su′bi-to (It.) (*soo′*-).
Sub-ja′cent.
Sub′ject, *n.* 103, 161.
Sub-ject′, *v.* 103, 161.
Sub-ject′ed [*not* sub′jekt-ed, 153.]
Sub-ject′ing.
Sub-jec′tion.
Sub′ject-ist, 106.
Sub-ject′ive, 84.
Sub-ject′ive-ly.
Sub-ject′iv-ism (-*izm*).
Sub-ject-iv′i-ty.
Sub-ject-mat′ter, 205.
Sub-join′.
Sub-joined′, 165.
Sub-join′ing.
Sub ju′di-ce (L.).
Sub′ju-gate.
Sub′ju-găt-ed, 183.
Sub′ju-găt-ing.
Sub-ju-ga′tion.
Sub′ju-găt-or.
Sub-junc′tion (-*jungk′*-).
Sub-junc′tive (-*jungk′*-).
Sub-lap-sa′ri-an.
Sub-lap′sa-ry, 72.
Sub-la′tion.
Sub′la-tive.
Sub-let′.
Sub-le-va′tion.
Sub-lĭ-ga′tion.
Sub-lim′a-ble, 164.
Sub′li-mate, 169.
Sub′li-măt-ed, 183.
Sub′li-măt-ing.
Sub-li-ma′tion, 169.
Sub′li-ma-to-ry, 72, 86.
Sub-lime′.
Sub-limed′.
Sub-lime′ly, 93.
Sub-lim′ing.
Sub-lim′i-ty, 169.
Sub-lĭ′tion (-*lish′un*).
Sub-lu′nar.
Sub′lu-na-ry, 72, 122.
Sub-ma-rine′ (-*rēn′*).
Sub-max′il-la-ry.
Sub-me′di-ant.
Sub-merge′, 21, N.
Sub-merged′, 165.
Sub-merg′ence (-*merj′*-), 183.
Sub-merg′ing (-*merj′*-).
Sub-merse′.
Sub-mersed′ (-*merst′*), Note C, p. 34.
Sub-mers′ing.
Sub-mer′sion.
Sub-mis′sion (-*mish′un*).
Sub-mis′sive, 84.
Sub-mis′sive-ly, 185.
Sub-mit′.
Sub-mit′ted, 176.
Sub-mit′ting.
Sub mo′do (L.).
Sub-mul′ti-ple, 164.
Sub-nas′cent.
Sub-or′di-na-cy, 169.

Sub-or′di-na-ry, 72.
Sub-or′di-nate.
Sub-or′di-nāt-ed.
Sub-or′di-nāt-ing.
Sub-or-di-na′tion.
Sub-or′di-na-tĭve.
Sub-orn′, 135.
Sub-or-na′tion.
Sub-orned′ (-ornd′), 165.
Sub-orn′ing.
Sub-o′val.
Sub-pœ′na (-pe′-) (189) [Subpena preferred by Gd. 203.]

☞ "Colloquially [pronounced] *sup-pe′na.*" *Smart.*

Sub-pœ′naed, 150, 188.
Sub-pœ′na-ing.
Sub-rep′tion.
Sub-ro-ga′tion.
Sub ro′sa (L.) (*-za*).
Sub′sâlt.
Sub-scribe′.
Sub-scribed′, 165.
Sub-scrīb′er.
Sub-scrīb′ing.
Sub′script.
Sub-scrip′tion.
Sub-sel′li-a (L.), *n. pl.*
Sub′se-quence.
Sub′se-quent.
Sub-serve′, 21, N.; 49.
Sub-served′ (*-servd′*).
Sub-serv′i-ence.
Sub-serv′i-en-cy.
Sub-serv′i-ent, 169.
Sub-side′.
Sub-sīd′ed.
Sub-sīd′ence, 122.
Sub-sīd′en-cy.
Sub-sid′i-a-ri-ly.
Sub-sid′i-a-ry (72) [so Wr. Wb. Gd.; *sub-sid′yŭr-y*, Sm.; *sub-sid′i-a-ry*, or *sub-sij′-i-a-ry*, Wk. 134, 155.]
Sub′si-dize, 202.
Sub′si-dized.
Sub′si-dīz-ing.
Sub′si-dy, 93, 233.
Sub sĭ-len′ti-o (L.) (*-len′shĭ-o*).
Sub-sist′, 103.
Sub-sist′ed.
Sub-sist′ence, 169.
Sub-sist′ent.
Sub-sist′ing.
Sub′soil.
Sub-spe′cies (*-shez*).
Sub′stance, 72.
Sub-stan′tial (*-shal*).
Sub-stan-ti-al′i-ty (*-shĭ-*) (171) [so Wk. Sm. Wr.; *sub-stan-shal′-i-ty*, Wb. Gd. 155.]
Sub-stan′tial-ly (*-shal-*).
Sub-stan′ti-ate (*-shĭ-*) [so Wk. Sm. Wr.; *sub-stan′shāt*, Wb. Gd. 155.]
Sub-stan′ti-āt-ed (*-shĭ-*), 171, 183.
Sub-stan′ti-āt-ing (*-shĭ-*).
Sub-stan-ti-a′tion (*-shĭ-*).
Sub′stan-tĭv-al, 106.
Sub′stan-tĭve, 84.
Sub′stan-tĭve-ly.
Sub′sti-tute, 26, 127.
Sub′sti-tūt-ed.
Sub′sti-tūt-ing.
Sub-sti-tu′tion.
Sub-sti-tu′tion-al.
Sub-sti-tu′tion-a-ry, 72.
Sub′sti-tūt-ĭve.
Sub-stract′.

☞ "*Substract* was formerly used in analogy with *abstract*. But in modern usage, it is written according to the Latin, *subtract*." *Webster.*

Sub′strate.
Sub-stra′tum (L.) [pl. Sub-stra′ta, 198.]
Sub-struc′tion.
Sub-struct′ure, 91.
Sub-sul′phate.
Sub′sul-to-ry, *or* Sub-sul′to-ry (86) [so Wr.; *sub′sul-tŭr y*, Wk.; *sub-sul′tŭr-y*, Sm. Wb. Gd. 155.]

☞ "Though the majority of authorities are against me, . . . I greatly mistake, if analogy is not clearly on my side." *Walker.*

Sub-sump′tion (*-sum′-shun*), 162.
Sub-sump′tĭve (*-sum′-*).
Sub-tan′gent.
Sub-tend′.
Sub-tend′ed.
Sub-tend′ing.
Sub-tense′.
Sub′ter-fuge.
Sub-ter-ra′ne-an, 110, 170.
Sub-ter-ra′ne-oŭs.
Sub′tĭle (81, 152), *a.* thin; rare; — delicate; — cunning; sly.

☞ In the latter sense, which is rare under this form of spelling, the pronunciation is *sut′l*. *See* Note under *Subtle.*

Sub-til-ĭ-za′tion.
Sub′til-ize, 202.
Sub′til-ized.
Sub′til-īz-ing.
Sub′til-ty, *n.* thinness; fineness. [*See* Subtlety, 148.]
Sub′tle (*sut′l*) (162), *a.* sly; artful; cunning. [*See* Suttle, 160.]

☞ "Such is now the mode of writing *subtile*, when it has this meaning; and such is the pronunciation, even under the original spelling, when the meaning is that here given." *Smart.*

Sub′tler (*sut′lur*), *a.* more subtle or crafty. [*See* Sutler, 160.]
Sub′tle-ty (*sut′l-ty*) (162, 171), *n.* slyness; artfulness. [*See* Subtilty, 148.]
Sub′tly (*sut′ly*), 162.
Sub-ton′ic.
Sub-tract′ [*not* sub-strakt′, 153. — *See* Note under *Substract.*]
Sub-tract′ed.
Sub-tract′ing.
Sub-trac′tion, 234.
Sub-trac′tĭve, 84.
Sub′tra-hend.
Su′bu-late, 108.
Su′bu-lāt-ed.
Su-bu′li-corn.
Su-bu′li-palp.
Sub′urb.
Sub-urb′an, 135.
Sub-urb-i-ca′ri-an.
Sub-urb′i-ca-ry, 72.
Sub-ven′tion, 169.
Sub-ver′sion, 169.
Sub-ver′sion-a-ry, 72.
Sub-ver′sĭve, 84.
Sub-vert′.
Sub-vert′ed.
Sub-vert′i-ble, 164, 169.
Sub-vert′ing.
Suc′cades (*-kādz*), *n. pl.*
Suc-ce-da′ne-oŭs.
Suc-ce-da′ne-um (L.) (111) [L. pl. Suc-ce-da′ne-a; Eng. pl. (rare) Suc-ce-da′ne-ums (*-umz*), 198.]

Suc-ceed′, 169.
Suc-ceed′ant, 169.
Suc-ceed′ed.
Suc-ceed′ing.
Suc-cen′tor.
Suc-cess′, 171.
Suc-cess′ful (*-fool*).
Suc-cess′ful-ly (*-fool-*).
Suc-ces′sion (*-sesh′un*).
Suc-ces′sion-al (*-sesh′-un-*).
Suc-ces′sion-ist (*-sesh′-un-*).
Suc-cess′ĭve, 228.
Suc-cess′or (88, 107) [so Sm. Wr. Wb. Gd.; *suk′ses-ur*, or *suk-ses′-ur*, Wk. 155.]

☞ "This is one of the words over which fashion now relaxes its sway in favor of the more consistent accentuation." *Smart. See* § 106.

Suc-cid′u-oŭs, 108.
Suc-cif′er-oŭs.
Suc′ci-nate.
Suc′ci-nāt-ed.
Suc-cinct′.
Suc-cin′ic, 109.
Suc′ci-nīte.
Suc′ci-noŭs.
Suc′cor (70), *v.* to relieve: — *n.* relief. [*See* Sucker, 160] [Succour, Sm. 203.]
Suc′cored (*-kurd*).
Suc′cor-er.
Suc′cor-ing.
Suc′co-ry.
Suc′cu-lence, 108.
Suc′cu-len-cy.
Suc′cu-lent, 89, 169.
Suc′cu-loŭs.
Suc-cumb′ (31, 32) [*not* suk-kum′, 153.]
Suc-cumbed′ (*-kumbd′*).
Suc-cumb′ing, 142.
Suc-cus′sion (*-kush′un*).
Suc-cus′sĭve.
Such (22, 44) [*not* sech, 127, 153.]
Suck, 22, 181.
Sucked (*sukt*), 165; Note C, p. 34.
Suck′er, *n.* he who, or that which, sucks; — a shoot from the roots of a plant; — a kind of fish. [*See* Succor, 160.]
Suck′ing.
Suck′le (*suk′l*), 164.
Suck′led (*suk′ld*).
Suck′ling, 183.
Su′crose.
Suc′tion.
Suc-to′ri-al, 49, N.
Suc-to′ri-an, 169.
Suc-to′ri-oŭs.
Su′da-to-ry, 86.
Sud′den (149) [*not* sud′ding, 141, 153.]
Sud′den-ness, 66, N.
[Sudder, 203. — *See* Sooder.]
Su-dor-if′er-oŭs.
Su-dor-if′ic, 109.
Su-dor-ip′a-rous, 108.
Su′dra [Soodra, 203.]
Suds, *n. pl.*

☞ "Webster considers this to be a noun singular; of this there are no authorities in proof, and common use makes it plural." *Smart.*

Sūe, 26, 39.
Sūed, 165, 183.
Su′ent.
Su′er, *n.* one who sues. [*See* Sewer, 148.]
Su′et, 76.
Su′et-y, 93.
Suf′fer, 77, 103.
Suf′fer-a-ble, 164, 169.
Suf′fer-a-bly.
Suf′fer-ance, 169.
Suf′fered (*-furd*), 150.
Suf′fer-er, 77.
Suf′fer-ing.
Suf-fice′ (*-fīz′*) (171) [*not* suf-fīs′, 153.]
Suf-ficed′ (*-fīzd′*), Note C, p. 34.
Suf-fĭ′cien-cy (*-fish′en-*), 169.
Suf-fĭ′cient (*-fish′ent*).
Suf-fīc′ing (*-fīz′-*).
Suf′fix, *n.* 103, 161.
Suf-fix′, *v.* 103, 165.
Suf-fixed′ (*-fikst′*).
Suf-fix′ing.
Suf-fix′ion (*-yun*).
Suf-fla′tion.
Suf′fo-cate, 105.
Suf′fo-cāt-ed.
Suf′fo-cāt-ing.
Suf-fo-ca′tion.
Suf′fo-cāt-ĭve.
Suf′fra-gan, 170.
Suf′frage, 70, 169.
Suf′fra-gist, 45.
Suf-fru-tes′cent (*-froo*), 171.
Suf-fru′ti-coŭs (*-froo′-*).
Suf-fu′mi-gate.
Suf-fu′mi-gāt-ed.
Suf-fu′mi-gāt-ing.
Suf-fu-mi-ga′tion.
Suf-fuse′ (*-fūz′*).
Suf-fused′ (*-fūzd′*).
Suf-fūs′ing (*-fūz′-*).
[Sufi, 203. — *See* Sofi.]
Sug′ar (*shoog′ur*), 20, 26, 46, 74, 171.
Sug′ar-cane (*shoog′-*).
Sug′ared (*shoog′urd*), 150, 171.
Sug′ar-i-ness (*shoog′-*).
Sug′ar-ing (*shoog′-*).
Sug′ar-y (*shoog′-*), 171.
Sug-gest′ (or *sud-jest′*) (45) [so Wr.; *sug-jest′*, Wk. Gd.; *sud-jest′*, Sm. 155.]

☞ Walker says of this word: "Though we sometimes hear it sounded as if written *sudjest*, the most correct speakers generally preserve the first and last *g* in their distinct and separate sounds.... As the accent is not on these consonants, there is not the same apology for pronouncing the first soft as there is in *exaggerate*." — Smart remarks: "It is possible, with a great deal of pains, to pronounce *suggest* .... so as to preserve to each *g* its regular sound; but surely the elegant, because the easy, pronunciation ... is that which runs both letters into the same sound, namely, that of *j*."

Sug-gest′ed (or *sud-jest′ed*).
Sug-gest′er (or *sud-jest′ur*).
Sug-gest′ing (or *sud-jest′ing*).
Sug-gest′ion (*sug-jest′-yun*, or *sud-jest′yun*).
Sug-gest′ĭve (or *sud-jest′iv*).
Sug-gil-la′tion (*sug-jil-*) [Wb. Gd. Wr.; *sud-jil-la′shun*, Sm. 155.]
Su′i-cīd-al (106) [so Sm. Wr.; *su-i-sī′dal*, Wb. Gd. 155.]
Su′i-cīde, 171.
Su′i-cīd-ism (*-izm*), 106.
Su′ī gen′er-is (L.).
Su′il-līne, 152.
Su′ing, 183.
Sūit, 26.
Sūit-a-bil′i-ty.
Sūit′a-ble, 164, 169.
Sūit′a-bly.

Suite (*swēt*) (Fr.) (154) [*not* sūt, *nor* soot, 153], *n.* a retinue; — a set, particularly of apartments opening into each other. [*See* Sweet, 160.]

☞ Webster prefers the Anglicized form of this word (*suit*), in the senses named; but general usage favors *suite*.

Sūit'ed.
Sūit'ing.
Sūit'or, 88, 169.
Sul'cate.
Sul'cāt-ed.
Sulk'i-ly.
Sulk'i-ness.
Sulks, *n. pl.*
Sulk'y, 169.
Sul'len, 149, 170.
Sul'len-ness, 66, N.
Sul'līed (*-lid*), 186.
Sul'ly, 93, 169.
Sul'ly-ing.
Sulph-aç'id.
Sul'phate.
Sul-phat'ic.
Sul'phīde.
Sul'phīte, 83, 152.
Sul'pho-sâlt.
Sul'pho-sel.
Sul'phur, 92, 169.
Sul'phu-rate [so Wr. Gd.; *sul'fur-āt*, Sm. 155.]
Sul'phu-rāt-ed.
Sul'phu-rāt-ing, 183.
Sul-phu-ra'tion.
Sul-phu're-oŭs, 169.
Sul'phu-ret.
Sul'phu-ret-ted (177) [Sulphureted, Wb. Gd. 203.]
Sul-phu'ric (109) [so Wr. Gd.; *sul-phur'-rik*, Sm. 155.]
Sul'phur-ing.
Sul'phur-oŭs, 106.
Sul'phur-y.
Sul'tan.
Sul-tä'na, *or* Sul-tā'na [*sul-tä'na*, Sm.; *sul-tā'na*, Wk. Wb. Gd.; *sul-tā'na*, or *sul-tä'-na*, Wr. 155.]
Sul'tan-ess.
Sul-tan'ic, 170.
Sul'tan-ry.
Sul'tri-ness, 186.
Sul'try, 230.
Sum (22, 33, 39), *n.* amount; — a question or problem: — *v.* to collect into an aggregate. [*See* Some, 160.]
Su'mach (*su'mak*, coll. *shoo'mak*) [so Sm.; *shū'mak*, Wb. Gd.; *shoo'mak*, or *su'mak*, Wr. 155] [Sumac, Shumac, 203.]
Su-mä'tran.
Sum'ma-ri-ly.
Sum'ma-ry, 72, 126.
Sum-ma'tion, 169.
Summed (*sumd*), 165.
Sum'mer.
Sum'mered (*-murd*).
Sum'mer-house.
Sum'mer-ing.
[Summersault, 203. — *See* Somersault.]
[Summerset, 203. — *See* Somerset.]
Sum'ming, 176.
Sum'mit, 170.
Sum'mon, 86.
Sum'moned (*-mund*).
Sum'mon-er.
Sum'mon-ing.
Sum'mons (*-munz*) [pl. Sum'mons-es (*-munz-ez*), 189.]
Sum'mum bo'num (L.).
Sump, 22.
Sump'ter (*sum'tur*), 162.
Sumpt'u-a-ry (*sumt'-*), 72, 162.
Sumpt'u-oŭs (*sumt'-*), 89, 108, 162.
Sun, 22, 39, 43.
Sun'bēam, 206.
Sun'bird.
Sun'burn.
Sun'burned (*-burnd*).
Sun'burn-ing.
Sun'burnt.
Sun'day (*-dy*).
Sun'der, 104.
Sun'-dī-al.
Sun'dog.
Sun'down.
Sun'-drīed, 206, Exc. 5.
Sun'drīes (*-driz*), *n. pl.* 171.
Sun'dry, 93.
Sun'fish.
Sun'flower (*-flour*).
Sung, 22, 54.
Sunk (*sungk*), 22, 54.
Sunk'en (*sungk'n*).
Sun'like.
Sun'na, or *Sun'nah* (*sŏŏn'-*) (203) [*sun'na*, Wr. 155.]
Sun'ni-ah (*sŏŏn'ni-ä*) [so Sm.; *sun-ne'a*, Gd. 155.]
[Sunnie, 203. — *See* Soonie.]
Sun'ni-ness, 66, N.
Sun'ning, 176.
Sun'nīte.
Sun'nud (*sŏŏn'nud*) [so Sm.; *soon'nud*, Wr. 155.]
Sun'ny, 93, 170.
Sun'rise (*-rīz*).
Sun'rīs-ing (*-rīz-*).
Sun'set.
Sun'shine.
Sun'shīn-y.
Sun'stroke.
Su'o ju're (L.).
Su'o mar'te (L.).
Sup, 22, 30, 39.
Su'per-a-ble, 164.
Su-per-a-bound', 116.
Su-per-a-bun'dance.
Su-per-a-bun'dant.
Su-per-add'.
Su-per-ad-dī'tion (*-dish'un*).
Su-per-an-gel'ic.
Su-per-an'nu-ate, 89.
Su-per-an'nu-āt-ed.
Su-per-an'nu-āt-ing.
Su-per-an-nu-a'tion.
Su-perb', 21, N.
Su-per-car'go [pl. Su-per-car'gōes (*-gōz*), 192.]
Su-per-cil'i-oŭs, *or* Su-per-cil'ioŭs (*-yus*) [so Wr.; *su-pur-sil'i-us*, Wb. Gd.; *su-pur-sil'-yus*, Wk. Sm. 155.]
Su-per-co-lum-ni-a'tion.
Su-per-cres'cence, 171.
Su-per-cres'cent.
Su-per-dom'i-nant.
Su-per-em'i-nence.
Su-per-em'i-nen-cy.
Su-per-em'i-nent.
Su-per-ĕr'ro-gate.
Su-per-ĕr-ro-ga'tion.
Su-per-ĕr'ro-ga-to-ry, 86, 126, 171.
Su-per-ex'cel-lence.
Su-per-ex'cel-lent.
Su-per-fī'cial (*-fish'al*), 171, 231.
Su-per-fī'cial-ist (*-fish'-al-*).
Su-per-fī'cial-ly (*-fish'-al-*), 170.

Su-per-fĭ'ci-a-ry (*-fish'-ĭ-*), 72, 171.
Su-per-fĭ'ci-es (*-fish'ĭ-ēz*), *or* Su-per-fĭ'ciēs (*-fish'ēz*) [so Wr.; *su-pur-fish'i-ēz*, Sm.; *su-pur-fish'ēz*, Wk. Wb. Gd. 155.]
Su-per-fine', 122.
Su-per-flu'i-ty.
Su-per'flu-oŭs, 108.
Su-per-hu'man.
Su-per-im-pose' (*-pōz'*).
Su-per-in-cum'bent.
Su-per-in-duce'.
Su-per-in-duced' (*-dūst'*).
Su-per-in-dūç'ing.
Su-per-in-duc'tion
Su-per-in-tend'.
Su-per-in-tend'ed.
Su-per-in-tend'ence.
Su-per-in-tend'en-cy.
Su-per-in-tend'ent, 169.
Su-per-in-tend'er.
Su-per-in-tend'ing.
Su-pe'ri-or, 49, N.
Su-pe-ri-ŏr'i-ty, 108.
Su-per'la-tĭve, 84.
Su-per-lu'nar.
Su-per-lu'na-ry, 72.
Su-per-mun'dane.
Su-per'nal, 72.
Su-per-na'tant.
Su-per-nat'u-ral.
Su-per-nat'u-ral-ism (*-izm*), 133.
Su-per-nat'u-ral-ist.
Su-per-nat-u-ral-ist'ic, 116.
Su-per-nat-u-ral'i-ty.
Su-per-nat'u-ral-ly.
Su-per-nu'mer-a-ry, 72.
Su-per-phos'phate.
Su-per-pose' (*-pōz'*).
Su-per-posed' (*-pōzd'*).
Su-per-po-sĭ'tion (*-zish'-un*).
Su-per-roy'al.
Su-per-sa'li-ent.
Su'per-sâlt.
Su-per-sat'u-rate.
Su-per-sat-u-ra'tion.
Su-per-scribe'.
Su-per-scribed', 165.
Su-per-scrīb'ing, 183.
Su-per-scrip'tion.
Su-per-sede', 169.
Su-per-se'de-as (L.).
Su-per-sēd'ed.
Su-per-sēd'ing.
Su-per-sēd'ure, 171.
Su-per-sens'u-al.
Su-per-ses'sion (*-sesh'-un*).
Su-per-stĭ'tion (*-stish'-un*).
Su-per-stĭ'tious (*-stish'-us*).
Su-per-stra'tum.
Su-per-struc'tion.
Su-per-struct'ure, 91.
Su-per-sub-stan'tial (*-shal*), 169.
Su-per-sul'phate.
Su-per-sul'phu-ret-ted. [*See* Sulphuretted.]
Su-per-ton'ic.
Su-per-vene'.
Su-per-vened', 165.
Su-per-ve'ni-ent.
Su-per-vēn'ing, 183.
Su-per-ven'tion.
Su-per-vi'sal (*-zal*).
Su-per-vise' (*-vīz'*).
Su-per-vised' (*-vīzd'*).
Su-per-vīs'ing (*-vīz'-*).
Su-per-vĭ'sion (*-vizh'-un*).
Su-per-vi'sor (*-zur*), 169.
Su-per-vi'sor-y (*-zur-*).
Su-per-vo-lute' [so Wr.; *su-pur-vo'lūt*, Gd. 155.]
Su-pi-na'tion, 112.
Su-pine', *a.* 161.
Su'pīne, *n.* 152, 161.
Su-pine'ly, 93.
Su-pine'ness, 66, N.
Supped (*supt*), 176; Note C, p. 34.
Sup'per, 66, 170.
Sup'ping.
Sup-plănt'.
Sup-plan-ta'tion.
Sup-plănt'ed.
Sup-plănt'ing.
Sup'ple (*sup'l*) (164, 170) [*not* soo'pl, 153.]
Sup'pled (*sup'ld*).
Sup'ple-ment, 169.
Sup-ple-ment'al.
Sup-ple-ment'a-ry, 72, 171.
Sup'ple-ness (*sup'l-*) [*not* soo'pl-nes, 153.]
Sup'ple-tĭve, 84.
Sup'ple-to-ry, 86.
Sup-pli'al, 186.
Sup'pli-ant, 169.
Sup'pli-cant, 72.
Sup'pli-cate, 108.
Sup'pli-cāt-ed.
Sup'pli-cāt-ing.
Sup-pli-ca'tion.
Sup'pli-cāt-or.
Sup'pli-ca-to-ry, 86.
Sup-pli-ca'vit (L.).
Sup-plied'.
Sup-pli'er.
Sup-ply'.
Sup-ply'ing.
Sup-pōrt'.
Sup-pōrt'a-ble, 164.
Sup-pōrt'a-bly.
Sup-pōrt'ed.
Sup-pōrt'er.
Sup-pōrt'ing.
Sup-pōs'a-ble (*-pōz'a-bl*), 164, 183.
Sup-pose' (*-pōz'*).
Sup-posed' (*-pōzd'*).
Sup-pōs'ing (*-pōz'-*).
Sup-po-sĭ'tion (*-zish'-un*), 170.
Sup-po-sĭ'tion-al (*-zish'un-*).
Sup-pos-i-ti'tious (*sup-(poz-i-tish'us*).
Sup-pos'i-tĭve (*-poz'-*).
Sup-pos'i-to-ry (*-poz'-*), 86, 171.
Sup-press'.
Sup-pressed' (*-prest'*), 165; Note C, p. 34.
Sup-press'ing.
Sup-pres'sion (*-presh'-un*).
Sup-press'ĭve, 228.
Sup-press'or.
Sup'pu-rate, 89.
Sup'pu-rāt-ed, 183.
Sup'pu-rāt-ing.
Sup-pu-ra'tion.
Sup'pu-rāt-ĭve.
Sup-pu-ta'tion.
Su-pra-ȧx'il-la-ry, 223.
Su-pra-cil'i-a-ry.
Su-pra-cre-ta'ceous (*-shus*).
Su-pra-lap-sa'ri-an.
Su-pra-lap-sa'ri-an-ism (*-izm*), 136.
Su-pra-lap'sa-ry, 72.
Su-pra-mun'dane.
Su-pra-nat'u-ral-ism (*-izm*), 133.
Su-pra-nat'u-ral-ist.
Su-pra-nat-u-ral-ist'ic, 109.
Su-pra-or'bit-al, 223.
Su-pra-or'bit-ar.
Su-pra-re'nal.
Su-pra-scap'u-lar.
Su-pra-scap'u-la-ry, 72.
Su-pra-spīn'al.
Su-prem'a-cy, 169.
Su-preme', 121.
Su-preme'ly, 185.

Su'ral, 49, N.
Sur'base.
Sur'based (-*bāst*).
Sur-base'ment.
Sur-bed'.
Sur-bed'ded.
Sur-bed'ding.
Sur-charge'.
Sur-charged', 165.
Sur-charg'ing (-*charj'*-),
Sur'cin-gle (-*sing-gl*) [so Wk. Wr. Wb. Gd.; *sur-sing'gl*, Sm. 155.]
Sur'cin-gled (-*sing-gld*).
Sur'cōat.
Sur'cu-lose [so Gd.; *sur-ku-lōs'*, Wr. 155.]
Surd, 21, 49, 135.
Sure (*shoor*) (46, 67) [so Sm. Wr.; *shŭr*, Wk. Wb. Gd. 155], *a.* firm; unfailing; certain. [*See* Shoer, 148.]
Sure'-fōōt-ed (*shoor'*-).
Sure'ly (*shoor'*-).
Sure'ness (*shoor'*-).
Sure'ty (*shoor'ty*), 145.
Surf (21), *n.* the swell of the sea breaking against rocks or shallows, or on the shore. [*See* Serf, 148.]
Sur'face.
Sur'feĭt, 97, 171.
Sur'feĭt-ed.
Sur'feĭt-ing.
Surge (21, 45), *n.* a large rolling wave: — *v.* to swell. [*See* Serge, 148.]
Surged, 165.
Sur'geon (-*jun*), 171; Note D, p. 37.
Sur'ger-y, 93.
Sur'gic-al.
Surg'ing (*surj'*-).
Surg'y (*surj'*-), 183.
Su'ri-cate.
Sur'li-ness, 186.
Sur'loin [Sirloin, 203. — *See* Note under *Sirloin.*]
Sur'ly, 93.
Sur-mise' (-*mīz'*).
Sur-mised' (-*mīzd'*).
Sur-mīs'ing (-*mīz'*-).
Sur-mount'.
Sur-mount'a-ble, 164, 169.
Sur-mount'ed.
Sur-mount'er.
Sur-mount'ing.
Sur-mul'let, 170.
Sur'name, *n.* (103, 161) [Sirname, 203. — *See* Note under *Sirname.*]
Sur-name', *v.* 103, 161.
Sur-named'.
Sur-nām'ing.
Sur-nom'i-nal.
Sur-pȧss'.
Sur-pȧss'a-ble, 164.
Sur-pȧssed' (-*pȧst'*).
Sur-pȧss'ing.
Sur'plĭce (169), *n.* a kind of ecclesiastical vestment. [*See* Surplus, 148.]
Sur'plus (169), *n.* residue. [*See* Surplice, 148.]
Sur'plus-age, 169.
Sur-prīs'al (-*prīz'*-).
Sur-prise' (-*prīz'*), *n.* & *v.* 202.
Sur-prised' (-*prīzd'*).
Sur-prīs'ing (-*prīz'*-).
Sŭr-re-but'.
Sŭr-re-but'ted.
Sŭr-re-but'ter.
Sŭr-re-but'ting.
Sŭr-re-join'.
Sŭr-re-join'der.
Sur-re'nal, 122.
Sur-ren'der.
Sur-ren'dered (-*durd*).
Sur-ren-der-ee' (118) [Law term, correlative of *Surrenderor.*]
Sur-ren'der-ing.
Sur-ren-der-or' (118) [so Sm.; *sur-ren'dur-or*, Wr. Wb. Gd. 155] [Law term, correlative of *Surrenderee.*]
Sur-rep'tion.
Sŭr-rep-tĭ'tious (-*tish'us*), 171.
Sŭr'ro-gate, 22.
Sur-round', 28.
Sur-round'ed.
Sur-round'ing.
Sur'sharp.
Sur-sol'id, 122.
Sur-tout' (-*toot'*), 19, 121, 171.
Sur'tur-brand.
Surveillance (Fr.) (*sur-vāl'yans*) [so Gd.; *soor-vāl-yäns'*, Wr. 154, 155.]
Sur-vey' (-*vā'*), *v.* 103, 161, 171.
Sur'vey (-*vā*), *n.* (98, 103, 161) [so Sm. Wb. Gd.; *sur-vā'*, or *sur'-vā*, Wk.; *sur'vā*, or *sur-vā'*, Wr. 155.]
Sur-vey'al (-*va'*-).
Sur-veyed' (-*vād'*).
Sur-vey'ing (-*vā'*-).
Sur-vey'or (-*va'*-), 169.
Sur-vīv'al.
Sur-vive'.
Sur-vived', 165.
Sur-vīv'ing.
Sur-vīv'or (88) [Surviver, 203.]
Sus-cep-ti-bil'i-ty, 171.
Sus-cep'ti-ble, 164, 169.
Sus-cep'ti-bly.
Sus-cep'tĭve, 39.
Sus-pect'.
Sus-pect'a-ble, 164, 169.
Sus-pect'ed.
Sus-pect'er.
Sus-pect'ing.
Sus-pend', 103.
Sus-pend'er, 169.
Sus-pend'ing.
Sus-pen-sa'tion, 169.
Sus-pense', 171.
Sus-pens-i-bil'i-ty.
Sus-pens'i-ble, 164.
Sus-pen'sion.
Sus-pen'so-ry.
Sus-pĭ'cion (-*pish'un*), 171, 231.
Sus-pĭ'cioŭs (-*pish'us*), 171, 231.
Sus-pi'ral, 49, N.
Sus-pi-ra'tion.
Sus-pire'.
Sus-pired', 165.
Sus-pīr'ing.
Sus-tāin'.
Sus-tāin'a-ble, 164.
Sus-tāined'.
Sus-tāin'er.
Sus-tāin'ing.
Sus'te-nance, 169.
Sus-ten-ta'tion.
Su'tĭle, 81, 152.
Sut'ler, *n.* a person who follows an army as a seller of provisions and liquors. [*See* Subtler, 160.]
Sut-tee', 121.
Sut-tee'ism (-*izm*), 136.
Sut'tle (*sut'l*), *a.* denoting weight after tare, and before tret, has been deducted. [*See* Subtle, 160.]
Sŭt'ur-al (-*yur*-), 91.
Sŭt'ure, 91.

Su'um cui'que (L.) (*-ki'kwe*).
Su'ze-räin.
Su'ze-räin-ty.
Swab (*swob*) (18) [S w o b, 203.]
Swabbed (*swobd*).
Swab'ber (*swob'-*).
Swab'bing (*swob'-*), 176.
Swad'dle (*swod'l*), 164.
Swad'dled (*swod'ld*).
Swad'dling (*swod'-*).
Swăg, 10.
Swage, 23, 45.
Swagged (*swagd*).
Swag'ger (*-gur*), 170.
Swag'gered (*-gurd*), 150.
Swag'ger-er (*-gur-*).
Swag'ger-ing (*-gur-*).
Swag'ging (*-ghing*).
Swag'gy (*-ghy̆*).
Swāin, 23.
Swāin'mote [S w a n i - m o t e, S w e i n - m o t e, 203.]
Swale, 23.
Swaled, 165.
Swāl'ing.
Swal'lōw (*swol'lo*), 101, 170.
Swal'lowed (*swol'lōd*).
Swal'lōw-er (*swol'-*).
Swal'lōw-ing (*swol'-*).
Swal'lōw-tāil (*swol'-*).
Swal'lōw-wort (*swol'lo-wurt*).
Swäm, 10.
Swamp (*swomp*), 18.
Swamped (*swompt*), Note C, p. 34.
Swamp'ing (*swomp'-*).
Swamp'-pink (*swomp'-pingk*), 206, Exc. 1.
Swamp'y (*swomp'-*), 169.
Swan (*swon*), 18.
[S w a n i m o t e, 203. — *See* Swainmote.]
Swăn'pan [so Gd.; *swon'pan*, Wr. 155.]
Swan's'-down (*swonz'-*).
Swap (*swop*) [S w o p, 203.]
Swapped (*swopt*).
Swap'ping (*swop'-*).
Swârd, 17.
Sware (*swêr*), 14, 49.
Swârm, 17, 49, 135.
Swârmed, 165.
Swârm'ing.
Swârth, 17, 37, 49.
Swârth'i-ly, 141.
Swârth'i-ness, 156.
Swârth'y (37, 140) [*not* swar<u>th</u>'y, 153.]
Swash (*swosh*), 18.
Swashed (*swosht*).
Swash'ing (*swosh'-*).
Swath (*swoth*, or *swawth*) [*swoth*, Sm. Wr.; *swawth*, Gd. 155.]
Swa<u>th</u>e, 163; Note D, p. 37.
Swa<u>th</u>ed (*swa<u>th</u>ed*).
Swā<u>th</u>'ing (*swā<u>th</u>'-*), 183.
Swāy, 56, Rem.
Swāyed (*swād*).
Swāy'ing.
Swēal, 13.
Swēaled, 165.
Swēal'ing.
Swêar (*swêr*), 14.
Swêar'er, 48, 49, N.
Swêar'ing.
Swĕat, 15.
Swĕat'ed.
Swĕat'i-ly, 186.
Swĕat'i-ness.
Swĕat'ing.
Swĕat'y.
Swede, 13.
Swe-den-bor'gi-an, 169.
Swe-den-bor'gi-an-ism (*-izm*), 133, 136.
Swēd'ish, 183.
Sweep, 13.
Sweep'er.
Sweep'ing.
Sweep'stakes, *n. sing. & pl.*
Sweep'y.
Sweet (13), *a.* pleasant to the taste, smell, ear, eye, or mind; — not sour nor bitter. [*See* Suite, 160.]
Sweet'brĕad, 216.
Sweet'bri-er.
Sweet'en (*sweet'n*), 149.
Sweet'ened (*-nd*), 165.
Sweet'en-er (*sweet'n-*).
Sweet'en-ing (*sweet'n-*).
Sweet'heärt.
Sweet'ing.
Sweet'ish.
Sweet'mēat.
Sweet'-scent-ed (*-sent-*), 206, Exc. 5.
Sweet'-smell-ing.
Sweet-will'iam (*-yam*).
[S w e i n m o t e, 203. — *See* Swainmote.]
Swell, 15, 172.
Swelled (*sweld*), 165.
Swell'ing.
Swel'ter, 77, 104.
Swel'tered, 150, 165.
Swel'ter-ing.
Swept (15, 41) [*not* swep, 141, 153.]
Swerve, 21, N.; 49, 135.
Swerved (*swervd*), 165.
Swerv'ing.
Swift, 16.
Swill, 16, 172.
Swilled (*swild*), 165.
Swill'er, 228.
Swill'ing.
Swim, 16.
Swim'mer, 66, 170.
Swim'ming, 176.
Swin'dle, 164.
Swin'dled (*-dld*), 61.
Swin'dler.
Swin'dling.
Swine, 25.
Swing, 16, 54.
Swinge (*swinj*), 16, 45; Note D, p. 37.
Swinged (*swinjd*).
Swinge'ing (171, 183) [S w i n g i n g, Sm. Wb. Gd. 203.]
Swin'gel (*swing'gl*) [so Gd.; *swin'jel*, Wr. 155.]
Swing'er.
Swing'ing.
Swin'gle (*swing'gl*).
Swin'gled (*swing'gld*).
Swin'gling (*swing'-*).
Swīn'ish, 183.
Swīpe, 25.
Swirl, 21, N.
Swirled, 165.
Swirl'ing.
Swiss, 16, 174.
Switch, 16, 44; Note D, p. 37.
Switched (*swicht*).
Switch'ing.
Switz'er (*swits'-*), Note C, p. 34.
Swiv'el (*swiv'l*), 149.
[S w o b, 203. — *See* Swab.]
Swōllen (*swōln*), *or* Swōln, 203.

☞ "The regular participle *swelled* is to be preferred." *Webster.* "*Swollen* and *swoln* are obsolescent." *Worcester.*

Swoon, 19.
Swooned, 165.
Swoon'ing.
Swoop, 19.
Swooped (*swoopt*).
Swoop'ing.

Swop [Swap, 203.]
Swopped (*swopt*), 41.
Swop'ping, 176.
Swōrd (*sord*) (162) [so Wk. Sm. Wr.; *swōrd*, or *sōrd*, Gd. 155], *n.* a weapon for cutting or for thrusting. [*See* Soared, 160.]
Swōrd'-cane (*sōrd'*-).
Swōrd'ed (*sōrd'*-).
Sword'-fish (*sōrd'*-).
Sword'-shaped (*sōrd'-shāpt*), 206, Exc. 5.
Swōrds'man (*sōrdz'*-), 196.
Swore, 24, 34, 49.
Swōrn, 135.
Swum, 22.
Swung, 22, 54.
Syb'a-rite, 152.
Syb-a-rit'ic, 109.
Syb-a-rit'ic-al, 108.
Syb'a-rit-ism (*-izm*), 106.
Syc'a-mīne, 82, 152.
Syc'a-more, 170.
Sȳ-cee', 121.
Sych-no-car'poŭs (*sik*-).
Syc'o-phan-cy, 169, 171.
Syc'o-phant.
Syc-o-phant'ic.
Syc-o-phant'ic-al.
Syc'o-phant-ism (*-izm*), 133, 136.
Sy'e-nite [Sienite, Siennite, 203.]

☞ Goodrich remarks: "As this word is from *Syene*, the proper spelling is *syenite*." The form *sienite*, however, is most in use.

Sy-e-nit'ic.
Syl'la-ba-ry, 72.
Syl-lab'ic, 122.
Syl-lab'ic-al.
Syl-lab'ic-al-ly.
Syl-lab'i-cate, 108.
Syl-lab'i-căt-ed.
Syl-lab'i-căt-ing.
Syl-lăb-i-ca'tion, 112, 116.
Syl-lab-i-fĭ-ca'tion.
Syl-lab'i-fīed, 186.
Syl-lab'i-fȳ, 94.
Syl-lab'i-fȳ-ing.
Syl'la-bist.
Syl'la-ble, 164.
Syl'la-bub [Sillabub, 203.]
Syl'la-bus (L.) [L. pl. *Syl'la-bī*; Eng. pl. Syl'la-bus-es (*-ez*), 198.]
Syl-lep'sis.
Syl-lep'tic-al.
Syl'lo-gism (*-jizm*), 86.
Syl-lo-gist'ic.
Syl-lo-gist'ic-al.
Syl-lo-gĭ-za'tion.
Syl'lo-gize, 202.
Syl'lo-gized, 186.
Syl'lo-gīz-er.
Syl'lo-gīz-ing.
Sylph, 16, 35.
Sylph'id.
Syl'va (L.) [pl. Syl'væ (*-ve*), 198.]
Syl'van [Silvan, 203.]
Sym'bol (86, 171), *n.* an emblem, type, or sign. [*See* Cymbal, 148.]
Sym-bol'ic.
Sym-bol'ic-al.
Sym-bol'ic-al-ly.
Sym'bol-ism (*-izm*), 136.
Sym'bol-ist.
Sym-bol-ĭ-za'tion.
Sym'bol-ize, 202.
Sym'bol-ized.
Sym'bol-īz-ing.
Sym-bo-log'ic-al(*-log'*-).
Sym-bol'o-gist, 45, 108.
Sym-bol'o-gy.
Sym-met'ric-al, 171.
Sym-met'ric-al-ly.
Sym'me-try, 169, 170.
Sym-pa-thet'ic.
Sym-pa-thet'ic-al.
Sym-pa-thet'ic-al-ly.
Sym'pa-thist.
Sym'pa-thize, 202.
Sym'pa-thized, 165.
Sym'pa-thīz-ing, 183.
Sym'pa-thy, 108.
Sym-phon'ic.
Sym-pho'ni-oŭs.
Sym'pho-nist.
Sym'pho-ny, 108.
Sym-phys'e-al (*-fiz'*-), 169.
Sym-phys-e-ot'o-my, *or* Sym-phys-ot'o-my (*-fiz*-), 108, 203.
Sym'phy-sis.
Sym-pī-e-som'e-ter (*-zom'*-) [so Gd.; *sim-pī-e-zom'e-tur*, Sm.; *sim-pī-e-som'e-tur*, Wr. 155.]
Sym'plo-ce, 163.
Sym-po'si-ac (*sim-po'-zi-ak*, coll. *sim-po'-zhi-ak*) [so Sm.; *sim-po'zi-ak*, Wb. Gd.; *sim-po'zhi-ak*, Wk.; *sim-po'zi-ak*, or *sim-po'zhi-ak*, Wr. 155.]
Sym-po'si-arch (*-zĭ-ark*, coll. *-zhĭ-ark*).
Sym-po'si-ast (*-zĭ-*, coll. *-zhĭ-*).
Sym-po'si-um (*sim-po'-zi-um*, coll. *sim-po'-zhĭ-um*).
Symp'tom (*sim'tum*), 86, 162.
Symp-tom-at'ic (*sim*-).
Symp-tom-at'ic-al (*sim*-).
Symp-tom-a-tol'o-gy (*sim*-), 45, 108.
Syn-ær'e-sis (*sin-ĕr'e-sis*), 171.
Syn-a-gog'ic-al (*-goj'*-).
Syn'a-gŏgue, 87, 171.
[Synalepha, 203.—*See* Synalœpha.]
Syn-al-lag-mat'ic.
Syn-a-lœ'pha (*-le'*-)(171) [Synalepha, 203.]
Syn-an'ther-oŭs.
Syn-an'thoŭs, 100.
Syn'ar-chy (*-kĭ*).
Syn-ar-thro'di-al.
Syn-ar-thro'sis, 109.
Syn-car'pi-um.
Syn-car'poŭs.
Syn-cat-e-gŏr-e-mat'ic, 116.
Syn-chon-drot'o-my (*-kon*-), 52, 108.
Syn-cho-re'sis(*sing-ko*-)
Syn'chro-nal(*sing'kro*-) [*See* Synchronism.]
Syn-chron'ic-al (*sin-kron'*-).
Syn'chro-nism (*sing'-kro-nizm*) [so Wk. Sm. Wr.; *sin'kro-nizm*, Wb. Gd. 155.]
Syn-chro-nist'ic (*sin-kro*-), 109.
Syn-chro-nĭ-za'tion (*sing-kro*-).
Syn'chro-nize (*sing'-kro-nīz*), 52, 54.
Syn'chro-nized (*sing'-kro*-), 165.
Syn'chro-nīz-ing (*sing'-kro*-).
Syn-chro-nol'o-gy (*sing-kro*-), 108.
Syn'chro-noŭs (*sing'-kro*-), 54, 141.
Syn-cli'nal.
Syn-clin'ic.
Syn-clin'ic-al.

Syn′co-pal (*sing′-*).
Syn′co-pate (*sing′-*).
Syn′co-pāt-ed (*sing′-*), 183.
Syn′co-pāt-ing (*sing′-*).
Syn-co-pa′tion (*sing-*).
Syn′co-pe (*sing′-*), 163.
Syn′co-pist (*sing′-*).
Syn-cret′ic (109) [so Sm.; *sin′kre-tik*, Wr. 155.]
Syn′cre-tism (*sing′kre-tizm*) (54) [so Sm.; *sin′kre-tizm*, Wr. Wb. Gd. 155] [Syncratism, 203.]
Syn′cre-tist (*sing′-*).
Syn-cre-tist′ic (*sing-*).
Syn-dac′tyl.
Syn-dac-tyl′ic (109) [so Gd.; *sin-dak′til-ik*, Wr. 155.]
Syn-des-mog′ra-phy.
Syn-des-mol′o-gy.
Syn-des-mot′o-my.
Syn′dic.
Syn′dro-me, 144, 163.
Syn-ec′do-che (*-ke-*), 52.
Syn-ec-doch′ic-al (*-dok′-*), 52.
Syn-ec-pho-ne′sis.
Syn-e′chi-a (*-kĭ-*).
Syn′e-py, 169.
Syn-er-get′ic, 45.
Syn-er′gism (*-jizm*).
Syn-er′gist [so Sm. Wr.; *sin′ur-jist*, Gd. 155.]
Syn-er-gist′ic, 109.
Syn′er-gy.
Syn-ge-ne′si-a (*-zhĭ-a*) [*sin-je-ne′zĭ-a*, Wr.; *sin-je-ne′sha*, Gd. 155.]
Syn-ge-ne′sian (*-zhan*).
Syn-ge-ne′sioŭs (*-zhus*) (171) [*sin-je-ne′zh′us*, Sm. (*See* § 26); *sin-je-ne′shus*, Wr. Gd. 155.]
Syn-gna′thi-an (*sin-na′-*), 162.
Syn′grăph (*sing′graf*) [*sin′graf*, Wr. Gd. 155]
Syn-i-ze′sis.
Syn-neū-ro′sis, 109.
Syn′od (Note F, p. 79) [*not* si′nŏd, 153.]
Syn-od′ic.
Syn-od′ic-al.
Syn′od-ist, 106.
Syn-om′o-sy, 105.
Syn′o-nўme, *or* Syn′o-nym, 203.
Syn-o-nym′ic.
Syn-on′y-mist, 169.
Syn-on′y-mize, 202.
Syn-on′y-mized, 165.
Syn-on′y-mīz-ing, 183.
Syn-on′y-moŭs, 171.
Syn-on′y my, 105.
Syn-op′sis (L.) [pl. Syn-op′sēs (*-sēz*), 198.]
Syn-op′tic.
Syn-op′tic-al.
Syn-op′tic-al-ly, 66.
Syn-os-te-og′ra-phy.
Syn-os-te-ol′o-gy, 171.
Syn-os-te-ot′o-my.
Syn-o′vi-a.
Syn-o′vi-al, 78, 169.
Syn-tac′tic.
Syn-tac′tic-al.
Syn-tac′tic-al-ly.
Syn′tăx.
Syn-tec′tic-al.
Syn-te-re′sis.
Syn-te-ret′ic.
Syn-tet′ic, 170.
Syn-tex′is.
Syn-ther′mal.
Syn′the-sis (L.) [pl. Syn′the-sēs (*-sēz*), 198.]
Syn-thet′ic.
Syn-thet′ic-al.
Syn-thet′ic-al-ly.
Syn′to-my, 108.
Syn-ton′ic.
[Syphon, 203. — *See* Siphon.]
[Syren, 203. — *See* Siren.]
Sўr′i-ac, 16, 48, 67, 231.
Sў-ri′a-cism (*-sizm*).
Sўr′i-an, 169.
Sўr′i-an-ism (*-izm*), 136.
Sўr′i-asm (*-azm*), 133.
Sў-rin′ga (*-ring′-*), 54.
Sўr′inge (*-inj*), 171.
Sўr′inged (*-injd*).
Sўr-ing-ing (*-inj-*).
Sўr-in-got′o-my [so Wr. Wb. Gd.; *sĭr-ing-got′-o-my*, Wk.; *sĭr-ing-ot′o-my*, Sm. 155.]
Sўr′inx (*-ingks*), 54.
Syrt, 21, N.
Syrt′ic.
Sўr′up [Sirup, 203.] [*See* Note under *Sirup.*]
Sys-tal′tic.
Sys′tem, 76.
Sys-tem-at′ic.
Sys-tem-at′ic-al.
Sys-tem-at′ic-al-ly.
Sys′tem-a-tism (*-tizm*).
Sys′tem-a-tist, 106.
Sys′tem-a-tize (202) [so Sm. Wr. Wb. Gd.; *sis-tem′a-tīz*, Wk. 155.]
Sys′tem-a-tized.
Sys′tem-a-tīz-er.
Sys′tem-a-tīz-ing.
Sys-tem-a-tol′o-gy.
Sys-tem′ic (109) [so Gd.; *sis′tem-ik*, Wr. 155.]
Sys-tem-ĭ-za′tion, 112.
Sys′tem-ize, 202.
Sys′tem-ized.
Sys′tem-īz-ing, 183.
Sys′tem-māk′er, 205.
Sys′to-le, 163.
Sys-tol′ic.
Sys′tўle, 171.
[Sythe, 203. — *See* Scythe.]
Syz′y-gy (93, 171) [pl. Syz′y-gies (*-jiz*), 190.]

T.

Tab′ard [Taberd, 203]
Tab′ard-er.
Tab′a-ret, *n.* a kind of stout silk. [*See* Taboret, *and* Tabouret, 148.]
Tab-a-sheer′ [Tabashir, 203.]
Tab′bīed (*-bid*).
Tab-bi-net′ (78) [so Sm.; *tab′bi-net*, Wr. Gd. 155.]
Tab′by, 66, 170.
Tab′by-ing.
Tab-e-fac′tion.
[Taberd, 203. — *See* Tabard.]
Tab′er-na-cle (72, 164) [so Wk. Wr. Wb. Gd.; *tab′ur-năk-l*, Sm. 155.]
Tab′er-na-cled (*-kld*).
Tab′er-na-cling.
Tab-er-nac′u-lar, 108.
Ta′bēs (L.) (*ta′bēz*).
Ta-bet′ic, 66, 170.
Tab′id, 171.
Ta-bif′ic.
Tab′la-ture, 26, 90.
Ta′ble, 164.
Tab′leau (*-lo*) [so Sm. Gd.; *tab-lo′*, Wr. 155] [pl. *Tab′leaux* (*tab′lo*, or *tab′lōz*), 198.]
Tableaux vivans (Fr.) (*tab′lo ve-vŏng′*) [so

Sm.; *tab'lo ve'văng*, Gd.; *tab'lo ve-văng'*, Wr. 155.]
Ta'ble-clŏth, 164.
Ta'bled (*ta'bld*).
Ta'ble d'hôte (Fr.) (*tä'-bl dōt*).
Ta'ble-land, 66, N.; 164.
Ta'ble-spoon.
Ta'ble-spoon'ful (*ta'bl-spoon'fŏŏl*), 197.
Tab'let.
Ta'ble-tâlk (*-tawk*).
Ta'bling.
Ta-boo'.
Ta-booed', 150, 171, 188.
Ta-boo'ing.
Ta'bor (88) [Tabour, Sm. 199, 203.]
Ta'bored (150, 165) [Taboured, Sm. 203.]
Tab'or-et, *n.* a small tabor. [Tabouret, Sm. 203] [*See* Tabaret, *and* Tabouret, 148.]
Ta'bor-īte (83, 152) [so Wr. Gd.; *tab'o-rĭt*, Sm. 155.]
Tab-ou-ret' (Fr.) (*tab-oo-rā'*) [so Wr.; *tab'-oo-ret*, Wb. Gd. 155], *n.* a kind of stool; — a frame for embroidery. [*See* Tabaret, *and* Taboret, 148.]
Tab'u-lar, 169.
Tab'u-la ra'sa (L.).
Tab-u-lar-ĭ-za'tion.
Tab'u-lar-ize, 202.
Tab'u-lar-ized.
Tab'u-lar-īz-ing.
Tab'u-late, 108.
Tab'u-lāt-ed.
Tab'u-lāt-ing.
Tab-u-la'tion, 112, 169.
Tac'a-ma-hac [so Wb. Gd.; *tak-a-ma-hak'*, Wr. 155.]
Tac-a-ma-ha'ca [so Wb. Gd.; *tak-a-ma-hak'a*, Wr. 155.]
Tăche (*tach*), 171.
Tach-e-og'ra-phy (*tak-*).
Ta-chom'e-ter (*-kom'-*), 108.
Tach'y-dĭ-dax-y (*tăk'-*) [*tak-ĭ-dĭ-daks'y*, Wr. Gd. 155.]
Tach-y-dro'mi-an(*tak-*).
Tach-y-graph'ic (*tak-*).
Tach-y-graph'ic-al (*tak-*).
Ta-chyg'ra-phy (*-kig'-*).
Tach'y-līte (*tak'-*).
Taç'it, 39, 235.
Taç'i-turn, 171.
Taç-i-turn'i-ty.
Tack (10, 181), *n.* & *v.* [pl. of *n.* Tacks, 189. — *See* Tax, 160.]
Tacked (*takt*) (Note C, p. 34), *v.* did tack. [*See* Tact, 160.]
Tack'ing.
Tack'le (*tak'l*, among seamen *ta'kl*), 164.
Tack'led (*tak'ld*).
Tack'ling, 183.
Tact (10), *n.* adroitness in adapting one's words or conduct to circumstances. [*See* Tacked, 160.]
Tac'tic.
Tac'tic-al.
Tac-tĭ'cian (*-tish'an*).
Tac'tics.
Tac'tĭle, 81, 152.
Tac-til'i-ty.
Tac'tion.
Tact'u-al, 108.
Tad'pole.
[Tædium, 203. — *See* Tedium.]
Tāel, 23.
Tā'en (*tān*), a poetical contraction of *taken*.
Tæ'ni-oid [Tenioid, 203.]
Taf'fe-ta, *or* Taf'fe-ty, 170, 203.
Taff'rāil [Tafferel, 203.]
Taf'fy.
Taf'i-a [so Gd.; *tä'fi-ä*, Wr. 155.]
Tag, 10.
Tagged (*tagd*), 165.
Tag'ging (*-ghing*), 138, 176.
Taglia (It.) (*täl'ya*).
Tagl-ia-co'tian (*tal-ya-ko'shan*) [so Sm. Gd.; *tal-yĭ-a-ko'shan*, Wr. 155] [Taliacotian, 203.]
Tāil, *n.* the protruding extremity of the vertebral column; — the hinder feathers of a bird; — the extremity, or hinder or lower part, of any thing; — limitation. [*See* Taille, *and* Tale, 160.]
[Tailage, Taillage, 203. — *See* Tallage.]
Taille (Fr.) (*tāl*), *n.* an imposition levied by the king upon his subjects. [*See* Tail, *and* Tale, 160.]
Tāil'less, 66, N.
Tāi'lor.
Tāi'lor-ess.
Tāi'lor-ing. [203.]
Tāil'zĭe (99) [Tailzee, 203.]
Tāint, 23.
Tāint'ed.
Tāint'ing.
Tāint'ure, 91.
Take, 23, 163.
Take'-in, 206, Exc. 4.
Tāk'en (*tāk'n*), 149.
Take'-off, 215.
Tāk'ing, 228.
Tal'a-poin [*tal'a-poin*, Wb. Gd.; *tal-a-poin'*, Wr.; *tal'a-po-in*, Sm. 155][Talapin, Telapoin, 203.]
Ta-la'ri-a (L.), *n. pl.*
Tâl'bot (86)[so Wr.Gd.]

☞ In Smart's notation of this word, the *a* is marked as having a sound intermediate between that of *a* in *all* and that of *o* in *on*. *See* § 18, N.

Talc (181) [*not* tawk, 153] [Talck, Talk, 203.]
Tal'cĭte.
Talck'y, 182.
Tal-cose' [so Wr.; *tal'-kōs*, Gd. 155.]
Talc'oŭs.
Tale (23), *n.* a story; a narrative. [*See* Tail, *and* Taille, 160.]
Tale'-bêar-er.
Tale'-bêar-ing.
Ta'led.
Tal'e-gal.
Tal'ent, 76, 127.
Tal'ent-ed.
Ta'lēs (L.)(*ta'lēz*), *n. pl.*
Tales'man (*tālz'-*), 196.
Tal-i-a-co'tian (*-shan*) [Tagliacotian, 203.]
Tal'is-man (or *tal'iz-man*) [*tal'is-man*, Sm.; *tal'iz-man*, Wk. Wr. Gd. 155.]
Tal-is-man'ic (or *tal-iz-man'ik*).

Tal-is-man′ic-al (or *tal-iz-man′ik-al*).
Tâlk (*tawk*), 162.
Tâlk′a-tĭve (*tawk′-*).
Tâlked (*tawkt*).
Tâlk′er (*tawk′-*).
Tâlk′ing (*tawk′-*).
Tâll, 17, 172.
Tăl′lage [Tailage, Taillage, Talliage, 203.]
Tal′lĭed (*-lid*).
Tal′lōw, 101.
Tal′lōw-y, 93.
Tal′ly, 66, 170.
Tal′ly-ing.
Tal′ly-man.
Tal′mud.
Tal-mud′ic (109) [so Sm. Gd.; *tal-mud′ik*, or *tal′mud-ik*, Wr. 155.]
Tal-mud′ic-al.
Tal′mud-ist, 106.
Tal-mud-ist′ic.
Tal′on, 86, 170.
Ta-look′ (India).
Ta-look′ah.
Ta-look′dar [so Sm.; *tal-ook-dar′*, Wr. 155.]
Ta′lus.
Tăm-a-bil′i-ty.
Tăm′a-ble, 164.
Tam′a-rack.
Tam′a-rin (148), *n.* a kind of monkey.
Tam′a-rind (142, 148), *n.* a kind of fruit.
Tam′a-risk, 171.
Tam′bac, *n.* a fragrant medicinal wood from the East Indies; — an alloy of copper [Tombac (in the latter sense), 203.]
Tam′bour (*tam′boor*, or *tam′bur*) [*tam′boor*, Wr. Gd.; *tam′bur*, Sm. 155] [Tambor, 203.]
Tam-bour-ine′ (*tam-boor-ēn′*, or *tam-bur-ēn′*), 122, 171.
Tam′breet.
Tame, 23.
Tamed, 165.
Tăm′er.
Tam′ĭne, 152.
Tăm′ing.
Tam′i-ny.
Tam′is.
[Tammuz, 203. — *See* Thammuz.]
Tam′my.
Tamp, 10.
Tamped (*tampt*), Note C, p. 34.
Tamp′er (228, N.), *n.* one who tamps.
Tam′per, *v.* 77, 169.
Tam′pered, 150.
Tam′per-ing.
Tamp′ing, 228.
Tam′pi-on (86) [Tompion, 203.]
Tam′pōe.
Tam′tam.
Tan, 10.
Tan′a-ger, 45.
Tan′dem.
Tang, 10, 54.
Tan′gen-cy.
Tan′gent.
Tan-gen′tial (*-shal*).
Tan′ghin (53, 160), *n.* a plant of Madagascar, the fruit of which is a very powerful poison.
Tan′ghĭne (160), *n.* a crystallizable poisonous principle obtained from tanghin.
Tan-gi-bil′i-ty, 169.
Tan′gi-ble, 164.
Tan′gi-bly.
Tan′gle (*tang′gl*).
Tan′gled (*tang′gld*).
Tan′gling (*tang′-*).
Tan′gly (*tang′-*).
Tan′ĭst, 66, 170.
Tan′ist-ry.
Tan′jib.
Tank (*tangk*), 10, 54.
Tank′ard (*tangk′-*).
Tan′nate, 170.
Tanned (*tand*), 165.
Tan′ner, 176.
Tan′ner-y, 233, Exc.
Tan′nic.
Tan′nin, 66, 170.
Tan′ning.
Tan′rec [Tenrec, 203.]
Tan′sy (*-zy*), 136, 169.
Tan′ta-lism (*-lizm*), 136.
Tan′ta-līte, 152.
Tan-ta-lĭ-za′tion, 112.
Tan′ta-lize, 202.
Tan′ta-lized, 165.
Tan′ta-līz-ing.
Tan′ta-mount, 171.
Tan-tiv′y [so Sm.; *tan′-tiv-y*, Wb. Gd.; *tan-tiv′y*, or *tan′tiv-y*, Wr. 155.]
Tan′trum, 169.
Tap, 10.
Tape, 23, 163.
Ta′per (77), *n.* a small wax candle; — a gradual diminution in diameter: — *a.* gradually diminishing in diameter: — *v.* to grow gradually smaller towards one end. [*See* Tapir, 160.]
Ta′pered (*-purd*), 150.
Ta′per-ing.
Tap′es-try [so Sm. Wr. Wb. Gd.; *taps′trў*, or *tap′es-trў*, Wk. 155.]

☞ "Though the first [*taps′try*] is the more common, the last [*tap′es-try*] is the more correct pronunciation." *Walker.*

Tap′e-tĭ, 191.
Tape′-worm (*-wurm*).
Tap′-house.
Tap-i-o′ca.
Ta′pir (85), *n.* a pachydermatous mammal allied to the rhinoceros and the hog. [*See* Taper, 160.]
Tapis (Fr.) (*tap′e*, or *ta′pis*) [so Wr.; *tap′e*, Sm.; *ta′pis*, Wb. Gd. 154, 155.]
Tăp′ist, 183.
Tap′ling.
Tap′net.
Tapped (*tapt*), 165; Note C, p. 34.
Tap′pet, 66, 170.
Tap′ping, 176.
Tap′ster.
Tar, 11, 41, 49.
Tăr′a-nis.
Tăr′an-tism (*-tizm*) [Tarentism, 203.]
Tăr-an-tis′mus (*-tiz′-*) [Tarentismus, 203.]
Ta-ran′tu-la (89) [Tarentula, 203.]
Tar-ax′a-cĭne, 152.
Tar′di-grade, 169.
Tar′di-grăd-oŭs, 100.
Tar′di-ly, 186.
Tar′di-ness.
Tar′dy, 135.
Tare (*têr*) (14), *n.* a weed growing among grain; — the common vetch; — an allowance in weight for the cask, box, or bag in which goods are contained. [*See* Têar, 160.]

[Tarentism, 203. — *See* Tarantism.]
[Tarentismus, 203. — *See* Tarantismus.]
[Tarentula, 203. — *See* Tarantula.]
Tar′get (*-ghet*), 138.
Tar-get-eer′ (*-ghet-*) (169) [Targetier, 203.]
Tar′gum, 169, 189.
Tar′gum-ist.
Tăr′iff, 171.
Tăr′in, 170.
Tar′la-tan, 72.
Tarn, 11, 49, 135.
Tar′nish, *n.* & *v.* 103, 104.
Tar′nished (*-nisht*).
Tar′nish-ing.
Tar-pâul′ing [Tarpaulin, Tarpawling, 203.]
Tar-pe′ian (*-yan*), 112, 171.
Tăr′ra-gon.
Tăr′ras [Terras, Trass, 203.]
Tarred (*tard*), 11, 165.
Tăr′ri-ance, 169.
Tăr′rĭed.
Tăr′ri-er, 186.
Tăr′ring, 176.
Tăr′rock.
Tär′ry (11, 161), *a.* of, or resembling, tar.
Tăr′ry (161), *v.* to delay.
Tăr′ry-ing.
Tar′sal, 49, 135.
Tarse, 11, 39; Note D, p. 37.
Tar′si-er.
Tar′so-met-a-tar′sal, 224.
Tar-sŏr′rha-phy (*-ra-fy̆*).
Tar-sot′o-my, 108.
Tar′sus (L.) [pl. *Tar′sī*, 198.]
Tart, 11, 49, 135.
Tar′tan, 72.
Tar′tar, 74.
Tar-ta′re-an, 49, N.; 110.
Tar′tar-e-met′ic.
Tar-ta′re-oŭs.
Tar-tăr′ic, 109.
Tar-tar-ĭ-za′tion, 169.
Tar′tar-ize.
Tar′tar-ized.
Tar′tar-īz-ing.
Tar′tar-oŭs (160), *a.* containing, or consisting of, tartar.

Tar′ta-rus (160), *n.* the nether world.
Tart′ish.
Tar′trate.
Tar-tuffe′ (*tar-tuf′*) [so Wr. Gd.; *tar′t′oof*, Sm. (*See* § 26), 155.]
Tar-tuff′ish.
Tȧsk, 12, 131.
Tȧsked (*tȧskt*), 165; Note C, p. 34.
Tȧsk′ing.
Tȧsk′mȧs-ter.
Tȧsk′work (*-wurk*).
Tas-ma′ni-an (*taz-*) [so Wr.; *tas-ma′ni-an*, Gd. 155.]
Tas′sel (127, 149) [so Wk. Sm. Wb. Gd.; *tas′sel*, or *tos′l*, Wr. 155.]
Tas′selled (*-seld*) [Tasseled, Wb. Gd. 203. — *See* 177, and Note E, p. 70.]
Tas′sel-ling (177) [Tasseling, Wb. Gd. 203.]
Tas′ses (*-sez*), *n. pl.*
Tāst′a-ble, 164, 169.
Taste, 23, 163.
Tāst′ed, 183.
Taste′ful (*-fŏŏl*), 180.
Taste′ful-ly (*-fŏŏl-*).
Taste′less, 185.
Tāst′er.
Tāst′i-ly, 186.
Tāst′ing.
Tāst′y, 169.
Tat′ter, 104.
Tat-ter-de-măl′ion (*-yun*) [*not* tat-tur-de-măl′yun, 127, 153.]
Tat′tered, 150.
Tat′ting, 170.
Tat′tle, 164.
Tat′tled, 150.
Tat′tler.
Tat′tling.
Tat-too′, *n.* & *v.*
Tat-tooed′, 188.
Tat-too′ing.
Tâught (*tawt*), *a.* & *v.* (162) [Taut (as an *a.* meaning *tense, tight*), 203.]
Täunt, *n.* & *v.* [so Sm. Wb. Gd.; *tänt*, or *tawnt*, Wk. Wr. 155.]

☞ Though Walker, in deference to other orthoëpists, admits *tawnt* as an alternative pronunciation, he says: "I see no good reason why this word should have the broad sound of *a*, and not *aunt, haunt, flaunt, jaunt*; . . . nor is my ear much accustomed to hear it so pronounced."

Täunt [so Wr. Gd.; *tawnt*, Sm. 155], *a.* very high or tall, as a ship's masts.
Täunt′ed.
Täunt′er.
Täunt′ing.
Tâu′ri-corn-oŭs [so Sm.; *taw-ri-korn′us*, Wr. Gd. 155.]
Tâu′ri-form, 108.
Tâu′rīne, *or* Tâu′rīne [*taw′rin*, Wr.; *taw′-rīn*, Gd. 155], *a.* pertaining to a bull.
Tâu′rīne (82, 152), *n.* a substance prepared from fresh bile.
Tâu′ro-col.
Tâu-ro-col′la.
Tâu-ro-ma′chi-an (*-ki-*).
Tâu-rom′a-chy (*-ky*), 52.
Tâu′rus (L.).
Tâut [Taught, 203.]
Tâu′to-chrone (*-krōn*).
Tâu-toch′ro-noŭs (*-tok′-*).
Tâu-tog′ [Tautaug, 203.]
Tâu′to-līte, 83, 152.
Tâu-to-log′ic (*-loj′-*).
Tâu-to-log′ic-al (*-loj′-*).
Tâu-tol′o-gist, 108.
Tâu-tol′o-gize, 202.
Tâu-tol′o-gized.
Tâu-tol′o-gīz-ing.
Tâu-tol′o-gy, 108.
Tâu-to-phon′ic-al.
Tâu-toph′o-ny.
Tav′ern, 135, 171.
Tav′ern-keep′er, 205.
Taw, 17.
Taw′dri-ly.
Taw′dri-ness, 186.
Taw′dry, 93.
Tawed, 150.
Taw′er.
Taw′er-y.
Taw′ing.
Taw′ny, 169.
Tax (10, 39, N.), *n.* an impost; a requisition: — *v.* to impose or assess a tax on; — to accuse. [*See* Tacks (pl. of Tack), 160.]

Tax-a-bil′i-ty.
Tax′a-ble, 164, 169.
Tax-a′tion.
Taxed (*takst*), 41.
Tax′er (77), *n.* one who taxes: — an officer in the University of Cambridge, who regulates the assize of bread, &c. [Taxor (in the latter sense), 203.]
Tax′-gath′er-er.
Tax′i-arch (*-ark*).
Tax′i-corn.
Tax-i-der′mic, 109.
Tax′i-der-mist [*not* taks-id′er-mist, 153.]
Tax′i-der-my, 126.
Tax′ing.
Tax-on′o-my, 108.
Tax′or (88) [Taxer, 203. — *See* Taxer.]
Tēa (13, 41) [pl. Teas (*tēz*), 189.— *See* Tease, 160.]
Tēach, 13, 44.
Tēach′a-ble, 164, 199.
Tēach′er.
Tēa′-chest, 206, Exc. 3.
Tēach′est, *v.* dost teach.
Tēach′ing.
Tēa′cup, 206.
Tēak, 13.
Tēa′ket-tle, 164, 206.
Tēal (13), *n.* a small natatorial bird of the duck family. [*See* Teil, 160.]
Tēam (13), *n.* two or more horses, oxen, or other beasts, harnessed for drawing. [*See* Teem, 160.]
Tēam′ing.
Tēam′ster.
Tēa′pot, 206.
Tēar (13, 161), *n.* a drop of the fluid which flows from the eyes, as in weeping. [*See* Tier, 160.]
Têar (*têr*) (14, 161), *v.* to rend: — *n.* a rent, or fissure. [*See* Tare, 160.]
Têar′er (*têr′-*).
Tēar′ful (*-fŏŏl*).
Têar′ing (*têr′-*).
Tēase (*tēz*) (13, 40), *v.* to comb or card, as wool or flax; — to scratch, as cloth, in order to raise a nap; — to annoy or torment. [*See* Teas (pl. of Tea), 160.]
Tēased (*tēzd*), Note C, p. 34.
Tēa′sel (*te′zl*) (149, 167) [Teasle, Teazle, Teazel, 203.]
Tēa′seled (*-zld*) [Teazled, 203.]
Tēa′sel-er (*te′zl-ur*) [so Gd.; *tēz′lur*, Sm. 155] [Teazler, 203.]
Tēa′sel-ing (*te′zl-ing*) [Teazling, 203.]
Tēas′er (*tēz′-*), *n.* one who teases. [*See* Teazer, 160.]
Tēas′ing (*tēz′-*).
[Teasle, 203. — *See* Teasel, Teazle.]
Tēa′spoon, 206.
Tēa′spoon-ful (*-fŏŏl*), 180, 197.
Tēat (12) [*not* tet, *nor* tit, 153.]
[Teatotal, 203. — *See* Teetotal.]
Tēa′-urn.
Tēaz′er, *n.* the stoker of a furnace. [*See* Teaser, 160.]
Tēa′zle (164) [Teazel, Teasel, 203.]
Tēa′zled (*te′zld*) [Teaseled, 203.]
Tēa′zler [Teaseler, 203.]
Tēa′zling [Teaseling, 203.]
Te′beth.
Tech′i-ly, 186.
Tech′i-ness.
Tech′nic (*tek′-*).
Tech′nic-al (*tek′-*).
Tech-ni-cal′i-ty (*tek′-*).
Tech′ni-cal-ly (*tek′-*).
Tech′ni-cist (*tek′-*).
Tech-ni-col′o-gy (*tek-*).
Tech-no-log′ic (*tek-no-loj′ik*), 109.
Tech-no-log′ic-al (*tek-no-loj′-*), 108.
Tech-nol′o-gist (*tek-*).
Tech′y [Tetchy, Touchy, 203.]
Tec-ti-bran′chi-ate (*-brang′ki-*).
Tec-ton′ic.
Tec-ton′ics, 109.
Tec′tri-cēs (*-sēs*), *n. pl.*
Ted, 15, 41, 42.
Ted′ded.
[Tedder, 203. — *See* Ted′ding. [Tether.]
Te De′um (L.).
Te′di-oŭs (or *tēd′yus*) [*te′di-us*, Sm. Wb. Gd.; *te′di-us*, or *te′ji-us*, Wk.; *tēd′yus*, Wr. 134, 155.]
Te′di-um (169) [Tædium, 203.]
Teem (13), *v.* to produce abundantly. [*See* Team, 160.]
Teemed (*tēmd*), 165.
Teem′ing.
Teens (*tēnz*), *n. pl.* 13, 39.
Teeth (13, 37, 161), *n. pl.* of Tooth.
Teeth (13, 38, 161), *v.* to breed teeth.
Tee-to′tal.

☞ "By some written *teatotal*, on the supposition that it implies the use of *tea*, instead of intoxicating liquors." *Worcester.*

Tee-to′tal-er.
Tee-to′tal-ism (*-izm*).
Tee-to′tum, 169.
Teg′men (L.) [pl. *Teg′mi-na*, 198.]
Teg-men′ta (L.), *n. pl.*
Tech′ni-cist (*tek′-*).
Teg′u-lar, 108.
Teg′u-lāt-ed.
Teg′u-ment, 89.
Teg-u-ment′a-ry, 72.
Te-hee′.
Tēil (13), *n.* the lime-tree, or linden. [*See* Teal, 160.]
Tei′no-scope.
Tel-a-mo′nès (L.)(*-nēz*), *n. pl.* [so Wr. Gd.; *tel′a-mō-nēz*, Sm. 155.]
[Telapoin, 203.— *See* Talapoin.]
Te′la-ry [*not* tel′a-ry, 127, 153.]
Tel′e-du [so Wr.; *tel-e-du′*, Gd. 155.]
Tel′e-gram, 171.
Tel′e-grăph, 127.
Tel′e-grăphed (*-grăft*).
Tel-e-graph′ic, 109.
Tel-e-graph′ic-al, 108.
Tel′e-grăph-ing.
Te-leg′ra-phist (108) [so Gd.; *tel′e-graf-ist*, Wr. 155.]
Te-leg′ra-phy (108) [so Gd.; *tel′e-graf-y*, Wr. 155.]

Tel-e-o-log'ic-al (-loj'-).
Tel-e-ol'o-gy [so Sm.; *te-le-ol'o-gy*, Wr. Gd. 155.]
Tel'e-o-sâur [so Sm.; *te'le-o-sawr*, Wr. 155.]
Tel-e-o-sâu'rus[so Sm.; *te-le-o-saw'rus*, Wr. Gd. 155.]
Tel'e-phone, 171.
Tel-e-phon'ic.
Tel'e-scope, 171.
Tel-e-scop'ic.
Tel-e-scop'ic-al.
Te-le'si-a(-*zhi-a*)[so Wr. *te-le'zha*, Gd. 155.]
Tel'esm (-*ezm*).
Tel-es-mat'ic (-*ez*-).
Tel-es-mat'ic-al (-*ez*-) [so Wr. Gd.; *tel-es-mat'ik-al*, Sm. 155.]
Tel-e-ste're-o-scope. [*See* Stereoscope.]
Te-les'tic, *a.*
Tel'es-tich (-*tik*), *or* Te-les'tich (-*tik*) [*tel'es-tik*, Sm.; *te-les'tik*, Wr. Gd. 155], *n.*
Tel'ic, 170.
Tell, 15, 172.
Tell'er.
Tell'ing.
Tell'-tale, 206, Exc. 4.
Tel'lu-rate.
Tel'lu-ret-ted [Tellureted, Wb. Gd. 203.]
Tel-lu'ri-an, 169.
Tel-lu'ric, 109.
Tel'lu-rīde.
Tel'lu-rīne, 82, 152.
Tel'lu-rīte, 83.
Tel-lu'ri-um, 26, 169.
Tel'lu-roŭs.
Tel'o-type.
Tem-er-a'ri-oŭs.
Te-mer'i-ty.
Tem-pe'an, 110.
Tem'per, 77.
Tem'per-a-ment, 106,169
Tem'per-ance, 169.
Tem'per-ate, 73.
Tem'per-a-tīve.
Tem'per-a-tūre (26, 171) [*not* tem'pur-a-toor, 127, 153.]
Tem'pered, 150.
Tem'per-ing.
Tem'pest, 76.
Tem-pest'u-oŭs, 108.
Tem'plar, 74, 169.
[Template, 203.—*See* Templet.]
Tem'ple, 164.
Tem'plet [Template, 203.]
Tem'po-ral, 105.
Tem-po-ral'i-ty, 190.
Tem'po-ral-ly, 170.
Tem'po-ra-ri-ly, 72.
Tem'po-ra-ry, 72.
Tem-po-rī-za'tion, 126.
Tem'po-rīze, 202.
Tem'po-rīzed.
Tem'po-rīz-er.
Tem'po-rīz-ing.
Tempt (*temt*), 162.
Tempt-a-bil'i-ty (*temt*-).
Tempt'a-ble (*temt'a-bl*), 164, 171.
Tempt-a'tion (*temt*-).
Tempt'ed (*temt'*-).
Tempt'er (*temt'*-).
Tempt'ing (*temt'*-).
Ten, 15, 41, 43.
Ten-a-bil'i-ty, 108.
Ten'a-ble (164) [*not* te'-na-bl, 153.]
Ten'ace.
Te-na'cious (-*shus*), 169.
Te-naç'i-ty, 171, 233.
Tenaille (Fr.) (*te-nāl'*) (154) [so Wr. Gd.; *ten'āl*, Sm. 155.]
Tenaillon (Fr.) (*te-nāl'-yun*), 154.
Ten'an-cy, 169.
Ten'ant, 66, 170.
Ten'ant-a-ble, 164.
Ten'ant-ed.
Ten'ant-ing.
Ten'ant-ry, 93.
Tench, 15, 44, Note 2.
Tend, 15.
Tend'ed.
Ten'den-cy.
Ten'der, 77.
Ten'dered (-*durd*), 150.
Ten'der-heärt'ed, 205.
Ten'der-ing.
Ten'der-loin.
Tend'ing.
Ten'di-noŭs, 108.
Ten'don, 86, 149.
Ten'dril, 80.
Ten-e-brif'ic.
Ten-e-brif'ic-oŭs, 108.
Te-ne'bri-oŭs.
Ten'e-brose [so Gd.; *ten-e-brōs'*, Wr. 155.]
Ten-e-bros'i-ty.
Ten'e-broŭs.
Ten'e-ment, 169.
Ten-e-ment'al, 109.
Ten-e-ment'a-ry, 72.
Ten'et (170) [*not* te'net, 127, 153.]
Ten'fold, 217.
Te'ni-oid [Tænioid, 203.]
Ten'nis, 170.
Ten'-o'-clock (221), *n.* a perennial plant, with a bulbous, fibrous root.
Ten'on, 86.
Ten'or, 88, 169.
Te-not'o-my, 108.
Ten'pen-ny, 217.
Ten'pins (-*pinz*).
Ten'rec [Tanrec, 203.]
Tense, 15, 39; Note D, p. 37.
Ten-si-bil'i-ty.
Ten'si-ble, 164.
Ten'sīle, 81, 152.
Ten-sil'i-ty.
Ten'sion, 169.
Ten'si-ty.
Ten'sor, 17, 88.
Tent, 15.
Ten'ta-cle (164)[*not* ten'-tăk-l, 126, 153.]
Ten-tac'u-lum (L.) [pl. *Ten-tac'u-la*, 198.]
Ten-tac'u-lar, 108.
Ten-tac'u-lāt-ed.
Ten-tac-u-lif'er-oŭs.
Ten-ta-cu'li-form.
Ten'ta-tīve, 72, 84.
Tent'ed.
Ten'ter.
Ten'ter-hōōk.
Tenth, 15, 37.
Tent'ing.
Tent'wort (-*wurt*).
Ten'u-es (L.) (-*ēz*), *n. pl.*
Ten-u-i-fo'li-oŭs.
Ten-u-i-ros'tral.
Ten-u-i-ros'ter.
Te-nu'i-ty, 169.
Ten'u-oŭs, 100.
Ten'ure (-*yur*) (91) [so Sm. Wb. Gd.; *te'nūr*, Wk.; *ten'yur*, or *te'-nūr*, Wr. 155.]
Te-o-cal'le (Mexican) [pl. *Te-o-cal'lī*, 198.]
Tep-e-fac'tion, 169.
Tep'e-fīed.
Tep'e-fȳ, 94, 171.
Tep'e-fȳ-ing.
Teph'ra-man-cy.
Tep'id (170) [*not* te'pid, 127, 153.]
Te-pid'i-ty, 108.
Te'por (88) [so Wk. Wr. Wb. Gd.; *tep'or*, Sm. 155.]

Tĕr'aph (171) [Eng. pl. Tĕr'aphs ; Heb. pl. Ter'a-phim, 198.]
Tĕr-a-tog'e-ny (*-toj'-*).
Tĕr-a-tol'o-gy, 108.
[Terce, 203. — *See* Tierce.]
[Tercel, 203. — *See* Tiercel.]
Ter-cen'te-na-ry, 72.
Tĕr'e-binth.
Tĕr-e-bin'thin-ate.
Tĕr-e-bin'thīne, 82, 152.
Ter-e-bra-tu'li-form.
Te-re'do (L.).
Te-rete', 121.
Ter'gal, 21, N.; 72.
Ter-gĕm'in-al.
Ter-gem'in-ate.
Ter-gem'in-oŭs.
Ter-gif'er-oŭs, 108.
Ter'gi-ver-sate (*ter'jĭ-*) [so Wr. Wb. Gd.; *ter-ji-ver'sāt*, Sm. 155.]
Ter'gi-ver-sāt-ed.
Ter'gi-ver-sāt-ing.
Ter-gĭ-ver-sa'tion (*ter-jĭ-*) [*not* ter-ghĭ-vur-sa'shun, 153.]
Ter'gi-ver-sāt-or [so Wr.; *ter-ji-ver-sāt'ur*, Gd. 155.]
Term, 21, N.; 49, 135.
Ter'ma-gan-cy, 169.
Ter'ma-gant, 21, N.
Termed (*termd*), 165.
Term'er, *n.* one who travels to attend a term of a court; — in law, one who holds an estate for a term of years, or for life. [Termor (in the latter sense), 203.]
Ter'mēs (L.) (*-mēz*) [pl. *Ter'mi-tēs* (*-tēz*), 198. — *See* Ter'mites, pl. of *Termite*, 161.]
Ter'mi-na-ble, 164.
Ter'mi-nal.
Ter'mi-nate, 73.
Ter'mi-nāt-ed, 183.
Ter'mi-nāt-ing.
Ter-mi-na'tion, 112.
Ter-mi-na'tion-al.
Ter'mi-na-tĭve, 84.
Ter'mi-nāt-or, 183.
Ter'mi-na-to-ry, 86.
Ter'mi-ner, 77.
Term'ing.
Ter'mi-nist, 169.
Ter-mi-nol'o-gy.
Ter-min'thus.
Ter'mi-nus (L.) (169) [pl. Ter'mi-nī, 198.]
Ter'mite [pl. Ter'mites (*-mīts*), 189. — *See* *Ter'mi-tēs*, pl. of *Termes*, 161.]
Term'or (88), *n.* in law, one who holds an estate for a term of years, or for life. [Termer, 203.]
Tern, 21, N.; 49.
Ter'na-ry, 72.
Ter'nate.
Terp-sich-o-re'an(*-sik-*), 110, 171.
Tĕr'race, 66, 170.
Tĕr'raced (*-rāst*), 41.
Tĕr'ra-cing, 183.
Tĕr'ra-cot'ta (It.).
Tĕr'ræ fil'i-us (L.).
Tĕr'ra fir'ma (L.).
Tĕr'ra in-cog'ni-ta(L.).
Tĕr'ra ja-pon'i-ca (L.).
Tĕr'ra-pin, 170.
Tĕr-ra'que-oŭs (17) [so Wk. Wr. Wb. Gd.; *tĕr-rak'we-us*, Sm. 155.]
[Terrass, 203. — *See* Terras.]
Tĕr-rene', 121.
Terre-plein (Fr.) (*têr-plān'*) [so Wr.; *têr'-plān*, Gd. 155.]
Tĕr-res'tri-al, 169.
Tĕr-res'tri-al-ly.
Têrre'-ten-aut (*têr'-*).
Terre'-verte (Fr.) (*têr'-vêrt*) [so Gd.; *têr'-vert*, Wr. 155.]
Tĕr'ri-ble, 164.
Tĕr'ri-bly.
Tĕr'ri-er, 77, 171.
Tĕr-rif'ic.
Tĕr-rif'ic-al.
Tĕr'ri-fīed, 99.
Tĕr'ri-fȳ-ing.
Tĕr-rig'e-noŭs (*-rij'-*).
Tĕr-ri-to'ri-al.
Tĕr'ri-to-ry, 86, 126.
Tĕr'ror, 88.
Tĕr'ror-ism (*-izm*).
Tĕr'ror-ist.
Terse, 21, N.; 135.
Ter'tial (*-shal*), 169.
Ter'tian (*-shan*).
Ter'tia-ry (*-sha-*) (72) [so Sm. Wb. Gd.; *ter'-shi-a-ry*, Wr. 155.]
Ter'ti-ate (*-shi-*) [so Sm. Wr.; *ter'shāt*, Wb. Gd. 155.]
Ter'ti-um quid (L.) (*ter'shi-um kwid*).
Terza rima (It.) (*tert'-sä re'mä*).
Terzetto (It.) (*tert-set'-to*), 154.
Tes'sel-lar.
Tes'sel-late, 170.
Tes'sel-lāt-ed, 183.
Tes'sel-lāt-ing.
Tes-sel-la'tion, 112.
Tes'ser-al.
Tes'su-lar, 108.
Test, 15.
Tes'ta (L.) [pl. *Tes'tæ*, 198.]
Tes'ta-ble, 164, 169.
Tes-ta'ce-a (*-she-a*) [so Wr.; *tes-ta'sha*, Gd. 155.]
Tes-ta'cean (*-shan*), 169.
Tes'ta-cel, 76.
Tes-tā-ce-og'ra-phy.
Tes-tā-ce-ol'o-gy, 108.
Tes-ta'ceoŭs (*-shus*), 169.
Tes'ta-cy, 171.
Tes'ta-ment, 169.
Tes-ta-ment'al.
Tes-ta-ment'a-ry, 72.
Tes-ta-ment-a'tion.
Tes'tate, 73.
Tes-ta'tor.
Tes-ta'trix.
Test'ed.
Tes'ter, 77.
Tes-ti-fĭ-ca'tion.
Tes'ti-fīed, 99.
Tes'ti-fī-er, 186.
Tes'ti-fȳ, 94.
Tes'ti-fȳ-ing, 186.
Tes'ti-ly.
Tes-ti-mo'ni al, 169.
Tes'ti-mo-ny, 86, 126.
Tes'ti-ness, 186.
Test'ing.
Tes-tone', 121.
Tes-toon', 121.
Test'-pa-per.
Tes-tu'di-nal, 169.
Tes-tu-di-na'ri-oŭs.
Tes-tu'di-nate.
Tes-tu'di-nāt-ed.
Tes-tu'do (L.).
Tes'ty, 93.
Te-tan'ic, 109, 170.
Tet'a-noid.
Tet'a-nus, 169.
Tet-ar-to-he'dral.
Tet-ar-to-he'drism (*-drizm*), 136.
[Tetchy, 203. — *See* Techy, Touchy.]

Tête-à-tête (Fr.) (*tāt′-a-tāt′*), 154.
Tête de pont (Fr.) (*tāt′-duh pong′*).
Teth′er, *n.* & *v.* [T e d-d e r , 203.]
Teth′ered, 150.
Teth′er-ing.
Te-thy′dan.
Tet-ra-bran′chi-ate (*-brang′ki-*), 171.
Tet′ra-chord (*-kord*).
Tet-ra-chot′o-moŭs (*-kot′-*).
Tet-ra-coc′cus.
Tet-ra-dac′tyl.
Tet-ra-dac′tyl-oŭs.
Tet-ra-di-a-pa′son.
Tet′ra-dīte, 152.
Tet′ra-drachm (*-dram*).
Tet-ra-dȳ-na′mi-an.
Tet-ra-dyn′a-moŭs.
[T e t r a e d r o n , 203.—*See* Tetrahedron.]
Tet′ra-gon.
Te-trag′o-nal.
Te-trag′o-nism (*-nizm*), 133, 136.
Tet-ra-gram′ma-ton.
Tet-ra-gyn′i-an (*-jin′-*) 169, 171.
Te-trag′y-noŭs (*-traj′-*).
Tet-ra-he′dral.
Tet-ra-he′dron [T e t-r a e d r o n , 203.]
Tet-ra-hex-a-he′dral.
Tet-ra-hex-a-he′dron.
Te-tral′o-gy, 108.
Te-tram′er-oŭs.
Te-tram′e-ter, 108.
Tet′ra-morph, 171.
Te-tram′y-ron, 171.
Te-tran′dri-an, 169.
Te-tran′droŭs.
Te-tra′o-nid.
Tet-ra-pet′al-oŭs.
Tet-ra-phar′ma-con (Gr.), *or* Tet-ra-phar′-ma-cum (L.), 203.
Tet-ra-phyl′loŭs, *or* Te-traph′yl-loŭs. [*See* Adenophyllous.]
Tet′ra-pla, 72.
Tet′ra-pod.
Te-trap′o-dy, 105.
Te-trap′ter-an, 72.
Te-trap′ter-oŭs.
Te-trap′tote [so Sm. ; *tet′rap-tōt*, Wr. Wb. Gd. 155.]
Te′trarch (*-trark*), *or* Tet′rarch (*-rark*) [so Wk. ; *te′trark*, Wr. Wb. Gd. ; *tet′rark*, Sm. 155.]
Te-trarch′ate (*te-trark′-*), *or* Tet′rarch-ate (*tet′rark-*) [*te-trark′āt* Wk. Wr. Gd.; *tet′rark-āt*, Sm. 155.]
Te-trarch′ic-al (*-trark′-*).
Tet′rarch-y (*tet′rark-*) [*not* te′trar-ky, 153.]
Tet-ra-sep′al-oŭs.
Tet′ra-spore.
Te-tras′tich (*-tik*), 156.
Tet′ra-style.
Tet-ra-syl-lab′ic.
Tet-ra-syl-lab′ic-al.
Tet-ra-syl′la-ble, 164.
Tet′ter, 66, 170.
Tet-ti-go′ni-an.
Teū′thi-dan.
Teū′ton (26, 86) [Eng. pl. Teū′tons (*-tunz*) ; L. pl. Teū′to-nēs (*-nēz*), 198.]
Teū-ton′i-cism (*-sizm*).
Tew′el (*tu′-*), 26, 76.
Tex′an.
Text, 15.
Text′-bo͝ok, 206, Exc. 4.
Tex′tīle, 81, 152.
Text-o′ri-al, 49, N.
Tex′trīne, 152.
Text′u-al, 108.
Text′u-al-ist.
Text′u-al-ly.
Text′u-a-ry, 72.
Text′ure, 91.
Thal′a-mus.
Tha-las′si-o-phyte.
Thā′ler (Ger.) (*tä′lur*) [so Wr. ; *thā′lur*, Wb. Gd. 155.]
Tha-li′a (L.).
Tha-li′an, 106, 122.
Thal′i-dan.
Thal′līte, 83, 170.
Thal′lo-gen, 45.
Thal′lo-phyte.
Thal′lus (L.) [pl. Thal′-lī, 198.]
Tham′muz [T a m m u z, 203.]
T͟han, 10, 38, 43.
Than′a-toid, 37, 140.
Than-a-tol′o-gy.
Than-a-top′sis.
Thane, 23, 37.
Thank (*thangk*), 10, 54.
Thanked (*thangkt*), 41.
Thank′ful (*thangk′fo͝ol*).
Thank′ful-ly (*thangk′-fo͝ol-*).
Thank′ful-ness (*thangk′fo͝ol-*).
Thank′ing (*thangk′-*).
Thank′-of-fer-ing (*thangk′-*).
Thanks′giv-ing (*thangks′ghiv-*) (54) [so Wk. Sm. Wr. ; *thanks-ghiv′ing*, Wb. Gd. 155.]
Thank′wor-t͟hy (*thangk′wur-*).
T͟hat, 10, 38.

☞ When used as a demonstrative pronoun, or pronominal adjective, this word is always emphasized, and the vowel has its distinct short sound, as in *mat* (No. 1, § 10); but when used as a relative pronoun or a conjunction, it is never emphasized, and the vowel is consequently corrupted, having nearly the sound of *u* in *up* (No. 13, § 22).

Thatch, 10, 37, 44.
Thatched (*thacht*), 165; Note C, p. 34.
Thatch′ing.
Thâu′ma-trope, 105.
Thâu-ma-tur′gic.
Thâu-ma-tur′gic-al.
Thâu-ma-tur′gics, 109.
Thâu-ma-tur′gist.
Thâu′ma-tur-gy.
Thaw, 17.
Thawed, 150.
Thaw′ing.
Thaw′y, 169.
T͟he (13, 69), the definite article. [*See* Thee, 160.]

☞ " The definite article, which, when it stands alone, we call *thē*, shortens and often changes its vowel sound in connection with other words (except when emphatic)." *Smart.* — " When *the* is prefixed to a word beginning with a consonant, it has a short sound, little more than the sound of *th* without the *e*; and when it precedes a word beginning with a vowel, the *e* is sounded plainly and distinctly. This difference will be perceptible, by comparing *the pen, the hand*, &c., with *the oil, the air*, &c." *Walker.*— In printed verse, the *e* is often cut off before a word beginning with a vowel, its place being supplied by an apostrophe; but in reading, the *e* should be sounded, so as to blend with the initial vowel, and form with it, or help to form, but a single syllable; as in the following line of Milton:

"Who durst defy *th'* Omnipotent to arms."

The-an-throp'ic-al.
The-an'thro-pism (*-pizm*), 133, 136.
The-an'thro-pist.
The-an'thro-py.
The'är-chy (*-ky*).
The'a-tīne (82, 152) [Theatin, 203.]
The'a-tre [Theater, Wb. Gd. 203. — *See* Note E, p. 70.]
The-at'ric, 109.
The-at'ric-al, 108.
The-at-ric-al'i-ty.
The-at'ric-al-ly.
The'ba-id, 72.
The'ban, 72.
The'ca (L.) [pl. *The'cæ* (*-se*), 198.]
The'ca-phore, 171.
The'co-dac-tyl.
The'co-dont, 105.
Thee (13), *pron.* objective case of *Thou.* [*See* The, 160.]
Theft, 15.
The'i-form, 108, 169.
The'ïne (152) [Thein, 203.]
Thêir (*thêr*) (14), *pron.* of, or belonging to, them. [*See* There, 160.]

☞ When this word is not emphatic, the vowel is shortened in quantity, and is liable to fall into the sound of the natural vowel (No. 12, § 21).

Thêirs (*thêrz*), 14, 38, 40.
The'ism (*-izm*), 136.
The'ist.
The-ist'ic.
The-ist'ic-al.
Thel-phu'sian (*-shan*).
Them, 15, 38.
Theme, 13, 37, 163.
The'mis, 169.
Them-selves' (*-selvz'*), *pron. pl.*
Then, 15, 38.
The'nal.
Thence, 15, 38.
Thence'fōrth, 206.
Thence-for'ward, 135.
The-o-bro'ma.
The-o-bro'mīne, 152.
The-o-chrĭst'ic(*-krist'-*).
The-oc'ra-cy (160, 169), *n.* government of a state by the immediate direction of God.
The-oc'ra-sy (160, 169), *n.* a mingling of the soul with God by means of contemplation.
The-o-crat'ic.
The-o-crat'ic-al.
The-od'i-cy, 169.
The-od'o-līte, 171.
The-od-o-lit'ic.
The-o-do'sian (*-shan*), 112.
The-o-gon'ic.
The-og'o-nist.
The-og'o-ny.
The-ol'o-gas-ter.
The-o-lo'gi-an, 169.
The-o-log'ic (*-loj'-*).
The-o-log'ic-al (*-loj'-*).
The-o-log'ic-al-ly (*-loj'-*).
The-ol'o-gist, 108.
The'o-lŏgue (*-log*), 87.
The-ol'o-gy, Note F, p. 79.
The-om'a-chist (*-kist*).
The-om'a-chy (*-ky*), 52.
The'o-man-cy.
The-o-pas'chite (*-kīt*).
The-o-pa-thet'ic.
The-o-path'ic, 109.
The-op'a-thy, 108.
The-oph'a-ny, 35, 190.
The-o-phil-an-throp'ic.
The-o-phi-lan'thro-pism (*-pizm*), 136.
The-o-phi-lan'thro-pist.
The-o-phil-o-soph'ic (*-sof'ik*, or *zof'ik*) [*See* Philosophic.]
The-op-neūs'tic, 171.
The-op-neūs'ty.
The-or'bist.
The-or'bo, 135.
The'o-rem.
The-o-rem-at'ic.
The-o-rem-at'ic-al.
The-o-rem'ic.
The-o-ret'ic, 109.
The-o-ret'ic-al, 108.
The-o-ret'ic-al-ly, 170.
The-ŏr'ic.
The'o-rist, 80.
The'o-rize, 202.
The'o-rized.
The'o-riz-ing, 183.
The'o-ry, 86, 93.
The-o-soph'ic.
The-o-soph'ic-al.
The-os'o-phism (*-fizm*).
The-os'o-phist.
The-os-o-phist'ic-al.
The-os'o-phy, 93.
Thĕr-a-peū'tic, 171.
Thĕr-a-peū'tic-al.
Thĕr-a-peū'tics.
Thĕr-a-peū'tist.
Thêre, 14, 38.

☞ When used as an adverb of place, opposed to *here*, it is pronounced with a distinct sound of the vowel (No. 5, § 14); but when it serves simply to introduce a verb or phrase, the vowel slides into the sound of *u* in *urn* (No. 12, § 21).

Thêre'a-bout, *or* Thêre'-a-bouts, 203.
Thêre-af'ter.
Thêre-at'.
Thêre-by'.
There'fore (*ther'fōr*, or *thêr'fōr*) [so Wr. Gd.; *ther'fōr*, Wk. Sm. (*See* No. 12, § 21, N.), 155.]

☞ "In *therefore* the *e* is generally shortened, as in *were*, but in my opinion improperly." *Walker.*

Thêre-from'.
Thêre-in'.
Thêre-of' (35) [*not* thêr-ov', 141, 153.]
Thêre-on'.
Thêre-up-on'.
Thêre-with' (37) [*not* thêr-with', 153.]
Thêre-with-âl', 180.
The'ri-ac, 49, N.
The-ri'ac-al, 108.
The-ri-ot'o-my.
Ther'mal, 21, N.
Ther-met'o-grăph, 127.
Ther'mic, 200.
Ther'mi-dor (Fr.), 154.
Ther-moch'ro-sy (*-mok'-*), 169.
Ther'mo-e-lec'tric, 224.
Ther'mo-e-lec-triç'i-ty.
Ther-mol'o-gy, 108.
Ther-mom'e-ter, 108.
Ther-mo-met'ric.
Ther-mo-met'ric-al.
Ther'mo-scope.
Ther-mo-scop'ic.
Ther-mo-scop'ic-al.
Ther'mo-stat.
Ther-mo-stat'ic.

Ther-mot'ic, 109.
Ther'mo-type.
Ther-mot'y-py.
The-sau'rus (L.).
These (*thēz*), 38, 40.
The'sis (L.) [pl. The'-sēs (-*sēz*), 198.]
Thes'mo-thete, 171.
Thes'pi-an, 169.
Thet'ic-al.
The'tis.
The-ur'gic.
The-ur'gic-al.
The'ur-gist, 45.
The'ur-gy.
Thews (*thūz*), *n. pl.*
They (*thā*), 23, 38.
Thĭ-be'tian (*tĭ-be'shan*) [*tĭ-be'shĭ-an*, Wr.; *thĭ-be'shan*, Gd. 155.]
Thick, 16, 181.
Thick'en (*thik'n*), 149.
Thick'ened (*thik'nd*).
Thick'en-ing (*thik'n-*).
Thick'et, 76.
Thick'hĕad, 216.
Thick'-hĕad-ed, 206, Exc. 5.
Thick'ish.
Thief (*thēf*) (13, 169, N.) [pl. Thiēves (*thēvz*), 193.]
Thiēve (*thēv*), 13, 36.
Thiēved (*thēvd*), 165.
Thiēv'er-y, 93.
Thiēves (*thēvz*), *n. pl.* [*See* Thief.]
Thiēv'ing.
Thiēv'ish, 183.
Thigh (*thī*), 37, 162.
Thill, 16, 172.
Thim'ble, 164.
Thim'ble-bĕr-ry (-*bl*-).
Thim'ble-ful (*thim'bl-fŏŏl*), 197.
Thim'ble-rig (-*bl*-).
Thin, 16, 37, 43.
Thine, 25, 38, 163.
Thing, 16, 54.
Think (*thingk*), 16.
Think'a-ble (*thingk'-*), 164, 169.
Think'er (*thingk'-*).
Think'ing (*thingk'-*).
Thinned (*thind*), 176.
Thin'ner, 66, 170.
Thin'ness, 66, N.
Thin'ning.
Thin'nish.
Third, 21, N.; 135.
Third'ings (-*ingz*), *n. pl.*
Thirl'age, 169.

Thirst, 21, N.; 49.
Thirst'ed.
Thirst'i-ly, 186.
Thirst'i-ness.
Thirst'ing.
Thirst'y, 169.
Thir'teen. [*See* Note under *Eighteen*.]
Thir-teenth'.
Thir'ti-eth, 186.
Thir'ty, 93.
This, 16, 38, 174.
This'tle (*this'l*), 162, 164.
This'tly (*this'ly*).
Thith'er, 140.
Thole'pin.
Thol'o-bate.
Tho-mæ'an [so Sm. Gd.; *to-me'an*, Wr. 155.]
Tho'ma-ism (-*izm*), 72.
Tho'mism (-*mizm*).
Tho'mist [so Sm. Wb. Gd.; *to'mist*, Wr. 155.]
Tho'mīte, 152.
Thomp-so'ni-an (*tom-*) (162) [T h o m s o n i a n, 203.]
Thomp-so'ni-an-ism (*tom-*) (136) [T h o m s o n i a n i s m, 203.]
Thong, 18, N.; 54.
Thor, 17, 37, 49.
Tho-raç'ic.
Tho'ral, 49, N.
Tho'rax.
Tho-rī'na.
Tho-rī'num.
Tho'rīte, 152.
Tho'ri-um.
Thorn, 17, 37.
Thorn'-ap-ple.
Thorn'back.
Thorn'but.
Thorn'y, 169.
Thor'ough (*thŭr'o*), 22, 162, 171.
Thor'ough-băss (*thŭr'-o-*), 171.
Thor'ough-bred (*thŭr'-o-*).
Thor'ough-fare (*thŭr'-o-*), 206.
Thor'ough-go'ing (*thŭr'o-*), 205.
Thor'ough-ly (*thŭr'o-*).
Thor'ough-wort (*thŭr'-o-wurt*), 171.
Thorp, 17, 49, 135.
Those (*thōz*), 24, 38, 40.
Thoth, 18, 37.

Thou, 28, 38.
Though (*tho*), 24, 162.
Thought (*thawt*), 17, 162.
Thought'ful (*thawt'-fŏŏl*), 171.
Thought'ful-ly (*thawt'-fŏŏl-*).
Thought'less (*thawt'-*).
Thou'sand (-*zand*).

☞ "The word *thousand*, as well as *hundred*, *million*, &c., assumes a plural termination, when not modified by an ordinal numeral adjective." *Worcester.*

Thou'sand-fōld (-*zand-*), 217.
Thou'sandth (-*zandth*), 42, 142.
[T h ō w l [so Sm. Wr. Wb. Gd.; *thoul*, Wk. 155, 203. — *See* Thole.]
Thra'cian (-*shan*), 169.
Thrâl'dom (169, 178) [T h r a l l d o m, Wb. Gd. 203. — *See* Note E, p. 70.]
Thra'nīte.
Thrash [T h r e s h, 203.]
Thrashed (*thrasht*) Note C, p. 34.
Thrash'er.
Thrash'ing.
Thra-son'ic-al.
Thrave, 23.
Thrĕad, 15.
Thrĕad'bare (-*bêr*).
Thrĕad'ed.
Thrĕad'en (*thred'n*), 149.
Thrĕad'ing.
Thrĕad'līke, 206.
Thrĕad'-shaped (-*shāpt*), 206, Exc. 5.
Thrĕad'y.
Thrĕat, 15.
Thrĕat'en (*thret'n*).
Thrĕat'ened (*thret'nd*).
Thrĕat'en-er (*thret'n-*).
Thrĕat'en-ing (*thret'-n-ing*).
Three, 13.
Three'-cor-nered (-*nurd*).
Three'-deck-er.
Three'fōld.
Three'-legged (-*legd*) [*not* thre'leg-ghed, 153.]
Three'pence (coll. *thrip'-*

ens) [so Sm. Wr.; *thrip'ens*, Wb. Gd.; *threp'ens*, Wk. 155.]
Three'pen-ny (coll. *thrip'en-y*) [so Sm.; *thrip'en-y*, Wr. Wb. Gd.; *threp'en-y*, Wk. 155.]
Three'-ply, *a.*
Three'score.
Threne, 13, 163.
Thre-net'ic, 109.
Thren'o-dist.
Thren'o-dy, 170.
Threp-sol'o-gy, 108.
Thresh (15, 46) [Thrash, 203.]

☞ "In the derivative sense, *to drub*, it generally takes the form *thrash.*" *Smart.*

Threshed (*thresht*).
Thresh'er.
Thresh'ing,
Thresh'ōld [so Sm. Wb. Gd.; *thresh'hōld*, Wk. Wr. 155.]
Threw (*throo*) (19, 37), *v.* did throw. [*See* Through, 160.]
Thrice, 25, 39.
Thrift, 16.
Thrift'i-ly, 93.
Thrift'i-ness.
Thrift'less.
Thrift'y.
Thrill, 16, 172.
Thrilled (*thrild*), 165.
Thrill'ing, 228.
Thrive, 25.
Thrived, 165.
Thriv'en (*thriv'n*), 149.
Thrīv'ing, 183.
Thro' (*throo*) [a contraction of *Through.*]
Thrōat, 24.
Thrōat'wort (*-wurt*).
Throb, 18.
Throbbed (*throbd*), 165.
Throb'bing, 176.
Thrōe (24) [pl. Throes (*thrōz*), 189. — *See* Throws, 160.]
Throne (24), *n.* the chair of state of a king or other sovereign. [*See* Thrown, 160.]
Throng, 18, N.
Thronged (*throngd*), 165.
Throng'ing.
Thros'tle (*thros'l*), 162.
Thros'tling (*thros'ling*).
Throt'tle, 164, 170.
Throt'tled (*throt'ld*).
Throt'tle-valve.
Throt'tling.
Through (*throo*) (19, 162) *prep.* from end to end, or from side to side, of: — *adv.* from one end or side to the other. [*See* Threw, 160.]
Through-out' (*throo-*).
Throve, 24.
Thrōw, 24.
Thrōw'ing.
Thrōwn, *part.* from *Throw.* [*See* Throne, 160.]
Thrōws (*thrōz*), *v.* does throw. [*See* Throes (pl. of Throe), 160.]
Thrōw'ster.
Thrum, 22.
Thrummed (*thrumd*), [165.
Thrum'ming, 176.
Thrush, 22.
Thrust, 22.
Thrust'ing.
Thug (22, 37, 53) [so Sm. Wb. Gd.; *thug*, or *tug*, Wr. 155.]

☞ "The sound of the first two letters [that of *th* in *thin*] is indicated for an English mouth; the Eastern pronunciation is that of a *t*, with a peculiar breathing." *Smart.*

Thug-gee' (*-ghe'*), 138.
Thug'ger-y (*-gur-*).
Thug'gism (*-ghizm*).
Thu'le (L.).
Thumb (*thum*), 162.
Thumbed (*thumd*).
Thumb'ing (*thum'-*).
Thumb'screw (*thum'-skroo*), 171.
Thumb'stâll (*thum'-*).
Thum'mim, *n. pl.*
Thump, 22.
Thumped (*thumpt*), 165; Note C, p. 34.
Thump'ing.
Thun'der, 230.
Thun'der-bōlt.
Thun'dered (*-durd*).
Thun'der-er, 77.
Thun'der-ing.
Thun'der-strike.
Thun'der-struck.
Thu'ri-ble, 49, N.; 164.
Thu-rif'er-oŭs.
Thu-ri-fĭ-ca'tion.
Thu-rin'gi-an.
Thurl, 21.
Thurs'day (*thurz'dy*).
Thus, 22, 38, 174.
Thwack, 10, 64, 181.
Thwacked (*thwakt*).
Thwack'ing.
Thwârt, 17.
Thwârt'ed.
Thwârt'ing.
Thy [so Wb. Gd.; *thī*, or *thĭ*, Wk. Wr.; *thī*, often *thĭ*, Sm.]

☞ "It is only in the most familiar style, and when the word is unemphatic, that the latter pronunciation [*thĭ*] should be used." *Smart.*

Thȳ'ine-wŏŏd [so Sm. Wr. Gd.; *the'in-wŏŏd*, Wk. 155.]
Thyme (*tīm*) (41), *n.* a kind of plant of an aromatic odor and pungent taste. [*See* Time, 160] [*not* thīm, 141, 153.]
Thy-me-la'ceoŭs (*-shus*) [so Sm.; *thim-e-la'-shus*, Wr. 155.]
Thym-i-a-tech'ny (*-tek'-*).
Thȳm'y (*tīm'y*), 171.
Thy'roid.
Thȳ-roid'e-al, 169.
Thyrse (*thirs*), 21, N.
Thyr'soid.
Thyr-soid'al.
Thyr'sus (L.).
Thys-an-u'ran [so Wb. Gd.; *this-a-nu'ran*, Wr.; *thī-san-u'ran*, Sm. 155.]
Thy-self'.
Tī-a'ra (49, N.) [so Wb. Gd.; *tī-ēr'ra*, Wk. Sm.; *tī-a'ra*, or *tī-ēr'ra*, Wr. 155.]
Tī-a'raed, 171, 188.
Tib'i-a, 72, 78.
Tib'i-al.
Tib'i-o-tar'sal.
Ti-câl', 121.
Tic douloureux (Fr.) (*tik-doo-loo-roo'*), 154.
Tich'or-rhine (*tik'or-rīn*) [Ticorrhine, (*tī'kor-rīn*, Sm.), 203.]
Tick, 16, 181.
Ticked (*tikt*), 165; Note C, p. 34.

Tick'en (149), *n.* cloth for bed-ticks. [T i c k - i n g, 203.]
Tick'et.
Tick'et-ed.
Tick'et-ing.
Tick'ing, *part.*
Tick'ing, *n.* [T i c k e n, 203.]
Tick'le (*tik'l*), 164.
Tick'led (*tik'ld*).
Tick'ler, 77, 183.
Tick'ling.
Tick'lish.
Tick'seed.
Tick'-tack.
Tīd'al, 72, 228.
Tid'bit [T i t b i t, 203.]
Tide (25), *n.* a periodic alternate rising and falling of the waters of the ocean. [*See* Tied, 160.]
Tide'-gāuge, 171.
Tide'-mill.
Ti'di-ly.
Ti'di-ness.
Ti'dings (*-dingz*), *n. pl.*
Tīd-ol'o-gy, 108.
Ti'dy, 93, 169.
Tīe, 25, 41.

☞ Webster says: "On account of the participle *tying*, it might be well to write the verb *tye*." He accordingly gives *tye* as an alternative orthography, and this form is retained by Dr. Goodrich in the revised edition of Webster's Dictionary published in 1859. It is to be observed, however, that the similar verbs, *die, hie, lie*, and *vie* — the participles of which, respectively, are *dying, hying, lying, vying* — are given by both these lexicographers in the common spelling only.

Tīed, *v.* did tie. [*See* Tide, 160.]
Tiēr (13, 41, 49), *n.* a row, or rank. [*See* Tēar, 160.]
Ti'er, *n.* one who ties; — a sort of child's apron, with sleeves, and covering the breast. [T i r e (in the latter sense), 203.]
Tiērce (*tērs*, or *ters*) [so Wr.; *tērs*, Sm.; *ters*, Wk.; *ters*, or *tērs*, Gd. 155] [T e r c e, 203.]

☞ "In *tierce*, and *fierce*, many speakers disregard the *i*." *Smart.*

Tiēr'cel (or *ter'sel*) [T e r c e l, 203.]
Tiērce'let (or *ters'let*).
Tiēr'cet (or *ter'set*) [so Wr.; *tēr'set*, Sm. Gd. 155.]
Tiers-état (Fr.) (*te-ērz'-ā-ta'*).
Tiff, 16, 173.
Tif'fa-ny, 169.
Tif'fin, 170.
Tiff'ish, 228.
Tig, 16.
Ti'ger (*-gur*) (138) [T y - g e r, 203.]
Ti'ger-cat (*-gur-*).
Ti'ger-ish (*-gur-*).
Ti'ger-lil'y, 53, 205.
Ti'ger-moth (*-gur-*).
Tīght (*tīt*), 162.
Tīght'en (*tīt'n*), 171.
Tīght'ened (*tīt'nd*).
Tīght'en-ing (*tīt'n-*).
Tīght'er (*tīt'-*).
Ti'gress.
Ti'grīne, 82, 152.
Tike, 25, 163.
Til'burgh (*-burg*).
Til'bu-ry (*-bĕr-y*).
Tile, 25.
Tiled, 165.
Tīl'er, 183.
Tīl'er-y, 233, Exc.
Tīl'ing.
Till, 16.
Till'a-ble, 164, 169.
Till'age, 70, 169.
Tilled (*tild*), 165.
Till'er.
Till'er-ing.
Till'ing.
Tilt, 16.
Tilt'ed.
Tilt'er, 169.
Tilth, 16, 37.
Tilt'ing.
[T i m b a l, 203. — *See* Tymbal.]
Tim'ber, *n.* wood, or a large piece of wood suitable for building; — the crest of a helmet; — a number of skins packed together: — *v.* to furnish with beams or timber. [T i m b r e (in the second and third senses of the noun), T i m m e r (in the third sense of the noun), 203.]
Tim'bered (*-burd*), 150.
Tim'ber-ing.
Tim'bre (*tim'bur*) (161), *n.* the crest of a helmet; — a number of skins packed together [T i m b e r (in the first sense), T i m m e r (in the second sense), 203.]
Timbre (Fr.) (*timbr*) (154, 161), *n.* quality of tone in the voice or in instruments.
Tim'brel, 76.
Time (25), *n.* measure of duration; — a limited portion of duration: — *v.* to adapt to the time or occasion; — to measure or regulate as to time. [*See* Thyme, 160.]
Tīmed, 165.
Time'-hon-ored (*-on-urd*).
Time'-keep-er.
Time'li-ness, 186.
Time'ly, 185.
Time'piēce.
Time'serv-er.
Time'serv-ing.
Time'-wōrn.
Tim'id, 66, 170.
Ti-mid'i-ty.
Tīm'ing, 183.
Tīm'ist.
Tim'mer [T i m b e r, T i m b r e, 203.]
Ti-moc'ra-cy [so Sm. Gd.; *tī-mok'ra-sy*, Wr. 155.]
Tim-o-neer' (122) [so Wr. Gd.; *tī-mo-nēr'*, Sm. 155.]
Tim'o-roŭs.
Ti-mo'the-an, 110, 169.
Tin, 16, 41, 43.
Tin'a-mou (*-moo*).
Tin'cal (*ting'-*), 54.
Tinc-to'ri-al (*tingk-*).
Tinct'ure (*tingkt'yur*), 91, 171.
Tinct'ured (*tingkt'-yurd*).
Tinct'ur-ing (*tingkt'-yur-*).
Tinder, 77, 169.
Tine, 25.
Ting, 16.
Ting'ing.

Tinge, 16, 45.
Tinged (*tinjd*).
Tinge′ing, 183.
Tin′gle (*ting′gl*), 54,164.
Tin′gled (*ting′gld*).
Tin′gling (*ting′-*), 183.
Tink (*tingk*), 16, 54.
Tinked (*tingkt*).
Tink′er (*tingk′-*).
Tink′ered (*tingk′urd*).
Tink′er-ing (*tingk′-*).
Tink′ing (*tingk′-*).
Tin′kle (*ting′kl*), 165.
Tin′kled (*ting′kld*).
Tin′kling (*ting′-*).
Tin′man, 193.
Tinned (*tind*), 165, 176.
Tin′ner, 170.
Tin′ning.
Tin′ny (93, 169), *a.* pertaining to tin. [*See* Tiny, 148.]
Tin′sel, 149.
Tin′selled (*-seld*) [Tinseled, Wb. Gd. 203. — *See* 177, and Note E, p. 70.]
Tin′sel-ling (177) [Tinseling, Wb. Gd. 203.]
Tin′smith.
Tint, 16.
Tint′ed.
Tint′ing.
Tin-tin-nab-u-la′tion.
Tin-tin-nab′u-loŭs, 108.
Tin-tin-nab′u-la-ry, 72.
Tin-tin-nab′u-lum (L.).
Tin′to, 86.
Tī′ny [so Wk. Sm. Wr.; *tin′y*, Wb. Gd. 155] [*not* te′ny, 127, 153], *a.* little. [*See* Tinny, 148]
Tip, 16, 30, 41.
Tipped (*tipt*), 176.
Tip′pet, 170.
Tip′ping.
Tip′ple, 164.
Tip′pled (*tip′ld*).
Tip′pler.
Tip′pling, 183.
Tip′si-ly, 186.
Tip′staff.
Tip′sy, 169.
Tip′tōe.
Tip′-top.
Tip′u-la-ry.
Tī-rāde′, *or* Tī-räde′ [*tĭ-rād′*, Wb. Gd.; *tĭ-räd′*, Sm. Wr. 155.]
Tirailleur (Fr.) (*te-rä′-il-yur*) [so Sm. Wr.; *te-rāl′yur*, Gd. 155.]

Tire (25, 49, 67), *n.* [Tier (in the sense of *a child's pinafore*), 203.]
Tire, *v.* 25, 49.
Tired, 165.
Tire′some (*-sum*), 169.
Tīr′ing, 49, N.
[Tiro, 203. — *See* Tyro.]
Tī-ro′ni-an.
Tir′wit (*ter′-*) (21, N.) [so Sm. Wr., *tĭr′-wit*, Gd. 155.]
'Tis (*tiz*) [a contraction for *it is.*]
Tis′rī (*tiz′-*).
Tis′sue (*tish′u*), 46, 171.
Tis′sued (*tish′ūd*).
Tis′su-ing (*tish′u-*).
Tit, 16, 41.
Tī′tan.
Tit′a-nate.
Tī-ta′ni-an [so Sm.; *tĭ-ta′ni-an*, Wr. 155.]
Tī-tan′ic, 109.
Tī-tan-if′er-oŭs, 108.
Tī-tan′īte, 152.
Tī-tan-it′ic.
Tī-ta′ni-um, 169.
Tit′bit [Tidbit, 203.]
Tith′a-ble, 164, 183.
Tithe (25, 38) [Tythe, 203.]
Tithed, 165, 183.
Tīth′er.
Tīth′ing.
Tīth′ing-man.
Tith′y-mal, 171.
Tit′il-late, 170.
Tit′il-lāt-ed.
Tit′il-lāt-ing.
Tit-il-la′tion, 112.
Tit′il-lāt-ĭve, 84.
Tit′lark, 206.
Tī′tle, 164.
Tī′tled (*tī′tld*).
Tī′tle-page (*tī′tl-*).
Tī′tling, 161, 228, N.
Tit′ling, 161, 228, N.
Tit′mouse [pl. Tit′mice, 195.]
Tit′ter, 104, 170.
Tit′tered, 150.
Tit′ter-ing.
Tit′tle, 66, 164.
Tit′tle-tat′tle, 164.
Tit′u-lar, 108.
Tit′u-la-ry, 72, 89.
Tme′sis (*me′-*) (162) [so Wr.; *tme′sis*, Sm. Wb. Gd. 155.]
To (*too*) (19, 69), *prep.* in the direction of towards. [*See* Too, *and* Two, 160.]
Tōad (24), *n.* a well-known batrachian animal. [*See* Towed, 160.]
Tōad′-ēat-er.
Tōad′ĭed.
Tōad′stōne, 24.
Tōad′stool.
Tōad′y, *n.* a base sycophant. [*See* Tody, 160.]
Tōad′y-ing.
Tōad′y-ism (*-izm*), 133.
Tōast, 24.
Tōast′ed.
Tōast′-mȧs′ter.
To-bac′co, 86, 170.
To-bac′co-nist.
Toc′sin, 149.
Tod, 18.
To-dāy′.

☞ "*To-day, to-night, to-morrow*, are almost universally printed with a hyphen." *Wilson.*

Tod′dle, 164.
Tod′dy.
To-do′ (*-doo′*).
To′dy, *n.* a kind of bird. [*See* Toady, 160.]
Tōe (24, 41), *n.* one of the small members which form the extremity of the foot. [*See* Tow, 160.]
To′ga (L.).
To′ga præ-tex′ta (L.).
To′ga-ted.
To′ga vĭ-ri′lis (L.).
To′ged (*-ghed*).
To-geth′er (*-gheth′-*).
Tog′ger-y (*-gur-*).
Tog′gle, 164, 170.
Toil, 27.
Toiled (*toild*), 165.
Toil′er, 228.
Toi′let (231) [Toilette, 203.]
Toil′ing.
Toi-li-nette′, 122.
Toil′less, 66, N.
Toil′some (*-sum*).
Toil′wōrn.
Toise (*toiz*), 27, 136.
To-kāy′.
To′ken (*to′kn*), 149.
Tōld, *v.* did tell. [*See* Toled, *and* Tolled, 160.]
Tole (24), *v.* to allure. [Toll, 203.]

Toled, *v.* did tole or allure. [T o l l e d, 203.] [*See* Told, 160.]
To-le′do.
Tol′er-a-ble, 164, 169.
Tol′er-a-bly.
Tol′er-ance, 169.
Tol′er-ant.
Tol′er-ate, 233, Exc.
Tol′er-āt-ed, 183
Tol′er-āt-ing.
Tol-er-a′tion.
Tōl′ing, *part.* from *Tole.* [T o l l i n g, 203.]
Tŏll (24), *n.* a tax, or duty; — the slow, regular sound or stroke of a bell: — *v.* to ring slowly; — to allure. [T o l e (in the last sense), 203.]
Tŏll [so Sm. Wb. Gd., *tŏl*, Wk.; *tŏl*, or *tōl*, Wr. 155], *v.* to take away; to defeat; to bar. [Law term.]
Tŏll′-booth, 38, 141.
Tŏll′-bridge.
Tōlled (*tōld*), *v.* did toll. [T o l e d (in the sense of *allured*), 203.] [*See* Told, 160.]
Tōll′ing [T o l i n g (in the sense of *alluring*), 203.]
Tŏll′man, 196.
Tōlt, 24.
To-lu′ (*-loo′*) [so Wr. Gd.; *tol′u*, Sm. 155.]
Tom′a-hawk, 171.
To-mā′to, *or* To-mä′to [so Wr. Gd.; *to-ma′-to*, Sm. 155.]
Tomb (*toom*), 162, 171.
Tom′bac.
Tom′boy.
Tomb′stōne (*toom′-*).
Tom′cat.
Tom′cod.
Tome, 24, 163.
To-men-tose′, 39, 136.
To-men′tous, 100.
Tom′fool.
Tom-fool′er-y [so Gd.; *tom′fool-er-y*, Wr. 155]
To-mŏr′rōw [*See* Note under *To-day*.]
Tom′pi-on [so Wr Wb. Gd.; *tomp′yŏn*, Sm. 155] [T a m p i o n, 203.]
Tom-tit′ [so Wk. Sm. Wr.; *tom′tit*, Wb. Gd. 155.]
Tŏn (Fr.), *n.* the prevailing fashion.
Ton (*tun*) (22), *n.* twenty hundred weight; forty cubic feet of round timber, or fifty cubic feet of hewn timber; — in the measurement of a ship, forty cubic feet. [T u n, 203.]

☞ Goodrich remarks: "The orthography *tun* would be preferable, as more accordant with the derivation." But, for the senses here given, *ton* is the usual spelling.

Tone, 24, 163.
Toned, 165.
Tongs (*tongz*), *n. pl.* 18, N.
Tongue (*tung*), 168, 171.
Tongued (*tungd*).
Tongue′-shaped (*tung′-shāpt*).
Tongue′-tīe (*tung′-*).
Tongue′-tīed (*tung′-*).
Tongu′ey (*tung′-*), 171.
Tongu′ing (*tung′-*).
Ton′ic, 170.
To-niç′i-ty, 108, 169.
To-night′ (*-nīt′*) [*See* Note under *To-day*.]
Ton′nage (*tun′-*), 170.
Tōn′oŭs.
Ton-quin-ese′ (*-ēz′*) [so Wr.; *ton-kwin-ēs′*, Gd. 155.]
Ton′sil (160), *n.* a gland at the base of the tongue.
Ton′sile (152, 160), *a.* that may be clipped or shaven.
Ton′sil-lar, 169.
Ton-sil-lit′ic, 109.
Ton-sil-li′tis.
Ton′sor, 88.
Ton-so′ri-al, 49, N.
Ton′sure (*-shur*), 91.
Ton′sured (*-shurd*).
Ton-tine′ (*-tēn′*), 121.
Too (19, 39), *adv.* overmuch, also. [*See* To, *and* Two, 160.]
Tŏŏk [so Sm. Wr. Wb. Gd.; *took*, Wk. 155. — *See* Note under *Book*.]
Tool, 19.
Toon′-wŏŏd.
Toot, 19.
Toot′ed.
Toot′er, 169.
Toot′ing.
Tooth, *n.* & *v.* [pl. of *n.* Teeth, 195.]
Tooth′ache (*-āk*), 171.
Tooth′brush, 206.
Toothed (*tootht*), 165; Note C, p. 34.
Tooth′ing.
Tooth′let-ted [T o o t h-l e t e d, Wb. Gd. 203.]
Tooth′pick.
Tooth′some (*-sum*).
Tooth′wort (*-wurt*).
Top, 18.
Top′ärch (*-ärk*) (171) [so Sm.; *to′park*, Wr. 155.]
Top′arch-y (*-ärk-*).
To′päz.
Tope, 24.
Toped (*tōpt*).
To′per.
Tōp′ing.
Top′-gal-lant.
To-pha′ceoŭs (*-shus*).
Top′-hēav-y.
To′phet.
To′phus, 169.
Top′i-a-ry, 72.
Top′ic, 200.
Top′ic-al, 108.
Top′māst.
Top′mōst.
Top-o-graph′ic.
Top-o-graph′ic-al.
To-pog′ra-phist.
To-pog′ra-phy, 108.
To-pol′o-gy.
Topped (*topt*) (Note C, p. 34) [T o p t, 203.]
Top′ping.
Top′ple, 164.
Top′pled (*top′ld*).
Top′pling, 183.
Top′sy-tur′vy.
[T o p t, 203. — *See* Topped.]
Toque (Fr.) (*tōk*).
Toquet (Fr.) (*to-kā′*).
Torch, 17, 49, 135.
Tore, 24, 49, 67.
To-reu-ma-tog′ra-phy (*-roo-*), 108.
To-reu-ma-tol′o-gy (*-roo-*), 171.
To-reu′tic (*-roo′-*), 19.
Tor′ment, *n.* 103, 161.
Tor-ment′, *v.* 103, 161.
Tor-ment′ed.
Tor-ment′er [T o r-m e n t o r, 203.]
Tor′men-til [so Sm. Wr.

Wb. Gd.; *tor-men'-til*, Wk. 155.]
Tor-ment'ing.
Tor-ment'or [Tormenter, 203.]

☞ Smart restricts this form of the word to the special sense of *one who inflicts penal tortures.*

Tor-ment'ress.
Tōrn, 24, 49, 135.
Tor-na'do [pl. Tor-na'dōes (*-dōz*), 192.]
To-rose'.
To-ros'i-ty, 169.
To'roŭs.
Tor-pe'do [pl. Tor-pe'dōes (*-dōz*), 192.]
Tor-pes'cence, 39.
Tor-pes'cent, 169.
Tor'pid, 135.
Tor-pid'i-ty, 108.
Tor'pi-fīed, 99.
Tor'pi-fȳ.
Tor'pi-fȳ-ing.
Tor'pi-tude, 78, 169.
Tor'por, 88.
Tor-por-if'ic, 109.
Tor'quāt-ed.
Torque (Fr.) (*tork*).
Torqued (*torkt*) [so Wr. Gd.; *tor'kwed*, Sm. 155.]
Tŏr-re-fac'tion.
Tŏr're-fīed, 169, 186.
Tŏr're-fȳ, 171.
Tŏr're-fȳ-ing.
Tor'rent, 66, 127.
Tor-ren'tial (*-shal*), 112.
Tŏr-ri-cel'li-an, 170.
Tŏr'rid, 48, 66.
Torse, 17.
Tor'sel, 76.
Tor-si-bil'i-ty.
Tor'sion.
Torsk, 17, 49, 135.
Tor'so [pl. Tor'sōs (*-sōz*), 192.]
Tort, 17.
Tor'teau (*-to*).
Tor'tĭle, 81, 152.
Tor-til'i-ty.
Tortilla (Sp.) (*tor-tēl'-ya.*)
Tor'tioŭs (*-shus*).
Tort'ĭve, 84.
Tor'toĭse (*tor'tiz*, or *tor'tis*) (171) [so Wr.; *tor'tiz*, Wk. Sm.; *tor'-tis*, Wb. Gd. 155.]
Tort'u-loŭs.
Tort-u-ose', 26, 89.
Tort-u-os'i-ty.
Tort'u-oŭs.
Tort'ure, 91.
Tort'ured (*-yurd*), 165.
Tort'ur-er (*-yur-*), 91.
Tort'ur-ing (*-yur-*).
Tŏr-u-lose', 89.
Tŏr'u-loŭs.
To'rus, 169.
To'ry, 49, N.
To'ry-ism (*-izm*), 136.
Toss, 18, 174.
Tossed (*tost*) (Note C, p. 34) [Tost, 203.]
Toss'ing, 228.
Tost [Tossed, 203.]
To'tal, 72.
To-tal'i-ty, 170.
To'tal-ly, 66.
To'tem.
T'oth'er (*tuth'-*) [a contraction of *the other.*]
Tot'i-dem ver'bis (L.).
To'ti-ēs quo'ti-ēs (L.) (*to'shĭ-ēz kwo'shĭ-ēz*).
To'to cœ'lo (L.).
Tot'ter, 104, 170.
Tot'tered, 150.
Tot'ter-ing.
Tot'tle, 164.
Tot'tled (*tot'ld*).
Tot'tling.
Tou'can (*tou'kan*, or *too'kan*) [*tou'can*, Sm. Wr.; *too'kan*, Gd. 155.]
Toŭch, 22.
Toŭched (*tucht*), 41.
Toŭch'i-ly, 186.
Toŭch'i-ness.
Toŭch'ing.
Toŭch'-me-nŏt, 221.
Toŭch'stone.
Toŭch'wŏŏd.
Toŭch'y [Techy, Tetchy, 203.]
Toŭgh (*tuf*), 22, 35.
Toŭgh'en (*tuf'n*), 149.
Toŭgh'ened (*tuf'nd*).
Toŭgh'en-ing (*tuf'n-*).
Toŭgh'ish (*tuf'-*).
Tough'ly (*tuf'-*).
Tou-pee' (*too-*) [so Wk. Sm. Wr.; *too-pā'*, Gd. 155.]
Toupet (Fr.) (*too-pā'*) [so Sm. Gd., *too-pet'*, Wk.; *too-pā'*, *too-pe'*, or *too-pet'*, Wr. 154, 155.]
Tour (*toor*) (19) [*not* tower, 153.]
Tour-bill'ion (*toor-bil'-yun*), 171.
Tour'ist (*toor'-*).
Tour'ma-lĭne (*toor'-*) [Tourmalin, Turmaline, Turmalin, 203.]
Tour'na-ment (*toor'-*, or *tur'-*) [so Wk. Wr.; *tur'na-ment*, Wb. Gd.; *tŏr'na-ment*, Sm. 155.]

☞ Walker refers to the pronunciation of *journey, nourish, courage*, and many other words from the French, as favoring *tur'-na-ment* rather than *toor'-na-ment.*

Tour'ney (*toor'*, or *tur'-*) (169) [so Wk. Wr.; *tur'ny*, Wb. Gd.; *tŏr'ny*, Sm. 155.]

☞ Walker thinks that general usage, as well as analogy, favors the pronunciation *tur'ny* rather than *toor'ny.* — Smart says: "*Our* . . . is sounded *oor* . . . by some speakers, in *tourney*."

Tourniquet (Fr.) (*tur'-ni-ket*) [so Sm. Wr. Wb. Gd., *tur'ni-kwet*, Wk. 154, 155.]
Tournure (Fr.) (*toor'-noor'*), 154.
Touse (*towz*), 28.
Toused (*towzd*).
Tous'ing (*towz'-*).
Tou'sle (*tow'zl*), 28.
Tou'sled (*tow'zld*).
Tou'sling (*tow'zling*).
Tout-ensemble (Fr.) (*toot'ong-som'bl*), 154.
Tōw (24, 41), *n.* short, loose fibres of flax: — *v.* to draw through the water by means of a rope. [*See* Toe, 160.]
Tōw'age, 70, 169.
Tōw'ard (*to'urd*), *or* Tōw'ards (*to'urdz*), *prep.* [*not* to-wârdz', 153.]

☞ "Notwithstanding our poets almost universally accent this word on the first syllable, and the poets are pretty generally followed by good speakers, there are some, and those not of the lowest order, who still place the accent on the second. These should be reminded that, as *inwards, outwards, backwards, forwards*, and every other word of the same form, have the accent on the first syllable, there is not the least reason for pronouncing *towards* with the accent on the last." *Walker.*

Tōw'ard, *a.* [so Sm. Gd.; *to'wurd*, Wk.; *to'urd*, or *to'wurd*, Wr. 155.]
Tōw'ard-ly.
Tōwed, *v.* did tow. [*See* Toad, 160.]
Tow'el, 28, 76.
Tow'el-ling [Towel-ing, Wb. Gd. 203. — *See* 177, and Note E, p. 70.]
Tower, 28, 67.
Towered (*tourd*), 28, 165.
Tower'ing.
Tower'y.
Tōw'ing.
Town, 28.
Town'-clerk (*-klerk*, or *-klark*) [*See* Clerk.]
Town'-cri-er.
Town'-hâll.
Town'-house.
Towns'folk (*townz'fōk*).
Town'ship.
Towns'man (*townz'-*), 196, 214.
Towns'pēo-ple (*townz'pe-pl*).
Tōw'y, 93.
Tox'ic-al.
Tox-i-co-log'ic-al (*-loj'-*), 108.
Tox-i-col'o-gist.
Tox-i-col'o-gy, 108.
Tox-oph'i-lite, 152.
Toy, 27, 41.
Toyed, 150, 165.
Toy'ing.
Tra'be-a (L.).
Tra'be-āt-ed.
Tra-be-a'tion.
Trace, 23, 163.
Trace'a-ble, 164, 183.
Trace'a-bly.
Traced (*trāst*), 41.
Trāç'er.
Trāç'er-y.
Tra'che-a (*-ke-*) (154, 169) [so Sm. Gd.; *tra'ke-a*, or *tra-ke'a*, Wr. 155.]

☞ "The original word is a *noun plural*, signifying rough parts or substances, with which signification its classical pronunciation would be *tra-ke'a*." *Smart.*

Tra'che-æ (*-ke-e*), *n. pl.*
Tra'che-al (*-ke-*).
Tra'che-a-ry (*-ke-*), 72.
Tra-chel'i-dan (*-kel'-*).
Tra-chel'i-pod (*-kel'-*).
Tra-chel-ip'o-doŭs (*-kel-*).
Tra'che-o-cele (*-ke-*).
Tra-che-ot'o-my.
Tra'chyte (*-kīt*), 171.
Trāç'ing, 228.
Trāç'ing-pa'per.
Track, 10, 181.
Tracked (*trakt*), *v.* did track. [*See* Tract, 160.]
Track'ing.
Tract, *n.* a district; — a dissertation in pamphlet form. [*See* Tracked, 160.]
Trac-ta-bil'i-ty, 108.
Trac'ta-ble, 164.
Trac'ta-bly.
Trac-ta'ri-an, 49, N.
Trac-ta'ri-an-ism(*-izm*).
Trac'tate.
Trac-ta'tor, 169.
Trac'tīle, 152.
Trac-til'i-ty.
Trac'tion, 169.
Tract'ite, 83.
Trac-ti'tioŭs (*-tish'us*).
Trac'tīve, 84.
Trac'tor.
Trac-tor-a'tion, 112.
Trac'to-ry, 86.
Trac'trix.
Trade, 23, 163.
Trād'ed.
Trade'-mark.
Trād'er.
Trade'-sale.
Trades'folk (*trādz'fōk*).
Trades'man (*trādz'-*), 196.
Trades'-ūn-ion (*trādz'-yoon-yun*).
Trade'-wind.
Trād'ing, 183.
Tra-dī'tion (*-dish'un*).
Tra-dī'tion-al(*-dish'un-*)
Tra-dī'tion-al-ism (*-dish'un-al-izm*), 171.
Tra-dī'tion-al-ist(*-dish'-un-*).
Tra-dī'tion-al-ly (*dish'-un-*).
Tra-dī'tion-a-ri-ly (*-dish'un-*).
Tra-di'tion-a-ry (*-dish'-un-*), 72.
Tra-dī'tion-ist (*-dish'un-*).
Trad'i-tīve, 84, 170.
Trad'i-tor.
Tra-duce', 72, 163.
Tra-duced' (*-dūst'*), 183; Note C, p. 34.
Tra-dūç'ent.
Tra-dūç'er.
Tra-dūç'i-ble, 164, 169.
Tra-dūç'ing.
Tra-duc'tion.
Tra-duc'tīve.
Traf'fic, 66, 200.
Traf'ficked (*-fikt*), 182.
Traf'fick-er, 182.
Traf'fick-ing, Note D, p. 37.
Trag'a-canth.
Trag'a-lism (*-lizm*), 136.
Tra-ge'di-an, 169.
Tra-ge-di-enne' (Fr.), *n. fem.* 154.
Trag'e-dy (*traj'-*), 169.
Trag'ic (*traj'-*).
Trag'ic-al (*traj'-*).
Trag'ic-al-ly (*traj'-*).
Trag-i-com'e-dy (*traj-*).
Trag-i-com'ic (*traj-*).
Trag-i-com'ic-al (*traj-*).
Trāil, 23.
Trāiled, 165.
Trāil'ing.
Trāil'net.
Trāin, 23.
Trāin'band.
Trāined, 150, 165.
Trāin'er, 77.
Trāin'ing, 141.
Trāit (*trāt*) [so Wb. Gd.; *trā*, Sm.; *trā*, or *trāt*, Wk.; *trāt*, or *trā*, Wr. 155.]

☞ "The *t* begins to be pronounced." *Walker*, 1806. — "It [*trait*] is now so fully Anglicized as to be properly pronounced as an English word." *Worcester.*

Trāi'tor, 88, 169.
Trāi'tor-oŭs, 105.
Trāi'tress.
Tra-ject', *v.* 103, 161.
Traj'ect, *n.* 103, 161.
Tra-jec'tion.
Tra-ject'o-ry, 86.
Tra-la'tion.
Tral-a-tī'tion (*-tish'un*).
Tral-a-tī'tioŭs(*-tish'us*).
Tram, 10.
Tram'ble, 164.
Tram'mel, 149, 170.
Tram'melled (*-eld*)

[Trammeled, Wb. Gd. 203.—*See* 177, and Note E, p. 70.]
Tram'mel-ling (177) [Trammeling, Wb. Gd. 203.]
Tra-mon'tane, *or* Tram'-on-tane [so Wr.; *tra-mon'tān*, Wb. Gd.; *tram'on-tān*, Sm. 155.]
Tramp, 10.
Tramped (*trampt*), 165; Note E, p. 70.
Tramp'ing.
Tram'ple, 164.
Tram'pled (*-pld*).
Tram'pler.
Tram'pling.
Tram'-rōad.
Trànce, 12, 131.
Tran'quil (*trang'kwil*), 54, 141.
Tran-quil'li-ty, 171.
Tran-quil-lĭ-za'tion (*trang-*).
Tran'quil-lize (*trang'-*), 202.
Tran'quil-lized(*trang'-*)
Tran'quil-liz-er (*trang'-*).
Tran'quil-līz-ing (*trang'-*).
Tran'quil-ly (*trang'-*).
Trans-act' [*not* tranz-akt', 153.]
Trans-act'ed.
Trans-act'ing.
Trans-ac'tion.
Trans-act'or, 169.
Trans-al'pīne, 152.
Trans-at-lan'tic.
Trans-ca'len-cy, 169.
Trans-ca'lent, 122.
Tran-scend', 171.
Tran-scend'ed.
Tran-scen'dence.
Tran-scen'den-cy.
Tran-scen'dent, 169.
Tran-scend-ent'al.
Tran-scend-ent'al-ism (*-izm*), 133, 136.
Tran-scend-ent'al-ist.
Tran-scend-ent'al-ly.
Tran-scend'ent-ly.
Tran-scend'ing.
Tran-scribe'.
Tran-scribed', 150.
Tran-scrīb'er.
Tran-scrīb'ing.
Tran'script, 230.
Tran-scrip'tion, 234.
Tran-scrip'tĭve, 84.
Trans-duc'tion, 228.
Tran'sept.
Trans-fer', *v.* 21, N.; 161.
Trans'fer, *n.* 77, 161.
Trans-fer-a-bil'i-ty.
Trans-fĕr'a-ble, *or* Trans'fer-a-ble (164) [so Wk.; *trans-fĕr'a-bl*, Wr. Wb. Gd.; *trans-fer'a-bl*, Sm. 155] [Transferrible, 203.]
Trans-fer-ee' (122) [Transferree, 203]
Trans'fer-ence [Transference, 203.]
Trans-fer-og'ra-phy, 108
Trans-fer'rence (21, N.; 169) [Transference, 203.]
Trans-ferred' (*-ferd'*).
Trans-fer'rer.
Trans-fer'ri-ble [Transferable, 203.]

☞ "A better spelling of *transferable*." *Smart.* —*See* Note under *Referrible.*

Trans-fer'ring.
Trans-fig-u-ra'tion.
Trans-fig'ure, 91.
Trans-fig'ured (*-yurd*).
Trans-fig'ur-ing (*-yur-*).
Trans-fix'.
Trans-fixed' (*-fikst'*).
Trans-fix'ing.
Trans-fix'ion (*-fik'-shun*), 46, Note 2.
Trans'flux.
Trans-form'.
Trans-form'a-ble, 164.
Trans-form-a'tion.
Trans-form'a-tĭve.
Trans-formed'.
Trans-form'ing.
Trans'fuge.
Trans-fu'gi-tĭve.
Trans-fuse' (*-fūz'*), 39, 40.
Trans-fused' (*-fūzd'*), 165, 183.
Trans-fūs'i-ble (*-fūz'i-bl*), 164, 169.
Trans-fūs'ing (*-fūz'-*).
Trans-fu'sion (*-zhun*), 47.
Trans-fu'sĭve, 84.
Trans-gress'.
Trans-gressed' (*-grest'*), Note C, p. 34.
Trans-gress'ing.
Trans-gres'sion (*-gresh'un*).
Trans-gres'sion-al (*-gresh'un-*).
Trans-gress'ĭve.
Trans-gress'or, 169.
Tran'sien-cy (*-shen-*).
Tran'sient (*-shent*), 46.
Tran-sil'ience(*-yens*)[so Sm. Wk. Wr.; *tran-sil'i-ens*, Wb. Gd. 155.]
Tran-sil'ien-cy (*-yen-*).
Trans-i're (L.).
Tran'sit, 80.
Tran-sĭ'tion (*-sizh'un*) [so Sm. Wr. Wb. Gd.; *tran-sizh'un*, or *tran-sish'un*, Wk. 155.]

☞ "*Abscission* and *transition* are commonly pronounced contrarily to rule, the element *sh*, which gives the short sound to the *i* in the second syllable, being vocalized. This occurs through the unconscious predetermination of the ear that since the syllable began with the hissing non-vocal consonant *s*, it ought, for the sake of variety, to finish with a consonant of a different kind." *Smart.*

Tran-sĭ'tion-al (*-sizh'-un-*).
Tran-sĭ'tion-a-ry (*sizh'-un-*), 72, 171.
Trans'i-tĭve, 84.
Trans'i-to-ri-ly, 86, 186.
Trans'i-to-ri-ness, 186.
Tran'si-to-ry, 86.
Trans-lāt'a-ble, 164.
Trans-late'.
Trans-lāt'ed, 183.
Trans-lāt'ing.
Trans-la'tion, 169.
Trans-lāt'ĭve.
Trans-lāt'or, 169.
Trans-lāt'o-ry [so Wk. Sm. Wr.; *trans'la-to-ry*, Wb. Gd. 155.]
Trans-la'tress.
Trans-lo-ca'tion.
Trans-lu'cence.
Trans-lu'cen-cy.
Trans-lu'cent, 171.
Trans-lu'cid.
Trans'lu-na-ry, 72.
Trans-ma-rine' (*-rēn'*).
Trans'mĭ-grate.
Trans'mĭ-grāt-ed.
Trans'mĭ-grāt-ing.
Trans-mĭ-gra'tion.
Trans'mĭ-grāt-or.
Trans-mi'gra-to-ry, 86.
Trans-mis-si-bil'i-ty.

Trans-mis′si-ble, 164.
Trans-mis′sion (*-mish′-un*).
Trans-mis′sĭve, 84, 170.
Trans-mit′.
Trans-mit′tal, 176.
Trans-mit′tance, 169.
Trans-mit′ted.
Trans-mit′ter.
Trans-mit′ti-ble, 164.
Trans-mit′ting.
Trans-mūt-a-bil′i-ty
Trans-mūt′a-ble, 164.
Trans-mu-ta′tion.
Trans-mu-ta′tion-ist.
Trans-mute′.
Trans-mūt′ed, 183.
Trans-mūt′er.
Trans-mūt′ing.
Tran′som, 86, 169.
Trans′pa-dane.
Trans-pâr′ence (*-pêr′-*).
Trans-par′en-cy (*-pêr′-*).
Trans-par′ent (*-pêr′-*) (171) [*not* trans-pa′-rent, 127, 153.]
Trans-piërce′ [*See* Pierce.]
Tran-spīr′a-ble, 169.
Tran-spĭ-ra′tion, 143.
Tran-spīr′a-to-ry, 86.
Tran-spire′.
Tran-spired′, 150.
Tran-spīr′ing.
Trans-plȧnt′.
Trans-plant-a′tion.
Trans-plȧnt′ed.
Trans-plȧnt′er.
Trans-plȧnt′ing.
Trans′pōrt, *n.* 103, 161.
Trans-pōrt′, *v.* 103, 161.
Trans-pōrt-a-bil′i-ty.
Trans-pōrt′a-ble, 164.
Trans-pōrt-a′tion.
Trans-pōrt′ed.
Trans-pōrt′ing.
Trans-pōs′al (*-poz′-*).
Trans-pose′ (*-poz′*).
Trans-posed′ (*-pōzd′*).
Trans-pōs′ing (*-pōz′-*).
Trans-po-sĭ′tion (*-zish′-un*), 112.
Trans-po-sĭ′tion-al (*-zish′un-*). [84.
Trans-pos′i-tĭve(*-poz′-*),
Trans-ship′.
Trans-ship′ment.
Trans-shipped′ (*-shipt′*).
Trans-ship′ping, 176.
Tran-sub-stan′ti-ate (*-shĭ-*).
Tran-sub-stan′ti-āt-ed (*-shĭ-*).
Tran-sub-stan′ti-āt-ing (*-shĭ-*).
Tran-sub-stan-ti-a′tion (*-shĭ-*), 171.
Tran-su-da′tion.
Tran-su′da-to-ry, 86.
Tran-sude′, 26.
Tran-sūd′ed.
Tran-sūd′ing, 183.
Trans-vec′tion.
Trans-vers′al.
Trans-verse′, 21, N.
Trans-verse′ly, 185.
Trans-vo-la′tion.
Trap, 10.
Tra-pan′, *v.* to lay a trap for: — *n.* a snare. [*See* Trepan, 148.]
Tra-panned′ (*-pand′*).
Tra-pan′ner.
Tra-pan′ning, 176.
Trap′-dōor (*-dōr*).
Trap′e-zate, 169.
Tra-pe′zi-an, 169.
Tra-pe′zi-form, 108.
Tra-pe′zi-um [so Sm. Wb. Gd; *tra-pe′zhĭ-um*, Wk.; *tra-pe′zhi-um*, or *tra-pe′zi-um*, Wr. 155.]
Trap-e-zo-he′dral, 116.
Trap-e-zo-he′dron.
Trap-e-zoid′ (122) [so Sm. Wb. Gd.; *tra-pe′-zoid*, Wk.; *trap-e-zoid′*, or *tra-pe′zoid*, Wr. 155.]
Trap-e-zoid′al.
Trap′pe-an, 110, 169.
Trapped (*trapt*), 165; Note C, p. 34.
Trap′per, 176.
Trap′ping.
Trap′pings (*-pingz*), *n. pl.*
Trap′pist.
Trap′poŭs.
Trap′py, 93.
Trap′-tu-fa, *or* Trap′-tuff.
Trash, 10, 46.
Trash′i-ly, 186.
Trash′i-ness.
Trash′y, 93.
Trass (10, 174) [Tarrass, 203.]
Trâu-mat′ic.
Trav′ăil, *n.* labor: — *v.* to labor; — to be in labor. [*See* Travel, 148.]
Trav′el (149), *v.* to journey: — *n.* act of journeying. [*See* Travail, 148.]
Trav′elled (*-eld*) [Traveled, Wb. Gd. 203. — *See* 177, and Note E, p. 70.]
Trav′el-ler (132, 177) [Traveler, Wb. Gd. 203.]
Trav′el-ling (132, 177) [Traveling, Wb. Gd. 203.]
Trav′ers-a-ble, 164.
Trav′erse, *adv.* [so Sm. Wr. Wb. Gd.; *tra-vers′*, Wk. 155.]
Trav′erse, *a. n.* & *v.*
Trav′ersed (*-erst*).
Trav′erse-săil′ing.
Trav′erse-ta′ble, 164.
Trav′ers-ing, 183.
Trav′er-tĭne (152) [Travertin, 203.]
Trav′es-tĭed (*-tid*).
Trav′es-ty, 93.
Trav′es-tȳ-ing.
Trav′is, 169.
Trawl, 17.
Trawl′ing.
Trawl′-net.
Trāy (23, 56, Rem.), *n.* a shallow vessel or stand; a waiter. [*See* Trey, 160.]
Trĕach′er-oŭs, 233, Exc.
Trĕach′er-y, 171.
Trē′cle, 164.
Trĕad, 15.
Trĕad′ing.
Trĕad′le (*tred′l*), 164.
Trĕad′mill, 206.
Trēa′son (*tre′zn*), 149.
Trēa′son-a-ble (*tre′zn-a-bl*), 164, 171.
Trēa′son-a-bly (*-zn-*).
Trĕas′ure (*trezh′ur*), 91.
Trĕas′ured (*trezh′urd*).
Trĕas′ur-er (*trezh′ur-*).
Treas′ure-trove (*trezh′-ur-*).
Treas′ur-ing (*trezh′ur-*).
Treas′ur-y (*trezh′ur-*).
Trēat, 13.
Trēat′ed.
Trēat′er.
Trēat′ing.
Trēat′ĭse (*trēt′iz*, or *trēt′is*) (169) [so Wr.; *trēt′iz*, Wk. Sm.; *trēt′is*, Wb. Gd. 155.]
Trēat′ment.
Trēat′y.
Treb′le (*treb′l*) (164) [so

Wk. Sm. Wr.; *trib′l*, Wb. Gd. 155.]
Treb′led (*treb′ld*).
Treb′ling.
Treb′ly, 93.
Treb′u-chet (*-shet*), *or* Tre′buck-et, 203.
Tre-chom′e-ter (*-kom′-*), 108.
Tree, 13, 189.
Treed, 188.
Tree′-frog.
Tree′ing.
Tree′nāil (commonly pronounced *trun′nel*) [Trunnel, 203.]
Tree′-tōad.
Tre′fal-lōw [Trifallow, 203.]
Tref′le (*tref′l*), 164.
Tre′foil, 171.
Treillage (Fr.) (*trel′āj*), 154.
Trel′lis, 169, 170.
Trel′lised (*-list*).
Trel′lis-ing.
Tre-män′do (It.) (*trā-*).
Trem′ble, 164.
Trem′bled (*bld*), 165.
Trem′bler.
Trem′bling, 183.
Tre-mel′la.
Tre-men′doŭs (100) [*not* tre-mend′u-us, *nor* tre-men′jus, 153.]
Trem′o-līte, 152.
Tre′mor, *or* Trem′or [*tre′mur*, Wk. Wr. Wb. Gd.; *trem′ur*, Sm. 155.]
Trem′u-loŭs, 108.
Trench, 15, 44, Note 2.
Trench′ant, 72.
Trenched (*trencht*), 165; Note C, p. 34.
Trench′er.
Trench′ing.
Trend, 15.
Trend′ed.
Trend′ing.
Tren′dle, 164.
Tren′tal, 72.
Tre-pan′, *n.* an instrument for removing portions of bone:— *v.* to perforate with a trepan. [*See* Trapan, 148.]
Tre-pang′ [so Wr.; *tre′-pang*, Gd. 155.]
Tre-panned′ (*-pand′*), 165.
Tre-pan′ner.
Tre-pan′ning, 176.
Tre-phine′ (*-fēn′*), *or* Tre-phīne′ [so Wr.; *tre-fēn′*, Sm.; *tre-fīn′*, or *tre-fēn′*, Gd. 155.]
Trep-i-da′tion.
Tres′āyle.
Tres′pass, 72, 171.
Tres′passed (*-past*).
Tres′pass-er.
Tres′pass-ing.
Tress, 15, 189.
Tressed (*trest*, or *tres′-ed*) [so Sm. Wr.; *trest*, Gd.; *tres′ed*, Wk. 155], *a.*
Tress′ure (*tresh′ur*), 91.
Tress′ured (*tresh′urd*).
Tress′y.
Tres′tle (*tres′l*), 162.
Tres′tle-tree (*tres′l-*).
Tret, 15, 41.
Trev′et [Trivet, 203.]
Trey (*trā*) (23), *n.* a card or a die with three spots. [*See* Tray, 160.]
Trī′a-ble, 164.
Tri-a-con-ta-he′dral.
Trī′ad.
Tri-a-del′phoŭs.
Trī′al, 72.
Trī-al′i-ty.
Trī′a-lŏgue (*-log*), 87.
Trī-an′der.
Trī-an′dri-a.
Trī-an′dri an, 169.
Trī-an′droŭs, 100.
Trī′an-gle (*-ang-gl*).
Trī′an-gled (*-ang-gld*).
Trī-an′gu-lar (*-ang′-*).
Trī-an-gu-lăr′i-ty (*-ang-*).
Trī an′gu-lar-ly (*-ang′-*).
Trī-an′gu-late (*-ang′-*), 108.
Trī-an′gu-lāt-ed (*-ang′-*).
Trī-an′gu-lāt-ing (*-ang′-*).
Trī-an-gu-la′tion (*-ang-*).
Trī′ärch-y (*-ärk-*), 52.
Trī′as, 72.
Trī-as′sic, 79, 109.
Trīb′al, 228.
Trī-ba′sic.
Tribe, 25, 163.
Trib′let [Tribolet, Triboulet, 203.]
Trĭ-bom′e-ter, 79, 108.
Trī′brach (*-brak*).
Trib-u-la′tion.
Trī-bu′nal, 72, 79.
Trib′u-na-ry, 72.
Trib′u-nate.
Trib′une (90) [*not* trī′-būn, 153.]
Trib-u-nĭ′tial (*-nish′al*), 231, 234.
Trib-u-nĭ′tian (*-nish′-an*).
Trib′u-ta-ri-ly.
Trib′u-ta-ry, 72.
Trib′ute, 90.
Trib′ūt-er.
Trī-cap′su-lar.
Trice, 25, 39; Note D, p. 37.
Trī-cen-na′ri-oŭs.
Trī-cen′ni-al.
Trī-cen′te-na-ry.
Trī′cho-cyst (*-ko-*).
Trī-chom′a-tose (*-kom′-*).
Trī-chop′ter-an (*-kop′-*).
Trī′chord (*-kord*), 88.
Trī-chot′o-moŭs(*-kot′-*).
Trī-chot′o-my (*-kot′-*).
Trī′chro-ism (*-kro-izm*).
Trick, 16, 181.
Tricked (*trikt*), 41.
Trick′er-y, 233, Exc.
Trick′ing.
Trick′ish.
Trick′le (*trik′l*), 164.
Trick′led (*trik′ld*).
Trick′ling, 183.
Trick′ster.
Trick′y, 93.
Tric′li-nate, 105.
Trī-clin′i-a-ry, 72.
Trĭ-clin′ic (109)[so Wr.; *trik′li-nik*, Gd. 155.]
Trī-coc′coŭs, 170.
Trī′col-or (*-kul-*) [Tricolour, 203.]
Trī′col-ored (*-kul-urd*) [Tricoloured, 203.]
Trī′corn.
Tri-cor-nig′er-oŭs (*-nij′-*), 108.
Trī-cor′po-ral.
Tri-cus′pid.
Trī-cus′pid-ate.
Trī-dac′tyl.
Trī-dac′tyl-oŭs.
Trī′dent, 76, 127.
Tri-dent′ate.
Tri-dent′āt-ed.
Trī′dent-ed.
Tri-dent-if′er-oŭs.
Trī-den′tĭne, 82, 152.
Trī-dī-a-pa′son (*-pa′-zun*).
Trī-dō-dec-a-he′dral.

Trīed, 186.
[T r i e d r a l, 203. — *See* Trihedral.]
Trī-en'ni-al (170) [so Sm. Wr. Wb. Gd.; *trī-en'yal*, Wk. 155.]
Trī-en'ni-al-ly.
Trī'er, *n.* one who tries. [*See* Trior.]
Trī'er-arch (*-ärk*).
Trī'fal-lōw [T r e f a l - l o w, 203.]
Trī-fā'ri-oŭs.
Trī-fas'ci-āt-ed(*-fash'ĭ-*)
Trī'fid [*not* trĭf'id, 153.]
Trī-fis'tu-la-ry, 72.
Trī'fle, 163, 230.
Trī'fled (*trī'fld*).
Trī'fler.
Trī'fling, 183.
Trī-flo'ral, 49, N.
Trī-flo'roŭs.
Trī-fo'li-ate.
Trī-fo'li-āt-ed.
Trī-fo'li-o-late.
Trī'fo-ly.
Trī-fo'ri-um (L.).
Trī'form.
Trī-form'i-ty, 108.
Trī-fur'cate.
Trī-fur'cāt-ed.
Trig, 16.
Trig'a-mist.
Trig'a-moŭs, 100.
Trig'a-my, 170.
Trī-gas'tric.
Trī-gem'i-noŭs, 45.
Trigged (*trigd*), 176.
Trig'ger (*-gur*), 138.
Trig'ging (*-ghing*).
Trī'glyph [so Wk. Sm. Wr.; *trig'lif*, Wb. Gd. 155.]
Trī-glyph'ic.
Trī-glyph'ic-al. [153.]
Trī'gon [*not* trig'un,
Trig'o-nal, 72.
Trig-o-noç'er-oŭs (*-nos'-*).
Trig-o-no-met'ric.
Trig-o-no-met'ric-al.
Trig-o-nom'e-try.
Trig'o-noŭs [so Gd.; *trī'go-nus*, Wr. 155.]
Trī'gram.
Trī-gram-mat'ic.
Trī-gram'mic.
Trī'graph.
Trī'gyn (*-jin*).
Trī-gyn'i-a (*-jin'-*), 78.
Trī-gyn'i-an (*-jin'-*).
Trī'gyn-oŭs (*-jin-*).
Trī-he'dral, 72.
Trī-he'dron.
Trī-ho'ral.
Trī-ju'goŭs [so Sm. Wr., *trij'u-gus*, Wb. Gd. 155.]
Trī-lat'er-al.
Trī-lat'er-al-ly.
Trī-lem'ma, 79.
Trī-lin'gual (*-ling'-*).
Trī-lit'er-al, 170.
Tril'i-thon.
Trill, 172.
Trilled (*trild*), 165.
Trill'ing.
Trill'ion (*-yun*), 51.
Trī'lo-bate [so Sm. Wr.; *trī-lo'bāt*, Gd. 155.]
Trī'lobed.
Trī'lo-bīte (83, 152) [*not* tril'o-bīt, 153.]
Trī-lo-bit'ic.
Trī-loc'u-lar, 108.
Tril'o-gy, 93, 108.
Trim, 16.
Trī-mac'u-lāt-ed.
Trī-mem'bral.
Trī'mer-an.
Trī'mer-oŭs [so Wr.; *trī-me'rus*, Gd. 155.]
Trī-mes'ter.
Trī-mes'tri-al.
Trim'e-ter, 108.
Trī-met'ric, 109.
Trī-met'ric-al, 108.
Trimmed (*trimd*), 165.
Trim'mer, 176.
Trim'ming.
Trī-morph'ism (*-izm*).
Trī'my-a-ry, 72, 190.
Trī'nal.
Trine, 163.
Trī-nerv'ate, 21, N.
Trī'nerved.
Trin'gle (*tring'gl*), 54.
Trin-i-ta'ri-an, 49, N.
Trin-i-ta'ri-an-ism (*-izm*), 133, 136.
Trin'i-ty, 170.
Trin'ket (*tring'-*), 54.
Trin'ket-ry (*tring'-*).
Trī-noc'tial (*-shal*), 112.
Trī-nōd'al.
Trī-no'mi-al, 169.
Trī-nom'i-nal, 108.
Trī'o [pl. Trī'os (*-ōz*), 192.]

☞ "Often pronounced *tre'o.*" *Goodrich.*

Trī-ob'o-lar.
Trī-ob'o-la-ry, 72.
Trī'oc-tīle, 81, 152.
Trī-oc-to-he'dral.
Trī-œ'cia (*-e'sha*).
Trī-œ'cioŭs (*-e'shus*), 112, 169.
Trī'or, *n.* a person appointed by the court to examine whether the challenge to a panel of jurors, or to any juror, is just or not. [Law term.] [T r i e r, 203.]
Trip, 16.
Trī-part'ed.
Trī-part'i-ble, 164, 169.
Trī-par'tient (*-shent*).
Trip'ar-tīte (83, 152)[*not* tri-par'tīt, 153.]
Trip-ar-tī'tion (*-tish'-un*).
Trī-pas'chal (*-kal*).
Tripe, 25, 163.
Trip'e-dal, *or* Trī-pe'-dal [*trip'e-dal*, Wk. Wr. Wb. Gd.; *trī-pe'-dal*, Sm. 155.]
Trī-pen'nate [T r i p i n - n a t e, 203.]
Trī-pen'na-tĭ-part-ed.
Trī-per'son-al, 21, N.
Trī-per'son-al-ist.
Trī-per-son-al'i-ty.
Trī-pet'al-oid.
Trī-pet'al-oŭs.
Trip'-ham-mer, 206, Exc. 3.
Triph'thong (*trip'-*) [so Wk. Sm. Wr.; *trif'-thong*, Wb. Gd. 155] [*See* Note under *Diphthong.*]
Triph-thon'gal (*trip-thong'gal*), 54, Note 2.
Triph'y-līne (152, 171) [so Gd.; *trif'i-līn*, Wr. 155.]
Trī-phyl'loŭs,*or*Triph'-yl-loŭs. [*See* Adeno-phyllous.]
Trī-pin'nate [T r i p e n - n a t e, 203.]
Trī-pin-nat'i-fid, *or* Trī-pin'na-ti-fid [*trī-pin-nat'i-fid*, Gd.; *trī-pin'na-ti-fid*, or *trī-pin-nat'i-fid*, Wr. 155.]
Trip'le (*trip'l*). 170.
Trip'led (*trip'ld*), 183.
Trip'let, 76.
Trip'li-cate, 169.
Trip-li-ca'tion.
Trī-pliç'i-ty.
Trip'ling.
Trip'līte, 83, 152.
Trī'pod [so Sm. Wr. Wb.

Gd.; *tri'pod*, or *trip'-od*, Wk. 155.]

☞ Though Walker gives *trip'od* as an alternative pronunciation of this word, he says: "I do not hesitate to pronounce the former [*trī'pod*] most agreeable to English analogy."

Trī-po'di-an.
Trip'o-dy, 66, 170.
Trip'o-lĭ [Tripoly, 203.]
Trip'o-lĭne, 82, 152.
Trĭ-pol'i-tan.
Trī'pŏs, 189.
Trip'pant.
Tripped (*tript*) (41) [Tript, 203.]
Trip'per.
Trip'ping, 176.
[Tript, 203.—*See* Tripped.]
Trip'tote.
Trip'tych (*-tik*), 171.
Trī-que'troŭs.
Trī-ra'di-ate, 169.
Trī-ra'di-āt-ed.
Trī'reme.
Trī-rhom-boid'al (*-rom-*), 171.
Trĭs-a'gi-on.
Trī-sect', 103.
Trī-sect'ed.
Trī-sect'ing.
Trī-sec'tion.
Trī-sep'al-oŭs.
Trī-se'ri-al, 49, N.
Trī-se'ri-ate.
Tris-oc-ta-he'dron.
Trī'spast, *or* Trī-spas'-ton, 203.
Trī-sperm'oŭs.
Tris'tich-oŭs (*-tik-*) [so Wr.; *trī-stik'us*, Gd. 203.]
Trī-stig-mat'ic.
Trī-stig'ma-tose.
Trī-sul'cate.
Tris-yl-lab'ic.
Tris-yl-lab'ic-al.
Tris-yl'la-ble, *or* Tris'-yl-la-ble (164) [*tris-il'la-bl*, Sm. Wb. Gd.; *tris'il-la-bl*, Wk. Wr. 155.]
Trite, 25, 163.
Trī-ter'nate, 21, N.
Trī'the-ism (*-izm*), 133.
Trī'the-ist.
Trī-the-ist'ic.
Trī-the-ist'ic-al.
Trī'thing [so Sm. Wb. Gd.; *trī'thing*, Wr. 155.]
Trī'ton.
Trī'tone.
Trī-tox'ĭde [Tritoxyd, Wb. Gd. 203.]
Trit'u-ra-ble, 164.
Trit'u-rate [so Wb. Gd. Wr.; *trī'tu-rāt*, Sm. 155.]
Trit'u-rāt-ed, 183.
Trit'u-rāt-ing.
Trit-u-ra'tion, 112.
Trī'umph.
Trī-umph'al.
Trī-umph'ant.
Trī'umphed (*-umft*), 41.
Trī'umph-er.
Trī'umph-ing.
Trī-um'vir (169) [L. pl. *Trī-um'vĭ-rī*; Eng.pl. Trī-um'virs (*-vurz*), 198.]
Trī-um'vĭ-rate.
Trī'une (90) [so Sm. Wr. Wb. Gd.; *trī-ūn'*, Wk. 155.]
Trī-u'ni-ty.
Trī'valve.
Trī-valv'u-lar, 108.
Trī-verb'i-al, 21, N.
Triv'et [Trevet, 203.]
Triv'i-al [so Sm. Wb. Gd.; *triv'yal*, Wk.; *triv'i-al*, or *triv'yal*, Wr. 155.]
Triv-i-al'i-ty.
Trī-week'ly.
Tro'car [Trochar, 203]
[Troch, 203.—*See* Troche.]
Tro-cha'ic (*-ka'-*), 171.
Tro-cha'ic-al (*-ka'-*).
Tro-chan'ter (*-kan'-*).
Tro-chan-te'ri-an (*-kan-*), 49, N.
Tro-chan-tin'i-an(*-kan-*)
[Trochar, 203.—*See* Trocar.]
Tro'che (*-ke*) (160), *n.* a circular cake of sugar, mucilage, and some kind of medicine, to be slowly dissolved in the mouth.
Tro'chee (*-ke*) (160), *n.* a poetic foot of two syllables, the first long or accented, the second short or unaccented.
Tro'chil (*-kil*).
Tro-chil'ic (*-kil'-*), 170.
Tro-chil'ics (*-kil'-*), 109.
Tro-chil'i-dist (*-kil'-*).
Troch'i-lus (*trok'-*), 169.
Tro'chings (*-kings*), *n.pl*
Troch'le-a (*trok'-*).
Troch'le-ar (*trok'-*), 169.
Troch'le-a-ry (*trok'-*), 72, 171.
Tro'choid (*-koid*), 52.
Tro-chom'e-ter (*-kom'-*).
Trod, 18.
Trod'den (*trod'n*), 149.
Trog'lo-dyte [so Wk. Wr. Wb. Gd.; *tro'-glo-dīt*, Sm. 155.]
Trog-lo-dyt'ic.
Trog-lo-dyt'ic-al.
Tro'jan, 72.
Trōll, 24, 172.
Trōlled (*trōld*), 165.
Trōll'ing.
Trol'lop, 170.
Trom'bone, *or* Trom-bo'ne (It.) (*-bo'nā*) [*trom'bōn*, Wb. Gd., *trom-bo'nā*, Sm., *trom-bo'ne*, or *trom'-bōn*, Wr. 154, 155.]
Tromp, 18.
Tromp'il.
Tro'na, 72.
Troop, 19.
Trooped (*troopt*), 41; Note C, p. 34.
Troop'er.
Troop'ing.
Trope, 24.
Tro'phĭed (*-fĭd*).
Tro-pho'ni-an.
Troph'o-sperm.
Tro'phy [*not* trof'y, 153.]
Trop'ic, 66, 170.
Trop'ic al, 228.
Trop'ic-al-ly.
Trōp'ist, 183.
Trop-o-log'ic-al (*-loj'-*).
Tro-pol'o-gy, 108.
Trot, 18.
Troth, 18, N.
Trot'ted, 176.
Trot'ter.
Trot'ting.
Trou'ba-dour (*troo'ba-door*) [so Wk. Wr. Gd.; *troo-ba-door'*, Sm. 155.]
Troŭb'le (*trub'l*), 171.
Troŭb'led (*trub'ld*), 183.
Troŭb'ler. 22, 77.
Troŭb'le-some (*trub'l-sum*), 171.
Troŭb'ling.

Troub'loŭs.
Trŏugh (*trof*), 18, N.; 35, 141.
Trounce, 28, 39.
Trounced (*trownst*).
Trounç'ing.
Trou'sers (*trou'zurz*), *n. pl.* (28) [Trowsers, 203.]
Trousseau (Fr.) (*troo-so'*) [so Wr. Gd.; *troo'so*, Sm. 155.]
Trout, 28, 41.
Tro'ver.
Trōw (24) [*not* trou, 127, 153.]
Trow'el, 28.
Trow'elled (*-eld*) [Troweled, Wb. Gd. 203. — *See* 177, and Note E, p. 70.
Troy, 27.
Tru'an-cy (*troo'-*), 169.
Tru'ant (*troo'-*), 19, 72.
Truce (*troos*), 19.
Truck, 22, 181.
Truck'age, 70, 169.
Trucked (*trukt*), 41.
Truck'er.
Truck'ing.
Truck'le (*truk'l*), 164.
Truck'le-bed (*truk'l-*).
Truck'led (*truk'ld*).
Truck'ling.
Truck'man, 196.
Tru'cu-lence (*troo'-*).
Tru'cu-len-cy (*troo'-*).
Tru'cu-lent (*troo'-*) (108) [*not* truk'u-lent, 153.]
Trudge, 22, 45.
Trudged, 165.
Trudg'ing, 45, 183.
True (*troo*), 19, 128.
Truf'fle (*trŏŏf'l*) (164) [so Sm.; *troof'l*, Wk. Wr.; *trŭ'fl*, Wb. Gd. (*See* § 26), 155.]
Truf'fled (*trŏŏf'ld*).
Tru'ism (*troo'izm*), 136.
Trul-li-za'tion.
Tru'ly (*troo'-*), 185.
Trump, 22.
Trumped (*trumpt*), 41.
Trump'er-y.
Trump'et.
Trump'et-ed.
Trump'et-er, 169.
Trump'et-fish.
Trump'et-shaped (*-shāpt*), 203, Exc. 5.
Trump'et-tongued (*-tungd*).
Trump'ing.
Trun'cate (*trung'-*), 54, 73.
Trun'cāt-ed (*trung'-*).
Trun'cāt-ing (*trung'-*).
Trun-ca'tion, 112.
Trun'cheon (*-shun*) [so Wk. Wr. Gd.; *trun'-chun*, Sm. 155.]
Trun'dle (*trun'dl*), 164.
Trun'dle-bed (*trun'dl-*).
Trun'dled (*trun'dld*).
Trun'dling, 183.
Trunk (*trungk*), 22, 54.
Trun'ket (*trung'-*).
Trunk'-fish (*trungk'-*).
Trunk'-hose (*trungk'-hōz*).
Trun'nel [Treenail, 203.]
Trunn'ion (*trun'yun*) [so Wk. Wr. Wb. Gd.; *trun'ni-un*, Sm. 155.]
Trunn'ioned (*trun'-yund*).
Truss, 22, 174.
Trussed (*trust*) (22, 41), *v.* did truss. [*See* Trust, 160.]
Truss'ing.
Trust (22), *n.* confidence: — *v.* to confide in. [*See* Trussed, 160.]
Trust'ed.
Trust-ee', 121.
Trust'er.
Trust'ful (*-fŏŏl*), 180.
Trust'ful-ly (*-fŏŏl-*).
Trust'i-ly, 186.
Trust'i-ness.
Trust'ing.
Trust'wor-thi-ness (*-wur-*).
Trust'wor-thy (*-wur-*), 206.
Trust'y, 93, 228.
Truth (*trooth*) (19, 37) [pl. Truths (*trooths*), 140, 189.]

☞ "Some go so far as to pronounce the plural of *truth*, *troothz*; but this must be carefully avoided." *Walker*.

Truth'ful (*trooth'fŏŏl*).
Truth'ful-ly (*trooth'-fŏŏl-*).
Truth'less (*trooth'-*).
Trut-ta'ceoŭs (*-shus*).
Try, 25, 41, 48.
Try'ing.
Try'sail.
Tryst, 16.
Tryst'ing.
Tub, 22, 31, 41.
Tu'ba, 26, 72.
Tub'bing, 176.
Tub'by, 93, 170.
Tube (26) [*not* toob, 127, 153.]
Tu'ber, 77.
Tu'ber-āt-ed.
Tu'ber-cle, 164.
Tu'ber-cled (*-kld*).
Tu-ber'cu-lar, 108.
Tu-ber'cu-late.
Tu-ber'cu-lāt-ed.
Tu'ber-cule, 90.
Tu-ber-cu-lĭ-za'tion.
Tu-ber'cu-lose.
Tu-ber'cu-loŭs.
Tu-ber-if'er-oŭs, 108.
Tu'ber-ose [so Sm.; *tūb'rōz*, Wk.; *tūb'rōz*, or *tu'bur-ōs*, Gd.; *tūb'rōz*, or *tu'bur-ōz*, Wr. 155], *n.*
Tu-ber-ose', *a.*
Tu-ber-os'i-ty.
Tu'ber-oŭs.
Tu-biç'i-nate, 108.
Tu'bi-cole.
Tu'bi-corn.
Tu'bi-fer.
Tu'bi-form, 108.
Tūb'ing, 183.
Tu'bi-pore.
Tu-bip'o-rite, 152.
Tu-bip'o-roŭs.
Tub'man, 196.
Tu'bu-lar, 26, 89.
Tu-bu-la'ri-an.
Tu'bu-late.
Tu'bu-lāt-ed.
Tu-bu-la'tion.
Tu'bule.
Tu-bu'li-cole.
Tu-bu'li-form, 108.
Tu'bu-lose [so Gd.; *tu-bu-lōs'*, Wr. 155.]
Tu'bu-loŭs.
Tu'bu-lure, 26.
Tuck, 22, 181.
Tucked (*tukt*), 41, 165.
Tuck'er.
Tuck'ing.
Tūes'day (*tūz'dy*) (26) [*not* tooz'dy, 127, 153.]
Tu'fa (26) [so Sm. Wb. Gd.; *too'fa*, Wr. 155.]
Tu-fa'ceoŭs (*-shus*), 112, 169.
Tuff, 22, 173.
Tuft, 22.

Tuft'ed.
Tuft'ing.
Tuft'y, 93.
Tug, 22, 41, 53.
Tugged (*tugd*).
Tug'ger (-*gur*). 138.
Tug'ging (-*ghing*).
Tu-ĭ'tion (-*ish'un*).
Tu-ĭ'tion-a-ry (-*ish'un-*), 72.
Tu'lip (26) [*not* too'lip, 127, 153.]
Tu'lip-ist.
Tu'lip-o-ma'ni-a.
Tu'lip-tree.
Tulle (Fr.) (*tool*), *n.* a kind of silk lace. [*See* Tool, 160.]
Tul'li-an, 169, 170.
Tum'ble, 164.
Tum'bled (*tum'bld*).
Tum'ble-down, *a.*
Tum'bler.
Tum'bling, 183.
Tum'brel.
Tu-me-fac'tion.
Tu'me-fied.
Tu'me-fȳ, 169.
Tu'me-fȳ-ing.
Tu'mid, 26.
Tu-mid'i-ty.
Tu'mor, 88.
Tu'mor-oŭs.
Tu'mu-lar.
Tu'mu-loŭs.
Tu'mult (26) [*not* too'-mult, 127, 153.]
Tu-mult'u-a-ri-ness.
Tu-mult'u-a-ry, 72.
Tu-mult'u-oŭs, 108, 228.
Tu'mu-lus (L.) [pl. *Tu'-mu-lī*, 198.]
Tun (22), *n.* a large cask; — the measure of four hogsheads; — any quantity proverbially large; — twenty hundred weight; — forty cubic feet of round timber, or fifty cubic feet of hewn timber; — in the measurement of a ship, forty cubic feet. [Ton (in the last three senses), 203] [*See* Note under *Ton.*]
Tūn'a-ble, 164, 183.
Tūn'a-bly.
Tune (26) [*not* toon, 127, 153.]
Tuned, 165.
Tune'ful (-*fŏŏl*).
Tune'ful-ly (-*fŏŏl-*).
Tune'less, 185.
Tung'state.
Tung'sten.
Tung'stic.
Tu'nic, 26, 200.
Tu'nic-a-ry, 72.
Tu'ni-cate.
Tu'ni-cāt-ed.
Tu'ni-cle, 164.
Tūn'ing, 183.
Tūn'ing-fork.
Tu-nĭ'si-an (-*nizh'ĭ-*).
Tunk'er (*tungk'-*).
[Tunnage, 203. — *See* Tonnage.]
Tun'nel, 170.
Tun'nelled (-*neld*) [Tunneled, Wb. Gd. 202. — *See* 177, and Note E, p. 70.]
Tun'nel-ling (177) [Tunneling, Wb. Gd. 203.]
Tun'ny, 66, 170.
Tu'pe-lo.
Tur'bȧn, 169.
Tur'ba-ry, 72.
Tur'bid, 49.
Tur-bid'i-ty, 108, 169.
Tur-bill'ion (-*bil'yun*).
Tur-bi-na'ceoŭs (-*shus*), 169.
Tur'bi-nate, 169.
Tur'bi-nāt-ed.
Tur'bīne, 82, 152.
Tur'bit, 135.
[Turbith, 203. — *See* Turpeth.]
Tur'bot, 86, 171.
Tur'bu-lence.
Tur'bu-len-cy, 169.
Tur'bu-lent, 108.
Tur'cism (-*sizm*), 136.
Turc'o-man [pl. Turc'-o-mans (-*manz*), 196.]
Tu-reen', 121.
Turf (21, 35), *n.* & *v.* [pl. of *n.* Turfs, 193.]

☞ Webster remarks: "Dryden and Addison wrote *turfs*, in the plural. But when turf or peat is cut into small pieces, the practice now is to call them *turves*." But Smart says: "The old plural, now obsolete, was *turves*." Worcester gives *turfs* as the plural now in use, marking *turves* as obsolete.

Turfed (*turft*), 41; Note C, p. 34.
Turf'i-ness, 186.
Turf'ing.
Turf'y, 93, 169.
Tur'gent, 45.
Tur-ges'cence, 171.
Tur-ges'cen-cy.
Tur-ges'cent, 39.
Tur-ges'ci-ble, 164.
Tur'gid.
Tur-gid'i-ty.
Tur'gīte, 152.
Tu-ri-o-nif'er-oŭs.
Turk, 21.
Tur'key, 98.
Tur'key-buz'zard, 205.
Turk'ish.
Turk'ism (-*izm*), 136.
Tur-kois' (*tur-kēz'*, or *tur-koiz'*) [so Wr.; *tur-kēz'*, Wk. Sm.; *tur-koiz'*, or *tur-kēz'*, Gd. 155] [Turquoise, 203.]
Turk's-cap, 213.
Tur'u-pin.
[Turmalin, Turmaline, 203. — *See* Tourmaline.]
Tur'mer-ic, 135, 169.
Tur'moil, *n.* (103, 161) [so Wk. Sm. Wr.; *tur-moil'*, Wb. Gd. 155.]
Tur-moil', *v.* 103, 161.
Tur-moiled'.
Tur-moil'ing.
Turn, 21.
Turn'cap, 206.
Turn'cōat, 24.
Turned (*turnd*), 165.
Turn'er, 228.
Turn'er-y.
Turn'ing.
Turn'ing-lathe.
Turn'ing-point.
Tur'nip, 169.
Turn'kēy, 171.
Turn'out.
Turn'o-ver.
Turn'pike.
Turn'plate.
Turn'sole [Turnsol, 203.]
Turn'spit.
Turn'stile.
Turn'stōne, 24.
Turn'-ta-ble, 164.
Tur'pen-tīne, 82, 169.
Tur'peth [Turbith, 203.]
Tur'pi-tude, 26.
Tur-quoise' (*tur-kēz'*, or *tur-koiz'*) [Turkois, 203.]

Tŭr'ret, 48, 66.
Tŭr'ret-ed.
Tŭr'ri-līte, 152.
Tur'tle, 21, 164.
Tur'tle-dove (*tur'tl-duv*).
Tur'tler.
Turves (*turvz*), *n.pl.* [*See* Note under *Turf.*]
Tus'can.
Tush, 22, 46.
Tusk, 22.
Tusk'ed (150) [so Wk. Wr.; *tuskt*, Sm. Gd. 155.]
Tusk'y, 93.
Tus'sac-grȧss [T u s-s o c k - g r a s s, 203.]
Tus-sic'u-lar, 108.
Tus'sle, 164, 170.
Tus'sock.
Tus'sock-grȧss [T u s-s a c - g r a s s, 203.]
Tus'sock-y.
Tut, 22, 41.
Tu'te-lage, 70, 169.
Tu'te-lar.
Tu'te-la-ry, 72.
Tu'te-nag.
Tu'tor, 88, 169.
Tu'tor-age.
Tu'tored, 150.
Tu'tor-ess.
Tu-to'ri-al.
Tu'tor-ing.
Tut'san.
Tut'ti (It.) (*toot'te*) [*See* Note under *Sgraffito.*]
Tut'ty, 93, 170.
Tuyère (Fr.) (*twēr*) (154) [so Gd.; *twe'êr*, Wr. 155] [T w e e r, 203.]
Twad'dle (*twod'l*).

☞ "A modern cant word, which seems to have nearly supplanted the similar word *twattle.*" *Worcester.*

Twad'dled (*twod'ld*).
Twad'dler (*twod'-*).
Twad'dling (*twod'-*).
Twāin, 23, 64.
Twāite [T w a i t, 203.]
Twang, 10, 54.
Twanged (*twangd*).
Twang'ing.
Twan'gle (*twang'gl*), 164.
Twan'gled (*twang'gld*).
Twan'gling (*twang'-*).
Twank (*twangk*), 54.
Twan'kāy.
Twank'ing (*twangk'-*).
'Twas (*twoz*) [a contraction of *it was.*]
Twat'tle (*twot'l*) [T w a d d l e, 203. — *See* Note under *Twaddle.*]
Twat'tled (*twot'ld*).
Twat'tler (*twot'-*).
Twat'tling (*twot'-*).
Twāy'blade.
Twēak, 13.
Twēaked (*twēkt*).
Twēak'ing.
Tweed, 13.
Twee'dle, 164.
Twee'dled (*-dld*).
Twee'dling.
[T w e e l, 203. — *See* Twill.]
[T w e e r, 203. — *See* Tuyère.]
Twee'zers (*-zurz*), *n. pl.*
Twelfth, *a.* & *n.* [pl. of *n.* Twelfths, 64, 189.]
Twelfth'-dāy.
Twelfth'-nīght (*-nīt*).
Twelve (*twelv*), 15.
Twelve'month (*twelv-munth*) [so Wr. Gd.; *twel'munth*, Wk.; *twelv'munth*, coll. *twel'munth*, Sm. 155.]

☞ "It [the letter *v*] is never irregular; and if ever silent, it is in the word *twelvemonth*, where both that letter and the *e* are, in colloquial pronunciation, generally dropped, as if written *twel'month.*" *Walker.*

Twelve'pence, 217.
Twelve'pen-ny, 217.
Twen'ti-eth, 186.
Twen'ty, 93.
Twen'ty-fōld, 217.
Twi'bil [T w i b i l l, 203.]
Twice, 25.
Twice'-told.
Twi'fal-lōw.
Twi'fal-lōwed.
Twi'fal-lōw-ing.
Twig, 16.
Twig'gy (*-ghy*), 138.
Twi'līght (*-līt*).
Twill (16, 172) [T w e e l, 203.]
Twilled (*twild*), 165.
Twil'ly, 170.
Twin, 16.
Twine, 25, 163.
Twined, 165.
Twinge, 16, 45.
Twinged, 165.
Twing'ing (*twinj'-*).
Twīn'ing, 183.
Twin'kle (*twing'kl*).
Twin'kled (*twing'kld*).
Twin'kler (*twing'-*).
Twin'kling (*twing'-*).
Twinned (*twīnd*), 176.
Twin'ning.
Twirl, 21, N.; 135.
Twirled (*twirld*), 150, 165.
Twirl'ing.
Twist, 16.
Twist'ed.
Twist'er.
Twist'ing.
Twit, 16.
Twitch, 16, 44; Note D, [p. 37.
Twitched (*twicht*), Note C, p. 34.
Twitch'ing.
Twit'ted, 176.
Twit'ter, *n.* & *v.* 103, 104.
Twit'tered, 150.
Twit'ter-ing.
Twit'ting, 176.
'Twixt [a contraction of *betwixt.*]
Two (*too*), *n.* & *a.* one and one. [*See* To, *and* Too, 160.]
Two'-deck-er (*too'-*).
Two'fōld (*too'-*), 217.
Two'-legged (*-legd*), 206, Exc. 5.
Two'-lobed (*too'lōbd*).
Two'pence (*too'pens*; in Eng. coll. *tup'ens*) (217) [so Sm.; *tup'ens*, Wk.; *too'pens*, Gd.; *too'pens*, or *tup'ens*, Wr. 155.]
Two'pen-ny (*too'pen-py*; in Eng. coll. *tup'-en-ny*) (217) [so Sm.; *too'pen-ny*, Gd.; *too'-pen-ny*, or *tup'en-ny*, Wr. 155.]
Tȳ-chon'ic (*-kon'-*), 52, 109.
[T y e, 203. — *See* Tie.]
[T y g e r, 203. — *See* Tiger.]
Ty'ing, 184.
Ty'ler.
Tym'bal (72) [T i m b a l, 203.]
Tymp, 16.
Tym'pan.
Tym'pan-al, 106.
Tym-pan'ic (109) [so Gd.; *tim'pan-ik*, Wr. 155.]

Tym'pan-ist.
Tym-pan-it'ic.
Tym'pan-ize, 202.
Tym'pan-ized, 165.
Tym'pan-īz-ing.
Tym'pa-num (169) [L. pl. *Tym'pa-na*; Eng. pl. Tym'pa-nums (*-numz*), 198.]
Tym'pa-ny.
Tўp'al, 228.
Type, 25.
Ty-phe'an, 110.
Ty'phoid.
Ty'phon.
Ty-phoon', 121.
Ty'phoŭs (100, 160), *a.* pertaining to typhus.
Ty'phus (35, 160, 169) [*not* ty'pus, 141, 153], *n.* a fever characterized by great debility.
Typ'ic.
Typ'ic-al.
Typ'ic-al-ly, 170.
Typ-i-fĭ-ca'tion, 112.
Typ'i-fied.
Typ'i-fy, 94.
Typ'i-fy-ing, 186.
Tў-pog'ra-pher, 108.
Tў-po-graph'ic, *or* Typ-o-graph'ic.
Tў-po-graph'ic-al, *or* Typ-o-graph'ic-al [so Wr.; *tī-po-graf'ik-al*, Wb. Gd.; *tip-o-graf'-ik-al*, Wk. Sm. 155.]
Tў-pog'ra-phy, 108.
Typ'o-līte, 152.
Tў-pol'o-gy.
Tў-ran'nic, *or* Tў-ran'-nic [*tī-ran'nik*, Wk. Wr. Gd.; *tĭ-ran'nik*, Sm. 155.]
Tў-ran'nic-al, *or* Tў-ran'nic-al.
Tў-ran-ni-cīd'al, *or* Tў-ran-ni-cīd'al.
Tў-ran'ni-cide, *or* Tў-ran'ni-cide.
Tўr'an-nize, 170, 202.
Tўr'an-nized, 165.
Tўr'an-nīz-ing.
Tўr'an-noŭs.
Tўr'an-ny, 171.
Ty'rant, 49, N.; 72.
Tўr'i-an, 169.
Ty'ro (49, N.) [pl. Ty'-rōs (*-rōz*), 192] [Ti-ro, 203.]
Tўr'ol-ese (*-ēz*)[so Wr.; *tĭr'ol-ēs*, Gd. 155], *n. sing. & pl.*
Tўr'o-man-cy.
Ty'ro-nism (*-nizm*).
Tyr-te'an (*tur-*), 110.
[Tythe, 203.—*See* Tithe.]
[Tzar, 203.—*See* Czar.]

U.

U-bi'e-ty, 108, 169.
U-bi-qua'ri-an, 49, N.
U'bi-quist, 34.
U-biq-ui-ta'ri-an (*-bik-wĭ-*).
U-biq'ui-ta-ry(*-bik'wĭ-*), 72.
U-biq'ui-toŭs (*-bik'wĭ-*).
U-biq'ui-ty (*-bik'wĭ-*), 171.
U'dal, 72.
Ud'der, 66, 170.
U-dom'e-ter, 108.
Ug'li-ness, 186.
Ug'ly, 93.
U-kase', 121.
U'lan.
Ul'cer, 77.
Ul'cer-ate.
Ul'cer-āt-ed, 183.
Ul'cer-āt-ing.
Ul-cer-a'tion, 169.
Ul'cer-a-tĭve, 84.
Ul'cer-oŭs, 100.
Ul'cus-cle (*-kus-l*), 162.
Ul-cus'cule.
U-le'ma [so Sm. Wb. Gd.; *oo-le'ma*, or *yoo-le'ma*, Wr. 155.]
Ul'lage, 170.
Ul-ma'ceous (*-shus*).
Ul'mic.
Ul'mĭne (82, 152) [Ul-min, 203.]
Ul'na, 72.
Ul'nar, 74.
Ul-te'ri-or, 49, N.
Ul'ti-ma ra'ti-o (L.) (*ra'shĭ-o*).
Ul'ti-mate.
Ul'ti-ma Thu'le (L.).
Ul-ti-ma'tion.
Ul-ti-ma'tum (L.) [pl. Ul-ti-ma'ta, 198.]
Ul'ti-mo (L.).

☞ Commonly abbreviated to *ult.*

Ul'tra.
Ul'tra-ism (*-izm*), 133, 136.
Ul'tra-ist.
Ul-tra-ma-rine' (*-rēn'*).
Ul-tra-mon'tane.
Ul-tra-mon'tan-ism (*-izm*), 136.
Ul-tra-mon'tan-ist.
Ul-tra-mun'dane.
Ul-tra-trop'ic-al.
Ul'u-late, 89.
Ul'u-lāt-ed.
Ul'u-lāt-ing.
Ul-u-la'tion, 112.
Um'bel, 76.
Um'bel-lar.
Um'bel-late, 170.
Um'bel-lāt-ed.
Um'bel-let.
Um-bel-lif'er-oŭs.
Um'ber.
Um'bered (*-burd*), 150.
Um-bil'ic, 109.
Um-bil'ic-al, 108.
Um-bil'i-cate.
Um-bil'i-cat-ed.
Um-bil'i-cus (L.).
Um'bles (*-blz*), *n. pl.*
Um'bo.
Um'bo-nate.
Um'bo-nāt-ed.
Um'bra.
Um-bra-cu'li-form.
Um'brage, 70, 169.
Um-bra'geoŭs (*-jus*), *or* Um-bra'ge-oŭs [*um-bra'jus*, Wb. Gd.; *um-bra'j'us*, Sm. (*See* § 26); *um-bra'jĭ-us*, Wk. Wr. 155.]
Um-brat'ic.
Um-brat'ic-al.
Um'bra-tĭle, 81, 152.
Um-brel'la (170) [*not* um-bril'la, 127, 153.]
Um-brif'er-oŭs, 233 Exc.
Um'pi-rage, 78, 169.
Um'pīre.
Um'quhĭle (*-kwil*), 171.
Un-, a prefix signifying *negation.*
U'nal-ist.
U-na-nim'i-ty, 108, 169.
U-nan'i moŭs, 100.
U'na vo'ce (L.).
U-nâu'.
Un'cial (*-shal*), 72.
Un'ci-form, 108, 169.
Un'ci-nate.
Un'cle (*ung'kl*), 54, 164.
Un-couth' (*-kooth'*), 140.
Unc'tion (*ungk'shun*), 54.
Ŭnc-tu-os'i-ty.
Unct'u-oŭs (89) [*not* ungk'shus, 153.]

Un′der, 205, Exc. 1; 230.
Un′der-dose, *n.* 161.
Un-der-dose′, *v.* 161.
Un′der-drāin, *n.* 161.
Un-der-drāin′, *v.* 161.
Un′der-ground, *n. a.* & *adv.*

☞ "The accents [primary and secondary] are interchangeable according to the rhythm of the context." *Smart.*

Un-der-neath′, 140.
Un-der-rate′, 205, Exc. 1.
Un-der-run′.
Un′der-shot.
Un-der-stand′.
Un-der-stand′ing.
Un′der-strap-per [so Wk. Sm. Wb. Gd.; *un-dur-strap′pur,* Wr. 155.]
Un-der-tāk′ing.
Un-der-val′ue.
Un-der-write′ (*-rīt′*).
Un′der-wrīt-er [so Sm. Wb. Gd.; *un-dur-rī′tur,* Wk. Wr. 155.]
Un-done′ (*-dun′*), 115.
Un-dress′, *v.* 103, 161.
Un′dress, *n.* 103, 161.
Un′du-lant, 89.
Un′du-la-ry, 72.
Un′du-late, 89.
Un′du-lāt-ed.
Un′du-lāt-ing.
Un-du-la′tion.
Un′du-la-to-ry (72, 86) [so Wr. Wb. Gd.; *un′ju-la-tŭr-y,* Wk.; *un′du-lā-tŭr-y,* Sm. 155.]
Un-e′qual.
Un-e′qualled (*-kwald*) [Unequaled, Wb. Gd. 203. — *See* 177, and Note E, p. 70.]
Un′gual (*ung′-*), 54.
Un′gue-al (*ung′gwe-*).
Un′guent (*ung′gwent*) (141) [so Wr.; *un′-gwent,* Wb. Gd.; *ung′went,* Sm. 155.]
Un′guent-a-ry (*ung′-*), 72, 171.
Un′guic-al (*ung′-*).
Un-guic′u-lar, 108.
Un-guic′u-late, 108.
Un-guic′u-lāt-ed.
Un-guif′er-oŭs, 108.
Un′gui-form, 108.
Un′gu-la (*ung′-*), 108.
Un′gu-late (*ung′-*), 108.
Un-hap′pi-ness, 106.
Un-hon′ored (*-on′urd*), 117, 171.
U-ni-ax′al.
U-ni-ba′sic.
U-ni-căr′i-nāt-ed.
U′ni-corn, 135.
U-ni-corn′oŭs [so Wr. Wb. Gd.; *u′ni-kor-nus,* Sm. 155.]
U-ni-fa′cial (*-shal*).
U-nif′ic, 109.
U-ni-fĭ-ca′tion.
U-ni-fi′lar.
U-ni-flo′roŭs [so Wr. Wb. Gd.; *u′ni-flō-rus,* Sm. 155.]
U-ni-fo′li-ate.
U-ni-fo′li-o-late.
U′ni-form, 89, 142.
U-ni-form′i-ty, 169.
U′ni-fȳ, 94.
U-ni-gen′i-ture.
U-ni-gen′i-tus (L.).
U-nig′e-noŭs (*-nij′-*).
U-ni-ju′gate, 156.
U-ni-la′bi-ate.
U-ni-lat′er-al.
U-ni-lin′e-āt-ed.
U-ni-lit′er-al, 108.
U-ni-loc′u-lar, 108.
Ūn′ion (*yoon′yun*) (26, 51) [so Wr. Wb. Gd.; *yoo′nĭ-un,* Wk.; *yoo′-nĭ-un,* or *yoon′yun,* Sm. 155.]
Ūn′ion-ist.
Ūn′ion-jack.
U-ni-o′vu-late (108) [so Gd.; *yoo-nĭ-ov′yoo-lāt,* Wr. 155.]
U-nip′a-roŭs, 108.
U′ni-ped, 78.
U-ni-per′son-al.
U-ni-per′son-al-ist.
U-nip′li-cate, 73.
U-nique′ (*-nēk′*), 168, 171.
U-ni-se′ri-al, 49, N.
U-ni-se′ri-ate.
U-ni-sex′u-al.
U′ni-son (*-sun,* or *-zun*) [*u′ni-sun,* Wk. Wr. Wb. Gd *yoo′ni-zun,* Sm. 155.]
U-nis′o-nance.
U-nis′o-nant.
U-nis′o-noŭs.
U′nit, 26, 80.
U-nīt′a-ble, 164, 183.
U-ni-ta′ri-an, 49, N.
U-ni-ta′ri-an-ism (*-izm*).
U-nite′.
U-nīt′ed, 183.
U-nīt′ing.
U-ni′tion (*-nish′un*).
U′ni-ty, 78, 108.
U′ni-valve
U′ni-valved, 165.
U-ni-valv′u-lar, 108.
U-ni-ver′sal, 21, N.
U-ni-ver′sal-ism (*-izm*).
U-ni-ver′sal-ist.
U-ni-ver-sal′i-ty.
U-ni-ver′sal-ize.
U-ni-ver′sal-ized, 183.
U-ni-ver′sal-iz-ing.
U-ni-ver′sal-ly.
U′ni-verse, 21, N.
U-ni-ver′si-ty.
U-niv′o-cal, 156.
Un-ken′nel.
Un-ken′nelled (*-neld*) [Unkenneled, Wb. Gd. 203. — *See* 177, and Note E, p. 70.]
Un-ken′nel-ling [Unkenneling, Wb. Gd. 203.]
Un-knelled′ (*-neld′*) [*See* Note under *Unnamed.*]
Un-knōwn′ (*-nōn′*) [*See* Note under *Unnamed.*]
Un-less′.
Un-named′, 66, Note; 165.

☞ In all words in which *un* is prefixed to a word beginning with the sound of *n*, as *unknown, unnatural, unnecessary, unnumbered,* &c., the two *n*'s, though representing only a single articulation, have the double effect described in the latter part of the Note under § 66.

Un-neigh′bor-ly (*-na′-*).
Un-nerve′.
Un-nerved′, 165.
Un-nŏt′ed.
Un-no′ticed (*-tist*).
Un-rav′el.
Un-rav′elled (*-eld*) [Unraveled, Wb. Gd. 203. — *See* 177, and Note E, p. 70.]
Un-rav′el-ling [Unraveling, Wb. Gd. 203.]
Un-ripe′, 121.
Un-rōll′ [Unrol, 179, 203.]
Un-sung′, 117.

Un-til′, 171, 179.
Un′to (*too*).
Un-wept′, 117.
Un-whōle′some (*-hōl′-sum*), 24.
Up, 22, 30.
U′pas, 26, 72.
Up-braid′.
Up-brăid′ed.
Up-braid′er.
Up-brăid′ing.
Up-cȧst′, *v.* 103, 161.
Up′cȧst, *n.* 103, 161.
Up′cast, *a.* [so Wb. Gd.; *up′kăst*, Sm.; *up-kăst′*, Wk.; *up-kȧst′*, or *up′kȧst*, Wr. 155.]
Up-hēav′al, 183.
Up-held′.
Up′her (*up′ur*) [so Sm. Wb. Gd.; *u′fur*, Wr. 155.]
Up′hĭll [so Wk. Sm. Wb. Gd.; *up′hil*, or *up-hil′*, Wr. 155.]
Up-hōld′.
Up-hōld′er.
Up-hōld′ing.
Up-hōl′ster-er, 24, 130.
Up-hōl′ster-y, 169.
Uph′rōe (*ūv′ro*) (171) [so Gd.; *ŭf′ro*, Wr. 155.]
Up′land.
Up-on′.
Up′per, 77, 170.
Up′right (*-rīt*), *a.* & *n.*

☞ "This word is often accented on the last syllable, especially when, as an adjective, it follows the noun; the derivatives are liable to the same diversity." *Smart.*

Up′rōar.

☞ "It is often accented on the latter syllable." *Smart.*

Up-rōar′i-oŭs, 49, N.
Up-set′, *v.* 103, 161.
Up′set, *n.* 103, 161.
Up′shot.
Up-start′, *v.* 103, 161.
Up′start, *n.* 103, 161.
U′pu-pa (L.) [so Gd. Wr.; *up′u-pā*, Sm. 155.]
Up′ward.
Up′wards (*-wardz*).
U-ra′li-an, 169.
U-ran′ic, 109.
U′ran-īte, 152.
U-ran-it′ic.
U-ra′ni-um, 169.
U-ran-o-graph′ic.
U-ran-o-graph′ic-al.
U-ran-og′ra-phy (108) [Ouranography, 203.]
U-ran-ol′o-gy, 108.
U-ran-os′co-py, 108.
U′ran-oŭs (156), *a.* composed of uranium,—denoting salts whose base is protoxide of uranium. [*See* Uranus, 160.]
U′ra-nus (156, 169), *n.* one of the planets of the solar system. [*See* Uranous, 160.]
U′rate.
Ur′ban, 135.
Ur-bane′, 121.
Ur-ban′i-ty, 108, 169.
Ur′ce-o-late, 156.
Ur-ce′o-lus.
Ur′chin.
U′re-a, 169.
U′re-ter, *or* U-re′ter [*u′re-ter*, Wk. Sm. Wr.; *u-re′tur*, Wb. Gd. 155.]
U-re′thra.
Urge, 21, 49, 142.
Urged, 165.
Ur′gen-cy, 169.
Ur′gent.
Urg′er (*urj′-*).
Urg′ing (*urj′-*).
U′ric.
U′rim (Heb.), 49, N.
U′rin-al.
U′rin-a-ry, 72.
U′rin-ate.
U′rin-āt-ed.
U′rin-āt-ing.
U′rin-a-tīve.
U′rīne, 82, 152.
U-rin-if′er-oŭs, 108.
U-rin-om′e-ter, 108.
U′rin-oŭs.
Urn, 21, 49, 135.
U-ros′co-py, 108.
Ur′sa Ma′jor (L.).
Ur′sa Mi′nor (L.).
Ur′si-form, 108.
Ur′sīne, 152.
Ur′su-līne, 82, 89.
Ur-ti-ca′ceous (*-shus*).
U′rus (L.).
Us, 22, 39, 174.
Ūs′a-ble (*yooz′-*), 164, 171, 183.
U′sage (*-zij*), 70, 136.
U′sance (*-zans*).
Use, *n.* 26, 161.
Use (*yooz*) (26, 161), *v.* to employ. [*See* Ewes, 160.]
Used (*yoozd*).
Use′ful (*yoos′fŏŏl*), 156.
Use′ful-ly (*-fŏŏl-*).
Ūs′er (*yooz′-*).
Ush′er, 77.
Ush′ered (*-urd*).
Ush′er-ing.
Ūs′ing (*yooz′-*), 183.
Us-que-bâugh′ (*-baw′*) (162, 171) [so Sm. Wr.; *us′kwe-baw*, Gd.; *us-kwe-bah′*, Wk. 155.]
Ust′ion (*-yun*), 44, N. 1.
Us-tu-la′tion, 112.
Ūs′u-al (*yoo′zhu-*).
U-su-cap′tion (*-zu-*) [so Sm. Wr.; *u-su-kap′-shun*, Wb. Gd. 155.]
U′su-fruct (*-zu-*) [so Sm. Wr.; *u-su-frukt′*, Wb. Gd. 155.]
U-su-fruct′u-a-ry (*-zu-*), 72, 171.
U′su-rer (*-zhu-*)
U-su′ri-oŭs (*-zu′-*) (49, N.) [so Wk. Sm. Wb. Gd.; *u-zhu′ri-us*, Wr. 155.]
U-surp′ (*-zurp′*), 89.
U-surp-a′tion (*-zurp-*), 112, 169.
U-surped′ (*-zurpt′*).
U-surp′er (*-zurp′-*).
U-surp′ing (*-zurp′-*).
U′su-ry (*-zhu-*).
U-ten′sil (107) [so Sm. Wb. Gd., *u′ten-sil*, Wk.; *u-ten′sil*, or *u′ten-sil*, Wr. 155.]
U′ter-īne, *or* U′ter-ĭne [*u′tur-in*, Sm. Wb. Gd.; *u′tur-īn*, Wk.; *u′tur-īn*, or *u′tur-in*, Wr. 155.]
U′te-rus (L.) [pl. *U′te-rī*, 198.]
U′ti-le dul′cī (L.).
U-til-i-ta′ri-an, 49, N.
U-til-i-ta′ri-an-ism (*-izm*), 133, 136.
U-til′i-ty, 170.
U′til-ize.
U′til-ized.
U′til-īz-ing, 183.
U′tī pos-si-de′tis (L.).
Ut′most, 24.
U-to′pi-a.

U-to'pi-an, 169.
U-to'pi-an-ism (-*izm*).
U'tri-cle, 164.
U-tric'u-lar, 108.
Ut'ter, 66, 77.
Ut'ter-a-ble, 164.
Ut'ter-ance, 169.
Ut'tered, 150, 165.
Ut'ter-ing.
Ut'ter-mōst.
U've-a, 169.
U've-oŭs, 100.
U'vu-la, 108.
U'vu-lar, 26, 89.
Ux-or'i-cide.
Ux-o'ri-oŭs (*ug-zo'-*) (49, N.) [so Wk. Sm. Wr.; *uk-so'ri-us*, Wb. Gd. 155.]

V.

Va'can-cy, 169.
Va'cant.
Va'cate.
Va'cāt-ed, 183.
Va'cāt-ing.
Va-ca'tion, 112.
Vac'ci-nate, 171.
Vac'ci-nāt-ed.
Vac'ci-nāt-ing.
Vac-ci-na'tion.
Vac'ci-nāt-or, 169
Vac'cīne, *or* Vac'cīne [so Wr.; *vak'sīn*, Wk. Sm.; *vak'sin*, Wb. Gd. 155.]
Vac'cin-ist.
Vach'er-y (*vash'*), 44.
Vaç'il-lan-cy.
Vaç'il-lant.
Vaç'il-late, 171.
Vaç'il-lāt-ed, 183.
Vaç'il-lāt-ing.
Vaç-il-la'tion.
Vac'u-ist, 89.
Va-cu'i-ty, 108, 169.
Vac'u-o-lāt-ed.
Vac-u-o-la'tion.
Vac'u-ole.
Vac'u-um, 169.
Va'de-me'cum (L.), *n.*
Vag'a-bŏnd, 171.
Vag'a-bŏnd-age.
Vag'a-bŏnd-ism (-*izm*).
Va-ga'ri-ous.
Va-ga'ry [*not* va'ga-ry, 153.]
Va-gi'na (L.) [pl. *Va-gi'næ*) (-*ne*), 198.]
Vag'i-nal (*vaj'-*), *or* Va-gi'nal [so Wr.; *vaj'i-nal*, Wb. Gd.; *va-ji'-nal*, Sm. 155.]
Vag'i-nant (*vaj'-*), *or* Va-gi'nant.
Vag'i-nate (*vaj'-*), *or* Va-gi'nate.
Vag'i-nāt-ed (*vaj'-*), *or* Va-gi'nāt-ed.
Vag-i-no-pen'noŭs (*vaj'-*) [Vaginipennous, 203.]
Va'gran-cy, 169.
Va'grant.
Vāgue, 23, 168.
[Vail, 203.—*See* Veil.]
Vāin (23), *a.* having no real substance, worth, or importance; — conceited. [*See* Vane, *and* Vein, 162.]
Vāin-glo'ri-oŭs.
Vāin-glo'ry, 216.
Vāin'ly, 93.
Vair (*vêr*), 14.
Vair'y (*vêr'ry*), 49, N.
Vāi'vode [Waiwode, 203.]
Val'ance, 170.
Vale (23), *n.* a valley. [*See* Veil, 160.]
Val-e-dic'tion, 169.
Val-e-dic-to'ri-an.
Val-e-dic'to-ry.
Val-en-ci-ennes' (Fr.) (-*enz'*), 154.
Va-len'ti-a (-*shĭ-*).
Val'en-tīne (82, 152) [so Sm. Wr. Gd.; *val'-en-tin*, Wk. 155.]
Val-en-tin'i-an [so Wr.; *val-en-tin'yan*, Sm. 155.]
Va-le'ri-an, 49, N.
Va-le-ri-an-a'ceoŭs (-*shus*).
Va-le-ri-an'ic.
Val'et (*val'et*, or *val'ā*) [so Gd.; *val'et*, Sm. Wr.; *val'et*, or *va-let'*, Wk. 155.]
Valet de chambre (Fr.) (*val'ā duh shäm'br*).
Val-e-tu-di-na'ri-an.
Val-e-tu-di-na'ri-an-ism (-*izm*), 116.
Val-e-tu-di-na'ri-oŭs.
Val-e-tu'di-na-ry, 72.
Val'hȧll.
Val-hal'la [Walhalla, 203.]
Val'iant (-*yant*), 51.
Val'id, 66, 170.
Va-lid'i-ty.
Va-lise' (*va-lēs'*, or *va-lēz'*) [*va-lēs'*, Wb. Gd.; *va-lēz'*, Sm.; *va-lēz'*, or *va-lēs'*, Wr. 155.]

☞ Sometimes incorrectly spelled *vallise*.

Val'kyr (-*kur*); 95.
Val-kȳr'i-a.
Val-kȳr'i-an, 48.
Val-la'tion.
Val'ley (98, 169) [pl. Val'leys (-*lĭz*), 187.]
Val'lum (L.).
Va-lo'ni-a.
Val'or (66, 170) [Valour, Sm. 203.]
Val'or-oŭs, 100.
Val'u-a-ble, 164, 169.
Val-u-a'tion, 112.
Val'u-ā-tor.
Val'ūe, 156.
Val'ūed (-*yood*).
Val'u-er, 183.
Val'u-ing.
Valv'ate.
Valve (*valv*), 10.
Valved, 164.
Valv'let, 171.
Valv'u-lar, 108, 183.
Valv'ule.
Vam'brace.
Vamp, 10, 64.
Vamped (*vampt*), 41.
Vamp'er.
Vamp'ing.
Vam'pīre [Vampyre, 203.]
Vam'pir-ism (-*izm*).
Vam'plate [Vamplet, 203.]
Van, 10, 36, 43.
Va-na'di-ate.
Va-nad'ic, 109.
Va-nad'i-nīte.
Va-na'di-um, 169.
Van-cou'ri-er (-*koo'-*) (49), *n.* [so Wr. Gd.; *van-koor'rĭ-ur*, Sm.; *van-koor-yēr'*, Wk. 155.]
Van'dal, 72.
Van-dal'ic, 109.
Van'dal-ism (-*izm*), 136.
Van-dyke', 121, 171.
Vane (23), *n.* a weather-cock. [*See* Vain, *and* Vein, 160.]
Van'foss.
Vang, 10, 54.
Van'glo (*vang'-*), 156.

---

fall; ê *as in* there; ŏŏ *as in* foot; ç *as in* facile; gh *as* g *in* go; th *as in* this.

Van′guärd.
Va-nil′la, 170.
Van′ish, 104.
Van′ished (*-isht*).
Van′ish-ing.
Van′i-ty, 169.
Van′quish, 54, 141.
Van′quish-a-ble, 164.
Van′quished (*-kwisht*), 41.
Van′quish-er.
Van′quish-ing.
Van′tage.
Van′tage-ground.
Vant′brace, *or* Vant′-bràss. [Vambrace, 203.]
Vap′id, 170.
Va-pid′i-ty, 169.
Va′por (199) [Vapour, Sm. 203.]
Vap′or-a-ble, 143, 164.
Va′pored (*-purd*) [Vapoured, Sm. 203.]
Vap-or-a′tion.
Va′por-er [Vapourer, Sm. 203.]
Va-por-if′er-oŭs.
Va-por-if′ic (109) [Vapourific, Sm. 203.]
Va′por-i-form, 106.
Va′por-ing [Vapouring, Sm. 203.]
Va′por-ish [Vapourish, Sm. 203.]
Vap′or-īz-a-ble [Vapourizable, Sm. 203.]
Vap-or-ĭ-za′tion [Vapourization, Sm. 203.]
Vap′or-īze [Vapourize, Sm. 203.]
Vap′or-īzed.
Vap′or-īz-ing.
Va′por-oŭs [Vapourous, Sm. 203.]
Va′por-y [Vapoury, Sm. 203.]
Va-ri-a-bil′i-ty.
Va′ri-a-ble, 164.
Va′ri-a-bly.
Va′ri-ance, 49, N.
Va′ri-ant.
Va-ri-a′tion.
Văr′i-cose [so Wb. Gd.; *vêr′i-kōs*, Sm.; *văr-i-kōs′*, Wr. 155.]
Văr′i-coŭs [so Wr. Wb. Gd.; *vêr′i-kus*, Sm. 155.]
Va′rĭed, 99.
Va′ri-e-gate (49, N.) [*not* va-ri′e-gāt, 153.]
Va′ri-e-gāt-ed.
Va′ri-e-gāt-ing.
Va-ri-e-ga′tion.
Va-ri′e-ty, 169.
Va′ri-form, 108.
Va′ri-formed.
Va-ri′o-la (L.).
Va-ri′o-lar.
Vā-ri-o-la′tion.
Va-ri-ol′ic.
Va′ri-o-līte.
Va′ri-o-loid [so Wr. Wb. Gd.; *va-ri′o-loid*, Sm. 155], *n.*
Va′ri-o-loid [so Wb. Gd.; *va-ri-o-loid′*, Wr.; *va-ri′o-loid*, Sm. 155], *a.*
Va-ri′o-loŭs.
Va-ri-o′rum (L.).
Va′ri-oŭs, 169.
Va′rix (L.) [pl. *Văr′i-cēs* (*sēz*), 198.]
Var′let.
Var′nish.
Var′nished (*-nisht*).
Var′nish-er.
Var′nish-ing.
Va′ry, 49, N.
Va′ry-ing.
Vas′cu-lar, 108.
Vas-cu-lăr′i-ty.
Vas-cu-lif′er-oŭs.
Vase (*vās*, or *vāz*) (23) [*vās*, Wb. Gd.; *vāz*, Wk. Sm.; *väz*, or *vās*, Wr. 155.]

☞ "Down to the time of Walker, this word was made to rhyme with *base*, *case*, &c., and is still so pronounced, to a great extent, in the United States. In England, it is more commonly pronounced as Walker gives it, *vaze*, though by some *väz*, and by a few *vawz*." *Goodrich.*

Vas′i-form, 108, 143.
Vas′sal, 72, 170.
Vas′sal-age, 70, 169.
Vas′sal-ry.
Vȧst, 12, 131.
Văs-ta′tion.
Vȧst′i-tude, 26.
Vȧst′y, 169.
Vat, 10.
Vat′i-căn, 78.
Vat′i-cide.
Va-tiç′i-nal [*not* vat-i-si′nal, 153.]
Va-tiç′i-nate, 108.
Va-tiç′i-nāt-ed.
Va-tiç′i-nāt-ing.
Va-tiç-i-na′tion.
Vaude′ville (*vōd′vil*) [Vaudevil, Vaudvil, 203.]
Vau-dois′ (*vo-dwaw′*) [so Sm. Gd.; *vo-dwä′*, Wr. 155.]
Vâult, 17.
Vâult′ed.
Vâult′er.
Vâult′ing, 228.
Vâunt, *or* Väunt [so Wr.; *vawnt*, Wk. Sm.; *vänt*, Wb. Gd. 155.]
Vâunt′ed, *or* Väunt′ed.
Vâunt′er, *or* Väunt′er.
Vâunt′ing, *or* Väunt′-ing.
Vâunt′mure.
Vauque′lin-ite (*vōk′-*).
Vav′a-sor, *or* Val′va-sor, 203.

☞ In old books also written Valvasour, Vavassor, Vavasour, Vavassour, Valvassour.

Vav′a-so-ry, 86.
Vēal, 13, 36, 50.
Vec′tor.
Ve′dä, *or* Ve-dâ′ [so Wr.; *ve′dä*, Wb. Gd.; *ve-daw′*, Sm. 155] [Vedam, 203.]
Ve-dette′, 121.
Veer, 13, 36, 49.
Veered, 165.
Veer′ing.
Ve′ga.
Veg′e-ta-ble (*vej′-*), 164, 169.
Veg′e-tal (*vej′-*).
Veg-e-ta′ri-an (*vej-*).
Veg-e-ta′ri-an-ism (*vej-e-ta′ri-an-izm*), 136.
Veg′e-tate (*vej′-*), 169.
Veg′e-tāt-ed (*vej′-*).
Veg′e-tāt-ing (*vej′-*).
Veg-e-ta′tion (*vej-*).
Veg′e-tāt-ĭve (*vej′-*).
Veg′e-to-an′i-mal (*vej′-*), 224.
Ve′he-mence, 156
Ve′he-men-cy, 169.
Ve′he-ment [*not* ve-he′-ment, 153.]
Ve′hi-cle, 164, 171.
Ve-hic′u-lar, 108.
Veh′mic (*va′mik*) [so Sm.; *ve′mik*, Wr. Wb. Gd. 155.]
Veil (*vāl*) (23), *n.* a thin

covering for the face: — *v.* to cover with a veil. [*See* Vale, 160.] [V a i l, 203.]
Veiled (*vāld*).
Veil'ing (*vāl'-*).
Vein (*vān*) (23), *n.* a vessel which returns the venous or black blood to the heart: — *v.* to variegate with veins. [*See* Vain, *and* Vane, 160.]
Veined (*vānd*), 165, 171.
Vein'ing (*vān'-*).
Vein'let (*vān'-*).
Vein'y (*vān'-*), 169.
Ve'late.
Vel-le'i-ty, 169.
Vel'li-cate, 170.
Vel'li-căt-ed.
Vel'li-căt-ing.
Vel-li-ca'tion.
Vel'lum, 66, 169.
Vel-o-cim'e-ter, 108.
Ve-loç'i-pēde, 171.
Ve-loç'i-ty, 169.
Ve-lu'ti-noŭs.
Vel'vet, 76.
Vel'vet-ed.
Vel-vet-een', 122, 171.
Vel'vet-y.
Ve'nal, 72.
Ve-nal'i-ty, 108.
Ven'a-ry, *a.* pertaining to hunting. [*See* Venery, 160.]
Ve-na'tion.
Vend, 15.
Vend'ed, 228.
Vend-ee' (118) [Law term, correlative of *Vendor.*]
Vend'er [*See* Vendor.]
Vend-i-bil'i-ty.
Vend'i-ble, 164.
Vend'ing.
Vend-ĭ'tion (*-ish'un*).
Vend'or (118) [Law term, correlative of *Vendee.*]
Ven-dūe', 26.
Ve-neer', 169.
Ve-neered', 165.
Ve-neer'ing.
Ven'er-a-ble, 164.
Ven'er-a-bly.
Ven'er-ate, 171.
Ven'er-āt-ed, 183.
Ven'er-āt-ing.
Ven-er-a'tion.
Ven'er-āt-or, 169.
Ven'er-y, *n.* the sport of hunting. [*See* Venary, 160.]
Ve-ne-sec'tion [so Wk. Sm. Wr.; *ven-e-sek'-shun*, Wb. Gd. 155.]
Ve-ne'tian (*-shan*), 112.
Ven'geance (*-jans*)(171), Note D, p. 37.
Ve'ni-al [*not* vēn'yal, 153.]
Ve-ni-al'i-ty, 169.
Ve-ni're-fa'ci-as (L.) (*-fa'shĭ-as*).
Ven'i-son (*ven'ĭ-zn*, or *ven'zn*) [so Wb. Gd.; *ven'ĭ-zn*, coll. *ven'zn*, Sm.; *ven'zn*, or *ven'-ĭ-zn*, Wk. Wr. 155.]
Ven'om, 169, 170.
Ven'omed (*-umd*), 150.
Ven'om-oŭs, 100.
Ve'nose.
Ve-nos'i-ty, 108.
Ve'noŭs (100), *a.* pertaining to the veins. [*See* Venus, 160.]
Vent, 15.
Ven'tāil.
Vent'ed.
Vent'i-duct.
Ven'ti-late, 169.
Ven'ti-lāt-ed, 183.
Ven'ti-lāt-ing.
Ven-ti-la'tion.
Ven'ti-lāt-or.
Vent'ing.
Ven'tral.
Ven'tri-cle, 164, 169.
Ven'tri-cose.
Ven'tri-coŭs.
Ven-tric'u-lar.
Ven-tric'u-loŭs, 89.
Ven-tri-lo'qui-al.
Ven-tril'o-quism (*-kwizm*), 133, 136.
Ven-tril'o-quist.
Ven-tril'o-quize, 202.
Ven-tril'o-quized.
Ven-tril'o-quiz-ing.
Ven-tril'o-quoŭs (*-kwus*), 171.
Ven-tril'o-quy.
Ven-tro-pla'noŭs.
Vent'ure, 91.
Vent'ured (*-yurd*), 165.
Vent'ur-er (*-yur-*), 91.
Vent'ure-some (*-yur-sum*), 169, 185.
Vent'ur-ing (*-yur-*), 91.
Vent'ur-oŭs (*-yur-*).
Ven'ūe, 170.
Ven'u-lose.
Ve'nus, *n.* one of the planets. [*See* Venous, 160.]
Ve-ra'cioŭs (*-shus*).
Ve-raç'i-ty.
Ve-ran'da.
Ve-ra'tri-a.
Ve-ra'trĭne (82, 152) [so Wb. Gd.; *ve-ra'trin*, or *vĕr'a-trin*, Wr. 155.]
Verb, 21, N.; 135.
Ver'bal, 72.
Ver'bal-ism (*-izm*), 133.
Ver'bal-ist.
Ver-bal'i-ty, 169.
Ver-bal-ĭ-za'tion.
Ver'bal-ize.
Ver'bal-ized.
Ver'bal-īz-ing.
Ver'bal-ly.
Ver-ba'tim (L.).
Ver-be'na, 72.
Ver'be-nate.
Ver-ber-a'tion.
Ver'bi-age, 70, 169.
Ver-bose', 121.
Ver-bos'i-ty, 169.
Ver'dan-cy.
Ver'dant, 72.
Verd'-an-tique' (Fr.) (*-tēk'*)
Ver'der-er, *or* Ver'der or, 70, 203.
Ver'dict, 21, N.; 171.
Ver'di-gris (*-grēs*), 156, 171.
Ver'di-ter, 171.
Ver'di-ture.
Verd'ure, 45, 91.
Verd'ured (*-yurd*).
Verd'ur-oŭs (*-yur-*), 91.
Ver-ga-loo' [V i r g a-l o o, 203.]
Verge, 21, N.; 135.
Verged, 165.
Ver'gen-cy̆, 169.
Verg'er (*verj'-*).
Ver-gette', 12?.
Verg'ing (*verj'-*).
Vĕr'i-fi-a-ble, 164.
Vĕr-i-fĭ-ca'tion, 112
Vĕr'i-fi-că-tĭve.
Vĕr'i-fīed.
Vĕr'i-fī-er.
Vĕr'i-fy̆, 94.
Vĕr'i-fy̆-ing.
Vĕr'i-ly, 78, 93.
Vĕr-i-sĭ-mil'i-tude.
Vĕr'i-ta-ble, 164.
Vĕr'i-ta-bly.
Vĕr'i-ty, 169.
Ver'juice (*-joos*).
Ver-me-ol'o-gist.
Ver-me-ol'o-gy.

Ver′mēs (L.)(-*mēz*), *n.pl.*
Ver-mi-cel′li (It.) (-*mi-chel′lĭ*) [so Wk. Sm. Wr.; *ver-mi-chel′lĭ*, or *ver-mi-cel′lĭ*, Gd. 155.]
Ver-mĭ′ceoŭs (-*mish′us*)
Ver-mic′u-lar, 108.
Ver-mic′u-late, 108.
Ver-mic′u-lāt-ed.
Ver-mic′u-lāt-ing.
Ver-mic-u-la′tion, 112.
Ver′mi-cule.
Ver-mic′u-lose.
Ver-mic′u-loŭs.
Ver′mi-form, 108, 169.
Ver′mi-fuge, 171.
Ver-mil′ion (-*yun*), 51, 171.
Ver′min (21, N.), *n. sing.* & *pl.*

☞ "It is seldom employed as a noun singular, in modern style, and it never takes a plural termination." *Smart.*

Ver-min-a′tion.
Ver′min-oŭs.
Ver-mip′a-roŭs, 108.
Ver-miv′o-roŭs, 108.
Ver-nac′u-lar.
Ver′nal, 72.
Ver-na′tion.
Ver′ni-cose.
Ver′ni-er, 63, 229.
Ve-ron′i-ca.
Vĕr′ru-cose (-*roo*-), 89.
Vĕr′ru-coŭs (-*roo*-).
Ver′sa-tĭle, 81, 152.
Ver-sa-til′i-ty, 171.
Verse, 21, N.; 135.
Versed (*verst*), *a.* skilled. [*See* Verst, 160.]
Ver′si-cle, 164.
Ver′si-col-or (-*kul*-).
Ver′si-col-ored (-*kul-urd.*)
Ver-si-fĭ-ca′tion.
Ver′si-fīed.
Ver′si-fī-er.
Ver′si-fȳ.
Ver′si-fȳ-ing, 186.
Ver′sion, 169.
Verst (21, N.), *n.* a Russian measure of 3501 feet. [*See* Versed, 160] [Werst, 203.]
Ver′sus (L.).
Ver-sute′, 121.
Vert, 21, N.
Ver′te-bra (L.) [pl. Ver′te-bræ, 198.]
Ver′te-bral.
Ver-te-bra′ta (L.), *n. pl.*
Ver′te-brate.
Ver′te-brāt-ed.
Ver′te-bre (-*bur*) (164, 189) [Verteber preferred by Gd. 203.— [*See* Note E, p. 70.]
Ver′tex (76) [L. pl. *Ver′ti-cēs* (-*sēz*); Eng. pl. Ver′tex-es (-*ez*), 198.]
Ver′ti-cal.
Ver′ti-cal-ly.
Ver′ti-cil [Verticel, 203.]
Ver-tiç′il-las-ter.
Ver-tiç′il-late, *or* Ver-ti-cil′late [so Wr.; *ver-tis′il-lāt*, Wb. Gd.; *ver-ti-sil′lāt*, Sm. 155.]
Ver-tiç′il-lāt-ed, *or* Ver-ti-cil′lāt-ed.
Ver-tiç′i-ty.
Ver′ti-cle, 164.
Ve-tig′i-noŭs (-*tij′*-).
Ver′ti-go, *or* Ver-ti′go (-*te′*-) [*ver′tĭ-go*, Wb. Gd.; *ver-te′go*, Sm.; *ver-tī′go*, *ver-te′go*, or *ver′tĭ-go*, Wk.; *ver′-tĭ-go*, *ver-tī′go*, or *ver-te′go*, Wr. 155.]

☞ Walker says of this word: "If we pronounce it learnedly, we must place the accent in the first manner [*ver-tī′go*]: if we pronounce it modishly, and wish to smack of the French or Italian, we must adopt the second [*ver-te′-go*]; but if we follow the genuine English analogy, we must pronounce it in the last manner [*ver′ti-go*]."

Ver′vāin [so Sm. Gd.; *ver′vin*, Wk.; *ver′vin*, or *ver′vān*, Wr. 155.]
Vĕr′y, 48, 66, 93.
Ves′i-cal.
Ves′i-cant.
Ves′i-cate.
Ves′i-cāt-ed.
Ves′i-cāt-ing.
Ves-i-ca′tion.
Ve-sic′a-to-ry, *or* Ves′i-ca-to-ry (86) [*ve-sik′a-to-ry*, Wk. Sm. Wr.; *ves′ĭ-ka-to-ry*, Wb. Gd. 155.]
Ves′i-cle, 164.
Ve-sic′u-lar.
Ve-sic′u-late.
Ve-sic′u-lose.
Ves′per, 77.
Ves′per-tīne, 82, 152.
Ves′pi-a-ry, 72.
Ves′sel, 149, 170.
Vest, 15.
Ves′ta.
Ves′tal.
Vest′ed.
Ves-ti-a′ri-an.
Ves′ti-a-ry, 72.
Ves-tib′u-lar.
Ves′ti-bule.
Ves′tige, 70, 169.
Vest′ing.
Ves′ti-ture.
Vest′ment.
Ves′try, 93, 230.
Vest′ure, 91.
Vest′ured (-*yurd*).
Ve-su′vi-an, 169.
Vetch, 15, 44; Note D, p. 37.
Vetch′y, 169.
Vet′er-an, 233, Exc.
Vet-er-i-na′ri-an.
Vet′er-i-na-ry, 72.
Ve′to, *n.* & *v.* [pl. of *n.* Ve′toes (-*tōz*), 192.]
Ve′tōed, 188.
Ve′to-ing.
Ve′to-ist.
Vet-tu′ra (It.) (-*too′*-).
Vet-tu-ri′no (It.) (-*too-re′*-).
Vex, 15, 39, N.
Vex-a′tion.
Vex-a′tioŭs (-*shus*), 169.
Vexed (*vekst*), *v.*
Vexed (*vekst*) (165) [so Gd.; *vekst*, or *veks′ed*, Wr. 155], *a.*
Vex′er.
Vex′il.
Vex′il-lar.
Vex′il-la-ry, 72.
Vex-il-la′tion, 169.
Vex-il′lum (L.).
Vex′ing.
Vi′a (L.).
Vi-a-bil′i-ty.
Vi′a-ble, 164.
Vi′a-duct.
Vi′al, *n.* a small bottle. [*See* Viol, 148.] [Phial, 203.]
Vi′a Lac′te-a (L.).
Vī-am′e-ter.
Vi′and, 72.
Vi′a-tect-ure, 91.
Vī-at′ic.
Vī-at′i-cum (L.).
Vi′brate.
Vi′brāt-ed, 183.
Vi′bra-tĭle, 81, 152.

Vī-bra-til'i-ty.
Vī'brāt-ing.
Vī-bra'tion.
Vī'bra-tīve, 84.
Vī'bra-to-ry, 86.
Vī-bur'num (L.).
Vic'ar, 74, 155.
Vic'ar-age, 70, 169.
Vī-ca'ri-al.
Vī-ca'ri-ate.
Vī-ca'ri-oŭs, 49, N.
Vice (25, 39, 161) [Vise (in the sense of *a griping machine, with jaws brought together by means of a screw*), 203.]
Vī'ce (L.), 161.
Vice-ad'mi-ral, 222, N.
Vice-chan'cel-lor.
Vice-con'sul.
Vice-ge'ren-cy, 169.
Vice-ge'rent, 49, N.; 222, N.
Viç'e-na-ry (72) [so Wr. Wb. Gd.; *vī'se-na-ry*, Sm. 155.]
Vī-cen'ni-al, 170.
Vice-pres'i-dent (*-prez'-*), 222, N.
Vice'roy, 222, N.
Vice-roy'al-ty.
Vī'ce ver'sa (L.).
[Viciate, 203. — *See* Vitiate.]
Viç'i-nage, 171.
Viç'i-nal, *or* Vī-ci'nal [so Wr.; *vis'i-nal*, Wk. Wb. Gd.; *vī-si'-nal*, Sm. 155.]
Vī-cin'i-ty (169) [so Sm. Wr. Wb. Gd.; *vī-sin'-i-ty*, or *vī-sin'i-ty*, Wk. 155.]
Vī'cioŭs (*vish'us*) (46, Note 2) [Vitious, 203.]
Vī-cis'si-tude, 171.
Vic'tim, 80.
Vic'tim-ize, 202.
Vic'tim-ized, 183.
Vic'tim-īz-ing.
Vic'tor, 88, 169.
Vic-to'ri-a, 49, N.
Vic-tor-ine' (*-ēn'*), 122.
Vic-to'ri-oŭs.
Vic'to-ry, 86, 93.
Vict'ual (*vit'l*), 162.
Vict'ualled (*vit'ld*) [Victualed, Wb. Gd. 203. — *See* 177, and Note E, p. 70.]
Vict'ual-ler (*vit'l-ur*) [Victualer, Wb. Gd. 203.]
Vict'ual-ling (*vit'l-ing*) [Victualing, Wb. Gd. 203.] [162.
Vict'uals (*vit'lz*), *n. pl.*
Vī'de (L.).
Vī-del'i-cet (L.).

☞ This word is usually abbreviated, in writing, to *viz.* In reading, the adverb *namely* is substituted for it.

Vid'u-age.
Vie, 25.
Vied.
Vī-en-nese' (*-nēz'*), *n. sing.* & *pl.* 171.
View (*vu*), 26, 36.
Viewed (*vūd*).
View'er (*vu'-*).
View'ing (*vu'-*).
Vig'il (*vij'-*).
Vig'il-ance (*vij'-*), 171.
Vig'il-an-cy (*vij'-*).
Vig'il-ant (*vij'-*).
Vignette (Fr.) (*vin-yet'*) [*vin'yet*, Wk.; *vēn-yet'*, Sm.; *vig-net'*, commonly *vin'yet*, Gd.; *vin'yet*, or *vin-yet'*, Wr. 154, 155.]
Vig'or, 88.
Vig'or-oŭs, 100.
Vi'king.
Vile, 25.
Vile'ly, 66, N.; 185.
Vil-i-fī-ca'tion.
Vil'i-fīed, 99.
Vil'i-fī-er.
Vil'i-fȳ, 94.
Vil'i-fȳ-ing.
Vil'la, 170, 189.
Vil'lage, 70, 170.
Vil'la-ger.
Vil'laĭn (96), *n.* in law, one who held lands by a base tenure; — a base person; a rascal. [Villan, Villein (in the former sense), 203.]

☞ The orthography *villein*, as Worcester remarks, "seems to be that which is best authorized, when used with reference to feudal manners and customs."

Vil'laĭn-oŭs [Villanous, 203.—*See* Note under *Villainy*.]
Vil'laĭn-y [Villany, 203.]

☞ In their modern sense, this word and the preceding are spelled, in most English dictionaries, *villanous*, and *villany*, with reference to the Low Latin *villanus*. Smart, however, allows only *villainous*, *villainy*, regarding the words as proper English derivatives from *villain*. Goodrich admits both modes of spelling, but says that *villainous*, *villainy*, are to be preferred, as coming regularly from *villain*.

Vil'lan-age [Villenage, Villeinage, 203.]

☞ The form *villenage* is best supported by the usage of writers upon the feudal system. *See* Note under *Villain*.

Vil'lan-oŭs [Villainous, 203. — *See* Note under *Villainy*.]
Vil'lan-y [Villainy, 203. — *See* Note under *Villainy*.]
Vil-lat'ic, 109.
Vil'leĭn, *n.* one who held lands by a base or servile tenure. [Villan, Villain, 203. — *See* Note under *Villain*.]
Vil'len-age [Villeinage, Villanage, 203. — *See* Note under *Villanage*.]
Vil'lī (L.), *n. pl.*
Vil-lose' [so Wr.; *vil'-lōs*, Gd. 155.]
Vil-los'i-ty.
Vil'loŭs, 100, 169.
Vim'i-nal [so Wr. Wb. Gd.; *vi'min-al*, Sm. 155.]
Vī-min'e-oŭs, *or* Vī-min'e-oŭs [so Wk.; *vī-min'e-us*, Wr.; *vī-min'e-us*, Sm. Gd. 155.]
Vī-na'ceous (*-shus*) [so Sm. Gd.; *vī-na'shus*, Wr. 155.]
Vin-āi-grette' (Fr.).
Vin-ci-bil'i-ty.
Vin'ci-ble, 164.
Vin'cu-lum (L.) (*ving'-*) [pl. Vin'cu-la (*ving'-*), 198.]
Vin-di-ca-bil'i-ty.
Vin'di-ca-ble, 164.
Vin'di-cate, 169.
Vin'di-cāt-ed, 183.

Vin'di-cāt-ing.
Vin-di-ca'tion, 112.
Vin'di-cā-tīve [so Wk. Sm. Wb. Gd.; *vin'di-kā-tiv*, or *vin-dik'a-tiv*, Wr. 155.]
Vin'di-cāt-or.
Vin'di-ca-to-ry, 86.
Vin-dic'tīve, 84.
Vine, 25, 163.
Vine'-clad, 206, Exc. 5.
Vin'e-gar, 169.
Vīn'er-y.
Vīne'yard.
Vin'ic, 143.
Vī-nose'.
Vī'noŭs.
Vin'tage, 70, 169.
Vin'ta-ger, 183.
Vint'ner.
Vīn'y, 93, 228.
Vī'ol, *n.* a stringed musical instrument, like the violin; — a large rope used in weighing anchor. [Voyal, Voyol (in the latter sense), 203] [*See* Vial, 148.]
Vī'o-la-ble, 164.
Vī-o-la'ceoŭs (*-shus*).
Vī-o-las'cent.
Vī'o-late.
Vī'o-lāt-ed, 183.
Vī'o-lāt-ing.
Vī-o-la'tion.
Vī'o-lāt-or.
Vī'o-lence, 156.
Vī'o-lent [*not* voi'lent, 153.]
Vī'o-let, 76.
Vī-o-lin' (122, 148), *n.* an instrument of the viol family; a fiddle.
Vī'o-līne (148, 152), *n.* a poisonous alkaline principle.
Vī-o-lin'ist, 106.
Vī'ol-ist.
Vi-o-lon-cel'list (*ve-*).
Vi-o-lon-cel'lo (It.) (*ve-o-lon-chel'lo*, or *ve-o-lon-sel'lo*) [so Wr. Gd.; *ve-o-lon-chel'lo*, Wk.; *ve-o-lŏn-chel'lo*, Sm. 154, 155.]
Vi-o-lo'ne (*ve-*), or *Vi-o-lo'no* (*ve-*) (It.).
Vī'per, 77.
Vī'per-īne [so Sm. Wr. Wb. Gd.; *vi'pur-īn*, Wk. 155.]
Vī'per-oŭs.
Vī-ra'go, *or* Vī-ra'go [so Wk.; *vī-ra'go*, Sm.; *vī-ra'go*, Gd.; *vī-ra'go*, or *vī-ra'go*, Wr. 155.]
Vīr'e-lāy.
Vī'rent, 49, N.
Vī-res'cent.
Vir-ga-loo' [Vergaloo, 203.]
Vir'gate, 21, N.
Vir-gil'i-an, 169.
Vir'gin, 21, N.; 135.
Vir'gin-al.
Vir-gin'i-ty.
Vir'go (L.).
Vir-gou-leuse' (Fr.) (*-goo-looz'*), 154.
Vir'gu-late, 108.
Vir'gule.
Vīr-ī-des'cence, 171.
Vīr-i-des'cent.
Vī-rid'i-ty, 169.
Vī'rīle, *or* Vīr'īle [so Wr.; *vi'ril*, Wk. Gd.; *vīr'il*, Sm. 155.]
Vī-ril'i-ty, *or* Vī-ril'i-ty [so Wk.; *vī-ril'i-ty*, Gd.; *vī-ril'i-ty*, Sm. Wr. 155.]
Vī'rose.
Vir-tu' (It.) (*vēr-too'*) [so Sm.; *ver-too'*, Wk. Wr.; *ver'tu*, Wb. Gd. 155.]
Virt'u-al, 89.
Virt'u-al-ly, 170.
Virt'ūe, 44, Note 1; 129.
Vir-tu-o'so (It.) (*ver-too-o'so*) [so Wk. Wr. Wb. Gd.; *vēr-too-o'zo*, Sm. 155] [It. pl. *Vir-tu-o'si* (*ver-too-o'se*); Eng. pl. Vir-tu-o'sōs (*-sōz*), 198.]
Virt'u-oŭs.
Vīr'u-lence, 89.
Vīr'u-len-cy.
Vīr'u-lent, 89.
Vī'rus.
Vis (L.).
Vi'sa (Fr.) (*ve'za*).
Vis'age (*viz'-*), 70.
Vis-à-vis' (Fr.) (*viz-a-ve'*).
Vis'ce-ra (L.), *n. pl.*
Vis'ce-ral.
Vis'cid, 39.
Vis-cid'i-ty, 171.
Vis-cos'i-ty.
Vis'count (*vi'-*), 162.
Vis'count-ess (*vi'-*).
Vis'count-y (*vi'-*).
Vis'coŭs, 100, 169.
[Vise, 203.—*See* Vice.]
Visé (Fr.) (*ve-zā'*) [so Gd.; *ve'zā*, Wr. 155.]
Vish'nu [so Wr. Gd.; *vēsh'noo*, Sm. 155.]
Vis-i-bil'i-ty (*viz-*).
Vis'i-ble (*viz'i-bl*).
Vis'i-bly (*viz'-*).
Vis'i-goth (*viz'-*).
Vis-i-goth'ic (*viz-*).
Vis in-er'ti-æ (L.) (*-shī-e*).
Vī'sion (*vizh'un*).
Vī'sion-a-ri-ness (*vizh'-un-*).
Vī'sion-a-ry (*vizh'un-*), 72, 171.
Vī'sion-ist (*vizh'un-*).
Vis'it (*viz'-*).
Vis'it-a-ble (*viz'it-a-bl*).
Vis'it-ant (*viz'-*).
Vis-it-a'tion (*viz-*).
Vis-it-a-to'ri-al (*viz-*).
Vi-site' (Fr.) (*vī-zēt'*).
Vis'it-ed (*viz'-*).
[Visiter, 203.— *See* Visitor.]
Vis'it-ing (*viz'-*).
Vis'it-or (*viz'-*) [Visiter, 203.]
Vis-it-o'ri-al (*viz-*).
Visne (*ve'ne*, or *vēn*) [*ve'ne*, Sm. Wr.; *vēn*, Wb. Gd. 155] [Law term.]
Vis'or (*viz'-*) [*not* vi'-zur, 127, 153.]
Vis'ored (*viz'urd*).
Vis'ta, 72, 189.
Vis'u-al (*vizh'-*), 47, N.
Vī'tal, 72.
Vī'tal-ism (*-izm*), 136.
Vī-tal'i-ty [so Wk. Sm. Gd.; *vī-tal'i-ty*, Wr. 155.]
Vī-tal-ī-za'tion.
Vī'tal-ize, 202.
Vī'tal-ized.
Vī'tal-īz-ing.
Vī'tal-ly.
Vī-tel'līne (152) [so Sm.; *vit'el-lin*, Gd. 155.]
Vī-tel'lus (L.).
Vī'ti-ate (*vish'ī-āt*) [so Wk. Sm. Wr.; *vish'-āt*, Wb. Gd. 155] [Viciate, 203.]

☞ "This verb is usually written *vitiate*; but as *vice*, from L. *vitium*, is established, it would be

well to write the verb *vici-ate*, as we write *appreciate* and *depreciate* from L. *pretium*." *Webster.*

Vĭ'ti-āt-ed (*vish'ĭ-*).
Vĭ'ti-āt-ing (*vish'ĭ*).
Vĭ-ti-a'tion (*vish-ĭ-*).
[V i t i o u s, 203. — *See* Vicious.]
Vit're-ous, 169.
Vĭ-tres'cence, 171.
Vĭ-tres'cent.
Vĭ-tres'ci-ble, 164.
Vit-ri-fac'tion.
Vit'ri-fi-a-ble, 164.
Vit'ri-fīed.
Vit'ri-form, 108.
Vit'ri-fȳ, 94, 169.
Vit'ri-fȳ-ing.
Vit'ri-ol.
Vit'ri-ol-ate.
Vit'ri-ol-āt-ed.
Vit-ri-ol-a'tion.
Vit-ri-ol'ic.
Vit-ri-ol-īz'a-ble, 164, 183.
Vit-ri-ol-ĭ-za'tion.
Vit'ri-ol-īze.
Vit'ri-ol-īzed.
Vit'ri-ol-īz-ing.
Vĭ-tru'vi-an (*-troo'-*).
Vit'tate.
Vit'tāt-ed.
Vit'u-līne [so Wk. Wr. Gd.; *vit'u-lĭn*, Sm. 155.]
Vĭ-tu'per-ate, *or* Vĭ-tu'-per-ate [so Wk. Wr.; *vĭ-tu'pur-āt*, Sm.; *vĭ-tu'pur-āt*, Gd. 155.]
Vĭ-tu'per-āt-ed, *or* Vĭ-tu'per-at-ed.
Vĭ-tu'per-āt-ing, *or* Vĭ-tu'per-āt-ing.
Vĭ-tu-per-a'tion, *or* Vĭ-tu-per-a'tion.
Vĭ-tu'per-a-tĭve, *or* Vĭ-tu'per-a-tĭve, 84.
Vĭ-tu'per-āt-or, *or* Vĭ-tu'per-āt-or.
Vi-vä'ce (It.) (*ve-vä'-chā*).
Vĭ-va'cioŭs, *or* Vĭ-va'-cioŭs (*-shus*) [so Wk. Wr.; *vĭ-va'shus*, Gd.; *vĭ-va'sh'us*, Sm. (*See* § 26), 155.]
Vĭ-vaç'i-ty, *or* Vĭ-vaç'i-ty [so Wk. Wr.; *vĭ vas'i-ty*, Sm.; *vĭ-vas'-i-ty*, Gd. 155.]
Vi'va-ry, 72.
Vi'va vo'ce (L.).

Vīves (*vīvz*), 25, 40.
Viv'i-an-īte.
Viv'id, 170.
Vĭ-vif'ic.
Vĭ-vif'ic-al.
Viv-i-fĭ-ca'tion.
Viv'i-fīed.
Viv'i-fȳ.
Viv'i-fȳ-ing.
Vĭ-vip'a-roŭs, 151.
Viv-i-sec'tion.
Vix'en (*viks'n*), 149.
Viz. [*See* Videlicet.]
Viz'ier (*-yur*) [so Sm. Wb. Gd.; *viz'yēr*, Wk.; *viz'yur*, or *viz'yēr*, Wr. 155] [V i z i r, 203.]
Viz'ier-ate (*-yur-*).
Vĭ-zĭr'i-al.
Vo'ca-ble (164) [*not* vok'a bl, 153.]
Vo-cab'u-la-ry, 72.
Vo-cab'u-list.
Vo'cal, 72.
Vo-cal'ic, 109.
Vo'cal-ist, 106.
Vo-cal'i-ty, 108.
Vo-cal-ĭ-za'tion.
Vo'cal-īze, 202.
Vo'cal-īzed, 165.
Vo'cal-īz-ing, 183.
Vo'cal-ly, 170.
Vo-ca'tion.
Voc'a-tĭve, 84.
Vo-cif'er-ate, 171.
Vo-cif'er-āt-ed.
Vo-cif'er-āt-ing.
Vo-cif-er-a'tion.
Vo-cif'er-oŭs, 108.
Vo'cule [*not* vok'yool, 153.]
Vogue (*vōg*), 87, 168.
Voice, 27, 39.
Voiced (*voist*).
Void, 27.
Void'a-ble, 164, 169.
Void'ance.
Void'ed.
Void'er.
Void'ing.
Voire-dire (Fr.) (*vwor-dēr'*).
Vo'lant [so Wk. Wr. Wb. Gd.; *vol'ant*, Sm. 155.]
Vo-lán'te (Sp.) (*-tā*).
[V o l a r y, 203. — *See* Volery.]
Vol'a-tĭle, 152.
Vol-a-til'i-ty.
Vol'a-til-īz-a-ble, 164.
Vol-a-til-ĭ-za'tion.

Vol'a-til-īze [*not* vo-lat'il-īz, 153.]
Vol'a-til-īzed.
Vol'a-til-īz-ing.
Vol-can'ic.
Vol-ca-niç'i-ty.
Vol'ca-nism (*-nizm*).
Vol'ca-nist.
Vol-can'i-ty.
Vol-ca-nĭ-za'tion.
Vol'ca-nīze.
Vol-ca'no [pl. Vol-ca'-nōes (*-nōz*), 192.]
Vole, 24.
Volée (Fr.) (*vo-lā'*).
Vol'er-y [so Wk. Wr.; *vo'ler-y*, Gd. 155] [V o l a r y, 203.]
Vŏl-i-ta'tion.
Vo-lĭ'tion (*-lish'un*)
Vol'i-tĭve, 84, 169.
Vol'ley (169), *n.* & *v.* [pl. of *n.* Vol'leys (*-liz*), 190.]
Vol'leyed (*-lid*).
Vol'leȳ-ing.
Vōlt, 18.
Vol-ta'ic.
Vol'ta-ism (*-izm*).
Vol-tam'e-ter, 108.
Vol'ta-plast.
Vol'ta-type.
Vŏl-ti-geur' (Fr.) (*-zhur'*), 154.
Vo-lu'bi-late.
Vol'u-bĭle.
Vol'u-ble, 164.
Vol'ume (*vol'yum*, or *vol'yoom*) [*vol'yum*, Wr. Gd.; *vol'yoom*, Wk. Sm. 155.]
Vol'umed (*-yumd*), 165.
Vol-u-met'ric.
Vo-lu'mi-noŭs.
Vol'un-ta-ri-ly, 186.
Vol'un-ta-ry, 72.
Vol-un-teer', 169.
Vol-un-teered', 165.
Vol-un-teer'ing.
Vo-lupt'u-a-ry, 72.
Vo-lupt'u-oŭs.
Vo-lute' [*not* vol'yoot, 153.]
Vo-lūt'ed.
Vo'mer (L.).
Vo'mer-īne.
Vom'it, 170.
Vom'it-ed.
Vom'it-ing.
Vo-mĭ'tion (*-mish'un*).
Vom'it-īve.
Vo-mi'to (Sp.) (*-me'-*).
Vom'it-o-ry.

Vom-it-u-rĭ′tion (*-rish′-un*).
Vo-ra′cioŭs (*-shus*).
Vo-raç′i-ty.
Vo-rag′i-noŭs (*-raj′-*).
Vor′tex [L. pl. *Vor′ti-cēs* (*-sēz*); Eng. pl. Vor′tex-es (*-ez*), 198.]
Vor′ti-cal.
Vor′ti-cel.
Vor-tig′i-noŭs (*-tij′-*).
Vo′ta-ress.
Vo′ta-rist.
Vo′ta-ry, 72.
Vote, 24.
Vōt′ed, 183.
Vōt′er.
Vōt′ing.
Vo′tīve, 84.
Vouch, 28.
Vouched (*voucht*).
Vouch-ee′ (118) [Law term, correlative of *Vouchor*.]
Vouch′er.
Vouch′ing.
Vouch′or (118) [so Wr. Wb. Gd.; *vouch-or′*, Sm. 155] [Law term, correlative of *Vouchee*.]
Vouch-safe′.
Vouch-safed′ (*-sāft′*).
Vouch-sāf′ing.
Vous-soir′ (Fr.) (*voos-swor′*).
Vow, 28.
Vowed, 150, 165.
Vow′el, 76.
Vow′elled (*-eld*) [Vow-eled, Wb. Gd. 203. — *See* 177, and Note E, p. 70.]
Vox pop′u-lī (L.).
Voy′age (coll. *vaw′ij*), 70, 169.
Voy′aged, 165.
Voy′a-ger.
Voy′a-ging (*-jing*).
Voyageur (Fr.) (*vwä-ya-zhur′*).
Voy′al [Viol, Voy-ol, 203.]
Vraisemblance (Fr.) (*vrā-säng-bläṅgs′*).
Vul-ca′ni-an, 169.
Vul-can′ic.
Vul′can-ist.
Vul-can-ĭ-za′tion.
Vul′can-ize, 202.
Vul′can-ized, 165.
Vul′can-iz-ing, 183.
Vul′gar, 72.
Vul′gar-ism (*-izm*).
Vul-găr′i-ty.
Vul′gar-ize, 202.
Vul′gar-ized.
Vul′gar-iz-ing.
Vul′gate.
Vul-ner-a bil′i-ty.
Vul′ner-a-ble, 164, 169.
Vul′ner-a-ry, 72.
Vul′ner-ose [so Gd.; *vul-ner-ōs′*, Wr. 155.]
Vul′nose.
Vul′pīne [so Sm. Wr. Wb. Gd.; *vul′pīn*, or *vul′pĭn*, Wk. 155.]
Vult′ure, 91.
Vult′u-rīne [so Sm. Wr. Wb. Gd., *vul′chu-rīn*, Wk. 155.]
Vul′vi-form, 108.
Vy′ing, 184.

W.

Wab′ble (*wob′l*), 18, 164.
Wab′bled (*wob′ld*).
Wab′bling (*wob′-*), 183.
Wack′e [so Sm. Wb. Gd.; *wak′e*, or *wak*, Wr. 155] [Wacky, 203.]
Wad (*wod*), 18.
Wad′ded (*wod′-*), 176.
Wad′ding (*wod′-*).
Wad′dle (*wod′l*), 164.
Wad′dled (*wod′ld*).
Wad′dler (*wod′lur*).
Wad′dling (*wod′-*), 183.
Wade (23), *v.* to walk through any yielding substance. [*See* Weighed, 160.]
Wād′ed, 183.
Wād′er.
Wād′ing.
Wa′fer, 77.
Wa′fered (*-furd*), 150.
Wa′fer-ing.
Waf′fle (*wof′l*), 164.
Wȧft, 12, 131.
Wȧft′age.
Wȧft′ed.
Wȧft′ing.
Wȧft′ure, 91.
Wag, 10, 34, 53.
Wage, 23, 45.
Waged (*wājd*), 165.
Wa′ger, 45.
Wa′gered (*-jurd*), 150.
Wa′ger-ing.
Wa′ges (*-jez*), *n. pl.*
Wagged (*wagd*), 165.
Wag′ging (*-ghing*).
Wag′gish, 53, 138.
Wag′gle, 164.
Wāg′ing (*wāj′-*). [203.
Wag′on, *or* Wag′gon, 86,

☞ This word is spelled *waggon* in most of the English dictionaries; and Smart says of *wagon*, that it "is a disused orthography." But this orthography, as Todd remarks, is "strictly conformable to the etymology [A. S. *wægen*: Dutch & Ger. *wagen*];" and Worcester says, that in the United States "*wagon* is perhaps the more common of the two forms."

Wag′on-age, *or* Wag′gon-age.
Wag′on-er, *or* Wag′gon-er.
Wag′tāil, 206.
Wä-hä′bee, *or* Wä-hä′by, 203.
Wāif, 23.
Wāil (23), *v.* to bemoan —*n.* loud lamentation. [*See* Wale, 160.]
Wāiled, 165.
Wāil′ing.
Wāin (23), *n.* a wagon. [*See* Wane, 160.]
Wāin′scot (coll. *wen′skut*) [*wān′skot*, Wr. Wb. Gd.; *wen′skut*, Wk. Sm. 155.]
Wāin′scot-ed (or *wen′skut-ed*).
Wāin′scot-ing (or *wen′skut-ing*).
Wāist (23), *n.* the narrowest part of the body just above the hips. [*See* Waste, 160.]
Wāist′band.
Wāist′cōat (coll. *wes′kut*) [so Sm.; *wāst′kōt*, Wb. Gd; *wes′kot*, Wk.; *wās′kōt*, or *wes′kot*, Wr. 155.]

☞ "This word has fallen into the general contraction observable in similar compounds, but, in my opinion, not so irrecoverably as some have done. It would scarcely sound pedantic if both parts of the word were pronounced with equal distinctness [*wāst′kōt*]." *Walker.*

Wāit (23), *n.* ambush:

— *v.* to delay, or tarry. [*See* Weight, 160.]
Wāit'ed.
Wāit'er.
Wāit'ing.
Wāive (23) [Wave, 203.]
Wāived, 165.
Wāiv'ing.
[Wāi'wode, 203. — *See* Vaivode.]
Wake, 23.
Waked (*wākt*), 41.
Wake'ful (-*fōōl*), 180.
Wāk'en (*wāk'n*), 149.
Wāk'ened (*wāk'nd*).
Wāk'en-er (*wāk'n-*).
Wāk'en-ing (*wāk'n-*).
Wāk'ing, 183.
Wal-den'sēs (*wawl-den'sēz*, or *wol'den-siz*) [*wawl-den'sēz*, Wr. Gd.; *wol'den-siz*, Sm. 155.]
Wale (23), *n.* a ridge on the skin made by the stroke of a whip; — one of the strong planks extending along the whole length of a ship's side: — *v.* to mark with stripes. [*See* Wail, 160.]
Wal-hal'la (*wol-*) [so Sm.; *wăl-hal'la*, Wr. 155] [Valhalla, 203.]
Walk (*wawk*), 17, 162.
Walked (*wawkt*).
Walk'ing (*wawk'-*).
Wâll (17, 172), *n.* a work of stone or other material for enclosure or defence; — the side of a building: — *v.* to surround with a wall. [*See* Waul, 160.]
Wal-la'chi-an (-*ki-*).
Wâlled, 165.
Wal'let (*wol'-*), 76.
Wâll'-eye.
Wâll'-eyed (-*īd*).
Wâll'-flower (-*flour*).
Wâll'ing.
Wâll'-knot (-*not*), 162.
Wal-loon', 121.
Wal'lop (*wol'-*), 103, 104.
Wal'loped (*wol'lupt*), 66.
Wal'lop-ing, 170.
Wal'lōw (*wol'-*), 101.
Wal'lōwed (*wol'lōd*).
Wal'lōw-er (*wol'-*).
Wal'lōw-ing (*wol'-*).
Wal'nut (*wol'nut*) [so Wb. Gd.; *wawl'nut*, Wk. Wr 155.]

☞ In Smart's notation of this word, as also of *walrus*, *waltz*, *wander*, *want*, *wanton*, the *a* is marked as having a sound intermediate between that of *a* in *all* and that of *o* in *on*.

Wal'rus (*wol'-*) [so Wb. Gd.; *wawl'rus*, Wr. 155.]

☞ *See* Note under *Walnut*.

Wâltz (*wawlts*), 17; Note C, p. 34.

☞ *See* Note under *Walnut*.

Wâltzed (*wawltst*).
Wâltz'ing (*wawlts'-*).
Wam'ble (*wom'bl*).
Wam-pee' (*wom-*), 121.
Wam'pum (*wom'-*) [so Wb. Gd. Sm.; *wawm'-pum*, Wr. 155.]
Wan (*wŏn*) (18) [*not* wăn, 153.]
Wand (*wŏnd*) (18) [*not* wănd, 153.]
Wan'der (*wŏn'-*).

☞ *See* Note under *Walnut*.

Wan'dered (*wŏn'durd*).
Wan'der-ing (*wŏn'-*).
Wane (23), *v.* to grow less: — *n.* decrease, as of the moon. [*See* Wain, 160.]
Waned, 165.
Wān'ing, 183.
Wang'hee [Wangee, (*wan-ghe'*, Wb. Gd.); Whanghee, 203.]
Wan'ness (*wŏn'-*), 66, N.
Wan'nish (*wŏn'ish*), 176.
Wânt (17) [so Wb. Gd.; *wŏnt*, Wk.; *wawnt*, or *wŏnt*, Wr. 155.]

☞ *See* Note under *Walnut*.

Wânt'ed.
Wânt'ing.
Wan'ton (*won'-*), 18, 86.

☞ *See* Note under *Walnut*.

Wan'toned (*wŏn'tund*).
Wan'ton-ing (*wŏn'-*).
Wan'ton-ness (*wŏn'-*).
Wânt'wit.
Wa'pen-take (*wa'pn-*) [so Sm.; *wap'en-tāk*, Wb. Gd.; *wap'en-tāk*, or *wa'pen-tāk*, Wr. 155.]
Wap'i-tī, 191.
Wâr, 17, 34, 49.
Wâr'ble, 135, 164.
War'bled (-*bld*), 150.
Wâr'bler, 183.
Wâr'bling.
Wâr'-cry.
Wârd, 17, 135.
Wârd'ed.
Wâr'den (-*dn*), 149, 167.
Wâr'den-ry (-*dn-*).
Wârd'er.
Wârd'ing.
Wârd'robe, 206.
Wârd'room, 19.
Ware (*wêr*) (67), *n.* merchandise. [*See* Weigher, 148; *and* Wear, 160.]
[Ware, *v.* (to veer), 203. — *See* Wear.]
Ware'house (*wêr'hous*), *n.* 161.
Ware'house (*wêr'houz*), *v.* 161.
Ware'housed (*wêr'-houzd*).
Ware'hous-ing (*wêr'-houz-*).
Wâr'fare (-*fêr*).
Wâr'-horse.
Wa'ri-ly [*See* Wary.]
Wa'ri-ness, 186.
Wâr'like, 206, Exc. 5.
Wârm, 17, 135.
Wârmed, 150, 165.
Wârm'ing.
Wârm'ing-pan, 215.
Wârm'ly, 93.
Wârmth, 17, 64.
Wârn, 17, 49.
Wârned (*wârnd*), 150.
Wârn'ing.
Wârp, 17.
Wârped (*wârpt*).
Wârp'ing.
War'rant (*wŏr'-*), 171.
War'rant-a-ble (*wŏr'-*), 164.
War'rant-a-bly (*wŏr'-*).
War'rant-ed (*wŏr'-*).
War-rant-ee' (*wŏr-*) (118) [Law term, correlative of *Warrantor*.]
War'rant-er (*wŏr'-*).
War'rant-ing (*wŏr'-*).
War-rant-or' (*wŏr-*) (118) [Law term, cor-

relative of *Warrantee.*]
War'rant-y (*wŏr'-*), 171.
Wârred (*wawrd*).
War'ren (*wŏr'-*), 48.
Wâr'ring, 171, 176.
Wâr'rior (*wawr'yur*) [so Wk. Wr. Wb. Gd.; *wŏr'ri-ur*, Sm. 155.]
Wârt, 17, 135.
Wârt'-hog', 206, Exc. 3.
Wârt'wort (*-wurt*).
Wârt'y, 169.
Wa'ry (49, N.) [so Wk. Sm. Wb. Gd.; *wêr'y*, or *wa'ry*, Wr. 155.]
Was (*woz*), 18, 174.
Wash (*wosh*), 18, 46.
Wash'bōard (*wosh'-*).
Wash'bōwl (*wosh'-*).
Washed (*wosht*).
Wash'er (*wosh'-*).
Wash'er-man (*wosh'-*).
Wash'ing (*wosh'-*).
Wash'-lĕath'er(*wosh'-*).
Wash'-stand (*wosh'-*).
Wash'y (*wosh'-*), 169.
Wasp (*wosp*), 18.
Wasp'ish (*wosp'-*).
Was'saĭl (*wos'sil*) [*not* wăs'sāl, 153.]
Was'saĭl-er (*wos'sil-*).
Wast (*wŏst*), 18.
Wāst'age, 183.
Wāste (23, 163), *n.* the act of squandering; — a wilderness: — *a.* destroyed; — desolate; — worthless: — *v.* to wear away; — to destroy; — to dwindle. [*See* Waist, 160.]
Wāste'-bŏŏk, 206, Exc. 4.
Wāst'ed.
Wāste'ful (*-fŏŏl*), 180.
Wāst'er.
Wāst'ing, 183.
Watch (*wŏch*), Note D, p. 37.
Watch'case (*wŏch'-*).
Watch'dog (*wŏch'-*).
Watched (*wŏcht*).
Watch'er (*wŏch'-*).
Watch'ful (*wŏch'fŏŏl*).
Watch'-house, 206, Exc. 1.
Watch'ing (*wŏch'-*).
Watch'man (*wŏch'-*), 196.
Watch'word (*wŏch'-wurd*).
Wâ'ter, *n.* & *v.* 103, 104.
Wâ'ter-age.
Wâ'ter-cōurse.
Wâ'tered, 150.
Wâ'ter-fâll.
Wâ'ter-fowl.
Wâ'ter-i-ness.
Wâ'ter-ing.
Wâ'ter-ing-place.
Wâ'ter-ish.
Wâ'ter-logged (*-logd*).
Wâ'ter-man.
Wâ'ter-mel-on.
Wâ'ter-pot.
Wâ'ter-ram.
Wâ'ter-ret.
Wâ'ter-ret-ted.
Wâ'ter-ret-ting.
Wâ'ter-rot.
Wâ'ter-rot-ted.
Wâ'ter-rot-ting.
Wâ'ter-shed.
Wâ'ter-spout.
Wâ'ter-tight (*-tīt*).
Wâ'ter-way.
Wâ'ter-work (*-wurk*).
Wâ'ter-wort (*-wurt*).
Wâ'ter-y, 93, 169.
Wat'tle (*wot'l*), 164.
Wat'tled (*wot'ld*).
Wat'tling (*wot'ling*).
Wâul (17), *v.* to cry as a cat. [*See* Wall, 160] [W a w l, 203.]
Wave, 23.
Waved, 165.
Wave'let.
Wave'like.
Wave'-of'fer-ing, 205.
Wa'ver.
Wa'vered, 150.
Wa'ver-ing.
Wave'son.
Wāv'ing, 183.
Wāv'y, 93.
[W a w l, 203. — *See* Waul.]
Wax, 10, 39, N.
Waxed (*wăkst*).
Wax'en (*wăks'n*), 149.
Wax'i-ness, 186.
Wax'ing.
Wax'wing, 206.
Wax'work (*-wurk*).
Wax'y, 93.
Wāy (23, 56, Rem.), *n.* a passage; — course. [*See* Weigh, 160.]
Wāy'-bill.
Wāy'brĕad [W a y-b r e d, 203.]

☞ "Properly *waybrede.*" *Smart.*

Wāy'far-er (*-fêr-*).
Wāy'far-ing (*-fêr-*).
Wāy'lāid.
Wāy'lāy [so Sm. Wb. Gd.; *wā-lā'*, Wk.; *wā'lā*, or *wā-lā'*, Wr. 155.]

☞ "In this word, there is little difference of accent." *Webster.*

Wāy'lāy-ing.
Wāy'side.
Wāy'ward.
[W a y w o d e, 203. — *See* Vaivode.]
Wāy'-wōrn, 206, Exc. 5.
We (13, 34), *pron.* pl. of *I.* [*See* Wee, 160.]
Wēak (13), *a.* feeble. [*See* Week, 160.]
Wēak'en (*wēk'n*), 149.
Wēak'ened (*wēk'nd*).
Wēak'en-ing (*wēk'n-*).
Wēak'eyed (*-īd*).
Wēak'ling.
Wēak'ly, *a.* feebly. [*See* Weekly, 160.]
Wēal (13), *n.* prosperity. [*See* Weel, 160.]
Wēald (13), *n.* a wood or grove. [*See* Wield, 160.]
Wēald'en (*wēld'n*) [so Gd.; *wēl'den*, Wr. 155.]
Wĕalth, 15, 37.
Wĕalth'y, 93.
Wēan (13), *v.* to accustom to a deprivation of the breast; — to disengage. [*See* Ween, 160.]
Wēaned (165), *v.* did wean. [*See* Weened, 160.]
Wēan'ing, *part.* from *Wean.* [*See* Weening, 160.]
Wēan'ling.
Wĕap'on (*wep'un*, or *wep'n*) [*wep'un*, Sm.; *wep'n*, Wk. Wr. Wb. Gd. 155.]
Wĕap'oned(*wep'und*, or *wep'nd*), 171.
Wêar (14), *v.* to have on the body; — to waste by friction or by time; — to veer: — *n.* the act of wearing; — vogue. [*See* Ware, 160] [W a r e (to veer), 203.]
Wēar (13) [so Sm. Gd.; *wêr*, Wk.; *wêr*,

or *wēr*, Wr. 155], *n.* a dam; — an enclosure of twigs set in a stream to catch fish. [Were, Weir, Wier, 203.]
Wêar'a-ble, 164.
Wêar'er.
Wēa'rïed, 49, N.
Wēa'ri-ness, 186.
Wêar'ing, 48, 49, N.
Wēa'ri-some (*-sum*).
Wēa'ry, 49, N.
Wēa'ry-ing.
Wēa'sand (*-zand*) (72) [so Sm. Wb. Gd.; *we'zn*, Wk.; *we'znd*, Wr. 155.] [Wesand, Wezand, 203.]
Wēa'sel (*-zl*), 149, 171.
Wĕath'er, *n.* the state of the atmosphere: — *v.* to pass to the windward of; — to bear up against. [*See* Wether, 160.]
Wĕath'er-bēat'en (*-bēt'n*).
Wĕath'er-bit.
Wĕath'er-bōard.
Wĕath'er-bound.
Wĕath'er-cock.
Wĕath'ered, 150, 165.
Wĕath'er-ing.
Wĕath'er-ly.
Wĕath'er-wise (*-wīz*).
Wēave, 13.
Wēav'er (77), *n.* one who weaves. [*See* Weever, 160.]
Wēav'ing, 183.
Web, 15, 31, 34.
Webbed (*webd*), 165.
Web'by.
Web'fŏŏt.
Web'-fŏŏt-ed.
Wed, 15.
Wed'ded, 176.
Wed'ding.
Wedge, 15, 45.
Wedged (*wejd*).
Wedg'ing (*wej'-*).
Wed'lock.
Wednes'day (*wenz'dy*), 162, 171.

☞ This word, according to Smart, was shortened in sound "first into *wen-es-day*, and then into *wensday*."

Wee (13), *a.* diminutive. [*See* We, 160.]
Weech'-elm (*wēch'elm*) [so Sm.; *wēch'elm*, Wk. Wb. Gd. 155] [Witch-elm, 203.]
Weed, 13.
Weed'ed.
Weed'er.
Weed'er-y.
Weed'ing.
Weed'ing-hŏŏk.
Weed'y, 93.
Week (13), *n.* seven days. [*See* Weak, 160.]
Week'-dāy.
Week'ly, *a.* occurring or produced once a week. [*See* Weakly, 160.]
Weel (13), *n.* a snare of twigs for catching fish. [*See* Weal, 160.]
Ween (13), *n.* to think. [*See* Wean, 160.]
Weened (165), *v.* did ween. [*See* Weaned, 160.]
Ween'ing, *part.* from *Ween.* [*See* Weaning, 160.]
Weep, 13, 30, 34.
Weep'er.
Weep'ing.
Weep'ing-wil'lōw.
Wee'ver, *n.* a fish of the perch kind. [*See* Weaver, 160.]
Wee'vil (*we'vl*), 149.
Wee'villed (*we'vld*) [Weeviled, Gd. 203. — *See* 177, and Note E, p. 70.]
Wee'vil-ly (*-vl-*) [Weevily, Gd. 203.]
Weft, 15.
Weigh (*wā*) (23, 162), *v.* to ascertain the weight of; — to have weight. [*See* Way, 160.]
Weigh'a-ble (*wa'a-bl*).
Weigh'age (*wa'-*).
Weighed (*wād*), *v.* did weigh. [*See* Wade, 160.]
Weigh'er (*wa'-*) (67), *n.* one who weighs. [*See* Ware, 148.]
Weigh'ing (*wa'-*).
Weight (*wāt*) (23, 162), *n.* the force with which a body tends to the centre of the earth; gravity. [*See* Wait, 160.]
Weight'ed (*wāt'-*).
Weight'i-ly (*wāt'-*).
Weight'i-ness (*wāt'-*).
Weight'y (*wāt'-*).
Weir (13) [Wear, 203.]
Weird, 13, 169.
[Welch, 203. — *See* Welsh.]
Wel'come (*-kum*), 169.
Wel'comed (*-kumd*).
Wel'com-er.
Wel'com-ing.
Weld (15), *n.* a kind of plant yielding a yellow dye: — *v.* to beat into firm union, as metals when heated. [*See* Welled, 160] [Wold, Woad (as a *n.*), 203.]
Weld'ed.
Weld'ing.
Wel'fare (*-fêr*), 180.
Wel'kin.
Well, 15, 172.
Well'-a-dāy.
Well'-be-ing.
Well'-bred, 180.
Well'-done (*-dun*).
Well-dressed' (*-drest*).
Welled (*weld*), *v.* did well, or spring. [*See* Weld, 160.]
Well'ing.
Well'-knōwn (*-nōn*), 206, Exc. 5.
Well-met'.
Well'-nīgh (*-nī*), 162.
Well-wish'er.
Welsh [Welch, 203.]
Welt, 15.
Welt'ed, 228.
Wel'ter, 230.
Wel'tered, 150, 165.
Wel'ter-ing.
Welt'ing.
Wen (15, 34), *n.* a hard, fleshy tumor. [*See* When, 148.]
Wend, 15.
Wend'ed.
Wend'ing.
Wen'ny, 170, 176.
Went, 15.
Wept, 15, 142.
Were (*wer*) (21, N.; 163) [*not* wêr, 127, 153.]
Wer-ne'ri-an, 169.
Werst (21, N.) [Verst, 203.]
Wert, 21, N.; 135.
[Wesand, 203. — *See* Weasand.]

Wes′leÿ-an, 171.
Wes′leÿ-an-ism (*-izm*).
West, 15.
West′er-ly.
West′ern, 135.
West′ing.
West′ward.
Wet (15, 34) [*See* Whet, 148.]
Weth′er, *n.* a kind of male sheep. [*See* Weather, 160.]
Wet′ted, 176.
Wet′ting.
Wet′tish.
[Wezand, 203. — *See* Weasand.]
Whack, 10, 33.
Whacked (*whakt*), Note C, p. 34.
Whack′ing.
Whale, 23, 33.
Whale′bōne, 206.
Whale′man, 196.
Whāl′er.
Whāl′ing, 183.
[Whangee, 203. — *See* Wangee.]
Whap (*whop*).
Whap′per (*whop′-*).
Whap′ping (*whop′-*).
Whârf (*whorf*) (135) [pl. Whârfs (Eng.), Whârves (*whorvz*) (U. S.), 193.]

☞ "The form of *wharves*, for the plural of *wharf*, has lately been used by some respectable English writers." *Worcester.*

Whârf′age, 70, 169.
Whârf′in-ger.
What (*whot*), 18, 33.
What-ev′er (*whot-*).
What′not (*whot′-*), 206.
What-so-ev′er (*whot-*), 205, Exc. 2.
Whēal (13, 33), *n.* a pustule or pimple. [*See* Wheel, 160.]
Whēat, 13, 33.
Whēat′-ēar, *n.* an ear of wheat; — a small warbling passerine bird.

☞ Walker gives this word only in the latter sense, and pronounces it *whit′yĕr*.

Whēat′en (*whēt′n*), 149.
Whee′dle, 164.
Whee′dled (*-dld*).
Whee′dler, 183.
Whee′dling.
Wheel (13, 33), *n.* a circular frame that turns round upon its axis: — *v.* to move on wheels; — to revolve. [*See* Wheal, 160.]
Wheel′băr-rōw.
Wheeled (*whēld*).
Wheel′-horse.
Wheel′-house.
Wheel′ing.
Wheel′wright (*-rīt*).
Wheeze, 13, 33, 171.
Wheezed, 150, 165.
Wheez′ing.
Wheez′y, 93, 169.
Whelk, 15, 33.
Whelk′y, 93.
Whelm, 15, 133.
Whelmed (*whelmd*).
Whelm′ing.
Whelp, 15, 33.
Whelped (*whelpt*).
Whelp′ing.
When (15, 33) [*See* Wen, 148.]
Whence, 15, 33, 39.
Whence-so-ev′er.
When-ev′er.
When-so-ev′er.
Whêre, 14, 33.
Whêre′a-bout.
Whêre′a-bouts.
Whêre-as′ (*-az′*).
Whêre-at′.
Whêre-by′.
Whêre′fore [*not* whur′-fŏr, 127, 153.]
Whêre-in′.
Whêre-of′ (35) [*not* whêr-ov′, 141, 153.]
Whêre-on′.
Whêre-so-ev′er.
Whêre-to′ (*-too′*).
Whêre-up-on′.
Whêr-ev′er, 180.
Whêre-with′ (37) [*not* whêr-with′, 141, 153.]
Whêre-with-âl′, 180.
Whĕr′ry, 48, 66.
Whet (15, 33) [*See* Wet, 148.]
Wheth′er (15,33,38) [*See* Weather, 148.]
Whet′slate.
Whet′stōne, 24.
Whet′ted, 176.
Whet′ter.
Whet′ting.
Whew (*whu*), 26, 33.
Whew′el-līte (*hu′-*), 171.
Whey (*whā*), 23, 33.
Whey′ey (*whā′-*), 98.
Whey′ish (*whā′-*).
Which (16, 33, 44) [*See* Witch, 148.]
Which′ev-er.
Which-so-ev′er.
Whiff, 16, 173.
Whiffed (*whift*), 165; Note C, p. 34.
Whiff′ing.
Whif′fle, 164.
Whif′fled (*-fld*), 165.
Whif′fler.
[Whiffle-tree, 203. — *See* Whippletree.]
Whif′fling, 183.
Whig, 16, 33.
Whig′gar-chy (*-ky*), 176.
Whig′ger-y (*-gur-*).
Whig′gish, 138.
Whig′gism (*-ghizm*).
While (25, 33) [*not* wīl, 153.]
Whiled, 150, 165.
Whīl′ing, 183.
Whīlst, 25, 33.
Whim, 16, 33.
Whim′brel, 76.
Whim′per.
Whim′pered, 150.
Whim′per-ing.
Whim′sey (*-zy*), 156, 169.
Whim′si-cal (*-zi-*).
Whim-si-cal′i-ty (*-zi-*), 108, 169.
Whim′wham.
Whin, 16, 33.
Whin′chat.
Whine, 25, 33.
Whined.
Whīn′er, 77.
Whīn′ing.
Whin′nīed.
Whin′ny, *a.* 176.
Whin′ny, *v.* 66, 170.
Whin′nÿ-ing, 186.
Whip, 16, 33.
Whip′cord.
Whipped (*whipt*) [Whipt, 203.]
Whip′per, 176.
Whip′per-in′, 205.
Whip′ping.
Whip′ping-pōst, 215.
Whip′ple-tree [Whiffle-tree, 203.]
Whip′poor-will (66) [so Sm.; *whip′poor-will′*, Wr. 155] [Whippowill, Wb.Gd.203]
Whip′snake, 206.
Whip′stâff.
Whip′ster, 77.

Whip'stick.
Whip'stitch.
Whip'stock.
[Whipt, 203.—*See* Whipped.]
Whir, 21, N.
Whirl, 21, N.
Whirl'a-bout.
Whirl'bat.
Whirl'bōne.
Whirled (*whirld*), 165.
Whirl'i-gig (*-ghig*), 138.
Whirl'ing.
Whirl'pool.
Whirl'wind.
Whirred (*whird*), 165.
Whir'ring, 21, N.
Whisk (16,33)[*not* wisk, 153.]
Whisked (*whiskt*), 41.
Whisk'er.
Whis'kered (*-kurd*), 150.
Whis'key (98, 169) [Whisky, 203.]
Whisk'ing.
Whis'per, 77, 141.
Whis'pered, 150.
Whis'per-er.
Whis'per-ing.
Whist, 16, 33.
Whis'tle (*whis'l*), 162.
Whis'tled (*whis'ld*).
Whis'tling (*whis'ling*).
Whit, 16, 33.
White, 25, 163.
Whīt'en(*whīt'n*),149,167
Whīt'ened (*whīt'nd*).
Whīt'en-er (*whīt'n-*).
White'ness, 185.
Whīt'en-ing (*whīt'n-*).
White'smith, 206.
White'wash (*-wosh*).
White'washed (*-wosht*).
White'wash-ing (*-wosh*)
White'weed, 206.
White'wŏŏd.
Whith'er (141) [*See* Wither, 148.]
Whith-er-so-ev'er, 205, Exc. 2.
Whīt'ing.
Whīt'ish.
Whit'lĕath-er.
Whit'lōw, 101.
Whit'sun.
Whit'sun-day (*-dy*).
Whit'sun-tide.
Whit'ten (*whīt'n*).
Whit'tle, 164.
Whit'tled (*whīt'ld*).
Whit'tling.
Whiz, 16, 33, 40.
Whizzed(*whizd*),165,176
Whiz'zing.
Who (*hoo*), 162.
Whole (*hōl*)(24,130,162), *a.* all;—entire;—complete:—*n.* the total. [*See* Hole, 160.]
Whole'sale (*hōl'-*), 24.
Whole'some (*hōl'sum*), 130, 169.
Whōl'ly (*hōl'-*), 130, 162.

☞ Walker says of this word, that "it ought undoubtedly to be written *wholely*, and pronounced like the adjective *holy*, and so as to correspond and rhyme with *solely*." But it is to be observed that, while *wholly* is identical in sound with *holy*, neither of these words rhymes with *solely*. In this word, the voice rests for an appreciable space of time on the sound signified by the two *l's*; whereas in the words *holy* and *wholly*, although the mode of articulating the sound of *l* is precisely the same as in *solely*, the sound is not dwelt upon at all, and a very different effect is produced upon the ear. *See* 66, N.

Whom (*hoom*), 19, 162.
Whom-so-ev'er(*hoom-*).
Whoop (*hoop*) (19, 162), *n.* a shout of pursuit:—*v.* to make a loud cry; to shout. [*See* Hoop, 160] [Hoop, 203.]
Whooped (*hoopt*), 41.
Whoop'ing (*hoop'-*).
Whoop'ing-cough (*hoop'ing-kŏf*)(18, N.) [Hooping-cough, 203.]
Whop, 18, 33.
Whop'per, 176.
Whop'ping.
Whorl (17, 135) [so Sm. Wr.; *whurl*, Gd. 155.]
Whorled, 165.
Whort (*whurt*), 21, 33.
Whor'tle-bĕr-ry(*whur'-tl-*) [so Wk. Wr. Wb. Gd.; *hor'tl-bĕr-ry*, Sm. 155.]
Whose (*hooz*), 19, 162.
Whose-so-ev'er (*hooz-*).
Who'so (*hoo'-*).
Who-so-ev'er (*hoo-*).
Why, 25, 33.
Wick, 16, 181.
Wick'ed.
Wick'er, 77.
Wick'ered (*-urd*).
Wick'et, 76.
Wick'liff-ite [Wicliffite, Wicliffite, Wycliffite, 203.]
Wide, 25, 34.
Wide-a-wake'.
Wīd'en (*wīd'n*) (149, 167) [*not* wĭd'n, 127, 153.]
Wīd'ened (*wīd'nd*).
Wīd'en-ing (*wīd'n-*).
Wide'-sprĕad.
Widge'on (86) [Wigeon (*wij'on*), 203.]
Wid'ōw, 101.
Wid'ōwed.
Wid'ōw-er.
Wid'ōw-hŏŏd.
Wid'ōw-ing.
Width, Note C, p. 34.
Wiēld (13, 169, N.), to handle;—to manage. [*See* Weald, 160.]
Wiēld'ed.
Wiēld'ing.
[Wiery, 203.—*See* Wiry.]
Wife (25, 163) [pl. Wives (*wīvz*), 193.]
Wife'like.
Wife'ly.
Wig, 16, 34, 53.
[Wigeon, 203.—*See* Widgeon.]
Wight (*wīt*), 25, 162.
Wig'wâm [so Wr.; *wig'-wŏm*, Wb. Gd.; *wig'-wum*, Sm. 155.]
Wīld, 25, 34.
Wīld'cat, 206.
Wil'der (161, 228, N.), *v.* to perplex.
Wīld'er (161, 228, N.), *a.* more wild.
Wil'dered, 150, 165.
Wil'der-ing.
Wil'der-ness.
Wīld'fire, 216.
Wīld'ing.
Wile.
Wil'ful (*-fŏŏl*) [Willful, Wb. Gd. 178,203.]
Wīl'i-ness, 186.
Will, 172.
Willed (*wĭld*), 165.
Will'ing.
Will'ing-ly, 93.
Wil'lōw, 101, 170.
Wil'lōwed, 165.
Wil'lōw-ing.
Wil'lōw-y.
Will'-with-a-wisp(221)

Will-o'-the-wisp, 203.]
Wil'ly, 66, 170.
Wilt, 16, 34.
Wilt'ed.
Wilt'ing.
Wil'y, 169.
Wim'ble, 164.
Wim'ple.
Win, 16, 34.
Wince, 16, 39.
Winced (*winst*), 165; Note C, p. 34.
Winç'er.
Winch, 16, 44, Note 2.
Winç'ing.
Wīnd (16, 161) [so Sm. Wr. Wb. Gd.; *wīnd*, or *wind*, Wk. 155], *n.* air in motion: — *v.* to perceive or follow by the wind; to nose;—to ride or drive so as to render scant of breath; — to rest, in order to recover wind or breath.

☞ Walker says: "These two modes of pronunciation [*wind* and *wīnd*] have been long contending for superiority, till at last the former seems to have gained a complete victory, except in the territory of rhyme. . . . But, in prose, the regular and analogical pronunciation borders on the antiquated and pedantic." Smart remarks: "He[Walker] gives no encouragement to the almost childish pedantry which insists on saying . . . *wīnd*, while others say *wind*."

Wīnd, *v.* (25,161), to cause to turn or revolve; — to twine or coil; — to sound, as a horn, so that the notes shall be prolonged and mutually involved; — to proceed in flexures.
Wĭnd'age, 156.
Wīnd'ed [*See* Wĭnd.]
Wīnd'er.
Wĭnd'fâll, 206.
Wĭnd'gâll.
Wĭnd'hov-er (*-huv-*).
Wĭnd'i-ness, 186.
Wĭnd'ing (161), *part.* from *Wĭnd.*
Wīnd'ing (161), *part.* from *Wīnd.*
Wīnd'ing-sheet.
Wĭnd'lass, 72.
Wĭnd'mill, 206.
Win'dōw (101) [*not* win'-dur, 153.]
Win'dōw-sēat.
Wĭnd'pipe [so Sm. Wb. Gd.; *wĭnd'pīp*, or *wīnd'pīp*, Wk. Wr. 155.]

☞ "Some speakers unnecessarily call it *wīnd'-pipe.*" *Smart. See* Note under *Wind.*

Wĭnd'row (*wĭnd'ro*, or *win'ro*) [*wĭnd'ro*, Wr.; *win'ro*, Gd. 155.]
Wĭnd'ward.
Wĭnd'y, 93.
Wine, 25, 163.
Wine'-bib-ber.
Wine'glȧss, 206.
Wing, 16, 54.
Wing'ed, *a.* (150) [so Wk. Sm.; *wing'ed*, or *wingd*, Wr. 155.]
Winged (*wingd*), *v.* 150.
Wing'ing.
Wing'y, 93.
Wink (*wingk*), 54.
Winked (*wingkt*).
Wink'ing (*wingk'-*).
Win'ner, 170.
Win'ning.
Win'nōw, 66, 170.
Win'nōwed, 165.
Win'nōw-ing.
Win'some (*-sum*), 169.
Win'ter, 77.
Win'tered, 150.
Win'ter-green.
Win'ter-ing.
Win'ter-kill.
Win'try [Wintery, 203.]
Wīn'y, 93, 183.
Winze (*winz*), 16, 40.
Wipe, 25, 163.
Wiped (*wīpt*), 41.
Wīp'er, 183.
Wīp'ing.
Wire, 25, 67.
Wire'drâw, 206.
Wire'drâw-er.
Wire'drâw-ing.
Wire'drew (*-droo*).
Wire'grȧss.
Wire'-worm (*-wurm*).
Wīr'i-ness, 186.
Wīr'y [Wiery, 203.]
Wis'dom (*wiz'-*), 86, 185.
Wise (*wīz*), 25, 40.
Wise'a-cre (*wīz'ā-kur*), 164, 171.
Wish, 16, 46.
Wish'a-ble, 164.
Wished (*wisht*), 41.
Wish'er, 77, 169.
Wish'ful (*-fŏŏl*), 180.
Wish'ful-ly (*-fŏŏl-*).
Wish'ing.
Wish'y-wash'y (*-wosh'-*).
Wisp, 16, 34.
Wist'ful (*-fŏŏl*).
Wis'ton-wish.
Wit, 16, 34, 41.
Witch, 16, 44; Note D, p. 37.
Witch'crȧft.
Witch'-elm [Weech-elm, 203.]
Witch'er-y, 233, Exc.
Witch'ing.
Wit'e-na-ge-mote' (*-ghe-*) [so Wr. Gd.; *wit-ten-aj'e-mōt*, Sm. 155.]
With, *prep.* 16, 38.
With (16, 37), *n.* an osier or willow twig. [Withe, Withy, 203.]
With-âl', 180.
With-drâw'.
With-drâw'al.
With-drâw'er.
With-drâw'ing.
With-drâwn'.
With-drew' (*-droo'*).
Wīthe (16, 37; Note D, p. 37) [so Wk. Wr. Wb. Gd.; *with*, Sm. 155] [With, Withy, 203.]
Withed (*witht*), 37, 41.
With'er, 77.
With'ered, 150.
With'er-ing.
With'er-năm.
With'ers (*-urz*), *n. pl.*
With-held'.
With-hold', 171.
With-hold'en (*-hōld'n*).
With-hold'ing.
With-in'.
With-out'.
With-stand'.
With-stand'ing.
With-stŏŏd'.
With'y (37, 93), *n.* a species of willow-tree; a withe; — *a.* made of, or resembling, withes; flexible and tough.
Wit'ling.

Wit′ness.
Wit′nessed (*-nest*).
Wit′ness-ing. [171.
Wit′ti-cism (*-sizm*), 78,
Wit′ti-ly, 186.
Wit′ti-ness.
Wit′ty, 93, 170, 176.
Wit′wâl [Witwall, 203.]
Wive, 25.
Wived, 165.
Wives (*wīvz*), *n. pl.* [*See* Wife.]
Wiv′ing, 183.
Wiz′ard, 72, 170.
Wiz′ard-ry.
Wōad (24) [Weld, Woald, Wold, 203.]
Wōe (24) [Wo, 203.]

☞ "It is with some repugnance that even [the] letter *o* is allowed to finish a word: we write *foe, doe, toe*, &c., and though Johnson writes *wo*, it is almost as frequently written with an *e* in the singular, and always in the plural." *Smart*. — "The termination in *o* belongs among monosyllables to the *other* parts of speech, as *go, so*, and to nouns of more than one syllable, as *motto, potato, tomato*, &c." *Goodrich*.

Wōe′-be-gōne, 18, N.
Wōe′ful, *or* Wo′ful (*-fōōl*), 203.

☞ These two forms are thus given by Goodrich. Smart and Worcester give only the form *woful*.

Wōld (24), *n.* a wood, or forest; — an open country; — a kind of plant yielding a yellow dye. [Weld, Woald, Woad, (in the last sense), 203.]
Wolf (*wōōlf*) (20) [pl. Wolves (*wōōlvz*), 193.]
Wolf′-fish (*wōōlf′-*), 66, N.; 206, Exc. 1.
Wolf′ish (*wōōlf′-*), 66.
Wŏl′fram [so Wr. Wb. Gd.; *wōōlf′ram*, Sm. 155.] [213.
Wolf′s′-bane (*wōōlfs′-*).
Wol-ver-ene′(*wōōl-*),122, 171.
Wom′an (*wōōm′an*) (20) [pl. Women (*wim′en*), 16, 195.]
Wom′an-hood (*wōōm′-*).
Wom′an-ish (*wōōm′-*).
Wom′an-kīnd (*woom′-*), 146.
Wom′an-li-ness (*wōōm′-*), 171, 186.
Wom′an-ly (*wōōm′-*).
Womb (*woom*), 19, 162.
Wom′bat [so Wr. Wb. Gd.; *woom′at*, Sm. 155]
Wom′en (*wim′en*), *n. pl.* (171) [*See* Woman.]
Won (*wun*) (22), *v.* did win. [*See* One, 160.]
Won′der (*wun′-*).
Won′dered (*wun′durd*).
Won′der-ful (*wun′dur-fōōl*), 171, 180.
Won′der-ing (*wun′-*).
Won′der-ment (*wun′-*).
Won′drous (*wun′-*), 171.
Wōn't (*wōnt*) (161) [so Wk. Sm. Wb. Gd.; *wōnt*, or *wŭnt*, Wr. 155.]

☞ "In New England commonly pronounced *wunt*." *Worcester*.

☞ "A contraction of *woll not*, that is, *will not*." *Webster*. — "A contraction of *would not*; — used for *will not*." *Worcester*. — "In *won't*, we drop *l*, and retain, instead of the short *i* in *will*, a long *o* from the Anglo-Saxon *wolde*." *Sir J. Stoddart*.

Wont (*wunt*) (22, 161), *n.* custom; habit: — *v.* to be accustomed [*not* wōnt, 127, 153.]
Wont′ed (*wunt′-*) [*not* wōnt′ed, 127, 153.]
Woo, 19, 34.
Wōōd (20), *n.* a large collection of trees; — the substance of trees. [*See* Would, 160.]
Wōōd′bine.

☞ This was originally *wood′bind*.

Wōōd′chat.
Wōōd′chuck [Woodchuk, 203.]
Wōōd′cock.
Wōōd′ed.
Wōōd′en (*wōōd′n*).
Wōōd′house.
Wōōd′i-ness, 186.
Wōōd′ing.
Wōōd′land.
Wōōd′man, 196. [214.
Wōōds′man (*wōōdz′-*),
Wōōd′-note.
Wōōd′peck-er.
Wōōd′roof, 19, 20.
Wōōd′wârd.
Wōōd′work (*-wurk*).
Wōōd′y, 169.
Wooed, 171, 188.
Woo′er.
Woof, 20.
Woof′y.
Woo′ing.
Wōōl, 19.
Woold, 20.
Woold′er.
Woold′ing.
Wōōl′-gath′er-ing, 205.
Wōōl′len (177) [Woolen, Wb. Gd. 203.]
Wōōl′li-ness [Wooliness, Wb. Gd. 203.]
Wōōl′ly [Wooly, Wb. Gd. 177, 203.]
Wōōl′man, 196.
Wōōl′sack.
Woor′a-ly [Woorali, Wourali, Wouri, 203.]
Wootz (*woots*), 19, 39; Note C, p. 34.
Word (*wurd*), 21, 49.
Word′-bōōk (*wurd′-*), 206, Exc. 4.
Word′ed (*wurd′-*).
Word′i-ly (*wurd′-*), 186.
Word′i-ness (*wurd′-*).
Word′ing (*wurd′-*).
Word′y (*wurd′-*), 93.
Wore, 24, 49, 67.
Work (*wurk*), 21, 49, 135.
Work′a-ble (*wurk′a-bl*).
Work′-dāy (*wurk′-*).
Worked (*wurkt*), 41.
Work′house (*wurk′-*).
Work′ing (*wurk′-*).
Work′ing-dāy (*wurk′-*).
Work′man (*wurk′-*),196.
Work′man-like (*wurk′-*), 206, Exc. 5.
Work′man-ly (*wurk′-*).
Work′shop (*wurk′-*).
World (*wurld*), 21, 135.
World′li-ness (*wurld′-*).
World′ly (*wurld′-*), 93.
World′ly-mīnd′ed (*wurld′-*), 205.
World′-wide (*wurld′-*), 206, Exc. 5.
Worm (*wurm*), 21, 49.
Worm′-eat-en (*wurm′-ēt-n*).
Wormed (*wurmd*).
Worm′ing (*wurm′-*).

Worm'wŏŏd (*wurm'-*).
Worm'y (*wurm'-*), 93.
Wōrn, 24, 49, 67.
Wor'nil [W o r n a l, W o r n e l, 203.]
Wōrn'-out, 203, Exc 5.
Wor'ri-er (*wŭr'-*), 171.
Wor'rĭed (*wŭr'rid*).
Wor'ry (*wŭr'-*), 22, 170.
Wor'ry-ing (*wŭr'-*).
Worse (*wurs*), 21, Note D, p. 37
Wor'ship (*wur'-*).
Wor'ship-ful (*wur'-ship-fŏŏl*), 180.
Wor'shipped (*wur'-shipt*) [W o r s h i p-e d, Wb. Gd. 177, 203.]
Wor'ship-per (*wur'-*) [W o r s h i p e r, Wb. Gd. 203.]
Wor'ship-ping (*wur'-*) [W o r s h i p i n g, Wb. Gd. 177, 203.]
Worst (*wurst*), *a.* & *v.*
Worst'ed (*wurst'-*) (161), *v.* did worst.
Wors'ted (*woors'ted*) (161) [so Sm. Wr.; *wŏŏst'ed*, Gd.; *wurs'-tid*, Wk. 155], *n.* a kind of yarn or thread made of wool.
Worst'ing (*wurst'-*).
Wort (*wurt*), 21, 49.
Worth (*wurth*), 21, 37.
Wor'thi-ly (*wur'-*).
Wor'thi-ness (*wur'-*).
Worth'less (*wurth'-*).
Wor'thy (*wur'-*).
Wot, 18, 34.
Would (*wŏŏd*) (20, 162), *v* from *Will*. [*See* Wood, 160.]
Would'-be (*wŏŏd'-*).
Wound (*woond*, or *wownd*), *n.* [so Wk. Wr., *woond*, Sm.; *wownd*, or *woond*, Gd. 155.]

☞ "The word *wound*, which, from its Saxon origin, ought to have the sound of *ow* [No 19, § 28], has, to a great extent, taken the French sound (*woond*): notwithstanding the remonstrances of Walker and other orthoëpists against it." *Goodrich.* — Walker styles *woond* "a capricious novelty," which "ought to be entirely banished." "But where," he asks, "is the man bold enough to risk the imputation of vulgarity by such an expulsion?" Smart speaks of *wownd* as "the old-fashioned pronunciation."

Wound (*wownd*) (28), *v.* did wind.
Wound'ed (*woond'ed*, or *wownd'ed*).
Wound'ing (*woond'ing*, or *wownd'ing*).
Wound'wort (*woond'-wurt*, or *wownd'wort*).
Wou'ra-lĭ (*woo'-*) [W o o r a l i, W o o-r a l y, W o u r i, 203.]
Wore, 24.
Wōv'en (*wōv'n*), 149, 167.
Wrack (*rak*) (162), *n.* a marine plant or kind of sea-weed. [*See* Rack, 160.]
Wrāith (*rāth*), 23, 162.
Wran'gle (*rang'gl*), 164.
Wran'gled (*rang'gld*).
Wran'gler (*rang'glur*).
Wran'gling (*rang'-gling*).
Wrap (*rap*) (10, 162), *v.* to roll together; — to cover with something rolled or thrown round. [*See* Rap, 160.]

☞ "This word is often pronounced *rop*, rhyming with *top*, even by speakers much above the vulgar. They have a confused idea that a preceding *w* makes the *a* broad, and do not attend to the intervening *r*, which bars the power of the *w*, and necessarily preserves the *a* in its short . . . sound." *Walker.*

Wrap'page (*rap'-*), 176.
Wrapped (*rapt*) (41) [W r a p t, 203.]
Wrap'per (*rap'-*).
Wrap'ping (*rap'-*).
Wrasse (*ras*), 162, 171.
Wrath (*räth*, or *rawth*), *n.* [so Wr.; *räth*, Wb. Gd.; *rawth*, Sm.; *roth*, or *răth*, Wk. 155]

☞ "In *wrath*, the *a* ought to be sounded *ah*, yet we sound it *aw*; which broader sound has no doubt been produced by the presence of *w* to the eye, though it is silent to the ear." *Smart.* — The word is generally pronounced *räth*, in the United States, in conformity to the analogy according to which, with hardly an exception, the Italian sound is given to *a* before *th*, as in *bath*, *path*, &c.

Wrath'ful (*räth'fŏŏl*, or *rawth'fŏŏl*), 180.
Wrēak (13), *v.* to inflict with violence. [*See* Reek, 160.]
Wrēaked (*rēkt*).
Wrēak'ing (*rēk'-*).
Wrēath (*rēth*) (13, 37, 162) [so Sm. Wr. Wb. Gd.; *rēth*, or *rēth*, Wk. 155] [pl. Wreaths (*rethz*), 189.]

☞ Walker considers *rēth* "much more agreeable to analogy" than *reth*. — "In *wreaths* [pl.], . . . the *th* is vocal." *Smart.*

Wrēathe (*rēth*), 38, 162 [W r e a t h, Wk. Sm. 203.]
Wrēathed (*rēthd*), 165.
Wrēath'ing (*rēth'-*).
Wrēath'y (*rēth'-*).
Wreck (*rek*) (15, 162), *n.* destruction of a vessel by being driven on rocks or shallows, or by foundering; — a vessel wrecked: — *v.* to cause to suffer shipwreck. [*See* Reck, 160.]
Wreck'age (*rek'-*), 169.
Wrecked (*rekt*), 165; Note C, p. 34.
Wreck'er (*rek'-*), 77.
Wreck'ing (*rek'-*).
Wren (*ren*), 15, 162.
Wrench (*rench*), 44, Note 2; 171.
Wrenched (*rencht*), 41, 165.
Wrench'ing (*rench'-*).
Wrest (*rest*) (15, 162), *v.* to pull with a violent turn or twist. [*See* Rest, 160.]
Wrest'ed (*rest'-*).
Wrest'er (*rest'-*).
Wrest'ing (*rest'-*).
Wres'tle (*res'l*), 162.
Wres'tled (*res'ld*).
Wres'tler (*res'lur*).
Wres'tling (*res'ling*).
Wretch (*rech*), 15, 162.
Wretch'ed (*rech'-*).
Wrig'gle (*rig'l*), 164.
Wrig'gled (*rig'ld*).

Wrig′gler (*rig′-*).
Wrig′gling (*rig′-*).
Wright (*rīt*) (25, 162), *n.* an artificer. [*See* Right, Rite, *and* Write, 160.]
Wring (*ring*) (16, 54, 162), *v.* to twist or turn round with violence; — to force by twisting or contortion; — to wrest. [*See* Ring, 160.]
Wring′-bōlt (*ring′-*).
Wring′ing (*ring′-*).
Wrin′kle (*ring′kl*), 164.
Wrin′kled (*ring′kld*).
Wrin′kling (*ring′-*), 183.
Wrin′kly (*ring′-*).
Wrist (*rist*), 16, 162.
Wrist′band (*rist′band*, coll. *riz′band*) [so Sm.; *rist′band*, Wk. Wr. Wb. Gd. 155.]
Wrist′let (*rist′-*).
Writ (*rit*), 16, 162.
Write (*rīt*) (25, 162), *v.* to form letters and words with a pen, pencil, or similar instrument; — to express by letters. [*See* Right, Rite, *and* Wright, 160.]
Wrīt′er(*rīt′-*),*n.*onewho writes. [*See* Righter, 160.]
Writhe (*rīth*).
Writhed (*rīthd*), 150, 165.
Wrīth′ing (*rīth′-*).
Wrīt′ing (*rīt′-*), *n.* act of one who writes; — any thing written. [*See* Righting, 160.]
Wrīt′ing-bŏŏk (*rīt′-*).
Wrīt′ing-desk (*rīt′-*).
Wrīt′ing-mȧs′ter (*rīt′-*), 205.
Wrīt′ing-pa′per (*rīt′-*).
Writ′ten (*rit′n*), 149, 170.
Wrong (*rong*), 18, 162.
Wrong′-do-er (*rong′doo-ur*).
Wrong′-do-ing (*rong′-doo-ing*).
Wronged (*rongd*).
Wrong′ful (*rong′fŏŏl*), 180.
Wrong′-hĕad-ed (*rong′-*).
Wrong′ing (*rong′-*).
Wrong′ly (*rong′-*), 93.
Wrote (*rōt*) (24, 162), *v.* did write. [*See* Rote, 160.]
Wroth (*rawth*, or *rŏth*) (162) [so Wr.; *rawth*, Wb. Gd.; *rŏth*, Wk.; *rŏth*, or *rawth* (nearly), Sm. 155.]
Wrought (*rawt*), 17, 162.
Wrung (*rung*) (22, 54, 162), *v.* did ring. [*See* Rung, 160.]
Wry (*rī*) (25, 162), crooked; distorted. [*See* Rye, 160.]
Wry′neck (*rī′-*).
Wy′vern.

X.

Xan′thi-an (*zan′-*).
Xan′thic (*zan′-*), 40.
Xan′thīne (*zan′-*) (82) [Xanthin, 203.]
Xan′tho-gen (*zan′-*).
Xan′thoŭs (*zan′-*).
Xan′tho-phyll (*zan′-*), 171.
Xe′bec (*ze′bek*) (40) [*not* ze-bek′, 153.]
Xe-ro-col-lȳr′i-um (*ze-*), 116, 171.
Xe-ro′dēs (*ze-ro′dēz*).
Xe-ro-my′rum (*ze-*) [so Sm. Wb. Gd.; *zĕr-o-mi′rum*,Wk.Wr.155.]
Xe-roph′a-gy (*ze-*).
Xe-roph′thal-my (*ze-rop′-*) [so Sm. Wr.; *ze-rof′thal-my*, Wb. Gd. 155.]
Xe-ro′tēs (*ze-ro′tēz*).
Xiph′i-as (*zif′-*).
Xiph′oid (*zif′-*) [so Sm. Wb. Gd.; *zif′oid*, or *zi′foid*, Wr. 155.]
Xi-phoi′dēs (*zī-foi′dēz*).
Xy′līte (*zi′-*).
Xy-lo-bal′sa-mum (L.), (*zī-*).
Xy-log′ra-pher (*zī-*).
Xy-lo-graph′ic (*zī-*).
Xy-lo-graph′ic-al (*zi-*), 108.
Xy-log′ra-phy (*zi-*), 108, 171.
Xy-loid′īne (*zi-*), 152.
Xy-loph′a gan (*zī-*).
Xy-loph′a-goŭs (*zī-*).
Xyst (*zist*), *or* Xys′tos (*zis′-*), 40, 203.
Xys′tarch(*zis′tark*),171.
Xys′ter (*zis′tur*).

Y.

Yacht (*yot*), 18, 156, 162.
Yacht′er (*yot′-*).
Yacht′ing (*yot′-*), 171.
Yâ′ger (*yaw′gur*), 156.
Yä′hoo, 189.
Yak, 10, 51, 52.
Yam, 10, 32, 51.
Yä′ma, *n.* a deity in Hindoo mythology.
Yan′kee (*yang′-*), 54.
Yan′kee-ism (*yang′ke-izm*), 133, 136.
Yä′pon, *or* Yā′pon [so Gd.; *yap′on*, Wr. 155] [Yaupon, Youpon, 203.]
Yard, 11, 49, 135.
Yard′-arm.
Yard′stick, 206.
Yare (*yêr*), 14, 49, 51.
Yarn, 11, 49, 142.
Yăr′rōw, 11, N.; 48.
Yat′a-ghan (53) [so Gd.; *yat-a-gan′*, Wr. 155] [Ataghan, 203.]
Yâup[Yaulp, Yawp, 203.]
Yâup′er.
[Yaupon, 203. — *See* Yapon.]
Yaw, 17.
Yawl, 17, 50, 51.
Yawn, 17.
Yawned (*yawnd*), 165.
Yawn′ing.
[Yawp, 203. — *See* Yaup.]
Yaws (*yawz*), *n. pl.*
Y-cleped′ (*ī-klept′*).
Ye, 13, 51.
Yea (*yā*, or *yē*) [so Wr.; *yā*, Sm.; *ye*, Wk.; *ye*, or *yā*, Gd. 155.]
Yēan, 13.
Yēaned, 165.
Yēan′ing.
Yēan′ling.
Yēar, 13, 49.
Yēar′-bŏŏk, 206, Exc. 4.
Yēar′ling.
Yearn (*yern*), 21, N.
Yearned (*yernd*), 165.
Yearn′ing.
Yēast, 13.

☞ "The old spelling and pronunciation, *yest*, seem to have quite yielded to those here given [*yēast*.]" *Smart.*

Yēast'y, 93, 169 [Y e s t y, 203.]
Yelk [Y o l k, 203.]

☞ This word is frequently written *yolk*. Johnson, Walker, and Webster, prefer *yelk*, as being more agreeable to etymology. Worcester gives both forms as having the sanction of good usage at the present time. Smart says: "The old form *yelk* appears to have gone out of use."

Yell, 172.
Yelled (*yeld*).
Yell'ing, 228.
Yel'lōw (101) [*not* yal'-ur, 127, 153.]
Yel'lōw-bird.
Yel'low-fe'ver.
Yel'lōw-ish.
Yelp, 15.
Yelped (*yelpt*), 165; Note C, p. 34.
Yelp'ing.
Ye'nīte, 152.
Yeō'man, 24, 171.
Yeō'man-ry.
Yerk, 21, N.
Yerked (*yerkt*), 41.
Yerk'ing.
Yes (174) [so Sm. Wr. Wb. Gd.; *yis*, Wk. 155.]
[Y e s t, 203.—*See* Yeast]
Yes'ter, 77.
Yes'ter-dāy [*not* yis'-tur-dā, 127, 153.]
[Y e s t y, 203. — *See* Yeasty.]
Yet (15, 51) [*not* yit, 127, 153.]
Yew (*yoo*) (26, 51), *n.* a kind of tree. [*See* You, 160.]
Yew'en (*yoo'*-).
Yew'-tree (*yoo'*-), 206, Exc. 4.
Yez-de-ger'di-an (*-jer'*-) (21, N.; 169) [so Sm.; *yez-de-gher'di-an*, Gd. 155.]
Yiēld, 13, 169, N.
Yiēld'ed.
Yiēld'ing.
Yoke (24, 163), *n.* a wooden frame by which oxen are connected for work: — *v.* to join by, or as by, a yoke. [*See* Yolk, 160.]
Yoked (*yōkt*), 41.
Yōk'ing, 183.
Yolk (*yōk*) (24, 162) [so Wk. Sm. Wr.; *yōlk*, Wb. Gd. 155], *n.* the yellow part of an egg. [*See* Yoke, 160] [Y e l k, 203. — *See* Note under *Yelk*.]
Yŏn, 18, 51.
Yŏn'der [*not* yen'der, *nor* yun'dur, 127, 153.]
[Y o n k e r, 203. — *See* Younker.]
Yore, 24, 49, 135.
You (*yoo*) (26, 51, 69), *pron.* pl. of *Thou.* [*See* Yew, 160.]
Yoŭng, 22, 54.
Yoŭn'ger (*yung'gur*), 54, Note 2.
Yoŭn'gest (*yung'ghest*).
Yoŭng'ish.
Yoŭng'ling.
Yoŭng'ster, 77.
Yoŭnk'er (*yungk'*-).
[Y o u p o n, 203. — *See* Yapon.]
Your (*yoor*, when emphatical; *yur*, when not so.)
Your-self' (*yoor*, or *yur*)

☞ When contrasted with one of the words *myself, himself, herself, itself, ourselves, themselves,* the first syllable of this word is pronounced *yoor*, and receives the chief stress of the voice, agreeably to the principle laid down in § 118.

Youth (*yooth*), 26, 37.
Youth'ful (*yooth'fōōl*).
Ўt'tri-a, 169, 170.
Ўt'tri-oŭs.
Ўt'tri-um.
Yule, 26.

Z.

Zac'cho (*-ko*).
Zaf'fre (*-fur*) (164) [Z a f f e r, Wb. Gd. 203. — *See* Note E, p. 70.]
Zāim, 23.
Zam'bo (86) [pl. Zam'-bōs (*-bōz*), 192.]
Zan'ti-ŏt.
Za'ny, 93, 169.
Za'ny-ism (*-izm*), 136.
Zar'nich (*-nik*), 52.
Zax, 10, 40.
Za'yat (Burmah).
Ze'a.
Zēal, 13.
Zēal'ot (143) [so Sm. Wr. Wb. Gd.; *zel'ut*, or *ze'lut*, Wk. 155.]
Zēal'ot-ism (*-izm*), 133.
Zēal'ot-ry.
Zēal'oŭs [*not* zēl'us, 143, 153.]
Ze'bra.
Ze'bu, 89.
Ze'chin (141) (*ze'kin*) [so Sm. Wb. Gd.; *che-kēn'*, Wk; *ze'kin*, or *che-kēn'*, Wr. 155] [C e c-c h i n, C h e q u i n, S e q u i n, 203.]
Zech'steīn (*zek'*-).
Zed.
Zed'o-a-ry, 72.
Zem-in-dar' [so Wr. Gd.; *zem'in-dar*, Sm. 155.]
Zem'in-da-ry, 72.
Zend, 15, 40.
Zend-a-ves'ta.
Ze'nik.
Ze'nith, *or* Zen'ith [*ze'-nith*, Wk. Wr. Wb. Gd.; *zen'ith*, Sm. 155.]
Ze'o-līte, 152.
Ze-o-lit'ic.
Ze-o-lit'i-form, 108.
Zeph'yr, 95, 169.
Zeph'y-rus (L.), 93.
Ze'ro (49, N.; 86) [pl. Ze'rōes (*-rōz*), 192.]
Zest, 15.
Ze'ta.
Ze-tet'ic.
Zeŭg'lo-don, 105.
Zeŭg'ma, 171.
Zib'et, 156.
Zic'ga, 13, 72.
Zig'zag.
Zig'zagged (*-zagd*), 165.
Zig'zag-ging.
Zim'ent-wâ'ter, 205.
Zinc (181) [Z i n k, 203.]
Zin-cif'er-oŭs (108) [Z i n c k i f e r o u s, 203.]
Zinck'y, 169.
Zinc-og'ra-pher (108) [so Gd.; *zin-kog'ra-fer*, Wr. 155.]
Zinc-o-graph'ic, 109.
Zinc-o-graph'ic-al.

Zinc-og′ra-phy.
Zinc′oid.
Zinc′oŭs.
Zi′on.
Zir′con, 21, N.
Zir-co′ni-a.
Zir-co′ni-um, 169.
Zo′cle, *or* Zoc′le (164) [*zō′kl*, Wr. Wb. Gd., *zok′l*, Sm. 155.]
Zo′di-ac [so Sm. Wr. Wb. Gd.; *zo′dī-ak*, or *zo′jī-ak*, Wk. 134, 155.]
Zo-di′ac-al, 108, 155.
Zo′hăr (Heb.).
Zo-il′e-an, 110, 169.
Zo′il-ism (*-izm*), 133, 136.
Zoll′ver-ein.
Zo′nar [Zonnar, 203.]
Zone, 24, 163.
Zōn′u-lar, 108, 183.
Zo-o-chem′ic-al(*-kem′-*).
Zo-och′e-my (*-ok′-*).
Zo-o-gen′ic.
Zo-og′e-ny (*-oj′-*).
Zo-og′ra-pher, 108.
Zo-o-graph′ic.
Zo-o-graph′ic-al, 108.
Zo-og′ra-phy, 93.
Zo-ol′a-try, 169.
Zo′o-līte, 83.
Zo-o-log′ic (*-loj′-*).
Zo-o-log′ic-al (*-loj′-*).
Zo-ol′o-gist.
Zo-ol′o-gy, 108, 144.
Zo-o-mor′phism (*-fizm*), 133, 136.
Zo-on′o-my, 108.
Zo-oph′a-gan.
Zo-oph′a-goŭs.
Zo-o-phŏr′ic (109) [*not* zo-of′o-rik, 153.]
Zo-oph′o-rŭs (L.).
Zo′o-phyte, 171.
Zo-o-phyt′ic.
Zo-o-phyt′ic-al.
Zo-o-phȳt-o-log′ic-al (*-loj′-*), 116.
Zo-o-phȳt-ol′o-gy [*zo-o-fī-tol′o-jy*, Gd.; *zo-ŏf-ī-tol′o-jy*, Wr. 155.]
Zo′o-sperm.
Zo′o-spore, 156.
Zo-o-tom′ic-al.
Zo-ot′o-mist.
Zo-ot′o-my, 108.
Zou-äve′ (*zoo-äv′*) [so Wr.; *zwav*, Gd. 155.]
Zounds (*zoundz*), 142; Note C, p. 34.
Zoutch (*zooch*) (91) [so Sm.; *zowch*, Wr. 155.]
Zu′fo-lo (It.) (*zoo′-*) [so Wr.; *zoof′o-lo*, Sm. 155] [Zuffolo (*zuf′fo-lo*, Gd. 203.]
Zum-boo′ruk.
[Zumologist, 203. — *See* Zymologist.]
[Zumology, 203. — *See* Zymology.]
[Zumometer, 203. — *See* Zymometer.]
[Zumosimeter, 203. *See* Zymosimeter.]
Zyg-o-dac-tyl′ic(109)[so Gd., *zī-go-dak′til-ik*, Wr. 155.]
Zyg-o-dac′tyl-oŭs.
Zyg-o-mat′ic.
Zȳ-mo-log′ic (*-loj′-*)
Zȳ-mo-log′ic-al (*-loj′-*).
Zy-mol′o-gist [Zumologist, 203.]
Zȳ-mol′o-gy (108) [Zumology, 203.]
Zȳ-mom′e-ter(108)[Zumometer, 203.]
Zȳ-mo-sim′e-ter [Zumosimeter, 203.]
Zȳ-mot′ic.
Zȳ-thep′sa-ry, 72.
Zy′thum.

www.ingramcontent.com/pod-product-compliance
Lightning Source LLC
LaVergne TN
LVHW020915110826
845150LV00004B/683